Hampton-Brown

EDGE

Reading, Writing & Language

PROGRAM AUTHORS

David W. Moore

Deborah J. Short

Michael W. Smith

Alfred W. Tatum

Literature Consultant

René Saldaña, Jr.

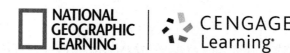

NATIONAL GEOGRAPHIC LEARNING | CENGAGE Learning

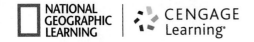

Acknowledgments

Grateful acknowledgment is given to the authors, artists, photographers, museums, publishers, and agents for permission to reprint copyrighted material. Every effort has been made to secure the appropriate permission. If any omissions have been made or if corrections are required, please contact the Publisher.

Photographic Credits

Cover: Avian Island, the Pantanal, Mato Grosso, Brazil, Mike Bueno. Photograph © Mike Bueno/National Geographic Stock.

Acknowledgments continue on page 986.

For product information and technology assistance, contact us at
Customer & Sales Support, 888-915-3276

For permission to use material from this text or product, submit all requests online at **www.cengage.com/permissions**
Further permissions questions can be emailed to
permissionrequest@cengage.com

National Geographic Learning | Cengage Learning
1 Lower Ragsdale Drive
Building 1, Suite 200
Monterey, CA 93940

Cengage Learning is a leading provider of customized learning solutions with office locations around the globe, including Singapore, the United Kingdom, Australia, Mexico, Brazil, and Japan. Locate your local office at **www.cengage.com/global**.

Visit National Geographic Learning online at **ngl.cengage.com**
Visit our corporate website at **www.cengage.com**

Printed in the USA.
Quad/Graphics, Versailles, KY

ISBN: 978-12854-39587

Printed in the United States of America
18 19 20 21 22
10 9 8 7 6 5

CONTENTS AT A GLANCE

UNIT	Essential Question	Genre Focus	Focus Strategy	Grammar	Writing
1	What Influences a Person's Choices?	Short Stories: Plot, Characterization, Setting	Plan and Monitor	Sentences Subjects and Predicates Subject-Verb Agreement	Autobiographical Narrative
2	Does Creativity Matter?	Nonfiction: Author's Purpose	Determine Importance	Subject Pronouns Present Tense Verbs Subject-Verb Agreement	Position Paper
3	What Makes a Hero?	Short Stories: Viewpoint	Make Inferences	Present, Past, and Future Tense Subject and Object Pronouns	Response to Literature
4	How Can Knowledge Open Doors?	Nonfiction: Text Structure	Ask Questions	Possessive Words Prepositions Pronoun Agreement	Research Report
5	What Makes Something Frightening?	Short Stories: Plot	Make Connections	Adjectives Adverbs	Short Story
6	How Do the Media Shape the Way People Think?	Nonfiction: Structure of Arguments	Synthesize	Infinitives and Gerunds Compound and Complex Sentences	Persuasive Essay
7	What Holds Us Together? What Keeps Us Apart?	Drama and Poetry	Visualize	Perfect Tenses Participles	Literary Analysis

REVIEWERS

We gratefully acknowledge the many contributions of the following dedicated educators in creating a program that is not only pedagogically sound, but also appealing to and motivating for high school students.

LITERATURE CONSULTANT

Dr. René Saldaña, Jr., Ph.D.

Assistant Professor
Texas Tech University

Dr. Saldaña teaches English and education at the university level and is the author of *The Jumping Tree* (2001) and *Finding Our Way: Stories* (Random House/Wendy Lamb Books, 2003). More recently, several of his stories have appeared in anthologies such as *Face Relations*, *Guys Write for GUYS READ*, *Every Man for Himself*, and *Make Me Over*, and in magazines such as *Boy's Life* and *READ*.

Teacher Reviewers

Felisa Araujo-Rodriguez
English Teacher
Highlands HS
San Antonio, TX

Barbara Barbin
Former HS ESL Teacher
Aldine ISD
Houston, TX

Joseph Berkowitz
ESOL Chairperson
John A. Ferguson Sr. HS
Miami, FL

Dr. LaQuanda Brown-Avery
Instructional Assistant Principal
McNair MS
Decatur, GA

Troy Campbell
Teacher
Lifelong Education Charter
Los Angeles, CA

John Oliver Cox
English Language
Development Teacher
Coronado USD
Coronado, CA

Clairin DeMartini
Reading Coordinator
Clark County SD
Las Vegas, NV

Lori Kite Eli
High School Reading Teacher
Pasadena HS
Pasadena, TX

Debra Elkins
ESOL Teamleader/Teacher
George Bush HS
Fort Bend, IN

Lisa Fretzin
Reading Consultant
Niles North HS
Skokie, IL

Karen H. Gouede
Asst. Principal, ESL
John Browne HS
Flushing, NY

Alison Hyde
ESOL Teacher
Morton Ranch HS
Katy, TX

Patricia James
Reading Specialist
Brevard County
Melbourne Beach, FL

Dr. Anna Leibovich
ESL Teacher
Forest Hills HS
New York, NY

Donna D. Mussulman
Teacher
Belleville West HS
Belleville, IL

Rohini A. Parikh
Educator
Seward Park School
New York, NY

Sally Nan Ruskin
English/Reading Teacher
Braddock SHS
Miami, FL

Pamela Sholly
Teacher
Oceanside USD
Oceanside, CA

Dilmit Singh
Teacher/EL Coordinator
Granada Hills Charter HS
Granada Hills, CA

Amanda E. Stewart
Reading Teacher
Winter Park High School
Winter Park, FL

Beverly Troiano
ESL Teacher
Chicago Discovery Academy
Chicago, IL

Dr. Varavarnee Vaddhanayana
ESOL Coordinator
Clarkston HS
Clarkston, GA

Donna Reese Wallace
Reading Coach
Alternative Education
Orange County
Orlando, FL

Bonnie Woelfel
Reading Specialist
Escondido HS
Escondido, CA

Pian Y. Wong
English Teacher
High School of American Studies
New York, NY

Izumi Yoshioka
English Teacher
Washington Irving HS
New York, NY

Student Reviewers

We also gratefully acknowledge the high school students who read and reviewed selections and tested the Online Coach.

PROGRAM AUTHORS

David W. Moore, Ph.D.
Arizona State University

Dr. Moore taught high school in Arizona public schools before becoming a professor of education. He co-chaired the International Reading Association's Commission on Adolescent Literacy and is actively involved with several professional associations. His thirty-year publication record balances research reports, professional articles, book chapter and books including *Developing Readers and Writers in the Content Areas, Teaching Adolescents Who Struggle with Reading, and Principled Practices for Adolescent Literacy.*

Deborah J. Short, Ph.D.
Center for Applied Linguistics

Dr. Short is a co-developer of the research-validated SIOP Model for sheltered instruction. She has directed scores of studies on English Language Learners and published scholarly articles in *TESOL Quarterly, The Journal of Educational Research, Language Teaching Research*, and many others. Dr. Short also co-wrote a policy report: *Double the Work: Challenges and Solutions to Acquiring Language and Academic Literacy for Adolescent English Language Learners.* She has conducted extensive research on secondary level newcomers programs and on long term English language learners.

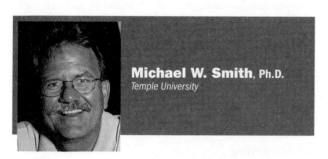

Michael W. Smith, Ph.D.
Temple University

Dr. Michael Smith joined the ranks of college teachers after eleven years teaching high school English. He has won awards for his teaching both at the high school and college level. He contributed to the Common Core State Standards initiative by serving on the Aspects of Text Complexity working group. His research focuses on how readers read and talk about texts and what motivates adolescents' reading and writing both in and out of school. His books include *"Reading Don't Fix No Chevys": Literacy in the Lives of Young Men, Fresh Takes on Teaching Literary Elements: How to Teach What Really Matters About Character, Setting, Point of View, and Theme,* and *Oh, Yeah?! Putting Argument to Work Both in School and Out.*

Alfred W. Tatum, Ph.D.
Northern Illinois University

Dr. Tatum began his career as an eighth-grade teacher and reading specialist. He conducts research on the power of texts and literacy to reshape the life outcomes of striving readers. His research focuses on the literacy development of African American adolescent males. He has served on the National Advisory Reading Committee of the National Assessment of Educational Progress (NAEP). Dr. Tatum's books include *Reading for Their Life: (Re)Building the Textual Lineages of African American Adolescent Males* and *Teaching Reading to Black Adolescent Males: Closing the Achievement Gap.*

CHOICES

EQ **ESSENTIAL QUESTION:**
What Influences a Person's Choices?

Unsafe Journey, near Dhaka, Bangladesh, Amy Helene Johansson. Photograph ©Amy Helene Johansson.

WRITING PROJECT   Good Writing Trait
Focus and Unity

THE ART OF
EXPRESSION

EQ ESSENTIAL QUESTION:
Does Creativity Matter?

A Boy Plays the Violin at Sulaimaniya Music Institute, Sulaimaniya, Iraq, 2009, Julie Adnan. Photograph ©REUTERS/Julie Adnan.

WRITING PROJECT

Good Writing Trait
Focus and Unity

THE HERO WITHIN

EQ **ESSENTIAL QUESTION:**
What Makes a Hero?

Rescuer Air Lifting Injured Hiker, Cumbria, England, 2005, Ashley Cooper. Photograph ©Ashley Cooper/Corbis.

WRITING PROJECT

**Good Writing Trait
Voice and Style**

UNIT 4

OPENING
DOORS

EQ ESSENTIAL QUESTION:
How Can Knowledge Open Doors?

A Buddhist Monk at the Angkor Wat Temple Complex, Siem Reap, Cambodia, Tino Soriano. Photograph ©Tino Soriano/National Geographic Stock.

WRITING PROJECT

Good Writing Trait
Development of Ideas

FEAR
THIS!

EQ ESSENTIAL QUESTION:
What Makes Something Frightening?

An Oceanic Whitetip Shark Swims Past a Diver, The Bahamas, Brian J. Skerry. Photograph ©Brian Skerry/National Geographic Stock.

WRITING PROJECT

Good Writing Trait
Organization

ARE YOU BUYING IT?

EQ ESSENTIAL QUESTION:
How Do the Media Shape the Way People Think?

Young Woman in Front of Soft Drink Advertising Sign, Ho Chi Minh City, Vietnam, Stu Smucker. Photograph ©Stu Smucker/Lonely Planet Images/Getty Images.

WRITING PROJECT

**Good Writing Trait
Voice and Style**

Genre Focus
Drama and Poetry

Reading Strategy
Visualize

WHERE WE
BELONG

EQ ESSENTIAL QUESTION:
What Holds Us Together? What Keeps Us Apart?

Design Within Reach, Heather Liebensohn. Photograph ©Heather Liebensohn.

Language and Learning Handbook
Language, Learning, Communication

Reading Handbook
Reading, Fluency, Vocabulary

Writing Handbook
Writing Process, Traits, Conventions

LITERATURE

Bicultural Tablesetting, 1998, Rolando Briseño. Serigraph, private collection.

A Refugee Near the Pakistani Border, Afghanistan, 1983, Reza Deghati. Photograph ©Reza.

EQ ESSENTIAL QUESTION:

What Influences a Person's Choices?

Everything is determined, the beginning as well as the end, by forces over which we have no control.

—ALBERT EINSTEIN

With every experience, you alone are painting your own canvas, thought by thought, choice by choice.

—OPRAH WINFREY

Critical Viewing ▷
A woman balances between the cars of a moving train in Bangladesh, Asia, on the day before an important religious holiday. What may have influenced her choice to take this life-threatening risk?

CHOICES

EQ ESSENTIAL QUESTION:
What Influences a Person's Choices?

Study the Facts

People make choices every day. What causes some people to make good choices? What influences others to make poor choices or harmful choices? Look at these facts:

Teen Choices	FEMALE	MALE
High school students who participate in sports**	32%	45%
High school students who said they had carried a weapon in the past 30 days**	7%	27%
High school students who said they had registered and voted*	21%	27%
High school students who said they had driven after drinking alcohol in the past 30 days**	9%	15%
High school students who said they had taken part in a physical fight in the past 12 months**	25%	41%
High school seniors who participated each month in community affairs or volunteer work***	39%	28%

* Data for 2002   ** Data for 2003   *** Data for 2004   Source: U.S. Dept. of Education, National Center for Education Statistics: *Youth Indicators 2005.*

Analyze and Debate

1. According to the data, young men and young women seem to be making different choices. What general statements can you make about these differences? What might influence a young man to behave differently from a young woman?

2. Which is the greatest influence on a person's choices—family, friends, culture, money, or wealth?

Talk with a group. Explain your opinions and support your ideas with evidence from your own experience.

EQ ESSENTIAL QUESTION

In this unit, you will explore the **Essential Question** in class through reading, discussion, research, and writing. Keep thinking about the question outside of school, too.

① Plan a Project

TV Talk Show

In this unit, you'll be producing a TV talk show about the Essential Question. Choose the kind of show, host, guests, and set to produce. To get started, watch a few different TV talk shows. When listening to a partner read, notice if you can understand the sound of each word. Then listen again to hear how your partner's intonation changes. Look for

- how the interviewer introduces each guest
- whether the interviewer reads from notes, talks from memory, or takes notes
- whether the guest and interviewer look directly at each other
- how the parts of the show relate to the topic.

myNGconnect.com
- ▶ Planning forms
- ▶ Scheduler
- ▶ Talk show sites
- ▶ Interview forms
- ▶ Rubric

Study Skills Start planning your talk show. Use the forms on myNGconnect.com.

② Choose More to Read

These readings provide different answers to the Essential Question. Choose a book and online selections to read during the unit.

Breaking Through
by Francisco Jiménez

Francisco "Panchito" Jiménez and his family worked day after day as migrant farm workers. Panchito was a good student and he wanted a better life. But his father wanted him to stay and help his family. How could Panchito please his father without giving up his future?
▶ NONFICTION

The Trojan Horse
by Justine and Ron Fontes

The beautiful Helen is married to the King of Sparta. When Helen runs away with a Trojan prince, her husband declares war on Troy! After ten years, the battle seems to have no end. But the Greek soldier Odysseus has a secret plan to defeat the Trojans. Will it work?
▶ GRAPHIC CLASSIC

Miracle's Boys
by Jacqueline Woodson

Ty'ree, Charlie, and Lafayette are Miracle's sons. When Miracle dies, the boys have to keep their family together. Staying together isn't easy. Charlie goes to jail, and Ty'ree has to work full-time to support them. How can Miracle's boys survive when so much is against them?
▶ NOVEL

myNGconnect.com
- ◐ Read biographies of celebrities and teens who have made difficult choices.
- ◐ Take a personality test to find out what traits and talents might influence your choices.
- ◐ Play a game to explore the consequences of different choices.

USING READING STRATEGIES

When you read fiction or nonfiction, you can use strategies to understand different parts of the text. Reading strategies are tools for thinking that help you interact with the text and take control of your reading comprehension.

Reading Strategies

Plan and Monitor	Set a purpose before you read.
	Make predictions and then read on to confirm them.
	Figure out confusing text by rereading or reading on.
Visualize	Picture sensory details in your mind.
Make Inferences	Combine what you read with what you know to figure out what the author doesn't say directly.
Ask Questions	Ask about things you don't know. Look for clues in the text.
Synthesize	Bring several ideas together to understand something new.
Make Connections	Connect what you read with what you have read or experienced.
Determine Importance	Identify and summarize the most important ideas.

Reading Handbook, page 733

Now read how one student applied reading strategies with this selection. As you read, pay attention to the reading strategies you use.

DEMO TEXT

HEALTHY CHOICES, HEALTHY TEENS
by Alicia Ramos

What Happened to Nina?

During PE today, a guest speaker discussed "Healthy Choices, Healthy Teens." Everyone usually messes around during health talks, but a lot more people paid attention this time. I think it's because of what happened to Nina.

Nina Kim is our school valedictorian, varsity softball player, and homecoming princess. In other words, she's smart, sporty, and gorgeous. Her life has always seemed so perfect. Then everything changed. Last week, Nina collapsed in the middle of the crowded girls' locker room. By the next morning, word was out: she was in the Intensive Care Unit being treated for an eating disorder and related health problems.

Before I read, I can **plan and monitor**. I preview the **title** and **headings**. I predict the text will be about "peer pressure."

I can use **details** to **visualize**, or picture, what Nina is like.

"They said she might die," my friend Ben said. "Is that true?"

I didn't know for sure. I also didn't know how someone with the perfect life could have made so many horrible choices.

Under the Influence

According to the speaker today, teens don't make important choices on their own. Whether they know it or not, many of their decisions—including how they look at themselves—are influenced by a variety of people and things, including family, friends, and the media.

Parents complain that kids never listen, but this is far from true. From a young age, children pick up signals from relatives about weight, appearance, and what makes someone attractive. They see how adults view their own bodies and hear the positive and negative comments they make about others. As a result, kids often make decisions about diet and appearance based on the qualities their own parents value.

Peers are another powerful force that affects teen decisions. According to statistics, 40–60% of teenage girls diet whether they are overweight or not. The everyday choices they make about food and exercise affect how their friends think and act. Even if peer pressure is not verbal, or spoken aloud, teens are influenced just by looking at the people around them. According to the Journal of Health and Social Behavior, teens in schools where the majority of students have a high body mass index do not feel a strong pressure to diet. But if the average body mass index of students at a school is low, kids are much more likely to diet.

Another major influence on teens is the media, including TV, movies, magazines, music, and blogs. The average teen watches 30 hours of TV a week. After spending 1560 hours a year watching unrealistic images of super-beautiful celebrities on TV, many teens are not satisfied by their own reflection in the mirror. More than 90% of girls 15–17 want to change at least one part of their appearance—usually their weight. For up to 11 million young people like Nina, this distorted image of beauty can lead to serious eating disorders.

Making Your Own Choices

The thought of so many outside influences on teens can be intimidating—but it doesn't have to be. Instead of accepting what the media has to say about beauty and self-worth, consider the qualities you value and find attractive. Have discussions with friends and family about how their attitudes affect your decisions. Most of all, use your own influence to encourage others to make healthy choices. Peer pressure isn't always negative. If more teens speak up, kids like Nina Kim might find the support they need to feel good about themselves—inside and out.

Based on what I read and know, I can make an inference that the writer had looked up to Nina.

I can ask questions about words or ideas. Clues in the text help me figure out what they mean.

I can synthesize the facts here and conclude that teens feel pressured to look like the people they see.

Sometimes, I wish I looked like people on T.V. I can make a connection to how many teens feel about themselves.

I can determine importance by finding the main idea: people should stand up to peer pressure.

Now let's learn about short stories. One way to find out how stories work is to think about how you make sense of a little story like this one. Read "On the Bus."

On the Bus

The first week of school was always a tough one for ninth-graders, at least for most ninth-graders. But not, it seemed, for James. From the first day of school he waltzed right to the back of the bus, a spot usually reserved for juniors and seniors. He talked with everyone and made fun of the other ninth-graders who shot quick looks to the back of the bus and then sank quietly into their seats up front.

Catherine had always admired James a little. She'd always been so shy that anybody who would draw attention to himself or herself would earn a little of Catherine's admiration. Because this was her first year at public school after having gone to a small church school all the way through eighth grade, she felt especially afraid to speak out.

Catherine didn't really like James, though. They'd lived in the same neighborhood for years, yet he hardly seemed to recognize her. And when he did, it was for all the wrong reasons. Once in eighth grade he saw her washing cars for a church fundraiser. He

was walking past her church with a group of friends and he shouted, "Hey, everybody, look. It's little Miss Missionary." Catherine didn't mind people's knowing that she was really religious because church was the most important thing in her life. It was just the way he had said it.

One day that first week James was doing more bragging than usual. He had just gotten the hottest new digital audio player. He came on the bus doing exaggerated dances and playing air guitar to songs he must have been hearing. Even the seniors in the back were impressed, or at least they pretended to be. Stefone, a kid who had a reputation as being a tough guy, asked James if he could hear a song. James handed him his player. Stefone listened, nodded his head, and looked hard at James. "This thing is great. I'm glad I got one. Too bad you lost yours. You understand what I'm saying? Too bad you lost yours." James slumped down in his seat.

Catherine saw the whole thing and felt queasy, or sick to her stomach. She looked at James and then at Stefone. Stefone stared hard at her and said in a threatening voice, "The poor kid lost his new toy. Don't worry about it, little girl. You wouldn't want to lose anything of yours, would you?"

■ Connect Reading to Your Life

What will Catherine do? First, think of all the possible choices she could make.

> I think she's going to try to get Stefone to give it back.

> I don't think so. I think she won't do anything, just like he said.

1. Catherine could _____
2. Or _____
3. Or _____

Now that you have thought about the alternatives, which one do you **predict** she will do? Explain your answer. Also tell what you want to know about Catherine that would give you more confidence in your prediction.

Focus Strategy ▶ Plan and Monitor

The kind of educated guesses you just made about Catherine and James are called **predictions**. In your life, you make predictions all the time. You predict how your teacher will react if you are late to class. You predict how a friend will like the gift you gave. You do this by thinking about what people are like, what they have done before, and what the current situation is like. Sometimes people surprise you, so you need to revise, or change, your predictions.

Making predictions is a key part of **monitoring**—or checking—your understanding as you read.

■ Your Job as a Reader

When you read, you first figure out what it is you are reading. You look at the title, a little of the text, and maybe the illustrations to figure out that you're reading a story. Then you pay attention to the characters, setting, and plot. For example, you had to learn as much as you could about Catherine in order to predict what she would do. If there were more to this little story, you would then read to find out whether your predictions were accurate.

Academic Vocabulary
- **predict** *v.*, to tell in advance; **prediction** *n.*, a statement of what someone thinks will happen
- **monitor** *v.*, to keep track of, to check

Reading Strategies

▶ Plan and Monitor
- Determine Importance
- Make Inferences
- Ask Questions
- Make Connections
- Synthesize
- Visualize

■ Unpack the Thinking Process

Characterization

Authors leave clues to let readers know what their characters are like. This is called characterization . For example, an author may include:

- **describing words** to tell what a character looks like
- **dialogue** to show how characters express themselves
- **actions** to show just what a character does
- **reactions** of other characters to show the impact of a character's actions.

Setting

Characters make choices because of who they are and the situations they are in. That's why the setting —where and when a story takes place—is so important. "On the Bus" is set during Catherine's first week at a public high school. You know that she is likely to act differently during her first week than in her senior year. If you notice the setting and use what you know, you can predict what she is likely to do.

Plot

The choices characters make determine the action in many stories. The way that authors select and arrange the choices and action is called the plot . These choices are affected by what the characters are like as well as when and where they live.

Plan and Monitor

Use the elements of short stories—character, setting, and plot—to plan and monitor your reading of short stories. Here's a way to do that:

Prediction Chart

I Notice	I Know	I Predict	Prediction Confirmed?
The title "On the Bus" The first sentence: "The first week of school..."	This sounds like a back-to-school story.	I think there will be some problem related to starting school.	[ ] yes [ ] no
Catherine is new to public school. She used to go to a small church school.	Public high schools are very different than small private schools.	Catherine will have a hard time adjusting.	[ ] yes [ ] no

Elements of Literature

characterization *n.,* the techniques an author uses to show what the characters are like

setting *n.,* the time and place of a story

plot *n.,* the series of events that make up a story

As you read, keep track of your predictions. Good readers actively keep track of their thinking while they read. Think about whether your predictions are confirmed, or whether you need to revise them based on new information. If you find that you're lost, take time to **clarify**, or get clear, so that you can keep reading. Here are just a few ways that you can get back on track:

- **reread** (or keep reading—sometimes you just need to read a bit more to know what's happening)
- **slow down** and read closely (or read faster—sometimes that helps)
- **paraphrase**, or say what's happening in your own words.

■ Try an Experiment

Pretend that the first part of the story is written like this:

DEMO TEXT *Take 2*

On the Bus

The first week of school was always a tough one for ninth-graders, at least for most ninth-graders. But not, it seemed, for James. From the first day of school he waltzed right to the back of the bus, a spot usually reserved for juniors and seniors. He talked with everyone and made fun of the other ninth-graders who shot quick looks to the back of the bus and then sank quietly into their seats up front.

Catherine had always admired James. People seemed to notice him. She wondered if they noticed her. She hoped so. After all, she had spent most of her savings to buy the trendiest new clothes she could find. This was her first year at public school after having gone to a small church school through eighth grade, and she wanted the new kids to think she was cool.

Think, Pair, Share Answer these questions with a partner.

1. What details about Catherine have changed? What do those new details tell you about the kind of person she is? Explain your answer.

2. Look back at your list of possible choices Catherine could make. Which one do you predict she will choose now? How do you expect the story to change if she does that?

Academic Vocabulary
- **clarify** v., to make clear and understandable, to get rid of confusion

☑ **Monitor Comprehension**

Characterization
What clues do authors give to help you understand characters? How do these help you make predictions?

EQ ## What Influences a Person's Choices?
Explore the effect of family and friends on choices.

Make a Connection

Rank Reasons Often our families, friends, and values or beliefs direct our actions. Read the **Ranking Chart** to see a list of reasons people help others. Rank each reason from 1 to 5 (1 means you agree with that reason the most). Then discuss these questions with a partner: Which reasons ranked highest? How did you rank your friends and family?

RANKING CHART Reasons for Helping Others	Rank (1 to 5)
"My parents taught me to do it."	_____
"My friends will respect me more."	_____
"Good works look good on a résumé or college application."	_____
"Changing the world starts with me."	_____

Learn Key Vocabulary

Study the Words Pronounce each word and learn its meaning. You may also want to look up the definitions in the Glossary.

● Academic Vocabulary

Key Words	Examples
● **affect** (u-**fekt**) *verb* ▸ pages 19, 35	When you **affect** something, you change it in some way. You can **affect** the environment by using more or less water.
● **conflict** (**kon**-flikt) *noun* ▸ pages 14, 25	When people or things are in **conflict**, they do not agree. A story's **conflict** is the main problem.
● **contribute** (kun-**tri**-byūt) *verb* ▸ page 30	When you **contribute**, you give something with others. Students **contribute** ideas to a group discussion. *Synonym:* give; *Antonym:* take
disrespect (dis-ri-**spekt**) *noun* ▸ pages 19, 25	When you are rude to someone, you show them **disrespect**. When children yell at their parents, they show **disrespect**. *Synonym:* rudeness; *Antonyms:* courtesy, respect
● **generation** (je-nu-**rā**-shun) *noun* ▸ pages 31, 33, 35	People who are about the same age belong to the same **generation**. We can learn a lot from our parents' **generation**.
● **motivation** (mō-tu-**vā**-shun) *noun* ▸ pages 29, 35	**Motivation** is the reason you act or think in a certain way. My **motivation** for volunteering is to help my neighbors. *Synonyms:* reason, drive
privilege (**pri**-vu-lij) *noun* ▸ page 19	A **privilege** is something special that someone is allowed to have, be, or do. The football team gets the **privilege** of leaving school early on game days. *Synonym:* favor
responsible (ri-**spon**-su-bul) *adjective* ▸ pages 18, 35	When you are **responsible** for something, it is your duty to take care of it. If you borrow a pen, you are **responsible** for returning it when you are done.

Practice the Words Write a sentence for each Key Vocabulary word. Then cover or erase the Key Vocabulary word and have a partner tell the word that fits.

Example: *Freedom of speech is a right, but driving a car is a privilege.*

BEFORE READING **The Good Samaritan**

short story by René Saldaña, Jr.

Reading Strategies

▶ **Plan and Monitor**
· Determine Importance
· Make Inferences
· Ask Questions
· Make Connections
· Sythesize
· Visualize

Analyze Plot

Plot is the sequence of events in a story. The story begins with the **exposition**, which introduces the characters and setting. Most plots have these parts:

- The **conflict** is the main problem that the characters face.
- **Complications** are events that make the conflict worse and lead to the climax.
- The **climax** is the turning point, or the most important event.
- The **resolution** is how the story ends and the problem is solved.

Look Into the Text

The characters make an agreement.

> Mr. Sánchez told us, "If you help clean up the yard, you boys can use the pool any time you want so long as one of us is here." . . . After a hard day's work cleaning his yard, I so looked forward to taking a dip. I'd even worn my trunks under my work clothes. Then Mr. Sánchez said, "Come by tomorrow. I don't want you fellas to track all this dirt into the pool."

How might this statement lead to a conflict between the characters?

Focus Strategy ▶ Plan and Monitor

Most stories include characters who have a conflict that will be resolved in some way. Events almost always lead to a climax. Use this information to **plan your reading**. Then as you read, make predictions, or guesses, about what will happen later in the story's plot.

HOW TO MAKE AND CONFIRM PREDICTIONS

Focus Strategy

Before you read a story:

1. **Read the story's title.** Also, look at any section introductions. You might find clues about the story's plot and characters.

2. **Look at art and quotations in large type.** They might contain clues about story events.

3. **Make predictions.** Put the clues together and predict what will happen next and what the characters will do, or how they will change.

4. **Confirm or change predictions.** As you read, notice details that either confirm your prediction or make you change your mind.

Prediction Chart

My Predictions	Confirmed or Changed Predictions
I think the story is about a basketball player and a man that he often helps.	I now think this story is about a conflict between a teenager and an older man.

René Saldaña, Jr.
(1968–)

> **Students teach me new things about my stories all the time. They have amazing insights.**

As a teenager, **René Saldaña, Jr.**, never guessed that he would become a writer. "In school, I hated literature!" It wasn't until college that Saldaña began to appreciate literature. "My friends taught me. They introduced me to books like *The Great Gatsby* and *The House on Mango Street*. But they weren't just reading; they were writing, too."

Still, Saldaña didn't begin writing until he became an English teacher. "I wanted my students to know that they could be writers. But they needed examples of writing that they could relate to, so I began to tell them my own stories." These stories grew into Saldaña's first novel, *The Jumping Tree*. The book is about a teenage boy struggling with what it means to be a real man. "The Good Samaritan" is about that same boy becoming an adult. "He is learning his own place in the world. He is realizing that he is part of a community."

Today, as a college professor, Dr. Saldaña continues to inspire students to write about their lives. "One of my favorite writers once

René Saldaña, Jr.

said that wherever there is a group of people, there is a group of writers. I've always believed that."

myNGconnect.com

◥ Read an excerpt from *The Jumping Tree*.
◥ Learn more about *The Great Gatsby* and *The House on Mango Street*.

The Good Samaritan

by René Saldaña, Jr.

I know he's in there, I thought. I saw the curtains of his bedroom move, only a little, yes, but they moved.

Yesterday Orlie told me, "Come over tomorrow afternoon. We'll **hang out** by the pool."

I rang the doorbell again. Then I knocked.

The door creaked open. The afternoon light crept into the dark living room inch by slow inch. Mrs. Sánchez, Orlie's mom, stuck her head through the narrow opening, her body hidden behind the door. "Hi, Rey, how can I help you?"

"Ah, Mrs. Sánchez, is Orlando here?" I tried looking past her but only saw a few pictures hanging on the wall. One of the Sánchez family all dressed up fancy and smiling, standing in front of a gray marble background.

"No, he's not. He went with his father to **Mission**."

"Oh, because Orlando said he would be here, and told me to come over."

"They won't be back until later tonight," she said. "You can come by tomorrow and see if he's here. You know how it is in the summer. He and his dad are always doing work here and there. Come back tomorrow, but call first."

"It's just that he said I could come by and swim in your pool. *Dijo*, 'Tomorrow, come over. I'll be here. We'll go swimming.' "

"I'm sorry he told you that, but without him or my husband here, you won't be able to use the pool," *me dijo Mrs. Sánchez*.

"Okay," I said.

"Maybe tomorrow?"

"Yeah, maybe." ▆

1 Plot/Predict
Based on what you've read so far, which characters do you predict might become involved in a **conflict**? Add this to your Prediction Chart.

Key Vocabulary
- **conflict** *n.*, disagreement or argument

In Other Words
hang out relax together
Mission a city at the southern tip of Texas
Dijo He said (in Spanish)
me dijo Mrs. Sánchez Mrs. Sánchez told me (in Spanish)

But there was no maybe about it. I wouldn't be coming back. Because I knew that Orlando was in the house, he just didn't want to hang out. ***Bien codo con su pool.*** **Plain stingy.** And tricky. This guy invited me and a few others over all summer to help his dad with some yard work because Mr. Sánchez told us, "If you help clean up the yard, you boys can use the pool any time you want so long as one of us is here." And we cleaned up his yard. On that hot day the water that smelled of chlorine looked delicious to me. And after a hard day's work cleaning his yard, I so looked forward to **taking a dip**. I'd even worn my trunks under my work clothes. Then Mr. Sánchez said, "Come by tomorrow. I don't want you fellas to track all this dirt into the pool." **2**

2 Language
Authors use language in ways that help us picture words. What does this paragraph help you see, hear, smell, taste, or touch?

◁ Critical Viewing: Design
The two shadows in this photo appear to be tilted. What does this **composition** make you think about the relationship between the two people who cast the shadows?

In Other Words
Bien codo con su pool. He's selfish about his pool. (Spanish slang)
Plain stingy. Not generous at all.
taking a dip going swimming
composition combination of images and ideas

"We can go home and shower and be back," said Hernando.

"No, *mejor que regresen mañana*. I'll be here tomorrow and we can swim. After lunch, okay. For sure we'll do it tomorrow," said Mr. Sánchez. **3**

The following day he was there, but he was headed out right after lunch and he didn't feel safe leaving us behind without supervision. "If one of you drowns, your parents will be angry at me and . . ." He didn't say it, but he didn't need to. One of our parents could sue him. And he needed that like I needed another F in my Geometry I class! Or, we figured out later, he could have just said, "I used you **saps** to do my dirty work. And I lied about the pool, suckers!"

I don't know why we hadn't learned our lesson. Twice before he had **gypped** us this way of our time and effort. Always **dangling the carrot in front of our eyes**, then snatching it away last second. **4**

One of those times he promised us soft drinks and snacks if we helped clean up a yard across the street from his house. It wasn't his yard to worry about, but I guess he just didn't like to see the weeds growing as tall as dogs. What if he had company? What would they think? And he was **angling for** a position on the school board. How could a *político* live in such filth!

3 Language
Some of the characters switch between English and Spanish. What can you guess about their community?

4 Plot/Confirm Prediction
Which characters will have a conflict? Do you want to change your prediction?

In Other Words

mejor que regresen mañana it's better if you come back tomorrow
saps foolish kids
gypped cheated, robbed (slang)
dangling the carrot in front of our eyes getting us to work by promising a reward

angling for making plans to get
político politician (in Spanish)

Well, we did get a soft drink and chips, only it was one two-liter bottle of Coke and one bag of chips for close to ten of us. We had no cups, and the older, stronger boys **got dibs on** most of the eats. "I didn't know there'd be so many of you," he said. "Well, share. And thanks. You all are good, strong boys."

The next time was real hard labor. He said, "Help me dig these holes here, then we can put up some basketball rims. Once the cement dries on the court itself, you all can come over and play anytime since it's kind of your court too. That is, if you help me dig the holes."

> ## "I didn't know there'd be so many of you," he said. "Well, share."

And we did. We dug and dug and dug for close to six hours straight until we got done, passing on the shovel from one of us to the next. But we got it done. We had our court. Mr. Sánchez **kept his word**. He reminded us we could come over to play anytime, and we took special care not to **dunk** and grab hold of the rim. Even the shortest kid could practically dunk it because the baskets were so low. But we'd seen the rims all bent down at the different yards at school. And we didn't want that for *our* court. 5

In Other Words

got dibs on had the first choice of
kept his word did what he had promised
dunk slam the basketball into the hoop

5 **Plot/Predict**
Mr. Sánchez keeps his promise. Do you think his relationship with Rey will change? Explain.

Monitor Comprehension

Summarize
How have Rey's feelings about Mr. Sánchez changed over time?

Predict

Will Mr. Sánchez keep his word to the boys who helped him?

One day, we wanted to play a **little three on three**. After knocking on the different doors several times and getting no answer, we figured the Sánchez family had gone out. We decided that it'd be okay to play. We weren't going to do anything wrong. The court was far enough from the house that we couldn't possibly break a window. And Mr. Sánchez had said we could come over any time we wanted. It was *our* court, after all. Those were his words exactly.

A little later in the afternoon, Mr. Sánchez drove up in his truck, honking and honking at us. "Here they come. Maybe Orlando and Marty can play with us," someone said.

Pues, it was not to be. The truck had just **come to a standstill** when Mr. Sánchez **shot out of** the driver's side. He ran up to us, waving his hands in the air like a crazy man, first saying, then screaming, "What are you guys doing here? You all can't be here when I'm not here." 6

"But you told us we could come over anytime. And we knocked and knocked, and we were being very careful."

"It doesn't matter. You all shouldn't be here when I'm not home. What if you had broken something?" he said.

"But we didn't," I said.

"But if you had, then who would have been **responsible** for paying to replace it? I'm sure every one of you would have denied breaking anything."

"***Este vato!***" said Hernando.

"*Vato*? Is that what you called me? I'm no street punk, no hoodlum. I'll have you know, I've worked my whole life, and I won't be called a *vato*. It's Mr. Sánchez. Got that? And you boys know what—from now on, you are not allowed to come here whether I'm home or not! You all

6 **Plot**
An event that makes the conflict worse is called a complication. What complication happens here?

Key Vocabulary
responsible *adj.*, have the duty of taking care of

In Other Words
little three on three small game of basketball with three players on each team
Pues Well (in Spanish)
come to a standstill stopped
shot out of jumped quickly from
Este vato! This dude! This guy! (Spanish slang)

messed it up for yourselves. You've shown me so much **disrespect** today you don't deserve to play on my court. It was a **privilege** and not **a right**, and you messed it up. Now leave!" **7**

Hernando, who was **fuming**, said, "*Orale*, guys, let's go." He took the ball from one of the smaller boys and began to run toward the nearest basket. He slowed down the closer he came to the basket and leapt in the air. I'd never seen him jump with such grace. He floated from the foul line, his long hair like wings, all the way to the basket. He grabbed the ball in both his hands and let go of it at the last moment. Instead of dunking the ball, he let it shoot up to the sky; then he wrapped his fingers around the rim and pulled down as hard as he could, hanging on for a few seconds. Then the rest of us walked after him, **dejected**. He hadn't bent the rim even a millimeter. **8** Eventually Orlie talked us into going back when his dad wasn't home. His baby brother, Marty, was small and slow, and Orlie wanted some competition on the court.

7 Plot
Mr. Sánchez thinks the boys have shown him disrespect. How do you think the boys feel about this?

8 Plot
How does Hernando's reaction to Mr. Sánchez **affect** the conflict in the story?

Key Vocabulary
disrespect *n.*, rudeness
privilege *n.*, something special that someone can have, be, or do
• **affect** *v.*, to change or influence

In Other Words
a right something you were allowed to do without questions or conditions
fuming very angry, furious
Orale Come on (Spanish slang)
dejected feeling sad and disappointed

Today was it for me, though. I made up my mind never to go back to the Sánchezes'. I walked to the little store for a Fanta Orange. That and a grape Popsicle would cool me down. I sat on the bench outside, finished off the drink, returned the bottle for my nickel refund, and headed for home.

9 Plot/Predict
Do you think Rey will keep this promise to himself? What evidence in the text makes you think so?

Monitor Comprehension

Confirm Prediction
Was your prediction accurate? If not, why? What happened that you did not expect?

Predict

Mr. Sánchez needs help again. What will Rey do?

As soon as I walked through our front door, my mother said, "*Mi'jo*, you need to go pick up your brother at summer school. He missed the bus."

"Again? He probably missed it on purpose, *'Amá*. He's always walking over to Leo's Grocery to talk to his little girlfriends, then he calls when he needs a ride." I turned toward the bedroom.

"Come back here," she said. So I turned and took a seat at the table. "Have you forgotten the times we had to go pick you up? Your brother always went with us, no matter what time it was."

"Yeah, but I was doing school stuff. Football, band. He's in summer school just **piddling his time away**!"

She looked at me as she brushed sweat away from her face with the back of her hand and said, "Just go pick him up, and hurry home. On the way back, stop at Circle Seven and buy some tortillas. There's money on the table."

I shook my head **in disgust**. Here I was, already a senior, having to be my baby brother's **chauffeur**. 🔟

I'd driven halfway to Leo's Grocery when I saw Mr. Sánchez's truck up ahead by the side of the road. I could **just make him out** sitting under the shade of his truck. Every time he heard a car coming his way, he'd raise his head slightly, try to catch the driver's attention by staring at him, then he'd hang his head again when the car didn't stop.

I slowed down as I approached. Could he tell it was me driving? When he looked up at my car, I could swear he almost smiled, thinking he had been saved. 🔢 He had been leaning his head between his bent knees, and I could tell he was tired; his white shirt stuck to him because of all the sweat. His sock on one leg was bunched up at his ankle like a

🔟 Plot
What do Rey's comments and thoughts tell you about how he feels about helping his brother? How is this similar to his feelings about helping Mr. Sánchez?

🔢 Predict
Do you think Rey will stop the car? Add this to your Chart.

In Other Words
Mi'jo My son (in Spanish)
'Amá Mom (in Spanish)
piddling his time away wasting his time
in disgust feeling angry and irritated
chauffeur paid driver
just make him out see him a little

The Good Samaritan **21**

carnation. He had the whitest legs I'd ever seen on a Mexican. Whiter than even my dad's. I kept on looking straight; that is, I **made like** I was looking ahead, not a care in the world, but out of the corner of my eye I saw that he had a flat tire, that he had gotten two of the lug nuts off but hadn't gotten to the others, that the crowbar lay half on his other foot and half on the ground beside him, that his hair was matted by sweat to his forehead. 🔢12

I knew that look. I'd probably looked just like that digging those holes for *our* basketball court, cleaning up his yard and the one across the street from his house. I wondered if he could use a cold two-liter Coke right about now! If he was dreaming of taking a dip in his pool!

I drove on. No way was I going to help him out again! Let him do his own dirty work for once. He could stay out there and melt in this heat for all I cared. And besides, someone else will stop, I thought. Someone who doesn't know him like I do.

> # No way was I going to help him out again!

And I knew that when Mr. Sánchez got home, he'd stop at my house on his walk around the *barrio*. My dad would be watering the plants, **his evening ritual** to relax from a hard day at work, and Mr. Sánchez would **mention in passing** that I had probably not seen him by the side of the road so I hadn't stopped to help him out; "Kids today," he would say to my dad, "not a care in the world, their heads up in the clouds somewhere." My dad would call me out and ask me to tell him and Mr. Sánchez why I hadn't helped out a neighbor when he needed it most. 🔢13 I'd say, to both of them, "That was you? I thought you and Orlie were in Mission taking care of some business, so it never occurred to me to stop to help a neighbor. Geez, I'm so sorry." Or I could say, "You know, I was in

12 Plot
Mr. Sánchez needs help again. How does this situation add to the conflict between Rey and him?

13 Plot/Character
What does Rey imagine about his dad? How does this add to the conflict he feels?

In Other Words
carnation folded-looking flower
made like pretended
barrio neighborhood (in Spanish)
his evening ritual the same thing he did every night

mention in passing say in a way that seemed unimportant

such a hurry to pick up my brother in La Joya that I didn't even notice you by the side of the road." 14

I'd be off the hook. Anyways, why should I be the one to **extend a helping hand** when he's done every one of us in the barrio wrong in one way or another! He deserves to sweat a little. A taste of his own bad medicine. Maybe he'll learn a lesson.

But I remembered the look in his eyes as I drove past him. That same tired look my father had when he'd get home from work and he didn't have the strength to take off his boots. My father always looked like he'd been working for centuries without any rest. He'd sit there in front of the television on his favorite green vinyl sofa chair and stare at whatever was on TV. He'd sit there for an hour before he could move, before he could eat his supper and take his shower, that same look on his face Mr. Sánchez had just now.

What if this were my dad **stranded** on the side of the road? I'd want someone to stop for him.

"My one **good deed** for today," I told myself. "And I'm doing it for my dad really, not for Mr. Sánchez."

14 Plot/Predict
Do you think the scene Rey is imagining will really take place? Explain.

In Other Words
I'd be off the hook. No one could blame me.
extend a helping hand help him
stranded left alone without help
good deed helpful act

I **made a U-turn**, drove back to where he was still sitting, turned around again, and pulled up behind him. [15]

"I thought that was you, Rey," he said. He wiped at his forehead with his shirtsleeve. "And when you drove past, I thought you hadn't seen me. Thank goodness you stopped. I've been here for close to forty-five minutes and nobody's stopped to help. Thank goodness you did. I just can't get the tire off."

Thank my father, I thought. If it weren't for my father, you'd still be out here.

I had that tire changed in no time. All the while Mr. Sánchez stood behind me and a bit to my left saying, "Yes, thank God you came by. Boy, it's hot out here. You're a good boy, Rey. You'll make a good man. How about some help there?"

[15] **Plot**
Why does Rey make his decision?

In Other Words
made a U-turn turned the car around

"No, I've got it," I answered. "I'm almost done."

"*Oyes*, Rey, what if you come over tomorrow night to my house? I'm having a little barbecue for some important people here in town. You should come over. We're even going to do some swimming. What do you say?"

I tightened the last of the nuts, replaced the jack, the flat tire, and the crowbar in the bed of his truck, looked at him, and said, "Thanks. But I'll be playing football with the *vatos*." 16 ❖

16 Plot/Character
Why does Rey refuse Mr. Sánchez's invitation?

ANALYZE The Good Samaritan

1. **Recall and Interpret** What does Rey do when Mr. Sánchez needs help at the end of the story? Were you surprised by Rey's response? Explain.

2. **Vocabulary** Do any characters show disrespect in the story? Explain.

3. **Analyze Plot** With a partner, create a map of the events in the story. Use a **Story Map** to describe the major events that lead to the main conflict.

   Story Map

Rey does yard work for Mr. Sánchez.	▶	The Sánchezes don't keep their promise.	▶	

4. **Focus Strategy Make and Confirm Predictions** Reread the **Prediction Chart** that you began on page 11. Show a partner the details in the story that confirmed your predictions or made you change them.

⟲ Return to the Text

Reread and Write How does Saldãna draw on the parable of the Good Samaritan for this story? Support your answer with evidence from the text.

In Other Words
Oyes Listen (in Spanish)

Don't Go Gentle Into That Good Expressway
by Luis J. Rodríguez

They say people in New York City are cold,
that they enter like the blackness of night
and rip into you when you shine with the
weakness of a smile. They say, you can't smile
5   in New York City because it could be
a death warrant. A kind word is a likely
ticket to a back-street mugging. Nobody
cares in New York City.

But I don't know . . . the city seemed refreshing
10   to me. People were upfront. They yelled,
they laughed, they had no qualms about your worth.
I could walk these streets and face anyone and be
crazier than the craziest dude
and ride the subways looking untouchable
15   and nobody knew whether to talk to me
or walk away. In most cities
madness seethes below the skin.
In New York City, it storms through the eyes.

And, at least once, New York City
20   showed me some heart.

In Other Words

be a death warrant invite someone to hurt you
upfront honest and real
had no qualms about did not worry about
seethes grows stronger, starts to boil

bobtail truck a small delivery truck
summon call for
getting sued being blamed if he got hurt
reasoned thought out loud

I had entered a packed expressway when a bobtail
truck in front of me rammed into a stalled car.
Fire then flared out of the truck's hood.
The truck driver dove out the side window
25 onto the asphalt and struck his head.
As he lay unconscious, we all got out
of our cars; somebody ran to an emergency phone
to summon help.
The rest of us rushed over to the driver.
30 We looked at each other and figured if we
didn't move him, the truck could explode
and break up over his body. But to move him
meant the risk of getting sued,
a New Yorker reasoned next to me.

35 In the seconds that followed,
we decided that everyone there
would take a hold of the guy.
Somebody got an arm, another a leg . . .
one guy just placed a hand on the dude's chest.

40 We carried the truck driver to the side
of the road. An ambulance finally came.
We continued to stand by the dude
until they laid him on a stretcher
and the truck in the distance
45 burst into a blaze.

About the Poet

Luis J. Rodríguez (1954–   ) is an award-winning poet, author, and
journalist. He captured the life of a gang member in his memoir *Always
Running: La Vida Loca—Gang Days in L.A.* He now commits his life
to helping kids stay out of gangs and empowering the local Latino
community through his cultural center in Los Angeles.

BEFORE READING **The World Is in Their Hands**

newspaper article by Eric Feil

Reading Strategies

▶ **Plan and Monitor**
· Determine Importance
· Make Inferences
· Ask Questions
· Make Connections
· Synthesize
· Visualize

Analyze Text Features: Article

Newspaper articles often use a combination of words and graphics to get a message across. Charts and other graphics can provide additional useful information. They can also restate or summarize what is in the text.

Look into the Text

Written text provides a main idea.

> Youth activism levels are at all-time highs. Nearly three-quarters of young adults say they have donated money, clothes, or food to a community or church organization over the past few years.

Graphics provide details that support the main idea.

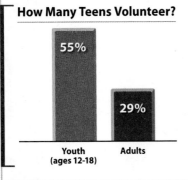

How Many Teens Volunteer?

Youth (ages 12-18): 55%
Adults: 29%

Source: Corporation for National and Community Service, 2005

The source for the information helps you decide if the data is reliable.

Focus Strategy ▶ Plan and Monitor

Reading nonfiction is different from reading a short story. Depending on your purpose, or reason, for reading, you may need to read slowly to understand all of the facts, numbers, and examples. Or you may read quickly if your purpose is to scan for one piece of information.

Focus Strategy

HOW TO PREVIEW AND SET A PURPOSE

1. **Look for clues about the text.** As you look over, or preview, a text, use visual clues to determine the type of text and its topic.

   - Title and headings show the text's main ideas.
   - Graphics show what subject the text deals with.
   - Photos can show whether the text discusses history or the present day.
   - The overall layout may give clues about the type of text.

2. **Set your purpose.** Think of the questions you want to answer and write them in a **5W/How Chart**. Then read the selection to find the answers. This is your purpose, or reason, for reading.

5W/How Chart

As I read, I want to find out

who . . .
what . . . kind of youth volunteer?
when . . .
where . . .
why . . . do they volunteer?
how . . .

The World Is in Their Hands

by Eric Feil

Connect Across Texts

In "The Good Samaritan," Rey must decide whether to help a neighbor. What makes people choose to help others?

Changing the World

With sincere apologies to that old song, the children are not the future.

They are the present.

They are not going to lead the way one day.

They are leading it right now.

Youth activism levels are at all-time highs. Nearly three-quarters of young adults say they have **donated** money, clothes, or food to a community or church organization over the past few years. They **get involved** at national and local levels, and their numbers are growing. Doing good, not **gaining recognition**, is their **motivation**. 1

"We've seen a huge demand from young people who want their voices

A volunteer helps out at an event for youth with special needs.

1 Text Features
What is the main idea of this paragraph?

Key Vocabulary
- **motivation** *n.*, reason for doing something or thinking a certain way

In Other Words

Youth activism levels The numbers of young people who help others
donated given
get involved join, offer to help
gaining recognition getting attention

heard and who feel they've got something to **contribute** to society," says **Youth Service America** president and CEO Steve Culbertson. "And they're not going to wait until they grow up to do it."

Clearly. Millions of youth volunteers will be out in force again this year, from five-year-olds visiting and decorating senior citizen homes to high school kids tutoring **peers**. Distributing HIV/AIDS educational materials, cleaning up the environment, **registering voters**—the list of projects is almost as limitless as the **enthusiasm** and energy of the people engaged in them. Young people are making a difference in their

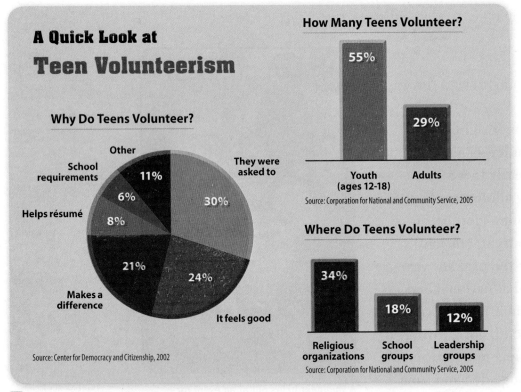

A Quick Look at Teen Volunteerism

Why Do Teens Volunteer?

- Other 11%
- School requirements 6%
- Helps résumé 8%
- Makes a difference 21%
- It feels good 24%
- They were asked to 30%

Source: Center for Democracy and Citizenship, 2002

How Many Teens Volunteer?

- Youth (ages 12-18) 55%
- Adults 29%

Source: Corporation for National and Community Service, 2005

Where Do Teens Volunteer?

- Religious organizations 34%
- School groups 18%
- Leadership groups 12%

Source: Corporation for National and Community Service, 2005

🔺 **Interpret the Data** The pie graph says 30% of teens volunteer because they were asked to. Who might have asked them? 2️⃣

2️⃣ **Text Features**
What are some of the ways people volunteer? What additional information do the graphs provide?

In Other Words
Youth Service America youth volunteer organization
peers people who are the same age
registering voters signing people up to vote
enthusiasm excitement, eagerness
Data Facts, Information

▲ Text Features **A volunteer paints a mural to celebrate Youth Service Day.** 3

3 **Text Features**
What does the photo lead you to think about volunteering?

communities. These volunteers also learn such life skills as planning events, raising funds, and holding leadership roles and responsibilities.

"Young people **have gotten sort of a negative rap**, when the majority of young people really are involved in their communities in very positive ways," says Carl Nelson. His company, State Farm, was the **Presenting Sponsor of** National Youth Service Day (NYSD) 2005, "a celebration of community service and service learning that goes on year-round."

Today's youth are building a unique background in **altruism**. And they are not going to leave their service history behind them when they enter the workforce. "We know that the one key predictor to lifetime service is whether you did it as a child," Culbertson states. "There's a whole **generation** of young people that have grown up giving back and

Key Vocabulary
• **generation** *n.*, people who are about the same age

In Other Words
have gotten sort of a negative rap are talked about in a bad way
Presenting Sponsor of company that paid for
altruism caring about the well-being of others

Monitor Comprehension

Summarize
On pages 29-31, what is the most important point the author makes about young volunteers in the U.S. today?

making that a **fundamental** part of their lives and it's not something you give up."

Not when they are so **engaged**, so passionate. Not where events like NYSD show them that there is a **diverse** group of peers striving for a common goal: a better world for everyone. "They're the most **tolerant** generation we've ever seen in history," Culbertson says. "They can't imagine that somebody should be left out of society simply because they're black or they're gay or they have a disability or they come from an ethnic background that's unusual. They just don't look at those differences as anything more than just part of what it means to be a

Volunteer Work:
By the Numbers

Teenagers volunteer 2.4 billion hours annually — worth $34.3 billion to the U.S. economy.
Source: Independent Sector/Gallup, 1996, and 1999 hourly value

82.6% of incoming college freshmen did volunteer work, compared to 66% in 1989.
Source: UCLA/Higher Education Research Institute Annual Freshmen Survey, 2001

The number of high school students involved in service learning increased 3,663% in the past decade from 81,000 to 2,967,000.
Source: U.S. Department of Education, 1999

A library volunteer keeps his audience's attention. 4

▲ **Interpret the Data** How do the numbers in this boxed feature support the main ideas of this article?

4 **Text Features** How do the picture and caption support the data in the boxed feature?

In Other Words
fundamental basic and important
engaged interested
diverse mixed
tolerant accepting, open-minded

human. They don't let those differences get in the way of progress. That's what makes this the greatest generation I think we've ever seen in this country, and nobody knows it."

They do now. ❖

ANALYZE The World Is in Their Hands

1. **Recall and Interpret** According to Steve Culbertson, why are more young people volunteering? Do the graphics support his idea? Explain.

2. **Vocabulary** What does the graph on page 30 say about the percentage of volunteers in the teen **generation** compared with adults?

3. **Analyze Text Features: Article** Which graphic gave you the most useful information about the article's topic? Why? Compare your choice with a partner's.

4. **Focus Strategy Preview and Set a Purpose** Reread the **5W/How Chart** you began on page 28. Did you find answers to all of your questions? Share your questions and answers with a partner.

Return to the Text

Reread and Write Steve Culbertson says that today's youth are the "greatest generation I think we've ever seen in this country." Find two examples in the text that support his opinion. Do you agree? Support your opinion.

Making a Difference

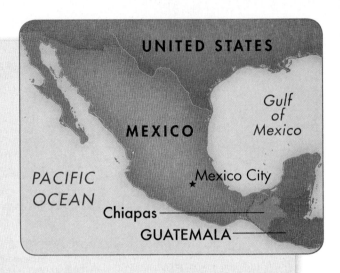

UNITED STATES

MEXICO

Gulf of Mexico

PACIFIC OCEAN

★ Mexico City

Chiapas —————

GUATEMALA —————

Schools for Indigenous Children
Chiapas, Mexico

Christina Fletes and Danny Acosta

In Chiapas, Mexico, on the border with Guatemala, thousands of Maya Indian children do not have easy **access** to schools. To get a formal education, children must walk miles. They are often **ridiculed** by teachers and classmates once they arrive. **In partnership with** the group Schools for Chiapas, Danny Acosta and Christina Fletes organized their high school to raise money to help build schools for these children. They feel **connected to** this issue, as their families are from Mexico and Central America. Through their work, they have created new educational opportunities for indigenous children.

Garden Angels
Brooklyn, New York

Planting the seeds of a better tomorrow is the perfect **metaphor for** youth volunteers. Shawn Henry **took it literally**. Today, neighborhoods throughout his hometown of Brooklyn are reaping the benefits of his Garden Angels project. Founded in 2002, Garden Angels is a group of 50 core members and some 200 other youths who are dedicated to improving life in New York. But Shawn wants to get even more young people involved in **civic activities**. He helps plan workshops and events for other students in NYC so that they too can build the skills to plant their own seeds for a better city.

Shawn Henry

In Other Words

Indigenous Native
access ways to get
ridiculed teased, made fun of
In partnership with Working together with
connected to felt especially close to

metaphor for way to describe
took it literally actually did it
civic activities things to help the community

EQ What Influences a Person's Choices?

Critical Thinking

EQ 1. Analyze Review the **Ranking Chart** on page 10. Then talk with a partner about how the statements relate to characters like Rey and the real-life volunteers in "The World Is in Their Hands."

2. Interpret Steve Culbertson says, "There's a whole generation of young people that have grown up giving back and making that a fundamental part of their lives." What does he mean? Explain whether this statement is true for Rey in "The Good Samaritan."

3. Compare What affects Rey's decision to help Mr. Sánchez clean a neighbor's yard? How does this compare with Shawn Henry's motivation to clean up his own neighborhood?

4. Speculate What would Mr. Sánchez say about the young people in his neighborhood? What do you think Steve Culbertson would say to Mr. Sánchez if he could?

EQ 5. Judge Is there ever a bad motivation for choosing to help others who are in need? Support your opinion with examples from the selections and your own experience.

EQ 6. Synthesize What do you think is the motivation for most people to do good deeds? Explain, using examples from both selections.

Write About Literature

Order-of-Importance Paragraph Brainstorm three or four reasons that teens choose to help others. Write a paragraph presenting these reasons in order of importance, ending with the reason that you think is most important. Use examples from both selections to support your ideas.

Key Vocabulary Review

Oral Review Work with a partner. Use these words to complete the paragraph.

affect	disrespect	privilege
conflicts	generation	responsible
contribute	motivations	

> Young people of today's __(1)__ are finding ways to give back or __(2)__ to their communities. The __(3)__ for volunteering are varied. Some may feel they enjoy more than their share of security and special __(4)__ in a world filled with violent __(5)__. Other youths volunteer because of values learned from their parents and grandparents. To avoid volunteering would seem like __(6)__ or rudeness for their families. Whatever makes them feel __(7)__ for helping others, "good samaritans" everywhere __(8)__ their communities in positive ways.

Writing Application Write your ideas about how teenagers can be responsible. Use at least five Key Vocabulary words.

Read with Ease: Expression

Assess your reading fluency with the passage in the Reading Handbook, p. 751. Then complete the self-check below.

1. My expression did/did not sound natural.

2. My words correct per minute: _____

Grammar

Write Complete Sentences

Sentences are the building blocks for most writing. In formal English, a sentence expresses a complete idea.

> The boy helps his neighbor.

A sentence is complete if it has two parts. The part called the **subject** tells whom or what the sentence is about. The complete subject may be one word or several words.

> **The boy** helps his neighbor.
> **Mr. Sánchez** needs help.

The part called the **predicate** tells what the subject *does*, *has*, or *is*. The complete predicate may be one word or several words.

> The boy **works for a reward**.
> He **is disappointed**.

Oral Practice (1–5) Find five complete sentences in the selections you just read. Tell a partner what the subject and predicate are in each sentence.

Written Practice (6–10) On your paper, use these phrases in complete sentences.

6. knocks on the door
7. Mrs. Sánchez
8. wants to swim
9. makes a promise
10. the friends

Language Development

Ask and Answer Questions

Role-Play Work with a partner to act out an interview with one of the people in the selections you read. Take turns asking the person questions that start with one of these words: *Who, What, When, Where, How, Why*. Listen to the person's answers. Then switch roles.

Literary Analysis

Analyze Theme

A **theme** is the central idea or message of a selection. The theme is a general statement that the author makes about people or life.

In some works, the theme is **stated** directly. But in most cases, the theme is **implied**, or hinted at, in the selection. The reader must infer what the truth or message is from what the writer provides. To discover the implied theme, look for clues in the events, characters, and dialogue.

Study the following details from "The Good Samaritan."

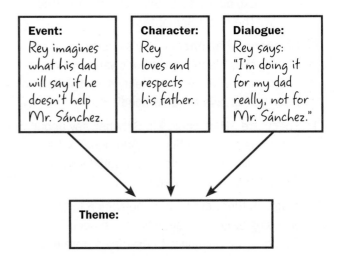

With a partner, identify the central theme of "The Good Samaritan." Add more evidence from the story that supports this theme. Share ideas with the class.

Language Development

Give and Follow Instructions

Pair Talk Think of something you have done to help someone. Give your partner instructions that tell how to do the same thing. Have your partner pantomime following your instructions. Then have your partner describe how he or she solved a similar problem. Listen and repeat as your partner gives instructions.

Prefixes

A **prefix** is a word part added to the beginning of a word. The prefix *pre-* means "before," so *preview* means "look *before.*" Here are more prefixes:

PREFIX	ORIGIN	MEANING
auto-	Greek	self
inter-	Latin	between
off-	Middle-English	from

Write the meaning of each word below. Check your definitions using a print or online dictionary. Then add entries for each prefix to a Prefix Chart.

1. intersect **2.** autocracy **3.** offspring

Write a Definition Paragraph

In a **definition paragraph**, you explain the meaning of a big concept. You restate the word's dictionary meaning and give examples that show what the word means to you. Write a definition paragraph for *responsibility*, *duty*, or a similar "big idea."

1 **Prewrite** Brainstorm a list of ideas about what the word means. Include examples from your life.

2 **Draft** Organize your ideas in a chart.

Word: duty
Dictionary Definition: what a person is required or expected to do (by law, family, friends, society)
Synonyms: responsibility, job, task, assignment
Example 1: taking care of my little brother
Example 2: staying in school
My Definition: doing what you have to do

3 **Revise** Think about whether your examples support your main definition. Add, move, or replace examples to make your definition clearer.

Oral Report

Social Studies: Good Samaritan Laws Find out what "Good Samaritan" laws are and the problems they are written to solve. Come up with a question you have about them. Then investigate these online sources:

> **myNGconnect.com**
> 🔎 **Search online for The Emerson Good Samaritan Food Donation Act.**
> 🔎 **Check out the topic on the American Medical Association's Web site.**

Write a definition of Good Samaritan laws, including examples of how they work. Then present your findings in an oral report to the class.

📖 **Language and Learning Handbook,** page 702

4 **Edit and Proofread** Work with a partner to correct spelling and grammar mistakes.

5 **Publish** Publish your definition paragraph by creating a class dictionary of terms.

Definition Paragraph Model

Duty — word

The dictionary says, "A duty is something you are required to do by law, family, friends, or society." — dictionary definition

I think duty also means doing something because it is right. For example, no one tells me that I have to look out for my little brother, but I still do it because I care about him. — example 1

Also, the law says I have to go to school until I'm older, but I feel like staying in school is my duty if I want a good education. — example 2

So, to me, duty is more than what others require of you. It's what you require of yourself. — conclusion with your definition

📖 **Writing Handbook,** page 784

Inside a Law Office

People in the legal profession work to apply local, state, or federal laws to protect people, businesses, and even ideas. Some people in this profession argue cases in a courtroom. Others do their work entirely in an office, preparing cases that are settled without a courtroom trial.

Jobs in the Legal Profession

To be successful, a law office needs people to do a variety of jobs. Each job requires specific training, education, and work experience.

Job	Responsibilities	Education/Training Required
Legal Secretary 1	• Types and files legal documents • Answers the telephone • Updates lawyers' calendars • Assists in legal research	• High school diploma • Computer training • On-the-job training
Paralegal 2	• Interviews witnesses • Investigates facts • Does legal research • Helps lawyers prepare agreements and get ready for court	• Associate's degree in paralegal studies or • College degree plus certificate of paralegal studies
Lawyer 3	• Writes legal contracts • May argue cases in court • Helps people and companies reach agreements	• College degree • Law school degree • Pass a state bar exam

Conduct an Informational Interview

Find out what a job in the legal profession would be like.

1. From the chart above, choose the job that interests you most. Then prepare five interview questions about the job you chose.

2. Call a law firm. You can find one under "Attorneys" in the yellow pages of your local telephone book, or search for local attorneys on the Internet.

3. Explain that you are a student interested in learning about a career in the legal profession. Ask if someone in that career would be willing to talk with you for a few minutes about his or her work.

4. Interview the person. Take notes and share what you learned with other students interested in the same career. Save the information in a professional career portfolio.

myNGconnect.com

🔵 Learn more about the legal profession.

🔵 Download a form to evaluate whether you would like to work in this field.

🔵 Download an interview form.

📖 **Language and Learning Handbook,** page 702

Use Word Parts

Bakers often prepare a big batch of basic dough. They can add sugar to the dough to change it into coffee cakes or other sweet pastries.

Many base words are like the basic dough. When you add an affix to the base word, you change its meaning. A prefix is an affix added to the beginning of the base word. A suffix is an affix added to the end. If you know what each part of the new word means, you can often figure out its meaning.

Make Meaning from Word Parts

Work with a partner to learn the meaning of some base words, prefixes, and suffixes.

1. Write each base word, prefix, and suffix on a separate card.
2. Mix and match cards to make a new word. Check a dictionary to confirm that you made a real word.
3. Have your partner give the meanings of the parts and the whole word.
4. Check the meaning in a print or online dictionary.
5. Switch roles. Continue until you cannot make any more words.

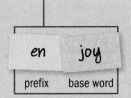

Base Word	Meaning
caution	care
connected	linked
history	past
joy	happiness
pay	give money

Prefix	Meaning
en-, em- (Latin)	to be in or to put in a certain way
inter- (Latin)	between
non- (Latin)	not
pre- (Latin)	before

Put the Strategy to Use

When you come to a word you do not know, use this strategy to check its parts.

1. Look for a prefix or suffix and cover it.
2. Define the base word.
3. Uncover the prefix or suffix and determine its meaning.
4. Put the meanings of the word parts together to define the whole word.

nonpayment
nonpayment

Suffix	Meaning
-ic (Greek)	relating to
-ful (Old English)	full of
-ment (Latin)	action or result
-less (Old English)	free from

TRY IT ▶ Read the following sentences. Use the strategy described above to write the meaning of the words printed in blue.

1. Dinosaurs are prehistoric.
2. The robin in the poem is symbolic of spring.
3. Coral and algae have an interdependent relationship.
4. Natural gas, coal, and oil are nonrenewable resources.
5. There is no such thing as a frictionless surface.

🔖 **Reading Handbook,** page 733

EQ ## What Influences a Person's Choices?
Find out how circumstances affect choices.

Make a Connection

Anticipation Guide Think about how circumstances, such as education, opportunities, and events, can affect a person's choice to break the law. Then tell whether you agree or disagree with these statements.

ANTICIPATION GUIDE	Agree or Disagree
1. Criminals choose to break the law, so they deserve their punishment.	_____
2. It is OK for hungry people to steal what they need.	_____
3. Everyone deserves a second chance.	_____

Learn Key Vocabulary

Study the Words Pronounce each word and learn its meaning. You may also want to look up the definitions in the Glossary.

• Academic Vocabulary

Key Words	Examples
• **circumstances** (**sur**-kum-stans-uz) *noun* ▸ pages 54, 58	**Circumstances** describe the situation a person is in. There are many **circumstances** that cause people to make bad choices.
• **commit** (ku-**mit**) *verb* ▸ pages 44, 53	A person who **commits** a crime is the one who carries it out, or does it. She **committed** the crime of robbery.
• **consequence** (**kon**-su-kwens) *noun* ▸ pages 44, 51, 54	A **consequence** is something that happens as a result of another action. If you lie to a friend, you may have to face a **consequence**, like losing your friendship.
• **contact** (**kon**-takt) *noun* ▸ page 46	When you are in **contact** with people or things, you connect with them in some way. I am still in **contact** with my friends from first grade.
empathy (**em**-pu-thē) *noun* ▸ pages 51, 53, 59	When you have **empathy** for people, you feel like you understand their problems, feelings, or behavior. I felt **empathy** for the lonely boy, and could feel his sadness.
juvenile (**joo**-vu-nīl) *adjective; noun* ▸ pages 53, 58, 59	A **juvenile** is a young person. [*noun*] Something **juvenile** is for young people. [*adjective*] The **juvenile** court is for people younger than eighteen.
maturity (mu-**choor**-u-tē) *noun* ▸ pages 54, 59	When people reach **maturity**, they are fully developed and have all the abilities of an adult. The girl's serious and responsible actions showed **maturity**.
salvage (**sal**-vuj) *verb* ▸ page 54	To **salvage** is to save someone or something from destruction. I **salvaged** my friendship by telling my friend I was sorry.

Practice the Words Work with a partner to write four sentences. Use at least two of the Key Vocabulary words in each sentence.

Example: Do you feel empathy for a person who commits a crime?

BEFORE READING **Thank You, M'am**

short story by Langston Hughes

Reading Strategies

▶ **Plan and Monitor**
· Determine Importance
· Make Inferences
· Ask Questions
· Make Connections
· Synthesize
· Visualize

Analyze Characterization

When you read a good story, you feel as if you know the characters. That's because authors use **characterization** to reveal, or show, what a character is like.

Look Into the Text

Hughes describes the woman's physical traits. Notice the way he structures his descriptive sentences.

> She was a large woman with a large purse that had everything in it but a hammer and nails. It had a long strap, and she carried it slung across her shoulder. It was about eleven o'clock at night, dark, and she was walking alone, when a boy ran up behind her and tried to snatch her purse. The strap broke with the sudden single tug the boy gave it from behind. But the boy's weight and the weight of the purse combined caused him to lose his balance. Instead of taking off full blast as he had hoped, the boy fell on his back on the sidewalk, and his legs flew up.

Hughes uses actions to show what she is like.

> The large woman simply turned around and kicked him right square in his blue-jeaned sitter. Then she reached down, picked the boy up by his shirt front, and shook him until his teeth rattled.

How does Hughes show the impact of her action on the boy?

Focus Strategy ▶ Plan and Monitor

When you **monitor your reading**, you check with yourself to see if you understand. Look into the text above and find something that isn't clear to you. Then, as you read the story, use these strategies to better understand, or clarify ideas.

HOW TO CLARIFY IDEAS

Focus Strategy

1. Reread If you are confused, go back to see if you missed something important.

NOT CLEAR TO YOU: I'm not sure why other people didn't stop to help the woman.

REREAD: It was about <u>eleven o'clock at night</u>, <u>dark</u>, and she was walking <u>alone</u>.

2. Read On Keep reading. The author may give more information later.

YOU THINK: The boy must have gotten hurt when he fell on his back.

READ ON: A few sentences later you'll come to this:

> "If I turn you loose, will you run?" asked the woman.
> "Yes'm," said the boy.

YOU THINK: The boy must be OK if he can run away.

Langston Hughes
(1902–1967)

Langston Hughes believed in equal opportunities for all Americans.

Langston Hughes wrote about the experience of being an African American in the early and middle 20th century. He was one of the most famous members of the "Harlem Renaissance," a group of writers, musicians, and artists who lived and worked in the Harlem neighborhood in New York City. Harlem became the setting, or location, for many of Hughes's works, including "Thank You, M'am."

When he was growing up, Hughes moved a lot. He lived in Missouri, Kansas, Illinois, Ohio, and Mexico. His parents were divorced, and he also spent time living with his grandmother and other relatives. In one essay, Hughes said that during these years he slept in "ten thousand beds."

Even though his home changed often, the one thing that never changed was his love of books and writing. Hughes wrote his first poem in the eighth grade, and he was named class poet. The *Central High School Monthly* in Cleveland, Ohio, was the first magazine to publish one of his poems.

Hughes went on to write three novels, nineteen books of poetry and short stories, twenty plays, and many newspaper articles and essays. Many of his poems were also set to music by the jazz musicians of his time.

myNGconnect.com

🔊 Listen to a jazz song with lyrics by Hughes.
🔊 Hear Hughes read and discuss his work.

THANK YOU, M'AM

by Langston Hughes

▲ Critical Viewing: Setting What is this neighborhood like?
How would the scene change late at night?

 Comprehension Coach

Find out the consequences for a young person who makes the choice to commit a crime.

She was a large woman with a large purse that had everything in it but a hammer and nails. It had a long strap, and she carried it **slung** across her shoulder. It was about eleven o'clock at night, dark, and she was walking alone, when a boy ran up behind her and tried to snatch her purse. The strap broke with the sudden single tug the boy gave it from behind. But the boy's weight and the weight of the purse combined caused him to lose his balance. Instead of **taking off full blast** as he had hoped, the boy fell on his back on the sidewalk and his legs flew up. The large woman simply turned around and kicked him **right square in his blue-jeaned sitter**. Then she reached down, picked the boy up by his shirt front, and shook him until his teeth rattled. **1**

After that, the woman said, "Pick up my pocketbook, boy, and give it here."

She still held him tightly. But she bent down enough to **permit him to stoop** and pick up her purse. Then she said, "Now ain't you ashamed of yourself?"

Firmly gripped by his shirt front, the boy said, "Yes'm."

The woman said, "What did you want to do it for?"

The boy said, "I didn't aim to." **2**

She said, "You a lie!"

By that time two or three people passed, stopped, turned to look, and some stood watching.

"If I turn you loose, will you run?" asked the woman.

"Yes'm," said the boy.

"Then I won't turn you loose," said the woman. She did not release him.

"Lady, I'm sorry," whispered the boy.

1 Characterization
What does this paragraph tell you about the two main characters?

2 Clarify Ideas
Are you surprised by the boy's answer? If so, try reading on to clarify what the boy means.

Key Vocabulary
- **consequence** *n.*, result of another action
- **commit** *v.*, to perform, do, or carry out something, often a crime

In Other Words
slung hanging
taking off full blast running away very fast
right square in his blue-jeaned sitter on his rear end, or backside
permit him to stoop let him lean down

"Um-hum! Your face is dirty. I **got a great mind** to wash your face for you. Ain't you got nobody home to tell you to wash your face?"

"No'm," said the boy.

"Then it will get washed this evening," said the large woman, starting up the street, dragging the frightened boy behind her.

He looked as if he were fourteen or fifteen, **frail and willow-wild**, in tennis shoes and blue jeans.

The woman said, "You ought to be my son. I would teach you **right from wrong**. Least I can do right now is to wash your face. Are you hungry?"

"No'm," said the being-dragged boy. ▣ "I just want you to turn me loose."

▣ **Language**
Authors often use familiar words in new ways. Here Hughes uses "being-dragged boy" to describe Roger. How does this help you picture what's happening?

The City from Greenwich Village, 1922, John Sloan. Oil on canvas, National Gallery of Art, Washington, D.C.

△ **Critical Viewing: Effect** Here is how one artist portrayed a New York City scene. What mood, or feeling, does the artist create?

In Other Words
got a great mind have a plan or desire
frail and willow-wild weak and small, with skinny arms and legs
right from wrong that stealing is wrong

"Was I bothering *you* when I turned that corner?" asked the woman. "No'm."

"But you put yourself in **contact** with *me*," said the woman. "If you think that that contact is not going to last awhile, **you got another thought coming**. When I get through with you, sir, you are going to remember Mrs. Luella Bates Washington Jones." ▪4

Sweat popped out on the boy's face and he began to struggle. Mrs. Jones stopped, jerked him around in front of her, put **a half nelson about** his neck, and continued to drag him up the street. When she got to her door, she dragged the boy inside, down a hall, and into a large **kitchenette-furnished room** at the rear of the house. She switched on the light and left the door open. The boy could hear other **roomers** laughing and talking in the large house. Some of their doors were open, too, so he knew he and the woman were not alone. The woman still had him by the neck in the middle of her room.

She said, "What is your name?"

"Roger," answered the boy.

"Then, Roger, you go to that sink and wash your face," said the woman, **whereupon** she turned him loose—at last. Roger looked at the door—looked at the woman—looked at the door—*and went to the sink.* ▪5

"Let the water run until it gets warm," she said. "Here's a clean towel."

"You gonna take me to jail?" asked the boy, bending over the sink.

"Not with that face, I would not take you nowhere," said the woman.

> # WHEN I GET THROUGH WITH YOU, SIR, YOU ARE GOING TO REMEMBER MRS. LUELLA BATES WASHINGTON JONES.

4 Characterization
Have you ever known a person who talks in a tough, bossy way like this? What does her language tell you about the character of Mrs. Jones?

5 Characterization
Hughes uses italics to draw your attention to what Roger did. What does this choice tell you about Roger?

Monitor Comprehension

Explain What consequences has Roger faced so far?

Key Vocabulary
● **contact** *n.*, connection

In Other Words
you got another thought coming think again
a half nelson about a strong hold around
kitchenette-furnished room room with a small kitchen
roomers boarders, people who lived there
whereupon and then

The Window, 1970, Bernard Safran. Oil on masonite, private collection.

▲ **Critical Viewing: Characterization** How does this picture compare to the picture you have in your mind of Mrs. Jones?

"Here I am trying to get home to cook me a bite to eat, and you snatch my pocketbook! Maybe you ain't been to your supper either, late as it be. Have you?"

"There's nobody home at my house," said the boy.

"Then we'll eat," said the woman. "I believe you're hungry—or been hungry—to try to snatch my pocketbook!"

"I want a pair of blue suede shoes," said the boy.

"Well, you didn't have to snatch *my* pocketbook to get some suede shoes," said Mrs. Luella Bates Washington Jones. "You could of asked me." 6

"M'am?"

The water dripping from his face the boy looked at her. There was a long pause. A very long pause. After he had dried his face and not knowing what else to do, dried it again, the boy turned around, wondering what next. The door was open. He could **make a dash for it** down the hall. He could run, run, run, *run!*

The woman was sitting on the daybed. After a while she said, "I were young once and I wanted things I could not get."

There was another long pause. The boy's mouth opened. Then he frowned, not knowing he frowned.

The woman said, "Um-hum! You thought I was going to say *but,* didn't you? You thought I was going to say, *but I didn't snatch people's pocketbooks.* Well, I wasn't going to say that." Pause. Silence. "I have done things, too, which I would not tell you, son—neither tell God, if He didn't already know. **Everybody's got something in common.** 7 So you set down while I fix us something to eat. You might run that comb through your hair so you will look **presentable**."

6 Characterization
What does this dialogue show about Mrs. Jones? From what you know of her so far, would she have helped Roger?

7 Clarify Ideas
Does what Mrs. Jones says here make sense to you? Reread the paragraph to clarify what she and Roger have in common.

In Other Words
make a dash for it try to run
Everybody's got something in common.
  All people are alike in some way.
presentable clean and neat

Cultural Background
"Blue Suede Shoes" was a song written by Carl Perkins in 1955. It was one of the first big rock and roll hits, and teens all over the U.S. listened to it. They also bought shoes like the ones shown here.

Jim, 1930, William H. Johnson. Oil on canvas, Smithsonian American Art Museum, Washington, D.C.

▲ **Critical Viewing: Characterization** Study the boy's look. What lines from the story could go with this look?

In another corner of the room behind a screen was a **gas plate** and **an icebox**. ⑧ Mrs. Jones got up and went behind the screen. The woman did not watch the boy to see if he was going to run now, nor did she watch her purse, which she left behind her on the daybed. But the boy took care to sit on the far side of the room, away from the purse, where he thought she could easily see him out of the corner of her eye

In Other Words
gas plate small stove
an icebox a refrigerator

⑧ **Access Vocabulary**
Do you know what *screen* means here? If not, look for clues. It must be big because an icebox, or refrigerator, is behind it.

Monitor Comprehension

Confirm Prediction
Were you right about what Mrs. Jones is teaching Roger? Explain.

if she wanted to. He did not trust the woman *not* to trust him. And he did not want **to be mistrusted** now.

"Do you need somebody to go to the store," asked the boy, "maybe to get some milk or something?" [9]

"Don't believe I do," said the woman, "unless you just want sweet milk yourself. I was going to make cocoa out of this canned milk I got here."

"That will be fine," said the boy.

She heated some lima beans and ham she had in the icebox, made the cocoa, and set the table. The woman did not ask the boy anything about where he lived, or his folks, or anything else that would embarrass him. Instead, as they ate, she told him about her job in a hotel beauty shop that stayed open late, what the work was like, and how all kinds of women came in and out, blondes, redheads, and Spanish. Then she cut him a half of her ten-cent cake. [10]

"Eat some more, son," she said.

When they were finished eating, she got up and said, "Now here, take this ten dollars and buy yourself some blue suede shoes. And next time, do not make the mistake of **latching onto** *my* pocketbook *nor nobody else's*—because shoes got by **devilish ways** will burn your feet. I got to get my rest now. But from here on in, son, I hope you will **behave yourself.**"

She led him down the hall to the front door and opened it. "Good night! Behave yourself, boy!" she said, looking out into the street as he went down the steps.

> ## HE DID NOT TRUST THE WOMAN *NOT* TO TRUST HIM. AND HE DID NOT WANT TO BE MISTRUSTED NOW.

9 Characterization
What do Roger's words tell about how he's feeling at this point in the story?

10 Clarify Ideas
Why does Mrs. Jones tell Roger so much about herself, instead of asking him questions? Reread the paragraph to find clues to her reason.

In Other Words
to be mistrusted her to stop trusting him
latching onto grabbing, taking
devilish ways bad behavior, wrong actions
behave yourself do the right thing, follow the rules

The boy wanted to say something other than, "Thank you, m'am," to Mrs. Luella Bates Washington Jones, but although his lips moved, he couldn't even say that as he turned at the foot of the **barren stoop** and looked up at the large woman in the door. Then she shut the door. ❖

ANALYZE Thank You, M'am

1. **Explain** Using details from the story, explain why Mrs. Jones wants Roger to learn the lessons she is teaching him. What might be the consequences of ignoring these lessons?
2. **Vocabulary** How does Mrs. Jones show that she has empathy for Roger?
3. **Analyze Characterization** Collect examples of characterization in a chart. Tell a partner what each character is like.

Type of Clue	Mrs. Jones	Roger
physical traits	large woman	frail, willow-wild
thoughts		wants to run
words		
actions		
reactions of others		

4. **Focus Strategy Clarify Ideas** As you read, the author may provide information that clarifies your ideas. Talk with a partner about a time when your ideas about the events or characters changed as you read on.

↩ Return to the Text

Reread and Write What do you think influenced Roger's choices? Reread to form an opinion and gather at least two pieces of evidence from the text. Then write your opinion. When you are finished, write a response in which you give your opinion of how Mrs. Jones treated Roger.

Key Vocabulary
empathy *n.*, understanding someone else's problems, feelings, or behavior

In Other Words
barren stoop empty staricase that led to her door

BEFORE READING **Juvenile Justice**

interviews by Janet Tobias and
Michael Martin

Analyze Text Features: Interview

You're about to read an excerpt from a TV show in which a number of people are
interviewed. In an **interview**, one person asks questions for another person to
answer. Interviews have specific kinds of features.

Reading Strategies

▶ **Plan and Monitor**
· Determine Importance
· Make Inferences
· Ask Questions
· Make Connections
· Synthesize
· Visualize

Look Into the Text

Judge LaDoris Cordell

*A state court trial judge since 1982, until
recently she served on the Superior Court of
Santa Clara County, where she heard both
juvenile and adult cases.*

Background
information often
appears in italics
at the beginning
of an article or
interview.

Questions and
answers make up
the interview.

Q. **Do you think any kid ever belongs in adult court?**

A. Yes. ... I have come across some young people who are so
sophisticated and who have committed such heinous crimes
that the adult system is the place for them to be. I haven't
come across a lot, but there have been some. ... It can happen,
and it does [happen].

Ellipses show
where the
speaker's words
have been
left out.

Brackets show that
a word has been
changed or added.

Focus Strategy ▶ Plan and Monitor

As you read, notice when you need to clarify ideas. One way to clarify is to
paraphrase the text, or restate what's happening in your own words.

HOW TO CLARIFY IDEAS

Focus Strategy

1. Read Judge Cordell's answer above.

2. Identify the main points in the text.

3. Paraphrase the text by putting those
main points into your own words.

4. Try it with a partner. Pick a new
paragraph and compare your
paraphrases.

The Text:

A. Yes. ... I have come across some young
people who are so sophisticated and who
have committed such heinous crimes that
the adult system is the place for them to be.

My Words:

Judge Cordell says that some kids act like adults, so
they belong in adult court.

Juvenile Justice
from Both Sides of the Bench
by Janet Tobias and Michael Martin

Connect Across Texts

In "Thank You, M'am," Mrs. Jones shows empathy *for Roger despite what he does. In these interviews, read how real-life judges and attorneys deal with teens who* commit *crimes.*

Recent legislation in many U.S. states makes it easier to try, or judge, juvenile offenders in adult criminal court and not in juvenile court. As a result, more and more teen offenders are **doing time** alongside adults in prison. **1**

Teens who are tried as adults can also receive longer sentences, or periods of punishment. Many people believe such punishment is a better fit for more serious crimes. They see this as more important than how old the person is.

Public opinion has changed over the last hundred years. In 1899, the first juvenile court was set up in Illinois. Then, most people believed juveniles were not as responsible for their actions as adults. Illinois wanted to protect each young person, even while it protected the public from crime. The goal of juvenile court was to help offenders make better choices about the future.

Today, however, many people believe that harsh punishment is the better way to stop teens from committing crimes in the future. To explore this topic, the Public Broadcasting System's *Frontline* TV news team interviewed **people from both sides of "the bench."**

1 Clarify Ideas
This paragraph has many difficult ideas and terms. Check **In Other Words**. Then tell the meaning of this paragraph in your own words.

Key Vocabulary
- empathy *n.*, the understanding of someone else's problems, feelings, or behavior
- commit *v.*, to perform, do, or carry out something, often a crime
- juvenile *adj.*, young; *n.*, young person

In Other Words
Recent legislation New laws
doing time being punished
people from both sides of "the bench" judges, who sit on one side of the bench, or desk, and lawyers, who stand on the other side

Judge Thomas Edwards

Until recently he was the presiding judge of the Juvenile Court of Santa Clara County, a division of the California Superior Court. He heard between 300 and 350 cases a month. 2

Q. Why should we treat a 14-year-old offender differently than a 24-year-old offender?

A. It depends on many, many <mark>circumstances</mark>. But very generally, the 14-year-old does not have the level of <mark>maturity</mark>, thought process, decision-making, experience, or wisdom that a 24-year-old presumably has.

Secondly, a 14-year-old is still growing, may not appreciate the <mark>consequences</mark> of that type of behavior, and **is susceptible to** change, at least to a higher degree than a 24-year-old is. . . . I think we have a real shot at trying to straighten out the 14-year-old, and even the people who are a little bit hard-nosed in the system, such as your average **prosecutor**, will sometimes grudgingly admit that, with a 14-year-old, given the proper level of accountability and the proper types of programs to change their behavior, we have a chance at <mark>salvaging</mark> these kids.

Q. Are there kids who don't belong in juvenile court?

A. Oh, sure. Yes. I've had **sociopaths** in court here. I've had only a few of them, and I've been doing this for a long time. I can only really count maybe a half a dozen, and only two in particular that I would be very frightened to see on the street. But I see them from time to time.

Key Vocabulary
- <mark>circumstances</mark> *n.*, situation
  <mark>maturity</mark> *n.*, the time when a person has all the abilities of an adult
- <mark>consequence</mark> *n.*, result
  <mark>salvage</mark> *v.*, to save or rescue

In Other Words
is susceptible to probably will
prosecutor lawyer whose job is to get punishment for criminals
sociopaths people who do not know right from wrong

Judge LaDoris Cordell
A state court trial judge since 1982, until recently she served on the Superior Court of Santa Clara County, where she heard both juvenile and adult cases.

Q. Why should we treat a 14-year-old offender differently than a 24-year-old offender? 3

A. The problem is that we're taking 14-year-olds, 15-year-olds, 16-year-olds, and we're giving up on them. We're saying, "You've committed a crime, and we're just going to give up on you. You're out of here; society has no use for you." We're throwing away these kids. And I have found, in my own experience, that there are salvageable young people. They have committed some very horrible kinds of crimes, but they are able to get their lives together and **be productive members of society**. I think it is a mistake to just . . . give up on these young people. There is so much more that goes into why that person got there at that point in time so young in their lives. 4

Q. Do you think any kid ever belongs in adult court?

A. Yes. . . . I have come across some young people who are so **sophisticated** and who have committed such **heinous** crimes that the adult system is the place for them to be. I haven't come across a lot, but there have been some. . . . It can happen, and it does [happen]. 5

In Other Words
be productive members of society work and be responsible like other people
sophisticated clever in a grown-up way
heinous horrible, evil

3 Text Features
The interviews repeat the same question for each person. How is this a good way to get information?

4 Clarify Ideas
What has the judge's experience shown her about how to treat most young offenders?

5 Language
A *logical fallacy* is an error in reasoning. A *rhetorical fallacy* is a way of persuading people with emotion or authority instead of with logic. Do you notice either type of fallacy in Judge Cordell's argument?

Monitor Comprehension

Summarize
According to these judges, why should teens be treated differently than adults in court?

Bridgett Jones
*Former supervisor of the Juvenile
Division of the Santa Clara County
Public Defender's Office*

**Q. Why should we treat a 14-year-old offender differently
than a 24-year-old offender?**

A. I think the community understands, or should understand, that the
younger a person is, the more likely it is that they can change. And
the best way I've heard it put is from a **victim** in a very serious case.

   This person had been **maimed** for life. He had **indicated to** the
young person who shot him, or was **alleged** to have shot him, that
he would rather meet up with this person ten years down the road
as a graduate from a college versus a graduate from [prison]. 6

   He [understood] that this person was eventually going to get back
out and be in our community. They don't go away. They come back.
And the younger they are, the more likely it is that they are going to
come back into our community. So I guess as a community we have to
decide what is it we're willing to get back in the long run.

   Children are not little adults. They think differently. They respond
and react to things differently than adults do. . . . So why should the
consequences be the same as for an adult? 7

   The only thing that's going to work with kids like [these] is a
willingness of the community to **redeem** them and saying, "Look,
your life's not over, there's still hope for you." 8

6 **Clarify Ideas**
What does the
judge's story show?
Put the meaning in
your own words.

7 **Content Area
Connections**
The teen brain
is biologically
different than
the adult brain.
How does this
fact support the
judge's argument?

8 **Text Features**
What do the
brackets mean in
this sentence?

In Other Words
victim person hurt by a crime
maimed physically hurt, wounded
indicated to told or shown
alleged suspected
redeem help and forgive

Social Studies Background
A district attorney prosecutes, or seeks
punishment for, someone charged with a
crime. If the person cannot afford a lawyer,
a public defender has the job of advising
and representing the person.

Kurt Kumli

The supervising deputy district attorney for the Juvenile Division of the Santa Clara County District Attorney's Office, he has practiced exclusively in juvenile court.

Q. Why should we treat a 14-year-old offender differently than a 24-year-old offender?

A. If we could take every kid and surround the kid with full-time staffs of psychologists and drug and alcohol counselors, then perhaps no kid should be in adult court. But the fact is, there are only a limited number of **resources** in the juvenile justice system. . . . You have to make **the hard call**, sometimes, as to whether or not the high-end offenders really are the **just recipients of** the [limited] resources that the juvenile justice system has available to it. 🔟

Q. What does it take to rehabilitate young offenders?

A. What works is different for every kid, but the one rule that I think is applicable, after years of seeing this, is "the sooner, the better." We need to reach these kids with **alternatives**, with opportunities, before they start to feel [like nobody cares]. If we took half of the money that we spend on **incarceration** and put it in **front-end programs** to give these kids alternatives, then we wouldn't have as many **back-end kids** that we needed to incarcerate. And I think that is the immediate answer. 🔟

9 Clarify Ideas
What does Mr. Kumli mean here? Put the meaning in your own words.

10 Language
Are Mr. Kumli's logic and rhetoric sound? Do you find any fallacies?

Monitor Comprehension

Explain
Tell what Kurt Kumli means by "the sooner, the better."

In Other Words

resources staff people and services
the hard call a difficult decision
just recipients of people who should receive
rehabilitate help, fix the problems of
alternatives other choices
incarceration keeping people in jail

front-end programs programs that help kids before they get into trouble
back-end kids kids who have already committed crimes

Judge Nancy Hoffman

Judge Hoffman served on the Superior Court of Santa Clara County, where she handled both juvenile and adult cases. She is currently retired.

Q. **What does it take to rehabilitate young offenders?**

A. I would like to see groups . . . working with troubled families and youth, before they get to middle school and . . . high school. Something is causing the **minor** to do things like not go to school, stay out till three o'clock in the morning . . . We **intervene** with a minor, but there's very little done with the family, and we're sending the minor right back in that situation. ❖

ANALYZE Juvenile Justice

1. **Recall and Interpret** What are some of the reasons that judges and attorneys decide not to try juveniles as adults? Are there any fallacies in the debate? Support your answer with text evidence.

2. **Vocabulary** According to Judge Cordell, under what circumstances should juveniles be tried as adults?

3. **Analyze Text Features: Interview** What text features in this selection show that it includes interviews? Why is this a good way to present the information?

4. **Focus Strategy Clarify Ideas** Paraphrase Judge Edwards's thoughts about how to treat teen offenders.

Return to the Text

Reread and Write Which person's ideas are closest to your own? Reread to confirm. Write a paragraph to tell why.

In Other Words

minor person under the age of 18
intervene get involved to prevent or
  solve problems

EQ What Influences a Person's Choices?

Reading
Critical Thinking

EQ 1. Analyze Complete the **Anticipation Guide** on page 40 again as if you were a character or person interviewed in the text. Defend your answers using ideas and quotations from the selections.

2. Compare How would Roger's treatment by today's court system be similar to how Mrs. Jones treats him? How would it be different?

3. Interpret Mrs. Jones tells Roger, "I have done things, too." Describe what she might have done in the past that helped her have **empathy** with Roger.

4. Speculate Imagine that Roger goes home that night and writes Mrs. Jones a letter. What does he say?

EQ 5. Draw Conclusions What things influence people's choices as **juveniles**? As adults? Give examples from both texts.

Writing
Write About Literature

Interpretive Response Why should we treat a 14-year-old offender differently than a 24-year-old offender? Identify the strongest reasons, and support them with examples and quotations from both texts. Embed the quotations in your writing. Gather text evidence in a T chart:

Thank You, M'am	Juvenile Justice

Vocabulary
Key Vocabulary Review

Oral Review Work with a partner. Use these words to complete the paragraph.

circumstances	contact	maturity
commit	empathy	salvage
consequences	juvenile	

Some young people grow up in difficult __(1)__ that influence the choices they make. Like Roger in "Thank You, M'am," some teens break the law, __(2)__ crimes, and come in __(3)__ with the law. They do not have the wisdom or __(4)__ to make different choices. Some do not understand the __(5)__ that result from breaking the law. They usually end up in the __(6)__ justice system for young people. Many judges and lawyers, however, have __(7)__ for troubled teens and understand their problems. They believe that they can __(8)__, or save, teens. These adults trust that teens can change their lives for the better.

Writing Application Recall a time when you or a friend showed **maturity** in a difficult situation. Write a paragraph that uses at least four Key Vocabulary words.

Fluency
Read with Ease: Phrasing

Assess your reading fluency with the passage in the Reading Handbook, p. 752. Then complete the self-check below.

1. I did/did not pause appropriately for punctuation and phrases.

2. My words correct per minute: _____

Make Subjects and Verbs Agree

The verb you use depends on your subject. These subjects and verbs go together. All the verbs are **forms of be**.

I **am**	We **are**
You **are**	You **are**
He, She, or It **is**	They **are**

Action verbs have two forms in the present:

I **work** a lot.   Mrs. Jones **works** every day.

Add **-s** to the action verb only when you talk about one other person, place, or thing. Find the subject in each sentence. How does the verb end?

Roger **pulls** at the pocketbook.
The strap **breaks**. The pocketbook **falls**.
Mrs. Jones **sees** Roger. She **shakes** him.

Oral Practice (1–5) Choose from each column to make five sentences. **Example:** Roger is hungry.

Roger	work	at home.
They	is	every day.
Mrs. Jones	are	respect.
The neighbors	eats	young.
Young people	need	hungry.

Written Practice (6–15) Write ten sentences to tell what happens when Mrs. Jones makes dinner for Roger. Start with these sentences and choose the correct verb. Then tell what else happens.

Mrs. Jones (take/takes) Roger home. He (is/are) scared and hungry. Mrs. Jones (decide/decides) to make dinner for Roger.

Express Ideas and Opinions

Group Talk What do you think happened to Roger after he left Mrs. Jones's apartment? Tell your ideas. Then tell what you think about Roger, Mrs. Jones, and all that happened.

Analyze Dialogue

An important part of characterization is how the characters talk, or their **dialogue**. A writer shows dialogue in several ways:

- Quotation marks are set at the beginning and end of the character's spoken words.

- Every time a different character speaks, a new paragraph starts.

- Speaker words such as *she said, he asked*, or *whispered the boy* tell who said the words and sometimes how the words were spoken.

Dialogue makes the characters seem real by revealing their thoughts, responses, and feelings. For example, in "Thank You, M'am," Mrs. Jones says, "You a lie!" Hughes could have written: "Mrs. Jones called the boy a liar." Her spoken words show more about her character than a simple description.

With a partner, rewrite these sentences as dialogue. Use quotation marks and add speaker words that tell how the words were spoken.

1. Roger said he wanted some blue suede shoes.
2. Mrs. Jones told Roger not to steal again.
3. Mrs. Jones told Roger to wash his face.
4. Roger explained that there was nobody home at his house.

"YES," SHE MUMBLED?...SIGHED?... MUTTERED?...SNARLED?... HISSED?...GROWLED?...

Source: ©C. Barsotti/The New Yorker

Word Roots

Many English words come from other languages. This chart shows some common roots.

ROOT	MEANING	ORIGIN
circum	around	Latin
dem	people	Greek
swer	proclaim	Anglo-Saxon

Knowing these roots can help you learn more words in various content areas in English. Find the root in each word, guess the word's meaning, and confirm your guess in a print or an online dictionary.

1. answer   **2.** democracy   **3.** circumference

Interview

History: Choices Interview a teacher about a person in history who made an important choice.

❶ **Prepare for the Interview** Think about what you want to know. Then write a list of open-ended questions you will ask, such as "Why do you think the person made that choice?"

❷ **Conduct the Interview** Ask your questions and listen respectfully to the answers. Make sure you understand the main ideas and details as well as the language your teacher uses. Ask clarifying questions, if necessary.

❸ **Share What You Learned** Tell the class about the highlights of your interview.

📖 **Language and Learning Handbook,** page 702

Write a Short Comparison Essay

A test may ask you to write a response to literature. The prompt often names the selection and asks you to think about some aspect of it.

❶ **Unpack the Prompt** Read the prompt and underline the key words.

> **Writing Prompt**
> In "Thank You, M'am," Roger learned an important lesson. Think about a lesson you have learned. Write an essay to compare the lessons. Use examples from the story and your life for support.

❷ **Plan Your Response** Choose a life lesson to write about. Then compare it to Roger's. Use a Venn diagram to help you plan.

Venn Diagram

My life lesson — Both — Roger's life lesson

❸ **Draft** Organize your essay like this.

> **Essay Organizer**
>
> In "Thank You, M'am," Roger learned [tell what his lesson was]. In my life, I have learned [tell what my lesson was].
>
> Our life lessons are alike because [tell how they are alike]. For example, in the story Roger [give an example from the story]. I also [give an example from my own life that is similar].
>
> However, our life lessons are different because [tell how they differ]. [give an example from the story], but [give an example from my own life that is different]. In conclusion, [summarize the comparison].

❹ **Check Your Work** Reread your essay. Ask:

- Does my essay address the writing prompt?
- Did I give examples to support my ideas?
- Are all my sentences complete?

📖 **Writing Handbook,** page 784

Oral Response to Literature

You've just finished reading a selection. Did you like it? Did you think it was boring? Did you identify with a character's point of view? Tell everyone what you think and why. Share your response to one of the selections in this unit with your classmates. Here is how to do it.

1. Plan Your Oral Response

Choose the selection about which you will present your oral response. Then do the following:

- Read the selection several times. Get to know it well.
- Think about how you feel about the selection. Did it move you, teach you something, or entertain you? What do you think it means?
- Look at the individual parts of the selection—the plot, the characters, and the setting. Decide what you like the most.
- Write down some notes about your response to the selection.

2. Practice Your Oral Response

Practice your oral response for another person who knows the selection.

- Begin by telling what you liked or disliked about the selection and why.
- Be sure to include a few examples from the selection to support your ideas.
- Make sure you give your response within the time limit.
- Get helpful suggestions from your listener.
- Edit your presentation by incorporating the listener's comments.

3. Present Your Oral Response

Keep your oral response focused and clear by doing the following:

- Clearly state your main points.
- Let your feelings about the selection show in your words, tone of voice, facial expressions, and body language.
- Establish eye contact with your audience.
- Look at your notes occasionally, but not too often.
- Speak clearly and loudly so that the audience can understand everything you say.

myNGconnect.com

🔊 **Download the rubric.**

4. Discuss and Rate the Oral Responses

Use the rubric to discuss and rate the oral responses, including your own.

Oral Response Rubric

Scale	Content of Oral Report	Student's Preparation	Student's Delivery
3 Great	• Expressed a clear, well-focused response to the selection • Was interesting and held my attention throughout	• Seemed to understand the selection very well • Included good support from the selection to develop the response	• Expressed feelings well and made eye contact • Spoke clearly and loudly
2 Good	• Expressed a fairly clear response to the selection • Held my interest much of the time	• Seemed to understand the selection fairly well • Included some support to develop the response	• Expressed feelings and made eye contact most of the time • Could be heard most of the time
1 Needs Work	• Didn't express a clear response to the selection • Was not very interesting	• Did not seem to understand the selection • Did not include support for the response	• Was stiff, not convincing, and did not make eye contact • Could not be heard or understood well

DO IT ▶ When you are finished preparing, present your oral response, and share your views with your audience.

📖 Language and Learning Handbook,
page 702

Which aspects of a good oral presentation is this speaker demonstrating?

EQ | ## What Influences a Person's Choices?
Discover how society influences choices.

Make a Connection

Quickwrite Imagine there is a club that you want to join. However, joining calls for a major change. Maybe you have to buy an expensive jacket or cut your hair very short. What would you do? Record your thoughts.

Learn Key Vocabulary

Study the Words Pronounce each word and learn its meaning. You may also want to look up definitions in the Glossary.

• Academic Vocabulary

Key Words	Examples
humiliating (hyū-**mi**-lē-ā-ting) *adjective* ▸ page 71	When someone teases you, it feels **humiliating**. A **humiliating** experience hurts your pride.
imitation (im-u-**tā**-shun) *noun* ▸ page 79	An **imitation** is something that looks or acts like something else. *Synonym:* fake; *Antonym:* real, genuine
inspire (in-**spīr**) *verb* ▸ pages 84, 86, 87	When something **inspires** you, it motivates you to do something. A movie about an Olympic athlete **inspired** me to start exercising.
luxury (**luk**-shu-rē) *noun* ▸ page 68	A **luxury** is something expensive that is nice to have, but not necessary. Is it a **luxury** to have two pairs of dress shoes?
• **perceive** (per-**sēv**) *verb* ▸ pages 79, 86	When you **perceive** something, you see it in a certain way. People with different points of view **perceive** things differently. *Synonym:* see; *Antonym:* ignore
poverty (**pov**-er-tē) *noun* ▸ page 76	**Poverty** is being very poor. People without enough money for food, shelter, or clothing live in **poverty**. *Synonym:* need; *Antonym:* wealth
• **symbol** (**sim**-bul) *noun* ▸ pages 73, 87	A **symbol** is something that represents, or stands for, something else. An eagle is a **symbol** of the United States. A dove is a **symbol** of peace.
value (**val**-ū) *verb* ▸ pages 79, 85	When you **value** something, you think it is important or useful. I **value** friends more than money.

Practice the Words Take notes about each Key Vocabulary word in a chart. Then quiz a partner about the words. For example:

Q: What is a synonym for *humiliating*?

A: embarrassing

Key Vocabulary Chart

Word	Synonym(s)	Definition	Sentence or Picture
humiliating	embarrassing	hurting your pride	Spilling my backpack at school was humiliating.
imitation			

BEFORE READING **The Necklace**

short story by Guy de Maupassant

Reading Strategies

▶ **Plan and Monitor**
· Determine Importance
· Make Inferences
· Ask Questions
· Make Connections
· Synthesize
· Visualize

Analyze Setting

The **setting** of a story includes the time and place in which the events happen and the circumstances of the characters' lives. The main setting of "The Necklace" is Paris, France, during the late 1800s. It is a time when wealthy people live in fancy homes and throw expensive parties. Within this main setting, there are other scenes, such as a shabby apartment and an elegant party. As you read, consider how the setting affects the characters and the choices they make.

Look Into the Text

The setting tells **when** and **where** this scene takes place.

> Then one evening, her husband came home and proudly handed her a large envelope . . .
>
> She . . . threw the invitation onto the table and murmured, "What do you want me to do with that?"
>
> "But, my dear, I thought you would be so pleased. This is a big event! I had a lot of trouble getting this invitation. All the clerks at the Ministry want to go, but there are only a few invitations reserved for workers. You will meet all the most important people there."
>
> She gave him an irritated look and said, impatiently, "I do not have anything I could wear. How could I go?"

She acts this way at home. How would she act in a setting like the party?

Is this party only for rich, important people? How can you tell?

Focus Strategy ▶ Plan and Monitor

When you come to a word that you don't know, ask yourself, "What could this mean?" Sometimes the context of the sentence will give you a clue. Some words are used regularly in different subjects. For example, *important* might be used in social studies, science, and math.

HOW TO CLARIFY VOCABULARY

Focus Strategy

1. **Look for context clues.** These words or phrases can give hints about the word's meaning.

   Unknown word: important
   Context clues: She did not even have a chance of meeting and marrying a <u>rich</u>, **important** man. <u>Instead</u>, she married a <u>lowly</u> clerk.

2. **Try to figure out what the word means.** Sometimes context clues will also tell you what the word *doesn't* mean.

   You think: A clerk is someone who is not rich or worth talking about. He must be poor.

3. **Try out the meaning.** See if the meaning makes sense in the sentence.

   New sentence: She did not even have a chance of meeting and marrying a rich man **of value, worth talking about**. Instead she married a lowly clerk.

Guy de Maupassant
(1850–1893)

Guy de Maupassant wrote his first short stories as a teenager.

Guy de Maupassant (gē du mō-pa-sahn) lived in France in the late 1800s. When he was a teenager, he worked with Gustave Flaubert, a famous novelist. Flaubert coached Maupassant in his writing and acted as a father figure to him. Flaubert also introduced him to other important writers of the day, including Emile Zola. In 1880, Zola helped Maupassant publish his story "Boule de Suif" ("Ball of Fat"). The story was so well received that Maupassant became an instant success.

During the next ten years, Maupassant published almost 300 short stories and six novels. He wrote about the Franco-German War (1870–1871) and about all kinds of people—rich and poor. Readers loved his stories for their realistic portrayal of French life.

Because of his success, Maupassant could afford the wealthy lifestyle that he wrote about in "The Necklace" and many of his other stories. He owned yachts and several homes throughout France, and he loved to travel.

Although Maupassant died more than one hundred years ago, he is still remembered as one of the greatest short story writers of all time.

myNGconnect.com

⊙ See photographs of Paris in the 1800s.
⊙ Read other stories by Guy de Maupassant.

The Necklace

by Guy de Maupassant

▲ **Critical Viewing: Design** This painting is a realistic portrait of a woman in the past. How does the artist use color, light, and texture to tell you more about the woman?

Comprehension Coach

She was one of those beautiful, charming women who are born, as if by accident, into a lower-class family. Because of this, she did not have even a chance of meeting and marrying a rich, important man. Instead, she married a lowly **clerk** from the Ministry of Education.

She had to dress plainly because she could not afford fine clothes or jewelry. This made her feel like someone of little **worth**. She thought that if she could dress well, other people might consider her more important.

She was miserable, feeling that she deserved a life of wealth and **luxury**. Her shabby apartment, with its dingy walls, worn furniture, and ugly upholstery was an embarrassment to her. Any other woman in her class would not have noticed these things, but for her they were a mark of her worthlessness. **1**

She dreamed of big rooms with thick carpets, bronze lamps, and fancy tapestries. She imagined two butlers napping in large, overstuffed chairs by a fire. She pictured silk draped from the walls, and priceless **knickknacks** cluttering delicate tables. She dreamed of tea with close friends and handsome men in stylish sitting rooms.

At dinner, she watched her husband lift the lid of the soup tureen and exclaim, with delight, "Ah! A good stew! There's nothing I like better. . . ." She imagined elegant dinner parties, shining silverware, dining rooms covered with tapestries of knights, ladies, and magical birds from fairy tales. She dreamed of delicious food served on expensive dishes and of **flattery** whispered and listened to with mysterious smiles.

But she had no fancy clothes, no jewels, nothing. Those were the things she loved; she felt she was made for them. She wanted to please, to **be envied**, to be admired, and to be popular. **2**

1 Setting
Picture Madame Loisel in her apartment. How does this setting make her feel?

2 Setting
Compare Madame Loisel's daydreams with her real surroundings. What kind of life does she want?

Key Vocabulary
luxury *n.*, expensive thing that you do not really need

In Other Words
clerk office worker
worth importance
knickknacks little decorations
flattery compliments to make her feel special
be envied make other people wish they had what she had

The Salon of Princess Mathilde (1820–1904), **1883, Giuseppe or Joseph de Nittis. Oil on canvas, Museo Civico, Barletta, Italy, The Bridgeman Art Library.**

▲ **Critical Viewing: Setting** How does this scene represent what Mathilde wants from life?

She had a rich friend from school, but she did not like to visit this friend. It made her so miserable. When she returned home, she would weep for days, feeling sad and hopeless about her own life.

Then one evening, her husband came home and proudly handed her a large envelope.

"Look," he said. "I have something for you."

She excitedly tore open the envelope. Inside was a printed card that said: "The Minister of Education and Madame Georges Ramponneau invite Monsieur and Madame Loisel to an evening **reception** on Monday, January 18th."

She was not delighted, as her husband had hoped. Instead, she threw the invitation onto the table and **murmured**, "What do you want me to do with that?"

"But, my dear, I thought you would be so pleased. This is a big event! I had a lot of trouble getting this invitation. All the clerks at the Ministry want to go, but there are only a few invitations reserved for workers. You will meet all the most important people there."

She gave him an **irritated** look and said, impatiently, "I do not have anything I could wear. How could I go?" ▣ 3

He had not thought about this. He stammered, "But what about the dress you wear to the theater? I think it looks quite nice."

He was amazed to see that his wife was sobbing. "What is it?" he gasped. "What is the matter?"

With great effort, she stopped crying. Wiping her wet cheeks, she replied, "It's nothing. I just don't have **an evening gown**, so I cannot go to the party. Give the

3 Setting
What does the invitation tell you about the kind of place where the party will be held? Why does Madame Loisel refuse to go?

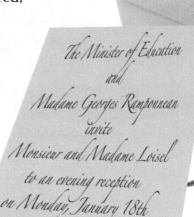

The Minister of Education and Madame Georges Ramponneau invite Monsieur and Madame Loisel to an evening reception on Monday, January 18th

In Other Words
reception party
murmured said very quietly
irritated angry, annoyed
an evening gown a long, expensive dress to wear to fancy parties

Historical Background
At the time of the story, the average French worker earned about 900 *francs* a year. It would be difficult for a clerk to afford expensive luxuries.

invitation to a friend at the office whose wife can dress better than I can."

He was stunned and said, "Mathilde, how much would it cost for a **suitable** dress that you could wear again?"

She thought for several seconds, wondering how much she could ask for without a shocked refusal from her **thrifty husband**.

Finally, she answered, "I am not sure exactly, but I think I could manage with four hundred *francs*."

His face turned pale because that was exactly the amount of money he had saved to buy a new rifle. He wanted to go hunting in Nanterre the next summer with some of his friends.

However, he said, "All right. I'll give you four hundred *francs*, but try to find a beautiful dress."

The day of the party approached. Madame Loisel's gown was ready, but she still seemed depressed and anxious. 🔳4

One evening, her husband asked, "What is wrong? You have been acting strangely for the past three days."

She answered, "I do not have a single jewel to wear. I will look like a **pauper**! I would rather not go to the party at all."

He replied, "You can wear some fresh flowers. They are very **fashionable** this season. For ten *francs*, you can buy two or three gorgeous roses."

She did not like his suggestion at all. "No . . . there is nothing more humiliating than to look poor among a lot of rich women." 🔳5

Then her husband exclaimed, "I know! Go see your friend Madame Forestier and ask her to lend you some jewelry. You two know each other well enough to do that."

She gave a cry of joy. "Yes! That did not occur to me!"

The next day, she went to visit her friend and told her about the

4 Clarify Vocabulary
What does *anxious* mean in this sentence? What surrounding words, or context clues, help you figure it out? What might Madame Loisel be anxious about?

5 Language
Mathilde thinks that looking poor is "humiliating." What other negative words on pages 68–70 does she use to describe being poor?

Key Vocabulary
humiliating *adj.*, very embarrassing

In Other Words
suitable nice enough, appropriate
thrifty husband husband who liked to save money
pauper person who is very poor
fashionable popular, stylish

problem. Madame Forestier went to her large closet with mirrored doors, took out a big jewelry box, brought it to Madame Loisel, opened it, and said, "Choose whatever you like, my dear."

Her eyes wandered over some bracelets, then a pearl necklace, then a gold Venetian cross set with stones. She tried on the jewelry in front of the mirror, but she could not decide what to choose.

Suddenly she discovered a superb diamond necklace in a black satin case. Her heart started beating faster, and her hands trembled as she picked it up. She fastened it around her neck and stood there, gazing at herself in **ecstasy**.

Her voice was hesitant and filled with **agony** when she asked, "Could you lend me this one—just this and nothing else?"

"Yes, of course."

She threw her arms around her friend, kissed her cheek, and then fled with her treasure. **6**

The day of the party arrived. Madame Loisel was a great success. She was the prettiest woman there. She was elegant, fashionable, and gracious, and she was beaming with happiness. All the men looked at her, asked who she was, and begged to be introduced. All the **Cabinet officials** wanted to **waltz** with her. Even the Minister noticed her.

She danced **madly**, thinking of nothing but her beauty and success. She was dazed by all the admiration and floated in a happy cloud brought on by all her awakened desires. She felt the complete victory that is so sweet to a woman's heart. **7**

She went to find her husband around four o'clock in the morning. Since midnight, he had been napping in a small sitting room along with

"Choose whatever you like, my dear."

6 Setting
How would Madame Loisel describe her friend's home and jewels? How does being in this new setting influence her choice?

7 Setting
How does Madame Loisel change in this setting? What does this tell you about her?

In Other Words

ecstasy extreme happiness
agony deep pain and sadness
Cabinet officials men who held important jobs in the government
waltz dance
madly wildly

three other gentlemen whose wives were having a wonderful time.

He covered her shoulders with her wraps. They were plain, from her everyday life, and their shabbiness clashed with the elegance of her evening gown. **8** She felt this and longed to escape quickly so that the other women, who were covered in expensive furs, would not see her.

Loisel held her back.

"Wait, you'll catch cold outside. I'll go for a cab."

But she wouldn't listen to him and went quickly down the stairs. When they reached the street, they did not see a carriage. They set out to find one, waving at the drivers they saw in the distance.

They walked toward **the Seine**, desperate and shivering. Finally, they found a cab on the wharf. It was one of those old carriages that are only seen at night in Paris, as if they are too **ashamed** to show their shabbiness during the daylight.

It took them to their door in the ***Rue des Martyrs***, and they climbed sadly up to their apartment. For her, it was all over. He was thinking that he had to be at the Ministry at ten o'clock. **9**

She took off her wraps in front of the mirror, so that she could see herself once again **in all her glory**. Suddenly, she cried out. There was nothing around her neck. The necklace was gone!

Her husband, who was already half undressed, asked, "What's the matter?"

She turned toward him in a panic. "I . . . I . . . I don't have Madame Forestier's necklace."

"What? That's impossible!"

8 Clarify Vocabulary
What words and phrases in this sentence give clues about the meaning of the word *elegance*?

9 Content Area Connections
Use a map of Paris to locate the places mentioned in the story.

Monitor Comprehension

Summarize
Explain what Mathilde wants in her life. How is the necklace a **symbol** of what she wants?

Key Vocabulary
- **symbol** *n.*, something that represents, or stands for, something else

In Other Words
the Seine the main river in Paris
ashamed embarrassed
Rue des Martyrs Street of the Martyrs (in French)
in all her glory looking so beautiful

They searched in the folds of her dress, in the folds of her wraps, in the pockets, everywhere. They found nothing.

He asked, "Are you sure you still had it when we left the ball?"

"Yes. I felt it in the hallway of the Ministry."

"But if you had lost it in the street, we would have heard it fall. It must be in the cab."

"Yes, most likely. Did you get its number?"

"No. What about you?"

"No."

They looked at each other in shock. Finally, Loisel got dressed again. "I'm going to retrace our steps on foot to see if I can find it," he said.

And he left the house. She slumped in her chair in the cold room, her mind a blank.

Her husband returned around seven o'clock. He had found nothing.

The next day he went to the police station, to the cab companies, and anywhere there was the slightest hope of finding it. He placed an advertisement in the paper offering a reward.

She spent the whole day waiting, feeling completely hopeless **in the face of** such an awful disaster.

When Loisel returned that evening, his face was pale and lined. He had learned nothing. "You must write to your friend," he said. "Tell her that you broke the **clasp** of the necklace and that you are having it repaired. That will give us time to think."

She wrote the letter **at his dictation**.

By the end of the week, they had lost all hope. 🔟

Loisel, who looked like he had aged five years, declared, "We must replace the necklace." The next day, they went to the jeweler whose

🔟 Language
The story includes phrases such as "her mind a blank" and "they had lost all hope." How do they add to your understanding of the characters' feelings?

Literature Background
A familiar archetype is the character whose actions lead to the downfall of another. Helen of Troy, from *The Trojan Horse*, is one example from classical literature. Madame Loisel is an example from 19th-century literature. Analyze how each character represents this archetype.

In Other Words
in the face of because she was thinking about
clasp hook, fastener
at his dictation with the words he told her to write

name they found inside the case. He looked through his **records**.

"I did not sell this necklace, madame," he said. "I only supplied the case."

Then they went from one jeweler to the next, trying to find a similar necklace. Both of them felt sick with worry and **anguish**.

In a shop in **the *Palais Royal***, they found a string of diamonds which looked exactly like the one they were seeking. It was worth 40,000 *francs*. They could have it for 36,000.

They begged the jeweler to hold it for them for three days. He agreed to take it back for 34,000 *francs* if they found the other necklace before the end of February.

Loisel had 18,000 *francs* that his father had left him. He would borrow the rest.

He borrowed, asking a thousand *francs* from one man, five hundred from another, a hundred here, fifty there. He signed **promissory notes** and made deals that could ruin him with all kinds of people. He compromised the rest of his life, agreeing to pay back money even when he wasn't sure that he would be able to do it. Then, terrified by a future of **anxiety and black misery**, he went to get the new necklace and placed 36,000 *francs* on the jeweler's counter. **11**

When Madame Loisel took the necklace back, Madame Forestier said, coldly, "You could have brought it back sooner! I might have needed it."

She did not open the case, as her friend had feared. If she had noticed the substitution, what would she have thought? What would she have said? Wouldn't she have thought Madame Loisel was a thief?

The Poor, 1896, Andre Collin. Oil on canvas, Musee des Beaux-Arts, Tournai, Belgium.

◤ **Critical Viewing: Effect**
How does use of shadow affect the feeling of this painting? How does the painting's feeling match the mood of the Loisel's home?

11 Clarify Vocabulary
What context clues in this paragraph help you understand what *compromised* means?

Monitor Comprehension

Confirm Prediction
Is your prediction correct, or is it still too soon to tell? Explain.

In Other Words

records papers that showed what he had sold and who he had sold it to
anguish suffering
the *Palais Royal* a building lined with shops

promissory notes papers that promised he would pay back the money he had borrowed
anxiety and black misery worrying and suffering

A Woman Ironing, 1873, Edgar Degas.
Oil on canvas, The Metropolitan Museum of Art.

▲ **Critical Viewing: Design** What feeling is expressed by the dark colors the artist used for the woman?

$\mathcal{M}$adame Loisel learned what it was like to live in **poverty**. She did it, however, with a sudden **heroism**. The dreadful **debt** had to be paid. She would pay it. They dismissed their maid and moved into an attic under the roof.

She learned to do all the heavy housework chores, all the hateful duties of cooking. She washed dishes, wearing down her pink fingernails by scouring grease from pots and pans. She scrubbed dirty linen, shirts, and cleaning rags, which she hung on the line to dry. She took the garbage down to the street each morning and carried up the water, stopping at each floor to catch her breath. Dressed like a **peasant woman**, she went to the fruit store, the grocer, and the butcher with a basket on her arm. There she argued for each *sou* of her tiny funds.

Each month, some bills had to be paid, and others were renewed to give more time to pay. Her husband worked in the evenings for a shopkeeper. At night, he copied documents for five *sous* a page.

And this went on for ten years. 12

After ten years, they had finally paid back the whole debt.

Madame Loisel looked like an old woman now. She had become hard, rough, and coarse like a peasant. With her hair uncombed, her skirts

12 **Setting**
Describe how Madame Loisel's surroundings and lifestyle have changed. How do you feel about her now?

Key Vocabulary
poverty *n.*, being very poor

In Other Words
heroism bravery, fearlessness
debt money that was owed
peasant woman poor woman who lived in the countryside
sou penny (in French)

askew, her hands red, and her voice loud, she slopped water over the floors and scrubbed them. But sometimes, when her husband was at the office, she would sit by the window and think of that party long ago, when she had been so beautiful and so admired.

What would have happened if she had not lost that necklace? Who knows? Who can say? How strange and unpredictable life is! How little there is between happiness and sorrow!

Then one Sunday, she went for a walk on **the *Champs Elysées*** to relax from the week's work. Suddenly, she noticed a woman taking a child for a walk. It was Madame Forestier, still young, still beautiful, and still charming.

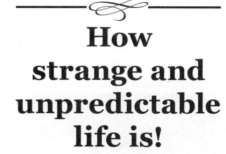

How strange and unpredictable life is!

Madame Loisel felt a rush of emotion. Should she speak to her? Yes, of course she should. And now that she had paid everything back she would tell Madame Forestier the whole story. Why not?

She went toward her.

"Hello, Jeanne."

The other did not recognize her and seemed surprised that this common woman would speak to her **so familiarly**. She stammered, "But . . . madame! . . . I don't recognize . . . You must be mistaken."

"No. I am Mathilde Loisel."

Her friend cried out, "Oh, my poor Mathilde! How you have changed!" **13**

"Yes, I've had a very hard time since I last saw you. I've had many troubles—and all because of you."

"Because of me? What do you mean?"

13 Setting
Why doesn't Madame Forestier recognize Mathilde? What does this tell you about the way people treated others at this time?

In Other Words
askew crooked, twisted around
the *Champs Elysées* a main street in Paris
so familiarly like a friend or family member

"Do you remember that diamond necklace you lent me to wear to the party at the Ministry?"

"Yes. What about it?"

"Well, I lost it."

"What do you mean? You returned it to me."

"I gave you another one that was just like it and it took us ten years to pay for it. You can imagine that wasn't easy for us, since we had nothing. Well, it's over now, and I am glad."

Madame Forestier stopped short. 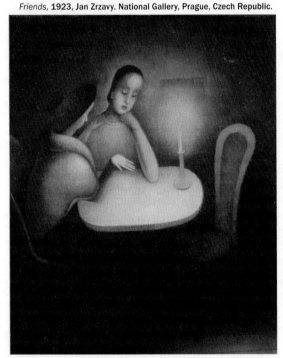 14 "You say that you bought a diamond necklace to replace mine?"

Friends, 1923, Jan Zrzavy. National Gallery, Prague, Czech Republic.

△ Critical Viewing: Effect What mood does the artist create with this painting? Explain.

14 Clarify Vocabulary What does the phrase "stopped short" mean? Why does Madame Forestier "stop short" when talking to Mathilde?

"Yes. You never noticed, then? They were exactly alike."

She smiled with proud, simple joy.

Madame Forestier, **quite moved**, took Mathilde's hands in her own.

"Oh, my poor Mathilde! Mine was an **imitation**. It was worth only five hundred francs at the most!" ❖

ANALYZE The Necklace

1. **Explain** How might the outcome of the story, or resolution, have changed if Madame Loisel had been more truthful? Support your response with details from the story.

2. **Vocabulary** How does the necklace change the way Madame Loisel **perceives** herself? Does it affect the way others at the party perceive her? Explain.

3. **Analyze Setting** With a partner, discuss how the settings and changing circumstances in the story affect Madame Loisel's choices. Record your ideas in a chart.

Setting/Circumstances	Choices
her shabby apartment	
the party	

4. **Focus Strategy Clarify Vocabulary** Tell a partner how you used a context clue to figure out a word's meaning.

🔲 Return to the Text

Reread and Write Madame Loisel's choices are influenced by what she **values** in life. Does her attitude toward these things change by the end of the story? Write your opinion using at least two pieces of evidence from the text.

Key Vocabulary
imitation *n.*, something that looks or acts like something else
• **perceive** *v.*, to see in a certain way
value *v.*, to think something is important or useful

In Other Words
quite moved feeling very emotional

BEFORE READING **The Fashion Show**

memoir by Farah Ahmedi with Tamim Ansary

Reading Strategies

▶ **Plan and Monitor**
- Determine Importance
- Make Inferences
- Ask Questions
- Make Connections
- Synthesize
- Visualize

Determine Viewpoint

A memoir is a writer's personal account of real events that happened in his or her life. It often has a plot like a short story. It also shares the writer's **viewpoint**, or thoughts and feelings about the events.

Look Into the Text

The author tells her own story. She is a **first-person narrator**. She uses *I* and *my* to tell the story. Many of the sentences have a similar structure.

> The first part of the show would be a dance performance by the kids from Mexico. The next part would be a fashion show. Kids from any country could be in the fashion show, and they would model clothes from their own culture, but no one had to do it.
>
> I felt torn and confused. I could not take part in the dance, of course, but should I be in the fashion show? I really wanted to do it. I had two beautiful Afghan outfits I could model. But I was also thinking, *My leg is damaged. What if I fall down?*

The writing shows the author's feelings and opinions.

Focus Strategy ▶ Plan and Monitor

Sometimes a context clue in the sentence can help you understand an unknown word. Most other times, though, you will need to look at more than one sentence to figure out what a word means.

HOW TO CLARIFY VOCABULARY
Focus Strategy

1. **Read the sentences around the unknown word.** Read the sentence before the word, the sentence the word is in, and the sentence after the word.

2. **Look for a relationship between sentences.** Notice how the second sentence below is connected to the first: It gives an example of what the writer means by "torn and confused."

   > I felt torn and confused. I could not take part in the dance, of course, but should I be in the fashion show?

   The author asks herself a question. Maybe <u>confused</u> means "questioning," or "unsure of the answer."

3. **Substitute your guess for the unknown word.** Check to see if it makes sense in the sentence.

   > I felt torn and unsure of the answer.

   That meaning makes sense.

Connect Across Texts

In "The Necklace," Madame Loisel makes a choice because she worries about what others think. Now read this memoir. How do the opinions of others affect Farah's decision?

THE FASHION SHOW

by Farah Ahmedi
with Tamim Ansary

At just 17, Farah Ahmedi entered an essay contest. Since then, her memoir, *The Other Side of the Sky*, has inspired people everywhere with her life story as a proud Afghan American.

▲ Farah Ahmedi was a junior in high school when she published *The Other Side of the Sky: A Memoir.*

Farah Ahmedi didn't have much of a childhood. She was still recovering from losing her leg in **a land mine accident** when a rocket attack destroyed her home in Kabul, Afghanistan. Four years and many challenges later, Farah and her mother found their way to a **suburb of** Chicago. Farah learned English, started high school, and began to make choices that would change her life. Despite her disability, she wanted to fit in. She wanted to "wear high-heeled shoes." Here, Farah remembers one of those choices.

During our second summer in America, I switched schools. The **ESL department** at my new high school had an international club. Kids from other countries met every Wednesday after school to play games, talk, and have fun. Ms. Ascadam, the teacher who sponsored this group, decided that the international kids should throw a party at the end of the year and present a show. 1 She told us each to bring food from our country to the party, and she encouraged us to think about participating in the show as well.

The first part of the show would be a dance performance by the kids from Mexico. The next part would be a **fashion show**. Kids from any country could be in the fashion show, and they would model clothes from their own culture, but no one had to do it.

From Kabul to Chicago

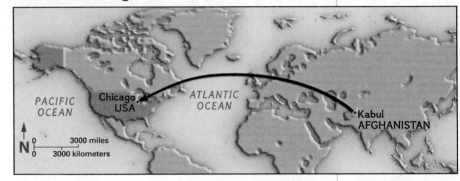

▲ Interpret the Map Use the scale to calculate how far Farah and her mother traveled to their new home.

1 **Clarify Vocabulary** What does *sponsored* mean? What clues in the sentences before and after the word can help you figure it out?

I felt **torn and confused**. I could not take part in the dance, of course, but should I be in the fashion show? I really wanted to do it. I had two beautiful **Afghan outfits** I could model. But I was also thinking, *My leg is damaged. What if I fall down?*

Finally, I said to myself, *Okay, next Wednesday I'll sit in on the practice session and see what it's like, and then I'll decide.*

That day the girl who always picked on me came to the practice session, because she was planning to be in the fashion show. The moment she saw me sitting there, she could tell I was thinking of entering the show, too. She didn't tell me to my face that I could not do it, but she immediately called out to the teacher. "Ms. Ascadam," she said, "when you model clothes at a fashion show, isn't this how you have to walk? Isn't this how models walk on a **runway**?"

Then she began to walk the way she thought a model should walk— with long strides, placing one foot in front of the other in a straight line that made her back end swing from side to side. "Is this the way you should walk?" she said. "If someone can't walk like this, should she be in the fashion show? She would just spoil the whole thing, wouldn't she?" And she kept walking back and forth, swinging from side to side.

It made me so angry, because I knew that she was really saying, *Farah can't do this. She has a problem with her legs. She shouldn't be in the fashion show.* She didn't say my name, but she was talking about me and only me, and everyone knew it.

That girl broke my heart. I felt as if somebody had punched me or slapped me. I felt as if someone had gotten into my throat and started pushing me and pressing me and choking me. I could not stay in that room. I turned and **fled**, my eyes stinging with tears. At home I

2 Clarify Vocabulary
What are some meanings for the word *model*? What context clues help you understand what the word means here?

3 Viewpoint
How is the author feeling? What images help you understand her feelings?

Monitor Comprehension

Summarize
How does Ahmedi feel about being a model in the fashion show?

In Other Words
torn and confused mixed up, upset
Afghan outfits sets of clothes from Afghanistan
runway stage
fled ran away

threw myself on my bed and just lay there, weeping and feeling sorry for myself—sorry about being only half a woman. I felt like everyone knew that I was not whole and that's what they thought about every time they looked at me. That girl had finally succeeded in getting through my defenses and poking me right where it hurt the most and where I would always hurt. **4**

Farah Ahmedi shares her memoir with First Lady Laura Bush.

And what happened just then?

My friend Alyce called.

"Hey," she said. "How are you, sweetie? Are you well?"

I started to **bawl**.

She said, "What is it? What are you crying about?"

I spilled the whole story.

Alyce said, "Now don't **get all hung up on** what other people say. You just go ahead and do it. You tell your teacher you want to be in the fashion show."

But I just went on crying. "You don't understand. It's not *just* what 'other people say.' The terrible thing is, that girl is right! I *can't* be in a fashion show! It's true. How can someone like me be in a fashion show? With my limp? I can't walk like a model." That girl's cruelty **wounded** me, to be sure, but what really hurt was the truth she was telling. "Why are you trying to **inspire** me to do something I should never even try?" I **ranted** at Alyce.

It was one of those moments, you see. And Alyce just let me rage.

4 Clarify Vocabulary
What does the author mean by the phrase "getting through my defenses"? To figure it out, look at the second part of this sentence. Remember to always use the context to help you figure out a word or a phrase's meaning.

Key Vocabulary
inspire *v.*, to encourage someone to take action

In Other Words
bawl cry hard
I spilled the whole story. I told her everything.
get all hung up on worry about, feel upset about
wounded hurt
ranted yelled angrily

But then she said, "No, people aren't looking at you that way. Here, we **value** who you are as a person. You go right ahead and enter the fashion show fearlessly."

Well, I thought about it. I thought I should do it just to **spite** the girl who tried to keep me out of the show. I decided I had to do it, even if it meant falling down in the middle of the runway—because if I let that girl get away with talking about me as if I were half human, she would never stop. She would make me **her scapegoat**, and others would take up her view as well. I had to stand up for myself, because this was not just about a fashion show. It was about claiming my humanity. I had to do it. **5**

I went to my teacher the next day and told her I wanted to enter the fashion show. She hugged me. "Farah," she said, "this makes me so, so happy!"

After that I started to practice walking. No, I started to practice *strutting* down a runway.

On the day of the fashion show, I hurried to the dressing room to get ready. I had two dresses to wear, an orange one and a purple

I HAD TO DO IT.

one. Backstage the makeup people put cosmetics on my face and curled my hair, so that I looked really different than usual. The teacher saw me and said, "Oh my gosh, you look so pretty!"

The fashion show began. Each model was supposed to go out and walk around the stage in a diamond-shaped pattern. At each point of the diamond we were supposed to pause, face the audience, and **strike a pose**.

When my turn came, I went strutting out. **6** I threw my shoulders back and held my head up high so that my neck stretched long. I didn't fall, and I didn't shake. I didn't even feel nervous.

5 Viewpoint
How does the author help you understand why she makes her decision?

6 Clarify Vocabulary
What does *strutting* mean? Look for clues in the paragraph.

Monitor Comprehension

Explain
What makes Ahmedi change her mind about the show?

Key Vocabulary
value *v.*, to think something is important or useful

In Other Words
spite annoy, get back at
her scapegoat the one everyone blamed
strike a pose stand boldly for everyone to see

Alyce told me later that no one could tell about my legs. I moved in time to the music, showed the clothes off well, and smiled—I did just fine! My mother **beamed**. She didn't say much at the time, but later on, at home, she told me she felt proud of me. Imagine that! Proud that her daughter stood up before an audience of strangers and modeled our beautiful Afghan clothes: She, too, has come a long way since we arrived in America.

After the show the party began. We had all brought special foods from our various cultures. My mother had cooked a fancy Afghan rice dish. We ate and chatted and felt happy. That night, though it wasn't **literally** true, I felt that I was wearing high-heeled shoes at last. ❖

ANALYZE The Fashion Show

1. **Explain** Who or what **inspires** Ahmedi's final decision about the show? Provide specific evidence from the text that helps explain her decision.

2. **Vocabulary** How does Ahmedi **perceive** herself at the start of the memoir? Do others agree? Explain.

3. **Determine Viewpoint** With a partner, discuss how the viewpoint of a newspaper article about the fashion show would be different from the viewpoint in the memoir.

4. **Focus Strategy Clarify Vocabulary** Share one example of how you used context clues to figure out a word's meaning.

Return to the Text

Reread and Write Decide who inspires Ahmedi more—her friend Alyce or the girl who picks on her. Write a thank-you note from Ahmedi to that person. Quote remarks that the person made that affected Ahmedi's decision.

Key Vocabulary
- **perceive** v., to see someone or something in a certain way

In Other Words
beamed smiled with joy
literally actually

EQ What Influences a Person's Choices?

Reading
Critical Thinking

EQ 1. Interpret What is Maupassant saying about the influence of society in "The Necklace"? Would Ahmedi agree with this message? Why or why not?

2. Compare The necklace in "The Necklace" and high-heeled shoes in "The Fashion Show" are both **symbols**. What is similar about the themes that the symbols represent? How are they different? Explain.

3. Analyze How do Ahmedi's and Madame Loisel's characters affect their decisions?

4. Speculate How would the theme of the memoir be different if it took place in France in the 1800s?

EQ 5. Evaluate Each of the selections in this unit deals with the things that influence us: our circumstances, our friends and families, and our communities. Which reason is the most positive? Use text examples to support your ideas.

Writing
Write About Literature

Response Log Write about a time when a choice you made had surprising consequences. Compare your experience to Madame Loisel's and Ahmedi's. Support your writing with examples from both texts.

Vocabulary
Key Vocabulary Review

Oral Review Work with a partner. Use these words to complete the paragraph.

humiliating	luxuries	symbols
imitations	perceive	value
inspire	poverty	

Some people think that money can buy happiness. They want __(1)__ that they don't really need, like big homes and cars. They think it's __(2)__ and embarrassing to wear inexpensive clothes. Some may even buy __(3)__ of other things because they are __(4)__ that represent happiness and wealth. But those things don't always make them happy. Sometimes, people who live in __(5)__ without enough money can be happier than rich people. It's because they __(6)__ things that are really important, like family and friends. They look at what they have and __(7)__ it as precious. These people __(8)__ me to be more like them.

Writing Application Write a paragraph about someone who **inspired** you. Use at least three Key Vocabulary words.

Fluency
Read with Ease: Intonation

Assess your reading fluency with the passage in the Reading Handbook, p. 753. Then complete the self-check below.

1. My intonation did/did not sound natural.

2. My words correct per minute: _____.

Grammar

Fix Sentence Fragments

This group of words begins with a capital letter and ends with a period, just like a sentence:

Dreams of a life of wealth.

The group of words looks like a sentence, but it is not complete. It is a **sentence fragment**. The fragment needs a **subject** :

The young wife dreams of a life of wealth.

A fragment may need a **verb** .

Fragment: The diamond necklace.
Sentence: The diamond necklace **sparkles** .

A fragment may need to become part of another sentence.

Fragment: Because she cannot afford fine clothes.
Sentence: Mathilde dresses plainly because she cannot afford fine clothes.

Oral Practice (1–5) Look at the selections you just read. Find five complete sentences. Break off a piece, and say it as a fragment. Ask your partner to change it back into a complete sentence.

Written Practice (6–10) Number your paper. Label each group of words with **S** for *Sentence* or **F** for *Fragment*. Then choose two fragments to write as complete sentences.

  6. Mathilde wants to dress well.
  7. To be envied and admired.
  8. Feels sad and hopeless about her life.
  9. A large envelope.
 10. The couple is invited to a fancy party.

Language Development

Express Feelings and Intentions

Role-Play Take the role of Monsieur or Madame Loisel and tell about something you plan to do in the future. Tell how you feel about it, too.

Literary Analysis

Analyze Setting and Theme

Setting is the time and place in which a story unfolds. A story's setting affects the characters and the **theme**, or message, of the story. Think about the setting of "The Necklace."

- "The Necklace" is set in nineteenth century Paris. During this period, people could move from the lower class to the upper class if they had enough money or knew the right people.

- Madame Loisel wants to be wealthy. The setting feeds her desire and affects her decisions.

- Since the setting affects her actions, it also affects the story's theme. Here's how:

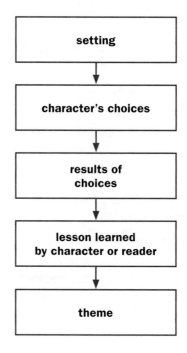

Discuss the following:

❶ Use the diagram above to trace the development of the story's theme, starting with its setting.

❷ State in your own words what you think the theme of this story is. How does the setting affect the theme?

Suffixes

A **suffix** is an affix, or word part, added at the end of a word. The suffix *-ify* comes from Latin. It means "to make." That's why the word *clarify* means "to make clear." Here are some other suffixes:

SUFFIX	ORIGIN	MEANING
-wise	Old English	in the direction of
-ion	Latin	act or process of
-logy	Greek	the study of

Copy each word below. Write what you think the word means based on the suffix. Then check the meaning in a dictionary. Use two of the words to tell a partner about "The Necklace."

1. biology **2.** attraction **3.** clockwise **4.** beautify

Focus and Unity: Thesis or Central Idea

Every time you write, keep your central idea, or **thesis**, at the center of attention. To do this:

- state your central idea clearly
- choose examples that support the idea
- leave out unnecessary details or ideas

Just OK	Much Better
Madame Loisel was influenced too much by society. She admired wealthy people. Her friend loaned her a fancy necklace. She should have been content with her life instead of trying to be like rich people.	Madame Loisel was influenced too much by society. She admired wealthy people, so she sacrificed everything she had to be like them. ~~Her friend loaned her a fancy necklace.~~ She should have been content with her life.

Research Report

Social Studies: Peers Under Pressure What is peer pressure—and are all of its influences bad? Work with a small group to brainstorm ideas, and then research the topic.

myNGconnect.com
- Learn more about good and bad peer pressure.
- Find ways to deal with peer pressure.

Pool your information to create a report about the positive and negative effects of peer pressure on teens today. Provide facts that support your thesis statement. Also tell stories with specific details that illustrate the influences of peer pressure.

📖 **Language and Learning Handbook,** page 702

📖 **Writing Handbook,** page 784

Read the paragraph below. Then brainstorm ways the writer could make the passage more focused. What would you add or take out?

> The most important lesson I've learned in high school is to always be myself. I used to try to be like the popular kids. They had expensive clothes and cars, and they all came from a school across town. Everybody thought they were cool. But whenever I tried to imitate them, I didn't feel right. They don't like to cook like me. I was really uncomfortable. I realized that to be really happy, I just had to be myself. I'm much happier now.

Identify the thesis. Then decide whether the details support or distract from the central idea.

Central Idea: It's important to be yourself.		
Detail	**Helps**	**Hurts**
She tried to be popular.	X	
They had expensive things.		

📖 **Writing Handbook,** page 784

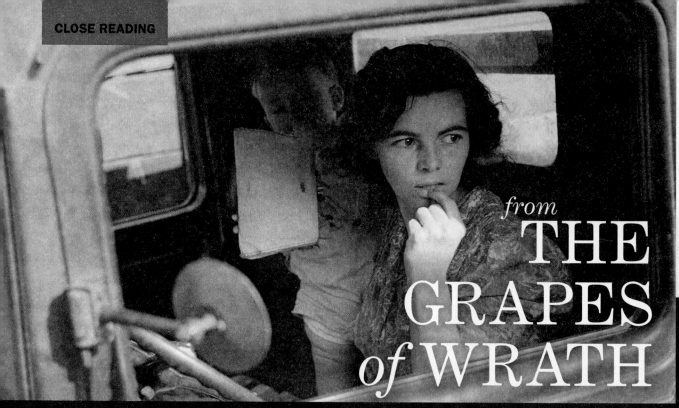

Farm wife waiting in the car while her husband attends the auction, Oskaloosa, Kansas, 1938, John Vachon. Photographic negative, Library of Congress

from
THE GRAPES *of* WRATH

By John Steinbeck

⚠ Critical Viewing: Mood What is the mood, or feeling, of this photograph? How did the photographer achieve the mood?

1 "...the road is full a them families goin' west. Never seen so many. Gets worse all a time. Wonder where the hell they all come from?"

2 "Wonder where they all go to," said Mae. "Come here for gas sometimes, but they don't hardly never buy nothin' else. People says they steal. We **ain't got nothin' layin'** around. They never stole nothin' from us."

3 Big Bill, munching his pie, looked up the road through the screened window. "Better tie your stuff down. I think you got some of 'em comin' now."

4 A 1926 Nash **sedan** pulled wearily off the highway. The back seat was piled nearly to the ceiling with sacks, with pots and pans, and on the very top, right up against the ceiling, two boys rode. On the top of the car, a mattress and a folded tent; tent poles tied along the running board. The car pulled up to the gas pumps. A dark-haired, hatchet-faced man got slowly out. And the two boys slid down from the load and hit the ground.

In Other Words

a them families goin' of those families going
ain't got nothin' layin' don't have anything lying
sedan medium-sized car

Historical Background

In the early 1930s, a drought hit the midwestern U.S. and farmers in the area lost all their crops. This area became known as the **Dust Bowl** because of the wind storms that swept dust over everything. Many families packed what little they had left and drove west to work in the fields of California.

5   Mae walked around the counter and stood in the door. The man was dressed in gray wool trousers and a blue shirt, dark blue with sweat on the back and under the arms. The boys in overalls and nothing else, ragged patched overalls. Their hair was light, and it stood up evenly all over their heads, for it had been **roached**. Their faces were streaked with dust. They went directly to the mud puddle under the hose and dug their toes into the mud.

6   The man asked, "Can we **git** some water, ma'am?"

7   A look of annoyance crossed Mae's face. "Sure, go ahead." She said softly over her shoulder, "I'll keep my eye on the hose." She watched while the man slowly unscrewed the radiator cap and ran the hose in.

8   A woman in the car, a flaxen-haired woman, said, "See if you can't git it here."

9   The man turned off the hose and screwed on the cap again. The little boys took the hose from him and they upended it and drank thirstily. The man took off his dark, stained hat and stood with a curious **humility** in front of the screen. "**Could you see your way to** sell us a loaf of bread, ma'am?"

> *The man…stood with a curious humility in front of the screen.*

10 Mae said, "This ain't a grocery store. We got bread to make **san'widges**."

11 "I know, ma'am." His humility was **insistent**. "We need bread and there **ain't nothin' for quite a piece**, they say."

12 " 'F we sell bread we gonna run out." Mae's tone was **faltering**.

13 "We're hungry," the man said.

14 "**Whyn't** you buy a san'widge? We got nice san'widges, hamburgs."

15 "We'd sure **admire** to do that, ma'am. But we can't. We got to make a dime do all of us." And he said embarrassedly, "We **ain't got but** a little."

16 Mae said, "You can't get no loaf a bread for a dime. We only got fifteen-cent loafs."

17 From behind her Al growled, "God Almighty, Mae, give 'em bread."

18 "We'll run out 'fore the bread truck comes."

In Other Words

roached brushed to stand upright
git get
humility modesty, lack of pride
Could you see your way to Would you
san'widges sandwiches
insistent demanding, persistent

ain't nothin' for quite a piece isn't anything for quite a while
faltering uncertain, hesitating
Whyn't Why don't
admire like
ain't got but only have

19   "Run out, then, goddamn it," said Al. And he looked sullenly down at the potato salad he was mixing.

20   Mae shrugged her plump shoulders and looked to the truck drivers to show them what she was up against.

21   She held the screen door open and the man came in, bringing a smell of sweat with him. The boys edged in behind him and they went immediately to the candy case and stared in—not with **craving** or with hope or even with desire, but just with a kind of wonder that such things could be. They were alike in size and their faces were alike. One scratched his dusty ankle with the toe nails of his other foot. The other whispered some soft message and then they straightened their arms so that their clenched fists in the overall pockets showed through the thin blue cloth.

The boys...went immediately to the candy case and stared in...

22   Mae opened a drawer and took out a long waxpaper-wrapped loaf. "This here is a fifteen-cent loaf."

23   The man put his hat back on his head. He answered with **inflexible** humility, "Won't you—can't you see your way to cut off ten cents' worth?"

24   Al said snarlingly, "Goddamn it, Mae. Give 'em the loaf."

25   The man turned toward Al. "No, we want ta buy ten cents' worth of it. We got it **figgered awful** close, mister, to get to California."

26   Mae said **resignedly**, "You can have this for ten cents."

27   "That'd be robbin' you, ma'am."

28   "Go ahead—Al says to take it." She pushed the waxpapered loaf across the counter. The man took a deep leather pouch from his rear pocket, untied the strings, and spread it open. It was heavy with silver and with greasy bills.

29   "May soun' funny to be so **tight**," he apologized. "We got a thousan' miles to go, an' we don' know if we'll make it." He dug in the pouch with a forefinger, located a dime, and pinched in for it. When he put it down on the counter he had a penny with it. He was about to drop the penny back into the pouch when **his eye fell on** the boys frozen before the candy counter. He moved slowly down to them. He pointed in the case at big long sticks of striped peppermint. "Is them penny candy, ma'am?"

In Other Words

craving want, hunger
inflexible unchanging
figgered awful counted very
resignedly giving up, yielding
tight worried about spending money
his eye fell on he saw

30   Mae moved down and looked in. "Which ones?"

31   "There, them stripy ones."

32   The little boys raised their eyes to her face and they stopped breathing; their mouths were partly opened, their half-naked bodies were **rigid**.

33   "Oh—them. Well, no—them's two for a penny."

34   "Well, gimme two then, ma'am." He placed the copper cent carefully on the counter. The boys **expelled** their held breath softly. Mae held the big sticks out.

35   "Take 'em," said the man.

36   They reached **timidly**, each took a stick, and they held them down at their sides and did not look at them. But they looked at each other, and their mouth corners smiled rigidly with embarrassment.

37   "Thank you, ma'am." The man picked up the bread and went out the door, and the little boys marched stiffly behind him, the red-striped sticks held tightly against their legs. They leaped like chipmunks over the front seat and onto the top of the load, and they burrowed back out of sight like chipmunks.

38   The man got in and started his car, and with a roaring motor and a cloud of blue oily smoke the ancient Nash climbed up on the highway and went on its way to the west.

39   From inside the restaurant the truck drivers and Mae and Al stared after them.

40   Big Bill **wheeled** back. "Them wasn't two-for-a-cent candy," he said.

41   "What's that to you?" Mae said fiercely.

42   "Them was nickel apiece candy," said Bill. ❖

Part of an impoverished family of nine on a New Mexico highway, 1936, Dorthea Lange. Photographic negative, Library of Congress.

Critical Viewing: Setting ▶
This photo was taken during the Dust Bowl. How do the setting details in the photo compare with the details in the story?

In Other Words

rigid stiff, not moving
expelled let out
timidly shyly, without confidence
wheeled turned the conversation

CHOICES

EQ **ESSENTIAL QUESTION:**
**What Influences
a Person's Choices?**

myNGconnect.com

⬇ Download the rubric.

EDGE LIBRARY

Present Your Project: TV Talk Show

It's time to host your TV talk show about the Essential Question for this unit:
What Influences a Person's Choices?

1 Review and Complete Your Plan

- How will the host introduce the guests and the Essential Question?
- How will the host keep the focus on the Essential Question?
- How long will the guests discuss the topic?

Practice your talk show at least once. Be sure that everyone is prepared.

2 Give Your Talk Show

Seat the host and the guests so that the audience can see and hear
them well. Follow the plan that you made to present the show.

3 Evaluate the Talk Shows

Use the online rubric to evaluate each of the talk shows, including yours.

Reflect on Your Reading

Many of the characters in the stories in this unit and in the Edge Library
made important choices.

Think back on your reading of the unit selections, including your choice
of Edge Library books. Then discuss the following with a partner or in a
small group.

Genre Focus Compare and contrast the elements of a short
story with the features of a memoir. Give examples, using the selections
in this unit.

Think about classical archetypes you encountered in *The Trojan Horse,*
such as the hero or the person who causes another's downfall. Did these
archetypes appear in any of the unit selections? Explain how
the archetypes in the selections are similar to the archetypes in
The Trojan Horse.

Focus Strategy Pick a selection in this unit that you think might be
difficult for some people to read. Choose three strategies that would help
a person clarify his or her understanding and explain them on a bookmark
that you can share with a partner. Use the bookmark as a reference as you
continue to read more selections in this program.

EQ Respond to the Essential Question

Throughout this unit, you have been thinking about how people make
choices. What have *you* decided? Support your response with evidence
from your reading, discussions, research, and writing.

Write an Autobiographical Narrative

Boston says hi!

Greetings from Miami

Writing Portfolio

Life is filled with choices. Some of them are easy to make. Some are hard. For this project, you will write about a choice that you made.

Study Autobiographical Narratives

Autobiographical narratives are stories about events in your own life. Whenever you describe something that happened to you, such as a choice you made, you are telling an autobiographical narrative.

❶ Connect Writing to Your Life

It is likely that you tell autobiographical narratives almost every day. You might tell classmates what you did over the weekend. You might tell friends about something funny that happened to you in school. You might trade stories with family about your day. This project builds on your personal storytelling skills.

❷ Understand the Form

Remember that you are not writing just for yourself. Other people will read your narrative. Make it clear and interesting to them. Like all good stories, it needs a beginning, a middle, and an end.

> **Beginning**
> Introduce the key choice that you made. Start with interesting background that leads to the decisions and choices that you made. Establish the **controlling idea** of your narrative.

> **Middle**
> Tell what happened in the **chronological order** that it happened. Use descriptive details and dialogue.

> **End**
> Tell what happened as a result of your choice.

Now look at these parts in action. Read an autobiographical narrative by a professional writer.

❸ Analyze a Professional Model

As you read, look for the three main parts of the story.

The Bike

by Gary Soto

I was scared of riding on Sarah Street. Mom said hungry dogs lived on that street, and red anger lived in their eyes. Their throats were hard with extra bones from biting kids on bikes, she said.

But I took the corner anyway. I didn't believe Mom. Once she had said that pointing at rainbows caused freckles, and after a rain had moved in and drenched the streets, a rainbow washed over the junkyard. I stood at the window, looking out, amazed and devious, with the devilish horns of my butch haircut standing up.

I pedaled my squeaky bike around the curve onto Sarah Street, but returned immediately. I braked and looked back at where I had gone. My face was hot, my hair sweaty, but nothing scary seemed to happen. There ain't no dogs, I told myself. I began to think that maybe this was like one of those false rainbow warnings.

I stopped when I saw a kid my age come down a porch. His bike was a tricycle. Big baby, I thought, and said, "You can run over my leg with your trike if you want." I laid down on the sidewalk, and the kid, with fingers in his mouth, said, "OK."

He backed up and slowly, like a tank, advanced. When the tire climbed over my ankle, I sat up quickly, my eyes flinging tears like a sprinkler.

The boy asked, "Did it hurt?"

"No," I said, almost crying.

I got on my bicycle and pedaled mostly with the good leg.

Then the sudden bark of a dog scared me, and my pants leg fed into the chain, the bike coming to an immediate stop. I tugged at the cuff, gnashed and oil-black, until ripping sounds made me quit trying. I fell to the ground, bike and all, and let the tears lather my face. I then dragged the bike home with the pants leg in the chain. There was nothing to do except lie in the dirt because Mom saw me round the corner from Sarah Street. I just lay there when she came out, and I didn't blame the dog or that stupid rainbow.

Interesting background introduces the choice.

The **choice** is stated here. The consequence of disbelieving and disobeying his mother is the **controlling idea**. Analyze the details that support and elaborate the controlling idea.

Descriptive details make the scene come alive, even if they aren't necessary to tell the story. Would you include them in a summary of the story? Why or why not?

The writer tells what happened in the order that it happened.

The writer includes actual dialogue.

What happened as a result of the narrator's choice?

▶ **Prompt** Write an autobiographical narrative about a choice you made. Be sure to tell:

- what the choice was
- how or why you made the choice
- how you felt about the choice
- what happened as a result of the choice

✎ Prewrite

Now that you know the basics of autobiographical narratives, plan one of your own. Planning will make it easier for you to write later on. Making a Writing Plan helps you avoid the "blank page blues," when you can't think of anything to say.

❶ Choose Your Topic

Here are some good ways to choose a topic:

- Pick a decision that you have strong feelings about, one that you're proud of, or one that you regret.
- Pick a decision that you wonder about. Why did you make the choice? What would have happened if you had made a different choice?
- Brainstorm ideas with a friend or family member.

❷ Clarify the Audience, Controlling Idea, and Purpose

If you do any blogging, you probably choose the audience for the entries you make. Who will you be writing this paper for? Jot down your ideas.

Then think about the main point or central idea you want to get across about your choice. Write your notes about the controlling idea.

Finally, think about your purpose, or reason, for writing. Is your purpose to tell a story about yourself? To entertain your audience? Make them understand how you felt? Jot down your purpose.

❸ Gather Supporting Details

Next, gather details to support, or explain, your choice. Recall what happened and how you felt. Take notes.

Then tell your story to a partner. Have your partner take notes and ask questions to

- get more details that are specific, important, and on target
- help you clarify your ideas
- fill in background information.

> **Prewriting Tip**
>
> Ask yourself these questions to find your controlling idea:
>
> - Was my choice good or bad?
> - Did it change my life? If so, how?
> - Did I learn something from the choice? If so, what?

❹ Organize the Details

Organize the details in chronological order, the order in which they happened. Make a list, or use a time line like the one below. Put the turning point of your choice in the middle. Then add events on the left and right in time order.

Technology Tip

List the details as phrases or sentences. Then use Cut and Paste from the Edit menu to move details around as you need to.

Time Line

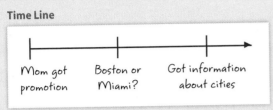

❺ Finish Your Writing Plan

Make a Writing Plan like the one below to capture all the planning you have done. Show which details will go in the beginning, the middle, and the end.

Writing Plan

Topic	how I helped Mom choose where we would move
Audience	my teacher and my classmates
Controlling Idea	choosing Miami gave me a fresh start
Purpose	to tell the story of a choice; to entertain
Time Frame	a week from Monday

Beginning
1. Mom received a promotion.
2. We had to choose where to move, Boston or Miami.
3. My mom broke the news of the move to me at a restaurant. (Interesting! Use this in the beginning.)

Middle
4. I was in my freshman year and wanted a change.
5. We gathered information about both cities.
6. We chose Miami.
7. I found out about the New World School in Miami.

End
8. I have applied to the New World School.
9. I am glad that we chose Miami.
10. Living here is a fresh start for me and my mom.

Reflect on Your Writing Plan

▶ Do you have enough details for the beginning, the middle, and the end? Are you pleased with your topic and controlling idea? If not, now's the time to change them!

✔ Write a Draft

Now you are ready to write. Use your Writing Plan as a guide while you write your narrative. It's OK to make mistakes. You'll have chances to improve your draft. Just keep writing!

❶ Keep Your Ideas Flowing

Sometimes writers get "stuck." They can't figure out what to say or how to say it. If you have trouble getting your ideas on paper, try these techniques:

- **Talk It Over** Tell someone what you want to say in your narrative. Together, find the words to say it.

- **Change Your Plan** If your plan is not helping, change it. Brainstorm, list, and organize new details.

- **Skip Over the Hard Part** If you have trouble writing one part of your paper, skip to a part that is easier to write. It will then be easier go back and finish it.

- **Do a Focused Freewrite** Write continuously about your topic for about five minutes. During that time, do not stop writing. If you can't think of anything to say, then say that. Then, reread what you wrote. Underline ideas that you might be able to use in your paper. Study the student example below.

> <u>I was not sure what choice to make</u>. I couldn't figure out what to do. What to do. What to do. I can't think of anything to say. Wait a minute. I remember. I remember. I felt as if I had <u>information overload</u>. Is there such a thing as <u>too much information</u>? There must be because I had it. I felt as if I were drowning in facts about Boston and Miami. <u>The more I knew, the harder it was to choose</u>.

Technology Tip

Make your text double- or triple-spaced, or as your teacher directs. (Use the Paragraph feature from the Format menu to change line spacing.) Print a copy of your draft to read later. The extra space between lines will give you room to mark changes.

❷ Create a Catchy Beginning

How will you hook your readers' attention? What is an interesting detail that you can start out with? Sometimes coming up with a great beginning can help the rest of the writing flow. Here's an example:

OK

> My mom and I went to dinner. My mom told me that she got a promotion at work. We had to move.

Better

> My mom and I were eating Italian food at our favorite place, Tedesco's, when she told me the big news.

Read this draft to see how the student used the Writing Plan to get ideas down on paper. This first draft does not have to be perfect. As you will see, the student fixed the mistakes later.

A Fresh Start

My mom and I were eating italian food at our favorite place, Tedesco's restaurant, when she told me the big news. I love Tedesco's because the lasagna is so good. I always order it. She said that she had received a promotion at work. The company was opening two new branch offices, and her boss had asked her to open one of them. The only thing was, both branches were kind of far away from Baltimore, where we lived. One was in Boston, and the other was in Miami.

"We won't go if you don't want to go" she said.

Did I want to go? I wasn't sure. Did I want to stay? I wasn't sure about that either.

"It doesn't really matter to me whether its Boston or Miami," she added. Pick the one that will make you happy. It would be a fresh start for both of us."

"A fresh start is just what I need!" I said.

Wow. Picking a city to live in was quite a challenge—and quite an opportunity. I had only a month to make the choice. I went on the Internet right away. Soon, I was overloaded with information. I knew a lot about each city, but I didn't feel any closer to choosing between them. The more I knew, the harder it was to choose. I was just about ready to tell my mother that she was going to have to make the choice when I found out about Miami's New World School of the Arts (NWSA).

The NWSA has special high school programs in music, dance, theater, and visual arts. I explored it online, and I immediately began to fantasize about going there. I couldn't apply their if we lived out of state, but if we were living in Miami, I could apply for the next school year. My choice was made. "I'm ready," I said to my mother.

I gave her the full presentation. Telling her everything I'd found out about Boston and Miami. I finished with the NWSA.

"What if you don't get in?" she asked.

"At least I will have tried," I said.

"Done," she said. "We're moving to Miami."

Reflect on Your Draft

▶ Is your controlling idea clear? Do you have enough details, and are they in chronological order? Talk it over with a partner.

Revise Your Draft

Your first draft is done. Now, polish it. Improve the focus and unity, and your choice of supporting details and words. Make what was just OK into something much better.

❶ Revise for Focus and Unity

Any kind of good writing has a **focus**—it has a central, controlling idea. In an autobiographical narrative, the focus is telling the story of an important experience in the writer's life.

Good writing also has **unity**—that means that all of the parts tell about, or support, that controlling idea. In an autobiographical narrative, that means that the facts and events, descriptive details, and dialogue all go with the controlling idea.

Don't expect to achieve focus and unity with your first draft. Every writer expects and needs to rewrite. Time spent revising helps you sharpen your focus. Cut out any word, sentence, or even paragraph that doesn't relate to your controlling idea.

TRY IT ▶ With a partner, discuss which parts of the draft below do not support or relate to the writer's controlling idea.

Student Draft

> My mom and I were eating italian food at our favorite place, Tedesco's restaurant, when she told me the big news. I love Tedesco's because the lasagna is so good. I always order it. She said that she had received a promotion at work. The company was opening two new branch offices, and her boss had asked her to open one of them. The only thing was, both branches were kind of far away from Baltimore, where we lived. One was in Boston, and the other was in Miami. I had never been to either place.
>
> "We won't go if you don't want to go" she said.
>
> I stopped eating. I started playing with my food and wondering how they get that lasagna to be so good. Then I started to wonder about going. Did I want to go? I wasn't sure. Did I want to stay? I wasn't sure about that either...

Writing Plan

Controlling Idea	Choosing Miami gave me a fresh start.

Now use the rubric to evaluate the focus and unity of your own draft. What score
do you give your draft and why?

Focus and Unity

myNGconnect.com

🔊 Rubric: Focus and Unity

🔊 Evaluate and practice
scoring other student
narratives.

	How clearly does the writing present a central idea or claim?	How well does everything go together?
4 **Wow!**	The writing expresses a <u>clear</u> central idea or claim about the topic.	<u>Everything</u> in the writing goes together. • The main idea of each paragraph goes with the central idea or claim of the paper. • The main idea and details within each paragraph are related. • The conclusion is about the central idea or claim.
3 **Ahh.**	The writing expresses <u>generally</u> clear central idea or claim about the topic.	<u>Most</u> parts of the writing go together. • The main idea of most paragraphs goes with the central idea or claim of the paper. • In most paragraphs, the main idea and details are related. • Most of the conclusion is about the central idea or claim.
2 **Hmm.**	The writing includes a topic, but the central idea or claim is <u>not</u> clear.	<u>Some</u> parts of the writing go together. • The main idea of some paragraphs goes with the central idea or claim of the paper. • In some paragraphs, the main idea and details are related. • Some of the conclusion is about the central idea or claim.
1 **Huh?**	The writing includes many topics and <u>does not</u> express one central idea or claim.	The parts of the writing <u>do not</u> go together. • Few paragraphs have a main idea, or the main idea does not go with the central idea or claim of the paper. • Few paragraphs contain a main idea and related details • None of the conclusion is about the central idea or claim.

Revise Your Draft, continued

2 Revise Your Draft

You've now evaluated the focus and unity of your own draft. If you scored 3 or lower, how can you improve your work? Use the checklist below to revise your draft.

Revision Checklist

Ask Yourself	Check It Out	How to Make It Better
Is my narrative focused?	If your score is 3 or lower, revise.	☐ If you are telling about more than one choice, focus on just one. ☐ Decide on one idea or opinion about the choice and cut any others. ☐ If there is no central, or controlling, idea, add one.
Is my narrative unified?	If your score is 3 or lower, revise.	☐ Remove or replace any sentence or paragraph that is not about the central event. ☐ Consider adding a topic sentence to each paragraph to tell the main idea of the paragraph. ☐ Cut, move, or replace any details that do not really support a paragraph's main idea.
Does my narrative have a beginning, a middle, and an end?	Find and mark the boundaries between these parts.	☐ Add any part that is missing. ☐ Move any paragraph or sentence that is in the wrong part.
Are the supporting details vivid and interesting?	Underline descriptive details. **Highlight** dialogue. Are there enough details to make the writing come alive?	☐ Add sensory details or dialogue.
Will readers be able to follow my story?	Read it to someone or ask someone to read it. Ask about any parts that were hard to follow.	☐ Add any missing details. ☐ Add sequence words and phrases.

📖 **Writing Handbook**, p. 784

❸ Conduct a Peer Conference

It helps to get a second opinion when you are revising your draft. Ask a partner to read your draft and look for

- any part of the draft that is confusing
- any place where something seems to be missing
- anything that the reader doesn't understand.

Then talk with your partner about the draft. Focus on the items in the Revision Checklist. Use your partner's comments to make your narrative clearer, more complete, and easier to understand.

❹ Make Revisions

Look at the revisions below and the peer-reviewer conversation on the right. Notice how the peer reviewer commented and asked questions. Notice how the writer used the comments and questions to revise.

Revised for Unity

My mom and I were eating italian food at our favorite place, Tedesco's restaurant, when she told me the big news. ~~I love Tedesco's because the lasagna is so good. I always order it.~~ While I was eating my lasagna, Mom told me she received a promotion. The company was opening two new branch offices.

Revised Ending

I gave her the full presentation. Telling her everything I'd found out about Boston and Miami. I finished with the New World School of the Arts.

"What if you don't get in?" she asked.

"At least I will have tried," I said.

"Done," she said. "We're moving to Miami."

Now we're here, and I'm glad. I have applied to the NWSA, and I think I will be admitted. I'm looking forward to a new adventure. My mom and I made a fresh start—and we did it together.

Peer Conference

Reviewer's Comment: I think you went off track in the first paragraph. Your paper is about choices, not lasagna, isn't it?

Writer's Answer: Oops. I see what you mean. I'll delete that.

Reviewer's Comment: This just sort of stops. Do you want to tell the result of the choice?

Writer's Answer: I was trying to be dramatic, but maybe it's not working. The assignment says to end with the result of the choice, so I'll add it.

Reflect on Your Revisions

► Think about the results of your peer conference. What are some of your strengths as a writer? What are some things that give you trouble?

Edit and Proofread Your Draft

Your revision should now be complete. Before you share it with others, find and fix any mistakes that you made.

❶ Capitalize Proper Nouns and Adjectives

Proper nouns are capitalized because they name specific people, places, and things. Common nouns, which are general, are not capitalized.

Common Noun	Proper Noun
teacher	Ms. Warner
city	Miami

Proper adjectives, which come from proper nouns, are also capitalized.

Proper Noun	Proper Adjective
Florida	Floridian
America	American

TRY IT ▶ Copy the sentences. Fix the two capitalization errors. Use proofreader's marks.

> My mom and I were eating italian food at our favorite place, Tedesco's restaurant, when she told me the big news.

❷ Punctuate Quotations Correctly

Put quotation marks (" ") around the exact words that people speak. Do not use quotation marks when you describe what people said.

Quotation: "I'm ready," she said.
Description: She said that she was ready.

Use a comma to set off tags, or words that identify who is quoted.

I replied, "I believe that I am ready to make a choice."
"I believe that I am ready to make a choice**," I replied.**
"I believe that I am ready**," I replied, "**to make a choice."

TRY IT ▶ Copy the sentences. Add any necessary quotation marks and commas.

> 1. We won't go if you don't want to go Mom said.
> 2. I answered I'm not sure how I feel.
> 3. She said that I should help her choose.

Proofreader's Marks

Use proofreader's marks to correct capitalization and punctuation errors.

Capitalize:
My mother is asian.

Do not capitalize:
I enjoy Asian Music.

Add quotation marks:
My teacher said,
Your narrative is good

Add comma:
"Thank you I replied.

Editing Tip

Quotation marks can also be used to show sarcasm or irony.

I found it hard to follow the "easy" directions.

Look in a style guide to find out more about how to use quotation marks.

❸ Check Your Spelling

Homonyms are words that sound alike but have different meanings and spellings. Spell these homonyms correctly when you proofread.

Homonyms and Their Meanings	Examples
it's (contraction) = it is; it has	**It's** hard to make a decision.
its (pronoun) = belonging to it	Every city has **its** good points.
there (adverb) = that place or position	I like Boston. I once lived **there**.
their (pronoun) = belonging to them	They sent me a map of **their** city.
they're (contraction) = they are	**They're** very friendly people.

TRY IT ▶ Copy the sentences. Find and fix the two homonym errors.

> Their are two cities where we might move. They're both nice places to live. Its nice in Boston, but Miami is nice, too.

❹ Check Sentences for Completeness

You use complete sentences in your writing every day. You also routinely see them in written classroom materials. The structure of a complete sentence includes a subject and a predicate. A complete sentence expresses a complete thought.

Problem

Sentence is missing a subject.
Had to choose a new home.

Sentence is missing a verb.
Mom glad about her promotion.

Sentence fragments do not express a complete thought.
I gave her the full presentation. Telling her everything.

Solution

Add the missing subject.
I had to choose a new home.

Add the missing verb.
Mom was glad about her promotion.

Join the fragments to express a complete thought.
I gave her the full presentation, telling her everything.

TRY IT ▶ Copy the paragraph. Find and fix the structure of four incomplete sentences.

> Life is full of choices. Some of them easy. Some of them hard. I recently made a hard choice. Changed high schools. I needed a change. To learn more and get better grades.

Writing Handbook, p. 850

Technology Tip

Most word-processing software includes a Spell-check feature and a Grammar feature. Always use these, but know their limits. Spell-checkers cannot find all homonym errors.

Proofreading Tip

Use a print or online dictionary to check your spelling and use of word endings.

Reflect on Your Corrections

▶ Look back over the changes you made. Do you see a pattern? If there are things you keep missing, make a checklist of what to watch in your writing.

Here's the student's draft, revised and edited. How did the writer improve it?

A Fresh Start

My mom and I were eating Italian food at our favorite place, Tedesco's Restaurant, when she told me the big news. She said that she had received a promotion at work. The company was opening two new branch offices, and her boss had asked her to open one of them. However, both branches were far away from Baltimore, where we lived. One was in Boston, and the other was in Miami.

"We won't go if you don't want to go," she said.

Did I want to go? I wasn't sure. Did I want to stay? I wasn't sure about that, either.

"It doesn't really matter to me whether it's Boston or Miami," she added. "Pick the one that will make you happy. It would be a fresh start for both of us."

"A fresh start is just what I need!" I said.

Wow. Picking a city to live in was quite a challenge—and quite an opportunity. I had only a month to make the choice. I went on the Internet right away. Soon, I was overloaded with information. I knew a lot about each city, but I didn't feel any closer to choosing between them. The more I knew, the harder it was to choose. That's when I found out about Miami's New World School of the Arts (NWSA).

The NWSA has special high school programs in music, dance, theater, and visual arts. I explored it online, and I immediately began to fantasize about going there. I couldn't apply there if we lived out of state, but if we were living in Miami, I could apply for the next school year. My choice was made. "I'm ready," I said to my mother.

I gave her the full presentation, telling her everything I'd found out about Boston and Miami. I finished with the NWSA.

"What if you don't get in?" she asked.

"At least I will have tried," I said.

"Done," she said. "We're moving to Miami."

Now we're here, and I'm glad. I have applied to the NWSA, and I think I will be admitted. I'm looking forward to a new adventure. My mom and I made a fresh start—and we did it together.

The writer capitalized the proper adjective and the complete name of the restaurant to fix the **capitalization** errors.

The writer deleted unrelated ideas.

The writer added the missing **comma** to the quotation.

The writer used the **right homonym** and added **quotation marks**.

The writer changed "their" to "there" to fix the **homonym error**.

The writer **fixed the fragment** to make a complete sentence.

✓ Publish and Present

Print or write a clean copy of your narrative. You are now ready to publish and present it. Give your audience a chance to read or hear what you have to say. You may also want to present your work in a different way.

Alternative Presentations

Do a Reading Read aloud your narrative to the class. Make it come alive by reading with expression.

1 Introduce Your Narrative Tell your audience the subject. For example, you might say, "My narrative tells about a time when I had to choose between _____ and _____ ."

2 Read with Expression Use your tone of voice to show how you felt.

3 Watch Your Pacing Don't rush your presentation. Speak at a pace that is comfortable for your audience. Look up from time to time to see people's reactions. Does anyone look puzzled? If so, slow down.

4 Make Eye Contact Don't hide your face behind paper. Look over the paper at your audience to make eye contact from time to time.

5 Ask for Feedback When you are finished, thank your audience. Then ask for feedback:

- Was the beginning interesting? If not, how could I improve it?
- Was it easy to understand what choice I had to make? If not, how could I make it clearer?
- Did the narrative feel complete? If not, what suggestions do you have for strengthening the ending?

Publish on the Internet Reach a wider audience. As your teacher directs, send your narrative to an appropriate Web site that publishes student writing.

1 Find a Good Web Site Post your paper on your own or the school's Web site, or another site.

myNGconnect.com

➲ Directory of Online Publishers

2 Send Your Writing Follow any instructions to submit your writing.

3 Ask for Feedback If there is a comment box, ask readers to comment on your work. Use their suggestions to improve your writing.

📖 Language and Learning Handbook, p. 702

Publishing Tip

Format your typed work according to your teacher's guidelines.

If you've handwritten your work, make sure your work is legible and clean.

Reflect on Your Work

▶ Ask for and use feedback from your audience and your teacher to evaluate your strengths as a writer.

- What parts of your narrative did your audience like?
- What parts of your narrative did your audience say need improvement?
- What would you like to do better the next time you write? Set a goal for your next writing project.

 Save a copy of your work in your portfolio.

EQ **ESSENTIAL QUESTION:**

Does Creativity Matter?

If you're an artist, you try to keep an ear to the ground and an ear to your heart.

—BRUCE SPRINGSTEEN

The function of art is to do more than tell it like it is—it's to imagine what's *possible*.

—BELL HOOKS

Critical Viewing ▶
A boy practices violin at a music school in Sulaimaniya, Iraq. The school has been damaged by war, but he continues to make music there. Does his creativity matter?

THE ART OF EXPRESSION

ESSENTIAL QUESTION:
Does Creativity Matter?

Study the Painting

A famous artist named Andy Warhol spent many years in the 1960s painting realistic images of canned soup, which he ate for lunch almost every day. Today, these paintings are displayed in important museums around the world and are considered very valuable. In May 2006, one of his soup can paintings was sold for $11,776,000. Study an example of Warhol's work.

Woman Admiring Andy Warhol's Campbell's Soup Cans, 2010, Museum of Modern Art, New York, New York, USA, Judie Long. Photograph ©Judie Long/Alamy.

Analyze and Debate

1. Art collectors believe that Warhol's paintings are important works of creativity. What do *you* think?

2. People express their creativity in many ways, including art, film, music, writing, dance, and more. Is creativity something that is necessary for society to survive? Or, is it something "extra" that we can live without?

With a small group, explain your opinions to others who may have a different point of view. Defend your ideas with reasons and examples from your own experience.

EQ **ESSENTIAL QUESTION**

In this unit, you will explore the **Essential Question** in class through reading, discussion, research, and writing. Keep thinking about the question outside of school, too.

① Plan a Project

Demonstration

In this unit, you will be giving a demonstration that relates to the Essential Question. Choose something creative to demonstrate, such as dancing, painting, or preparing a special food. To get started, choose an activity you enjoy and know about. Then think about

- steps needed to demonstrate the process
- materials or equipment you will need
- information and ideas you want to present.

Study Skills Start planning your demonstration. Use the forms on myNGconnect.com to plan your time and to prepare the content.

myNGconnect.com
▶ Planning forms
▶ Scheduler
▶ Steps in the Demonstration Diagram
▶ Rubric

② Choose More to Read

These readings provide different answers to the Essential Question. Choose a book and online selections to read during the unit.

Hole in My Life
by Jack Gantos

Jack wanted a writer's life of adventure and excitement. But instead of traveling around the world, he went to prison for smuggling drugs. By making the biggest mistake of his life, did Jack ruin his dream forever? Or did prison help him see what was really important?
▶ **NONFICTION**

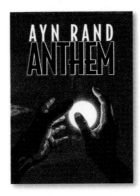

Anthem
by Ayn Rand

It is the future. Society as we know it was destroyed long ago. There is no "I" in this new society, only "we." But Equality 7-2521 seeks knowledge. Can he survive in a society that considers individual thought and creativity a crime?
▶ **NOVEL**

The Stone Goddess
by Minfong Ho

Cambodian sisters Nakri and Teeda love to dance. But life changes when a cruel rebel army takes control of Cambodia. The new government punishes Cambodians who dance. How will Nakri and Teeda survive when everything they love is at risk?
▶ **NOVEL**

myNGconnect.com

- ◗ **Read biographies of people who have found unique ways to express their creativity.**
- ◗ **Visit galleries of art, poetry, and music created by teens.**
- ◗ **Use programs that help you create your own artistic expressions.**

One of the challenges of nonfiction is that there are so many kinds. Experienced readers approach each kind in a different way. Read these three nonfiction texts. Think about how the same topic works in each one.

DEMO TEXT #1

Lee Krasner first met Jackson Pollock in 1941. Like Pollock, she was a painter living and working in New York City. One day, she saw Pollock's canvases. "How could there be a painter like that who I didn't know about?" she wondered. Immediately recognizing his talent, she knew she had to meet him. As the two artists got to know one another, they soon fell in love. Four years later, they were married. The couple moved to the east end of Long Island and settled into a peaceful life on a farm. It was here that Jackson Pollock created the unusual paintings that made him famous. As for Lee, she became known as one of the best abstract painters of her generation.

DEMO TEXT #2

In the middle of the 20th century, a group of young artists in New York created a style that stunned the world. These painters brought new ideas to painting. They decided that a painting did not have to be a picture of something. A painting could just be colors and shapes. They also decided that a painting should show how the artist had put paint on the surface. If the artist used a brush, the viewer should see the brushstrokes.

The best-known artist in the group was Jackson Pollock. He won fame creating paintings by dripping paint onto canvas. The new style of art that he and these other young artists developed is often called *action painting*.

DEMO TEXT #3

Jackson Pollock is one of the greatest painters of all time. The way Pollock worked was truly amazing. He would run back and forth beside a huge canvas on the floor, dipping a brush in a can and flinging paint at the canvas. His method seems incredibly original. What other artist ever painted like that before? It is truly amazing to behold. He looks more like an athlete than an artist. Watching him surely would make anyone excited about the process of creating art.

■ Connect Reading to Your Life

Each of the following sentences belongs with one of the preceding Demo Texts. With a partner, figure out which sentences go with which texts.

I think the first sentence goes with Demo Text 2.

You're right. It gives information about action painting.

	Demo Text #1	Demo Text #2	Demo Text #3
1. Action painting was an important art style throughout the 1950s.			
2. Some people say that Jackson Pollock's paintings are nothing special, but I disagree.			
3. Krasner worked hard to promote her husband's career.			

Focus Strategy ▶ Determine Importance

In the activity you just completed, your purpose was to match sentences with the Demo Texts. So you looked for important details in the sentences to help you.

You do this kind of thinking all the time in your life. Suppose that you're driving to Centerville. You see many road signs, but you only need to pay attention to the ones that point to Centerville. Experienced readers know that they can't pay attention to *everything* as they read. They only keep track of the important details.

■ Your Job as a Reader

What is important depends on why you are reading. You might, for example, be reading to prepare for a test. Then you need to determine what the author **emphasizes**, or says is important, and remember that. Or, you might be reading in order to solve a problem with a computer. In that case, you need to determine what is important to solving *your* problem. Your job as a reader of nonfiction is to know *why* you are reading and to determine what is important to help you meet your purpose.

Academic Vocabulary
- **emphasize** *v.*, to give special importance to, to stress;
  emphasis *n.*, special importance, force, stress

■ Unpack the Thinking Process

Determine the Kind of Nonfiction

When you read the Demo Texts, you were probably looking to see what was different about each text. Try looking at what the sentences are mostly about.

- **Demo Text #1:** The sentences tell a story about people. The events are told in time order. This usually means that the nonfiction text is a **narrative**. Its purpose is to tell a story—a biography—of a real person or group of people.
- **Demo Text #2:** These sentences sound pretty formal: "new style of art" and "best-known artist." Because they give facts and explain things, they are clues that the text is **expository**—or written to inform. Other clues include graphs, tables, and headings.
- **Demo Text #3:** Words like "one of the greatest" and "truly amazing" show strong opinions. The many opinions are clues that the nonfiction is an **argument**—written to argue a position.

Doing this is just like what you do when you go into a new store or restaurant. If you walk into a fast-food restaurant, you know that you have to go up to the counter and place your order. If you go into a fancier restaurant, you know that a waiter will come to take your order. It's the same principle with reading: if you know what kind of writing you're dealing with, you can figure out how to read it more effectively.

Determine Author's Purpose

There's another way to determine the kind of nonfiction you're about to read: figure out the **author's purpose**. Here are some of the most common purposes for writing nonfiction. Which Demo Text matches each purpose?

Author's Purpose	Type of Text	Demo Text #
To narrate	Narrative	
To explain	Expository	
To argue	Argument	

Elements of Literature

narrative *adj.*, that tells a story

expository *adj.*, that informs and explains

argument *n.*, a stated opinion or position defended with reasons

author's purpose *n.*, the reason an author has for writing a text

Determine What's Important

You've just learned some ways to approach nonfiction as you're reading. You pay attention to the kind of nonfiction it is, why the author wrote it, and your purpose for reading. But then what? The goal of determining importance as you read is to focus on important information. And how do you do that? You **summarize**. Here's one way to do that:

How to Summarize	
1. Tell what the passage is mostly about (the topic).	action painting
2. Tell what the passage is mostly saying about the topic.	how it brought new life to art
3. Combine your ideas into a complete sentence. Add details to make it complete.	Action painting, especially by Jackson Pollock, brought new life to art in the middle of the twentieth century.

■ Try an Experiment

Read this passage about the art world.

DEMO TEXT #4

Action painting is a unique style which began in New York around 1950. Unlike many other artistic styles, action painting does not require mastery of skills, such as showing perspective or rendering light. Instead, artists are concerned with the physical act of painting. They drip, splash, and splatter paint on a canvas. Jackson Pollock, the most famous of the action painters, even rode a bicycle across some of his canvases. Although these techniques were unusual, action painting played an important role in American art.

1. **Think:** What type of information is in this text? What is the author's purpose in writing it?

2. **Pair:** What is the main idea of the passage? Summarize it with a partner.

3. **Share:** Share your summary sentence with the class. Compare main ideas.

Academic Vocabulary
- **summarize** *v.*, to briefly give the main points, to sum up;
  summary *n.*, a short statement that gives the main points

Monitor Comprehension

Expository Nonfiction
How can you tell when you're reading this kind of text?

EQ **Does Creativity Matter?**
Consider ways to express your creativity.

Make a Connection

Anticipation Guide Think about all the ways that people express creativity, such as art, music, poetry, and drama. Then tell whether you agree or disagree with these statements. After reading the selections, see if you feel the same way.

ANTICIPATION GUIDE	Agree or Disagree
1. Creativity is important in everyday life.	_____
2. You are either born creative, or you're not.	_____
3. Some kinds of art are better than others.	_____
4. Students should be required to take a class like art or music.	_____

Learn Key Vocabulary

Study the Words Pronounce each word and learn its meaning. You may also want to look up the definitions in the Glossary.

● Academic Vocabulary

Key Words	Examples
career (ku-**rear**) noun ▸ page 122	A **career** is the kind of work a person does. The artist began her **career** by drawing comics in high school.
collaborate (ku-**lab**-u-rāt) verb ▸ pages 122, 133	To **collaborate** is to work together with one or more people on a specific task or project. My friends and I **collaborate** on group projects for class. 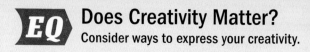
● **commitment** (ku-**mit**-munt) noun ▸ page 123	You show your **commitment** by continuing to work on something, even when it is difficult. He shows his **commitment** to work by coming early every day.
● **evaluate** (i-**val**-ū-āt) verb ▸ page 131	When you **evaluate** something, you decide how good or valuable it is. The teacher will **evaluate** your presentation and then give you a final grade.
expectation (ek-spek-**tā**-shun) noun ▸ pages 122, 127	**Expectations** are beliefs about how things will turn out. If you have high **expectations,** you expect something to turn out well.
● **insight** (**in**-sīt) noun ▸ pages 129, 132, 133	When you have **insight,** you have a new or special understanding about something. The instruction sheet gave me **insight** into how to use the machine.
talent (**tal**-unt) noun ▸ page 124	Having **talent** means showing special ability or skill. She has a wonderful **talent** in music.
● **transform** (trans-**form**) verb ▸ page 125	To **transform** something means to change it in an important way, or completely. I **transformed** my sketch into a painting.

Practice the Words Work with a partner to find synonyms for each of the Key Vocabulary words. Use a thesaurus for ideas.

Example: *Career = job, work, profession*

BEFORE READING Creativity at Work

news article by Abe Louise Young

Reading Strategies

- Plan and Monitor
- ▶ **Determine Importance**
- Make Inferences
- Ask Questions
- Make Connections
- Synthesize
- Visualize

Analyze Author's Purpose

The purpose of a **news article** is to give information. The author describes people, places, and events using facts and supporting details from reliable sources.

Look Into the Text

Headlines and **heads** catch the reader's attention and give clues about the information in a section.

PUSHING THE LIMITS

The program began in 1991 as a collaboration between Susan Rodgerson—a white, middle-class artist—and five African American teen friends who started painting in her studio. The friends needed to sell their artwork in order to buy supplies and make more art. Sheer economics inspired an entrepreneurial zeal, and they approached Boston colleges, nonprofits, and corporations as potential customers. An audience was found and a program bloomed—with youth at the helm.

Details answer the 5Ws: *Who?*, *What?, Where? When?,* and *Why?* Which answers can you find?

Focus Strategy ▶ Determine Importance

A news article is filled with a lot of information and ideas, but not every fact has the same importance as others. As you read each paragraph, look for the important facts and details. They can help you identify the writer's most important idea.

HOW TO IDENTIFY MAIN IDEAS AND DETAILS

Focus Strategy

1. **Find the Important Details** Add them to a 5Ws Chart.

2. **State the Main Idea** Ask yourself: If the author could say only one general thing in this paragraph, what would it be? Sometimes, this is very clear. Other times, it is implied, or hinted. In these cases, look at all the facts and say the idea in a few of your own words.

5Ws Chart

Who? Name the people.	What? Name the topic.	Where? Name the location.

Why? Name the reason.	When? Name the time period.

Main Idea
State the topic and make a comment on what the author is saying about it.

An Accidental Cartoonist

*Almost all my comics
are about stupidity . . .
I think most people
can identify with being
a loser. We've all been
in that situation.*

Cartoonist Tony Carrillo draws a
character from his comic strip,
"F Minus."

Like many artists who
are just starting their
careers, Tony Carrillo
had an interesting
series of day jobs. They
included pizza server,
camel ride attendant, and orange cone-waver guy,
directing planes at the airport.

Carillo didn't start out to be a professional
cartoonist; he entered Arizona State University as
an arts major. One day, he saw an ad in the student
paper. That's when he discovered his creativity. The ad
said, "'Can you draw—even just a little bit?'" recalls
Carrillo. "It sounded like a fun job and I needed the
money, so I drew three little cartoons and sent them
in. They hired me over the phone, and I've been doing
cartoons ever since."

And what's one of the secrets to Carrillo's
success? "The rule is: If it's funny, I'll do it."

myNGconnect.com

See "F Minus" online.
Read Tony Carrillo's biography.

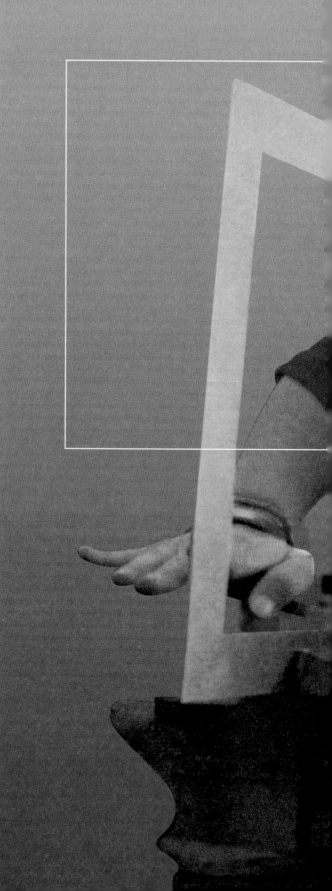

CREATIVITY
AT WORK

by Abe Louise Young

 Comprehension Coach

"Art" is an **elusive** idea of a career for people young and old—a bit like basketball fame or becoming an astronaut. Yet for the hundreds of public high school students who **collaborate** on projects at Artists for Humanity (AFH), art careers are becoming a thrilling reality. ▣

▣ Main Ideas and Details
What clues tell you that the subject of "art careers" is important in this article?

CREATIVE ENERGY

The **nonprofit's mission** is to create meaningful employment for urban youth through creative arts. AFH is a study in **attainable dreams**: about what happens when high **expectations** for performance, discipline, and creativity meet the raw and eager energy of youth.

"Most of our participants come in off the sidewalk having never held a paintbrush," says Shane Hassey, who started at AFH when he was 15 years old and now works as the office manager. "After a few months, they are making full-scale paintings, selling their work, and developing their own visions."

At 3 p.m., teenagers from public schools all over Boston set up easels, mix their paints and photo developing chemicals, **rev up** woodcrafting tools, and settle down to sculpture tables and graphic-design computers. Hip-hop beats pulse through the studios, and small groups gather in the hallways to plan collaborative projects. Participants begin in the painting studio, and can branch out into sculpture, woodcrafting, photography, design, fashion, and **silkscreening**.

Portrait of an AFH Artist: Jose Guardarrama

"Here, I get to learn how to paint, draw, socialize. I wouldn't be able to do this anywhere else."

Key Vocabulary
career *n.*, job, occupation
collaborate *v.*, to work together with one or more people
expectations *n.*, beliefs about what will happen in the future

In Other Words
elusive difficult, challenging
nonprofit's mission goal of this people-centered group
attainable dreams dreams that can come true
rev up start
silkscreening printing art on cloth

Painters at work in the studio of AFH's EpiCenter building.

PUSHING THE LIMITS

The program began in 1991 as a collaboration between Susan Rodgerson—a white, middle-class artist—and five African American teen friends who started painting in her studio. The friends needed to sell their artwork in order to buy supplies and make more art. **Sheer economics inspired an entrepreneurial zeal**, and they approached Boston colleges, nonprofits, and corporations as potential customers. An audience was found, and a program bloomed—with youth at the helm.

Mars, 17, expresses his **commitment** this way: "You've just got to give all your might and create as much as you can. Do something that people have never seen before. That's what makes you an artist. Do something different."

Any public high school student in Boston can join AFH. After a period of **apprenticeship**, participants are paid seven dollars an hour to create. They clock in, clock out, and get a regular paycheck. When their art is sold, half of the **profit** goes to the program, and half to the artist's pocket. "We charge a fair dollar for the kids' work. We ask **market value**. We don't give it away or de-value the work," Rodgerson says. **2**

Massiel Grullon began the program when she was 12 years old. "This is my home," she said. "To make art and get paid for it is the best job in the world. You can feel the love and creativity when you come in here." At 17, Grullon has sold thousands of dollars worth of her high-contrast, hyper-realistic paintings—and after

2 Main Ideas and Details
These details describe AFH. Using only a few words, how would you say AFH works?

Monitor Comprehension

Explain
What are some ways that AFH helps teens?

Key Vocabulary
- **commitment** *n.*, dedication, determination

In Other Words
Sheer economics inspired an entrepreneurial zeal The need for money encouraged them to start a business
apprenticeship practice and training
profit money made by selling the art
market value the price people are willing to pay

taking a fashion workshop at AFH, is outfitted in her own designs. **3**

"You don't really know you're a visual artist until somebody pushes your limits," says Omar, a third-year participant. Christie, 17, reflects, "It's good to be able to get into a certain form of art. It makes you think, it makes you feel relaxed. It's a talent that you have for yourself that you earn and you don't have to give it to anyone. It feels like you own it. It gives you something to be proud of."

Rather than **formal instruction**, participants have a master artist as a **mentor** for each **medium** they choose to study. Mentor Ryan Conley says, "**Teaching here is very intuitive.** Every student has their own ideas and themes, and we work with everyone individually." Mentors also produce their own artwork side-by-side. Conley adds, "I work on my paintings right here; it shows that I'm focusing on my work. It's better to paint together than for me to just tell them things. And, the kids need a lot of room to make their own discoveries."

3 Author's Purpose
Why do you think the author adds the detail that "Grullon has sold thousands of dollars worth" of her art?

Portrait of two **AFH Artists:**
Michael Guardarrama and Massiel Grullon

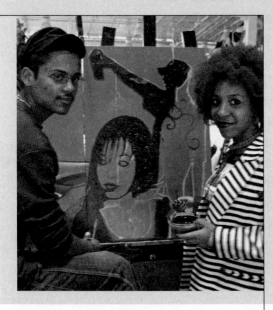

"I come here every single day. I got involved exactly one year ago—I fell in love with this place. I can't get enough of it. There's so much potential in it. One year ago today, I wouldn't have thought I'd do something like this painting—especially with her!"
    —Michael

"We decided to collaborate because our styles are very different. He does more of a graffiti-influenced style, and I do more of a graphic, high-contrast realism thing." **4**
    —Massiel

4 Author's Purpose
The article includes quotes from AFH students. What do they help you understand?

Key Vocabulary
talent *n.*, ability or skill

In Other Words
formal instruction being taught in a classroom
mentor coach and teacher
medium different type of artwork
Teaching here is very intuitive. Teachers create lessons based on what they think will work best.

AFH artists created a painting based on Paul Gauguin's work. Their finished painting now hangs in Boston's Logan Airport.

BEAUTIFYING BOSTON

The artwork that **emerges from** these discoveries beautifies buildings all over Boston. When a department store **commissioned** a store window for Black History Month this year, AFH students welded larger-than-life steel human figures in clothes **depicting** the history of black fashion.

Last year, a large Boston bank commissioned a large-scale painting of modern Boston. It was based on Paul Gauguin's signature masterpiece, *Where Do We Come From? What Are We? Where Are We Going?* After hanging alongside the colorful Gauguin original in the Museum of Fine Arts, this painting now greets travelers at Logan Airport, where it is on permanent display.

The very building that houses the program is perhaps the most **arresting** example of Boston urban landscape **transformed** in the hands of Artists for Humanity. The method of dreaming big—and collaborating with youth to make dreams into reality—resulted in the $6.8 million EpiCenter, the most environmentally-friendly building in Boston. **5** The EpiCenter **utilizes** solar panels, rainwater collection, and recycled

Yinetta Fuertes adds details to one of her paintings.

5 Main Ideas and Details
The author says that AFH "beautifies buildings all over Boston." What details support the main idea of this section?

Monitor Comprehension

Explain
How do AFH teens work together to help each other and their neighborhood?

Key Vocabulary
- **transform** *v.*, to change from one thing to another

In Other Words
emerges from comes out of
commissioned hired them to create
depicting showing
arresting shocking, amazing
utilizes uses

materials. Gallery balconies are lined with car windshields from **old Crown Victorias**. Industrial-sized toilet paper dispensers are cut from the bottoms of 5-gallon plastic water jugs. "The building represents who we are and what we do," says Susan Rodgerson.

Though most come from low-income families, 95 percent of AFH participants go on to college, and two-thirds of them **pursue careers in commercial or fine arts**. "I have the highest expectations for young people, and they have the highest expectations of me. Our entire **philosophy** is built on Respect, Responsibility, and Relationships," says Founding Director Susan Rodgerson. That, it appears, is a simple formula for brilliant success in **social entrepreneurship** with youth. ⑥ ❖

⑥ **Main Ideas and Details**
Read for this paragraph's main idea. Then state it in your own words.

Portrait of an **AFH Artist:** **Rassan Charles**

"This painting reminds me of my homeland in Haiti. I left Haiti in June of 2003. In Haiti, after high school, I wouldn't be able to make any money at art. Art is the only thing I can do—I knew I wanted to be an artist since I was 11 [years old]! Working at AFH helps me a lot . . . By practicing painting every day, I'll be more skillful. I want to go to college, to the School of the Museum of Fine Arts." ⑦

⑦ **Author's Purpose**
Which of the 5W questions does this quote answer?

In Other Words
old Crown Victorias fancy old cars
pursue careers in commercial or fine arts look for jobs in the arts
philosophy belief about how to do things
social entrepreneurship creating positive businesses together

Geographic Background
Haiti a nation on an island in the Caribbean. It is one of the oldest countries in the Americas. Haiti has had many recent troubles. Jobs of any type can be difficult to find there.

ANALYZE Creativity at Work

1. **Explain** What do most of the students from Artists for Humanity do after high school? Why do you think the program is so successful? Provide details from the article to support your answers.

2. **Vocabulary** What kind of **expectations** does Susan Rodgerson have for students in the program? What expectations should they have for *her*?

3. **Analyze Author's Purpose** In a news article, a reporter tries to provide the most important information about the article's subject. With a partner, compare the **5Ws Charts** you began on page 119. Then work together to create a **5Ws Chart** that identifies the most important details and main idea for the entire news article.

4. **Focus Strategy Determine Importance** Often, a main idea is implied, instead of stated directly in the text. With a partner, review a paragraph where you had difficulty deciding about the main idea. Find clues that point to the main idea that is implied.

Return to the Text

Reread and Write For kids in AFH, art is more than something to look at. Look back at the article and read all the things they say art does for them. List reasons why these students want and need to express themselves through art.

BEFORE READING The Hidden Secrets of the Creative Mind

interview by Francine Russo

Reading Strategies

- Plan and Monitor
- ▶ **Determine Importance**
- Make Inferences
- Ask Questions
- Make Connections
- Synthesize
- Visualize

Analyze Development of Ideas

An **interview** is a printed a conversation between an interviewer and someone who has something interesting to say. The interviewer develops ideas by asking questions designed to get information from the person interviewed.

Look Into the Text

The interviewer asks questions. The answers give the exact words of the person being interviewed.

Q: Has new research changed any of our popular ideas about creativity?

A: Virtually all of them. Many people believe creativity comes in a sudden moment of insight and that this "magical" burst of an idea is different from our everyday thinking. But research has shown that when you're creative, your brain is using the same mental building blocks you use every day—like when you figure out a way around a traffic jam.

Q: Then how do you explain the "aha!" moment we've all had in the shower or the gym—or anywhere but at work?

What information can you learn from this answer?

Answers can lead to new questions.

Focus Strategy ▶ Determine Importance

In an interview, you can often find main ideas in the questions and supporting details in the answers. As you read, find the main idea for each question-answer pair.

HOW TO IDENTIFY MAIN IDEA AND DETAILS

Focus Strategy

1. **Identify the Topic** Look for clues to find out what the passage is mostly about.

2. **Read for the Main Idea** Decide upon the writer's topic and look for details that give information about it. Use these to create a **Main Idea and Details Diagram** for each section.

3. **Sum Up the Information** Review all of your diagrams. Then decide upon one main idea for the entire interview.

4. **Think Beyond the Text** Ask yourself: What have I learned?

Main Idea and Details Diagram

Main Idea:
Research has changed what we know about creativity.

Detail 1:
People used to think that creativity was different from regular thinking.

Detail 2:

The Hidden SECRETS of the Creative Mind

by Francine Russo

Connect Across Texts

"Creativity at Work" describes teens who use their creativity to begin careers in art. In this interview, a psychologist tells artists, inventors—and all of us—how to make the most of our creativity.

What is creativity? Where does it come from? The workings of the creative mind have been studied over the past twenty-five years by an army of researchers. But no one has a better **overview** of this mysterious mental process than Washington University psychologist R. Keith Sawyer. In an interview with journalist Francine Russo, he suggests ways in which we can **enhance** our creativity, not just in art and science, but in everyday life.

Q: Has new research changed any of our popular ideas about creativity?

A: **Virtually** all of them. Many people believe creativity comes in a sudden moment of insight and that this "magical" burst of an idea is different from our everyday thinking. But research has shown that when you're creative, your brain is using the same **mental building blocks** you use every day—like when you figure out a way around a traffic jam.

Q: Then how do you explain the "aha!" moment we've all had in the shower or the gym—or anywhere but at work? [1]

A: In creativity research, we refer to the three Bs—for the bathtub, the bed, and the bus. They are places where ideas have famously and suddenly emerged. When we take time off from working on a problem, we change what we're doing and **our context**. That can

[1] **Development of Ideas**
What idea from the first answer leads to the second question?

Key Vocabulary
• insight *n.*, understanding

In Other Words
overview understanding
enhance improve
Virtually Almost
mental building blocks ways of thinking
our context where and how we are doing it

activate different areas of our brain. If the answer wasn't in the part of the brain we were using, it might be in another. If we're lucky, in the next context we may hear or see something that relates to the problem that we had temporarily put aside.

Q: Can you give us an example of that? ▣2

A: In 1990 a team of NASA scientists was trying to fix the lenses in the Hubble telescope, while it was already in orbit. An expert suggested that tiny mirrors could correct the images, but nobody could figure out how to fit them into the hard-to-reach space inside. Then

▣2 **Development of Ideas**
Why do you think the interviewer asks Sawyer for an example of what he just said?

▣3 **Access Vocabulary**
Many scientific experts use specialized words, or jargon, to describe ideas in their field. What clues do the text and diagram give about what the specialized term *hemisphere* means?

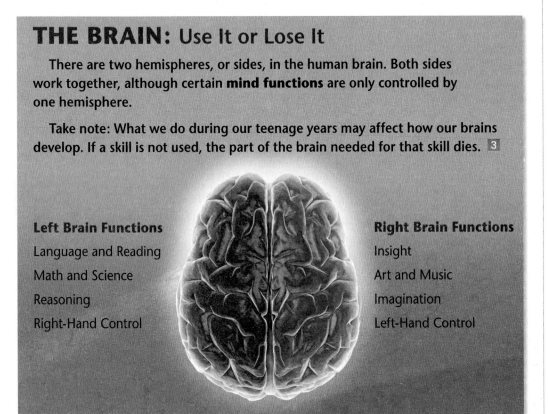

THE BRAIN: Use It or Lose It

There are two hemispheres, or sides, in the human brain. Both sides work together, although certain **mind functions** are only controlled by one hemisphere.

Take note: What we do during our teenage years may affect how our brains develop. If a skill is not used, the part of the brain needed for that skill dies. ▣3

Left Brain Functions

Language and Reading

Math and Science

Reasoning

Right-Hand Control

Right Brain Functions

Insight

Art and Music

Imagination

Left-Hand Control

🔺 **Interpret the Diagram** How does the diagram help you understand how the brain functions?

In Other Words
activate turn on
mind functions jobs done by the brain

engineer Jim Crocker, taking a shower in a German hotel, noticed the European-style showerhead on **adjustable rods**. He realized the Hubble's little mirrors could be **mounted onto** similar folding arms. And this **flash** was the key to fixing the problem.

Q: How have researchers studied this creative flash?

A: Some psychologists set up video cameras to watch creative people work, asking them to describe their thought processes out loud or interrupting them frequently to ask how close they were to a solution. In other experiments, subjects worked on problems that, when solved, tend to result in the sensation of sudden insight. In one experiment, they were asked to look at words that came up one at a time on a computer screen and to think of the one word that was associated with all of them. After each word they had to give their best guess. Although many swore they had no idea until a sudden burst of insight at about the twelfth word, their guesses got closer to the solution. Even when an idea seems sudden, our minds have actually been working on it all along.

Q: Are there other generalizations you can make about creative people?

A: Yes. They have tons of ideas, many of them bad. The trick is to evaluate them and **purge** the bad ones. But even bad ideas can be useful. Sometimes you don't know which sparks are important until later. But the more ideas you have, the better. 4

Q: So how can the average person get more ideas?

A: Ideas don't magically appear from nowhere. They always build on what came before. And collaboration is key. Look at what others are doing. Brainstorm with different people. Research and evidence suggest that this leads to new ideas.

4 **Main Idea and Details**
What is the main idea of this question-and-answer set?

Monitor Comprehension

Summarize
Summarize the important ideas and information in this passage.

Key Vocabulary
• evaluate *v.*, to decide how good or valuable something is

In Other Words
adjustable rods metal bars that can move back and forth
mounted onto placed on
flash idea, understanding
purge get rid of

Q: What advice can you give us nongeniuses to help us be more creative?

A: Take risks, and expect to make lots of mistakes. Work hard, and take frequent breaks, but stay with it over time. Do what you love, because creative breakthroughs take years of hard work. Develop a **network of colleagues**, and schedule time for free, unstructured discussions. Most of all, forget those romantic myths that creativity is all about being artsy and gifted and not about hard work. They **discourage** us because we're waiting for that one full-blown moment of inspiration. And while we're waiting, we may never start working on what we might someday create. **5** ❖

> **5** **Main Idea and Details**
> In a few words, state the main idea of the advice offered here.

ANALYZE The Hidden Secrets of the Creative Mind

1. **Explain** According to the diagram on page 130, why is it important to use all of your skills during your teen years?

2. **Vocabulary** What sudden `insight` came to engineer Jim Crocker in a hotel room? How does this example support the author's ideas?

3. **Analyze Development of Ideas** Are interviews a good way to present information? Share your opinions with a partner.

4. **Focus Strategy Determine Importance** In a few words, state the main idea of this interview and find two facts from the selection that support this idea. Compare your work with a partner's and discuss which facts best support the main ideas each of you found.

↪ Return to the Text

Reread and Write Choose a question and answer from the interview where you had difficulty finding the main idea. Reread the question and answer. Then try to write a sentence expressing the main idea.

In Other Words

network of colleagues group of people who are interested in working on the same things

discourage take hope away from

EQ Does Creativity Matter?

Reading

Critical Thinking

EQ 1. **Analyze** Review the **Anticipation Guide** on page 118. Explain how the selections supported or challenged your opinions.

2. **Interpret** According to the two selections, is it possible for people to improve their creativity? Give examples from both texts.

3. **Compare** What elements of the AFH program match R. Keith Sawyer's ideas about creativity?

4. **Generalize** Sawyer says that "collaboration is key." Consider what both selections say. Then explain how **collaborating** with others changes the creative experience.

5. **Draw Conclusions** Is creativity only useful in the **EQ** arts? Base your conclusion on specific evidence from the text.

Writing

Write About Literature

Opinion Paragraph Choose one of the statements from the **Anticipation Guide** on page 118. Have your thoughts changed? Write a paragraph that explains your thoughts and feelings about the topic. Be sure to include support from both texts and your own experience.

Vocabulary

Key Vocabulary Review

Oral Review Work with a partner. Use these words to complete the paragraph.

career	evaluate	talent
collaborate	expectations	transform
commitment	insight	

It isn't easy to have a successful __(1)__ working as an artist. You need more than just natural skills and artistic __(2)__. You also need dedication and a __(3)__ to hard work. And forget about working alone. __(4)__ with other artists often so that you can study and __(5)__ the good and bad in each other's work. This can give you flashes of __(6)__ and understanding about how to improve. Above all, set high __(7)__ for a bright future. Over time, you will see yourself __(8)__ from a dreamer into a successful artist.

Writing Application Write about a time when you used your creativity or had a moment of sudden **insight**. Use at least 3–4 Key Vocabulary words.

Fluency

Read with Ease: Phrasing

Assess your reading fluency with the passage in the Reading Handbook, p. 754. Then complete the self-check below.

1. I did/did not pause appropriately for punctuation and phrases.

2. My words correct per minute: _____

INTEGRATE THE LANGUAGE ARTS

Use Subject Pronouns

A **subject pronoun** is used in the subject of a sentence.

- Use **I** to talk about yourself.
- Use **we** to talk about yourself and one or more than one other person.
- Use **you** to talk to one or more than one other person.
- Use **he**, **she**, **it**, and **they** to talk about other people or things. To choose which of these pronouns to use, think about number and gender.

One	More Than One	Male	Female
he she it	they	he	she

Oral Practice (1–5) Say each sentence with the correct subject pronoun.

1. Jill and I set out paints. ____ also set out paper.
2. Many artists work hard. ____ hope for success.
3. Maria is a sculptor. ____ loves to work with clay.
4. This painting is odd. ____ has only two colors.
5. Paul Gauguin was an artist. ____ was French.

Written Practice (6–10) Fix three more pronouns and rewrite the paragraph. Add two sentences.

> **They**
> Teens in Boston create art. ~~She~~ earn money, too. An art piece is sold for a fair price. They is not sold for less. Susan Rodgerson started Artists for Humanity. He worked with five teens. Companies became interested. It gave AFH money.

Describe People, Places, and Things

Pair Talk Describe an artist from the selection or an artist you know. Describe the places where the artist works and what he or she produces.

Analyze Description

When writers use **description**, they carefully choose words that will:

- help readers imagine people, places, and events.
- appeal to readers' senses of sight, smell, taste, touch, and hearing.
- give the selection a specific tone, or feeling.

In "Creativity at Work," the writer paints a picture of the sights and sounds at the AFH studio:

> teenagers…rev up wood-crafting tools and settle down to sculpture tables and graphic design computers. Hip-hop beats pulse through the studios…

Find three more descriptions in the selections where the writer's word choice helps you picture something or identify a certain tone.

Interview

In "The Hidden Secrets of the Creative Mind," the writer interviews an expert on creativity. Now it's your turn. Interview a creative person you know.

❶ Prepare Interview Questions Use what you learned in the articles to brainstorm questions you can ask about how the person uses creativity.

❷ Conduct the Interview Take notes or ask for permission to record the conversation. Add follow-up questions if you need more information.

❸ Share Your Interview Review your work. Then share the main ideas of what you learned with the class. If you recorded the interview, play short excerpts that support your ideas.

Context Clues

Whenever you read an unfamiliar word, look for **context clues** in the words and phrases that are nearby. Many times, these will include:

- definitions of the word: "There are two **hemispheres**, or sides, in the human brain."

- examples of the word: "And **collaboration** is key. Look at what others are doing. Brainstorm with different people."

Work with a partner to review any unfamiliar words and phrases you have found in the two selections. Reread the context and find any definitions and examples that will make the meanings more clear.

Oral Presentation

Science: Parts of the Brain Learn more about the parts of the brain and the functions of each section.

myNGconnect.com

- ➲ Study the PBS special, *The Secret Life of the Brain*.
- ➲ Use magazine index databases to find articles about the brain in your local library.

Use a computer program to create a web or a Venn diagram that organizes the results of your research. Then present your information to the class.

📖 **Language and Learning Handbook**, page 702

Writing a Test Essay

A test may ask you to write about a topic using examples from your own experience.

1 **Unpack the Prompt** Study the writing prompt. As you read, underline words or phrases that show what you need to include in your essay.

> **Writing Prompt**
>
> What is creativity? Why is it important in our everyday lives? Write a short essay that gives your ideas about creativity. Include three examples of how people express themselves in creative ways.

2 **Plan** Organize your ideas in a cluster.

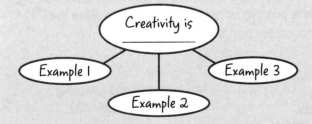

3 **Draft** Use these ideas to write your essay:

> **Essay Organizer**
>
> I believe that creativity is [give your definition]. It is an important part of our lives because [give your reason].
>
> There are many ways to express your creativity. Some people [give example 1]. This helps them [support example 1].
>
> People also show creativity by [give example 2]. This helps them [support example 2].
>
> Other people express themselves through [give example 3]. This helps them show [support example 3].
>
> In conclusion, [summarize your ideas].

4 **Check Your Work** Reread your essay. Ask:

- Does my essay address the writing prompt?
- Do I give examples to support my ideas?
- Do I use the correct subject pronouns?

📖 **Writing Handbook**, page 784

Inside an Art Museum

People who work in art museums are responsible for preserving and displaying valuable works of art. Museum employees organize exhibitions and provide educational services to the public.

Jobs in Art Museums

Art museums hire people for a variety of positions that require specific education and skills. Many employees are experts in a specific type of art or period of cultural history.

Job	Responsibilities	Education/Training Required
Museum Technician **1**	• Builds, installs, and removes exhibits • Hangs and mounts works of art • Constructs cabinets and other displays for artwork • Moves, packs, and uncrates art shipments	• High school diploma • Shop or carpentry courses • Experience in designing and installing exhibits
Conservator **2**	• Performs lab tests and uses special equipment to evaluate condition of art objects • Treats and repairs artwork	• College degree • Special knowledge about one kind of art • On-the-job training
Curator **3**	• Researches and catalogs art collections • Directs purchases and exchanges of art objects and collection loans • Organizes exhibitions • Coordinates tours, lectures, and fundraisers	• Master's degree in art history or museum studies • Ph.D. desirable • Related work experience or internship in a museum

Research the Job Outlook

Analyze the job outlook for a job in an art gallery or museum.

1. Prepare a four-column chart with the following headings: *Job, Number of Employees in the Industry, Salary,* and *Job Outlook.*

2. Consult the Occupational Outlook Handbook. Read about your chosen job.

3. Fill in information about your chosen job in the chart. Work with a partner to determine if your job has a positive or negative job outlook. Save the information in a professional career portfolio.

myNGconnect.com

⊙ **Learn more about museum jobs.**

⊙ **Download a form to evaluate whether you would like to work in this field.**

▼ **Language and Learning Handbook,** page 702

Use Context Clues

Suppose you read the following in your school's newspaper: *The basketball star tore his anterior cruciate ligament. He will not return to the court until the tissue around his knee heals.* Can you figure out what the basketball player tore?

One way to figure out what unfamiliar words mean is to use **word clues** in the context of the sentence or paragraph where the unfamiliar words appear. Context clues are often **synonyms**. For example:

> Exercise has a number of **beneficial** results. One **positive** result is sleeping better.

Positive is a synonym clue for *beneficial*. You can often, but not always, identify synonyms by signal words such as *like, another, also, as, for example,* and *likewise.*

Explore Words and Context Clues

Work with a partner to use context clues to determine word meanings.

1. Read the sentences on the right.
2. Look for context clues to determine the meaning of each highlighted word.
3. Check the meaning in a dictionary.

Put the Strategy to Work

When you see a word you don't know, use this strategy to look for context clues.

1. Look for punctuation clues or familiar words or ideas in the surrounding text that may mean something similar.
2. Look for signal words such as *or, like, also, as,* or *for example.*
3. Replace the unfamiliar word with the known one and see if it makes sense.

TRY IT ▶ Read the following sentence and use context clues to understand the meaning. Then rewrite the sentence using your own words.

> ▶ The middens of ancient people provide clues to their daily life, just as the trash heaps of today show how people live in modern times.

---

1. The river was full of **noxious**, dangerous materials such as chemicals from factories.

2. When going to a party, you should show your best **decorum**. For example, dress your best and thank the host.

3. As she got on the **off-roader**, she realized that the bicycle's tires were flat.

🔖 Reading Handbook, page 733

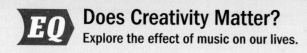

EQ **Does Creativity Matter?**
Explore the effect of music on our lives.

Make a Connection

Discussion Sometimes music can have a big influence on its listeners. With a group, talk about whether and how different kinds of music can affect the way people dress, talk, and even think.

Learn Key Vocabulary

Study the Words Pronounce each word and learn its meaning. You may also want to look up the definitions in the Glossary.

• Academic Vocabulary

Key Words	Examples
• **achieve** (u-**chēv**) verb ▸ pages 149, 153	To **achieve** means to succeed or do well. If you work hard, you can **achieve** your goals.
assert (u-**surt**) verb ▸ page 145	When you **assert** something, you insist on having your opinions and ideas heard. The song lyrics **assert** the band's ideas about the power of music.
• **culture** (**kul**-chur) noun ▸ pages 142, 149, 155	**Culture** includes the beliefs, attitudes, and behaviors that are shared by a group of people. Young people have a **culture** that appreciates creativity and independence.
evolve (ē-**valv**) verb ▸ page 144, 155	When something **evolves**, it changes over time. My taste in music has **evolved** over the years.
heritage (**her**-u-tij) noun ▸ page 152	Your **heritage** is your background. **Heritage** includes the traditions and beliefs given to you by your family, culture, and society.
innovator (in-nu-**vā**-tur) noun ▸ page 144	An **innovator** is someone who introduces something new. The new styles and sounds the musician uses make her an **innovator** of music.
• **perspective** (pur-**spek**-tiv) noun ▸ page 142	Your **perspective** is your point of view. Our teacher's background in classical music gives him a unique **perspective** when he hears our music.
self-esteem (self es-**tēm**) noun ▸ pages 153, 154	**Self-esteem** is the feeling that you are valuable. The confident girl has high **self-esteem**. *Synonyms:* confidence, self-respect

Practice the Words Complete a **Word Square** for each Key Vocabulary word.

Word Square

Definition: beliefs, attitudes, and behaviors shared by a group	Important Characteristics: large group of people
Examples: trick or treating for Halloween	Non-Examples: painting

(culture)

BEFORE READING Hip-Hop as Culture

essay by Efrem Smith

Reading Strategies

- Plan and Monitor
- ▶ **Determine Importance**
- Make Inferences
- Ask Questions
- Make Connections
- Synthesize
- Visualize

Analyze Author's Purpose

An **essay** is a short piece of writing about a subject. The author's **purpose** is usually to entertain, inform, persuade, or share opinions and ideas. The author presents details in a way that effectively achieves one or more of these purposes.

Look Into the Text

Smith gives facts to inform the reader about how hip-hop is often used.

> Hip-hop has taken over the music industry in the same way the Williams sisters have taken over tennis. Look at the way the National Basketball Association uses hip-hop players like Shaquille O'Neal and Allen Iverson—and hip-hop culture in general—to sell soda, candy, and clothes to young people. To see hip-hop as simply rap is to not understand the impact and influence of a greater movement.
>
> Rap music is just one element of hip-hop. In fact, true hip-hop heads understand that hip-hop isn't just about music. It's a culture, a way of life, a language, a fashion, a set of values, and a unique perspective.

What opinions does Smith include about hip-hop?

Focus Strategy ▶ Determine Importance

Once you have found the author's main ideas, it often helps to put them in your own words. As you read the rest of the essay, summarize the most important ideas.

HOW TO SUMMARIZE NONFICTION

Focus Strategy

1. **Identify the Topic** Repeated words and ideas often point to the main topic.

2. **Read Carefully** Try to picture what the author is describing. Take notes.

3. **Summarize Each Section** Pause at the end of each section to decide upon the important details. Produce main idea statements.

Detail #1		Detail #2		Main Idea for Section 1
Hip-hop influences many industries.	+	It includes language, fashion, and values.	=	Hip-hop is an important culture today.

4. **Think Beyond the Text** After reading, ask yourself: What have I learned about the topic? How does this change my thinking?

Hip-Hop High School

Chris "Kharma Kazi" Rolle created the Hip-Hop Project in 1999 when he was still a teenager. His goal was to create a "last chance" arts program for New York City teens. And the teens who come to the program have almost run out of second chances. Most of them are thinking about dropping out of high school. Some are homeless or have just been released from prison. Although these teens come from a variety of backgrounds, they do have something in common: hip-hop is a second language to them. Its rich poetry and power inspire their creativity and passion.

Recognizing the power of hip-hop to change lives, Rolle designed the Hip-Hop Project as a way to give students confidence in their abilities. It also gives them knowledge and skills they can use in the future. The intensive program brings students together with professionals in the music industry who help them write, produce, market, and distribute their own collective hip-hop album. The money made from the album and all the related marketing materials they create—such as music videos, T-shirts, and posters—go into a special Scholarship/Enterprise Fund set up for the students.

In addition to recording their own music, the kids have performed at dozens of open-microphone and performance events. In 2000, they wrote, produced, and performed their own show to sold-out audiences in Manhattan. They also recorded their first demo album. Thanks to one teenager's vision, the kids of the Hip-Hop Project share the life-changing experience of transforming their own stories into powerful works of art.

myNGconnect.com

🔊 Listen to a song by members of the Hip-Hop Project.
🔊 Read more about teens and the arts.

Hip-Hop as Culture

by Efrem Smith

Comprehension Coach

Hip-Hop Today

Hip-hop has taken over the music industry in the same way **the Williams sisters** have taken over tennis. Look at the way the National Basketball Association uses hip-hop players like Shaquille O'Neal and Allen Iverson—and hip-hop **culture** in general—to sell soda, candy, and clothes to young people. To see hip-hop as simply rap is to not understand the impact and influence of a greater movement.

Rap music is just one element of hip-hop. In fact, true hip-hop heads understand that hip-hop isn't just about music. It's a culture, a way of life, a language, a fashion, a set of values, and a unique **perspective**. Hip-hop is an **economy**. It's the ability to take the inner-city system and turn it into a multi-million—or possibly even billion—dollar business. Hip-hop **encompasses** groups like Public Enemy who use rap to address racism, oppression, and poverty. Their leader, "Chuck D," turned it into a new political movement that gets **urban young adults** active in ways **reminiscent of** the days of the civil rights movement. **1**

1 Author's Purpose
What does Smith do in the first two paragraphs to help establish the purpose of his essay? Explain.

2 Access Vocabulary
How do the photo and caption give clues about what *breaking, popping,* and *locking* mean?

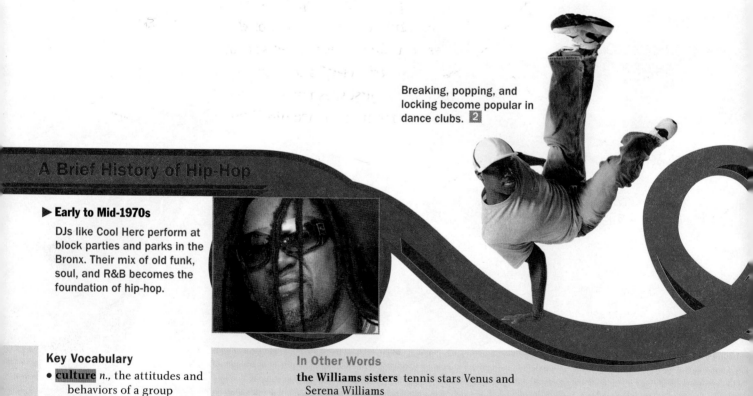

Breaking, popping, and locking become popular in dance clubs. **2**

A Brief History of Hip-Hop

▶ **Early to Mid-1970s**

DJs like Cool Herc perform at block parties and parks in the Bronx. Their mix of old funk, soul, and R&B becomes the foundation of hip-hop.

Key Vocabulary
- **culture** *n.,* the attitudes and behaviors of a group
- **perspective** *n.,* point of view

In Other Words

the Williams sisters tennis stars Venus and Serena Williams
economy organization of money and resources
encompasses includes
urban young adults young people in large cities
reminiscent of that are like

Hip-hop culture is worldwide. Here, the group De La Soul performs in England.

Hip-Hop History

Hip-hop tells the stories of the **multiethnic** urban youth and the communities they live in. Hip-hop is about **inner-city and lower-class life**. It's about trying to live out the **American dream** from the bottom up. It's about trying to make something out of nothing. Hip-hop is about the youth culture of New York City taking over the world. Hip-hop is about dance, art, expression, pain, love, racism, sexism, broken families, hard times, **overcoming adversity**, and even the search for God. Anyone who looks at hip-hop and just sees rap music doesn't truly understand the history and the current influence hip-hop has on the whole youth culture. ▣

▶ **Late 1970s**

The focus of hip-hop moves from DJs to MCs, or rappers.

The Sugarhill Gang releases "Rapper's Delight," an early rap hit.

In Other Words

multiethnic varied backgrounds of
inner-city and lower-class life the lives of people in poor areas of large cities
American dream hope of being successful
overcoming adversity succeeding in spite of challenges

3 Summarize Nonfiction
What is the author's main idea in this paragraph?

Monitor Comprehension

Explain
According to the author, what are some examples of today's hip-hop culture?

I was born in 1969, so I am a part of the original hip-hop generation. I watched hip-hop **evolve** from **underground** house parties in the basements of my friends' houses, to the first Run DMC video on cable television, to today's rap millionaires like Sean "Diddy" Combs, Master P, Suge Knight, and Russell Simmons. **4** These successful African Americans are more than just rappers. As a matter of fact, Russell Simmons doesn't even rap. Simmons has been **behind the scenes of** hip-hop—developing it from rap artists and groups to films and clothing lines. Simmons, a true **pioneer** of the culture, opened the door so that others in the movement could start their own record labels and develop their own clothing lines.

These **innovators** are the **architects of** culture. **5** They started from the streets of the city and now influence suburban areas and even small rural towns. They took the hustle of the street and turned it into a Wall Street economy. It doesn't matter if you're in a city or suburb. It doesn't matter if you are Latino, Asian, or Irish. Hip-hop is influencing your situation.

I am part of the hip-hop generation

4 **Author's Purpose**
Why does the author include his own experience with hip-hop? Explain.

5 **Language**
Smith describes Russell Simmons as a "pioneer." What other words does he use to describe early hip-hop leaders? How is this different from calling them "artists" and "producers"?

▶ **Early to Mid-1980s**
Kurtis Blow's song, "The Breaks," becomes hip-hop's first gold single.

Rick Rubin and Russell Simmons form Def Jam Records, one of the top labels in hip-hop.

Key Vocabulary
evolve *v.*, to develop over time
innovator *n.*, person who introduces something new

In Other Words
underground secret
behind the scenes of working to support and help
pioneer early leader
architects of designers who plan and build

The Hip-Hop Influence

Kids may not love hip-hop, but they're being influenced by it. If teens are wearing oversized jeans with the tops of their boxers showing, oversized athletic jerseys, or long chains around their necks, this is hip-hop. Girls on a bus braiding their hair in the style of an Ethiopian queen, that's hip-hop. There are things around you that daily scream at you, "Long live hip-hop!" If you want to understand the culture teens live in today, it's important to understand hip-hop and understand it as culture, not just music.

In the book *Hip-Hop America*, Nelson George writes this:

"Now we know that rap music, and hip-hop style as a whole, has utterly broken through from **its ghetto roots** to **assert** a lasting influence on American clothing, magazine publishing, television, language, . . . and **social policy** as well as its obvious presence in records and movies. . . . [A]dvertisers, magazines, [television], fashion companies, . . . soft drink manufacturers, and **multimedia conglomerates** . . . have embraced hip-hop as a way to reach not just black young people, but *all* young people." **6**

> **6 Summarize Nonfiction**
> What is the main idea of this paragraph from *Hip-Hop America*?

▶ **Mid to Late 1980s**

The Beastie Boys release the first rap album to reach #1 and the best-selling rap album of the decade.

DJ Jazzy Jeff & the Fresh Prince win the first Grammy Award for rap music.

Key Vocabulary
assert *v.*, to insist on having one's opinions and rights recognized

In Other Words
its ghetto roots where it began in poor areas
social policy the way the government and leaders treat different groups
multimedia conglomerates organizations that control TV, film, news, and advertising

Monitor Comprehension

Explain
According to Smith, how did leaders like Russell Simmons help later hip-hop artists?

Interview
with a Hip-Hop Legend

Russell Simmons

*Excerpt from Terry Gross's interview
with Russell Simmons,
from the program "Fresh Air,"
produced by WHYY, Philadelphia.*

Terry Gross: Have you ever been concerned about the promotion of a gangster lifestyle through rap?

Russell Simmons: People are always surprised to know that I'm really proud of all of what rap stands for today. And I believe that what people say in their closed doors, they're shocked to hear it on the radio. They're shocked to hear a reflection of this reality, you know, broadcast. . . .

   Almost all the records that people perceive as "gangster records" are about people frustrated—who don't perceive themselves as having any other opportunity—and it's a *description* of their lifestyle more than it is **an endorsement of** it. And so that's something that, you know, people who listen closely to the music can tell. And people from the outside, all they can hear is the language. Well, *real* language is OK by me, and descriptions of *real* situations and a *real* reflection of our society, a part of our society, is important by me.

◀ **Early to Mid-1990s**

Cypress Hill becomes one of the first Latino hip-hop groups to sell more than a million records.

In Other Words
an endorsement of a way to promote

A rap artist who goes by the name KRS-One (Knowledge **Reigns Supreme** Over Nearly Everyone) presents the elements and history of hip-hop in his book, *Ruminations*. To him, hip-hop connects to philosophy, religion, government, and corporate America. It's a commentary from **the 'hood,** with urban artists serving as inner-city journalists who use their rap, dance, and urban art to report what's going on in the city and in the world at large. **7** KRS-One describes hip-hop as culture this way:

> "True hip-hop is a term that describes the **independent collective consciousness of** a specific group of inner-city people. Ever growing, it is commonly expressed through such elements as: Breakin' (dance), Emceein' (rap), . . . Deejayin', Beatboxin', Street Fashion, Street Knowledge, and **Street Entrepreneurialism**. Discovered by Kool DJ Herc in the Bronx, New York around 1972, and established as a community of peace, love, unity, and having fun by Afrika Bambaataa through Zulu Nation in 1974, hip-hop is an independent and unique community, **an empowering behavior,** and an international culture." **8**

7 Access Vocabulary
What is a "commentary"? First, decode the word by its syllables and word parts. Pronounce the word aloud. Look for words and phrases in the sentence that give you context clues about the word's meaning.

8 Author's Purpose
Why do you think the author includes this excerpt from KRS-One's book? Does it add or take away from the essay? Explain.

▶ **Mid to Late 1990s**
Queen Latifah wins the Grammy for best rap solo performance.

Lauryn Hill wins 5 Grammys. Her album is the first hip-hop album to win Album of the Year.

In Other Words

Reigns Supreme Has the Most Power
the 'hood neighborhood
independent collective consciousness of unique point of view that is shared by
Street Entrepreneurialism Business that began in the street

an empowering behavior a way to give people power and confidence

Beyond Hip-Hop

The *American Heritage College Dictionary* gives hip-hop the following definition: "A popular urban youth culture, closely **associated with** rap music and with the style and fashions of African American inner-city residents."

Hip-hop moves beyond music into other forms: D.J., the M.C., dance, visual art, fashion, language, and big business. It's also culture because it encompasses the culture of African Americans, Latinos, and urban America. When I was in middle school and high school, hip-hop was more than just music for me—it was finally feeling like my voice, and the voice of urban youth culture, was **in the mainstream of** American culture. **9**

Take into consideration that hip-hop evolved after a movement for civil rights, which had young people on the front lines. That isn't to say that hip-hop was the first movement to use the arts to speak to political, social, and spiritual issues. But it did so representing the underclass of urban America in a new way.

Things have changed since those early days. For today's teens, hip-hop is the mainstream culture—one that affects what they see, hear, and experience every day. The question is: What issues can hip-hop address today? How can its message reflect the realities of today's world? The answer is now, as it was then, for today's youth to decide. ❖

9 **Summarize Nonfiction** Summarize the main idea of this paragraph in your own words. How does it fit in with the rest of the essay?

▶ **Early to Mid-2000s**
Kanye West bursts onto the scene, delivering street-rap with a spirited message.

In Other Words
associated with related to
in the mainstream of accepted as an important part of

ANALYZE Hip-Hop as Culture

1. **Explain** According to Efrem Smith, why is it important to understand hip-hop? Use examples from the text to support your answer.

2. **Vocabulary** What are the important parts of the hip-hop culture? How do these things influence our society?

3. **Analyze Author's Purpose** The goal of most essayists is to entertain, inform, persuade, and/or present opinions. Does Efrem Smith achieve each of these goals? Give examples from the text to support your analysis.

4. **Focus Strategy Determine Importance** Find a paragraph where the author's main idea was difficult to understand. Work with a partner to identify and summarize the main idea.

Return to the Text

Reread and Write Efrem Smith says, "If you want to understand the culture teens live in today, it's important to understand hip-hop and understand it as culture, not just music." Reread the text to find examples and details that support and elaborate this idea. Then summarize his idea in your own words and explain whether you agree.

▶ **Mid-2000s**

Grammy-winner Jill Scott establishes the Blues Babe Foundation, a program founded to help minority students between the ages of 16 and 21 pay for college.

Key Vocabulary
• **achieve** *v.*, to succeed or do well

BEFORE READING I Am Somebody

song lyrics by Grandmaster Flash

Reading Strategies

- Plan and Monitor
▶ Determine Importance
- Make Inferences
- Ask Questions
- Make Connections
- Synthesize
- Visualize

Analyze Structure: Song Lyrics

You're about to read the **lyrics**, or words, to a hip-hop song. Like most songs, "I Am Somebody" has a specific set of features that are very similar to poetry.

Look Into the Text

A verse is a set of lines in a song or poem. Here each verse is four lines long.

Hey people
We got a little something that we wanna tell you all, so listen, understand
Yo, God made one no better than the other
Every girl becomes a woman, every boy a man

Rhyme is a common structural element of song lyrics.

While you're livin' in your mansion, drivin' big cars
There's another on the street, cold sleepin' on the ground
And when you walk by, yo, don't act cold-blooded
'Cause it just ain't fair to kick a man when he's down

The chorus is a verse that is repeated at different times in the song.

'Cause he is somebody (Say it loud)
Like I am somebody
You are somebody
Like I am someone (Say it loud)

Imagery helps readers picture the writer's ideas. How do the images in the first line of verse 2 contrast with the image in the next line?

Focus Strategy ▶ Determine Importance

Song lyrics, like other texts, contain main ideas. Identify the main ideas in the song, and summarize them in your own words.

HOW TO SUMMARIZE LYRICS

Focus Strategy

1. **Look for the clues about what's important.** Read for words or phrases that are repeated or very emotional words. Then determine the main idea that unites the important material. Record these in a **Main Idea Chart**.

2. **Check your understanding.** Compare your statement of the main idea against the other details of the song lyrics.

Main Idea Chart

Writer's Words	Main Idea
"don't act cold-blooded 'Cause it just ain't fair to kick a man when he's down" (lines 7-8)	Always treat others with respect.

I AM SOMEBODY

BY GRANDMASTER FLASH

Connect Across Texts

In "Hip-Hop as Culture," Efrem Smith says that hip-hop tells the stories of "youth and the communities they live in." The following song lyrics describe how a legendary hip-hop artist feels about his own community.

Hey people
We got a little something that we wanna tell you all,
    so listen, understand
Yo, God made one no better than the other
Every girl becomes a woman, every boy a man

5   While you're livin' in your mansion, drivin' big cars
There's another on the street, cold sleepin' on the ground
And when you walk by, yo, don't act cold-blooded
'Cause it just ain't fair to kick a man when he's down   **1**

'Cause he is somebody (Say it loud)
10 Like I am somebody
You are somebody
Like I am someone **(Say it loud)**

> **1 Summarize Lyrics**
> What is the main idea of verse 2? State it in your own words.

In Other Words
mansion big, expensive house
cold-blooded in a rude, heartless way
kick a man when he's down treat a man badly
  when he is already hurting

Whether you're here or you're gone, you're right or you're wrong
You were meant to be somebody from the second you were born
15 Don't criticize and knock one another
It ain't really that hard to just be a brother **2**

So be good, speak up, don't wait for it to happen
Life is passing you by, and homeboy, you're cold nappin'
Don't be gettin' hung up on what you're not
20 Be proud of what you are and whatever you got

'Cause it's a cold, cruel world causing kids to cry
If you're hangin' your head, cold kiss it goodbye
Stand up for your heritage, rejoice in the fact
Whether you're red, white, tan, yellow, brown, or black **3**

25 **'Cause you are somebody (Say it loud)**
Like I am somebody
He is somebody
Like I am someone (Say it loud)

There are firemen, bankers, messengers, preachers
30 Brokers, policemen, executives, teachers,
Journalists, janitors, architects, doctors,
Restaurant workers, nurses, chief rockers

Key Vocabulary
heritage *n.*, background, race, or ethnic group you belong to

In Other Words
criticize talk badly about
cold nappin' wasting your time
Don't be gettin' hung up on Don't worry about
rejoice in be happy about
Brokers People who trade stocks
Journalists News writers and reporters

If you feel you're somebody, be proud, and show it

'Cause everybody's somebody, (ugh) and ya know it

35 It doesn't matter if you're black, white, or Chinese

Livin' in the States or reside overseas

'Cause you and I are special, same as everyone else

If you don't believe me, you're only cheating yourself

We all got a purpose in life to achieve

40 That's a fact, and here's another that you better believe

That I am somebody (Say it loud)

Like you are somebody

He is somebody

Like I am someone (Say it loud) ▣

45 You got wealth, good health, and you're stuck on yourself

Well let me tell you that you're better than nobody else

'Cause you got no self-esteem, so I'm richer

And when you leave this earth, you can't take money witcha

So play your dumb game, call me out my name,

50 But nothing you can do could make me feel shame

We're all created equal, we live and we die

So when you try to bring me down, I keep my head up high

▣ **Structure**
The words "I am somebody" are repeated in each chorus. Why do you think the author includes the direction to "Say it loud"?

Key Vocabulary
- **achieve** *v.*, to succeed or do well
  self-esteem *n.*, feeling that you are valuable, confidence in yourself

In Other Words
reside overseas living in another country
stuck on yourself too proud of yourself
call me out my name speak rudely about me

Don't judge a book by its cover
'Cause it's never what it seems
55 Now I know what I'm sayin',
And I feel I gotta scream

That I am somebody (Say it loud)
Like you are somebody
He is somebody
60 Like I am someone

So be yourself, HUH! ❖

ANALYZE I Am Somebody

1. **Explain** What is the theme, or message, of the chorus?
2. **Vocabulary** According to Grandmaster Flash, what is important about self-esteem? What are the dangers of low self-esteem?
3. **Analyze Structure: Song Lyrics** Identify examples of imagery from the song. How do they help you understand the author's ideas?
4. **Focus Strategy Determine Importance** With a group, summarize the song's main idea. Discuss whether it is easier or harder to summarize ideas in song lyrics than in an essay.

⮌ Return to the Text
Reread and Write What message does the song have for the different people in our society? Write a letter from Grandmaster Flash to one of the people he mentions. What ideas does he want them to know?

About the Songwriter

Grandmaster Flash (1958–), born Joseph Saddler, was one of the first musicians during rap and hip-hop music's early days. With his group, Grandmaster Flash and the Furious Five, he created some of the distinctive hip-hop sound effects that are still used today. In 2003, he received the Founder's Award for his achievements in hip-hop at the *Billboard* R&B/Hip-Hop Awards.

EQ Does Creativity Matter?

Reading
Critical Thinking

EQ 1. **Analyze** Think back to your discussion on page 138 about ways that music influences our lives. Explain whether the two selections support your ideas.

2. **Compare** Many people might think that hip-hop culture is all about clothes and money. Would Efrem Smith and Grandmaster Flash agree? Give examples from both selections.

3. **Interpret** Smith believes that no matter who you are, "Hip-hop is influencing your situation." What does he mean? Do you think Grandmaster Flash would agree?

4. **Predict** Over time, hip-hop evolved into an important culture. Do you think hip-hop will continue to be very popular? Why or why not?

EQ 5. **Evaluate** Music can have many effects on our lives. What effects might "I Am Somebody" have on a listener? Discuss your ideas with a group.

Writing
Writing: Write About Literature

Song Lyrics Think about the authors' important ideas in "Hip-Hop as Culture" and "I Am Somebody." Work with a partner to decide on one main idea that fits both texts. Then write a four-line verse that expresses the main idea. Read or perform your lyrics for the class.

Vocabulary
Key Vocabulary Review

Oral Review Work with a partner. Use these words to complete the paragraph.

achieve	evolved	perspective
asserts	heritage	self-esteem
culture	innovator	

Hip-hop style has __(1)__ and changed in many ways over the past few decades. It began in the 1970s with an __(2)__ who introduced a new way to combine many styles of music. Its __(3)__ includes influences from disco, funk, and reggae music. In the past, hip-hop lyrics included some negative messages. But much of today's hip-hop __(4)__ important ideas that come from the __(5)__, or point of view, of urban youth. It encourages young people to work hard in order to __(6)__ their goals, to have high __(7)__ and to believe that they are valuable. Hip-hop has become a __(8)__ that includes the beliefs, attitudes, and behaviors of many young people today.

Writing Application Write a short journal entry about a time when music had an effect on you. Use at least four Key Vocabulary words.

Fluency
Read with Ease: Intonation

Assess your reading fluency with the passage in the Reading Handbook, p. 755. Then complete the self-check below.

1. My intonation did/did not sound natural.

2. My words correct per minute: _____

Grammar

Use Action Verbs in the Present Tense

An **action verb** tells what the subject does. An action verb in the **present tense** tells what the subject does now or does often.

My friends and I **listen** to music every day.
We **dance** to the beat.

Add **-s** to the action verb only when you talk about one other person, place, or thing.

That new song **amazes** me.
The singer **struts**.

An action verb can have a helping verb and a **main verb**. The helping verbs **can**, **could**, **may**, or **might** come before the main verb. Never add **-s** to them.

Music **can change** the world.
He **may write** a song.

Oral Practice (1–5) With a partner, take turns completing each sentence with a present tense verb.

1. Music ____ from the radio.
2. The DJ can ____ the songs.
3. Dancers ____ to the music.
4. Lyrics ____ a message.
5. I might ____ with my friends.

Written Practice (6–10) Rewrite the paragraph. Choose the correct present tense verb. Then add two sentences. Use action verbs in the present tense.

Today, many teens (listen/listens) to music on the Internet. Music (unite/unites) people from different cultures. A song (can help/cans help) people speak a common language.

Language Development

Describe Experiences

Group Talk What kind of music do you like? In a group with others who agree with you, describe a dance or music event you have experienced.

Literary Analysis

Analyze Style and Word Choice

Word choice is the kind of language a writer uses. It plays a big part in helping a writer develop his or her own **style**, or particular way of writing. Word choice often changes based on a writer's audience.

A hip-hop artist like Grandmaster Flash uses lots of informal language, or slang, choosing words and phrases that relate to his listeners:

• "yo, don't act cold-blooded"

An essayist like Efrem Smith mainly uses more formal writing to describe his experiences:

• "Hip-hop tells the stories of the multiethnic urban youth ..."

Smith also adds slang that helps readers understand the time he is describing:

• "It's a commentary from the 'hood ..."

Work with a partner to find more examples of the type of word choice that contributes to each writer's style. Discuss whether the author's message would be more effective with different style or word choice.

Research/Speaking

Oral Presentation

Teens and Trends Research how teens get their music today, such as: music stores and radio stations, over the Internet, or other ways.

1 Survey Ask students at your school where they get their music. Record your responses.

2 Research Find more information in newspaper, magazine, and online articles.

3 Analyze Compare your survey with research results. What trends or patterns do you see?

4 Report Share your findings with the class in a short oral report.

Language and Learning Handbook, page 702

Context Clues for Idioms

Expressions like "you're stuck on yourself" are called **idioms**. Idioms mean something different from the literal, or exact, meaning of their words.

To figure out the meaning of an unfamiliar idiom:

1. **Study the context of the phrase** The next line of the song says: "You're better than nobody else."

2. **Guess the meaning** The verse is about an overly proud or self-centered person.

3. **Test your guess** If it fits, you may have found your definition! If not, revise your guess.

4. **Use a resource** If all else fails, look up the phrase or ask a friend or teacher for help.

There may be times when these techniques do not work, and context clues may not always help you. Sometimes, it may help to skip over the phrase. The meaning may become clearer as you read on.

With a partner, find four unfamiliar idioms from both selections and add their meanings to a chart. You may even find more modern idioms that mean the same thing.

PAGE	IDIOM	CONTEXT	MEANING
153	you're stuck on yourself	"you're better than nobody else"	You're too proud of yourself.

Focus and Unity

Whenever you write, you want to keep the reader focused on your main idea. To do this:

- avoid repeating yourself
- leave out unnecessary details
- remove ideas that take away from your point.

Just OK

> Music is important to my family. Two of my four grandparents were singers. They have photos of tours to Europe. My parents fill our house with music all day. My sisters and I all take piano lessons, but I play sports, too.

Much Better

> Music is important to my family. Two of my four grandparents were singers. ~~They have photos of tours to Europe.~~ My parents fill our house with music all day. My sisters and I all take piano lessons~~, but I play sports, too~~. Music is what brings our family together.

With a partner, analyze how to make the passage below more focused and unified.

> Music is one way that people express their feelings and ideas. Other people may like to write letters or paint things to express their feelings and ideas. Loud music with a heavy beat shows strong emotions, such as anger and jealousy. Soft, slow music shows love or sadness. You don't have to be able to play an instrument to express yourself through music, either. There are times when I can tell how my friends are feeling by hearing what they're listening to. Just listening makes me know how they feel.

Sometimes a diagram helps you decide which details are focused and which are not.

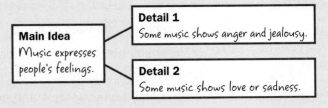

| **Main Idea** Music expresses people's feelings. | **Detail 1** Some music shows anger and jealousy. |
| | **Detail 2** Some music shows love or sadness. |

📖 **Writing Handbook,** page 784

Descriptive Presentation

Have you ever heard a speaker describe an event in a way that was so interesting, you could imagine the event as if you were there? You can be just as interesting of a speaker! All you need is the right subject, some great language, and a little practice. Here's how to give a great descriptive presentation:

1. Plan Your Presentation

Think about a memorable event, such as a dance or a sporting event that you have gone to or been a part of. Then do the following:

- List the most important details about the event.
- Write descriptive words or phrases about how the event looked, how being there made you feel, or what made it memorable.
- Choose details that support the impression you want to make.
- Write your presentation, including factual descriptions and sensory details.

2. Practice Your Presentation

Rehearse your presentation a few times to keep it smooth and interesting.

- Think of interesting ways to start—by role-playing a scenario, showing a photograph, or having the audience guess the event from your description.
- Practice using your voice and gestures in a way that keeps the audience focused on what you are saying.
- Practice speaking without your notes.
- Ask a classmate for helpful suggestions.

myNGconnect.com
Download the rubric.

3. Give Your Presentation

Keep your audience interested by doing the following:

- Make eye contact with your audience.
- Use your voice and gestures to keep your audience's attention.
- Stay focused on your topic and purpose.
- Speak clearly and loudly enough for the audience to understand.
- Look at your notes if you need to, but try to use them as little as possible.

4. Discuss and Rate the Presentation

Use the rubric to discuss and rate the descriptive presentations, including your own. Make sure your style and structure support your meaning and purpose.

Descriptive Presentation Rubric

Scale	Content of Descriptive Presentation	Student's Preparation	Student's Delivery
3 Great	• Made me really see the event • Was lively and held my attention throughout	• Included precise details about the event • Created a very clear impression of the event	• Spoke clearly and was easy to follow • Stayed focused on the purpose of describing the event
2 Good	• Gave me a fairly good picture of the event • Held my interest much of the time	• Included some details about the event • Created a general impression of the event	• Spoke clearly most of the time and was usually easy to follow • Was often focused on describing the event
1 Needs Work	• Did not help me imagine the event • Was not very interesting	• Included hardly any details about the event • Did not create an impression	• Was hard to hear and understand • Seemed to have no purpose

DO IT ▶ When you are finished preparing and practicing, give your descriptive presentation!

📖 Language and Learning Handbook, page 702

> How can you make a presentation even more descriptive?

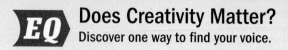

EQ **Does Creativity Matter?**
Discover one way to find your voice.

Make a Connection

Quickwrite As a student, you have encountered many kinds of poetry. Think about the different characteristics (if any) that they share. Then do a quickwrite about what you think poetry should and shouldn't be.

Learn Key Vocabulary

Study the Words Pronounce each word and learn its meaning. You may also want to look up the definitions in the Glossary.

• Academic Vocabulary

Key Words	Examples
compose (kum-**pōz**) verb ▸ pages 167, 177	To **compose** means to create something by writing it. If you **compose** a poem, I'll compose music to go with it.
euphoria (ū-**for**-ē-u) noun ▸ pages 175, 176	**Euphoria** is great joy and happiness. Our team was filled with **euphoria** after we won the art contest. *Antonym*: depression
expression (eks-**pre**-shun) noun ▸ pages 166, 176, 179	The art of **expression** is the ability to communicate in a creative way. Poetry is one form of creative **expression**.
improvisation (im-prah-vu-**zā**-shun) noun ▸ page 171	**Improvisation** means something done without pre-planning. When I forgot to prepare a speech for class, **improvisation** was my only option.
• **phenomenon** (fi-**nahm**-u-nahn) noun ▸ pages 171, 173, 177	A **phenomenon** is something different that people get really excited about. The new music video is a real **phenomenon**; people everywhere are watching it.
recitation (re-su-**tā**-shun) noun ▸ page 164	A **recitation** involves speaking a poem or other text aloud in front of other people. For my class project, I will give a poetry **recitation**.
• **structure** (**struk**-chur) noun ▸ pages 166, 174, 175, 176	**Structure** is the way something is set up or organized. My poem has a **structure** that includes lots of rhyme.
transcend (tran-**send**) verb ▸ page 166	To **transcend** means to rise above or go beyond. Art is something that **transcends** the limits of language. *Synonyms*: outdo, exceed

Practice the Words Work with a partner to add a **Connotation Chart** entry for each Key Vocabulary word. If you think the word has a positive meaning, write +. If you think the word has a negative meaning, write –. If the word is neither, write =. Write your reason in the last column.

Connotation Chart

Word	Positive (+), Negative (–), or Neither (=)	Reason
compose	+	I always think it's good to create something new.

• Plan and Monitor
▶ Determine Importance
• Make Inferences
• Ask Questions
• Make Connections
• Synthesize
• Visualize

BEFORE READING Slam: Performance Poetry Lives On

essay by Pooja Makhijani

Analyze Author's Purpose

An **essay** is short piece of nonfiction writing that is about a single subject. The author writes from a limited point of view to inform, persuade, or entertain you about a certain topic. Be sure to think about the author's purpose for writing this essay and use it to decide whether he or she meets these goals effectively.

Look Into the Text

The author gives information about poetry.

> Poetry doesn't have to be the twelve lines on a page in a book that is sitting in the dustiest corner of the library. Poetry doesn't have to be something you don't understand. Poetry is moving, breathing, ever changing.

How does the author want to persuade you to feel about poetry?

Want proof? Take a trip to the Urban Word Annual Teen Poetry Slam at the Nuyorican Poets Cafe in New York City.

Gathered in this tight space are hundreds of teens from every corner of the city. They've come together to compete for one of five top spots in Brave New Voices, the Eighth Annual National Youth Poetry Slam Festival.

The author informs you about an event.

Focus Strategy ▶ Determine Importance

Every text has a main idea. Details in the text help to support or explain that idea. As you read, ask yourself: Why is this detail important? How does it support the main idea of the text?

HOW TO DETERMINE IMPORTANCE

1. **Read Carefully** As you read, pause to ask yourself:
   - What is the main point of this section?
   - How do the details support this main idea?

Response Journal

Page	Details	Importance
164	"The slam is about words, rhythm, and performance, and it's a lot of fun."	The author includes this to show the important parts of slam.

2. **Record Your Ideas** Use a **Response Journal** to add details from the text and tell how they support the main idea. Note where you found the idea in the text.

3. **Summarize the Important Ideas** Retell the most important ideas in your own words.

Never a Dull Friday Night

by Katy Murphy, Oakland Tribune

It was a Friday night, and sounds of an electric guitar traveled down the hallways of San Leandro High School in San Leandro, CA.

But the music was just a warm-up. The teenagers who filled all the available chairs, desks, and tables of the drama room came for something else.

Poetry.

They came for Dylan Thomas and Bob Dylan. Langston Hughes and Marianne Moore. But most of all, they came to hear original works being read and sung by people they see every day and to share their art with a friendly audience.

"Love is like waking up on a beautiful Saturday morning because your house is on fire," Nicholas Morales, 16, delivered in perfect deadpan as the drumming stopped.

He strummed his guitar for a few beats.

Friday nights in San Leandro haven't been the same in the past few months, since Jesse Ibarra and his friends got tired of having nothing to do and nowhere to play their music.

Ibarra, a senior at San Leandro High School who says he writes "on a continuous basis," managed to secure a classroom with an adult chaperone. He called the monthly event "Friday Night of the Arts."

About 15 people showed up for the first run. The second drew about 20. By the fourth night more than 50 people—almost all high school students—came to whoop and laugh and cheer for anyone brave enough to take the stage, until it was their turn.

Ibarra advertises the event with signs asking people to help "break the mold of bad poetry," with strict instructions to leave all unicorn and rainbow poems at home. Poetry can be a powerful weapon, he said, and more young people need to realize that it's not all about rhyme and structure.

Increasingly, they do.

"I like that it's informal and completely unplanned for the most part," Morales said. "It's not like a show that you have to put on. It's like hanging out with friends."

myNGconnect.com

◐ **Read about the founder of slam poetry.**
◐ **Listen to readings of poems by new and classic poets.**

SLAM

Performance Poetry Lives On

by Dana Malkwine

Poet Aja Monet performs at the Nuyorican Poets Cafe.

Comprehension Coach

What Is Poetry?

Poetry doesn't have to be the twelve lines on a page in a book that is sitting in the dustiest corner of the library. Poetry doesn't have to be something you don't understand. Poetry is moving, breathing, ever changing. **1**

Want proof? Take a trip to the **Urban** Word Annual Teen Poetry Slam at the Nuyorican Poets Cafe in New York City.

Gathered in this tight space are hundreds of teens from every corner of the city. They've come together to compete for one of five top spots in Brave New Voices, the Eighth Annual National Youth Poetry Slam Festival.

Sitting in the cafe feels like being at a sporting event. A DJ **revs up the crowd** with upbeat music. Young people erupt into wild applause as one of their own **hollers** his latest creation of slam before the microphone. **2**

Take a listen to this **excerpt** from "Elementary Invasion," by 16-year-old slam poet Kai Zhang:

Zhang's **recitation** is a mix of **rant**, **rhetoric**, and stand-up comedy, with dashes of hip-hop and rap. Judges in the front row hold up cards with scores—10, 9.5, 10— as the crowd cheers her on, voting to keep her in the race.

The slam is about words, rhythm, and performance, and it's a lot of fun.

1 Author's Purpose
The author begins by describing what poetry is not. What do you think is the author's purpose for starting this way?

2 Author's Purpose
Why do you think Makhijani includes this lively scene near the beginning of the essay?

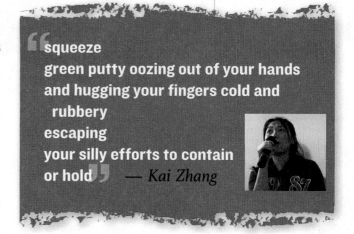

"squeeze
green putty oozing out of your hands
and hugging your fingers cold and
    rubbery
escaping
your silly efforts to contain
or hold" — *Kai Zhang*

Key Vocabulary
recitation *n.*, speaking a poem or other text aloud in front of other people

In Other Words
Urban Big city
revs up the crowd gets the crowd excited
hollers shouts out
excerpt small part
rant, rhetoric opinion, argumentative style

Slamming sequence at the Nuyorican Poets Cafe Friday Night Slam, performed by poet Ryler Dustin

Slam poet Ricardo Perez Gonzalez

What Is Slam?

As the founders of the literary organization Youth Speaks put it, slam is a form of expression. It's "a generation of young people speaking for themselves; a generation . . . reciting struggles and successes on open microphones . . . transcending traditional stereotypes by speaking their truths and listening to the truths of others."

"A poetry slam is like a lyrical boxing match that pits poets against other poets in a bout," according to journalist Shilanda L. Woolridge. In simpler words, a slam is a competition in which poets perform original works alone or in teams. They recite their poems for an audience that boos and cheers as it votes on the best performers. Each poet's work is judged as much on the manner of its performance as on its content or style.

The structure of the traditional slam is a spoken-word performance of three minutes plus a ten-second grace period. This was started by construction worker and poet Marc Smith in 1984. **3** The emphasis on performance soon led to the energetic brand of poetry known as slam. Similar competitions quickly spread across the country and finally found a home at the Nuyorican Poets Cafe and in similar "slam cafes" around the country.

Really, though, the roots of slam can be traced from hip-hop back to the first storytellers, through Shakespeare, and to the Beat poets of the 1960s. **4**

3 Author's Purpose/
Determine
Importance
What key moment in slam history is described here? Why does the writer include it?

4 Determine
Importance
What's an important way slam relates to older forms of poetry? How does the author show it's important?

Key Vocabulary
expression *n.*, way to get thoughts or feelings across to another person
transcend *v.*, to rise above or go beyond
• **structure** *n.*, way something is set up

In Other Words
traditional stereotypes old beliefs about other groups of people
bout contest
grace period time to think and get ready
emphasis focus

From Spoken Word to Written Word

Although slam draws on urban street rhythms like hip-hop, it is first a modern version of the oral **roots** of storytelling and poetry.

Oral storytelling is older than the written word. In ancient times, stories were passed from lips to ears and traveled from place to place. They changed as different storytellers forgot details, deliberately left things out, and added their own details. In ancient Greece, traveling **bards** performed to audiences across their land, reciting **epic poems**.

Over the course of history, there has been a change from the oral tradition to a written one. The earliest example of written poetry is Homer's *Odyssey*. **Composed** around the eighth century B.C.E., this epic poem was most likely the combination of several oral stories about the journey of **Odysseus**.

Perhaps the most famous poet of all is William Shakespeare. His written work was meant to be performed rather than read. He wrote 37 plays and 154 **sonnets** between 1588 and 1613. Like the ancient Greeks, Shakespeare wrote his plays in verse.

It is said that the beat of Shakespeare's poetry is modeled on the rhythm of the human heartbeat—bom-BOM bom-BOM bom-BOM bom-BOM bom-BOM. This separated it from the language of every day. **5**

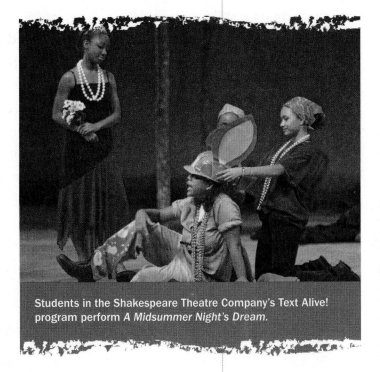

Students in the Shakespeare Theatre Company's Text Alive! program perform *A Midsummer Night's Dream*.

5 Author's Purpose
Why do you think the author "sounds out" the bom-BOM bom-BOM rhythm that Shakespeare used?

Monitor Comprehension

Explain
Does the author say slam is a totally new concept? Explain.

Key Vocabulary
compose *v.*, to write a poem or song

In Other Words
roots tradition
bards poets
epic poems long poems about heroes
Odysseus an Ancient Greek war hero
sonnets 14-line poems

Beating to the Sound of the Times

Although poetry has moved in many different directions since the time of Shakespeare, it has always kept a deep connection to the oral tradition. ◻6

In the 1950s and '60s, the Beat poets brought poetry directly to the people using the ancient ways of the traveling storyteller. Like today's slam artists, the Beats came to be known for their **unique** performance styles.

Allen Ginsberg is one of the most **celebrated** poets of the Beat generation. He first read his most well-known poem, "Howl," in a series of famous readings in October 1955 in San Francisco. ◻7

It was Ginsberg's first **public performance**, and it made him instantly famous at the age of 29. After starting his recitation in a calm tone, the story goes, he soon gained confidence. He began to **sway rhythmically** with the music of his poetry, responding to the enthusiasm of the audience.

Beat poet Allen Ginsberg once said, "Poetry is the one place where people can speak their original human mind. It is the outlet for people to say in public what is known in private."

◻6 **Determine Importance**
What is the main idea of paragraph 1? Explain how one detail on page 168 supports this main idea.

◻7 **Language**
The author describes Ginsberg as a "celebrated" poet. What words in this paragraph are synonyms for *celebrated*?

In Other Words
unique special, unusual
celebrated famous
public performance poetry reading in front of other people
sway rhythmically move back and forth to the beat

Ginsberg and other Beat poets, such as Jack Kerouac, were heavily influenced by jazz music. This is most obvious if you listen closely to the music of their words as you read them aloud. ▣

▣ **Author's Purpose**
The author says a lot about the Beats. How are they connected with slam?

Poetry for the People

Slam has a **mission** for poetry that is similar to Ginsberg's. It seeks to bring poetry back to the people through rhythm, rhyme, and music. "What poetry is about is people," says Mike Henry. He **coordinates** the Austin National Slams, of Austin, Texas. "Slams have put the voice back into . . . the hands of the people."

Although the Beat poets were more influenced by jazz, slam poets have turned to hip-hop for inspiration. The godfather of popular slam, as we know it, is Russell Simmons. In 2001, the father figure to such rappers as Ludacris and Jay-Z created Def Poetry Jam (later called Def Poetry), a slam shown on television. The series **showcased** such artists as poet Ursula Rucker; the hip-hop spoken-word performer Saul Williams; and the British musical diva duo Floetry.

The first season of "def" (slang for *excellent*) poetry was hosted by hip-hop superstar Mos Def. He often opened the

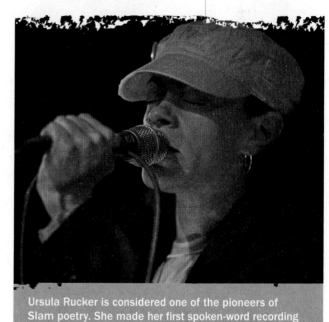

Ursula Rucker is considered one of the pioneers of Slam poetry. She made her first spoken-word recording in 1994, and has performed all over the world.

In Other Words

mission goal, purpose
coordinates is in charge of, organizes
showcased gave the audience a chance to meet

Monitor Comprehension

Summarize
How did music influence both the Beats and slam?

night with a classic poem by **Byron, Shelley, Keats, or Wordsworth**. After that, the audience was treated to slam poetry such as Saul Williams's "Said the Shotgun to the Head": 9

9 **Determine Importance**
What is "slam's mission for poetry"? How does the Def Poetry Jam help to support this concept?

CURRENTLY
MOON MARKED
AND
SUN SPARKED
UNMARKED BILLS
WILL I AM
CERTAIN
I SPEAK A NEW LANGUAGE
as is ALWAYS
THE FIRST SIGN
of a
NEW AGE — *Saul Williams*

Poet Saul Williams performs. He also records music and acts in films.

Def Poetry brought slam to **center stage**. In 2002, it **made its Broadway debut**. The show brought together a cast of poets as diverse as the United States itself: from Chinese American Beau Sia to Palestinian American Suheir Hammad.

The success of DPJ has made people all around the country appreciate this form of expression. Theater critic Matthew Murray put it best when he wrote, "Def Poetry Jam on Broadway [is] dedicated to proving that poetry **needn't be ancient or stodgy**, but that it can still prove . . . inspiring to the current generation."

Whether it is being recited on Broadway, in a classroom, or in a local coffeehouse, the same is true of slam. 10

10 **Author's Purpose**
Why does the author include Murry's quote? How does this quote support the author's main idea about poetry?

In Other Words

Byron, Shelley, Keats, or Wordsworth famous poets from hundreds of years ago
center stage everyone's attention
made its Broadway debut was first performed in one of New York City's famous theaters

needn't be ancient or stodgy doesn't have to be old and boring

Slam Poetry FAQs by Cecily von Ziegesar

What's the difference between slam poetry and performance art?

Like performance art, slam poetry is entertaining. It makes you think, and, like all art, it tries to say something meaningful about **the human experience.** But a slam is a competition, so unlike presenting a set performance art piece, you have to do your best to win! In a slam there's always an element of **improvisation**. A good slam poet thinks on her feet and **delivers straight from the heart**.

Cecily von Ziegesar

Do slam poets really make a living doing this?

Writing poetry is **a labor of love**. Poets aren't paid to write or to slam, although there are sometimes cash prizes at slams. And there are always chances to get published, recorded, or filmed, especially at the bigger slam venues. Most slam poets have day jobs. But they make time to write poetry and to slam, because they love it. **11**

11 Determine Importance
Why do slam poets write and perform for little or no pay? What important idea does this detail tell you about slam poets?

Do you have to memorize your poems to compete in slams?

No. But the judges will be more impressed if you do. There's an actor inside of every successful slam poet. They love to *perform*.

Where can I find a slam near me?

Check out listings in your local paper or weekly area magazine. The poetry slam is a rapidly growing **phenomenon**, so there are most likely slams happening within a short traveling distance.

Monitor Comprehension

Describe
What are slam poets like? Why do they choose to participate in slam?

Key Vocabulary
improvisation *n.,* something done without pre-planning
• **phenomenon** *n.,* something new that people get really excited about

In Other Words
FAQs Frequently Asked Questions
the human experience people and their lives
delivers straight from the heart says exactly what she really thinks and feels
a labor of love work that you do because you love it

How Do You Have Your Own Slam?

by Felice Belle, *host of the Friday Night Slam at the Nuyorican Poets Cafe*

Felice Belle

A typical slam is five poets competing in three **rounds**. One poem per round. The highest **cumulative** score wins. So . . .

1. **You need poets.** You cannot have a poetry slam without poets.

2. **You need judges.** Judges should be **chosen at random** from the audience. Judges will score each poem on a scale of 0 to 10, 10 being the highest. Decimals are encouraged, because they prevent ties. A score of 30 is the highest score in slam. Larger slams usually have five judges and in calculating the score, the highest and lowest scores are dropped. If you select three judges all the scores should count. **12**

3. **You need a scorekeeper.** Preferably a math major.

4. **Poets choose numbers to decide the order.** So as not to be unfair to the poet who has to perform first, we **sacrifice a poet on the altar of judgely ignorance**. This poet is not in the slam. She is called the sacrificial goat. Her purpose is to warm up the judges.

Now, you are ready to slam.

12 Determine Importance
At a slam, anyone can be a judge and "expert." Why is this detail important? What does it show about slam?

How Do You Win a Slam?

by Beau Sia, *award-winning slam poet* **13**

That's easy. Be yourself. Once you get your **raw** self on stage, start to shape, mold, and **perfect it**. Most of the people who win slams are their poems **to the core**. And remember: it really isn't about the scores. It's about your voice and your poetry and having a stage to speak from.

Beau Sia

13 Author's Purpose
Why does the author mention Sia's awards?

In Other Words
rounds turns
cumulative total
chosen at random picked by chance

sacrifice a poet on the altar of judgely ignorance have a different poet read for the judges without getting a score that counts
raw true
perfect it make it the best it can be
to the core 100%, all the way

How Do You Find Your Voice?

by Ishle Park, *2004 Poet Laureate, Queens, New York*

Ishle Park

I write out of a fierce love for the people and places I care deeply about; I want them remembered, I want me remembered. No one else will speak for us if we don't do it ourselves.

ANALYZE Slam: Performance Poetry Lives On

1. **Explain** What happens at a typical poetry slam? Include details from the text to describe the event and the people.

2. **Vocabulary** Slam may be a new **phenomenon**, but it is linked to older forms of poetry. Explain how traditional poetry contributed to slam.

3. **Analyze Author's Purpose** One purpose of this essay is to present information about the subject. Complete the sentences below with information from the article.

   - Slam poetry is _____.
   - Slam poetry has its roots in _____.
   - The mission of slam poetry is to _____.

4. **Focus Strategy Determine Importance** Look back at the **Response Journal** you began on page 161 about the essay's important ideas and details. With a partner, discuss the ideas and details you both listed and the reasons you found them important.

◀ Return to the Text

Reread and Write Look back at the statements that describe how different people feel about slam poetry. Then write a short summary of reasons why people are attracted to creative expressions like slam.

In Other Words
Poet Laureate official poet

BEFORE READING Euphoria

poem by Lauren Brown

Reading Strategies

- Plan and Monitor
- ► Determine Importance
- Make Inferences
- Ask Questions
- Make Connections
- Synthesize
- Visualize

Analyze Structure: Free Verse

Poetry comes in many forms. Some poems have a specific **structure** with rhythms (like bom-BOM) and regular rhymes. **Free verse poems** usually do not have set rhythms and regular rhymes. The poet is free to structure the free verse poem in any way. However, you will still read the poem in the usual way, from top to bottom and left to right.

Look Into the Text

Lines can be long or short.

Text doesn't always follow grammar rules.

> today I'm filled with such a feeling of greatness and immortality
> I must sit on my hands to control them from dancing
> I find blinking a hazard
> it takes too much time and leaves me in the darkness
> when I could be seeing and living the manic colors

The poet chooses words that show her feelings.

Images paint pictures in the reader's mind.

Focus Strategy ► Determine Importance

Like other literature, poems have main ideas. As you read a poem, think about how the details and images relate to the poet's main idea.

HOW TO DETERMINE IMPORTANCE

Focus Strategy

1. Read the poem once.

2. Read it again, pausing often to let the words linger, or stay, in your mind.

3. Think about the main idea of the poem.

4. Use a **Reading Journal** to record how details and images relate to the main idea of the poem.

Reading Journal

The speaker says:
"I must sit on my hands to control them from dancing"
(line 2)

This supports the main idea by:
showing how excited and happy the speaker feels

Connect Across Texts

The article "Slam: Performance Poetry Lives On" describes how performance poetry has become a modern creative art. How does the author of the following slam poem show the ways that creativity matters to her?

Euphoria

by Lauren Brown

today I'm filled with such a feeling of greatness and immortality
I must sit on my hands to control them from dancing
I find blinking a hazard
it takes too much time and leaves me in the darkness
5 when I could be seeing and living the manic colors
everything in me is magnified and exposed
but no one seems to notice
the air caresses my flesh
and my heart beats faster
10 and my pulse pulses with the concrete rhythm of the song
permanently playing [1]

in my mind
I want to write everything I have ever felt before in my whole existence and

15 paste them on
the walls
I want to dance with such balance and magnificence
that the whole world will want to dance too

[1] Structure
What features of free verse does the author use? How would the poem be different if it had a strict **structure** of rhythm and rhyme?

Key Vocabulary
euphoria *n.*, great joy and happiness
● **structure** *n.*, the way something is set up, organization

In Other Words
immortality the ability to live forever
hazard danger
manic wild, excited
magnified and exposed made bigger and visible for everyone to see
caresses softly touches

I want to sing like the angels
20   to part my lips and have the loveliness of my song drip out of
the corners of

my mouth
and to echo into everyone's ears and have a piece of my song
glued into their minds
25   I want to be able to use my hands in ways I never have before
and to feel other people's emotions like sandpaper on my tongue . . .
. . . maybe I will **2**

2 Determine Importance
What is the speaker's most important idea? How do the details and images in the poem support this idea?

ANALYZE Euphoria

1. **Explain** At the end of the poem, the speaker says, ". . . maybe I will."
   What do you think she plans to do? Why?

2. **Vocabulary** What do you think has caused the speaker's euphoria?
   How does she plan to express this?

3. **Analyze Structure: Free Verse** How does the free verse structure
   help the speaker express her ideas and feelings?

4. **Focus Strategy Determine Importance** With a partner, discuss two
   details from the poem that you recorded in your Response Journal.
   Consider how each detail supports the main idea of "euphoria."

Return to the Text

Reread and Write Reread the poem. Then write about how the speaker
wants to show her feelings and ideas through different forms of expression.

Key Vocabulary
expression *n.*, creative
  communication

In Other Words
sandpaper rough paper used to make
  wood smooth

EQ Does Creativity Matter?

Reading

Critical Thinking

EQ 1. **Explain** Return to the Quickwrite about poetry that you did before reading. Have your ideas changed? Discuss your responses with a partner.

EQ 2. **Analyze** Based on your reading of the essay and the poem, explain whether you think poetry matters in today's world.

3. **Compare** The author of "Slam: Performance Poetry Lives On" says "Poetry is moving, breathing, ever changing." Would the speaker of "Euphoria" agree? Why or why not?

4. **Predict** The recent **phenomenon** of slam poetry has its roots in many older forms of poetry. Do you think slam is here to stay? Why or why not?

5. **Evaluate** Why do you think popular kinds of poetry change over the years? How do they reflect the creativity of different times?

Writing

Write Poetry

Slam Poetry Imagine you are holding a poetry slam at your school. Write a slam poem using information from both texts for ideas. Try a variety of **structures** and styles, such as free verse or rhyme, for your slam poems. Highlight phrases you think will spark your listeners' interest. Then post the poems and judge them based on effectiveness and creativity. Which ones capture the joys of slam? Read or perform your poem for the class.

Vocabulary

Key Vocabulary Review

Oral Review Work with a partner. Use these words to complete the paragraph. You might see words like *structure*, *expression*, and *recitation* used in classroom materials in other subject areas.

compose	improvisation	structure
euphoria	phenomenon	transcend
expression	recitation	

Writing poetry is an exciting new __(1)__ that I just discovered. I love having a new form of __(2)__ that communicates my ideas and feelings. When I sit down at my computer to __(3)__ the words to a brand new poem, I usually use __(4)__ —which doesn't require a lot of pre-planning. Every time a poem comes out well, I feel great happiness, or __(5)__. Other times, I run into problems that I must rise above and __(6)__ through hard work. I think about my word choice and change the __(7)__ and organization of my poem until it looks just right. Next month, I'm reading two poems at a __(8)__ in front of my class.

Writing Application If you were to **compose** a song or poem, what would it be like? Use at least two Key Vocabulary words to write a song or poem.

Fluency

Read with Ease: Expression

Assess your reading fluency with the passage in the Reading Handbook, p. 756. Then complete the self-check below.

1. My expression did/did not sound natural.

2. My words correct per minute: _____

Grammar

Use Verbs to Talk About the Present

The verb **have** has two forms in the present.

I **have** poetry class today. You **have** class, too.
He **has** three favorite poets. She **has** four.

The verb **be** has three forms in the present.

I **am** a poet. She **is** a poet, too. We **are** creative.

Am, **is**, and **are** can also be **helping verbs**. A helping verb can come before a main verb that ends with **-ing**. The helping verb agrees with the subject.

I **am** performing my poetry.
The judge **is** listening.
They **are** enjoying the contest.

Oral Practice (1–5) With a partner, say each sentence with the correct helping verb.

1. The poetry contest ____ starting now.
2. We ____ waiting for the first poet.
3. The audience ____ applauding the poet.
4. She ____ reciting her poem with emotion.
5. The new poets ____ learning the art.

Written Practice (6–10) Rewrite the paragraph. Choose the correct present tense form of the verb. Add two more sentences. Use present tense verbs.

> Poetry (have/has) rhythm. Poetry slams (have/has) action. Poets (is speaking/are speaking) their minds.

Language Development

Give and Follow Commands

Role-Play Using commands, write instructions telling a poet how to perform slam poetry. Start your commands with verbs such as *speak* and *express*. With a partner, take turns being the poet and the instructor. The instructor tells the poet what to do. The poet follows the directions. Each should ask and answer questions to clarify the directions.

Literary Analysis

Literary Movements: Poetry Across Cultures

In "Slam: Performance Poetry Lives On," author Pooja Makhijani says, "Poetry is living, moving, ever changing." That's because poetry, like many other forms of literature, changes across different times and cultures.

With a partner, reread the essay to find the many roots of slam poetry. Create a chart to track how these trends have led to the slam we know today.

Type of Poetry	Place and Time Period	Influence on Slam
epic poems	Ancient Greece c. 8th century B.C.E.	started the tradition of reciting poetry

Media Study

Judging Panel

Performance Evaluation With a group, conduct your own poetry slam or find video of a slam poetry performer. Search online poetry sites or check out the video collections of local libraries. Have each group member assign the performer a score from 1 to 10. Then take turns with group members in presenting and justifying the scores you gave. Discuss differences in opinion.

7   9

▼ **Language and Learning Handbook,** page 702

Context Clues for Idioms

An idiomatic expression is a word or phrase that has a meaning beyond its literal definition. Consider this example from "Euphoria":

I want to ... have the loveliness of my song ... echo into everyone's ears and have a piece of my song glued into their minds

1. **Study the context of the** expression The poet thinks her song is lovely.

2. **Make a guess about the meaning** If something is lovely or memorable, it sticks like glue. I think the poet wants people to remember her song.

3. **Test your guess** with the original passage. If it fits, you may have found your definition.

4. If all else fails, **look up the phrase or ask a friend or teacher for help**.

Use context to figure out the meaning of this idiom: The poet's voice filled the room as he screamed out his poem at the top of his lungs.

Write a How-To Paragraph

Imagine that you want to explain something to another person, like how to do well at a poetry slam. One way to do so is by writing an expository how-to paragraph. Read how to do it below. Then write a paragraph explaining how to do something you can do well.

1 **Identify the Topic** Be sure to include the main idea you want to express about the topic.

> **Topic:** Performing at a poetry slam
> **Main Idea:** There are specific things you can do to perform at a poetry slam.

2 **Brainstorm Details** Include ideas that support your main idea.

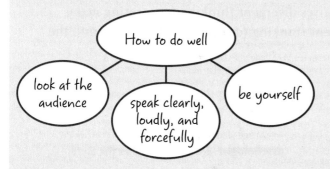

3 **Draft** First, introduce the topic and main idea. Then include supporting details. Use transition words to move from one detail to the next. Finally, sum up with a concluding sentence. Be aware that you have twenty minutes to complete your draft.

Model

> If you want to do well at a poetry slam, there are things you can do to improve your chances. First, look at the audience while you perform. This will keep people focused on you. Second, be sure to speak loudly and clearly. You will not win if no one can hear your poems. Finally, relax and be yourself. If you like to move, move. Following these rules will help you do the best you can at a slam.

4 **Check Your Work** Reread your paragraph. Ask:

- Do I identify my topic and main idea?
- Do the details support the main idea?

5 **Publish** Share your work with others in written or oral form. Provide feedback.

🔖 **Writing Handbook,** page 784

from
THE CREATIVITY CRISIS

BY
PO BRONSON
AND ASHLEY
MERRYMAN

1   Back in 1958, Ted Schwarzrock was an 8-year-old third grader when he became one of the "Torrance kids," a group of nearly 400 Minneapolis children who completed a series of creativity tasks newly designed by professor E. Paul Torrance. Schwarzrock still vividly remembers the moment when a **psychologist** handed him a fire truck and asked, "How could you improve this toy to make it better and more fun to play with?" He recalls the psychologist being excited by his answers. In fact, the psychologist's session notes indicate Schwarzrock rattled off 25 improvements, such as adding a removable ladder and springs to the wheels. That wasn't the only time he impressed the scholars, who judged Schwarzrock to have "unusual visual perspective" and "an ability to synthesize diverse elements into meaningful products."

2   The accepted definition of creativity is production of something original and useful, and that's what's reflected in the tests. There is never one right answer. To be creative requires divergent thinking (generating many unique ideas) and then convergent thinking (combining those ideas into the best result).

In Other Words
psychologist doctor who studies the mind

3   Nobody would argue that Torrance's tasks, which have become **the gold standard** in creativity assessment, measure creativity perfectly. What's shocking is how incredibly well Torrance's creativity index predicted those kids' creative accomplishments as adults. Those who came up with more good ideas on Torrance's tasks grew up to be **entrepreneurs**, inventors, college presidents, authors, doctors, diplomats, and software developers. The **correlation** to lifetime creative accomplishment was more than three times stronger for childhood creativity than childhood **IQ**.

4   Like intelligence tests, Torrance's test—a 90-minute series of discrete tasks, administered by a psychologist—has been taken by millions worldwide in 50 languages. Yet there is one crucial difference between IQ and CQ scores. With intelligence, there is a **phenomenon** called the Flynn effect—each generation, scores go up about 10 points. Enriched environments are making kids smarter. With creativity, a reverse trend has just been identified and is being reported for the first time here: American creativity scores are falling.

5   The potential consequences are sweeping. The necessity of human ingenuity is undisputed. A recent IBM poll of 1,500 CEOs identified creativity as the No. 1 "leadership competency" of the future. Yet it's not just about sustaining our nation's economic growth. All around us are matters of national and international importance that are crying out for creative solutions. Such solutions emerge from a healthy marketplace of ideas, sustained by a populace constantly contributing original ideas and receptive to the ideas of others.

American creativity scores are falling.

6   To understand exactly what should be done requires first understanding the new story emerging from **neuroscience**. The lore of pop psychology is that creativity occurs on the right side of the brain. But we now know that if you tried to be creative using only the right side of your brain, it'd be like living with ideas perpetually at the tip of your tongue, just beyond reach.

7   When you try to solve a problem, you begin by concentrating on obvious facts and familiar solutions, to see if the answer lies there. This is a mostly left-brain stage of attack. If the answer doesn't come, the right and left hemispheres of the brain activate together. **Neural networks** on the right side scan remote memories that could be vaguely relevant. A wide range of

Key Vocabulary
- **phenomenon** *n.*, something different that people get really excited about

The Creativity Crisis   **181**

distant information that is normally **tuned out** becomes available to the left hemisphere, which searches for unseen patterns, alternative meanings, and **high-level abstractions**.

8   Having glimpsed such a connection, the left brain must quickly lock in on it before it escapes. The attention system must radically reverse gears, going from defocused attention to extremely focused attention. In a flash, the brain pulls together these **disparate shreds of thought** and binds them into a new single idea that enters consciousness. This is the "aha!" moment of <mark>insight</mark>, often followed by a spark of pleasure as the brain recognizes the **novelty** of what it's come up with.

9   Is this learnable? Well, think of it like basketball. Being tall does help to be a pro basketball player, but the rest of us can still get quite good at the sport through practice. In the same way, there are certain innate features of the brain that make some people naturally prone to divergent thinking. But convergent thinking and focused attention are necessary, too, and those require different neural gifts. Crucially, rapidly shifting between these modes is a top-down function under your mental control. University of New Mexico neuroscientist Rex Jung has concluded that those who diligently practice creative activities learn to recruit their brains' creative networks quicker and better. A lifetime of consistent habits gradually changes the neurological pattern.

This is the "aha!" moment of insight...

10   In early childhood, distinct types of free play are associated with high creativity. Preschoolers who spend more time in role-play (acting out characters) have higher measures of creativity: voicing someone else's point of view helps develop their ability to analyze situations from different <mark>perspectives</mark>. When playing alone, highly creative first graders may act out strong negative emotions: they'll be angry, hostile, anguished. **The hypothesis is** that play is a safe harbor to work through forbidden thoughts and emotions.

11   In middle childhood, kids sometimes create paracosms—fantasies of entire alternative worlds.

Iker Ayestaran.

 Critical Viewing: Theme What comparison does the artist make here? What message does that send?

Key Vocabulary
- <mark>insight</mark> *n.*, understanding
- <mark>perspective</mark> *n.*, point of view

In Other Words
tuned out ignored
high-level abstractions complicated ideas
disparate shreds of thoughts separate ideas
novelty creative newness
The hypothesis is This may mean

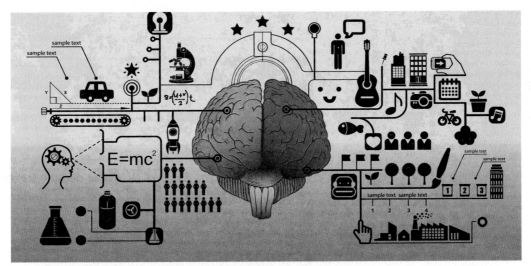

Left and right brain functions. Vector illustration, Doggygraph(alias)/Shutterstock.com.

◁ Critical Viewing: Design What is the artist saying about the two parts of the brain?

Kids revisit their paracosms repeatedly, sometimes for months, and even create languages spoken there. This type of play peaks at age 9 or 10, and it's a very strong sign of future creativity. A Michigan State University study of MacArthur "genius award" winners found a remarkably high rate of paracosm creation in their childhoods.

12   From fourth grade on, creativity no longer occurs **in a vacuum**; researching and studying become an integral part of coming up with useful solutions. But this transition isn't easy. As school stuffs more complex information into their heads, kids get overloaded, and creativity suffers. When creative children have a supportive teacher—someone **tolerant of unconventional** answers, occasional disruptions, or detours of curiosity— they tend to **excel**. When they don't, they tend to underperform and drop out of high school or don't finish college at high rates.

13   Creativity has always been prized in American society, but it's never really been understood. While our creativity scores **decline unchecked**, the current national strategy for creativity consists of little more than praying for a Greek muse to drop by our houses. The problems we face now, and in the future, simply demand that we do more than just hope for inspiration to strike. Fortunately, the science can help: we know the steps to lead that **elusive muse** right to our doors. ❖

In Other Words

in a vacuum only when playing
tolerant of unconventional who likes unusual
excel succeed, do very well
decline unchecked keep going down
elusive muse difficult to find source of creativity

THE ART OF EXPRESSION

EQ ESSENTIAL QUESTION:
Does Creativity Matter?

myNGconnect.com
⬥ Download the rubric.

EDGE LIBRARY

Present Your Project: Demonstration

It's time to present your demonstration about the Essential Question for this unit: Does Creativity Matter?

1 Review and Complete Your Plan

Consider these points as you complete your project:

- What steps in the process will you emphasize in your demonstration?
- Will you need help? Can you get a volunteer from the class, or do you need someone to practice with you?
- How much time do you have for your demonstration?

Practice your demonstration at least once before you present it.

2 Give Your Demonstration

Position yourself so your audience can follow the demonstration clearly. Have any equipment or materials within easy reach.

3 Evaluate the Demonstrations

Use the online rubric to evaluate each of the demonstrations, including the one you presented.

Reflect on Your Reading

Many of the people in the selections in this unit and in the Edge Library expressed themselves through creativity.

Think back on your reading of the unit selections, including your choice of Edge Library books. Then discuss the following with a partner or in a small group.

Genre Focus   Compare and contrast the author's purpose in a news article and an essay. Give examples, using the selections in this unit.

Focus Strategy   Choose a selection in this unit to describe to a family member or friend. Identify strategies that would help you determine the most important ideas and details. Then summarize the selection in your own words.

EQ Respond to the Essential Question

Throughout this unit, you have been thinking about whether creativity matters. What have *you* decided? Support your response with evidence from your reading, discussions, research, and writing.

Write a Position Paper

Writing Mode
Argument

Writing Trait Focus
Focus and Unity

What issues make you want to speak out?
Present an argument about an issue that
matters to you by writing a position paper.

Study Position Papers

Position papers contain claims, or positions, on important issues. Writers of position papers give reasons for their claims to make them sound credible, or believable, to the reader. They want the reader to fully understand and consider the issue.

❶ Connect Writing to Your Life

You probably have argued for or against many things in your life. From debating a new school rule to convincing your parents to let you stay out late, you have stated your case many times. But how do you make a case believable? How do you get your point across? Learning to support an argument, or claim, with evidence will help you become a more convincing speaker and writer.

❷ Understand the Form

A good position paper contains the following elements:

Introduction

Present the issue. Identify both sides. One side is your position, or claim. The other side is the opposing position. Your position is the **controlling idea** of your paper.

Body

Explain why you believe your position.

Support

Provide **reasons** to support your position and **evidence** to support your reasons. Address the **opposing position**, or other side of the argument, and provide reasons why that position is wrong.

Conclusion

Summarize your position in a memorable way.

Now look at these parts in action. Read a position paper by a professional writer.

❸ Analyze a Professional Model

As you read, look for the writer's position and supporting evidence.

Why Teens Need the Arts

by Oscar Delgado

Picture an environment in which young people do not dance or make music. Imagine a school where students do not put on plays, paint pictures, or take photographs. This situation may become a reality if the school board cannot balance its budget. To save money, the board has gone out on a limb and proposed cutting all arts funding for city high schools. While we must balance the budget and not spend more than we have, we should try to look elsewhere for the money. Visual and performing arts are a necessary part of our children's education.

The writer states the issue and gives his **position**, as well as an **opposing position**, in the introduction.

For many students, art has helped them stay interested in school. Tara Sossa, for example, is a West High graduate who had planned to drop out as soon as she turned sixteen. A few months before her sixteenth birthday, an art teacher got her involved with oil painting. This opened up a bright new world to her—a world in which she could succeed. Little by little, she built self-confidence, and she stayed in school. In fact, she went on to get a degree in graphic design and a job at a magazine.

These **reasons** support the writer's position. The writer elaborates on the reasons by providing examples as evidence.

The arts not only help keep teens in school but also teach them useful skills while they are there. Student artists learn problem-solving skills. Student actors, directors, and stage workers learn about teamwork. So do students in orchestra, chorus, and band. Student dancers learn the meaning of hard work, determination, and focus. Students involved in the arts learn the same skills as those who are members of a sports team.

The writer uses **transition words** to connect ideas.

Perhaps most important of all, the arts encourage inventiveness and creative thinking. These are qualities our young people need if they are to become active members of government, business, and society. So, while many people think of the arts as a luxury we cannot afford, the truth is that the arts are as essential to students' learning as academics are.

The writing style has a formal, academic **tone**.

The writer addresses the **opposing position**.

The painter Robert Motherwell once said, "Art is much less important than life, but what a poor life without it!" For many of today's youth, art is the *only* chance they have for a successful life.

What does the writer do to summarize his position in a memorable way?

▶ **Prompt** Write a position paper about an issue that affects your school or your community. Be sure to:

- state your position on the issue
- give reasons to support your position
- address the opposing position
- use a formal writing style
- end in a memorable way

✔ Prewrite

Now that you know the basics of position papers, plan one of your own. Planning will make it easier for you to write later on. When you are finished, you will have a detailed Writing Plan to guide you as you write.

❶ Choose Your Topic

Think of an issue to write about. Here are some good ways to choose a topic:

- With a small group of students, brainstorm a list of issues that affect your school or community. Brainstorm questions related to this issue. Choose the issue that is most important to you.

- Skim the headlines of a school or community newspaper. What issues are in the news? Which could you write about?

❷ Clarify the Audience, Controlling Idea, and Purpose

Your teacher and classmates will probably be your main audience. Who else might be interested in reading your paper? Jot down your ideas.

What is your position on the situation you are writing about? Do you want to encourage it or stop it? In a sentence or two, state your position. That is your **controlling idea**.

Finally, think about your reason for writing. What do you want your audience to understand? Your answer will be your purpose for writing.

❸ Gather Your Support

Next, gather reasons to support your position. List every reason your position is credible. Then choose the reasons that would be most understandable to your audience. Also think of the reasons someone might not support your position and then provide evidence to refute them, or prove them wrong. Remember, your purpose for writing is to make the audience understand and consider your position. Research the full range of information on the topic and determine which information best supports your position.

4 Organize the Details

Build up to a strong conclusion. Present supporting information in order of importance. You can put your least important reason first and your most important reason last. Or you can put your most important reason first and your least important reason last. How can you tell which one is the most important? Decide which reason you have the most to say about. Presenting your data and factual support in this way will help to strengthen your position.

> *Reasons Why Uniforms Are Not for Us*
>
> 2   Expensive
> 1   Not in other schools
> 3   Loss of freedom of expression

5 Finish Your Writing Plan

Choose a graphic organizer, such as an outline, to create a Writing Plan. Show which ideas will go in the introduction, the body, and the conclusion.

Writing Plan

Topic	uniform policy in district schools
Audience	my teacher, principal, and all students
Controlling Idea	school uniforms are not for us
Purpose	to explain why uniforms are not for us
Time Frame	one week from today

I. Introduction

    A. District wants to make students wear uniforms.

    B. School uniforms are not for us.

II. Body

    A. No other public school districts have uniforms.

    B. Uniforms are expensive.

    C. Uniforms equal loss of freedom of expression.

    D. Opposing position: Uniforms look neater, prevent kids from bad appearance. But we could have strict dress code instead.

III. Conclusion

    A. Summarize position.

    B. Ask a question.

Technology Tip

For help creating an outline, use the outline function of your word-processing program. Click on Outline from the View menu. To close the outline view, click on a different view, such as Page Layout.

Reflect on Your Writing Plan

Are your reasons likely to appeal to your audience? Are they organized by order of importance? If not, now is the time to change them.

✓ Write a Draft

Now you are ready to write. Use your Writing Plan as a guide. You'll have chances to improve your draft later.

❶ Put Ideas into Words

Sometimes writers look at a blank page and freeze. They do not know how to put their ideas into words. If you have this trouble, try these techniques:

- **Talk to Your Audience** Tell your ideas to one of your classmates. Ask the person to take notes. Use the notes to get your ideas down on paper.

- **Picture Your Audience** Choose one real person who will read your paper. Picture this person in your mind. Begin writing to this person alone. If it helps, you might write in the form of a letter. Underline the parts you can use in your draft.

- **Send Yourself an E-mail** If you are used to writing e-mails, begin your draft in an e-mail. It can be easier to write because it is less formal. Send yourself the e-mail. Underline the text you think you might use; then cut and paste the text into a document.

Technology Tip

Turn your outline into your draft. Copy your outline. Delete the numbers and letters and turn the list into a draft. Make each line a complete sentence. Combine related sentences into paragraphs.

❷ Use Evidence for Support

One way to make your audience believe your position is to provide good supporting evidence. Supporting evidence should be clear and exact. Evidence that is presented objectively, or fairly, and is related to your position will help your audience better understand and believe it. Here are some kinds of evidence that you can use to support your position:

- **Facts** are statements that are proved to be true.

- **Examples** illustrate why your position is believable.

- **Analogies** are rhetorical devices that allow you to compare your position to something the audience might better understand.

OK

> The worst consequence of a school uniform policy, however, would be the loss of freedom of expression. Clothing is an expression of students' personal identity, and it should stay that way.

Better

> The worst consequence of a school uniform policy, however, would be the loss of freedom of expression. Clothes and jewelry allow us to be creative and confident about who we are as individuals. Putting us in uniforms would take away our personal identities. It would be like making everyone in the city paint their buildings the same color.

❸ Student Model

Read this draft to see how the student used the Writing Plan to get ideas down on paper. This first draft does not have to be perfect. As you will see, the student fixed the mistakes later.

School Uniforms: Not Our Style

Because of a few students with bad judgment, all students in our school district may soon suffer the consequences. Administrators of South Regional school district 101 are considering adopting a school uniform policy to eliminate the problem of students dressing improperly. While something does need to be done, issuing school uniforms is a bad idea that would cause more harm than good.

First, having a school uniform will make us stand out from other School Districts. Most other districts have tackled the clothing problem by issuing dress codes like this one "You must dress in a manner that shows respect for other students and the school. You may not wear you're hats or caps indoors, and you may not wear clothing that could offend others." That is a sensible code. Choosing what students can wear, on the other hand, is *not* sensible, and that is why other districts does not do it.

Another problem with school uniforms is their cost. For many families in the area, school uniforms would be an additional strain on a budget that is already stretched to thin. What if a family have several children in high school at the same time? What if these children has a growth spurt? My friend Isaiah grew five inches in one year! The cost of new uniforms could grow out of control.

The worst consequence of a school uniform policy, however, would be the loss of our freedom of expression. Clothes and jewelry allow us to be creative and confident about who we are as individuals. Putting us in uniforms would take away our personal identities. It would be like making everyone in the city paint their buildings the same color.

It is true that uniforms are one way to prevent the distraction that could be caused by inappropriate clothing. However, a strictly enforced dress code could be just as effective, without costing students money and taking away their right to personal expression. Isn't rules supposed to help students instead of harm them? And on that note, how about getting rid of the "no-food-or-drink-in-class" policy, too?

Reflect on Your Draft

▶ What gave you trouble when you were writing? Was it hard to start? Was it hard to keep going? Think about what you might do differently next time.

✔ Revise Your Draft

Your first draft is done. Now, you need to polish it. Improve the focus and unity. Make what was just OK into something much better.

❶ Revise for Focus and Unity

Good writing has a **focus**—it has a central, controlling idea. In a position paper, the focus is the writer's position, or claim.

Good writing also has **unity**—that means that all of the parts support the controlling idea. In a position paper, that means that the reasons and evidence all relate to the writer's position. Good evidence is clear and exact. It is also related to your position.

Don't expect to have perfect focus and unity in your first draft. Time spent revising helps you sharpen your focus. Cut out any word, sentence, or even paragraph that doesn't relate to your controlling idea. It also helps to use transition words such as *first, also,* or *another* to unify your ideas.

TRY IT▶ With a partner, discuss which parts of the draft below do not support or relate to the writer's controlling idea.

Student Draft

> Another problem with school uniforms is their cost. For many families in the area, school uniforms would be an additional strain on a budget that is already stretched to thin. What if a family have several children in high school at the same time? What if these children has a growth spurt? My friend Isaiah grew five inches in one year! The cost of new uniforms could grow out of control.

Now use the rubric to evaluate the focus and unity of your own draft. What score do you give your draft and why?

Focus and Unity

myNGconnect.com

🔘 Rubric: Focus and Unity

🔘 Evaluate and practice scoring other student papers.

	How clearly does the writing present a central idea or claim?	How well does everything go together?
4 Wow!	The writing expresses a <u>clear</u> central idea or claim about the topic.	<u>Everything</u> in the writing goes together. • The main idea of each paragraph goes with the central idea or claim of the paper. • The main idea and details within each paragraph are related. • The conclusion is about the central idea or claim.
3 Ahh.	The writing expresses a <u>generally</u> clear central idea or claim about the topic.	<u>Most</u> parts of the writing go together. • The main idea of most paragraphs goes with the central idea or claim of the paper. • In most paragraphs, the main idea and details are related. • Most of the conclusion is about the central idea or claim.
2 Hmm.	The writing includes a topic, but the central idea or claim is <u>not</u> clear.	<u>Some</u> parts of the writing go together. • The main idea of some paragraphs goes with the central idea or claim of the paper. • In some paragraphs, the main idea and details are related. • Some of the conclusion is about the central idea or claim.
1 Huh?	The writing includes many topics and <u>does not</u> express one central idea or claim.	The parts of the writing <u>do not</u> go together. • Few paragraphs have a main idea, or the main idea does not go with the central idea or claim of the paper. • Few paragraphs contain a main idea and related details • None of the conclusion is about the central idea or claim.

✒ Revise Your Draft, continued

❷ Revise Your Draft

You've now evaluated the focus and unity of your own draft. If you scored 3 or lower, how can you improve your work? Use the checklist below to revise your draft.

Revision Checklist

Ask Yourself	Check It Out	How to Make It Better
Is my paper focused?	Underline your controlling idea. Check that it states your position.	☐ Add a controlling idea if you don't have one. ☐ Rewrite your controlling idea if it is not clear.
Is my paper unified?	Check every paragraph to make sure you stay on topic.	☐ Cut or rewrite sections that do not support the controlling idea.
Does my position paper have an introduction, a body, and a conclusion?	Draw a box around each part.	☐ Add any part that is missing.
Do I address both sides of the issue?	Underline each side.	☐ State the opposing position in your introduction if you haven't done so. ☐ In the body, add reasons that explain why the opposing position is wrong.
Does the body contain two or more supporting reasons?	Underline each main reason. Count them.	☐ Add more reasons if you have just one.
Do I provide specific evidence to support those reasons?	Underline any examples, facts, or analogies that elaborate on your reasons.	☐ Add more specific evidence if needed.
Is my organizing structure appropriate to the purpose of the paper?	Check to see that you put your reasons in order of importance.	☐ Put your reasons in order from least to most important, or vice versa.
Have I used a formal style and presented my claims fairly?	Look for informal or overly emotional language.	☐ Replace informal language with academic-sounding language. ☐ Eliminate language that sounds emotional or exaggerated.
Can readers follow my train of thought?	Ask a classmate to read your paper.	☐ Reorganize your reasons. ☐ Add more supporting evidence. ☐ Add transition words and phrases.

🔖 **Writing Handbook**, p. 784

❸ Conduct a Peer Conference

It helps to get a second opinion when you are revising your draft. Ask a partner to read your draft and look for the following:

- any part of the draft that is confusing
- any place where something seems to be missing
- anything that the person doesn't understand

Then talk with your partner about the draft. Focus on the items in the Revision Checklist. Use your partner's comments to make your position paper clearer, more complete, and easier to understand.

❹ Make Revisions

Look at the revisions below and the peer-reviewer conversation on the right. Notice how the peer reviewer commented and asked questions. Notice how the writer used the comments and questions to revise.

Revised for Unity

> Another problem with school uniforms is their cost. For many families in the area, school uniforms would be an additional strain on a budget that is already stretched to thin. ~~This would be particularly hard on a family that~~ ~~What if a family~~ have several children in high school at the same time? ~~It would also be a problem~~ ~~What~~ if these children has a growth spurt? ~~My friend Isaiah grew five inches in one year.~~ The cost of new uniforms could grow out of control.

Revised for Focus

> It is true that uniforms are one way to prevent the distraction that could be caused by inappropriate clothing. However, a strictly enforced dress code could be just as effective, without costing students money and taking away their right to personal expression. Isn't rules supposed to help students instead of harm them? ~~And on that note, how about getting rid of the "no food or drink in class" policy, too?~~

Edit and Proofread Your Draft

Your revision should now be complete. Before you share it with others, find and fix any mistakes that you made.

❶ Capitalize the Names of Groups

The names of some groups are proper nouns. These include organizations and businesses. These also include institutions and government agencies.

Institution: First Bank of Newberg
Business: Cape Fuel Company
Organization: American Medical Association

The names of nonspecific groups should not be capitalized.

a bank   a company   an association

TRY IT ▶ Copy the sentences. Fix the capitalization errors. Use proofreader's marks.

> 1. Administrators of South Regional school district 101 are currently considering adopting a school uniform policy.
> 2. Having a school uniform will make us stand out from other School Districts.

❷ Use Colons Correctly

A colon (:) is used to set off a list, an explanation, or a quotation. It usually signals that important information is going to follow.

Students are forbidden to wear the following: baseball caps, sleeveless shirts, and ripped jeans.

There is only one solution to this problem: to require that students wear uniforms.

The principal read from a page in the student handbook: "Students must obey the dress code at all times, including during school-sponsored outings."

The first word after a colon is usually capitalized only if it is a proper noun or the first word of a complete sentence.

TRY IT ▶ Copy the sentence. Add a colon where necessary.

> Most other districts have tackled the clothing problem by issuing dress codes like this one "You must dress in a manner that shows respect for other students and the school."

Proofreader's Marks

Use proofreader's marks to correct errors.

Capitalize:
I joined the National Students' union.

Do not capitalize:
There are many different kinds of Unions in this country.

Add colon:
Your new uniform will consist of the following a white shirt, a red vest, and a blue skirt or blue pants.

Proofreading Tip

If you are unsure of when to use a colon, look in a style manual for help and examples.

❸ Check Your Spelling

Homonyms are words that sound alike but have different meanings and spellings. Spell these homonyms correctly when you proofread.

Homonyms and Their Meanings	Examples
to (preposition) = toward **two** (adjective) = the number 2 **too** (adverb) = also, very	I walk **to** school. The rule has **two** parts. Your paper is **too** short.
your (adjective) = belonging to you **you're** (contraction) = you are	**Your** boots are like mine. **You're** in my art class.

TRY IT ▶ Copy the sentences. Find and fix the homonym errors.

> 1. You may not wear you're hats or caps indoors.
> 2. School uniforms would be an additional strain on a budget that is already stretched to thin.

❹ Use Correct Verb Forms in the Present Tense

The verbs *have*, *be*, and *do* are irregular verbs. They have different forms in the present tense than regular verbs do.

Have		Be		Do	
I have	we have	I am	we are	I do	we do
you have	you have	you are	you are	you do	you do
he, she, it has	they have	he, she, it is	they are	he, she, it does	they do

The key to using these verbs correctly in the present tense is to be sure the verb form agrees with the subject of the sentence.

I **have** a school uniform. She **has** one, too.

Are you angry about the decision? I definitely **am**.

I **do** not want to wear a uniform. Neither **does** he.

TRY IT ▶ Copy the sentences. Find and fix any verb errors.

> 1. That is why other districts does not do it.
> 2. It would be a problem if the children has a growth spurt.
> 3. Isn't rules supposed to help students instead of harm them?

Writing Handbook, pp. 840–841; 851

Reflect on Your Corrections

▶ How many errors did you find and fix? Notice what kinds of errors they were. If there are things you keep missing, make a checklist of what to watch in your writing.

Here's the student's draft, revised and edited. How did the writer improve it?

School Uniforms: Not Our Style

Because of a few students with bad judgment, all students in our school district may soon suffer the consequences. Administrators of South Regional School District 101 are considering adopting a school uniform policy to eliminate the problem of students dressing improperly. While something does need to be done, issuing school uniforms is a bad idea that would cause more harm than good.

> The writer fixed the **capitalization** error.

First, having a school uniform will make us stand out from other school districts. Most other districts have tackled the clothing problem by issuing dress codes like this one: "You must dress in a manner that shows respect for other students and the school. You may not wear your hats or caps indoors, and you may not wear clothing that could offend others." That is a sensible code. Choosing what students can wear, on the other hand, is *not* sensible, and that is why other districts do not do it.

> The writer fixed the **capitalization** error.
>
> The writer added a **colon** to separate the quotation and used the correct **homonym**.
>
> The writer used the correct **verb form**.

Another problem with school uniforms is their cost. For many families in the area, school uniforms would be an additional strain on a budget that is already stretched too thin. This would be particularly hard on a family that has several children in high school at the same time. It would also be a problem if these children have a growth spurt. The cost of new uniforms could grow out of control.

> The writer used the correct **homonym** and **verb forms**. The writer also deleted the sentence that doesn't belong and revised the "What if...?" questions.

The worst consequence of a school uniform policy, however, would be the loss of our freedom of expression. Clothes and jewelry allow us to be creative and confident about who we are as individuals. Putting us in uniforms would take away our personal identities. It would be like making everyone in the city paint their buildings the same color.

It is true that uniforms are one way to prevent the distraction that could be caused by inappropriate clothing. However, a strictly enforced dress code could be just as effective, without costing students money and taking away their right to personal expression. After all, aren't rules supposed to help students instead of harm them?

> The writer added a **transitional phrase** and used the correct **verb form**. She also deleted the sentence that introduced a new controlling idea.

Publish and Present

You are now ready to publish and present your position paper. Print out your paper or write a clean copy by hand. You may also want to present your work in a different way.

Alternative Presentations

Submit a Guest Editorial Many publications have guest editorials. Most editorials are a type of position paper.

1 Find a Publication You are writing about a local issue, so check newspapers and magazines in your school and community.

2 Check the Guidelines Many publications have guidelines for writers. Ask for them if you can't find any.

3 Send Your Work Mail or e-mail your work. Include a way for the publisher to contact you. Ask for feedback on your work.

Create a Podcast A podcast is a radio-style program that is published on the Internet. Listeners subscribe to a podcast and can then download it to their computers or portable listening devices. You can easily reorganize and turn your position paper into a mini-podcast.

1 Practice Practice reading aloud before you record your podcast. Check with a dictionary if you are not sure how to pronounce a word.

2 Record and Edit Use a computer with a microphone and recording software to record your podcast. Speak clearly and slowly so your listeners can understand you. Use features of your software to add special effects, such as background noise and music.

3 Listen Carefully listen to your recording. Be sure it is clear and easy to follow. Ask a friend or classmate to listen and give feedback.

4 Convert Look at the file extension of your recording. If it is a WAV file, you need to convert it to a smaller file, such as an MP3. Certain recording software or media players will allow you to do this.

5 Publish Many schools provide free Web space to students who wish to publish school-related projects online. Check with your teacher or school Web administrator to see if your school has this policy.

📖 **Language and Learning Handbook**, p. 714

Publishing Tip

Include a cover letter when you submit your position paper. Begin it with a highlight from the paper that will grab the publisher's attention. You want to stand out among all other submissions.

Reflect on Your Work

▶ Ask for and use feedback from your audience and your teacher to evaluate your strengths as a writer.

• Did your audience clearly understand your position?

• Did your audience think you supported your position with strong reasons?

• What would you like to do better the next time you write? Set a goal for your next writing project.

 Save a copy of your work in your portfolio.

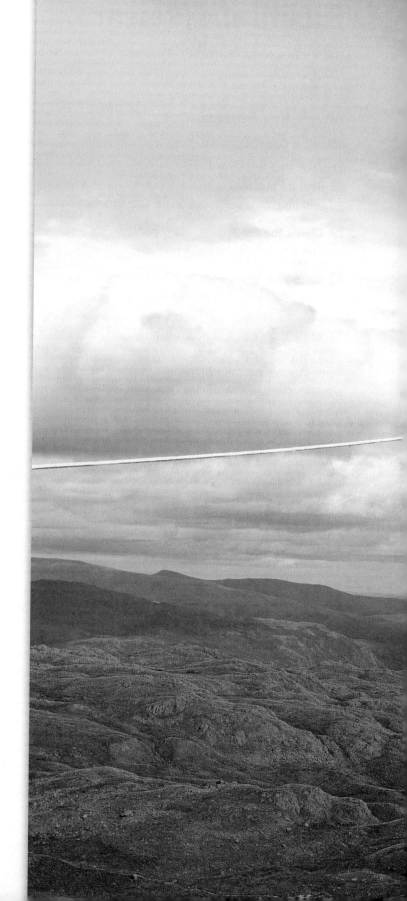

EQ ESSENTIAL QUESTION:

What Makes a Hero?

True heroism is remarkably sober, very undramatic. It is not the urge to surpass all others at whatever cost, but the urge to serve others at whatever cost.

—ARTHUR ASHE

Show me a hero and I will write you a tragedy.

—F. SCOTT FITZGERALD

Critical Viewing ▷
Suspended in mid-air, a rescuer in Cumbria, England, guides an injured hiker to the safety of a helicopter overhead. What makes this airman a hero?

THE HERO WITHIN

EQ **ESSENTIAL QUESTION:**
What Makes a Hero?

Study the Facts

Most people have heroes, people whom they admire and respect. They may be world leaders, explorers, adventurers, sports stars, family members, or friends. When asked in a poll who their heroes were, people gave these responses:

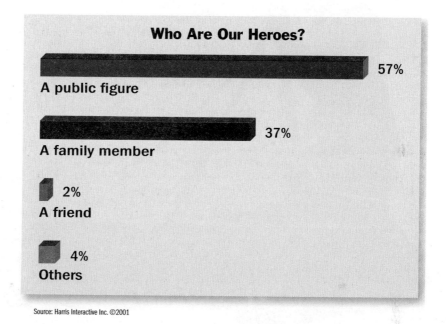

Who Are Our Heroes?

A public figure — 57%

A family member — 37%

A friend — 2%

Others — 4%

Source: Harris Interactive Inc. ©2001

Debate and Vote

1. Make a list of heroes that *you* admire. How does your list compare with the data in the bar graph above?

2. What are the most important qualities of a hero?

Share your list with a small group and use the information to make a bar graph that reflects the heroes you all admire. Analyze the results and discuss the qualities that make a hero. Then vote for the most important quality a hero must have. Defend your ideas with reasons and examples from your own knowledge, experience, and observations.

EQ **ESSENTIAL QUESTION**

In this unit, you will explore the **Essential Question** in class through reading, discussion, research, and writing. Keep thinking about the question outside of school, too.

① Plan a Project

Documentary

In this unit, you will be creating a documentary about the Essential Question. Choose a hero of yours and create a documentary that presents a glimpse of the person's life and what makes the person a hero. To get started, watch a few documentaries on TV. Look for

- the types of information presented, such as interviews, photographs, and time lines
- the order in which information is given
- the narrator's role in the documentary.

Study Skills Start planning your documentary. Use the forms on myNGconnect.com to plan your time and to prepare the content.

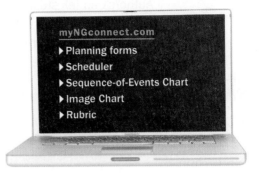

myNGconnect.com
- ▶ Planning forms
- ▶ Scheduler
- ▶ Sequence-of-Events Chart
- ▶ Image Chart
- ▶ Rubric

② Choose More to Read

These readings provide different answers to the Essential Question. Choose a book and online selections to read during the unit.

September 11, 2001: Attack on New York City
by Wilborn Hampton

Wilborn Hampton describes the events of September 11, 2001, through the stories of those who lived through the attack on the World Trade Center. Their stories show that everyday people can turn into heroes and even the saddest stories can be full of hope.

▶ NONFICTION

Hercules
by Paul Storrie

Hercules is a hero of ancient Greece. His strength is legendary. But Hercules has a powerful enemy—the goddess Hera. She will do anything to defeat him. Hercules may be the strongest human alive, but is he stronger and more clever than an angry goddess?

▶ GRAPHIC CLASSIC

Left Behind
by Velma Wallis

Fighting to survive the harsh Alaskan winter, a Native American chief has to decide: Should he leave two old women behind or risk the lives of the entire group? The choice is a cruel one, but the decision is clear. Can the women survive alone?

▶ LEGEND

myNGconnect.com
- 🔗 Read about everyday heroes in your community and nominate some of your own.
- 🔗 Take a personality quiz to find out how you match up to heroes of the past.
- 🔗 Play an online game that takes you on a heroic adventure.

SHORT STORIES

Authors can tell stories in many ways. One way to think about the way a story is told is to look at different versions of a familiar story.

DEMO TEXT #1

Humpty Dumpty sat on a wall.
Humpty Dumpty had a great fall.
All the King's horses
And all the King's men
Couldn't put Humpty together again.

DEMO TEXT #2

Humpty Dumpty sat on a wall. Thoughts raced through his mind: "You old fool. What is an egg like you doing on a wall? You always have to be the one to take risks. You always have to be the one who thinks that being fragile is no big deal."

Humpty looked out and saw the King's men sitting on their horses, waiting. Waiting for what? "For you to take a risk that will get you scrambled, that's what," Humpty thought. He sighed. He asked himself whether the view from the wall was worth it. Looking at the fields below him, he thought it was. Then the wind started to blow. He wondered what the King's men would think if he just climbed down. "I'll never give them the satisfaction."

Soon, Humpty felt himself tipping, then falling. As he fell, he thought that it hadn't been a bad life at all. At least not for an egg.

DEMO TEXT #3

Humpty Dumpty sat on a wall. Thoughts raced through his mind: "You old fool. What is an egg like you doing on a wall? You always have to be the one to take risks."

Humpty wasn't the only one whose mind was racing. For many of the King's men, the Humpty Dumpty job was no big deal. They had seen splattered eggs before. They made jokes about cracked eggs. For Joshua Jones, though, this was his first time. He was nervous. And queasy. He thought about all of the training he had received in fixing cracked eggs.

Joshua looked up. He saw Humpty teeter and then fall. His heart went out to the great egg. "He must be so frightened! He must be so disappointed to have it end this way," Joshua thought.

The crash echoed through the kingdom. People were concerned and rushed out of their houses. Joshua and the other King's men raced to fix Humpty. As he raced to the egg, he was certain he could help.

He rushed to the front to try some of the techniques he had learned. But nothing worked. The King's horses and King's men stood defeated. They couldn't put Humpty back together.

Connect Reading to Your Life

Look at all three Demo Texts. Then rank the following statements. One (1) means you are *most sure* it is true. Five (5) means that you are *least sure* it is true.

Reading Strategies
- Plan and Monitor
- Determine Importance
▶ **Make Inferences**
- Ask Questions
- Make Connections
- Synthesize
- Visualize

Rank

_____ Humpty Dumpty sat on a wall.

_____ The view was worth the risks.

_____ The King's men were very careful as they tried to put Humpty back together.

_____ Humpty was frightened as he sat on the wall.

_____ Joshua had learned many techniques for putting eggs back together.

Focus Strategy ▶ Make Inferences

To do that ranking, you had to make **inferences**. All the stories were told by a narrator. Some of the information came from the viewpoint of the characters. Some seemed to come from the author. Experienced readers make inferences about which information is **reliable**, or able to be trusted.

Think about two little kids playing with action figures. One kid says, "He's the greatest" and marches the action figure around. The other says, "He's the strongest" and marches the second action figure into battle with the first. After they fight for a while, one kid says, "There was an earthquake and the people were scared."

Like authors do, the little kids sometimes tell the story from the point of view of a character, even though they say *he* instead of *I*. They also make decisions about the plot—like the earthquake—that are beyond the scope of the characters to make.

Your Job as a Reader

One of your most important jobs as a reader is to figure out where you get your information from and which information to believe. You'll need to make a lot of inferences to do that.

Elements of Literature
narrator *n.*, the person who tells a story

Academic Vocabulary
- **inference** *n.*, good guess based on evidence and knowledge; **infer** *v.*, to make a good guess based on evidence and knowledge
- **reliable** *adj.*, trustworthy or believable; **rely** *v.*, to put trust in someone or something, to depend

■ Unpack the Thinking Process

Viewpoint

Some stories are told by a narrator but focus on the **perceptions** of one character. These stories are told from the **third-person** limited point of view. When you read one of these stories, you have to make inferences about how that character's viewpoint affects the information, just as you have to do when one of the characters is telling the story (first-person point of view). A character's experiences and attitudes play a role in shaping his or her viewpoint. This is also true of an author's viewpoint. For example, authors from different cultures may have different ways of looking at the world, which can affect the way a story is told.

Stories told by narrators who can see into the minds of all of the characters are told from the **third-person** omniscient point of view. Even in these stories, the viewpoints of characters or the author may affect the information we learn and the way it is presented. So no matter what the point of view, you also have to figure out what you're *not* being told. It is your job as a reader to make inferences to fill in those blanks.

In the nursery rhyme version (Demo Text #1), the narrator only tells the facts. You trust that those facts are true, but there is a lot of information missing. If the nursery rhyme continued, experienced readers would look for details that would help them make inferences to fill in information such as:

- how Humpty got up on that wall in the first place
- why the King was so concerned about Humpty's safety.

You learn a lot more in Demo Text #2. The narrator chooses to let the reader in on Humpty's thoughts, so you know what Humpty thinks about himself. As a reader making inferences, you need to consider how Humpty's viewpoint affects the information. For example, Humpty considers it worth risking his life to see the view from the wall. You may wonder if the view is really so magnificent or if he is simply being stubborn because of his attitude toward the King's men.

Elements of Literature
third-person *adj.*, referring to a narrator who describes the action from outside the story
omniscient *adj.*, all-knowing

Academic Vocabulary
- **perception** *n.*, knowledge that comes from understanding or being aware; **perceive** *v.*, to be aware of, to observe, to notice

You get to see even more in Demo Text #3. You get to see *into* the thoughts of another character. Sometimes the narrator tells us the thoughts directly: Joshua was nervous.

But when things are told from Joshua's **perspective**, be careful. He thinks that he'll be able to put Humpty back together. That turns out not to be true.

Sometimes an omniscient narrator tells us things about the plot or setting that are beyond the knowledge of an individual character. When you read that the people in the kingdom rushed out in concern, you are learning information that neither Humpty Dumpty nor Joshua know.

■ Try an Experiment

Imagine that the story continues. Read on.

DEMO TEXT #3 *(continued)*

Someone would have to tell the Dumpty family about Humpty's accident. None of the King's men wanted that terrible job. Everyone knew that the Dumpty family was the most famous and well-loved family in the entire kingdom. The task fell to Joshua, since he was the newest of the King's men. Joshua was not happy, but he would do his duty.

Joshua rode swiftly to the family's house. As he neared their home, he slowed down so that he didn't scare the family. He took a deep breath and walked up to the enormous door. He knocked softly. Mrs. Dumpty and Humpty's young son looked at Joshua and then at each other. "They know," thought Joshua. "They already know."

Retell the Story Work with a small group to retell this new section of Demo Text #3. Use third-person *limited* point of view. Tell the story from the perspective of Joshua, Mrs. Dumpty, or the young son. Remember to use *he* or *she*, not *I,* to refer to the characters. Include illustrations to go along with your retelling.

Debrief After you retell the story, answer these questions:

1. What information did you leave out?
2. Which version requires you to make more inferences?

Academic Vocabulary
- **perspective** *n.*, a specific angle from which something is viewed or observed

Monitor Comprehension

Viewpoint Why is knowing a narrator's viewpoint important?

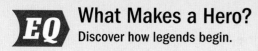

EQ ## What Makes a Hero?
Discover how legends begin.

Make a Connection

Quickwrite A writer named Bernard Malamud once said, "Without heroes, we are all plain people and don't know how far we can go." Write a response that explains what you think Malamud means and whether you agree or disagree. Then share your writing to see if others feel the same way.

Learn Key Vocabulary

Study the Words Pronounce each word and learn its meaning. You may also want to look up the definitions in the Glossary.

• Academic Vocabulary

Key Words	Examples
conscientiously (kon-shē-**en**-shus-lē) *adverb* ▶ page 213	When you work **conscientiously**, you work carefully and thoroughly. Maribel **conscientiously** researched all the facts before writing her history essay.
endure (in-**dyur**) *verb* ▶ pages 223, 230, 233	Something **endures** if it continues to exist for a long time. Some old stories **endure** for centuries because people love to read and hear them.
• **evidence** (**e**-vu-duns) *noun* ▶ pages 221, 226, 230	**Evidence** is information that helps prove something. The detective looks for **evidence** that supports her ideas.
genuine (**jen**-yū-win) *adjective* ▶ pages 228, 231	Something is **genuine** if it is real and not fake. He thought that the statue was **genuine** gold, but it was really made of brass.
historian (hi-**stor**-ē-un) *noun* ▶ pages 223, 230	A **historian** is someone who studies the events of the past and interprets them. The **historian** wrote an article about World War II.
• **investigation** (in-ves-ti-**gā**-shun) *noun* ▶ page 227	An **investigation** is a careful search or study that looks for facts. We only found out the truth about the event after we conducted our own **investigation**.
just (**just**) *adjective* ▶ pages 219, 221	A **just** person is guided by truth and fairness. I admire leaders who make decisions that are reasonable, fair, and **just**.
skeptic (**skep**-tik) *noun* ▶ page 229	A **skeptic** is someone who doubts beliefs that are generally accepted by others. My friends believe in the legend, but I'm a **skeptic** who needs more proof.

Practice the Words Work with a partner. Make a **Definition Map** for each Key Vocabulary word. Use a dictionary to find other forms of the word.

Definition Map

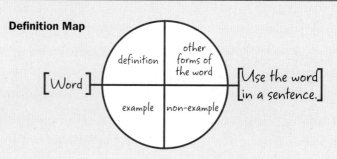

Reading Strategies
- Plan and Monitor
- Determine Importance
▶ **Make Inferences**
- Ask Questions
- Make Connections
- Synthesize
- Visualize

Analyze Cultural Perspective

Most stories are told from a **cultural perspective** that reflects the customs and attitudes of a particular society and era. "The Sword in the Stone" takes place in England during the Middle Ages. The cultural perspective of this time and place affects story elements, including plot, character, setting, and theme.

Look Into the Text

Farming is an important part of the culture in which the story takes place. It affects the plot, characters, and setting.

> Everyone in the household had to get up early that morning because they were starting the hay-making.
>
> This was Arthur's favorite time of year. Lessons were suspended so that he and Kay could join the men out in the fields. . . .
>
> Tossing the hay onto the wagon was men's work. Arthur was not yet strong enough to lift a sheaf, but Kay had grown several inches in the last few months and was almost a man. In a few weeks' time he would leave the schoolroom for good to take up his duties as a squire.

Duties and roles are important in Arthur's society.

Focus Strategy ▶ Make Inferences

Sometimes understanding a text is like fitting together the pieces of a puzzle. Some pieces come from the author, who includes ideas and information about the subject. As a reader, you add your own experiences with the subject. You **make inferences** when you put these pieces together.

HOW TO MAKE INFERENCES

Focus Strategy

1. As you read about a subject, record the author's details in an **Inference Chart**.

2. Think about what you already know about the subject. Add your knowledge to the chart.

3. Consider all the information you now have about the subject. What new ideas can you infer, or put together, about the subject?

4. As you continue to read, see if the text proves or changes your inferences.

Inference Chart

Author's Details	My Knowledge	My Inferences
"Lessons were suspended so that he and Kay could join the men out in the fields."	School is suspended only for something important.	Hay-making is important to the characters and their society.

A Legend Takes New Forms

Your grandparents' generation may have first met the hero King Arthur in books with elegant illustrations by artists like Howard Pyle and Arthur Rackham.

Today's generation is discovering the King Arthur legend through computer games. In these games the players control the actions of characters with plenty of swordplay, archery, and fights on horseback. Some of the games let you play from Arthur's perspective, while others make you a character in his world.

Stories about King Arthur and his knights, or soldiers, have been part of popular culture for hundreds of years. Beginning in the 1900s, modern media have made it possible to enjoy his story in many forms besides books. For instance, Arthur's character has appeared in comic strips since the 1930s. One of the earliest and most successful strips was *Prince Valiant in the Days of King Arthur*, created by Harold Foster. A number of other comic books and strips are based on characters and events from the Arthur story.

The Arthur legend has been adapted in dozens of live-action and animated films. These movies deal not only with the central hero, Arthur, but also with his knights of the Round Table and the ladies of his court. There have been animated films for younger audiences, including *The Sword in the Stone*, released in 1963, and cartoon television series based on the legend.

Each generation finds ways to retell the story and interpret its events in new ways. What form will Arthur's story take for future generations?

myNGconnect.com

◐ Read an encyclopedia entry about King Arthur.
◐ View classic illustrations of the Arthur legend.

The Sword in the Stone

by Molly Perham

King Arthur's Sword in Stone, Richard T. Nowitz, ©1996.

▲ Critical Viewing: Effect How does the photographer use light
and dark in this image? What effect does he create?

Comprehension Coach

Set a Purpose
**Find out what change is on its way
for Arthur and all of England.**

The dragon loomed large in front of Arthur's eyes, **1** then **wavered and disintegrated** and the smoke faded away.

Arthur sat up in his own bed and rubbed his eyes. He had been having the most wonderful dream. He started to tell his brother Kay about his strange adventures but just then someone knocked loudly at the door. Everyone in the household had to get up early that morning because they were starting the hay-making.

This was Arthur's favorite time of year. Lessons were suspended so that he and Kay could join the men out in the fields. **It was all hands to the wheel** to get the harvest in before the autumn rains.

Arthur loved to follow the men as they moved up and down with their scythes, cutting great swathes through the waist-high grass and sending scores of rabbits scurrying for cover into the nearby woods. He loved the smell of the new-mown hay, and the heat of the sun burning through the thin shirt on his back. He and Kay were responsible for tying the hay into **sheaves** and stacking them into stooks. Later these would be collected up and taken back to the barn just inside the castle gates.

Tossing the hay onto the wagon was men's work. Arthur was not yet strong enough to lift a sheaf, but Kay had grown several inches in the last few months and was almost a man. In a few weeks' time he would leave the schoolroom for good to take up his duties as a **squire**. Kay could toss the heavy sheaves as well as any of the farmhands. **2** At the end of the day he would climb up on top, pulling Arthur after him, and together they would ride back to the hay barn for supper—a splendid feast of rabbit stew and apple pies which the women had been preparing for most of the day, washed down with jugs of **frothing cider**.

1 Language
A dragon *loomed* large; it appeared in a frightening way. How does this help you picture Arthur's dream?

2 Cultural Perspective
What do the details show about the value this culture places on size and strength? Why is it so important to the boys of this era?

In Other Words

wavered and disintegrated went blurry and broke into small pieces
It was all hands to the wheel Everyone was hard at work
sheaves large piles

squire person who helped a knight or soldier get ready to fight
frothing cider bubbly apple juice

And so several more harvests came and went, and life went on much the same as usual, though it was a little dull for Arthur without his childhood companion. Kay was often away from the castle, acting as a squire to various knights at **tournaments** all over the country. A squire's task was to dress and **arm** his knight before an event, to carry all the **lances**, and generally to make sure that everything was kept in good order. Kay had been well trained in Sir Ector's household, and performed these tasks **conscientiously**. Rumor had it that Sir Ector was considering the possibility of making Kay a knight. **3**

Meanwhile, Arthur grew tall and strong and waited impatiently for his school days to be over. This happened sooner than he expected. One day **an envoy** from the Archbishop arrived breathless at the castle gate with news from London.

On Christmas Day all the great **nobles** and knights had assembled in St. Paul's Cathedral to pray for a sign that would show who was the rightful King of England. When the service was over and they came out of the church they saw an amazing sight. There was a huge stone in the middle of the churchyard with

3 Make Inferences
Using the text and what you know already, what is Kay learning? Make a note in your Inference Chart.

Mountain Dragon, 1992, Bob Eggleton. Acrylic on illustration board, private collection of Pat Wilshire, Pennsylvania.

▲ **Critical Viewing: Effect** How do you think the artist wants the viewer to feel about this image? How does he create this mood?

Key Vocabulary
conscientiously *adv.*, very carefully and thoroughly

In Other Words
tournaments contests for knights, or soldiers
arm give weapons to
lances long-handled weapons with sharp metal points
an envoy a messenger
nobles people with high rank in royal society

an anvil embedded in it. Pushed into the anvil was a magnificent sword, and written in golden letters were the words:

> *Whoever pulls this sword out of this stone*
> *is born to be King of all England.*

The nobles stood around the stone wondering about the words that were written on the sword. One of them went back to tell the Archbishop, who hurried out to see the **miracle**.

"God has given us a sign," he said. "We must pray once more and then those who think they are fit to be king may try to pull the sword out of the stone." **4**

One by one the nobles tried to pull out the sword, but none of them succeeded.

"The man who will be King of England is not here," said the Archbishop. "But God will send him in his own good time."

Ten nobles were chosen to guard the sword until the right man was found. Then the Archbishop sent out messengers to all the knights in the land to invite them to a tournament.

Kay had just been made a knight, and Sir Ector agreed that this was a good opportunity for him to show off his skills. Arthur was to ride with them so he could act as Sir Kay's squire.

A very excited and expectant **party** set off for London that cold winter's morning. **5** The city was crowded with visitors and they had to **take lodgings** some distance from the center.

On New Year's Day Sir Ector, Sir Kay, and Arthur rode into town. But before they reached the field where the tournament was to be held, Kay discovered that he had forgotten his sword.

"Arthur," he gasped in horror, "I have left my sword at the house where we spent the night. I cannot fight without it. If I ride back, I will

4 Make Inferences
Heroes in legends often pass tests. In this story, what do the characters believe this test will show about the man who will become king? Make a note in your Inference Chart.

5 Access Vocabulary
What does the word *expectant* mean? Look for a root word and context clues that may give you an idea.

In Other Words

an anvil embedded in it a steel block stuck deep into the stone
miracle extraordinary event
party group of people
take lodgings find a place to stay

be tired before the tournament starts. Please go and get it for me."

"Of course I will," said Arthur, who was always willing to help other people. In any case, it was his duty as a squire to serve his brother. 6

He rode back along the road as quickly as he could, but when he reached the lodging house he found that **it was locked and shuttered**. The landlady and all the other people who lived there had gone to watch the **jousting**.

Arthur was very upset. He rode slowly back to the jousting field wondering what he could do. Without a sword Kay would not be able to take part in the tournament.

Passing St. Paul's churchyard Arthur saw a magnificent sword gleaming in the sunlight. As he drew closer he saw that it was sticking out of an anvil on top of a huge stone. Arthur looked around but saw no one. The ten knights who were supposed to be keeping watch had also gone to the tournament.

"Well," thought Arthur, "whoever owns this sword can't want it very much if they leave it lying around like that."

He dismounted from his horse and climbed onto the stone. Grasping the sword by the **hilt** he pulled it out of the anvil. Then, delighted to have found a sword for his brother, Arthur spurred on his horse to catch up with Sir Ector's party.

> ... Arthur saw a magnificent sword gleaming in the sunlight.

6 Cultural Perspective
How does Arthur's cultural perspective affect his actions?

Monitor Comprehension

Explain
How will the sword in the stone change the lives of everyone in England?

In Other Words
it was locked and shuttered the doors were shut and the windows were covered
jousting contests between knights riding on horses
hilt handle

"**K**ay! Kay!" he called. "The lodging house was all locked up, so I couldn't fetch your sword. But I found this one pushed into an anvil. It doesn't seem to belong to anyone. Will it be all right?"

When Kay saw the sword he realized immediately what it was and the **temptation** was too much for him. He took it to Sir Ector.

"Father," he said, "I have the sword from the stone. Therefore I must be King of England."

Sir Ector looked at the sword and looked at Kay. He knew that his son had no right to be king. He turned and took the two boys back to the churchyard.

Putting a Bible into Kay's hand he said, "Now, my son, tell me how you got the sword."

Kay sighed. "Arthur brought it to me," he said. ▣ 7

"And how did you get the sword, Arthur?"

"Kay forgot his sword, and I rode back to the lodging house to get it for him," Arthur explained, hoping that he was not going to get into trouble. "But the house was all locked up. On the way back I saw this sword in the churchyard. It didn't seem to belong to anyone, so I thought that Kay might as well have it. I'm sorry if I did wrong."

"Did anyone see you take the sword?"

"No, sir, there was no one there."

"Put the sword back and let us all try to pull it out."

"But it's easy," said Arthur, "anyone could do it."

"Just do as I say," said Sir Ector **sternly**. ▣ 8

Arthur was **puzzled** by all this fuss over a sword, but he did as he was told and pushed it back into the anvil. Kay **seized** it by the hilt,

▣ 7 **Make Inferences**
What inference did you make about Kay when he took the sword? Has your idea about him changed? Explain.

▣ 8 **Make Inferences**
Choose one word to describe Sir Ector's character. What details in this scene help you make this inference?

In Other Words

temptation wish to do something wrong
sternly very seriously
puzzled confused
seized grabbed

but though he pulled as hard as he could with both hands, he couldn't move it.

Then Sir Ector tried, but with no more success. "You try it, Arthur," he said.

So Arthur, wondering what this was all about, got hold of the sword and pulled it out easily.

Sir Ector stared in amazement at the boy he had brought up as his own. Then he dropped to his knees and motioned to Kay to do the same.

"Father!" Arthur cried in alarm. "Why are you kneeling before me?"

"**It is God's will** that whoever pulls the sword from the stone must be King of England," said Sir Ector. "You know that I am not your real father, and Kay is not your brother, although we both love you dearly. **Merlin** brought you to me when you were a tiny baby, wrapped in a cloth of gold. I knew you were of noble blood, but I had no idea that you were born to be King." **9**

"If I am really King," said Arthur **solemnly**, "then I swear to serve God and my people, to **put right any wrongs**, and to bring peace to the land. But please do not leave me, Father, for I will need your support and advice. And Kay, I want you to be a knight of my court and governor of my lands."

Merlin and Arthur, Sir William Goscombe John (1860–1952), Bronze, National Museum and Gallery of Wales, Cardiff, The Bridgeman Art Library.

9 Cultural Perspective
Why is Arthur surprised when Sir Ector kneels before him? What do Sir Ector's words and actions show about his culture?

◁ Critical Viewing: Effect
Look at the sculpture of Merlin holding Arthur as a baby. What does the artist show about their relationship?

In Other Words
It is God's will God's plan is
Merlin A wise wizard
solemnly seriously
put right any wrongs correct any problems or crimes

Sir Ector and Kay promised to stay with Arthur as long as he needed them.

Then they went to the Archbishop and told him what had happened. Arthur put the sword back into the stone again and invited anyone who wished to try and pull it out. No one succeeded. Only Arthur could pull it free.

The great nobles and knights refused to agree that this unknown youth should be king over them.

"We will come again **at Candlemas**," they said, as they mounted their horses and rode away. "Perhaps by then a man will have been found who is more worthy to be our King."

So at Candlemas there was another great gathering, but though all the nobles tried their hardest to draw the sword, none of them could move it. Once again Arthur put his hand on the hilt and at his touch it came out as easily as though it had never been stuck **fast** in the stone. Yet still the nobles would not accept such a boy for their king.

"We will pray to God again," they said. And at Easter, they made another trial, but none of them could move the sword except Arthur. By now the ordinary people, who had heard of the miracle and watched the trials eagerly, would be held back no longer.

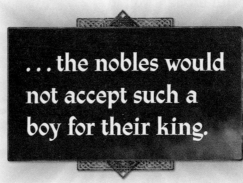

...the nobles would not accept such a boy for their king.

"It is God's will that Arthur should be King—we will have Arthur for our King," they cried. And so the great nobles and knights **were obliged to** give in.

10 Cultural Perspective
What does the nobles' and knights' behavior toward Arthur show about attitudes in their society?

11 Make Inferences
Why do you think the nobles refuse to accept Arthur as King?

Monitor Comprehension

Draw Conclusions
Who helped Arthur become a hero? Would he have become a hero without help from other people?

In Other Words
at Candlemas on February 2, a Christian holiday
fast completely
were obliged to were forced to, had to

Predict
**Arthur faces many new challenges.
How will he work to win his people's support?**

Arthur went into the church and placed the sword on the **high altar**. The Archbishop took it up and touched Arthur on the shoulder with it to make him a knight. Then Arthur forgave the great nobles and knights for doubting him and swore an oath that he would be a ▮just▮ and true king for all his days.

He ordered the lords who held their land from the crown to fulfil the duties they owed him. Each one knelt before him in turn and promised to **abide by** the laws of the king. After this ceremony, Arthur said he would hear complaints about **injustices** and crimes committed in the land since the death of his father, **Uther Pendragon**. They told him of how lands and castles had been taken by force, and men murdered, and of how knights and ladies and common people were robbed and assaulted.

Arthur ordered that all lands and properties should be returned to their rightful owners and that everyone should respect the rights of others. 🔢 When that was done, Arthur organized his government. Sir Kay was made High Steward of all Britain and the most trustworthy knights were **appointed to high office**. Merlin was **confirmed** as chief counsellor to the King.

🔢 **Make Inferences**
Think about the decisions Arthur makes as king. How do they help you understand him?

Roman sword, Hod Hill fort, Dorset, Roman Britain, first century

Key Vocabulary
▮just▮ *adj.*, guided by truth and fairness

In Other Words
high altar table in the church
abide by follow
injustices unfair actions
Uther Pendragon the old King
appointed to high office given important jobs
confirmed named

King Arthur, 1903, Charles Ernest Butler. Oil on canvas, private collection.
Christopher Wood Gallery, London, The Bridgeman Art Library.

▲ **Critical Viewing: Design** Why has the artist used so much gold in this painting? What is it
a symbol for?

Then Arthur proclaimed that the **Feast of Pentecost** would be his **coronation day**. When that day came, the Archbishop crowned him King of all **Britain**. He ruled his kingdom from **Camelot**, and everyone rejoiced that Britain once more had a King. ❖

ANALYZE The Sword in the Stone

1. **Explain** How do the nobles and the ordinary people treat Arthur at first? How do their attitudes compare by the end of the story? Cite evidence from the story to support your answer.

2. **Vocabulary** How does Arthur show that he will be a `just` and fair king?

3. **Analyze Cultural Perspective** With a partner, record how cultural perspectives affect the plot, characters, setting, and theme of the story.

Cultural Perspective	How It Affects the Story
Farming is important.	Everyone helps with the hay-making.

How would the story be different if it was told from a different cultural perspective?

4. **Focus Strategy Make Inferences** Do you think Arthur will make a good king? Consider what you know about kings or other leaders from stories you have read and heard. Then work with a partner to gather `evidence` from the story and make an inference about Arthur.

🔄 **Return to the Text**
Reread and Write Is Arthur a hero? Reread "The Sword in the Stone," and write your opinion. Include at least two details from the text to serve as evidence to support your ideas.

Key Vocabulary
• **evidence** *n.*, information that helps prove something

In Other Words
Feast of Pentecost Christian festival held on the seventh Sunday after Easter
coronation day day to become king
Britain England and all its lands
Camelot the capital city

BEFORE READING Was There a Real King Arthur?

historical analysis by Robert Stewart

Reading Strategies

- Plan and Monitor
- Determine Importance
- ▶ **Make Inferences**
- Ask Questions
- Make Connections
- Synthesize
- Visualize

Analyze Text Structures

Nonfiction authors often organize their ideas into **text structures** that share information in a clear and interesting way. As you read, look for common signal words that show which text structure the author is using. These signal words will help you follow the author's thinking and find the information you need to know.

- Description: *for example, such as, one such, most important*
- Sequence or Time Order: *first, then, before, after, meanwhile, finally, on, in*
- Compare and Contrast: *like, while, but, on one hand, however, both, also*
- Cause and Effect: *therefore, so, because of, if . . . then, this led to, as a result*

Look Into the Text

Signal words can show how the author organizes events by time.

A historian usually starts by looking for written evidence. The first mention of someone who might be Arthur is in a book called *The Overthrow of Britain* compiled by the British monk Saint Gildas (c. 516–570 C.E.)....

At the same time, bards in Wales and Brittany, in France, were entertaining their hosts with stories of a hero named Arthur. This one had a personality much like that of the Arthur we know, and he slew monsters and wicked giants.

Which date does the author include to help you understand the order of events?

Focus Strategy ▶ Make Inferences

Most nonfiction authors provide evidence to support a big idea. But sometimes, reading the evidence is not enough. The reader must put together evidence to **make inferences** about the big idea.

HOW TO MAKE INFERENCES

Focus Strategy

1. As you read nonfiction, note important evidence from each section in an **Inference Diagram**.

2. Think about what the evidence proves. Sometimes, the author will state this directly.

3. If the big idea is not stated, summarize the evidence to make an inference about the author's big idea.

4. As you read on, make more inferences. See if the text supports or changes your inferences.

Inference Diagram

Evidence 1: Historians look for clues about Arthur.
  +
Evidence 2: Early written stories told about a hero like Arthur.
  +
Evidence 3: Bards told stories about a hero named Arthur.
  ↓
Inference: Many old written and oral stories were about a hero like Arthur.

Was There a Real King Arthur?

by Robert Stewart

Connect Across Texts

The short story "The Sword in the Stone" retells a heroic legend that has been told for centuries. The following article about history examines its lasting appeal. What makes this hero's legend **endure***?*

King Arthur is a mysterious figure, and his tale has a long and complex history. Writers from every age have constructed their own version of Arthur, tailored to suit the spirit of their times. But was there a real King Arthur? If so, exactly who was the **historical figure** behind the folk tale? How did the world-famous legend **emerge**? It is one of history's greatest unsolved riddles.

Almost everyone has heard of King Arthur. He was the ancient British king who pulled the sword from the stone. He consulted the magician Merlin, led the knights of the Round Table, married the beautiful Guinevere, and set an example of bravery and chivalry. According to British legend, though he is long dead, he lies somewhere in the hills, waiting for the moment when his countrymen need him most. Then he will awake and save them.

Is this history? Much of it certainly is not. The magical Merlin sounds **suspect**, and how could a sword possibly be embedded in a stone in the first place? That all sounds like **folklore**. But just because the story is folklore now does not necessarily mean that it did not have a historical seed. It is for that seed that **historians** and **archaeologists** have long been looking.

Head of King Arthur, from the *Beautiful Fountain*, Nuremberg, Germany, fourteenth century **1**

1 Make Inferences This photo and caption show a very old statue. How does this add to the text?

Key Vocabulary
endure *v.*, to continue or go on
historian *n.*, person who studies the past and interprets it

In Other Words
historical figure real person from the past
emerge come about
suspect hard to believe
folklore tales or beliefs shared by many people
archaeologists scientists who study past cultures

British and World History Before 1100

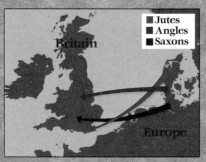

Map legend:
- ■ Jutes
- ■ Angles
- ■ Saxons

Britain
Europe

Anglo-Saxon helmet, Sutton Hoo, England, early seventh century

c. 500
Ambrosius, a Christian Roman-British leader, **makes a last stand** against an army of invading Saxons at the battle of Mount Badon.

c. 390 C.E. (Common Era)
Tribes of Angles, Saxons, and Jutes start to flood into Britain.

410
The Romans abandon Britain.

c. 547
The monk Gildas mentions Ambrosius in *The Overthrow of Britain*.

c. 540
Buddhism reaches Japan.

Ethiopian monks **translate the Bible**.

c. 700
Ancestors of the Maori reach New Zealand.

Seated Buddha, Japan, Asuka Period, seventh century

570
Mohammed is born in Mecca.

Detail from an early twentieth-century Maori carving

Mosque, Baghdad, Iraq, Abbasid dynasty (749–1258)

711
Muslim **forces** cross the Straits of Gibraltar and conquer Spain.

The World

In Other Words

c. about (abbreviation used for estimated dates)
makes a last stand fights to defend his land
translate the Bible change the Bible from one language to another

Ancestors Family members from past generations
forces armies, soldiers

Portrait of Alfred the Great, 849–899

Anglo-Saxons

Danes

Norman coat of arms, c. 1066

886
England is split between Danish **territory** to the east (the Danelaw), and Anglo-Saxon land to the west.

1066
Normans from early France conquer Britain. The Norman Conquest leads to many changes in English language, culture, and government.

c. 870
An army of Danes moving across England is defeated by Alfred the Great of Wessex.

Nennius names King Arthur as the hero of the Battle of Mt. Badon in his *History of the Britons*.

1013
King Swein of Denmark takes control of England. The Anglo-Saxon King Ethelred **flees** to Normandy.

800
Charlemagne, king of the Franks, is crowned Holy Roman Emperor. His lands cover much of Europe.

873
Arab mathematicians invent the **concept** of zero.

1031
Christians begin to reconquer Spain.

1045
Printing with movable type is invented in China.

Charlemagne is crowned by Pope Leo III, December 25, 800.

A doorway in the Alhambra Palace, Granada, Spain, c. 1300

▲ **Interpret the Time Line** This time line shows major world events that occurred at the same time. What does this show about the legend of Arthur?

In Other Words
concept idea or notion
territory land
flees escapes

Where Is Arthur?

A historian usually starts by looking for written **evidence**. The first mention of someone who might be Arthur is in a book called *The Overthrow of Britain* **compiled** by the British monk Saint Gildas (c. 516–570 C.E.). In this book, a British leader named Ambrosius slows the **advance** of the invading Angles and Saxons, who are later defeated at the Battle of Mount Badon in about 500 C.E. Gildas does not mention Arthur, nor say that Ambrosius fought at Badon. However, some historians have wondered if Ambrosius and Arthur are **one and the same**. This is historical evidence, but was it Arthur? **2**

At the same time, **bards** in Wales and Brittany, in France, were entertaining their hosts with stories of a hero named Arthur. This one had a personality much like that of

2 Make Inferences How does the author feel about the evidence that Arthur and Ambrosius are the same person? How do you know?

Europe in the Early Middle Ages (c. 500–800 C.E.)

THE ORIGINS OF ARTHUR

800 C.E. Nennius writes about Arthur.

500 C.E. Bards tell of Arthur.

British Isles

NORTH SEA

ATLANTIC OCEAN

Wales

Mt. Badon

Winchester

English Channel

500 C.E. St. Gildas describes Ambrosius.

Brittany

N W E S

0   300 mi
0   300 km

⚔ Castle
📍 Battle site

▲ Interpret the Map What do the captions on the map show?

Key Vocabulary
• **evidence** *n.*, information that helps prove something

In Other Words

compiled put together from different sources
advance forward movement
one and the same the same person
bards storytellers from ancient times

the Arthur we know, and he **slew** monsters and wicked giants. Folk heroes are sometimes based on history. But was this Arthur real?

The next piece of written evidence comes from the early ninth century, when Arthur was named by the Welsh monk Nennius in his *History of the Britons*. According to Nennius, Arthur was a British war leader who fought a series of twelve battles against the Angles and Saxons, of which Badon was the last. The similarities with Ambrosius are unmistakable. **3**

And that, together with poems and a few other writings of the same time, is all of the written evidence we have for King Arthur. All of the details—Lancelot, Guinevere, the sword in the stone, Camelot and the Round Table, Merlin the magician—appear only in literature. Much of it was written long after the Norman Conquest of 1066.

For hundreds of years after that, people were **content** to leave Arthur as a legend. Then, in the early twentieth century, some historians began to wonder. Could Arthur

possibly be real after all? One popular view held by many scholars was that Arthur was actually a late-Roman **cavalry commander** who had led British forces against the invading Anglo-Saxons.

Archaeologists have also been looking around Britain for evidence of the real Arthur. One such **investigation** took place in 1976 in the city of Winchester in southern England. Hanging there, in the Great Hall of Winchester Castle, is an enormous round table-top. It is made of solid oak, is eighteen feet (5.4 meters) in diameter, weighs one-and-a-quarter tons (1,138 kilograms), and has places for twenty-five people marked on it. Many argued that it was the actual Round Table of legend. Historically, Winchester had become the capital of the Saxon kings of Wessex in the seventh century. Could the Saxons possibly have turned Arthur's capital into their own? **4**

Unfortunately, the belief did not stand up to modern scientific investigation. **Tree-ring and radiocarbon dating**, plus a study

3 Make Inferences
What does this written evidence add to what you already know?

4 Make Inferences
How do the facts about the table support the inference that Arthur was real?

Monitor Comprehension

Explain
Why do some historians believe Arthur and Ambrosius are the same person?

In Other Words
slew killed
content happy, satisfied
cavalry commander leader of a group of soldiers riding on horses
Tree-ring and radiocarbon dating Scientific methods used to measure time

of **medieval carpentry practices**, revealed that the table was actually constructed in the 1270s at the start of Edward I's **reign**. This was during a time when the king himself was taking a great interest in everything associated with Arthur. Experts now think that the table at Winchester was probably made to be used at the many knightly tournaments that Edward himself liked to hold.

Although no **genuine** Arthurian objects have ever been discovered, many possible Arthurian places have been investigated. Geoffrey of Monmouth, an author of the 1100s, said that Tintagel in Cornwall was Arthur's birthplace, and there is even a suitably ruined castle perched on a cliff there. But, unfortunately, the castle is no older than Geof-

frey himself. Writers choose places as settings for their books for many different reasons. Geoffrey may have added the reference to Tintagel simply to please a rich local nobleman. **5**

In the 1960s, the search for Camelot heated up when archaeologists **excavated** an **Iron Age hill fort** at Cadbury Castle in southern England. Local legend held that Arthur and his knights lay sleeping under the hill. John Leland, a historian writing during King Henry VIII's reign, had stated that the local people often called the **fortified remains** "Camalat—King Arthur's palace."

Exhaustive excavations conducted by the archaeologist Leslie Alcock yielded evidence dating from about Arthur's time of a wall encircling an extensive hilltop

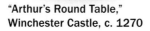
"Arthur's Round Table,"
Winchester Castle, c. 1270

5 **Text Structures**
Find the signal words in this paragraph. What do they tell you about how the author feels about Geoffrey of Monmouth's claim?

Key Vocabulary
genuine *adj.*, real, true

In Other Words
medieval carpentry practices ways carpenters worked in the Middle Ages
reign rule, time as king
excavated dug up
Iron Age hill fort fort built c. 1000 B.C.E.
fortified remains ruins

Local legends held that Arthur and his knights lay sleeping under the hill at Cadbury Castle (left). Geoffrey of Monmouth claimed that Tintagel Castle (right) was Arthur's birthplace.

compound. At its center was a large aisled hall. Some see the remains of a stout defensive wall around a great feasting hall such as might befit a king named Arthur. But skeptics see only a moderately sized barn surrounded by walls barely able to contain horses and cattle, let alone keep determined enemies away.

So King Arthur remains a mystery. Though archaeologists can find no evidence for Arthur, this fact alone does not disprove his existence. Archaeologists are the first to explain that lack of proof is not a convincing argument against the existence of a person, place, or event. All it takes is one small piece of evidence—one small "voice"—to overcome the **accumulated** weight of silence. Such a discovery may well lie in the future. 6

6 **Make Inferences**
Do you think the author believes that we will find proof of Arthur? What parts of the text give you clues?

Monitor Comprehension

Explain
What did the researchers at Cadbury Castle find? Explain their different ideas about the find.

Key Vocabulary
skeptic *n.*, person who doubts facts and beliefs that are generally accepted by others

In Other Words
compound group of buildings in an enclosed space
accumulated piled up

Why Do We Need Arthur?

But there is another Arthurian mystery. Why is it that we so much want King Arthur to be real? Why do historians and archaeologists continue this search? One of the great attractions of the Arthur story is that it contains something for everyone—action, mystery, romance, the struggle between good and evil. And the tales **have a ring of truth** because some have their roots in genuine ancient traditions.

And the idea of a once and future king, sleeping somewhere, awaiting his time to return, is not **unique to** the Arthur story. In Denmark, the knight Holger Danske sleeps. In Spain it is El Cid. In Germany it is Frederick Barbarossa. Arthur **embodies** real human needs and desires. We *want* him to be real. 7 ❖

> **7 Text Structures**
> List three reasons the author feels we need Arthur. What signal word or phrase introduces each one?

ANALYZE Was There a Real King Arthur?

1. **Recall and Interpret** According to the article, what kinds of evidence do historians study in the search for Arthur? What makes this evidence important?

2. **Vocabulary** What questions about King Arthur have endured over the centuries?

3. **Analyze Text Structures** With a partner, review the text and look for signal words that the author uses. What structure does the author use? How do you know?

4. **Focus Strategy Make Inferences** Does the author believe that King Arthur was real? Work with a partner to find details in the text to support your inference.

Return to the Text

Reread and Write Which information in the selection gives the most convincing evidence about a real King Arthur? Review that section and write a paragraph to explain why the evidence supports the belief that Arthur was real.

In Other Words

have a ring of truth sound like they might be true
unique to found only in
embodies represents, stands for

EQ What Makes a Hero?

Critical Thinking

1. **Analyze** Reread the **Quickwrite** you wrote about the quotation on page 208. How did the selection affect your thinking? Explain.

EQ 2. **Compare** How might a modern news story show a hero such as King Arthur differently than a legend from the Middle Ages?

3. **Interpret** According to Robert Stewart, "Arthur embodies real human needs and desires." Explain how Arthur's story influences the stories of other real heroes who have come after him.

4. **Speculate** Imagine that someone discovers **genuine** evidence proving that Arthur was a real person. Would this make people more or less interested in reading legends such as "The Sword in the Stone"? Explain.

EQ 5. **Draw Conclusions** Author Robert Stewart concludes his article by asking why we need heroes like Arthur to be real. What conclusions can you draw about whether *you* need heroes to be real?

Write About Literature

Interpretive Response Think about King Arthur's heroic qualities. Find specific examples from both texts that show these qualities. Then answer this question: What makes King Arthur such an appealing hero? Give evidence and embed quotations in your response.

Key Vocabulary Review

Oral Review Work with a partner. Use these words to complete the paragraph.

conscientiously	genuine	just
endured	historians	skeptics
evidence	investigations	

The legend of King Arthur has __(1)__ over time because Arthur represents the qualities of a true hero. He is a __(2)__ and fair ruler who respects all of his people. Scientists and __(3)__ who study the past have begun many __(4)__ to see whether the legend is true. They look carefully and __(5)__ for any __(6)__ that would prove that Arthur was a real person. On the other hand, doubting __(7)__ do not believe that a __(8)__ object that proves Arthur's existence will ever be discovered.

Writing Application Think about a puzzle or problem you solved by making inferences. Write a paragraph about your experience. Use at least two Key Vocabulary words.

Read with Ease: Phrasing

Assess your reading fluency with the passage in the Reading Handbook, p. 757. Then complete the self-check below.

1. I did/did not pause appropriately for punctuation and phrases.

2. My words correct per minute: _____

INTEGRATE THE LANGUAGE ARTS

Grammar

Use Verb Tenses

Use the **present tense** to talk about an action that happens now or happens often. Use the **past tense** to talk about an action that already happened. If you use two or more verbs in the same sentence, they must all be in the same tense.

- **Present:** Archaeologists **search** for artifacts, **uncover** evidence, and **draw** conclusions.

  Past: In the 1960s, they **searched** for Camelot, **excavated** a hill, and **found** a hall.

The verbs **be** and **have** are irregular. They have special forms to show the past tense.

- **Present:** The story of Ambrosius **is** exciting.

  Past: Ambrosius **was** a real commander.

- **Present:** People **have** many ideas about Arthur.

  Past: In the legend, King Arthur **had** a palace.

In a list, all the verbs must be in the same tense.

  Past: Arthur **ruled** fairly and **was** a just king.

Oral Practice (1–5) Tell a partner about a hero in history. Use at least five past tense verbs, with three in one sentence.

Written Practice (6–10) Rewrite the paragraph. Correct the underlined verbs to reflect parallel structure.

Arthur <u>is</u> an ancient British king. Today, scientists still search for sites, <u>excavated</u> hills, and uncover ruins. In 1976, a group <u>study</u> a round table, found places for 25 people, and <u>argue</u> that it was Arthur's. But even then, other scientists <u>have</u> their doubts.

Language Development

Ask for and Give Information

Pair Talk Ask a partner questions about King Arthur. For example, *Why do people want King Arthur to be real?* Give information to support your answer.

Literary Analysis

Compare Character's Motives and Traits

Just as there are many ways to get to know someone new, there are many ways to get to know a character in a story. These include:

- **actions:** what the character does
- **dialogue:** what the character says
- **motives:** why the character says and does certain things
- **traits:** how you describe the character and what makes him or her unique.

Study how Kay's motives and traits are shown in "The Sword in the Stone":

Character Chart

Character	Kay
Actions	He takes the sword from Arthur and pretends that he got it from the stone.
Dialogue	"I have the sword from the stone. Therefore I must be King of England."
Motives	He wants to be king, even if he must lie to do it.
Traits	ambitious, dishonest

Talk with a partner about Kay. How does his motivation affect what he does next? What are the consequences of his actions? As you read on, see if your understanding of the character changes.

Then create **Character Charts** for Arthur, Sir Ector, and the nobles in the story. Compare the characters from the text and discuss how their motivations affect what will happen in the story.

Word Families

Word families are similar word forms related by meaning. While you read, a word may seem unfamiliar. But take a closer look. Sometimes, knowing the meaning of another member of a word family can help you understand the unfamiliar word.

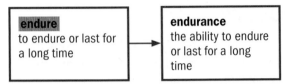

endure to endure or last for a long time	→	**endurance** the ability to endure or last for a long time

The word *skeptical* is related to a Key Vocabulary word from this unit. What do you think the word means, based on what you already know? Check the meaning in a dictionary.

Compare Visuals

Arthur Art Gallery Collect and display Arthurian images from books, magazines, and Web sites.

1 **Focus Your Search** Find two pieces of art that show an event or a character from the legend.

2 **Write Captions** Identify the images by title, artist, date created, and medium, such as painting or cartoon.

3 **Compare** Share the art that you found. Then compare how the different artists, times, or media affect how the art is presented.

▼ **Language and Learning Handbook,** page 702

▼ **Writing Handbook,** page 784

Write a Test Essay

An essay test may ask you to write a short response to a specific prompt.

1 **Unpack the Prompt** Underline key words that show what your response should include.

> **Writing Prompt**
>
> What makes a hero? In a short response, define the archetype of the hero. Then describe a character in traditional literature (such as the legend *Left Behind* from the Edge Library) whose heroic traits meet your definition.

2 **Plan Your Response** Choose a hero from traditional literature to write about. Then use a planning chart to organize your ideas in a clear way.

Hero	Ch'idzigyaak in *Left Behind*
Traits	courage and strength
Examples	She was brave in the face of certain death. Her determination helped her to survive.

3 **Draft** Organize your short response like this. Include specific ideas from your chart.

> **Short Response Organizer**
>
> To me, a hero is someone who is [name the traits here]. One person who is heroic is [hero's name]. He/She is [describe the hero].
>
> [Your hero] is heroic because he/she is [give trait]. For example, [give an example of trait].
> Another example of [your hero's] heroic traits is [give trait]. This was very important when [give examples of trait].
>
> In conclusion, [restate the main idea of how the person fits your idea of a hero.]

4 **Check Your Work** Reread your response. Ask:

- Do I address the writing prompt?
- Do I give examples to support my ideas?
- Do I use the correct past tense verbs?

▼ **Writing Handbook,** page 784

Inside an Airport

Each year, millions of people pass through airports on business trips and vacations. Hundreds of people work inside an airport to help these travelers reach their destinations safely.

Jobs in the Airport Industry

Most jobs in an airport require workers to have a high school diploma. Jobs that involve the safety of airline passengers also require on-the-job training and the completion of off-site classes and certification programs.

Job	Responsibilities	Education/Training Required
Ticket Agent 1	• Accepts tickets from passengers • Checks in passengers and baggage • Makes seat assignments • Answers customers' questions	• High school diploma • Company training programs and on-the-job training
Airport Security Screener 2	• Screens passengers, baggage, and cargo for dangerous or illegal objects using special equipment • Performs physical searches of passengers, baggage, and cargo	• High school diploma • Certification exam • On-the-job and off-site training
Air Traffic Controller 3	• Organizes flow of aircraft into and out of airport • Informs pilots of changes in weather conditions • Coordinates movement of air traffic to make sure planes stay a safe distance apart	• Pre-employment test • Three years of full-time work experience *or* • College degree • Twelve-week training program and two to four years of on-the-job training

Explore the Job Market

Find out what other jobs are available in the airport industry.

1. Visit the Web site of a major U.S. airline. Click the "Careers" link. Check for information about careers available at that airline, other than those listed above.
2. Create a chart listing three or four available jobs. Include job description, responsibilities, and necessary qualifications. Share the chart with your classmates. Discuss which career you think is most interesting and why. Save the information in a professional career portfolio.

myNGconnect.com

🌐 **Learn more about careers in the airport industry.**

🌐 **Download a form to evaluate whether you would like to work in this field.**

🔖 **Language and Learning Handbook,** page 702

Find Familiar Words

You probably know more words than you think. Even if you see a word you do not know, you have most likely seen part of the word before. **Word families** are words that share the same root word. For example, you may not know the word *dishonor*. However, you probably know the root word *honor*. You can then use your knowledge of prefixes and suffixes to get an idea of the word's meaning. The prefix *dis-* = *not* or *opposite*, so *dishonor* = *the loss of honor*.

Sometimes the root word has a slightly different spelling when a suffix is added. For example, *depth* = ~~deep~~ + pth. Usually, though, the spelling is close enough to recognize the root.

Use Word Families to Find Meaning

Work with another student to find familiar parts of words to figure out their meanings.

1. Copy the chart to the right onto a piece of paper.
2. Discuss what each word in the *honor* word family may mean.
3. Look up each word in the dictionary.
4. Think of other words in the *honor* word family and add them to the chart.

Words in the **Honor** Family	
honorable	honorary
dishonor	dishonorably

Put the Strategy to Use

When you come to a word you don't know, use this strategy to figure out its meaning:

1. Look for a root word.
2. Identify the other part or parts of the word.
3. Figure out how the part you know fits with the other part or parts.
4. Take a guess at the word's meaning.

TRY IT▸ Explore the words *untruthful* and *director*. Use a chart like the one below to define the word, determine the word family, and add additional words from the family. Look at the example for the word *dishonor*.

Word	Definition	Word Family	Additional Words
dishonor	the loss of honor	honor	honorable, honorary

▶ Reading Handbook, page 733

EQ   What Makes a Hero?
Consider the everyday heroes in your community.

Make a Connection

Anticipation Guide Write whether you agree or disagree with the statements. After reading the three selections, see if you still feel the same way.

ANTICIPATION GUIDE	Agree or Disagree
1. Anyone can become a hero in special circumstances.	_____
2. A hero is someone who is never afraid.	_____
3. Heroes are born, not made.	_____

Learn Key Vocabulary

Study the Words Pronounce each word and learn its meaning. You may also want to look up the definitions in the Glossary.

• Academic Vocabulary

Key Words	Examples
anxiety (ang-**zī**-ut-ē) noun ▶ pages 246, 250, 257	If people are nervous or worried they may show **anxiety**. I felt great **anxiety** before I started my new job. *Synonyms:* nervousness, worry; *Antonym:* calm
distracted (di-**strakt**-id) adjective ▶ page 241	A person who is **distracted** isn't able to pay attention. If you are **distracted** by too many activities after school, you may not have time for homework.
• **inherent** (in-**hair**-unt) adjective ▶ pages 255, 256, 257	Something that is **inherent** is something that you are born with. She has always had an **inherent** sense of courage.
• **inhibit** (in-**hib**-it) verb ▶ pages 255, 257	When something **inhibits** you, it stops or holds you back from doing something. I want to swim but my fear of water **inhibits** me. *Antonym:* open
prejudiced (**prej**-u-dist) adjective ▶ page 241	**Prejudiced** people form opinions about others without thinking about the facts. I try not to be **prejudiced** about people who are different than me. *Antonym:* open-minded
protest (**prō**-test) verb ▶ page 242	When you **protest** something, you say or show that you are against it. We **protest** the unfair way the students are being treated. *Synonym:* object; *Antonym:* agree with
• **survivor** (sur-**vī**-vur) noun ▶ page 253	A person who overcomes some hardship or manages to live through a disaster is a **survivor**. The police rescued the **survivors** of the car accident.
tragedy (**tra**-ju-dē) noun ▶ page 253	A **tragedy** is a terrible event or disaster. The earthquake **tragedy** left people homeless and many children became orphans. *Synonym:* misfortune; *Antonym:* good fortune

Practice the Words With a group, make a **Vocabulary Study Card** for each Key Vocabulary word. Write the word on the front of the card. On the back, write its definition, a synonym or antonym, and an example sentence. Take turns quizzing each other on the words.

Before Reading **A Job for Valentín**

short story by Judith Ortiz Cofer

Reading Strategies

• Plan and Monitor
• Determine Importance
▶ **Make Inferences**
• Ask Questions
• Make Connections
• Synthesize
• Visualize

Analyze Viewpoint

A narrator's **viewpoint** is what he or she thinks and says about a situation. The viewpoint may be different depending on who is telling the story and can affect the way information is shared. If a story is told by one of the characters, it is called **first-person point of view**. First-person narrators tell the story using pronouns such as *I* and *me*. The reader sees everything through just that one person's eyes, so the information is limited by what the narrator knows and may be affected by the character's thoughts, experiences, and attitudes.

Look Into the Text

The narrator uses first-person pronouns.

The narrator reports only what she sees, hears, and feels.

> Bob Dylan laughs and kisses my hand.
> "My Chiquita banana," he says, "stay true to me. Don't give my whereabouts out to the enemy. I shall return."
> "Bye," I say. I am such a great conversationalist, inside my own head.
> But he's already looking away. We have both heard familiar giggles. It's Clarissa and Anne. I see him waving to them, letting them get a view of his entire, glorious self. He looks over his shoulder at me and winks, covering all the bases.

The narrator's viewpoint affects the information shared.

Focus Strategy ▶ Make Inferences

When you read fiction, you add information from your own knowledge and experiences. Use this information to **make inferences** that help you understand the text.

HOW TO MAKE INFERENCES

Focus Strategy

1. **Record Information and Ideas** Note things the narrator thinks, says, or does in an **"I Read," "I Know," "And So" Chart**. Then think about your own experience. Finally, make an inference by combining the information and ideas.

2. **Connect the Inferences** By adding up your inferences, you can form big ideas about the narrator.

3. **Read On** If your inferences turn out to be wrong, revise them.

"I Read," "I Know," "And So" Chart

I Read …	I Know …	And So …
"I am such a great conversationalist, inside my own head." (page 244)	When I don't know what to say, I get all confused.	The narrator often feels confused when talking to people—especially boys.

Judith Ortiz Cofer
(1952–)

The women in my family were wonderful storytellers who infected me at a very early age with the desire to tell stories.

For Judith Ortiz Cofer, storytelling is a family tradition.

Judith Ortiz Cofer uses growing up in two different worlds as the inspiration for much of her work.

Born in Puerto Rico, Cofer and her family moved to the United States when she was two years old. Although most of her school years were spent in the United States, she often returned to Puerto Rico, where she lived with her grandmother, or *abuela*, who was a great storyteller. She remembers, "When my *abuela* sat us down to tell a story, we learned something from it, even though we always laughed."

Living in two countries led Cofer to see herself as "never quite belonging, because, after all, I speak English with a Spanish accent and Spanish with an American accent."

When Cofer began writing, her double heritage gave her many ideas for stories. In her fiction, Cofer deals with the challenges of moving between cultures and the possibility of using creativity to fit in. She says she often thinks about how being bilingual affects her understanding of the world. "Why do words have such an impact in one culture and not in another? Without being bilingual and bicultural I wouldn't know these things."

myNGconnect.com

◐ **Visit the author's Web site.**
◐ **Read a blog about being bilingual.**

A Job for Valentin

by Judith Ortiz Cofer

▲ Critical Viewing: Effect What details in this scene remind you of summer? How do you think this artist feels about the place shown in the painting?

 Comprehension Coach

A teenager gets a summer job, but it isn't perfect.
Read to find out what challenges come up.

I can't swim very well, mainly because my eyesight is

so bad. The minute I take off my glasses to get in the pool, everything becomes a blob of color and I freeze. But I **managed** to talk my way into a summer job at the city pool anyway. All I'll be doing is selling drinks and snacks, and I get to talk to everyone since the little **concession stand** faces the pool and the cute lifeguard, Bob Dylan Kalinowski. His mother named him after the old singer from the sixties. **1**

It's a good first day. Mrs. O'Brien says I don't need any training. I can run a cash register, I can **take inventory**, and I am very friendly with customers. The only thing I don't really like is that Mrs. O'Brien expects to be told if I ever see Bob Dylan messing around on the job.

"People's lives, *children's* lives, are in that young man's hands," she says. "Keep an eye on him, Teresa, and use that phone to call me, if you need to."

I say, "Yes, ma'am," even though I feel funny about being asked to spy on Bob Dylan. He's a senior at my school and, yeah, a crazy man sometimes. But if they gave him the job as a lifeguard, they ought to trust him to do it right.

That was the first day. Except for O'Brien asking me to fink on Bob Dylan, I had a good time. **2** And one thing nobody knows: I'm interested in Bob Dylan, too. He flirts with every girl in school. Even me.

The second day is bad news. A disaster. I got assigned a **"mentally challenged" assistant** by the city. There's a new program to put retarded people to work at simple jobs so they can make some money, learn a skill, or something.

I don't have anything against these handicapped people, but I don't

1 Viewpoint
Who is the narrator of this story? What do you find out about him or her?

2 Language
The narrator uses slang, or informal language. What are some examples of slang used in the story so far? What do the words and phrases mean?

In Other Words
managed was able
concession stand stall for selling snacks and drinks
take inventory keep a record of things to be sold

"mentally challenged" assistant helper with mental disabilities

want to spend my whole summer with one. Besides, how is it going to look to Bob Dylan and my other friends? They're not going to want to hang around the store with someone like that around. **3**

But there he is. My new *partner* is being led in by Mrs. O'Brien. He is Puerto Rican like me, thirty years old, and mildly challenged. He has the **IQ** of a third grader, she tells me. A *bright* third grader. And he is an artist. I can't help but wonder what others are going to say about this guy. It's hard enough to get people to believe that you have normal intelligence when you're Puerto Rican, and my "assistant" will be a living proof for prejudiced people.

"He's brought some of his creations," Mrs. O'Brien told me in a cheerful voice. "We're letting him sell them at the store. Valentín is gifted in art."

Old Valentín **has the posture of** a gorilla. And so much hair on his head and his arms that he is furry. And he's carrying a huge shopping bag that seems to drag him down. Great. Wonderful.

Mrs. O'Brien takes Valentín's hand and guides him in. But then she is distracted by yelling and running at poolside. No running is allowed. Bob Dylan is nowhere in sight. Mrs. O'Brien takes off for the pool, and I'm left facing Valentín. He's standing there like a big hairy child waiting to be told what to do.

> **I can't help but wonder what others are going to say about this guy.**

3 Make Inferences
How would you describe Teresa's relationships with her friends? Look for evidence to support your inferences.

Key Vocabulary
prejudiced *adj.*, ready to form opinions about others without thinking about the facts
distracted *adj.*, unable to pay attention

In Other Words
IQ level of intelligence
has the posture of stands like

Monitor Comprehension

Describe
What unexpected challenge does Teresa face at her new job?

Predict

Teresa and Valentín start working together. How do you think they will get along?

"I'm Terry," I say. Nothing. He doesn't even look up. This is going to be even worse than I thought.

"What's your name?" I say it real slow and loud.

"*Soy* Valentín," he says in Spanish. His deep voice surprises me. Then he starts taking out these little animals. They are strange-looking things, all tan in color. They are made from rubber bands. Valentín takes them out one at a time: a giraffe, a teddy bear, an elephant, a dog, a fish, all kinds of animals. They are really kind of cute.

"Do you speak English?" I ask him. I can speak Spanish, but not that good.

"*Sí*," Valentín says. **4**

This is going to be even worse than I thought.

He arranges his rubber-band **menagerie** on the counter, taking a long time to decide what goes next to what. Mrs. O'Brien walks in looking very upset.

"Teresa, does he do this often?"

I know she's talking about Bob Dylan taking off.

"This is only my second day here," I **protest**. And maybe my last, I think.

"Teresa, someone could drown while that boy is away from **his post**."

I don't say anything. **5** I was not hired to spy on Bob Dylan. Although I do plan to keep my eyes on him a lot for my own reasons. He's fun to watch.

Mrs. O'Brien turns to Valentín. "I see you two have met. Teresa, it is Valentín's goal to sell his art and make enough money to buy himself a bicycle. He lives in a **group home** on Green Street and he wants to have

4 Make Inferences
What can you tell about Valentín from this first conversation? Read on to see if your inference is correct.

5 Make Inferences
Why doesn't Teresa answer Mrs. O'Brien? Use what you already know to make sense of her silence.

Key Vocabulary
protest *v.*, to say or show that you are against something

In Other Words
Soy I am (in Spanish)
Sí Yes (in Spanish)
menagerie collection of animals
his post his station or place (the lifeguard's chair)
group home home for people with special needs

transportation so that he can get a job in town. I think it's a wonderful idea, don't you?"

Mrs. O'Brien sighs, looking out at the pool again. Bob Dylan is back in his lifeguard chair. She says again, "Teresa, if anything goes wrong, use that phone there to call me. At five I'll come get Valentín. See if you can get your friends to buy his art. It's for a **worthy cause**!" 6

Valentín watches her leave the store with the look of a child left at school for the first time. His hands are **trembling** a little as he continues to line up his little rubber-band zoo.

Valentín moves around me cautiously. He acts like he's afraid I'm going to bite his head off. It's really annoying. He shows me a bunch of thick rubber bands. He smiles.

"*Trabajo*," he says. Work. It is his job.

"Yes. Make more ***animales***," I say. That will keep him busy and out of my way. I watch him wind a rubber band around his index finger into a tight little ball. He does it so slowly and carefully that it makes me want to scream.

6 **Viewpoint**
You see other characters from Teresa's point of view. What impression does she give you of Mrs. O'Brien?

Studies for a portrait, Federico Barocci (1526–1612)/Scala/Ministero per i Beni e le Attività culturali/Art Resource, NY

Critical Viewing: Effect ▶
Why might the artist have chosen to use hands as the focus of this art? What feeling do these hands express?

In Other Words

worthy cause good goal
trembling shaking
animales animals (in Spanish)

Monitor Comprehension

Confirm Prediction
Was your prediction right? Why or why not?

Predict

Teresa is unhappy with Valentín and wants him out of her way. Do you think her attitude will change?

Bob Dylan's deep voice startles me.

"Hey, is that your new boyfriend there, Terry? I thought you were my girl." He pulls himself up onto the counter. The muscles on his arms are awesome.

"Hi." I cannot think of anything else to say.

"Give me **an o. j. on the rocks**, little mama. And introduce me to *el hombre* over there. And what are these . . . ?"

"This is Valentín." I point to him, and Valentín quickly ducks his head like someone's going to punish him. "He makes them to sell."

Bob Dylan picks up the fish and makes his eyes cross. I have to laugh.

Valentín stops what he's doing to stare at us. He looks afraid. But he doesn't move. I take the fish back and put it in its place on the counter.

"VERY NICE, MY MAN!" Bob Dylan says, too loud. Valentín drops the little ball, and it bounces and rolls under the counter. I can tell that he's upset.

Bob Dylan laughs and kisses my hand.

"My Chiquita banana," he says, "stay true to me. Don't **give my whereabouts out to the enemy**. I shall return."

"Bye," I say. I am **such a great conversationalist**, inside my own head.

But he's already looking away. We have both heard familiar giggles. It's Clarissa and Anne. I see him waving to them, letting them get a view of his entire, glorious self. He looks over his shoulder at me and winks, covering all the bases. **7**

Valentín has finally retrieved his rubber ball out from behind some cartons. He looks a little embarrassed, and I guess that he's really been hiding.

"Valentín, let me show you how to pour drinks. Those two girls will

7 Make Inferences
Use evidence from the text and what you already know about people to describe the type of person Bob Dylan is.

In Other Words
an o.j. on the rocks orange juice with ice
el hombre the man (in Spanish)
give my whereabouts out to the enemy tell the boss where I am
such a great conversationalist so good at talking to people

order a root beer and a diet cola. I'll do the cola and then you do the root beer. Watch."

He watches me very closely, following my hands with his eyes.

"Hey, Terry. How's the job going?" Clarissa booms out. I hear a crash behind me and see that Valentín has dropped ice all over everything. Both my friends start giggling. Valentín's turning red from his neck up. Embarrassed. [8]

"This is Valentín," I say, not smiling. "He's helping me out, and he's selling these so that he can buy himself a bicycle."

"You make them yourself, right?" Anne is trying to be nice.

"**Dos dólares**," Valentín says to Anne.

Anne takes the giraffe and hands me a five-dollar bill. Valentín follows me to the cash register while I make change. I hand him two one-dollar bills. He smiles at me. Then he starts to pick up the ice cubes he dropped, one by one.

When I turn back to my friends, they are both grinning.

"Well, Teresa, you're going to have a *very interesting* summer," Clarissa says, looking pointedly in Valentín's direction.

Soon I get a crowd of kids all at once, so I have to get to work. Valentín really **gets the hang of** pouring drinks, but I'm hoping that he'll get tired of the work and quit. After we fill the orders, he sits down and closes his eyes. It must be tough to have to work so hard at every little thing you do. He takes the rubber-band ball he's been working on and starts a tail on it. But he just smiles at me and a peaceful look **settles over** his face. I guess that means he's happy. [9]

8 **Make Inferences**
What do most people think about Valentín? From what you have read, do you think they are right? Explain.

◁ **Critical Viewing: Design**
What animal does this rubber-band art represent? Tell what clues you used to identify it.

9 **Viewpoint**
How does Teresa feel about Valentín now? How do you know?

In Other Words
Dos dólares Two dollars (in Spanish)
gets the hang of becomes good at
settles over appears on

Everything settles into a routine for Valentín and me for the next few days. The only problem I have is Mrs. O'Brien, who calls me a lot to ask me about him and about Bob Dylan. I just say everything's okay, even though Bob Dylan has **zeroed in on** an older girl, and he's disappeared with her at least once that I know of. I found out after she left her two-year-old son alone, asleep on a lounge chair. When he woke up, he started crying so loud that I had to go out there and get him before someone called Mrs. O'Brien. I brought him into the store, and it was instant friendship between the kid and Valentín. The two of them played with the rubber-band animals until his mother, Maricela Nuñez, finally showed up looking like she'd been having a good time. I was furious.

"Is Pablito having fun with his new friend?" she says in a fake-friendly voice. She showed no <mark>anxiety</mark> over the fact that the kid could have drowned or just walked off into traffic while she was fooling around with Bob Dylan. **10**

"Look at them," she says, laughing at the way Pablito and Valentín are lining up the animals back on the counter. "I think Pablito is teaching the dummy a few things."

Valentín looks at me with such a hurt **expression** that I honestly had to count to five or I would have punched her. I lift

... the kid could have drowned ...

Pablito over the counter to his mother. "Maricela, you are the dummy. You listen up. If we hadn't been here to take care of your son, someone would have called **the family services** and they would have taken him away—which may be the best thing for him anyway." **11**

She **storms off** and behind me I hear soft laughter. It's Valentín, apparently amusing himself with his new toy.

---

10 Viewpoint
What does Teresa assume about Maricela? Do you think Teresa's comments about her are reliable? Explain.

11 Make Inferences
Think about Teresa's reaction to Maricela's remarks. How does this help you understand Teresa?

Monitor Comprehension

Confirm Prediction
Did your prediction turn out to be correct? What did you learn about Teresa and Valentín?

Key Vocabulary
<mark>anxiety</mark> *n.*, nervousness, worry

In Other Words
zeroed in on concentrated his attention on
expression look on his face
the family services an agency for helping and checking on families
storms off walks away angrily

Predict

Think about the different things you have learned so far about Teresa and Valentín. What will they do if there's a problem?

By Friday afternoon, Maricela has been here every afternoon, and she, Pablito, and Bob Dylan leave together. Valentín is getting good at pouring drinks and cleaning up, so at least the job is easier. He works with his rubber bands and only talks when Maricela brings Pablito over for a snack.

Valentín is teaching Pablito the names of his animals in Spanish. "*Elefante, caballo, oso*"—Valentín points to each animal. Then Pablito tries to repeat the words. This makes Valentín smile big. I guess it makes him feel good to be able to teach someone else something for a change. 🔢

It's almost closing time on Friday when we hear a kind of little scream. It doesn't last very long, so I almost ignore it. I think it's some kid out in the street, since the pool is closed for the day. But Valentín has come out with a really scared look on his face. He is trying to see something in the water. I don't see anything, but Valentín is flapping his arms and stuttering "Pa . . . Pa . . . Pa . . ." His eyes look terrified. I start thinking he may be about to **have a fit** or something.

"What is it, Valentín? What do you see out there?"

"Pablito. Pablito." He is trembling so much I fear he's going to go out of control. But I don't have time to think. The water *is* moving, and it could be the kid. I don't see Bob Dylan anywhere.

"Get Mrs. O'Brien!" I yell to Valentín. But he **is frozen on the spot**.

When I get to the pool, I see the kid is **thrashing wildly** near the edge. He's really scared and his kicking is only forcing him away toward the deep water. I jump into the shallow end and start walking in his direction. I cannot tell how deep it will be, and I feel scared that I may drown, but I have to reach Pablito. I keep going toward his voice.

🔢 **Viewpoint**
As a narrator, Teresa can only describe what she sees and thinks. What does she guess about Valentín?

In Other Words
Elefante, caballo, oso Elephant, horse, bear (in Spanish)
have a fit lose control
is frozen on the spot can't move
thrashing wildly moving his arms violently

But I feel that I'm moving in slow motion, so I finally dive into the water. My glasses get wet and I can't see, so I throw them off, which makes it worse. I can't see a thing. I start screaming for help. I'm sinking and pushing up, stretching my hands in front of me to feel his body. **13**

Just when I feel that my lungs are going to burst, I feel Pablito and pull him up. I hear splashing behind me, and it's Valentín heading for us. He carries Pablito out of the pool in one arm and pulls me out with his free hand.

When I take him from Valentín's arms, his body **feels limp**, so I put him on the ground and push on his tiny chest until water comes out. Soon he is coughing and crying. **14**

Then I see Bob Dylan and Maricela run up. Bob Dylan takes over while I run to call Mrs. O'Brien and the emergency rescue. Maricela **goes nuts** until Valentín guides her to a bench, where they sit holding hands until the ambulance drives up. She and Bob Dylan ride with Pablito to the hospital.

It's all over in minutes, but I feel like it's days while Valentín and I sit in Mrs. O'Brien's office, waiting for word from the hospital. I also expect to get fired for not **reporting** that Bob Dylan was not at his post. She comes in in a very solemn mood, and I look over at Valentín, who is

13 Viewpoint
What does Teresa tell the reader about her feelings that an outsider couldn't know?

14 Make Inferences
What do Teresa's actions with Pablito tell you about her?

Reaching Hands, 2007, Jerry Lindemann. Digital illustration.

▲ **Critical Viewing: Effect** Explain how this image reflects how Teresa feels when she is underwater.

In Other Words
feels limp is weak and lifeless
goes nuts is very upset (slang)
reporting telling someone

wringing his hands. I know he's only thinking of Pablito, and I feel a little guilty for worrying about myself so much.

"The boy is going to be fine," Mrs. O'Brien says, "thanks to both of you."

Then she does something that really surprises me. She kisses me on the forehead. She **fishes** my glasses out of her skirt pocket.

Then she goes over to Valentín.

"Valentín, you did a very good thing today. You and Teresa saved a little boy's life. You are a hero. Do you understand me?"

"*Sí*," Valentín says. But I'm not sure about his English, so I start to translate: "Valentín, *ella dice que eres un héroe*."

"I know," Valentín says, and smiles real big.

"You speak English?" I cannot believe he's fooled me into thinking that he can barely speak a few words of Spanish, and here he understands two languages.

> # It's all over in minutes, but I feel like it's days . . .

"*Sí*," Valentín answers, and laughs his funny quiet laugh. **15**

Mrs. O'Brien looks at Valentín in a motherly way. "Valentín, how would you like to keep your job here year-round?"

Valentín slowly glances over at me, as if asking me what I think. He can communicate in total silence, and I'm learning his language.

"When the pool closes at the end of the summer, we are going to ask you, and yes, Teresa too, to come work in my office. We have many things that you both can do, such as helping out with after-school programs and **supervising** the playground. Are you interested?"

Valentín looks at me for an answer again. I can tell that we have

15 Make Inferences
Why do you think Valentín hasn't spoken English before? How does this change what you think about Valentín?

In Other Words
wringing his hands twisting his hands together
fishes pulls
ella dice que eres un héroe she says that you are a hero (in Spanish)
supervising watching over

to take the job as partners or he won't do it. I sneeze loudly and he practically falls out of his chair. Really, he's the most nervous human being I've ever met. I see that I'm going to have to put up with him in this new job, too. I don't think anyone else would have the patience. 16 ❖

16 **Make Inferences**
Why does Teresa say she takes the job? Why do you think she takes it?

ANALYZE A Job for Valentín

1. **Explain** What qualities does Valentín have? Think about his friendship with Pablito and his behavior during the accident. Include examples from the text to support your answer.

2. **Vocabulary** Why does Teresa experience anxiety when she learns that she is to work with Valentín? Do her fears come true? Explain.

3. **Analyze Viewpoint** Make a chart to compare the way Teresa describes Valentín at the beginning of the story with her ideas about him after the accident. How does Teresa's viewpoint affect the way we see him?

Before	After
"Valentín has the posture of a gorilla." (page 241)	"He can communicate in total silence, and I'm learning his language." (page 249)

4. **Focus Strategy Make Inferences** Find a passage where you as a reader understand something that the narrator doesn't realize. Tell a partner how you used evidence to make your inference.

▶ **Return to the Text**
Reread and Write Is Valentín a hero? What does the story say about how challenged individuals can become everyday heroes? Write your opinion in a paragraph. Include two or three examples from the story to support your ideas.

Hero

by Mariah Carey

There's a hero,
  if you look inside your heart.
You don't have to be afraid,
  of what you are.

There's an answer,
  if you reach into your soul.
And the sorrow that you know,
  will melt away.

Chorus
And then a hero comes along,
  with the strength to carry on.
And you cast your fears aside,
  and you know you can survive.
So when you feel like hope is gone,
  look inside you and be strong.
And you'll finally see the truth,
  that a hero lies in you.

It's a long road,
  when you face the world alone.
No one reaches out a hand
  for you to hold.

You can find love,
  if you search within yourself.
And the emptiness you felt,
  will disappear.

[Chorus]

Lord knows,
  dreams are hard to follow.
But don't let anyone
  tear them away.

Hold on,
  there will be tomorrow.
In time
  you'll find the way.

[Chorus]
…that a hero lies in you…
…that a hero lies in you…

BEFORE READING **In the Heart of a Hero**

feature article by Johnny Dwyer

Reading Strategies

· Plan and Monitor
· Determine Importance
▶ **Make Inferences**
· Ask Questions
· Make Connections
· Synthesize
· Visualize

Analyze Structure: Feature Article

A **feature article**, or human interest story, is different from a **news story**, which reports just the facts about a current event. Feature articles go into more detail about real people and their emotions, opinions, and problems. There is often something dramatic or surprising about the stories feature articles tell.

Look Into the Text

These facts tell who, what, where, and when.

> On a sunny Sunday last month, the glass-like surface of Lake George, in New York's Adirondack Mountains, was dotted with boats. Just before three, the afternoon's tranquility shattered. The *Ethan Allen*, a tour boat carrying almost fifty senior citizens, tipped crazily. Within thirty seconds, it had capsized and its passengers were struggling for their lives.
>
> Brian Hart was on the lake that day, paddling a canoe with Brianna, his youngest daughter, and three of her cousins. When he saw the boat overturn, he didn't hesitate, immediately calling 911—"Get to the lake real quick"—even as he headed for the nearest dock. There, he dropped the girls and phoned his brother, Eric. Two minutes later, Eric, 42, and his son, E.J., scooped up Brian in the family fishing boat, and the three of them sped to the scene.

The emotional hook pulls in the reader.

A quotation gives the exact words of a witness.

How does the author use words and phrases that give a dramatic feeling to the story?

Focus Strategy ▶ Make Inferences

When you read nonfiction, like a feature article, you add information from your own knowledge and experiences. Use this information to **make inferences** that help you understand the text.

HOW TO MAKE INFERENCES

Focus Strategy

1. Think about what happens in the selection. Compare this to your own experiences, and record your thoughts in an **Inference Chart**.

2. Make an inference about a person or event in the selection.

3. Keep updating your ideas and inferences as you read.

Inference Chart

Think about what happened.	A boat turned over in the lake.
Think about what most people would do.	Most would call for help.
Think about what the hero did.	He called 911 and his family. Then they all jumped into a boat and sped to the scene.
My inference about the hero: Hart cares about other people and is a quick and clear thinker.	

In the Heart of a Hero

by Johnny Dwyer

Connect Across Texts
In "A Job for Valentín," the hero is not who we expect. This feature article explores why some people act as heroes when others cannot.

On a sunny Sunday last month, the glass-like surface of Lake George, in New York's Adirondack Mountains, was dotted with boats. Just before three, the afternoon's **tranquility shattered**. The *Ethan Allen*, a tour boat carrying almost fifty senior citizens, tipped crazily. Within thirty seconds, it had **capsized** and its passengers were struggling for their lives. **1**

Brian Hart was on the lake that day, paddling a canoe with Brianna, his youngest daughter, and three of her cousins. When he saw the boat overturn, he didn't hesitate, immediately calling 911—"Get to the lake real quick"—even as he headed for the nearest dock. There, he dropped the girls and phoned his brother, Eric. Two minutes later, Eric, 42, and his son, E.J., scooped up Brian in the family fishing boat, and the three of them sped to the scene. Brian and Eric dove straight in and started **hauling survivors** onto life preservers, seat cushions—anything that would float. When other boats arrived, the Hart brothers **hoisted** victims into them for nearly half an hour.

Onlookers gasped in horror, watching the **tragedy unfold**; many

1 Feature Article
What information in the opening paragraph tells who, what, when, and where?

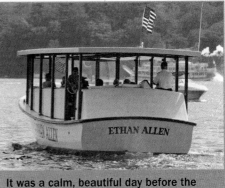
It was a calm, beautiful day before the *Ethan Allen* capsized on Oct. 2, 2005.

Key Vocabulary
- **survivor** *n.*, person who lives through a hardship or disaster
- **tragedy** *n.*, terrible disaster

In Other Words
tranquility shattered calmness was wrecked
capsized turned upside down
hauling pulling
hoisted lifted
unfold happen over time

called for help. Those who saw the brothers' actions surely wondered at their uncommon courage: *Do they know what they're doing? Will they be able to save anyone? Will they die trying?* Later—over dinner, perhaps, or just before they drifted off to sleep—these **bystanders** likely pondered another set of questions both simple and complex: *What makes a hero? Why do some of us dive in when others simply cannot?*

In Brian's case, the answer may lie in his **biological makeup**. "I guess my boys were always fearless," says Donald Hart, 71, Brian and Eric's father. "Not only that day, but in childhood, with the motorbikes, snowmobiles. I wasn't surprised they would do something like that."

Dr. Frank Farley, a psychologist who has studied heroic behavior, says that something literally in a hero's **DNA** may contribute to brave actions. Heroes, he says, often have what he calls "Big T"—or thrill-seeking, risk-taking personalities. "They're not satisfied with normal levels of **stimulation**, so they seek out more of it," says Farley. **2**

New York

Recovery divers prepare to search for the *Ethan Allen* after it sank in Lake George, New York, in October 2005.

▲ **Interpret the Visuals** What additional information do the map and caption give you about the photo?

2 Feature Article
What ideas does the quotation support?

In Other Words
bystanders people who stood by and watched
biological makeup nature
DNA genetic code
stimulation excitement

When Brian plunged into the lake and swam into the crowd of struggling passengers, he remained calm and focused. "Situational heroes," as Farley refers to regular people who **rise to the occasion** in emergencies, simply aren't **inhibited** by "**uncertainty**, which is one of the biggest sources of human fear." 3

Brian had something else, too, that **complemented** his **inherent** fearlessness: his comfort in the water, particularly this water. As a boy, he'd learned to paddle and fish on Lake George, and later scuba dived and piloted his first motorboat there. "We always used to horse around, brothers grabbing you in the water. I'm sure a lot of people who came [to the scene] in boats didn't jump in because they didn't have the comfort level I had."

And beyond that? Perhaps empathy. 4

Is it **a coincidence** that this man who dove into the water had once been rescued on Lake George? In 1978, Brian was thrown from a motorboat. He floated dazed—but uninjured—for fifteen minutes until a boater fished him out.

Donald wonders about the circumstances of rescues—a man with the heart of a hero finding himself in the right place at the right time—and **speculates on** what his boys might have taken from hearing about his own experience: "Something like this, it's a series of events that happens, and if there's

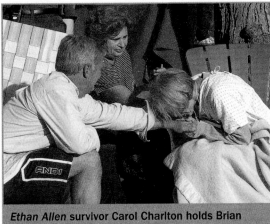

Ethan Allen survivor Carol Charlton holds Brian Hart's hand.

3 **Access Vocabulary**
Why are people like Brian called "situational heroes"? Look for root words and context clues for ideas.

4 **Make Inferences**
Use what you already know about rescuers. Do they "dive in" with the same kind of attitude presented here?

Key Vocabulary
- **inhibit** *v.*, to stop or hold a person back from doing something
- **inherent** *adj.*, natural, basic

In Other Words
rise to the occasion do more than they thought they could
uncertainty doubt
complemented added to
a coincidence just chance
speculates on guesses about

a lesson, maybe it's that there's an outside source, a God above."

Whether **Providence** or circumstance, when Hart, exhausted, finally returned to shore, Brianna asked, "Did you save everybody?"

"Yes," he lied. She's 8 years old; there's time yet for truth.

"Daddy, why did you go back?" she asked.

"The people needed my help."

For some—for heroes—it's as simple as that. 5 ❖

5 Make Inferences
Think about Hart's answers to his daughter's questions. What does it tell you about him?

ANALYZE In the Heart of a Hero

1. **Recall and Interpret** Would Brian Hart consider himself to be a hero? Include examples of his words and actions to explain your answer.

2. **Vocabulary** What information in the article supports the idea that heroic behavior is inherent? Do you agree? Explain.

3. **Analyze Structure: Feature Article** Review the article and identify several ways that the author gives information. Explain the information and tell how it helps you understand the selection.

4. **Focus Strategy Make Inferences** Why would the author include the word *heart* in the title of this article? Explain your reasons to a partner.

↩ Return to the Text

Reread and Write What explanations does the author give for heroic behavior? Write a paragraph to describe the explanation that you agree with most. Support your opinion with examples from the text.

In Other Words
Providence God's plan

What Makes a Hero?

Critical Thinking

1. **Analyze** Review the **Anticipation Guide** on page 236 and explain whether you still agree or disagree with the statements after reading the selections. Use examples from the selections to support your answer.

2. **Interpret** Do you think Valentín fits the description of a "situational hero" who acts bravely in emergencies? Review the definition on page 255, then give reasons to support your answers to a group.

3. **Compare** The author of "In the Heart of a Hero" compares people with **inherent** courage to others who are **inhibited** by fear and **anxiety**. How would Brian Hart, Teresa, and Valentín respond to this idea? Support your ideas with details from the texts.

4. **Imagine** Think of the scene that takes place between Mrs. O'Brien and Bob Dylan after the pool accident. Choose a partner and role-play the scene, using what you have learned about both characters in the story.

5. **Synthesize** Imagine Brian Hart wasn't successful in saving anyone. Would he still be a hero? Include details from the article to help you explain your answer.

Write About Literature

Comparison In "A Job for Valentín," the hero is not who we expect. The unlikely hero is a common archetype that appears often in traditional literature. Think about the two old women in the legend *Left Behind* or the characters in a familiar fable, such as "The Tortoise and the Hare." Write a paragraph explaining how the "heroes" in these stories are like Valentín.

Key Vocabulary Review

Oral Review Work with a partner. Use these words to complete the paragraph.

anxiety	inhibited	survivor
distracted	prejudiced	tragedy
inherent	protest	

My friend believes that heroes are different from everyone else. He says that ordinary people get too __(1)__ by the excitement around them to think clearly and help. He thinks that their __(2)__, or nervousness, will cause more harm than good. Some people may want to help, but they are too __(3)__ by their own doubts to step forward and help. However, I disagree and __(4)__ this idea because it gives a negative opinion that is __(5)__ against everyday people. Just ask a __(6)__, like Pablito, who lived through an accident. I bet he'd say that although some people are born with the __(7)__ qualities of a hero, almost anyone can be trained to help in a disaster or __(8)__.

Writing Application Recall a time when you felt anxiety. Write a paragraph about the situation that uses at least three Key Vocabulary words.

Read with Ease: Expression

Assess your reading fluency with the passage in the Reading Handbook, p. 758. Then complete the self-check below.

1. My expression did/did not sound natural.

2. My words correct per minute: _____

Use Verb Tenses

Regular past tense verbs end in **-ed**. Irregular verbs have special forms to show the past tense.

Present: Lifeguards **do** an important job.

Past: In the story, Valentín **did** something heroic.

Here are some common irregular verbs.

Present	Past	Present	Past
am, is, are	was, were	make	made
do, does	did	say	said
eat	ate	see	saw
have, has	had	write	wrote

Use the **future tense** to tell about an action that has not yet happened. Use **will** before the main verb to tell about the future. If there is more than one main verb in a sentence, use **will** only before the first verb.

Present: Valentín **works** at the pool, **makes** toys, and **saves** a child.

Future: Later, Valentín **will buy** a bike, **ride** to the pool, and **work** in the office.

Oral Practice (1–5) With a partner, find one or two examples of parallel structure on pages 243–245. Tell the tense of each verb.

Written Practice (6–8) Rewrite each sentence. Change the verb to the tense shown in parentheses.

6. Valentín showed his animal art. (present)
7. He makes animals and works. (future)
8. Teresa and Valentín did a good job. (future)

Engage in Discussion

Group Talk Discuss and list Teresa and Vaentín's strengths and faults. Make ground rules for the discussion and decide what to add to your list.

Multiple Themes in a Text

A **theme** is a main idea or lesson in a story. The author uses characters, dialogue, and plot events to make a general statement that is true about people or life.

Many stories include more than one theme. Study these examples from "A Job for Valentín":

Theme	Examples
Don't judge others by their appearance.	• Teresa assumes that Valentín can't speak English, even though he says he can. • People treat Valentín as if he doesn't understand anything, although he does.
Even ordinary people can be heroes.	• Teresa overcomes her fears to try to save Pablito. • Valentín jumps into the water to save Pablito and Teresa.

With a partner, add at least two more themes that you can find from the story. Include evidence and examples that support your ideas.

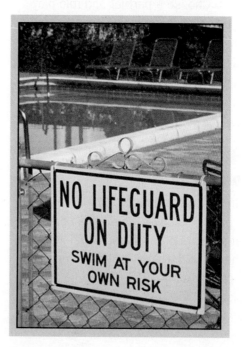

Borrowed Words

Borrowed words come into one language from another language. Dictionaries tell you the language or languages a word has been borrowed from. For example, the entry below describes the word *banana*. It originated in Africa. Portuguese borrowed it; then Spanish borrowed it from Portuguese. English borrowed it from one of those languages.

> **banana** [< Sp or Pg; Sp from Pg of African origin]

Use a print or online dictionary, glossary, or thesaurus to trace the source of these borrowed words: *chic, patio, chocolate.*

Profile

Historical Hero Who are the historical heroes in your community? Research local sources, such as newspaper archives, regional histories, and Internet articles to identify local, historical heroes.

myNGconnect.com

🌐 **Find biographies of courageous people in history.**

Write a profile of your local hero that you can share with your class. Be sure to use specific details to describe the person and explain why he or she is a hero.

🐾 **Language and Learning Handbook**, page 702

🐾 **Writing Handbook**, page 784

Voice and Style

Think about the **voice and style** of your work. Ask:

- **Voice:** Is my voice clear and interesting? Does it express who I am and what I think?

- **Style:** Is the style right for my audience and purpose? How can I improve my word choice and sentence structure?

Just OK

> **News Report for Older Readers**
> Brian Hart is a total hero in New York. Brian saw a boat tip over. He jumped right in. He helped a lot of people.

Much Better

> **News Report for Older Readers**
> Brian Hart is one of New York's many heroes. When Hart saw the *Ethan Allen* tour boat capsize in Lake George, he immediately dove in and pulled many of the elderly passengers to safety. Thanks to Hart, there were many more survivors of this dreadful tragedy.

Read the paragraph below. Talk with a partner about what the writer can do to improve the voice and style.

> **Personal Narrative for Your Classmates**
> I think that a hero is someone who tries to help others. Even when it's dangerous. I was three years old when I fell in the pool. No one noticed except for my neighbor, Nia. She dove in and pulled me out. She made sure I was breathing. She said that she couldn't just stand by and do nothing. Nia is my biggest hero. I wouldn't even be here without her.

After you make your revisions, use a chart to evaluate the voice and style.

The voice and style...	Yes	Not Yet
are clear and interesting		
don't change too much		
are right for the audience and purpose		
show great word choices		
show sentence variety		

🐾 **Writing Handbook**, page 784

Panel Discussion

A panel discussion offers the perfect forum to explore different sides of a topic, such as "What makes a hero?" In a panel discussion, each group member focuses on a different part of a given topic. After the panelists present their views, the moderator opens the discussion to the audience. Here is how to plan and conduct a panel discussion:

1. Plan Your Panel Discussion

Discuss the question "What makes a hero?" with a group of four or five classmates. Then do the following:

- Set the ground rules your group will follow to reach agreements and make decisions. Then, decide on an approach. For example, each panelist might give his or her own definition of a hero.
- Choose a moderator, who will introduce the speakers and take questions from the audience afterward.
- Have each panelist write notes on his or her main idea about heroism with supporting examples and other information.

myNGconnect.com

🔊 **Download the rubric.**

How can practicing and providing feedback to your group improve your panel discussion?

2. Practice Your Panel Discussion

Work together to make the presentations go as smoothly as possible.

- Make sure each panelist speaks within the amount of time given.
- Practice speaking without your notes.
- Provide positive feedback about how the panelists explain their ideas.
- Ask questions and make comments to clarify and elaborate on others' ideas.

3. Hold Your Panel Discussion

Have the panelists sit at a long table, with the moderator in the center, in front of the audience. Keep your presentation interesting and lively by doing the following:

- Make eye contact with your audience.
- Speak clearly and loudly enough for the audience to understand.
- Look at your notes if you need to, but try to use them as little as possible.
- Listen attentively and respectfully to the rest of your group, so that you can help answer the audience's questions.

4. Discuss and Rate the Panel Discussion

Use the rubric to discuss and rate the discussions, including your own.

Panel Discussion Rubric

Scale	Content of Panel Discussion	Participants' Preparation	Participants' Delivery
3 Great	• Thoroughly covered the topic with many good examples • Taught me something and made me think	• Seemed to know a lot about the topic • Presentation was well coordinated	• All spoke clearly and were easy to follow • Responded to questions and comments very well
2 Good	• Gave good coverage of the topic with some good examples • Had some effect on my ideas	• Seemed somewhat well-informed about the topic • Presentation was fairly well coordinated	• Most spoke clearly and were usually easy to follow • Responded to questions and comments fairly well
1 Needs Work	• Gave little coverage of the topic • Didn't make me think and didn't influence my opinions	• Did not seem familiar with subject • Presentation was disorganized	• Most were hard to understand • Did not respond to questions and comments well

DO IT ▶ When your group is finished preparing and practicing, hold your panel discussion, and keep it lively!

❤ Language and Learning Handbook, page 702

EQ **What Makes a Hero?**
Explore how heroes change the world around them.

Make a Connection

Brainstorming List the names of people who have helped break down barriers in such fields as sports, education, and employment. Work in small groups to explore how these heroes have changed the world around them.

Learn Key Vocabulary

Study the Words Pronounce each word and learn its meaning. You may also want to look up the definitions in the Glossary.

• Academic Vocabulary

Key Words	Examples
• **authority** (u-**thor**-u-tē) noun ▶ pages 282, 285, 287	People in **authority** can have power over others. Government leaders have the **authority** to make laws. *Synonym:* power
boycott (**boi**-kot) noun ▶ page 266	A **boycott** is a way to punish an organization by refusing to use its product or service. We will hold a **boycott** of the company's products because we don't like the way it treats its workers.
compassion (kum-**pash**-un) noun ▶ pages 274, 277	When you show **compassion** for others, you care deeply about their suffering and troubles. I felt **compassion** for the sad, lonely girl. *Synonym:* pity; *Antonym:* unkindness
desperately (**des**-pur-it-lē) adverb ▶ page 270	When you act **desperately**, you make a big effort because you feel a great need. The doctors worked **desperately** to save the child's life. *Synonym:* frantically; *Antonym:* calmly
• **discrimination** (di-skrim-u-**nā**-shun) noun ▶ pages 266, 284, 285	**Discrimination** is treating people in a particular group unfairly. Racism is a form of **discrimination** that focuses on a person's skin color.
• **persistent** (pur-**sis**-tunt) adjective ▶ page 282	If you are **persistent**, you keep trying in spite of challenges. The **persistent** woman kept asking for help even though everyone ignored her.
provoke (pru-**vōk**) verb ▶ page 283	To **provoke** means to force a person or thing to act. We hope our protests against the unfair law will **provoke** the government to make a change. *Synonym:* stir up
segregation (seg-ri-**ga**-shun) noun ▶ page 280	**Segregation** keeps some people apart from others because of race. In the past, **segregation** didn't allow black and white children to go to the same schools. *Synonyms:* divided, separated; *Antonym:* united

Practice the Words Create a **Vocabulary Study Card** for each Key Vocabulary word. Write the word on one side. On the other side, write an example sentence for the word, but leave the word out. Then take turns quizzing a partner.

Vocabulary Study Card

_____
_____ authority _____
_____
_____

Police officers, judges, and mayors are some people who have _____ in a community.

BEFORE READING **The Woman in the Snow**

short story by Patricia C. McKissack

Reading Strategies

- Plan and Monitor
- Determine Importance
▶ **Make Inferences**
- Ask Questions
- Make Connections
- Synthesize
- Visualize

Analyze Viewpoint

The **third-person omniscient** narrator tells the story as an outsider. Because the narrator is omniscient, or all-knowing, he or she can reveal what the characters think and feel, include information that the characters do not know, and describe past and future events.

Although a third-person narrator does not reflect the thoughts and feelings of one character, he or she may reflect a cultural **viewpoint**. For example, this story is set in the South, before African Americans had equal rights. The culture affects how the narrator shares information with the reader.

Look Into the Text

The narrator knows how characters feel and what they think.

Why does the narrator explain who Billy is?

> Grady Bishop had just been hired as a driver for Metro Bus Service. When he put on the gray uniform and boarded his bus, nothing mattered, not his obesity, not his poor education, not growing up the eleventh child of the town drunk. Driving gave him power. And power mattered.
>
> One cold November afternoon Grady clocked in for the three-to-eleven shift. "You've got Hall tonight," Billy, the route manager, said matter-of-factly.

What does the narrator tell about Grady that other characters might not know?

Focus Strategy ▶ Make Inferences

As you read, look for new ideas and information that the author provides. Use this to build on the inferences you have already made.

HOW TO MAKE INFERENCES

Focus Strategy

1. As you read, make an inference about a character or an event in the story. Record this in an **Inference Chart**.

2. Add information from the story that supports your inferences.

3. Add ideas and information from the text to form a new, revised inference.

Inference Chart

Initial Inference	Grady Bishop doesn't feel good about himself.
New Information	"Driving gave him power."
New Inference	Having power makes him feel good.

Patricia C. McKissack
(1944–)

Patricia McKissack says, "It's quite interesting how your youth shapes how you think in the future."

Patricia C. McKissack was born in Nashville, Tennessee, in the 1940s, and lived through both segregation and the civil rights movement. Although the outside world might have been challenging, her family life was full of wonderful stories and poems. "Long before I became a writer," she says, "I was a listener and an observer."

Her family gathered on the porch during the hot summer evenings of her childhood. They took turns telling ghost stories, reciting poetry, or remembering their own younger days. The ghost stories took place during the "dark-thirty," the thirty minutes just before darkness falls, and they made a big impression on McKissack.

As an adult, McKissack felt drawn to create stories that have their roots in the experiences of her youth, both good and bad. "I write because there's a need to have books for, by, and about the African American experience and how we helped to develop this country," she has said.

McKissack has written over 100 books, many of which deal with the lives and contributions of African Americans. "The Woman in the Snow" first appeared in her award-winning book *The Dark-Thirty: Southern Tales of the Supernatural*, which draws on the African American oral traditions she grew up with.

myNGconnect.com

🌐 Listen to a traditional African American story.
🌐 Explore the world of oral traditions.

The Woman in the Snow

by Patricia C. McKissack

Standing Mother and Child, 1978, Elizabeth Catlett. Bronze sculpture with bronze patina, © Photograph by David Finn.

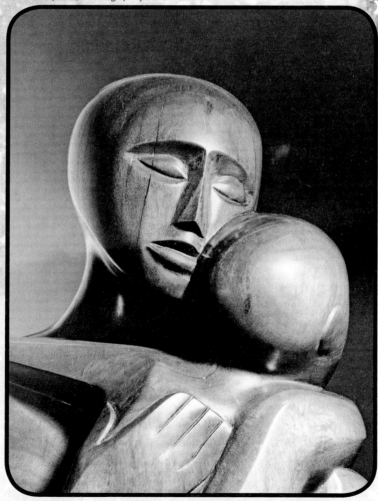

▲ **Critical Viewing: Effect** How does the artist's use of shapes and expression create a mood for this image?

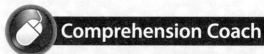
Comprehension Coach

The year-long Montgomery, Alabama, bus **boycott** in 1955–56 was a **pivotal** event in the **American civil rights movement**. Blacks refused to ride the buses until their demand of fair and equal treatment for all **fare-paying passengers** was met. Today the right to sit anywhere on a public bus may seem a small victory over racism and **discrimination**. But that single issue changed the lives of African Americans everywhere. After the successful boycott in Montgomery, blacks in other cities challenged bus companies, demanding not only the right to sit wherever they chose but also employment opportunities for black bus drivers. Many cities had their own "bus" stories. **1** Some are in history books, but this story is best enjoyed by the fireplace on the night of the first snowfall.

Pools of Defiance, Colin Bootman, 2001. Oil on canvas, private collection. The Bridgeman Art Library.

△ **Critical Viewing: Effect** Why do you think the artist chose to show these men and women from the back? What emotions does the artist want the viewer to feel?

1 **Make Inferences**
The author has provided you with necessary background information. What might this "bus story" be about? Form an initial inference.

Key Vocabulary
boycott *n.,* punishment of an organization by refusing to use its services
• **discrimination** *n.,* unfair treatment of people in a particular group

In Other Words
pivotal very important, key
American civil rights movement effort to gain equal rights for all Americans
fare-paying passengers riders who paid to ride the bus

Find out what happens when a bus driver goes down a lonely road one snowy night.

Grady Bishop had just been hired as a driver for Metro Bus Service. When he put on the gray uniform and **boarded** his bus, nothing mattered, not his **obesity**, not his poor education, not growing up the eleventh child of the town drunk. Driving gave him power. And power mattered. **2**

One cold November afternoon Grady **clocked in** for the three-to-eleven shift. "You've got Hall tonight," Billy, the route manager, said **matter-of-factly**.

"The Blackbird Express." Grady didn't care who knew about his nickname for the route. "Not again." He turned around, slapping his hat against his leg.

"Try the *Hall Street Express*," Billy corrected Grady, then hurried on, cutting their conversation short. "Snow's predicted. Try to keep on schedule, but if it gets too bad out there, forget it. Come on in."

Grady popped a fresh stick of gum into his mouth. "You're the boss. But tell me. How am I s'posed to stay on schedule? What do those people care about time?"

Most Metro drivers didn't like the Hall Street assignment in the best weather, because the road twisted and turned back on itself like a retreating snake. When slick with ice and snow, it was even more **hazardous**. But Grady had his own reason for hating the route. The Hall Street Express serviced black **domestics** who rode out to the fashionable west end in the mornings and back down to the lower east side in the evenings.

"You know I can't stand being a chauffeur for a bunch of colored maids and cooks," he **groused**. **3**

2 Viewpoint
What does the omniscient narrator tell about the driver's character in the first paragraph?

3 Make Inferences
What does this sentence add to your initial inference of what the story is about?

In Other Words
boarded got on
obesity heavy weight
clocked in got to work
matter-of-factly without emotion
hazardous dangerous

domestics maids or cooks
groused complained

The Woman in the Snow **267**

"Take it or leave it," Billy said, walking away in disgust.

Grady started to say something but thought better of it. He was still **on probation**, lucky even to have a job, especially during such hard times.

Snow had already begun to fall when Grady pulled out of the garage at 3:01. It fell steadily all afternoon, creating a frosted wonderland on the **manicured** lawns that lined West Hall. But by nightfall the winding, twisting, and bending street was a driver's nightmare.

The temperature **plummeted**, too, adding a new challenge to the mounting snow. "Hurry up! Hurry up! I can't wait all day," Grady snapped at the boarding passengers. "Get to the back of the bus," he **hustled** them on impatiently. "You people know the rules."

The regulars recognized Grady, but except for a few muffled groans they paid **their fares** and rode **in sullen silence** out to the east side loop.

"Auntie! Now, just why are you taking your own good time getting off this bus?" Grady grumbled at the last passenger.

The woman struggled down the wet, slippery steps. At the bottom she looked over her shoulder. Her dark face held no clue of any emotion. "Auntie? Did you really call me *Auntie?*" she said, laughing **sarcastically**. "Well, well, well! I never knew

> **4 Make Inferences**
> The narrator describes the bus route in detail. How might the setting affect the plot of the story?

The Country Girl, Lester J. Ambrose (1879–1949), Oil on canvas, private collection.

▲ **Critical Viewing: Design** How would you describe this image? Are there features in the image that tell you how the passengers feel? Explain.

In Other Words

on probation in danger of being fired if he did anything wrong
manicured carefully and evenly trimmed
plummeted dropped quickly
hustled hurried

their fares the price for the bus ride
in sullen silence angrily but quietly
sarcastically in a rude way

my brother had a white son." And she hurried away, chuckling.

Grady's face flushed with surprise and anger. He shouted out the door, "Don't get **uppity** with me! Y'all know *Auntie* is what we call all you old colored women." Furious, he slammed the door against the bitter cold. He shook his head in disgust. "It's a waste of time trying to be nice," he told himself. **5**

But one look out the window made Grady refocus his attention to a more immediate problem. The weather had worsened. He checked his watch. It was a little past nine. Remarkably, he was still on schedule, but that didn't matter. He had decided to close down the route and take the bus in.

> ## "It's a waste of time trying to be nice," he told himself.

That's when his headlights picked up the **figure** of a woman running in the snow, without a hat, gloves, or boots. Although she'd pulled a shawl over the lightweight jacket and **flimsy** dress she was wearing, her clothing offered very little protection against the **elements**. As she pressed forward against the driving snow and wind, Grady saw that the woman was very young, no more than twenty. And she was clutching something close to her body. What was it? Then Grady saw the baby, a small bundle wrapped in a faded pink blanket. **6**

"These people," Grady sighed, opening the door. The woman stumbled up the steps, escaping the wind that **mercilessly** ripped at her **petite frame**.

"Look here. I've closed down the route. I'm taking the bus in."

In big gulping sobs the woman laid her story before him. "I need help, please. My husband's gone to Memphis looking for work. Our baby's

5 Viewpoint
Explain how Grady's remarks reflect a cultural viewpoint about African Americans. Use specific examples.

6 Make Inferences
Think about the inferences you have made about Grady so far. What do you think he will do?

In Other Words
uppity too bold
figure shape
flimsy thin and poorly made
elements weather

mercilessly cruelly, harshly
petite frame slim body

sick, real sick. She needs to get to the hospital. I know she'll die if I don't get help."

"Well, I got to go by the hospital on the way back to the garage. You can ride that far." Grady nodded for her to pay. The woman looked at the floor. "Well? Pay up and get on to the back of the bus so I can get out of here."

"I—I don't have the fare," she said, quickly adding, "but if you let me ride, I promise to bring it to you in the morning."

"**Give an inch, y'all want a mile.** You know the rules. No money, no ride!" **7**

"Oh, please!" the young woman cried. "Feel her little head. It's so hot." She held out the baby to him. Grady **recoiled**.

Desperately the woman looked for something to bargain with. "Here," she said, taking off her wedding ring. "Take this. It's gold. But please don't make me get off this bus."

He opened the door. The winds howled savagely. "Please," the woman begged.

"Go on home, now. You young gals get **hysterical** over a little fever. Nothing. It'll be fine in the morning." As he shut the door the last sounds he heard were the mother's sobs, the baby's wail, and the moaning wind.

Grady **dismissed** the incident until the next morning, when he read that it had been a record snowfall. His eyes were drawn to a small article about a colored woman and child found frozen to death on Hall Street. No one seemed to know where the woman was going or why. No one but Grady.

"That gal should have done like I told her and gone on home," he said, turning to the comics.

7 Make Inferences
Is Grady's answer consistent with the inferences you have made about him so far? Why or why not? Add the new information to your Inference Chart.

Monitor Comprehension

Explain
What does Grady discover happened on Hall Street that snowy night?

Key Vocabulary
desperately *adv.*, frantically, with great need

In Other Words
Give an inch, y'all want a mile. If I do you a small favor, you will want even more.
recoiled pulled back in disgust
hysterical very upset
dismissed forgot about

Predict
A year later Grady is assigned to the same bus route. What do you think will happen?

It was exactly one year later, on the anniversary of the record snowstorm, that Grady was assigned the Hall Street Express again. Just as before, a storm heaped several inches of snow onto the city in a matter of hours, making driving extremely hazardous. **8**

By nightfall Grady decided to close the route. But just as he was making the turnaround at the east side loop, his headlight picked up a woman running in the snow—the same woman he'd seen the previous year. Death hadn't **altered** her desperation.

8 Language
What words and phrases give clues about what might happen next?

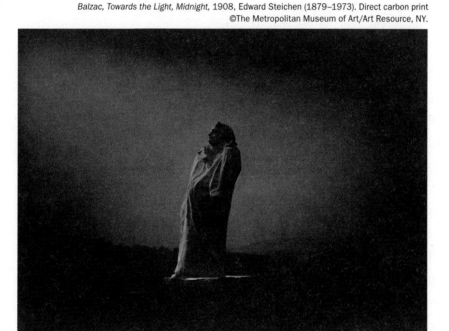

Balzac, Towards the Light, Midnight, 1908, Edward Steichen (1879–1973). Direct carbon print
©The Metropolitan Museum of Art/Art Resource, NY.

△ Critical Viewing: Effect How does this image express the feeling and mood of the story?

In Other Words
altered changed

Still holding on to the blanketed baby, the small-framed woman **pathetically** struggled to reach the bus.

Grady closed his eyes but couldn't keep them shut. She was still coming, but from where? The answer was too horrible to consider, so he chose to let his mind find a more reasonable explanation. **9** From some dark corner of his childhood he heard his father's voice, **slurred** by alcohol, **mocking** him. *It ain't the same woman, dummy. You know how they all look alike!*

Grady remembered his father with bitterness and swore at the thought of him. This *was* the same woman, Grady argued with his father's memory, taking no comfort in being right. Grady watched the woman's movements breathlessly as she stepped out of the headlight beam and approached the door. She stood outside the door waiting . . . waiting.

The gray coldness of Fear slipped into the driver's seat. Grady sucked air into his lungs in big gulps, feeling out of control. Fear moved his foot to the gas pedal, **careening** the bus out into oncoming traffic. Headlights. A truck. Fear made Grady hit the brakes. The back of the bus went into a sliding spin, slamming into a tree. Grady's stomach crushed against the steering wheel, **rupturing** his liver and spleen. *You've really done it now, lunkhead.* As he drifted into the final darkness, he heard a woman's sobs, a baby **wailing**—or was it just the wind? **10**

> ## She stood outside the door waiting . . . waiting.

In Other Words
pathetically pitifully
slurred made unclear
mocking making fun of
careening wildly swaying, tilting

rupturing cutting a hole in
wailing crying loudly

9 Make Inferences
What clues tell you that these events are unusual?

10 Viewpoint
How would this part of the story be different if the narrator had been the truck driver, rather than a third-person omniscient narrator? Explain.

Monitor Comprehension

Confirm Prediction
Was your prediction accurate? Explain whether it met or didn't meet your expectations.

Predict

What will happen now that a new driver has been assigned to the Hall Street Express?

Twenty-five years later, Ray Hammond, a war hero with two years of college, became the first black driver Metro hired. A lot of things had happened during those two and a half decades to pave the way for Ray's new job. The military had **integrated its forces** during the Korean War. In 1954 the Supreme Court had ruled that **segregated** schools were unequal. And one by one, unfair laws were being challenged by civil rights groups all over the South. Ray had watched the Montgomery bus boycott with interest, especially the boycott's leader, Dr. Martin Luther King, Jr.

Ray soon found out that progress on the day-to-day level can be painfully slow. Ray was given the Hall Street Express.

"The white drivers call my route the Blackbird Express," Ray told his wife. "I'm the first driver to be given that route as a permanent assignment. The others wouldn't take it." **11**

"What more did you expect?" his wife answered, tying his bow tie. "Just do your best so it'll be easier for the ones who come behind you."

In November, Ray worked the three-to-eleven shift. "Snow's predicted," the route manager barked one afternoon. "Close it down if it gets bad out there, Ray."

The last shift on the Hall Street Express.

Since he was a boy, Ray had heard the story of the haunting of that bus route. Every first snowfall passengers and drivers testified that they'd seen the ghost of Eula Mae Daniels clutching her baby as she ran through the snow.

"Good luck with Eula Mae tonight," one of the drivers said, **snickering**.

"I didn't know white folk believed in **haints**," Ray shot back.

But parked at the east side loop, staring into the swirling snow mixed

11 Make Inferences
Think about the information on this page. What initial inferences can you make about Ray Hammond?

In Other Words

integrated its forces allowed soldiers of different races to serve together
segregated racially separate
snickering laughing meanly
haints spirits or ghosts

with ice, Ray felt tingly, as if he were dangerously close to an electrical charge. He'd just made up his mind to close down the route and head back to the garage when he saw her. Every hair on his head stood on end.

He wished her away, but she kept coming. He tried to think, but his thoughts were jumbled and confused. He wanted to look away, but curiosity fixed his gaze on the advancing horror.

Just as the old porch stories had described her, Eula Mae Daniels was a small-framed woman frozen forever in youth. "So young," Ray whispered. "Could be my Carolyn in a few more years." He watched as the ghost came around to the doors. She was out there, waiting in the cold. Ray heard the baby crying. "**There but for the grace of God goes one of mine**," he said, <mark>compassion</mark> overruling his fear. "Nobody deserves to be left out in this weather. Ghost or not, she deserves better." And he swung open the doors.

The woman had form but **no substance**. Ray could see the snow falling *through* her. He pushed fear aside. "Come on, honey, get out of the cold," Ray said, waving her on board. 🔟2️⃣

Eula Mae stood stony still, looking up at Ray with dark, questioning eyes. The driver understood. He'd seen that look before, not from a dead woman but from plenty of his passengers. "It's okay. I'm for real. Ray Hammond, the first Negro to drive for Metro. Come on, now, get on," he coaxed her gently.

Eula Mae moved soundlessly up the steps. She held the infant to her body. Ray couldn't remember ever feeling so cold, not even the Christmas he'd spent in a Korean **foxhole**. He'd seen so much death, but never anything like this. 🔟3️⃣

The ghost mother consoled her crying baby. Then with her head bowed she told her story in quick bursts of sorrow, just as she had twenty-five years earlier. "My husband is in Memphis looking for

12 Viewpoint
How does the narrator explain the difference between Ray's and Grady's responses to the woman?

13 Viewpoint
What does the narrator tell you about Ray's past? Why do you think the narrator chooses to share this information?

Key Vocabulary
compassion *n.*, care for the suffering and troubles of others

In Other Words
There but for the grace of God goes one of mine That could be someone in my family
no substance no body or flesh
foxhole hole that protects a soldier in battle

work. Our baby is sick. She'll die if I don't get help."

"First off," said Ray. "Hold your head up. **You got no cause for shame.**"

"I don't have any money," she said. "But if you let me ride, I promise to bring it to you tomorrow. I promise."

Ray sighed deeply. "The rule book says no money, no ride. But the book doesn't say a word about a personal loan." He took a handful of change out of his pocket, fished around for a dime, and dropped it into the pay box. "**You're all paid up.** Now, go sit yourself down while I try to get this bus back to town."

Eula Mae started to the back of the bus.

"No you don't," Ray stopped her. "You don't have to sit in the back anymore. You can sit right up front."

The ghost woman moved to a seat closer, but still not too close up front. The baby **fretted**. The young mother comforted her as best she could.

> The rule book says no money, no ride.

They rode in silence for a while. Ray checked in the rearview mirror every now and then. She gave no reflection, but when he looked over his shoulder, she was there, all right. "Nobody will ever believe this," he mumbled. "*I* don't believe it. 🔢14

"Things have gotten much better since you've been . . . away," he said, wishing immediately that he hadn't opened his mouth. Still he couldn't—or wouldn't—stop talking.

"I owe this job to a little woman just about your size named Mrs. Rosa Parks. Down in Montgomery, Alabama, one day, Mrs. Parks refused to give up a seat she'd paid for just because she was a colored woman."

14 Make Inferences
Think about the new information on these pages. What more can you infer about Ray Hammond?

In Other Words
You got no cause for shame. You have no reason to be embarrassed.
You're all paid up. Your ticket is paid for.
fretted cried and moved around

Eula Mae sat **motionless**. There was no way of telling if she had heard or not. Ray kept talking. "Well, they arrested her. So the colored people decided to boycott the buses. Nobody rode for over a year. Walked everywhere, formed **carpools**, or just didn't go, rather than ride a bus. The man who led the boycott was named Reverend King. Smart man. We're sure to hear more about him in the future. . . . You still with me?" Ray looked around. Yes, she was there. The baby had quieted. It was much warmer on the bus now.

Slowly Ray **inched along** the icy road, holding the bus steady, trying to keep the back wheels from racing out of control. "Where was I?" he continued. "Oh yeah, things changed after that Montgomery bus boycott. This job opened up. More changes are on the way. Get this: They got an Irish Catholic running for President. Now, what do you think of that?"

About that time Ray pulled the bus over at Seventeenth Street. The lights at Gale Hospital sent a welcome message to those in need on such a frosty night. "This is it." 15

Eula Mae raised her head. "You're a kind man," she said. "Thank you."

Ray opened the door. The night air **gusted** up the steps and **nipped** at his ankles. Soundlessly, Eula Mae stepped off the bus with her baby.

"Excuse me," Ray called politely. "About the bus fare. No need for you to make a special trip . . . back. Consider it a gift."

He thought he saw Eula Mae Daniels smile as she vanished into the swirling snow, never to be seen again. ❖

15 **Make Inferences**
Review the inferences you have made about Ray. Are his actions consistent? Explain.

In Other Words
motionless without moving
carpools groups to share rides
inched along moved a little at a time on
gusted blew strongly
nipped felt like little bites

Historical Background
The Reverend Martin Luther King Jr., organized the Montgomery bus boycott and eventually became the leader of the civil rights movement. He was shot and killed in 1968.

ANALYZE The Woman in the Snow

1. **Recall and Interpret** What happens to Eula Mae after her bus ride with Ray? What is responsible for the change? Use details from the text to support your answer.

2. **Vocabulary** How does Grady's background explain his lack of **compassion**? Does he show any signs of feeling guilty or sorry? Explain.

3. **Analyze Viewpoint** Talk with a partner about how having a third-person omniscient narrator affects the story. How would the story be different if the author had written it using a first-person narrator?

4. **Focus Strategy Make Inferences** Choose a passage that you think suggests the story's message, or theme. Explain to a partner the theme you infer and the details that support your inference.

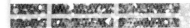 Return to the Text

Reread and Write What qualities make Ray Hammond a hero? Reread the story and find at least two details from the text. Write your opinion.

BEFORE READING Rosa Parks

magazine profile and poem by Rita Dove

Reading Strategies

- Plan and Monitor
- Determine Importance
- ▶ **Make Inferences**
- Ask Questions
- Make Connections
- Synthesize
- Visualize

Analyze Development of Ideas

A **magazine profile** is a short article that tells about one aspect, or part, of a person's life. Authors usually tell events in time order and use facts, quotations, and other details to develop important ideas about the person's life. In this profile of Rosa Parks, the writer focuses on Parks's role in the civil rights movement.

Look Into the Text

The profile shows the sequence of events with time order words.

> Parks was not the first to be detained for this offense. Eight months earlier, Claudette Colvin, 15, refused to give up her seat and was arrested. And then in October, a young woman named Mary Louise Smith was arrested. Smith paid the fine and was released.
>
> Six weeks later, the time was ripe. The facts, rubbed shiny for retelling, are these: On December 1, 1955, Mrs. Rosa Parks, seamstress for a department store, boarded the Cleveland Avenue bus. She took a seat in the fifth row—the first row of the "Colored Section." … [H]ad her work in the N.A.A.C.P. sharpened her sensibilities so that she knew what to do—or more precisely, what not to do: Don't frown, don't struggle, don't shout, don't pay the fine?

What facts develop the idea in the first sentence?

What names, events, and details do these two paragraphs include?

Focus Strategy ▶ Make Inferences

As you read, ask yourself why the author includes certain details. Use your own knowledge and experience to **make inferences** about Parks and the civil rights movement.

HOW TO MAKE INFERENCES

Focus Strategy

Use an **Inference Map** to collect information from the key points of the text and your own experience. Then use that information to make an inference.

1. Jot down an important idea from the text.
2. Identify details that support that idea.
3. Add what you know about the idea from your own experience.
4. Combine the information to make an inference.

Inference Map

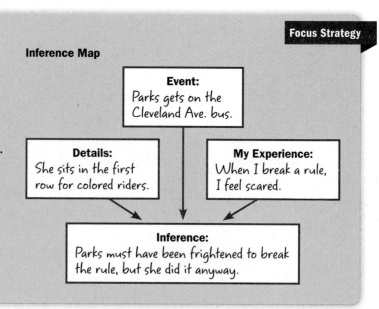

Connect Across Texts

In "The Woman in the Snow," an ordinary person makes an extraordinary choice. Read this profile about another person's extraordinary choice.

Rosa Parks

by Rita Dove

"Our mistreatment was just not right, and I was tired of it."

—Rosa Parks

We know the story.

One December evening, a woman left work and boarded a bus for home. She was tired; her feet ached. But this was Montgomery, Alabama, in 1955. As the bus became crowded, the woman, a black woman, was ordered to give up her seat to a white passenger. When she remained seated, that simple decision eventually led to the end of **segregation** in the South, **ushering in** a new era of the civil rights movement. **1**

This, anyway, was the story I had heard from the time I was curious enough to **eavesdrop on** adult conversations. I was 3 years old when a white bus driver warned Rosa Parks, "Well, I'm going to have you arrested," and she replied, "You may go on and do so." As a child, I didn't understand how doing nothing had caused so much activity, but I recognized the **template**: David slaying the giant Goliath, or the boy who saved his village by sticking his finger in the **dike**. **2** And perhaps it is the **lure of fairy-tale retribution** that colors the lens we look back through. Parks was 42 years old when she refused to give up her seat. She has insisted that her feet were not aching; she was, by her own testimony, no more tired than usual. And she did not plan her fateful act: "I did not get on the bus to get arrested," she has said. "I got on the bus to go home."

Montgomery's segregation laws were complex. Blacks were required to pay their fare to the driver, then get off and reboard through the back door. Sometimes the bus would drive off before the paid-up customers made it to the back entrance. If the white section was full and another white customer entered, blacks were

In Alabama in the 1950s, by law, if the white section of the bus was full, blacks had to give up their seats to allow whites to sit down.

Key Vocabulary
segregation *n.*, the act of separating or keeping apart

In Other Words
ushering in introducing, beginning
eavesdrop on listen secretly to
template pattern, model
dike barrier to prevent flooding
lure of fairy-tale retribution appeal of evil people being punished

required to give up their seats and move farther to the back. A black person was not even allowed to sit across the aisle from whites. At the time, two-thirds of the bus riders in Montgomery were black. ▣

Parks was not the first to be **detained for this offense**. Eight months earlier, Claudette Colvin, 15, refused to give up her seat and was arrested. And then in October, a young woman named Mary Louise Smith was arrested. Smith paid the fine and was released.

Six weeks later, the time was ripe. The facts, rubbed shiny for retelling, are these: On December 1, 1955, Mrs. Rosa Parks, **seamstress** for a department store, boarded the Cleveland Avenue bus. She took a seat in the fifth row—the first row of the "Colored Section." The driver was the same one who had put her off a bus twelve years earlier for refusing to get off and reboard through the back door. ("He was still mean-looking," she has said.) Did that make her stubborn? Or had her work in the N.A.A.C.P. sharpened her **sensibilities** so that she knew what to do—or more precisely, what not to do: Don't frown, don't struggle, don't shout, don't pay the fine?

She was arrested on a Thursday; **bail was posted** by Clifford Durr, the white lawyer whose wife had employed Parks as a seamstress.

After her first arrest in December, 1955, Rosa Parks was arrested again in February, 1956. This time the charge was helping organize a bus boycott.

▣ **Make Inferences**
The author says the laws "were complex." How else could the laws be described?

Monitor Comprehension

Explain
Why was Rosa Parks arrested?

In Other Words
detained for this offense held in jail for breaking this law
seamstress a woman who sewed clothes
sensibilities awareness and understanding
bail was posted money to release Rosa from jail was paid

Cultural Background
The **National Association for the Advancement of Colored People** (N.A.A.C.P.) was founded in 1909. Over the years, it has fought for the civil rights of schoolchildren, leaders, and ordinary men and women.

That evening, after talking it over with her mother and husband, Rosa Parks agreed to challenge Montgomery's segregation laws. Thirty-five thousand handbills were distributed to all black schools the next morning. The message was simple:

"We are . . . asking every Negro to stay off the buses Monday in protest of the arrest and trial . . . You can afford to stay out of school for one day. If you work, take a cab, or walk. But please, children and grown-ups, don't ride the bus at all on Monday. Please stay off the buses Monday."

Monday came. Rain threatened, yet the black population of Montgomery stayed off the buses, either walking or catching one of the black cabs stopping at every **municipal** bus stop for ten cents per customer—standard bus fare. Meanwhile, Parks was scheduled to appear in court. As she made her way through the throngs at the courthouse, a girl in the crowd caught sight of her and cried out, "Oh, she's so sweet. They've messed with the wrong one now!"

Yes, indeed. The trial lasted thirty minutes, with the expected **conviction and penalty**. That afternoon, the Montgomery Improvement Association was formed. The members elected as their president a **relative newcomer to** Montgomery, the young minister of Dexter Avenue Baptist Church: the Reverend Martin Luther King Jr. That evening, addressing a crowd, King declared in that ringing voice millions the world over would soon thrill to: "There comes a time that people get tired." When he was finished, Parks stood up so the audience could see her. She did not speak; there was no need to. Here I am, her silence said, among you. **4**

And she has been with us ever since—a **persistent** symbol of human dignity in the face of brutal **authority**. The famous **U.P.I.** photo (actually taken more than a year later, on December 21, 1956, the day

4 Development of Ideas
Dove gives facts and comments about Rosa Parks's life. What does she add to help you understand Parks's actions?

Key Vocabulary
- **persistent** *adj.*, continuing in spite of challenges, unchanging
- **authority** *n.*, people with power over others

In Other Words
municipal city
conviction and penalty decision and punishment
relative newcomer to person who hadn't lived long in
U.P.I. United Press International (a news agency)

Montgomery's public transportation system was legally integrated) is a study of calm strength. She is looking out the bus window, her hands resting in the folds of her checked dress. **5** A white man sits calmly in the row behind her. That clear profile, the neat eyeglasses and sensible coat—she could have been my mother, anybody's favorite aunt. History is often portrayed **as a grand opera, all baritone intrigues and tenor heroics**. Some of the most **tumultuous** events, however, have been **provoked** by **serendipity**—the assassination of an archduke spawned World War I, a kicked-over lantern may have sparked the Great Chicago

5 Make Inferences
What do Rosa Parks's actions tell you about her?

Rosa

How she sat there,
the time right inside a place
so wrong it was ready.

That trim name with
its dream of a bench
to rest on. Her sensible coat.

Doing nothing was the doing:
the clean flame of her gaze
carved by a camera flash.

How she stood up
when they bent down to retrieve
her purse. That courtesy. **6**

—Rita Dove

6 Make Inferences
Study the poem. What words or phrases can you use from it to describe this picture?

Monitor Comprehension

Explain
How did blacks in Montgomery show that they supported the fight against segregation?

Key Vocabulary
provoke *v.*, to force a person or thing to act

In Other Words
as a grand opera, all baritone intrigues and tenor heroics as if it were an exciting drama played out on a stage
tumultuous wild and noisy
serendipity a lucky accident

Fire. One cannot help wondering what role Martin Luther King Jr. would have played in the civil rights movement if the opportunity had not presented itself that first evening of the boycott—if Rosa Parks had chosen a row farther back from the outset, or if she had missed the bus altogether. Today, it is the modesty of Rosa Parks's example that **sustains us**. It is no less than the belief in the power of the individual, that **cornerstone** of the American Dream, that she inspires, along with the hope that all of us—even the least of us—could be that brave, that **serenely** human, when crunch time comes. ❖

ANALYZE Rosa Parks

1. **Recall and Interpret** According to author Rita Dove, what is it about Rosa Parks's actions that makes them important? Include evidence from the profile to support your ideas.

2. **Vocabulary** How were segregated buses an example of **discrimination** against African Americans?

3. **Analyze Development of Ideas** What facts does Dove use to develop ideas about Rosa Parks and her achievement?

4. **Focus Strategy Make Inferences** List a few of the inferences you made while reading the profile. Which ones changed as you gained new information about Parks?

Return to the Text

Reread and Write When Rita Dove was a child, she heard about Rosa Parks as a traditional hero. Write a letter to young Rita Dove to explain why Rosa Parks's protest on the bus was so important to so many people. Use at least two examples from the selection.

About the Writer

Rita Dove (1952–) is one of the best-known modern American poets. She has published seven books of poetry as well as a novel and a short story collection. In 1993 she became the youngest person ever to be named the Poet Laureate of the United States.

In Other Words
sustains us gives us hope and support
cornerstone foundation
serenely calmly

EQ What Makes a Hero?

Critical Thinking

1. **Interpret** In the poem "Rosa," Rita Dove writes, "Doing nothing was the doing." Tell what you think she means. Reread the profile to find details that support your interpretation.

EQ 2. **Analyze** What conditions in people's lives can lead them to show **discrimination** against a particular group of people? Find details in both texts that suggest explanations.

3. **Compare** Identify the different types of narrators in "The Sword in the Stone," "A Job for Valentín," and "The Woman in the Snow." How does the choice of a narrator affect each story's character, plot, and tone? How does it influence the story's credibility? Explain.

4. **Speculate** How is Eula Mae's experience similar to Rosa Parks's? How would Parks respond to a driver like Grady Bishop?

EQ 5. **Synthesize** How does the traditional heroism of Rosa Parks affect Ray Hammond? Discuss how one individual's courage or heroism can influence the world.

Write About Literature

Theme Statement What do both selections say about the struggle to overcome prejudice? Write a brief statement of their shared theme and support it with examples from both texts. Use a **T Chart** to keep track of your examples.

T Chart

Overcoming Prejudice	
"The Woman in the Snow"	"Rosa Parks"

Key Vocabulary Review

Oral Review Work with a partner. Use these words to complete the paragraph.

authority	desperately	provoke
boycott	discrimination	segregation
compassion	persistent	

During the Montgomery bus __(1)__ , African American passengers refused to use city buses. This fought the __(2)__ laws that kept black passengers separated from white passengers. After this protest, the civil rights movement went on to fight racial __(3)__ that treated people differently in schools and jobs. They were determined and __(4)__ , working for long, hard years to improve the lives of __(5)__ poor people who felt sad and helpless. These leaders felt great __(6)__ for others in need. They did not hesitate to __(7)__ the anger of the leaders in __(8)__ who wished to keep things the way they were.

Writing Application Write a paragraph about when you think it is right to challenge people in **authority**. Use at least two Key Vocabulary words in your paragraph.

Read with Ease: Intonation

Assess your reading fluency with the passage in the Reading Handbook, p. 759. Then complete the self-check below.

1. My intonation did/did not sound natural.

2. My words correct per minute: _____

Use Subject and Object Pronouns

Pronouns can take the place of nouns. Use a **subject pronoun** to replace a subject. Use an **object pronoun** to replace an object.

Rosa Parks started **the boycott**.
subject   object

She started **it** in 1955.

Subject Pronouns	I, you, he, she, it, we, they
Object Pronouns	me, you, him, her, it, us, them

Oral Practice (1–5) With a partner, change the underlined subject or object to the correct pronoun.

1. <u>Rosa Parks</u> boarded the bus. (She/Her)
2. She rode <u>the bus</u> every day. (it/them)
3. The passengers paid <u>the driver</u>. (he/him)
4. <u>My friends and I</u> admire Rosa Parks. (We/Us)
5. She inspires <u>my friends and me</u>. (them/us)

Written Practice (6–9) Fix four more pronouns and rewrite the paragraph below. Then add a sentence about the boycott.

They

 The laws were unjust. ~~Them~~ treated people differently. One day, Rosa Parks took a seat on a bus. He refused to give up her seat. They was arrested. Citizens boycotted buses. Them won. The boycott changed the law. They changed America.

Elaborate During a Discussion

Pair Talk Tell what Rosa Parks did on the bus. Then tell more about what the event meant.

Compare Themes

Theme is the most important idea in a work of literature. Many themes are universal, which means that they deal with issues that all people can relate to, such as looking for love or experiencing loss.

Both "The Sword in the Stone" and "The Woman in the Snow" deal with the universal theme of heroism, but each selection focuses on a different aspect of heroism.

Read these lines from "The Sword and the Stone." How do they help express the theme that true heroes are honest and trustworthy?

> Arthur … got hold of the sword and pulled it out easily.

> Arthur … swore an oath that he would be a just and true king for all his days.

Now read these lines from "The Woman in the Snow." How do they support the theme that an everyday act of kindness can turn an ordinary person into a hero?

> Eula Mae raised her head. "You're a kind man," she said. "Thank you."

In a small group, discuss these questions:

- Why is heroism a universal theme?
- What do *you* think the author says about heroism in each story?

Word Families

Knowing the meaning of one word can help you understand other related words. For example, you know that **authority** means "power" or "control." When you see the new word *authoritarian*, you can guess that it means "showing a lot of power or control."

Here are some words related to words in the selections. Guess what each word means before confirming the definition in a dictionary.

WORD	WHAT I THINK IT MEANS	WHAT IT MEANS
desperation		
compassionate		
persist		

Oral Interpretation

Literature: Poetry Presentation Prepare Rita Dove's poem "Rosa" for an oral presentation to classmates or a group of friends. You might practice with a partner or tape your reading as you rehearse before your recitation.

❶ Practice reading the poem aloud, paying attention to the meaning of the words as well as their sound. The punctuation of the poem will give you clues about where to pause.

❷ Think about your intonation. Decide where you should raise or lower your voice. How will you emphasize key words or change the tone in your voice?

❸ Ask your audience to review your performance.

🔖 **Language and Learning Handbook**, page 702

Write an Opinion Paragraph

In an **opinion paragraph**, you tell what you think about a subject. Write an opinion paragraph about this quote by James A. Autry: "I believe it is the nature of people to be heroes, given the chance."

❶ **Prewrite** Organize your ideas by completing these sentences:

- The quote means that _____.
- I agree/disagree because _____.
- An example of this is _____.

❷ **Draft** Arrange your sentences into a paragraph that states your opinion clearly.

❸ **Revise** Add, move, or replace examples to make your opinion clearer.

❹ **Edit and Proofread** With a partner, fix spelling and grammar mistakes. Match sounds to letters or use rules to make corrections.

❺ **Publish** Share your work with the class. Then compare opinions in a group discussion.

Model Opinion Paragraph

James A. Autry once said: "I believe it is the nature of people to be heroes, given the chance." The quote means that everyone is brave enough to be a hero, we just don't have many chances to be heroic in our everyday lives. I agree with Autry that we all can be heroes, but I disagree that we don't have chances to be heroes. I think that we can be heroes all the time—in big and small ways. My mom and grandma are always making sacrifices for our family. My best friend spends a lot of his free time helping out at a homeless shelter. Sure, one of them might save someone from a speeding bus someday, but even if they don't, they'll still be heroes to me.

> The writer gives his opinion.

> These examples support the main opinion.

> The conclusion restates the writer's opinion.

🔖 **Writing Handbook**, page 784

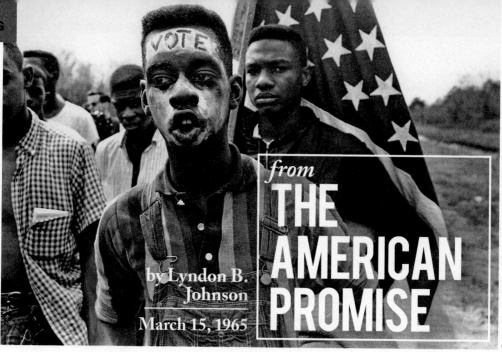

from

THE AMERICAN PROMISE

by Lyndon B. Johnson

March 15, 1965

Selma March, Selma, Alabama, USA, 1965, Bruce Davidson. Photograph © Bruce Davidson/Magnum Photos.

1 . . . **At** times history and fate meet at a single time in a single place to shape a turning point in man's unending search for freedom. So it was at **Lexington and Concord**. So it was a century ago at **Appomattox**. So it was last week in Selma, Alabama.

2 There, long-suffering men and women peacefully **protested** the denial of their rights as Americans. Many were brutally assaulted. One good man, a man of God, was killed. . . .

3 In our time we have come to live with moments of great crisis. Our lives have been marked with debate about great issues; issues of war and peace, issues of prosperity and depression. But rarely in any time does an issue lay bare the secret heart of America itself. Rarely are we met with a challenge, not to our growth or abundance, our welfare or our security, but rather to the values and the purposes and the meaning of our beloved nation.

4 The issue of equal rights for American Negroes is such an issue. And should we defeat every enemy, should we double our wealth and conquer the stars, and still be unequal to this issue, then we will have failed as a people and as a nation. . . .

5 This was the first nation in the history of the world to be founded with a purpose. The great phrases of that purpose still sound in every American

Key Vocabulary
protest *v.*, to say or show you are against something

In Other Words
Lexington and Concord the first battles of the American Revolution
Appomattox the last battle of the Civil War

Historical Background
In March 1965, African Americans in Selma, Alabama marched to protest laws preventing them from voting. Authorities attacked the marchers, killing one of them.

heart, North and South: "All men are created equal"—"government by consent of the governed"—"give me liberty or give me death." Well, those are not just clever words, or those are not just empty theories. In their name Americans have fought and died for two centuries, and tonight around the world they stand there as guardians of our liberty, risking their lives.

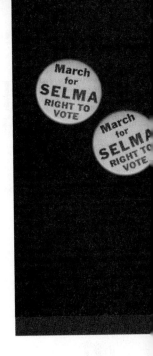

6   Those words are a promise to every citizen that he shall share in the **dignity** of man. This dignity cannot be found in a man's possessions; it cannot be found in his power, or in his position. It really rests on his right to be treated as a man equal in opportunity to all others. It says that he shall share in freedom, he shall choose his leaders, educate his children, and provide for his family according to his ability and his merits as a human being.

7   To apply any other test—to deny a man his hopes because of his color or race, his religion or the place of his birth—is not only to do injustice, it is to **deny** America and to dishonor the dead who gave their lives for American freedom. . . .

8   Every American citizen must have an equal right to vote. . . .

9   Wednesday I will send to Congress a law designed to eliminate illegal barriers to the right to vote. . . .

10   But even if we pass this bill, the battle will not be over. What happened in Selma is part of a far larger movement which reaches into every section and state of America. It is the effort of American Negroes to secure for themselves the full blessings of American life.

11   Their cause must be our cause too. Because it is not just Negroes, but really it is all of us, who must overcome the crippling legacy of **bigotry** and injustice.

12   And we shall overcome.

13   The real hero of this struggle is the American Negro. His actions and protests, his courage to risk safety and even to risk his life, have awakened the **conscience** of this nation. His demonstrations have been designed to call attention to injustice, designed to provoke change, designed to stir reform.

14   He has called upon us to make good the promise of America. And who among us can say that we would have made the same progress were it not for his **persistent** bravery, and his faith in American democracy. . . . ❖

Key Vocabulary
- **persistent** *adj.*, continuing in spite of challenges, unchanging

In Other Words
dignity value and worthiness
deny reject
bigotry hating another person because of ethnic background, racism
conscience sense of right and wrong

THE HERO WITHIN

EQ ESSENTIAL QUESTION:
What Makes a Hero?

myNGconnect.com
🌐 Download the rubric.

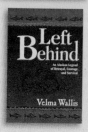

Present Your Project: Documentary

It's time to present your documentary about the Essential Question for this unit: What Makes a Hero?

1 Review and Complete Your Plan

Consider these points as you complete your project:

- How will you present your documentary? Will you show it as a movie or perform it live?
- Is your script organized in a logical order, and does it answer the Essential Question?
- What materials, such as photographs and interviews, do you need?

2 Give Your Documentary

Present your documentary to your classmates. Be prepared to answer questions afterward.

3 Evaluate the Documentaries

Use the online rubric to evaluate each of the documentaries, including the one you presented.

Reflect on Your Reading

Many of the characters in the selections in this unit and in the Edge Library showed heroic qualities.

Think back on your reading of the unit selections, including your choice of Edge Library books. Then discuss the following with a partner or in a small group.

Genre Focus   Compare and contrast the different perspectives used in first-person and third-person omniscient narrators. Give examples, using the selections in this unit.

Focus Strategy   Choose a selection in this unit that doesn't reveal everything about a character or event. Identify three strategies that would help you make inferences and write them on an index card that you can share with a partner.

EQ Respond to the Essential Question

Throughout this unit, you have been thinking about the archetype of the hero. What different types of heroes have you come across in contemporary and traditional literature? Support your response with evidence from the unit selections and Edge Library books.

Response to Literature

Writing Mode
Informative/Explanatory

Writing Trait Focus
Voice and Style

Thinking about great literature can give you new insight into life, other people—and yourself. For this project, you will write an essay in response to a work of literature.

Study a Response to Literature

When you write an essay about something you have read, you are writing a response to literature. You summarize the main ideas in the text and you share your personal thoughts about the writer's work.

❶ Connect Writing to Your Life

Sometimes an interesting article opens your eyes to a whole new way of looking at the world, or a work of fiction prompts you to think about a similar experience in your own life. When you write an essay in response to literature, you carefully consider ideas and details in the text and then share your personal interpretation of their significance.

❷ Understand the Form

When you write a response to literature, be sure to:

Introduction
- Write in the first person.
- Identify the work of literature.
- Briefly state the significant idea in the literature and its impact on you.

Body of Essay
- Tell how that idea or event relates to your experience.
- Support your interpretation with accurate and detailed examples from the literature.
- Identify any uncertainty the literature created in your mind and show how you dealt with that.

Conclusion
- Make a personal observation about life based on the author's work and the effect the author's ideas and style created.

Now look at an essay by a professional writer, writing in response to a short story, "The Woman in the Snow."

❸ Analyze a Professional Model

In this essay, the writer reflects on the significance of a short story in her own life.

Response to "The Woman in the Snow"

by Ana Jacobs

Sometimes in life we must rely on the kindness of others. In the short story "The Woman in the Snow" by Patricia McKissack, a young mother cannot get the help she needs to save her baby. Even though she desperately pleads for a ride to the hospital, a prejudiced bus driver turns her away. This story reminded me of a time when my family was also turned away unfairly.

Several years ago, a landlord had refused to rent to us. He claimed that the vacant apartment we had an appointment to see had just been rented by someone else. Yet, it stood empty for months.

Likewise, the racist bus driver of McKissack's short story wields power instead of practicing fairness. When Grady Bishop "put on the gray uniform and boarded his bus, nothing mattered, not his obesity, not his poor education, not growing up the eleventh child of the town drunk. Driving gave him power. And power mattered."

Grady treats "his bus" as if it were his own exclusive world. Perhaps this demonstrates how excluded Grady feels from the larger world, but I think what's most important is that in the narrow world of Grady's bus, there is no room for kindness. "It's a waste of time," he says.

By contrast, Ray Hammond, "the first black driver Metro hired," welcomes the title character onboard. By this point in the story, 25 years have passed and the woman in the snow is a ghost. But with "compassion overruling his fear," Hammond grasps what Grady cannot or will not—that "nobody deserves to be left out in this weather."

Reading this story again, I realize that life offers us all the chance to be kind, and that refusing to be kind hurts us as well as others. After all, the man who shut the door on my family will never know the friendship that we would gladly have shown him. Fortunately, just two blocks away, we were able to rent an apartment from a kind woman who became a lifelong family friend.

After all, what matters most, McKissack suggests, is that nobody deserves to be left out, period.

The writer states a **significant idea** and identifies the **literary work** that prompted it.

The writer relates the literature to a **personal experience**.

The writer supports her interpretation with detailed examples from the literature.

The writer deals with an **uncertainty** the literature created in her mind.

The writer concludes with an insight she gained through **further reflection** on the literature.

▶ **Prompt** Write an essay in response to literature. Make sure to:

- show that you grasp the significant ideas in the text
- support your interpretation with detailed examples
- identify any uncertainty the literature created in your mind and show how you dealt with that

✔ Prewrite

Now that you have analyzed the elements of an effective essay in response to literature, make a Writing Plan. This will help you demonstrate your grasp of significant ideas about the literature as you write.

❶ Choose Your Topic

Try these strategies to find a topic for your essay:

- List works of literature that made a strong impression on you.
- Note which literature has the strongest connection to your life, and why.
- Review any written responses you have already made to the literature.

❷ Clarify the Audience, Controlling Idea, and Purpose

Are your readers familiar with the literary work? If not, consider what information they will need and what details should be kept a surprise.

Turn your first impression and later reflections into a clear **controlling idea**. This main point should be true to the literature as well as to your own experience.

Remember that your purpose is to demonstrate your grasp of a significant idea in a literary work and to show what effect the work has on you, and why.

❸ Gather Supporting Details

To trap details from the story that support your controlling, or main idea, you can use a **Cluster Map** like the one shown. It's based on a student's response to "A Job for Valentín" (pp. 238–250). The controlling idea is in the center. Supporting details surround the main idea.

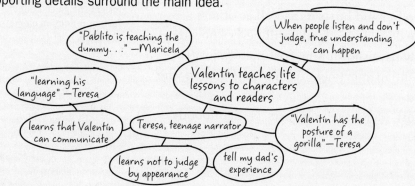

Prewriting Tip

To clarify significant ideas in the literature:

- List details about the characters, the conflict, and the plot.
- Accurately note quotations that make an impression on you.
- State what is important about each item on your list.
- Write the message, or idea, about the literature that best sums up your details.

❹ Organize the Details

Organize the details in a way that best supports your controlling idea.
The student writer organized details in order of importance.

❺ Finish Your Writing Plan

Before you actually begin drafting your essay, make a final plan. Decide how you
will begin your essay, how you will organize it, and how you will conclude. Your
Cluster Map will provide information for the body of your essay.

Technology Tip

If you use a computer,
save your Writing Plan,
draft, and other notes
for the essay in one
folder. That way, you
can quickly locate
everything you need.

Writing Plan

Topic	response to "A Job for Valentín"
Audience	my teacher and my classmates
Controlling Idea	Valentín teaches other characters and readers valuable life lessons.
Purpose	to reflect on the story's significant ideas
Time Frame	due in ten days
Organization	order of importance
Introduction Include least important detail	Briefly summarize the story; connect to my life; engage readers' attention with dramatic example from story. State controlling idea.
Body Include more important details	Valentín teaches the other characters; present my ideas in order of importance; support them with detailed examples and accurate quotations.
Conclusion Include most important detail	When people listen and stop judging, true understanding can take place.

**Reflect on
Your Plan**

▶ Does your plan include
accurate and detailed
examples from the
literature? Do you make
a clear observation?
Share your plan with
a partner. Ask for
suggestions. Make
any changes you think
would improve the plan
for your essay.

✒ Write a Draft

Let your Writing Plan guide you as you write your essay. Don't worry if you're still thinking over some of the details. You'll have a chance to clarify your writing later.

❶ Keep Your Ideas Flowing

Sometimes a literary work evokes strong feelings in you, yet you aren't sure how to turn those feelings into more considered thought. If so, try these techniques:

- **Save Those First Impressions** Reread the literary work, pausing to jot down whatever impressions come to mind. Use sticky notes to attach your responses to important examples in the text. Then go back and see what your responses have in common. Write notes about it.

- **Link Impressions to Your Life** What personal experience or connection comes to mind as you read the literature, and why? Has the writer established a viewpoint you share? Jot down your ideas.

- **Go Deeper** Reflect further on your first impressions. Make notes. Then discuss your ideas with another student who has read the literary work. Upon further reflection, what seems most significant to you about the literature? How does this idea apply to life in general?

- **Do a Focused Freewrite** If you're on the verge of an idea and aren't sure how to say it, just freewrite to talk to yourself about it.

❷ Create a Compelling Opening

How will you engage the attention of readers who may not have read the literature? A compelling, or strong, opening is one that makes readers want to find out more. Consider using different rhetorical devices in the introduction of your essay, as shown below. Choose the one that will lead most easily to the main point that you want to make and that will help your readers grasp the effect the literature had on you.

Rhetorical Device	Example
Start with a simile.	Pablito was like a fish without fins
Start with a question.	Why are people so quick to see differences between themselves and others?
Start with a thought-provoking quotation.	"I think Pablito is teaching the dummy a few things." —Maricela

Drafting Tip

Use transition words to help readers better understand your ideas and experiences. For example:

- Use time order words such as *several years ago, at first, afterward,* and *later* to show when an experience took place.
- Use transitions such as *likewise, in the same way,* and *after all* to show how two ideas go together or are similar.
- Use transitions like *however, instead,* and *yet* to emphasize a contrast or difference.

Technology Tip

If you try two different ways to begin your essay, save them both. You might want to name one file *Intro1* and another *Intro2*. You can later determine which version works better for you and then delete the one you don't want.

❸ Student Model

Here is the first draft of the essay written in response to "A Job for Valentín."
There are some mistakes. Those can be fixed later.

Lessons to Learn

This story is called "A Job for Valentín." This story is about a man named Valentín. This man is disabled. A Summer job at a pool is gotten by him. This man looks after a little boy. The boy's mother says something mean. She says how Valentín is a dummy. But it is Valentín who teaches the other characters.

For example, Teresa the teenage narrator of the story learns not to judge others by their appearance. At the beginning of the story, Teresa says, "Valentín has the posture of a gorilla." She assumes that he is helpless. My dad who uses a wheelchair sometimes deals with similar assumptions. Last tuesday a new neighbor expressed surprise that Dad manages the city animal shelter. He was spoken to loudly and slowly by her as if he could not hear or comprehend.

As this experience and Cofer's story show, assumptions can get in the way of real communication. For example, Teresa thinks that Valentín has trouble understanding things and that he can't speak English even after he tells her he can. At first I was uncertain about him, too. When he sees Pablito in the water and tries to tell her, Teresa says, "I guess he's having a fit or something."

Teresa changed. She will change at end of the story. Teresa realized that Valentín can do something she thinks he can't. Communicate in total silence. Teresa will learn something from this. In both of the two things I'm thinking about the significance of this is clear. Only when people listened actively and stopped judging others by their appearance can true understanding take place.

Reflect on Your Draft

▶ Does your paper have a clear introduction, body, and conclusion? Did you provide details from the story that demonstrate the significant ideas and style of the writer and the effects on you? Talk them over with a partner.

✐ Revise Your Draft

The word *revise* is made from word parts that mean "see again." Look at your draft with fresh eyes. You can then improve your essay's voice and style.

❶ Revise for Voice and Style

Because a response to literature is a type of informative writing that also presents your personal thoughts, ideas, and experiences, it is important to let your writing sound like you. This doesn't just happen. A good writer uses **voice** to make the writing sound real and unique. Writing with an effective voice shows a mature command of language and has freshness of expression. Just as an engaging speaking voice makes someone want to keep listening, effective voice in writing fully engages the reader and lets the writer's personality shine through.

Good writing also has **style**. That means that the words and sentences are appropriate to the purpose and the audience. The word choices are vivid and precise. As for the sentences, they don't all begin in the same way, have the same end punctuation, or run the same length. The writer can vary the sentence length and structure by using a longer sentence to discuss a complex aspect of the text or a shorter sentence to emphasize a point.

Revising Tip

Make sure that your ending fits your purpose and reflects your voice and style. For example, if you want to share an insight, state it clearly and in your own words.

TRY IT ▶ With a partner, evaluate the voice and style of the two drafts below. Which draft uses words that are more powerful and engaging? Explain.

Draft 1

> This story is called "A Job for Valentín." This story is about a man named Valentín. This man is disabled. A Summer job at a pool is gotten by him. This man looks after a little boy. The boy's mother says something mean. She says how Valentín is a dummy.

Draft 2

> In "A Job for Valentín," a story by Judith Ortiz Cofer, the main character is a developmentally disabled man who gets a summer job at a pool. The man makes friends with a 2-year-old boy, Pablito. But others are not so kind. How does the boy's mother, Maricela, respond? She laughs. "I think Pablito is teaching the dummy a few things," she says meanly.

Now use the rubric to evaluate the voice and style of your own draft. What score do you give your draft and why?

Voice and Style

	Does the writing have a clear voice and is it the best style for the type of writing?	Is the language interesting and are the words and sentences appropriate for the purpose, audience, and type of writing?
4 Wow!	The writing **fully** engages the reader with its individual voice. The writing style is best for the type of writing.	The words and sentences are interesting and appropriate to the purpose and audience. • The words are precise and engaging. • The sentences are varied and flow together smoothly.
3 Ahh.	Most of the writing engages the reader with an individual voice. The writing style is mostly best for the type of writing.	**Most** of the words and sentences are interesting and appropriate to the purpose and audience. • Most words are precise and engaging. • Most sentences are varied and flow together.
2 Hmm.	**Some** of the writing engages the reader, but it has no individual voice and the style is not best for the writing type.	**Some** of the words and sentences are interesting and appropriate to the purpose and audience. • Some words are precise and engaging. • Some sentences are varied, but the flow could be smoother.
1 Huh?	The writing does **not** engage the reader.	**Few or none** of the words and sentences are appropriate to the purpose and audience. • The words are often vague and dull. • The sentences lack variety and do not flow together.

myNGconnect.com
● **Rubric: Voice and Style**
● **Evaluate and practice scoring other student responses to literature.**

📖 **Writing Handbook**, p. 784

⬤Revise Your Draft, continued

❷ Revise Your Draft

You've now evaluated the voice and style of your own draft. If you scored 3 or lower, use the checklist below to revise your draft.

Revision Checklist

Ask Yourself	Check It Out	How to Make It Better
Does my introduction: • **introduce the work and the author?** • **state my main idea?** • **engage readers' attention?**	Put a checkmark by the author's name, the name of the work, and your main idea.	☐ Add missing details. ☐ Rewrite the opening to be more compelling.
Does the body of my essay refer to significant ideas in the literature? **Do I refer to my own experience?**	Read each paragraph. Look for a reference to an idea in the literary work. Reread the body to find a reference to your experience.	☐ If specific ideas from the literature are missing, add them. ☐ State the link between the literature and your life.
Do I support significant ideas with accurate and detailed examples from the literature, including quotations?	Read each body paragraph. Underline examples. Compare quotations in your essay with quotations in the text.	☐ If examples are missing, or lack detail, add them. ☐ Match the wording and punctuation of your quotations to the literature.
Does my essay reflect effective voice? **Did I adjust the style to fit the purpose and the audience?**	Examine the sentence length and structure for sameness. Mark word choices that are dull or vague. Read the essay aloud to a partner. Ask for feedback.	☐ Rewrite some sentences to vary the structure and length. ☐ Replace weak language with precise and vivid words. ☐ Rewrite some parts to be clearer and more interesting.
Does my conclusion show the progress of my thinking?	Read the conclusion aloud. Find a sentence that leaves readers with your most important idea.	☐ Write the conclusion to include the idea you want readers to remember. ☐ Briefly sum up the content of your essay.

📖 **Writing Handbook,** p. 784

❸ Conduct a Peer Conference

Exchanging essays with a partner will help each of you revise your draft. Look for any part that:

- seems to be missing important details
- is difficult to understand
- seems very different from the rest of the writing

Discuss the draft with your partner. Focus on the items in the Revision Checklist. Use your partner's comments to make your essay more engaging, more complete, and easier to understand.

❹ Make Revisions

Look at the revisions below and the peer-reviewer conversation on the right. Notice how the peer reviewer commented and asked questions. Notice how the writer used the comments and questions to revise the essay.

Revised for Voice and Style

> Teresa ^has^ changed. She ~~will change at the end of the story.~~
>
> ~~Teresa~~ realize^s^d that Valentín can ~~do something she thinks he can't.~~
>
> ^∅^Communicate in total silence. ^and I'm learning his language."^ ~~Teresa will learn something from this.~~
>
> ^life and literature,^ In both ~~of the two things I'm thinking about~~ the significance of this
>
> is clear. Only when people listened actively and stopped judging
>
> others by their appearance can true understanding take place.

Revised for Accuracy and Detail

> As this experience and Cofer's story show, assumptions can get
>
> in the way of real communication. For example, Teresa thinks that
>
> Valentín has trouble understanding things and that he can't speak
>
> English even after he tells her he can. At first I was uncertain about
>
> him, too. When he sees Pablito in the water and tries to tell her,
>
> ^start thinking he may be about to have^
> Teresa says, "I ~~guess he's having~~ a fit or something."
>
> └ Upon further reflection, I realize that it's Teresa who
> misunderstands Valentín.

Peer Conference

Reviewer's Comment: I don't hear your voice, because the sentences are repetitive and the word choice is vague.

Writer's Answer: I'll vary the structure and length of sentences. I'll also add specific details.

Reviewer's Comment: You say you were uncertain about Valentín as you first read this. Can you show how you dealt with that?

Writer's Answer: Yes. I'll also fix the quotation so that it accurately reflects the text.

Reflect on Your Revisions

▶ Think about the results of your peer conference. Then, in a journal or notebook, write down what you think are your strengths and where you can improve. What did you learn by revising this essay that you can use again?

Edit and Proofread Your Draft

When you have revised your draft, find and fix any mistakes that you made.

❶ Capitalize Days of the Week and Months

Capitalize specific days of the week and the names of months because they are proper nouns.

Common Nouns	Proper Nouns
day, night, today, summer, spring, autumn, winter	**Days of the Week**: Monday, Tuesday, Wednesday, Thursday, Friday, Saturday, Sunday
	Months: January, February, March, April, May, June, July, August, September, October, November, December

TRY IT ▶ Copy the sentences. Fix the two capitalization errors. Use proofreader's marks.

> 1. Last tuesday, a new neighbor visited.
> 2. In the story, Valentín gets a Summer job.

❷ Punctuate Appositives and Nouns of Direct Address Correctly

An appositive is a noun or pronoun placed next to another noun to identify it or to give more information about it. An appositive phrase is an appositive plus any words that modify it. You should usually use commas to set off an appositive or an appositive phrase.

> "A Job for Valentín," a story by Judith Ortiz Cofer, is about a mentally challenged man.

Use commas to set off a noun of direct address, or the person to whom one is speaking.

> Pablito, stay away from the water!
>
> I'm coming to help you, Pablito!

TRY IT ▶ Copy the sentences. Add commas where they are needed.

> 1. The narrator a teenage girl named Teresa learns a lesson.
> 2. Valentín could you please help me?

Proofreader's Marks

Use proofreader's marks to correct capitalization and punctuation errors.

Capitalize:
School lets out in june.

Do not capitalize:
The Winter of 2006 was unusually cold.

Add comma:
Valentín's animals all made from rubber bands, were on display.

Proofreading Tip

If you are unsure of whether you need to set off a word or phrase with commas, look in a style manual for help.

❸ Check Sentences for Active Voice

Use the **active voice** when the subject of the sentence performs the action described by the verb. Use the **passive voice** when you want to focus on the result (or the receiver) of the action. Read the following sentences aloud.

Passive Voice	Active Voice
He was **spoken** to by her.	She **spoke** to him.
It **has been decided** by the group to see a movie.	The group **has decided** to see a movie.
The test **had been given** before by the teacher.	The teacher **has given** the test before.

The passive voice can be awkward and hard to follow. It also drains energy from the writing. Use it only when it is necessary.

TRY IT ▶ Copy the sentences. Identify whether the sentence is active or passive voice. Rewrite each sentence, using the active voice if passive, and passive voice if active.

1. A wheelchair is used by Dad.
2. The way we gather information has been changed by the Internet.
3. The teacher had already helped him.
4. The family agreed to get a dog.

❹ Check for Consistency of Verb Tense

Check that you have used the correct verb tense and that you haven't switched from tense to tense. Change tense only if you talk about something that happened before or after the time you are writing about. The present tense of a verb tells about an action that is happening now. The past tense of a verb tells about an action that happened earlier or in the past.

present   past   past
I remember what I learned, last June, when I volunteered at the animal shelter.

TRY IT ▶ Copy these sentences. Rewrite them, using the correct verb tense.

1. I remembered now that last year we travel to California.
2. Yesterday I check the computer and it work.

🔖 **Writing Handbook**, p. 835

Editing Tip

Ask someone to read your essay aloud, or read it aloud yourself. You can often notice choppy sentences more clearly when they are read aloud.

Reflect on Your Corrections

▶ Proofread your essay more than once. You can often find mistakes you missed the first time. If there are things you keep missing, make a checklist of what to watch in your writing.

5 Edited Student Draft

Here's the student's draft, revised and edited. Read the draft aloud. How did the writer improve it? Copy the sentences highlighted in blue and underline the complete verb.

Lessons to Learn

In "A Job for Valentín," a short story by Judith Ortiz Cofer, a developmentally disabled man gets a summer job at a pool. The man makes friends with a 2-year-old boy, Pablito. But others are not so kind. How does the boy's mother, Maricela, respond? She laughs. "I think Pablito is teaching the dummy a few things," she says meanly. In my opinion, it is Valentín who teaches the other characters—and readers, too.

For example, Teresa, the teenage narrator of the story, learns not to judge others by their appearance. At the beginning of the story, Teresa says, "Valentín has the posture of a gorilla." She assumes that he is helpless. My dad, who uses a wheelchair, sometimes deals with similar assumptions. Last Tuesday, a new neighbor expressed surprise that Dad manages the city animal shelter. She spoke to him loudly and slowly as if he could not hear or comprehend her.

As this experience and Cofer's story show, assumptions can get in the way of real communication. For example, Teresa thinks that Valentín has trouble understanding things and that he can't speak English even after he tells her he can. At first, I was uncertain about him, too. Upon further reflection, I realize that it's Teresa who has been misunderstanding Valentín. When he sees Pablito in the water and tries to tell her, using verbal and body language, Teresa says, "I start thinking he may be about to have a fit or something."

By the end of the story, Teresa has changed. She realizes that Valentín "can communicate in total silence, and I'm learning his language." In both life and the literature, the significance of this is clear. Only when people listen actively and stop judging others by their appearance can true understanding take place.

The writer created a compelling opening and improved the voice and style by using precise word choices and varying sentence structure.

The writer used **commas** to set off appositives.

The writer **capitalized** a day of the week.

The writer replaced passive voice with **active voice** and more complex tenses to make sentences stronger.

To convey the significant ideas in the literature, the writer added detailed examples from the text. The writer also fixed a **quotation** for accuracy.

The writer fixed the **verb tenses** for consistency.

✓ Publish and Present

You are now ready to publish and present your work. Print out your essay or write a clean copy by hand. You may also want to present your work in a different way.

Alternative Presentations

Make an Illustrated Booklet Create a booklet that presents your essay along with quotations from the work of literature. Add illustrations that complement the work.

❶ Create a Cover Put the title of your essay on a cover page. Find or make an illustration from the work of literature for the cover as well.

❷ Body Print a clean copy of your essay. If you like, leave room to add illustrations.

❸ About the Writer On the inside back cover, write a paragraph or two to share what you know about the writer. Include biographical details and titles of some of his or her other writing.

❹ Share Your Booklet Exchange booklets with another student, or share your booklet with a friend or family member. Ask for feedback.

Create a Web Site With your teacher's supervision, make a class Web site to showcase each student's essay. Follow school rules. Work in groups to complete the following steps.

❶ Design a Home Page Find out if your school computer lab has Web authoring software, or work with an online template from a source approved by your teacher. Make sure the content of your home page is organized and easy to follow. Don't use a lot of different font styles or divide the page into too many sections. Include links to each student's essay on the home page.

❷ Prepare a Template Create a model page for the essays. Have each essay follow that design. Decide what font to use, how many lines to run on each page, and whether to add graphics.

❸ Publicize Your Web Site Send out an e-mail to friends and family with the link to the Web site. Check with your teacher about school guidelines.

❹ Ask for Feedback If appropriate, invite readers to e-mail comments about the Web site to your teacher that he or she can share with the class. Be sure to ask your teacher's permission.

📖 **Language and Learning Handbook**, p. 702

Publishing Tip

You can design, lay out, and print a cover using desktop publishing software.

Technology Tip

Choose the booklet, pamphlet, guide, or photo-essay format on the computer to access graphic features. These features let you set up the size, spacing, and layout of elements on a page. Create three different layouts and then discuss them with a group to evaluate which layout is best.

Reflect on Your Work

▶ Use the feedback from your teacher and peers to improve your ongoing writing. Write a brief summary of the positive comments you got.

☑ **In your portfolio, save a copy of your essay in response to literature.**

EQ ESSENTIAL QUESTION:

How Can Knowledge Open Doors?

I change myself, I change the world.

—GLORIA ANZALDUA

Sometimes it is more important to discover what one cannot do, than what one can.

—LIN YUTANG

Critical Viewing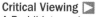
A Buddhist monk enters part of an ancient temple in Angkor, Cambodia. This site is part of a large city that was mysteriously abandoned in the mid-1500s. How does knowledge about the past open doors today?

OPENING
DOORS

EQ ESSENTIAL QUESTION:
How Can Knowledge Open Doors?

Study the Facts

More and more teens are choosing college as an option after high school. Study the numbers of U.S. students who enrolled in college in one decade.

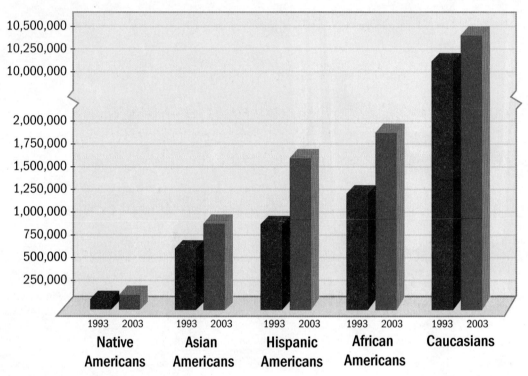

Source: American Council on Education, 2006

Analyze and Debate

1. How did college enrollment change between 1993 and 2003? Why do you think so many more students were able to attend college in 2003?

2. Overall, minority enrollment increased 50.7% during these years. How might the increase in the number of minority students who attended college affect our society?

3. How can a college education affect a person's life after high school? Is getting an education the same thing as getting knowledge?

Talk about the facts and the questions with a group. Give reasons to support your opinions. Identify how your opinions differ from the viewpoints of others in your group.

ESSENTIAL QUESTION

EQ In this unit, you will explore the **Essential Question** in class through reading, discussion, research, and writing.

① Plan a Project

Class Newspaper or Magazine

In this unit, you'll be creating a class newspaper or magazine about the Essential Question. Choose the subjects you'll develop in your articles. To get started, review some magazines and newspapers. Look for

- the kinds of subjects that are covered
- how the headlines capture readers' interest
- how the articles are organized
- how images and diagrams help tell the story.

Study Skills Start planning your newspaper or magazine. Use the forms on myNGconnect.com to plan your time and to prepare the content.

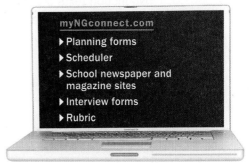

myNGconnect.com
- ▶ Planning forms
- ▶ Scheduler
- ▶ School newspaper and magazine sites
- ▶ Interview forms
- ▶ Rubric

② Choose More to Read

These readings provide different answers to the Essential Question. Choose a book and online selections to read during the unit.

Narrative of the Life of Frederick Douglass: An American Slave
by Frederick Douglass

Frederick Douglass was born a slave in 1817, but he never stopped dreaming of freedom. Douglass discovered that education was the key to overcoming the obstacles that stood in his way. Education also gave Douglass the voice to help others.

▶ **NONFICTION**

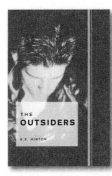

The Outsiders
by S. E. Hinton

Life has been hard for Ponyboy and his brothers ever since their parents died. But they are not alone as long as "the Greasers" are there to protect them from their enemies, the Socs. Will Ponyboy be trapped in a life of violence, or will he learn to open doors to a new future?

▶ **NOVEL**

Parrot in the Oven: Mi Vida
by Victor Martínez

Manny's friends think school is not the place to get the kind of education they need. To them, gangs are the best teachers. That's where they learn the really valuable lesson—how to get respect. But is that really the education Manny wants?

▶ **NOVEL**

myNGconnect.com
- 🌐 Read about men and women whose lives have opened doors for others.
- 🌐 Learn how educational options can change your life.
- 🌐 Play a game to explore how your choices can open doors to success.

Nonfiction texts organize information in certain ways.
One way to make sense of a nonfiction text is to read
one like this.

How to Complete a College Application

Filling out a college application can be a time-consuming and difficult
task, but you can make the process easier by following a few suggestions.

Before you begin, skim the application to find out whether an essay
is required. If so, leave plenty of time to write your essay. Organize your
ideas and be concise. Be honest about yourself, too. Don't exaggerate your
accomplishments.

The next step is to gather all the information and materials you will need
to complete the application:

- personal and family information (names, addresses,
  Social Security numbers)
- educational information (schools you've attended and when,
  courses you've taken)
- test scores
- honors and awards
- information about extracurricular activities
- examples of outstanding work that you have done
- personal essay
- recommendations from teachers and counselors
- high school transcript
- check or credit card information for the processing fee

Now that you have everything you need, choose a time and a
place to complete the application. Allow plenty of time. Read
all the directions carefully. Answer every question. Don't leave
anything blank unless you are given the option to do so.

After you finish, proofread your application. Then sign
your name. Finally, attach all supporting materials (letters of
recommendation, your transcript, examples of your work, etc.).
Make sure you also include payment for the processing fee.

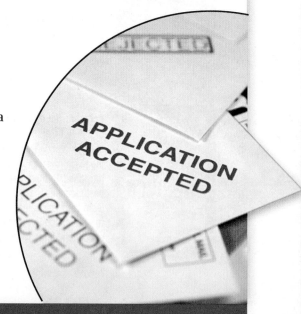

■ Connect Reading to Your Life

Here are some extra steps for completing an application. Work with a partner to decide where each one could go in Demo Text #1.

Where do you think item A belongs?

I think it should go at the very end.

A. Make a copy for your records.
B. Ask a parent or friend to proofread your application as well.
C. Be sure to edit and proofread your essay so that the final version is ready to attach to your application.
D. Select a workspace that is quiet and uncluttered.

Focus Strategy ▶ Ask Questions

When you placed the steps, you and your partner probably asked each other questions like these: Where does this go? Where does it make sense? What should this come after? You also probably figured out that the text is organized in a logical **sequence**. This helped you figure out where to insert the extra steps.

When you read, you also ask questions—of the author, yourself, and the text. Asking questions is an important reading strategy. It helps you understand what you're reading, as well as how the information in a text is organized.

Reading Strategies

· Plan and Monitor
· Determine Importance
· Make Inferences
▶ Ask Questions
· Make Connections
· Synthesize
· Visualize

■ Your Job as a Reader

Experienced readers know that one of the best ways to read is to question the author, themselves, and the text. Your job as a reader is to get involved with the text and think along with the author. *Who? What? When? Where? How?* and *Why?* are some of a good reader's favorite questions.

Academic Vocabulary

● **sequence** *n.*, an arrangement, or order, in which one thing comes after another; **sequential** *adj.*, forming a sequence

■ Unpack the Thinking Process

Authors can organize nonfiction texts in many ways. Experienced readers know that authors put their ideas together in certain patterns, or text structures, and that analyzing those text structures can help them understand the ideas.

Text Structure: Sequence

Sequence is one kind of text structure. Writers use a **chronological** (by time) or sequential (by steps in a process) text structure when they want to explain how to do something or show how or why something happened.

To identify a sequential text structure, look for:

☑ **Numbered Steps**

1. Write, edit, and proofread your essay.
2. Gather the information and materials you will need.
3. Choose a time and a place to complete the application.

☑ **Signal Words**

after	first	next	soon
afterward	following	not long after	then
as soon as	immediately	now	third
before	initially	on [date]	today
during	later	preceding	until
finally	meanwhile	second	when

Signal words are useful during all stages of the reading process.

- Before Reading: Skim for signal words to help you identify the text structure.
- During Reading: Use the signal words as anchors to keep track of all the steps or events.
- After Reading: Use the signal words to review.

Elements of Literature
chronological *adj.*, in the order in which events occur

Asking Questions

Experienced readers also ask questions to help identify the text structure and to **clarify** a sequence of steps or events in their minds. Here are some questions a reader might ask about Demo Text #1:

Question the Author	*Why did you organize the text like this?* *Why are you telling about this now?*
Question Yourself	*Do I understand that step?* *What will I read about next?*
Question the Text	*Where is the signal word in this sentence?* *Why is this a new paragraph?*

With a partner, take turns reading aloud Demo Text #1. As you listen, imagine you are following the instructions in the text. Then, ask questions to clarify the sequence of steps.

■ Try an Experiment

Here are two texts that explain how to do something.

DEMO TEXT #2

Dear Elena:

Your **orientation** date for Rutherford College is September 12. Please follow the instructions in this letter carefully. First, complete the attached form and mail it back with the $50 fee by July 31. Then wait for a confirmation letter. It will be sent along with information about check-in and the day's activities. After receiving confirmation, you can finalize your travel plans. We look forward to meeting you.

DEMO TEXT #3

When you read a textbook, do you have trouble remembering all the information? These steps can help you study effectively:

1. When you come to each chapter, glance at headings, pictures, and captions to get an idea of what the text is about.
2. Read the first and last paragraphs of the chapter and the chapter questions.
3. Describe each passage in your own words.
4. Review the entire chapter. Refer to the book if you need help.

Think, Pair, Share With a partner, reread Demo Text #2 and #3. Identify the structure of each text. Tell what signal words helped you identify the structure.

Monitor Comprehension

Text Structure Describe two ways to identify sequential text structure.

Academic Vocabulary
- **clarify** *v.*, to make something clear or understandable
- **orient** *v.*, to adjust yourself to a new situation; **orientation** *n.*, the act or process of orienting

PREPARE TO READ

▷ **Curtis Aikens and the American Dream**
▷ **Think You Don't Need an Education?**
▷ **Go For It!**

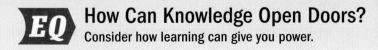

EQ How Can Knowledge Open Doors?
Consider how learning can give you power.

Make a Connection

Think-Pair-Share An English writer named Francis Bacon once said, "Knowledge is power." What does this statement mean to you? With a partner, talk about people who have used knowledge as power. Then share your example with the class.

Learn Key Vocabulary

Study the Words Pronounce each word and learn its meaning. You may also want to look up the definitions in the Glossary.

● Academic Vocabulary

Key Words	Examples
ambitious (am-**bi**-shus) *adjective* ▸ page 332	If you are **ambitious**, you have big goals that you want to achieve. The **ambitious** student studied day and night to win the science prize.
cause (**kawz**) *noun* ▸ page 327	A **cause** is an idea you believe in and are willing to fight for. I volunteer my time and money to the **cause** of helping the homeless. *Synonym:* goal
confession (kun-**fe**-shun) *noun* ▸ pages 326, 328	You make a **confession** when you tell someone something private or secret. *Synonyms:* telling the truth, owning up; *Antonyms:* keeping a secret, denial
discourage (dis-**kur**-ej) *verb* ▸ pages 332, 334	When someone or something **discourages** you, it makes you not want to do something. His laughter **discouraged** me from painting any more pictures.
fate (**fāt**) *noun* ▸ page 322	**Fate** is the future that is expected to happen. Many people believe that you cannot change your **fate**, while others think that you can change it with hard work.
literacy (**li**-tu-ru-sē) *noun* ▸ pages 318, 328, 335, 336	**Literacy** is the ability to read and write. Without **literacy**, it is difficult to complete a job application, use the Internet, or read a map.
● **profession** (pru-**fe**-shun) *noun* ▸ pages 332, 334	A **profession** is a job that you need special training to do. Because he chose the medical **profession**, he spent years studying to be a doctor. *Synonyms:* career, work
reputation (re-pyu-**tā**-shun) *noun* ▸ pages 321, 335	Your **reputation** is the way people think about you. He had a **reputation** as a shy person because he was always so quiet in class.

Practice the Words Complete a **Vocabulary T Chart** to compare whether the Key Vocabulary words mean something positive or negative to you. Then share your chart with a group, and discuss how you grouped the words in similar or different ways.

Vocabulary T Chart

Positive (+)	Negative (–)
ambitious	discourage

BEFORE READING Curtis Aikens and the American Dream

biography by Dan Rather

Reading Strategies

- Plan and Monitor
- Determine Importance
- Make Inferences
- ▶ **Ask Questions**
- Make Connections
- Synthesize
- Visualize

Analyze Text Structure: Chronology

A biography is the true story of someone's life. It includes information about the most important events and people in the person's life. Authors often organize biographies in **chronological order**. This describes the events in the order that they happened.

Look Into the Text

Dates and times tell when events happened.

Sequence words, such as *first*, *then*, *later*, signal the order of events.

> In the third grade, Curtis made a decision that would determine the course of his life. As he sat through a parent-teacher conference, he heard his teacher praise him: "'I just love having your boy in my class,'" Curtis remembers her saying. "'He's a great kid, he's sweet,' and then I heard a 'but.' And I thought, 'Oh no. What's this? But he's dumb? He's stupid?'" Well, no. She didn't say anything close to that, but she did say that he had some reading trouble, and she thought it would be best for him to repeat the third grade.

What happens here? Who are the people involved?

Focus Strategy ▶ Ask Questions

It's natural to have questions about what you're reading. In fact, learning to ask useful questions is a good way to find new information, solve problems, and learn more. As you read, ask yourself about the people, places, and events in each section.

HOW TO SELF-QUESTION

Focus Strategy

1. As you read, ask yourself questions to add to your understanding of the passage.

2. Ask questions about the passage based on the 5Ws and H: *Who?*, *What?*, *Where?*, *When?*, *Why?*, and *How?* Record these on a **Question-Answer Chart**.

3. Reread the text to see if you can find the answers. If you don't find them, ask a classmate or teacher.

Question-Answer Chart

My Questions	My Answers
Curtis seems really worried about what his teacher tells his parents. <u>Why</u> is he so worried?	The author includes Curtis's thoughts. Curtis is scared that people will think that he is "dumb" and "stupid."

Literacy Volunteers

TEENS *for* LITERACY!

Dear **Teens for Literacy! Volunteer**,

Thank you for your interest in Teens for Literacy! You are making a difference in the world by helping an adult or child learn to read.

By volunteering each week, you are helping to change these statistics:

- 38% of American 4th graders read below the "basic" level.

- Forty million adults in the U.S. aren't able to read a simple story to a child.

- From 1983 to 1999, over ten million Americans reached the 12th grade without learning to read at a basic level. In the same time period, six million Americans dropped out of high school.

Though these numbers are scary, we can do something about them! The time you spend teaching others to read will change their lives and make sure that they don't become another statistic.

Again, thank you for your interest in Teens for Literacy! We're looking forward to seeing you at our orientation. If you have any questions, please contact me, Jenny Ramirez, at (650) 555-6545.

Sincerely,

Jenny

myNGconnect.com

🔘 Learn about the problem of illiteracy in the U.S.
🔘 Read stories about adults who learned to read.

Curtis Aikens
and the
American Dream

by Dan Rather

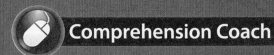
Comprehension Coach

Hiding
the Truth

Curtis Aikens puts a face to **statistics about literacy** that we hear but sometimes cannot believe: he went through high school and five semesters of college without learning how to read or write, one of millions of Americans who **fall through the cracks and keep falling**. Curtis believes today that he would have disappeared completely if he hadn't, at age twenty-six, finally asked for help. Now, at age forty-one, he's **molded himself into a celebrity chef**, with three cookbooks to his name and his own show on the Food Network. Of his literacy tutors, he says, "They didn't change my life, they *saved* my life."

Elementary School Days

Conyers, Georgia, was a small rural town when Curtis was growing up, but he says his parents always encouraged their children to think beyond the way their lives were then.

In the third grade, Curtis made a decision that would determine the course of his life. As he sat through a parent-teacher conference, he heard his teacher praise him: "'I just love having your boy in my class,'" Curtis remembers her saying. "'He's a great kid, he's sweet,' and then I heard a 'but.' And I thought, 'Oh no. What's this? But he's dumb? He's stupid?'" Well, no. She didn't say anything close to that, but she did say that he had some reading trouble, and she thought it would be best for him to repeat the third grade. 1

1 **Text Structure: Chronology**
When do the main events of Curtis's story start? How do you know?

Key Vocabulary
literacy *n.*, ability to read and write

In Other Words
statistics about literacy studies showing numbers of people who cannot read
fall through the cracks and keep falling have problems but never get the help they need
molded himself into a celebrity chef turned himself into a famous cook on television

"I was shocked. I was floored. **2** I'm thinking to myself, 'Well, I'm not gonna let anyone ever call me dumb or stupid again.' So instead of learning to read, I learned to hide the fact that I couldn't read." Bad choice, as Curtis would find out. Faking it took a good deal more effort than if he had simply asked for help. As he grew older, he felt that if anyone found out his secret, the label "stupid, dumb" would be much bigger and harder to shake. So he dug himself deeper and deeper into a hole.

We've all heard of children graduating from high school, and even going on to college, with little or no reading and writing skills, and most often it is the schools that get blamed. Curtis, however, **declines to point a finger, except at himself**. Most of his teachers, he feels, were ready to give him a hand if he asked. But they were also completely fooled by what Curtis calls "the tricks of the trade." The trade, in this case, was about **conning** everyone. "I had two things going for me," the younger Curtis realized. "I remembered stuff—I had pretty much total recall—and I had a likeable personality." **3**

"One of the things I remember thinking about was, if you sound smart, people think you're smart. So I had this great **facade** of being this smart, confident boy." He says he built his vocabulary and **charisma** by watching TV and listening to recordings of great black entertainers—Flip Wilson, Richard Pryor, Bill Cosby, Redd Foxx, Sidney Poitier. They used big words, they were likeable, and they projected the confidence that Curtis needed to **pull off his scam**. And, Curtis adds,

I learned to hide the fact that I COULDN'T READ.

2 Language
The phrase "I was floored" is an idiom. Find clues that tell you what it means. Where do you think this expression comes from?

3 Ask Questions
Pause here. Think of a *what* question that will help you understand this paragraph. Record it in your Question-Answer Chart.

Monitor Comprehension

Explain
What secret does Curtis hide? Why doesn't he ask someone for help?

In Other Words

declines to point a finger, except at himself only blames himself
conning fooling
facade fake appearance

charisma charm
pull off his scam make people believe he could read

"When they really wanted to **do the Anglo talk,** they did it."

Most of his grade school teachers **were completely taken**. In the fifth grade, however, Curtis met up with a teacher who wouldn't be fooled. So he adjusted his game plan—he started acting up. He realized that being a pain in the neck was also a sure way to be passed over. Once again, he advanced, and went on to high school with **no one the wiser**. Sadly, Curtis was no wiser himself.

The High School Years

The game changed in high school, with Curtis discovering that a course load **heavy on electives and light on academics**, coupled with athletics and student government, could bring him a diploma. He could do basic math, he could guess at multiple choice. 🔲

It would have been hard indeed to fail Curtis Aikens: star football player, student council member, winner of a statewide cooking competition (he was the only boy in his **Home Economics class**). And now, though he doesn't blame his teachers, he does have some lessons for them. "Now when I talk to teachers," he explains, "I say, listen, it's not just the bad kids that you gotta worry about. Sometimes it's those sugar sweet kids who are having problems, too, but they're afraid to talk to you about

4 Text Structure: Chronology
The biography begins when Curtis is a child. How old is Curtis now? What clues on the page let you know this?

Conyers High School 1975–1976 Student Schedule

Name: **AIKENS, CURTIS**
Student ID: **472344**

Course	Days	Time	Room	Instructor
HOME ECONOMICS	MTWRF	8:15 – 9:05 AM	F35	MORRIS
BASIC MATH	MTWRF	9:10 – 10:00 AM	M122	MCCRACKEN
PHYSICAL EDUCATION	MWF	10:05 – 10:55 AM	GYM	SCHMIDT
BAND	TR	10:05 – 10:55 AM	MUS	BENSON
READING 2	MTWRF	11:00 – 11:50 AM	B17	GOLDBERG
LUNCH	ALL	12:00 – 12:50 PM	CAF	LILLY
NUTRITION	MTWRF	12:55 – 1:45 PM	F38	TAYLOR
STUDY HALL	MTWRF	2:00 – 2:50 PM	LIB	SANTINI

🔺 **Interpret the Schedule** Curtis's course load is "heavy on electives and light on academics." What examples of these can you find on the course schedule?

In Other Words
do the Anglo talk talk like many successful white people do
were completely taken never knew he couldn't read
no one the wiser no one knowing the truth

heavy on electives and light on academics filled with easy classes
Home Economics class class that taught students how to cook and sew

it because they have the **reputation** of being a nice kid. That was me. I was that nice kid, who really wanted a teacher to grab him and say, 'What's up?'"

On top of being nice, Curtis was headed for a football scholarship. He remembers a photograph of himself signing his **letter of intent** to Southern University, **ringed by** his beaming family. He was supposed to be the first in the family to graduate from college, and he represented their hopes and dreams. Curtis should have been beaming along with them. "But my face just looked like this sheer face of horror: 'Oh, no. Here I go again. Four more years of having to fake this.'" 5

Facing the Facts

College and Work

The ploys of high school were **evidently not going to play** in college. He barely made it through his first year at Southern, and halfway through his sophomore year, he dropped out. 6

"My dad, he was so heartbroken that I had left college. . . Everybody thought I was supposed to be a success, but no one knew I couldn't read. Not my mom, not my dad, not my brothers and sisters, not my school. And I remember, I wanted to say, 'Dad, you know what, your kid can't read, man. I can't read! I'm just faking.'"

The American dream seemingly out of reach, Curtis thought he could settle for a California dream instead. The Golden State's promise

5 **Ask Questions**
Ask and answer a *why* question to check your understanding of this paragraph. Record the question and answer in your chart.

6 **Access Vocabulary**
What is a *ploy*? Look for clues in the text. Then check your guess in a dictionary.

Monitor Comprehension

Explain
What does Curtis want to tell teachers? Why doesn't he tell them this?

Key Vocabulary
reputation *n.*, what people think about another person

In Other Words
letter of intent acceptance letter
ringed by surrounded by
evidently not going to play not going to work
The American dream The idea that anyone can succeed through hard work and determination

of **rebirth had strong appeal**, and with both San Diego and the San Francisco Bay area tugging on him, he flipped a coin to decide. His **fate** settled, he headed north and got a job in a grocery store. **7**

Life should have been much easier than it was in school. Curtis says he had little trouble telling the difference between smooth and chunky peanut butter, between two-percent and nonfat milk. It was all in the packaging. But his manager turned out to be one of the few people he wasn't able to win over, and the two fought constantly. After one particularly bad argument, he went home to plot a new course. When he got there, he did something strange.

"I got a pad and paper like I could write something. I don't know why I took it out, but that's what smart people do. They write down their ideas. This is one of the things I'd learned—that smart people write down their ideas. And the first idea that came to my head was to start a **produce company**. I wrote the number one down. But I never wrote the idea out. I didn't know how in the world to write that." **8**

I DIDN'T KNOW HOW in the world to write that.

His idea was to go into a business that he could run on, as he says, "a handshake and a smile," with a minimum of letters. He'd noticed buyers from restaurants coming in for produce. He could do that. He could selectively pick produce from **wholesalers** and deliver it to restaurants. He knew little about produce, but he knew plenty about talking to people. The grocers at the produce market were happy to share:

7 Text Structure: Chronology
What is life like for Curtis after leaving college? What decision does he make next?

8 Ask Questions
Use *wh–* questions to check your understanding of Curtis's actions after he leaves school. Make notes in your Question-Answer Chart.

Key Vocabulary
fate *n.*, the future that will happen

In Other Words
rebirth had strong appeal a new beginning seemed like a good idea
produce company company that sells fruits and vegetables
wholesalers other companies that sell things in large amounts

"These guys taught me everything about buying mushrooms and onions and tomatoes. It was like being in the college of fruits and vegetables."

Curtis even developed a **microlanguage of produce** to help him deal with crates. He learned to recognize that two Ps meant the box contained apples, two Ts meant lettuce. An apex followed by a vertex, AV, stood for avocados. Curtis couldn't sound out the letters, but he didn't make many mistakes.

△ Interpret the Graphic
Use the visual details to help you comprehend the language. What does Curtis use to identify what is inside crates?

At the wholesale end, he couldn't have run his business without trust. He could pretend to read **an invoice** but ultimately had to believe that it was right. To pay the wholesalers, he usually had to leave a blank check: "There's no way I could have pulled off my scam if I had to write a check to [for example] Crescent Produce. I couldn't spell 'crescent,'" Curtis recalls, adding, "but every single **purveyor** had become a friend. They wanted to help me, they wanted me to succeed. They trusted me and I had to trust them." **9**

As Curtis says, he could have **strung this tiny enterprise along indefinitely** as long as it remained tiny. But he soon found himself with seven employees, serving seventy-five **accounts**. The larger companies in the business started to **take notice**. They could afford to lower their prices. Curtis couldn't, and more quickly than it had grown, his business crumbled.

9 Ask Questions
What questions will deepen your understanding of this part of the selection? Record them in your Question-Answer chart.

Monitor Comprehension

Describe
How does Curtis's business succeed even when he cannot read?

In Other Words
microlanguage of produce special way to read the boxes of fruits and vegetables
an invoice a bill
purveyor seller

strung this tiny enterprise along indefinitely kept his small business going forever
accounts customers, companies he worked with
take notice pay attention, know about

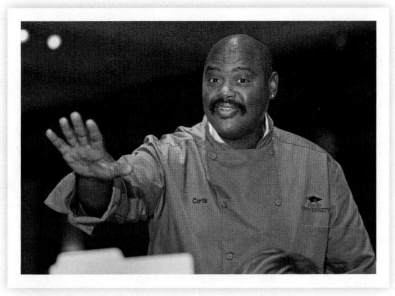

Curtis Aikens works with businesses and organizations around the U.S. to promote literacy.

Reaching Out for Help

At the same time, Curtis was feeling the **undertow of his illiteracy**. Driving across the country, he found himself stuck on the side of the road, unsure if he was headed in the right direction, simply because he couldn't read the word "Arkansas." In the airport, he found himself staring at the **arrival and departure monitors** until he got the courage to ask someone where his connecting flight was. The world started to look like a very limited place. 🔟

Deep in debt, with all his employees let go, Curtis seldom left his apartment except to **service** his few remaining accounts or work his part-time job: "You don't date anyone when you don't feel good about yourself. You don't really have friends to **socialize** with. . . . So a bag of chips and a Coke and my television were my friends." One night, a **public service announcement from Literacy Volunteers of America**

🔟 **Text Structure: Chronology**
When does Curtis finally realize that not being able to read is a problem? What makes him realize it?

In Other Words
undertow of his illiteracy effects of not being able to read and write
arrival and departure monitors TV screens that show when planes land and take off
service work on
socialize spend time
public service announcement from Literacy Volunteers of America TV commercial about an organization that teaches people how to read

came on that spoke directly to Curtis: "It said, 'Don't be ashamed, don't be embarrassed. We can teach you how to read.'" And, Curtis adds, they knew the secret to getting him to make that call when they said: "'And we won't tell anybody.'" **11**

He was hooked up with a husband-and-wife team he only remembers as "Steve and Ginny." Steve was a student, Ginny a nurse. They were the first people Curtis felt he could tell his secret to: "It was like the world was lifted off my shoulders when I said 'You know what? I can't read, and I want to be able to read.' To be able to say that to somebody and not have them laugh or pick at me or think I was dumb or stupid . . . was my biggest fear, and they didn't do it." **12**

Sharing the Lessons

Building a New Life

Curtis flew through the literacy training program, in part, he was told, because he already had a large vocabulary. But he could also feel the way his life was about to change, and that, more than anything, **impelled him forward**. He says he now reads about a book a week and has read maybe close to a thousand books since he learned how it's done. He carries a **laptop** with him on his frequent trips. He enjoys a laugh every time a conversation turns to books because he can participate without faking it.

On the surface, Curtis's life changed little. He didn't tell anyone that he had just learned how to read—it was still **a stigma**. After a few years in New York, working for a market that **catered to upscale** restaurants,

11 Ask Questions
The ad for the literacy organization says, "And we won't tell anybody." What questions will help you understand this more fully? Record them in your chart.

12 Ask Questions
Ask questions to understand more about Curtis's tutors. Record the questions in your chart.

In Other Words
impelled him forward made him continue, motivated him
laptop light, moveable computer
a stigma something he was ashamed of
catered to upscale sold things to expensive

Monitor Comprehension

Describe
How does literacy change Curtis's life?

he returned to Georgia. Once back in Conyers, he started a produce company with his family and took French lessons. Before he could read, he says, his confidence was just for show. Now it was brimming over, looking for **an outlet**.

Eventually, he sold himself as a **food columnist** to the editor of the local paper. He wrote his first column on how to pick the perfect fig. 🔢13

13 Text Structure: Chronology
What are two things Curtis does *after* he goes back to Georgia?

Helping Others

As his writing developed, Curtis started to see how he could use it as a **platform for** more than just his ideas about produce. He decided to become a celebrity, to help those who couldn't read. Curtis knew enough about the game to use his connections. He called an old high school friend who was then in theater in Atlanta, and told her everything: how he fooled her and everyone else, how he finally learned to read and write, and why he wanted to get on television. His tearful **confession** moved her to call and write every station in Atlanta, and one called back. 🔢14

14 Ask Questions
What *wh–* questions will help you fully understand what Curtis is doing here? Record the questions in your chart.

. . . he **FOOLED** her and everyone else . . .

The personality he had developed to hide his illiteracy made him perfect for television. He was outgoing, funny, **somewhat self-effacing**. His appearances kept getting longer and went out to larger audiences, especially after he published his first cookbook. His audiences were growing, as was his confidence. But it took years before he could muster the courage to confess his own illiteracy on camera. He finally talked

Key Vocabulary
confession *n.*, something you say about a thing you have kept private or secret

In Other Words
an outlet a new way to use and express itself
food columnist person who writes about food
platform for way to tell others about
somewhat self-effacing and sometimes made fun of himself

a producer into doing **a segment** on illiteracy, and he felt he was ready to let the world know that he had learned to read in his twenty-sixth year. He did it on *The Home Show* on ABC, as a guest host with Sarah Purcell.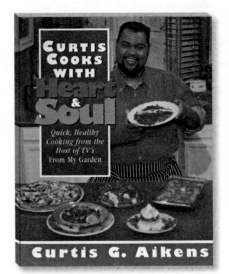

15 Text Structure: Chronology
When does Curtis finally feel he's ready to talk about his problem on TV?

"We were doing a story on how television can help people learn to read. It was about using **closed captioning**. And I actually misread the **teleprompter**. On live television. I actually asked Sarah Purcell a word on TV. . . . I wasn't even thinking about the fact that I asked until two or three seconds after I did it. I broke down and started crying on national TV." There was nothing left to hide, and no way to hide it: "The whole thing just blew up."

Aikens donates part of the profits from his cookbook sales to literacy programs across the country.

Curtis thought he had really screwed up, that no one would listen to him, that his television career was over, and that if the show had reached any illiterate adults, they would only be more convinced to hide their problem. But the opposite was true. Curtis's "screwup" had been one of those moments where television was at its best, where everything was real. The phone lines lit up, at the station and at literacy centers across the country. "It was a great day for literacy," Curtis concludes, without a hint of embarrassment or regret.

His story finished, the TV chef **climbs up on his soapbox**. The only reason he wanted to share all of this is because he has a **cause**: "Illiteracy is a problem that all of America can unite around. It doesn't

Monitor Comprehension

Explain
How is Curtis able to help others in an unexpected way?

Key Vocabulary
cause *n.*, an idea you believe in and are willing to fight for

In Other Words
a segment part of a TV show
closed captioning a feature that shows the words the people on TV are saying
teleprompter script
climbs up on his soapbox tells people about the importance of learning to read

know race, it doesn't know money, it doesn't know **boundaries**. This is one thing we can all get together on." That cause fully and completely contains Curtis's version of the American dream: "I don't get bored anymore, because I can read. I don't get lonely anymore, because I can read. I'm never out of friends anymore, because I can read. But I'm still trying to **obtain the American dream**, because I want to give everybody the ability to read. I know that sounds **hokey**, but there it is." 16 ❖

16 **Ask Questions**
What questions help you think deeply about Curtis and the American dream? Record the questions in your chart.

ANALYZE Curtis Aikens and the American Dream

1. **Explain** How does literacy change Curtis's life? What kind of power does he gain by learning how to read? Cite evidence from the text to support your answers.

2. **Vocabulary** How does Curtis's confession help other people?

3. **Analyze Text Structure: Chronology** This **Sequence Chain** shows some events in Curtis's life in the order that they happened. Add more events, including signal words or phrases to show the order of events.

Sequence Chain

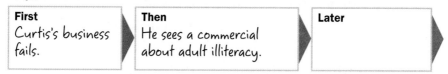

First	Then	Later
Curtis's business fails.	He sees a commercial about adult illiteracy.	

4. **Focus Strategy Ask Questions** Review the **Question-Answer Chart** you began on page 315 and add any answers you may have found. Then put a star by questions that helped you understand the biography. Put an "X" by any questions that weren't so helpful.

↩ Return to the Text

Reread and Write Many doors were closed to Curtis because he couldn't read. Reread the section "Facing the Facts" to find and describe several everyday things that Curtis could not do because of his illiteracy.

In Other Words
boundaries the imaginary lines that divide people or things into groups
obtain the American dream make my dreams of success come true
hokey silly and cheerful

Think You Don't Need an Education?

There are many options for your life after high school. Your education is one choice that makes a big difference—a difference that can add up to millions of dollars over your lifetime.

Here are some of your choices:

Technical/Vocational School

1–2 years for an applied degree or certificate in computers, mechanics, firefighting, etc.

Community/Junior College

(high school diploma required) 2 years for an associate's degree in electronics, healthcare, social work, etc.

College or University

(high school diploma required) 4 years for a bachelor's degree in most fields

Graduate School

(bachelor's degree required) 1–4 years for a master's degree, 4–8 years for a doctorate in most fields

Other

time varies for a professional degree in architecture, law, medicine, etc.

For most people in the United States, education may decide whether or not they will have a job—and how much that job will pay. What is that difference worth to you? Think about it.

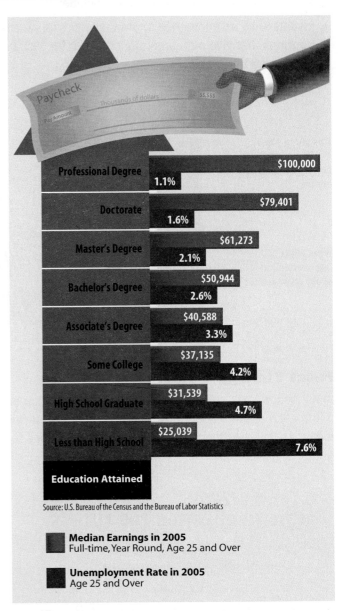

Source: U.S. Bureau of the Census and the Bureau of Labor Statistics

Education Attained	Median Earnings in 2005	Unemployment Rate in 2005
Professional Degree	$100,000	1.1%
Doctorate	$79,401	1.6%
Master's Degree	$61,273	2.1%
Bachelor's Degree	$50,944	2.6%
Associate's Degree	$40,588	3.3%
Some College	$37,135	4.2%
High School Graduate	$31,539	4.7%
Less than High School	$25,039	7.6%

Median Earnings in 2005
Full-time, Year Round, Age 25 and Over

Unemployment Rate in 2005
Age 25 and Over

In Other Words
Median Average

BEFORE READING **Go For It!**

opinion essay by Earvin "Magic" Johnson

Reading Strategies

· Plan and Monitor
· Determine Importance
· Make Inferences
▶ **Ask Questions**
· Make Connections
· Synthesize
· Visualize

Analyze Text Features

Nonfiction writers can use many devices to develop and present their ideas. Many writers use a variety of **text features**. These are simple ways to give information clearly and quickly. Some text features include:

- **visuals** such as photographs, drawings, diagrams, charts, and graphs
- **captions** that give more information about the visuals
- **text boxes** that add or highlight information.

Look Into the Text

This photo shows Magic working with teens at a computer center.

Magic Johnson spends time with students at his computer center in Philadelphia, PA.

What kinds of information can a photo show easily?

A caption explains what is shown in the photo. What information does this caption give?

Focus Strategy ▶ Ask Questions

In nonfiction texts such as opinion essays, the author provides more than just information or facts about a topic. The author also includes his or her beliefs and ideas. As you read this type of writing, **ask questions** to see if you understand the author's opinion.

HOW TO QUESTION THE AUTHOR

Focus Strategy

1. Read the selection carefully.

2. Use a **Question the Author Chart** to list questions you have about the author and the selection.

3. Find evidence in the text to support your answers. This evidence may be clearly stated, or it may be hinted at in words and phrases.

4. Review your chart to decide if the author effectively gives information, ideas, and opinions.

Question the Author Chart

What is the author's most important message?	Go to college.
How does the author state his beliefs and ideas?	
Why does the author include this detail?	
Does the author change opinions in the selection?	

Connect Across Texts

"Curtis Aikens and the American Dream" describes how one person reaches for success by learning. In this essay, what does basketball star Magic Johnson say to people about success in life?

Go For It!

by Earvin "Magic" Johnson

with William Novak

Basketball was my ticket to success. But if I hadn't been good enough at basketball, I would have been successful in something else.

Magic Johnson at the 1992 Olympics in Barcelona, Spain

I would have gone to college, and worked hard, and made something of myself. You can do that, too. Basketball is not the best way to get ahead. It's probably the most difficult path you could take. There are thirty teams in the **NBA**, and each team has twelve players. That makes 360 players who are in the league at any one time. In a country as big as ours, that's not a big number. There are about 1,800 college seniors who play ball, and only a few of them are good enough to be **drafted**. So even if you're good enough and fortunate enough to play in college, what makes you think you're going to play in the NBA? You have to understand that your chances of playing basketball for a living are **miniscule**. 1

The black community already has enough basketball players. And enough baseball players, and football players. But there are a lot of other people we could really use. We need more teachers. We need more lawyers. We need more doctors. We need more accountants. We need more nurses. We need more pilots. And more scientists.

> # We need more teachers . . . And more scientists.

And more carpenters. And more professors. And more police officers. And more bankers. And more computer programmers. And more mechanics. And more **social workers**. And more car dealers. And more politicians. 2

And every single one of these **professions**—*including doctor and lawyer—is easier to get into than the NBA.*

If you can possibly go to college, go! I know it's hard. I know that some kids you know will **discourage** you. If you're **ambitious**, if you

1 **Ask Questions**
What questions help you fully understand Johnson's message? Record them in your Question the Author Chart.

2 **Syntax**
How does Johnson's use of repetitive phrases, such as "We need..." affect the tone of the essay?

Key Vocabulary
- **profession** *n.*, job that requires education or training
- **discourage** *v.*, to make someone not want to do something
- **ambitious** *adj.*, having big goals

In Other Words
NBA National Basketball Association
drafted chosen to play on a professional team
miniscule tiny
social workers people who work for a city or state to help other people

Magic lives up to his name.

Earvin "Magic" Johnson got his nickname in high school after a local sportswriter saw him in action on the basketball court. Johnson went on to play basketball for two years at Michigan State University in East Lansing. Then in 1979, he was drafted by the NBA to play for the Los Angeles Lakers. From there, he went on to make NBA history. He was named to the NBA All-Star team twelve times and was voted both league and NBA Finals Most Valuable Player three times. He retired from the NBA in 1991. Johnson was a member of the USA's famous "Dream Team," which won a gold medal at the 1992 Olympics. He was voted into the Naismith Memorial Basketball Hall of Fame in 2002.

Magic Johnson spends time with students at his computer center in Philadelphia, PA. **3**

His basketball career over, Johnson continues to amaze. He is the head of Magic Johnson Enterprises, a company that tries to bring business to urban areas. It is estimated that he is worth $800 million from his post-basketball activities. But Johnson gives back to the community through his charity, The Magic Johnson Foundation. He provides scholarships and develops community centers and technology training centers. Johnson lives up to his own advice: Go for it! **4 5**

3 Text Features
What information do the photo and caption give about Johnson?

4 Text Features
What kind of information does this text box provide? How can you tell that it was not written by Johnson?

5 Ask Questions
What *wh-* questions do you still have for the author of the text box? Record them in your chart.

study hard, if your goals are high, some people may tell you you're "acting white." Stay away from these people! They are not your friends. If the people around you aren't going anywhere, if their dreams are no bigger than hanging out on the corner, or if they're **dragging you down**, get rid of them. Negative people can **sap your energy** so fast, and they can take your dreams from you, too.

In Other Words
dragging you down making it harder for you to succeed
sap your energy take away your desire to reach your goals

I don't mean to tell you it's easy. It's *not* easy. Growing up today is hard. I know that. It's much harder than when I was your age. We've got to quit making excuses. Quit feeling sorry for ourselves. We have to go to college. Think about business. Work hard. Support one another, like other groups do.

The government will not save you.

The black leadership will not save you.

You're the only one who can make the difference.

Whatever your dream is, go for it. ❖

ANALYZE Go For It!

1. **Explain** What reasons does Magic Johnson give for continuing one's education?

2. **Vocabulary** Why does Johnson **discourage** readers from seeking a career in basketball? What does he say about other **professions**?

3. **Analyze Text Features** Talk with a partner about the photos used in this essay. Explain whether the pictures support the text or add new information. What other photo ideas would you have included to help readers understand Johnson's opinions?

4. **Focus Strategy Ask Questions** Share your **Question the Author Chart** with a small group. Did these questions help you? Were you able to find answers?

⟲ Return to the Text

Reread and Write According to Magic Johnson, there are many things that either help us or distract us from achieving our goals. Find one of these examples in the text and write a paragraph about how this relates to your own experiences with education.

REFLECT AND ASSESS

▶ Curtis Aikens and the American Dream
▶ Think You Don't Need an Education?
▶ Go For It!

EQ How Can Knowledge Open Doors?

Critical Thinking

EQ 1. Analyze Think back to the quotation: "Knowledge is power." Give examples of how Curtis Aikens's experiences and Magic Johnson's opinions support this idea.

2. Compare Find evidence in both selections that shows how Aikens and Johnson have used their fame and success to help others.

3. Interpret Curtis Aikens says that his literacy coaches "didn't change my life, they *saved* my life." What do you think he means by this? In what way does Magic Johnson try to do the same thing for others?

EQ 4. Speculate Do you think Curtis Aikens would agree with Magic Johnson that college is the best way to open doors? Explain.

EQ 5. Evaluate Explain whether the selections give convincing reasons for learning to read and going to college. Describe the ideas that connected most to your own experiences and opinions.

Write About Literature

Public Service Announcement Watching a public service announcement about **literacy** changed Curtis Aikens's life. Work with a partner to write a public service announcement that encourages high school students to go to a technical school or college. Include information and quotations from both texts to describe how knowledge can open doors to success in the future.

Key Vocabulary Review

Oral Review Work with a partner. Use these words to complete the paragraph.

ambitious	discouraged	profession
cause	fate	reputation
confession	literacy	

Last year, my cousin Amy made a __(1)__ about a secret she had hidden for years. "I can't read," she said. "In school, I got a __(2)__ as a lazy student because that's how everyone saw me. This __(3)__ me so much that I didn't want to tell anyone the truth. Now I'll never have a good job or a __(4)__ that I like." After that, Amy and I found a program for adult __(5)__ that taught her to read and write. Soon she saw that her __(6)__ was not set—she is very __(7)__ and filled with big goals for the future. I've also changed because now I have a __(8)__ that I am dedicated to help: I'm working with schools to teach teens how to read!

Writing Application What are some things you can do to earn a good **reputation** with classmates or teachers? Write a paragraph about it. Use at least five Key Vocabulary words.

Read with Ease: Phrasing

Assess your reading fluency with the passage in the Reading Handbook, p. 760. Then complete the self-check below.

1. I did/did not pause appropriately for punctuation and phrases.

2. My words correct per minute: _____ .

INTEGRATE THE LANGUAGE ARTS

Show Possession

Use **possessives** to show who owns something.

	Possessive Nouns	Possessive Adjectives	Possessive Pronouns
One Owner	Curtis's Ginny's teacher's school's	my your his, her, its	mine yours his, hers, its
More Than One Owner	teachers' schools'	our your their	ours yours theirs

Curtis's problem was hidden. **His** family didn't know.

Illiteracy is **our** problem. The problem is **ours**.

Ask your **teachers'** help. Ask for **their** help.

This is **your** choice. The choice is **yours**.

Oral Practice (1–5) With a partner, say each sentence with the correct possessive word.

1. Curtis tried to fool (his/their) teachers.
2. He watched actors and copied (his/their) speech.
3. Many adults cannot read. The problem is often (their/theirs) secret.
4. My aunt learned how to read as an adult. This story reminds me of (his/hers).
5. Curtis's story and (its/our) message are powerful.

Written Practice (6–10) Choose the correct possessive word. Rewrite the paragraph. Add two more sentences. Use possessive words.

Curtis's problem of illiteracy held him back. He lost (his/her) business. (His/Their) secret was too big. He found literacy coaches. (Our/Their) help changed his life.

Language Development

Define and Explain

Pair Talk What is literacy? Give a simple definition of literacy, and explain why it is so important.

Research / Writing

Visual Presentation

Social Studies: Literacy in the United States
Curtis Aikens helps fight the problem of illiteracy. How widespread is this problem? And what are people doing to solve it?

Work with a small group to research the problems and solutions for illiteracy. Then create a poster that uses illustrations, photos, and text. Try to include images that connect to your school, home, or town.

myNGconnect.com
- Look for statistics and data about illiteracy in the U.S.
- Search for literacy programs in your community or state.

Display your poster in your neighborhood to provide information for people who may need help.

Language and Learning Handbook, page 702

Media Study

Evaluate Public Service Announcements

Media Presentation Celebrities often participate in public service announcements (PSAs), which inform the public about different causes, like literacy, education, and health issues.

With a partner, create a media presentation that evaluates different public service announcements:

1. Research PSAs on the Internet. Choose three causes that are meaningful to you.
2. Evaluate the effectiveness of the PSAs. What kind of language, tone, and voice do they use? How do you think they affect the viewers?
3. Present your findings to the class. If possible, role-play or show each PSA, and see if your classmates agree with your critiques.

Language and Learning Handbook, page 702

Dictionary and Jargon

An English **dictionary** gives the meanings of words in the English language. Many English words have an everyday meaning and a specialized meaning in a career field. The meanings of words also vary according to part of speech.

produce (pruh-**düs**) *v.* to make

produce (**prö**-düs) *n.* fruit and vegetables

Jargon is the specialized language of a career field. The following words have special meanings related to cooking: *beat, batter, dress, fold, skim, toss.*

With a partner, look up each of the six words in a print or online dictionary. Then answer the following questions:

- How many meanings does the word have?
- Which meaning relates to the field of cooking?
- What part of speech is it?

With your partner, research and list jargon in other fields, such as sports, education, or government. For each word, give an everyday meaning and the specialized meaning.

Development of Ideas

Good writers develop their ideas in organized and creative ways. They begin by stating a clear main idea. Then they add thoughtful, relevant details that help support the main idea.

Just OK

> Education is one of the most important things that will influence your future. Some other things are your family and your interests. Education gives you the skills you need for a successful career, and it prepares you to face the world with confidence.

Much Better

> Education is one of the most important things that will influence your future. ~~Some other things are your family and your interests.~~ Doing well in school shows that you are willing to sacrifice your time and energy to achieve goals that you set for yourself. Education gives you the skills you need for a successful career, and it prepares you to face the world with confidence. Education can open doors to a brighter future.

With a partner, revise the student model below. Look for ways to state the main idea clearly, include more details to support the main idea, and remove details that are unnecessary or distracting.

Model Paragraph

> Something that people should think about is literacy. People graduate from high school and can't read—there are even statistics that show this. But even if you get through school without learning how to read, that doesn't mean that you will do well. A few people probably do it, but most people need to read in order to survive in daily life. There are many times you can't do things if you can't read. It's important to have good math skills, too, because you may get cheated when you shop. Reading is also very fun. We should all do what we can to help people become literate because reading is something we should all be able to do well.

Write your own paragraph that describes another way that people can open doors to the future. State a clear main idea, and then add details that develop your main idea in a clear, thoughtful way.

📕 **Writing Handbook**, page 784

1

2

3

Inside a Restaurant

In a full-service restaurant, a greeter seats customers at a table where menus, drinks, and food are provided. Some full-service restaurants are part of a national chain. Others are run independently.

Jobs in the Restaurant Industry

A restaurant employs a team of workers for different responsibilities. The amount of training and experience each employee needs depends on the type of restaurant. Here are some jobs found in a typical full-service restaurant.

Job	Responsibilities	Education/Training Required
Greeter 1	• Greets customers and shows them to tables • Takes phone reservations • Acts as cashier when necessary	• On-the-job training
Assistant Manager 2	• Supervises servers and kitchen staff • Ensures quality of food preparation and service	• Previous experience working in food service • On-the-job training
Manager 3	• Hires, trains, and supervises all staff • Performs clerical and financial tasks • Handles customer complaints	• Experience in food service (often as an assistant manager) • Completion of a restaurant management program

Write a Business Memo

Practice writing a general business memo to the staff at a restaurant.

1. Imagine you are an assistant manager at a restaurant. You need to write a memo to your staff telling them about a new policy. Choose a topic for your memo: new uniforms, how to greet customers, or telling customers about daily specials.

2. Write your memo. Include the date the memo was written and when the new policy will start. Make sure you use a professional tone.

3. Read your memo to a classmate. Ask for feedback about how to improve it. Save the information in a professional career portfolio.

myNGconnect.com

🔁 Learn more about the restaurant industry.

🔁 Download a form to evaluate whether you would like to work in this field.

🔁 Download a memo form.

📕 **Writing Handbook,** page 784

Access Words During Reading

When you read, you may not understand some parts of the text. Use this set of strategies to help you access the meaning.

Use Strategies During Reading

1. What unfamiliar word should I figure out in order to understand the selection? Can I decode the word by sounding out the letters or breaking up the word by its parts?

2. Have I seen this word before? What do I know about it already?
   Now do I understand the word well enough to continue?

3. Does this part of the selection help me understand the word? Do other parts of the selection help me understand the word?
   Now do I understand the word well enough to continue?

4. Do any parts of the word help me understand it?
   Now do I understand the word well enough to continue?

5. Who or what can help me understand the word right away?
   If I still don't understand the word, I'll mark it and come back to it later.

TRY IT▶ Read the passage below and apply the five strategies above. Then answer these questions: What does it take to become a paramedic? Why do you think turnover, or the number of people who leave this job, is high?

> ▶ Paramedics go through a lot of training to become certified. Some are called upon to perform difficult prehospital procedures. Paramedics put in long hours and do not get much pay. Job turnover is fairly high, so there are often job openings.

✎ Reading Handbook, page 733

EQ How Can Knowledge Open Doors?
Consider how books can take you places.

Make a Connection

Anticipation Guide People read for many reasons. Some read for school or work, while others only read for entertainment. What do you think about reading? Tell whether you agree or disagree with the statements in the **Anticipation Guide**.

ANTICIPATION GUIDE	Agree or Disagree
1. Reading books is more important than reading papers or magazines.	_____
2. Magazines are more interesting than books.	_____
3. It's more important to read a lot about one topic than a little about many topics.	_____

Learn Key Vocabulary

Study the Words Pronounce each word and learn its meaning. You may also want to look up the definitions in the Glossary.

• Academic Vocabulary

Key Words	Examples
arrogant (ar-u-gunt) *adjective* ▸ pages 347, 357	If you are **arrogant**, you are overly proud. That **arrogant** girl acts like she is better than everyone else.
• **assume** (u-sūm) *verb* ▸ page 346	When you **assume** something, you think it is true even though you do not know that it is. He **assumes** that I am poor because my clothes are old.
• **constant** (kon-stunt) *adjective* ▸ pages 355, 356	Something that is **constant** stays the same. No matter what else changes, my love for my family will always stay **constant**.
disgusted (di-skus-tid) *adjective* ▸ pages 352, 356	If you are **disgusted**, you feel turned off or very upset. I felt **disgusted** when I saw the rude way he treated others.
prodigy (prah-du-jē) *noun* ▸ page 346	A **prodigy** is a young person who has unusual skills for his or her age. The **prodigy** could play the violin when she was four years old.
recall (rē-kawl) *verb* ▸ pages 344, 357, 359	To **recall** means to remember something from the past. I **recall** many happy memories from my childhood.
shame (shām) *noun* ▸ page 352	**Shame** is a painful feeling that is caused by embarrassment or guilt. He felt **shame** about a mistake that he had made.
standard (stan-durd) *noun* ▸ pages 344, 349	A **standard** is a way of judging or measuring things. According to the teacher's high **standards**, she was a great student.

Practice the Words Work with a small group to complete a **Synonym-Antonym Chart** for the Key Vocabulary words. Use a thesaurus to find ideas and check your work.

Synonym-Antonym Chart

Word	Synonyms	Antonyms
arrogant	proud, stuck up	humble, modest

BEFORE READING Superman and Me
essay by Sherman Alexie

Reading Strategies

· Plan and Monitor
· Determine Importance
· Make Inferences
▶ Ask Questions
· Make Connections
· Synthesize
· Visualize

Analyze Text Structure: Cause and Effect

Some nonfiction writers use **cause and effect** to structure, or organize, their ideas. A **cause** is an event that leads to another event, which is called the **effect**. Authors use cause and effect to explain why something happens and how one thing leads to another.

Look Into the Text

> In a fit of unemployment-inspired creative energy, my father built a set of bookshelves and soon filled them with a random assortment of books about the Kennedy assassination, Watergate, the Vietnam War, and the entire twenty-three-book series of the Apache westerns. My father loved books, and since I loved my father with an aching devotion, I decided to love books as well.

This effect has more than one cause.

Signal words like *since*, *so*, and *because* show how events relate.

You can begin a **Cause-and-Effect Chart** to show how events relate.

Cause-and-Effect Chart

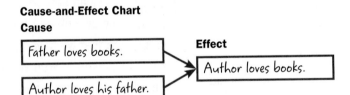

Cause

Father loves books.

Author loves his father.

Effect

Author loves books.

Focus Strategy ▶ Ask Questions

It's not only important to ask questions about a text. When you read, you also need to find the answers. Sometimes the answer to a question is "right there" in the text.

Focus Strategy

HOW TO FIND QUESTION–ANSWER RELATIONSHIPS

1. As you read, ask yourself how important events relate. Your questions may begin with *Who, What, Where, When, Why,* and *How.*

   QUESTION: Why does Alexie explain that his father loved books?

2. Reread the section to find any answers that are "right there."

   IN THE TEXT: "My father loved books, and since I loved my father … I decided to love books as well."

   ANSWER: He explains that his father's love of books causes him to love books, too. Record these relationships on your **Cause-and-Effect Chart.**

3. If the answer cannot be found in this section, keep reading. You may find the answer you need in later sections.

Sherman Alexie
(1966–   )

Sherman Alexie has said, "I have no answers. I just hope I'm asking the right questions."

Sherman Alexie says, "The percentage of Indian kids doing some sort of artistic work is much higher than in the general population—painting, drawing, dancing, singing . . . It's not a big leap from a kid who dances to a kid who writes poems. It's the same impulse. It just needs a little push."

Alexie should know. He was born into a poor Native American community on the Spokane Indian Reservation in Washington. As described in the essay, "Superman and Me," Alexie took it upon himself to improve his situation. He developed an early love of books and later decided to attend high school off the reservation, where he says, "I was the only Indian, besides the mascot."

In a literary world with few Native American authors, Alexie has created his own place. "It's selfish in a sense that we haven't had our Emily Dickinson or Walt Whitman; we haven't had our Shakespeare or Denis Johnson or James Wright."

However, that doesn't stop him from looking to the future to motivate the next generation. "There's a kid out there, some boy or girl who will be that great writer, and hopefully they'll see what I do and get inspired by that."

myNGconnect.com

🔊 **Listen** to interviews with the writer.
🔊 **Read** reviews of films the writer has written, such as *Smoke Signals*.

SUPERMAN
and Me

by Sherman Alexie

Superman from the *Myths* series, Andy Warhol © 1981.

▲ **Critical Viewing: Cause and Effect** Think of what you know about Superman. What feelings does this image and title create?

POOR BY MOST STANDARDS

I learned to read with a *Superman* comic book. Simple enough, I suppose. I cannot **recall** which particular *Superman* comic book I read, nor can I remember which villain he fought in that issue. I cannot remember the plot, nor **the means by which I obtained** the comic book. What I can remember is this: I was three years old, a Spokane Indian boy living with his family on the **Spokane Indian Reservation** in eastern Washington state. We were poor by most **standards**, but one of my parents usually managed to find some **minimum-wage job** or another, which made us middle-class by reservation standards. I had a brother and three sisters. We lived on a combination of irregular paychecks, hope, fear, and **government-surplus food**. ▪1

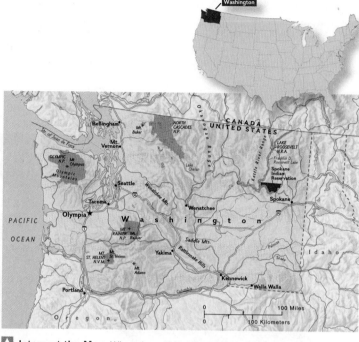

▲ **Interpret the Map** What does this map show you about the cities and land near the Spokane Indian Reservation?

CRAZY PILES

My father, who is one of the few Indians who went to Catholic school on purpose, was an **avid** reader of westerns, spy thrillers, murder mysteries, gangster epics, basketball-player biographies, and anything else he could find. He bought his books by the pound at Dutch's Pawn

1 Ask Questions
Check your understanding by asking a question about this section with an answer that is "Right There" on the page.

Key Vocabulary
recall *v.*, to remember something from the past
standard *n.*, way of judging or measuring things

In Other Words
the means by which I obtained the way I got
Spokane Indian Reservation land where the Spokane Tribe lives
minimum-wage job low-paying job
government-surplus food free food
avid eager, regular

Shop, Goodwill, Salvation Army, and Value Village. When he had extra money, he bought new novels at supermarkets, convenience stores, and hospital gift shops. Our house was filled with books. They were stacked in crazy piles in the bathroom, bedrooms, and living room. **In a fit of unemployment-inspired creative energy,** my father built a set of bookshelves and soon filled them with a random assortment of books about the Kennedy assassination, Watergate, the Vietnam War, and the entire twenty-three-book series of the Apache westerns. My father loved books, and since I loved my father with an aching devotion, I decided to love books as well. **2**

Our house was filled with books.

BREAKING DOWN THE DOOR

I can remember picking up my father's books before I could read. The words themselves were mostly **foreign**, but I still remember the exact moment when I first understood, **with a sudden clarity,** the purpose of a paragraph. I didn't have the vocabulary to say "paragraph," but I realized that a paragraph was a fence that held words. The words inside a paragraph worked together for a common purpose. They had some specific reason for being inside the same fence. This knowledge delighted me. I began to think of everything in terms of paragraphs. Our reservation was a small paragraph within the United States. My family's house was a paragraph, distinct from the other paragraphs of the LeBrets to the north, the Fords to our south, and the Tribal School

2 Cause and Effect
What changes in Alexie's life because of his father's love of books? Give two examples. Add them to your Cause-and-Effect Chart.

Monitor Comprehension

Describe
What is the author's childhood like on the reservation?

In Other Words
In a fit of unemployment-inspired creative energy, Once, when he was unemployed,
foreign impossible to understand
with a sudden clarity, and it was suddenly clear,

Historical Background
The **Kennedy assassination, Watergate,** and the **Vietnam War** were important events in U.S. history. In 1963, President Kennedy was killed. In the 1970s, President Nixon was forced to quit because of the Watergate scandal. The U.S. was also fighting a very unpopular war in Vietnam.

to the west. Inside our house, each family member existed as a separate paragraph, but still had **genetics** and common experiences to link us. Now, using this logic, I can see my changed family as an essay of seven paragraphs: mother, father, older brother, the deceased sister, my younger twin sisters, and our adopted little brother. ▨3

At the same time I was seeing the world in paragraphs, I also picked up that *Superman* comic book. Each **panel, complete with picture, dialogue, and narrative, was a three-dimensional paragraph**. In one panel, Superman breaks through a door. His suit is red, blue, and yellow. The brown door shatters into many pieces. I look at the narrative above the picture. I cannot read the words, but I `assume` it tells me that Superman is breaking down the door. Aloud, I pretend to read the words and say "Superman is breaking down the door." Words, dialogue, also float out of Superman's mouth. Because he is breaking down the door, I assume he says, "I am breaking down the door." Once again, I pretend to read the words and say aloud, "I am breaking down the door." In this way, I learned to read. ▨4

PRODIGY OR ODDITY?

This might be an interesting story all by itself. A little Indian boy teaches himself to read at an early age and advances quickly. He reads *Grapes of Wrath* in kindergarten when other children are struggling through Dick and Jane. If he'd been anything but an Indian boy living on the reservation, he might have been called a `prodigy`. But he is an Indian boy living on the reservation, and is simply **an oddity**. He grows into a man who often speaks of his childhood in the third-person, as if it will somehow dull the pain and make him sound more modest about his talents.

▨3 **Cause and Effect**
The author learns what paragraphs are. What effect does this have on the way he looks at the world? Add it to your Cause-and-Effect Chart.

▨4 **Ask Questions**
Ask *wh–* questions about Alexie learning how to read. How do asking and answering these questions add to your understanding? Find clues in this paragraph.

Key Vocabulary
- `assume` *v.*, to think that something is true even if you're not sure
- `prodigy` *n.*, young person with advanced (or specialized) skills

In Other Words
genetics the same family
panel, complete with picture, dialogue, and narrative, was a three-dimensional paragraph square of the comic had a picture, words, and a story that went together like a paragraph
an oddity someone who is very strange

A smart Indian is a dangerous person, widely feared and **ridiculed by** Indians and non-Indians alike. I fought with my classmates on a daily basis. They wanted me to stay quiet when the non-Indian teacher asked for answers, for volunteers, for help. We were Indian children who were expected to be stupid. Most lived up to those expectations inside the classroom, but **subverted them** on the outside. They struggled with basic reading in school, but could remember how to sing a few dozen **powwow songs**. They **were monosyllabic** in front of their non-Indian teachers, but could tell complicated stories and jokes at the dinner table. They **submissively** ducked their heads when confronted by a non-Indian adult, but would slug it out with the Indian bully who was ten years older. As Indian children, we were expected to fail in the non-Indian world. Those who failed were ceremonially accepted by other Indians and appropriately pitied by non-Indians. ⑤

WITH JOY AND DESPERATION

I refused to fail. I was smart. I was arrogant. I was lucky. I read books late into the night, until I could barely keep my eyes open. I read books at recess, then during lunch, and in the few minutes left after I had finished my classroom assignments. I read books in the car when my family traveled to powwows or basketball games. In shopping malls, I ran to the bookstores and read bits and pieces of as many books as I could. I read the books my father brought home from the pawnshops and

I refused to fail.

⑤ **Cause and Effect**
How do the other Indian boys at school react to Alexie's talent for reading? What causes their reaction towards him? Add this to your Cause-and-Effect Chart.

✓
Monitor Comprehension

Explain
Why was Alexie considered an "oddity" at his school?

Key Vocabulary
arrogant *adj.*, overly proud

In Other Words
ridiculed by teased by
subverted them went against them
powwow songs traditional Native American songs
were monosyllabic hardly spoke at all
submissively meekly, timidly

secondhand stores. I read the books I borrowed from the library. I read the backs of cereal boxes. I read the newspaper. I read the **bulletins** posted on the walls of the school, the clinic, the **tribal offices**, the post office. I read junk mail. I read auto-repair manuals. I read magazines. I read anything that had words and paragraphs. I read **with equal parts joy and desperation**. I loved those books, but I also knew that love had only one purpose. I was trying to save my life. **6**

Despite all the books I read, I am still surprised I became a writer. I was going to be a **pediatrician**. These days, I write novels, short stories, and poems. I visit schools and teach creative writing to Indian kids. In all my years in the reservation school system, I was never taught how to write poetry, short stories, or novels. I was certainly never taught that Indians wrote poetry, short stories, and novels. Writing was something beyond Indians. **7** I cannot recall a single time that a guest teacher visited the reservation. There must have been visiting teachers. Who were they? Where are they now? Do they exist? I visit the schools as often as possible. The Indian kids crowd the classroom. Many are writing their own poems, short stories, and novels. They have read my books. They have read many other books. They look at me with bright eyes and arrogant wonder. They are trying to save their lives. Then there are the **sullen** and already defeated Indian kids who sit in the back rows and ignore me **with theatrical precision**.

> *I was trying to save my life.*

6 Language
Notice the common structures the author uses in this paragraph. What effect does the author create by repeating the phrase *I read* so many times in this paragraph?

7 Ask Questions
Ask yourself questions about Alexie's surprise at becoming a writer. As you read this, what do you learn about how some people viewed Native Americans?

In Other Words
bulletins announcements, fliers
tribal offices buildings where the leaders of the Spokane Indians worked
with equal parts joy and desperation out of love and out of need
pediatrician doctor for children

sullen quiet and angry
with theatrical precision as if they are playing bad students in a play

The pages of their notebooks are empty. They carry neither pencil nor pen. They stare out the window. They refuse and **resist**. "Books," I say to them. "Books," I say. I throw my weight against their locked doors. The door **holds**. I am smart. I am arrogant. I am lucky. I am trying to save our lives. **8** ❖

8 **Language**
What might the metaphor of the locked door suggest about Native American culture in the present day?

ANALYZE Superman and Me

1. **Explain** Why does Sherman Alexie return to reservation schools as an adult? What is his hope for the young students there? Cite evidence from the text to support your responses.

2. **Vocabulary** According to Alexie, why did many of his childhood classmates resist books and have low **standards** for their schoolwork?

3. **Analyze Text Structure: Cause and Effect** Review the **Cause-and-Effect Chart** you began on page 341. Name two causes and two effects that Alexie gives for his love of reading.

4. **Focus Strategy Ask Questions** As you read, there may be times when you ask yourself: "Why does the author include this?" or "Why is this event or detail important?" Talk with a partner about which questions most helped you understand Alexie's essay. Make a rule about what makes good and bad questions.

🔙 Return to the Text

Reread and Write Sherman Alexie believes that reading can save people's lives. Do you agree? Reread the text to see how Alexie supports his ideas and consider your own experiences. Then write a short opinion statement about whether reading really has the power to save lives.

In Other Words
resist fight against me
holds stays shut against me

BEFORE READING A Smart Cookie/ It's Our Story, Too

short fiction by Sandra Cisneros
memoir by Yvette Cabrera

Reading Strategies

· Plan and Monitor
· Determine Importance
· Make Inferences
▶ **Ask Questions**
· Make Connections
· Synthesize
· Visualize

Analyze Text Structure: Chronology

As you have seen, writers choose from a variety of text structures, such as cause and effect, chronological order, or problem-solution, to organize their writing. In **chronological order**, writers describe the events in the order that they happened. Other writers may use **flashback**, which is a kind of chronological order that tells about events further in the past, often by relating memories, dreams, or conversations. Or writers may shift to the present time to tell about what is happening now. Signal words and phrases are good clues that the events are heading in a different direction.

Look Into the Text

The author describes time passing.

She uses flashback to tell about a time before high school.

It was that way all through high school. Then one day in college I was assigned to read *The House on Mango Street.*

Mango. The word alone evoked memories of childhood weekends. Back then my family and I would pile into our sky-blue Chevrolet Malibu and head to Olvera Street's plaza in downtown Los Angeles.

Signal words and phrases show how time changes.

Focus Strategy ▶ Ask Questions

As you **ask questions** about a selection, you may find that some answers are "right there" in the text. Other answers may not be so easy to answer. In many cases, you will need to consider how different ideas in a text are connected before you think and search for the answer you are looking for.

HOW TO FIND QUESTION-ANSWER RELATIONSHIPS

Focus Strategy

1. As you read, record questions you have about the text in a **Question-Answer Journal**.

2. Record any answers that can be found "right there" in the text.

3. For other questions, find the part of the selection that the question is asking about. Consider how the information or ideas fit together and see if you can find an answer.

4. If you cannot find an answer, keep reading. You may find an answer later.

Question-Answer Journal

Question	Answer
When did the author read *The House on Mango Street?*	Right There: in college
Why did the book remind the author of her childhood?	Think and Search: The people, places, and things (like mangos) were like her memories of the past.

Connect Across Texts

In "Superman and Me," Sherman Alexie describes how a comic book changed his life. Read "A Smart Cookie" and "It's Our Story, Too" to learn how Cisneros's book changed the life of one of her readers.

A Smart Cookie

by Sandra Cisneros

Do words have the power to change lives? Author Sandra Cisneros's characters (and her readers) certainly think so.

I could've been somebody, you know? my mother says and sighs. 🟦**1** She has lived in this city her whole life. She can speak two languages. She can sing an opera. She knows how to fix a T.V. But she doesn't know which subway train to take to get downtown. I hold her hand very tight while we wait for the right train to arrive.

She used to draw when she had time. Now she draws with a needle and thread, little knotted rosebuds, tulips made of silk thread. Someday she would like to go to the ballet. Someday she would like to see a play. She borrows opera records from the public library and sings with **velvety lungs powerful as morning glories**.

Today while cooking oatmeal she is **Madame Butterfly** until she sighs and points the wooden spoon at me. I could've been somebody, you know? Esperanza, you go to school. Study hard. That Madame Butterfly was a fool. She stirs the oatmeal. Look at my *comadres*. She means Izaura whose husband left and Yolanda whose husband is dead. Got to take care all your own, she says shaking her head.

Then out of nowhere:

Shame is a bad thing, you know. **It keeps you down**. You want to know why I quit school? Because I didn't have nice clothes. No clothes, but I had brains.

Yup, she says disgusted, stirring again. I was a smart cookie then. 🟦**2**

🔺 **Critical Viewing: Design**
What is the title of this work? How do the colors and light contribute to its meaning?

🟦**1** **Ask Questions**
What *wh–* questions help you understand this sentence better? Record them in your Question-Answer Journal.

🟦**2** **Chronology**
Which signal words tell you when the mother talks about the past and the present?

Monitor Comprehension

Explain
The mother in "A Smart Cookie" remembers her youth. How did she see herself then? How does she see herself now?

Key Vocabulary
shame *n.*, a painful feeling that is caused by embarrassment or guilt
disgusted *adj.*, feeling very upset

In Other Words
velvety lungs powerful as morning glories a strong and beautiful voice
Madame Butterfly a famous opera character
comadres very good friends (in Spanish)
It keeps you down. It keeps you from being happy and doing what you want to do.

It's Our Story, Too

by Yvette Cabrera

The Orange County Register (Santa Ana, California)
April 15, 2002

Growing up, I studied books my high school English teachers said were must reads for a well-rounded education. Books like J. D. Salinger's *Catcher in the Rye*, Fyodor Dostoyevsky's *Crime and Punishment*, and Thomas Hardy's *Tess of the d'Urbervilles*.

It was literature with great meaning that taught important lessons. But still, I **felt a disconnection**. *Beowulf* was an epic poem. But as my high school teacher went into great detail explaining what **a mail shirt** was, I wondered what that had to do with my life.

It was that way all through high school. Then one day in college I was assigned to read *The House on Mango Street*.

Mango. The word alone **evoked memories** of childhood weekends. Back then my family and I would pile into our sky-blue Chevrolet Malibu and head to **Olvera Street's plaza** in downtown Los Angeles. **3**

For my sisters and me, the treat for behaving ourselves was a juicy mango on a stick sold at a fruit stand in the plaza. We would squeeze lemon and sprinkle chile and salt over the bright yellow slices.

As an adult, whenever I had a reporting assignment near Olvera Street, I'd always take a minute to stop. Standing amid the smell of sizzling *carne asada*, the sounds of **vendors negotiating** prices in Spanish, and children licking a rainbow of *raspados* (shaved ice treats), I would bite into my mango and feel at home. **4**

That's what *The House on Mango Street* did for me.

Fresh fruit from a fruit stand at the Olvera Street plaza in Los Angeles, California

3 Chronology
Look for the phrases that signal what time periods the author is describing.

4 Author's Purpose
Why does the author switch to Spanish words?

In Other Words

felt a disconnection couldn't relate to the stories
a mail shirt armor in old battles
evoked memories reminded me

Olvera Street's plaza an outdoor shopping area that is famous for its Hispanic products
carne asada grilled steak (in Spanish)
vendors negotiating sellers arguing about

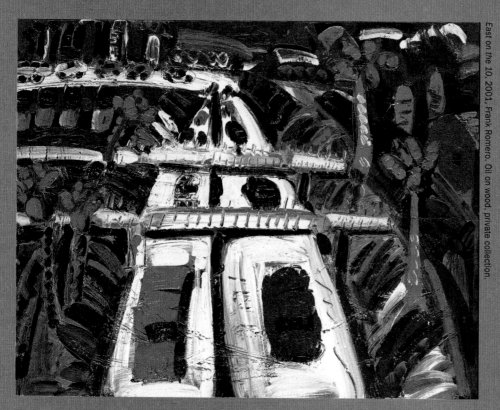

East on the 10, 2001, Frank Romero. Oil on wood, private collection.

▲ Critical Viewing: Effect What mood do the colors and lines create? How might this reflect the feeling of a large city like Los Angeles?

On the first page, Esperanza explains how at school they say her name funny, "as if the syllables were made out of tin and hurt the roof of your mouth." I was **hooked**.

I knew nothing of the East Coast **prep schools** or the English **shires** of the books I had read before. But like Esperanza, I could remember how different my last name sounded when it was **pronounced melodically** by my parents but **so haltingly** by everyone else. 5

Cisneros's hometown of Chicago may have been hundreds of miles away from the palm-tree lined streets of Santa Barbara, California, where I grew up. But in her world I was no longer **the minority**.

5 Ask Questions
Check your understanding by asking questions about this text. Reread the text to find the answer. Record them in your Question-Answer Journal.

In Other Words

hooked so interested I couldn't stop reading it
prep schools expensive private schools
shires villages
pronounced melodically said in a musical way

so haltingly said in a jerky, ugly way
the minority part of the small group that no one seemed to notice or care about

That was a dozen years ago. Today, Latinos are the **majority** in cities like Santa Ana, California, where Cisneros spoke at Valley High School.

Today, these students can pick from bookstore shelves filled with authors such as Julia Álvarez, Victor Villaseñor, and Judith Ortiz Cofer. These are authors who go beyond **census numbers** to explain what U.S. Latino life is about. **6**

Cisneros provided an hour of humorous storytelling that had the students busting with laughter. They crowded in line afterward, **giddily** waiting to get her autograph.

"Everything she explains, what she says is true," Jessica Cordova, a 10th-grader at Valley High School, says of *The House on Mango Street.* "She puts a lot of emotion, feeling, and thought into the book." **7**

Later, as I talk to Cisneros, she explains how much **the literary world** has changed since she finished writing *The House on Mango Street* twenty years ago. Back then, forget trying to get *The New York Times* to review your book if you were Latino—or getting a major bookseller to carry it, she says.

One thing has remained **constant**, something that Cisneros can see by the question that's most asked by students.

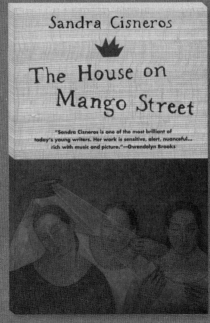

The House on Mango Street is a book by Sandra Cisneros. The narrator is a Latina girl named Esperanza, who describes people and events in her neighborhood.

6 Chronology
How have schools, students, and books changed since the author first read the book?

7 Ask Questions
What questions might the students have asked Cisneros? Record them in your Question-Answer Journal.

Key Vocabulary
- **constant** *adj.*, the same, without any change

In Other Words
majority group which has the most people
census numbers the official number of people who live in the country
giddily excitedly
the literary world the book-selling and publishing businesses

"They want to know, 'Is this real? Did this happen to you?'" Cisneros says. "They're so concerned and want to make sure this is my story, because it's their story, too."

ANALYZE A Smart Cookie/It's Our Story, Too

1. **Explain** How does the idea of reading change for Yvette Cabrera after she reads *The House on Mango Street*? Support your answer with details from the text.

2. **Vocabulary** Why does the mother in "A Smart Cookie" feel **disgusted**? Who or what is she upset about?

3. **Analyze Text Structure: Chronology** According to Cabrera, how have schools changed since her childhood? What has remained **constant**?

4. **Focus Strategy Ask Questions** Work with a group to share your questions from the **Question-Answer Journal** you began on page 350. Discuss how you found details and connected ideas to answer your questions.

Return to the Text

Reread and Write Reread "A Smart Cookie" by Sandra Cisneros. Then write a journal entry from the daughter's point of view. Describe the advice she has gotten from her mother and how it has opened doors.

About the Writer

Sandra Cisneros (1954–) is one of the leading Latina voices in contemporary American literature. She has published two novels, a collection of short stories, and three books of poetry. "A Smart Cookie" is from her famous book, *The House on Mango Street*, which is often taught in high schools and colleges today.

EQ How Can Knowledge Open Doors?

Critical Thinking

EQ 1. Analyze How does reading have the power to open doors in people's lives? Support your ideas with examples from each selection.

2. Compare Both Sandra Cisneros and Sherman Alexie talk with high school students about writing. How are the students' responses similar or different? Explain.

3. Interpret According to the selections, why do some students resist reading or working hard in school? What do you think can be done to change the way these students view school?

4. Speculate What might Esperanza's mother tell the "sullen" and "defeated" students at Alexie's school? What advice do you think Alexie and Yvette Cabrera would give these students?

EQ 5. Assess Each of these authors addresses the importance of education and reading. Which selection do you relate to the most? Why?

Write About Literature

E-mail Message Write an e-mail to one of the struggling students you have read about, such as one of Alexie's students, Esperanza's mother, and young Yvette Cabrera. Offer advice from one of the three authors about what the student can do to change his or her attitude toward school and reading.

Key Vocabulary Review

Oral Review Work with a partner. Use these words to complete the paragraph.

arrogant	disgusted	shame
assumed	prodigy	standards
constant	recall	

My little brother Eddie is a true __(1)__ who could read and write when he was only three years old. As I __(2)__ from memories of his childhood, he was a __(3)__ reader who always had a book open. People who didn't know the truth __(4)__ that everything came easily for him. But he just set such high __(5)__ for himself that he worked harder than everyone else. He became __(6)__ and upset if he made one mistake on a test. If he made two mistakes, he'd feel great __(7)__, guilt, and embarrassment. But even though Eddie is a really smart kid, he's always humble and never __(8)__. It's just another reason why I'm so proud of my little brother.

Writing Application **Recall** a time when you met someone who was **arrogant**. Write a paragraph about it. Use at least four Key Vocabulary words.

Read with Ease: Intonation

Assess your reading fluency with the passage in the Reading Handbook, p. 761. Then complete the self-check below.

1. My intonation did/did not sound natural.

2. My words correct per minute: _____ .

Grammar

Use Pronouns in Prepositional Phrases

Prepositions show how words relate. Some common prepositions are **about**, **for**, **from**, **in**, **on**, **to**, and **with**.

A **prepositional phrase** is a group of words that begins with a preposition and ends with a noun or an object pronoun. **Object pronouns** are **me**, **you**, **him**, **her**, **it**, **us**, and **them**.

> The books were **for Sherman Alexie**.

> The books were **for** him.

When a prepositional phrase ends with both a noun and an object pronoun, put the object pronoun last.

> Books were important **to our father and** us.

> I wrote **about Superman and** me.

Oral Practice (1–5) With a partner, replace the underlined word or words with an object pronoun.

1. Sherman Alexie tells about his home.
2. The house was filled with books.
3. The boy learned from both his father and mother.
4. Many of the books came from his father.
5. What does Alexie's message mean to my friends and me?

Written Practice (6–10) Fix three more pronouns and rewrite the paragraph. Then add two more sentences. Use prepositional phrases.

                                            him

    Sherman Alexie's culture is important to ~~he~~. Alexie wants young Indians to learn from them. He talks to students. He hopes to be a help to her. Alexie visits schools and wants other speakers to go to us, too.

Language Development

Clarify

Pair Talk Read a paragraph from "Superman and Me." Use everyday, informal English to ask questions to clarify its meaning.

Literary Analysis

Analyze Imagery

Imagery is language that appeals to the senses. Authors use imagery to help readers

- "picture" what is being described
- imagine how things taste, smell, look, feel, and sound
- understand how characters feel or what they experience
- experience ideas or emotions.

In "It's Our Story, Too," Cabrera uses imagery to show readers what her childhood was like and to help readers imagine the trips her family took to Olvera Street's plaza. She uses phrases that appeal to the five senses to help readers

- smell the "sizzling *carne asada*"
- see the "bright yellow slices" of mango
- taste the slices of mango sprinkled with "chile and salt."

With a partner, create an **Imagery Chart** to record examples of how Alexie, Cisneros, and Cabrera use imagery in their selections. Discuss and write about how the images help you understand and relate to the text.

Imagery Chart

Author	Imagery	Sense	Effect
Cabrera	"children licking a rainbow of raspados" (p. 353)	sight, taste, touch	I can picture what it's like to be at Olvera Street.

Multiple-Meaning Words

Many English words have more than one meaning. In the dictionary, these meanings are numbered.

recall (verb):
1. to remember something
2. to take something back

Since *recall* is always spelled the same way, the best way to figure out the correct meaning is to study the context clues near the word. Which meaning of *recall* is used on page 344?

Look up the words below in a dictionary and list the meanings for each word. Then find the words on page 344 and tell which meaning applies.

1. plot
2. state
3. reservation
4. pound

Oral Presentation

Book Recommendation Share about a book that you would recommend, or suggest, for others.

1. **Choose a Book** Think of a book that has affected your life.

2. **Share** Display the book and describe it to the class. Include your opinions, ideas, and how it has affected you in some way.

3. **Discuss** Listen respectfully to other presentations. Pay attention to the way your classmates describe their books. Then talk about the books you have each read and heard about. Make a reading list of books you would like to read.

📖 **Language and Learning Handbook**, page 702

Social Science: Write a Case Study

A **case study** presents research information about how a specific person, event, or situation relates to a larger issue. Write a short case study about the role of education in the life of someone you know.

1. **Prewrite** Interview your subject about how education has affected his or her life.

2. **Draft** Write a topic sentence that explains why the person is a good subject for a case study. Describe events and ideas in a logical way, such as chronological order. Use specific details in your description.

3. **Revise** Ask yourself:
   - Is my topic sentence clear?
   - Do I use specific details to describe events and ideas?

4. **Edit and Proofread** Check your work carefully for spelling, grammar, and punctuation.

5. **Publish** Add your paragraph to a class case study book about education.

Model Case Study

My cousin Lenny's life was changed by a great teacher. He never was a good student. Then he took Ms. Gonzalez's Spanish class. She didn't just teach Spanish grammar and vocabulary. She brought the culture alive for Lenny and the other students. Lenny loved the field trips to museums and historical sites. He started going to Spanish music concerts, where he enjoyed the fast-paced rhythms. After graduation, Lenny got a job with a health care organization in Mexico City. Now every year he visits Ms. Gonzalez's class and tells how what he learned has helped both himself and others.

> The topic sentence gives the main idea.

> Events are presented in chronolgical order.

> Specific details add to the description.

📖 **Writing Handbook**, page 784

ORAL REPORT

It would be very difficult to imagine our lives without most of the technology tools we take for granted—the automobile, the telephone, the television, the computer. Choose one invention that is really important to you, and learn as much as you can about it. You can impress your classmates with your special knowledge by giving an oral report about it. Here is how to plan and give an oral report:

1. PLAN YOUR ORAL REPORT

Brainstorm about various inventions that you use and that interest you. Then do the following:

- Choose an invention you want to tell your audience about.
- Summarize how the invention contributes to your life.
- Write questions you have about the invention: who created it, how it works, and what need it fulfills. Do research to answer your questions.
- Use your notes to write your report. Focus on three or four important points, and write facts and examples to develop each point.
- Use multimedia in your report, if appropriate.

2. PRACTICE YOUR ORAL REPORT

Rehearse your report several times before your presentation.

- Experiment with different ways to introduce your subject. If the invention is portable, you might demonstrate it.
- Look at your notes if you need to, but try to use them as little as possible.
- If you include multimedia, practice with that, too.
- Ask a friend to listen to your report and ask you questions.
- Use formal English, but avoid lengthy technical explanations.
- Make sure you speak within the given time limit.

3. GIVE YOUR ORAL REPORT

Keep your presentation lively by doing the following:

- Make eye contact with your audience.
- Speak clearly and loudly enough for the audience to understand. Use your notes as little as possible.
- Answer questions and comments from the audience.

4. DISCUSS AND RATE THE ORAL REPORT

Use the rubric to discuss and rate the oral reports, including your own.

ORAL REPORT RUBRIC

Scale	Content of Oral Report	Student's Preparation	Student's Delivery
3 Great	• Thoroughly covered the invention • Taught me a lot about the invention	• Gathered good information about the invention • Presented a clear, well-focused explanation of the invention	• Spoke clearly and was easy to follow • Responded to questions and comments very well
2 Good	• Gave somewhat good coverage about the invention • Taught me a few new things about the invention	• Gathered an adequate amount of information about the invention • Presented a reasonably focused explanation of the invention	• Spoke clearly most of the time and was usually easy to follow • Responded to questions and comments fairly well
1 Needs Work	• Gave poor coverage about the invention • Taught me nothing new	• Did not seem very familiar with the invention • Presented confusing or disorganized explanations of the invention	• Was hard to hear and understand • Was not able to handle questions and comments well

DO IT ▶ When you are finished preparing and practicing, give your oral report, and be informative!

❤ Language and Learning Handbook, page 702

How can showing the invention help your presentation?

myNGconnect.com
🌐 **Download the rubric.**

EQ How Can Knowledge Open Doors?
Explore how knowledge changes the world.

Make a Connection

Brainstorm Advances in areas like science and medicine help to make life easier, keep people healthier, and make the world a better place. Work with a group to brainstorm a list of specific ways that technology opens doors to the future.

Learn Key Vocabulary

Study the Words Pronounce each word and learn its meaning. You may also want to look up the definitions in the Glossary.

● Academic Vocabulary

Key Words	Examples
aggressive (u-**gre**-siv) *adjective* ▶ page 374	**Aggressive** means forceful, bold, and willing to take strong action. She is an **aggressive** soccer player who scores lots of goals. *Synonym*: assertive; *Antonym*: shy
● **assemble** (u-**sem**-bul) *verb* ▶ pages 371, 380	When you **assemble** something, you put it together. **Assemble** the model car out of the pieces in the box. *Synonym*: build
● **device** (di-**vīs**) *noun* ▶ pages 378, 380, 382	A **device** is a machine or tool that is used to do a particular job. A cell phone is a **device** that makes it easy to communicate.
efficient (i-**fi**-shunt) *adjective* ▶ pages 366, 374, 381	Someone or something that is **efficient** works well without wasting energy. My **efficient** car gets 35 miles per gallon of gas. *Antonym*: wasteful
● **environment** (in-**vī**-ru-munt) *noun* ▶ page 368	Your **environment** includes all the things that surround you. The race car driver's work **environment** is noisy and stressful.
obstacle (**ahb**-sti-kul) *noun* ▶ pages 368, 374, 380, 381	An **obstacle** is something that gets in your way or causes trouble for you. The fallen tree was an **obstacle** on the road.
solution (su-**lü**-shun) *noun* ▶ pages 363, 366, 380, 381, 383	A **solution** is an answer that solves, or fixes, a problem. My team found a **solution** to our problem with the project. *Antonym*: problem
● **technology** (tek-**nah**-lu-jē) *noun* ▶ pages 374, 377, 380, 381	**Technology** is scientific knowledge as it is used in the world. **Technology** can include machines, equipment, and systems that are created by science. The car doesn't run on gas; it uses a battery-powered **technology**.

Practice the Words Write each Key Vocabulary word on an index card. Then take turns with a partner to group two or more words at a time. Explain how the words go together.

assemble

device

Some <u>devices</u> must be <u>assembled</u> before they can work.

The Fast and the Fuel-Efficient

news feature by Akweli Parker

Analyze Text Structure: Problem and Solution

Some nonfiction authors use a **problem and** solution text structure. The author introduces a problem and then describes how the problem is solved. Some selections also include smaller problems that must be solved along the way.

Look Into the Text

This paragraph describes the team's problem.

A student got under the car to pop the axle in. Kinsler yanked on the suspension to create clearance. But , after many tries, it hadn't connected.

Quietly, Calvin Cheeseboro … took over.…

First, the wheel-facing side popped into place. Then, with Kinsler again pulling on the suspension, the inboard side connected with the transmission with a satisfying clunk.…

The team had hopefully resolved their most difficult problem. They'd find out soon if their solution had worked.

Signal words help to show how the passage is organized.

Begin a **Problem-and-Solution Chart** to record information as you read.

Problem-and-Solution Chart

Problem	Solution	Question
The team needs to connect an axle.	Calvin sets it in place.	Why was he able to do it?

Focus Strategy ▶ Ask Questions

There are many times when the answer isn't something you can find in the text. In these cases, look for ways to figure out the answers for yourself.

HOW TO FIND QUESTION-ANSWER RELATIONSHIPS

Focus Strategy

As you read the selection, add notes to your **Problem-and-Solution Chart**. Include questions you have about each problem-and-solution pair. To answer:

1. **"Right There" or "Think and Search" questions:** Look in the text.

2. **"Author and You" questions:** Use what you have already read. Your answers should make sense with the rest of the author's ideas.

You read: There could be scholarships and well-paying jobs—and badly needed grants.

How does the author feel about the team's goal?

He says money is "badly needed." He wants them to win.

Alternatives and Hybrids

What Is Alternative Fuel? An *alternative* fuel is any fuel other than the traditional options, such as gasoline and diesel. Many alternative fuels are also renewable, so they'll never run out.

- **Alcohols** are mainly methanol and ethanol. They are made mostly from coal and grain.

- **Blends** are mixtures of traditional and alternative fuels, such as E85 (85% ethanol and 15% gasoline).

- **Hydrogen** is mostly made from petroleum. It can also be made by passing electricity through water.

- **Electricity** is created by traditional or alternative fuel sources. It is stored in a rechargeable battery.

- **Biodiesel** is a diesel fuel replacement or additive. It is made from vegetable oil or animal fat.

Why Go Alternative? Alternative fuels reduce exhaust emissions like carbon monoxide and carbon dioxide, which cause air pollution and contribute to global warming. Some alternative fuels also cost less.

What Is a Hybrid? A hybrid car uses at least two different fuel sources. For example, it can combine gasoline with electricity.

Why Go Hybrid? Because of their special technology, hybrid cars get much higher gas mileage than the average U.S. vehicle and they are better for the environment.

myNGconnect.com

- Discover how hybrid cars work.
- Learn more about alternative fuels.

THE FAST AND THE
Fuel-Efficient

by Akweli Parker

 Comprehension Coach

The Tour de Sol is an annual competition that honors the "greenest vehicles." The goal is to produce a vehicle that reduces gasoline use and greenhouse gas emissions by 100%. West Philadelphia High School's Electric Vehicle Team won the Tour's category for student-built vehicles in 2002 and 2005—could they win again in 2006? **1**

A Test Run

Clayton Kinsler, auto mechanics teacher at West Philadelphia High School, scanned Locust Street to make sure there were no **pedestrians**. Then he hammered the throttle, rocketing the mean little coupe down the block. The car was the Attack— the country's fastest, most **efficient**, **eco-friendly** sports car. And it was created by a West Philadelphia High School team.

The asphalt-hugging, gunmetal-gray roadster was preparing for the Olympics of environmental auto competitions—the Tour de Sol in upstate New York. And much was riding on this car.

The car had won the race in 2002 and 2005, earning national attention for the team of about a dozen mostly African American **vocational education students**. If it won more Tour de Sol victories, there could be **scholarships** and well-paying jobs in the auto industry for the students— and badly needed **grants**, sponsorships, or even partnerships with major automakers for the city school's auto-motive academy.

Maybe Hollywood would come knocking. **2**

For the moment, though, on Locust Street, it was time to cut loose and show off. At each high-speed pass by Kinsler, 47, the car's student builders whooped and cheered. Then, zooming down Locust, Kinsler suddenly felt a loss of power. When he pushed the pedal, the engine revved, but nothing happened at the wheels. He coasted to a stop at 48th Street. And sat there.

The Attack in the shop. It is arguably the country's fastest, most efficient sports car.

1 Problem and Solution
The author begins by introducing the team's main problem. What is it? Add this to your Problem-and-Solution Chart.

2 Ask Questions
What questions and answers help you understand this section more fully?

Key Vocabulary
efficient *adj.*, working well without wasting energy
solution *n.*, the answer that solves or fixes a problem

In Other Words
pedestrians people walking on the street
eco-friendly environmentally safe
vocational education students students learning technical skills
scholarships awards that help pay for college
grants money to pay for the project

The students looked at one another and began walking, then running toward the car, as they realized that something had gone horribly wrong. They moved around the car **with pit crew precision** and removed the engine cover. 3

Simon Hauger, 36-year-old head of the school's Electric Vehicle Team and mastermind of the project, looked into the tangle of wires, pipes, and hoses. "The axle's done," he announced. As he had feared might happen, the car's axle had broken in two.

3 **Problem and Solution**
How do the students realize there is a problem with the car before they even get there?

Under the Hood

West Philadelphia High School's **hybrid electric and biodiesel car** goes from 0 to 60 m.p.h. in under 4 seconds and gets over 50 miles to the gallon. It is built mainly from a car kit, **donor parts**, and also has a number of **custom innovations**.

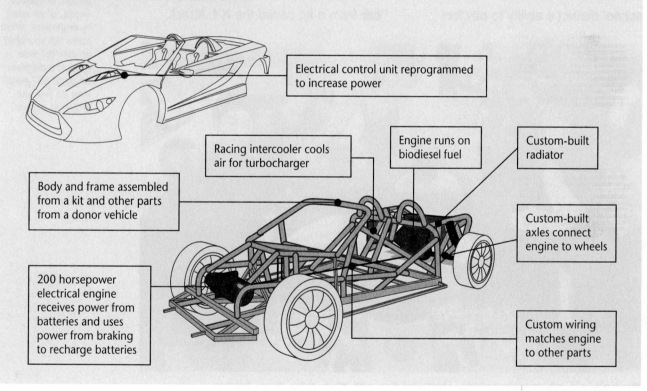

Electrical control unit reprogrammed to increase power

Racing intercooler cools air for turbocharger

Engine runs on biodiesel fuel

Custom-built radiator

Body and frame assembled from a kit and other parts from a donor vehicle

Custom-built axles connect engine to wheels

200 horsepower electrical engine receives power from batteries and uses power from braking to recharge batteries

Custom wiring matches engine to other parts

⚠ **Interpret the Diagram** What does the diagram show about the amount of work the students put into the car?

Monitor Comprehension

Explain
What is the Attack? What happens during its test run on Locust Street?

In Other Words

with pit crew precision like expert teams that work on racecars during races
hybrid electric and biodiesel car car that runs on battery power and fuel made from vegetable oils and/or animal fats
donor parts parts from other cars

custom innovations special features designed for this particular car

Overcoming Obstacles

Over the last year, the team and their instructors—Kinsler, Hauger, and shop teacher Ron Preiss—had overcome all kinds of **obstacles**:

How to **instill in these urban students** the value of hard work, responsibility, and a passion for learning when their **environment** outside of school often encouraged the opposite.

How to get the money to support the **endeavor**, which was beyond the school district's ability to pay for.

And how to use **unconventional** thinking not just to succeed, but to blow away the world's expectations of them. **4**

The axle—a thick metal rod that transfers engine power to the wheels—had required a lot of unconventional thinking. This was the fourth time in less than a year that it had broken. **5**

The team had **custom built the car** from a kit called the K-1 Attack,

4 Problem and Solution
What are some of the **obstacles** that the team leaders face if they want the team to succeed?

5 Language
This article uses jargon, or special words, often used by engineers. What clues tell you what an *axle* is? How does the diagram on page 367 help? How do you use jargon at school?

The team, in a rare moment together (clockwise from left): Terrie Gabe, Bruce Harmon, Oceansey Tete, Victor Webster, Tyson Drummond (in passenger seat), teacher Clayton Kinsler (rear), Calvin Cheeseboro (in driver's seat), Tyshona Lovett, Joseph Pak, and Kevin McKnight.

Key Vocabulary
- **obstacle** *n.*, something that gets in the way or causes trouble
- **environment** *n.*, the surroundings or conditions a person lives in

In Other Words
instill in these urban students make these city kids believe in
endeavor project
unconventional unusual, creative
custom built the car worked together to build their unique car

with parts coming from different car manufacturers. The axle presented a peculiar engineering challenge—the car's Volkswagen engine needed a way to spin its Honda rear wheels.

And so, the two rear axles are a combination of Volkswagen, Honda, and other parts welded together. The left one, shorter and less flexible, is constantly breaking. A section of cheap steel pipe held its VW and Honda ends together, but the pipe tore during acceleration. (The car goes from zero to sixty in four seconds.) A thicker, higher-quality sleeve might do the trick, Hauger thought.

A half-dozen team members pushed the car backwards, uphill to the school's garage, and gently rolled it onto a **power car lift**. The only thing to do now was saw off new axle halves from whole VW and Honda units, send them out to be welded . . . and wait. **6**

"We didn't expect it to break again," said a disappointed Joseph Pak, a **lanky**, earringed tenth-grader with gel-spiked hair. Still, he said, he was re-lieved that it had happened well before the May competition.

For Pak and other team members who'd struggled with school, the car was **an "in-your-face" affirmation of**

Student Tyson Drummond cuts pipe for a roof frame he and classmates will affix to the hybrid car they're assembling. Winning the national Tour de Sol race for eco-friendly cars could fulfill their dreams.

their talents and dreams. Pak, the team's only Asian member, admits he used to skip more school than he attended. "I was just hanging out." Now he gets straight As and wants to be an engineer.

"I've seen the **extreme** of not doing things when you should," Pak said. With the Attack, he said he's seen the extreme of what happens when you **stay the course**.

Hauger, though, was optimistic. "This is actually pretty good news," Hauger said. Their more complex engineering of the axle had held. This was a simple weld.

6 Problem and Solution
Why has the axle been a challenging problem? How has the team worked to solve it?

Monitor Comprehension

Explain
How does the Electric Vehicle program help students?

A Lesson for Detroit Automakers

The ideas that come out of West Philly's auto shop aren't **rocket science**, Hauger says, but they do require imagination and some risk-taking—traits he thinks Detroit could use. He dreams of the high school program sharing the team's know-how of building hybrid cars cheaply. No major automaker sells a performance car that **gets such outrageously high mileage**. With oil prices high and demand for hybrids soaring, the timing could not be better.

Developing a car model costs automakers about $1 billion. Even adding back the discounts and **freebies** the school team received—such as carbon-fiber body panels and custom wheels—the Attack would still have **clocked in well under** $100,000. Hauger estimated their two-seater, if **mass-produced**, could sell for about $50,000.

But before **such lofty ambitions** could become reality, the Attack's axle had to be repaired. **7**

7 Ask Questions
Ask yourself, "What does the author mean by 'lofty ambitions'? Which ambitions are they?" How do your answers add to your understanding?

Do Hybrid Cars Make A Difference?

A hybrid car combines a gas engine with one or more electric motors. This limits the amount of gas used and the emissions that are released into the environment. This chart shows the difference in fuel consumption between a regular engine and a hybrid engine.

Type	Model	Miles Per Gallon City	Hwy	Emissions Category
SUV	2006 Brand A Standard	13	17	LEV II (Low)
	2006 Brand A Hybrid	31	27	SULEV (Super-Ultra-Low)
sedan	2006 Brand B Standard	22	31	U-LEV II (Ultra-Low)
	2006 Brand B Hybrid	60	51	AT-PZEV (Advanced Technology Partial Zero)
coupe	2006 Brand C Standard	23	33	U-LEV II
	2006 Brand C Hybrid	60	66	SULEV

Sources: The California Air Resources Board
The U.S. Environmental Protection Agency

▲ **Interpret the Chart** According to this chart, what are the main differences between standard models and hybrids?

In Other Words

rocket science too difficult for everyday people to think of or understand
gets such outrageously high mileage can drive so many miles on such little gas
freebies free things
clocked in well under cost much less than

mass-produced built in large numbers by car companies
such lofty ambitions his great dreams

Students Terrie Gabe (left) and Tyson Drummond (right) peering under the hood for some last minute inspections and troubleshooting during the beginning of the Tour de Sol.

One Solution at a Time

Sixteen days later, during fourth-period auto mechanics class, a handful of team members gathered in the school shop. On a metal worktable sat the newly welded axle assembly.

A student got under the car to pop the axle in. Kinsler **yanked on the suspension to create clearance**. But, after many tries, it hadn't connected.

Quietly, Calvin Cheeseboro, a tall, athletic-looking eleventh-grader with neatly twisted braids, took over. Cheeseboro, who'd twice **installed** axles in the Attack and can practically **assemble** some of its complicated parts in his sleep, now wrestled with the greasy metal rod.

First, the wheel-facing side popped into place. Then, with Kinsler again pulling on the suspension, the inboard side connected with the transmission with a satisfying clunk. **8**

Cheeseboro, who has struggled to maintain passing grades so he can work with the team, said it felt good to be the guy to put in the **critical part**. Still, he said, he'd sooner not face such drama, especially with the May race coming up soon. "I don't want to break another axle."

The team had hopefully resolved their most difficult problem.

They'd find out soon if their solution had worked. **9**

8 Ask Questions
Ask yourself questions to add to your understanding of what the article says about Calvin. Read on to look for the answers.

9 Access Vocabulary
What do you think the word *resolved* means? What root word and context clues help you figure it out?

Monitor Comprehension

Explain
How does the team solve the axle problem?

Key Vocabulary
- **assemble** *v.*, to put something together

In Other Words
yanked on the suspension to create clearance made room to work
installed put in
critical part important piece

The Final Test of Mind, Spirit—and Car

The three-day Tour de Sol competition had begun.

Of the sixty or so Tour de Sol **entrants**, West Philadelphia was directly competing with only four others, all in the powerful **"prototype alternative fuel and hybrids" division**. But the team aimed to earn the most points overall as well—as it had done last year.

Between Wednesday and Friday, the team's **ranking** had never dropped beyond third, and it had **dominated** the driving event. The point spread was narrow. With each challenge, though, the team had found ways to stay in the running.

On Thursday night, Hauger explained the next day's 200-mile run to his team. They'd have to do a good job

The Tour de Sol Competition: How It Works

Vehicles entered in the Tour de Sol Championship participate in four days of events that **assess the "green-ness" of the vehicle** and give points for accomplishment. Events also assess **conventional** vehicle performance such as acceleration, braking, and handling. 🔟

Category / WPHS 2006 Results	Maximum Possible Points	Points Scored by "Attack"
Technology / Internal Combustion Engine: Biodiesel	100	64
Range (total distance covered) / 198 miles	100	100
Acceleration / 5 seconds	75	73
Hill climb / 10 seconds	75	72
41-mile trip to STEP* & back / 41 miles	100	100
Efficiency event / 55 mpg	250	105
Greenhouse gas per mile / 58 GHG per mile	250	242
Autocross (handling) / 31 seconds	100	100
TOTAL POINTS	1050	865.8

*STEP = Saratoga Technology + Energy Park

🔺 **Interpret the Chart** Which categories does the Attack score well in?

🔟 **Ask Questions** Ask and answer questions to develop your understanding of the Tour de Sol's events.

In Other Words

entrants competing teams, competitors
"prototype alternative fuel and hybrids" division category of cars that don't run on regular gasoline
ranking place in the competition
dominated easily beat the others in

assess the "green-ness" of the vehicle test how the car protects the environment
conventional regular, typical

of attaching the Plexiglas top to their open-air car. **Navigation** had to be perfect. And **conserving** fuel would challenge the **lead-footed** Hauger.

"The idea is to drive as slowly as possible," Hauger would say. "Without losing your sanity."

The next day, **fatigue**, cold, wet weather, and **inconsiderate** drivers all threatened Hauger and student Joseph Pak on their trip. A scary **hydroplaning incident** brought Hauger to attention around the 150-mile mark.

"I was praying, praying, 'God, please let us finish,'" he said later.

After Hauger and Pak pulled into the parking lot, a Tour official measured the biodiesel fuel left in their tank to calculate miles per gallon.

With the race tight, West Philly had one event still to complete. It was the afternoon's autocross, which involved zipping through a cone-marked path.

It was the Attack's **strong suit**, provided the car could hold together. The event could decide the overall winner.

Amazingly, West Philadelphia's **miniature muscle car** had logged the highest mileage out of its closest competitors in the total points standings—55 miles per gallon.

In total points, West Philly stood at 665.8 points, compared with the next team's 652.6.

Shortly before the race, Hauger pointed to the number "1" under the "Position" heading next to his team's listing on the score sheet.

"Heh, heh," he said. "It's ours to lose."

After the West Philly student crew helped him into the cramped Attack, Hauger pulled up to the start line. An official dropped his arm and the Attack sprang to life, with its characteristic whistling roar.

On the first run, Hauger seemed **tentative**, but managed to complete the course in a respectable 32.3 seconds.

West Philadelphia High School teacher Simon Hauger drives the Attack during the technical test of the 2006 Tour de Sol in Saratoga Springs, NY.

---

11 Ask Questions
What questions help you better understand this test of mind, spirit, and car?

12 Problem and Solution
What is the main challenge that the team has to meet? How is the team doing so far? What does Hauger mean when he says "It's ours to lose"?

✔ Monitor Comprehension

Describe
What are some of the challenges that the team faces at the competition?

In Other Words

Navigation The car's direction
conserving not using too much
lead-footed fast-driving
fatigue exhaustion
inconsiderate rude, impatient

hydroplaning incident moment when the car skidded on a wet road
strong suit best category
miniature muscle car tiny sports car
tentative cautious, hesitant

Moritz, the Jetta from St. Mark's High School in Southborough, Massachusetts, took to the course. Its driver navigated expertly, hitting 32.2 seconds on his second try.

Viking 32 of Western Washington University, a top car-design school, **snared** the low 30s.

Again, West Philly's Attack sprinted out onto the course. As Hauger swung it around each corner and accelerated, the gray missile seemed to grow more **aggressive** and confident.

With a final grunt, it shot through the finish line, and the announcer said, "30.895."

West Philly's team **erupted**. The numbers didn't lie. West Philly had won itself another Tour de Sol championship. **13** ❖

13 Problem and Solution Consider the team's original goal. Do the team members meet it? How? Add these notes to your Problem-and-Solution Chart.

ANALYZE The Fast and the Fuel-Efficient

1. **Explain** What is the Tour de Sol competition like? How does the West Philly team perform in the different challenges? Use evidence from the text to find details.

2. **Vocabulary** What makes West Philly's Attack an **efficient** car? What kind of **technology** does the car use?

3. **Analyze Text Structure: Problem and Solution** What was the continuing mechanical problem that became an **obstacle** for the team? Explain how you used the structure of the text to identify the problem.

4. **Focus Strategy Ask Questions** Talk with a partner about how your knowledge of the topic and your own experiences helped you to answer a question you had about the news feature.

⤺ Return to the Text
Reread and Write Simon Hauger and the West Philly team have dreams that go beyond winning the Tour de Sol. Identify more examples of things the team wants to achieve and write a paragraph that describes their dreams.

Key Vocabulary
aggressive *adj.*, forceful and bold

In Other Words
snared completed the course in
erupted cheered

by Mick Stevens

"It runs on its conventional gasoline-powered engine until it senses guilt, at which point it switches over to battery power."

◀ **Critical Viewing**
What is happening in the comic? Describe it to a partner.

BEFORE READING Teens Open Doors

article by Richard Thompson

Reading Strategies

· Plan and Monitor
· Determine Importance
· Make Inferences
▶ **Ask Questions**
· Make Connections
· Synthesize
· Visualize

Analyze Development of Ideas

Nonfiction writers often include **quotations** in order to develop their ideas. Quotations show the exact words a person says about a subject. Writers use quotations in nonfiction articles to:

• provide facts and opinions from a reliable expert
• add details and elaborate on ideas
• help the reader relate to the subject and person
• give the viewpoint of someone who was there.

Compare how the speaker's words are presented in the first two paragraphs below.

Look Into the Text

Quotation marks signal where the quotation begins and ends.

"We tried to run this like it was a real-world project that an engineering company would go through," said Paul Moskevitz, a machine technology instructor who was a mentor to the group.

More than a dozen students at Whittier contributed to the final product, Moskevitz said. He added that he liked how a variety of the school's programs, including carpentry, electronics, robotics, and metal fabrication were involved.

"We have lots of capabilities at this school, and it was good for folks to see the other disciplines," Moskevitz said.

The text explains who the speaker is and why you can believe him.

Focus Strategy ▶ Ask Questions

You've learned many ways to **ask questions** as you read. Now choose the strategy that works best for each question.

HOW TO FIND QUESTION-ANSWER RELATIONSHIPS

Focus Strategy

As you read, record your questions in a **Question Chart**. Then identify the strategy or strategies you can use to find each answer. Use the following strategies:

• **Right There:** when the answer is found in the text
• **Think and Search:** when you need to relate separate information you find in the text
• **Author and You:** when the answer is not in the text, use what you know about the text to form new ideas
• **On My Own:** when you can answer the question based on what you already know

Question Chart

Question	Strategy
How could the different school programs contribute to the project?	I can use "Author and You" to combine clues in the text with what I know to find an answer.

Teens Open Doors

by Richard Thompson

Connect Across Texts

The students in "The Fast and the Fuel-Efficient" found that the **technology** they used could change the world. As you read this article, consider how technology can open all sorts of doors.

Getting through high school can be challenging for any teenager. For junior Molly Rizk, who has **cerebral palsy**, one of the most difficult tasks is not taking tests at Whittier Regional Vocational Technical High School. It's opening her locker. **1**

That should change in the fall, thanks to the skill of four classmates who have designed and produced a locker remote control. It will allow Rizk to get into her locker as quickly as other students.

Assistive Technology: Resources that help people with disabilities to become more independent.
Examples:
• wheelchairs, crutches, and other equipment
• hearing aids, text phones, and captioned TV

The wheels of the iBot wheelchair can lift a person to standing height.

The remote control took less than two months to complete. It was one of four entries last month at the University of Massachusetts-Lowell's Assistive Technology Design Fair. The fair is a noncompetitive event that gives **engineering experience** to high school students who complete projects that help people with special needs or disabilities.

Since it began in 2002, the fair has grown. Now it includes more than 100 students from a dozen schools across the country.

1 Ask Questions
Ask yourself a question about Molly Rizk. What strategy will help you answer it as you read? Record the question and strategy in your Question Chart.

Key Vocabulary
• **technology** *n.*, scientific knowledge as it is used in the world

In Other Words
cerebral palsy a condition that affects the central nervous system
engineering experience experience in designing, building, and using machines

For juniors Zachary Drapeau and Tom Smallwood, and seniors Casey Hansen and Nathan Lindberg, their work could make getting through college easier to afford. If they choose to **enroll** at University of Massachusetts-Lowell, each student will be able to apply for a $2,000 grant for each of the four years.

"We tried to run this like it was a real-world project that an engineering company would go through," said Paul Moskevitz, **2** a machine technology instructor who was a **mentor** to the group.

More than a dozen students at Whittier contributed to the final product, Moskevitz said. He added that he liked how a variety of the school's programs, including carpentry, electronics, robotics, and metal fabrication, were involved.

"We have lots of capabilities at this school, and it was good for folks to see the other **disciplines**," Moskevitz said.

Students must use keys to unlock their lockers at Whittier. The **device** developed by the four students lets Rizk use a remote control. It automatically slides the bolt out of the lock. They have also given her a specially designed key. It is molded to fit her grasp, in case the batteries in the remote stop working.

The remote control uses **an infrared signal**. It ensures that if more than one is used in a hallway, the signal will only be able to open the locker **programmed to the same encryption**. **3**

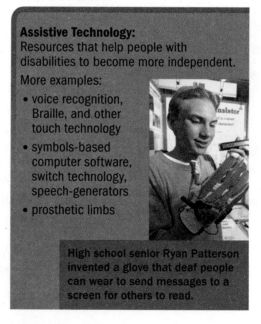

Assistive Technology: Resources that help people with disabilities to become more independent.

More examples:

- voice recognition, Braille, and other touch technology
- symbols-based computer software, switch technology, speech-generators
- prosthetic limbs

High school senior Ryan Patterson invented a glove that deaf people can wear to send messages to a screen for others to read.

2 Development of Ideas
How does this quotation help you understand what it is like to be a part of the project?

3 Ask Questions
Ask and answer "Think and Search" questions to deepen your understanding of this part of the selection. Record the question and how you use the strategy in your chart.

Key Vocabulary
- **device** *n.*, machine or tool that is used to do a particular job

In Other Words

enroll go to school
mentor teacher and guide
disciplines types of classes and studies
an infrared signal a powerful beam of light
programmed to the same encryption that has the same code

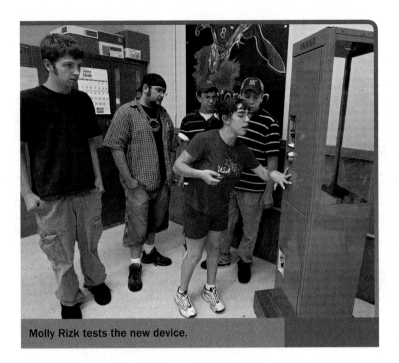

Molly Rizk tests the new device.

"There was a lot of **trial and error** along the way," Smallwood said. "Especially trying to fit the parts together and trying to get things to work and to have everything centered so the **deadbolt** would come across and strike the plate at the right time." 4

In the last few weeks, the students have been in the process of **patenting** their device. David Cunningham, the school's technology chairman, said he hopes that the device could have **broader application**. It's a realistic possibility, he said, given that the setup can be easily **duplicated and maintained**.

Next year, school officials plan to "check with local **nursing homes** . . . to see if this device could be used" to help **their residents**, Cunningham said.

Mike Hart, president of the Haverhill Rotary Club, saw the remote control in action last month when the students sat in on one of his

4 **Development of Ideas**
What does this quotation tell you about Smallwood? Why do you think he worked so hard?

In Other Words

trial and error testing new ideas and then fixing them if they didn't work
deadbolt metal bar in the lock
patenting getting ownership of
broader application many more uses

duplicated and maintained made again and taken care of
nursing homes homes for people with very serious health problems
their residents the people who live there

group's weekly meetings. Hart said he was "very impressed." The presentation "really added a lot to the meeting . . . I was amazed at **the sophistication and the complexity of** the device," he said. "It was just beyond what you would've expected their achievements to be."

Rizk said she was moved by the commitment of her classmates.

"When I first saw the actual locker, I was touched that the kids had built this for me," said Rizk. "I really appreciated that they took the time out of their busy schedules to do this for me, and I've learned that people can be very caring once you get to know them." **5** ❖

5 **Development of Ideas**
Why does the author end with a quotation by Molly Rizk? What effect does this have on the article?

ANALYZE Teens Open Doors

1. **Explain** What inspired the students to invent their device? How does the device also help the students who invented it? Support your answer with details from the text.

2. **Vocabulary** How long did it take the students to assemble the locker device? What kinds of technology did they use?

3. **Analyze Development of Ideas** Many nonfiction authors include quotations from witnesses, experts, and other people involved in the events. Find two quotations in the article and think about why the author includes them. Look at the list on page 376 for the possible reasons.

4. **Focus Strategy Ask Questions** Share your **Question Chart** with a partner. Discuss the strategies you used to answer each question. Ask your partner whether he or she would have used the same strategies.

Return to the Text
Reread and Write Return to the section that describes Molly Rizk and her disability. Then brainstorm a list of other challenges that going to high school might pose for Rizk. Write a paragraph that describes one obstacle in detail and suggest solutions that would help her overcome it.

In Other Words

the sophistication and the complexity of
the professional quality and hard work that was shown in

EQ How Can Knowledge Open Doors?

Critical Thinking

EQ 1. Analyze Review the brainstorm you began on page 362 and consider the students you read about in both selections. Why are people motivated to use **technology** to make improvements?

2. Interpret In "The Fast and the Fuel-**Efficient**," student Joseph Pak says: "I've seen the extreme of not doing things when you should" (page 369). What does he mean? How does this idea also apply to "Teens Open Doors"?

3. Compare How does each team overcome **obstacles** to find **solutions** to their problems? How are their experiences different?

4. Speculate How do you think these students' experiences will affect them in the future? What have they learned from the process of finding solutions for their problems?

EQ 5. Synthesize Considering the examples in these two selections, describe ways that technology can help open doors for people in the future.

Write About Literature

Opinion Statement Consider the work both groups of students are doing. Which do you think is more important? Write an opinion statement that explains your choice and support it with examples from both texts. Use the cluster below to organize your ideas.

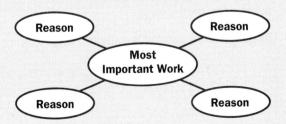

Key Vocabulary Review

Oral Review Work with a partner. Use these words to complete the paragraph.

aggressive	efficient	solutions
assembling	environment	technology
devices	obstacles	

Advances in science and __(1)__ improve our lives in many ways. Many __(2)__ car companies are taking strong action to help protect the __(3)__ that surrounds us. They are __(4)__, or putting together, new hybrid cars that are more __(5)__ because they use less gas and release fewer emissions. New machines and __(6)__ also help people with disabilities overcome __(7)__ and difficulties that get in their way. Our world still isn't perfect, but if we continue to identify problems and find __(8)__, tomorrow will be even better than today.

Writing Application What example of technology would you have trouble living without? Write a paragraph about it that uses at least four Key Vocabulary words.

Read with Ease: Expression

Assess your reading fluency with the passage in the Reading Handbook, p. 762. Then complete the self-check below.

1. I did/did not sound natural.

2. My words correct per minute: _____.

Use the Correct Pronoun

The pronoun you use depends on the **noun** it refers to. To choose the correct pronoun, ask yourself:

- Does the noun name a male, a female, or a thing?
- Does the noun name one or more than one?
- Do you need a **subject pronoun** or an **object pronoun** ?
- Do you need a **reciprocal pronoun** : **each other** or **one another**?

Study these examples:

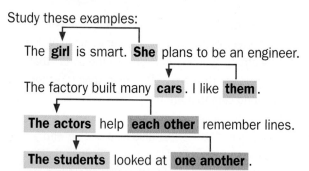

The **girl** is smart. **She** plans to be an engineer.

The factory built many **cars** . I like **them** .

The actors help **each other** remember lines.

The students looked at **one another** .

Oral Practice (1–5) With a partner, take turns using each pair of words below in sentences about "The Fast and the Fuel-Efficient." **Example:** *Mr. Preiss is the shop teacher. Students talk to him about cars.*

teacher, him	girl, her
race, it	future, they

Written Practice (6–10) Rewrite the paragraph using the correct pronouns. Add one sentence.

Clayton Kinsler test drove the car. (He/Him) sped down the street. Students who built (them/ it) cheered. (They/He) were shocked when the car stopped. The axle was broken. Students whispered to (it/each other).

Verify or Confirm Information

Pair Talk What do you think are the most fuel-efficient cars on the road today? Check a reliable source and report your findings: *I thought _____, and found out that it was (true/not true).*

Descriptive Diagram

Science: Assistive Technology Assistive technology helps improve the lives of many people with disabilities. Work with a group to research one important assistive **device**, such as text-to-speech software, Braille printers, or text telephones.

myNGconnect.com

- 🌐 Find information about how the device looks and works.
- 🌐 Read firsthand accounts by people who have used it.

Create a diagram that explains the different parts of the device and how the device works. Then write a paragraph describing the device. Be sure to use specific details and technical language in your paragraph.

Speech

Tech Talk Imagine that you are Simon Hauger and you have been asked to give a presentation about the Attack to auto company executives. What would you say about your project?

1. **Brainstorm Ideas** Jot down the ideas that are most important to discuss, such as the dream of building inexpensive hybrids.

2. **Outline Ideas** Organize your ideas into a point-by-point outline.

3. **Rehearse** Practice your speech. Remember your audience. Use formal language and jargon from the selection. Speak clearly and be polite.

4. **Speech** Deliver your speech to your classmates. Then, listen to their speeches and take notes to summarize their ideas.

🔖 **Language and Learning Handbook**, page 702

Multiple-Meaning Words

Many **multiple-meaning words** have specialized meanings in different subject areas. Review the chart. What does the word *power* mean in each subject area?

Copy the chart. For each word below, look in a dictionary to find specialized definitions in two or more subject areas. Add the definitions to the chart.

1. ruler   2. landslide   3. revolution   4. solution

Word	Social Studies	Science	Math
power	authority, influence, control	a source of energy, such as electricity	the result of a number multiplied by itself one or more times

Write a Problem-Solution Essay

An essay test in a social science class may ask you to find a solution for a problem that is described in a prompt.

1 Unpack the Prompt Read the prompt and underline key words.

> Your school library cannot afford to provide a large selection of audio books for blind and disabled students. Describe the best solution to the problem. Explain why your solution is the best.

2 Plan Your Response Put your ideas in a chart. First, describe the problem. Then list possible solutions. Provide specific details to describe why each solution will or won't work. Finally, choose the best solution. Add additional specific details to make the solution strong.

Problem	
Possible Solutions	**Why They Work or Don't Work**
1.	1.
2.	2.
3.	3.
Best Solution and Reasons	

3 Draft Use this organizer to plan your essay. Keep in mind that your paragraphs should flow from one idea to another. Limit your writing time to fifteen minutes, as if it was a test.

Essay Organizer

> A current problem in our school is [describe the problem]. This is important to solve because [explain].
>
> I believe the best way to solve this problem is to [describe your solution]. This solution would work because [explain how the solution solves the problem].
>
> My solution is better than other options because [give specific reasons and examples].
>
> In conclusion, I believe the best solution is to [restate the best option].

4 Check Your Work Reread your work. Ask:

- Does my response address the prompt?
- Does my essay suggest good solutions?
- Do I use the correct pronouns?
- Do I use rhetorical devices?

❧ **Writing Handbook**, page 784

The Sky Is Not the Limit

110th CONGRESS
   1st Session
H. RES. 661

House Calendar No. 158

RESOLUTION

1   *Honoring the accomplishments of Barrington Antonio Irving, the youngest pilot and first person of African descent ever to fly solo around the world.*

2   **Whereas** Barrington Irving was born in 1983 in Kingston, Jamaica, and raised in inner-city Miami, Florida;

3   Whereas Irving discovered his passion for aviation at the age of 15 when Captain Gary Robinson, a Jamaican airline pilot who has since served as his mentor, took him to tour the **cockpit of a Boeing 777**;

4   Whereas Irving overcame financial hardship to pursue his dream to become a pilot by working miscellaneous jobs and working for private aircraft owners in exchange for flying lessons;

5   Whereas Irving was the recipient of a joint Air Force/Florida Memorial University Flight Awareness Scholarship to cover college tuition and flying lessons for his tireless volunteer efforts and commitment to community service;

6   Whereas in 2003, Irving contacted companies including aircraft manufacturer Columbia, which agreed to provide him with a plane to fly around the world if he could secure **donations and components**;

7   Whereas over several years, Irving visited **aviation trade shows** throughout the country and secured more than $300,000 of cash and donated components including the engine, tires, cockpit systems, and seats for a Columbia 400, one of the world's fastest single-engine piston airplanes;

In Other Words

Whereas Since
cockpit of a Boeing 777 steering area of a large airplane
donations and components money and parts
aviation trade shows meetings of companies that sell airplane parts

Social Studies Background

Resolutions are documents created by members of the United States Congress. Unlike bills, simple resolutions are not laws. Instead, they may give advice, honors, or opinions.

8   Whereas in the process of pursuing his dream of an around the world flight, Irving founded a nonprofit organization in 2005 to address the significant shortage of youth pursuing careers in aviation and aerospace;

9   Whereas Irving's efforts have **garnered** widespread community support and sponsorship as an effective model to expose young people and underrepresented groups to opportunities in aviation;

10   Whereas on March 23, 2007, Irving embarked from Miami, Florida, on a 24,600-mile flight around the world in an airplane named "Inspiration" at 23-years of age while still a senior majoring in aerospace at Florida Memorial University;

11   Whereas on June 27, 2007, Irving concluded his flight in Miami, Florida, after stopping in 27 cities throughout the world; and

12   Whereas Irving continues to inspire youth and adults alike with his achievements and work to increase the accessibility of opportunities in aviation and aerospace: Now, therefore, be it

13   Resolved, that the House of Representatives—

14   (1) honors the accomplishments of Barrington Irving, the youngest pilot and first person of African **descent** ever to fly solo around the world and founder of a nonprofit organization that inspires youth to pursue careers in aviation and aerospace;

15   (2) encourages young people and minorities to pursue educational opportunities in preparation for careers in aviation and related industries; and

16   (3) encourages museums throughout the Nation related to aviation to commemorate the historic achievements of Captain Barrington Irving.

In Other Words
garnered gotten
descent ancestry

Miami Pilot Makes History, Inspires Others

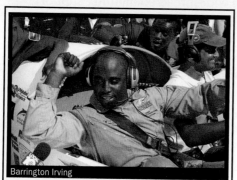

2007, John Ross.

Barrington Irving

BY DANIELA GUZMAN
The Miami Herald

1 As a young man at Miami Northwestern Senior High School, Barrington Irving knew he had **potential**. He imagined a football scholarship to a state school would fulfill that potential. When the Opa-locka **native** was offered a full **ride** to the University of Florida, he was set.

2 But another dream took off. Before turning 29 years old, Irving became the youngest person and the first black pilot to fly around the world, the founder of a non-profit organization and most recently, one of 15 National Geographic Emerging Explorers in 2012.

3 His journey began in Miami, long before he took off on his first flight.

4 Irving was sixteen and working at his parents' bookstore in Miami Gardens when he met Gary Robinson, a customer and a commercial pilot. Robinson told Irving about the life of a pilot. Although the **salary was intriguing**, Irving didn't feel he was smart enough.

5 "I never had that confidence," Irving said.

6 But his confidence soared when Robinson invited Irving to take a test flight with him in a training plane from the Opa-locka airport. Flying above his own neighborhood, from the airport he lived so close to, Irving **became enamored** with aviation. Robinson gave Irving a handheld radio that could tune into airport traffic control, helping Irving tune into his own calling. Upon graduating, Irving rejected the UF football scholarship and started working odd jobs. He cleaned pools. He bagged groceries. But he dreamed of the skies. While he saved up, Irving started studying aeronautical science at Florida Memorial University in Miami Gardens.

In Other Words

potential the ability to become successful
native resident
ride scholarship
salary was intriguing pay was interesting
became enamored fell in love

7   With the help of his mentor, Irving started learning how to fly planes, first with simulator software, which he now uses with students grades 3 through 12 in his after-school and summer camp program, Experience Aviation. The non-profit educational program is based at Opa-locka Airport and the newly restored Glen Curtiss Mansion in Miami Springs. Through the program, which he started in 2008, he has mentored hundreds of students in the South Florida area. Because of Irving's success in aviation, he decided to give back by encouraging young people to pursue careers in science, **technology**, engineering and mathematics.

8   "My ultimate goal is to show young people that they can do amazing things," said Irving.

9   It's something that Irving showed the world when he flew around the world in a plane put together from over $300,000 worth of donated parts. Irving reached out to aviation companies, telling them about his passion for flying and aerospace engineering. The companies saw the young man's effort as remarkable. The airplane, a Cessna 400, is named the "Inspiration," and was manufactured and **assembled** by the Columbia Aircraft Mfg. Co. in 2005. Without a de-icing system or weather radar, the 23-year-old pilot took off from Miami making the unprecedented journey around the globe.

10   Upon landing, Irving felt the accomplishment would not be complete without teaching minority youth that they could do the same. Under his guidance, 60 high school students built a plane in 10 weeks—from scratch. Then, Barrington tested it out with a flight over Miami. The program evolved into Experience Aviation. There are some students in the program that are coming straight from jail, and some that are straight-A students. But according to Irving, you wouldn't be able to tell the difference when they're learning how to fly on a simulator, or building an engine.

11   Daniel Diaz, 14, an incoming ninth-grader at Coral Park Senior High, has participated in Experience Aviation for three years. While he had never seen aviation as a **field** before, he has his mind set on being an aeronautical engineer.

12   "I have a chance to do things that a lot of people my age don't have," said Diaz, who flew with Irving in a small plane last year, sealing his love for flying. "I never thought I could feel what it's like to be in the sky. Now that's all I want to do." ❖

Key Vocabulary
- **technology** *n.*, scientific knowledge as it is used in the world
- **assemble** *v.*, to put something together

In Other Words
field career option

OPENING DOORS

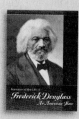

EQ ESSENTIAL QUESTION:
How Can Knowledge Open Doors?

myNGconnect.com
◎ Download the rubric.

Present Your Project: Class Newspaper or Magazine

It's time to present your class newspaper or magazine about the Essential Question for this unit: How Can Knowledge Open Doors?

1 Review and Complete Your Plan

Consider these points as you complete your project:

- What kinds of stories interest your readers?
- What materials, such as photographs and interviews, do you need?
- What are the best ways to present the information?

2 Publish Your Newspaper or Magazine

Consider ways to get your newspaper or magazine out. You might publish it electronically on your school computer network. You could also photocopy and distribute it to classmates.

3 Evaluate the Newspaper or Magazine

Use the online rubric to evaluate the class newspaper or magazine.

Reflect on Your Reading

Many of the people in the selections in this unit and in the Edge Library found ways that knowledge could open doors to success.

Think back on your reading of the unit selections, including your choice of Edge Library books. Then discuss the following with a partner or in a small group.

Genre Focus Compare and contrast the elements of a biography with an essay. Write your interpretive response using quotations and relevant evidence from the selections. Give examples, using the selections in this unit.

Focus Strategy Choose a selection in this unit that might be difficult for someone to read. Think of three places where asking questions about self, the text, or the author could help readers understand the text. Mark these places with self-stick notes to remind readers to ask questions as they read.

EQ Respond to the Essential Question

Throughout this unit, you have been thinking about how knowledge can open doors. What have you decided? Support your response with evidence from your reading, discussions, research, and writing.

Write a Research Report

Writing Mode
Informative/Explanatory

Writing Trait Focus
Development of Ideas

How do you find out more about something that interests you? You do research, or gather information about it. You also ask research questions that can be changed as you go along. Here's your chance to learn more about technology as you write a research report.

Study Research Reports

Research reports present a synthesis, or compilation, of information about a topic. In a research report, you combine and organize facts from different sources. You put the information in your own words and let your readers know where you found it.

❶ Connect Writing to Your Life

How do you find the location of a new restaurant? You look it up on the Internet or in the phone book. How do you find a part-time job? You read the want ads in the paper or look for "now hiring" signs in store windows. All of these methods, no matter how simple, are a form of research. What other kinds of research do you perform in everyday life?

❷ Understand the Form

Like other kinds of informative/explanatory writing, a research report has an introduction, a body, and a conclusion. It is written with a formal voice that presents the information clearly and objectively. An additional feature of a research report is a list of Works Cited at the end. This list includes the sources of information you cite, or use, in your report. A good research report must contain the following elements.

1. Thesis Statement	A **thesis statement** consists of one or two sentences that state the **controlling**, or main, **idea** that you will develop in your report or essay. It usually appears in the introduction and is restated in the conclusion.
2. Supporting Information and Evidence	Supporting information and evidence come from your research on your topic and make up the body of the paper. They should both relate to the thesis statement and provide background or proof.
3. Citations	Citations are references to the sources from which you gathered your information and evidence. They appear with the supporting information and evidence you are citing, or using, in your paper.
4. Conclusion	In the conclusion, you restate your thesis statement and briefly summarize your supporting ideas.
5. Works Cited	This list appears after the conclusion and shows all the sources you used to write your report. Use a style guide to learn how to format and arrange your sources.

Before you get started, you need to become familiar with the research process.

Thesis Tip

A good thesis statement should be thoughtful and interesting. It should make your audience want to learn more about your topic.

The following are examples of what to avoid when writing your thesis:

- a long list of everything you are going to cover in the paper
- a statement that most people already know to be true

❸ Understand the Research Process

When you research a topic, you look for useful, accurate, and trustworthy information about it.

- **Decide What You Need to Know** What do you want to know about your topic? Make a list of questions that you would like to answer. Look at the most important words in your questions. Those are **key words** that you can use to find information.

- **Locate Resources** Find sources of information about your topic. Typical resources are print materials, such as books, magazines, and newspapers, and electronic media, such as documentaries or Web sites.

- **Include Primary and Secondary Resources** There are two kinds of resources: primary and secondary sources. **Primary sources** give firsthand information about a topic. Some examples are historical documents, diaries, and letters. **Secondary sources** give explanations and interpretations of a topic. Some examples are encyclopedias, books, and journal articles.

- **Evaluate the Resources** Not everything in print or online is useful, accurate, and trustworthy. To check the validity of your resources, answer the questions below. The more you can answer with a "yes," the more likely that you can use the resource.

  1. Will this resource answer at least some of my questions?
  2. Does this resource explain my topic in ways that I can understand?
  3. Can I tell who the author is?
  4. Is the author an expert on my topic?
  5. Is the information up to date?

- **Gather Information and Take Notes** Use tables of contents, indexes, and Internet search engines to locate your key words. This will help you save time as you look for information. While you read, jot down important ideas on note cards along with their sources.

📖 **Language and Learning Handbook**, pp. 725–727

> ### Research Tip
>
> Paraphrase, or take notes in your own words, to avoid **plagiarizing**. This occurs when you use someone else's words or ideas without giving the person credit.

Prompt Write a research report about the origin or history of an everyday invention. Be sure to tell:

- what the invention is and how it originated
- how it developed into what we use today
- how it has changed the way people live and why it matters

Tip

Throughout this project, refer to the Writing Handbook, pp. 812–815.

Prewrite

Once you know the basics of research reports, you can plan one of your own. Planning will make it easier for you to write later on.

❶ Choose Your Topic

Think of an everyday tool or gadget that you want to learn more about.

- Pick something that you enjoy using.
- Pick something that puzzles or interests you.
- Brainstorm with friends or family members about which inventions interest them.

❷ Clarify the Audience, Thesis Statement, and Purpose

Your teacher and your classmates will probably be part of your audience. Who else would like to know about your topic? Jot down your ideas.

What aspect of your topic will you focus on? Write one or two sentences that summarize what your research will be about. These sentences will form your **thesis statement**.

Think about your purpose for writing. Is it to inform? Why else might you write about your topic? Write down your ideas.

❸ Do Your Research

Use questions to drive your research. How did the invention originate? How has it changed everyday life? If you are unable to find sources based on your research questions, revise your questions and refocus your research. Be sure to take detailed notes on cards. Use a separate card for each piece of information. Remember to paraphrase. Use quotation marks if you write an exact quotation. Include the source information, too.

Prewriting Tip

Be sure that your topic isn't too broad, or general, to cover in a short report.

Also be sure that your topic will be of interest to your audience. Ask the question "Why should we care?" about your topic. If you can't come up with a reason, you might want to choose a different topic.

Prewriting Tip

Read your note cards carefully and pull out the ones that are related to your thesis statement. Sort these note cards into groups based on common ideas. The idea for each group will become a main point in your research paper.

author	*Robert V. Bellamy, Jr., and James R. Walker*
title	*Television and the Remote Control*
where and when published	*New York: Guilford Press, 1996*
	Zenith Space Command first sold in 1956 (p. 50)

➍ Evaluate Your Sources

As you conduct your research and choose your sources, evaluate the credibility, or believability, of the source and what is said. To check the validity of your sources, consider the following:

- Who wrote the information? Is the source written by an authority on the topic?
- How recent is the information? Check the publication date to see if the source reflects the most current research on your topic.
- Is it a reliable resource? Some popular-interest magazines or Web sites may not be considered credible sources. More reliable sources include an approved encyclopedia, a scholarly Web site, or a respected newspaper or magazine.

Refer to the **Language and Learning Handbook** on page 727 for information about evaluating and citing sources.

➎ Finish Your Writing Plan

Choose a graphic organizer, such as an outline, to create a Writing Plan. Use your groupings to help organize your main points.

Technology Tip

Use the Outline feature in a word-processing program to help create your plan.

Writing Plan

Topic	the history of the remote control
Audience	my teacher and classmates
Thesis Statement	Many people deserve credit for inventing the remote control.
Purpose	to inform
Time Frame	two weeks from today

I. Introduction
   A. remotes used for many things today
   B. who's responsible
II. Body
   A. Eugene McDonald's invention
   B. Eugene Polley's improvement
   C. Robert Adler's invention
III. Conclusion
   A. restate thesis
   B. summarize key points

Reflect on Your Writing Plan

▶ Are your main points organized in a way that will make your report easy to understand? Do you have enough research to support your thesis statement?

✔ Write a Draft

Use your Writing Plan as a guide while you write your report. It's OK to make mistakes. You'll have chances to improve your draft later on.

❶ Keep Your Ideas Flowing

If you took good notes during your research, you have a head start on the writing. Use your notes to write your draft. As you write each section, your draft will grow. Also, keep in mind the way your paragraphs work together. You want your draft to flow smoothly from one idea to another and one paragraph to another.

❷ Cite Your Sources

As you write, cite your sources. That is, tell where you got information, ideas, or words that are not your own. For example, put the author's name in parentheses after the information, along with the page number on which the information was found. This is called the parenthetical method. Check with your teacher to find out what citation style you should use.

> Robert Adler is known as "the father of the remote" (Gregory 3).

After you finish writing, create your Works Cited list. Include all the sources that you cited in your paper. Sources are listed in alphabetical order by authors' last names.

🔖 **Language and Learning Handbook**, p. 729.

❸ Student Model

Read this draft to see how the student used the Writing Plan to get ideas down on paper. The student will fix any mistakes later.

Drafting Tip

Some of your sources may not have a listed author. In this case, you should use part of the title in your parenthetical element. You can also use it when alphabetizing your Works Cited list.

Format the titles of books, journals, Web sites, and newspapers with underlining or italics. The MLA format (shown in the student model) gives preference to underlining, but if you type your research paper, you may use italics instead, if your teacher allows it.

A History of the Remote Control

Today, a person can turn on the TV, adjust the volume, play a video game, or fast-forward through a movie without ever getting out of their chair. One revolutionary device has made this possible. What is it? Duh, they're remote controls! Several people deserve credit for this life-changing invention.

The story of the remote's development begins with Eugene McDonald, founder of Zenith Radio Corporation now known as Zenith

Electronics Corporation. Late in the 1940s, McDonald decided that Zenith ought to give people a way to control their TVs from their couches. By 1950, Zenith's engineers had created a device that McDonald called the Lazy Bones.

McDonald wanted something better. He specifically told his engineers that it should enable viewers to avoid commercials. ("Five Decades" 1) One engineer, Eugene Polley, created a remote that used a light beam. It became known as the Flashmatic. The viewer pointed their Flashmatic at the TV controls and pressed a button, and flashes of light turned the picture on or off and the sound up or down. The Flashmatic's drawback was that they would not work in bright light. If sunlight hit the targets, the TV might turn on and off by itself.

McDonald again called on Zenith's engineers to come up with something better. This time, Robert Adler invented a remote that uses sound instead of light. It is a small box with a number of keys on top. In some ways it is like a miniature piano. By pressing the keys, the user played musical tones. A receiver in the TV detected the sounds and responds to them. People do not notice the sounds because they were too high-pitched for the human ear. Adler's device went on sale in 1956 as the Zenith Space Command (Bellamy and Walker 50).

In the end, Polley's invention was the one that led to the modern remote. Today's remotes use light, not sound, to communicate with the TV. The light it uses is infrared, so bright light is not a problem anymore. In popular histories of television, Adler is known as "the father of the remote (Gregory 3)". Polley has said that his invention was first and he should have gotten more recognition. Adler seems to have agreed. When he was interviewed in 2006 at the age of 92, Adler said, "I don't believe that it has a single father" (3).

Works Cited

Bellamy, Robert V., Jr., and James R. Walker. Television and the Remote
    Control: grazing on a vast wasteland. New York: Guilford, 1996.
Gregory, Ted. "Meet your Maker, Couch Potatoes." Chicago Tribune
    5 Feb. 2006: 1.
"Five Decades Of Channel Surfing: History Of The TV Remote Control."
    Zenith.com. 2006. Zenith Electronics Corp. 14 Dec. 2006
    <http://www.zenith.com/sub_about/about_remote.html>.

Reflect on Your Draft

▶ Is your thesis statement clear? Have you used your note cards and followed your Writing Plan?

✔ Revise Your Draft

Your first draft is done. Now, you need to polish it. Improve the development of ideas and your choice of supporting details.

❶ Revise for Development of Ideas

Good writing contains **well-developed ideas**. A good writer **elaborates**, or builds, on his or her ideas by providing specific details for support.

In a good research report, the writer elaborates on the thesis statement by supporting it with specific facts and data gathered from his or her research. The writer also makes sure that each piece of information supports the thesis statement and removes any information that does not.

Don't expect to fully develop all of your ideas in your first draft. As you read your draft, you may notice that some of your body paragraphs need more details. Adding specific facts such as names, dates, and places will help you better narrate the story of the scientific invention you chose to write about.

TRY IT ▶ Evaluate the drafts below. Does either one contain facts or data that do not support the thesis statement? Which one needs more development? Discuss them with a partner, using the rubric to decide.

Draft 1

> The story of the remote's development begins with Eugene McDonald, founder of Zenith Radio Corporation now known as Zenith Electronics Corporation. Late in the 1940s, McDonald decided that Zenith ought to give people a way to control their TVs from their couches. By 1950, Zenith's engineers had created a device that McDonald called the Lazy Bones.

Draft 2

> The story of the remote's development begins with Eugene McDonald, founder of Zenith Radio Corporation. He had Zenith's engineers create a device that he called the Lazy Bones.

Now use the rubric to evaluate the development of ideas in your own draft. What score do you give your draft and why?

Development of Ideas

myNGconnect.com

- Rubric: Development of Ideas
- Evaluate and practice scoring other student reports.

	How thoughtful and interesting is the writing?	How well are the ideas or claims explained and supported?
4 Wow!	The writing engages the reader with meaningful ideas or claims and presents them in a way that is interesting and appropriate to the audience, purpose, and type of writing.	The ideas or claims are fully explained and supported. • The ideas or claims are well developed with important details, evidence, and/or description. • The writing feels complete, and the reader is satisfied.
3 Ahh.	**Most** of the writing engages the reader with meaningful ideas or claims and presents them in a way that is interesting and appropriate to the audience, purpose, and type of writing.	**Most** of the ideas or claims are explained and supported. • Most of the ideas or claims are developed with important details, evidence, and/or description. • The writing feels mostly complete, but the reader still has some questions.
2 Hmm.	**Some** of the writing engages the reader with meaningful ideas or claims and presents them in a way that is interesting and appropriate to the audience, purpose, and type of writing.	**Some** of the ideas or claims are explained and supported. • Only some of the ideas or claims are developed. Details, evidence, and/or description are limited or not relevant. • The writing leaves the reader with many questions.
1 Huh?	The writing does <u>not</u> engage the reader. It is not appropriate to the audience, purpose, and type of writing.	The ideas or claims are <u>not</u> explained or supported. The ideas or claims lack details, evidence, and/or description, and the writing leaves the reader unsatisfied.

❷ Revise Your Draft

You've now evaluated the development of ideas in your own draft. If you scored 3 or lower, how can you improve your work? Use the checklist below to revise your draft.

Revision Checklist

Ask Yourself	Check It Out	How to Make It Better
Are the ideas in my report clear?	If your score is 3 or lower, revise.	☐ If your report does not have a thesis statement, add one. ☐ Be sure that each body paragraph relates to the thesis. ☐ Make the main idea of each paragraph easy to identify. If necessary, add topic sentences.
Have I answered my major research question?	If your score is 3 or lower, revise.	☐ Look back at your note cards and see if there is information you may have overlooked while writing your draft. ☐ Add more specific details appropriate to the content area, such as scientific or technical facts, names, dates, and places. ☐ If necessary, change your question and do more research.
Does my report have an introduction, a body, and a conclusion?	Find and mark the boundaries between the parts.	☐ Add any part that is missing.
Have I used a formal tone?	Look for informal language, including contractions.	☐ Spell out contractions. ☐ Replace slang with more formal language and academic terms.
Do I cite everything that I need to cite in my report?	Reread your report to be sure that any ideas or words that are not your own are properly cited.	☐ Add citations where necessary. These should be included for quotations and information that you summarized or paraphrased. ☐ Use a style manual to make sure you have correctly formatted your citations.
Is every source cited included on a Works Cited list?	Compare your Works Cited list with your citations.	☐ Add any missing information.

📖 **Writing Handbook**, pp. 785–802; 812–815

❸ Conduct a Peer Conference

It helps to get a second opinion when you are revising your draft. Ask a partner to read your draft and look for the following:

- any part of the draft that is confusing
- any element that seems to be missing or out of place
- any place where the tone seems inappropriate for a research report
- anything that the person doesn't understand

Then talk with your partner about the draft. Focus on the items in the Revision Checklist. Use your partner's comments to make your report clearer, more complete, and easier to understand.

❹ Make Revisions

Look at the revisions below and the peer-reviewer conversation on the right. Notice how the peer reviewer commented and asked questions. Notice how the writer used the comments and questions to revise.

Revised for Development of Ideas and Tone

> The story of the remote's development begins with Eugene McDonald, founder of Zenith Radio Corporation now known as Zenith Electronics Corporation. Late in the 1940s, McDonald decided that Zenith ought to give people a way to control their TVs from their couches. By 1950, Zenith's engineers had created a device that McDonald called the Lazy Bones. The Lazy Bones worked, but it had one big drawback: It was connected to the TV by a cable.
>
> McDonald wanted something better. He specifically told ~~his engineers~~ them that it should enable viewers to avoid commercials. ("Five Decades" 1) One engineer, Eugene Polley, created a remote that used a light beam. It became known as the Flashmatic. The viewer pointed their Flashmatic at the TV controls and pressed a button, and flashes of light turned the picture on or off and the sound up or down. The Flashmatic's drawback was that they ~~wouldn't~~ would not work in bright light. If sunlight hit the targets, the TV might turn on and off by itself, ~~which was pretty weird~~. He challenged his engineers to come up with a remote that worked without wires.

Peer Conference

Reviewer's Comment: I'm a little confused. Why did McDonald want something better? What was wrong with the Lazy Bones?

Writer's Answer: That's a good question I hadn't really thought about. I'll need to do some more research to answer it.

Reviewer's Comment: Do you really need to say that it "was pretty weird" in the last sentence? It doesn't sound very academic, and I don't think it adds much.

Writer's Answer: You're right. I'll also spell out the contraction "wouldn't," since "would not" will sound more formal.

Reflect on Your Revisions

▶ Which revisions improved your paper the most? Take note of them. The next time you write, refer to your notes to remember which areas you most want to improve.

✔ Edit and Proofread Your Draft

Your revision should now be complete. Before you share it with others, find and fix any mistakes that you made.

❶ Capitalize the Titles of Publications

Capitalize all main words in the titles of resources. Do not capitalize small words such as *a*, *on*, *the*, and *of*. The first word in a title should always be capitalized, even if it's a small word.

Book: *Television: Critical Methods*
Magazine: *TV Guide*
Newspaper: *The Washington Post*
Article: "You Watched It!"

TRY IT ▶ Copy the titles. Fix the capitalization errors. Use proofreader's marks.

> 1. *Television and the Remote Control: grazing on a vast wasteland*
> 2. "Five Decades Of Channel Surfing: History Of The TV Remote"

❷ Use Parentheses Correctly

Parentheses ( ) can be used to set off a sentence, phrase, or citation.

- If the words in parentheses interrupt the train of thought or are a citation, the end punctuation goes after the end parenthesis.

  Half a billion remote controls are in use (Bellamy and Walker 1–2**).**

  Many different devices can now be operated with one remote control (called a universal remote**).**

- When you are citing a direct quotation, the citation comes after the end quotation and before the end punctuation.

  He is "the greatest inventor on the planet**" (Smith 53).**

TRY IT ▶ Copy the sentences. Correct any errors with parentheses.

> 1. The story of the remote's development begins with Eugene McDonald, founder of Zenith Radio Corporation now known as Zenith Electronics Corporation.
> 2. He specifically told his engineers that it should enable viewers to avoid commercials. ("Five Decades" 1)
> 3. In popular histories of television, Adler is known as "the father of the remote (Gregory 3)".

Proofreading Tip

If you are unsure about whether a word in a title should be capitalized or not, look in a style manual to see if there is a similar example.

Proofreader's Marks

Use proofreader's marks to correct errors.

Capitalize:
An article in ̲newsweek discussed the remote control.

Do not capitalize:
The book *How ⁄The Remote Changed TV* mentioned Adler.

Add parentheses:
Polley is the real father of the remote (Gregory 3).

❸ Use Consistent Verb Tense

A paragraph or essay that has shifting verb tenses can be difficult to follow. When you write, you need to choose a tense and stick to it. Change tense only to talk about something that happened before or after the time that you are writing about. Here are some general tips:

- Use the past tense to tell a story and to talk about historical events.
- Use the present tense to talk about facts, literary works, actions that continually happen, and your own ideas.

TRY IT ▶ Rewrite the paragraph, correcting any inconsistencies in verb tense.

> McDonald again called on Zenith's engineers to come up with something better. This time, Robert Adler invented a remote that uses sound instead of light. It is a small box with a number of keys on top. In some ways it is like a miniature piano. By pressing the keys, the user played musical tones. A receiver in the TV detected the sounds and responds to them. People do not notice the sounds because they were too high-pitched for the human ear. Adler's device went on sale in 1956 as the Zenith Space Command (Bellamy and Walker 50).

❹ Make Pronouns Agree with Their Antecedents

A pronoun takes the place of a noun. The pronoun you use depends on its antecedent, or the noun it replaces. To choose the correct pronoun, you need to decide if the antecedent is male or female and if it is singular or plural.

The **man** said **he** broke the TV's remote.

The **remote** is broken. **It** needs to be repaired.

In paragraphs and essays, the antecedent may not always appear in the same sentence as the pronoun. Check your work to be sure you are not switching from singular to plural pronouns, or vice versa, to describe the same antecedent.

TRY IT ▶ Copy the sentences. Correct any pronoun agreement errors.

> 1. What is it? They're remote controls.
> 2. The viewer pointed their Flashmatic at the TV controls and pressed a button.
> 3. The Flashmatic's drawback was that they would not work in bright light.

🔖 **Writing Handbook**, p. 784

Reflect on Your Corrections

▶ Look back at any edits you made. Do you see a pattern? If there are things you keep missing, make a list of what to watch in your writing. Then review the grammar concepts to make sure you understand them and can use them correctly in your writing.

5 Edited Student Draft

Here's the student's draft, revised and edited. How did the writer improve it?

A History of the Remote Control

Today, a person can turn on the TV, adjust the volume, play a video game, or fast-forward through a movie without ever getting out of his or her chair. One revolutionary device has made this possible. What is it? It is the remote control, and several people deserve credit for this life-changing invention.

The story of the remote's development begins with Eugene McDonald, founder of the Zenith Radio Corporation (now known as Zenith Electronics Corporation). Late in the 1940s, McDonald decided that Zenith ought to give people a way to control their TVs from their couches. By 1950, Zenith's engineers had created a device that McDonald called the Lazy Bones. The Lazy Bones worked, but it had one big drawback. It was connected to the TV by a cable.

McDonald wanted something better. He challenged his engineers to come up with a remote that worked without wires. He specifically told them that it should enable viewers to avoid commercials ("Five Decades" 1). One engineer, Eugene Polley, created a remote that used a light beam. It became known as the Flashmatic. The viewer pointed his or her Flashmatic at the TV controls and pressed a button, and flashes of light turned the picture on or off and the sound up or down. The Flashmatic's drawback was that it would not work in bright light. If sunlight hit the targets, the TV might turn on and off by itself.

McDonald again called on Zenith's engineers to come up with something better. This time, Robert Adler invented a remote that used sound instead of light. It was a small box with a number of keys on top. In some ways it was like a miniature piano. By pressing the keys, the user played musical tones. A receiver in the TV detected the sounds and responded to them. People did not notice the sounds because they were too high-pitched for the human ear. Adler's device went on sale in 1956 as the Zenith Space Command (Bellamy and Walker 50).

In the end, Polley's invention was the one that led to the modern remote. Today's remotes use light, not sound, to communicate with the TV. The light they use is infrared, so bright light is not a problem anymore. In popular histories of television, Adler is known as "the father of the remote" (Gregory 3). Polley has said that his invention was first and he should have

---

The writer corrected the **pronoun agreement** error and changed the **tone** to make it more formal.

The writer used **parentheses** to set apart a phrase that interrupts the train of thought.

The writer added more details to develop an idea.

The writer correctly used end punctuation with **parentheses**.

The writer corrected the **pronoun agreement** error.

The writer used **consistent verb tense**.

The writer corrected the **pronoun agreement** error (and changed the verb form).

The writer correctly used quotation marks and end punctuation with **parentheses**.

gotten more recognition. Adler seems to have agreed. When he was interviewed in 2006 at the age of 92, Adler said, "I don't believe that it has a single father" (3).

Works Cited

Bellamy, Robert V., Jr., and James R. Walker. Television and the Remote Control: Grazing on a Vast Wasteland. New York: Guilford, 1996.

Gregory, Ted. "Meet Your Maker, Couch Potatoes." Chicago Tribune 5 Feb. 2006: 1.

"Five Decades of Channel Surfing: History of the TV Remote Control." Zenith.com. 2006 Zenith Electronics Corp. 14 Dec. 2006 <http://www.zenith.com/sub_about/about_remote.html>.

The writer corrected capitalization errors in the titles.

✔Publish and Present

You are now ready to publish and present your report. Print out your research report or write a clean copy by hand. You may also want to present your work in a different way.

Alternative Presentations

Read Your Written Report Read your research report aloud to your class.

1 Print a hard copy of your report.

2 Bind it using a folder, binder, or adhesive.

3 Read the report to your class.

4 Lead a question-and-answer session about your report.

Deliver a Presentation Use information from your report to give a presentation on your topic.

1 Use presentation software to create a slide show.

2 Gather images to illustrate your presentation.

3 Use your report as a script as you present the slide show.

4 Lead a question-and-answer session about your presentation.

▼ **Language and Learning Handbook**, pp. 719; 724

Publishing Tip

Format your typed work according to your teacher's guidelines.

If you've handwritten your work, be sure your work is legible and clean.

Reflect on Your Work

▶ Ask for and use feedback from your audience and your teacher to evaluate your strengths as a writer.

• Did your audience find your report to be interesting? What did they learn?

• What did your audience think was the strongest point of your report? What did they think was the weakest point?

• What would you like to do better the next time you write? Set a goal for your next writing project.

☑ Save a copy of your work in your portfolio.

ESSENTIAL QUESTION:

What Makes Something Frightening?

Nothing in life is to be feared.
It is only to be understood.

—MARIE CURIE

Fear has many eyes and can see things underground.

—MIGUEL DE CERVANTES

Critical Viewing ▷
Biologist Wes Pratt grips his camera as one of the ocean's fiercest predators, the oceanic whitetip shark, approaches. Sharks are essential to healthy ocean ecosystems, and their threat to humans is considered very small. Just what is it that makes them so frightening?

FEAR
THIS!

EQ ESSENTIAL QUESTION:
What Makes Something Frightening?

Study the Painting
The painting below is by Francisco de Goya. Study the details in the painting, including the men's expressions and their positions. What do you think Goya wants you to feel when you look at this scene?

Old Men Eating Soup, Francisco de Goya. oil on plaster, transferred to canvas, 1819-23, Prado Museum, Spain.

Analyze and Vote
1. Looking at the painting above, many people see a dark scene filled with fear, disgust, or even terror. What does the artist do to encourage these emotions?

2. Other people look at the same painting and see a harmless scene that matches its title, *Old Men Eating Soup*. Why do you think people have such different responses to the same scene?

3. What makes something frightening? Is fear always something that depends on a person's point of view? Are there some things that *everyone* fears?

Discuss Goya's painting with a group and vote on whether it is frightening or harmless. Then discuss the questions, and give reasons for your answers based on your knowledge and experience.

EQ ESSENTIAL QUESTION
In this unit, you will explore the **Essential Question** in class through reading, discussion, research, and writing. Keep thinking about the question outside of school, too.

1 Plan a Project

Radio Drama or Podcast

In this unit, you'll be writing a radio drama or podcast about the Essential Question. Choose the characters and setting and develop a plot. To get started, review one or two scary radio broadcasts on the Internet, such as *The War of the Worlds*, by Orson Welles. Look for

- how the writers catch and keep your interest
- how the writers develop suspense
- what you like or don't like about the way the drama is presented.

Study Skills Start planning your drama. Use the forms on myNGconnect.com to plan your time and to prepare the content.

myNGconnect.com
- ▶ Planning forms
- ▶ Scheduler
- ▶ Archives of old radio broadcasts
- ▶ Story map
- ▶ Rubric

2 Choose More to Read

These readings provide different answers to the Essential Question. Choose a book and online selections to read during the unit.

Dr. Jenner and the Speckled Monster
by Albert Marrin

Throughout history, everyone in the world feared smallpox. Millions died from the "Speckled Monster"—a horrible disease that no one could cure. Then Edward Jenner made a lucky discovery that would change history.

▶ **NONFICTION**

Dance Hall of the Dead
by Tony Hillerman

Two boys have disappeared, and Joe Leaphorn of the Navajo Tribal Police must find out what happened. Soon, a mysterious masked creature is following him. Could it be a Zuñi ancestor spirit? Should Leaphorn search deeper? Or should some mysteries be left unsolved?

▶ **NOVEL**

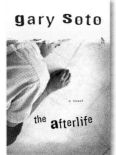

The Afterlife
by Gary Soto

Seventeen-year-old Chuy dies suddenly. As a ghost, Chuy has a new understanding about life and learns more about himself. He even falls in love. But Chuy's life as a ghost is almost over. Which should he fear more—losing the life he left behind or his next unknown journey?

▶ **NOVEL**

myNGconnect.com
- Read classic horror stories by famous writers like Edgar Allan Poe, H. P. Lovecraft, and H. G. Wells.
- Learn what science has to say about fear and where it comes from.
- Read frightening and funny urban legends that prey on the fears we all share.

One way to see just how much you already know about the way stories work is to take a look at the beginning of a few stories and then think about how those stories might continue.

DEMO TEXT #1

They'll never catch me. After all, I am the smartest, cleverest criminal ever. The crimes I commit are perfect crimes. Nothing ever left to chance. No evidence ever left behind. I'll never be caught. I'm too careful. Too intelligent. And the police? Too sloppy. Too dull.

DEMO TEXT #2

The wind howled and the moon cast ghostly shadows across the lawn leading up to the long-deserted house. A window shutter crashed wildly in the wind. And the weather vane, a black raven, spun squeakily around.

Tom and Gloria stood on the sidewalk. A black cat ran by them. They both jumped, looked at each other, and giggled.

"Oh, man," Tom said. "For a minute there I was getting the creeps. But there's nothing to be afraid of. It's just a house."

"Yeah," Gloria agreed. "It's just a house. Let's go in and get this dare over with. I want us to get back to the party as soon as we can. You got the camera? Remember, we have to take pictures to prove we really did it."

"Piece of cake," Tom thought. "Piece of cake."

DEMO TEXT #3

"Oh, no," thought Jenny as her car rattled to a stop. "My radiator is overheated. I guess it could be worse, though. Even though I haven't seen a car for hours, it looks like there is a gas station just ahead."

She got out of the car and started walking. She passed a sign that said "Terror Canyon, 1 mile." Jenny smiled. She said to herself, "I guess it's more than a gas station. I guess it's a whole town. Not much of a town, though. And "Terror Canyon"? What a silly name. Look at how beautiful everything is. After hours of driving through the desert, it's great to see so many flowers. It's kind of weird that they're all blooming in what look like seven-by-three-foot rectangles, but hey, I'll take color any way I can get it. They shouldn't call this place Terror Canyon. They should call it Oasis in the Desert. It's just beautiful. And anyone who takes such great care of so many flowers is someone I'm dying to meet."

■ Connect Reading to Your Life

Choose one of the Demo Texts and join other students who chose the same text. In your group, decide:

- What do you think will happen as the story continues?
- Why do you think that? What knowledge did you draw on when you thought about how the story might continue? Give evidence from the text and other stories or movies that support your prediction.

Reading Strategies

· Plan and Monitor
· Determine Importance
· Make Inferences
· Ask Questions
▶ **Make Connections**
· Synthesize
· Visualize

Focus Strategy ▶ Make Connections

When you made your prediction about what would happen, you didn't have very much to go on—just a paragraph or two. In order to make your prediction, you had to **make connections** between other stories that you've read or seen and the Demo Texts.

Making connections is something you do all the time. At the end of many TV shows, you'll see a few seconds of next week's show. Even after just those few seconds, you usually have a good idea of how the whole show will play out because you know how that kind of show typically works.

When you go to the movies and watch the previews of new movies, you probably have a pretty good idea about whether you want to see the film. You know whether it's your kind of movie. You probably even have a pretty good sense of what will happen. Of course, you won't know every detail (otherwise you might not bother to see it), but you probably have a good sense of the general direction of the movie, especially if you've seen a lot of movies of that type.

■ Your Job as a Reader

As a reader, your job is to recognize just what *kind* of story you're reading—the genre—and then to make predictions about what will happen in that story (the story's plot), based on what you know about other stories of that type. For example:

- If you identify a story as a mystery, you know that a crime will occur, that there will be multiple suspects, and that the crime will be solved in the end.
- If you identify the story as a horror story, you are **guaranteed** that something bad will happen to some of the characters.

Elements of Literature

genre *n.*, a type or kind of artistic work
plot *n.*, the series of events that make up a story

Academic Vocabulary

- **guarantee** *v.*, to promise or pledge that something will be done; to assure

■ Unpack the Thinking Process

Plot Structure

Authors count on readers to make predictions about what will happen in a story. One great pleasure in reading is finding out that your prediction is right. We base some of our predictions on our knowledge of how stories in general work.

For example, we know that if a character starts out by making a really strong statement about herself, the story will probably prove that statement wrong. If a story begins with a character saying "I'm the smartest," the story will probably show the opposite. We can make these predictions because that's the way most stories work.

Almost all stories have a general pattern of events that make up the plot.

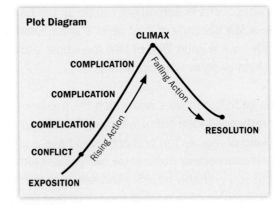

- Stories begin with **exposition**. You meet the characters and find out about the setting. You get a sense of the problem.
- Then the **conflict** develops. There are **complications**. The main character struggles, and tension mounts.
- The conflict builds until the tension reaches the **climax**, or turning point of the story.
- The remaining events lead to the **resolution**. The conflict ends or is resolved.

Plot Structure in Different Genres

Experienced readers know that different genres work in different ways.

- In comedies, everything turns out all right in the end. Also, the **mood**, or feeling, of the story is funny.
- In mysteries, the most likely suspect is probably not the person who committed the crime. The mood of these stories is usually tense, or edgy.
- In horror stories, it's usually one scary thing after another. The mood usually changes from ordinary, everyday calm to nail-bitingly scary.

Elements of Literature

exposition *n.*, background information given at the beginning of a story

conflict *n.*, the problem or struggle that drives a story's plot

complication *n.*, an event that makes the conflict worse

climax *n.*, the turning point, or most important event

resolution *n.*, the solution to the problem in a story

mood *n.*, the feeling a reader gets from a piece of writing

Let's look back at the beginnings of the Demo Texts.

DEMO TEXT #1: We know right from the start that the first story is told by a narrator who is very full of himself and immoral. Stories like that typically show how the narrator is taught a lesson.

DEMO TEXT #2: This seems to be a **suspense story** . After all, it has a scary house, a black cat, and a raven. That means it's *not* going to be a "piece of cake" for Tom and Gloria.

DEMO TEXT #3: This seems to be a little different—perhaps a horror story. The place name *Terror Canyon* is a big clue. Once you see the story as a horror story, you might be able to make a guess about what the seven-by-three-feet plots of flowers are. When Jenny says that the person who planted the flowers is someone she's "dying" to meet, experienced readers say, "Uh, oh."

One way that authors can surprise readers is when they write a story that ends up not working the way that stories of that genre typically do.

- If you're reading a mystery, and it turns out that the first and most likely suspect *did* indeed commit the crime, you'll be surprised.
- If it turns out that the person who planted the flowers in Demo Text 3 is just a gardener, you'll be surprised and will know that the author is playing with your expectations.

■ Try an Experiment

Find the comics section in a newspaper. Cut out each of the comic strips separately. Then sort them into **categories**.

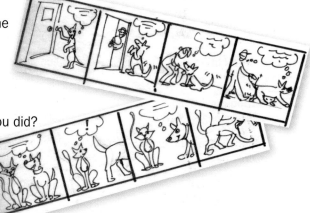

Think, Pair, Share Answer these questions and share your thoughts with a partner:

1. Why did you **categorize** the comic strips the way that you did? What factors were most important? The artwork? The mood? Or something else?

2. Choose one group of comic strips. What do you expect tomorrow's comic strips to be about?

Monitor Comprehension

Elements of Literature
suspense story *n.*, a story full of tension and excitement

Academic Vocabulary
- **category** *n.*, a group or division that is classified in a certain way; **categorize** *v.*, to put into a category or group; to classify

Make Connections
How can recognizing a story's genre help you read?

EQ What Makes Something Frightening?

Think about the power of the unexpected.

Make a Connection

Rank Fears Study this list of things that many teens fear, and rank them from scariest (1) to least scary (6). Share your rankings with a partner and add more things to the list.

COMMON FEARS OF TEENS
Rank (1 to 6)

_____ the unknown   _____ animals or insects

_____ failure   _____ high places

_____ death and injury _____ crime and violence

Learn Key Vocabulary

Study the Words Pronounce each word, and learn its meaning. You may also want to look up the meaning in the Glossary.

• Academic Vocabulary

Key Words	Examples
boundary (**bown**-du-rē) noun ▸ page 416	A **boundary** is a line that separates two places. This fence marks the **boundary** between our yard and yours. *Synonym:* border
feud (**fyūd**) noun ▸ pages 416, 423, 433	A **feud** is an ongoing argument between two people, groups, families, or tribes. The **feud** between our families lasted for years.
• **grant** (**grant**) verb ▸ page 416	To **grant** something means to give or allow. My teacher **granted** us extra time to complete the project. *Synonyms:* give, offer; *Antonym:* take
identification (ī-den-tu-fu-**kā**-shun) noun ▸ pages 427, 430	When you feel an **identification** with people, you feel that you understand them. I felt an **identification** with the characters in the movie. *Synonym:* connection
• **obvious** (**ob**-vē-us) adjective page ▸ 418	Something that is **obvious** is very easy to see or understand. The answer to the riddle is **obvious** because everyone knows it.
reconciliation (re-kun-si-lē-**ā**-shun) noun ▸ page 422	When people have a **reconciliation**, they agree to make up after an argument. The men reached a **reconciliation** by talking about their problem.
• **release** (rē-**lēs**) verb ▸ page 417	When you **release** something, you let it go or set it free. *Antonyms:* catch, hold
terror (**ter**-rur) noun ▸ pages 423, 425, 430, 431	When you feel **terror**, you feel great fear. The actress in the horror movie had a look of **terror** on her face.

Practice the Words Work with a partner to complete a **Word Square** for each of the Key Vocabulary words.

Word Square

Definition: *an argument that keeps going*	Important Characteristics: *lasts a long time*
feud	
Examples: *a fight*	Non-Examples: *peace*

BEFORE READING The Interlopers
short story by Saki

Reading Strategies

· Plan and Monitor
· Determine Importance
· Make Inferences
· Ask Questions
▶ **Make Connections**
· Synthesize
· Visualize

Analyze Structure: Plot

Fiction writers often organize story events around a **plot structure**, or pattern. As you read the selection, record details about the story on a **Plot Diagram**.

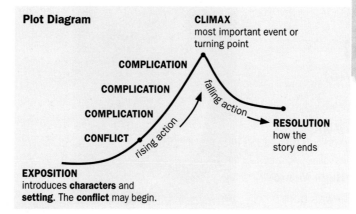

Plot Diagram

CLIMAX
most important event or turning point

COMPLICATION

COMPLICATION

COMPLICATION

CONFLICT

rising action

falling action

RESOLUTION
how the story ends

EXPOSITION
introduces **characters** and **setting**. The **conflict** may begin.

Look Into the Text

This exposition describes the story's setting.

> In a forest of mixed growth somewhere in the eastern Carpathian Mountains, a man stood one winter night. He was watching and listening, as though waiting for some beast of the woods to come within the range of his vision … and his rifle. But the game he sought could not be found in any sportsman's guide. Ulrich von Gradwitz searched the dark forest on the hunt for a human enemy.

Which main character is introduced? What do you know about him?

Focus Strategy ▶ Make Connections

All stories have some sort of connection to our lives. It's important to work to find the connections, since they aren't always obvious. In fact, research shows that connecting the things we read with our own thoughts and experiences helps us understand the text even better. As you read, **make connections** with the text.

HOW TO MAKE CONNECTIONS

Focus Strategy

1. As you read the selection, pause often to ask yourself questions like these:

   · *How does this relate to my life and experiences?*
   · *How does this relate to what I know about others in my neighborhood, my country, or the world?*
   · *How does this relate to other things I have read?*

2. Make more connections and ask yourself: How do these connections help me understand the story?

Exposition: Ulrich waits in the forest to attack his enemy.

At night, forests can be quiet and creepy.

If Ulrich is like me, he's alert and anxious now.

Saki
(1870–1916)

There is such a thing as writing oneself out.

British writer **Hector Hugh Munro**— better known as **Saki**—was born in the Asian country of Burma, now called Myanmar.

Though he was sickly, Saki had "an adventurer's soul."

A small and sickly child, he was sent back to England, along with his brother and sister, to live with his aunts. His aunts were very strict, rarely opened the windows, and seldom let the children go outside.

Later, Saki turned his aunts into characters and used other childhood experiences in his stories. Though Saki did not have many friends his own age, he had a great love of animals. He even kept a tiger cub as a pet and often featured animals in his writing.

Despite his poor health and lonely childhood, he developed what one biographer has called "an adventurer's soul."

When Saki turned twenty-three, he still had not chosen a career. His father got him a job with the Burma police force, which he hated because of the heat and the dirt. Illness again forced him back to England, where he began a career as a journalist.

When World War I began in 1914, Saki joined the British army. He was killed during a battle in France.

Saki is famous for his eerie stories which rely on humorous language, odd twists, and strange characters. Many of these elements are present in "The Interlopers."

myNGconnect.com

🌐 **Read more of Saki's work.**
🌐 **Listen to a reading of "Interlopers."**

The
Interlopers
by Saki

▲ **Critical Viewing: Effect** What is the effect of the dark colors, mist, and shadows in this image? How would it feel to be deep in this forest?

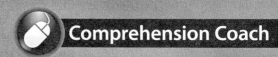
Comprehension Coach

In a forest of mixed growth somewhere in the **eastern Carpathian Mountains**, a man stood one winter night. He was watching and listening, as though waiting for some beast of the woods to come within the range of his vision . . . and his rifle. But the **game he sought** could not be found in any sportsman's guide. Ulrich von Gradwitz searched the dark forest on the hunt for a human enemy.

The narrow strip of woodland around the edge of the Gradwitz forest was not remarkable, but its owner guarded it more jealously than all his other possessions. Long ago, the court had **granted** the land to his grandfather, taking it away from the illegal possession of a neighboring family. The family who had lost the land had never agreed with the court's decision. Over time, they began **poaching trips** and **caused scandals** that started a **feud** between the families which had lasted for three generations.

The neighbor feud became personal once Ulrich became the head of his family. If there was a man in the world whom he hated and wished ill to, it was Georg Znaeym. The feud might have died down if the two men's hatred had not stood in the way. As boys, each had thirsted for one another's blood. As men, each prayed that **misfortune** might fall on the other. **1**

So, on this wind-scourged winter night, Ulrich and his men were on the lookout—not for four-footed game, but for thieves prowling across the **boundary**. The deer, which usually hid during a storm, were running wildly tonight, and the other animals were restless. Yes, something was disturbing the forest, and Ulrich could guess where the trouble had begun. **2**

1 Make Connections
Two families have been feuding for years. What kinds of arguments do you know about that might last this long? Add their feud to your Plot Diagram.

2 Plot Structure
What setting and characters have been introduced in this exposition? What is the main conflict so far? Record this information in your Plot Diagram.

Key Vocabulary
- **grant** *v.*, to give or allow
- **feud** *n.*, an ongoing argument between two people or groups
- **boundary** *n.*, a line or border that separates two places

In Other Words
eastern Carpathian Mountains mountains in central Europe
game he sought thing he hunted
poaching trips hunting illegally
caused scandals acted in upsetting ways
misfortune bad luck

He ordered his men to wait on the crest of the hill while he wandered far down the steep slopes into the wild tangle of the forest. Peering through the tree trunks and listening through the whistling wind, he hoped to find a trace of the poachers. If only on this wild night, in this dark, lone spot, he might come across Georg Znaeym, man to man, with no one to witness! That was his dearest wish. And as he stepped around a large beech tree, he came face to face with the man he sought.

The two enemies glared at each other for a long, silent moment. Each had a rifle in his hand; each had hate in his heart and murder in his mind. The chance had come to **release** the violence and anger that had grown over a lifetime. But **civilized** men cannot easily shoot down their neighbors in cold blood, and during this moment of hesitation, Nature's own violence **overwhelmed** them both. There was a splitting crash over their heads, and before they could leap aside, a huge section of the beech tree thundered down on them. ⬛3

Large Tense Hand (Grande Main Crispe), After 1886, Auguste Rodin (1840-1917), Bronze brown patina, Christie's Images/SuperStock.

⬛ **Critical Viewing: Design** What do you think this sculpture and its title mean? How would its effect be different if it was a drawing or a painting?

⬛3 **Plot Structure**
Why does Saki treat "Nature" as a character in the story? How has Nature affected the plot, so far? Make notes in your Plot Diagram.

Monitor Comprehension

Explain
How is Ulrich's hunting trip unusual? What happens when he finds his prey?

Key Vocabulary
● **release** v., to let go or set free

In Other Words
civilized normal and reasonable
overwhelmed defeated, overpowered

Ulrich von Gradwitz found himself stretched on the ground. One arm lay numb beneath him and the other was **pinned helplessly in** a tight tangle of forked branches. Both his legs were pinned beneath the fallen branches and it was **obvious** that he could not move without someone releasing him. The falling branches had slashed his face, and he had to wink away blood from his eyelashes before he could see the full disaster. At his side, near enough to touch, lay Georg Znaeym, who was alive and struggling, but obviously as helplessly pinned down as himself. All around them lay the thick wreckage of splintered branches and broken twigs. **4**

Feeling a mixture of relief at being alive and **exasperation** at being trapped, Ulrich muttered a strange **medley** of thankful prayers and sharp curses. Georg, who was blinded by the blood in his eyes, stopped struggling for a moment to listen. Then he gave a short, snarling laugh.

"So you're not killed, as you ought to be, but you're caught, anyway," he cried. "Trapped. What a joke! Ulrich von Gradwitz trapped in his stolen forest. That's justice for you!"

And he laughed again, **mockingly and savagely**.

"I'm caught on my own land," retorted Ulrich. "When my men come to release us, you will wish you hadn't been caught poaching on a neighbor's land. Shame on you." **5**

Georg was silent for a moment. Then he answered quietly: "Are you sure that your men will find much to release? I also have men in the forest tonight who are close behind me, and *they* will be here first and do the releasing. When they drag me out from under these damned branches, they might be clumsy enough to roll this trunk right on

4 Access Vocabulary
Do you know what *wreckage* means? Look for parts of the word that you already know. These can give you clues about what the unfamiliar word means.

5 Make Connections
Consider the different feelings that Ulrich and Georg have. Think of a time you felt many different emotions at once. How does this help you understand the story? Explain.

Key Vocabulary
- **obvious** *adj.*, easy to see or understand

In Other Words
pinned helplessly in trapped under
exasperation anger, frustration
medley mixture, combination
mockingly and savagely in an insulting and mean way

top of you. Your men will find you dead under a fallen beech tree."

"What a useful idea," said Ulrich fiercely. "My men have orders to follow me. When they get me out, I will remember your idea."

"Good," snarled Georg, "good. We will **fight this quarrel out** to the death, you and I and our men, with no cursed **interlopers** to come between us. Death and damnation to you, Ulrich von Gradwitz."

"The same to you, Georg Znaeym."

Both men spoke bitterly, knowing that **defeat could be near**. It might be a long time before their men would begin the search, and it was only a matter of chance whose men would find them first. ⑥

Eventually, both gave up the useless struggle to free themselves from the wood that held them down. Ulrich concentrated on bringing his wounded arm near enough to reach the wine flask in his coat pocket. Even when he had accomplished this, it was a long time before he could unscrew the cap or get any of the liquid down

We will fight this quarrel out to the death...

his throat. Oh, but the wine seemed Heaven-sent! It warmed and **revived him**, and he looked over with something like pity to where his enemy lay, wounded and weary.

"Could you reach this flask if I threw it over to you?" asked Ulrich suddenly. "We may as well be as comfortable as we can. Let us drink, even if tonight one of us dies."

"No, I can scarcely see anything; there is so much blood caked around my eyes," said Georg. "In any case, I don't drink wine with an enemy."

⑥ **Plot Structure**
How might this conversation affect the rising action of the plot? Make a note about it in your Plot Diagram.

In Other Words
fight this quarrel out keep fighting
interlopers strangers and outsiders
defeat could be near they could soon lose everything
revived him made him feel stronger

Untitled, 1910, Emily Carr. Watercolor, graphite on paper, Collection of the Vancouver Art Gallery, Emily Carr Trust, VAG 42.3.87, Photo: Trevor Mills, Vancouver Art Gallery.

◁ **Critical Viewing: Effect**
How is this forest scene different from the one on page 415? What is the effect of the colors and light?

Ulrich was silent for a few minutes, listening to the weary **screeching** of the wind. An idea was slowly forming and growing in his brain, an idea that gained strength every time that he looked across at the man who was fighting **so grimly** against pain and exhaustion. With the pain and weakness that Ulrich himself was feeling, the old, fierce hatred seemed to be dying down.

In Other Words

screeching high-pitched sound
so grimly with sudden determination

Monitor Comprehension

Confirm Prediction
Did you correctly predict how the falling tree would affect the story? What story details led you to make your prediction?

Predict
How do you think the situation will change the two men's futures?

"Neighbor," Ulrich said after awhile, "do as you please if your men come first. It was a fair **compact**. But as for me, I've changed my mind. If my men are the first to come, you shall be the first to be helped, as though you were my guest. We have quarreled like devils all our lives over this stupid strip of forest, where the trees can't even stand upright in a breath of wind. Lying here tonight thinking, I've come to realize that we've been fools. There are better things in life than winning a **boundary dispute**. Neighbor, if you will help me to bury the old quarrel, I—I will ask you to be my friend." **7**

Georg Znaeym was silent for so long that Ulrich thought he might have fainted from his injuries. Then he spoke slowly.

"How everyone would stare and gossip if we rode into the market square together. No one living can remember seeing a Znaeym and a von Gradwitz talking to one another in friendship. And our people would

...we've been fools.

have peace if we ended our feud tonight. If we chose to make peace, no one could **interfere**, there would be no interlopers from outside . . . I would never fire a shot on your land, unless you invited me as a guest. And you should come and shoot with me down in the marshes where the wild birds are. In all the countryside, no one could stop us if we decided to make peace. I always thought I would hate you for the rest of my life, but I think I have changed my mind about things, too, this last half-hour. You offered me your wine flask . . . Ulrich von Gradwitz, I will be your friend." **8**

7 Make Connections
Think about a time you apologized to someone. How do you think Ulrich felt as he apologized? How does this help you understand the story?

8 Plot Structure
In what ways are the two men's attitudes toward their conflict changing? What effect will this have on the plot? Make a note about it in your Plot Diagram.

In Other Words
compact agreement, deal
boundary dispute fight over who owns land
interfere stop us

For a while, both men were silent, turning over in their minds the wonderful changes that their **dramatic reconciliation** would bring about. In the cold, gloomy forest, with the wind tearing through the naked branches and whistling round the tree trunks, they lay and waited for the help that would now bring release and aid to both men. Each man privately prayed that his men might be the first to arrive, so that he might be the first to show **honorable attention** to the enemy that had become a friend. 🔲

As the wind dropped for a moment, Ulrich broke the silence.

"Let's shout for help," he said. "In this **lull**, our voices may **carry a little way**."

"They won't carry far through the trees and undergrowth," said Georg, "but we can try. Together, then."

The two raised their voices in a long hunting call.

"Together again," said Ulrich a few minutes later, after listening **in vain** for an answering call.

"I heard nothing but the damned wind," said Georg hoarsely.

There was silence again for some minutes. Then Ulrich gave a joyful cry.

"I can see figures coming through the wood. They are following the path I took down the hillside."

Both men shouted as loudly as they could.

"They hear us! They've stopped. Now they see us. They're running down the hill towards us," cried Ulrich.

"How many of them are there?" asked Georg.

"I can't see clearly," said Ulrich. "Nine or ten,"

"Then they are yours," said Georg. "I had only seven men with me."

"They are coming as quickly as they can, brave lads," said Ulrich gladly.

9 Plot Structure
How do the two men try to resolve their conflict? What resolution do they expect to their problem? Make notes in your Plot Diagram.

Key Vocabulary
reconciliation *n.*, agreement to make up after an argument

In Other Words
dramatic surprising and exciting
honorable attention respect
lull quiet moment during the storm
carry a little way reach farther
in vain unsuccessfully

"Are they your men?" asked Georg. "Are they your men?" he repeated impatiently when Ulrich did not answer.

"No," said Ulrich with a laugh, the crazed, chattering laugh of a man **unstrung with hideous fear**.

"Who are they?" asked Georg quickly, straining his eyes to see what the other man would gladly not have seen.

"Wolves." 🔟 ❖

🔟 **Plot Structure**
When does the climax of this story happen? Is there a resolution? Explain.

ANALYZE The Interlopers

1. **Explain** What is the story's surprise ending? Why doesn't Saki describe what happens next?

2. **Vocabulary** How does the men's feud shape the plot?

3. **Analyze Structure: Plot** Review the **Plot Diagram** you began on page 413. Then talk with a partner about specific parts of the story where Saki built a sense of fear, or terror.

4. **Focus Strategy Make Connections** Share your **Plot Diagram** with a partner, and discuss the strongest connections you each made with the text. Explain to one another how these connections added to your understanding of the story.

🔙 Return to the Text

Reread and Write How did unexpected events throughout the story frighten the characters? Reread the story, and then write about the different parts where the characters became frightened.

Key Vocabulary
terror *n.*, feeling of great fear

In Other Words
unstrung with hideous fear who was losing control because of great fear

BEFORE READING An Interview with the King of Terror

magomeni interview by Bryon Cahill

Reading Strategies

• Plan and Monitor
• Determine Importance
• Make Inferences
• Ask Questions
▶ **Make Connections**
• Synthesize
• Visualize

Analyze Word Choice: Analogy

Writers and speakers often use analogies to help make their meanings clear. An **analogy** is a comparison. It explains what one thing is like by showing how it is similar to something else.

Look Into the Text

This **analogy** compares Stephen King to something else.

> **BC:** You once said, "_I am the literary equivalent of a Big Mac and fries_."
>
> **SK:** _Yeah, and I'm still paying for that. What I meant by that is I'm tasty. I go down smooth. And I don't think that a steady diet of Stephen King would make anybody a healthy human being._

What are two ways that King is like a Big Mac and fries?

Focus Strategy ▶ Make Connections

As you read interviews, **make connections** with your own experiences, with things you know, and with other things you've read or seen. These will help you better understand and enjoy the interview.

HOW TO MAKE CONNECTIONS

Focus Strategy

1. As you read, ask yourself: How does this connect to me, the world, or other texts? Record these in a **Connections Chart**.

2. Review each connection, and describe how it is useful in helping you understand the text.

Connections Chart

Idea from the Text	Type of Connection	Usefulness
Stephen King is like a Big Mac and fries.	I love fast food, but Mom always says I need a balanced diet.	I guess he means that his readers need to read "healthier" books, too.

An Interview with the King of Terror

by Bryon Cahill

Connect Across Texts

In "The Interlopers," two enemies come face to face with the unexpected. As you read this interview, think about how writers can use the unexpected to reach our greatest fears.

Stephen King is one of the world's most famous horror writers. Over his career he has sold more than 80 million copies of his spine-tingling books, and the movies based on his stories chill audiences in their seats. His subjects range from the outright **terror** of *Carrie* and *The Shining* to the mysteries of the **supernatural** in *The Dead Zone* and *The Green Mile*. The "King of Terror" has said, "I am Halloween's answer to Santa Claus." What makes him so popular? **1**

1 Analogy
What analogy does King make in this paragraph? What is he trying to do?

Q: What makes a scary story really scary?

A: I don't know. That's a really tough question. That's like asking someone: "What makes a funny story really funny?" Scary things are personal. People come up to me sometimes and say, "You know I really love that book *IT* because I was always terrified of clowns." But other people come up to me and say, "Why would you say such mean things about clowns? I'm married to a guy who's a clown. Children love [them]! It's so mean to say that about clowns." When I was a kid, clowns just scared me and I've seen other kids cry about clowns and to me there's something scary, something **sinister** about such a figure of happiness and fun being evil. **Lon Chaney** once said,

Key Vocabulary
terror *n.*, feeling of great fear

In Other Words
supernatural things that are not part of this world, like unusual powers and abilities
sinister threatening and evil
Lon Chaney An actor who starred in many classic horror movies

"Nobody laughs at a clown at midnight." So I guess that sometimes what makes a scary thing scary is that when we realize there's something sinister behind a nice face.

I think things are scarier when there's some sensory deprivation, when we take away our ability to sense things, when we take away escape—that makes things scary. We're afraid of things that are different than we are. A lot of times what somebody does when they're writing scary stories is they're giving us permission to **be politically incorrect**, to say, "It's all right to be afraid of things that are different than you are." And people will say, "You have to be nice to people that are different than you are." And we understand that that's true and we try to do it but **nevertheless**, there's always that little bit of fear that says, "Maybe they're going to eat us up." And the person who writes a scary story says that it's all right to feel that way because you have to find a place to get rid of that. 2

Friendly or scary? The clown from the movie *IT* may change your mind.

Q: What, if anything, scares you? 3

A: Well clowns **freak me out** and scare me. I think that any kind of situation that I'm trapped in, certainly

2 **Make Connections**
A clown is one thing that people can view in different ways. When have you been afraid of something that did not scare other people? How does this help you understand King's point? Add your ideas to your Connections Chart.

3 **Make Connections**
How would you answer this interview question? Read on to see how your answers relate to King's.

In Other Words
be politically incorrect say or do things that might insult other people
nevertheless even though we know it's wrong
freak me out terrify me

claustrophobia or turbulence at 40,000 feet, freaks me out a lot. I hate that. Any kind of a situation where I'm not in control and somebody else is. Those things freak me out.

Q: Would you like to talk about building suspense in a book?

A: The most important thing about building suspense is building **identification** with character. You have to take some time and make your reader care about the characters in the story. There's a difference between horror and terror. You can go to a movie and you can be horrified because you don't know what terrible things are going to happen or who's going to get their head chopped off and that's horrible. But you don't necessarily know any of those people. They're very **two-dimensional**.

But if you take somebody and you put them in a situation . . . and little by little you get to know this guy and you get to understand him a little bit and you get to see different **aspects** of him and you start to feel for him . . . this person. Then you start to **empathize with** him and you start to put yourself in his shoes and then you start to be very, very afraid because you don't want anything to happen to him. It isn't a question anymore of *when* will something happen to him. It's a question that you're saying, "I don't want anything to happen." But because it's the kind of story that it is, you know that something **is gonna**, so one by one you close off the exits and things get more and more nerve wracking until finally there's an explosion. You know that's going to

> ## There's a difference between horror and **terror.**

Key Vocabulary
identification *n.*, feeling that you know and understand someone else's experiences and feelings

In Other Words
claustrophobia or turbulence feeling trapped on a small, bumpy plane ride
two-dimensional unrealistic
aspects sides
empathize with care about and understand
is gonna is going to happen

4 Access Vocabulary
Do you know what *nerve wracking* means? Look for clues in the sentence to tell you more.

Monitor Comprehension

Explain
According to King, why do readers need to feel an identification with the characters? How does this help the story?

happen. **5** The other thing is that there's a **format to** these stories where we all understand that things are going to build up to some kind of climax. And that adds to the suspense.

Q: What is the most important element of storytelling to you?

A: They all have their part to play but for me the most important thing is I want the reader to turn the page. So I would say that it's **an almost intangible thing that adds up to readability**. That makes somebody want to sit down and read the story that you wrote. It's a kind of modesty almost where you say to yourself this is not about me, this is about the person who reads my stories. It's not **psychoanalysis**, it's not about showing off (although it always is, we know that). You just hope that it goes out to somebody who's going to connect with what you said. And that you're going to tell them the story that makes them want to continue to read. Different writers feel different ways about this. I want to make a connection with them that's emotional. I want them to read the story and I want to make them sweat a little bit, laugh, and cry. I'm less interested in their thought processes than I am **their lower emotion**. **6**

I want the reader to turn the page.

Q: You once said, "I am the literary equivalent of a Big Mac and fries."

A: Yeah, and I'm still paying for that. What I meant by that is I'm tasty. I go down smooth. And I don't think that a steady diet of Stephen King

5 **Make Connections**
King describes a difference between horror and terror. What movies or books do you know that belong to these groups? Add your ideas to your Connections Chart.

6 **Make Connections**
Think about the books and stories that make *you* want to keep reading. What do they have in common with King's ideas?

In Other Words
format to set pattern for
an almost intangible thing that adds up to readability something about a good story that is hard to describe
psychoanalysis figuring out how the mind works
their lower emotion in how they feel
the literary equivalent of a writer who is like

would make anybody a healthy human being. I think that you **oughtta** eat your vegetables, and you oughtta find other things, you oughtta **find some Dickens, some Ian McEwan** . . . you oughtta range widely and read all kinds of different stuff. You shouldn't just settle on one thing. I'd feel the same way about people that said they didn't read

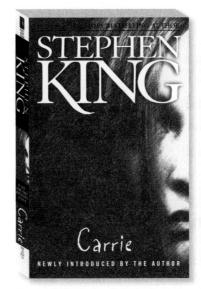
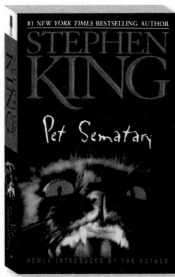

Many of King's books have been made into movies and TV shows.

anything but *Harry Potter.* I'd say, "There's something wrong with you, buddy." If you're gonna read fiction, read all kinds of things and challenge yourself, read some stuff that's really tough. ▧7

Q: **If you were a teacher, what is the most important lesson you would impart to your students? What writing advice do you have for our readers?** ▧8

A: As writers, I'd say write every day. If you want to write and you want to write well, do it a lot. Practice it. The same way that you would anything else that you want to do all the time. Baseball players know about it, trombone players know about it, swimmers know about it. Use it or lose it. Get better. Work at it. Feel comfortable with it. Feel comfortable with sentences, feel comfortable with paragraphs until those things just roll off your fingertips. And the better you feel about it, the better it's going to go for you.

▧7 **Analogy**
What two things does King compare with this analogy? How does it help you to understand his advice?

▧8 **Text Features**
Why did this passage include the interviewer's questions and not just King's words?

Monitor Comprehension

Summarize
According to King, what is the most important part of writing? Summarize his ideas in your own words.

In Other Words

oughtta should (slang)
find some Dickens, some Ian McEwan read a mix of classics and good modern books
Harry Potter popular books for young people
impart teach, share with

Q: After you were hit by a van in '99, rumors were circulating that you would never write again. If that tragedy couldn't stop you, do you think you'll ever retire?

A: Sure, I'll die. Or I'll get a horrible disease, or something. You see, I'm a horror writer, I can think of all sorts of nasty reasons to stop. ❖

ANALYZE An Interview with the King of Terror

1. **Explain** What advice does Stephen King have for readers? Include specific examples from the interview.

2. **Vocabulary** King says that readers' **identification** with characters is important for building tension or suspense. What does he mean? Use an example from the text to explain.

3. **Analyze Word Choice: Analogy** Find examples of analogies in the interview. Then use a chart to show how they add to your understanding of the ideas in the interview.

Analogy	Comparison	How It Adds to the Meaning
"I am Halloween's answer to Santa Claus."	King compares himself to Santa.	He's a symbol of scary things.

4. **Focus Strategy Make Connections** Which of King's ideas would be most useful to you in writing your own tales of **terror**? Explain.

↩ Return to the Text

Reread and Write King says, "I am Halloween's answer to Santa Claus." Review the selection and describe in a paragraph how King brings terror to people.

In Other Words
rumors were circulating people were saying
retire stop writing as your job

EQ What Makes Something Frightening?

Reading

Critical Thinking

EQ 1. Analyze Think back to your discussion about fear on page 412. How have the selections supported or changed your ideas?

2. Interpret According to Stephen King, "There is a difference between horror and **terror**." Describe this in your own words. Then explain whether "The Interlopers" is a tale of horror, terror, or neither.

3. Compare King says, "I think things are scarier . . . when we take away escape." How is this true in "The Interlopers"?

EQ 4. Generalize What do these selections say about fear?

5. Judge King describes ways that authors can build suspense in a book. Explain whether Saki's story succeeds as a suspense story.

Writing

Write About Literature

Story Starter Use this story starter to begin your own tale of terror. Reread both selections to get ideas about how to tell a scary story.

> Nick tightened his grip on his bag and started walking faster. For weeks, he'd had the feeling that someone was watching him, hidden just out of sight. Tonight, that feeling was stronger than ever. Nick glanced quickly behind him, but like always, there was no one there. He looked around. When had the neighborhood gotten so quiet and empty?
>
> "There's nothing there," Nick reassured himself. "Don't be an idiot!" Then he heard it—a pair of heavy footsteps.
>
> Nick dropped his bag and ran.

Vocabulary

Key Vocabulary Review

Oral Review Work with a partner. Use these words to complete the paragraph.

boundaries	identification	released
feuds	obvious	terror
granted	reconciliation	

> The scariest tales of __(1)__ give readers a sense of __(2)__ that helps them relate to the characters. But what can we have in common with "The Interlopers"—a story that was written almost a hundred years ago? The connection may not be __(3)__ for everyone to see at first, but we have all heard of __(4)__, or long arguments, between people. We know that people shouldn't cross the personal __(5)__ that separate us from others. And who wouldn't feel frightened if they were trapped and not __(6)__ from a scary situation? By telling a story about a __(7)__ that brings two enemies together, Saki has __(8)__ us a story that we can still relate to, decades later.

Writing Application Write a paragraph describing how a screenwriter created terror in a scary movie you've seen. Use three Key Vocabulary words.

Fluency

Read with Ease: Phrasing

Assess your reading fluency with the passage in the Reading Handbook, p. 763. Then complete the self-check below.

1. I did/did not pause appropriately for punctuation and phrases.

2. My words correct per minute: _____ .

INTEGRATE THE LANGUAGE ARTS

Use Adjectives to Elaborate

An **adjective** is a describing word. Use adjectives to elaborate, or tell more about, people, places, and things.

Some adjectives tell how someone or something looks, smells, sounds, feels, or tastes.

The **forest** was **dark** and **spooky**.

The **air** smelled **salty**.

The men heard a **thundering crash** above them.

They felt the **heavy tree** upon them.

Use adjectives to make your writing more interesting. Choose lively, descriptive adjectives to elaborate. Which sentence below provides the most detail?

The men heard sounds.

The men heard **strange** sounds.

The men heard **loud, blood-chilling** sounds.

Oral Practice (1–5) With a partner, look at one of the paintings in "The Interlopers." Describe the art in five sentences. Use at least one adjective in each sentence to elaborate and add detail.

Written Practice (6–10) Rewrite the paragraph to add detail. Add adjectives that appeal to the senses.

Ulrich hunted for his _____ enemy. The night was _____ . Ulrich and Georg listened to the _____ , _____ wind. They felt _____ .

Tell a Story

Group Talk With a partner, make up the beginning of a scary story. Tell your story to a group. Use interesting adjectives to help your listeners picture the people and places in your story.

Analyze Irony

Authors Saki and Guy de Maupassant, who wrote "The Necklace," are famous for writing short stories that include stylistic and rhetorical devices, such as irony. Think about the aesthetic effect irony has on the story.

Verbal irony is one type of irony used by authors as a stylistic device. Verbal irony contrasts what a character says with what he or she really means. Characters may exaggerate or say things that are the opposite of what they mean. For example, if the weather in the story is bad, a character might say "today is a beautiful day."

Situational irony is another type of irony. Using this stylistic device, the author contrasts what we expect to happen with what really happens. In "The Interlopers," we expect the two enemies to fight when they meet. Instead, they are stopped by an unexpected accident.

Writers use irony to:

- surprise the reader
- show something about the character
- make a story funny, sad, or frightening
- show that life is unpredictable and often beyond our control

Review the key events in "The Interlopers" to find examples where Saki uses verbal or situational irony. Then discuss and write about how irony adds to the story.

Page	Quotation or Event	Type of Irony	Impact
416	Ulrich hunts for his enemy in the forest.		

Irony plays an important role in many scary stories. As you read more selections in this unit, look for ways that the authors use irony.

Synonyms

Synonyms are related words that have the same, or nearly the same, meaning. Most synonyms, however, do not mean *exactly* the same thing. Knowing the exact meaning of a synonym helps you use words more precisely.

Use a dictionary to find the meanings of these synonyms for the word *fight*. Write the definition in your own words in the chart below. Then rank the words from 1 (most serious) to 3 (least serious).

SYNONYM	MEANING	RANK
dispute (page 421)		
feud (page 416)		
quarrel (page 419)		

Dramatization

Work with a small group to dramatize, or perform, a scene from "The Interlopers."

1 **Before the Performance** Plan how your group will show the story's events and actions. Decide which parts will be spoken, acted, or described by a narrator.

2 **During the Performance** Have "characters" perform dialogue from the story, using intonation and expression. Make sure to match each character's personality in the text.

3 **After the Performance** Have the audience respond to what they saw and heard. Listen carefully to their comments—they may give you useful ideas for future performances.

◥ **Language and Learning Handbook**, page 702

Write a Character Sketch

A **character sketch** is like a snapshot of a character that shows how he or she looks, behaves, and talks. Write a character sketch of a scientific or historical person.

1 **Prewrite** Choose a person to describe. Think about what you know about that person.

2 **Draft** Think of a brief story scene that shows a good example of what the person is like. Include detailed descriptions and dialogue. Be sure to include explanations of why the person is famous.

3 **Revise** Focus on details that show what the person is like.

4 **Edit and Proofread** Identify and correct any spelling or grammar mistakes.

5 **Publish** Read aloud your character sketch to "introduce" the person to your classmates.

Model Character Sketch: Scientist

Edward Jenner was a surgeon who developed the smallpox vaccine in the 1790s. The vaccine helped stop the spread of the deadly disease.

One day Jenner was studying a medical problem with the brilliant Dr. John Hunter. He had been up for hours but still couldn't solve it. Dr. Hunter said, "Why think? Experiment."

"Experiment?" Jenner asked confusedly. He had a puzzled look on his face.

"Find ways to prove or disprove what you're thinking—make a guess at what to do and check to see if you're right."

By learning how to experiment, Jenner was able to test new ideas and eventually create the smallpox vaccine.

The writer describes how the person looks, acts, and sounds.

Explanation details how and why the person became famous.

◥ **Writing Handbook**, page 784

1

2

3

Inside a Newspaper Office

Newspapers report on events that take place locally or around the world. There are many different types of newspapers. Some publish every day. Others publish weekly. Some newspapers specialize in a specific field, such as financial news.

Jobs in the Newspaper Profession

Major newspapers tend to hire a large staff that includes writers, reporters, and editors. They also hire people who work in marketing, advertising, and production. At small newspapers, one person may have several different jobs.

Job	Responsibilities	Education/Training Required
Press Operator 1	• Prepares, operates, and maintains the printing presses in a pressroom • Performs minor repairs to machines • Monitors the printing process to make sure deadlines are met	• High school diploma • Good math and computer skills • On-the-job training
Reporter 2	• Gathers information, observes events, and interviews people • Writes news stories • May specialize in a specific type of reporting	• Proven ability to write well • College degree in journalism or communications
Copy Editor 3	• Reviews and edits reporters' stories • Checks stories for newspaper style and suggests revisions • Does research to verify facts	• College degree in English, journalism, or communications

Request Information About Internships

Write a business letter to a newspaper requesting internship information.

1. Go online to research high school student internships offered by news organizations. Or locate a newspaper in your area that participates in journalism programs for students.

2. Write a business letter to the newspaper requesting information about internships for high school students and how you can apply. Share your letter with a classmate who can help you check your work. Save the information in a professional career portfolio.

myNGconnect.com

○ Learn more about the newspaper profession.

○ Download a form to evaluate whether you would like to work in this field.

○ Download a model business letter.

▼ Writing Handbook, page 784

Make Word Connections

How do you describe a movie to make your friends want to see it? You can explain what kind of movie it is, such as a comedy. You can compare it to other movies. In both cases, you describe the movie by relating it to other movies you know that are alike.

You can learn new words by relating them to words you already know, too. One way to relate words is to create a **word map**.

Explore Word Relationships

Work with a partner to complete the word map.

1. Check the definition of *exuberant* in a dictionary.

2. Think of other words you know that are similar. Look at the words from the list on the right. Find a word that is similar to *exuberant* and an example of the word. Fill in the synonym and example boxes. Do the same for antonym and nonexample.

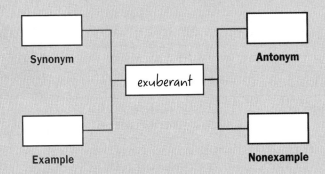

Words and Phrases for Word Map

- dejected
- a cheering crowd
- a losing team
- joyous

Put the Strategy to Use

When you learn a new word, relate it to others you know that are like it.

1. Identify the new word and determine its meaning. Use a dictionary if necessary.

2. Relate it to other words you know. Think of a synonym and an antonym.

3. Think of an example that expresses the word's meaning.

4. Think of a nonexample that expresses the opposite meaning.

TRY IT▶ Draw more word maps like the one above and complete a word map for each of these words: *avaricious, predominant, compatible,* and *contemporary.*

📖 Reading Handbook, page 733

EQ What Makes Something Frightening?
Explore how fears can become reality.

Make a Connection

Discussion President Franklin D. Roosevelt once said: "We have nothing to fear but fear itself." What do you think he meant? Share your ideas with a small group. Then discuss what you think causes fear.

Learn Key Vocabulary

Study the Words Pronounce each word and learn its meaning. You may also want to look up the definitions in the Glossary.

• Academic Vocabulary

Key Words	Examples
• **capable** (**kā**-pu-bul) *adjective* ▶ pages 448, 456, 459	If you are **capable** of something, you can do it. We are all **capable** of doing good and bad things with our lives. *Synonym*: able
• **precision** (pri-**si**-zhun) *noun* ▶ pages 442, 459	When you do something with **precision**, you do it exactly and correctly. A stopwatch keeps track of time with great **precision**.
• **rely** (ri-**lī**) *verb* ▶ pages 442, 457, 459	When you **rely** on something, you depend upon it. Do you **rely** on your alarm clock to wake you up in the morning? *Synonym*: count on
resist (ri-**zist**) *verb* ▶ pages 455, 457, 459	If you **resist** something, you fight against it. I **resisted** the urge to scream during the scary movie. *Synonym*: oppose; *Antonyms*: surrender, give in
ritual (**ri**-chu-wul) *noun* ▶ pages 440, 450, 457	A **ritual** is a set plan for or formal way of doing something. Many cultures have **rituals** to protect children from danger. *Synonyms*: ceremony, custom
subside (sub-**sīd**) *verb* ▶ page 449	When things **subside**, they become less strong. When a storm **subsides**, the wind and rain slow down. *Antonym*: increase
• **trace** (**trās**) *noun* ▶ pages 455, 456	A **trace** is a small sign that shows that someone or something has been in a place. The police searched for fingerprints or any other **trace** of the man at the crime scene. *Synonyms*: mark, evidence
vulnerable (**vul**-nu-ru-bul) *adjective* ▶ pages 445, 450	When you are **vulnerable**, you are weak and could be easily hurt. The small child was lost and **vulnerable** without his mother. *Synonym*: helpless

Practice the Words Complete a **Vocabulary Example Chart**. Connect your own experiences with at least four of the Key Vocabulary words.

Vocabulary Example Chart

Word	Definition	Example from My Life
capable	able to do things	My uncle is a very capable cook.

BEFORE READING The Baby-Sitter

short story by Jane Yolen

Reading Strategies

- Plan and Monitor
- Determine Importance
- Make Inferences
- Ask Questions
- ▶ **Make Connections**
- Synthesize
- Visualize

Analyze Word Choice: Mood and Tone

As you read, think about how the story changes.

- The **mood** is the feeling you get from reading a story. Does a story make you feel angry, sad, or frightened? Good authors encourage these feelings through word choice and techniques such as foreshadowing, which hints about what will happen later. Often, a story's mood changes as the plot unfolds.
- The **tone** is how the author feels about the subject, the character, and you, the reader. The writing can be serious, funny, respectful, or even insulting.

Look Into the Text

Descriptive details can help create a spooky mood. What other words and phrases add to this mood?

Hilary hated baby-sitting at the Mitchells' house, though she loved the Mitchell twins. The house was one of those old, creaky Victorian horrors, with a dozen rooms and two sets of stairs....

There was a long, dark hallway upstairs, and the twins slept at the end of it. Each time Hilary checked on them, she felt as if there were things watching her from behind the closed doors of the other rooms or from the walls. She couldn't say what exactly, just *things*.

The author uses a serious tone to describe Hilary's feelings.

Focus Strategy ▶ Make Connections

We all make connections to the stories that we read. A character may remind you of a friend or the setting may make you think of a song. But not all of the connections we make are useful in helping us understand the text. Some may even distract us from the story itself. As you read, try to focus on making connections that count.

Focus Strategy

HOW TO MAKE CONNECTIONS

1. Read the passage aloud with a partner.

2. As you read, pause to make connections to the text.

   The Mitchells live in a scary, old house. This reminds me of every horror movie I've ever seen—there's always a scary, old house! Why would anyone go in one?

3. Talk with your partner about your connections.

   I think the story will be like a horror movie.

4. Discuss whether the connection helps you understand the story. If it doesn't, move on to form new connections.

5. As you continue to read, help each other make and evaluate connections.

The Writer and Her Influences

Jane Yolen
(1939–)

*I am a person in love …
with words. I wake up, and
I have to write.*

Many of Yolen's stories deal with strange and eerie situations.

Jane Yolen says, "I remember practically nothing about my early childhood." With her father overseas during World War II, Yolen went to live with her grandparents in Virginia. When her grandfather died, one of many deaths that would influence her writing, Yolen recalls that "the house seemed haunted and cold."

While she was growing up, Yolen wrote everything from school musicals to fiction and nonfiction stories. "I was a writer from the time I learned to write." She found her inspiration early as well. "If I had to point to my primary source of inspiration, it would be to the folk culture. My earliest readings were the folk tales and fairy stories I took home from the library by the dozens. Even when I was old enough to make the trip across Central Park by myself, I was still not too old for those folk fantasies."

As in "The Baby-Sitter," many of Yolen's stories deal with strange and eerie situations. Yet whatever she writes, her motivation is clear: "I don't care if the story is real or fantastical. I tell the story that needs to be told."

myNGconnect.com

◎ Visit the writer's Web site.
◎ Listen to storytellers perform scary stories.

The Baby-Sitter

by Jane Yolen

Critical Viewing: Effect What images does the artist combine in this picture? Describe the mood that this combination creates.

Comprehension Coach

What would it feel like to be a baby-sitter in a big, creepy house?

Hilary hated baby-sitting at the Mitchells' house, though she loved the Mitchell twins. The house was one of those old, creaky **Victorian horrors**, with a dozen rooms and two sets of stairs. One set led from the front hall, and one, which the servants had used back in the 1890s, led up from the kitchen.

There was a long, dark hallway upstairs, and the twins slept at the end of it. Each time Hilary checked on them, she felt as if there were things watching her from behind the closed doors of the other rooms or from the walls. She couldn't say what exactly, just *things*. 1

"Do this," Adam Mitchell had said to her the first time she'd taken them up to bed. He touched one door with his right hand, the next with his left, spun around twice on his right leg, then kissed his fingers one after another. He repeated this **ritual** three times down the hall to the room he shared with his brother, Andrew.

Once a night, and you're all right, he sang in a **Munchkin voice**. Andrew did the same.

Hilary laughed at their **antics**. They looked so cute, like a pair of six-year-old wizards or pale little **clones**, she couldn't decide which. 2

"You do it, Hilary," they urged.

"There's no music, guys," she said. "And I don't dance without music."

"But it's not dancing, Hilly," Adam said. "It's magic."

"It keeps *Them* away," Andrew added. "We don't like *Them*. Grandma showed us how. This was her house first. And her grandmother's before her. If you do it, *They* won't bother you."

1 **Make Connections**
Think about other stories like this with spooky houses. What can you expect to happen here? How does this help you understand the story?

2 **Tone**
Study the way the narrator describes the twins. How does the author feel about them?

Key Vocabulary
ritual *n.*, set plan for or formal way of doing things

In Other Words
Victorian horrors big, spooky houses built in the late 1800s
Munchkin voice high, squeaky voice
antics playful and silly behavior
clones identical copies of each other

"Well, don't worry about *Them*," Hilary said. "Or anything else. That's what I'm hired for, to make sure nothing bad happens to you while your mom and dad are out." 3

But her promises hadn't satisfied them, and in the end, to keep them happy, she banged on each door and spun around on her right leg, and kissed her fingers, too. It was a lot of fun, actually. She had taught it to her best friend, Brenda, the next day in school, and pretty soon half the kids in the ninth grade had picked it up. They called it the Mitchell March, but secretly Hilary called it the **Spell**.

The first night's baby-sitting, after they had danced the Spell all the way down the long hall, Hilary had tucked the boys into their beds and pulled up a rocking chair between. Then she told them stories for almost an hour until first Adam and then Andrew fell asleep. In one night she'd become their favorite baby-sitter.

She had told them baby stories that time—"The Three Bears" and "The Three Billy Goats Gruff" and "The Three Little Pigs," all with sound effects and a different voice for each character. After that she

3 **Mood**
What feeling does the author want you to get when you read about *Them*? How would you say the word *Them* out loud?

In Other Words
Spell Magical words

relied on TV plots and the books she'd read in school for **her material**. Luckily she was a great reader.

The twins hated to ever hear a story a second time. Except for "The Golden Arm," the **jump story** that she'd learned on a camping trip when she was nine. Adam and Andrew asked for *that* one every time.

When she had asked them why, Adam had replied solemnly, his green eyes wide, "Because it scares *Them*."

After she smoothed the covers over the sleeping boys, Hilary always drew in a deep breath before heading down the long, uncarpeted hall. It didn't matter which stairs she headed for, there was always a strange echo as she walked along, each footstep **articulated** with **precision**, and then a slight *tap-tapping* afterward. She never failed to turn around after the first few steps. She never saw anything behind her. **4**

4 Mood
What words or phrases help set the mood for this page? Has the mood changed so far? Explain.

Key Vocabulary
- **rely** *v.*, to depend on
- **precision** *n.*, exactness and correctness

In Other Words
her material ideas for her stories
jump story scary, surprising story
articulated placed

The Mitchells called her at least three times a month, and though she always **hesitated to accept**, she always went. Part of it was she really loved the twins. They were bright, polite, and funny **in equal measure**. And they were not shy about telling her how much they liked her. But there was something else, too. Hilary was a stubborn girl. You couldn't tell from the set of her jaw; she had a sweet, rounded jaw. And her nose was too snubbed to be taken seriously. But when she thought someone was treating her badly or trying to threaten her, she always **dug in and made a fuss**. 5

Like the time the school principal had tried to **ban** miniskirts and had sent Brenda home for wearing one. Hilary had changed into her junior varsity cheerleading uniform and walked into Mr. Golden's office.

"Do you like our uniforms, sir?" she had said, quietly.

"Of course, Hilary," Mr. Golden had answered, being too sure of himself to know a trap when he was walking into it.

"Well, we **represent** the school in these uniforms, don't we?" she had asked.

"And you do a wonderful job, too," he said.

Snap. The sound of the closing trap. "Well, they are shorter than any miniskirt," she said. "And when we do cartwheels, our **bloomers** show! Brenda never does cartwheels." She'd smiled then, but there was a deep challenge in her eyes.

Mr. Golden **rescinded** the ban the next day.

So Hilary didn't like the idea that any *Them*, real or imagined, would make her afraid to sit with her favorite six-year-olds. She always said yes to Mrs. Mitchell in the end. 6

5 Make Connections
What does this description tell you about Hilary? Use what you know about someone like Hilary to help understand her.

6 Tone
Why does the author include a long description of Hilary at school? What does this reflect about the author's attitude about Hilary?

Monitor Comprehension

Explain
How would Hilary describe baby-sitting at the Mitchells'? Why does she always agree to watch the twins?

In Other Words
hesitated to accept stopped to think before agreeing
in equal measure all at the same time
dug in and made a fuss became stubborn and tried to fight it
ban make a rule against

represent stand for
bloomers small shorts worn under cheerleading skirts
rescinded took back, cancelled

Predict

Hilary baby-sits at the Mitchells' the night before Halloween. Will this be a quiet evening with the twins?

It was on the night before Halloween, a Sunday, the moon hanging ripely over the Mitchells' front yard, that Hilary went to **sit for** the twins. Dressed as a wolf in a sheep's clothing, Mr. Mitchell let her in. 7

"I said they could stay up and watch the Disney special," he said. "It's two hours, and lasts well past their bedtime. But we are **making an exception** tonight. I hope you don't mind." His sheep ears bobbed.

She had no homework and had just finished reading Shirley Jackson's *The Haunting of Hill House,* which was scary enough for her to prefer having the extra company.

"No problem, Mr. Mitchell," she said.

Mrs. Mitchell came out of the kitchen carrying a pumpkin pie. Her costume was a **traditional witch's**. A black stringy wig covered her blond hair. She had blackened one of her front teeth. The twins trailed behind her, each eating a cookie.

"Now, no more cookies," Mrs. Mitchell said, more to Hilary than to the boys.

Hilary winked at them. Adam grinned, but Andrew, **intent on** trying to step on the long black hem of his mother's skirt, missed the wink.

"Good-bye," Hilary called, shutting the door behind the Mitchells. She had a glimpse of the moon, which reminded her of the Jackson book, and made a face at it. Then she turned to the twins. "Now, what about those cookies?" she asked. 8

They raced to the kitchen, and each had one of the fresh-baked chocolate-chip cookies, the kind with the real runny chocolate.

"Crumbs don't count," Hilary said. She scraped around the dish for the crumbs, and having counted what cookies remained—there were thirteen—she shooed the boys back into the living room. They turned

7 Mood
Why do you think the writer chose the night before Halloween as the setting for this part of the story?

8 Make Connections
Hilary connects the setting with a book she is reading. What does the setting remind you of?

In Other Words
sit for baby-sit, take care of
making an exception allowing them to stay up
traditional witch's black dress and pointed hat that people think witches wore
intent on thinking only about

Literary Background
Shirley Jackson's famous 1959 novel *The Haunting of Hill House* is set in a house full of whispers and strange sounds. Readers may wonder if the house is haunted, or if the characters are.

on the TV and settled down to watch the show, sharing the handful of crumbs slowly through the **opening credits**.

Adam lasted through the first hour but was fast asleep in Hilary's lap before the second. Andrew stayed awake until nearly the end, but his eyes kept closing through the commercials. At the final ad, for vitamins, he fell asleep for good.

Hilary sighed. She would have to carry them upstairs to bed. Since she wanted to watch *Friday the Thirteenth, Part II*—or at least she thought she wanted to watch it—she needed to get them upstairs. **It wouldn't do** for either one to wake up and be scared by the show. And if she woke them, they'd want to know the end of the Disney movie and hear at least one other story. She would miss her show. So she hoisted Adam in her arms and went up the stairs. 9

He nuzzled against her shoulder and looked so vulnerable and sweet as she walked down the creaky hall, she smiled. Playfully she touched the doors in the proper order, turning around heavily on one leg. She couldn't quite reach her fingers with her mouth until she dumped him on his bed. After covering him with his quilt, she kissed his forehead and then, with a grin, kissed each of her fingers in turn, whispering, "So there," to the walls when she was done.

She ran down the stairs for Andrew and carried him up as well. He opened his eyes just before they reached the top step.

"Don't forget," he whispered. To **placate him**, she touched the doors,

> She would have to carry them upstairs to bed.

9 **Access Vocabulary**
Do you know what *hoisted* means? Look for clues in the paragraph. Then check your guess in a dictionary.

Key Vocabulary
vulnerable *adj.*, helpless, easily hurt

In Other Words
opening credits beginning of the movie before the action starts
It wouldn't do It would not be good
placate him make him feel better

The Baby-Sitter **445**

turned, and kissed her fingers one at a time.

He smiled sleepily and **murmured**, "All right. All right now."

He was fast asleep when she put him under the covers. She straightened up, watched them both for a moment more, listened to their quiet breathing, and went out of the room.

As she went down the stairs, the hollow *tap-tapping* echo behind her had a **furtive sound**. She turned quickly but saw nothing. Still, she was happy to be downstairs again.

In Other Words

murmured said very softly

furtive sound sneaky sound, as though someone or something didn't want to be noticed

Monitor Comprehension

Confirm Prediction
Was your prediction accurate? Describe any events that you did not expect.

The first half of the show was scary enough. Hilary sat with her feet tucked under a blanket, arms wrapped around her legs. She liked scary stuff usually. She had seen *Alien* and *Aliens* and even *Jaws* without **blanching**, and had finished a giant box of popcorn with Brenda at *Night of the Living Dead.* But somehow, watching a scary movie alone in the Mitchells' spooky house was too much. Remembering the popcorn, she thought that eating might help. There were still those thirteen chocolate-chip cookies left. Mrs. Mitchell had meant the boys weren't supposed to eat them. Hilary knew she hadn't meant the baby-sitter to starve.

During the commercial break, she threw off the blanket and **padded** into the kitchen. **10** Mrs. Mitchell had just had new **linoleum** put on the floor. With a little run, Hilary slid halfway across in her socks.

The plate of cookies was sitting on the counter, next to the stove. Hilary looked at it strangely. There were no longer thirteen cookies. She counted quickly. Seven—no, eight. Someone had eaten five.

"Those twins!" she said aloud. But she knew it couldn't have been them. They never disobeyed, except when she let them, and their mother had said specifically that they could have no more. Besides, they had never left the sofa once the movie had started. And the only time she had left either one of them alone had been when she had taken Adam upstairs, leaving Andrew asleep. . . . She stopped. Andrew hadn't been asleep. Not entirely. Still, she couldn't imagine Andrew **polishing off** five chocolate-chip cookies in the time it had taken her to tuck Adam into bed. **11**

"Now . . ." she said to herself, "if it had been Dana Jankowitz!"

10 Language
Threw and *through* are homophones, or words that sound alike, though they have different spellings and meanings. Which one is the verb? This helps you know the meaning.

11 Mood
What mood is created when Hilary slides across the floor? How does the mood change when she sees the cookies? Explain.

In Other Words
blanching becoming pale with fear
padded walked softly
linoleum kitchen flooring
polishing off quickly eating

Cultural Background
Night of the Living Dead (1968), *Jaws* (1975), *Alien* (1979), and *Aliens* (1986) are classic horror films that people continue to watch today.

She'd baby-sat Dana for almost a year before they moved away, and *that* kid was **capable** of anything.

Still puzzled, she went over to the plate of cookies, and as she got close, she stepped into something cold and wet. She looked down. There was a puddle on the floor, soaking into her right sock. An icy-cold puddle. Hilary looked out the kitchen window. It was raining.

Someone was in the house. 🔢12

She didn't want to believe it, but there was no other explanation. Her whole body felt cold, and she could feel her heart **stuttering** in her chest. She thought about the twins sleeping upstairs, how she had told them she was hired to make sure nothing bad happened to them. But what if something bad happened to *her*? She **shuddered** and looked across the room. The telephone was hanging by the refrigerator. She could try and phone for help, or she could run outside and go to the nearest house. The Mitchells lived down a long driveway, and it was about a quarter mile to the next home. And dark. And wet. And she didn't know how many someones were in the house. Or outside. And maybe it was all her imagination.

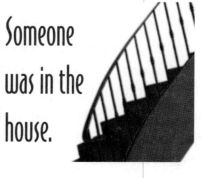

Someone was in the house.

But—and if her jaw trembled just the slightest she didn't think anyone could **fault her**—what if the someones wanted to hurt the twins? She was the only one home to protect them. 🔢13

As silently as possible, she slid open the knife drawer and took out a long, sharp, carving knife. Then slowly she opened the door to the back stairs . . .

. . . and the man hiding there leaped at her. His face was hidden behind a gorilla mask. He was at least six feet tall, wearing blue jeans

🔢12 **Mood**
How does the author use word choice and sensory details to help to add suspense to this scene?

🔢13 **Mood and Tone**
The narrator describes Hilary's thoughts about what to do next. What does the author want to show about Hilary?

and a green shirt. She was so frightened she dropped the knife and ran through the dining room, into the living room, and up the front stairs.

Calling, "Girly, girly, girly, come here," the man ran after her.

Hilary took the steps two at a time, shot around the corner, and ran down the hall. If only she could get to the twins' room, she thought, she could lock and **barricade** the door by pushing the dressers in front of it. And then she'd wake up the twins and they'd go through the trapdoor in the closet up to the attic. They'd be safe there.

But the man was pounding behind her, laughing oddly and calling out.

Hilary heard the **chittering** only after she passed the third door. And the man's screaming as she got to the twins' room. She didn't take time to look behind her but slid into the room, slammed the door, **rammed the bolt home**, and slipped the desk chair under the doorknob. She didn't bother waking the twins or moving anything else in front of the door. 14 The man's high screams **subsided** to a low, horrifying moan. Then at last they stopped altogether. After all, he hadn't taken time to touch the doors or turn on his leg or kiss his fingers one at a time. He hadn't known the **warding spell**. *Once a night and you're …*

She waited a long time before opening the door and peeking out. When she did, all she could see was a crumpled gorilla mask, a piece out of a green shirt, and a dark stain on the floor that was rapidly disappearing, as if someone—or something—were licking it up.

▲ **Critical Viewing: Effect**
What feelings from the story best match this picture?

14 Make Connections
What does this chase remind you of? How does this help you better understand Hilary's situation?

Key Vocabulary
subside *v.*, to grow weaker or less strong

In Other Words
barricade block
chittering strange little animal noises
rammed the bolt home locked it
warding spell magic ritual

Hilary closed the door quietly. She took a deep breath and lay down on top of the covers by Andrew's side. Next time she came to baby-sit, she wouldn't tell the "Golden Arm" story. Not next time or ever. After all, she owed *Them* a favor. ❖

ANALYZE The Baby-Sitter

1. **Explain** How does Hilary feel about what happens at the end of the story? How do you know? Use examples from the story.

2. **Vocabulary** Why was the `ritual` the twins taught Hilary so important to the plot? How does it help them feel less `vulnerable`?

3. **Analyze Word Choice: Mood and Tone** With a partner, discuss how the mood and tone shift during the story. Then discuss how the author uses mood and tone to make the story more frightening.

	Beginning	Middle	End
Mood	calm, like a normal night of baby-sitting		
Tone			

4. **Focus Strategy Make Connections** Analyze "Interview with the King of Terror" for Stephen King's ideas about scary stories. How does this help you understand the techniques Jane Yolen uses in "The Baby-Sitter"? Share the connections you made with a partner.

⟲ Return to the Text

Reread and Write How do Hilary's fears become realities to her? Reread the events and then write a journal entry that expresses them from Hilary's point of view. Be sure to include thoughts and feelings about the events. When you have finished writing, create a multimedia presentation using images and sound to convey Hilary's point of view to your classmates.

by Gahan Wilson

"Shouldn't Willis be in the bed and his imaginary monster under it?"

BEFORE READING Beware: Do Not Read This Poem

poem by Ishmael Reed

Reading Strategies

· Plan and Monitor
· Determine Importance
· Make Inferences
· Ask Questions
► **Make Connections**
· Synthesize
· Visualize

Analyze Word Choice: Repetition and Syntax

Mood is an important part of poetry because it affects how we feel about the poem. Poets use different techniques to help create a mood. These techniques include **repetition of words** and **word choice**. Some poets also vary their **syntax**, which is the way sentences and phrases are formed. As you read the poem, study the way the poet uses words, repetition, and syntax to build a unique mood.

Look Into the Text

What is unusual about some of the words in these lines? How do they affect the mood of the poem?

> tonite, *thriller* was
> abt an ol woman, so vain she
> surrounded her self w/
>   many mirrors
> It got so bad that finally she
> locked herself indoors & her
> whole life became the
>   mirrors

The poem doesn't include much punctuation. What do you notice about how words are formed and joined?

Focus Strategy ► Make Connections

Look for connections as you read a poem. Which connections help you understand the poem?

HOW TO MAKE CONNECTIONS

Focus Strategy

1. Read the poem several times, focusing on words, ideas, and images that connect to your own experiences. Mark these places with self-stick notes.

2. Reread the sections you marked and write about the connections you made to the text.

   > abt an ol woman, so vain she
   > surrounded her self w/
   >   many mirrors

   I saw a film once where dead people lived inside mirrors.

   My notes helped me form images of what was happening.

3. Talk about your notes with a partner. Decide if the connections you made are helpful in understanding the poem or not. Remove the notes that distract from the poem.

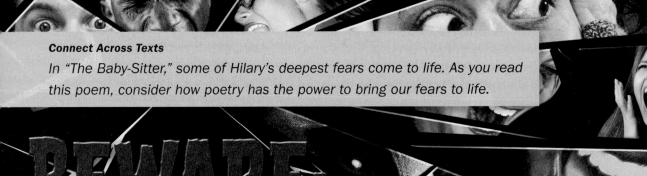

Connect Across Texts

In "The Baby-Sitter," some of Hilary's deepest fears come to life. As you read this poem, consider how poetry has the power to bring our fears to life.

BEWARE:
Do Not Read This Poem
by Ishmael Reed

tonite, *thriller* was
abt an ol woman, so vain she
surrounded her self w/
   many mirrors

5 It got so bad that finally she
locked herself indoors & her
whole life became the
   mirrors **1**
one day the villagers broke
10 into her house, but she was too
swift for them. she disappeared
    into a mirror
each tenant who bought the house
after that, lost a loved one to
15   the ol woman in the mirror:
      first a little girl
      then a young woman
      then the young woman/s husband
the hunger of this poem is legendary
20 it has taken in many victims

1 Make Connections
What do you know about people's beliefs about mirrors? What connections might these beliefs have to this poem?

In Other Words
thriller the spooky TV show
vain pleased with herself, focused on her looks
swift quick
tenant person living there
legendary so famous, well-known

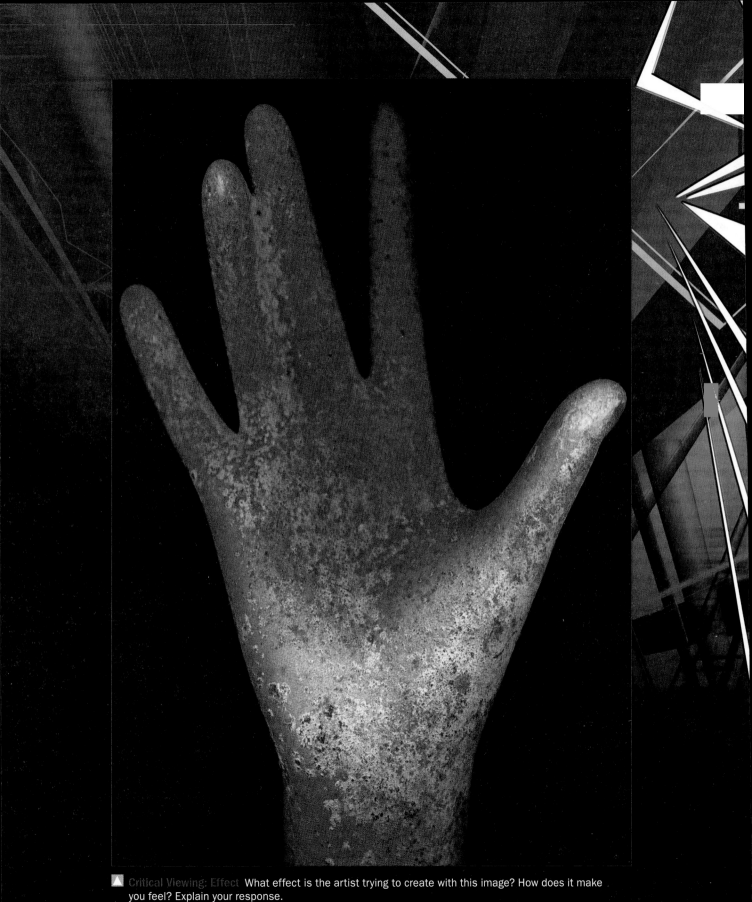

▲ Critical Viewing: Effect What effect is the artist trying to create with this image? How does it make
you feel? Explain your response.

back off from this poem
it has drawn in yr feet
back off from this poem
it has drawn in yr legs
25   back off from this poem
it is a greedy mirror 2️⃣
you are into this poem. from
    the waist down
nobody can hear you can they?
30   this poem has had you up to here
       belch
this poem aint got no manners
you cant call out frm this poem
relax now & go w/ this poem
35   move & roll on to this poem

       do not resist this poem
       this poem has yr eyes
       this poem has his head
       this poem has his arms
40   this poem has his fingers
       this poem has his fingertips

this poem is the reader & the
      reader this poem

statistic: the us bureau of missing persons reports

45   that in 1968 over 100,000 people disappeared
        leaving no solid clues
          nor trace   only
   a space   in the lives of their friends 3️⃣

2️⃣ **Make Connections**
In what kinds of situations do people usually order you to "back off," or move away? Why is that order unusual here?

3️⃣ **Mood**
How do the syntax, or the way phrases are formed, and the way the words are spaced on the page affect the mood of the poem?

Key Vocabulary

resist *v.*, to fight against
• trace *n.*, small sign that something or someone was in a place

In Other Words

belch   burp
us bureau of missing persons   government agency that looks for people who have disappeared
no solid clues   no evidence that would tell people where they were

ANALYZE Beware: Do Not Read This Poem

1. **Recall and Explain** According to the speaker, what happened to over 100,000 people who disappeared without a `trace` in 1968?

2. **Vocabulary** The speaker warns the reader to beware. What does he suggest that the poem is `capable` of?

3. **Analyze Word Choice: Repetition and Syntax** Many poets use techniques like repetition, word choice, and syntax to create a certain mood. With a partner, find examples of each technique in the poem and figure out the mood that Ishmael Reed creates.

4. **Focus Strategy Make Connections** Talk with a partner about the connections you made with this poem. Discuss how those connections helped you understand the poem's meaning.

Return to the Text
Reread and Write What makes this poem frightening? Write a paragraph explaining how the poet creates fear.

About the Poet

Ishmael Reed (1938–   ) is a novelist, journalist, poet, and playwright. He has been called one of the greatest African American writers of his generation. Reed uses a lively style in his poetry that reflects everyday conversation, slang, and popular music.

EQ What Makes Something Frightening?

Critical Thinking

EQ 1. Analyze How do the two selections show the ways that our fears become reality?

2. Interpret What is the central theme, or message, of "The Baby-Sitter"? Use examples from the selection to support your answer.

3. Compare What is Hilary's attitude toward legends and rituals? How is it different from the attitude of the woman in the poem?

4. Judge Are the stories successful in creating a frightening mood and tone? Use examples from both texts to support your opinions.

EQ 5. Speculate Think back to the quotation, "We have nothing to fear but fear itself." How would the characters in the story and the speaker in the poem respond to this idea?

Write About Literature

Opinion Statement Think about the frightening events that the writers choose to show and the events they only refer to.

Selection	Events That Are Shown	Events That Aren't Shown
The Baby-Sitter		
Beware: Do Not Read This Poem		

Write your opinion about which events are more frightening—scenes that are shown, or scenes that rely on the reader's imagination. Support your opinion using examples from your chart.

Key Vocabulary Review

Oral Review Work with a partner. Use these words to complete the paragraph.

capable	resist	trace
precision	ritual	vulnerable
relies	subsides	

The scariest stories are difficult to __(1)__ because their effect on you is so strong. For example, "The Baby-Sitter" tells about an old __(2)__ and tradition that carries frightening powers. The author chooses her words with careful __(3)__ to build suspense and leave you feeling as helpless and __(4)__ as the children. "Beware: Do Not Read This Poem" __(5)__ on, or counts on, our common fears about people who disappear without the smallest sign or __(6)__. Both of these selections have power and are __(7)__ of stirring up our fears. Fortunately, the stories come to an end and the terror __(8)__ until it is just a memory.

Writing Application Recall a scary story, book, or movie you could not resist. Write a paragraph describing how the writer created a mood of fear. Use at least three Key Vocabulary words.

Read with Ease: Expression

Assess your reading fluency with the passage in the Reading Handbook, p. 764. Then complete the self-check below.

1. My expression did/did not sound natural.

2. My words correct per minute: _____.

INTEGRATE THE LANGUAGE ARTS

Comparative Adjectives

Add -er to one-syllable adjectives to compare **two** people, places, or things.

Her house is **old**, but their house is **older**.

If a two-syllable adjective ends in a consonant + **y**, change the **y** to **i** before you add -**er**.

The first story of the house was **scary**.

The second story was **scarier** than the first.

Add -**est** to one-syllable adjectives to compare **three or more** people, places, or things.

The hallways were the **strangest** part of the house.

For adjectives of three or more syllables, use **more** instead of -**er** and **most** instead of -**est**.

Hilary felt **more confident** before the movie.

It was the **most terrifying** movie she had seen!

Most other two-syllable adjectives take **more** and **most** to compare.

That night was the **most starless** night we've had.

Oral Practice (1–5) Say five sentences that compare the people, places, or things in "The Baby-Sitter."

Written Practice (6–10) Fix three adjectives below and rewrite the paragraph. Add two more sentences.

cutest
The twins were the ~~most cute~~ kids Hilary knew. Their house was the stranger one Hilary knew. On Halloween, Adam was most exhausted than Andrew. The house was more scarier than the movie.

Make Comparisons

Pair Talk Compare Hilary's behavior in "The Baby-Sitter" to the way you would react in the same situation. Use adjectives such as *braver* and *more frightened* to make comparisons.

Analyze Foreshadowing

Authors use **foreshadowing** when they leave hints about events that will happen later in the story.

- Foreshadowing encourages the reader to make predictions about the rest of the plot.
- It builds suspense as the reader waits to see if the prediction will come true.

For example, in "The Baby-Sitter," the narrator says that Hilary "felt as if there were things watching her from behind … the walls. She couldn't say what exactly, just *things*." The narrator foreshadows, or hints about, a mystery that will be solved later. In some cases, foreshadowing is easy to identify. Other times, it isn't until later that the reader can recognize the clues that were given along the way.

With a partner, identify more examples of foreshadowing in "The Baby-Sitter."

Page	Clue	What the Clue Foreshadows
440	Hilary hears strange noises.	She learns firsthand about the "things" that live in the walls.

Then discuss and write about how well the foreshadowing builds suspense.

"Those aren't buzzards, are they?"

Source: ©Mick Stevens/*The New Yorker*

Many people believe that buzzards foreshadow death. Why would they believe this?

Thesaurus

A **thesaurus** lists words with their synonyms and antonyms. Writers often use a thesaurus so they can avoid repeating the same words in nearby sentences.

> **OK:** The poet is very **capable**. She shows that she is **capable** because she chooses just the right words.

> **Better:** The poet is very **capable**. She shows that she is **skilled** because she chooses just the right words.

For each word, use a thesaurus to find at least two other words or phrases that have similar meanings.

1. precision   2. rely   3. resist

Storytelling

Jump Stories In "The Baby-Sitter," the twins love hearing Hilary's "jump stories." These are frightening tales that have surprising twists that make listeners "jump" in fright.

What jump stories do you know? Take turns sharing your scariest stories with a small group, and then discuss the factors that make them scary. Work together to create an original jump story that you can share with the class.

Listen to other groups' stories. Then, ask questions to clarify and build on their ideas. Discuss ways to improve the mood and tone of each story.

⬗ **Language and Learning Handbook**, page 702

Write a Literary Analysis

A test may ask you to analyze, or look closely at, a specific part of a selection of literature.

1 **Unpack the Prompt** Underline words that show what your response should include.

> **Writing Prompt**
> Write a literary analysis of the plot of "The Baby-Sitter." What techniques does the author use to build suspense? Does she succeed? Use specific story passages to support your analysis.

2 **Plan Your Response** Use a **Plot Diagram** to track examples where the author worked to build suspense.

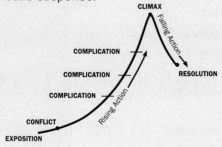

3 **Draft** Use an **Essay Organizer**. Limit your writing time to 15 minutes.

> **Essay Organizer**
>
> "The Baby-Sitter" is a scary story in which the author builds suspense. To do this, Yolen uses [list techniques the author uses].
>
> The author first uses suspense when [add example from the exposition]. As the story goes on, [add example from the conflict section]. The conflict rises to a climax when [add example from the climax]. When the story is finally resolved, the suspense [explain whether the building suspense works].
>
> In conclusion, [give your opinion about whether the author succeeds in building suspense in the story].

4 **Check Your Work** Reread your analysis. Ask:

- Does my work address the prompt?
- Do I cover all aspects of the literary element?
- Do I use adjectives correctly?
- Do I use rhetorical devices?

⬗ **Writing Handbook**, page 784

Perform and Evaluate a Dramatic Reading

Some stories can be just as thrilling when they are dramatized as the stories you have been reading. Do a dramatic reading of a short story for another class, your family, or a group of friends. Here is how to do it.

1. Plan Your Dramatic Reading

Choose a story that

- fits your audience and occasion
- is highly emotional, or one you think will have a powerful effect on the audience's emotions
- can be read within your time limit.

2. Practice the Dramatic Reading

Practice reading the story until you can

- create a mood or tone that is appropriate to the story
- emphasize the story's elements—the characters' voices or personalities, or the setting description
- as you read, hold the story in a way that won't distract the audience.

3. Perform the Dramatic Reading

As you perform your dramatic reading, stay connected to the audience.

- Speak clearly enough that your listeners can easily understand each word and hear changes in your intonation.
- Make eye contact with your audience as you read.
- Read so that you build tension, or find humor, in the right places.
- Adjust your reading if the audience is not responding to the story's tension, mood, or emotions.
- Use your voice, facial expressions, and body movements to make the story sad, exciting, frightening, or humorous.
- After your presentation, ask your audience for feedback. Incorporate their suggestions into a future presentation.

4. Rate the Dramatic Readings

Use the rubric to discuss and rate the dramatic readings, including your own.

Dramatic Reading Rubric

Scale	Content of Short Story	Speaker's Preparation	Speaker's Delivery
3 Great	• Strongly affected my feelings • Was perfect for the audience and occasion	• Understood the story well	• Made me feel the story's mood • Helped me visualize the story elements
2 Good	• Affected me somewhat • Seemed appropriate to the audience and occasion	• Understood the story for the most part	• Gave some sense of the story's mood • Sometimes helped me visualize the story
1 Needs Work	• Did not affect me • Did not match the audience and occasion	• Did not seem to understand the story	• Did not convey the mood of the story • Did not help me visualize the story

DO IT ▶ Now, perform a dramatic reading. Keep it interesting and full of emotion!

📕 Language and Learning Handbook, page 702

myNGconnect.com
🔊 Download the rubric.

> How can you use the audience's feedback to improve future readings?

EQ ## What Makes Something Frightening?
Consider the role of imagination.

Make a Connection

Quickwrite What is more frightening—the dangers that we can see, or the dangers that we can only imagine? Think about your own experiences, including stories you've seen and read. Then write down some ideas about how the imagination affects our fears. Don't spend more than three minutes writing.

Learn Key Vocabulary

Study the Words Pronounce each word and learn its meaning. You may also want to look up the meaning in the Glossary.

• Academic Vocabulary

Key Words	Examples
burden (**bur**-din) *noun* ▸ page 479	A **burden** is a heavy thing that you must carry or something difficult you have to do or know about. Keeping my brother's secret was a great **burden** to me. *Synonym:* weight
• **cease** (sēs) *verb* ▸ page 475, 485	When something **ceases**, it stops. The voices **ceased** when he entered. It got completely quiet.
dread (dred) *noun* ▸ pages 468, 483, 485	Someone who is filled with **dread** is very afraid. The thought of death fills me with **dread**. *Synonym:* fear
ominous (**ah**-mu-nus) *adjective* ▸ page 479	An **ominous** sign hints that something evil or dangerous is coming. The dark, cloudy sky looked **ominous**. *Synonym:* threatening
ponder (**pon**-dur) *verb* ▸ pages 475, 485	When you **ponder** something, you think about it very carefully. I **pondered** the meaning of the poem for hours.
prophet (**pro**-fut) *noun* ▸ pages 480, 481, 485	A **prophet** is someone who can predict what will happen in the future. The **prophet** warned us about the coming disaster.
• **relevance** (**re**-lu-vuns) *noun* ▸ pages 473, 477, 481, 483	When an idea has **relevance**, it is important and connects to another thing. The news story has **relevance** to my own life.
suspect (su-**spekt**) *verb* ▸ pages 466, 485	To **suspect** is to believe that something may be different from what it seems. I **suspect** that she is lying.

Practice the Words Work with a partner to write four sentences. Use at least two Key Vocabulary words in each sentence.

> The ominous cloud on the
> horizon gave me a feeling of
> dread.

BEFORE READING **The Tell-Tale Heart**

short story by Edgar Allan Poe

Reading Strategies

· Plan and Monitor
· Determine Importance
· Make Inferences
· Ask Questions
▶ **Make Connections**
· Synthesize
· Visualize

Analyze Structure: Suspense

Writers often build **suspense** in their stories. They want their readers to feel uncertain of what will happen next because it keeps readers interested. Writers use different techniques to build this sense of suspense, such as

- slowing down or speeding up the action of a story
- putting characters in dangerous situations
- hinting that the narrator is not trustworthy or reliable
- giving clues about good or bad things that may happen later in the story.

Look Into the Text

These opening lines from the story introduce the narrator. Can you trust his point of view?

> True! I had been and still am very nervous—very, very dreadfully nervous. But why *will* you say that I am mad? The disease had made my senses sharper. It had not destroyed or dulled them. Above all, my sense of hearing was sharp. I heard all things in the heaven and in the earth. How, then, can you say I am mad? Listen! You shall see how healthy and calm I am as I tell you the whole story.

How does the narration or voice add to a feeling of suspense?

Focus Strategy ▶ Make Connections

Suspense draws you into a story. Another way to become involved in a story is to **make connections**. With a partner, read the story, and ask each other questions about it. What are your ideas, feelings, and reactions to the story?

HOW TO MAKE CONNECTIONS

Focus Strategy

1. As you read, look for words, phrases, and ideas that seem important to understanding the story. Record these in a **Triple-Entry Journal**.

2. Consider how these parts of the story connect to your life, to other texts, and to the world. Add your ideas to the chart.

3. Explain how the connections help you to understand the text. Review the text and think of more connections you can make.

Triple-Entry Journal

Important Ideas in the Text	My Connection	What This Helps Me Understand
"You shall see how healthy and calm I am as I tell you the whole story."	In TV shows, whenever someone says he is healthy and calm, he's usually just the opposite.	I know that I can't trust this narrator's version of the story.

Edgar Allan Poe
(1809–1849)

All that we see or seem
Is but a dream within a dream.

Edgar Allan Poe was one
of America's first Gothic
horror writers.

American writer and poet **Edgar Allan Poe** was born in Boston, Massachusetts, to parents who were traveling actors. Poe's father disappeared soon after Poe's birth and later died from tuberculosis. His mother died soon after in 1811. This deeply affected Poe, who was a very young boy at the time. The image of his dead mother lying in her coffin in her best gown and surrounded by candles was one the most haunting images of Poe's childhood.

After his mother's death, Poe was adopted by John and Frances Allan, who lived in Richmond, Virginia. From an early age, Poe often entertained his adopted parents' friends by reciting poetry at dinner parties. In 1815 the Allans moved to England, where Poe entered boarding school. He began to spend more of his time reading and writing, eventually deciding to make it his career.

Although Poe's own short life ended in 1849, he has remained popular with readers throughout the years. He is said to be the creator of the modern mystery and detective story. However, he is known first and most importantly as a Gothic horror writer. Stories like "The Tell-Tale Heart" show his writing at its spine-chilling best.

myNGconnect.com

◯ Read more of Poe's work.
◯ Learn more about Gothic horror stories.

THE TELL-TALE HEART

by Edgar Allan Poe

retold by Emily Hutchinson

Critical Viewing: Suspense How do the colors and subjects of this image create a feeling of suspense?

 Comprehension Coach

True! I had been and still am very **nervous**—very, very dreadfully nervous. But why *will* you say that I am **mad**? The disease had made my senses sharper. It had not destroyed or dulled them. Above all, my sense of hearing was sharp. I heard all things in the heaven and in the earth. How, then, can you say I am mad? Listen! You shall see how healthy and calm I am as I tell you the whole story. 🔢

It is impossible to say how I first got the idea. But once I had the thought, it haunted me day and night. There was no good reason for it. I didn't hate the old man. I loved him. He had never done anything against me. And he had never insulted me. I had no wish at all to take his gold.

I think it was his eye! Yes, that's what it was. One of his eyes looked like a vulture's eye. It was a pale blue eye, with a **film over it**. Whenever he looked at me, my blood ran cold. And so bit by bit, very slowly, I made up my mind to take the life of the old man. That way, I would rid myself of the eye forever.

Now this is the point. You think I am mad. But a person who is mad knows nothing. You should have seen *me* and how wisely I acted. I was **cautious**, and I planned ahead. I never gave the old man any reason to **suspect**. In fact, I was never kinder to him than during the whole week before I killed him.

Every night, about midnight, I turned the handle of his door and opened it—oh, so gently! When I had opened it just wide enough, I pushed a dark lantern through the crack. The lantern was covered, so that no light shone

1 Suspense
After reading this paragraph, what expectations do you have for the story?

Théodore Géricault (1791–1824) Dying, Alexandre Correard. Oil on canvas, Musee des Beaux-Arts, Rouen, France, The Bridgeman Art Library.

🔺 **Critical Viewing: Effect** What do you think the old man looks like? Does this painting match your image of him? Explain.

Key Vocabulary
suspect *v.*, to believe that something may be hidden or different from what it seems

In Other Words
nervous emotional, worried, and tense
mad crazy, insane
film over it thin, skin-like covering
cautious very careful

from it. Then I put my head in the door opening.

Oh, you would have laughed to see how I did it! I moved slowly—very, very slowly, so that I would not **disturb** the old man's sleep. It took me an hour to put my whole head inside the opening far enough so I could see the old man. Ha! Would someone who is mad have been this smart? And then, when my head was well in the room, I uncovered the lantern. I did this very cautiously, for the hinges creaked. I uncovered it just enough so that a single long ray of light fell upon the vulture eye. **2**

I did this for seven long nights, every night just at midnight. But I found the eye was always closed. That made it impossible to do the work. You see, it was not the old man who upset me, but his Evil Eye. Every morning, when the day broke, I went boldly into his room, calling him by name in a friendly voice. I asked him how he had passed the night. I knew he had no idea that every night, just at midnight, I **looked upon** him while he slept.

On the eighth night, I was more cautious than usual. A watch's minute hand moves more quickly than my hand did. Never before that night had I *felt* just how powerful and wise I really was. I could hardly control my feelings of **triumph**. There I was, opening the door, little by little. I knew that the old man couldn't even dream of my secret actions or thoughts. The very idea just about made me laugh out loud.

Perhaps he heard me, for he moved on the bed suddenly. It was as if he were surprised by something. Now you may think that I moved back, but I did not. The room was as black as tar, for the **window shutters** were closed tight. I knew that he could not see the opening of the door. So I kept pushing on it—slowly, slowly. **3**

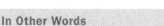

Would someone who is mad have been this smart?

2 Make Connections
What do you know about vultures? What do they symbolize? Why do you think the narrator calls the old man's eye a "vulture eye"?

3 Suspense
How do the narrator's slow and careful movements build suspense?

Monitor Comprehension

Explain
What reason does the narrator give for wanting to murder the old man? Is he a trustworthy narrator? Explain.

In Other Words
disturb interrupt, bother
looked upon watched
triumph great success
window shutters covers over the windows

Predict
The narrator has been planning his crime for a week.
Will his plan work, or will he be stopped?

I had my head inside, and was about to uncover the lantern, when my thumb slipped. This small noise caused the old man to sit up in bed. I heard him cry out, "Who's there?" but I kept quite still and said nothing. For a whole hour, I did not move a muscle. In the meantime, I did not hear him lie down. He was still sitting up in the bed, listening.

After a time, I heard a slight groan. I knew it was a groan of deathly terror. It was not a groan of pain or sorrow. Oh, no! It was the low sound that comes from the bottom of the soul when it is filled with **dread**. I knew the sound well. Many a night, just at midnight, I have made such a sound myself. As I did so, that very sound made my terrors even worse. Oh, yes, I knew that sound well. **4**

I knew what the old man felt, and I **pitied** him—even though I was laughing in my heart. I knew that he had been lying awake since the first slight noise. His fears had been growing ever since he had turned in the bed. He had been trying to talk himself out of being afraid, but he could not. He had been saying to himself, "It is nothing but the wind in the chimney. It is nothing but a mouse crossing the floor. It is only a cricket that has made a single chirp."

Yes, I knew very well that he had been trying to talk himself out of being afraid. But it wasn't working. Death, in coming near him, had cast its black shadow before him. Now the victim was surrounded. It was the unseen shadow of Death that made the old man feel my closeness. He could neither see nor hear me, but he could feel the presence of my head in that room. **5**

After waiting a long time, I decided to open the lantern a tiny bit. You cannot imagine how carefully I did so. Finally, a single dim ray,

4 Suspense
What is the effect of this detailed description of the old man's reaction?

5 Make Connections
The narrator thinks he knows the old man's feelings. Use what you know to decide whether you think he's right or not. Add this to your Triple-Entry Journal.

Key Vocabulary
dread *n.*, great fear

In Other Words
pitied felt sorry for

like the thread of a spider, shot out and fell upon the vulture eye.

The eye was open—wide, wide open. I grew very angry as I looked at it. I saw it with perfect clearness. It was all a dull blue, with an ugly film over it. The sight of it chilled my very bones. I could see nothing else of the old man's face. The ray of light was pointing right at his eye.

Didn't I already tell you that what you think is madness is only a sharpness in my senses? Now, I say, I started to hear a low, dull, quick sound. It sounded like a watch wrapped in cotton. I knew *that* sound well, too. It was the beating of the old man's heart. Somehow that sound made me even angrier—just as the beating of a drum makes a soldier feel brave.

But even then I kept still. I hardly even breathed. I tried to see how steadily I could keep the lantern's ray shining on the eye. I heard the beating of the heart increase. It grew quicker and quicker, and louder and louder with every beat. The old man's terror *must* have been growing by the minute! His heartbeat grew louder, I say, louder every moment! Do you hear me? ⑥

I have told you that I am nervous.

⑥ **Suspense**
What techniques does Poe use here to build suspense?

Head III, Francis Bacon (1909–1992). Oil on canvas, private collection, ©2013 The Estate of Francis Bacon. All rights reserved. ARS, New York/DACS, London/Bridgeman Art Library.

◣ **Critical Viewing: Effect** Study the expression on the man's face in this image. What feelings does he show? What mood does the artist create with the man's expression and the streaked background?

It is true. And now, in the awful silence of that old house, this noise terrified me. Yet, for some minutes longer, I stood still. But the beating of the heart grew louder, louder! His heart sounded as if it might burst. Suddenly a new terror came upon me. I thought that the sound would be heard by a neighbor!

The old man's hour had come! With a loud yell, I opened the lantern and leaped into the room. He screamed once—once only. In an instant, I dragged him to the floor and pulled the heavy bed over him. Then I smiled, to find the **deed** so close to being done. But, for many minutes, the heart beat on **with a muffled sound**. This, however, did not bother me. Under the heavy bed, the sound would not be heard through the wall.

He screamed once—once only.

Finally it stopped. The old man was dead. I moved the bed and looked at the body. Yes, he was stone, stone dead. I placed my hand on his heart and held it there for a few minutes. There was no beating. He was stone dead. That horrible eye would bother me no more. **7**

If you still think I am mad, you will no longer think so when I tell you what I did next. I thought about the best way to hide the body. Then I cut it into pieces. I cut off the head and the arms and the legs.

Next I took up three boards from the floor of the bedroom. I put the body under the floor, and then put the boards back in place. I did this so well that no human eye—not even his—could have noticed anything wrong. There was nothing to wash out. There was no stain of any kind. There were no spots of blood anywhere. I had been too careful for that. A tub had caught all—ha! ha!

7 Make Connections
Use what you know from movies and books to explain the narrator's actions. Why would someone do what he did? Add your ideas to your Triple-Entry Journal.

Monitor Comprehension

Confirm Prediction
Did you accurately predict the crime would happen? What reasons led you to make an accurate or inaccurate prediction?

In Other Words
deed old man's murder
with a muffled sound as though the
    heart were wrapped or covered to keep
    it quiet

When I had finished all this work, it was four o'clock. It was still as dark as midnight. As the clock struck four, I heard a knocking at the street door. **With a light heart**, I went down to open it. The Evil Eye was gone. There was nothing now to fear. Three men entered the house. They introduced themselves as police officers. They said a scream had been heard by a neighbor during the night. **Foul play was suspected.** A report had been made at the police station. The police officers had been sent out to search the house.

I smiled—for what did I have to fear? I greeted the officers **warmly**. The scream, I said, was my own. I had had a bad dream. The old man, I said, was on vacation in the country. I took my visitors all over the house. I told them to search—search *well*. Finally, I took them to *his* room. I showed them his belongings, safe and undisturbed. Feeling very confident, I even brought chairs into the room. I told the officers to rest for a while. Quite sure of myself, I even put my own chair right over the old man's body. **8**

The officers believed me. I was **at ease**. They sat there for a while, chatting about everyday things. But, before long, I felt myself **getting pale**. I wished they would go. My head ached, and I thought I heard a ringing in my ears. Yet still they sat and talked. The ringing in my ears became louder. I talked more to get rid of the feeling. But the noise kept getting louder. Finally, I realized that the noise was not within my ears. **9**

8 Make Connections
Have you seen movies or read stories in which criminals believed they would not get caught? What usually happens?

9 Suspense
How does the narrator's behavior build suspense? What do you expect will happen next?

In Other Words

With a light heart Without worries
Foul play was suspected. They thought a crime had been committed.
warmly in a friendly way
at ease relaxed, calm
getting pale turning white

I started to grow very pale. I began to talk even faster, and in a louder voice. Yet the sound got louder. What could I do? It was a low, dull, quick sound. It sounded like a watch wrapped in cotton. I gasped for breath. Still, the police officers did not hear it. I talked faster and louder, but the noise kept increasing. I stood up and moved around. I talked about things that were not important. I spoke in a high voice and I **used violent gestures**—but the noise kept getting louder.

Why *would* they not be gone? I walked back and forth on the floor with heavy steps, but the noise kept getting louder. Oh, God! What *could* I do? The noise grew louder—louder—*louder!* And still the men chatted pleasantly and smiled. Was it possible that they didn't hear the sound? Almighty God! No, no! They heard! They suspected! They knew! They were making fun of me! This is what I thought, and it is what I still think.

But anything was better than this **agony**! Anything was better than to let them go on making a fool of me! I could look at their smiles no

Man with Blue Head, John Ritter © CORBIS.

▲ **Critical Viewing: Suspense** How does the expression on the face resemble the narrator's sense of agony?

In Other Words
used violent gestures moved my hands and arms around wildly
agony great mental pain

longer! I felt that I must scream or die! And now, again, listen! The sound is louder! *Louder!*

"**Villains!**" I screamed. "Pretend no more! I admit the deed! Tear up the floor boards! Here, here! It is the beating of his **hideous** heart!" ▨ ❖

▨ **Suspense**
How does the author speed up the action to build suspense? At what point does the suspense finally end?

ANALYZE The Tell-Tale Heart

1. **Explain** How is the narrator's evil crime discovered? Is this a surprise for the police? Use details from the text to explain your answer.

2. **Vocabulary** What is the `relevance` of the title to the story? What does the heart represent?

3. **Analyze Structure: Suspense** Review the list of techniques that authors use to build suspense (page 463). Record examples of the techniques that Poe uses. Then discuss how these add to a growing sense of suspense in the story.

Technique	Example	Effect
slowing down the action	The narrator takes hours to attack the old man.	You know that something terrible is getting closer and closer.

4. **Focus Strategy Make Connections** Talk with a partner about the types of connections that were most useful in helping you understand Poe's story. Provide specific examples from the **Triple-Entry Journal** you began on page 463.

⟲ Return to the Text
Reread and Write What role does imagination play in making "The Tell-Tale Heart" frightening? Reread the story, and then write a short story that builds suspense to make the mood frightening.

Key Vocabulary
- **relevance** *n.*, importance that connects to something else

BEFORE READING The Raven

poem by Edgar Allan Poe

Reading Strategies

· Plan and Monitor
· Determine Importance
· Make Inferences
· Ask Questions
▶ **Make Connections**
· Synthesize
· Visualize

Analyze Word Choice: Imagery and Repetition

Poets use a variety of techniques to create a mood or build suspense.

- **Repetition** involves the use of certain sounds, words, and phrases over and over again.
- **Imagery** is the use of words and phrases to create pictures in the reader's mind.

Look Into the Text

Try to see the **image** in your mind.

Once upon a midnight dreary, while I pondered, weak and weary,
Over many an old and curious book filled with forgotten lore—
While I sat there, nearly napping, suddenly there came a tapping,
As of someone gently rapping, rapping at my bedroom door.
"It is some visitor," I muttered, "tapping at my bedroom door—
Only this, and nothing more."

How does the **repetition** of sounds and words help build suspense?

As you read the poem, create a **Suspense Chart** to study the poet's use of repetition and imagery and how it builds suspense.

Suspense Chart

Technique	How Does This Build Suspense?
The raven repeats "Nevermore."	The word sounds more final every time the raven repeats it.

Focus Strategy ▶ Make Connections

As you read poetry, the images and repetition that the poet includes can often spark connections with your own experiences. Because not all connections are useful in understanding the text, it's important to learn to evaluate the connections you make.

HOW TO MAKE CONNECTIONS

Focus Strategy

1. As you read the poem, look for ideas, images, and repeated phrases that connect to yourself, to other texts, and to the world.

2. Record your connections on self-stick notes and place them by the text.

   While I sat there, nearly napping, suddenly there came a tapping,

   When I'm half-asleep, sudden noises can really surprise me.

3. Compare your notes with a partner's. Does reading your partner's connections help you?

4. Explain how your connections help you to understand the text. If you cannot do this, the connection may not be useful.

Connect Across Texts

In "The Tell-Tale Heart," Edgar Allan Poe brings readers into the narrator's twisted imagination. As you read this classic poem by Poe, consider the role of the imagination on our deepest fears.

The Raven
by Edgar Allan Poe

Once upon a midnight dreary, while I pondered, weak and weary,
Over many an old and curious book filled with forgotten lore—
While I sat there, nearly napping, suddenly there came a tapping,
As of someone gently rapping, rapping at my bedroom door.
5 "It is some visitor," I muttered, "tapping at my bedroom door—
              Only this, and nothing more."

Ah, clearly I remember it was in cold and dark December,
And each separate dying ember formed a ghost upon the floor.
Eagerly I wished for tomorrow—I had tried but failed to borrow
10 Help from books to cease my sorrow—sorrow for the lost Lenore—
For the rare and beautiful maiden whom the angels name Lenore—
              Nameless here for evermore. **1**

1 Repetition
What words does the speaker repeat in this stanza? What mood and feeling does this show?

Key Vocabulary
ponder *v.*, to think carefully about
● **cease** *v.*, to stop

In Other Words
dreary that was gloomy, dark, and sad
forgotten lore knowledge that was taught long ago
rapping knocking
ember glowing coal
for evermore forever

And the silken, sad, uncertain rustling of each purple curtain

Thrilled me—filled me with fantastic terrors never felt before;

15 So that now, to still the beating of my heart, I stood repeating,

"It's some visitor entreating entrance at my bedroom door—

Some late visitor entreating entrance at my bedroom door—

That is it and nothing more." **2**

Very soon my soul grew stronger; hesitating then no longer,

20 "Sir," said I, "or Madam, truly your forgiveness I ask for;

The fact is that I was napping, and so gently you came rapping,

And so faintly you came tapping, tapping at my bedroom door,

That I was not sure I heard you." Then I opened wide the door—

Darkness there and nothing more.

25 Deep into that darkness peering, long I stood there wondering, fearing,

Doubting, dreaming dreams no man had ever dared to dream before;

But the silence was unbroken, and the stillness gave no token,

And the only word there spoken was the whispered word, "Lenore!"

This I whispered, and an echo murmured back the word "Lenore!"

30 Only this and nothing more.

Back into the bedroom turning, all my soul within me burning,

Soon again I heard a tapping somewhat louder than before.

"Surely," I said, "surely that is something at my glass pane;

Let me see, then, what could be there, and this mystery explore—

35 Let my heart be still a moment and this mystery explore—

It is the wind and nothing more!" **3**

2 Repetition
The speaker repeats several long phrases. What can you guess about the speaker at this point?

3 Make Connections
Have you ever heard a noise at night and not been able to explain it? How does that help you understand the speaker's reactions? Add this to a self-stick note.

In Other Words
entreating asking for
hesitating pausing, waiting
peering looking and searching
token hint of what was out there

Open wide I flung the shutter, when, with many a flit and flutter,

In there stepped a noble Raven from the ancient days of yore.

Not the smallest greeting made he; not a minute stopped or stayed he;

40 But, with look of lord or lady, perched above my bedroom door—

Perched upon a bust of Pallas just above my bedroom door—

Perched, and sat, and nothing more. **4**

Then this ebony bird beguiling my sad spirit into smiling,

By the serious appearance of the expression that it wore,

45 "Though your crown is short and shaven, you," I said, "are sure no craven,

Terrible, grim, and ancient Raven wandering from the Nightly shore—

Tell me what your lordly name is on the Night's so ghostly shore!"

Said the Raven, "Nevermore."

I was amazed by this ungainly bird to hear it speak so plainly,

50 Though its answer little meaning—little relevance it bore;

For we cannot help agreeing that no living human being

Ever yet was blessed with seeing bird above his bedroom door—

Bird or beast upon the sculptured bust above his bedroom door,

With such name as "Nevermore."

4 Imagery
Picture the image of the raven described in this stanza. What kind of mood does this image create? Add this to your Suspense Chart.

Key Vocabulary
- **relevance** *n.*, importance that connects to something else

In Other Words
days of yore past
bust of Pallas statue of the head of the Greek goddess, Athena
beguiling charming
craven coward
Nevermore Never again

Australian Raven, 2005, Kate Breakey. Handcolored silver gelatin photograph, Courtesy of Stephen Clark Gallery.

▲ **Critical Viewing: Mood** Study the artist's use of color, shadow, and light. What mood do these elements make you feel?

55　But the Raven, sitting lonely on the silent bust, spoke only

That one word, as if his soul in that one word he did outpour.

Nothing further then he uttered—not a feather then he fluttered—

Till I scarcely more than muttered "Other friends have flown before—

On the morrow *he* will leave me, as my hopes have flown before."

60　　　　　　　　　Then the bird said, "Nevermore."

Startled at the stillness broken by reply so clearly spoken,

"Surely," I said, "what it utters is a trick and nothing more,

Caught from some unhappy master whom a terrible Disaster

Followed fast and followed faster till his songs one burden bore—

65　Till the sad songs of his Hope that even sadder burden bore

　　　　　　　　　Of 'Never—nevermore.'"

But the Raven still beguiling all my spirit into smiling,

Soon I wheeled a cushioned seat in front of bird and bust and door;

Then, while into the cushion sinking, in my mind I started linking

70　Idea to idea, all the time thinking what this ominous bird of yore—

What this grim, ungainly, ghastly, gaunt and ominous bird of yore　**5**

　　　　　　　　　Meant in croaking, "Nevermore."

So I sat engaged in guessing, but without a word expressing

To the bird whose fiery eyes now burned into my spirit's core;

75　This and more I sat divining, with my head at ease reclining

On the cushion's velvet lining which the lamp-light shined all over,

But whose velvet violet lining with the lamp-light shining o'er,

　　　　　　　She shall touch, ah, nevermore!　**6**

**5　Vocabulary/
Repetition**
The speaker uses alliteration, that is, words with similar beginning sounds. Read the line aloud. What effect do the sounds create?

6　Make Connections
Think about a time you pondered a question that you could not answer. How does this help you understand the speaker?

Key Vocabulary
burden *n.*, something heavy or difficult that one has to carry
ominous *adj.*, threatening

In Other Words
uttered said
On the morrow Tomorrow
bore carried
divining guessing

Then, I thought, the air grew denser, perfumed from an unseen censer
80   Swung by angels whose soft foot-falls tapped so lightly on the floor.
"Wretch," I cried "your God has lent you—by these angels he has sent you
Relief—relief and cure from your memories of Lenore;
Drink, oh drink this kind cure and forget this lost Lenore!"
                              Said the Raven, "Nevermore." **7**

85   "Prophet!" I said, "thing of evil!—still a prophet, bird or devil!—
Did the Tempter or the tempest storm toss you to this shore?
All alone yet all undaunted, on this desert land enchanted— **8**
On this home by Horror haunted—tell me truly, I ask for—
Is there—is there relief from sorrow? tell me—truth, I ask you for!"
90   Said the Raven, "Nevermore."

"Prophet! I said, "thing of evil!—still a prophet, bird or devil!
By that Heaven that bends above us—by that God we both adore—
Tell this soul with sorrow laden if, within the distant Aidenn,
It shall clasp again a maiden whom the angels name Lenore—
95   Clasp a rare and beautiful maiden whom the angels name Lenore."
                              Said the Raven, "Nevermore." **9**

"Be that word our sign of parting, bird or fiend!" I yelled, upstarting—
"Then get yourself back into the tempest and the Night's ghostly shore!
Leave no feather as a token of that lie your soul has spoken!
100 Leave my loneliness unbroken!—leave the bust above my door!
Take your beak out of my heart, and take your form off of my door!"
                              Said the Raven, "Nevermore."

Key Vocabulary
prophet *n.*, someone who predicts what will happen in the future

In Other Words
censer container for burning incense
Wretch Poor, unhappy person
distant Aidenn long-ago Garden of Eden
fiend evil creature, devil
tempest storm

And the Raven, never flitting, still is sitting, *still* is sitting

On the pale bust of Pallas just above my bedroom door;

105 And his eyes have all the seeming of a demon's that is dreaming,

And the lamp-light over him streaming throws his shadow on the floor;

And my soul from out of that shadow that lies floating on the floor

Shall be lifted—nevermore! **10**

10 Imagery
What is the final image of the raven? How does it reflect the speaker's feelings?

ANALYZE The Raven

1. **Explain** What happens to the speaker at the end of the poem? Use specific details from the poem to support your ideas.

2. **Vocabulary** Is the raven truly a **prophet**? What is the **relevance** of its answer, "Nevermore"?

3. **Analyze Word Choice: Imagery and Repetition** Review the **Suspense Chart** you began on page 474. Select the most memorable image and example of repetition in the poem. How do they help create suspense? Discuss your answers with other classmates.

4. **Focus Strategy Make Connections** Think about how the poem relates to Poe's short story, "The Tell-Tale Heart." Look for connections between the characters, plots, settings, themes, and styles. Which of these connections made the most difference to your understanding of the poem?

Return to the Text

Reread and Write The speaker requires readers to imagine what happened to Lenore. Does this make the poem frightening? Reread the poem, and then write your opinion. Include details from the poem that support your point of view.

In Other Words

over him streaming throws shining on him sends

⊷═ The Mysterious Edgar Allan Poe ═⊷

Edgar Allan Poe is often called the father of the modern detective story. So, it's no surprise that everything from the date of Poe's birth to the cause of his death is **shadowed by** mystery.

Mystery 1: *Poe's Birth*

No birth certificate for Edgar Allan Poe has ever been found. For many years, biographers believed that he was born in 1811, even though Poe himself said that he was born in 1809. Later, Poe claimed that he was born in 1813—something that would have been difficult, since his mother had died two years earlier.

Mystery 2: *Poe's Death*

On October 3, 1849, Edgar Allan Poe was found lying in a gutter in Baltimore. He was sent to Washington College Hospital where he **lapsed** in and out of consciousness for several days. No one could explain where he had been or why he was found wearing someone else's clothes. He died on October 7.

Mystery 3: *Poe's Burial*

Even after his death, Edgar Allan Poe remained a mystery. He originally was buried in his family plot in 1849, but many years later, his body was reburied in a new memorial tomb. Although the church committee was satisfied that they had removed the correct body, they were never able to explain why the Edgar Allan Poe they later reburied was taller, wore different clothes, had better teeth, and rested in a completely different coffin than the one he had been buried in.

Although the facts about Poe's life and death may never be fully known, Poe's fans know that the writer would have enjoyed the mystery.

In Other Words
shadowed by filled with
lapsed faded

EQ ## What Makes Something Frightening?

Critical Thinking

EQ 1. **Analyze** Consider what you know about Edgar Allan Poe and his writing. How does he use the imagination to create stories that frighten readers?

EQ 2. **Compare** How does imagination inspire fear in Poe's narrator in "The Tell-Tale Heart" and the speaker in "The Raven"?

3. **Interpret** Why do you think Poe called his poem "The Raven" instead of "Lenore"? What is the relevance of the title to the poem?

4. **Assess** Explain whether Poe succeeds in building suspense in the two selections.

EQ 5. **Evaluate** Which is more frightening, the beating heart in "The Tell-Tale Heart" or the raven in the poem? Why do you think so?

Write About Literature

Opinion How do you think Poe would answer the question "What makes something frightening?" Write a short response giving your opinion. Give details from both texts to support your answer.

Key Vocabulary Review

Oral Review Work with a partner. Use these words to complete the paragraph.

burdens   ominous   relevance
cease   ponder   suspected
dread   prophet

When Edgar Allan Poe died in 1849, no one guessed or __(1)__ that he'd be known as a great writer. Since then, his tales of great fear and __(2)__ have become the standard for scary stories. Today's writers study his works and __(3)__ what makes them great. Is it the __(4)__ feelings he creates that warn the reader that something terrible is coming? Do his narrators' heavy __(5)__ of fear and insanity touch something in us and give them __(6)__ that connects to our own lives? Perhaps he was a __(7)__ who looked into the future and predicted that our greatest fears would never change, or __(8)__. They are with us always, just as Poe's work stands the test of time.

Writing Application Write a paragraph describing the dread and fright you felt as you watched a scary movie. Use at least four Key Vocabulary words.

Read with Ease: Intonation

Assess your reading fluency with the passage in the Reading Handbook, p. 765. Then complete the self-check below.

1. My intonation did/did not sound natural.

2. My words correct per minute: _____ .

Use Adverbs Correctly

Use **adverbs** to tell *how, when,* or *where.* Adverbs often end in **-ly**.

- An **adverb** can describe a <u>verb</u>.

  I **gently** <u>open</u> the door.

- An **adverb** can also describe an <u>adjective</u> or another adverb.

  I am **amazingly** <u>calm</u>. I move **very** <u>cautiously</u>.

- Some adverbs compare. Use **more** or **-er** to compare two actions. Use **most** or **-est** to compare three or more actions.

  I speak **loudly**. Then I speak **even more loudly**. They run **fast**, but I run the **fastest** of all.

Oral Practice (1–5) With a partner, say five sentences using adverbs. Choose from each column. Use words more than once.

The old man	moved	more slowly	of all
The narrator	waited	the most cautiously	than him
The police	entered	more patiently	than them

Written Practice (6–10) Fix three more adverbs below and rewrite the paragraph. Then add two more sentences about the story. Use adverbs.

> terribly
> The old man's eye upset me ~~terrible~~. I planned my crime careful. I behaved strange than usual that week. I paced quick than before.

Compare and Contrast

Group Talk Discuss the murderer in "The Tell-Tale Heart." Compare his thoughts and actions from the beginning of the story to the end. Write sentences that compare and contrast his thoughts. As you write, be sure you are using commas correctly. A comma is required between the two contrasting expressions, before a word like *not* or *but*: *First the murderer is confident, not afraid.*

Analyze Mood and Tone

Mood is the feeling that a reader gets from a story. **Tone** is the author's attitude toward his or her topic. In the stories you read in this unit, each author creates a frightening mood and uses a unique tone.

Make a chart like this one with a partner. Include excerpts from the stories and tell how the writing made you feel. Then collect story words that illustrate the mood and tone.

The Interlopers	The Baby-Sitter	The Tell-Tale Heart
p. 417: "...each had hate in his heart..." *I feel like something bad will happen.*	p. 440: "The house was one of those old, creaky Victorian horrors..." *This sounds spooky!*	p. 468: Poe repeats: "I knew the sound well." *This gives me a creepy feeling.*
Mood:	Mood:	Mood:
Tone:	Tone:	Tone:

Using examples from your chart, tell how

- word choice created mood and tone in each story
- the mood and tone made you feel.

Analyze Symbolism

A **symbol** is something that stands for something else. For example, a raven is a symbol of death in many cultures. Writers use symbolism to make their stories richer and more interesting by adding layers of meaning.

In "The Tell-Tale Heart," the beating heart symbolizes the murderer's conscience. With a group, discuss why this symbol is effective. Why would the story be less exciting without it?

Analogies

An **analogy** is a comparison between two pairs of words to show relationships. For example: thunder is to hearing as lightning is to seeing. This analogy can also be written: thunder : hearing :: lightning : seeing.

In this analogy, the first word in each pair names something frightening, and the second word tells how you perceive the fear. Work with a partner to complete the following two analogies. Then explain the relationship between the pairs of words.

1. begin : **cease** :: ___
   a. start : stop
   b. **dread** : fear
   c. danger : death

2. **prophet** : predict :: ___
   a. criminal : crime
   b. poet : **ponder**
   c. detective : investigate

Dramatization

Police Story Dramatize the final scene of "The Tell-Tale Heart" with three classmates.

① Discuss the scene and decide what the police know or **suspect**. How do they behave? How is the narrator acting? What is he saying?

② Write a script for the dramatization. Decide who will play each role.

③ Practice your dramatization. Think about the characters' facial expressions and gestures. Consider how they would speak.

④ Perform your dramatization for the class.

🔖 **Language and Learning Handbook**, page 702

Organization

You may have an engaging story to tell, but if your ideas aren't organized well, the story will be hard for readers to follow. When you write, ask:

- Does the organization fit my purpose for writing?
- Will the beginning "hook" readers and make them want to read more?
- Are there clear transitions to help readers move from one part of the story to another?
- What techniques can I use to build suspense and keep my readers interested?

As you read the two examples, study what the writer does to organize her ideas.

Just OK

> I decided last summer that I would prove that the house on Oak Street wasn't haunted. Everyone says it is haunted and that scary things happen there. Have you ever heard of the haunted house on Oak Street? I bet my friend John that I could spend the night in the house.

Much Better

> Have you heard the rumors about the spooky old house on Oak Street? My friends and I grew up hearing about the eerie sights and mysterious sounds there. This summer, I decided to face my fears head on. I interrupted my friend John in the middle of one of his ghost stories and declared, "I'm spending the night at the house on Oak Street!"

Here are the next events in the story. Work with a partner to organize them into a paragraph that would keep your readers' attention.

- The night before I went to Oak Street, I talked with old Mr. Lee.
- Talking to him scared me!
- He was the last person who lived in the house.
- He heard strange sounds there.
- Doors in the house slammed at night.

Share your stories with your class. Use the information and checklist for stories on page 808 to guide your writing and to provide feedback to classmates.

🔖 **Writing Handbook**, page 808

Puddle

by Arthur Porges

1   A great poet promised to show us fear in a handful of dust. If ever I doubted that such a thing were possible, I know better now. In the past few weeks **a vague**, terrible memory of my childhood suddenly came into sharp focus after staying **tantalizingly** just beyond the edge of recall for decades. Perhaps the high fever from a recent virus attack opened some blocked pathways in my brain, but whatever the explanation, I have come to understand for the first time why I see fear not in dust, but water.

2   It must seem quite absurd: fear in a shallow puddle made by rain; but think about it for a moment. Haven't you ever, as a child, gazed down at such a little pool on the street, seen the reflected sky, and experienced the illusion, very strongly, so that it brought a **shudder**, of endless depth a mere step away—**a chasm** extending downward somehow to the heavens? A single stride to the center of the glassy puddle, and you would fall right through. Down? Up? The direction was indefinable, a weird blend of both. There were clouds beneath your feet, and nothing but that shining surface between. Did you dare to take that critical step and **shatter the illusion**? Not I. Now that memory has returned, I recall being far too scared of the consequences. I carefully skirted such wet patches, no matter how casually my playmates splashed through.

In Other Words
a vague an unclear
tantalizingly in a teasing way
shudder fearful shaking
a chasm an opening
shatter the illusion prove yourself wrong

Literary Background
"I will show you fear in a handful of dust" is a line from the famous poem "The Wasteland," by T.S. Eliot.

3   Most of my acquaintances tolerated this weakness in me. After all, I was a sturdy, active child, and **held my own** in the games we played. It was only after Joe Carma appeared in town that my own little hell materialized, and I lost status.

4   He was three years older than I, and much stronger; thickset, muscular, dark—and perpetually surly. He was never known to smile in any joyous way, but only to laugh with a kind of *schadenfreude*, the German word for **mirth** provoked by another's misfortunes. Few could stand up to him when he **hunched his blocky frame** and bored in with big fists **flailing**, and I wasn't one of the elect; he terrified me as much by his **demeanor** as his physical power.

5   Looking back now, I discern something grim and evil about the boy, fatherless, with a weak and **querulous** mother. What he did was not the thoughtless, basically merry mischief of the other kids, but full of malice and cruelty.

6   Somehow Joe Carma learned of my phobia about puddles, and my torment began. On several occasions he meant to go so far as to **collar me**, hold my writhing body over one of the bigger pools, and pretend to drop me through—into that terribly distant sky beyond the sidewalk.

7   Each time I was saved at the last moment, nearly hysterical with fright, by Larry Dumont, who was taller than the bully, at least as strong, and thought to be more agile. They were bound to clash eventually, but so far Carma had **sheered off**, hoping, perhaps, to find and exploit some weakness in his opponent that would give him an edge. Not that he was a coward but just coldly careful; one who always **played the odds**.

8   As for Larry, he was good-natured, and not likely to fight at all unless pushed into it. By grabbing Carma with his lean, wiry fingers that could bend thick nails, and half-jokingly arguing with him, Dumont would bring about my release without forcing a **showdown**. Then they might scuffle a bit, with Larry smiling and Joe darkly sullen as ever, only to separate, newly respectful of each other's strength.

9   One day, after a heavy rain, Carma caught me near a giant puddle—almost a pond—that had appeared behind the Johnson barn at the north end of town. It was a lonely spot, the hour was rather early, and ordinarily

In Other Words

held my own was a strong participant
mirth happiness, laughter
hunched his blocky frame bent his large body
flailing moving wildly
demeanor personality
querulous complaining

collar me grab me by the neck
sheered off gotten away
played the odds made sure he would win
showdown fight

Joe would not have been about, as he liked to sleep late on weekends. If I had **suspected** he might be around, that was the last place in the world I'd have picked to visit alone.

10   Fear and fascination often go together. I stood by the huge puddle, but well away from the edge, peering down at the blue sky, quite cloudless and so far beneath the ground where it should not have been at all; and for the thousandth time tried to gather enough nerve to step in. I *knew* there had to be solid land below—jabs with a stick had proved this much before in similar cases—yet I simply could not make my feet move.

11   At that instant brawny arms seized me, lifted my body into the air, and tilted it so that my **contorted** face was parallel to the pool and right over the glittering surface.

12   "Gonna count to ten, and then drop you right through!" a rasping voice taunted me. "You been right all along: it's a long way down. You're gonna fall and fall, with the wind whistling past your ears; turning, tumbling, faster and faster. You'll be gone for good, kid, just sailing down forever. You're gonna scream like crazy all the way, and it'll get fainter and fainter. Here we go: one! two! three!—"

13   I tried to scream but my throat was sealed. I just made husky noises while squirming desperately, but Carma **held me fast**. I could feel the heavy muscles in his arms all knotted with the effort.

14   "—four! five! Won't be long now. Six! seven!—"

15   A thin, whimpering sound broke from my lips, and he laughed. My vision was blurring; I was going into shock, it seems to me now, years later.

16   Then help came, swift and effective. Carma was jerked back, away from the water, and I fell free. Larry Dumont stood there, white with fury.

17   "You're a dirty skunk, Joe!" he gritted angrily. "You need a lesson, your own kind."

18   Then he did an amazing thing. Although Carma was heavier than he, if shorter, Larry whipped those lean arms around the bully, snatched him clear of the ground and with a single magnificent heave threw him fully six feet into the middle of the water.

Key Vocabulary
suspect *v.*, to believe that something may be different from what it seems

In Other Words
contorted fearful
held me fast kept hold of me

19   Now I wonder about my memory; I have to. Did I actually see what I now recall so clearly? It's quite impossible, but the vision persists. Carma fell full-length, face down, in the puddle, and surely the water could not have been more than a few inches deep. But he went on through! I saw his body twisting, turning, and shrinking in size as it dropped away into that cloudless sky. He screamed, and it was exactly as he had described it to me moments earlier. The terrible, shrill cries grew fainter, as if dying away in the distance; the flailing figure became first a tiny doll, and then a mere dot; an unforgettable thing, surely, yet only a dream-memory for so long.

20   I looked at Larry; he was **gaping**, his face drained of all blood. His long fingers were still hooked and tense from that mighty toss.

21   That's how I remember it. Perhaps we **probed** the puddle; I'm not sure, but if we did, surely it was inches deep.

22   On recovering from my illness three weeks ago, I hired a good private detective to make a check. The files of the local paper are unfortunately not complete, but one item for August 20, 1937, when I was eight, begins:

23   NO CLUES ON DISAPPEARANCE OF CARMA BOY
       After ten days of police investigation, no trace has been found of Joe Carma, who vanished completely on the ninth of this month. It is not even known how he left town, if he did, since there is no evidence that he went by either bus or train. Martin's Pond, the only deep water within many miles, was **dragged**, but without any result.

24   The detective assures me that Joe Carma never returned to town and that the name is unlisted in army records, with the FBI, or indeed any national roster from 1937 to date.

25   These days, I skin dive, sail my own little **sloop**, and have even **shot** some of the worst Colorado River rapids in a rubber boat. Yet it still takes almost more courage than I have to slosh through a shallow puddle that mirrors the sky. ❖

In Other Words
gaping staring
probed poked
dragged searched
sloop sailboat
shot floated down

FEAR THIS!

EQ ESSENTIAL QUESTION:
What Makes Something Frightening?

myNGconnect.com
🟢 **Download the rubric.**

EDGE LIBRARY

Present Your Project: Radio Drama or Podcast

It's time to present your radio drama or podcast about the Essential Question for this unit: What Makes Something Frightening?

1 Review and Complete Your Plan

Consider these points as you complete your project:

- How will you present your drama? Will you produce it as a podcast? Will you present it live? Will you record it and play it for your class?
- Does your script immediately capture your listeners' interest?
- Does your script develop and maintain suspense throughout?

Practice your drama several times. You might record it and critique it as a group before your final presentation.

2 Present Your Radio Drama or Podcast

Present your drama. If you're presenting it live, take your time. Do not let any nervousness cause you to rush through the performance.

3 Evaluate the Radio Dramas or Podcasts

Use the online rubric to evaluate each of the radio dramas or podcasts, including the one you presented.

Reflect on Your Reading

Many of the characters in the stories in this unit and in the Edge Library had to face their fears.

Think back on your reading of the unit selections, including your choice of Edge Library books. Then discuss the following with a partner or in a small group.

Genre Focus Compare and contrast how different genres like short stories and poems are able to create the feelings of fear and suspense. Write your interpretive response using quotations from the selections and specific examples and ideas from the text. Give examples, using the selections in this unit.

Focus Strategy Choose the selection in this unit that you found the most frightening. List the techniques the writer used to create this mood, such as unexpected plot twists, repetition, and word choice. Find a classmate who chose a different selection and use your card to explain your choice. Listen to your partner's ideas.

EQ Respond to the Essential Question

Throughout this unit, you have been thinking about what makes something frightening. What have *you* decided? Support your response with evidence from your reading, discussions, research, and writing.

Write a Short Story

What do you like best in a short story—an intriguing conflict, a memorable setting and characters, or a plot that twists and turns? For this project, you will write a short story with a surprise ending.

Study Short Stories

Short stories are narratives about imaginary people, places, and events. Writers use vivid details and dialogue to bring the characters and conflicts to life.

❶ Connect Writing to Your Life

You've probably heard people tell stories at home or at school. Writing stories down is a way to keep them forever yet share them with others.

❷ Understand the Form

A short story is highly organized. It usually has two or more characters, including a protagonist, or main character, and an antagonist. The protagonist faces a **conflict**, or struggle, which can include or lead to complications. This sequence of events, or the **plot**, rises to a climax, the turning point of the story. After that, the conflict gets resolved. In stories with a twist, the plot may include unexpected events or lead to a surprise ending.

Plot Diagram

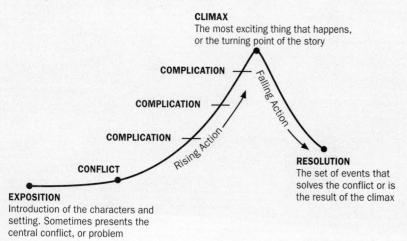

CLIMAX
The most exciting thing that happens, or the turning point of the story

COMPLICATION

COMPLICATION

COMPLICATION

Falling Action

Rising Action

CONFLICT

RESOLUTION
The set of events that solves the conflict or is the result of the climax

EXPOSITION
Introduction of the characters and setting. Sometimes presents the central conflict, or problem

Along with dialogue, a writer may use **interior monologue**, passages that let readers "hear" the character's thoughts. The writer also shows changes in the story's mood, its atmosphere or feeling, and shifts in time.

Now read a short story by a professional writer. Using the plot diagram and the margin notes, identify the conflict and analyze the development of the plot.

❸ Analyze a Professional Model

In this short story, the unknown may be the most surprising thing of all. As you read, look for ways the writer builds suspense.

Please Stand By

by Luke Samuelson

"There has been a serious situation," the authorities announced mysteriously over the radio and on television. "Please stand by. Await further instructions. Do not panic." Within minutes, I joined my neighbors on the crowded urban sidewalks, unsure of what to do or think.

> The exposition introduces the **conflict**, the **protagonist**, and the **antagonist**.

We are not the kind of people who stand by for anything. We are people who act quickly. *Just tell us where to go and what to do.* The authorities always knew.

> The writer uses **interior monologue** so readers "hear" the character's thoughts.

Or did they? What was this situation? A chemical leak? A fire? Why was the power cut off? Surely the authorities would have directed us away from such danger. After all, that's what authorities do. "But what if," one nervous looking man speculated, "the situation is with the authorities themselves?"

> **Dialogue** and **description** bring the scene to life.

A young woman in the anxious crowd began to tremble. Her mouth was open, and her eyes were wide. "Where are the police?" she cried, her voice hoarse with fear. "Why aren't there any police?"

> Mysterious events, or **complications**, make the conflict worse.

Now that was odd, we had to admit. Thousands of people had gathered in one place. Yet not an officer was in sight.

Our mood began to change. Night was falling. People raised their voices. Scuffles broke out. Somebody had to do something.

> The writer paces the action to show a change in time and mood.

"I'm going to the Capitol," I announced, looking with desperate hope toward its gleaming white dome. "Our leaders know what's happening." I pushed my way through the crowd, toward the enormous, concrete building. I knew no better than the rest of them, but it seemed like a good idea. Others agreed, and began following me.

> The protagonist's decision is the **turning point**.

Together we marched in the growing darkness toward the Capitol. We would find the authorities there. We would find answers. Wouldn't we?

But as we opened door after door, we made a terrifying discovery. The building was completely deserted.

> How does the writer end his story of suspense?

▶ **Prompt** Write a suspenseful short story with a twist.
Make sure you include:

- characters' actions, dialogue, and interior monologue
- a beginning, a middle, and an end
- rising action, climax, and falling action
- a surprise ending

✔ Prewrite

You have studied a professional writer's suspenseful short story. Now write one of your own. A Writing Plan helps you organize all the elements.

❶ Choose Your Topic

Try the following strategies to generate great ideas for a short story:

- Use what you know. What frightens or fascinates you? How would the main character feel, think, speak, and act in such circumstances? Jot down your ideas.
- Ask "What if?" questions. What if a mysterious event disrupts life in a community? What if someone discovers something mysterious? What if the main character is suddenly transported in time?
- Brainstorm ideas with a friend or family member.

❷ Clarify the Audience, Theme, and Purpose

Good writers know who is reading their work, and they write for that audience. Will your friends, family, and teacher be reading your story?

To engage your readers, clarify what your story is all about. This is the **theme**. The theme can be serious or lighthearted. For example, the theme of "Please Stand By" is that a sudden, unexplained event can throw people into uncertainty and confusion.

Finally, decide why you are writing this story. Is it to entertain with a suspenseful mood or a surprise ending? Write down your purpose.

❸ Gather Supporting Details

Gather supporting details by making notes about the conflict and the plot. Discuss your story with a partner. Take notes. Make sure to brainstorm:

- complications that might worsen the conflict
- character traits, setting, and mood—the story's atmosphere or feeling
- two or three possible resolutions
- the most interesting or surprising resolution

❹ Organize the Plot

Organize your supporting details in a way that helps you build a suspenseful mood and advance the plot. Although a writer of suspense may deliberately withhold some information, such as by saving critical details for a surprise ending, each part of the story must still be complete and easy for readers to follow. Here is how the writer organized the events and details of "The Watcher."

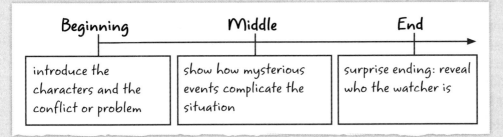

Beginning	Middle	End
introduce the characters and the conflict or problem	show how mysterious events complicate the situation	surprise ending: reveal who the watcher is

❺ Finish Your Writing Plan

Use your prewriting ideas to make a Writing Plan like the one below.

Writing Plan

Title	"The Watcher"
Audience	my classmates, friends, and teacher
Theme	things are not always what they seem
Purpose	to entertain, to surprise
Beginning	1. introduce characters: a girl (Jan) and a mysterious woman (the gray lady) 2. introduce conflict: Jan fears the gray lady has mistaken her for a thief. 3. describe setting: bookstore; cramped, twisting aisles
Middle	4. Jan picks up an unusual red book. 5. Everywhere Jan looks, the gray lady is watching, following. 6. add complication: the book keeps falling off shelf into Jan's bag 7. show Jan's fear; build up a mood of suspense 8. turning point: Jan takes decisive action.
End	9. reveal identity of the watcher

Technology Tip

Use a computer to try out two versions of your Writing Plan. Take a break between developing the two versions, so you will clearly see which one you like better.

Reflect on Your Writing Plan

▶ Does the way you organized the details flow from one idea to the next? Will events in the story have rising action, climax, and falling action? Will it suit your purpose? Talk it over with a partner.

✔ Write a Draft

Now write your first draft. It doesn't have to be perfect. Just follow your Writing Plan and get your ideas down on paper. You can make changes later.

❶ Keep Your Ideas Flowing

Even the best writers sometimes find it a bit scary to face a blank page! Use these techniques to get the words flowing.

- **Look Again** As you write the story draft, keep the conflict in mind and structure your plot around it. Use your Writing Plan and the plot diagram on page 492 to guide you. Introduce the conflict in the first paragraph. Then, keep moving the plot forward by adding events and details that intensify, or compound, the conflict. Pace the events of your story:

  1. First, elaborate on, or build the tension of events to create the **rising action**.
  2. Next, show how events lead to a turning point, or **climax**.
  3. Then, in the **falling action**, show how events lead to the surprise ending, or other **resolution**.

- **Freewrite** Sometimes writers get stuck trying to write a perfect first sentence. If you're stuck, just start writing about your characters and your idea and don't stop for five minutes. Don't think about punctuation or complete sentences. Write what comes to mind. Then, read what you wrote, and underline or circle the ideas, descriptions, or phrases you like and can use in your story. Freewriting is also an excellent way to brainstorm ideas for **interior monologue**. Put yourself in a character's place and "think on paper" from his or her point of view.

- **Storyboard** When movie directors prepare to film a script, they often create a storyboard, drawings of the different scenes. You can try the same technique for your story. If you prefer, cut and paste images from magazines or Web sites into a storyboard. Or create a poster that reflects the mood and other elements of your story.

Here's how the student made notes about what to draw on a storyboard.

> - I'll show a magazine photo of a bookstore filled with old books.
> - Then, I'll draw a girl in a bookstore reaching for a red book.
> - Next, I'll draw a mysterious gray-haired woman.

📖 **Writing Handbook**, p. 808

Notice how the student used a Writing Plan to develop the draft below.
It's a good start. The student revised the draft later.

The Watcher

Jan glanced back to see if the lady was still there. She was. Jan saw the lady in old-fashioned clothing. They never spoke, but Jan knew that the gray lady was watching.

When the shy, quiet teen entered the bookstore, it was raining, she wanted to get out of the rain.

Something real strange had happened as she wandered the cramped aisles. The book with the red cover looked unusualer than all the other books. The gold lettering on the cover glittered as if signaling Jan. She had moved closer, and then whoosh the book tumbled into her bag. Quick, she fished it out, her face turning as red as the cover.

Then she spied her.

Watching her.

Following Jan's every move. Jan's thoughts raced. For every time Jan put the book on the shelf, it fell back into her bag. All the while, the gray lady was watching.

To calm her pounding heart, she studied the book. But that was after Jan moved frantic along the aisles for the next several minutes.

She felt trapped. It was filled with splendid illustrations and stories. Jan wrote stories also, but was too shy to tell anyone. She gazed at the book. Something that rare must cost a lot.

She realized there was only one thing to do. Took a deep breath. She moved purposeful toward the door. She placed the book onto the counter. i'd like this book if you will sell it for $5.37. That's all I've got. The cashier looked at Jan.

it's a deal. My grandmother wrote those stories. I found them after she died and published them. They practical fly off the shelves he said.

I know what you mean, Jan said, trying not to laugh. She looked around. There was no one else in the store.

That's when Jan saw the photo on the wall. It was a woman with a shy smile. The gray lady.

Reflect on Your Draft

▶ Did you introduce your characters and setting in the beginning? Does the order of events make sense, and do they build to a climax? Is the conflict resolved?

Revise Your Draft

Your story is starting to take shape. Now organize it carefully to make it easier to follow and more interesting. Read your work carefully. Check every word, sentence, and paragraph to see what you can improve.

❶ Revise for Organization

A reader's understanding of a short story depends on its **organization**. In a well-organized story, ideas about the characters, conflict, plot, and other details progress in a logical way. For example, a great story seems to flow from paragraph to paragraph, and from one sentence to the next. The order of events makes sense.

In addition, organized writers make effective use of transitional devices. Transition words like *then*, *next*, and *finally*, along with introductory phrases, keep the story rolling along.

TRY IT ▶ Evaluate the drafts below. Which one is better organized? Discuss them with a partner, using the rubric to decide.

Draft 1

> To calm her pounding heart, she studied the book. But that was after Jan moved frantic along the aisles for the next several minutes.
>
> She felt trapped. It was filled with splendid illustrations and stories. Jan wrote stories also, but was too shy to tell anyone. She gazed at the book. Something that rare must cost a lot.

Draft 2

> Anxious to get away, Jan moved frantically along the twisting aisles. She felt trapped.
>
> Then, to calm her pounding heart, Jan studied the book. It was filled with splendid illustrations and stories. Jan wrote stories also, but was too shy to tell anyone. She gazed at the book. Something that rare must cost a lot.

Now use the rubric to evaluate the organization of your own draft. What score would you give your draft and why?

Organization

myNGconnect.com

- Rubric: Organization
- Evaluate and practice scoring other student short stories.

	Does the writing have a clear structure, and is it appropriate for the writer's audience, purpose, and type of writing?	How smoothly do the ideas flow together?
4 Wow!	The writing has a structure that is <u>clear</u> and appropriate for the writer's audience, purpose, and type of writing.	The ideas progress in a smooth and orderly way. • The introduction is strong. • The ideas flow well from paragraph to paragraph. • The ideas in each paragraph flow well from one sentence to the next. • Effective transitions connect ideas. • The conclusion is strong.
3 Ahh.	The writing has a structure that is <u>generally</u> clear and appropriate for the writer's audience, purpose, and type of writing.	<u>Most</u> of the ideas progress in a smooth and orderly way. • The introduction is adequate. • Most of the ideas flow well from paragraph to paragraph. • Most ideas in each paragraph flow from one sentence to the next. • Effective transitions connect most of the ideas. • The conclusion is adequate.
2 Hmm.	The structure of the writing is <u>not</u> clear or <u>not</u> appropriate for the writer's audience, purpose, and type of writing.	<u>Some</u> of the ideas progress in a smooth and orderly way. • The introduction is weak. • Some of the ideas flow well from paragraph to paragraph. • Some ideas in each paragraph flow from one sentence to the next. • Transitions connect some ideas. • The conclusion is weak.
1 Huh?	The writing is not clear or organized.	<u>Few or none</u> of the ideas progress in a smooth and orderly way.

✔ Revise Your Draft, continued

❷ Revise Your Draft

You've now evaluated the organization of your draft. If you scored 3 or lower, how can you improve your work? The checklist below will help you revise your draft.

Revision Checklist

Ask Yourself	Check It Out	How to Make It Better
Does my story have a clear structure that supports my purpose?	Underline sentences that introduce the characters, the setting, and the conflict.	☐ At the beginning of the story, introduce the protagonist and the antagonist. Clearly state the conflict. ☐ Cut, move, or replace paragraphs that do not fit or have a clear purpose.
Are the ideas and events clearly connected? Does the story move forward smoothly?	If your score is 3 or lower, revise.	☐ Move sentences or paragraphs around to tell about events in logical order. ☐ Add transitions to clearly connect ideas and actions.
Does my story have rising and falling action?	Underline the climax and the resolution.	☐ Add complications that lead to the climax. ☐ Rewrite the ending so the resolution is clear.
Does my story have figurative language or other rhetorical devices to make the characters and the setting vivid?	Underline dialogue and descriptions.	☐ Add figurative language to make characters and setting seem as vivid as possible.
Is the mood of my story suspenseful?	Read aloud to see if sentence length and structure are too repetitive. Underline word choices that support the suspenseful mood.	☐ Rewrite to include shorter and longer sentences. Use a variety of sentence types. ☐ Add details and dialogue that support the suspenseful mood.

📖 **Writing Handbook**, p. 784; 808

❸ Conduct a Peer Conference

A peer conference gives you the opportunity to present your work to a reader for the first time. Have a partner read your draft and check for the following:

- any part of the draft that is confusing
- any place where something seems to be missing
- anything that the reader does not understand

Discuss your draft with your partner. Focus on the items in the Revision Checklist on the previous page. Then use your partner's comments to improve the organization of your story.

❹ Make Revisions

Read the revisions below and the peer-reviewer conversation on the right. Notice the questions the peer reviewer asked and the revisions that were made. How does the writer respond to the reviewer's ideas?

Revised for Organization

> Jan   the gray lady
> Then, she spied her.
>
> Watching her.
>
> Following her Jan's every move. Jan's thoughts raced. For every
>
> time Jan put the book on the shelf, it fell back into her bag. All the
>
> while, the gray lady was watching. ¶ Anxious to get away, Jan moved
>
> frantically along the twisting aisles.

Revised for Mood

> *Does that woman think I was trying to*
> *steal? I'll put the book back on the shelf.*
> *There. Oh, no. What's going on?*
>
> Jan's thoughts raced. For every time Jan put the book on
>
> the shelf, it fell back into her bag. All the while, the gray lady
>
> was watching.

📖 **Writing Handbook**, p. 784; 808

Peer Conference

Reviewer's Comment: This is hard to follow. Who saw whom? Which details belong together?

Writer's Answer: I'll fix the paragraph structure to show which details tell about the same thing.

Reviewer's Comment: What are Jan's thoughts? "Hearing" what the character is thinking adds to the suspense.

Writer's Answer: Oh, you mean interior monologue! I'll add that and use italics to make it stand out.

Reflect on Your Revisions

▶ Think about the results of your peer conference. What are some of your strengths as a writer? What are some things that give you trouble?

Edit and Proofread Your Draft

Now that you have a revised draft, it's time to polish it for presentation to your readers. Find and fix any mistakes that you made.

❶ Capitalize Quotations Correctly

Capitalize the first word in a direct quotation.

> "**Who** wrote this book?" asked Jan.

> He smiled and said, "**Her** name is on the book cover."

TRY IT ▶ Copy the sentences. Fix the capitalization errors. Use proofreader's marks.

> 1. "hi. I would like to buy this book," She said.
> 2. "it's a deal," he said.

❷ Use Punctuation Correctly

Put quotation marks (" ") around the exact words that characters speak or to show sarcasm or irony. Use a comma before someone's exact words. Use a comma after someone's exact words if the sentence continues. Do not use commas or quotation marks when you explain what a character said without quoting him or her directly.

> **Irony:** The "**warmest**" the temperature ever gets is 20 degrees.

> **Quotations:** He said, "The book is for sale."
>   "I have $5.37," Jan said.

> **Explanation:** Jan said that she had $5.37.

TRY IT ▶ Copy the sentences. Add any necessary quotation marks and commas. Delete quotation marks that aren't necessary.

> 1. Read this book he said.
> 2. Jan said that "she wrote stories, too."

Use commas to punctuate nonrestrictive phrases or clauses. A nonrestrictive clause has a subject and a verb, while a nonrestrictive phrase does not. A nonrestrictive phrase or clause does not change the basic meaning of a sentence, but it does add a relevant detail.

TRY IT ▶ Copy the sentences and add any necessary commas.

> 1. The picture is in my wallet which you can find in my dresser drawer.
> 2. The dog a brown German Shepherd is only two years old.

Proofreading Tip

If you are unsure of whether you need to set off a phrase or clause with commas, look in a style manual for help.

❸ Use Correct Paragraph Structure

A paragraph is a group of sentences that all tell about the same idea. The topic sentence tells about the main, or controlling, idea.

Incorrect	Correct
"I know what you mean," Jan said, trying not to laugh. She looked around. There was no one else in the store. That's when Jan saw the photo on the wall. It was the gray lady.	"I know what you mean," Jan said, trying not to laugh. She looked around. There was no one else in the store. That's when Jan saw the photo on the wall. It was the gray lady.

❹ Use Adjectives and Adverbs Correctly

Use a comparative adjective to show how things are alike or different. Add **–er** to most adjectives followed by *than*. Use *more than* or *less than* with the adjective or adverb if it has three or more syllables.

Incorrect	Correct
She felt **more brave then** she did before.	She felt **braver than** she did before.
The red book looked **unusualer** than all the other books.	The red book looked more **unusual** than all the other books.

> **Technology Tip**
>
> Most word-processing software includes a Spell-check feature and a grammar feature. Always use these, but know their limits. New words—such as technological terms—are not always recognized by a Spell-checker. It's always a good idea to keep a dictionary nearby when you write.

Use an adverb to make an adjective or another adverb stronger.

Incorrect	Correct
adj. Something **real** *adj.* **strange** happened.	*adv.* Something **really** *adj.* **strange** happened.

TRY IT ▶ Rewrite the following sentences correctly.

The store was mysteriouser than other stores. The real tall woman was there. She was more tall than Jan.

🔖 **Writing Handbook**, pp. 832, 843

> **Reflect on Your Corrections**
>
> ▶ Note the errors you made on your draft. Make a list so you remember them the next time you have a writing assignment.

5 Edited Student Draft

Here's the student's revised and edited draft. How did the writer improve it?

The Watcher

Jan glanced back to see if the gray lady was still there. She was. Wherever she turned, Jan saw the gray hair and ghostly skin of a woman in old-fashioned clothing. They never spoke, but Jan knew that the gray lady was watching.

When the shy, quiet teen had ducked into the bookstore, it was only to get out of the rain. Something really strange happened as she wandered the cramped aisles. The book with a red cover looked more unusual than the other books. The gold lettering on the cover glittered as if signaling Jan. She moved closer, and—whoosh!—the book tumbled into her bag. Quickly, she fished it out, her face turning as red as the cover.

Then, Jan spied the gray lady. Watching her. Following her every move. Jan's thoughts raced. *Does that woman think I'm a thief? I'll put the book back on the shelf. There. Oh, no. What's going on?* For every time Jan put the book on the shelf, it fell back into her bag. All the while, the gray lady was watching.

Anxious to get away, Jan moved frantically along the twisting aisles. She felt trapped.

Then, to calm her pounding heart, Jan studied the book. It was filled with splendid illustrations and stories. Jan wrote stories also, but was too shy to tell anyone. She gazed at the book. Something that rare must cost a lot. *What do I do? I can't put it back. Yet I can't leave. The gray lady will call me a thief.*

Finally, Jan realized there was only one thing to do. Taking a deep breath, she moved with sudden purpose toward the door. "I'd like this book," she said to the cashier in a firm voice, "if you will sell it for $5.37. That's all I've got."

The cashier looked surprised. "Such confidence!" he said. "It's a deal. You see, my grandmother wrote those stories. Unlike you, she was shy. Never told anyone. I found them after she died and published them. They practically fly off the shelves," he said.

"I know what you mean," Jan said, trying not to laugh.

She looked around. There was no one else in the store.

That's when Jan saw the photo on the wall. It was a woman with a shy smile—the gray lady. Feeling braver than ever, Jan smiled back.

The writer used **adverbs** and **adjectives** correctly.

The writer reorganized the sentences to show one main idea in each paragraph.

The writer added **details** to show Jan's thoughts.

The writer used transition words like *finally* and introductory phrases to guide the reader along.

The writer **capitalized** the first word in direct quotations and added **quotation marks**.

Publish and Present

You are now ready to publish and present your short story. Print out your story or write a clean copy by hand. Give your audience a chance to read or hear what you have to say. Ask for and use feedback from your peers and teacher. You may also want to present your work in a different way.

Alternative Presentations

Record a Reading of Your Story Gather a group of students to help you record a reading of your story.

1 Plan How to Record Decide how you will record it. Will you make an audio or videotape recording, copy it onto a compact disc to share with others, or create an audio file that can be uploaded onto a Web site? Be sure to check with your teacher to see what recording equipment is available. Follow school rules about sharing your work.

2 Cast the Characters Assign roles to yourself and other students. You will need one student to read aloud each character's dialogue, plus one more reader to narrate the part in between. Make photocopies of your story. Ask the actors to highlight the lines they will read aloud.

3 Rehearse Start with a "cold reading." This is when the actors first read aloud a text together. Don't worry if you occasionally make mistakes, such as reading the wrong line or skipping a line. Practice a few more times and you'll soon know each line by heart.

4 Perform You can use your copies of the story when you perform. But don't hide behind them! Remember, people will hear, and perhaps view, your recorded performance. Read with expression and vary the tone of your voice.

Compile Stories into a Book In "The Watcher," someone discovers a collection of stories and has them published. With your classmates, compile your short stories into a book, too.

1 Gather the Content Have each writer submit a clean, formatted copy of a story, following a standard format. Ask students not to show page numbers as you may change them once all the stories have been collected into the book. Check that each manuscript has a name and a title.

2 Organize the Content Decide how to group the stories. Will you follow the alphabetical order of students' last names? Group them by similar themes or settings? Add a table of contents that matches the order of the stories.

3 Print Copies Make photocopies of the book, and keep one book for your classroom. Donate your other books to a library or another classroom.

📖 **Language and Learning Handbook**, p. 702

Publishing Tip

When you read aloud, don't hurry! Make sure to pause for commas, periods, and paragraph breaks.

Reflect on Your Work

▶ **Think back on your experience in the writing process.**

- Which step in the process was the easiest? Which was the most difficult?
- What one thing would you most like to change about your finished story?
- What will you do differently next time?

☑ Save a copy of your work in your portfolio.

UNIT **6**   NONFICTION

EQ **ESSENTIAL QUESTION:**

How Do the Media Shape the Way People Think?

You can tell the ideals of a nation by its advertisements.

—NORMAN DOUGLAS

All television is educational television. The only question is, what is it teaching?

—NICHOLAS JOHNSON

Critical Viewing
A young woman in a traditional Vietnamese *nón lá*, or leaf hat, stands in front of an advertisement in Ho Chi Minh City, Vietnam. What does this photo suggest about the media's influence on young people throughout the world?

BANG BONG

ARE YOU BUYING IT?

EQ ESSENTIAL QUESTION:
How Do the Media Shape the Way People Think?

Study the Facts

The media—TV, newspapers, the Internet, and so on—are everywhere. We use aspects of the media every day in many different ways. Something that is such a big part of our lives shapes what we do, what we think, and, maybe, who we are. Look at these facts:

Television in the United States

Number of thirty-second commercials the average American teen sees
   each year: 20,000

Number of dollars American teens spend each year: 175 billion

Number of violent crimes the average American sees on TV by age 18: 200,000

Number of arrests of Americans under 18 for violent crimes in 2005: 66,748

Number of hours the average American spends watching TV each year: 1,745

Number of hours an American teen attends school each year: 900

Sources: U.S. Census Bureau *Statistical Abstract*, Tables 1116 and 1117; Norman Herr, *Sourcebook for Teaching Science*, 2001; U.S. Department of Justice, *Statistical Briefing Book*, 2003; Lueg, J.E. and Ponder, N. (2006) "Understanding the Socialization Process of Teen Consumers Across Shopping Channels," *International Journal of Electronic Marketing and Retailing*, Vol., 1, No. 1, pp. 83-97; www.fbi.gov.

Analyze and Debate

1. Do you think the information presented in each pair of statistics is related? For example, does advertising affect the spending habits of teens? Does watching crime on TV or playing violent video games make teens more violent? Do teens learn more from TV than from school?

2. Do the media decide what is most important for Americans to know about?

In a class debate, argue your point of view about one or more of the issues in Item 1. Support your opinions with reasons and evidence from your experience.

EQ ESSENTIAL QUESTION

In this unit, you will explore the **Essential Question** in class through reading, discussion, research, and writing. Keep thinking about the question outside of school, too.

1 Plan a Project

Ad Campaign

In this unit, you'll be creating an ad campaign that will inform your understanding of the Essential Question. Choose a product or service and develop ads to sell it. To get started, analyze some ads on TV, in magazines and newspapers, and on the radio. Look for

- the audience the ads try to reach
- techniques used to shape how people feel and think about the products
- how the ads present the products' benefits
- what the ads *don't* say about the products.

Study Skills Start planning your ad campaign. Use the forms on myNGconnect.com to plan your time and to prepare the content.

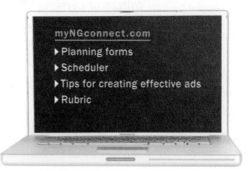

myNGconnect.com
▶ Planning forms
▶ Scheduler
▶ Tips for creating effective ads
▶ Rubric

2 Choose More to Read

These readings provide different answers to the Essential Question. Choose a book and online selections to read during the unit.

Warriors Don't Cry
by Melba Pattillo Beals

In 1957, millions of Americans watched as nine African American students enrolled in the all-white Central High School in Little Rock, Arkansas. Years later, one of the "Little Rock Nine" reconstructs the events of that year with diary entries and newspaper stories.

▶ **NONFICTION**

Picture Bride
by Yoshiko Uchida

It is 1917 in Japan. Hana's family finds a Japanese man for her to marry in the United States. She has seen only an old picture of him. Now Hana must journey to a foreign land to begin her life with a stranger. Are a picture and few letters enough to start a marriage?

▶ **NOVEL**

Keeper
by Mal Peet

How does a poor boy from the jungle become El Gato, soccer's greatest player? Reporter Paul Faustino discovers the truth. But who will believe it? Who could believe that El Gato's trainer was a ghost? Maybe no one except the Keeper.

▶ **NOVEL**

myNGconnect.com
- Read opinions about the positive and negative effects of the media on society.
- Learn about ways that advertisers target teens.
- Find out ways that young people are using the media to their advantage.

Writers of persuasive nonfiction want to convince readers to agree with their position, or viewpoint. Read these passages. Decide whether you think violence on TV should be controlled.

DEMO TEXT #1

Fifty Years of TV Violence

Violence on television is not real. So how can it be dangerous? But for more than fifty years, we have studied the effect television has on violence in our society. We have learned that violence inspires violence.

In 1952, Congress held hearings on the issue and decided that violence on radio and television had a "negative impact on children and youth." In the 1960s, the University of Pennsylvania began tracking violence in television programs. In the 1970s, the American Medical Association called TV violence an "environmental hazard" that could harm children. Some regulations were put in place.

In the 1980s, however, government relaxed its regulation of television. The number of violent programs increased. So did the level of violence on those programs. The networks agreed to a policy limiting violent programs. However, cable TV did not have to follow the rules that the networks had set for themselves. Cable TV violence increased rapidly.

Now we are in a time of rising violence. We have seen the evidence. Think of the harm this is doing to children. Isn't it time to protect children and act on what we have learned? It's the right thing to do.

—Dr. Bernadette R. Hillock
Child psychologist

DEMO TEXT #2

End the Violence

Television executives claim that television shows are violent because they reflect violence in real life. Yet we know that TV violence breeds violence in the street. And we let it continue. It's time to say, "Enough!"

Television is a breeding ground for violence. Congress has been holding hearings about TV violence since 1952. What good has all that talking done? No good at all! Academics have been studying TV violence since the 1960s. What good has that done? No good at all! Children see far more TV violence now than they did back then.

Today, all TV broadcasters freely broadcast the most horrible violence. We must put an end to this assault on our young people. Violent TV creates a violent society. There is no doubt about it any longer. Stand up for decency. Get the violence off TV. You owe it to your children.

—Mr. Asa Jones
Business owner and father

■ Connect Reading to Your Life

Do you agree with the authors of the Demo Texts that TV violence is a problem? Take a vote. Then, think about why you voted the way that you did. With a partner, look in the text for reasons for and against the argument that TV violence is a problem that should be controlled.

Reading Strategies

· Plan and Monitor
· Determine Importance
· Make Inferences
· Ask Questions
· Make Connections
▶ **Synthesize**
· Visualize

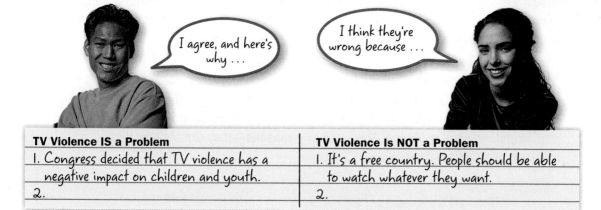

TV Violence IS a Problem	TV Violence Is NOT a Problem
1. Congress decided that TV violence has a negative impact on children and youth.	1. It's a free country. People should be able to watch whatever they want.
2.	2.

Focus Strategy ▶ Synthesize

To decide what you think about the issue of TV violence, you bring together many ideas. You think about the different reasons for restricting TV violence. You add what you already know about the issue. You also think about who is presenting the arguments. Then you decide what *you* think. Any time you bring together many different ideas like this, you are synthesizing.

Persuasion is everywhere. Think about all the commercials, advertisements, speeches, and other times when someone tries to get you to do something. The goal of persuasion is to get you to do (or not do) or believe (or not believe) something. People who write persuasive nonfiction use many techniques to try to get you to think one way or another. When you read persuasive nonfiction, you need to synthesize the information and decide whether you agree or not. That's why reading persuasive nonfiction can be a challenge.

■ Your Job as a Reader

The first thing to recognize when you read persuasive nonfiction is that the author is trying to convince you of something. That's the author's goal. Once you understand that, you can synthesize the information and decide whether you agree. For example, you may have thought about all of the different reasons for controlling violence on TV and still have decided that people should be free to watch what they want.

■ Unpack the Thinking Process

Whenever you try to convince anyone of anything, you're making an argument. You're making an argument when you try to convince your parents to raise your allowance. You're making an argument when you try to convince your teacher not to assign weekend homework. And you're making an argument when you write a paper to convince your reader that your understanding of a text is right. Although there are many different kinds of arguments, they all have the same structure.

The Structure of Arguments

All arguments start with **claims**. Claims are statements that give the writer's position, or the point a writer is trying to make. Good writers support their claims with strong, relevant **evidence**. They also give **reasons**—they explain how their evidence connects to their claim.

Claim	Reasons	Evidence
I think_____. The point you are trying to make	*So what?* A clear explanation of why the evidence supports the claim	*What makes you say so?* • Facts • Statistics • Expert Opinions • Personal Experience

Responding to Counterclaims

There are often different opinions or ideas about a topic. A **counterclaim** is what someone who disagrees might say. Good writers often include counterclaims and then explain why their claim is better than a counterclaim.

Evaluate the Argument

Reread the Demo Texts and figure out whether you agree. Ask yourself:

- **Reliability:** Is the evidence reliable and relevant to the topic?
- **Connection to Claim:** Does the writer clearly explain how the evidence supports the claim?
- **Possible Counterclaims:** Think about other options or counterclaims. Does the writer predict and defend against them?

Elements of Persuasion

claim *n.*, a statement defining an idea as true or false, right or wrong, good or bad

Academic Vocabulary

- **evidence** *n.*, ideas that support or prove a point; **evident** *adj.*, clearly seen; apparent

Read this persuasive text.

DEMO TEXT #3

It's Not TV's Fault

America is a nation of free speech and free expression. Yet many people today feel free speech has gone too far. They want to control the kinds of programs that TV networks show and regulate TV by restricting violent programming, which they believe is harmful to young people.

I agree that the amount of violence on TV should be restricted. However, it is the parents' job to do this. Many parents are too busy today to supervise what their children watch on TV. They want the government to do their job for them.

I remember when I was a kid. My parents always controlled what I watched on TV. I wasn't allowed to watch shows that contained violence. This is what parents should do today if they want to restrict TV violence.

Furthermore, if the government regulates TV violence, what else will it try to control in the media? Dr. Helen Lopez, a media executive, states that "once the government enters an area of our lives, it doesn't leave. Do you want the government in your house, telling you what you can watch on TV or listen to on the radio?"

In the past, the government has placed restrictions on TV violence. Yet society doesn't seem any less violent. Only individuals can create a less violent society. Adults must take responsibility for their behavior and for the TV-viewing habits of their children.

—William Yeng
Founder and owner of KYEH-TV

Partner Talk Answer these questions with a partner.

1. What is the author's claim?

2. What evidence does the author use to support the claim?

3. Does the author explain why his argument is better than the counterclaims? Give examples from the text.

4. Does it matter who the author is? Explain your thinking.

Revote Take another vote about regulating violence on TV. Did your vote change?

Monitor Comprehension

Persuasion What types of evidence do authors use to persuade readers? What should readers do before deciding if they agree?

How Do the Media Shape the Way People Think?
Explore how advertising changes our opinions.

Make a Connection

Debate Study the two quotations about advertising. Then work with a group to support one of the ideas while another group represents the other point of view. While working together, listen carefully to group members' ideas and questions and respond appropriately.

> "Advertising is the art of convincing people to spend money they don't have for something they don't need."
> —Will Rogers, American actor

> "Advertising says to people, 'Here's what we've got. Here's what it will do for you. Here's how to get it.'"
> —Leo Burnett, advertising expert

Learn Key Vocabulary

Study the Words Pronounce each word and learn its meaning. You may also want to look up the definitions in the Glossary.

● Academic Vocabulary

Key Words	Examples
advertising (**ad**-vur-tīz-ing) *noun* ▸ pages 518, 526, 531, 536, 537, 539	**Advertising** is a kind of media that encourages people to buy, use, or do something. The company uses **advertising** like TV commercials and Internet ads to sell its new product.
appeal (u-**pēl**) *verb; noun* ▸ pages 521, 531	When something **appeals** to you, it asks for a good reaction from you. [*verb*] When a person makes an **appeal** he or she is asking for a good response. [*noun*]
● **consumer** (kun-**sū**-mur) *noun* ▸ pages 520, 526, 532, 536, 537, 539	A **consumer** is someone who buys or uses something. Stores want **consumers** to buy their products.
● **convince** (kun-**vins**) *verb* ▸ pages 518, 526, 536	To **convince** means to make someone believe something. My friend **convinced** me to buy the expensive magazine.
● **impact** (**im**-pakt) *verb* ▸ pages 521, 531, 537	When something **impacts** you, it has an influence or effect on you. Do movies and celebrities **impact** the things you choose to buy?
● **manipulate** (mu-**ni**-pyū-lāt) *verb* ▸ pages 524, 537, 539	To **manipulate** means to influence or control someone or something in a negative way. That toy commercial uses popular cartoon characters to **manipulate** kids into wanting new toys.
persuasive (pur-**swā**-siv) *adjective* ▸ pages 518, 526	A person or thing is **persuasive** if it gives reasons that are good enough to make you do or believe something. The **persuasive** man always gets people to help him.
profit (**prah**-fut) *noun* ▸ page 534, 539	**Profit** is the money you make when you sell something, after expenses are subtracted. The bookstore increased its **profits** by selling more books.

Practice the Words With a partner, group Key Vocabulary into categories. Share with the class why you put certain words together.

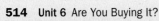

BEFORE READING Ad Power

persuasive text by Shari Graydon

Reading Strategies

· Plan and Monitor
· Determine Importance
· Make Inferences
· Ask Questions
· Make Connections
▶ **Synthesize**
· Visualize

Evaluate Evidence

An **argument** gives a writer's point of view about an issue or a problem. The writer states his or her idea and then supports it with **evidence**, such as facts, statistics, data, and quotations. The more reliable and relevant the evidence is, the more you'll be willing to believe the writer's argument.

Look Into the Text

The author uses an old saying to make a point about advertising.

People in Ghana, a country in West Africa, have a saying: *To the fish, the water is invisible*. In other words, when you're surrounded by something all the time, you don't notice it....

In parts of the world where people have a lot of modern conveniences and up-to-date technology, you could say that advertising has become "the water in which we swim." There's so much of it that we hardly notice it anymore. In fact, some experts estimate that a young person growing up in North America is likely to see between 20,000 and 40,000 TV commercials every year. When you add in all the advertisements from other media—up to 16,000 a day!—it's easy to see how you'd begin to stop noticing, and just keep swimming.

She adds relevant statistics and facts from experts to support her argument.

Focus Strategy ▶ Synthesize

When you **synthesize**, you put together ideas and information to form new understandings. You can read a writer's argument, combine it with what you already know, and use this to draw a conclusion about the text.

HOW TO DRAW CONCLUSIONS

Focus Strategy

1. As you read, note the writer's claims in a **Conclusion Chart**.

2. Add evidence from the text that supports each claim.

3. Add your own background knowledge and experience with the claim.

4. Synthesize, or combine, your ideas with the writer's.

5. Draw a conclusion that makes a judgment, gives an opinion, or shows new understanding. As you read on, synthesize the new information and draw more conclusions.

Conclusion Chart

Writer's Claim: There are so many ads that we don't notice them anymore.
Evidence: Experts say that teens see up to 40,000 commercials a year.
My Experience: I see ads everywhere—even in our school.
My Conclusion: I agree with the author's claim.

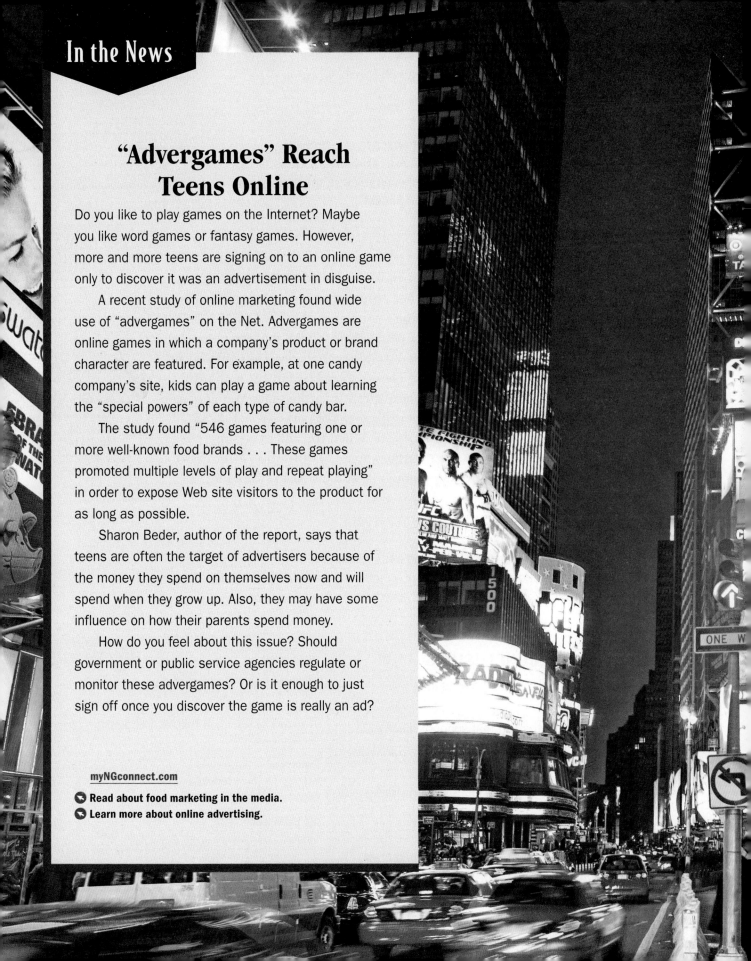

"Advergames" Reach Teens Online

Do you like to play games on the Internet? Maybe you like word games or fantasy games. However, more and more teens are signing on to an online game only to discover it was an advertisement in disguise.

A recent study of online marketing found wide use of "advergames" on the Net. Advergames are online games in which a company's product or brand character are featured. For example, at one candy company's site, kids can play a game about learning the "special powers" of each type of candy bar.

The study found "546 games featuring one or more well-known food brands . . . These games promoted multiple levels of play and repeat playing" in order to expose Web site visitors to the product for as long as possible.

Sharon Beder, author of the report, says that teens are often the target of advertisers because of the money they spend on themselves now and will spend when they grow up. Also, they may have some influence on how their parents spend money.

How do you feel about this issue? Should government or public service agencies regulate or monitor these advergames? Or is it enough to just sign off once you discover the game is really an ad?

myNGconnect.com

🌐 **Read about food marketing in the media.**
🌐 **Learn more about online advertising.**

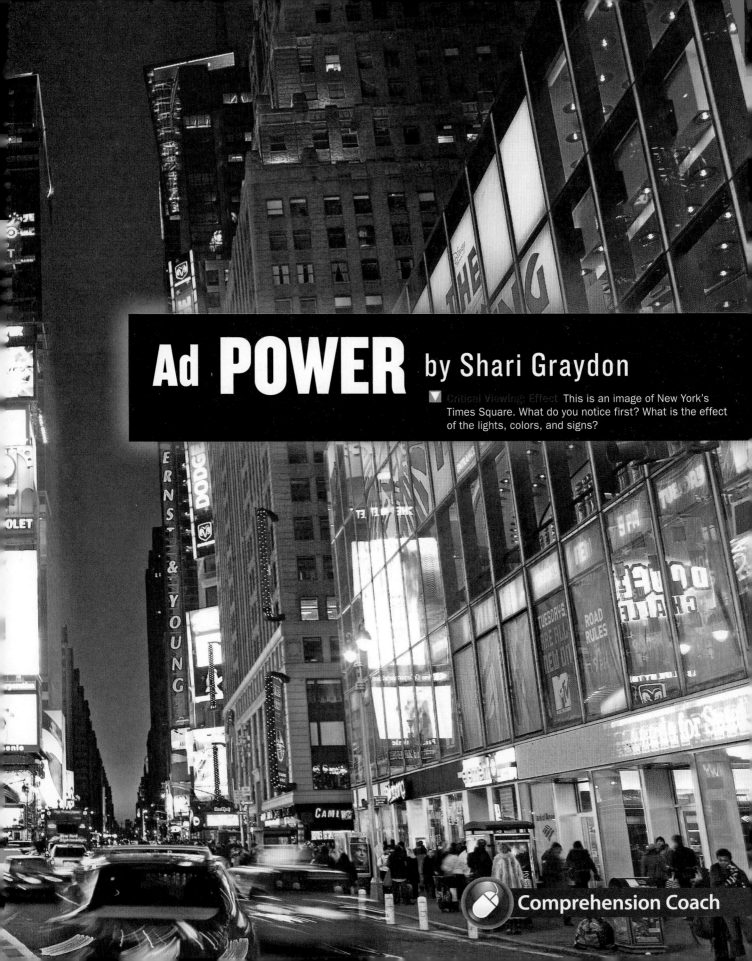

Ad POWER by Shari Graydon

▼ Critical Viewing: Effect This is an image of New York's Times Square. What do you notice first? What is the effect of the lights, colors, and signs?

Comprehension Coach

Advertising: You're Swimming In It

Do you remember the day one of your parents sat you down to have a serious talk about advertising?

Me neither. And it's not something they ever test you on at school. That's too bad. Given how easy it is to remember **jingles and slogans**, an ad exam might be the one test all year you wouldn't have to study for.

Really, you've been "studying" the subject almost since the day you were born. Every time you got parked in front of the TV or carried past a billboard, you were absorbing the art—or some would say science—of persuasive communication.

Advertising is basically anything someone does to grab your attention and hold on to it long enough to tell you how cool, fast, cheap, tasty, fun, rockin', or rad whatever they're selling is. Some people have a different definition. They argue that advertising is trickery used to shut down your brain just long enough to convince you to open your wallet! **1**

People in Ghana, a country in West Africa, have a saying: *To the fish, the water is invisible.* In other words, when you're surrounded by something all the time, you don't notice it. **You take it for granted and assume** that it's natural. Or, you think that it's always been there. You don't think about whether it's good or bad, or how it's affecting your life. **2**

In parts of the world where people have a lot of **modern conveniences** and up-to-date technology, you could say that advertising has become "the water in which we swim." There's so much of it that we hardly notice it anymore. In fact, some experts estimate that a young person growing up in North America is likely to see between 20,000 and 40,000 TV commercials every year. When you add

1 Draw Conclusions
Graydon claims there are two ways to look at advertising. Which one best matches your experience with ads? Draw a conclusion that combines your ideas with the author's in your Conclusions Chart.

2 Evidence
What does this saying mean? How does it support Graydon's argument about advertising?

Key Vocabulary
advertising *n.*, work that encourages people to buy, do, or use things
persuasive *adj.*, believable enough to make you do or believe something
• **convince** *v.*, to make someone believe

In Other Words
jingles and slogans songs and phrases used in ads
You take it for granted and assume You think that it's just normal and
modern conveniences things that make life easy

in all the advertisements from **other media**—up to 16,000 a day!—it's easy to see how you'd begin to stop noticing, and just keep swimming.

Think about it...

The mind boggles trying to imagine 16,000 ads in a single day. But what if you tested the estimate? What if, from the time you got up one morning, till the time you went to bed that night, you counted every single commercial message that showed up **in your surroundings**? If you try this, don't forget to include:

- Radio jingles
- The neon signs of local stores
- Outdoor billboards
- Posters in school hallways
- **Logos** on your friends' clothing
- **Blurbs** on your favorite Internet sites
- Ads in magazines—not to mention commercials on television! **3**

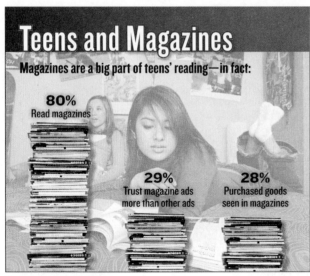

Teens and Magazines

Magazines are a big part of teens' reading—in fact:

80%
Read magazines

29%
Trust magazine ads more than other ads

28%
Purchased goods seen in magazines

◀ **Interpret the Graph**
According to the graph, what is the relationship between what teens read and what they buy?

Sources, from left to right:
Magazine Publishers of America;
Nonprofit Youth Study;
Neopets Youth Society

3 Evidence
How does the writer support the claim that people are surrounded by ads? Does this convince you that what she says is true?

Monitor Comprehension

Explain
What claim does the author make about advertising?

In Other Words

other media more types of communication like magazines, newspapers, and radio programs
The mind boggles trying to imagine We can't even imagine what it's like to see
in your surroundings everywhere you went

Logos Symbols and brand names
Blurbs Information about products

Is Advertising Good For You?

Are sugared breakfast foods **a subject of debate** in your house? Do you beg for sugary cereal, while your dad insists on high fiber cereal? My mom called the **heavily promoted sugary stuff** "candy— **with no redeeming food value**," but I always argued it was nutritious, and pointed to the vitamin chart on the back of the box. Was one of us right, or was it just two ways of looking at the same thing?

Advertisers say that people make thoughtful decisions about what they're going to buy—that **consumers** think about their choices and make decisions using their minds. Others argue that a lot of advertising is aimed at people's hearts, not their minds. They suggest that ads affect us emotionally and trick us into buying products for the wrong reasons. **4**

4 Evidence
How does the debate about sugary cereal help explain the different points of view about advertising? Make a note in your Conclusions Chart.

Ads in the Past

Ads have been around for as long as people have had things to sell. Some merchants advertised by showing their products and calling out to shoppers. Others painted pictures on walls and hanging signs. After the printing press was invented, ads included posters, flyers, and newspapers. The Hamlin's Wizard Oil Company used wall thermometers, posters, and traveling shows to sell what they called "the greatest pain remedy on Earth."

Hamlin's Wizard Oil ad, circa 1900

Key Vocabulary
- **consumer** *n.*, someone who buys or uses something

a subject of debate something you argue about
heavily promoted sugary stuff cereals with a lot of sugar that are advertised everywhere
with no redeeming food value that was completely unhealthy

Think about it...

Consider how advertising **impacts** your life:

- What forms of advertising do you notice the most?

- What kinds of advertising do you enjoy?

- Have you ever felt interrupted or annoyed by advertising?

- Can you think of an ad that made you want to run out and buy the product? What was it that convinced you?

- Do the ads you see give you facts about the product, or **appeal** more to your emotions?

- If you hear or see things in an advertisement that you don't believe or agree with, how do you react?

- Have you ever bought something just because you saw it advertised? **Did the product live up to the ad?** ⑤

5 Draw Conclusions
How do Graydon's questions help you draw a conclusion about advertising?

Ads Today

Just as technology has changed the way we live, it has changed the way advertisers sell. Television and radio commercials present ads with music and visuals that are hard to avoid. Moviemakers are paid to display products for audiences to see. And it's almost impossible to surf the Internet without having banner and pop-up ads interrupt your concentration. All of these ads catch our attention and put product names in our minds. ⑥

6 Evidence
How do the two advertisements on pages 520 and 521 support the writer's ideas? Make a note in your Conclusion Chart.

Monitor Comprehension

Summarize
How do advertisers and their critics think consumers make their decisions?

Key Vocabulary
- **impact** *v.*, to influence and affect
  appeal *v.*, to ask for a good reaction

In Other Words
Did the product live up to the ad? Was the product as good as the ad made it seem?

Slogans and Logos

Do you know how diamonds came to be the gem of choice for engagement rings? You might imagine that it's an old tradition that was handed down for generations. In fact, diamond engagement rings are an invention of advertising. For centuries, opals, rubies, and sapphires were often featured in women's engagement rings. But in 1947, a big diamond producer began advertising the glittering white stones as the symbol of love.

The company's slogan, "Diamonds are forever," cleverly connected the hardness and **durability** of diamonds with the **notion** of permanent love. Diamonds quickly **became synonymous with** engagement rings. Isn't it strange that a few words, repeated many times, can change how people think and act? **7**

PLEASE!

SMOKEY

Only you can prevent forest fires **8**

Smokey Bear and his famous slogan represented the U.S. Forest Service for decades.

What Makes a Good Slogan?

A good **slogan**:

- gets your attention. It can be funny or serious, but never boring.

- makes a good point—and convinces you to do something.

- is unforgettable and timeless.

7 Draw Conclusions
Does this information change your understanding of diamond engagement rings? Explain and add notes to your Conclusion Chart.

8 Draw Conclusions
Read this slogan and think about other slogans you know. Where do you see these slogans in your surroundings? What types of messages do they convey? Draw a conclusion about what makes a good slogan.

In Other Words
durability lasting quality and strength, permanence
notion idea
became synonymous with started to mean the same thing as

Think about it...

Every time you put on a T-shirt or a pair of jeans that shows a company's logo, you become a walking billboard. You're "advertising" the company's products.

Think about the **exchange**. You get a T-shirt. The company gets the money you paid for the shirt plus the **exposure** that comes from you wearing it. Your willingness to wear the company's name on your body is the same as you personally **endorsing** the product. 9

Also, think about how some fashion trends support the goals of advertisers. When kids started to wear their pants so low that the tops of their underwear showed, which clothing **manufacturer** got more "exposure"?

9 Evidence
What does Graydon say about logos on clothes? Does her explanation convince you? Explain.

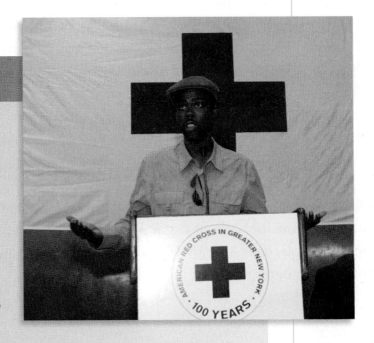

What Is a Logo?

A **logo** is an organization's identifying "signature." It can simply be the company's name or a symbol. Do you recognize the logo shown here? What organization does it represent?

Companies and organizations use logos that people will recognize quickly. Some organizations, like the Red Cross, ask celebrities like Chris Rock, shown here, to endorse their cause.

In Other Words

exchange trade
exposure chance to be seen by many people
endorsing approving and supporting
manufacturer maker

Monitor Comprehension

Explain
How do slogans and logos help advertisers?

How to Evaluate Ads Critically
by Nancy Day

Is advertising a way for businesses to **manipulate** people? Or is it something that helps consumers choose products and encourages companies to improve products? It is probably all of these things. The next time you see an ad, keep these things in mind:

1. Remember that the purpose of an advertisement is to make you want to buy something.

2. Ask yourself whether the product will actually provide the **benefits shown** in the advertisement. See if the benefits are social or psychological (happiness, popularity, success, etc.). 🔟

3. Remember that the product is being shown **under the best possible conditions**.

4. Realize that sports figures, movie and TV stars, singers, and even "experts" in commercials are simply being paid to read scripts.

5. Be aware that most brands of products shown in movies or on TV have been placed there for a fee by an advertiser.

6. Keep in mind that people appearing in advertisements are almost always professional actors or models playing a role.

7. Remember that if something seems too good to be true, it probably is. 🔢

Whichever way you look at it, advertising is a huge part of our world. Trying to imagine life without it starts to sound like a science-fiction movie: *Black Holes and Other Mysteries of Life Before Advertising*. And what do you want to bet it would be in black and white?

🔟 **Access Vocabulary**
Study the examples to find out what the word *psychological* means in this sentence.

🔢 **Draw Conclusions**
What information presented here adds to your understanding of advertising? Make a note in your Conclusion Chart.

Key Vocabulary
• **manipulate** *v.*, to influence or control someone in a negative way

In Other Words
benefits shown good things promised
under the best possible conditions with none of the problems that might happen

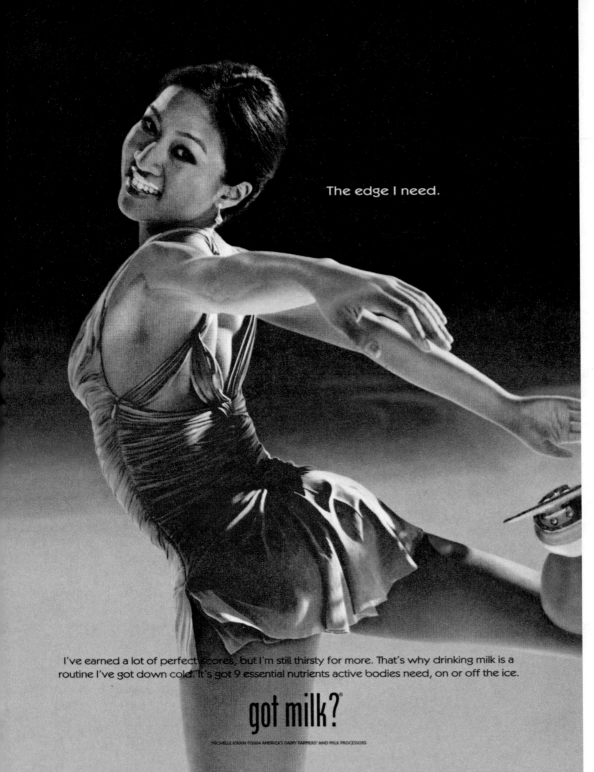

The edge I need.

I've earned a lot of perfect scores, but I'm still thirsty for more. That's why drinking milk is a routine I've got down cold. It's got 9 essential nutrients active bodies need, on or off the ice.

got milk?

MICHELLE KWAN ©2004 AMERICA'S DAIRY FARMERS® AND MILK PROCESSORS

◀ **Critical Viewing: Effect**
You are probably familiar with ads like this one. They appear all around you in your environment. Read this ad. Make sure you read it from top to bottom. What message is this ad trying to convey? Is it important for the reader to know that the skater is Michelle Kwan, an Olympic medalist?

The fact is that advertising is an unavoidable part of our daily lives. Fortunately, the more **critical** you can be when you look at ads, the more you will see them for what they really are. Your decisions about what you really want to buy, do, and be may even change. If this happens—don't worry! It just means that you're ready to take charge of your wallet, your mind . . . and your life! ❖

ANALYZE Ad Power

1. **Explain** What are three things that Shari Graydon wants readers to know about advertising? Cite specific examples from the text in your response.

2. **Vocabulary** According to Graydon's argument, how can consumers protect themselves from the persuasive ads that surround them?

3. **Evaluate Evidence** One way to judge a writer's argument is to see whether you believe the evidence he or she gives. Work with a small group to review each section. Then discuss whether the evidence convinces you to believe the author's ideas.

4. **Focus Strategy Draw Conclusions** With a partner, review the **Conclusion Chart** you began on page 515. Identify the author's overall claim about advertising. Combine this with what you know about the subject, and then draw your own conclusion about advertising.

Return to the Text

Reread and Write Review the selection to find one of Graydon's most valid claims about how the media shape the way people think. Write this claim in your own words and support it with evidence from Graydon and your own experience.

In Other Words
critical careful and aware

and talking about
fishbelly
5 white.
The color white
is not bad at all.
There are white mornings
that bring us days.
10 Or, if you must,
tan only because
it makes you happy
to be brown,
to be able to see
15 for a summer
the whole world's
darker
face
reflected
20 in your own.

Your eyes are
beautiful.
25 Sometimes
seeing you in the street
the fold zany
and unexpected
I want to kiss
30 them
and usually
it is only
old
gorgeous
35 black people's eyes
I want
to kiss.

Stop trimming
your nose.
40 When you
diminish
your nose
your songs
become little
45 tinny, muted
and snub.
Better you should
have a nose
impertinent
50 as a flower,
sensitive
as a root;
wise, elegant,
serious and deep.
55 A nose that
sniffs
the essence
of Earth. And knows
the message
60 of every
leaf.

Stop bleaching
your skin
and talking
65 about
so much black
is not beautiful.
The color black
is not bad
70 at all.
There are black nights
that rock
us
in dreams.
75 Or, if you must,
bleach only
because it pleases you
to be brown,
to be able to see
80 for as long
as you can bear it
the whole world's
lighter face
reflected
85 in your own.

In Other Words

trimming your nose using surgery to
change the shape of your nose
diminish change, reduce
muted quiet, dull
impertinent bold, confident

the essence of Earth what is real
and beautiful
bleaching your skin making your
skin lighter

As for me,
I have learned
to worship
the sun
90 again.
To affirm
the adventures
of hair.

For we are all
95 *splendid*
descendants
of Wilderness,
Eden:
needing only
100 to see
each other
without
commercials
to believe.

105 Copied skillfully
as Adam.

Original

as Eve.

About the Poet

Alice Walker (1944–) is best known for her Pulitzer Prize-winning novel *The Color Purple* (1982), which was made into a successful film. In addition to novels, she has written short stories, poetry, nonfiction, and children's books. Walker's writing reflects her African American roots. She coined the word "womanist" to refer to the focus in her work. Although she has written chiefly about the black woman's experience, Walker's work is concerned with all of humanity.

What's Wrong with Advertising?

essay by David Ogilvy

Analyze Viewpoint: Word Choice

Some writers use evidence and logic to convince readers that their ideas are true. Other writers appeal to the reader's emotions or beliefs. These **persuasive appeals** are words that create strong feelings in the reader. An appeal that does not use evidence or logic is called a **logical fallacy**, or a **rhetorical fallacy**.

Look Into the Text

According to the writer, who benefits from toothpaste ads?

> Few of us advertising professionals lie awake nights feeling guilty about the way we earn our living. We don't feel bad when we write advertisements for toothpaste. If we do it well, children may not have to go to the dentist so often.
>
> I did not feel bad when I wrote advertisements promoting travel to Puerto Rico. They helped attract industry and tourists to a country that had been in poverty for 400 years.

What words does the writer choose in order to appeal to the reader's emotions?

As you read David Ogilvy's essay, look for words, phrases, or examples that appeal to the reader's emotions or beliefs. Write them in an **Appeals Chart**.

Appeals Chart

Text	Appeals to	Conclusion
"My children were grateful when I wrote an ad that recovered their dog from dognappers."	emotions because I was sad when my dog was lost	The writer wants me to think that ads can be used for good reasons.

Focus Strategy ▶ Synthesize

When you read a persuasive essay, synthesize the writer's ideas with your own experiences. Then draw conclusions about the writer's ideas.

HOW TO DRAW CONCLUSIONS

Focus Strategy

1. As you read, continue the **Appeals Chart** you began above. Record the words, phrases, and examples that show the writer's ideas.

2. Add what you know about the topic from your own experiences.

3. Synthesize the information in the first two columns by stating a judgment, opinion, or new idea based on this evidence.

4. As you read on, see how the new information fits the conclusions you have made.

What's Wrong with Advertising?
by David Ogilvy

Connect Across Texts

"Ad Power" examines how **advertising** **impacts** our lives. In this essay, an ad executive explains how he feels about the work he does.

David Ogilvy, the "Father of Advertising," began his career by selling kitchen stoves door-to-door. In 1949, Ogilvy only had $6,000, but he used it to open **an advertising agency** with two partners. Their company went on to create advertising for many of the world's largest companies. Forty years later, the Ogilvy Group was sold for $864 million. *Time* magazine called Ogilvy "the most sought-after wizard in the advertising industry."

Ogilvy once said, "Never write an advertisement which you wouldn't want your family to read. You wouldn't tell lies to your own wife. Don't tell them to mine." **1** Here are more of David Ogilvy's ideas from his book *Ogilvy on Advertising*.

Is Advertising Evil?

A professor in New York teaches his students that "advertising is . . . **intellectual and moral pollution**. . . . It is **undermining** our faith in our nation and in ourselves."

Holy smoke, is *that* what I do for a living?

Some of the defenders of advertising are equally guilty of **overstating** their case. Said Leo Burnett, the great Chicago advertising man: "Advertising is not the noblest creation of man's mind . . . It does not,

1 Word Choice
What type of **appeal** is Ogilvy making with this quotation? Make a note in your Appeals Chart.

Key Vocabulary

advertising *n.*, work that encourages people to buy, do, or use things
- **impact** *v.*, to influence and affect
appeal *n.*, request for a good reaction

In Other Words

an advertising agency a company that creates advertisements
intellectual and moral pollution destroying our minds and values
undermining weakening and damaging
overstating exaggerating

single-handedly, **sustain the whole structure of capitalism and democracy and the free world**. . . . We are merely human, trying to do a necessary human job **with dignity, with decency, and with competence**."

My view is that advertising is no more and no less than a reasonably efficient way to sell. Procter & Gamble spends about $600,000,000* a year on advertising. Howard Morgens, their former president, is quoted as saying, "We believe that advertising is the most effective and efficient way to sell to the consumer. If we should ever find better methods of selling our type of products to the consumer, we'll leave advertising and turn to these other methods." 2

Few of us advertising professionals lie awake nights feeling guilty about the way we earn our living. We don't feel bad when we write advertisements for toothpaste. If we do it well, children may not have to go to the dentist so often.

*This was Proctor & Gamble's advertising **budget** in 1983. Today, the manufacturing company spends about $2 billion a year on advertising.

2 Draw Conclusions Consider this quotation. Based on your knowledge and experience, do you think there is a better way to sell products? Explain.

ADVERTISING DOLLARS SPENT

Large companies spend a large percentage of their budgets on advertising. Look at these products. Do they sound familar to you? Have you bought or used any of them yourself? Maybe these advertising dollars are well spent after all.

Top Advertising Categories
January–September 2005

Industry	Ad Expenditure (billions)
Automobile (foreign and domestic brands)	$12.4
Financial Services (banks, credit cards, car loans, etc.)	$5.7
Telecommunications (phone, Internet)	$5.5
Personal Care Products (cosmetics, shampoo, etc.)	$4.2
Travel and Tourism	$4.0

Source: TNS Media Intelligence Report, December 2005

Interpret the Chart Why do you think automobile companies spend more on advertising than companies that sell personal care products?

Key Vocabulary
• **consumer** *n.*, someone who buys or uses something

In Other Words
sustain the whole structure of capitalism and democracy in the free world keep the free world running
with dignity, with decency, and with competence with pride, good taste, and skill
budget cost

I did not feel bad when I wrote advertisements promoting travel to Puerto Rico. They helped **attract industry** and tourists to a country that had been in poverty for 400 years.

I do not think that I am wasting my time when I write advertisements for the World Wildlife Fund.

My children were grateful when I wrote an advertisement that recovered their dog Teddy from **dognappers**.

Nobody suggests that the printing press is evil because it is used to print pornography. It is also used to print the Bible. Advertising is only evil when it advertises evil things.

Some **economists** say that advertising tempts people to waste money on things they don't need. Who are they to decide what you need? Do you *need* a dishwasher? Do you *need* a deodorant? Do you *need* a trip to Rome? I **feel no qualms of conscience** about persuading you that you do. What the economists don't seem to know is that buying things can be one of life's more innocent pleasures, whether you need them or not.

If advertising were **abolished**, what would be done with the money? Would it be spent on public works? Or **distributed to stockholders**? Or given to the media for the loss of **their largest source of revenue**? Perhaps it could be used to reduce prices to the consumer—*by about 3 percent.*

Reports show that Americans spent more money than they earned in 2005. Advertisers fight for their attention—and their money.

3 Word Choice
Why is this an example of a fallacy? What words give you clues?

4 Word Choice
Ogilvy argues that advertising can help others. Which words does he use to appeal to people's emotions and beliefs? Make a note in your Appeals Chart

Monitor Comprehension

Explain
How does Ogilvy feel about the benefits of, and problems with, advertising?

In Other Words
attract industry bring businesses, jobs
dognappers the people who stole him
economists experts who study how people spend money
feel no qualms of conscience don't feel ashamed or guilty

abolished stopped
distributed to stockholders given to people who own parts of a company
their largest source of revenue the way they make most of their money

Can Advertising Sell Bad Products?

It is often charged that advertising can persuade people to buy inferior products. So it can—*once*. But the consumer sees that the product is inferior and never buys it again. This is expensive for the manufacturer, whose **profits** come from *repeat* purchases.

The best way to increase the sale of a product is to *improve the product*. This is particularly true of food products. The consumer is amazingly quick to notice an improvement in taste and buy the product more often. **5**

Manipulation?

You may have heard it said that advertising is "manipulation." I know of only two examples, and neither of them actually happened. In 1957, a **market researcher** called James Vicary **hypothesized** that it might be possible to flash commands on television screens so fast that the viewer would not **be conscious of** seeing them. However, the viewer's *unconscious* mind *would* see the commands—and obey them. He called this gimmick "subliminal" advertising, but he never even got around to testing it, and no advertiser has ever used it.

I myself once came near to doing something so diabolical **6**

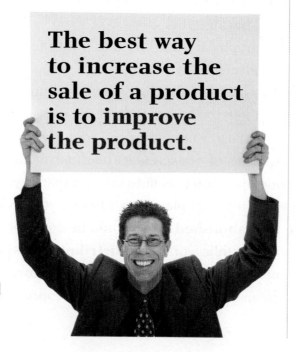

The best way to increase the sale of a product is to improve the product.

5 Draw Conclusions
How does Ogilvy's claim about advertising bad products match your own experience? What conclusion can you draw about the topic?

6 Access Vocabulary
Do you know what *diabolical* means? Read on to gather clues. Then give a definition of the word.

Key Vocabulary
profit *n.*, the money a company makes after expenses

In Other Words
market researcher man who studied how consumers spend their money
hypothesized guessed
be conscious of realize he or she was

534 Unit 6 Are You Buying It?

that I hesitate to confess it even now, thirty years later. Suspecting that **hypnotism** might be an element in successful advertising, I hired a professional hypnotist to make a commercial. When I saw it in the projection room, it was so powerful that I had visions of millions of **suggestible consumers** getting up from their armchairs and rushing like **zombies** through the traffic on their way to buy the product at the nearest store. **7** Had I invented the *ultimate* advertisement? I burned it,

7 Draw Conclusions
Draw a conclusion about this retelling. What is your opinion of it?

TRUTH IN ADVERTISING?

Advertisers want their products to appear attractive and appealing. Many times, this includes removing distracting objects and "touching up" photos. Which of these photos gives a more appealing glimpse of a vacation getaway?

Original Photo

Touched-Up Photo

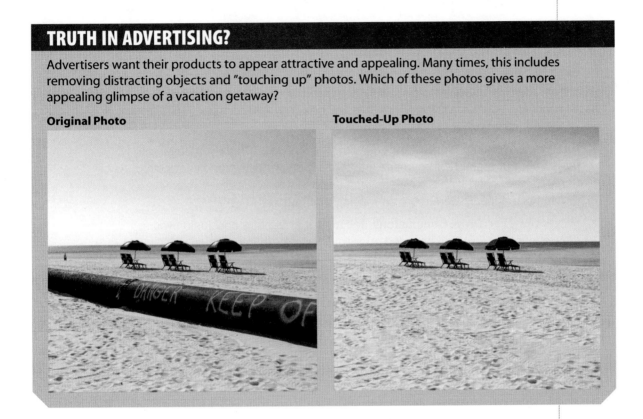

In Other Words

hypnotism controlling people's unconscious so they will do whatever they are told to do
suggestible consumers buyers who didn't know what they were doing
zombies half-dead people

Monitor Comprehension

Summarize
How does Ogilvy feel about the idea that advertising is dishonest or manipulative?

and never told my client how close I had come to **landing him in a national scandal**.

One way or another, the odds against your being manipulated by advertising are now very long indeed. Even if I wanted to manipulate you, I wouldn't know how to get around the **legal regulations**. ❖ ■8

■8 **Word Choice**
What is the author's final argument supporting advertising? Make a note in your Appeals Chart, explaining whether you are persuaded by it.

ANALYZE What's Wrong with Advertising?

1. **Explain** What is David Ogilvy's attitude toward advertising? Give specific examples of how he supports his opinions.

2. **Vocabulary** According to Ogilvy, what is the best way for a company to convince consumers to buy its products?

3. **Analyze Viewpoint: Word Choice** Review the **Appeals Chart** you began on page 530. Put a star next to appeals that you found effective and convincing. Compare your chart with a partner's, and discuss why some of the author's appeals were more convincing than others.

4. **Focus Strategy Draw Conclusions** Tell a partner about a conclusion you drew about the topic that changed after you found more information in the selection.

Return to the Text

Reread and Write How would you respond to Ogilvy's claims about how the media shape the way people think? Write a letter to Ogilvy that explains some of your conclusions about the essay. Support your ideas with your background knowledge and details from the text.

In Other Words
landing him in a national scandal making him and his company look bad
legal regulations laws that prevent untruthful or deceptive ads

EQ How Do the Media Shape the Way People Think?

Critical Thinking

EQ 1. **Analyze** According to Shari Graydon and David Ogilvy, how does advertising impact the way people think? Support your ideas with evidence from both texts.

2. **Compare** Describe Graydon's point of view about advertising and Ogilvy's point of view. Which view convinces you?

3. **Interpret** Look back at the end of Alice Walker's poem "Without Commercials." What does Walker say about commercials? How would Graydon and Ogilvy respond?

4. **Speculate** What would Ogilvy say about the advice for consumers in "How to Evaluate Ads Critically"? Explain.

EQ 5. **Draw Conclusions** Does advertising manipulate or help young people? Consider your own experience and evidence from both selections to draw your own conclusions.

Write About Literature

Definition What is advertising? Collect the definitions given in both texts, add what you know, and synthesize your own definition.

"Ad Power"	"What's Wrong with Advertising?"
"...anything someone does to grab your attention..." (p. 518)	"...a reasonably efficient way to sell" (p. 532)

My definition _____

Key Vocabulary Review

Oral Review Work with a partner. Use these words to complete the paragraph.

advertising   convince   persuasive
appeal   impact   profit
consumers   manipulate

As __(1)__ who buy many products, we need to recognize the way companies use __(2)__ to encourage us to buy and use their products. Some ads are __(3)__ because they give us good reasons to buy the product. But other ads try to control and __(4)__ us in negative ways. They __(5)__ to our beliefs and emotions in order to __(6)__ us that we should believe what they say. These companies just want to make a __(7)__ by selling more products. Whether they are good or bad, all of these ads __(8)__, or influence, us in some way.

Writing Application Think of a persuasive advertisement that got you to buy a certain product. Write a paragraph about the experience. Use at least five Key Vocabulary words.

Read with Ease: Expression

Assess your reading fluency with the passage in the Reading Handbook, p. 766. Then complete the self-check below.

1. I did/did not pause appropriately for phrases and punctuation.

2. My words correct per minute: _____ .

Vary Your Sentences

Writing that uses a variety of sentence patterns can be more interesting to read. In a simple sentence, the **subject** usually comes before the **verb**.

Ads **are** all around us.

How can you vary your sentences?

- Change the word order. Use the **verb** before the **subject**.

  All around us **are** **ads**.

- Add an **infinitive phrase**.

  Companies advertise.

  Companies advertise **to sell their products**.

- Start some sentences with a **gerund**.

  Advertising sells products.

Oral Practice (1–5) With a partner, read each sentence. Then say the sentence in another way.

1. Radio jingles are easy to remember.
2. The mind boggles trying to imagine 16,000 ads per day.
3. Outdoor billboards sit above the streets.
4. Companies create clever ads.
5. A way to be safe is to read critically.

Written Practice (6–10) Write a paragraph. Start with this sentence:

It is impossible to escape commercial messages.

Add five sentences with details about the topics below. Remember to vary your sentences.

- television and radio
- Web sites
- store windows
- clothing logos

Persuade

Pair Talk Name a product that you like. Persuade your partner to buy this product.

Compare Authors' Purposes and Viewpoints

The reason an author writes a selection is known as the **author's purpose**. An author might write to entertain, inform, or persuade. The author's perspective reflects his or her background, experiences, and **viewpoint**. It affects the ideas and opinions the author expresses.

In persuasive writing, authors often write in the first-person so they can directly state their opinions.

When you read persuasive writing, there are several things you should look for to decide whether the writer is convincing and credible, or believable. These include:

- **Agenda**: Does the author have an agenda, or a hidden idea or belief, that he or she wants to get across? What does the writer want to accomplish by writing?

- **Bias**: Does the author have a bias, or strong opinion, that affects how he or she presents the subject? You can get clues by looking at his or her background, including political or religious beliefs.

Compare "Ad Power" and "What's Wrong with Advertising?"

1. Identify each author's purpose and perspective.

2. Identify any bias or a possible agenda that the writer might have. The author's background may give you clues.

3. Identify any effects that the author's purpose, viewpoint, bias, or agenda has on the writing and on the argument used in the writing.

4. Then sum up your ideas: Compare the bias and agenda of both authors. How do they affect whether you think each author is convincing and credible? As you give your analysis, cite examples from the selections to prove your points.

Latin and Greek Roots

Many English words are made up of Latin and Greek roots with other word parts added. Knowing the meaning of the roots can help you understand the meaning of the entire word.

ROOT	MEANING	EXAMPLE
fit	to make	**profit**
man	hand	**manipulate**
merc	trade	merchant
psych	spirit or soul	psychology
sume	to take	**consumer**
techn	art, skill	technical
vert	to turn	**advertising**

Read the paragraph. Use the list of roots to figure out the meaning of each underlined word. Check the definition by looking up the word in the dictionary.

My cousin wanted to buy a used car. We saw a <u>commercial</u> on TV for a car dealer, so we checked out the place. We found a red <u>convertible</u> with a manual shift. The car looked good but cost too much. Besides, the dealer wanted my cousin to <u>assume</u> the loan. Next, we looked at online car ads. One <u>benefit</u> to using this <u>technology</u> is that you can check out lots of cars from home!

Write a Letter to the Editor

You may feel strongly about a social issue, such as the ban of cell phones in your school. In a social science class, you may be asked to to write a **letter to the editor** of a school or local newspaper to express your opinion.

❶ **Prewrite** Decide where you stand on the issue. Organize your thoughts and the reasoning behind your opinion.

❷ **Draft** Compose a letter that explains the issue briefly and states the most important reasons for your stance.

❸ **Revise** Add, move, or replace details to make your explanation clearer or more effective.

❹ **Proofread** Work with a partner to identify and correct any spelling or grammar mistakes.

❺ **Publish** Share your work with the class. Compare all of the letters and opinions in a group discussion.

Model Letter to the Editor

To the Editor:

    Recently, student use of cell phones has been banned in my school. Although these devices occasionally disturb a class, they should still be allowed.

    I feel that students using the devices secretly and getting caught will cause as much of a disturbance as if they were allowed.

    Many parents also give their children phones to be used during emergencies. If this is approved by parents, I don't think that schools should complain.

    I hope the school will reconsider its decision to ban these devices. This decision will only cause more disturbances and remove technology that parents approve of.

Sincerely,
Joe Flores

> The writer gives his opinion.

> These examples give support for the opinion.

> The conclusion restates the writer's opinion.

🔖 **Writing Handbook**, page 784

1

Inside a Department Store

People who work in department stores are part of the retail industry. Department stores are large retail stores that sell many different kinds of goods. They are arranged in departments such as clothing, cosmetics, and household appliances.

Jobs in the Retail Industry

Most jobs in the retail industry are for salespersons. There are also positions for customer service representatives, sales managers, buyers, store managers, and administrators.

Job	Responsibilities	Education/Training Required
Salesperson 1	• Assists customers in purchasing merchandise • Deals courteously with customers • Receives and processes payment for purchases from customers	• On-the-job training
Sales Supervisor 2	• Interviews, hires, and trains salespersons • Supervises sales staff • Reviews inventory and sales records	• Work experience as a salesperson and knowledge of management practices • On-the-job training
Buyer 3	• Predicts products consumers will want to buy and purchases goods for resale • Keeps track of sales and stock inventory • Works with suppliers to develop products consumers will want	• College degree • Knowledge of merchandising • On-the-job training

2

Create a Résumé

A résumé is a summary of your education, skills, and work history. Many employers require that you submit a résumé to be considered for a job.

1. Gather the information you will need for your résumé. Include your personal contact information, education and job history, and any skills you can bring to the job. Such skills might include professional phone skills, experience as a cashier, or knowledge of other languages.

2. Use this information to create your résumé. Share your résumé with a classmate. Ask for feedback about how you might improve it. Then create your final draft and the information in a professional career portfolio.

3

myNGconnect.com

🔊 Learn more about working in a department store.

🔊 Download a form to evaluate whether you would like to work in this field.

🔊 Download a résumé worksheet.

💟 **Writing Handbook**, page 784

Build Word Knowledge

Do you have your grandmother's eyes or your uncle's hair? Like everyone else, your face probably includes a combination of features from different family members. Languages are also combinations from different sources.

Latin, Greek, and Anglo-Saxon Roots

Many English words include a root that came from Latin, Greek, or Anglo-Saxon. You have probably come across them many times in your studies of different content areas. If you know the meanings of these roots, you can often figure out the meaning of an unfamiliar word.

Work with a partner to learn the meanings of some Latin, Greek, and Anglo-Saxon roots. Then use what you know about the meanings of the roots to figure out these words.

| equivalent | | landmark | | metamorphosis |

Once you know the meaning of these roots, you should be able to recognize them by sight. This will help you to recognize whole words by sight rather than having to decode them. You will find that words used in classroom materials are based on these roots. For example, *credit* and *audio* are words you should know by sight. What other words can you think of using the roots on the right?

Put the Strategy to Use

When you come to a word you don't know, try this strategy to figure out its meaning:

1. Look for a Latin, Greek, or Anglo-Saxon root in the word.
2. Identify the other part or parts of the word.
3. Figure out how the root you know fits with the other part or parts.
4. Take a guess at the word's meaning.

TRY IT▶ Read the following passage. Use the strategy described above to write the meaning of the words printed in blue.

▶ A **politician** visited our government class today. She explained how our government is based on the **democracy** of Ancient Greece. I thought that her ideas were **credible** and truthful. She took questions from the **audience** after her talk, and we were all **satisfied** by her wisdom.

Greek Root	Meaning
dem	people
ethn	nation
morph	form
polit	city, state

Latin Root	Meaning
aud	to hear
cred	belief, trust
equi	equal
sat	to please

Anglo-Saxon Root	Meaning
mark	boundary, sign
reck	care, regard
tru	faithful
wit/wis	know

◀ **Reading Handbook,** page 733

EQ ## How Do the Media Shape the Way People Think?
Consider the ways media shape our worldview.

Make a Connection

Anticipation Guide Talk with a small group about each of these statements. Explain your opinions with examples from your own life.

ANTICIPATION GUIDE

	Agree or Disagree
1. Watching a lot of TV can affect the way a person thinks.	_____
2. TV shows do a good job of showing people from different ethnic groups.	_____
3. Some TV shows show races in negative and insulting ways.	_____

Learn Key Vocabulary

Study the Words Pronounce each word and learn its meaning. You may also want to look up the definition in the Glossary.

● Academic Vocabulary

Key Words	Examples
● **alternative** (awl-**tur**-nu-tiv) *adjective* ▶ page 550	An **alternative** choice offers something that is different from what is usual or expected. The **alternative** movie was created and filmed in a unique way.
● **expand** (ik-**spand**) *verb* ▶ page 551	When something **expands**, it increases or grows larger in some way. Our group will **expand** if more members join. *Antonym:* contract
influence (**in**-flū-uns) *verb* ▶ pages 547, 553, 557	When you **influence** a person, you affect him or her in some way. Some people believe that violence on TV can **influence** teens in harmful ways.
● **media** (**mē**-dē-u) *noun* ▶ pages 546, 551, 553, 557	The **media** are all the different ways people use to communicate, inform, and entertain. Newspapers, radio, and TV are mass **media** that provide news and entertainment to many people.
minority (mu-**nor**-u-tē) *noun; adjective* ▶ pages 547, 551, 557	A **minority** is a group that has fewer members than most of the people. [*noun*] Many **minority** groups feel they are treated unfairly by groups with more people. [*adjective*] *Antonym:* majority
racism (**rā**-si-zum) *noun* ▶ page 551	**Racism** is the belief that some races, or ethnic groups, are better than others. The man shows **racism** when he judges others by their skin color.
stereotype (**ster**-ē-u-tīp) *noun* ▶ pages 546, 551, 559	A **stereotype** is an idea people have about an entire group of people. People say that all teens are lazy and rude, but that **stereotype** doesn't fit me.
token (**tō**-kun) *adjective* ▶ pages 553, 556, 559	A **token** is one person or thing that is included to supposedly represent a larger group. A **token** female on the all-male team was supposed to show that the group included both sexes.

Practice the Words Work with a partner to write four sentences. Use at least two Key Vocabulary words in each sentence.

Example: <u>Racism</u> treats people in <u>minority</u> groups differently than others.

BEFORE READING A Long Way to Go: Minorities and the Media

essay by Carlos Cortés

Reading Strategies

· Plan and Monitor
· Determine Importance
· Make Inferences
· Ask Questions
· Make Connections
▶ Synthesize
· Visualize

Evaluate Evidence

Most persuasive writers depend on **evidence** to support their claims. They include facts, specific examples, data, and statistics that prove their point. As a reader, you must determine whether the evidence you read is effective and convincing. To do this, ask:

- Is the evidence relevant to the topic?
- Is the evidence sufficient to support the author's beliefs and viewpoints?
- Is the evidence accurate and from a reliable, or trustworthy, source?

Look Into the Text

The writer uses sufficient examples to show his point.

Minorities have traditionally had only a small presence in the media. The national popularity of Bryant Gumbel, Connie Chung, and Geraldo Rivera on television is very recent. While these breakthroughs are certainly welcome, progress is slow. For example, only about 40 percent of the nation's 1,600 daily newspapers have *any* minorities as editors.

Reliable, accurate statistics support his position.

Focus Strategy ▶ Synthesize

It can be hard to understand a topic when you have only what one writer says. In these cases, it helps to see how the topic is treated by another writer. When comparing the texts, look for the similarities and differences, and then combine the ideas that fit together. You'll complete the comparison after you read the next selection, "Reza: Warrior of Peace."

Focus Strategy

HOW TO COMPARE OPINIONS

1. **Record Ideas** As you read, begin a **Perspectives Chart** for each important claim. Add the first author's opinions.

2. **Add Texts** Later you will read another selection about the same topic.

3. **Compare** Determine how the claims are alike and different. Then combine the ideas.

4. **Read On** As you continue to read the selection, add more entries for important claims.

Perspectives Chart

"A Long Way to Go" says:	The media should show more minorities.
"Reza: Warrior of Peace" says:	
My experience says:	
My new idea:	

On-Demand Television

Imagine that your favorite TV show is on tonight, but you've got other plans. How can you be in two places at once? A few years ago, your only option would have been to videotape the show so you could watch it later, if you had the equipment to do it. While that's still possible, today there are more TV viewing options than ever.

The hottest trend is downloading or streaming TV shows over the Internet, using services that provide on-demand TV. For a couple of dollars, viewers can own a TV program soon after it is aired and watch it when and where they want.

You might think that this would be a problem for television networks, but that's not what experts say. According to most estimates, the current trend in on-demand TV will continue to grow and will allow the networks to make even more money than traditional advertising does.

In addition, experts believe that on-demand TV will give viewers more options, since networks can produce shows only for on-demand audiences. They predict that viewers will be willing to pay a "subscription fee" for their favorite shows, in the same way that readers can subscribe to their favorite magazines and newspapers.

So if you have plans for the evening, don't worry. Modern technology is developing more and more options for you to see your favorite show wherever and whenever you want it. The latest episode is just a click away.

myNGconnect.com

🌐 Consult websites about media awareness.
🌐 Read more about the future of TV.

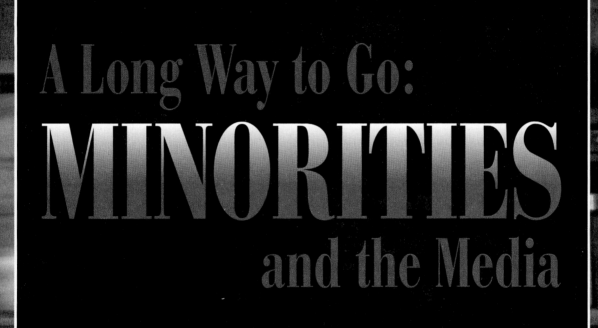

A Long Way to Go:
MINORITIES
and the Media

by Carlos Cortés

Teaching **Stereotypes**

In one episode of *The $25,000 Pyramid*, a remarkable **exchange** occurred. In this TV game show, a word appears on a screen in front of one contestant. He then gives clues to try to get his partner to identify the correct word.

On that special day, the word "gangs" came up on the clue-giver's screen. Without hesitation, he **fired out** the first thing that came to his mind: "They have lots of these in East L.A." (a heavily Mexican American area of Los Angeles). His partner immediately answered, "gangs."

Under pressure, two strangers had linked "East L.A." with "gangs." Why? What force could have brought these two strangers to the same idea?

The answer is obvious—the mass **media**. The entertainment media have a fascination with Latino gangs. The news media also like to show them often. At the same time, the entertainment media rarely show other Latino characters. And the news media rarely show other Hispanic topics, except for such "problem" issues as immigration and language. The result has been **a Latino public image**—better yet, a **stereotype**—in which gangs are an important part. **1**

First, both the news and the entertainment media "teach" the public about minorities and other groups in society, such as women and the elderly. Second, mass media have a powerful educational impact on

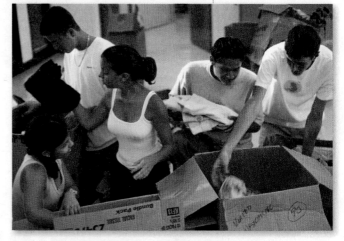

Teen volunteers sort donated clothes at a community center in Miami Beach, Florida.

1 Compare Opinions
How do you think the audience is "taught," or influenced, by this? What claim about the mass media would benefit from being compared with other claims?

Key Vocabulary
- **media** *n.*, ways people communicate, inform, and entertain; mass media reaches many people at once
- **stereotype** *n.*, an idea people have about an entire group of people

In Other Words

exchange conversation
fired out quickly said
a Latino public image the way many people see Latinos

people who have little or no direct contact with the groups being shown. This example is important for **minority** and other **ethnic groups.**

Minorities have long recognized the media's power to **influence** their lives. And they have struggled to achieve greater influence over **their own media destinies**.

That's why Asian Americans protested against Chinatown-bashing movies. That's why black actors have protested against the lack of good black film roles. That's why Native Americans have started their own newspapers throughout the country. **2**

Minorities realize that the media influence not only how others view them, but even how they view themselves. So they have long attempted to **seek better balance** in news coverage of minorities. They want to improve the treatment of minorities by the media.

2 Access Vocabulary
How do the examples in this paragraph help you understand what the word *protested* means?

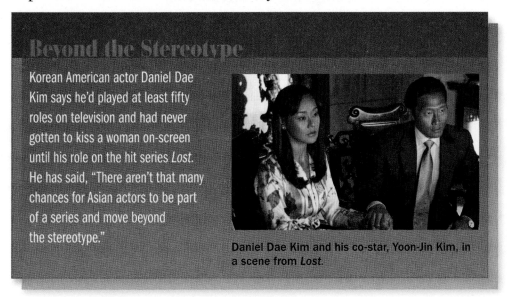

Beyond the Stereotype

Korean American actor Daniel Dae Kim says he'd played at least fifty roles on television and had never gotten to kiss a woman on-screen until his role on the hit series *Lost*. He has said, "There aren't that many chances for Asian actors to be part of a series and move beyond the stereotype."

Daniel Dae Kim and his co-star, Yoon-Jin Kim, in a scene from *Lost*.

Likewise, they have called for the media presentation of better minority role models—in news, in entertainment, even in advertising.

Monitor Comprehension

Summarize
How does the author feel about the media's treatment of minorities?

Key Vocabulary
minority *adj.*, a group that has fewer members than most of the people
influence *v.*, to affect in some way

In Other Words
ethnic groups people from the same race or cultural background
their own media destinies the way they are shown by the media
seek better balance be shown equally and fairly

This would **set standards** for minority people and reduce the negative stereotypes in the media. ▣

Decision Makers

Minorities have traditionally had only a small **presence** in the media. The national popularity of **Bryant Gumbel, Connie Chung, and Geraldo Rivera** on television is very recent. While these **breakthroughs** are certainly welcome, progress is slow. For example, only about 40 percent of the nation's 1,600 daily newspapers have *any* minorities as editors.

In the entertainment media, the successes of such stars as Bill Cosby, Oprah Winfrey, and Edward James Olmos are **cause for satisfaction**. But it still must be remembered that in six decades of Academy Awards, only nine blacks (Hattie McDaniel, Sidney Poitier, Louis Gossett, Jr.,

3 Evidence
Are the photos, captions, and quotations on pages 546 and 547 reliable evidence? Do they sufficiently support the writer's opinions? Explain.

Minorities Employed by Newspapers

Year	Total Newsroom Workforce*	Minority Newsroom Workforce*	Percent of Minority Employees	Total U.S. Population**	Minority U.S. Population**	Percent of Minority Residents
1980	47,000	2,300	4.89	226,545,805	38,174,183	16.9
1990	56,000	4,500	7.86	248,708,873	49,023,803	19.7
2000	56,200	6,700	11.85	281,421,906	69,961,280	24.9

Sources: * American Society of Newspaper Editors, 2004
**U.S. Census Bureau, 2000

▲ **Interpret the Chart** How does the percentage of minorities in the U.S. population compare to the percentage in the newsroom? How did these numbers change between 1980 and 2000?

In Other Words

set standards provide positive role models
presence role, part
Bryant Gumbel, Connie Chung, and Geraldo Rivera a few minority news reporters
breakthroughs important advances

cause for satisfaction reason to be pleased
workforce employees

Denzel Washington, Whoopi Goldberg, Cuba Gooding, Jr., Halle Berry, Morgan Freeman, and Jamie Foxx), three Asians (Miyoshi Umeki, Dr. Haing S. Ngor, and Ben Kingsley, who is English of half-Indian ancestry), three Puerto Ricans (José Ferrer, Rita Moreno, and Benicio Del Toro), and one Chicano (the half-Irish, half-Mexican Anthony Quinn) have won Oscars for acting—Quinn and Washington twice. That makes an average of just over two per decade. **4**

4 Evidence
Why does the author include specific information about minority actors who have won Oscars?

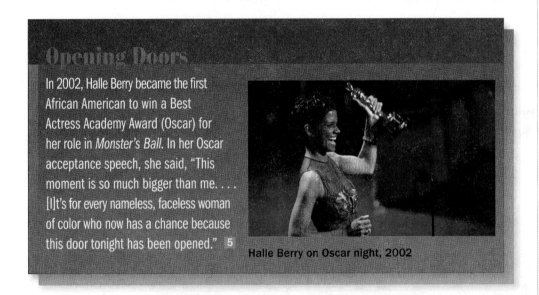

Opening Doors

In 2002, Halle Berry became the first African American to win a Best Actress Academy Award (Oscar) for her role in *Monster's Ball*. In her Oscar acceptance speech, she said, "This moment is so much bigger than me. . . . [I]t's for every nameless, faceless woman of color who now has a chance because this door tonight has been opened." **5**

Halle Berry on Oscar night, 2002

5 Compare Opinions
What do the quotations by Halle Berry and Daniel Dae Kim (on page 547) show about minorities in the media?

But the presence of minority news people, **television personalities**, and movie stars in the media is still relatively small. **Gaining admission into** the media has not been easy.

And once inside the door, problems continue. Minority journalists often have to balance their commitment to provide better **coverage** of minorities against their fears of failure. Minority actors are caught between needing to find roles and seeing that many of these roles may add to negative stereotyping.

In Other Words
television personalities TV actors and talk show hosts
Gaining admission into Getting jobs in
coverage representation

Monitor Comprehension

Explain
How does the author prove that progress for minorities in the media has been slow?

Image Making

This is what comes **with the absence of** power. For this reason, some minority people have formed their own media. In this way, they **select their own themes**, express their own views, and influence their own public images. They have established their own newspapers and magazines, set up their own radio and television stations, and created their own film production companies. Some have even formed their own advertising agencies to help companies reach **a "minority market."** 6

As a result, magazines now range from *Ebony* and *Essence* to *Nuestro* and *Hispanic Business*, from *China Spring* to the American Indian *Talking Leaf.* Many television and radio stations now provide programming in languages from Spanish to Korean. Ethnic people have been making alternative movies.

But the road has not been easy. Most minority filmmaking does not have the money to create high quality movies. Some minority

6 **Evidence**
What examples does the author give of how "minority people have formed their own media"? Explain whether these examples are reliable enough to persuade you to believe the author's opinions.

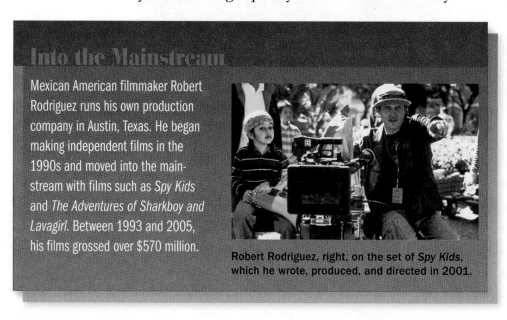

Into the Mainstream

Mexican American filmmaker Robert Rodriguez runs his own production company in Austin, Texas. He began making independent films in the 1990s and moved into the mainstream with films such as *Spy Kids* and *The Adventures of Sharkboy and Lavagirl.* Between 1993 and 2005, his films grossed over $570 million.

Robert Rodriguez, right, on the set of *Spy Kids*, which he wrote, produced, and directed in 2001.

Key Vocabulary
- **alternative** *adj.*, offering a choice that is different from what is usual or expected

In Other Words
with the absence of when you don't have
select their own themes choose what messages they want to send
a "minority market" customers who are minorities

newspapers and magazines do make money, but they do not always last long. Radio and television stations may **broadcast** in many languages, but ownership often does not rest in minority hands.

Minorities have long been aware of the influence of the mass media on their lives and they have struggled to increase their own impact on the media. The results have often been frustrating and depressing.

But there have been victories and successes. With increasing media experience, minorities are determined to **expand** their media influence, just as they are expanding their presence in our **multiethnic society**. ❖

ANALYZE A Long Way to Go

1. **Explain** What are some ways that **minority** groups have increased their influence on the **media**? Based on the evidence provided in the text, does the writer believe this is enough?

2. **Vocabulary** According to Carlos Cortés, how do the media create **stereotypes** that encourage **racism** and **influence** the way people see ethnic groups?

3. **Evaluate Evidence** Choose a key fact from the essay that shows how the influence of minorities in the media is **expanding**. Explain how it supports Cortés's opinions.

4. **Focus Strategy Synthesize** How do the writer's opinions compare with your own opinions and experience with TV and the media? Explain.

⮐ Return to the Text
Reread and Rewrite How far do minorities in the media need to go in order to present themselves without stereotype? Write an editorial expressing your opinion. Reread the selection for evidence to support your claims.

Key Vocabulary
- **expand** *v.*, to increase or get larger
  racism *n.*, the belief that some groups of people are better than others

In Other Words
broadcast be shown
multiethnic society country that is made up of people from many different cultural and racial backgrounds

BEFORE READING Reza: Warrior of Peace

photo-essay by Amy Ostenso

Reading Strategies

· Plan and Monitor
· Determine Importance
· Make Inferences
· Ask Questions
· Make Connections
▶ **Synthesize**
· Visualize

Evaluate Arguments

The goal of persuasive writing is to convince readers that a claim is valid, or true. To do this, persuasive writers must provide **reasons** that explain how their evidence connects with and supports their claim.

Good persuasive writers also anticipate **counterclaims**, or what someone who disagrees might say, and provide a **response** that explains why their claim is better.

Look Into the Text

The writer states a counterclaim and then provides a response to support her position.

> Photographs are just pretty pictures, right? Not always! Photographs have the power to change the way people see the world.
>
> Photojournalist Reza Deghati has been using the power of photography to change people's minds for 40 years. Reza captures images that portray suffering and injustice and show people the whole truth about the events of our world. In this way, his images influence the way people see the world and move them to seek solutions to the world's problems. Reza felt compelled to pursue this line of work because, he says, "As a witness, I could make a difference."

The writer gives a reason and a quote to support her claim.

Focus Strategy ▶ Synthesize

The author of "A Long Way to Go" presents his opinions about the way television and movies influence the way people think. The author of "Reza: Warrior of Peace" shares her opinions about another kind of media—photography—and how it can shape people's worldview. Compare the authors' opinions and **synthesize** the information to draw conclusions about the topic.

HOW TO COMPARE OPINIONS

Focus Strategy

1. Review the **Perspectives Chart** you began on page 543. Add the important claims from the second selection to the chart.

2. Find similarities and differences in the two authors' opinions.

3. Combine what you've read with what you know. Then combine your ideas into new opinions about the topic.

Perspectives Chart

"A Long Way to Go" says:	The media shapes the way people think about minorities.
"Reza: Warrior of Peace" says:	
My experience says:	
My new idea:	

Connect Across Texts

"A Long Way to Go" argues that the **media** have a negative effect on people's perception by casting minorities only in **token** roles. This photo-essay shows how photography can change people's minds.

Reza: WARRIOR OF PEACE

by AMY OSTENSO

Photographs are just pretty pictures, right? Not always! Photographs have the power to change the way people see the world.

Photojournalist Reza Deghati has been using the power of photography to change people's minds for 40 years. Reza captures images that portray suffering and injustice and show people the whole truth about the events of our world. In this way, his images **influence** the way people see the world and move them to seek solutions to the world's problems. **1** Reza felt compelled to pursue this line of work because, he says, "As a **witness**, I could make a difference."

1 Compare Opinions What claim does the author make about how photography can shape people's worldview? How does it compare to Carlos Cortés's claim about media in "A Long Way to Go"?

April 1983, Afghanistan. An old man sitting on a bench reads the Koran near the Pakistani border. He and his family are refugees fleeing the Soviet invasion.

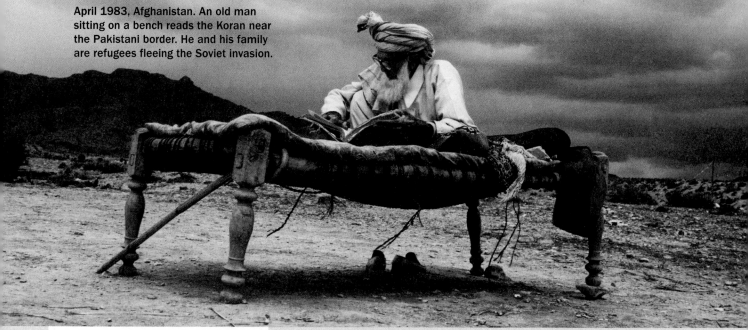

Key Vocabulary
- **media** *n.*, ways people communicate
- **token** *adj.*, only symbolic
- **influence** *v.*, to affect

In Other Words
Photojournalist A person who takes photographs in order to tell about events
witness person who sees an event

As a student in the 1970s, Reza began to photograph the political struggles in Iran, his native country. He used only his first name to remain anonymous. The Iranian government felt threatened by the images he displayed and felt that the photos could jeopardize their power. They arrested him and sent him to prison. Then, in 1981, Reza was **exiled from** his home country because of his photography. 2

عکسبرداری ممنوع

PHOTOGRAPHY PROHIBITED

A sign prohibiting photography

2 **Argument**
What evidence does the author give to support her claim?

▽ **Critical Viewing: Effect**
Why would this photograph be threatening to the government?

1980, Banneh, Kurdistan, Iran. Following a bombing by the Iranian army, a family learns of the death of their nine-year-old son, Payman, and his twelve-year-old sister.

In Other Words
exiled from forced to leave and never return to

2010–2011, Luxembourg Metro Station, Paris, France. This exhibition presents the work of Reza and his son Delazad. It is an invitation to think about the importance of education and commitment in a changing society.

Now Reza takes his camera around the world to **document** and report the horrors of war and disaster by capturing the suffering of the people. One place he returns to again and again is Afghanistan.

In 1991, a United Nations official told Reza, "Your photographs are the reason why we're so drawn to Afghanistan." Reza's images portray the whole story of events in Afghanistan. They show people's joys and the sorrows, not just events from the latest news headlines. Because of this, the photos help the viewer to connect with and to show care towards the people there. 3

3 Argument
The author says that "Reza's images portray the whole story of events in Afghanistan." How does she support the argument?

In Other Words
document make a record of

But Reza's influence doesn't stop with his own photos. He **founded an NGO** called *Aina* (Mirror), enabling the women and children of Afghanistan to tell their own stories in photographs and other visual media. Giving these people their own voice **empowers** them to join the fight for equality, freedom, and peace. ▪4

One day an Aina photographer may change the world through her photos, just as Reza has done with his images. ❖

2007, Kabul, Afghanistan. Camerawoman Mehria Azizi was trained by the NGO Ainaworld, founded by Reza in 2001. Azizi is also a camera crew member of the film "Afghanistan Unveiled," which was nominated for an Emmy Award in 2005.

4 Argument
What reason does the author give to support the claim that "Reza's influence doesn't stop with his own photos"?

ANALYZE Reza: Warrior of Peace

1. **Explain** What is the author's opinion about Reza's photographs? Cite evidence from the photo-essay to support your response.

2. **Vocabulary** Are Reza's photographs token representations? Why or why not?

3. **Evaluate Arguments** What reasons does the author give to support her claim that photographs can be powerful weapons?

4. **Focus Strategy Synthesize** With a partner, review the **Perspectives Chart** you began on page 543 and added to with notes about this selection. Discuss which author influenced your ideas about the topic more.

Return to the Text
Reread and Rewrite How does Reza's photography influence people? Write an email to Reza to tell him what impact his photography has. Include text evidence.

In Other Words
founded an NGO began a non-governmental organization or group
empowers gives power to

EQ ## How Do the Media Shape the Way People Think?

Critical Thinking

EQ 1. **Analyze** Review the **Anticipation Guide** you completed on page 542. Explain whether and how the two selections **influenced** the way you look at the statements now.

2. **Interpret** What does Carlos Cortés mean on page 549 when he says that, for **minorities**, "gaining admission into the **media** has not been easy"? How would author Amy Ostenso reply to this idea?

3. **Compare** Study the facts that both writers use to support their claims. What facts do you find the most persuasive? Explain.

4. **Assess** Each author has an idea about how to use media to shape the way people think. Summarize each opinion in your own words. Then explain whether you think their ideas would work.

EQ 5. **Synthesize** How do the media shape the way people think? Use examples from both selections to support your statement.

Write About Literature

Opinion Statement Why should people care about the way different people are represented in the media? Consider examples from both texts in developing your response. Use the chart below to organize your writing. Then write an opinion that includes at least two of your reasons for support.

Reasons	Examples from Texts
1.	
2.	

Key Vocabulary Review

Oral Review Work with a partner. Use these words to complete the paragraph.

alternative	media	stereotypes
expand	minority	token
influence	racism	

Television is one example of how the __(1)__ can __(2)__, or affect, people in positive and negative ways. For this reason, __(3)__ groups, who have fewer members than most of the population, are worried about their image on TV. They complain when one __(4)__ character is added to a show to represent their entire race. They also object to __(5)__ about their entire ethnic group. They say that it is __(6)__ to show that some people are better or worse than others. Because of this, many groups are creating their own __(7)__ shows that are different from other shows. In this way, the number of ethnic groups on TV can __(8)__ and grow in positive ways.

Writing Application Think of a TV program that presents minority groups well. Describe the strong points of the program in a paragraph. Use at least three Key Vocabulary words.

Read with Ease: Intonation

Assess your reading fluency with the passage in the Reading Handbook, p. 767. Then complete the self-check below.

1. I did/did not express feelings as I read.

2. My words correct per minute: _____.

INTEGRATE THE LANGUAGE ARTS

Use Compound Sentences

A **clause** is a group of words with a **subject** and a **verb**. Some clauses are complete sentences.

People **have** different roles on TV.

A **compound sentence** has two clauses that are complete sentences joined by a **conjunction**. The words **and**, **but**, and **or** are conjunctions. Use a comma (,) before the conjunction.

- Use **and** to join ideas that are alike.

  Actors are on TV, **and** some are famous.

- Use **but** to join ideas that are different.

  Latino actors have roles on TV, **but** the characters are often criminals.

- Use **or** to show a choice between two ideas.

  Is this harmful, **or** does it have no effect?

Oral Practice (1–5) With a partner, say five sentences about the media. Take turns adding **and**, **but**, or **or** and another clause to make a compound sentence.

Written Practice (6–10) Rewrite the paragraph to create four compound sentences. Use conjunctions. Add another compound sentence.

> Minority television roles have changed. Roles did not change until recently. Minorities need personal success. They need to avoid negative stereotyping. Minority media allows people more choices. Minorities can also develop their own public images. Minority filmmaking offers alternative movies. Some films do not make money.

Evaluate

Group Talk In the selections you read, the writers expressed opinions about how the **media influence** people. Which argument do you think is strongest? Why?

Persuasive Text Structures

Persuasive writing is often organized into **text structures** that make the writer's ideas easy to follow. There are many ways to organize an argument, but here are a few common structures:

- **Strength of Reasons**: Writers give their weakest ideas first and lead up to their strongest reasons at the end, or vice versa.

- **Claim-Counterclaim**: Writers present an opposing claim and explain their reasons against it. They continue until they prove that their own claim is the strongest.

- **Problem/Solution**: Writers present a problem and then explain how their solution is the best way to fix the problem.

To make their arguments as convincing as possible, writers may use several structures at once. With a partner, complete a chart that identifies the persuasive text structures used in the selections. Share your chart with the class and explain how you categorized each selection.

Title	Text Structure		
	Strength of Reasons	Claim-Counterclaim	Problem/Solution
"Reza: Warrior of Peace"	X	X	X

Report on Minorities and the Media

Social Studies: Minorities and the Media Many groups protest that minority characters are not represented well on prime time, or evening, television. Talk with a small group to find out how the media influences your opinions. How do these compare with the opinions in "A Long Way to Go" and "Reza: Warrior of Peace"?

◥ **Language and Learning Handbook**, page 702

Latin and Greek Roots

Many English words come from Latin and Greek, as well as other languages. Root words can help you understand what a word means in English.

ROOT	MEANING	EXAMPLE
flu	to flow	fluent
gram	written	programs
jour	day	journalists
popul	people	popularity
tele	far off, distant	television

Use a word from the chart to complete each sentence.

> Professionals who report the news are called (1). Some reporters write articles for newspapers or magazines. Others appear on (2). Most U.S. cities have news (3) in Spanish and other languages. Those shows are gaining (4) as the nation changes. The reporters must be (5) in those languages.

Organization

When you write, always consider the best way to present and develop your main ideas. For persuasive writing, you can use a text structure to organize your ideas.

To use a **claim-counterclaim** text structure, introduce the topic and present a common argument that others make about it. Explain why the opposing argument doesn't work. Then continue to argue against other viewpoints until you prove that your ideas are the best.

Just OK

> There are many ways to deal with the lack of minority representation on television. I think that television producers should do more to show what our society is really like. Not just a few token characters in minor roles. And not minority actors in stereotypical roles. I'm tired of seeing these sad attempts that are not enough.

Much Better

> There are many ways to deal with the lack of minority representation on television. Some people feel that it's enough to show a few token minority characters. But that doesn't make a cast ethnically diverse. Others think it's enough to cast minority actors in stereotypical roles. But showing people as servants or criminals isn't right. Instead, I think television producers should create multicultural shows that really reflect our society—where different kinds of people live and work together.

Use a text structure from page 558 to develop the paragraph below in a clearer, more organized way.

Just OK

> Television producers need to know that we're interested in seeing higher quality shows. Minorities deserve to have good parts that reflect their importance to our society. Producers think that what they're doing is already enough. We should encourage them to create more multicultural shows. It will give the producers bigger audiences.

◥ **Writing Handbook**, page 784

Debate

Have you ever watched a political program that shows people arguing that their opinion makes more sense than someone else's? A formal, respectful way of arguing your opinion in front of an audience is called a debate. Here is your chance to debate the question, "How much do the media shape our opinions?"

1. Plan the Debate

Prepare teams and topics for the debate.

- Set some rules for making decisions and reaching agreements. Then, assign who will moderate and who will debate. Divide the debaters into two teams.
- Brainstorm with your group about the role of the media in today's society. Create a clear opening statement that includes strong supporting evidence—details based on facts or appropriate appeals to the audience's emotions.
- Think of what the opposing team's opening statement may include, and write responses. Use facts and reliable sources to strengthen your response.

2. Practice Your Debate

Each team should practice arguing its side smoothly.

- Get helpful suggestions about the strength of the supporting details and the delivery from your team members.
- Practice persuasive responses based on what the opposing team might say.
- The debate can follow this order, introduced by the moderator:
  - –opening statement by Team A
  - –response by Team B
  - –opening statement by Team B
  - –response by Team A

> **myNGconnect.com**
> ↘ **Download the rubric.**

3. Hold Your Debate

Keep your debate focused and respectful by doing the following:

- Listen actively. Take notes during the opponent's opening statement to summarize their ideas and prepare your response.
- If you have trouble following along, try to connect the speaker's ideas to the research you conducted, or ask a group member for clarification.
- Speak clearly and with appropriate emotion to make your points.
- Glance at your notes occasionally. Maintain eye contact with your opponent as you speak to show that you are respectful of your opponent's views.

4. Discuss and Rate the Debate

Use the rubric to discuss and rate each team, including your own.

Debate Rubric

Scale	Content of Debate	Team's Preparation	Team's Performance
3 Great	• Had strong arguments supported by clear details • Really influenced my thinking about the issue	• Stayed on the subject • Opening statement was direct and polished	• All arguments were clear, logical and easy to follow • Team members worked well together
2 Good	• Had a few good arguments supported by some details • Made me think about the issue somewhat	• Stayed on the subject most of the time • Opening statement was not very clear	• Arguments were clear most of the time and were usually logical and easy to follow • Team members worked fairly well together
1 Needs Work	• Did not have strong arguments supported by any details • Did not influence my thinking about the issue	• Spoke off the subject most of the time • Opening statement was not clear at all	• Most arguments were hard to understand and were not logical at all • Did not work well together

DO IT ▶ Now that you know how to debate an issue, organize your team and speak in a way that gets people thinking!

📖 Language and Learning Handbook, page 702

What can you do to provide a complete response to your opponent?

EQ How Do the Media Shape the Way People Think?

Discover how the news media affect our understanding of events.

Make a Connection

Interpret the Cartoon The news media surround us. Newspapers, Web sites, TV shows, and even entire television networks are dedicated to bringing you constant information about the day's events. But who creates the news? And how do they influence us? Examine the cartoon. What is the cartoonist saying about news coverage?

Source: ©Mick Stevens/*The New Yorker*

Learn Key Vocabulary

Study the Words Pronounce each word and learn its meaning. You may also want to look up the definitions in the Glossary.

● Academic Vocabulary

Key Words	Examples
● **access** (**ak**-ses) *noun* ▶ pages 566, 573	When you have **access** to something, you are able to get and use it. Our school computer lab gives us **access** to the Internet.
● **bias** (**bī**-us) *noun* ▶ pages 572, 575, 578	You show **bias** when your opinions affect the way you see or present things. The insulting article showed the reporter's **bias** against teens.
deliberate (di-**lib**-u-rut) *adjective* ▶ page 573	Something is **deliberate** if it is planned or done on purpose. We thought she made a mistake, but it was a **deliberate** choice.
● **detect** (di-**tekt**) *verb* ▶ page 575	To **detect** means to discover or notice something that was not clear before. It wasn't easy to **detect** his attitude about the topic because he hid his opinion very well.
distorted (dis-**tor**-tid) *adjective* ▶ page 570	When something is **distorted**, it gives a false or misleading representation of reality. Her **distorted** description of the man made him seem meaner than he really was.
engaged (en-**gājd**) *adjective* ▶ page 567	An **engaged** person is interested and involved with something. She was very **engaged** in our conversation about current events.
● **objectivity** (ub-jek-**tiv**-u-tē) *noun* ▶ pages 575, 578, 579	**Objectivity** is a view or judgment of things that is not influenced by personal opinions. It is difficult for reporters to show **objectivity** when they report on events that they feel strongly about.
● **priority** (prī-**or**-u-tē) *noun* ▶ page 569	When something is a **priority**, it has high importance. One main **priority** of our school newspaper is to report our teams' sports scores.

Practice the Words Use a thesaurus to identify at least one synonym or antonym for each of the Key Vocabulary words. Record these in a **Synonym-Antonym Chart**.

Synonym-Antonym Chart

Word	Synonyms	Antonyms
bias	prejudice, favoritism	fairness, open-mindedness

BEFORE READING **What Is News?**

persuasive text from PBS's *My Journey Home*

Reading Strategies

· Plan and Monitor
· Determine Importance
· Make Inferences
· Ask Questions
· Make Connections
▶ **Synthesize**
· Visualize

Analyze Viewpoint: Tone

Tone is the writer's attitude toward the topic or the reader. A persuasive writer often chooses a tone that will convince the audience to believe the writer's opinions and ideas.

Look Into the Text

The writer states an **opinion** with a clear and logical tone.

> With the pervasiveness of news today, it is important to take a look at how news affects our lives. We have come a long way from the days when the nightly news was reported at 6 p.m. on the "Big 3" broadcast networks.
>
> Today, we have access to news whenever we want—from a variety of 24-hour cable news channels, to "news when you want it" from the Internet, to instant news on one's PDA device. Instant news is just part of our lives.

The writer's **word choice** creates a friendly tone. Words like *we* and *our* include readers and involve them in the topic.

Focus Strategy ▶ Synthesize

When you make a generalization, you gather many pieces of information about the topic and synthesize, or combine, them in a broad statement.

HOW TO FORM GENERALIZATIONS

Focus Strategy

1. Begin a **Generalization Map**. As you read, record clues about the author's tone and purpose for writing. These can include:

   • word choice, details, and images the author uses
   • the way the author organizes his or her argument.

2. After reading, combine all the pieces of information. Form a statement about the author's purpose and tone.

Generalization Map

Clues About Tone	Clues About Purpose
• "the pervasiveness of news today" • "we have come a long way"	• "it is important to take a look at how news affects our lives"

Generalization: The author is writing informally while making a major point about the news.

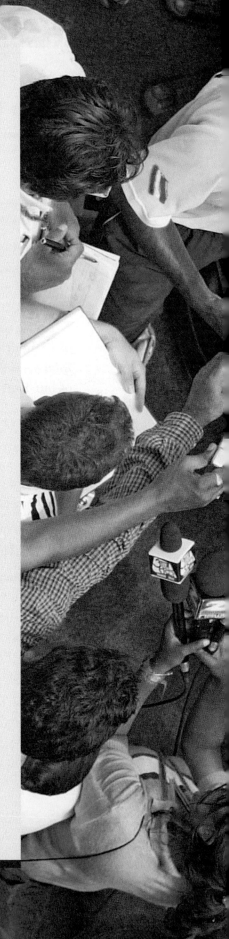

A New Kind of News

USA Today is a daily newspaper that was started in 1982 and now calls itself "America's Newspaper." Its success changed the way newspapers look, as well as what and how much is covered in newspapers.

At first, USA Today was criticized by media critics and the newspaper industry. Its articles were considered too short and general. In-depth reporting was kept to a minimum. Also, articles about celebrities and upbeat topics came first over hard news. An article about a 1982 plane crash in Spain focused on the "miracle" of its 327 survivors, rather than on the 55 passengers who were killed in the crash.

Additionally, the paper's news stories had endless charts and tables. Critics complained that this approach made important issues seem trivial or less signifcant. The paper also published many lists, poll results, and short informational elements called sidebars. USA Today was mockingly compared to fast food, earning the nickname "McPaper."

Today, many of USA Today's techniques have become the standard in the newspaper industry. Poll results have virtually taken over the news. Stories about celebrities have become the focus throughout most of the media. USA Today was one of the first daily newspapers to be divided into four sections: "News," "Life," "Money," and "Sports," with full-color photographs printed on the front pages of each. These practices became popular with USA Today readers and were eventually adopted by other papers.

In the early 1990s, USA Today began emphasizing news content over visual presentation. In 1997, media reporter Ben Bagdikian noted, "It has become a much more serious newspaper. . . . I don't think it's a joke anymore."

—Rob Edelman

myNGconnect.com
- Visit online news sites.
- View current news videos.

What Is NEWS?

from PBS's *My Journey Home*

We depend on the news media to provide news about the world around us. But where does the news come from? And how reliable is the news we read and see every day?

Comprehension Coach

Examining the News

With the **pervasiveness** of news today, it is important to take a look at how news affects our lives. We have come a long way from the days when the nightly news was reported at 6 p.m. on the **"Big 3" broadcast networks**. [1]

Today, we have **access** to news whenever we want—from a variety of 24-hour cable news channels, to "news when you want it" from the Internet, to instant news on one's **PDA device**. Instant news is just part of our lives. [2]

Examining the news is important, not only because of our access to it, but because so many elements, resources, and dollars go toward supporting the news. The news also directly impacts our opinions about others' behavior, celebrity, and **relevance** to our day-to-day activities.

1 Author's Tone
What is the author's attitude toward the news? What words or phrases suggest this tone?

2 Author's Tone
Does the author continue the first paragraph's tone in this paragraph? What clues from the text support your response?

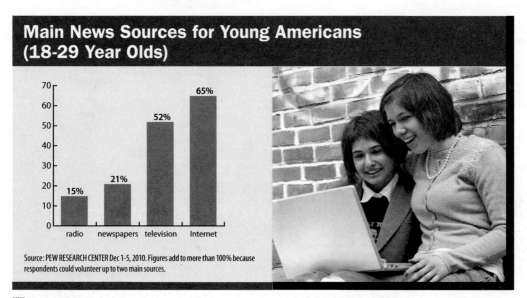

Main News Sources for Young Americans (18-29 Year Olds)

- radio: 15%
- newspapers: 21%
- television: 52%
- Internet: 65%

Source: PEW RESEARCH CENTER Dec 1-5, 2010. Figures add to more than 100% because respondents could volunteer up to two main sources.

Interpret the Data According to the information, where do young Americans choose to get their news?

Key Vocabulary
- **access** *n.,* ability to get and use something

In Other Words

pervasiveness spread
"Big 3" broadcast networks top three television companies
PDA device (personal digital assistant) handheld organizer that can be used for email or the internet
relevance how they apply

Young People's Interest in the News

Research **indicates** that students get most of their political information from watching **David Letterman, Jay Leno,** *The Daily Show,* **MTV**, and from surfing the Web. As recent elections reveal, candidates gain appeal by reaching out to youth through the media. In 1994, former president Bill Clinton made his case to youth on MTV as part of their "Rock the Vote" campaign. And in 2003, California Governor Arnold Schwarzenegger announced his candidacy on Leno's show. ▣

From online chats, instant messaging, blog writing, and market research, candidates know exactly how to find young people on the Internet who are engaged in news and current events activities.

Politicians and advertisers are using the media and **"hipper" methods** to attract young people. **This bears close scrutiny of** how youth react to the media messages they see and hear. ▣

3 Generalizations
Based on what you have read, form a statement about the writer's purpose and tone so far in this selection.

4 Reasons and Evidence
What reasons and evidence does the writer use in this section to support the claim?

The *New* News

Barbara Walters was the first female evening news anchor. Like most traditional news reporters, she described world events from behind a desk.

MTV News Correspondent Gideon Yago reports from places like Iraq, Pakistan, and India. Here he is interviewing Secretary of State Condoleezza Rice at MTV Studios in New York.

Monitor Comprehension

Key Vocabulary
engaged *adj.,* to be interested and involved in something

In Other Words
indicates shows
David Letterman, Jay Leno, *The Daily Show,*
  MTV a mix of talk shows, comedy news shows, and music video stations
"hipper" methods trendy ways
This bears close scrutiny of We should study

Summarize
According to the author, how does the news media reach out to younger viewers?

The Importance of Being Informed

The free reporting on the activities of government and the events of civic life is a major foundation of our democracy—one that our **founding fathers** felt very strongly about.

Thomas Jefferson was the third U.S. president and cowriter of the Constitution. He once said: "Were it left to me to decide whether we should have a government without newspapers, or newspapers without a government, I should not hesitate to **prefer the latter**."

Having informed citizens is as important today as it was in Thomas Jefferson's day. But with all the sources of news and information **at our disposal**, how informed *are* young people? 5

A recent survey compared teens' knowledge of American history to their knowledge of **pop culture**. Look at the percentages of participants who could correctly answer these two questions:

Survey
- What is the name of the town where Abraham Lincoln lived for most of his adult life and that he represented when in Congress? (Springfield) 12.2%
- What is the name of the town where Bart Simpson lives? (Springfield) 74.3%

Source: National Constitution Center

This poll illustrates that when teens feel something is interesting and **relevant** to their lives, they are open and ready to learn.

The stories behind our country's history are interesting and relevant. But the poll shows that the media have a greater impact on young people's lives than historical knowledge about our country. History needs to be presented in an interesting way. And there is still work to be done in order for print and electronic news to be effective. 6

5 **Generalizations**
Form a statement about the author's purpose for quoting Thomas Jefferson in this section.

6 **Author's Tone**
Why does the author include information about the survey? What does this reveal about the author's attitude?

In Other Words
founding fathers country's first leaders
prefer the latter choose the second option
at our disposal available whenever we want it
pop culture life today
relevant important, applies

What Is News?

News is the information about recent events or happenings, especially as reported by newspapers, **periodicals**, radio, or television.

News has two `priorities`: it must be current, and it must mean something to people. A story about the environment and a story about the Super Bowl are both newsworthy, but for different reasons.

On the surface at least, the **objective** of news is to inform the audience. It's the job of all the news media to tell people what's going on in their community—locally, nationally, or globally. In this sense, the news media provide a valuable public service. 7

7 Author's Tone
What does the phrase "valuable public service" suggest about the author's attitude toward the news? What clues show that the author's attitude may change on the next page?

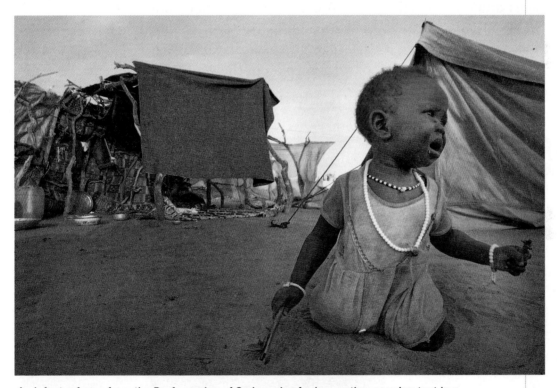

An infant refugee from the Darfur region of Sudan cries for her mother near her tent in a refugee camp, on August 31, 2004, in Oure Cassoni, northeastern Chad.

Key Vocabulary
- **priority** *n.,* something that has high importance

In Other Words
periodicals magazines
objective goal

Monitor Comprehension

Explain
According to the text, what makes the news interesting and important to the public?

What Is News? **569**

Understanding the News

What sorts of stories make it into the news, and why? Who decides which stories get reported, and from what angle? What challenges do reporters face, and how do these challenges affect the news we read and watch?

Media **cater to** their audiences. **8** They report stories they think their consumers want to see, hear, or read about. Most news stories are honest and factual. But the competitive nature of news reporting can also lead to shorter, more exciting stories that grab the audience's attention.

Many stories can then become flashy and sexy. They show shocking images that **depict** crime, death, disaster, violence, or controversy. When taken to these extremes, "news" can become just another type of **sensational entertainment**. Understanding the use of the media then becomes even more important to viewers. Car crashes and shootings are sure-fire attention grabbers. But **a steady exposure to** these images can give us a **distorted** view of what goes on in the world. **9**

8 Language and Tone
What does this sentence show about the author's attitude toward the media? What are other ways to say the same idea?

9 Organization of Ideas
How does the author organize his arguments on this page?

How do stories become today's news?

News editors consider questions like these:

- Will the news have a great *effect* on the reader's life?
- Is it *timely* and *important* enough to follow?
- Will it capture the reader's *interest* and *emotion*?

Then it might just become news!

Key Vocabulary
- **distorted** *adj.,* false or misleading

In Other Words
cater to do things that will appeal to
depict show, present
sensational entertainment entertainment that causes superficial curiosity
a steady exposure to constantly seeing

Millions of people each day flip open a newspaper to get the latest news. Think about ways that news writers and editors design their pages—and their news—to match the way their customers read and buy their newspapers.

Many readers skim the top half of the newspaper before they read or buy.

Editors use space "above the fold" for stories they feel are important—and likely to sell papers. Other stories are placed lower, or further back in the newpaper.

Many readers only skim the titles, or headlines, of stories.

Writers make sure that headlines catch—and hold—readers' interest.

Many readers are attracted to photos and captions.

Editors of many newspapers include large color photos on the front page.

Many readers don't read an article all the way to the end. (Especially if it continues on another page.)

Writers arrange facts in a "pyramid" with important information at the beginning. This gives readers information before they lose interest. It also helps editors cut unimportant information if they need more space.

The Edge Times

Tuesday March 13, 2007

Celebrity Homes Threatened

Landslide warnings issued for the homes of the rich and famous

by Greta Shirley
Edge Staff Writer

MALIBU—High rains in southern California are threatening landslides for some of the most expensive coastline homes in Malibu, the Pacific Palisades, and neighboring Ventura counties.

According to expert Phyllis Jackson, the unusually high amount of rainfall that has fallen during winter and spring has weakened the land around the coast.

"The soil is saturated across the county," Jackson explained. "But the areas along the coast are the most susceptible to landslides due to the high cliffs and the mixture of sand and soil near the foundations of homes."

This dangerous combination usually creates delays along major roadways, such as the Pacific Coast Highway, where lanes are closed each year due to minor landslides.

But for many of the celebrities who have built

see LANDSLIDES, A4

ALSO ON THE EDGE TODAY
• Pasadena City Council Votes to Extend Freeway ......*LOCAL C1*
• Downtown Museums Get a Facelift ....*ARTS G1*
• Weather Chance of rain 40% increasing to 80% in the evening ....*LOCAL C6*

Firefighters battle blaze in early morning hours.

Dramatic Rescue for Family of Four

Crews quickly contain home fire.

by Amy Mortezai
Edge Staff Writer

EAGLE ROCK—Local firefighters rescued a family of four from a home fire last night in the 2300 block of Colorado Boulevard.

According to Fire Department Captian Shane McDowd, fire dispatch was contacted at 2:03 a.m. when a caller reported a blaze in a single-family home. Firefighters reported to the scene within minutes to contain the fire and remove Branson Chan, 43, Melody Chan, 36, and their two children, Emma, 12, and Scott, 6. All were transported to an area hospital for precautionary reasons.

According to McDowd, the fire crew acted with trained precision to prevent the fire from destroying more property and endangering more lives. "This is the kind of [positive] outcome that we spend years training for."

Although causes of the fire are still under investigation, McDowd says that the fire began somewhere in the rear of

see FIREFIGHTERS, C3

Local Underdogs Advance to Basketball Nationals!

Wilson Wildcats defeat Hamilton Eagles 82–77 to advance to the 2007 National playoffs

by Joe Ignacio
Edge Staff Writer

LOS ANGELES—In what could be the upset of the high school basketball season, the Wilson Wildcats defeated the top-ranked Hamilton High Eagles to earn a place at the upcoming national playoffs.

Celebrations could be heard across Los Angeles County as the Wilson Wildcat team advanced to the finals for the first time in the school's history.

"It's a dream come true," said Wilson head coach Lee Buchanan. "My team has overcome a huge number of obstacles this year, including injuries and personal setbacks. So this is more than a sports victory."

Jordan Fray led the game with 22 points.

see WILDCATS, A2

Monitor Comprehension

Explain
How can the public's opinions change the way news is selected and reported?

Hundreds of stories are reported in the news each day. But how much of what we see is an **objective** view of the facts, and how much is based on the stereotypes and bias of others? Study the images to see what these news stories reveal about the news and the culture we live in.

Ernst Van Dyk wins the 2006 Boston Marathon Wheelchair division.

Firefighters battle a 2006 wildfire in California.

Actors Will and Jada Pinkett Smith arrive at the 2006 Academy Awards.

Stereotypes and Bias in the News

The **negative slant of the news** often means that when young people (and members of minority groups) do appear in the head-lines, it is often **in the context of** crime, drugs, violence, death, or some other alarming issue.

By knowing how the news in-dustry works, we can find out how to reach the people who shape the news. Then we can begin to change reporting that reflects stereotyping or bias.

Most journalists try to be objective and factual in reporting events. But all news stories have a point of view. Each story is influenced by the attitudes and beliefs of the reporters or the photographers who select the images. 🔟

Most reporters are adults who see the world from an adult's point of view. They may also as-

🔟 **Author's Tone**
What words and phrases show the author's attitude about stereotypes in the news?

Key Vocabulary
● **bias** *n.,* opinions that affect the way something is seen or presented

In Other Words
objective fair and unprejudiced
negative slant of the news way the news shows more bad stories than good ones
in the context of in a story about

sume that their audiences are mostly adults who share similar views. So, age bias affects how they report an event—from an "adult" point of view.

Not all bias is **deliberate**. But you can become more aware as a news reader or viewer by watching for **journalistic techniques that** allow bias to "creep" into the news. 11 ❖

11 **Generalizations**
Now that you have read the entire text, form a statement about the writer's purpose and tone in this selection. Add the information to your Generalization Map.

ANALYZE What Is News?

1. **Explain** How does the author answer the question in the title, "What is news?"

2. **Vocabulary** What are some ways that we have access to the news today? Include examples from the selection.

3. **Analyze Viewpoint: Tone** Find examples in the selection that show the attitude of the author toward the subject and toward the reader. Record these examples and identify the tone on the chart.

Attitude of Author	Example	Tone
Toward the Subject	"This bears close scrutiny of how youth react to the media messages they see and hear." (p. 567)	Serious
Toward the Reader	"We have come a long way from the days when the nightly news was reported at 6 p.m." (p. 566)	Conversational

4. **Focus Strategy Form Generalizations** Work with one or two other students to record a generalization about the overall tone and purpose of the selection. Compare your answer with that of others in the class.

⤺ Return to the Text
Reread and Write Did the author persuade you to think differently about how the media shape the way people think? Express your opinion in writing and support it with reasons and evidence from the selection.

Key Vocabulary
deliberate *adj.,* planned or done on purpose

In Other Words
journalistic techniques that ways that journalists

BEFORE READING How to Detect Bias in the News

how-to article by Jeffrey Schank

Reading Strategies

· Plan and Monitor
· Determine Importance
· Make Inferences
· Ask Questions
· Make Connections
▶ Synthesize
· Visualize

Analyze Structure: Logical Order

A **how-to article** gives step-by-step instructions that explain how to do something. A how-to article arranges information logically, often in sequential order, or by order of importance. Read the passage below. Remember to monitor your comprehension. *(Which words and structures can I recognize by sight? Which do I have to decode?)*

Look Into the Text

In this how-to article, numbers show the sequence of steps.

How to Detect Bias in the News

3. Consider headlines.

Many people read only the headlines of a news item. Most people scan nearly all the headlines in a newspaper. Headlines are the most-read part of a paper. They also can present carefully hidden bias and prejudices. They can convey excitement where little exists. They can express approval or condemnation....

4. Look at names and titles.

News media often use labels and titles to describe people, places, and events. A person can be called an "ex-convict" or someone who "served time for a minor offense." Whether a person is described as a "terrorist" or a "freedom fighter" is another example of bias.

Steps in a how-to article tell the reader what to do.

Sight words might include *people* or *often*. These are words you recognize by sight and don't have to decode.

Focus Strategy ▶ Synthesize

When you form a generalization, you **synthesize**, or put together, different pieces of evidence. Be sure to look at various elements of a how-to article in order to make a generalization about the purpose of the article or the procedure it describes. **Synthesize** is a word you will see regularly in classroom materials.

HOW TO FORM GENERALIZATIONS

Focus Strategy

1. Consider the title of the article and record this on a **How-To Chart**.

2. As you read, summarize each of the article's steps in your own words.

3. Form a statement that combines the purpose of the article and the procedure it describes.

How-To Chart

How to Detect Bias in the News
1. Consider headlines.
2. Because headlines attract lots of attention, they should be examined critically.
3. Because newspaper photos can make a person look good or bad, they should be examined, too.
Generalization: If you are looking for bias in the news, look at headlines and pay attention to how people are described.

How to Detect Bias in the News

by Jeffrey Schank

Connect Across Texts

*"What Is News?" raises questions about **objectivity** in today's news coverage. This how-to article gives tips on how to **detect** and judge **bias** in the news that comes our way.*

Bias or Objectivity?

At one time or other we all complain about "bias in the news." Despite the journalistic goal of "objectivity," every news story is influenced by the attitudes and background of its interviewers, writers, photographers, and editors. Not all bias is deliberate. But you can watch for journalistic techniques that allow bias to "creep in" to the news.

1. Study selections and omissions.

An editor can express a bias by choosing to use or not to use specific information. These decisions give readers or viewers a different opinion about the events reported. If a few people boo during a speech, the reaction can be described as "remarks greeted by **jeers**." On the other hand, they can be ignored as "a handful of **dissidents**." Bias through omission is difficult to identify. In many cases, it can only be observed by comparing multiple news reports. **1**

1 Logical Order
What does the author emphasize as the first step to detecting bias?

Key Vocabulary
- **objectivity** *n.*, view that is not influenced by opinions
- **detect** *v.*, to discover or notice
- **bias** *n.*, opinions that affect the way you see or present things

In Other Words
journalistic techniques that the ways that journalists
omissions the things that are left out
jeers rude comments
dissidents people who make it known they don't agree with the speaker

When filmmaker Michael Moore gave a **controversial speech** at the 2003 Academy Awards, the news gave very different reports:

• •

> *The London Daily: "He was both applauded and booed by the assembled celebrities."*
>
> *CNN: "The speech won him icy stares and undeniable celebrity . . . "*
>
> *ABC News: "Moore achieved what some may have considered impossible—getting a largely Democratic Hollywood crowd to boo."*
>
> *TV Guide: "That's not what I saw," Moore insisted. "I saw the entire place stand up and applaud . . . "* 2

• •

2. Look at item placement.

Readers of papers judge first-page stories to be more significant than those in the back. Television and radio newscasts run the most important stories first and leave the less significant for later. Where a story is placed influences what a reader or viewer thinks about its importance. 3

3. Consider headlines.

Many people read only the headlines of a news item. Most people **scan** nearly all the headlines in a newspaper. Headlines are the most-read part of a paper. They also can present carefully hidden bias and prejudices. They can **convey excitement where little exists**. They can express approval or **condemnation**.

In 2005, Kellenberg Memorial High School in New York canceled its prom. How do these different headlines show bias?

2 **Generalizations**
How do these examples of selections and omissions add to the author's emphasis in Step 1? Make a note in your How-To Chart.

3 **Logical Order**
According to Step 2, how can the placement of news express bias?

In Other Words
controversial speech speech that made some people upset and others happy
scan quickly look over, skim over
convey excitement where little exists make a story sound exciting even if it isn't
condemnation strong disapproval

4. Look at names and titles.

News media often use labels and titles to describe people, places, and events. A person can be called an "ex-convict" or someone who "served time for **a minor offense**." Whether a person is described as a "terrorist" or a "freedom fighter" is another example of bias.

5. Study photos, camera angles, and captions.

Some pictures **flatter a person**. Others make the person look unpleasant. For example, a paper can choose photos to influence opinion about a candidate for election. The captions newspapers run below photos are also sources of bias. **4**

4 Generalizations
How can photos and captions show different attitudes towards people and events in the news?

▲ **Interpret the Photo** Photos can indicate a newswriter's attitude about a subject. Which photo might go with a positive article about actress Jennifer Lopez? Explain.

In Other Words

Institutes Establishes, Sets up
a minor offense a crime that is not too serious
flatter a person make a person look good

6. Consider sources.

To detect bias, always consider where the news item "comes from."
Is the information from a reporter, an eyewitness, police or fire officials,
executives, or government officials? Each may have a particular bias
that influences the story. Companies often supply **news outlets** with
news releases, photos, or videos. ❖ 5

5 **Logical Order**
Step 6 in the process is to consider sources. Summarize this step in detecting bias in the news. Make a note in your How-To Chart.

ANALYZE How to Detect Bias in the News

1. **Recall and Interpret** According to the article, why is it difficult for news reports to show objectivity in the way they present information?

2. **Vocabulary** What are some examples of bias that can be found in portrayals of people and events in the news?

3. **Analyze Structure: Logical Order** The how-to article includes examples to illustrate each step in the process. Which step does the author think is the most important in teaching you how to recognize bias in the news? Explain.

4. **Focus Strategy Form Generalizations** Return to the **How-To Chart** you began on page 574. Compare your chart with others in a small group. Then work together with a group to form a generalization about the way that how-to articles give information.

⤺ Return to the Text

Reread and Write Why is it important for news reporters to show objectivity? Write a short response that includes strong text evidence from the how-to article.

In Other Words

news outlets newspapers, magazines, and TV stations

news releases statements or stories they want the media to cover

EQ How Do the Media Shape the Way People Think?

Reading

Critical Thinking

EQ 1. Analyze What does each selection say about the way the news media influence the way people think about society?

2. Compare Explain how the writers' tone and organization in each article help them achieve their purposes.

3. Interpret In "What Is News?" the author says that "media cater to their audience." Explain this idea and describe how this applies to both selections. Cite specific evidence from the texts.

4. Evaluate Both articles mention **bias** in the news media. Which selection do you think is more successful in proving the claim that the news is biased? Assess how well the reasons and evidence support this claim.

EQ 5. Speculate Do you think it's possible to present news in a way that shows **objectivity**? Give examples from both texts to support your opinion.

Writing

Write About Literature

Which news medium—newspaper, TV news show, radio broadcast—does the best job of covering the news? Reread both selections. Then find text evidence of advantages and disadvantages of each and write a sentence stating your conclusion.

Medium	Advantages	Disadvantages
Newspaper		
Radio		
Television		

Conclusion I think that _____
because _____ .

Vocabulary

Key Vocabulary Review

Oral Review Work with a partner. Use these words to complete the paragraph.

access	detect	objectivity
bias	distorted	priority
deliberate	engaged	

Most news media try to present information with an __(1)__ that is not influenced by personal opinions. But many people believe that news stories always show a __(2)__ that is affected by the reporter's opinions. Our class is going to study all the news media we have __(3)__ to, such as newspapers and the Internet. We'll examine whether photos and captions are fair, or if they are __(4)__ and misleading. We'll find out if stereotypes are accidental, or if they are __(5)__ and planned by the reporter. These things can be difficult to __(6)__ at first. But this is an important __(7)__ for us to study because we want to be __(8)__ citizens who are interested in world events.

Writing Application Choose a news commentator on TV or radio. Briefly describe his or her reporting of the news. Use at least three Key Vocabulary words.

Fluency

Read with Ease: Phrasing

Assess your reading fluency with the passage in the Reading Handbook, p. 768. Then complete the self-check below.

1. I did/did not pause appropriately for punctuation and phrases.

2. My words correct per minute: _____

Grammar

Use Complex Sentences

A **complex sentence** has one independent clause and at least one dependent clause.

An **independent clause** expresses a complete idea. It can stand alone as a sentence.

   The news is important.

A **dependent clause** depends on the independent clause to make sense. It cannot stand alone.

   Because it affects us.

Subordinating conjunctions like **because**, **although**, **if**, and **since** start a dependent clause. If the dependent clause is at the beginning of the sentence, use a comma after it.

   The news is important because it affects us.

   Because the news affects us, it is important.

Oral Practice (1–5) Use the conjunctions in parentheses to create complex sentences. Be sure to use correct punctuation.

1. Reports can show bias. Most journalists try to report events factually. (although)
2. People enjoy popular culture. They see many reports about celebrities. (because)
3. Viewers can have a distorted image of events. Reports feature sensational stories. (if)
4. Reporters consider their audience. They report on their audience's interests. (because)
5. Current events are posted on the Web. Teens read fewer newspapers. (since)

Written Practice (6–10) Use conjunctions to create two complex sentences. Then add three more.

   We have many sources for news. Many people are uninformed. Young people like news that relates to them. The media should think of ways to interest young people.

Language Development

Justify

Pair Talk State an opinion expressed in this unit. Give two reasons the author gave to justify the opinion.

Media Study

Evaluate Bias in the Media

News Coverage Comparison Newspapers, TV news, and Web sites often cover the same events with different techniques, biases, and purposes. Which version is the most reliable?

Work with a small group to study how different news sources present the same news story.

1. Choose a current event that has received a lot of news coverage. Find examples of how it is presented by different media. At least one of your examples should be an audio and/or visual program.

2. Use the steps in "How to Detect Bias in the News" as a way to compare how the news is presented. Record your ideas in a comparison chart.

News Medium	Examples of Positive Bias	Examples of Negative Bias
Newspaper article		
TV news broadcast		
Internet blog		

3. As a group, discuss your completed chart and evaluate how each source covers the news item. Vote on which news medium is the most reliable, useful, and objective. Give each other feedback on word choice, and decide whether to use formal or informal English when presenting to the class.

📕 **Language and Learning Handbook**, page 702

Denotations and Connotations

The **denotation** of a word is its dictionary meaning. The **connotations** of a word are the various feelings, images, and memories that may be associated with it. For example, the words *home* and *house* have the same denotation but different connotations that arouse certain feelings or emotions in a reader.

Match the words in the two columns that have similar denotations. Consider how the connotations have slightly different meanings.

1. insulted   a. influence
2. manipulate   b. serene
3. calm   c. distorted
4. changed   d. attacked

Write a Response

An essay for a social science class may ask you to explain someone's statement about an issue.

1 **Unpack the Prompt** Read the prompt and underline key words.

> **Writing Prompt**
> CBS President Les Moonves once said, "Anyone who thinks the media [have] nothing to do with [youth violence] is an idiot." Write a short response that gives your opinion about this statement. Support your opinion with reasons and evidence.

2 **Plan Your Response** Use a mind map to organize specific reasons or evidence.

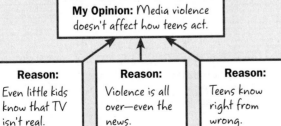

| My Opinion: Media violence doesn't affect how teens act. |

| Reason: Even little kids know that TV isn't real. | Reason: Violence is all over—even the news. | Reason: Teens know right from wrong. |

Oral Report

News Survey Work with a group to find out about news trends in your school.

1 **Brainstorm** Think of questions, such as:
- Where and how often do you check the news?
- How reliable is your news source?

2 **Survey** Talk to students. Record what they say.

3 **Analyze** Study the data and organize the information in a logical way. Create a chart or a graph that represents any trends.

4 **Share** Make a generalization and give an oral report to present your findings. Show your visuals.

🔖 **Language and Learning Handbook**, page 702

3 **Draft** Use an organizer to draft your argument.

> **Response Organizer**
>
> [Name of the person] once said, "[write the original quotation here]." I think the statement means [paraphrase the quotation in your own words].
>
> I [agree/disagree] with this statement for many reasons. First, I believe that [give one reason or piece of evidence]. I also think that [give another reason]. I have also found that [give your strongest reason or more evidence].
>
> In conclusion, I think that [restate your opinion about the quotation in a new way].

4 **Check Your Work** Reread your response. Ask:
- Are my opinions and ideas clear?
- Do I support my opinion with convincing reasons and evidence?
- Do I use complex sentences correctly?

🔖 **Writing Handbook**, page 784

Eyes, Darren Hopes. Collage ©Darren Hopes/
Illustration Works/Corbis.

IS GOOGLE MAKING US STUPID?

by Nicholas Carr

▲ **Critical Viewing: Design** What argument do you think this image makes about people and technology? Support your answer with details from the design.

1   Over the past few years I've had an uncomfortable sense that someone, or something, has been tinkering with my brain, remapping the **neural circuitry**, reprogramming the memory. My mind isn't going—so far as I can tell—but it's changing. I'm not thinking the way I used to think. I can feel it most strongly when I'm reading. Immersing myself in a book or a lengthy article used to be easy. My mind would get caught up in the narrative or the turns of the argument, and I'd spend hours strolling through long stretches of prose. That's rarely the case anymore. Now my concentration often starts to drift after two or three pages. I get **fidgety**, lose **the thread**, begin looking for something else to do. I feel as if I'm always dragging my wayward brain back to the text. The deep reading that used to come naturally has become a struggle.

In Other Words
neural circuitry nerve pathways
fidgety restless
the thread focus

2   I think I know what's going on. For more than a decade now, I've been spending a lot of time online, searching and surfing and sometimes adding to the great databases of the Internet. The Web has been a **godsend** to me as a writer. Research that once required days in the stacks or periodical rooms of libraries can now be done in minutes. A few Google searches, some quick clicks on hyperlinks, and I've got the telltale fact or pithy quote I was after. Even when I'm not working, I'm as likely as not to be foraging in the Web's info-thickets, reading and writing e-mails, scanning headlines and blog posts, watching videos and listening to podcasts, or just tripping from link to link to link. (Unlike footnotes, to which they're sometimes likened, hyperlinks don't merely point to related works; they propel you toward them.)

3   For me, as for others, the Net is becoming a universal medium, the **conduit** for most of the information that flows through my eyes and ears and into my mind. The advantages of having immediate **access** to such an incredibly rich store of information are many, and they've been widely described and duly applauded. "The perfect recall of silicon memory," *Wired's* Clive Thompson has written, "can be an enormous **boon** to thinking." But that boon comes at a price. As the **media** theorist Marshall McLuhan pointed out in the 1960s, **media** are not just passive channels of information. They supply the stuff of thought, but they also shape the process of thought. And what the Net seems to be doing is chipping away my capacity for concentration and contemplation. My mind now expects to take in information the way the Net distributes it: in a swiftly moving stream of particles. Once I was a scuba diver in the sea of words. Now I zip along the surface like a guy on a Jet Ski.

4   I'm not the only one. Some of the bloggers I follow have also begun mentioning the phenomenon. Scott Karp, who writes a blog about online media, recently confessed that he has stopped reading books altogether. "I was a **lit** major in college, and used to be [a] **voracious** book reader," he wrote. "What happened?" He speculates on the answer: "What if I do all my reading on the Web not so much because the way I read has changed, **i.e.** I'm just seeking convenience, but because the way I THINK has changed?"

Key Vocabulary
- **access** *n.*, the ability to get and use something
- **media** *n.*, different ways people use to communicate, inform, and entertain

In Other Words
godsend huge benefit
conduit passageway
boon help, benefit
lit literature
voracious very enthusiastic
i.e. in other words

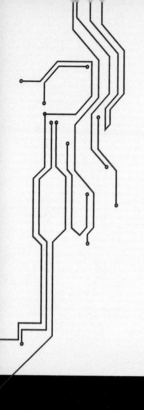

5 **Anecdotes** alone don't prove much. And we still await the long-term **neurological and psychological** experiments that will provide a definitive picture of how Internet use affects **cognition**. But a recently published study of online research habits, conducted by scholars from University College London, suggests that we may well be in the **midst of a sea change** in the way we read and think. The authors of the study report:

6 It is clear that users are not reading online in the traditional sense; indeed there are signs that new forms of "reading" are emerging as users "power browse" horizontally through titles, contents, pages, and abstracts going for quick wins. It almost seems that they go online to avoid reading in the traditional sense.

7 The idea that our minds should operate as high-speed data-processing machines is not only built into the workings of the Internet, it is the network's **reigning** business model as well. The faster we surf across the Web—the more links we click and pages we view—the more opportunities Google and other companies gain to collect information about us and to feed us advertisements. Most of the proprietors of the commercial Internet

> ...users "power browse" horizontally through titles, contents, pages, and abstracts going for quick wins.

have a **financial stake in** collecting the crumbs of data we leave behind as we flit from link to link—the more crumbs, the better. The last thing these companies want is to encourage leisurely reading or slow, concentrated thought. It's in their economic interest to drive us to distraction.

8 Maybe I'm just a **worrywart**.

9 Just as there's a tendency to glorify technological progress, there's a countertendency to expect the worst of every new tool or machine. In Plato's *Phaedrus*, Socrates **bemoaned** the development of writing. He feared that, as

In Other Words

Anecdotes Personal stories
neurological and psychological physical and mental
cognition thought
midst of a sea change middle of a big change

reigning ruling, governing
financial stake in money-related reason for
worrywart person who worries unnecessarily
bemoaned complained about

people came to rely on the written word as a substitute for the knowledge they used to carry inside their heads, they would, in the words of one of the dialogue's characters, "cease to exercise their memory and become forgetful." And because they would be able to "receive a quantity of information without proper instruction," they would "be thought very knowledgeable when they are for the most part quite ignorant." They would be "filled with the conceit of wisdom instead of real wisdom." Socrates wasn't wrong—the new technology did often have the effects he feared—but he was shortsighted. He couldn't foresee the many ways that writing and reading would serve to spread information, spur fresh ideas, and **expand** human knowledge (if not wisdom).

10   Then again, the Net isn't the alphabet, and although it may replace the printing press, it produces something altogether different. The kind of deep reading that a sequence of printed pages promotes is valuable not just for the knowledge we acquire from the author's words but for the intellectual vibrations those words set off within our own minds. In the quiet spaces opened up by the sustained, undistracted reading of a book, or by any other act of contemplation, for that matter, we make our own associations, draw our own inferences and analogies, foster our own ideas. Deep reading, as Maryanne Wolf argues, is indistinguishable from deep thinking.

11   If we lose those quiet spaces, or fill them up with "content," we will **sacrifice** something important not only in our selves but in our culture. ❖

National Public Works Week 2007 Poster ©Gordon Studer.

▶ **Critical Viewing: Theme** How does the artist connect people and machines in this painting? Do you think the artist sees these connections as positive? Why or why not?

In Other Words
sacrifice give up

ARE YOU BUYING IT?

How Do the Media Shape the Way People Think?

myNGconnect.com

Download the rubric.

Present Your Project: Ad Campaign

It's time to present your ad campaign related to the Essential Question for this unit: How Do the Media Shape the Way People Think?

1 Review and Complete Your Plan

Consider these points as you complete your project:

- Who is the target audience for your ad campaign? What would make them want your product?
- How does your ad campaign appeal to your audience?
- What media are you using? Will the media influence your audience?

2 Present Your Ad Campaign

Present your ad campaign. Show examples of your ads, and explain your plan for distributing them to reach your target audience.

3 Evaluate the Ad Campaign

Use the online rubric to evaluate each of the ad campaigns, including your own.

Reflect on Your Reading

Many of the selections in this unit and in the Edge Library showed examples of how the media shape the way people think.

Think back on your reading of the unit selections, including your choice of Edge Library books. Then discuss the following with a partner or in a small group.

Genre Focus Compare and contrast the techniques effective writers use to present their arguments. Write your interpretive response using quotations and rhetorical devices from the selections to illustrate writers' techniques. Give examples, using the selections in this unit.

Focus Strategy Choose two selections in this unit that present different opinions about the same topic. Synthesize the ideas of each selection into a generalization or conclusion that you can share with a friend or family member. Then discuss which opinion you agree with most.

EQ Respond to the Essential Question

Throughout this unit, you have been thinking about how the media shape the way people think. What have *you* decided? Support your response with evidence from your reading, discussions, research, and writing.

Write a Persuasive Essay

Writing Portfolio

How do you get your friends to see the movie you want to see? You persuade them. This project gives you a chance to see how convincing you can be as you write a persuasive essay.

Study Persuasive Essays

A persuasive essay, like other forms of argument, presents a position and anticipates readers' concerns and counterclaims. Unlike other types of argument, however, a persuasive essay uses strong language, emotional appeal, and other persuasive techniques to get the reader to take a particular action.

❶ Connect Writing to Your Life

You probably try to persuade other people almost every day. You might persuade your sister or brother to trade chores with you. You might persuade your classmates to support your campaign for class president. This project will help you build your persuasive powers.

❷ Understand the Form

The **controlling idea** of a persuasive essay is the argument, or **claim**. Usually, the claim is either *for* or *against* some type of issue. The claim is stated in the introduction and is supported by **reasons** and **evidence**. A strong persuasive essay must contain the following parts:

1. Claim	Introduce the issue by giving some background information. Then, state your opinion of the issue.
2. Reasons	List several reasons to support your claim. Why do you think your opinion is correct?
3. Evidence	Give facts, statistics, expert opinions, and examples that illustrate each reason. How do you prove that your reasons are good ones?
4. Counterclaim	Think of what someone on the opposite side of the issue might say. Why isn't your opinion correct? Why aren't your reasons good ones?
5. Rebuttal	Tell why the counterclaim is incorrect. What reasons can you give? What evidence can you show?
6. Call to Action	Restate your claim. What do you want your readers to do?

Now look at how these parts come together.
Read a persuasive essay by a professional writer.

As you read, look for the important parts of a persuasive essay.

Graduated Licenses Save Lives

by Lisa Desai

If you are like many teenagers, you want to get your driver's license on your 16th birthday. However, many states now have laws limiting teens' ability to get full licensing. Most states require a number of supervised driving hours before a teen can take a licensing test. These states also limit the number of passengers teens can have as well as the amount of night driving they can do. The laws are part of a graduated license process, and if your state has them, you should obey them. If it does not, work to get them passed, because they are lifesavers.

The writer gives background information about the **issue** *and clearly states her* **claim**.

Car accidents are the leading cause of death among people ages 16 to 20. These young people have a much higher accident rate than other drivers. Sixteen-year-olds are also twice as likely to die in a car crash as older drivers.

Furthermore, the teen accident rate increases when one or more teens are passengers. The Insurance Institute for Highway Safety has collected the grim facts. Drivers who are 16 and 17 years old have more than three times as many crashes when they drive with three or more other teens than when they drive alone. Drivers ages 16 and 17 are also three times more likely to be involved in a crash at night than are older drivers.

The writer gives solid reasons to support her claim. Notice the use of numbers, or **statistics,** *to back up her argument.*

Critics of graduated licensing argue that limiting the number of teen passengers that teens can have increases the number of cars on the road. The more cars on the road, they feel, the more accidents there will be. However, the studies show that even with more cars on the road, there are fewer teen fatalities when teens drive alone.

The writer states a **counterclaim,** *or different appeal, and gives a rebuttal.*

If you live in one of the many states with teen driving restrictions, be thankful. Follow the laws—they work. If your state does not have restrictions, get together with your friends and family and ask your lawmakers to enact them. Your life may very well depend on it.

At the end, the writer uses different types of sentences, or syntax, to appeal to readers' emotions.

▶**Prompt** Write a persuasive essay on an issue about which you have strong feelings. Be sure to:
- tell what the issue is and state your claim
- give reasons and support them with evidence
- answer at least one opposing claim
- tell readers what action to take

✔ Prewrite

Now that you know the basics of a persuasive essay, you are ready to plan one of your own. A good Writing Plan will help you as you draft your essay.

❶ Choose Your Topic

These activities will help you find and choose your topic:

- Complete this sentence five different ways: "The world (or our school or community) would be a better place if _____."

- Ask friends and family these questions: What is an important issue you care about? What change could you or I make to improve the world? What issues have you heard me talk about lately? After talking with others, write the one question that you want to answer in your essay.

Technology Tip

Look on the Web sites of well-known news organizations or newspapers. This will give you a good idea of current issues that are on the public's mind.

❷ Clarify the Audience, Controlling Idea, and Purpose

Who are your readers? What background do they need to understand your topic? What opinions do they already have? Jot down your ideas.

Then, write your argument, or **controlling idea**. Fit it into one of these sentences: "We should do X" or "We should not do Z."

Finally, think about your purpose. What do you want your audience to believe? What do you want your audience to do? Write down your ideas.

❸ Develop Reasons and Gather Evidence

Your next step is to think of reasons and compile evidence and data to support your claim. Here are some helpful suggestions:

- Brainstorm a list of reasons that support your claim.

- Interview other students to get their opinions and ideas. When students disagree, make careful note of their reasons.

- Research the topic. Note evidence that supports your position. Also note any evidence that goes against your opinion. Be sure to use authoritative sources: for example, books and articles written by experts.

📖 **Language and Learning Handbook**, p. 702

Prewriting Tip

Think about the following questions as you research evidence:

- Who wrote this evidence?
- Will my audience think my sources are reliable?
- Is this information fact or opinion?
- What are some opposing facts or views from experts that I should consider?

4 Organize Your Reasons

Each reason will require one or more paragraphs to present it. Arrange these paragraphs in the order that builds the most convincing argument. Organize your reasons to support your argument. Build up to a strong finish by putting reasons in order of importance. Start with a good reason; then move to a better one. End with your best reason.

5 Finish Your Writing Plan

Choose a graphic organizer, such as a chart, to create a Writing Plan. Remember to organize your reasons from most important to least important.

Writing Plan

Topic	limiting teens' working hours
Audience	my teacher, other students, and parents
Controlling Idea or Claim	Teens should work no more than 10 hours per week during the school year.
Purpose	to persuade students to cut back on excessive working hours
Time Frame	due one week from today
Reason 1 Too much work affects sleep.	**Evidence** Teens only get about 6.8 hours of sleep a night, which leads to harmful side-effects.
Reason 2 Too much work affects grades.	**Evidence** Students who worked more than 15 hours a week showed a decline in grades and test performance.
Counterclaim	Some kids need to work more hours to save for college or help with household expenses.
Rebuttal	Most kids spend their money on nonessential things.
Call to Action	think of school as your main job

Reflect on Your Writing Plan

▶ Will your reasons be persuasive to your audience? Talk them over with a partner.

✓ Write a Draft

Now you are ready to write. Use your Writing Plan as a guide. Spend the most time developing persuasive techniques to convey meaning. You'll have chances to improve your draft. Just keep writing!

❶ Use Persuasive Techniques

In a persuasive essay, you want to get your audience on your side. Rhetorical devices will help you form a convincing argument:

- **Logical Appeal** This technique involves the use of evidence such as facts, statistics, and examples to support your argument. The more exact and related your facts and statistics, the better your viewpoint will be supported.

   According to the National Sleep Foundation, most teens only get about 6.8 hours of sleep per night.

- **Emotional Appeal** This technique involves the use of strong words that appeal to the audience's needs, values, and attitudes.

   Teens are paying a price for all those hours they aren't sleeping, studying, and pursuing hobbies or interests!

- **Ethical Appeal** This technique involves convincing the audience that you are fair, honest, and well-informed about the issue.

   Some teens do need to work a lot of hours to save money for college or to help out with household expenses, but most teens spend their money on nonessentials.

❷ Write a Strong Conclusion

You want your conclusion to be memorable. A good way to end an essay is to quote somebody. The quotation does not have to be from a famous person, but it should relate specifically to the issue.

OK

> Be sensible and limit your job to ten hours a week. Remember—school is the job that will take you somewhere.

Better

> "Teens have to realize their primary job is getting a good education," says Bryna Shore Fraser, associate director of the National Institute for Work and Learning in Washington, D.C. So be sensible and limit your job to ten hours a week. School is the job that will grant you opportunities.

Technology Tip

Save your first draft under two different file names. The second name might simply be "persuasive.essay.2." That way, you have a backup file if you decide you like the first version of a paragraph better.

Drafting Tip

Strengthen your position paper by using transitional words. They help guide readers from idea to idea. Use transitions such as the following:

- *First, in addition, furthermore, in conclusion* to convey ideas in logical order;
- *However, instead, yet* to emphasize a contrast or difference

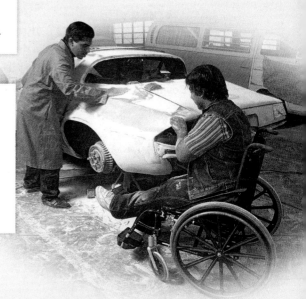

❸ Student Model

Read this draft to see how the student used the Writing Plan to get ideas down on paper. Remember that this first draft does not have to be perfect. Later, you will see how the student fixed the mistakes.

Work—But Not Too Much

Getting a driver's license is one of the best things that happens in high school. So's getting a part-time job. It provides extra pocket money, you know? I think it also teaches responsibility and time and money management. But do you think we pay a price? According to the government, teens ages 15–17 years old work an average of 17 hours a week during school months. This is 7 hours too much. Studies have shown that working more than 10 hours a week has more negative than positive effects.

One aspect of a teen's life affected by excessive work is sleep. The average teen needs a lot of sleep each night, however, according to the National Sleep Foundation most teens only get about 6.8 hours. Teens who work too much have to find time to finish their homework. This causes them to stay up later. A lack of sleep can lead to harmful scenarios.

Grades are also negatively affected by too much work. In 2000, Kusum Singh, an Education professor at Virginia Tech, conducted a study on the effect of part-time work on students' academic achievement. She discovered that students who worked more than 15 hours per week showed a decline in grades and didn't perform as well on standardized tests. She also found that these students were less likely to take challenging courses, such as upper-level Math and Science classes.

Of course, there are those of you who may argue that some teens need to work as many hours as possible to save money for college or to help out with household expenses. This may be true for some; but according to David Walsh, author of *Selling Out America's Children: How America Puts Profits Before Values—and What Parents Can Do*, most teens today spend the money they earn on nonessentials.

"Teens have to realize their primary job is getting a good education," says Bryna Shore Fraser, associate director of the National Institute for Work and Learning in Washington, D.C. So be sensible and limit your job to 10 hours a week. School is the job that will grant you opportunities.

Reflect on Your Draft

▶ Think about the process that you used to write your draft. Which parts of the drafting process did you find most difficult? Can you think of any ways to work more efficiently next time?

Revise Your Draft

Your first draft is done. Now, you need to polish it. Improve the voice and style. Make your writing flow with varied sentence structure and word choice.

Revising Tip

As you revise your essay, think about your purpose. Is it to persuade? Then you want to adopt a persuasive style. Use words like *should* and *must* to sound more convincing.

1 Revise for Voice and Style

When you speak, you have a voice. The same is true when you write. Your **voice** shows your own personality through the following traits:

- your tone
- your word choice
- your sentence structure

Your **tone** shows how you feel about your topic. The tone can be serious, friendly, questioning, and persuasive. In a persuasive essay, you are most likely to use a persuasive tone.

The **word choice** and **sentence structure** you use make up your **style**. Do you use mostly big or little words? Are your sentences long or short? Good writers use a variety of words and sentences to make their writing style more interesting to their audience. They also might adopt a certain style to fit a certain purpose.

Don't worry if you're not sure about your voice and style. It takes practice to develop them. When you look over your draft, see if you notice any patterns in your writing. Is there some word or phrase you keep using? Is there a common sentence structure in your writing? Once you notice these patterns, you can decide if they work with the audience and purpose of your essay.

TRY IT ▶ With a partner, decide how the voice and style of the draft below could be improved.

Student Draft

> Getting a driver's license is one of the best things that happens in high school. So's getting a part-time job. It provides extra pocket money, you know? I think it also teaches responsibility and time and money management. But do you think we pay a price? According to the government, teens ages 15–17 years old work an average of 17 hours a week during school months. This is 7 hours too much. Studies have shown that working more than 10 hours a week has more negative than positive effects.

Now use the rubric to evaluate the voice and style of your own draft. What score do you give your draft and why?

Voice and Style

	Does the writing have a clear voice and is it the best style for the type of writing?	Is the language interesting and are the words and sentences appropriate for the purpose, audience, and type of writing?
4 Wow!	The writing <u>fully</u> engages the reader with its individual voice. The writing style is best for the type of writing.	The words and sentences are interesting and appropriate to the purpose and audience. • The words are precise and engaging. • The sentences are varied and flow together smoothly.
3 Ahh.	<u>Most</u> of the writing engages the reader with an individual voice. The writing style is mostly best for the type of writing.	<u>Most</u> of the words and sentences are interesting and appropriate to the purpose and audience. • Most words are precise and engaging. • Most sentences are varied and flow together.
2 Hmm.	<u>Some</u> of the writing engages the reader, but it has no individual voice and the style is not best for the writing type.	<u>Some</u> of the words and sentences are interesting and appropriate to the purpose and audience. • Some words are precise and engaging. • Some sentences are varied, but the flow could be smoother.
1 Huh?	The writing does <u>not</u> engage the reader.	<u>Few or none</u> of the words and sentences are appropriate to the purpose and audience. • The words are often vague and dull. • The sentences lack variety and do not flow together.

myNGconnect.com
- Rubric: Voice and Style
- Evaluate and practice scoring other student essays.

❷ Revise Your Draft

You have now evaluated the voice and style of your own draft. If you scored
3 or lower, how can you improve your work? Use the checklist below to revise
your draft.

Revision Checklist

Ask Yourself	Check It Out	How to Make It Better
Does the essay sound like me?	If your score is 3 or lower, revise.	☐ Read your essay aloud. Listen for any words that do not sound natural. ☐ Write as you speak.
Does the tone stay the same?	If your score is 3 or lower, revise.	☐ Read your essay aloud. Listen for changes in tone. ☐ Choose new words that make the tone consistent.
Does the style fit the audience?	If your score is 3 or lower, revise.	☐ Look for words that your audience may not relate to. ☐ Be sure sentences are varied.
Do I state my claim clearly, along with background information on the issue?	Read your essay to someone else. See if you provide enough information for your classmate to understand the issue and your argument.	☐ Research more background information, and rewrite your claim statement.
Do I support my claim with enough evidence?	Do you provide at least one type of evidence for each reason?	☐ Research the issue to find more evidence for your reasons.
Do I include at least one counterclaim or different viewpoint and a rebuttal?	Underline parts where you gave the opinion of people who disagree with you. Also underline your response.	☐ Add the missing counterclaim or different viewpoint. ☐ Add the missing rebuttal.
Did I restate the claim and include a call to action?	Read your conclusion. Does it tell the reader to do something?	☐ Add a sentence that tells readers what action to take.

📖 **Writing Handbook**, p. 784

3 Conduct a Peer Conference

It is useful to get a second opinion when you are revising your draft.
Ask a partner to read your draft and look for the following:

- a voice that does not sound real and accurate
- reasons are not precise or relevant to their arguments
- anything that seems to be missing
- any ideas that need more support

Then talk with your partner about the draft. Discuss the items in the Revision
Checklist. Revise your essay based on your partner's comments.

4 Make Revisions

Look at the revisions below and the peer-reviewer conversation on the right.
Notice how the peer reviewer commented and asked questions. Notice how
the writer used the comments and questions to revise.

Revised for Voice and Style

~~Getting a driver's license is one of the best things that happens~~
~~in high school. So's getting a part-time job. It provides extra~~
~~pocket money, you know? I think it also teaches responsibility and~~
~~time and money management. But do you think we pay a price?~~
According to the government, teens ages 15–17 years old work an
average of 17 hours a week during school months. This is 7 hours
too much. Studies have shown that working more than 10 hours a
week has more negative than positive effects.

Aside from getting a driver's license, a part-time job is one of the
most liberating aspects of your high school experience. In addition to the
extra pocket money it provides, a job can teach you responsibility and
time and money management skills. But do you pay a price for all those
hours you aren't sleeping or studying?

Peer Conference

Reviewer's Comment:
Your tone in the first part
of the paragraph is very
informal. It doesn't match
the formal tone at the
end.

Writer's Answer You're
right. I'll rewrite the first
part of the paragraph so it
has a more formal tone.

Reflect on Your Revisions

► Think about the results
of your peer conference.
What did your partner
like and dislike about
your essay?

✒ Edit and Proofread Your Draft

Your revision should now be complete. Read it over one more time to fix any mistakes you might have missed.

❶ Capitalize Specific School Courses

Capitalize the names of courses in school only when they are languages or names of specific courses. Do not capitalize general course names.

Capitalize	Do Not Capitalize
English	art
French	geometry
Biology 101	biology

TRY IT ▶ Copy the sentences. Fix the capitalization errors. Use proofreader's marks.

1. Kusum Singh, an Education professor at Virginia Tech, conducted a study on the effect of part-time work on students' academic achievement.

2. She found that these students were less likely to take challenging courses, such as upper-level Math and Science classes.

❷ Use Semicolons and Commas Correctly

A semicolon (;) is used to join two complete sentences that are related. Often the semicolon comes before the conjunctive adverb *however*. A comma (,) is used with a coordinating conjunction to join two complete sentences. Common coordinating conjunctions are *and*, *or*, and *but*.

Working after school gives me less time to do my homework**;** however, I really enjoy the extra spending money.

Working after school gives me less time to do my homework**, but** I really enjoy the extra spending money.

TRY IT ▶ Copy the sentences. Add or remove commas and semicolons where needed.

1. Teens need a lot of sleep each night, however, most teens only get about 6.8 hours.

2. This may be true for some; but according to David Walsh, most teens today spend the money they earn on nonessentials.

Proofreader's Marks

Use proofreader's marks to correct errors.

Capitalize:
I passed my chemistry 3 midterm and my japanese test.

Do not capitalize:
Have you read your Science assignment yet?

Add a comma or semicolon:
I have a job but I still have no money.

I have a job I still have no money.

Proofreading Tip

If you are unsure of whether to use a semicolon or a comma, look in a style manual for help.

3 Use Precise Language

In a persuasive essay, you want to present a clear point of view and sound convincing. One way to do this is to use precise language. Check each sentence that contains supporting evidence in your essay. Can you:

- substitute a word or phrase with a word or phrase that is more specific?
- replace words like *few*, *many*, and *some* with specific amounts?
- add a word or phrase to provide more information about another word?

TRY IT ▶ Read each sentence. Decide whether it contains precise language. If not, think of ideas about how the sentence could be improved.

> 1. The average teen needs lots of sleep each night.
> 2. A lack of sleep can lead to harmful scenarios.
> 3. Most teens today spend their money on nonessentials.

4 Build Effective Sentences

Sentence combining can add variety to your writing. For instance, you can join two sentences with a subordinating conjunction to form a complex sentence. Make sure you put the conjunction at the beginning of the less important sentence. That way the less important sentence supports the main sentence.

> **Incorrect:** I got a job **because** I have more money.
> **Correct:** I have more money **because** I got a job.

Also check that the structure of the new sentence is parallel. For instance, if you form a compound predicate with two or more ideas in it, make sure they have the same word pattern.

> **Incorrect:** I like **waiting** on tables and **to cook** at the restaurant.
> **Correct:** I like **waiting** on tables and **cooking** at the restaurant.
> **Correct:** I like **to wait** on tables and **to cook** at the restaurant.

TRY IT ▶ Copy each pair of sentences. Combine one pair with a subordinating conjunction and the other pair by creating a compound predicate. Be sure to use the correct sentence structure.

> 1. Teens who work too much have to find time to finish their homework. This causes them to stay up later.
> 2. These teens have to find time for studying. They also have to find time to sleep.

📖 **Writing Handbook**, pp. 819; 821–822

Reflect on Your Corrections

▶ Read over your essay one more time to check for errors in grammar and punctuation. Make a list of your problem areas. You can use it when you edit and proofread in the future.

5 Edited Student Draft

Here's the student's draft, revised and edited. How did the writer improve it?

Work—But Not Too Much

Aside from getting a driver's license, a part-time job is one of the most liberating aspects of your high school experience. In addition to the extra pocket money it provides, a job can teach you responsibility and time and money management skills. But do you pay a price for all those hours you aren't sleeping or studying? According to the U.S. Department of Labor, teens ages 15–17-years-old work an average of 17 hours a week during school months. This is 7 hours too much. Studies have shown that working more than 10 hours a week has more negative than positive effects.

One aspect of a teen's life affected by excessive work is sleep. The average teen needs 8.5–9.5 hours of sleep each night; however, according to the National Sleep Foundation most teens only get about 6.8 hours. Because teens who work too much have to find time to finish their homework, they tend to stay up later. A lack of sleep can lead to depression, mood swings, and carelessness on the job and behind the wheel.

Grades are also negatively affected by too much work. In 2000, Kusum Singh, an education professor at Virginia Tech, conducted a study on the effect of part-time work on students' academic achievement. She discovered that students who worked more than 15 hours per week showed a decline in grades and didn't perform as well on standardized tests. She also found that these students were less likely to take challenging courses, such as upper-level math and science classes.

Of course, there are those of you who may argue that some teens need to work as many hours as possible to save money for college or to help out with household expenses. This may be true for some, but according to David Walsh, author of *Selling Out America's Children: How America Puts Profits Before Values—and What Parents Can Do*, most teens today spend the money they earn on nonessentials such as designer clothing and entertainment.

"Teens have to realize their primary job is getting a good education," says Bryna Shore Fraser, associate director of the National Institute for Work and Learning in Washington, D.C. So be sensible and limit your job to ten hours a week. School is the job that will grant you opportunities.

The writer revised the introduction to improve the tone.

The writer replaced the general word *government* with more **precise language**.

The writer correctly replaced the comma with a **semicolon** to join the two sentences.

The writer joined two sentences with a **subordinating conjunction** and replaced phrases with more **precise language**.

The writer corrected the **capitalization** errors in the names of general school subjects.

The writer correctly replaced the semicolon with a **comma**.

The writer used **precise language** to describe the word *nonessentials*.

✒Publish and Present

You are now ready to publish and present your essay. Print out your essay or write a clean copy by hand. You may also want to present your work in a different way.

Alternative Presentations

Publish Online Reach out to a wider audience. You never know whom you might persuade.

❶ Find a Good Web Site With your teacher's permission, do a search to find a Web site that will be interested in your essay. Look for sites designed for student writing, as well as sites that address your topic.

❷ Edit, Then E-mail Go over your essay one last time. Then submit it, following the directions on the site.

❸ Get Feedback If there is a comment box, ask readers to comment on your essay. Ask them to be specific about what they liked and disliked. Use their suggestions to improve your writing. Don't forget to tell all your friends where they can read your work.

Put on a Debate Debate the subject of your essay in front of an audience. You will need to cover both sides of the issue.

❶ Adapt Your Essay Rewrite it so that two people can argue the points of view you've covered. You will need to reorganize your essay into clear, debatable points. Further develop the objections people might make to your opinion. You will probably need to do some additional research.

❷ Choose Debaters Present your opinions yourself. Ask a classmate to present the opinions of people who disagree with you. You will each need to prepare an opening statement to present your argument. You will also have to prepare a rebuttal to the opposing argument.

❸ Present the Debate Practice debating your topic with the classmate you've chosen. Then debate your topic for your class.

- Take notes while the opposing side is talking so you can address what has been said in your response.
- Speak clearly so the audience and your opponent can understand you.

Refer to the **Listening and Speaking Workshop** on p. 560 for more information about debates.

📖 **Language and Learning Handbook**, p. 702

Publishing Tip

If your teacher has you publish your article on the Internet, format it to make it easy to read on a computer screen. When you write for the Web, you do not indent paragraphs. Instead, you leave a space between them.

Reflect on Your Work

▶ **Ask for and use feedback from your audience and your teacher to evaluate your strengths as a writer.**

- Did your audience come away with a clearer understanding of your opinion?
- Did you get feedback from anywhere else that made you reconsider your opinion?
- What did you learn that you can apply to other writing you do? Set a goal or two for yourself.

☑ **Save a copy of your work in your portfolio.**

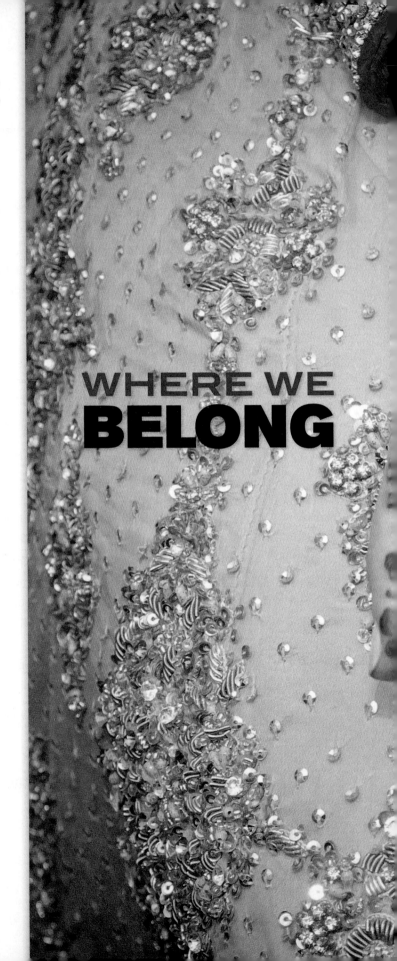

EQ ESSENTIAL QUESTION:

What Holds Us Together? What Keeps Us Apart?

A man is, in the long run, his own circumstances.
—JORGE LUIS BORGES

You cannot shake hands with a fist.
—INDIRA GANDHI

WHERE WE BELONG

Critical Viewing ▶
A temporary henna "tattoo" decorates the hands of a bride at an Indian-Pakistani wedding in New Jersey, United States. What do you think the design represents? What might it suggest about what holds people together?

EQ ESSENTIAL QUESTION:
What Holds Us Together? What Keeps Us Apart?

Study the Images
You have probably heard of the term "melting pot" used to refer to the United States. What does the term mean to you? In what ways is the United States a melting pot of people from all around the world? How else could you describe the combination of cultures?

Sunday 10th, P. J. Crook, 2006. Acrylic on canvas, private collection.

The Museum of Modern Art, Malcah Zeldis, 1973.

Compare and Discuss

1. How do the artists' interpretations of the United States differ? How are they alike? Do the differences between the characters in the illustrations keep them apart or hold them together? Explain.

2. Do the differences between people in your community hurt or strengthen the community? Would it be better to live in a place where people are all the same?

Talk with a group and explain your response to these questions. Give reasons and draw on your experiences and knowledge to support your opinion.

EQ ESSENTIAL QUESTION
In this unit, you will explore the **Essential Question** in class through reading, discussion, research, and writing. Keep thinking about the question outside of school, too.

① Plan a Project

Poetry Anthology

In this unit, you'll be creating a poetry anthology about the Essential Question. Choose a subject and theme connected to the Essential Question and write a poem. Then work with classmates to compile an anthology, or collection, of everyone's work. To get started, review some poetry anthologies. Look for

- how poems are organized in the anthology, such as by poet, subject, time period, or theme
- how poems are placed on the page
- how poems are introduced.

Study Skills Start planning your poetry anthology. Use the forms on myNGconnect.com to plan your time and to prepare the content.

> myNGconnect.com
> ▶ Planning forms
> ▶ Scheduler
> ▶ Book map
> ▶ Imagery graphic organizer
> ▶ Rubric

② Choose More to Read

These readings provide different answers to the Essential Question. Choose a book and online selections to read during the unit.

The Other Side of the Sky
by Farah Ahmedi with Tamim Ansary

Farah Ahmedi had a happy life with her family in Afghanistan. Then war destroyed everything. Searching for a better future, she and her mother moved to the United States. How does she adjust to her new community? What does she have to do to build a new life?

▶ **NONFICTION**

Romiette and Julio
by Sharon M. Draper

Romiette and Julio are from different worlds. She is African American. He is Hispanic. They do not care what other people think. But gang members threaten violence if they do not end their relationship. Are Romiette and Julio strong enough to survive?

▶ **NOVEL**

A Raisin in the Sun
by Lorraine Hansberry

It is Chicago after World War II. Living in a tiny, old apartment and working at jobs they hate, each member of the Younger family dreams of a better future. Then Mama inherits $10,000. Will the money make all of their dreams come true? Or will it tear the Younger family apart?

▶ **DRAMA**

myNGconnect.com

- Read about the experiences of teens who have come to America.
- Use a role-playing game to learn about conflict resolution.
- Learn about ways that you can be active in your community.

Plays are stories brought to life by actors. Read this script.
Bring it to life in your mind as you read.

DEMO TEXT

Found Out

Act 1, Scene 3

SETTING: *Outside Principal DeLuca's office*

RONNIE. I don't like this, Ty. I don't like it at all.

TY. Cut the drama, Ronnie. We're fine.

RONNIE. Fine? For now. But what happens when we walk through that door?

TY. Just be cool. It's probably nothing.

RONNIE. When was the last time a visit to Principal DeLuca was "nothing"?

TY. She doesn't know anything. Trust me.

RONNIE. Trusting you is how I ended up here! [*Mockingly*] "We'll just steal a semester's worth of answer keys…"

TY. First of all, it was one answer key. Second, you agreed that we already knew all the algebra that was going to be on the test, so no harm done, right? Third, how could Ms. Jackson figure it out? She's just a substitute.

RONNIE. Breathing in, breathing out…

MS. JACKSON. [*Appears at the door*] We're ready for you, boys.

[*All enter Principal DeLuca's office*]

PRINCIPAL DELUCA. You boys must like this office. I see you here often enough.

RONNIE. Yes. I mean, no. I mean, sorry.

PRINCIPAL DELUCA. Easy, Ronnie. Ms. Jackson just has a question for you.

MS. JACKSON. Boys, I may be a substitute, but I know talent when I see it.

TY. Talent?

MS. JACKSON. Your work on the last algebra test was outstanding. How would you two like to join the math team?

RONNIE. No! I mean, yes! I mean, Ty?

PRINCIPAL DELUCA. Let me put it this way: I just had a chat with your parents. They thought it sounded like a great idea. A lot better than the alternative. Unless I'm missing something here, it seems you two would be great mathletes. Is there anything else I should know about?

RONNIE. I… I…

TY. Principal DeLuca, Ms. Jackson, I thought you would never ask.

[*Lights down*]

■ Connect Reading to Your Life

Let your imagination go to work on "Found Out." Picture the characters, the setting, and the action. You may want to close your eyes.

- What do you think Ronnie, Ty, Ms. Jackson, and Principal DeLuca look like?
- Where does the action take place? What does the setting look like?
- How do Ms. Jackson and Principal DeLuca act as they speak to Ronnie and Ty?

How did you manage to answer these questions? Not all of the answers were in the text. You used your imagination to bring the scene to life. You staged the **drama** in the theater of your mind.

Focus Strategy ▶ Visualize

Imagine that you are sitting on a bus. The people in the seat behind you are having an argument. You cannot see them, but you can hear them. As you listen to their conversation, you begin to form ideas about them. In your mind, you create the following:

- what they look like
- their age
- how they feel toward each other

You have no information except what they are saying. Your imagination creates a **mental** picture, or **image**, of the people. Reading drama requires that you use your imagination. When you read drama, you have only the characters' words and the stage directions to work with. These help you "see" what's going on.

■ Your Job as a Reader

Slow down as you read a play. Stop after a character speaks and let an impression form in your mind. How is the character saying the line? How does he or she look and move? What are the other characters doing? As you read, be the director in your mind:

- Build the set. Imagine the setting fully enough so that you can "walk around" on stage.
- Choose the cast. Select actors to play the characters in your mind. You might think of professional actors, or you might cast family, friends, or imaginary people.

Reading Strategies

· Plan and Monitor
· Determine Importance
· Make Inferences
· Ask Questions
· Make Connections
· Synthesize
▶ **Visualize**

Elements of Literature

drama *n.*, plays, or stories that are acted out, for theater, radio, and television

Academic Vocabulary
- **mental** *adj.*, existing in the mind
- **image** *n.*, a picture

■ Unpack the Thinking Process

On stage, actors make the characters in a drama real. They move, they speak, and they **interact** according to the script. They perform on a set that someone designed.

When you are reading a play, the actors and the set do not exist. All you have is **dialogue**, the words the characters speak, and stage directions, or short descriptions of the set and the action. From those words you learn everything the author has to say about the characters, the setting, and the plot.

Setting and Stage Directions

If "Found Out" had been a short story, it might have started like this:

> Ronnie and his friend Ty stood outside the wooden door of Principal DeLuca's huge office. Ronnie nervously shoved his hands into the pockets of his jeans, but Ty looked cool—as if everything was going to be OK.

Notice how much the writer tells the reader about the setting and the characters' actions. The **playwright** leaves more to the reader's imagination.

Characters and Plot

At the heart of any story are characters and a **conflict**. The difference between short stories and plays is how much the author tells you. Now look at the way a writer might introduce the conflict in a short story.

> "I know talent when I see it," Ms. Jackson said with a smile.
> Talent! Ronnie couldn't believe his ears. Ms. Jackson chirped on. "Your work on the last algebra test was outstanding. How would you two like to join the math team?"
> Ronnie's mind scrambled to make sense of what was happening. How could two guys who had cheated on an algebra test join a math team?

In the drama, you learn about the conflict only through the characters' dialogue.

Elements of Literature
dialogue *n.*, the words that characters in a play speak to each other
playwright *n.*, a person who writes a play
conflict *n.*, the problem or struggle that drives a story's plot

Academic Vocabulary
● **interact** *v.*, to be involved with people or things; **interactive** *adj.*, having to do with people or things that act upon one another

■ Try an Experiment

Drama is meant to be performed. When the actors portray the characters, they bring them to life. Each performance is different. Maybe new actors **interpret** the characters differently, or new sets change the look and feel of the play.

Here's the beginning of the last scene of "Found Out."

DEMO TEXT *continued*

Act 2, Scene 3

    SETTING: *Inside the living room of Ty's home*

TY'S FATHER. I never expected this of you, Ty. I'm proud that you owned up to what you and Ronnie did. Still, you're not off the hook. You have to do what Principal DeLuca says.

TY. [*Looking down*] I know, Dad.

    [*Phone rings*]

TY'S SISTER. [*Calling from kitchen*] It's Principal DeLuca. She wants to speak to Ty.

Create an Ending How do you think the play will end? In a group, create an ending.

- Brainstorm possible endings. Take notes to record your best ideas.
- Choose the ending that the group likes best.
- Write the script for your ending, based on your notes.
- Revise your writing, making sure you've included elements of drama.
- Assign roles and choose a director.
- Rehearse the scene, including your ending, and perform it for the class.

Debrief After each group has presented its scene, discuss the performances.

1. How was watching the scene different from reading the script? Which details in the script helped the actors and director make decisions about the performance?

2. What changes or additions did the actors and director make to the script? For example, what gestures or movements, facial expressions, and tones of voice did the actors use?

3. Which ending did you like best? Explain.

Academic Vocabulary

- **interpret** *v.*, to express your understanding of something in a personal way; **interpretation** *n.*, the act of expressing your personal understanding of something

Monitor Comprehension

Visualize Why do readers have to use their imaginations fully when they read drama?

This picture and poem use different tools to express a similar idea about friendship. The picture uses colors, shapes, and other visual details. The poem uses rhythm and the sounds of the words. Think about how the picture and the poem create a similar mood, or feeling.

DEMO TEXT

Forever Friends

Where I begin and you do end,
I cannot hope to comprehend.
When one and one make one again,
They're twice as strong; forever friends.

Gypsy Maidens, circa 1839, Thomas Sully. Watercolor on paper, Brooklyn Museum

■ Connect Reading to Your Life

Do you like to read or listen to poetry? Perhaps you don't think poetry has much to do with your life, but think about your favorite song. The words of a song, or song lyrics, are a lot like poetry. Both are meant to be heard, and both say a lot in a few words. Song lyrics also follow patterns, just as many poems do. They may have **verses** , lines that **rhyme** , and lines that repeat.

■ Your Job as a Reader

Slow down when you read a poem. Listen to the "music" of the words. "See" the images. "Feel" the emotions the poem makes you experience. Your job as a reader is to get involved in the poem. Poetry is meant to cause you to think *and* feel.

Elements of Literature
verse *n.*, a group of lines in a poem or a song
rhyme *n.*, a repetition of the final sounds of
   words, as in the words *end* and *comprehend*

■ Unpack the Thinking Process

Experienced readers know that there are many **aspects** to poetry. Just as art is more than lines and colors, poems are not just words—those words are carefully chosen and arranged in a certain way.

Look at the Form

Poets choose different forms, or ways to organize their poems. Some poets divide poems into **stanzas** and follow patterns of line length and rhyme. Other poets choose a loose **structure**; the arrangement of the words follows the flow of their feelings and thoughts. A poet can even arrange his or her words in a shape.

Listen to the Sound

Appreciating the sounds in a poem draws you into a deeper experience with the poem. It helps you visualize the images and understand the meaning. Here are some devices poets use to create sound:

- Rhythm, or beat. Try tapping or snapping your fingers as you read a rhythmic poem, as you would do with a song.
- Rhyme, or the repetition of sounds at the ends of lines. Find the rhymes in "Forever Friends."
- Consonance, or the repetition of consonant sounds, such as in *begin* and *end* in the first line of "Forever Friends."

Visualize the Language

The Demo Text is a short poem that says big things about friendship and loyalty. Create mental images of the poet's words to help you understand the ideas. Then compare those mental images to the picture on page 610. How are they similar and different?

Words or phrase from poem:	Makes me visualize:
Where I begin and you do end	My friend is like my shadow: always there with me, through good and bad
One and one make one again	People working together, like on a sports team

■ Try an Experiment

Take turns reading the Demo Text with two or three classmates. Each of you should use a different rate of speed, pause in different places, and emphasize different words. How does each reading change the meaning or effect of the poem? Discuss which reading comes closest to the mood of the picture on page 610 and why.

Monitor Comprehension

Poetry Describe three devices that poets often use.

Elements of Literature
stanza *n.*, a section, or verse, of a poem

Academic Vocabulary
- **aspect** *n.*, part
- **structure** *n.*, the way in which something is organized or put together

EQ ## What Holds Us Together? What Keeps Us Apart?
Consider how families hold us together.

Make a Connection

Rank Priorities Different things hold people together. Rank the ideas in the **Priority Chart** from most to least important. Then compare your rankings with a small group to see what you have in common.

Priority Chart

Rank these priorities in order of importance.
_____ shared interests
_____ family
_____ shared beliefs
_____ ethnicity

Learn Key Vocabulary

Study the Words Pronounce each word and learn its meaning. You may also want to look up the meaning in the Glossary.

● Academic Vocabulary

Key Words	Examples
● **bond** (bond) *noun* ▸ pages 635, 640, 641	A **bond** is a kind of connection between people or things. My sister and I are held together by the strong **bonds** of family and love. *Synonyms:* link, tie
● **collapse** (ku-**laps**) *verb* ▸ page 628	To **collapse** means to fall down suddenly. The man **collapsed** to the floor when he heard the bad news about his son's accident.
● **integrity** (in-**te**-gru-tē) *noun* ▸ pages 630, 641	People who have **integrity** are honest and trustworthy. I trust her because she shows **integrity** in everything she says and does. *Antonym:* dishonesty
● **invest** (in-**vest**) *verb* ▸ page 618	When you **invest** in something, you provide time, money, or attention for it to grow. I **invest** money in this business because I know it will pay me back more money later.
loyalty (**loi**-ul-tē) *noun* ▸ pages 630, 641	When you have **loyalty**, you are faithful to someone or something. The friends showed **loyalty** to each other by staying together no matter what happened.
pretense (**prē**-tens) *noun* ▸ page 637	When people show **pretense**, they pretend to do or be something. Some people try to act tough, but my brother never shows any **pretense**.
provider (pru-**vī**-dur) *noun* ▸ pages 637, 641	A **provider** is someone who gives necessary things to someone else. My mother is an excellent **provider**, because she provides us with food, shelter, and love.
successful (suk-**ses**-ful) *adjective* ▸ pages 618, 633	When you are **successful**, you have done well. The parents at the graduation were proud of their **successful** children. 

Practice the Words Work with a partner to write four sentences. Use at least two Key Vocabulary words in each sentence.

Example: Our <u>bond</u> of friendship was so strong that I never questioned his <u>loyalty</u>.

BEFORE READING A Raisin in the Sun
play by Lorraine Hansberry

Reading Strategies

- Plan and Monitor
- Determine Importance
- Make Inferences
- Ask Questions
- Make Connections
- Synthesize
▶ **Visualize**

Compare Representations: Script and Performance

A **drama** is a story that actors perform. It is written as a **script** that includes:

- **dialogue:** words that characters say
- **stage directions:** instructions about how the stage should look and how the actors should talk, act, and move.

Actors interpret the script when they put on a live **performance** of the drama for an audience. Read this passage from a script, and study the photograph of a performance of the same passage.

Look Into the Text

Based on details in the dialogue, how do you think Travis feels as he speaks his first line?

What do the stage directions show about Travis's feelings?

TRAVIS. Mama, my teacher says we're supposed to bring fifty cents to school today for our field trip.

RUTH. We don't have it, baby.

TRAVIS. Aw, come on.

RUTH. I'm sorry, honey. Here, give me a hug.

[TRAVIS *hugs his mom and hurries off to school.*]

In this photo of the performance, what can you tell about Travis's feelings based on the expression on his face?

Focus Strategy ▶ Visualize

When you read a script, you don't always have photos of the performance to compare to the script. Instead, you need to **visualize**, or form mental images, to understand what you read.

HOW TO FORM MENTAL IMAGES

Focus Strategy

1. As you read, pay attention to the dialogue and stage directions. These describe characters, setting, and actions.

2. Look for descriptive words and phrases that appeal to the senses. Use these details to help you form mental images.

3. Make a simple sketch of how you see the characters and action.

YOU READ: "RUTH ... *shakes her 10-year-old son,* TRAVIS, *who's sleeping on the sofa.*"

YOU PICTURE:

Lorraine Hansberry
(1930–1965)

*Never be afraid to sit
awhile and think.*

**Lorraine Hansberry drew from
her own experiences of growing
up in a segregated neighborhood.**

Lorraine Hansberry was born in Chicago, Illinois, and grew up on the city's South Side. Her award-winning play, *A Raisin in the Sun*, is based on her family's experiences moving to a white neighborhood. Their struggles with segregation led to the Supreme Court case of *Hansberry v. Lee* (1940), which the Hansberry family won.

After attending a university performance of a play, she decided to become a writer. Hansberry moved to New York City in 1950, and began working for a newspaper there. She also wrote short stories, poetry, and plays.

A Raisin in the Sun was the first play written by an African American woman to be produced on Broadway. It opened in 1959 and became an instant hit. Since then, it has been shown on stage, film, and television. In 2004, a revival starring Phylicia Rashad and Sean "Diddy" Combs was a critical success; two cast members received Tony awards for their roles.

Although Lorraine Hansberry was only 34 when she died of cancer, she was one of the most famous writers of her time. Her plays are still performed, and her words continue to encourage people to believe in themselves even in the most difficult situations.

myNGconnect.com

◔ **Watch a scene from this play.**
◔ **Listen to an interview with Lorraine Hansberry.**

A Raisin in the Sun

by Lorraine Hansberry

adapted by Rachel Waugh

◀ Critical Viewing: Effect Describe the actors' body language. What feelings do they express?

 Comprehension Coach

Mama is expecting money from her late husband's life insurance. Read to find out what the different members of the Younger family plan to do with the money.

CHARACTERS

WALTER LEE YOUNGER, JR., a limo driver

RUTH YOUNGER, Walter's wife, a maid

TRAVIS YOUNGER, Walter and Ruth's 10-year-old son

BENEATHA YOUNGER, Walter's younger sister

MAMA, Walter and Beneatha's mother

KARL LINDNER, a man from a white neighborhood

BOBO, Walter's friend

WILLY, Walter's friend

MRS. JOHNSON, a nosy neighbor

SCENE 1

SETTING: *It's a gray Friday morning in 1950s Chicago. In a tiny, **run-down apartment**, a family begins to **stir**. The apartment has two bedrooms. The bathroom is in the hall and is shared with neighbors.*

[RUTH, *a young working mother, is the first one up. She shakes her 10-year-old son, TRAVIS, who's sleeping on the sofa.*] **1**

RUTH. Come on now, it's seven-thirty. Wake up! Hurry to the bathroom while it's free.

[*Half asleep,* TRAVIS *stumbles toward the bathroom.*]

RUTH. Walter Lee, get up!

[RUTH's *husband,* WALTER LEE, *comes out of their bedroom.*]

WALTER. Is Mama's check coming today?

1 **Description**
If you were summarizing the play, would you include the detail from the stage directions that Travis was sleeping on the sofa? Why or why not?

In Other Words
run-down apartment older apartment that needs repairs
stir wake up

Background Note
This selection is illustrated with images from the 2004 stage production. It starred Sean "Diddy" Combs (as Walter), Audra McDonald (as Ruth), and Phylicia Rashad (as Mama).

RUTH. Don't start talking about money this early in the morning.

[TRAVIS *comes back from the bathroom, and* WALTER *flies into the hall. He gets to the bathroom just before a neighbor does.*] **2**

TRAVIS. Mama, my teacher says we're supposed to bring fifty cents to school today for our field trip.

RUTH. We don't have it, baby.

TRAVIS. Aw, come on.

RUTH. I'm sorry, honey. Here, give me a hug. **3**

[TRAVIS *hugs his mom and hurries off to school.*]

2 Form Mental Images
How do you visualize the action in the hall outside the bathroom?

3 Compare Representations
Compare the dialogue between Travis and Ruth to the photo of the same scene with Travis, Ruth, and Mama from the stage performance. What can you tell about Ruth's feelings based on her dialogue? What can you tell from the expression on her face?

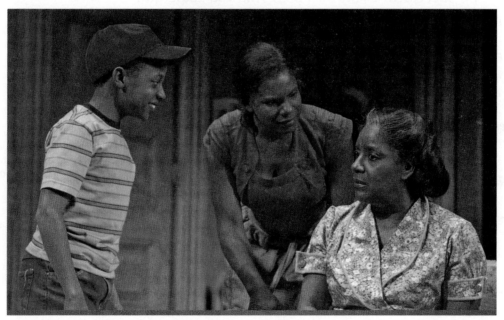

Actors play Travis, Ruth, and Mama from the 2004 Broadway production of *A Raisin in the Sun*.

SCENE 2

[WALTER *returns*.] **4**

WALTER. Willy, Bobo, and I were talking last night . . .

RUTH. Yes, I know. You kept Travis awake until after ten! The living room is also his bedroom, you know.

WALTER. This is important, Ruth. Willy found a liquor store we can buy if we each **invest** $10,000. Please talk to Mama for me?

RUTH. It's *her* money, from your daddy's life insurance.

WALTER. If I had my own business, I could quit being Mr. Arnold's driver. I know I'd be **successful** as my own boss. And you could quit cleaning other people's clothes for a living!

RUTH. Honey, eat your eggs.

WALTER. [*frustrated*] I say, "I have a dream." You say, "Eat your eggs." **5**

[WALTER's *sister*, BENEATHA, *comes out of the bedroom she shares with her mother.*]

WALTER. [*grumpily*] You're horrible-looking at this hour.

BENEATHA. [*equally grumpy*] Good morning to you, too.

WALTER. How's college?

BENEATHA. Biology is the greatest. Yesterday I had to **dissect a thing** that looked just like you.

4 Dramatic Elements
Writers often begin a new scene to show that the time, setting, or characters have changed. What has changed in Scene 2?

5 Compare Representations
Compare the dialogue between Walter and Ruth with the photo of the characters on page 619. What stage direction does the photo show? What does the dialogue reveal about the reason for Walter's feelings?

Key Vocabulary
- **invest** *v.*, to provide time, money, or attention to help something grow
- **successful** *adj.*, doing well

In Other Words
frustrated discouraged and angry
dissect a thing cut apart and examine the pieces of an animal

WALTER. So, you're still **set on going** to medical school? How much is that going to cost?

BENEATHA. I'm not asking you for anything.

WALTER. No, but if Mama spends her check to help you graduate, that's just fine with you.

BENEATHA. It's Mama's money. She can spend it however she wants.

WALTER. Why do you have to be a doctor? Why can't you be a nurse like other women?

BENEATHA. Picking on me won't make Mama give you money for your liquor store.

WALTER. [*to* RUTH] Did you hear that? No one in this family understands me!

BENEATHA. Because you're a **nut**! 6

[WALTER *frowns at* BENEATHA, *kisses* RUTH, *and leaves for work.*]

6 **Dramatic Elements**
What does the dialogue reveal about Walter, Beneatha, and their relationship?

In Other Words
set on going determined to go
nut crazy person (slang)

SCENE 3

[BENEATHA *leaves for the bathroom.* MAMA *enters.*]

MAMA. Who's slamming doors at this hour? **7**

RUTH. Walter and Beneatha were at it again.

MAMA. My children and their **tempers**—what were they **fussing** about this time?

RUTH. Walter **has his heart set on** that store.

MAMA. I don't feel right about selling liquor, honey.

RUTH. It *is* your money. Just think—$10,000! What would *you* like to do with it?

MAMA. Maybe we can buy a little house somewhere, with a yard for Travis.

RUTH. Lord knows we've put enough rent into this rattrap to pay for four houses by now.

[MAMA *looks around sadly.*]

MAMA. A rattrap. Yes, that's all it is. I remember when Big Walter and I moved in here. We didn't plan to stay more than a year. I guess dreams sometimes get **put on hold**.

[RUTH *starts ironing a big pile of clothes.* MAMA *washes the breakfast dishes. It's the beginning of another busy day.*]

7 Dramatic Elements
Write a stage direction showing how you think Mama should say her line.

Monitor Comprehension

Summarize
What does each person want to do with the check that Mama is expecting?

In Other Words

tempers bad moods, anger
fussing fighting, arguing
has his heart set on really wants to buy
put on hold delayed

SCENE 4

[*The next morning is Saturday. The family waits for* MAMA's *check to arrive. Brrringg! The mailman rings the doorbell.* TRAVIS *runs and brings back an envelope.*]

TRAVIS. Open it, Grandmama!

[MAMA *nervously opens the envelope. The check is inside. She holds it up.*] 8

> 8 **Form Mental Images**
> Draw a sketch to show how you picture Mama's facial expression and body movements.

MAMA. Is that the right number of zeros, Travis?

TRAVIS. Yes ma'am, $10,000. You're rich!

[WALTER *tries to hand* MAMA *a piece of paper.*]

WALTER. Mama, look at this—Willy wrote everything down . . .

MAMA. Walter Lee, I will not invest in a liquor store.

WALTER. But you didn't even look!

MAMA. **I'm the head of this family**, and I said "no." 9

[WALTER *is very disappointed.* MAMA *feels bad.*]

> 9 **Dramatic Elements**
> What do you learn about Mama and Walter from this dialogue?

MAMA. Honey, you have a job.

WALTER. A job! I drive a man around and I say "yes, sir; no, sir" all day. You call that a job?

MAMA. In my time, we worried about how to stay alive.

In Other Words
I'm the head of this family I make the decisions for this family

WALTER. I have bigger dreams, Mama. I want to be more!

MAMA. *I know what this family needs.*

[*She grabs her bag, and hurries out. The family looks at each other. Where can she be going?*] 10

SCENE 5

[*A few hours later,* MAMA *comes home. Everyone gathers in the living room.*]

MAMA. Family, do you know what I just did? I bought a house!

TRAVIS. Yay! I always wanted to live in a house!

RUTH. Praise God!

[RUTH *notices* WALTER's *sad face.*]

RUTH. Walter, honey, be glad . . .

MAMA. It's a little house, but it's ours. The address is 406 Clybourne Park.

BENEATHA. But Mama, that's a white neighborhood.

MAMA. I just tried to find the nicest house for the least amount of money.

BENEATHA. Goodbye, ugly old apartment! 11

MAMA. Walter, say something.

10 **Dramatic Elements**
Why do you think the stage directions ask a question? How should the characters act while Mama leaves?

11 **Dramatic Elements/Form Mental Images**
Study the dialogue and stage directions to see how each character responds to Mama's announcement. How do you picture them showing their feelings?

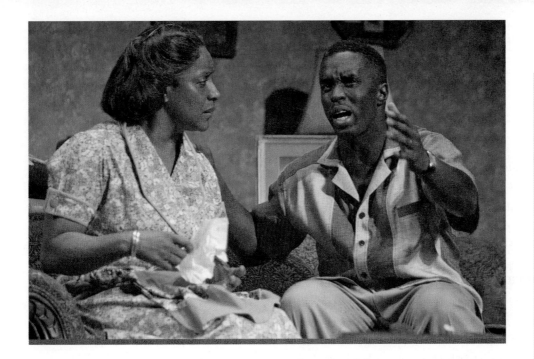

WALTER. What for? You're the head of this family. You make all the decisions. You killed my dream, that's all.

MAMA. Baby, don't say that. I **put down** $3,500 on the house. That leaves $6,500.

[MAMA *takes an envelope out of her purse and places it in* WALTER'*s hands.*]

MAMA. Put $3,000 in the bank **for Beneatha's tuition**. The rest is for you. You decide what to do with it. *You're* the head of the family now.

WALTER. [*smiling*] Mama, I can make a wonderful life for all of us. I just need this chance.

[WALTER *and* MAMA *hug. The family goes to bed feeling excited and happy about the future.*] 12

In Other Words

put down spent
for Beneatha's tuition to pay for Beneatha to go to college

12 **Form Mental Images/Compare Representations** Which part of Walter's dialogue in Scene 5 is represented in the photo at the top of this page? Does it match the mental images you had of Walter during this scene? Explain.

Monitor Comprehension

Confirm Prediction Was your prediction about Mama correct? What clues helped you make your prediction?

SCENE 6

[*The next day is Sunday.* MAMA *and* TRAVIS *are at church.* WALTER, BENEATHA, *and* RUTH *are at home. There's a knock at the door.* WALTER *answers it. In the doorway stands an embarrassed-looking white man.*]

LINDNER. Um, how do you do? My name is Karl Lindner.

WALTER. What can I do for you, Mr. Lindner?

LINDNER. I'm from the Clybourne Park Improvement Association. I understand you people are planning to move into our neighborhood. We think that you'd be happier **in your *own* community.**

BENEATHA. What a welcome!

LINDNER. We're prepared to **make you a very generous offer.**

RUTH. You have some nerve!

LINDNER. Let me tell you how much . . .

WALTER. We don't want to know. Get out of my house, man. 🔳

LINDNER. Why move to a neighborhood where you aren't wanted? Some people are going to get very upset about this . . .

WALTER. [*angrily*] Is that a threat?

[WALTER *stares hard at* LINDNER. *Finally* LINDNER *puts his business card on the table and leaves.*] 🔳

🔳 **Dramatic Elements**
What does this dialogue tell you about how the Youngers feel about Lindner's offer?

🔳 **Form Mental Images**
What mental images do you have of this meeting between the Youngers and Lindner? How do Walter and Lindner look?

In Other Words

in your *own* community with other African Americans
make you a very generous offer pay you a lot of money to stay out of our neighborhood
You have some nerve! How dare you say that!

Historical Background

During the 1950s, neighborhoods in Chicago and other cities were often segregated by race. Some white neighborhoods were violent or threatening toward minority families who wanted to live in their communities.

SCENE 7

[*Later that day,* WALTER *meets his friends* WILLY *and* BOBO *in a smoky jazz cafe.*]

WILLY. Walter Lee, my man!

BOBO. Hey, Walt.

[WALTER *throws a fat envelope on the table.*]

WALTER. I got the money for the liquor store!

[WILLY *opens the envelope and counts the bills inside. He looks at* WALTER.]

WILLY. Man, there's only $6,500 here.

WALTER. [*pleading*] It's all I've got. This is my big chance, Willy.

[WILLY *pauses.* WALTER *holds his breath. Finally* WILLY *smiles.*]

WILLY. OK. Let's **shake on it**!

[*The three men shake hands.* WILLY *puts on his hat and takes the envelope.*] 15

WILLY. I'm going to go buy us a liquor store! We'll meet here next week and make plans.

[WILLY *leaves as* WALTER *and* BOBO *talk and dream about their new store.*]

15 Form Mental Images
How do you picture this handshake between the three partners? How does each man feel?

In Other Words
pleading begging
shake on it shake hands to show that we have a deal

SCENE 8

[A week later, it's finally moving day. MAMA and RUTH are happily packing. There's a knock at the door. It's their nosy neighbor, MRS. JOHNSON.]

MRS. JOHNSON. Oooh, I knew it. You're moving! I saw all the boxes in the hallway and I said to myself, those Youngers are **moving up**! Clybourne Park is such a nice neighborhood . . .

MAMA. *[tensely]* Thank you. Ruth, give Mrs. Johnson a cup of coffee, please.

MRS. JOHNSON. *[sweetly]* I guess you saw the news in the paper?

MAMA. No, I don't believe so.

[MRS. JOHNSON stops sipping her coffee and pretends to be surprised.]

MRS. JOHNSON. You didn't read about that black family that **was bombed out of their house** in Clybourne Park?

RUTH. Oh my!

MRS. JOHNSON. Some folks might say don't go where you're not wanted. But I think it's wonderful that you all are so . . . brave. **16**

[MAMA reaches for MRS. JOHNSON's coffee cup.]

MAMA. If you'll excuse us, we're very busy.

MRS. JOHNSON. Oh yes, yes. Well, I'll look out for your name in the paper!

[MRS. JOHNSON leaves. MAMA and RUTH return to their work, a little less cheerful.] **17**

16 **Form Mental Images**
On the surface, Mrs. Johnson's words sound encouraging. What mental image do you have of her?

17 **Compare Representations**
What do the stage directions show about Mama and Ruth's feelings after Mrs. Johnson leaves? How can you tell that the photo of Mama, Ruth, and Beneatha on page 627 takes place after Mrs. Johnson's visit?

In Other Words
moving up doing well, going to a better place
tensely annoyed
was bombed out of their house was forced to move when someone blew up their house

SCENE 9

[*Later,* BENEATHA *and* WALTER *help* MAMA *and* RUTH *pack.* TRAVIS *plays outside. There's a knock at the door. It's* BOBO. *He looks upset.*]

WALTER. Hi Bobo. Where's Willy?

BOBO. I went to meet Willy, like we planned. Man, Willy didn't show up.

[*At first* WALTER *is* ***puzzled.*** *Then he begins to* ***panic.***]

WALTER. Why? Where is he?

In Other Words
puzzled confused
panic get very upset

BOBO. [*starting to cry*] Willy is *gone.*

[WALTER **collapses** *and beats the floor with his fists.*]

WALTER. [*sobbing*] Willy robbed us!

BOBO. I'm sorry, Walter. That was all the money I had in the world, too . . .

[BOBO *quietly leaves.*]

MAMA. Son, is it *all* gone? Beneatha's money, too?

WALTER. Yes! All of it! It's all gone! **19**

MAMA. Your father worked himself to death for that money . . . and you! You gave it all away in a day! **20**

[WALTER *rushes out.* BENEATHA *and* RUTH *try to comfort* MAMA.]

Key Vocabulary
• **collapse** *v.*, to fall down suddenly

19 Compare Representations
What does the photo of the performance on this page show you about Walter's feelings as he says this line of the script? Explain.

20 Form Mental Images
The author doesn't include stage directions about how Mama should say these lines. How do you picture her response?

Monitor Comprehension

Confirm Prediction
Did you accurately predict what kind of leader Walter would be? Explain why you made the prediction that you did.

Set a Purpose

What will happen to the Youngers? Will their dreams come true?

SCENE 10

[*After a while,* MAMA *calms down.*]

MAMA. Well, one of you'd better call the moving men and tell them not to come.

RUTH. No, Mama! We can still **make the monthly payments**!

MAMA. Maybe we just **aimed too high**. We've never been **landowning folk**.

RUTH. I'll scrub all the floors in America if I have to! We've got to get *out* of here!

[WALTER *enters the apartment.*]

MAMA. Where have you been, son?

WALTER. [*breathing hard*] I made a call.

MAMA. Who to?

WALTER. Lindner. We're going to do business with him.

RUTH. Are you talking about taking those people's money to keep us out of their neighborhood?

WALTER. I'm not just *talking* about it, baby, I'm telling you: That's what's going to happen! 21

MAMA. You're making something inside me cry, son!

21 **Form Mental Images** Describe the mental image you form of Walter as he makes his announcement.

In Other Words
make the monthly payments have enough money to pay for the house each month
aimed too high set impossible goals
landowning folk people who owned houses or land

WALTER. Don't cry, Mama. Understand. That man is going to write us a check for more money than we ever had. You and Ruth can stop doing other people's housework.

MAMA. Son, I come from five generations of people who were slaves and **sharecroppers**. We did work nobody wanted to do. But we *never* took money that was a way of telling us we **weren't fit to walk the earth**. We've never been *that* poor.

WALTER. That thief Willy taught me something today. Forget pride, forget loyalty. The only thing that matters is money. That's **the bottom line**.

BENEATHA. You've reached the bottom. You have no integrity, Walter. 22

WALTER. I'll do whatever it takes to put some pearls around my wife's neck! I'll tell Lindner whatever he wants to hear!

MAMA. [*crushed*] But baby, how are you going to feel inside?

WALTER. I'll feel fine! Fine!

[WALTER *stomps into his bedroom and slams the door.*]

SCENE 11

[*Later that day,* TRAVIS *bursts in.*]

TRAVIS. Grandmama, the moving men are downstairs!

[LINDNER *arrives a moment later.* RUTH *calls* WALTER *from the bedroom.*]

22 **Dramatic Elements**
Give two examples of how the writer reveals the characters' emotions to the reader without using stage directions.

Key Vocabulary
loyalty *n.*, being faithful
• integrity *n.*, being honest and trustworthy

In Other Words
sharecroppers people who farmed land without making very much money
weren't fit to walk the earth didn't deserve to be alive
the bottom line what it all means

RUTH. Travis, go downstairs.

MAMA. No, Travis, you stay right here. Walter, I want your son to see what you're about to do.

WALTER. Mr. Lindner. I called you because, well, my family and I . . .

[WALTER *pauses and looks around at his family. He struggles to continue.*] 23

LINDNER. Yes?

WALTER. Well, my father was not an educated or wealthy man, but he never let anyone insult him, or call him a bad name.

LINDNER. So?

WALTER. So, we come from people who had a lot of pride. That's my sister and she's going to be a doctor and we are very proud . . .

LINDNER. That's very nice, but . . .

[WALTER *sees that* TRAVIS *is looking up at him. At that moment he knows what he must do. He pulls* TRAVIS *close.*]

WALTER. This is my son, and he makes the sixth generation of our family in this country. We all thought about your offer . . .

LINDNER. [*impatiently*] Yes, yes.

WALTER. And we've decided to move into our house. Because my father, he earned it for us brick by brick. 24 We don't want to make any trouble, and we will try to be good neighbors. And that's all we have to say.

23 Dramatic Elements
Based on the dialogue and stage directions in this scene, why do you think Mama tells Travis to stay in the room? How do you think Travis will affect Walter?

24 Language
What does Walter mean when he says that his father earned the house "brick by brick"?

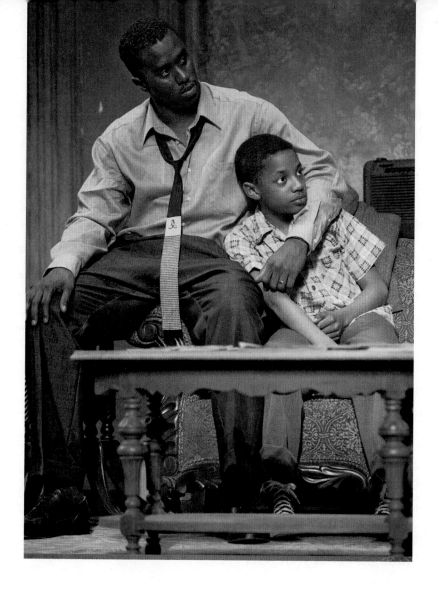

LINDNER. [*coldly*] Well, I sure hope you people know what you're getting into.

[*As* LINDNER *leaves, the family is quiet. Then everyone comes to life.*] 25 26

RUTH. Well, for goodness sake—if the moving men are here, let's get moving!

25 **Compare Representations**
In this final photo from the performance, what does the actors' body language tell you about Walter's relationship with his son? How does the body language convey the same ideas as Walter's dialogue with Linder?

26 **Form Mental Images**
What mental picture do you form of the Youngers after Lindner leaves?

MAMA. **Hallelujah**, Walter Lee!

WALTER. I'll find another way to reach my dream.

[*Everyone hugs WALTER. He finally feels proud. Smiling and laughing, the family walks down the stairs, out of their old apartment and toward a new life.*] ❖

ANALYZE A Raisin in the Sun

1. **Explain** What is Walter's final decision for the family? What does this show about how his character has changed?

2. **Vocabulary** Walter wants to be successful . What does he do to achieve his dream? How does his behavior affect the plot of the play?

3. **Compare Representations: Script and Performance** Choose one photo of the performance and explain how the actors go beyond the stage directions to convey emotions that support the plot or dialogue.

Character	Dialogue or Stage Direction	What It Reveals About the Character
Walter	"Yes! All of it! It's all gone!" (page 628)	The photo shows how the actor expresses Walter's feelings by throwing up his hands and looking miserable and unhappy.

4. **Focus Strategy Visualize: Form Mental Images** Page through the selection and see how the photos show scenes from the story. Talk with a partner about an important scene that is not pictured. Find details in the text about how the scene looks. Then sketch the mental image you have formed together.

◎ Return to the Text

Reread and Write Reread "A Raisin in the Sun." Choose two members of the family. Write a paragraph to tell how they are alike and different. Be sure to support your ideas with details from the play.

In Other Words
Hallelujah Thank goodness

BEFORE READING **Family Bonds**

poems by Luis Omar Salinas
and Teresa Palomo Acosta

Reading Strategies

- Plan and Monitor
- Determine Importance
- Make Inferences
- Ask Questions
- Make Connections
- Synthesize
▶ **Visualize**

Analyze Word Choice: Imagery

Poets use **imagery** to help readers "see" what the words describe.

- **Sensory imagery** reaches the reader's sense of sight, sound, touch, taste, and smell.
- **Literal imagery** describes things exactly as they are.
- **Figurative imagery** describes what things are like in a creative way.

Look Into the Text

Literal imagery describes what the speaker sees and hears. What other literal images can you find in this passage?

I walk to town with my father
to buy a newspaper. He walks slower
than I do so I must slow up.
The street is filled with children.
We argue about the price
of pomegranates, I convince
him it is the fruit of scholars.
He has taken me on this journey
and it's been lifelong.

The poet uses figurative imagery to describe life as a journey.

Focus Strategy ▶ Visualize

You can use your imagination to **visualize**, or picture, the scenes a poet describes.

HOW TO FORM MENTAL IMAGES

Focus Strategy

1. As you read a poem, pause and study the details the poet uses. How does he or she describe the person, place, or thing?

   YOU READ: The street is filled with children.

2. Picture in your mind what the poet describes.

   YOU VISUALIZE: In my mind, I can see a street where children are laughing, playing, and running around.

3. Think about how visualizing this image helps you understand the feelings and scenes that the poet describes.

   YOU THINK: The father and son are walking slowly while the children run by. The son cares for his aged father.

Connect Across Texts

"A Raisin in the Sun" describes what happens when a family deals with sudden wealth. In these poems, parents share lessons about a different kind of wealth.

Family BONDS

My Father Is a
Simple Man

by Luis Omar Salinas

I walk to town with my father
to buy a newspaper. He walks slower
than I do so I must slow up.
The street is filled with children.
5   We argue about the price
of pomegranates, I convince
him it is the fruit of scholars.
He has taken me on this journey
and it's been lifelong. **1**
10 He's sure I'll be healthy
so long as I eat more oranges,
and tells me the orange
has seeds and so is perpetual;
and we too will come back
15 like the orange trees. **2**
I ask him what he thinks
about death and he says
he will gladly face it when
it comes but won't jump
20 out in front of a car.
I'd gladly give my life
for this man with a sixth
grade education, whose kindness
and patience are true . . .

1 Form Mental Images
How do the speaker's words and phrases help you visualize the father and son?

Still Life with Oranges and Lemons in a Wan-Li Porcelain Dish, Jacob van Hulsdonck. Oil on panel, private collection.

▲ **Critical Viewing: Effect** The artist painted these oranges in a highly realistic style. Which senses do you think he wanted to appeal to?

2 Imagery
Picture what the speaker says about oranges. How does this imagery add to your understanding of the poem?

In Other Words
Simple Plain, Ordinary
scholars smart people who have a lot of education
is perpetual will go on forever because it produces new fruits

25 The truth of it is, he's the scholar,
and when the bitter-hard reality
comes at me like a punishing
evil stranger, I can always ③
remember that here was a man
30 who was a worker and provider,
who learned the simple facts
in life and lived by them,
who held no pretense.
And when he leaves without
35 benefit of fanfare or applause
I shall have learned what little
there is about greatness.

③ Form Mental Images
What things might make reality "bitter-hard"? What does the phrase make you visualize?

About the Poet

Luis Omar Salinas (1937–2008) is internationally recognized as one of the leading figures in Mexican American poetry. Born near the Texas-Mexico border, Salinas emerged as one of the most important writers in the "Fresno School" of poets in the 1970s and wrote nine books of poetry.

Key Vocabulary
provider *n.*, someone who gives necessary things to someone else
pretense *n.*, the act of pretending to do or be something

In Other Words
benefit of fanfare or applause the world celebrating the great things about his life

My Mother Pieced Quilts

by Teresa Palomo Acosta

Blocks-and-Strips Quilt, 2003, Mary Lee Bendolph. Corduroy quilted fabric, collection of Tinwood Alliance, Atlanta, Georgia.

they were just meant as covers
in winters
as weapons
against pounding january winds

5   but it was just that every morning I awoke
      to these
october ripened canvases
passed my hand across their cloth faces
and began to wonder how you pieced
all these together
10 these strips of gentle communion cotton
      and flannel nightgowns
wedding organdies
dime store velvets

how you shaped patterns square and oblong
      and round
positioned
15 balanced
then cemented them
with your thread
a steel needle
a thimble **4**

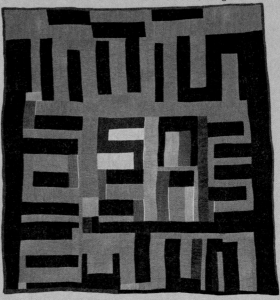

▲ Critical Viewing: Design and Effect What do the colors and shapes of this quilt make you think of? How do they make you feel?

4 Imagery
What do these images tell you about the woman who makes the quilts?

In Other Words
Pieced Planned, Created
october ripened canvases quilts that we used
  when the weather turned cold
oblong rectangular
a thimble and other sewing tools

20 how the thread darted in and out
    galloping along the frayed edges, tucking them in
    as you did us at night
    oh how you stretched and turned and re-arranged
    your michigan spring faded curtain pieces
25 my father's santa fe work shirt
    the summer denims, the tweeds of fall

    in the evening you sat at your canvas
    —our cracked linoleum floor the drawing board
    me lounging on your arm
30 and you staking out the plan:
    whether to put the lilac purple of easter against the red plaid of winter-going-
        into-spring
    whether to mix a yellow with blue and white and paint the
    corpus christi noon when my father held your hand
    whether to shape a five-point star from the
35 somber black silk you wore to grandmother's funeral 5

    you were the river current
    carrying the roaring notes
    forming them into pictures of a little boy reclining
    a swallow flying
40 you were the caravan master at the reins
    driving your threaded needle artillery across the mosaic cloth bridges
    delivering yourself in separate testimonies.

    oh mother you plunged me sobbing and laughing
    into our past 6

5 Form Mental Images
How do you visualize the mother designing the quilt? What details in the poem helped you form this mental picture?

6 Imagery
What imagery does the poet include in lines 43–44? How does this image appeal to the senses?

In Other Words

frayed old and worn
staking out the plan planning where each piece would go
corpus christi noon hot day
river current flowing stream
reclining relaxing

caravan master at the reins one in control
needle artillery weapons
mosaic cloth bridges combinations of cloth
testimonies stories

45 into the river crossing at five
    into the spinach fields
    into the plainview cotton rows
    into tuberculosis wards
    into braids and muslin dresses
50 sewn hard and taut to withstand the
        thrashings of twenty-five years

    stretched out they lay
    armed/ready/shouting/celebrating

    knotted with love
    the quilts sing on

About the Poet

Teresa Palomo Acosta (1949–   ) grew up in the cotton country of Central Texas. She has published three books of poetry and co-authored *Las Tejanas: 300 Years of History*, about the contributions Mexican American women have made to American life.

ANALYZE Family Bonds

1. **Explain** Both poems describe a person or a thing that is more than what it seems. Cite examples from the poems and explain what they mean.

2. **Vocabulary** In lines 22–23 of "My Father Is a Simple Man," the speaker says that his father only had a sixth grade education. Later he adds: "The truth of it is, he's the scholar." What does the speaker mean by these two ideas?

3. **Analyze Word Choice: Imagery** Which written image best shows the close bond between children and parents? How does the image help you picture this relationship?

4. **Focus Strategy Visualize: Form Mental Images** Find a description in either poem that is easy to visualize. Sketch the image and describe the details to a partner.

Return to the Text

Reread and Write Choose one of the poems. Write a letter from the speaker to the parent to describe what holds the speaker and parent close. Include examples from the poem. Then write a poem about another parent-child relationship. Try a variety of poetic forms for your poem, and include imagery so that readers can form mental images.

In Other Words
plainview wide
tuberculosis wards hospital areas
taut to withstand the thrashing strong
    to survive the hard daily use

EQ What Holds Us Together? What Keeps Us Apart?

Critical Thinking

EQ 1. Analyze Review the **Priority Chart** on page 612. Would you rank the priorities the same way after reading the selections? Consider whether each priority would hold a family together or keep it apart.

2. Compare Both Mama in "A Raisin in the Sun" and the father in "My Father Is a Simple Man" are **providers** for their families. What kinds of things do they give to their children?

3. Interpret How does the speaker in "My Mother Pieced Quilts" see quilt making as a way to hold a family together? How does this compare to the way Mama holds her family together in "A Raisin in the Sun"? Cite examples from the text to support your answers.

4. Assess Which character in the selections shows the most **integrity**? How does he or she treat the other members of the family?

EQ 5. Synthesize Write a definition of "family **bond**" that synthesizes, or puts together, the views and feelings expressed in the three selections.

Write About Literature

Comparison Paragraph How are the parents in the three selections similar? Use a **Venn Diagram** to record your ideas. Then write a paragraph that describes the similarities using specific examples from the three selections.

Venn Diagram

"A Raisin in the Sun"   "My Father Is a Simple Man"   "My Mother Pieced Quilts"

Key Vocabulary Review

Oral Review Work with a partner. Use these words to complete the paragraph.

bonds	invests	provider
collapse	loyalty	successful
integrity	pretense	

"A Raisin in the Sun" is a play about the close __(1)__ of love that connect a family. When Walter loses the money he __(2)__ in a new business, he sees his dreams __(3)__ around him. But Mama reminds Walter of the example of his own father. Walter's father showed great __(4)__ as an honest man. He was without __(5)__, never pretending to be better than he was. He worked hard every day to be a good __(6)__ and support his family. In the end, Walter learns that business is not the only way to become a __(7)__ man. The love and __(8)__, or faithfulness, he feels for his family are enough to make him rich.

Writing Application Is integrity, love, **loyalty**, duty, or something else the most important bond that holds families together? Write a paragraph about the bond. Use at least three Key Vocabulary words.

Read with Ease: Phrasing

Assess your reading fluency with the passage in the Reading Handbook, page 769. Then complete the self-check below.

1. I did/did not pause appropriately for punctuation and phrases.

2. My words correct per minute: _____

Grammar

Write in the Present Perfect Tense

The **present perfect tense** can show an action that happened at some point in the past.

We **have decided** to move.

The present perfect tense can also tell about an action that began in the past and may still be going on.

Mama **has worked** hard her whole life.

To form the present perfect tense, use **have** or **has** plus the **past participle** form of the main verb. For most verbs, add **-ed** to form the past participle.

She and Walter **have talked** about the money.

Irregular verbs have special forms for the past participle. Here are some irregular verbs.

Present	Past	Present Perfect
go	went	has gone, have gone
see	saw	has seen, have seen
take	took	has taken, have taken

Oral Practice (1–5) Choose from each column to make five sentences. Use words more than once.

Example: *They have packed the truck.*

Mama	have	gone	to college.
Beneatha	has	waited	the truck.
They		packed	a long time.

Written Practice (6–10) Choose the correct form of the verb. Rewrite the paragraph. Then add two more sentences about the story. Use present perfect verbs.

Walter (have made/has made) plans to buy a store. Mama and Walter (has argued/have argued) about how to spend the money. Mama (has seen/have seen) the house she wants to buy.

Language Development

Negotiate

Role-Play Act out a scene in which Mama and Walter try to agree on how to spend the $10,000.

Literary Analysis

Analyze and Compare Poetry

Consider this cartoon about poetry.

Source: ©Tom Prisk/CartoonStock, Ltd.

Poetry is more than just words that rhyme. **Poetry** often uses carefully controlled language, figures of speech, and imagery to appeal to a reader's senses, emotions, and imagination. As you read a poem, consider these poetic elements:

- **Speaker** The speaker is the narrator of the poem. This can be the voice of the poet or a character that the poet has created.

- **Sound Devices** Language in a poem is very different from the way we communicate in everyday life. Poets use rhythm, rhyme, meter, and repetition to give the poem a sense of life, movement, and intensity.

- **Imagery** Descriptive words and phrases help the reader form mental images.

- **Punctuation and Line Breaks** These can affect the poem's sound, rhythm, and meaning.

Critique Work with a small group to analyze and compare poems from this unit. Think about how each poet creates sounds, feelings, and themes. Is the poet's technique effective? Is one poem better than another? Explain your opinions and cite evidence from the poems to support your critique.

Interpret Figurative Language

You can sometimes use context clues to help you understand the meaning of figurative language, such as hyperbole, or extreme exaggeration. In "A Raisin in the Sun," Beneatha calls Walter "a nut." She doesn't literally think he is a nut, but instead uses the word figuratively. The context clue, their argument, helps you to realize this. Use context clues to help you explain the meaning of the following expressions.

1. ... we've put enough money into **this rattrap** to pay for four houses now. (p. 620)

2. Your father **worked himself to death** for that money. (p. 628)

Write About Theme

Most writing includes **themes**—general statements about people or life. An essay test may ask you to analyze a theme found in several selections.

❶ **Unpack the Prompt** Read the prompt and underline the key words.

> **Writing Prompt**
>
> Analyze a theme that is common in the selections "A Raisin in the Sun," "My Father Is a Simple Man," and "My Mother Pieced Quilts." Give examples of how the theme is expressed in each selection.

❷ **Plan Your Response** Begin by identifying themes in each selection, and then list one theme they all share. Identify specific examples that develop the theme.

Common Theme: _____

Selection	Two Examples That Develop the Theme
"Raisin"	
"Father"	
"Mother"	

Dramatization

Drama: Perform a Scene With a small group, perform a scene from "A Raisin in the Sun."

❶ Study the dialogue and stage directions. See if there are props, such as objects, that you need.

❷ Rehearse your scene. Using the stage directions as a guide, ask a group member to direct the scene. Think about how your movements and expression can show your character's thoughts, feelings, and actions.

❸ Perform your scene, and then watch as other groups perform. Compare how each group interprets the characters and story differently.

◆ **Language and Learning Handbook**, page 702

❸ **Draft** Use a **Response Organizer** to present your ideas. Since you are writing an analysis involving three selections, you may wish to organize your essay by allowing one paragraph for each selection.

> "A Raisin in the Sun," "My Father Is a Simple Man," and "My Mother Pieced Quilts" all include the theme: [give the theme].
>
> This theme is clear in "A Raisin in the Sun" when [give two examples from the play].
>
> In "My Father Is a Simple Man," the theme is clear when [give two examples].
>
> The theme is also seen in "My Mother Pieced Quilts," when [give two examples].
>
> These three selections show that [restate the theme in a way that relates to each selection].

❹ **Check Your Work** Reread your response. Ask:
- Does my work address the writing prompt?
- Do I give examples that illustrate the theme?
- Do I write in the present perfect tense?

◆ **Writing Handbook**, page 784

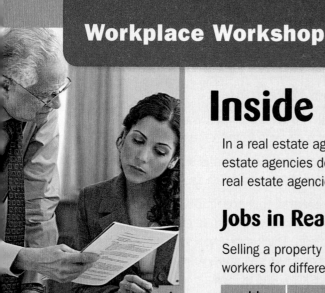

Inside a Real Estate Agency

In a real estate agency, people buy and sell property for their clients. Some real estate agencies deal with houses. Others deal with commercial buildings. Some real estate agencies also rent properties to people to live or work in.

Jobs in Real Estate

Selling a property takes more than sales skills. Many real estate agencies employ workers for different roles to make sure deals are a success.

Job	Responsibilities	Education/Training Required
Agency Assistant **1**	• Enters data into databases • Delivers, faxes, and scans documents • Answers telephones	• High school diploma • Knowledge of computers and other office equipment • On-the-job training
Agent **2**	• Writes descriptions of properties for sale to use in advertisements • Shows properties to possible buyers • Helps buyers and sellers make deals	• High school diploma • Thirty hours of classroom training • Successful completion of a real estate license exam
Broker **3**	• Finds properties to sell • Advertises to improve business • Calculates the price of properties	• Some college • Ninety hours of classroom training • Successful completion of brokerage license exam

Create a Property Listing

Explore what a job as a real estate agent would be like by writing a property listing for a home you know well.

1. Look at the real estate listings in your local newspaper to see how properties are listed.

2. Imagine you are a real estate agent. Write a property listing for a house or apartment you know well. Make your listing as interesting as possible, so that people will want to see the property.

3. Share your listing with the class. Discuss what makes it interesting. Save the information in a professional career portfolio.

myNGconnect.com

🌐 Learn more about real estate jobs.
🌐 Download a form to evaluate whether you would like to work in this field.

📖 **Writing Handbook**, page 784

Interpret Figurative Language

Read the following sentences. Think about the meanings of the highlighted phrases.

1. James was **as excited as a kid in a candy store**.
2. **Marisa is a solid rock** that I lean on during trouble.
3. **The air was heavy with spices and aromas** from her home country.

Each of these includes figurative, or nonliteral, language.

1. A **simile** compares two unlike things using the words *like* or *as*. The two things being compared, like James and an excited child, are different people, but they are alike in one important way—they're both excited.

2. A **metaphor** also compares two unlike things, but a metaphor says that one thing *is* the other thing.

3. A **sensory image** is language a writer adds to help you imagine an image by appealing to one of the five senses. The phrase "heavy with spices and aromas" uses the sense of smell.

Understand Figurative Language

Work with a partner. Identify each highlighted phrase as a simile, a metaphor, or a sensory image. Then match it with its meaning in the box to the right.

1. The crowded market was **a beehive of activity**.
2. Her flushed face was **hot with embarrassment**.
3. He stalked into the room **like a lion on the hunt**.
4. Their friendship was **an iron chain that couldn't be broken**.

A. strong and lasting

B. warm

C. crowded and busy

D. in a forceful way

Put the Strategy to Use

Use the strategy to figure out the meanings of figurative expressions.

1. Identify clues in the context around the phrase.
2. Form a mental picture of the phrase.
3. Guess the meaning from the context clues and your mental picture.

TRY IT ▶ Use the strategy to identify and figure out the figurative expressions in the sentences below. (Hint: There are five.)

▶ Mia sat alone. Around her, the party was a whirlwind of sights and sounds. Voices and laughter filled the air, but Mia was a lonely island in the sea of activity. When she saw her friend walk in at last, Mia's face shone like a star. She wouldn't be alone.

Make a Connection

Debate Should you be loyal to a friend even if he or she commits a crime? Debate this question in a small group. Then read "Pass It On" and two poems to see how they affect your ideas about loyalty to friends.

Learn Key Vocabulary

Study the Words Pronounce each word and learn its meaning. You may also want to look up the definitions in the Glossary.

● Academic Vocabulary

Key Words	Examples
conquer (kon-kur) *verb* ▶ pages 668, 672, 673	To **conquer** means to defeat or beat a person or a thing. The army **conquered** its enemy after a long battle.
● **devotion** (di-vō-shun) *noun* ▶ pages 667, 673	**Devotion** is the love and dedication you feel toward someone or something. Her poetry tells about the great **devotion** she feels for her family and friends.
grief (grēf) *noun* ▶ pages 670, 672	When you feel **grief**, you feel sorrow and sadness. He felt great **grief** when his good friend died. *Antonym:* joy
● **issue** (i-shoo) *noun* ▶ pages 665, 667, 673	An **issue** is an important topic or idea that people often are concerned about. How to stop school violence is an important **issue** that affects many teens.
refuge (re-fyūj) *noun* ▶ pages 657, 665	A **refuge** is a place of safety. My bedroom is my private **refuge** when I want to be alone.
● **restore** (ri-stor) *verb* ▶ page 670	When you **restore** something, you return it to the way it was before. After we talked about our problems, our friendship was **restored** to the way it used to be. *Synonyms:* mend, rebuild
subside (sub-sīd) *verb* ▶ page 651	When something **subsides**, it falls or loses strength. The loud noise of the car radio **subsided** as the car drove away. *Synonyms:* decline, lessen; *Antonyms:* increase, rise
territory (ter-u-tor-ē) *noun* ▶ pages 650, 675	Your **territory** is a specific area of land that belongs to you. A long fence marks the edges of our farm's **territory**.

Practice the Words Complete a **Vocabulary Example Chart** for each Key Vocabulary word. Add examples of how you have seen or experienced the words in your own life.

Vocabulary Example Chart

Word	Definition	Example from My Life
conquer	beat, defeat, win	Our soccer team conquered the other team at the game last Saturday.

BEFORE READING Pass It On

play by Franklin Just

Reading Strategies

· Plan and Monitor
· Determine Importance
· Make Inferences
· Ask Questions
· Make Connections
· Synthesize
▶ **Visualize**

Analyze Elements of Drama: Characterization

Playwrights use different techniques to bring their characters to life.

- **Dialogue** shows characters' thoughts through the words they say. The language they use can also give background information about the characters.
- **Stage directions** include details about how characters speak, move, and act. Some stage directions also tell what characters look like.

Look Into the Text

Judge's dialogue includes repetition. It shows that his character is surprised and upset.

JUDGE. Where's Echo?

TAILLIGHT. As if you didn't know.

WHISPER. He's at the courthouse.

DOC. [*sarcastically*] "Somebody" filed an assault charge.

JUDGE. [*looking upset*] Oh, I, I mean, Dawn just said she told the police what happened to Gram. She didn't tell me . . . I mean, with everything that happened, I didn't think about . . .

[DOC, WHISPER, *and* TAILLIGHT *look at each other and shake their heads.*]

DOC. We have to go.

[DOC, WHISPER, *and* TAILLIGHT *leave.*]

JUDGE. [*speaking to himself*] I have to go, too.

Stage directions show that the boys question whether or not Judge is sincere.

Focus Strategy ▶ Visualize

When you read, your imagination helps you to **visualize** the scene in your mind. Your imagination also helps you to **respond** emotionally to the characters and events.

HOW TO IDENTIFY EMOTIONAL RESPONSES

Focus Strategy

1. As you read, look for details that help you visualize the scene, characters, and events.

2. Think about how this relates to your own life. How would you feel if you experienced these events?

3. Record your emotional responses in a **Response Journal**.

Response Journal

I Read	I Feel
Judge tells Doc, "I didn't think. . . ."	Something like this happened to me once, so I felt proud of Judge when he realized what he had done.

Shadows of the Vietnam War

During the 1980s, the United States was still recovering from the effects of the Vietnam War. Thousands of U.S. troops had been killed, wounded, or emotionally scarred. Many families were left without husbands and fathers. Children had to deal with crisis situations. Moreover, the U.S. economy was still suffering from the cost of the war. "Inflation," a term that refers to rising costs of certain goods and services, and rising prices made it difficult for some people to buy what they needed.

In addition, an unfair practice known as "redlining" made matters worse. For largely self-serving reasons, businessmen and politicians would draw an imaginary red line around certain neighborhoods, declaring them unfit for financial assistance. Redlining made it difficult for people who lived in those neighborhoods to get bank loans and mortgages.

For that reason, many people could not remain in their homes and were forced to move to other neighborhoods. Unfortunately, cheaper housing was often found in unsafe areas. Both adults and children found it difficult to adjust to their new surroundings. As some neighborhoods emptied out, abandoned homes and businesses became targets for crime and destruction. Because of this shift in population, many large cities in the United States experienced what came to be known as "urban decay," a painful challenge for families and communities.

Pass It On

by Franklin Just

▲ What is the mood of this photograph? What does it suggest about the play to come?

CHARACTERS

ECHO, 17, lead basketball player for team eventually known as the Tigers

WHISPER, 14, Echo's brother

TAILLIGHT, 17, Echo's friend, watches people's backs

DOC, 17, Echo's friend, team "manager"

ROY, a middle-aged man who manages the playground where the boys play basketball

JUDGE, 17, leader of the Hatchets. Judge and Echo used to be friends when they were small.

DETAILS, 17, "manager" of the Hatchets

SLEEPWALKER, 17, member of the Hatchets

DAWN, 14, Judge's sister

DELILAH, 10, Judge's sister

GRAM, older woman, grandmother to Judge, Dawn, Delilah

POLICEMEN

SCENE 1

SETTING: *All of the action takes place in a neighborhood in Boston, during the mid-1980s.*

[WHISPER *is shooting baskets at a basketball court on a public playground. JUDGE approaches and catches the ball when it rebounds off the rim.*]

JUDGE. Time's up. **Beat it.**

WHISPER. Echo!

[ECHO *approaches, followed by* DOC *and* TAILLIGHT.]

ECHO. We still have fifteen minutes. Give him the ball back.

JUDGE. Not your neighborhood anymore, not your territory, not your court. Now, I said beat it. 1

TAILLIGHT. This is a public playground. We have a right to be here.

1 **Characterization in Drama**
How does the author introduce the character of Judge? How do you know what he is like?

In Other Words
Beat it. Go away.

Key Vocabulary
territory *n.*, a specific area of land that belongs to someone

Literature Note
Pass It On is an allegory about growing up. An allegory is a story with both a literal meaning and a deeper, symbolic meaning.

[JUDGE *bounces the ball once, hard. He is joined by* DETAILS *and* SLEEPWALKER.]

JUDGE. Don't they teach you any manners where you live? When somebody tells you to leave, you leave.

[*The boys argue. A whistle blows and* ROY *approaches.*]

ROY. Okay, **simmer down**. [*waits for the shouting to* subside*, then says to* ECHO] I said it was okay to bring your [*looks at* TAILLIGHT] friends as long as there wasn't any trouble. I think you're done for today.

JUDGE. You're done, period. **2**

ECHO. I want my ball back.

ROY. Give him his ball back, Judge. It was his Dad's. **3**

[JUDGE *bounces the ball and* **flings** *it towards* ECHO'S *chest, but* ECHO *catches it and bounces it.*]

DOC. It's getting pretty hot, anyway. We should be going.

[JUDGE *laughs, but* ECHO *stares at* JUDGE.]

ECHO. We're not done.

[ECHO, WHISPER, DOC, *and* TAILLIGHT *leave.*]

2 Emotional Responses
How do you feel about the way Judge treats Echo? What makes you respond this way?

3 Characterization in Drama
How would you describe Roy? Which words and actions make you see him this way?

△ Critical Viewing: Characterization How do you think the players in this photo feel about playing basketball? What details help you reach your conclusion?

In Other Words
simmer down quiet down
flings throws

Key Vocabulary
subside *v.*, to fall or lose strength

SCENE 2

[ECHO, WHISPER, DOC, *and* TAILLIGHT *walk together on a street behind the playground.*]

TAILLIGHT. Judge! Who told him he could be a judge! You know him, Echo? 4

ECHO. We knew each other a long time ago.

DOC. Back when you used to live around here?

[DAWN *and* DELILAH *approach.*]

TAILLIGHT. Well, well, well! Two lovely ladies out for a stroll!

DAWN. [*to* DELILAH] Take my hand.

TAILLIGHT. Oh, you think you're too good, princess? Afraid of some **riff raff**? 5

DAWN. We don't talk to [*she looks* TAILLIGHT *up and down*] strange boys.

[TAILLIGHT *says* "Who," *but* DOC *pulls him back.*]

DOC. C'mon. It's lunchtime and I'm hungry.

[DOC *and* TAILLIGHT *leave.* ECHO *and* WHISPER *start to follow.*]

DAWN. [*to* ECHO] I've seen you play. You're pretty good. Where did you learn to play basketball like that?

ECHO. From my dad.

DAWN. He must be proud.

WHISPER. He died in **'Nam**. 6

DAWN. [*to* WHISPER] I'm really sorry. Are you guys brothers?

WHISPER. [*heatedly*] **Yeah**, and yeah, my dad would be proud.

4 **Emotional Responses**
What do you know about people like Taillight? Describe your response to his character.

5 **Access Vocabulary**
Does the word *princess* have a positive or negative connotation in this passage? Explain.

6 **Characterization in Drama**
Why do you think Whisper tells Dawn about his father? What does this tell you about Whisper?

In Other Words
riff raff tough kids
'Nam Vietnam
Yeah Yes

Cultural Background
By the time the Vietnam War ended in 1975, there were more than 68,000 U.S. casualties. The remains of servicemen lost in the war are being discovered even today.

Providence:

10 If there be pain
Reach out for a helping hand
If there be pain
And I shall hold you wherever I am . . .

Together:

Wherever I am
15 Every breath I breathe will be into you
For without you here my joy is through
My life was lived through falling rain
So call on me if there be pain [2]

RasDaveed El Harar:

(chanting)

Providence:

Every breath I breathe will be into you
20 For without you here my joy is through
My life was lived through falling rain
So call on me . . .

Together:

If there be pain [3]

[2] **Emotional Responses**
What do you think the phrase "my life was lived through falling rain" means? How does this make you feel about the lyrics and the writer?

[3] **Emotional Responses**
Which words and phrases stand out to you? How do these lyrics make you feel?

In Other Words
(chanting) (adds more lyrics of his own)

Sonnet 30

by William Shakespeare

When to the sessions of sweet silent thought
I summon up remembrance of things past,
I sigh the lack of many a thing I sought,
And with old woes new wail my dear time's waste:
5   Then can I drown an eye, unused to flow,
For precious friends hid in death's dateless night,
And weep afresh love's long since cancell'd woe,
And moan the expense of many a vanish'd sight:
Then can I grieve at grievances foregone,   **4**
10   And heavily from woe to woe tell o'er
The sad account of fore-bemoaned moan,
Which I new pay as if not paid before.
But if the while I think on thee, dear friend,
All losses are restor'd and sorrows end.   **5**

4 **Access Vocabulary**
Use what you know about the Key Vocabulary word **grief** to define the words *grieve* and *grievances*.

5 **Form and Style**
How does the rhyming pattern of the sonnet change in this last couplet?

Key Vocabulary
grief *n.*, sorrow and sadness
• restore *v.*, to return something to the way it was before

Sonnet 30

A Modern Paraphrase

When in moments of quiet thoughtfulness

I think about the past,

I regret that I did not achieve all that I wanted,

And it saddens me to think of the years that I wasted:

5   Then I cry, though I am not one who cries often,

For my good friends who have died,

And I cry again over heartbreaks that ended long ago,

And mourn the loss of many things that I have seen and loved:

Then I grieve again over past troubles,

10   And sadly I remind myself, one regret after another,

Of all the sorrows and disappointments in my life,

And they hurt me more than ever before.

But if I think of you at this time, dear friend,

I regain all that I have lost and my sadness ends. 6

6 **Emotional Responses** Can you relate to the speaker's experiences and feelings? Explain how this deepens your understanding of the poem.

In Other Words
achieve do, accomplish
mourn am saddened by, grieve
disappointments failures, frustrations

ANALYZE Standing Together

1. **Summarize** Paraphrase "Sonnet 30." Describe the speaker's thoughts in your own words.

2. **Vocabulary** What do the song lyrics and the sonnet suggest about love's ability to conquer grief? Do you agree? Why or why not?

3. **Analyze Form and Style** Compare and contrast the form and style of the lyrics and the sonnet. Which speaks more directly to you and why?

4. **Focus Strategy Visualize: Identify Emotional Responses** Share your emotional response to the song lyrics or the sonnet with a partner. Point out specific words and phrases that influenced your response.

Return to the Text

Reread and Write Shakur's and Shakespeare's words show that writers have written about friendship over the past 400 years. Reread the selections and write a short paragraph that describes the similarities between the song lyrics and the sonnet.

About the Songwriter

Tupac Shakur (1971–1996) was one of the best-selling and most controversial hip-hop artists of all time. "If There Be Pain" is from an album of Shakur's poetry titled *The Rose That Grew From Concrete* (2000), recorded by friends and fellow artists after his death.

About the Poet

William Shakespeare (1564–1616) is England's most famous poet and playwright. He wrote more than thirty plays, three major works of poetry, and over one hundred fifty sonnets. His plays, such as *Hamlet* and *Romeo and Juliet*, are still performed throughout the world and have been made into many motion pictures.

EQ ## What Holds Us Together? What Keeps Us Apart?

Critical Thinking

EQ 1. **Analyze** Think about your debate about what it means to be a friend during a difficult time. (page 646) How is this **issue** addressed in the selections?

2. **Compare** Which selection shows the most realistic view of friendship? Use specific examples from the selection to support your opinion.

3. **Interpret** Details tells Doc, "What your man did was excellent." (page 664) Explain what he means. How is this idea of **devotion** expressed in the song lyrics and sonnet?

4. **Judge** Which character or speaker best represents your idea of a true friend? Explain your opinion with support from the text.

EQ 5. **Generalize** What are the things that hold friends together? What keeps some groups apart? Can these things be overcome? Answer each question with evidence from the selections.

Write About Literature

Theme Study Tupac Shakur wrote: "Together we can never fall / Because our love will **conquer** all." Write a paragraph that explains how this theme applies to each of the selections. Then add your opinion about this idea of friendship.

Key Vocabulary Review

Oral Review Work with a partner. Use these words to complete the paragraph.

conquer	issue	subside
devotion	refuge	territory
grief	restore	

In "Pass It On," Echo and Whisper share a strong love and __(1)__ for one another. They want to play basketball in their old neighborhood, although it is no longer their __(2)__. Once, their home in this neighborhood was their __(3)__, but now it does not feel safe. The death of the boys' father is an __(4)__ for them. Whisper, especially, feels __(5)__ because he doesn't remember his father well. But their friends help them __(6)__ their loneliness. Visits to the old neighborhood seem to help their homesickness __(7)__, even though they can never __(8)__ their old lives.

Writing Application Write a letter to a friend about an issue that resulted in a quarrel. Use at least three Key Vocabulary words.

Read with Ease: Expression

Assess your reading fluency with the passage in the Reading Handbook, p. 770. Then complete the self-check below.

1. My expression did/did not sound natural.

2. My words correct per minute: _____

Write with the Perfect Tenses

When you write, choose the verb tense that best expresses your meaning.

Use the **present perfect tense** to tell about an action that happened at some point in the past or that began in the past and may still be happening.

Echo **has come** back before. So far, the visits **have gone** well.

Use the **past perfect tense** to write about an action that happened before some other action in the past.

Before he moved, Echo and Judge **had been** friends.

Use the **future perfect tense** to tell about an action that will be completed at some point in the future.

By the time Judge and his friends are adults, they **will have seen** plenty of trouble.

Oral Practice (1–5) With a partner, use these verbs in sentences about events in "Pass It On."

has talked	had hidden	has left
have saved	will have become	

Written Practice (6–10) Write this paragraph, using the correct verbs. Then add two more sentences. Use perfect tenses.

Before going home, Tommy (has gone/had gone) to the movies. J.J. was angry, and he (will have shown/had shown) his anger before. Willis was scared. He (have asked/had asked) his brothers to stop fighting many times in the past.

Use Appropriate Language

Role-Play Act out a scene in which you have dinner with Judge and Echo. Then act out the same scene with Tupac Shakur and William Shakespeare.

Literary Criticism

Literary criticism is the evaluation, analysis, description, or interpretation of literary works. A literary criticism usually follows one of these approaches:

- **Biographical:** The writer shows how the author's life affects the work.
- **Aesthetic:** The writer focuses on what makes a work appealing to the reader.
- **Historical:** The writer researches a specific time period and shows how it influenced the work.

In describing Franklin Just's play "Pass It On," critic Alison Pauley uses an historical approach. She says, "Just researched the effects of the Vietnam War at home. In the 1960s and 70s, nearly every working-class city or town in the United States was touched by the war. It is clear that Just was well-informed about the emotional and financial suffering of families who lost brothers, fathers, and sons in Vietnam." Do you agree with Pauley's opinion?

With a partner, gather information that could help you write a literary criticism about one of the poems.

🌐 **myNGconnect.com**

Then create a chart showing how biographical or historical facts influenced the work.

Historical Influences

In History	In "Pass It On"
More than two million American men and women served in Vietnam. Military personnel and their families experienced high rates of divorce, drug abuse, and homelessness.	Echo and his family are examples of how some families of military personnel show war "scars" many years after the war has ended.

Denotation and Connotation

Denotation is the exact meaning, or definition, of a word. **Connotation** is a meaning or feeling that is commonly added or attached to the word. For example, study the difference between denotation and connotation for the word territory.

WORD	DENOTATION	CONNOTATION
territory	a specific area of land that belongs to someone	land that you should protect and defend

With a partner, add four more Key Vocabulary words to the chart. Read the passages where they appear and decide each word's connotation. Then discuss why authors choose to use words that carry certain connotations.

Compare Media

Evaluate Techniques in Print, Plays, and Film

Plays like "Pass It On" are often performed in theaters, recorded for television, or filmed as movies. Work with a small group to study how a media version compares with the written text.

1 Choose a play. Get the script and then view a live or video performance of the play.

2 Take notes comparing the performance with the written play. What was changed, emphasized, or left out? How did the actors interpret the lines?

3 Discuss why the changes may have been made. Were the changes effective? Explain.

4 Share your ideas with the class. Play film clips or read excerpts to show the differences.

🔖 **Language and Learning Handbook**, page 702

Write a Literary Critique

A **literary critique** is a critical analysis of a work of literature. You can choose to evaluate the work with an approach that focuses on its biographical influences, aesthetic success, or historical context. Use one of these approaches to write a literary critique of "Pass It On" by Franklin Just.

1 **Prewrite** Write a topic sentence that states your opinion about the play. Then decide which approach to take in your critique. This will help you organize your ideas.

2 **Draft** Use a chart to list your opinions and examples from the play that support them.

Aesthetic Review of "Pass It On"

Opinions	Examples
Franklin Just is successful in presenting realistic characters.	Echo's family is in a tough situation, so he is often angry and sad.

3 **Revise** Make sure that your thesis clearly states your opinion. Each example you include should support this opinion.

> "Pass It On" is a touching play that represents realistic characters in difficult situations. For example, since Echo and Whisper's father died in Vietnam, they and their mother have had a difficult life. Their mother couldn't keep up with payments on their house, and they had to leave their neighborhood and their friends behind. Whisper has done better than his brother. Echo's anger and sadness has landed him in trouble in the past, and it threatens to land him in trouble again.

4 **Edit and Proofread** Working with a partner, reread your critique and correct any errors in spelling or grammar. Match sounds to letters or use rules to make spelling corrections.

5 **Publish** Print out your critique and prepare to read it in front of your class.

🔖 **Writing Handbook**, page 784

Narrative Presentation

Speaking in front of an audience can be uncomfortable. But if you are speaking about something you know a lot about, it can also be fun. Talking about a personal experience, such as a real-life family story, is an easy way to make a presentation interesting. Here is how to give a narrative presentation people will remember:

1. Plan Your Narrative Presentation

Choose a story a family member has told you about your family, or an experience you have had with your family. Then do the following:

- List as many details as you can remember, and arrange the details in the order they happened.
- Think of appropriate language to use.
- Think of ways to use your voice, such as characters' voices or dialogue, that might make the narrative more interesting.

2. Practice Your Narrative Presentation

Rehearse your presentation with a partner, so that you are familiar with your story.

- Start with the setting, or time and place, then introduce the people.
- Use your voice and nonverbal language, such as gestures, to make the narrative interesting.
- Practice pausing and emphasizing certain words. Incorporate humor into the story, if appropriate.
- Make sure you speak within the given time limit.

3. Give Your Narrative Presentation

Keep your audience focused by doing the following:

- Make eye contact with your audience.
- Speak clearly and loudly.
- Look at your notes if you need to, but try to use them as little as possible.
- Monitor your audience's interest as you speak. Adjust your speaking style if needed.

myNGconnect.com

↘ **Download the rubric.**

4. Discuss and Rate the Narrative Presentations

Use the rubric to discuss and rate the narrative presentations, including your own.

Narrative Presentation Rubric

Scale	Content of Presentation	Student's Preparation	Student's Delivery
3 Great	• Made me really see what happened • Expressed why the story was so memorable	• Presented events in an easy-to-follow order • Used hardly any notes	• Spoke clearly and was easy to follow • Used facial expressions and gestures very well to keep the presentation lively
2 Good	• Gave me a fairly good idea of what happened • Gave me some idea of why the story was memorable	• Presented events in order most of the time • Used notes a lot	• Spoke clearly most of the time and was usually easy to follow • Used facial expressions and gestures fairly well
1 Needs Work	• Did not really tell what happened • Did not express why the story was memorable	• Presented events in a confusing sequence • Read directly from notes	• Was hard to hear and understand • Did not use facial expressions and gestures well

DO IT ▶ When you are finished preparing and practicing, give your presentation and keep the audience listening!

📖 Language and Learning Handbook, page 702

How is this student bringing her narrative to life?

EQ What Holds Us Together? What Keeps Us Apart?

Discover what it means to belong to a community.

Make a Connection

Discussion What does it mean to belong to a community? List the different types of communities you belong to—whether they are your friendships and school clubs or something larger like your state, country, or culture. Then talk with a small group about the communities you share. Which communities are the most important? Why?

Learn Key Vocabulary

Study the Words Pronounce each word and learn its meaning. You may also want to look up the definitions in the Glossary.

• Academic Vocabulary

Key Words	Examples
alien (ā-lē-un) *noun* ▸ pages 688, 689, 695	An **alien** is a person who comes from another country. When she moved to the U.S., she was an **alien** in a strange, new culture. *Synonym:* foreigner
ashamed (u-shāmd) *adjective* ▸ page 684	When you are **ashamed**, you feel guilty or embarrassed. I felt **ashamed** about the way I had treated my friend when I was angry.
• **feature** (fē-chur) *noun* ▸ pages 686, 687	Your **features** are the parts of your face. His big, brown eyes are his best **feature**.
• **interpret** (in-**ter**-prut) *verb* ▸ page 686	When you **interpret** something, you translate it from one language to another. I often **interpret** letters and notices for my parents, who don't read English.
• **major** (mā-jur) *adjective* ▸ pages 693, 694	**Major** means great in size or importance. We have a **major** problem that is too big for us to solve without help. *Synonyms:* serious, large
melodious (me-lō-dē-us) *adjective* ▸ page 682	A sound is **melodious** if it is pleasant to hear, like music. Whenever she sings, everyone enjoys her **melodious** songs.
• **minor** (mī-nur) *adjective* ▸ pages 693, 694	**Minor** means small or unimportant. My twin and I differ in **minor** ways, but we think alike and are interested in the same things.
variety (vu-rī-u-tē) *noun* ▸ page 692	Things show **variety** if they represent many different things. The people in the group represent a **variety** of backgrounds from all over the world.

Practice the Words Write each Key Vocabulary word on an index card. Then, with a partner, take turns grouping two or more words at a time. Explain how the words go together.

> Example: Some people feel <u>ashamed</u> of the way the <u>features</u> on their faces look.

ashamed

feature

BEFORE READING Voices of America

poems by Walt Whitman, Langston Hughes, Nellie Wong, and Pat Mora

Reading Strategies

· Plan and Monitor
· Determine Importance
· Make Inferences
· Ask Questions
· Make Connections
· Synthesize
▶ **Visualize**

Analyze Word Choice: Figurative Language

Poets use figurative language to create images and appeal to the reader's senses and emotions. **Figurative language** is the use of words and phrases in imaginative ways to express ideas beyond the words' direct meanings.

- **Metaphors** compare two different things by stating that one thing is the other thing.
- **Personification** describes animals, objects, or ideas as having human abilities or emotions.

Look Into the Text

America is a country, not a living creature that can sing. This is an example of personification.

I hear America singing, the varied
   carols I hear,
Those of mechanics, each one
   singing his as it should be
   blithe and strong,
The carpenter singing his as he
   measures his plank or beam,
The mason singing his as he
   makes ready for work, or leaves
   off work.
            —Walt Whitman

I, too, sing America.
I am the darker brother.
They send me to eat in the kitchen
When company comes,
But I laugh
And eat well.
            —Langston Hughes

The speaker is not literally America's "brother." What type of figurative language is this?

Focus Strategy ▶ Visualize

Poets often include **sensory images** that appeal to the reader's five senses. These words and phrases help the reader imagine how something looks, sounds, tastes, smells, and feels.

HOW TO IDENTIFY SENSORY IMAGES

Focus Strategy

1. **Read** As you read, look for details and descriptions that appeal to your senses. Record these in a **Sensory Image Chart**.

2. **Reflect** Think about what sense the image appeals to. Add this to the chart.

3. **Respond** Describe how the image makes you feel or what it makes you think.

Sensory Image Chart

Read	Reflect	Respond
"I hear America singing, the varied carols I hear"	I _hear_ different people singing together.	I worry that some people's songs are not being heard.

E PLURIBUS UNUM

Have you ever taken a look at the change you have in your pocket? If you look closely, you will see that all of the coins have the words *E PLURIBUS UNUM* on them. It means "out of many, one" and it represents America and its people.

Ever since the United States was founded, immigrants have come from all over the world looking for freedom, opportunity, and a better life. There have been challenges to be faced, but there is also hope.

Just where in the world is everyone coming from? From 1900 to 1920, over 10 million people came to the U.S. from Italy, Mexico, Austria-Hungary, Germany, Great Britain, Ireland, and Sweden. In recent years, many people have come to the U.S. from countries in Central and South America as well as from many countries in Asia such as China, the Philippines, Vietnam, and India.

Over the years, American society has been called a "melting pot" and a "mosaic." Both terms refer to the diversity and uniqueness of the people of America. All Americans bring their own backgrounds, cultures, beliefs, and experiences to our society. This is what makes American culture so special and so challenging at the same time. No matter where our families come from—*E PLURIBUS UNUM*.

myNGconnect.com

◐ **Learn more about the immigrant experience.**
◐ **Find out how *E PLURIBUS UNUM* became part of American history.**

Voices OF AMERICA

▲ **Critical Viewing: Design** What do the colors and combinations of this collage say about America and the people who live here?

Comprehension Coach

I Hear Singing

by Walt Whitman

I hear America singing, the varied carols I hear, **1**

Those of mechanics, each one singing his as it should be blithe
and strong,

The carpenter singing his as he measures his plank or beam,

The mason singing his as he makes ready for work, or leaves off work,

5　The boatman singing what belongs to him in his boat, the deckhand
singing on the steamboat deck,

The shoemaker singing as he sits on his bench, the hatter singing
as he stands,

The wood-cutter's song, the ploughboy's on his way in the morning,
or at noon intermission or at sundown,

The delicious singing of the mother, or of the young wife at work,
or of the girl sewing or washing, **2**

Each singing what belongs to him or her and to none else,

10　The day what belongs to the day—at night the party of young fellows,
robust, friendly,

Singing with open mouths their strong melodious songs.

1

Look at the title and first line of the poem. Who is singing? Read on to find out what this personification means.

2

Find descriptions that the poet uses. What senses do they appeal to? Add the ideas to your Sensory Image Chart.

Key Vocabulary
melodious *adj.*, having a pleasant sound, like music

In Other Words
varied carols different songs
blithe joyful, happy
mason stone worker, bricklayer
noon intermission lunch
robust healthy and strong

People of Colors, 2004, Elizabeth Rosen. Acrylic on board, private collection.

How does the artist's use of color contribute to the message of the poem?

About the Poet

Walt Whitman (1819–1892) worked as a teacher and journalist before beginning to write poetry. Often treated as an outsider in his lifetime, he is now viewed as the first and greatest poet of individuality and American democracy.

I, too

BY LANGSTON HUGHES

I, too, sing America.

I am the darker brother.
They send me to eat in the kitchen
When company comes,
5   But I laugh,
And eat well,
And grow strong.

Tomorrow,
I'll be at the table **3**
10   When company comes.
Nobody'll dare
Say to me,
"Eat in the kitchen,"
Then.

15   Besides,
They'll see how beautiful I am
And be ashamed—

I, too, am America. **4**

3 Figurative Language
The speaker says that he will be "at the table." What does this metaphor mean?

4 Figurative Language
How would the poem be different if the last line were, "I, too, am an American."

Key Vocabulary
ashamed *adj.*, feeling guilty and embarrassed

Double Trouble, 2006, Morgan Lockamy. Scratch board drawing, Scholastic Art and Writing Awards at the Alliance for Young Artists and Writers, Inc. collection.

▲ Critical Viewing: Design Study the artist's use of line and shading. How do those design elements emphasize the question in the young man's eyes?

About the Poet

Langston Hughes (1902–1967) had his first breakthrough as a professional poet while working as a busboy in a restaurant. He went on to become one of the leading figures in the Harlem Renaissance. He is an internationally known voice of the African American experience.

WHERE IS
MY COUNTRY?

by Nellie Wong

Where is my country?
Where does it lie?

The 4th of July approaches
and I am asked for firecrackers.
5   Is it because of my skin color?
Surely not because
of my husband's name.

In these skyways
I dart in and out.
10 One store sells rich ice cream
and I pick bittersweet nuggets. 5

In the office someone asks me
to interpret Korean,
my own Cantonese netted
15 in steel, my own saliva. 6

Where is my country?
Where does it lie?

5 **Figurative Language**
Why does the speaker use this example to describe feeling out of place?

6 **Sensory Images**
What senses do lines 8-15 appeal to? How do they help you experience the speaker's feelings? Add the ideas to your Sensory Image Chart.

Key Vocabulary
- **interpret** v., to translate something from one language to another
- **features** n., the parts of your face

In Other Words
skyways modern highways
dart move quickly
Cantonese Chinese language
netted caught and trapped

Tucked between boundaries
striated between dark dance floors
20 and whispering lanterns
smoking of indistinguishable features?

Salted in Mexico
where a policeman speaks to me in Spanish?
In the voice of a Chinese grocer
25 who asks if I am Filipino?

Channeled in the white businessman
who discovers that I do not sound Chinese?
Garbled in a white woman
who tells me I speak perfect English?
30 Webbed in another
who tells me I speak with an accent?

Where is my country?
Where does it lie?

Now the dress designers flood us
35 with the Chinese look,
quilting our bodies in satin
stitching our eyes with silk.

Where is my country?
Where does it lie? 7

7 Figurative
Language
Look at the verbs
in lines 18–31 that
the author uses to
describe where her
country is. What
images do they
suggest?

Asian Wind, 2004, Nicole Cardiff. Colored pencil and watercolor, collection of the artist.

▲ Critical Viewing: Mood Explain how the mood of the painting reflects the mood of the poem. What elements in the painting help to create this mood?

In Other Words
striated marked with lines
indistinguishable features parts that all look the same
Channeled Found
Garbled in Confused by, Distorted by

About the Poet

Nellie Wong (1934–) grew up in Chinatown in Oakland, California. In the 1970s she began writing poetry and staging public readings with a group of politically active Chinese American female poets. Her work often addresses issues of gender, race, and class.

LEGAL ALIEN
by Pat Mora

Bi-lingual, Bi-cultural,
able to slip from "How's life?"
to *"Me'stan volviendo loca,"* 8
able to sit in a paneled office
5   drafting memos in smooth English,
able to order in fluent Spanish
at a Mexican restaurant,
American but hyphenated,
viewed by Anglos as perhaps exotic,

8   Why do you think the poet includes this Spanish phrase? How does it add to the meaning of her poem?

Bicultural Tablesetting, 1998, Rolando Briseño. Serigraph, private collection.

◀ Critical Viewing

What is the effect of the layered images and the division of the background? How do these elements reflect the theme of the poem?

Key Vocabulary
alien *n.*, someone who comes from another country

In Other Words
Bi-lingual Able to speak two languages
Me'stan volviendo loca They're making me crazy (Spanish)
but hyphenated both Mexican and American
inferior less important
Bi-laterally By both sides

10 perhaps inferior, definitely different,
    viewed by Mexicans as alien,
    (their eyes say, "You may speak
    Spanish but you're not like me")
    an American to Mexicans
15 a Mexican to Americans
    a handy token
    sliding back and forth
    between the fringes of both worlds
    by smiling
20 by masking the discomfort
    of being pre-judged
    Bi-laterally.

About the Poet

Pat Mora (1942–   ) was born in the border town of El Paso, Texas, and grew up speaking both English and Spanish. Her bilingual experience continues to influence her work as an award-winning author. Mora has published five books of poetry, a memoir, a collection of essays, and many children's books.

ANALYZE Voices of America

1. **Explain** What is the main idea of "I Hear America Singing"? How does this theme compare with the main ideas of the other three poems?

2. **Vocabulary** The speakers in the final three poems describe themselves as aliens in American society. Give examples that show this feeling from each of the poems.

3. **Analyze Word Choice: Figurative Language** The speaker in "I, Too" finishes with a metaphor. What is it? How does this reflect how he feels about his role in the community?

4. **Focus Strategy Visualize: Identify Sensory Images** With a partner, review the **Sensory Image Chart** you began on page 679. Discuss which poem appeals most to your senses, then describe how the images help you understand the poem better.

Return to the Text

Reread and Write Which poem best expresses what it means for people to belong to a community? Write a note to the poet explaining your choice. Include specific examples to support your ideas.

BEFORE READING Human Family
poem by Maya Angelou

Reading Strategies

• Plan and Monitor
• Determine Importance
• Make Inferences
• Ask Questions
• Make Connections
• Synthesize
▶ Visualize

Analyze Structure: Rhythm and Rhyme

Like many of the songs you know, poetry often has a special rhythm and rhyme.

• **Rhythm** is a musical quality that poets create by repeating sounds, words, and lines. Rhythm also helps poets emphasize certain words.

• **Rhymes** create a musical effect by repeating sounds. Some poets use a **rhyme scheme**, or a pattern of rhymes, in their poems. Other poets write **free verse** poems which do not include any rhythm or rhyme. The poet instead tries to capture the natural rhymes found in ordinary speech.

Look Into the Text

In this poem, each stanza has four lines.

```
        The variety of our skin tones
  10    can confuse, bemuse, delight,
        brown and pink and beige and purple,
        tan and blue and white.

        I've sailed upon the seven seas
        and stopped in every land,
  15    I've seen the wonders of the world,
        not yet one common man.
```

The last word of every other line rhymes in each stanza. This rhyme scheme adds rhythm to the poem.

Focus Strategy ▶ Visualize

Sensory images help you experience the details that a writer describes. Visualizing these images will help you understand and experience the text in new ways.

HOW TO USE SENSORY IMAGES

Focus Strategy

1. As you read, focus your attention on words and phrases that appeal to your senses.

YOU NOTICE: I've sailed upon the seven seas ... / I've seen the wonders of the world, / not yet one common man.

2. Imagine the scene, character, or event using all five senses.

YOU VISUALIZE: I feel the rocking motion of a boat. I see many amazing sights that I've only seen in books. I imagine the faces of people all over the world.

3. Think about how this helps you understand the selection.

YOU THINK: The speaker has seen all the amazing sights of the world, but nothing is as amazing as people.

Connect Across Texts

The poems in "Voices of America" describe what it means to belong to a country. As you read this poem by Maya Angelou, think about what it means to belong to the "Human Family."

HUMAN FAMILY

BY MAYA ANGELOU

All Human Beings are Born Free and Equal in Dignity and Rights, 1998, Ron Waddams. Acrylic on board, private collection, The Bridgeman Art Library.

▲ Critical Viewing: Effect Study the effect of the curved arms in this painting.

I note the obvious differences
in the human family.
Some of us are serious,
some thrive on comedy.

5   Some declare their lives are lived
as true profundity,
and others claim they really live
the real reality.

The variety of our skin tones
10   can confuse, bemuse, delight,
brown and pink and beige and purple,
tan and blue and white. **1**

I've sailed upon the seven seas
and stopped in every land,
15   I've seen the wonders of the world,
not yet one common man. **2**

1 Sensory Images
What do you
visualize as you
read this stanza?
How do these
sensory images
add to your
understanding
of the poem?

2 Rhythm
and Rhyme
Describe the rhyme
scheme of this
poem. How does
it contribute to
the rhythm?

Key Vocabulary
variety *n.*, mix of different things

In Other Words
declare insist, say
as true profundity in a great, meaningful way
bemuse confuse, puzzle
one common man a person who is
   totally ordinary

I know ten thousand women
called Jane and Mary Jane,
but I've not seen any two
who really were the same.

Mirror twins are different
although their features jibe,
and lovers think quite different thoughts
while lying side by side.

We love and lose in China,
we weep on England's moors,
and laugh and moan in Guinea,
and thrive on Spanish shores.

We seek success in Finland,
are born and die in Maine. 3
In minor ways we differ,
in major we're the same.

3 **Sensory Images**
What details in lines 25–30 help you visualize the places mentioned? How does this help you understand the poet's message?

Key Vocabulary

- **minor** *adj.*, small or unimportant
- **major** *adj.*, great in size or importance

In Other Words

jibe match, go together
moors open, empty land

I note the obvious differences
between each sort and type,
35 but we are more alike, my friends,
than we are unalike.

We are more alike, my friends,
than we are unalike.

We are more alike, my friends,
40 than we are unalike.

ANALYZE Human Family

1. **Summarize** What is the main idea of "Human Family"? Use details from the poem to support your answer.

2. **Vocabulary** Lines 31 and 32 say: "In minor ways we differ, / in major we're the same." What examples does the speaker give to support this idea? What examples can you find in your own life?

3. **Analyze Structure: Rhythm and Rhyme** How does the rhythm and rhyme scheme change in the last stanza? Why do you think Maya Angelou chooses to repeat the same lines at the end?

4. **Focus Strategy Visualize: Use Sensory Images** How does the poet's use of sensory images help convey her message? Use specific details from the poem in your answer.

Return to the Text

Reread and Write According to Angelou, all people are members of the "human family." Reread the poem and write a short paragraph that describes Angelou's thinking about what holds the human family together and what keeps the human family apart. Note specific details from the poem to support your answer.

About the Poet

Maya Angelou (1928–   ) is recognized as one of the important voices of modern American literature. A poet, educator, historian, and civil rights activist, she explores the many ways in which people view themselves and others through the lens of gender and race.

EQ What Holds Us Together? What Keeps Us Apart?

Reading

Critical Thinking

EQ 1. Analyze Think back on the discussion you had on page 678 about what it means to belong to a community. Then consider the themes of the five poems you have read. What do they have in common?

2. Interpret In Nellie Wong's poem, what does the speaker mean when she says, "Where is my country? Where does it lie?" How would the speakers in the other poems answer this question?

3. Compare Which two speakers have the most different views of community? Compare the two speakers' viewpoints.

4. Speculate How would Maya Angelou respond to the idea that you can feel like an **alien** in your own country?

EQ 5. Opinion Do you think it is possible to have a community in which every person feels that he or she belongs? Is community always a good thing? Explain, using examples from the selections to support your answer.

Writing

Write About Literature

Judgment Which poem speaks most directly to you about what it means to be an American? Write a paragraph that explains your choice. Include specific examples from the poems to support your opinions. When you have finished writing your paragraph, create a multimedia presentation using images and sound to convey your viewpoint.

Vocabulary

Key Vocabulary Review

Oral Review Work with a partner. Use these words to complete the paragraph.

aliens	interpret	minor
ashamed	major	variety
features	melodious	

For centuries, poets have written about the theme of community. Walt Whitman once saw America as a __(1)__ and pleasing song that was sung by people from a __(2)__ of different walks of life. Modern poets with different backgrounds feel differently. They are sometimes embarrassed and __(3)__ to be __(4)__ who have come from other countries. They notice that the __(5)__ on their faces look different, and they find it difficult to __(6)__ what others say. Maya Angelou, however, doesn't feel that these are __(7)__ problems. She believes that our differences are __(8)__ and unimportant compared to the joys of being together.

Writing Application Write a journal entry about a time you felt like an alien in a group. Use at least three Key Vocabulary words.

Fluency

Read with Ease: Intonation

Assess your reading fluency with the passage in the Reading Handbook, p. 771. Then complete the self-check below.

1. My intonation did/did not sound natural.

2. My words correct per minute: _____

INTEGRATE THE LANGUAGE ARTS

Enrich Your Sentences

Phrases with **participles** can enrich your sentences. A participle is a verb form that usually ends with **-ing** or **-ed**. A phrase that describes a noun or a pronoun can begin with a participle.

Walt Whitman heard Americans. They were singing their varied songs.

Walt Whitman heard Americans **singing** their varied songs.

Walt Whitman wrote poetry. It was admired for its musical sounds.

Walt Whitman wrote poetry **admired** for its musical sounds.

One longer sentence that includes a **participial phrase** can be more interesting than two short, choppy sentences.

Oral Practice (1–5) Say each sentence, adding a participle in the blank.

1. Langston Hughes wrote poems _____ Harlem. (describe)
2. _____ about her country, Nellie Wong wonders where it can be found. (write)
3. Walt Whitman wrote a new kind of poetry _____ with images of American workers. (fill)
4. _____ to his environment, the speaker of the poem feels like an alien. (respond)
5. _____ our similarities and differences, Maya Angelou describes the human family. (celebrate)

Written Practice (6–10) Use participles to combine each pair of sentences.

6. Maya Angelou is a famous poet. She is celebrated around the world.
7. She writes poems. She uses meter and rhyme.
8. She uses many images. They include pictures of people and places.
9. She writes poems. They are filled with hope.
10. She creates work. It is respected by other poets.

Allusions

An **allusion** is a reference to a well-known person, place, event, artwork, or work of literature. Understanding what the writer is alluding to can help you understand his or her meaning.

The title of the play *A Raisin in the Sun* is an allusion to the poem "Harlem" by Langston Hughes.

With a partner, reread "I, Too" by Langston Hughes. Which other poem in the unit is Hughes alluding to? Discuss how recognizing this allusion helps you understand the poem.

Source: ©Edward Frascino/*The New Yorker*

DOG WALKER TO THE STARS

What famous "stars" does this cartoon allude to? How does your knowledge of the characters help you understand the humor?

Use Appropriate Language

Formal Introductions Suppose one of the poets visited your school. Read the biographies on pages 683, 685, 687, 689, and 694. Choose a poet to introduce to a schoolwide assembly.

Figurative Language

Figurative language helps readers create images in their minds.

- A **simile** uses *like* or *as* to make a comparison. How are the two things in this simile alike?

  Whitman is **as joyful as a child**.

- A **metaphor** compares by saying one thing *is* another thing. A mosaic is art made from pieces of glass or tile. How is America a mosaic?

  America **is a mosaic** of people.

Find these examples of figurative language in poems you just read and tell what they mean.

1. varied carols (page 682)

2. my own saliva (page 686)

3. handy token (page 689)

Historical Figure Biography

A **biography** tells the story of a person's life. Study the biographies of the poets in this unit. Then write a biography for a historical figure you admire.

1 **Research** Use the Internet or library resources to find information on the historical figure.

2 **Take Notes** Record information about people and events in the figure's life. Find interesting quotes.

3 **Write and Present** Be sure to include specific details as you narrate the life of your historical figure. Share your biography with the class.

🔖 **Language and Learning Handbook**, page 702

🔖 **Writing Handbook**, page 784

Voice and Style

Every writer makes decisions about voice and style.

- **Voice** is the language, tone, and word choice that makes the writing uniquely yours.

- **Style** is how you use words and sentences to address your purpose and audience. You would use a different style for a note to a friend than for an essay.

Study the paragraph. Are the voice and style right for a short answer essay response?

Just OK

> I think the speaker in "Legal Alien" is totally right! People shouldn't say "I know who you are" when they have no idea about it! People from Mexico shouldn't make fun of her. And Caucasians shouldn't either. It's not even fair.

Here is how the writer improved the paragraph:

Much Better

> I agree with the speaker in "Legal Alien." People judge others too easily. They assume that they know what she is like based on her appearance or ethnicity. But each person is unique. Instead of criticizing her, they should learn who she really is.

Revise the paragraph below to use an appropriate voice and style for a short answer essay response.

> "Human Family" is totally cool. It shows how we are all really the same deep down inside. We should look at the way everyone on Earth is part of the same big, happy family of people. This is more important than the small stuff that keeps us apart.

After you rewrite the paragraph, check your work.

- Are my voice and style appropriate?
- Do I keep the main ideas from the original?
- Do I use participial phrases correctly?

🔖 **Writing Handbook**, page 784

Mending Wall

BY ROBERT FROST

Something there is that doesn't love a wall,
That sends the frozen-ground-swell under it,
And spills the upper boulders in the sun;
And makes gaps even two can pass abreast.
5 The work of hunters is another thing:
I have come after them and made repair
Where they have left not one stone on a stone,
But they would have the rabbit out of hiding,
To please the yelping dogs. The gaps I mean,
10 No one has seen them made or heard them made,
But at spring mending-time we find them there.
I let my neighbor know beyond the hill;
And on a day we meet to walk the line
And set the wall between us once again.

In Other Words
Something there is There is something
gaps spaces so
abreast side by side

15 We keep the wall between us as we go.
     To each the boulders that have fallen to each.
     And some are loaves and some so nearly balls
     We have to use a spell to make them balance:
     'Stay where you are until our backs are turned!'
20 We wear our fingers rough with handling them.
     Oh, just another kind of outdoor game,
     One on a side. It comes to little more:
     There where it is we do not need the wall:
     He is all pine and I am apple orchard.
25 My apple trees will never get across
     And eat the cones under his pines, I tell him.
     He only says, 'Good fences make good neighbors.'
     Spring is the mischief in me, and I wonder
     If I could put a notion in his head:
30 '*Why* do they make good neighbors? Isn't it
     Where there are cows? But here there are no cows.
     Before I built a wall I'd ask to know
     What I was walling in or walling out,
     And to whom I was like to give offense.
35 Something there is that doesn't love a wall,
     That wants it down.' I could say 'Elves' to him,
     But it's not elves exactly, and I'd rather
     He said it for himself. I see him there
     Bringing a stone grasped firmly by the top
40 In each hand, like an old-stone savage armed.
     He moves in darkness as it seems to me,
     Not of woods only and the shade of trees.
     He will not go behind his father's saying,
     And he likes having thought of it so well
45 He says again, 'Good fences make good neighbors.'

Stonewall with pines, Vermont, John Churchman.

In Other Words

There where it is In fact
is all pine has all pine trees
a notion an idea

WHERE WE BELONG

EQ ESSENTIAL QUESTION:
What Holds Us Together? What Keeps Us Apart?

myNGconnect.com

🌐 Download the rubric.

EDGE LIBRARY

Present Your Project: Poetry Anthology

It's time to publish and present your poetry anthology about the Essential Question for this unit: What Holds Us Together? What Keeps Us Apart?

1 Review and Complete Your Plan

Consider these points as you finish preparing your poetry anthology:

- How will you organize your anthology—by theme, subject, or writer?
- Will you include illustrations, photographs, or other images?
- Does the anthology or each poem need an introduction?

2 Publish Your Poetry Anthology

Publish your poetry anthology on your school Web site or photocopy and distribute it to other classes or your school library.

3 Evaluate the Anthology

Use the rubric to evaluate your poetry anthology.

Reflect on Your Reading

Many of the plays in this unit and in the Edge Library examine the things that keep people together and the things that can drive them apart.

Think back on your reading of the unit selections, including your choice of Edge Library books. Then discuss the following with a partner or in a small group.

Genre Focus Compare and contrast the elements of drama with the elements of poetry. Give examples, using the selections in this unit.

Focus Strategy Choose a selection in this unit that might be difficult for someone to understand. Write a list of ways that they can visualize images in the text. Share the strategies with a partner and discuss how visualizing details can help you understand the text.

EQ Respond to the Essential Question

Throughout this unit, you have been thinking about what holds people together and what keeps them apart. What have *you* decided? Support your response with evidence from your reading, discussions, research, and writing.

Language and Learning Handbook
Language, Learning, Communication

Reading Handbook
Reading, Fluency, Vocabulary

Writing Handbook
Writing Process, Traits, Conventions

Learning and Developing Language

How Do I *Learn* Language?

1 **Listen actively and try out language.**

What to Do	Examples
Listen to others and use their language.	**You hear:** "When did our teacher say that the assignment is due?" **You say:** "Our teacher said that the assignment is due May 1."
Listen to yourself to perfect pronunciation of new words.	**You say:** "I see the word *privacy*. *Privacy* has a long *i* sound. Let me practice the long i sound to make sure I'm saying the word correctly."
Incorporate language chunks into your speech.	**You hear:** "Send me an e-mail or a text message on my cell." **You think:** *I know what an e-mail is. So a text message must be an e-mail that you send on a phone.* **You say:** "I'll e-mail you. I don't think I can send text messages on my cell."
Make connections across content areas. Use the language you learn in one subject area in other subject areas and outside of school.	**You read this in science class:** Studies show that each person in the U.S. produces more than 4 pounds of garbage each day. We don't have enough landfill space. Recycling is essential. **You write this in your reading journal:** Maybe I'll do my persuasive paper for English class on recycling. I have strong feelings about why it is good to recycle. **At home, you might say:** Mom, did you recycle the empty cans and bottles?
Take risks. Use words or phrases you know and use them in another way.	**All of these statements mean the same thing:** My teacher helps me push my thinking. My teacher helps me stretch my mind to see different viewpoints. Before I make a decision, my teacher suggests I role-play different choices in my imagination.
Memorize new words. They will help you build the background knowledge you need to understand more difficult language.	**Make flash cards:** Flash cards are a great way to memorize new words, phrases, or expressions. Write the English meaning on one side of a note card and the meaning in your language on the other side. Look at the words or phrases in your language and try to say the English meaning. Flip the card over to check your answer.

2 Ask for help, feedback, and clarification.

What to Do	Examples
Ask questions about how to use language.	Did I say that right? Did I use that word the right way? Which is right: "brang" or "brought"?
Use your native language or English to ask for clarification. Use what you learned to correct your mistakes.	**You say:** "Wait! Could you go over that point again, a little more slowly, please?" **Other examples:** "Does 'have a heart' mean 'to be kind'?" "Is 'paper' another word for 'essay'?"
Use context clues to confirm your understanding of difficult words.	**You hear:** "The team united, or came together, after they lost the game." **You think:** "I hear the word *or* after the word *united*, so *united* must mean 'came together.'"

3 Use nonverbal clues.

What to Do	Examples
Use gestures and mime to show an idea.	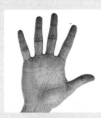 I will hold up five fingers to show that I need five minutes.
Look for nonverbal clues.	 Maria invited me to a concert where her favorite band will be playing. They are electrifying! *Electrifying* must mean "good." She looks good.
Identify and respond appropriately to nonverbal and verbal clues.	Let's give him a hand. Everyone is clapping. "Give him a hand" must mean to clap for him. I should clap for him, too.

4 Verify how language works.

What to Do	Examples
Test hypotheses about how language works.	**You can try out what you learned:** I can add -ation to the verb observe to get the noun observation. So maybe I can make a noun by adding -ation to some verbs that end in -e. Let's see. Prepare and preparation. Yes, that is right! Compare and comparation. That doesn't sound correct. I will see what the dictionary says ... Now I understand—it's comparison.
Use spell-checkers, dictionaries, and other available reference aids, such as the Internet.	**You just finished your draft of an essay, so you think:** Now I'll use spell-check to see what words I need to fix.
Use prior knowledge.	You can figure out unfamiliar words by looking for or remembering words you do know or experiences you've learned about previously. Use this prior knowledge to figure out new words. **Example:** We felt embarrassed for Tom when he behaved like a clown. I know the word "clown." Maybe "embarrassed" means the way I feel when one of my friends starts acting like a clown.
Use contrastive analysis to compare how your language works to how English works.	**You hear:** "She is a doctor." **You think:** In English, an article, such as a or an, is used before the title of a job. In my native language, no article is used: "She is doctor."
Use semantic mapping to determine the relationship between the meanings of words.	jogging — tennis — football exercising weightlifting — swimming — water / goggles / pool **You think:** Where should I place the word ball? It can attach to football or tennis because both activities use a kind of ball.
Use imagery.	Use descriptive language to form a picture in your imagination in order to figure out a word you don't know. You can draw pictures of what you imagined to remind you of the meaning of the word. Say the words while looking at the pictures to make connections.

5 | **Monitor and evaluate your learning.**

What to Do	Examples
Self-monitor and self-assess language use.	*Did I use the correct verb form to tell what my plans are for the future?* *Was it all right to use informal language only? Did I use transitions to show how my ideas were connected?*
Take notes about language.	Active Voice Compared to Passive Voice • I should write most sentences in active voice. This is the most common way to construct sentences. The "doer," or actor, of the verb in the sentence should be the subject. **Incorrect**: The race was won by Jon. **Correct**: Jon won the race.
Use visuals to construct or clarify meaning.	*This paragraph is confusing. Maybe I can use a graphic organizer to organize the main ideas.*
Review.	*Do I understand everything that was taught? I should review my notes and graphic organizers.*

How Do I *Use* Language?

Sometimes you use language to clarify ideas or to find out about something. Other times you will want to share information.

How to Ask Questions

Ask about a person: *Who* is the girl in the photograph?

Ask about a place: *Where* are the people standing?

Ask about a thing: *What* is she holding?

Ask about a time: *When* do you think Anna plays tennis?

Ask about reasons: *Why* is the woman interviewing Anna?

How to Express Feelings

Name an event: I won the game.

Name a feeling: I was so happy when I won the game.

Tell more: I held the trophy over my head with pride!

Use the subjunctive mood: If you weren't here, I would be concerned.

How to Express Likes and Dislikes

Tell what you think: I like this painting. I think this painting is creative. In my opinion, this is a great painting.

How to Express Ideas, Needs, Intentions, and Opinions

Use words that express your needs: I need (require, must have) something to eat.

Be specific about what you need: I need a fire extinguisher now!

Elaborate on why you need something: I need some tape because I need to attach these two pieces of paper.

Use words that signal your intentions: I plan (intend, expect) to arrive at 6:00 p.m.

Use words that tell your opinions: I believe (think) the movie is great.

How to Give Oral Directions

Tell the first thing to do: Go to the board.

Tell the next step. Use a time order word: Now pick up the chalk.

Tell another step. Use another time order word: Next, write your name.

Tell the last thing to do: Go back to your seat.

Receive feedback on directions: Ask listeners if they were able to follow the directions. Repeat directions as needed.

How to Give Directions

Give information: The meeting begins at 3:15 p.m. at the library on Main Street.

Give one step directions: Go south on Ridge Road, then turn left on Main Street.

Provide directions to peers: The meeting is at the library on Main Street. It is on the same block as the school where last week's football game was held.

How to Give and Respond to Requests and Commands

Make **polite requests**: Could you please give me a pen? May I read aloud?

Respond to a **request**: Of course. You're welcome.

Make a **polite command**: Please listen carefully.

Make a **strong command**: Do not follow me!

Respond to a **command**: Of course. Certainly.

How to Engage in Conversation and Small Talk

Engage in small talk: How are you today? Nice weather we're having, isn't it?

Use social courtesies: May I borrow your pen, please? Thank you.

Ask and answer questions: Do you play baseball? Yes, I do.

Use verbal cues to show that you are listening: Uh-huh. Yes, I see. OK.

Use nonverbal language skills: For example, nod your head, smile at something funny, or make eye contact.

How to Tell an Original Story

Give the main idea of the story first: I want to tell you about my trip to Chicago.

Tell the important events of the story: I visited my cousin at her office. She showed me what her job is like.

Use transition words: First, I got off the bus. Then, I walked down into a tall, modern building.

Give details to make the story interesting: It was very cold that day. I remember I was wearing a big, warm jacket.

Retell a story: Maria said she was on her way to the library when she noticed something strange. Someone was following her.

How to Describe

Be specific by using descriptive words or phrases: I like the actor with the bright red hair.

Use descriptive imagery when possible: The room was as dark as a mountain cave. The butterfly floated gracefully through the air.

Describe a **favorite activity**: Playing volleyball is exciting and competitive.

Describe **people**: Marta has long, brown hair. She is wearing a blue t-shirt.

Describe **places**: The building on the corner had its windows covered with wood, and its yard was filled with trash.

Describe **things**: My house is large and brown. It looks like a barn.

Describe **events**: The jazz band is playing in the auditorium tonight.

Describe **ideas**: We plan to have a car wash next Saturday.

Describe **feelings**: I was bored, but happy.

Describe **experiences**: Playing guitar is relaxing for me.

Describe **immediate surroundings**: There are 28 desks in my English classroom.

Describe **wishes using the subjunctive mood**: I wish that my brother were nicer to me.

How to Elaborate an Idea

Give examples to support your ideas: All students should participate in an activity to fully experience their high school years. For example, people could join the chess club, a sports team, or the school band.

Give details about your ideas: I want to organize a group trip to the museum. We can take the city bus there. We will bring our own lunches to save money. There are many new, exciting exhibits to see at the museum.

Be as specific as possible: It takes several years of school to become a lawyer. First, you have to get a college degree. Then, you need to go to law school. Getting a law degree usually takes about three years.

How to Ask for and Give Information

Use polite requests to ask for information: Can you please tell me your name again?

Give the exact information someone is asking for: To get to the bus stop, walk down this street, then turn left at Carter Avenue.

How to Recognize, Express, and Respond Appropriately to Humor

Listen and watch for clues: For example, a change in a person's voice or facial expression might mean that the person is joking or using humor. Also, watch for more obvious clues such as smiling and laughing.

Use verbal or nonverbal responses to recognize humor: A smile or a nod of the head is a good nonverbal response to humor. You might also respond by saying, "I get it!" or "That's funny!"

Watch others to see how they react: If other people are responding to a humorous situation, then it is usually appropriate to respond to the humor, too.

How to Make Comparisons

Use compare and contrast words: The eagle is a majestic animal. Similarly, many people love dolphins. On the contrary, rats are pests and have few admirers.

Explain with details: The first math problem was difficult. But the second math problem was much more difficult. It required students to read a graph with data.

How to Define and Explain

Give a clear definition: A peacock is a large bird that is known for its colorful feathers.

Give details or examples to clarify: The large tail feathers of the male peacock are often bright green, gold, and blue.

Use a logical order for explanations: The house needs to be cleaned. First, pick up all of the toys and clothes and put them away. Then, vacuum and mop the floors.

Use graphic organizers to help explain: See the Index of Graphic Organizers on p. 772 for graphic organizers you can use to explain and define words and ideas.

How to Clarify Information

Restate your words with new words: The job is a volunteer position. In other words, you do not receive payment for doing the work.

Define some confusing words: Math class is intriguing, meaning it is very interesting.

Use synonyms and antonyms: The information in the memo is confidential, or secret. It is not public information, or common knowledge.

How to Verify and Confirm Information

Ask for repetition: Could you repeat that, please? Would you rephrase that for me?

Restate what you just heard: So, you're saying that it is OK to wear jeans to school?

How to Express Doubts, Wishes, and Possibilities

Understand the subjective mood: Verbs in the subjunctive mood describe doubts, wishes, and possibilities.

Use the subjunctive mood correctly:

- In the present tense, third-person singular verbs in the subjunctive mood do not have the usual *-s* or *-es* ending: She demands that he *play* outside.
- In present tense, the subjunctive mood of *be* is *be* (instead of *is* or *are*): She insists that the boys be quiet.
- In past tense, the subjunctive mood of *be* is *were*, regardless of the subject: If she *were* kinder, the boys might listen to her.

How to Understand Basic Expressions

Consider the social context:
This video game is so cool!
It's rather cool out today. It's 55 degrees.

Consider the language context: Turn right on Maple Street. The gas station will be just ahead on the left.

How to Justify with Reasons

State your claim clearly: I should be the class president.

Support your claim with evidence: This year I created a scholarship drive, organized career night, and spoke up for students at a school board meeting.

Give clear reasons that connect the evidence and your claim: My actions show that I can be a strong class president.

Combine your sentences to make the logic clear: I should be voted president of our class because I have worked hard to give students new opportunities this year.

How to Persuade or Convince

Use persuasive words: You can be a positive force in your community.

Give suggestions to others: You should listen to what the people in your community believe. You ought to consider all options available.

Give strong support for your persuasive idea: Everyone should ride his or her bicycle to work or school. It will lessen pollution and give people daily exercise.

How to Negotiate

Show that you know both sides of an issue: I see your point about the need for a new parking lot, but a park and soccer field would be more useful.

Use persuasive language: I believe you will agree with me if you consider these facts.

Clearly state your goals: We want to raise $2,000 by April and donate the money to the park fund.

How to Adjust Communication for Your Audience, Purpose, Occasion, and Task

Make sure your language is appropriate for your audience and the situation: You should choose a formal or informal manner of speaking depending on whom you are speaking to and the situation.

If you are addressing your teacher, an employer, or another adult, you might speak in this manner:

> Excuse me, Mr. Johnson. May we please talk about my research paper?

If you are speaking to a friend, you can be less formal:

> Hey Bob, can we talk about my research paper?

If you do not know whether a situation will call for formal or informal language, ask your teacher to help you.

Focus on your purpose: I want to make it very clear to you why that behavior could be hazardous to your health.

How to Engage in an Academic Discussion

Use formal speech: Please review the information at your convenience.

Refer to evidence: In the article we read, the author says that only 40 percent of newspapers have minorities as editors.

Ask questions: Why do you think that? What other options are there? What might have caused that?

Involve others: What do you think?

Express respect for what others say: I understand your opinion. Thank you for sharing that information.

Clarify and verify what others say: Can you explain that in another way? What evidence supports that opinion?

How to Express Social Courtesies

Listen politely and show interest: Yes, I see. Oh, what a good idea!

Wait your turn to speak: May I ask a question? I would just like to say that I disagree.

Use polite terms: Please. Thank you. That was nice of you. You are so welcome.

Use informal language when interacting with friends and family: Hi! How's it going? Thanks! No problem. Bye!

How to Conduct a Transaction or Business Deal

Clearly state numbers, dollar amounts, and other important details: Yes, I would like three textbooks. I cannot spend more than $50.

Be polite and professional: Thank you for your time. I appreciate your help.

Consider the context of the situation: Consider where you are and what is going on. For example, you can infer that when you are asked for your identification at a bank, the teller means your driver's license rather than a school ID.

How to Demonstrate and Interpret Nonverbal Communication

Watch for and use gestures, eye contact, or other visual or nonverbal communication.
Some examples include the following:

- waving to say "hello" or "good-bye"
- direct eye contact to show attention
- nodding to show understanding or approval
- using hands to show a number or a sign, like "stop"
- winking or smiling to show you are joking

Look for clues by combining verbal and nonverbal communication. You can often guess what someone means by watching how they communicate nonverbally while they speak. For example, you will have an easier time understanding someone's directions by watching where he or she points.

Listening and Speaking

Listening

Good listeners are able to learn new information and avoid confusion.

How to Listen Actively and Respectfully

- Set a purpose and prepare for listening.
- Pay close attention to the speaker. Demonstrate appropriate body language by sitting up straight and looking at the speaker as you listen.
- Connect texts or ideas that you are hearing to personal knowledge and experience—this will help you understand.
- Don't interrupt, unless you need to ask the speaker to speak more loudly.
- When the speaker is finished, ask him or her to explain things you did not understand. If the speaker did not talk enough about a topic, ask him or her to tell you more about it.

How to Overcome Barriers to Listening

- Pay close attention to the speaker.
- Try to ignore other noises or distractions around you.
- Politely ask any other people who are talking to be quiet.
- Close the classroom door or any windows if outdoor noises are distracting.
- Raise your hand, and ask the speaker to speak louder if necessary.
- Take notes on the topic being discussed. This will help you stay focused and self-monitor what you hear and track your understanding.
- In your notes, summarize the speaker's main idea and details. Were they effective enough to keep you interested? Was the speech's main idea easy to understand? Did the supporting ideas confirm the speech's main idea?

How to Use Choral Reading and Readers Theater

Choral Reading is a group activity that involves people reading a selection aloud, together. Readers Theater takes a story and treats it like a play. Students are assigned to read different parts, such as the narrator or a character.

During Choral Reading

- Listen carefully to how other readers pronounce words and phrases.
- Listen to how the intonation of the words changes.
- Listen to hear if your pitch and pronunciation sound like everyone else's.

During Readers Theater

- Listen to how different characters have different voices and expressions.
- Watch the speakers for gestures or acting.
- If you are the one who narrates or reads the stage directions, focus on describing where the action takes place.

Speaking

Speaking is saying aloud what you are thinking. Good speakers choose their words and use language effectively. They also choose an appropriate organizational strategy for their ideas. You may be required to speak in class during a discussion or when giving a presentation. Always speak responsibly and ethically. When you speak ethically, you are careful not to offend or upset anyone who is listening to you.

How to Manage Discussions and Presentations

To be a good speaker, you need to effectively share your ideas in class, in a group, or with a partner. There will be times when it is necessary to have a conference with your teacher or another student. In any discussion, whether it is formal or informal, there are things you can do to make it a productive meeting. Discussions are good ways to find information, check your understanding, and share ideas.

- In discussions, make positive comments about the ideas of others. Connect your ideas to what others say.

> Interesting point! That is a good idea. Thank you for sharing your opinion.

> I agree that people should recycle and I also think we should focus on saving water.

- Think about the topic that is being discussed. Give ideas about that topic, and exclude nonessential information.

> He is talking about how climate and weather are different in other parts of the world.

> There are many tropical climates near the equator.

- Ask questions if you need more information.
- Ask questions to verify or challenge ideas.

> Can you please repeat that? I do not understand. Can you explain that again?

> Can you give me evidence to support that idea? I respect your opinion but I think the character was shy, not scared.

- Anticipate, recognize, and adjust to listeners' needs and concerns.

> He looks confused. I should stop and explain that concept again.

How to Give Presentations

Choose an interesting topic that will engage listeners' attention. You may make a speech, share a poem, or give a performance or report to share your ideas. Be sure to justify your choice of performance technique. That is, does it fit your purpose and audience?

Use an engaging and effective introduction and conclusion. Keep your audience interested by changing your tone and volume and by using varied sentence structure to emphasize meaning. Speak using standard English grammar and syntax. It is fine to make your audience laugh, but be careful to use effective and appropriate humor that does not upset or offend your listeners. Use audience feedback to improve future presentations.

- Change your rate and volume for your audience or purpose. Be sure to speak with appropriate pitch, stress, intonation, and enunciation.

  I will be speaking about how dangerous chemicals are in the chemistry lab. I should use a serious tone during the presentation.

- Use body language such as gestures, facial expressions, and posture while you are speaking to show what you mean.

  I want to show how tall and wide a hockey goal is. I'll use my hands.

- Occasionally make eye contact with specific audience members.

  I do not want to appear nervous or unprepared. If I make eye contact with my audience, my presentation will be natural and relaxed.

How to Overcome Anxiety

Some people get a bit nervous or anxious about speaking in front of others. There are simple ways you can avoid this.

- **Be prepared**. If you plan your presentation well, you can be confident that you will speak well. Practice presenting in front of a mirror or a family member.

- **Use notes**. Use notes, graphic aids, and props as memory aids and to support the message. Notes can guide your speech or presentation. You can refer to the notes if you get confused or forget a topic you want to discuss. See the example on the right for the type of information you can keep track of in notes.

  Civil Wars Around the World
  — Mexico, 1857–1861
  — U.S., 1861–1865
  — Greece, 1946–1949
  — Yugoslavia, 1991–2001

How to Self-Monitor

Monitoring is watching or noticing what is happening as you speak. It is important to monitor your audience's reactions, so you can adjust your presentation if necessary. If possible, tape your speech so you can listen to it before you give it. Analyze the tape to discover anything that might be confusing or inappropriate for the listeners. Use a rubric to prepare, critique, and improve your speech. Create a scoring guide that you can use to self-monitor. For sample rubrics and scoring guides, see page 720–722 and 792–800.

How to Use Rhetorical Devices

Rhetorical devices are ways to use language to make your presentation more interesting, engaging, or effective. Look at the examples below. Then produce one or two examples of your own.

Rhetorical Device	Example
Alliteration: The repetition of the same consonant sounds at the beginning of words.	Pablo prefers pecan pie.
Allusion: A form of literary language in which one text makes the reader think about another text that was written before it.	When Hannah wrote in her essay that vanity was the main character's weak point, or "Achilles' heel," her teacher understood that Hannah was referring to a character in a Greek myth.
Analogy: A way of illustrating or explaining a thing or an idea by comparing it with a more familiar thing or idea.	*Blogs* are to the *Internet* as *journals* are to *paper*.
Irony: When you say one thing, but want the listeners to understand something different. You may say the opposite of what is really true.	Your friend says to you after you trip and fall, "Today must be your lucky day!"
Mood: The attitude or feeling of your presentation. You create this for your listeners with the words you choose.	Slowly the car approached. It rolled to a stop, and a strange looking character stepped out of the back seat.
Quotation: Repeating the exact words of someone using quotation marks.	As Franklin D. Roosevelt said, "The only thing we have to fear is fear itself."
Pun: A humorous use of words that have more than one meaning.	To write with a broken pencil is *point*-less.
Parallelism: Similarity of structure in a pair or series of related words, phrases, or sentences.	We can change our school. We can make a difference. We can do this together.
Repetition: Repeating words, phrases, or ideas. Using this device shows your listeners that you believe the idea is very important.	All people are entitled to freedom. Freedom is something everyone deserves. Freedom will make the world a better place.
Tone: A speaker's attitude toward the topic, audience, or self.	I am definitely not in favor of a shorter lunch period.

Viewing and Representing

Monitoring Your Understanding of Visuals

You encounter visual elements constantly—in print, on TV, on the Internet, and in movies. How can you make sure you accurately understand and interpret what you see? Does the visual enhance your understanding of the oral presentation? Use the following strategies to self-monitor, or check that you understand, what you are viewing.

How to View and Look for Details

Study the image below. Ask these kinds of questions:

- Who or what does the image show? Are there other details that answer *when*, *where*, *why*, or *how* questions about the image?
- How does the image make me feel? Do I enjoy looking at it? Does it worry me, make me laugh, or give me a good or bad feeling?
- What do the details and elements (such as shape, color, and size of the image) add to the meaning?

How to Respond to and Interpret Visuals and Informational Graphics

When you view visuals and informational graphics, think about why they are included and what information they provide. Informational graphics often present facts or statistics. For example, you will sometimes see illustrations or informational graphics used in an oral presentation. Ask yourself:

- What message or information is the visual showing?
- Why did the artist, designer, or illustrator create and include the visual?
- Does the visual represent information accurately and fairly? What information did the creator choose to include or leave out? Why?

How to Self-Correct Your Thoughts as You View

Examine your understanding of visuals to correct any faulty thinking. Always question the validity and accuracy of visuals.

- Be aware of racial, cultural, and gender stereotyping. A **stereotype** is a general opinion that is not always true. A stereotype does not look at the differences between individual people or things. For example, "All cats are lazy." This is a stereotype because although some cats are lazy, some are very active.
- Look again at the image or graphic for more information and details that may change your understanding and for things you did not notice at first.
- Watch for **bias**. Is the writer or creator presenting information that is slanted or manipulated to show a particular point of view?

How to Understand Different Kinds of Visuals

It is important to be familiar with the different kinds of visuals that illustrate ideas for a text or spoken presentation. You will be expected to respond to and interpret these different visuals. Some examples are maps, charts, graphs, photographs, illustrations, and other artwork. As you look at a visual, decide what it is telling you. Visuals should help you better understand the information, especially if the language is elaborate or complex.

Map

A map is a visual layout of a specific location. Maps are an excellent way to gain more information about an idea presented in text.

Graphic Displays

A chart or a graph can show comparisons or provide information more clearly than if the same statistics were only presented in a text. Be sure to evaluate the credibility of the source of the data.

Chart

Number of Endangered Species in the United States	
Classification	Number of Species
Mammals	70
Birds	76
Reptiles	13
Fish	74
Insects	47

Graph

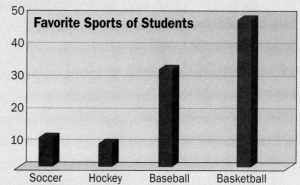

Favorite Sports of Students

Photographs, Illustrations, Video, Sound, and Artwork

Photographs, illustrations, and other artwork can have a variety of purposes:

- to share an opinion
- to elicit, or draw out, emotions
- to make people think
- to entertain

Multimedia resources include sound, motion, special effects, audio, and visuals. Use what you see and hear. Think about how the creator of a video or media presentation uses music or effects to make a point. Animations and other interactive media change based on what you click or touch.

Using Visuals and Multimedia in Writing and Presenting

Here are some key points to keep in mind when you choose to represent your ideas by using a visual or other media.

Representing Your Ideas Through Visuals

Using visuals in your writing and oral presentations can help you make your point more clearly. Choose visuals that match your purpose and your topic. Strong visuals will make a strong impression. Music and sound effects in multimedia presentations also impact tone and can be used to emphasize ideas or information. For example, if you choose to illustrate a poem about nature, include a picture that will help readers picture the place or feel the mood of the poem.

How Key Elements of Design Create Meaning and Influence the Message

Different visuals share information in different ways.

- If your goal is to entertain, choose a humorous picture.

Source: ©Terry Warner/Cartoon Stock, Ltd.

"Is this seat taken?"

- If your goal is to inform, use a visual that gives additional information about your topic or clarifies the information in some way. See the Index of Graphic Organizers on page 886 for ideas of ways to share information in graphic form.

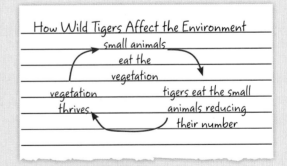

How Wild Tigers Affect the Environment

small animals eat the vegetation

vegetation thrives

tigers eat the small animals reducing their number

- If your goal is to persuade, or to make people feel or think a certain way, you may want to choose a visual that will appeal to emotions.
- If you use a visual from another source, be sure to identify the source.

Source: ©Jeff Rotman/Getty Images.

The Effects of Visual Arts on Mood

When you choose a visual to represent information in an essay or an oral presentation, make sure it is a visual that your particular audience will understand. A complex graph may not work well if your viewers do not know a lot about your topic. Creating a simple visual is especially important if you have an elaborate presentation. Your audience should be able to use the visual to make sense of the presentation. Make sure it is a visual you would want to view yourself.

In addition, consider the mood that you want the visual to create. The mood should be appropriate to your purpose and audience, such as a classroom of students listening to your oral presentation. If the mood of a presentation or essay is serious, do not use humorous or distracting visuals. For example, if you are giving a presentation on the United States government, you might display a graphic showing the legislative, executive, and judicial branches of government.

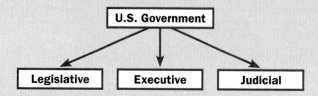

Interpreting and Analyzing Media

Media is the term used to describe the many forms of technology used today to provide communication to a large number of people. As you view media around you, such as the Internet, television, movies, magazines, and newspapers, make sure you remember the key points that are presented. What information is being presented in the visuals that are used? How is it presented? Make decisions about the information you are presented with by the media.

The information and visuals presented may be trustworthy, or they may be suspicious. In today's world, we are surrounded by images and information that we need to analyze and make decisions about. Keep in mind that visual media can easily influence our cultural and social expectations because it is much more visual than traditional texts. Be aware that you can make judgments and decisions while viewing the images and form your own opinions about the information they present.

Sometimes, the same event can be interpreted differently, based on the way the event is covered and the medium in which it is shown. Find a news event discussed in a newspaper and the same event on the Internet or TV. Then compare what is similar and what is different.

- What is the message?
- How do I know it is believable or valid?
- What information is included and what is left out?
- Is the information objective, or is it biased?

Technology and Media

How to Use Technology to Communicate

This section provides examples of the technology used today to communicate in school, in the workplace, and with friends and family.

Cell Phone

A **cell phone** does not need a wire connection to a phone network. It can be used anywhere there is a wireless phone network signal. It is completely portable. Cell phones can allow you to send text messages, connect to the Internet, play music, take photos, and make phone calls.

Personal Computer

A **personal computer** is an electronic tool that helps you create, save, and use information. You can also use a computer to communicate with e-mail, browse the Internet, work with digital photos or movies, or listen to music.

A **desktop computer** is not portable. It has several parts, including a monitor, a mouse, a keyboard, and a CD drive.

A **laptop computer** is smaller than a desktop computer. It is designed to be portable. A laptop computer usually fits in a travel case.

stylus

A **tablet computer** is typically even smaller than a laptop computer. You can use your fingers or a stylus pen to make most tablet computers work.

How to Select and Use Media to Research Information

Modern technology allows us to access a wide range of information. The Internet is a popular source for research and finding information for academic, professional, and personal reasons. Another source for research is your local library. It contains databases where you can gain access to many forms of print and nonprint resources, including audio and video recordings and many other sources of information.

The Internet

The **Internet** is an international network, or connection, of computers that share information with each other. The **World Wide Web** is a part of the Internet that allows you to find, read, and organize information. Using the Web is a fast way to get the most current information about many topics.

Any series of words or phrases can be typed into the "search" section of a search engine, and multiple Web sites with those words will be listed for you to investigate. Once you are at a Web site, you can perform a word or phrase search of the page you are on. This will help direct you to the information you are researching.

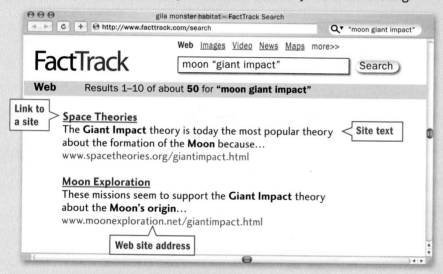

Other Sources of Information

There are many other reliable print and nonprint sources of information to use in your research. For example:

- magazines
- newspapers
- professional or scholarly journal articles
- experts
- political speeches
- press conferences

Most of the information from these sources is also available on the Internet. You should be careful to evaluate and choose the best sources for this information. It is important to double-check the source. Does the source show a bias? Is the source from a professor or from an anonymous blog post?

How to Evaluate the Quality of Information

There is so much information available on the Internet it can be hard to comprehend. It is important to be sure that the information you use as support or evidence is reliable and can be trusted. Use the following checklist as a guideline to decide if a Web page you are reading is reliable and a credible source.

Checklist to Determine Reliable Web Sites

☑ The information is from a well-known and trusted source. For example, Web sites that end in ".edu" are part of an educational institution and usually can be trusted. Other cues for reliable Web sites are sites that end in ".org" for "organization" or ".gov" for "government."

☑ The people who write or are quoted on the Web site are experts, not just everyday people expressing ideas or opinions.

☑ The Web site gives evidence, not just opinions.

☑ The Web site is free of grammatical and spelling errors. This is often a hint that the site was carefully constructed and will not have factual errors.

☑ The Web site is not trying to sell a product or persuade people. It is trying to provide accurate information.

If you are uncertain about the quality of a Web site, contact your teacher for advice.

How to Organize and Discuss Information From Various Media

Devise a system to organize the information you find from various forms of media, such as newspapers, books, and the Internet. You can make photocopies of important newspaper and magazine articles or pages from books and keep them in labeled folders. Web pages can be printed out or bookmarked on your computer for reference. You can discuss the information you find from various media with your classmates or teachers to evaluate its reliability. In fact, explaining aloud what you've gathered from a variety of media is one way to better understand the information. It will also help you to learn how to use specific language and vocabulary related to certain types of media.

How to Analyze and Interpret Information from Various Media

You should always try to analyze and interpret the information you find from various media sources. Many times the same event can be interpreted differently depending on the medium in which it is presented. Ask yourself if the source is reliable or if the information you find shows any bias or opinion. Some writers may only mention facts that support their ideas or opinions and not mention details that are not supportive of their arguments. Find an event that is covered both in your local newspaper and on television. Compare the differences between the coverage in the two media. Do you notice a difference in bias or opinion? Comparing two sources of information about the same topic may help you see that one is more biased than the other. It can help you see ways that different people present similar information.

How to Use Technology to Create Final Products

Technology allows people to create interesting final products to share information. Once you become comfortable with the appropriate equipment and software, there are many ways to create, change, and individualize your work using technology. Here are two examples of products that can be made with technology today.

Electronic Media

Electronic media, or a **word-processing document**, allows you to create and save written work. You can use it to:

- store ideas, plans, and essays
- write drafts of your work
- revise, edit, and proofread your writing
- format, publish, and share your work

There are many different kinds of word-processing programs. If you are not familiar with word-processing programs, talk to your teacher about learning one that will work well for you in class. Review or learn the following basic steps:

1 **Start a File or Document** Open a new document, and choose a place to save it.

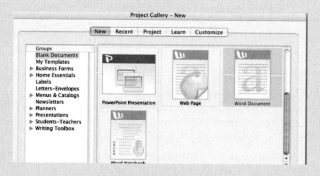

2 **Type and Format Your Work** Review how to do basic tasks, such as change a font, highlight words in color, and make type bold or underlined.

3 **Save and Share Your Work** Continually click the Save icon on the toolbar to ensure your work is not lost by computer error. Once you have a finished document, talk to your teacher about printing or using e-mail options.

Multimedia Presentation

A **multimedia presentation** allows your audience to read, see, and hear your work. You may choose to include visuals, videos, photographs, or audio recordings in your presentation to make the information more interesting for your audience. Be sure to carefully plan and practice your presentation. This will help you avoid errors during your presentation.

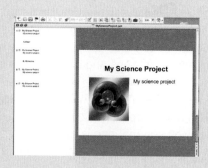

What Is Research?

Research is collecting information about a specific subject. When you research, you are trying to find the answer to a question.

How to Use the Research Process

When you research, you search for information about a specific topic. You can use the information you find to write a story, an article, or a research report.

Choose and Narrow Your Topic

The best way to choose your research topic is to think of something you want to learn more about and that interests you. Make sure your teacher approves your topic. Pick a topic that is not too general. A specific topic is easier to research and write about. It also is more interesting to read about in a report.

Discover What Is Known and What Needs to Be Learned

Get to know your topic. Are there recent articles or reports in the news that relate to your topic? What are researchers and scientists currently working on that relates to the topic?

Formulate Research Questions

What do you know about your topic? What do you want to learn? Write down some questions about your topic that you want to find the answers to. Look at the most important words in your questions, or the key words. These are the words that will be the focus of your research.

> Is there life on Mars?
> Is water or oxygen found on Mars?
> Can life forms live on the surface of Mars?
> What have space missions to Mars discovered about possible life there?

Narrowing the Topic

> Outer Space: This is a very large topic. There are too many things to research in outer space, such as planets, stars, and meteors. There is too much information to cover in one report.

> Planets: This topic is better, but it is still too large. There are many planets in our solar system. It is best to pick a specific planet, and decide on one thing you want to learn about that planet.

> Life on Mars: This topic is more specific than researching the entire planet of Mars. The research can focus just on whether or not plants and animals exist on Mars, or if they ever existed there in the past.

Choose Appropriate Resources to Support Your Topic

Resources can be people you interview, such as experts or teachers. Textbooks, magazines, newspapers, videos, photographs, and the Internet are also resources. The four main types of resources are:

- print
- electronic
- audio visual
- graphic aids

Create a rubric to rate the reliability of your sources. Rate each source on a scale of 1 to 4; 4 is the most reliable, 1 is the least reliable. If you are unsure of the reliability of your sources, ask your teacher, your parents, or a partner.

Gather Information

You may need to survey, skim, or scan a variety of sources to pick the best ones. Use the research questions you formulated to guide your reading.

To Skim   Read the title to see if the article is useful for your topic. Read the beginning sentences of the main paragraphs, or any subheads. See if the article may give details about your topic. Read the last paragraph. At the end, there is usually a conclusion that will summarize the main points of the article.

To Scan   Look for key words or details. They may be underlined or in bold type. This will tell you if the article will discuss your topic.

Take Notes

As you read, take notes. You will gather the specific information you need from each source. For each resource:

1. Include the key words or important phrases about your topic.

2. Write down the source to record where you found the facts.
   - For a book, list the title, author, page number, publisher, and year of publication.
   - For a magazine or newspaper article, list the name, date, volume, and issue number of the source. Also list the title of the article and the author.
   - For an Internet site, list the Web address, the name of the site, the author (if there is one listed), and the date of the latest site update.

3. List the details and facts that are important to your topic. Be certain to summarize or paraphrase the information in your own words. If you use exact words from a source, you must put the words in quotation marks and note the page you copied it from. If you exactly copy someone else's words, you will be plagiarizing. **Plagiarism** is illegal and can be punished by law.

Notecard for a book

Is there life on Mars?
Mars by Seymour Simon, page 27
—Viking spacecraft supposed to find out if
there's life
—Some think experiments showed there isn't

Organize Information from Multiple Sources

After you have taken notes from several sources, **organize** them to see what information is the most important. See how the information from different sources is related.

One of the best ways to organize your information is to use a graphic organizer called an outline. You can also organize your information by using technology. For example, you could type up your notes and save them in a word processing document. It also allows you to choose which data (like dates or times), facts, or ideas are the most relevant.

Analyze, Evaluate, and Use Information

Review your rubric that showed which sources were the most reliable. After you check the reliability, usefulness, relevance, and accuracy of the information, **analyze** and **evaluate** the information. All resources are either primary or secondary sources. A **primary source** is an account of an event by someone who was actually there. A primary source might be a journal, letter, or photograph. A **secondary source** is an account of an event by someone who was not present at the event but that describes the event for other people. A secondary source could be a textbook or an article.

Primary Sources	Secondary Sources
• a soldier's journal	• a book about World War I
• a photograph of a volcano erupting	• a documentary that tells the story of a day a volcano erupted

Synthesize Information from Multiple Sources

Convert your data into graphic aids. Make an outline to **synthesize**, or organize and summarize, your research findings and draw conclusions. Doing this will allow you to identify complexities and discrepancies. You can also use your outline and notes to organize your Works Cited page at the end of your paper. Include the author, title, and page number or Web address.

How to Make an Outline:

1. Put all your notes that have the same keywords or phrases together.

2. Make the first question from your notes into a main idea statement. This will be Roman numeral I.

3. Each of your key research questions will be a Roman numeral heading.

4. Find details that explain each main idea statement. Each important detail about that idea should go below it, and be listed with capital letters.

5. More specific details can be listed with numbers under each capital letter detail.

6. Give your outline a title. This title should state the overall or main idea. It may be a good title to use for your report.

Sample Outline

The Mystery of Life on Mars
I. Life on Mars
  A. How Mars is like Earth
    1. Volcanoes
    2. Giant canyons
  B. Fact-finding missions
    1. Viking
    2. Pathfinder
II. Signs of life on Mars
  A. Studied by David McKay's team
  B. Meteorite
    1. Might contain bacteria fossils
    2. Found in Antarctica
    3. Probably from Mars
III. Continued search for life on Mars
  A. Look underground
  B. More study
    1. Mission planned for future
    2. Gases in atmosphere
    3. What rocks are made of.

Design and Write a Research Report

Before you write, ask your teacher to show you which style guide to use. Follow the style guide to learn the proper formatting of the paper. It will also show you how to format your sources into a works cited page. Use the following techniques to complete your research paper.

Write the Title and Introduction

Copy the **title** from your outline. You can make it more interesting if you want. Make sure it gives the main idea of your topic. Next you should write an interesting **introduction** that will explain what the rest of your report will be about. Write an introduction that will get your readers' attention.

Outline

The Mystery of Life on Mars

Title and Introduction

The Mystery of Life on Mars
Perhaps you have heard stories about life on other planets. Or perhaps, you may have only thought about life here on Earth. I am going to explore the research on the planet Mars and discuss with you the studies that have been done to see if there is life on "the red planet."

Write the Body

The body is the main portion of your report. Use your main ideas to write topic sentences for each paragraph. Then use your research details to write sentences about each topic.

Outline

I. Life on Mars
  A. How Mars is like Earth
    1. Volcanoes
    2. Giant canyons

Topic Sentence and Detail

People have always wondered if there is life on other planets, especially Mars. Because Mars is similar to Earth with features like volcanoes and giant canyons, it seems possible that there is life on Mars.

Write the Conclusion

Write about the main ideas of your report in the **conclusion**. This will summarize your report. You can also include an interesting fact or opinion to end your report. This will keep your audience thinking after they have finished reading. For example, "I believe that with all the research still being done on Mars, perhaps in the near future, we will learn more about life on that mysterious planet."

Design Your Report: Graphic and Multimedia Aids

After you write your report, you should consider its **design**, or how it will look on a printed page. This includes choosing the font of the text and deciding whether you will use **graphic aids** to make the information in your report easier to understand or more interesting. Do you want to include illustrations or photographs? Does your audience need a time line or diagram to understand the text better? Is there a video or audio file that might support your ideas? Choose visuals or media that will make your presentation more effective.

Integrate Quotations and Citations

Adding **quotations** and including **citations** are important ways of sharing the information you find during your research. Any words that are not your own must be in quotation marks and the source must be given in the running text in order to avoid plagiarism. If you use an idea that is not your own, even if you paraphrase it in your own words, you must **cite** the source for that information.

To cite a source means to list the information of your source. This helps you to properly note where you found your information. Citing allows other readers to look at the source, too. Use the citation style your teacher tells you to use. Two commonly used citation styles were developed by the Modern Language Association (MLA) and the American Psychological Association (APA). Both of these associations publish style manuals that can help you write research papers. They are available at **www.mla.org** and **www.apastyle.org**.

A common way to cite is to use the MLA style for author and page citation. List the author and the page number of your source right after you use the words or idea of that author. The author's name should be either in the sentence itself or in parentheses following the quotation or paraphrase. The page number(s) should always appear in parentheses, not in the text of your sentence. For example:

> The writer T. S. Eliot has said that poetry expresses an "overflow of powerful feelings" (263).

> Poetry expresses an "overflow of powerful feelings" (Eliot 263).

At the end of your report create a separate **"Works Cited"** page.

> Works Cited
>
> Ackroyd, Peter. *T. S. Eliot: A Life.* London: Simon and Schuster, 1985.
>
> Vendler, Helen. "T. S. Eliot." *Time* 8 June 1998. 70–72.
>
> "T. S. Eliot." *Microsoft Encarta Online Encyclopedia.* 2006.
>
> <http://encarta.msn.com>

Evaluate Your Research Report and Draw Conclusions

After you complete your research report, you should **evaluate** it, or check its quality. Ask questions about how well you did each step of the report. Look at the paper overall. Does it accomplish what you want it to do? Do you have to do more research or adjust your main idea to achieve the goal of your paper? This will help you to decide if the end product is presented correctly.

Checklist to Evaluate

- ☑ The title tells what the report is about.
- ☑ The introduction is interesting, gets the attention of the reader, and gives the main idea of the report.
- ☑ The body gives the facts you found.
- ☑ Each paragraph covers a specific topic from your outline.
- ☑ Each topic in the body paragraphs is connected to the main idea.
- ☑ Other sentences give specific details about the topic.
- ☑ The conclusion is a summary of the most important information on your topic.
- ☑ The conclusion is interesting for the reader.
- ☑ The paper is formatted according to the style guide used.
- ☑ All sources are properly formatted per the style guide used.

Share Your Report

Publish your report. You can choose different media for publishing. You can print the final report in paper, put it online, create a poster or display of your final paper, or attach it to an email and send it to trusted friends or adults. Be sure to check your school's Acceptable Use Policy before posting your work.

Questions for Further Study

Now that you have finished the report, you may have questions based on the conclusions you drew. You can consider these questions as other research ideas for the future.

During Your Research

I see that there were space missions to Mars such as the Viking. How are those machines created? Who designs them? I would like to know more about space technology.

Now

Maybe my next research report will be about space technology. I could study who designs the machines that go into space and how they work.

Test-Taking Strategies

What Are Test-Taking Strategies?

Test-taking strategies are skills to help you effectively complete a test. These strategies will help you to show what you know on a test without making mistakes.

What to Do Before a Test

Use the following strategies to help you prepare for a test.

- Find out if the test will be multiple-choice, short answers, or essay. Noting the format will allow you to select an appropriate strategy.
- Ask your teacher for practice tests or examples to try before the test day.
- Carefully study the material that will be on the test.
- Make sure you get a good night of rest before a test. This will help you focus.
- Eat a nutritious meal before the test. This will give you energy to get through the test.

What to Do During a Test

Use the following strategies as you complete the test.

Relax: Relax and think carefully during the test. If you feel stressed, take a few deep breaths. Remind yourself that you are prepared.

Plan Your Time: Survey the test to estimate difficulty and plan time. See what questions you can answer easily. Do not work on one question for too long because you might not have enough time to finish the test if you only focus on one question.

Read: Read the directions for each section of the test. Then, read each question carefully. Underline key words in the directions and questions to focus on the most important information. Be certain that you are doing what the question asks. For example, if a question says to "describe," give more than a definition. You may need to give specific details.

Clarify: Tests ask logical questions. If something seems strange, reread the directions, question, or passage to clarify information. Think about words carefully to be certain you understand their meaning. Use typographic and visual clues to find meaning.

Mark Answers: Carefully mark your answers on the test and check for legibility. This can affect your test grade! Be sure to use the correct writing utensil. For example, some multiple choice tests require the use of a #2 pencil.

Check Completeness: Check to make sure all questions are answered (if there is no penalty for guessing). Always reread your answers or answer choices, if you have time. Finish any questions you may not have finished before.

You think:

This question is difficult. I cannot answer this right now.

Then you decide:

I will return to this question later. I will answer the questions I do know first.

Tips for Objective Tests

Use the following strategies to help you complete objective tests.

Easy First: Answer the easy questions first. Leave the most difficult ones for last.

Narrow the Choices: If you are uncertain of an answer, determine which choices are definitely not correct. Choose the two that are closest to correct. This will narrow your number of answers to choose from to only two.

Rephrase Questions and Answer Them Mentally: Try to put the question in your own words and think about how you will answer. Then, look at the answer choices to see which one matches your own answer the best.

Make Changes If Needed: Ask yourself if you answered each question correctly. Check your work by reading through the test a second time. Change your answer only if the question was initially misunderstood.

Shuttle Among the Passage, the Question, the Choices: Read the passage, the questions, and the choices until you fully understand what is being asked.

Tips for Essay Tests

Use the following strategies to help you complete essay tests.

Outline: Make an outline of your answer before you write. This way, you can make sure you discuss all the important points of your essay.

Plan: Plan the time for your essay. Know how long you have to write your essay. Mark on your outline how long you plan to spend writing each section of your essay.

Write: Only include information in your essay that you know is accurate and is about your topic. If you are uncertain if it is factual or important, do not include it. Use a topic sentence and supporting details for each paragraph.

Proofread: Carefully proofread your writing. Check for grammar, punctuation, and capitalization. Most importantly, make sure all parts of your essay can be read clearly.

Tips for Online Tests

Use the following strategies to help you complete tests on a computer.

- Find out how the test is designed—Can you go back to questions you have already answered? Can you change your answers? Is there a time limit? Is there a glossary? Audio? Some tests will show you this information on the introduction screen. You can also ask your teacher.

- Find out if this is an adaptive test. When you take adaptive tests, the questions get harder or easier based on whether you are getting answers correct or incorrect. So when you take an adaptive test, take your time and be careful as you answer the first several questions.

- Have a pencil and paper in addition to your computer test. Use your paper to jot down an idea or organize your thoughts with a graphic organizer.

Reading Strategies

Reading Fluency

Study Skills and Strategies

Vocabulary

What Are Reading Strategies?

Reading strategies are hints or techniques you can use to help you become a better reader. They help you interact with the text and take control of your own reading comprehension. Reading strategies can be used before, during, and after you read.

Plan and Monitor

Before you read, plan how to approach the selection by using prereading strategies. **Preview** the selection to see what it is about and try to make a prediction about its content. Keep in mind that English is read from left to right, and that text moves from the top of the page to the bottom. **Set a purpose** for reading, or decide why you will read the selection. You might want or need to adjust your purpose for reading as you read. Monitor your reading to check how well you understand and remember what you read.

How to Select and Use Prereading Strategies	
Title:	Surfing the Pipeline
Author:	Christina Rodriguez
Preview the Text	• Look at the title: Surfing the Pipeline. • Look at the organization of the text, including any chapter titles, heads, and subheads. • Look at any photos and captions. • Think about what the selection is about.
Activate Prior Knowledge	• I know many people surf in the ocean on surfboards. • I've seen a film about people trying to surf on huge waves in California.
Ask Questions	• What is the pipeline? • Where is the pipeline? • Who surfs the pipeline? • Why do people try to surf the pipeline?
Set a Purpose for Reading	• I want to read to find out how people surf the pipeline.

How to Make and Confirm Predictions

Making **predictions** about a selection will help you understand and remember what you read. As you preview a selection, **ask questions** and think about any **prior knowledge** you have about the subject. If you do not learn enough additional information from these steps, read the first few paragraphs of the selection.

Think about the events taking place, and then predict what will happen next. If you are reading fiction or drama, you can use what you know about common plot patterns to help you predict what may happen in the story. After you read each section, confirm your predictions, or see if they were correct. Sometimes you will need to revise your predictions for the next section based on what you read.

Preview to Anticipate Read the title. Think about what the selection will be about as you read the first few paragraphs. Look for clues about the selection's content.

Make and Confirm Predictions As you read, predict what will happen next in the selection based on text evidence or personal experience. Take notes while you are reading, and use a **Prediction Chart** to record your ideas. As you continue to read the selection, confirm your predictions. If a prediction is incorrect, revise it.

Surfing the Pipeline

There Uli was, standing on the white, sandy shores of Oahu, Hawaii. Right in front of her was the famous Banzai Pipeline—one of the most difficult and dangerous places to surf in the world. Uli looked out and saw twelve-foot waves crashing toward her.

Uli had been waiting for this day for a long time. She was ready.

Uli grabbed her surfboard and entered the water. The waves were fierce and strong that morning. It took all of Uli's energy to swim out to the surfing location. Uli could see rocks sticking up through the water. She finally found the perfect starting point and waited anxiously to begin surfing.

Prediction Chart

Prediction	Did It Happen?	Evidence
Uli is going to surf at the Banzai Pipeline.	Not yet, but she will soon.	She is at the starting point to begin surfing. (text evidence)
Surfing the Banzai Pipeline will be hard for Uli.	Not yet, but it will soon.	New activities are always hard when I try them for the first time. (personal experience)

How to Monitor Your Reading

When you **monitor your reading**, you are checking to make sure you understand the information you read. You can check your understanding by keeping track of your thinking while reading. Pause while reading to think about images you may be creating in your mind, connections you are making between words or topics within the text, or problems you are having with understanding the text. When you read something that doesn't make sense to you, use these monitoring strategies to help you.

Strategy	How to Use It	Example Text
Reread to Clarify Ideas	Reread silently the passage you do not understand. Then reread the passage aloud. Continue rereading until you feel more confident about your understanding of the passage.	I will silently reread the first paragraph. Then I will read it aloud. The paragraph is more understandable now.
Use Resources to Clarify Vocabulary	Look up confusing words in a dictionary or thesaurus, or ask a classmate for help.	"... dangerous places to surf ..." I'm not sure what "surf" means. I'll look it up.
Read On and Use Context Clues to Clarify Ideas and Vocabulary	Read past the part of the text where you are confused. What does the rest of the information tell you? Are there nearby words or phrases, context clues or visuals that help you understand?	"... looked out and saw twelve-foot waves ..." Maybe "surf" means riding ocean waves.
Adjust Your Reading Rate	Read slowly when something is confusing or difficult. Keep in mind that English is read from left to right and that text runs down the page from the top. If you are having a difficult time understanding what you're reading, first make sure that you're reading it in the right order.	"Right in front of her was the famous Banzai Pipeline ..." I've never heard of the Banzai Pipeline. I'll read slower to find out what it is.
Adjust Your Purpose for Reading	Think of the purpose you set for reading before you started to read. Have you found a new purpose, or reason to read? If so, adjust your purpose and read on.	I originally wanted to read to find out how people surf the pipeline. Now I want to read to see if Uli actually does it.

How to Use Graphic Organizers

Before you read, you can use graphic organizers to prepare for better comprehension. For example, use a **KWL Chart** to record your prior knowledge about the topic.

KWL Chart

WHAT I <u>K</u>NOW	WHAT I <u>WANT</u> TO KNOW	WHAT I <u>L</u>EARNED

As you read, use a variety of graphic organizers such as diagrams and charts to help keep track of your thinking. Take notes about any ideas or vocabulary that confuse you. Writing down ideas keeps you actively involved in your reading. It also can help clear up any confusion you may have about information in a selection.

Use graphic organizers to capture your thoughts and to help you remember information based on how it was described in the text or based on the text structure. Here are some more examples of graphic organizers:

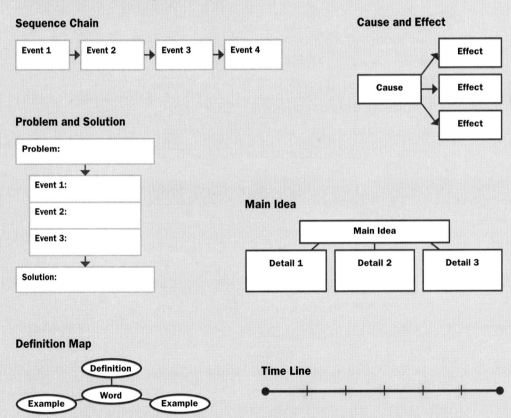

Sequence Chain

Event 1 → Event 2 → Event 3 → Event 4

Cause and Effect

Cause → Effect, Effect, Effect

Problem and Solution

Problem: → Event 1: Event 2: Event 3: → Solution:

Main Idea

Main Idea → Detail 1, Detail 2, Detail 3

Definition Map

Definition, Word, Example, Example

Time Line

For more graphic organizers, see the Index of Graphic Organizers on page 886.

Determine Importance

Determining importance is a reading strategy you can use to find the most important details or ideas in a selection. A good way to think about what is important in the selections you read is to **summarize**. When you summarize, you state the main idea and only the most important details in a selection, usually in a sentence or two. To summarize, identify the topic of a paragraph or selection, find the main idea and the most important details, and put them in your own words.

Stated Main Ideas

The main idea of a selection is the most important point a writer wants to relate to readers. Writers often state the main idea in a topic sentence near the beginning of a selection.

What's in a Name?

All college sports teams have special names. Many of these names are common, such as the Bears or the Tigers. However, more teams should have names that are unique and express the school's individuality. The University of Arkansas team names are Razorbacks and Lady Razorbacks. Virginia Tech athletes are called Hokies. Purdue has the Boilermakers. My favorite is the University of California at Santa Cruz's Banana Slugs and Lady Slugs. Slugs are unusual creatures. They have soft, slimy bodies and enjoy moist environments. These unique names make the college sports world a more interesting and fun place.

How to Identify Stated Main Ideas	
What is the paragraph about?	• names of college teams
Look for supporting details.	• Some teams have unique names like Razorbacks, Hokies, Boilermakers, and Lady Slugs. • The author feels these names make the college sports world more fun.
Eliminate unnecessary information or details.	• Slugs are slimy and enjoy moist environments.
Summarize the main idea.	• Unique sports team names are better and more fun than common names.

Implied Main Ideas

Sometimes a main idea is implied, or not directly stated. Readers have to figure out the main idea by studying all of the details in a selection.

The Future of Humankind

Many people agree that space exploration is important. However, when government spending is discussed, many people insist there are problems on Earth that need attention and money first. Don't they realize that the future of the human race depends on space exploration? Someday, the Earth's resources may run out. Paying for more exploration will allow us to learn more about space and how we can better care for our planet.

How to Identify Implied Main Ideas	
What is the paragraph about?	• space exploration
Find and list details.	• Many people feel other issues are more important than space exploration. • Our future depends on exploration.
What message is the author trying to convey?	• If we explore space now, we can better take care of ourselves and Earth.
Summarize the implied main idea.	• Space exploration should be paid for because it is just as important as any other issue. We could die without it.

Personal Relevance

An additional way to determine importance while reading a selection is to look for details that have personal relevance to you. These details may be important to you because they remind you of someone or something in your own life. For example, you might relate to "What's in a Name?" because you have a favorite sports team name. You might understand the main point that the writer is trying to make because you might agree that sports team names should be unique.

Make Connections

Making connections is a reading strategy you can use to better understand or enjoy the information presented in a selection.

As you read, think about what the information reminds you of. Have you seen or heard something like this before? Have you read or experienced something like this? Thinking about what you already know helps you make a connection to the new information.

Type of Connection	Description	Example
Text to Self	A connection between the text you are reading and something that has happened in your own life. A text-to-self connection can also be a feeling, such as happiness or excitement, that you feel as you are reading.	This part of the story reminds me of the first time I drove a car. My dad showed me how to turn and stop. I remember how scared I was. Thinking about this memory helps me better understand how the character is feeling as he learns how to drive.
Text to Text	A connection between the text you are reading and another selection you have read, a film you have seen, or a song you have heard. Sometimes the text you are reading might have a similar theme, or message, to something you've read, seen, or heard before. A text may also belong to a genre, such as mystery or biography, that you are familiar with.	This part of the news article reminds me of a movie I saw about space. Astronauts were taking a trip to the moon, but their spaceship lost all power. I can think about the movie as I read about the most recent space shuttle mission.
Text to World	A connection between something you read in the text and something that is happening or has happened in the world. You might also make a connection with the time period or era that a selection takes place in, such as the Great Depression or the 1980s. The setting may also be familiar.	This part of the text reminds me of presidential elections. I remember candidates giving speeches to tell why they should be president. Thinking about this helps me understand why the characters in the selection give speeches.

Use a chart like the one below to help make and record text-to-self, text-to-text, or text-to-world connections as you read.

Make Connections Chart

The text says ...	This reminds me of ...	This helps me because ...

Make Inferences

Making inferences is a reading strategy in which you make educated guesses about the text's content based on experiences that you've had in everyday life or on facts or details that you read.

Sometimes people call making inferences "reading between the lines." This means looking at *how* the text was written along with what is being discussed. When you "read between the lines," you pay attention to the writer's tone, voice, use of punctuation, or emphasis on certain words. Writers can also use irony, dialogue, or descriptions to infer messages.

When you add your prior knowledge or personal experiences to what you are reading, you can make inferences by reading all the clues and making your best guesses.

How to Make Inferences Using Your Own Experience

Read the following paragraph and chart to learn how to make an inference using your own experiences.

The Waiting

Rain pounded against the windows as Sarah stomped up and down the stairs. She only stopped going up and down to check the time on the clock downstairs every five minutes. She had been dressed and ready to go for more than an hour! Sarah had spent weeks picking out her dress and shoes, and she had even paid $50 to have her hair styled. She threw the flower she had so excitedly bought yesterday in the corner beside the camera. Sarah wondered, "Where is he? Will I have to go alone tonight?"

Inferences Based on Your Own Experience	
You read	Sarah had been dressed and ready to go somewhere for more than an hour. She spent a lot of time selecting her dress and shoes. She threw her flower in the corner by the camera.
You know	I know that people spend a lot of time choosing special outfits for events like dances, weddings, or parties. I know that my parents took a photo of me and my date for the prom last year. My date and I both had flowers for our outfits that night.
You infer	Sarah had a date to a special event that night. She was upset because she cared a lot about the event she was going to and didn't want to be late or go alone.

How to Make Inferences Using Text Evidence

Read the following paragraph and chart to learn how to make an inference by using clues that appear in the text.

The Waiting

Rain pounded against the windows as Sarah stomped up and down the stairs. She only stopped going up and down to check the time on the clock downstairs every five minutes. She had been dressed and ready to go for more than an hour! Sarah had spent weeks picking out her dress and shoes, and she had even paid $50 to have her hair styled. She threw the flower she had so excitedly bought yesterday in the corner beside the camera. Sarah wondered, "Where is he? Will I have to go alone tonight?"

Inferences Based on Text Evidence	
You read	Sarah had been dressed and ready to go somewhere for more than an hour. She spent a lot of time selecting her dress and shoes. She threw her flower in the corner by the camera.
You infer	Sarah had plans to go somewhere special that evening and was waiting for her date. She cared a lot about the event she was going to. Someone is late, and she is angry at him.

Ask Questions

You can **ask questions** to learn new information, to clarify, and to understand or figure out what is important in a selection. Asking questions of yourself and the author while reading can help you locate information you might otherwise miss.

How to Self-Question

Ask yourself questions to understand something that is confusing, keep track of what is happening, or think about what you know.

Ask and Write Questions Use a question word such as *Who, What, When, Where, Why,* or *How* to write your questions.

Examples: *How can I figure out what this word means? What are the characters doing? Why is this important? Do I agree with this?*

Answer the Questions and Follow Up Use the text, photographs, or other visuals to answer your questions. Write your answer next to the question. Include the page number where you found the answer.

How to Question the Author

Sometimes, you may have questions about what the author is trying to tell you in a selection. Write these types of questions, and then try to answer them by reading the text. The answers to these questions are known as "author and you" answers.

Questions to Ask the Author

- What is the author trying to say here?
- Does the author explain his or her ideas clearly?
- What is the author talking about?
- Does the author support his or her ideas or opinions with facts?

How to Find Question-Answer Relationships

Where you find the answers to your questions is very important. Sometimes the answers are located right in the text. Other times, your questions require you to use ideas and information that are not in the text. Some questions can be answered by using your background knowledge on a topic. Read the chart to learn about question-answer relationships.

Type of Answer	How to Find the Answers
"Right There"	Sometimes you can simply point to the text and say that an answer to one of your questions is "right there."
"Think and Search"	Look back at the selection. Find the information the question is asking about. Think about how the information fits together to answer the question.
"Author and You"	Use ideas and information that are not stated directly in the text. Think about what you have read, and create your own ideas or opinions based on what you know about the author.
"On Your Own"	Use your feelings, what you already know, and your own experiences to find these answers.

Synthesize

When you **synthesize**, you gather your thoughts about what you have read to draw conclusions, make generalizations, and compare the information to information you've read in other texts. You form new overall understandings by putting together ideas and events.

How to Draw Conclusions

Reading is like putting a puzzle together. There are many different parts that come together to make up the whole selection. Synthesizing is the process of putting the pieces together while we read. We combine new information with what we already know to create an original idea or to form new understandings.

Read this passage and the text that follows to help you understand how to synthesize what you read.

Distracted Drivers

Cell phone use in cars has steadily risen in the past decade. Studies from the Departments of Highway Safety show that the more distracted drivers are, the more likely they are to be in an accident. Lawmakers in some states have successfully passed laws requiring drivers to use hands-free accessories while a vehicle is moving. This means they may use an earpiece or a speaker-phone device but not hold the phone in their hands. Many people feel that talking on cell phones is not the only distracting activity that should be illegal for drivers.

Use text evidence from the selection and your own experience to draw conclusions as you read.

Drawing Conclusions	
Look for Details	The more distracted a driver is, the more likely he or she is to be involved in an accident. Cell phones are distracting.
Think About What You Know	I know people who have been in car accidents while talking on their cell phones.
Decide What You Believe	Lawmakers should continue to work on laws to stop drivers from being distracted.

How to Make Generalizations

Generalizations are broad statements that apply to a group of people, a set of ideas, or the way things happen. You can make generalizations as you read, using experience and text evidence from a selection to help you.

- **Take notes about the facts or opinions** Look for the overall theme or message of the selection.

- **Add examples** Think about what you know about the topic from your own knowledge and experience.

- **Construct a generalization** Write a statement that combines the author's statements and your own.

  Example: Using a cell phone while driving can make you have an accident.

How to Compare Across Texts

Comparing two or more texts helps you combine ideas, develop judgments, and draw conclusions. Read the following paragraph, and think about how it connects to the paragraph on page 630.

Graduated Driver's License Programs

More and more states are creating graduated driver's license (GDL) laws. Studies show that these programs help teen driver accidents and deaths to decline. The programs differ from state to state, but most GDL programs require an adult with a valid driver's license to be present when a teen is driving, and a teen driver must enroll in a certified driver's education and training course. Each state has various restrictions for teen drivers and punishments for when those restrictions are ignored.

Think About Something You Have Already Read In "Distracted Drivers," you read that cell phones are distracting to drivers and that many people feel it should be illegal to use one while driving.

Think About What You Are Reading Right Now Many states have graduated driver's license programs. Accidents involving teen drivers have declined.

Compare Across Texts and Draw Conclusions Both articles are about laws related to driving. Lawmakers hope that all of the laws they pass related to driving will create safer driving conditions for everyone.

Comparing across texts can help you foster an argument or advance an opinion. Having multiple opinions and facts from different sources makes your argument or opinion more credible.

Visualize

When you **visualize**, you use your imagination to better understand what the author is describing. While reading, create an image or picture in your mind that represents what you are reading about. Look for words that tell how things look, sound, smell, taste, and feel.

My Favorite Car Is a Truck

My name is Stephen, and today was a magical day. I've been working hard and saving money all summer. I finally have enough money for a down payment on a new car. Today my father took me to a car dealership to pick out my car. I immediately found my favorite vehicle. It was a red, shiny pickup truck with gleaming wheels. I climbed inside and looked around. The brown seats were sparkling clean, and the truck still had that new car smell inside the cab. I put the key in the ignition and turned it on. The quiet hum of the engine made me so happy. After a long test-drive, my father and I agreed this was the truck for me.

How to Visualize Using Sketches

- **Read the Text** Look for words that help create pictures in your mind about the characters, setting, and events.
- **Picture the Information in Your Mind** Stop and focus on the descriptive words. Create pictures in your mind using these words.
- **Draw the Events** Sketch pictures to show what is happening. You could draw Stephen climbing inside the pickup truck.

How to Visualize Using Senses

- **Look for Words** Find adjectives and sensory words: smell, look, sound, taste, and feel. Stephen uses the words *red, shiny, with gleaming wheels; brown seats, sparkling clean; new car smell;* and *quiet hum of the engine* to talk about the truck.
- **Create a Picture in Your Mind of the Scene** What do you hear, feel, see, smell, and taste? Examine how these details improve your understanding.

  I smell: new car smell   **I hear**: engine humming
  I see: red, shiny truck   **I feel**: texture of the seats, the key

How to Recognize Emotional Responses

Do any of the words in the selection make you feel certain emotions? Asking yourself how you feel when you read can help you remember the information.

Example: I feel excited for the main character because I know what it's like to pick out something new.

Reading Fluency

What Is Reading Fluency?

Reading fluency is the ability to read smoothly and expressively with clear understanding. Fluent readers are able to better understand and enjoy what they read. Use the strategies that follow to build your fluency in these four key areas:

- accuracy and rate
- phrasing
- intonation
- expression

How to Improve Accuracy and Rate

Accuracy is the correctness of your reading. Rate is the speed of your reading.

How to read accurately:

- Use correct pronunciation.
- Emphasize correct syllables.

How to read with proper rate:

- Match your reading speed to what you are reading. For example, if you are reading an exciting story, read slightly faster. If you are reading a sad story, read slightly slower.
- Recognize and use punctuation.

Test your accuracy and rate:

- Choose a text you are familiar with, and practice reading it aloud or silently multiple times.
- Ask a friend to use a watch or clock to time you while you read a passage.
- Ask a friend or family member to read a passage for you, so you know what it should sound like.

Use the formula below to measure a reader's accuracy and rate while reading aloud. For passages to practice with, see **Reading Fluency Practice**, pp. 751–771.

Accuracy and Rate Formula

| words read in one minute | − | number of errors | = | words correct per minute (wcpm) |

How to Improve Intonation

Intonation is the rise and fall in the tone of your voice as you read aloud. It means the highness or lowness of the sound.

How to read with proper intonation:

- Change the sound of your voice to match what you are reading.
- Make your voice flow, or sound smooth, while you read.
- Make sure you are pronouncing words correctly.
- Raise the sound of your voice for words that should be stressed, or emphasized.
- Use visual clues. (see box below)

Visual Clue and Meaning	Example	How to Read It
Italics: draw attention to a word to show special importance	She is *smart*.	Emphasize "smart."
Dash: shows a quick break in a sentence	She is—smart.	Pause before saying "smart."
Exclamation: can represent energy, excitement, or anger	She is smart!	Make your voice louder at the end of the sentence.
All capital letters: can represent strong emphasis, or yelling	SHE IS SMART.	Emphasize the whole sentence.
Bold facing: draws attention to a word to show importance	She is **smart**.	Emphasize "smart."
Question mark: shows curiosity or confusion	She is smart?	Raise the pitch of your voice slightly at the end of the sentence.

Use the rubric below to measure how well a reader uses intonation while reading aloud. For intonation passages, see **Reading Fluency Practice**, pp. 751–771.

Intonation Rubric		
1	**2**	**3**
The reader's tone does not change. The reading all sounds the same.	The reader's tone changes sometimes to match what is being read.	The reader's tone always changes to match what is being read.

How to Improve Phrasing

Phrasing is how you use your voice to group words together.

How to read with proper phrasing:

- Don't read too quickly or too slowly.
- Pause for key words within the text.
- Make sure your sentences sound smooth, not choppy.
- Make sure you sound like you are reading a sentence instead of a list.
- Use punctuation to tell you when to stop, pause, or emphasize. (see box below)

Punctuation	How to Use It
. period	stop at the end of the sentence
, comma	pause within the sentence
! exclamation point	emphasize the sentence and pause at the end
? question mark	emphasize the end of the sentence and pause at the end
; semicolon	pause within the sentence between two related thoughts
: colon	pause within the sentence before giving an example or explanation

One way to practice phrasing is to copy a passage, then place a slash (/), or pause mark, within a sentence where there should be a pause. One slash (/) means a short pause. Two slashes (//) mean a longer pause, such as a pause at the end of a sentence.

Read aloud the passage below, pausing at each pause mark. Then try reading the passage again without any pauses. Compare how you sound each time.

There are many ways to get involved / in your school and community. // Joining a club / or trying out for a sports team / are a few of the options. // Volunteer work can also be very rewarding. // You can volunteer at community centers, / nursing homes, / or animal shelters. //

Use the rubric below to measure how well a reader uses phrasing while reading aloud. For phrasing passages, see **Reading Fluency Practice**, pp. 751–771.

Phrasing Rubric

1	2	3
Reading is choppy. There are few pauses for punctuation.	Reading is mostly smooth. There are some pauses for punctuation.	Reading is very smooth. Punctuation is being used properly.

How to Improve Expression

Expression in reading is how you use your voice to express feeling.

How to read with proper expression:

- Match the sound of your voice to what you are reading. For example, read louder and faster to show strong feeling. Read slower and quieter to show sadness or seriousness.
- Match the sound of your voice to the genre. For example, read a fun, fictional story using a fun, friendly voice. Read an informative, nonfiction article using an even tone and a more serious voice.
- Avoid speaking in monotone, or using only one tone in your voice.
- Pause for emphasis and exaggerate letter sounds to match the mood or theme of what you are reading.

Practice incorrect expression by reading this sentence without changing the tone of your voice: *I am so excited!* Now read the sentence again with proper expression: *I am so excited!* The way you use your voice while reading can help you to better understand what is happening in the text.

For additional practice, read the sentences below aloud with and without changing your expression. Compare how you sound each time.

- I am very sad.
- That was the most *boring* movie I have ever seen.
- We won the game!

Use the rubric below to measure how well a reader uses expression while reading aloud. For expression passages, see **Reading Fluency Practice**, pp. 751–771.

Expression Rubric

1	2	3
The reader sounds monotone. The reader's voice does not match the subject of what is being read.	The reader is making some tone changes. Sometimes, the reader's voice matches what is being read.	The reader is using proper tones and pauses. The reader's voice matches what is being read.

Reading Fluency Practice

Practice Expression: "The Good Samaritan"

Expression in reading is how you use your voice to express feeling. Use this passage to practice reading with proper expression. Print a copy of this passage from myNGconnect.com to help you monitor your progress. Practice independently and participate in shared reading to improve your expression. To use an Expression Rubric, see page 750.

A little later in the afternoon, Mr. Sánchez drove up in his truck, honking and honking at us. "Here they come. Maybe Orlando and Marty can play with us," someone said.

Pues, it was not to be. The truck had just come to a standstill when Mr. Sánchez shot out of the driver's side. He ran up to us, waving his hands in the air like a crazy man, first saying, then screaming, "What are you guys doing here? You all can't be here when I'm not here."

"But you told us we could come over anytime. And we knocked and knocked, and we were being very careful."

"It doesn't matter. You all shouldn't be here when I'm not home. What if you had broken something?" he said.

"But we didn't," I said.

"But if you had, then who would have been responsible for paying to replace it? I'm sure every one of you would have denied breaking anything."

"*Este vato!*" said Hernando.

"*Vato?* Is that what you called me? I'm no street punk, no hoodlum. I'll have you know, I've worked my whole life, and I won't be called a *vato*. It's Mr. Sánchez. Got that? And you boys know what—from now on, you are not allowed to come here whether I'm home or not! You all messed it up for yourselves. You've shown me so much disrespect today you don't deserve to play on my court. It was a privilege and not a right, and you messed it up. Now leave!"

From "The Good Samaritan," page 13

Practice Phrasing: "Thank You, M'am"

Phrasing is how you use your voice to group words together. Use this passage to practice reading with proper phrasing. Print a copy of this passage from <u>myNGconnect.com</u> to help you monitor your progress. To use a Phrasing Rubric, see page 749.

Sweat popped out on the boy's face and he began to struggle. Mrs. Jones stopped, jerked him around in front of her, put a half nelson about his neck, and continued to drag him up the street. When she got to her door, she dragged the boy inside, down a hall, and into a large kitchenette-furnished room at the rear of the house. She switched on the light and left the door open. The boy could hear other roomers laughing and talking in the large house. Some of their doors were open, too, so he knew he and the woman were not alone. The woman still had him by the neck in the middle of her room.

She said, "What is your name?"

"Roger," answered the boy.

"Then, Roger, you go to that sink and wash your face," said the woman, whereupon she turned him loose—at last. Roger looked at the door—looked at the woman—looked at the door—*and went to the sink.*

From "Thank You, M'am," page 43

Practice Intonation: "The Fashion Show"

Intonation is the rise and fall in the pitch or tone of your voice as you read aloud. Use this passage to practice reading with proper intonation. Print a copy of this passage from myNGconnect.com to help you monitor your progress. To use an Intonation Rubric, see page 748. When listening to a partner read, notice if you can understand the sound of each word. Then listen again to hear how your partner's intonation changes.

I felt torn and confused. I could not take part in the dance, of course, but should I be in the fashion show? I really wanted to do it. I had two beautiful Afghan outfits I could model. But I was also thinking, *My leg is damaged. What if I fall down?*

Finally, I said to myself, *Okay, next Wednesday I'll sit in on the practice session and see what it's like, and then I'll decide.*

That day the girl who always picked on me came to the practice session, because she was planning to be in the fashion show. The moment she saw me sitting there, she could tell I was thinking of entering the show, too. She didn't tell me to my face that I could not do it, but she immediately called out to the teacher. "Ms. Ascadam," she said, "when you model clothes at a fashion show, isn't this how you have to walk? Isn't this how models walk on a runway?"

Then she began to walk the way she thought a model should walk—with long strides, placing one foot in front of the other in a straight line that made her back end swing from side to side. "Is this the way you should walk?" she said. "If someone can't walk like this, should she be in the fashion show? She would just spoil the whole thing, wouldn't she?" And she kept walking back and forth, swinging from side to side.

From "The Fashion Show," page 81

Practice Phrasing: "The Hidden Secrets of the Creative Mind"

Phrasing is how you use your voice to group words together. Use this passage to practice reading with proper phrasing. Print a copy of this passage from myNGconnect.com to help you monitor your progress. To use a Phrasing Rubric, see page 749.

Q: How have researchers studied this creative flash?

A: Some psychologists set up video cameras to watch creative people work, asking them to describe their thought processes out loud or interrupting them frequently to ask how close they were to a solution. In other experiments, subjects worked on problems that, when solved, tend to result in the sensation of sudden insight. In one experiment, they were asked to look at words that came up one at a time on a computer screen and to think of the one word that was associated with all of them. After each word they had to give their best guess. Although many swore they had no idea until a sudden burst of insight at about the twelfth word, their guesses got closer to the solution. Even when an idea seems sudden, our minds have actually been working on it all along.

From "The Hidden Secrets of the Creative Mind," page 129

Practice Intonation: "Hip-Hop as Culture"

Intonation is the rise and fall in the pitch or tone of your voice as you read aloud. Use this passage to practice reading with proper intonation. Print a copy of this passage from myNGconnect.com to help you monitor your progress. Practice independently and participate in shared reading to improve your intonation. To use an Intonation Rubric, see page 748.

These innovators are the architects of culture. They started from the streets of the city and now influence suburban areas and even small rural towns. They took the hustle of the street and turned it into a Wall Street economy. It doesn't matter if you're in a city or suburb. It doesn't matter if you are Latino, Asian, or Irish. Hip-hop is influencing your situation.

Kids may not love hip-hop, but they're being influenced by it. If teens are wearing oversized jeans with the tops of their boxers showing, oversized athletic jerseys, or long chains around their necks, this is hip-hop. Girls on a bus braiding their hair in the style of an Ethiopian queen, that's hip-hop. There are things around you that daily scream at you, "long live hip-hop!" If you want to understand the culture teens live in today, it's important to understand hip-hop and understand it as culture, not just music.

From "Hip-Hop as Culture," page 141

Practice Expression: "Slam: Performance Poetry Lives On"

Expression in reading is how you use your voice to express feeling. Use this passage to practice reading with proper expression. Print a copy of this passage from myNGconnect.com to help you monitor your progress. To use an Expression Rubric, see page 750.

Poetry doesn't have to be the twelve lines on a page in a book that is sitting in the dustiest corner of the library. Poetry doesn't have to be something you don't understand. Poetry is moving, breathing, ever changing.

Want proof? Take a trip to the Urban Word Annual Teen Poetry Slam at the Nuyorican Poets Cafe in New York City.

Gathered in this tight space are hundreds of teens from every corner of the city. They've come together to compete for one of five top spots in Brave New Voices, the Eighth Annual National Youth Poetry Slam Festival.

Sitting in the cafe feels like being at a sporting event. A DJ revs up the crowd with upbeat music. Young people erupt into wild applause as one of their own hollers his latest creation of slam before the microphone.

Take a listen to this excerpt from "Elementary Invasion," by 16-year-old slam poet Kai Zhang:

> *squeeze*
> *green putty oozing out of your hands*
> *and hugging your fingers cold and rubbery*
> *escaping*
> *your silly efforts to contain*
> *or hold . . .*

From "Slam: Performance Poetry Lives On," page 163

Practice Phrasing: "The Sword in the Stone"

Phrasing is how you use your voice to group words together. Use this passage to practice reading with proper phrasing. Print a copy of this passage from myNGconnect.com to help you monitor your progress. To use a Phrasing Rubric, see page 749.

Arthur went into the church and placed the sword on the high altar. The Archbishop took it up and touched Arthur on the shoulder with it to make him a knight. Then Arthur forgave the great nobles and knights for doubting him and swore an oath that he would be a just and true king for all his days.

He ordered the lords who held their land from the crown to fulfil the duties they owed him. Each one knelt before him in turn and promised to abide by the laws of the king. After this ceremony, Arthur said he would hear complaints about injustices and crimes committed in the land since the death of his father, Uther Pendragon. They told him of how lands and castles had been taken by force, and men murdered, and of how knights and ladies and common people were robbed and assaulted.

Arthur ordered that all lands and properties should be returned to their rightful owners and that everyone should respect the rights of others. When that was done, Arthur organized his government. Sir Kay was made High Steward of all Britain and the most trustworthy knights were appointed to high office. Merlin was confirmed as chief counsellor to the King.

From "The Sword in the Stone," page 211

Practice Expression: "A Job for Valentín"

Expression in reading is how you use your voice to express feeling. Use this passage to practice reading with proper expression. Print a copy of this passage from myNGconnect.com to help you monitor your progress. To use an Expression Rubric, see page 750.

I can't swim very well, mainly because my eyesight is so bad. The minute I take off my glasses to get in the pool, everything becomes a blob of color and I freeze. But I managed to talk my way into a summer job at the city pool anyway. All I'll be doing is selling drinks and snacks, and I get to talk to everyone since the little concession stand faces the pool and the cute lifeguard, Bob Dylan Kalinowski. His mother named him after the old singer from the sixties.

It's a good first day. Mrs. O'Brien says I don't need any training. I can run a cash register, I can take inventory, and I am very friendly with customers. The only thing I don't really like is that Mrs. O'Brien expects to be told if I ever see Bob Dylan messing around on the job.

"People's lives, *children's* lives, are in that young man's hands," she says. "Keep an eye on him, Teresa, and use that phone to call me, if you need to."

I say, "Yes, ma'am," even though I feel funny about being asked to spy on Bob Dylan. He's a senior at my school and, yeah, a crazy man sometimes. But if they gave him the job as a lifeguard, they ought to trust him to do it right.

From "A Job for Valentín," page 239

Practice Intonation: "The Woman in the Snow"

Intonation is the rise and fall in the pitch or tone of your voice as you read aloud. Use this passage to practice reading with proper intonation. Print a copy of this passage from myNGconnect.com to help you monitor your progress. To use an Intonation Rubric, see page 748.

Grady closed his eyes but couldn't keep them shut. She was still coming, but from where? The answer was too horrible to consider, so he chose to let his mind find a more reasonable explanation. From some dark corner of his childhood he heard his father's voice, slurred by alcohol, mocking him. *It ain't the same woman, dummy. You know how they all look alike!*

Grady remembered his father with bitterness and swore at the thought of him. This *was* the same woman, Grady argued with his father's memory, taking no comfort in being right. Grady watched the woman's movements breathlessly as she stepped out of the headlight beam and approached the door. She stood outside the door waiting … waiting.

The gray coldness of Fear slipped into the driver's seat. Grady sucked air into his lungs in big gulps, feeling out of control. Fear moved his foot to the gas pedal, careening the bus out into oncoming traffic. Headlights. A truck. Fear made Grady hit the brakes. The back of the bus went into a sliding spin, slamming into a tree. Grady's stomach crushed against the steering wheel, rupturing his liver and spleen. *You've really done it now, lunkhead.* As he drifted into the final darkness, he heard a woman's sobs, a baby wailing—or was it just the wind?

From "The Woman in the Snow," page 265

Practice Phrasing: "Curtis Aikens and the American Dream"

Phrasing is how you use your voice to group words together. Use this passage to practice reading with proper phrasing. Print a copy of this passage from myNGconnect.com to help you monitor your progress. To use a Phrasing Rubric, see page 749.

Curtis thought he had really screwed up, that no one would listen to him, that his television career was over, and that if the show had reached any illiterate adults, they would only be more convinced to hide their problem. But the opposite was true. Curtis's "screwup" had been one of those moments where television was at its best, where everything was real. The phone lines lit up, at the station and at literacy centers across the country. "It was a great day for literacy," Curtis concludes, without a hint of embarrassment or regret.

His story finished, the TV chef climbs up on his soapbox. The only reason he wanted to share all of this is because he has a cause: "Illiteracy is a problem that all of America can unite around. It doesn't know race, it doesn't know money, it doesn't know boundaries. This is one thing we can all get together on." That cause fully and completely contains Curtis's version of the American dream: "I don't get bored anymore, because I can read. I don't get lonely anymore, because I can read. I'm never out of friends anymore, because I can read. But I'm still trying to obtain the American dream, because I want to give everybody the ability to read. I know that sounds hokey, but there it is."

From "Curtis Aikens and the American Dream," page 317

Practice Intonation: "It's Our Story, Too"

Intonation is the rise and fall in the pitch or tone of your voice as you read aloud. Use this passage to practice reading with proper intonation. Print a copy of this passage from myNGconnect.com to help you monitor your progress. To use an Intonation Rubric, see page 748.

On the first page, Esperanza explains how at school they say her name funny, "as if the syllables were made out of tin and hurt the roof of your mouth." I was hooked.

I knew nothing of the East Coast prep schools or the English shires of the books I had read before. But like Esperanza, I could remember how different my last name sounded when it was pronounced melodically by my parents but so haltingly by everyone else.

Cisneros's hometown of Chicago may have been hundreds of miles away from the palm-tree lined streets of Santa Barbara, California, where I grew up. But in her world I was no longer the minority.

That was a dozen years ago. Today, Latinos are the majority in cities like Santa Ana, California, where Cisneros spoke at Valley High School.

Today, these students can pick from bookstore shelves filled with authors such as Julia Álvarez, Victor Villaseñor, and Judith Ortiz Cofer. These are authors who go beyond census numbers to explain what U.S. Latino life is about.

Cisneros provided an hour of humorous storytelling that had the students busting with laughter. They crowded in line afterward, giddily waiting to get her autograph.

From "It's Our Story, Too," page 353

Practice Expression: "The Fast and the Fuel-Efficient"

Expression in reading is how you use your voice to express feeling. Use this passage to practice reading with proper expression. Print a copy of this passage from myNGconnect.com to help you monitor your progress. To use an Expression Rubric, see page 750.

A half-dozen team members pushed the car backwards, uphill to the school's garage, and gently rolled it onto a power car lift. The only thing to do now was saw off new axle halves from whole VW and Honda units, send them out to be welded … and wait.

"We didn't expect it to break again," said a disappointed Joseph Pak, a lanky, earringed 10th grader with gel-spiked hair. Still, he said, he was relieved that it had happened well before the May competition.

For Pak and other team members who'd struggled with school, the car was an "in-your-face" affirmation of their talents and dreams. Pak, the team's only Asian member, admits he used to skip more school than he attended. "I was just hanging out." Now he gets straight As and wants to be an engineer.

"I've seen the extreme of not doing things when you should," Pak said. With the Attack, he said he's seen the extreme of what happens when you stay the course.

Hauger, though, was optimistic. "This is actually pretty good news," Hauger said. Their more complex engineering of the axle had held. This was a simple weld.

From "The Fast and the Fuel-Efficient," page 365

Practice Phrasing: "The Interlopers"

Phrasing is how you use your voice to group words together. Use this passage to practice reading with proper phrasing. Print a copy of this passage from myNGconnect.com to help you monitor your progress. Practice independently and participate in shared reading to improve your phrasing. To use a Phrasing Rubric, see page 749.

Ulrich von Gradwitz found himself stretched on the ground. One arm lay numb beneath him and the other was pinned helplessly in a tight tangle of forked branches. Both his legs were pinned beneath the fallen branches and it was obvious that he could not move without someone releasing him. The falling branches had slashed his face, and he had to wink away blood from his eyelashes before he could see the full disaster. At his side, near enough to touch, lay Georg Znaeym, who was alive and struggling, but obviously as helplessly pinned down as himself. All around them lay the thick wreckage of splintered branches and broken twigs.

Feeling a mixture of relief at being alive and exasperation at being trapped, Ulrich muttered a strange medley of thankful prayers and sharp curses. Georg, who was blinded by the blood in his eyes, stopped struggling for a moment to listen. Then he gave a short, snarling laugh.

"So you're not killed, as you ought to be, but you're caught, anyway," he cried. "Trapped. What a joke! Ulrich von Gradwitz trapped in his stolen forest. That's justice for you!"

And he laughed again, mockingly and savagely.

"I'm caught on my own land," retorted Ulrich. "When my men come to release us, you will wish you hadn't been caught poaching on a neighbor's land. Shame on you."

From "The Interlopers," page 415

Practice Expression: "The Baby-Sitter"

Expression in reading is how you use your voice to express feeling. Use this passage to practice reading with proper expression. Print a copy of this passage from myNGconnect.com to help you monitor your progress. To use an Expression Rubric, see page 750.

Still puzzled, she went over to the plate of cookies, and as she got close, she stepped into something cold and wet. She looked down. There was a puddle on the floor, soaking into her right sock. An icy-cold puddle. Hilary looked out the kitchen window. It was raining.

Someone was in the house.

She didn't want to believe it, but there was no other explanation. Her whole body felt cold, and she could feel her heart stuttering in her chest. She thought about the twins sleeping upstairs, how she had told them she was hired to make sure nothing bad happened to them. But what if something bad happened to *her*? She shuddered and looked across the room. The telephone was hanging by the refrigerator. She could try and phone for help, or she could run outside and go to the nearest house. The Mitchells lived down a long driveway, and it was about a quarter mile to the next home. And dark. And wet. And she didn't know how many someones were in the house. Or outside. And maybe it was all her imagination.

But—and if her jaw trembled just the slightest she didn't think anyone could fault her—what if the someones wanted to hurt the twins? She was the only one home to protect them.

From "The Baby-Sitter," page 439

Practice Intonation: "The Tell-Tale Heart"

Intonation is the rise and fall in the pitch or tone of your voice as you read aloud. Use this passage to practice reading with proper intonation. Print a copy of this passage from myNGconnect.com to help you monitor your progress. To use an Intonation Rubric, see page 748.

It was a low, dull, quick sound. It sounded like a watch wrapped in cotton. I gasped for breath. Still, the police officers did not hear it. I talked faster and louder, but the noise kept increasing. I stood up and moved around. I talked about things that were not important. I spoke in a high voice and I used violent gestures—but the noise kept getting louder.

Why *would* they not be gone? I walked back and forth on the floor with heavy steps, but the noise kept getting louder. Oh, God! What *could* I do? The noise grew louder—louder—*louder!* And still the men chatted pleasantly and smiled. Was it possible that they didn't hear the sound? Almighty God! No, no! They heard! They suspected! They knew! They were making fun of me! This is what I thought, and it is what I still think.

But anything was better than this agony! Anything was better than to let them go on making a fool of me! I could look at their smiles no longer! I felt that I must scream or die! And now, again, listen! The sound is louder! *Louder!*

"Villains!" I screamed. "Pretend no more! I admit the deed! Tear up the floor boards! Here, here! It is the beating of his hideous heart!"

From "The Tell-Tale Heart," page 465

Practice Expression: "Ad Power"

Expression in reading is how you use your voice to express feeling. Use this passage to practice reading with proper expression. Print a copy of this passage from myNGconnect.com to help you monitor your progress. To use an Expression Rubric, see page 750.

Do you remember the day one of your parents sat you down to have a serious talk about advertising?

Me neither. And it's not something they ever test you on at school. That's too bad. Given how easy it is to remember jingles and slogans, an ad exam might be the one test all year you wouldn't have to study for.

Really, you've been "studying" the subject almost since the day you were born. Every time you got parked in front of the TV or carried past a billboard, you were absorbing the art—or some would say science—of persuasive communication.

Advertising is basically anything someone does to grab your attention and hold onto it long enough to tell you how cool, fast, cheap, tasty, fun, rockin', or rad whatever they're selling is. Some people have a different definition. They argue that advertising is trickery used to shut down your brain just long enough to convince you to open your wallet!

From "Ad Power," page 517

Practice Intonation: "A Long Way to Go: Minorities and the Media"

Intonation is the rise and fall in the pitch or tone of your voice as you read aloud. Use this passage to practice reading with proper intonation. Print a copy of this passage from myNGconnect.com to help you monitor your progress. To use an Intonation Rubric, see page 748.

In one episode of *The $25,000 Pyramid*, a remarkable exchange occurred. In this TV game show, a word appears on a screen in front of one contestant. He then gives clues to try to get his partner to identify the correct word.

On that special day, the word "gangs" came up on the clue-giver's screen. Without hesitation, he fired out the first thing that came to his mind: "They have lots of these in East L.A." (a heavily Mexican American area of Los Angeles). His partner immediately answered, "gangs."

Under pressure, two strangers had linked "East L.A." with "gangs." Why? What force could have brought these two strangers to the same idea?

The answer is obvious—the mass media. The entertainment media have a fascination with Latino gangs. The news media also like to show them often. At the same time, the entertainment media rarely show other Latino characters. And the news media rarely show other Hispanic topics, except for such "problem" issues as immigration and language. The result has been a Latino public image—better yet, a stereotype—in which gangs are an important part.

From "A Long Way to Go: Minorities and the Media," page 545

Practice Phrasing: "What Is News?"

Phrasing is how you use your voice to group words together. Use this passage to practice reading with proper phrasing. Print a copy of this passage from myNGconnect.com to help you monitor your progress. To use a Phrasing Rubric, see page 749.

Research indicates that students get most of their political information from watching David Letterman, Jay Leno, *The Daily Show*, MTV, and from surfing the Web. As recent elections reveal, candidates gain appeal by reaching out to youth through the media. In 1994, former president Bill Clinton made his case to youth on MTV as part of their "Rock the Vote" campaign. And in 2003, California Governor Arnold Schwarzenegger announced his candidacy on Leno's show.

From online chats, instant messaging, blog writing, and market research, candidates know exactly how to find young people on the Internet who are engaged in news and current events activities.

Politicians and advertisers are using the media and "hipper" methods to attract young people. This bears close scrutiny of how youth react to the media messages they see and hear.

From "What Is News?," page 565

Practice Phrasing: "My Mother Pieced Quilts"

Phrasing is how you use your voice to group words together. Use this passage to practice reading with proper phrasing. Print a copy of this passage from myNGconnect.com to help you monitor your progress. To use a Phrasing Rubric, see page 749.

they were just meant as covers
in winters
as weapons
against pounding january winds

but it was just that every morning I awoke to these
october ripened canvases
passed my hand across their cloth faces
and began to wonder how you pieced
all these together
these strips of gentle communion cotton and flannel nightgowns
wedding organdies
dime store velvets

how you shaped patterns square and oblong and round
positioned
balanced
then cemented them
with your thread
a steel needle
a thimble

From "My Mother Pieced Quilts," page 638

Practice Expression: "Sonnet 30: A Modern Paraphrase"

Expression in reading is how you use your voice to express feeling. Use this passage to practice reading with proper expression. Print a copy of this passage from myNGconnect.com to help you monitor your progress. To use an Expression Rubric, see page 750.

When in moments of quiet thoughtfulness

I think about the past,

I regret that I did not achieve all that I wanted,

And it saddens me to think of the years that I wasted:

Then I cry, though I am not one who cries often,

For my good friends who have died,

And I cry again over heartbreaks that ended long ago,

And mourn the loss of many things that I have seen and loved:

Then I grieve again over past troubles,

And sadly I remind myself, one regret after another,

Of all the sorrows and disappointments in my life,

And they hurt me more than ever before.

But if I think of you at this time, dear friend,

I regain all that I have lost and my sadness ends.

From "Sonnet 30: A Modern Paraphrase," page 671

Practice Intonation: "I Hear America Singing"

Intonation is the rise and fall in the pitch or tone of your voice as you read aloud. Use this passage to practice reading with proper intonation. Print a copy of this passage from myNGconnect.com to help you monitor your progress. To use an Intonation Rubric, see page 748.

I hear America singing, the varied carols I hear,

Those of mechanics, each one singing his as it should be blithe
and strong,

The carpenter singing his as he measures his plank or beam,

The mason singing his as he makes ready for work, or leaves off work,

The boatman singing what belongs to him in his boat, the deckhand
singing on the steamboat deck,

The shoemaker singing as he sits on his bench, the hatter singing
as he stands,

The wood-cutter's song, the ploughboy's on his way in the morning,
or at noon intermission or at sundown,

The delicious singing of the mother, or of the young wife at work,
or of the girl sewing or washing,

Each singing what belongs to him or her and to none else,

The day what belongs to the day—at night the party of young
fellows, robust, friendly,

Singing with open mouths their strong melodious songs.

From "I Hear America Singing," page 682

Study Skills and Strategies

Before You Study

Studying can be difficult, especially when you are distracted or have many subjects you need to study all at the same time. There are several ways to prepare to study, including creating a routine and establishing a productive study environment. You can also make studying easier by studying subjects in a specific order and creating a schedule.

How to Create and Maintain a Study Routine

Before you begin studying, create a routine.

- Study at the same time and place for each session.
- Mark the study time in your calendar as an appointment, like going to the doctor. For example, *Tuesday: 3:30–4:30: Study English.*
- Set small, specific goals for each study session.
- Pay attention to what works best for you and repeat that method.
- Give yourself a small reward when you are finished. For example, call a friend or listen to your favorite music.

How to Create a Productive Study Environment

Setting up a study area will help you follow your routine. Find an area where you are comfortable that you can claim as your own.

Set Up Your Workplace

- Make sure your area is quiet or has background noise, depending on which you prefer.
- Make sure you have enough light—get an extra lamp if your area is too dark.
- Have everything you need for studying available beforehand.
- Designate certain places for each necessary item. Don't waste valuable time looking for books, notes, writing materials, self-stick notes, or information.
- After you have assembled the items you need, put them where you can easily access them.
- Keep a calendar and a watch or clock in your study area to help you stay focused on your available time and on your priorities.
- Keep your study area clean.

How to Create an Efficient Study Order

Creating priorities for study time will help you complete your tasks in an efficient order. Making a list of the things you need to do can help you organize your priorities. Look at the chart to understand how to create an efficient order for your study time.

Study Order Tips	
Label Your Assignments by Priority	• **Urgent** Must be done immediately • **Important** Must be done soon • **Upcoming** Must be done in the near future
Make a List	• List the things you have to do in order of importance. • Once you complete a task, cross it off your list.
Stay Organized	• Keep your list nearby to record new tasks or updates.

How to Complete Tasks on Schedule

A good schedule can help you stay focused and complete assignments on time. Create a schedule or purchase a day planner and record homework due dates, quizzes, and tests.

Think about events that might affect your schedule, such as appointments or extracurricular activities. You may need to postpone or cancel other plans to help you stay on schedule. If you are concerned about missing a date, circle the task.

Weekly Schedule					
Subject	**Monday**	**Tuesday**	**Wednesday**	**Thursday**	**Friday**
Math	Chapter 6: Problems 1-10	None	Chapter 6: Problems 11-20	None	Chapter 7: Problems 1-15
Science	Study for Test	Review for Test	Test	Read Chapter 8	None
History	None	Read Chapter 11	Read Chapter 12	Study for Quiz	Quiz: Chapters 11 and 12
English	Read Chapter 3	Read Chapter 4 Study for Quiz	Quiz: Chapters 3 and 4	Read Chapter 5	None

While You Study

There are many different ways to study. Talk with classmates and your teachers to learn new study techniques and strategies that might work for you, too. No matter which study strategies you use, you should use a variety, such as writing and using graphic organizers, until you figure out which strategies work best for you.

How to Use Writing as a Study Tool

Use writing as a tool to assist you:

- Write your own questions about the topic, and practice answering them.
- Condense your classroom notes onto note cards or into charts for easier reviewing.
- Create an outline from your notes, and then write a summary of the information.
- Write notes on self-stick notes as you read. Later, attach the self-stick notes in an organized manner to a sheet of notebook paper for at-a-glance study.

How to Use Graphic Organizers as a Study Tool

Graphic organizers are effective study tools. For example, a time line can be used to organize the events covered in a nonfiction selection. A word web can be used to learn new vocabulary words. See the Index of Graphic Organizers on page Index 1 for more examples of graphic organizers you can use as study tools.

How to Review

It is very important to review material. The best time to review is right after you have finished reading something for the first time. Reviewing gives you an opportunity to figure out anything you do not understand and to better remember information in the future.

Review Effectively

- When you read something new, review the information on the same day.
- Reread information to measure what you have learned.
- Go over notes in detail to clarify information you may have missed or don't understand. Combine your notes with any outlines or study guides that you have about the topic.
- Write down any new questions you may have.
- Plan a time to review each day. This will help you learn to review information regularly as part of your daily study schedule.

How to Use a Learning Log and Set Goals

You can use learning logs to record what you have learned, what you found interesting, and questions you have about the text. The purpose of a learning log is to think about your understanding of the material and to clarify your knowledge for further study. Use the **What parts am I struggling with?** and **What will I do next?** columns in the learning log to set future learning goals.

Learning Log Title of Selection:				
Dates and page numbers	What have I learned?	What parts am I struggling with?	What will I do next?	

How to Seek Help

There will be times when you don't understand certain information, even after studying and careful note taking. You will need to seek help to understand the information. Make a list of the topics or problems that you don't understand. Include the page numbers where they are located in your textbooks. Make a chart that lists people and places you can seek help from. Then use these resources to help clarify confusing information.

Resources for Help

People: teachers, parents, siblings, classmates, librarians, tutors

Places: libraries, museums, study centers, school

Reference Sources: dictionaries, thesauruses, encyclopedias, atlases, newspapers, magazines, Web sites, television programs

How to Make Words Your Own Routine

When you cook, you follow the steps of a recipe. This helps you make the food correctly. When you read, there are also steps you can follow to learn new words. The following steps will help you practice the words in different ways and make the words your own.

Learning a Word

Follow these steps to add new words to your vocabulary.

1. **Pronounce the Word** Write and say the word one syllable at a time.
   - **realize**: re-a-lize
   - Think about what looks familiar in the word. For example, *real* is part of *realize*.

2. **Study Examples** When you are given examples, read them carefully and think about how and why the word is being used.
   - **Example**: *Marietta did not **realize** that Lupe was so busy.* What does this sentence tell you about Marietta and Lupe?
   - Look for more examples to study in books or magazines.

3. **Elaborate** Create new sentences to check your understanding of the word.
   - Finish these sentence frames for practice:
   - I **realized** I was happy when _____.
   - Steve's mom **realized** he was growing up when _____.
   - How did your teacher **realize** that you _____?

4. **Practice the Words** Use the new word to write sentences.
   - Use the word in many different ways. This will help you remember the word and understand its meaning.

How to Relate Words

A good way to build your vocabulary is to **relate new words** to words or concepts you already know. Think about how the new word is similar to or different from words you are already familiar with. You can also create a **semantic map** to help you study the new word.

Semantic Map

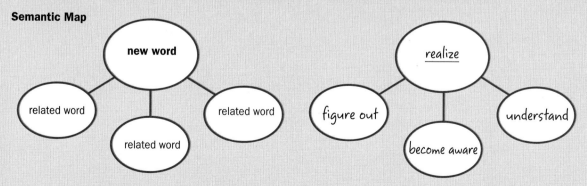

How to Use Context to Understand Words

Context is the surrounding text near a word or phrase that helps explain the meaning of the word or phrase.

Unfamiliar Words

Context clues are hints in a sentence or paragraph that can help define unknown or unfamiliar words. Context clues can include synonyms, antonyms, explanations, definitions, examples, sensory images, or punctuation, such as commas and dashes.

- **Example**: *My fascination with* <u>celestial bodies</u>—*such as* **stars***,* **planets***, and* **moons**—*made me want to buy a* **telescope***.* The words *stars*, *planets*, and *moons* are clues that tell me *celestial bodies* are objects in the universe. The word *telescope* tells me I can see these objects from Earth, probably at night.

Multiple-Meaning Words

Some words have different meanings depending on how they are used in a sentence. Check what context the words are used in to help determine which meaning is correct in the material you are reading. Substitute each meaning you know in the context of the sentence until you find the use that makes the best sense.

- **Example**: *Please sign your name before entering the museum.* The word *sign* has more than one meaning. Which meaning is correct in this sentence? *Sign* can mean "to write" or it can mean "something that hangs on a wall to provide information." The first meaning is correct.

Figurative Language

Figurative language is a tool that writers use to help you visualize or relate to what is happening in a selection. This type of language is nonliteral because it does not mean exactly what it looks like it says, or it is using a special meaning. Idioms, similes, and metaphors are common types of nonliteral, or figurative language. It is helpful to use mental images or context clues to better understand what you are reading.

Idioms

An **idiom** is a phrase or an expression that can only be understood as a complete sentence or phrase. The individual words have separate meanings and they will not make sense if they are thought of literally. Read the words before or after the idiom to figure out the meaning. Remember to think about an idiom as a group of words, not as individual words.

- **Example**: Don't *bite off more than you can chew* or you will never finish the job. This is an idiom used to advise people against agreeing to do more work than they are capable of doing. It is not a phrase about biting or chewing.

Similes and Metaphors

Similes use *like* or *as* to compare two things.

- **Example:** *The willow tree's branches are like silken thread.* This simile is comparing a tree's branches to silk thread. Think about the things that are being compared and what they each mean. Silk is very soft and smooth. The simile means the willow's branches are also very soft and smooth.

Metaphors compare two things without using *like* or *as*.

- **Example:** *The night sky is a black curtain.* This metaphor compares the night sky to a black curtain. A black curtain would block out light from coming in a window. This metaphor means the night sky is very dark.

- **Example:** *The company planned an advertising blitz to promote its new product.* The word *blitz* comes from the German word *blitzkrieg*, which refers to the bombing of London, England, by Germany during World War II. The term *advertising blitz*, therefore, is a metaphor that expresses the way advertisements will overwhelm the public.

You can also use sensory images to learn new words by asking yourself or others: What does it look like? Feel like? Sound like?

Technical and Specialized Language

Technical, or specialized, language provides important information about a topic. Many words in English have an everyday meaning and a special meaning in a career field. For example, the word *shift* can mean "to move something from one place to another." In the workplace, however, *shift* can mean "a time period for work."

Example: *Be sure to clean your mouse regularly to make the cursor move smoothly on the computer monitor.*

- Read the sentence to determine the specialized subject.
- Identify technical vocabulary: *mouse, cursor, computer monitor.*
- Use context clues to help you figure out the meaning of the technical language, or jargon.

Denotation and Connotation

Denotation is the actual meaning of a word that you would find in a dictionary. For example, if you looked up the word *snake* in the dictionary, you could find that one of its meanings is "a limbless scaled reptile with a long tapering body."

Connotation is the suggested meaning of the word in addition to its literal meaning. Connotations can be positive or negative. For example, the word *snake* can be used in a positive or negative way.

- **Example:** *Jenny was caught sneaking around Maria's locker. She wanted to steal Maria's homework and copy Maria's answers. Nobody could believe that Jenny would be such a snake.*

By using the context of the paragraph (*sneaking around, steal*), you can understand that the connotation of *snake* in this usage is negative.

Analogies

An **analogy** is a comparison. Think of analogies as word problems. To solve the analogy, figure out what the connection is. Use context to see how the word pairs are related.

- **Example**: *Hard* is to *rocks* as *soft* is to _____. *Hard* describes the feeling of *rocks*. Rocks are hard. What does *soft* describe the feeling of? *Hard* is to *rocks* as *soft* is to *blankets*.

Use the relationships between words in an analogy to infer the meaning of an unfamiliar word. For example, in the analogy "*sparse* is to *meager* as *quarrel* is to *argue*," you can infer that *sparse* and *meager* mean the same thing.

Allusions

An **allusion** is a reference to another text. If you know or can find out about the source that the writer is alluding to, you can better understand the word or phrase.

- **Example**: "It took a herculean effort, but she finally made it to graduation." *Herculean* refers to a character from Greek mythology named Hercules. He fought monsters and faced many dangers. So the character must have faced challenges too.

How to Analyze Word Parts

Each piece in a puzzle fits together to make a picture. Words have pieces that come together, too. Analyzing the parts, or structures, of words will help you learn the meaning of entire words. Use a print or electronic dictionary to confirm your word analysis.

Compound Words

Compound words are made when two separate words are combined to make a new word. To learn the meaning of a compound word, study its parts individually. For example, *doghouse* is one word made from two smaller words, *dog* and *house*. Since you know that *dog* is an animal and *house* is a structure where people live, you can figure out that *doghouse* means a house for a dog.

Greek and Latin Roots

Many words in the English language derived from, or came from, other languages, especially Greek and Latin. It is helpful to know the **origins**, or **roots**, of English words. You may be able to figure out the meaning of an unknown word if you know the meaning of its root. Roots can form many different words and can't be broken into smaller parts. The chart below has examples of roots.

Root Chart		
Root	**Meaning**	**English Example**
crit (Greek)	to judge	*Criticize* means "to find fault." *Critique* means "an act of judgment."
mal (Latin)	bad	*Malady* means "an illness." *Malice* means "desire to harm another."

Prefixes and Suffixes

If you know common roots, **prefixes**, and **suffixes**, you can figure out the meanings of many words. The chart below shows how to analyze the word *constellation*.

Word Part	Definition	Example
Root	The main part of a word	*stella* means "star"
Prefix	A word part placed in front of the root to create a new meaning	*con-* means "together"
Suffix	A word part placed after the root to create a new meaning	*-tion* means "the act of"

Example: A *constellation* is a group of stars.

Inflected Forms

An **inflection** is a change in the form of a word to show its usage. You can learn new words by analyzing what type of inflection is being used.

Inflection	Meaning	Examples
-er	more	cold**er**, fast**er**
-ed	in the past	call**ed**, talk**ed**
-s	plural	pen**s**, dog**s**

Word Families

A word family is a group of words that all share the same root but have different forms. For example, look at the word family for *success*: success**ful**, success**fully**, **un**success**ful**, **un**success**fully**. If you know the meaning of the root word *success*, you can use what you know to help you understand the rest of the meanings in the word family.

Cognates and False Cognates

Cognates are words that come from two different languages but that are very similar because they share root origins. Cognates have similar spellings and meanings. For example, the English word *artist* and the Spanish word *artista* both mean "a person who creates art."

False cognates seem like they share a meaning but they do not. For example, the English word *rope* means "a cord to tie things with," but the Spanish word *ropa* means "clothing."

How to Use Cognates to Determine Word Meaning

- Think about what the word means in the language you are most familiar with.
- Substitute the meaning of the word with your language's definition.
- If your language's definition does not make sense, you may be using a false cognate. Try to learn the word using a different resource.

Foreign Words in English

Some foreign words come directly into English, without changes in spelling. For example, the French phrase *avant-garde*, referring to a cutting-edge movement in art or music, is often used in English. Use a print or online dictionary to identify other foreign words in English.

How to Use a Reference

Dictionary

A dictionary lists words with correct spellings, pronunciations, meanings, and uses. It can be used to find the denotation, or exact meaning, of a word. Sometimes a dictionary definition may be helpful in determining the connotation, or feelings associated with a word.

- Read all the definitions of the new word to find the use and meaning you need. Use the dictionary's key to understand any abbreviations or symbols.
- Go back to the selection and reread the paragraph. Substitute the meaning you found for the original word. Check to make sure it is the correct use of the word.

fraud·u·lent

(frȯ' jə lənt), *adj.*: based on or done by fraud or trickery; deceitful. [ME *fraude* fr. L *fraud-*] –fraud'u·lent·ness, *n.* –fraud'u·lent·ly, *adv.*

Key	
ME	Middle English (an old version of English)
L	Latin
fr.	from
ȯ	pronounced like the *a* in *saw*
ə	pronounced like *uh*
'	accented syllable

Thesaurus

A thesaurus lists words with their synonyms and antonyms. Use a thesaurus to confirm word meanings.

- Try to identify a familiar word from the synonyms listed for the new word.
- Go back to the selection and reread the paragraph. Substitute the synonym you chose for the original word. Keep trying synonyms until the words make sense.

Glossary

A glossary is like a dictionary but only defines words found in a specific book.

- Check to see whether there is a glossary at the end of the book you are reading.
- Read the definition of the new word in the glossary.
- Reread the sentence and substitute the definition for the word.

Technology

The Internet links computers and information sites electronically.

Web Sites to Use for Vocabulary Support

- myNGConnect.com This Web site has links to reference sources.
- m-w.com The Merriam-Webster Dictionary Web site includes a dictionary, a thesaurus, Spanish-English translation, and word activities.

Practice Your Vocabulary

When you are trying to learn something new, like a musical instrument, you practice. The more you practice, the better you become. Practicing vocabulary words is an important step in learning new words.

Memorize New Words

- Read the word and its definition silently and aloud.
- Cover the definition and try to restate the word's meaning.
- Write words on one side of index cards and their meanings on the opposite sides to make flashcards. Have someone show you the words, and try to recite their definitions from memory.
- Ask yourself questions using the definition and the word.
- Think of clues or mental images to associate with the new word to help you better remember its definition. You can also use real images to help you remember. For example, look around the classroom. Point to an object and say what it is. Use this to describe the entire classroom.

Review New Words

- Reread the definition of each word.
- Create sentences expressing the correct meaning of each word.
- Make lists of new words with their definitions in a notebook to periodically review.
- Study each word until you are confident you understand its meaning and how to use the word properly.

Word Awareness

It is important to choose the right words in order to clearly say what you mean. You need to be aware of different kinds of words and how they work. For example, remember that some words have multiple meanings. If you are not aware of this as you read, you might use the wrong meaning or misunderstand a sentence.

Synonyms and Antonyms

Synonyms are words that have the same or similar meanings.

- Think of a different word that has the same meaning of the word you want to use. For example, synonyms for the word *loud* include *noisy* and *roaring*.
- Use a thesaurus when trying to identify synonyms.

Antonyms are words that have opposite meanings.

- Think of words that are the exact opposite of the word you want to use. For example, antonyms for the word *break* include *fix* and *repair*.
- Remember that antonyms are usually listed at the end of an entry for a word in a thesaurus.

Homonyms and Homophones

Homonyms are words that are spelled the same but have different meanings.

- **Example**: *I* rose *out of my chair to pick the* rose *from the top of the bush*. In this sentence, *rose* has two meanings. One *rose* is a verb (past tense of *rise*), and the other *rose* is a noun (a type of flower). Using context clues, you can see that *out of my chair* signals that "the past tense of rise" comes at the beginning of the sentence. You can then conclude that "the flower" is the second *rose*.

Homophones are words that sound the same but have different meanings and spellings.

- **Example**: *The wind* blew *the clouds across the* blue *sky*. *Blew* and *blue* sound alike, but they are spelled differently. *Blew* is a verb (the past tense of *blow*), and *blue* is an adjective (a color). Using context clues, you can see that *the clouds* signals that "the past tense of blow" comes at the beginning of the sentence. You can then conclude that "a color" is the second *blue*.

When you hear a homonym or a homophone read aloud, it is easy to become confused. Visualizing the word can help you figure out its correct meaning and spelling.

Phrasal Verbs, or Two-Word Verbs

Phrasal verbs combine a particle such as *out*, *up*, or *on* with a verb. These phrases are often idiomatic because the two words on their own mean something different than the phrase.

- **Example**: *I* brought up *my fight with Leon during dinner*. *Brought* is the past tense of *bring*, and *up* is a direction. But when the words are combined in the context shown in the sample sentence, they mean "mentioned." *I mentioned my fight with Leon during dinner*.

You may be able to find some phrasal verbs in a dictionary. If you do not understand a certain phrase, ask for help or look for English usage resources in the library.

Slang

Slang is language that is informal and specific to certain groups.

- Slang words are created and used in place of standard terms. Popular culture and the media heavily impact slang words and usage.

- Learning when to use slang is important. Slang is OK for casual situations, but not for more formal ones, like school discussions, writing, or presentations.

- If you become familiar with common slang words and phrases, it may help you to better understand everyday conversations. Special dictionaries for slang can help you learn more terms.

Dialect and Regionalism

A **dialect** is a way people in a specific region or area use a language.

- People in different locations often have different ways to express or pronounce words from the same language.

- If you are unfamiliar with a dialect, try to find out more about the way local people use their language. You can use the Internet or library resources to study dialects.

WRITING HANDBOOK

The Writing Process

What Is the Writing Process?

Writing is like anything else—if you want to do it well, you have to work at it. This work doesn't happen all at once, though. Good writers often follow a series of steps called the Writing Process. This process helps the writer break the writing into manageable tasks.

Prewrite

Prewriting is what you do before you write. In this step, you gather ideas, choose your topic, make a plan, and gather details.

❶ Gather Ideas

Great writing ideas are all around you. What interests do you have that other people might want to read about? Think about recent events or things you've read or seen. Brainstorm ideas with your classmates, teachers, and family. Then record your ideas in an "idea bank," such as a notebook, journal, or **word processing** file. Add to your idea bank regularly and draw from it whenever you are given a writing assignment.

❷ Choose Your Topic

Your teacher may give you a topic to write about, or you may have to choose one for yourself. Find several suitable topics in your idea bank; then ask these questions:

- What do I know about this topic?
- Who might want to read about this topic and why?
- Which topic do I feel most strongly about?
- Which topic best fits the assignment?
- What important question can I ask about the topic?

> Writing Ideas
>   visiting my family in Mexico
> ✓ my first job
>   teens and peer pressure

❸ Make a Plan

Create a Writing Plan to focus and organize your ideas.

Writing Plan
Topic: What will I write about? my first job
Purpose: Why am I writing? to share a lesson with others
Audience: Who will read this? my teacher and classmates
Form: What form works best for my topic, audience, and purpose? autobiographical narrative
Controlling Idea: What is this mainly about? learning to do things for myself
Voice/Tone: What attitude and feeling do I want my writing to express? serious, with a little humor

❹ Gather Details

A 5Ws and H chart will help you gather details for many kinds of writing assignments.

5Ws and H Chart	
Who?	my dad, my boss, and I
What?	first job
Where?	Garcia's Restaurant
When?	last summer to now
Why?	spending money, save for college
How?	fill out application, use bus to get to and from my job

⑤ Research

Some writing forms and topics require research. Use these resources to find out more about your topic:

- **Internet** Develop a list of terms to enter into a search engine. Use sites that end in .edu or .gov for the most reliable information. For more on Internet research, see p. 608.

- **Library** Search the library's catalog and databases for books and articles about your topic. Ask a librarian for help.

- **Interview** You may want to interview a person who has knowledge about your topic. Prepare questions ahead of time and take notes on the responses.

⑥ Get Organized

Review your details and choose a way to organize your writing. Use an appropriate graphic organizer such as a topic outline to show the main idea and details of your paragraphs in order. List your main ideas next to the roman numerals. List any supporting details underneath the main ideas, next to the capital letters.

Topic Outline

My First Job

I. Introduction: I joined the workforce.
   A. Many teens work.
   B. Work taught me responsibility.
II. Body: I looked for and got a job.
   A. I searched want ads.
   B. I applied for jobs.
   C. I interviewed.
III. Body: I learned the job.
   A. My first day was hard.
   B. I improved over time.
IV. Conclusion: I learned a lesson.
   A. I earned money for college.
   B. I learned responsibility.

For another sample outline, see **Language and Learning Handbook**, page 641.

Draft

The drafting stage is when you put your Writing Plan into action. Don't worry about making things perfect at this point. Drafts are meant to be changed. Instead, concentrate on writing out your ideas in complete sentences and paragraphs. The following ideas will help you organize your main idea and supporting details into a draft.

❶ Remember Purpose, Form, and Audience

Remember, you already made many important decisions about your work during the prewriting stage. Return to your Writing Plan often. Remind yourself of your purpose, form, and controlling idea as you organize your paragraphs. Think carefully about your audience, voice, and tone as you choose words and craft sentences.

❷ Introduce the Controlling Idea and Use Literary Devices

Your first paragraph should introduce your controlling idea and draw readers into your work. You can use any of the following literary devices to begin your paper in a clear and interesting way. Each device is an example of a **topic sentence**, which lets readers know what the text will be about.

- **Position Statement**: *Few things teach responsibility better than a part-time job.*

- **Question**: *Do you remember your first paycheck?*

- **Quotation**: *My dad always says, "If you really want something, you'll work for it."*

- **Statistic**: *In July 2006, almost 22 million teens in the United States held a job. I was one of them. It was my first job.*

The controlling idea is the main thing you are writing about, or the idea you want to express. It is more specific than the topic. The topic is the general area or subject of your writing. For example, if the topic of an article is baseball, the controlling idea could be learning how to hit home runs.

❸ Work Collaboratively

Involve other people in the writing of your draft early and often. Teachers, classmates, and family members can help you improve what you have written and determine what needs to be done. Listen carefully to what they have to say, and take notes on their suggestions.

❹ Use Technology to Draft

Continue writing until you have a complete draft. You can write your draft with a pen and paper or with a **word processor**. In either case, be sure to save a copy of your work.

Draft

My First Job

In July 2006, almost 22 million teens in the United States held a job (Bureau of Labor Statistics). I was one of them. It was my first job. That summer I learned lessons about responsibility that will last me the rest of my life.

The first thing I learned is that knowing how to find, apply for, and interview for a job is as important as knowing how to do the job itself. I searched the want ads in our local newspaper and on the Internet. In fact, I even filled out and submitted applications for several places online. I was sure to fill out each application as completely and honestly as possible. This work proved useful when two restaurants asked me to interview for busboy, or assistant server, positions. I dressed neatly and gave myself plenty of time to make it to the interviews on schedule. When I met the managers, I shook their hands, then listened closely to their questions before responding.

Revise

After you have written a draft, you need to revise it, or make changes. Revision is what takes your writing from good to great.

❶ Revise for Traits of Good Writing

Focus and Unity

- ☑ Do you have a clearly stated controlling idea or opinion?
- ☑ Is your controlling idea supported?
- ☑ Do your ideas and details flow logically?

Organization

- ☑ Do you have a title and an introductory paragraph?
- ☑ Do you transition between ideas?
- ☑ Are your ideas in a sensible order?
- ☑ Do you have a conclusion or ending?
- ☑ Does the organization match your purpose and audience?

Development of Ideas

- ☑ Are your ideas meaningful?
- ☑ Are your details vivid?
- ☑ Do your details answer questions that readers may have about the topic?
- ☑ Have you addressed purpose, audience, and genre to improve subtlety of meaning?

Voice and Style

- ☑ Is your writing unique and engaging?
- ☑ Are most of your sentences in active voice?
- ☑ Do the style and language used match your purpose and audience?
- ☑ Do you use figurative language to address purpose, audience, and genre?

Written Conventions

- ☑ Are your spelling, punctuation, capitalization, grammar, and usage correct?

See pages 706–715 for more information.

❷ Use Technology

The word processing software found on most computers will help you develop and make changes to your work quickly and easily. Here are some hints to help you get the most out of your computer:

- Save your work often. This will prevent the loss of your work in case of a computer malfunction.

- Create a "scrap file" of sentences and paragraphs you deleted as you revised. This deleted material may contain other ideas and details you can use in later writing.

- Think about how you will move your document from computer to computer. For example, if you e-mail yourself a copy, make sure the next computer you plan to use has Internet access.

❸ Hold a Peer Conference

Work with your classmates to improve each other's work.

Peer Review Guidelines

As Writer ...

- Read your draft aloud or supply copies for each member of your group.

- Ask for help on specific points related to the traits of good writing.

- Listen carefully and take notes on your reviewers' comments.

As Reviewer ...

- Read or listen to the complete writing. Take notes as you read or listen.

- Compliment the strong parts of the draft before you criticize weak points.

- Offer specific suggestions.

Edit and Proofread

After you have revised your draft for content, organization, and wording, it is time to check it for mistakes.

❶ Take Your Time

Successful editing and proofreading require attention to detail. The following hints will help you do your best work:

- Use a printed copy of your work. Text looks different on paper than on a computer screen. Many people catch more mistakes when they edit a printed version of their work.

- Set your work aside for a while. Your review may be more effective if you are rested.

- Read line by line. Use a ruler or piece of paper to cover the lines below the one you are reading. This will help you concentrate on the text in front of you.

❷ Check Your Sentences

Make sure your sentences are clear, complete, and correct. Ask yourself:

- Did I include a subject and a predicate in each sentence?

- Did I break up run-on sentences?

- Did I use a variety of sentence structures to keep my writing interesting?

- Did I combine short sentences, when possible, to create longer sentences?

- Did I use the active voice in most of my sentences?

❸ Check for Mistakes

Proofread to find errors in capitalization, punctuation, grammar, and spelling. Look especially for:

- capital letters, end marks, apostrophes, and quotation marks

- subject-verb agreement

- misspelled words

4 Use Reference Tools

Reference tools are an important part of every writer's tool kit. Dictionaries, thesauruses, and electronic sources such as Web sites and the spell-checking features of most word processing programs are all reference tools available to the good writer. When in doubt, check different versions of several sources.

Use a **dictionary** to check the meaning and spelling of your words.

> I worked **diligently** that summer.
> *Is that spelled correctly?*

Use a **thesaurus** to find words that are livelier or more appropriate for your audience.

> I worked ~~diligently~~ **hard** that summer.
> *Maybe this word is clearer to my audience.*

Use a **grammar handbook** to fix sentences and punctuation errors.

> We ~~was~~ **were** cleaning the grill.
> *That's the correct verb.*

Use a **style guide** or **style manual**, which is a publication containing rules and suggestions about grammar, writing, and publishing, for help in **citing** your sources. When you use information and ideas from other authors, you need to give them credit for their work. **Plagiarism** is using someone's words or ideas without giving the person credit. When you reword another author's ideas, you still have to give the author credit for his or her ideas.

> In July 2006, almost 22 million teens in the United States held a job. (Bureau of Labor Statistics)
> *Now the statistic is properly cited, according to the method I found in the style guide.*

5 Mark Your Changes

Use proofreader's marks to show changes on a printout of your draft. Then make changes to your word processed document.

> ¶ The first thing I learned is that knowing ~~how~~ how to find, apply for, and interview for a job is as important as knowing how to do the job itself. I ^{searched} the want ads in our local newspaper and on the Internet⊙ In fact, I even filled out and submitted applications for several places online. I was sure to fill out each application as completely and honestly as possible.¶ dressed neatly and gave myself plenty of time to make it to the interviews on schedule. This work proved useful when two restaurants asked me to interview for busboy, or assistant server, positions. when I met the Managers, I shook their hands, then listened closely to their questions before responding.

Proofreader's Marks	
ϱ	Delete
∧	Add text
⊃→	Move to here
⊙	Add period
⋏	Add comma
≡	Capitalize
/	Make lowercase
¶	Start new paragraph

Publish and Evaluate

You've made it! You're now ready for the last step in the Writing Process. First, prepare your final document for your readers. Then, reflect back on what you've done well and what you could do better next time.

❶ Print Your Work

The final version of your work should be neat and easy to read. It should be visually appealing. You can increase the visual impact of the final version of your work by using different font types and sizes, headings, bullet points, or even diagrams and charts as a way to present data. Use the information below to format your document for final publication. Then print out and make copies of your work to share with others. Be sure to keep a copy for yourself.

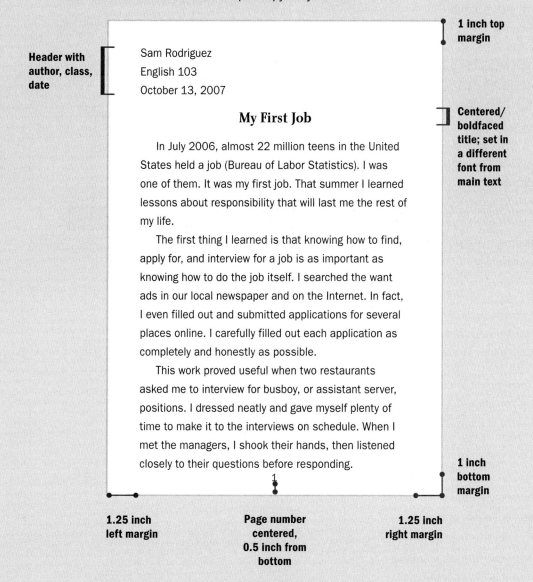

1 inch top margin

Header with author, class, date

Sam Rodriguez

English 103

October 13, 2007

Centered/ boldfaced title; set in a different font from main text

My First Job

In July 2006, almost 22 million teens in the United States held a job (Bureau of Labor Statistics). I was one of them. It was my first job. That summer I learned lessons about responsibility that will last me the rest of my life.

The first thing I learned is that knowing how to find, apply for, and interview for a job is as important as knowing how to do the job itself. I searched the want ads in our local newspaper and on the Internet. In fact, I even filled out and submitted applications for several places online. I carefully filled out each application as completely and honestly as possible.

This work proved useful when two restaurants asked me to interview for busboy, or assistant server, positions. I dressed neatly and gave myself plenty of time to make it to the interviews on schedule. When I met the managers, I shook their hands, then listened closely to their questions before responding.

1

1 inch bottom margin

1.25 inch left margin

Page number centered, 0.5 inch from bottom

1.25 inch right margin

❷ Publish Your Work

Take your work beyond the classroom and share it in new ways.

- Save examples of your writing in a portfolio. This will allow you to see the improvement in your writing over time. Organize your portfolio by date or form. Each time you add pieces to your portfolio, take some time to self-reflect and compare the new piece to your older work.

Portfolio Review

- ☑ How does this writing compare to other work I've done?
- ☑ What traits am I getting better at?
- ☑ What traits do I need to work on?
- ☑ What is my style? What kinds of sentences and words do I often use?
- ☑ What makes me a super writer?

- Expand your work by making it into a poster or other visual display, such as a video or a Web site. What images best express your ideas? How will the text appear?

- Many newspapers and Web sites publish teen writing. Ask a teacher or librarian for examples, or research them yourself. For writers, there are few things more satisfying than sharing their ideas with as wide an audience as possible.

❸ Evaluate Your Work

Now that you have completed your work, look to see what you can improve.

- Use rubrics to evaluate the quality and effectiveness of your writing. Rubrics contain criteria for evaluating your work. Review the rubrics on pages 706–715.

- Discuss your work with your teacher and classmates, then ask yourself:

What did I do well?

I added some description. My details were sequential and organized.

What are some weaknesses that I could improve on easily?

It lacks uniqueness. I need to vary my sentence structures.

How will I make sure I improve on those weaker areas?

I could pick topics that I feel strongly about. During revision I can check my sentence structure.

What are some weaknesses that may take time to improve?

Expanding my ideas, making my voice more mature.

- Set goals based on your evaluation. Make a list of goals; cross them out as you accomplish them. Then set new goals.

Goals to Improve My Writing
1. ~~I am going to use more descriptive sentences in my next narrative piece.~~
2. I am going to check all my sentence beginnings and make sure they are different.
3. I am going to add more "important" facts to my expository nonfiction pieces.

What Are Writing Traits?

Writing traits are the characteristics of good writing. Use the traits and writing examples on the following pages to plan, evaluate, and improve your writing.

Focus and Unity

All the ideas in a piece of writing should be related, or go together well. **Focus** your writing by selecting a single central or **controlling idea**. Then give your work **unity** by relating each main idea and detail to that controlling idea. Use the rubric below to help maintain focus and unity in your writing.

	How clearly does the writing present a central idea or claim?	How well does everything go together?
4 Wow!	**The writing expresses a <u>clear</u> central idea or claim about the topic.**	<u>Everything</u> in the writing goes together. • The main idea of each paragraph goes with the central idea or claim of the paper. • The main idea and details within each paragraph are related. • The conclusion is about the central idea or claim.
3 Ahh.	**The writing expresses a <u>generally</u> clear central idea or claim about the topic.**	<u>Most</u> parts of the writing go together. • The main idea of most paragraphs goes with the central idea or claim of the paper. • In most paragraphs, the main idea and details are related. • Most of the conclusion is about the central idea or claim.
2 Hmm.	**The writing includes a topic, but the central idea or claim is <u>not</u> clear.**	<u>Some</u> parts of the writing go together. • The main idea of some paragraphs goes with the central idea or claim of the paper. • In some paragraphs, the main idea and details are related. • Some of the conclusion is about the central idea or claim.
1 Huh?	**The writing includes many topics and <u>does not</u> express one central idea or claim.**	The parts of the writing <u>do not</u> go together. • Few paragraphs have a main idea, or the main idea does not go with the central idea or claim of the paper. • Few paragraphs contain a main idea and related details • None of the conclusion is about the central idea or claim.

Focus and Unity: Strong Example, score of 3 or 4

"Mother to Son"—An Amazing Poem

Nobody writes poetry like Langston Hughes. In the poem "Mother to Son," he shows why he is such an amazing poet. He is a master of theme, rhythm, and figurative language.

The theme of "Mother to Son" is about life's difficulties and the need to keep going. The voice in the poem is that of a mother. She talks about how her life has been such a struggle. The mother shares with her son that he is going to go through some tough times, too, but he has to stay strong and focused when life is hard.

Langston Hughes is also great at creating rhythm with words. His poems read like songs in your head, and "Mother to Son" is no different. He uses quick, short lines with repetitive beginnings to make the poem very rhythmic. Hughes also creates rhythm by adding just a couple of lines that rhyme.

This poem is all about figurative language. The poem really is one big metaphor. The mother compares her life to a rough, worn-out staircase. The metaphor helps me to picture what the mother means about life being difficult sometimes. It also symbolizes that in order to get somewhere, you have to keep trying and working until you get to where you want to be.

Langston Hughes is an amazing poet. He is able to write poems that affect me by making them about something I can relate to and by making them rhythmic and creative.

The beginning states the controlling idea.

The main idea of each paragraph is about the controlling idea.

Details support the main idea.

The end connects to the beginning.

Focus and Unity: Weak Example, score of 1 or 2

An Amazing Poem

The narrator of the poem is that of a mother. She talks about how her life has been such a struggle. The mother shares with her son that he is going to go through some tough times, too, but he has to stay strong and focused when life is hard.

Langston Hughes is a great poet. His poems have theme, figurative language, and rhythm. This poem is all about figurative language. The poem really is one big metaphor. The mother compares her life to a rough, worn-out staircase. The metaphor helps me to picture what the mother means about life being difficult sometimes. It also symbolizes that in order to get somewhere you have to keep trying and working until you get to where you want to be.

He uses quick, short lines with repetitive beginnings to make the poem very rhythmic. Hughes also creates rhythm by adding just a couple of lines that rhyme.

Langston Hughes is an amazing poet.

The controlling idea is unclear.

The paragraphs have no clear main idea.

The conclusion is vague and abrupt.

Organization

Having a clear central idea and supporting details is important, but in order for your audience to understand your ideas, make sure your writing is organized. Good **organization** helps readers move through your writing easily. In a well-organized work, all paragraphs work together to fulfill the author's purpose clearly and smoothly.

Organization

Scale	Does the writing have a clear and appropriate structure?	How smoothly do the ideas flow together?
4 Wow!	**The writing has a structure that is <u>clear</u> and appropriate for the writer's audience, purpose, and type of writing.**	**The ideas progress in a smooth and orderly way.** • The introduction is strong. • The ideas flow well from paragraph to paragraph. • The ideas in each paragraph flow well from one sentence to the next. • Effective transitions connect ideas. • The conclusion is strong.
3 Ahh.	**The writing has a structure that is <u>generally</u> clear and appropriate for the writer's audience, purpose, and type of writing.**	<u>**Most**</u> **of the ideas progress in a smooth and orderly way.** • The introduction is adequate. • Most of the ideas flow well from paragraph to paragraph. • Most ideas in each paragraph flow from one sentence to the next. • Effective transitions connect most of the ideas. • The conclusion is adequate.
2 Hmm.	**The structure of the writing is <u>not</u> clear or <u>not</u> appropriate for the writer's audience, purpose, and type of writing.**	<u>**Some**</u> **of the ideas progress in a smooth and orderly way.** • The introduction is weak. • Some of the ideas flow well from paragraph to paragraph. • Some ideas in each paragraph flow from one sentence to the next. • Transitions connect some ideas. • The conclusion is weak.
1 Huh?	**The writing is not clear or organized.**	<u>**Few or none**</u> **of the ideas progress in a smooth and orderly way.**

Common patterns of organization include:

- **chronological order**, in which details are told in time order
- **compare and contrast**, in which similarities and differences between two or more things are discussed
- **problem-solution**, in which a problem is discussed first and then one or more solutions are presented
- **order of importance**, in which the writer presents the strongest arguments first and last, and presents weaker arguments in the middle.

Organization: Strong Example, score of 3 or 4

Say No to Raising the Legal Driving Age

For teens in the United States, receiving a driver's license at age sixteen is an important part of growing up. However, some states are considering raising the legal driving age to eighteen years old. I believe that this idea would negatively affect teens and parents.

One reason teens need to be able to drive at the age of sixteen is so they can get a job. Many teens need to get jobs to have money for food, clothes, and entertainment. Often, a teen who has a job must have a car and be able to drive it to work.

Teens also want to be able to date and do other social activities on their own. Teens need the opportunity to be responsible and feel trusted. Being able to drive at sixteen helps teens earn this trust.

Perhaps most importantly, teen students have to be able to drive to and from school. A lot of parents and guardians go to work before school starts and have to work until after school is out. The only way for some students to get to school or get to school events and practices is to drive. Without driver's licenses, students may end up missing a lot of school and school activities.

While there may be some good reasons why the legal driving age should be raised, it is important to teens and parents that it stays the same. Sixteen-year-olds need to be able to drive to work, to social events, and to school functions.

The beginning makes the purpose clear: to persuade.

There are effective transitions between paragraphs.

Details support the main idea.

Each paragraph gives reasons that support the author's opinion.

Organization: Weak Example, score of 1 or 2

Teens and Driving

Can you imagine having your mom drive you to your high school graduation or to prom? How would you feel if you couldn't get a job? Many states want to make eighteen the legal driving age.

Many teens do not reach age eighteen until after they have been graduated from high school. It wouldn't be fun waiting until eighteen before you could drive. My friends and I drove once when we were fifteen. Many kids need to work to earn money. It would be difficult to get a job if the legal driving age was eighteen.

Students need to be able to drive to school. If the driving age is eighteen, lots of kids will have to take the bus. My friends and I rode the bus for many years. There are thousands of students who have to ride the bus each year.

Can you imagine going on a date with your parents in the front seat? My mom drove me to a dance once, and I was so embarrassed. Students need to be able to go on dates.

The legal driving age needs to stay the same so teens can drive to school, work, and on dates.

The purpose is not clear.

Paragraphs lack transitions.

The details here do not support the author's opinion.

Development of Ideas

Good ideas are important, but so are the details that describe the ideas. Details develop your ideas, or help your reader to understand them. They also make your writing much more interesting to read. When you are writing, there may be many ideas to choose from, so consider which ideas are most important to your audience and support your purpose for writing.

Development of Ideas

Scale	How thoughtful and interesting is the writing?	How well are the ideas or claims explained and supported?
4 Wow!	The writing engages the reader with meaningful ideas or claims and presents them in a way that is interesting and appropriate to the audience, purpose, and type of writing.	**The ideas or claims are fully explained and supported.** • The ideas or claims are well developed with important details, evidence, and/or description. • The writing feels complete, and the reader is satisfied.
3 Ahh.	<u>Most</u> of the writing engages the reader with meaningful ideas or claims and presents them in a way that is interesting and appropriate to the audience, purpose, and type of writing.	<u>Most</u> **of the ideas or claims are explained and supported.** • Most of the ideas or claims are developed with important details, evidence, and/or description. • The writing feels mostly complete, but the reader still has some questions.
2 Hmm.	<u>Some</u> of the writing engages the reader with meaningful ideas or claims and presents them in a way that is interesting and appropriate to the audience, purpose, and type of writing.	<u>Some</u> **of the ideas or claims are explained and supported.** • Only some of the ideas or claims are developed. Details, evidence, and/or description are limited or not relevant. • The writing leaves the reader with many questions.
1 Huh?	The writing does <u>not</u> engage the reader. It is not appropriate to the audience, purpose, and type of writing.	**The ideas or claims are <u>not</u> explained or supported.** The ideas or claims lack details, evidence, and/or description, and the writing leaves the reader unsatisfied.

Development of Ideas: Strong Example, score of 3 or 4

Parent-for-a-Day

Have you ever wondered what it would be like if we could change places with our parents just for the day? I have, and there are a few things I would like to do.

No school! Making my parents go to school for me would be the first thing I would do as parent for the day. Oh, what fun to be the one to tell my parents to "wake up, eat your breakfast, get to school!" Off they would go to sit in classrooms while I headed to the park for a long game of soccer.

No chores! When my parents got home from school, they would take out the trash, they would do the dishes, and they would clean the house. Meanwhile, I would sit in front of the television and watch my favorite shows.

No bedtime! The last and best part of being a parent for the day is that there would be no bedtime. I would stay up until the wee hours of the morning watching television and finishing my favorite mystery novel.

I have my "parent-for-a-day" all planned out, but the hardest part remains. I still need to convince my parents it is a good idea.

The writer asks a question to engage the audience.

Each paragraph explains and supports the main idea.

The end returns to the topic in a new way.

Development of Ideas: Weak Example, score of 1 or 2

Parent-for-a-Day

Have you ever wondered what it would be like if we could change places with our parents just for the day?

No school! Making my parents go to school for me would be the first thing I would do as parent for the day.

No chores! When my parents got home from school, I would make them do all the chores.

No bedtime! The last and best part of being a parent for the day is that there would be no bedtime.

Now I just need to talk my parents into the idea.

Paragraphs offer little explanation or support.

The ending is abrupt.

Voice and Style

Voice and **style** in writing contribute to communicating the meaning of writing. These qualities make each writer and piece of writing unique.

- **Voice** in writing is the quality that makes the words sound as if they are being spoken by someone. Voice communicates the author's or speaker's attitude.

- **Style** is the characteristic way a writer expresses his or her ideas. Part of that style is the author's **tone**, or attitude toward his or her subject as reflected in word choice. Tone, word choice, and sentence structure are all parts of a writer's style.

Matching Voice and Style to Audience

Because writing is intended to communicate, it is important to match voice and style to the audience. A serious subject may require a serious tone. The intended audience may also dictate whether you can use informal English. If the audience is your classmates, you might be able to use informal or casual English as you would in everyday conversation. If your audience is your teacher or other adults, use formal English in your writing. Whoever the audience, choose vivid words, and vary your sentence patterns.

Voice and Style

Scale	Does the writing have a clear voice and is it the best style for the type of writing?	Is the language interesting and are the words and sentences appropriate for the purpose, audience, and type of writing?
4 Wow!	The writing <u>fully</u> engages the reader with its individual voice. The writing style is best for the type of writing.	The words and sentences are interesting and appropriate to the purpose and audience. • The words are precise and engaging. • The sentences are varied and flow together smoothly.
3 Ahh.	<u>Most</u> of the writing engages the reader with an individual voice. The writing style is mostly best for the type of writing	<u>Most</u> of the words and sentences are interesting and appropriate to the purpose and audience. • Most words are precise and engaging. • Most sentences are varied and flow together.
2 Hmm.	<u>Some</u> of the writing engages the reader, but it has no individual voice and the style is not best for the writing type.	<u>Some</u> of the words and sentences are interesting and appropriate to the purpose and audience. • Some words are precise and engaging. • Some sentences are varied, but the flow could be smoother.
1 Huh?	The writing does <u>not</u> engage the reader.	<u>Few or none</u> of the words and sentences are appropriate to the purpose and audience. • The words are often vague and dull. • The sentences lack variety and do not flow together.

Voice and Style: Strong Example, score of 3 or 4

> ### Dried Up
>
> Some people are meant to make speeches, and others are meant to listen. I learned the hard way that I am definitely a listener.
>
> I have always been comfortable speaking out in class, so when my friend Heather joined the speech team, I decided to give it a try. This kind of activity looks great on college applications, I figured. Moreover, how hard could it be?
>
> I learned just how hard on the afternoon of the regional speech competition. Preparation certainly wasn't a problem. I had spent hours crafting my words. Each of us had rehearsed time and time again in front of our coach and each other. The rhythm and accents of my speech had been drilled into my mind and body.
>
> When I stepped on stage, however, all that preparation dried up under the hot lights. My mouth felt as if it were filled with cotton, and I thought even the packed auditorium could hear my dry bones tremble. As I began to speak, my voice creaked like a rusty door.
>
> I would like to say that I overcame that rough start, but I barely recall giving the rest of my speech. I slouched off stage and took my seat to the sound of weak applause, eager to take my place as the quietest, most intent listener in the room.

The voice is light-hearted and clear.

The sentence lengths are varied.

Vivid verbs and modifiers make the scene seem real and exciting.

Voice and Style: Weak Example, score of 1 or 2

> ### A Bad Day
>
> It was one of the worst days of my life. I tried to give a speech in front of a lot of people and ended up a failure.
>
> This is what happened. My friend was part of the speech team. She talked me into trying out. I thought that it would be easy and it was, at least in front of my classmates.
>
> At our first competition, I sat waiting until the judge called my name. I went on stage, and I could see a lot of people in the audience. I couldn't move, and then I almost passed out. The speech didn't go well at all.
>
> It was an embarrassing moment, but I am glad I at least tried.

The voice is flat and lifeless.

Sentences have little variety.

Words are general and uninteresting.

Written Conventions

You want readers to focus on your ideas, but errors can make it hard to understand what you mean. Good writers pay attention to **written conventions**, that is, the accepted methods and rules for grammar, punctuation, spelling, and capitalization that are commonly used to write English.

Written Conventions Rubric

Scale	Grammar: Are the sentences grammatically correct?	Mechanics and Spelling: Are there errors in spelling, punctuation, or capitalization that affect understanding?
4 Wow!	**The writing contains grammatically correct sentences throughout.**	There are few or no mistakes in spelling, punctuation, or capitalization.
3 Looks Good.	**Most of the sentences contain proper grammar.**	There are mistakes in spelling, punctuation, or capitalization, but they do not affect understanding.
2 Hmm.	**Some of the sentences contain grammar errors.**	There are some mistakes in spelling, punctuation, and capitalization that affect understanding.
1 Huh?	**Many sentences contain grammar errors.**	There are many mistakes in spelling, punctuation, and capitalization that make the writing difficult to understand.

Written conventions also include using **complete sentences**, **organization**, and **text features** that people understand. Complete sentences have a subject and a predicate and express a complete thought. For more help with written conventions, see Grammar, Usage, Mechanics, and Spelling on page 738.

Written Conventions: Strong Example, score of 3 or 4

A True Hispanic Hero

There are many Hispanic heroes, but my favorite is Miriam Colon Valle. With hard work and a strong belief in herself and her profession, she has become a role model for all.

Early Years

Miriam Colon Valle grew up in Puerto Rico in the 1940s. She participated in drama in high school, and her teacher saw that she had a lot of talent. Valle was then asked to take part in the drama program at the University of Puerto Rico. Her work at the university earned her scholarships that allowed her to attend the Lee Strasberg Acting Studio in the United States.

Rise to Stardom

In the United States, Valle worked hard. She played roles in more than thirty movies; one of her most famous was as the mother of Al Pacino in the movie *Scarface*. Valle was also on television shows, such as the soap opera *The Guiding Light*.

Valle also loved the theater. In the 1950s she started her own theater group. She also acted in numerous Broadway productions. Her drive to help other Hispanic actors and to share theater with poor people inspired her to start the Puerto Rican Traveling Theater.

Because of her love for acting and her love for Hispanic culture and theater, she was awarded a Lifetime Achievement Award in Theater. Miriam Colon Valle is an inspiration to Hispanics and people of all races.

Grammar is correct throughout.

Heads separate sections and give information.

Readers can easily understand the sequence of events.

Names and titles are properly formatted.

Punctuation occurs in the proper places throughout.

Written Conventions: Weak Example, score of 1 or 2

A true Hispanic Hero

There are many hispanic heroes. My favorite is Miriam Colon Valle. She is a role model for evrybody.

Miriam Colon Valle grew up in puerto rico in the 1940s she participated in drama in high school. Valle then taken part in the drama program at the "university of puerto rico." Her work at the university lead her to The United States eventually.

Valle also loved the theater. In the 1950s she started her own theater group. She also acted in a bunch of Broadway productions. She also started the Puerto Rican Traveling Theater. She was awarded a "Lifetime Achievement Award in Theater." Because of her love for acting and her love for hispanic culture and theater. Miriam Colon Valle is an inspiration to hispanics and people of all races.

In The United States, Valle worked hard. She played roles in more than thirty movies. Valle was also on television shows. Including the soap opera The Guiding Light.

There are many misspellings.

Names and titles are not properly capitalized or formatted.

Poor organization and lack of heads make it difficult to follow information.

Sentences are incorrectly punctuated or too long.

Writing Purposes, Modes, and Forms

There are many **forms** of writing, which appear in a number of **modes**, or types, based on the author's purpose and audience. Some writing is meant strictly to inform; other writing is meant to entertain. Other writing forms are intended to persuade or convince readers or listeners to act in certain ways or change their opinions or beliefs. Writing forms can often be categorized into more than one mode.

Writing Modes

A writing mode, or type, is defined by its purpose. Most of your writing tasks will occur in one of the modes described below.

Write to Inform or Explain

The purpose of **expository writing** is to present information or explanations about a topic. Many academic writing forms, such as research papers and literary response papers, are expository. Expository texts usually include a strong controlling idea or thesis in the first paragraph. Each of the body paragraphs presents a main idea and details related to the controlling idea. The final paragraph, or conclusion, restates, or sums up, the controlling idea.

Write Narratives

The purpose of **narrative writing** is to tell readers something they can follow in story form. Narratives can be fiction or nonfiction. They are often used for entertainment or to explain something that really happened. They offer a way of making sense of the world by ordering events into a clear beginning, middle, and end. Strong characters and interesting settings are usually key parts of narrative fiction. Most short stories are narratives, as are autobiographical and biographical essays.

Write Arguments

You can argue to defend your own ideas or opinions or you can try to influence the thinking or actions of other people. When you try to convince others, it's called **persuasive writing**. All arguments include a claim. A claim clearly states the writer's idea or opinion. Good arguments include evidence like facts, statistics, expert opinions, or personal experiences. Clear explanations, or reasons, connect evidence to claims. The reasons may appeal to the reader's emotions, ethics (sense of right and wrong), or to logic and understanding of facts. Persuasive texts should have an appropriate voice and tone for the intended audience, clear organization of ideas, and strong supporting details.

Common Academic Writing Forms

The following pages explain the most common writing forms you will use in school. You may be asked to write, read, evaluate, and respond to any of these forms while you are a student.

Cause-and-Effect Essay

A **cause-and-effect essay** traces the relationship between events. A cause is the reason something happens. An effect is the result of that cause.

Use a graphic organizer like the one below to develop your cause-and-effect essays.

Single Cause/Multiple Effects

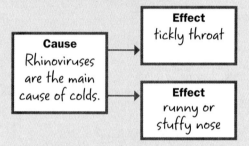

Multiple Causes/Single Effect

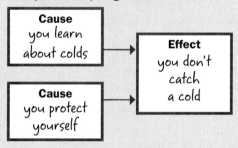

Check your essay for the following:

- A clear statement of the relationship that is being analyzed and discussed.
- A clear main idea for each paragraph.
- Appropriate supporting details.
- Signal words like *if/then* and *because*.

> Most colds are caused by rhinoviruses. There are more than one hundred kinds of these tiny, disease-causing organisms. If a rhinovirus infects the lining of your nose or throat, then you have a cold.
>
> The first effects of a cold are a tickling feeling in the throat and a runny or stuffy nose. Other symptoms include sneezing, headaches, and achiness.
>
> A severe cold may cause further effects. For example, the cold sufferer may develop a low-grade temperature, or fever. If his or her chest becomes congested, then the person may also develop a cough.

College Entry Essay

If you apply to a college or university, you may be asked to submit an **entrance essay** as part of the application. A college entrance essay is a kind of **reflective essay**, in which a person tells stories about their experiences. Your essay should do more than introduce who you are to the college board. It should detail specific events in your life and how these events impacted you. Choose words that show your personality, point out your skills and talents, and outline your future plans. A good college entrance essay should explain how your unique talents and personality will make you a successful student.

A college may provide you with a topic to write about, or it may ask you to select your own topic.

> **Causes and Effects of Colds**
>
> Cold season is almost here. It's a good time to review the causes and symptoms, or effects, of colds. The more you know, the better prepared you will be to protect yourself from catching a cold.

Use the graphic organizer below to develop your college entry essay.

College Entry Essay Overview

Beginning
Introduce yourself by writing in your own conversational tone. Get the reader interested with a good story or description. You might also present your controlling idea here.

Middle
Develop your main ideas with clearly organized supporting details. These details should help readers understand how your experiences have helped you grow as a person. Focus on how one or a few experiences helped you grow in one very important way.

End
Lead the reader back to the controlling idea. Leave a lasting, positive impression with a strong ending that tells who you are and why you should be accepted at the college.

Check your college entry essay for the following elements:

- clear focus on your own experience
- a personal voice and tone
- interesting details
- correct grammar, spelling, and punctuation

"Travel broadens the mind," my dad always says just before our summer road trip. Every June, he piles Mom, me, my sisters, and our dog into the car, and away we go. Though I used to dread our trips, I now realize how much I have gained from them. Our road trips have broadened my mind in many ways.

Comparison-Contrast Essay

A **comparison-contrast essay** tells how things are similar and different. Comparisons show how two or more things are alike. Contrasts show how they differ.

Use a Venn diagram to collect information for your comparison-contrast essay. List characteristics of each thing being described. Then, in the center, list the characteristics they share.

Venn Diagram

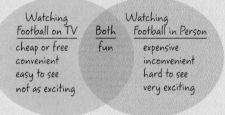

Watching Football on TV
cheap or free
convenient
easy to see
not as exciting

Both
fun

Watching Football in Person
expensive
inconvenient
hard to see
very exciting

Check your essay for the following:

- A clear statement of what is being compared and contrasted
- A clear main idea for each paragraph
- Appropriate supporting details
- Signal words like *both/and*, *similar*, and *like* for comparisons; signal words like *but*, *however*, and *on the other hand* for contrasts

At Home or at the Stadium?

If you really like football, you probably watch it on TV every chance you get. You may even go to the stadium to see your home team play. Though both ways of watching football are fun, there are some important differences between the two.

The first big difference is cost. Watching a football game on TV costs little or nothing. If the game is on network TV, it's free. If the game is on cable, it may be included in the cable package. But a ticket to a professional football game is expensive. The average price for a ticket to an NFL game is $50.

Descriptive Essay

A **descriptive essay** provides the reader with a strong impression of a setting, event, person, animal, or object. The essay may contain many different sensory details, but all the details should work together to support the author's controlling idea.

Use a details web to gather and organize sensory details for your descriptive essay.

Details Web

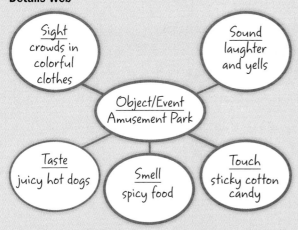

Check your descriptive essay for the following elements:

- a controlling idea that presents a single, strong impression that appeals to the five senses
- Information about how the subject affects more than one of the senses
- Vivid verbs, adjectives, and adverbs
- Clear organization of information, using a pattern such as spatial order (describing items from left to right, top to bottom, etc.)
- A unique style and appropriate tone for the audience

An Amusing Mixture

When summer vacation starts, I want to go to Alman's Amusement Park. Of course, I enjoy the thrilling rides there. But I enjoy the mixture of sights, sounds, smells, tastes, and feelings even more.

As I stroll past the Tilt-A-Whirl, I always see a blur of colors. People in bright summer clothes madly twirl, staining the sky with swirls of red, blue, green, and yellow. I hear the kids laughing and giggling, and I want to stop and watch. But I can't. The tempting scent of spicy food is in the air. I follow my nose to the Food Court for a juicy hot dog.

How-To Essay

A **how-to essay** explains a process. This kind of essay is also known as a process description or a technical document. A how-to essay describes the equipment, materials, and steps needed to complete a task. It answers any possible questions readers might have in order to make the process clear. The essay also often explains why the process is worth doing.

Use the chart below to collect information for your how-to essay.

How-To Planner

Task: Making a grilled cheese sandwich	
Materials:	Steps:
2 slices rye bread	First, butter one side of each piece of bread.
1 tablespoon butter	Next, place the cheese between the bread.
1, one ounce slice sharp cheddar cheese	Next, fry the sandwich until brown.
1 slice tomato	Then, add the tomato to the sandwich.
1 nonstick frying pan	Finally, serve the sandwich with chips.

Check your **how-to essay** for the following elements:

- a clear statement of the process
- a complete list of materials and equipment needed to complete the process
- chronological organization of steps
- signal words such as *first*, *next*, and *then*
- complete description of the actions to take during each step
- benefits of performing the process

Deluxe Grilled Cheese Sandwich

A grilled cheese sandwich is delicious and easy to make. Try this simple but yummy recipe. All you need are two pieces of rye bread, a tablespoon of butter, a one-ounce slice of sharp cheddar cheese, a slice of tomato, and a nonstick frying pan.

First, spread half a tablespoon of butter on one side of each slice of bread. Be sure to spread the butter evenly, from corner to corner, so that the sandwich browns evenly when you fry it.

Next, place the unbuttered sides of the bread slices together. Put the piece of cheese inside the slices to form a sandwich. Make sure that the cheese slice is not larger than the bread. If it is, trim the cheese so that it fits inside the bread. Otherwise, when the cheese melts it will drip over the sides of the bread.

Literary Response Essay

In a **literary response essay**, you present your reactions to and analysis of a text. In an analysis, you look at elements that make up the text. For an analysis of fiction, for example, you might look at characters and conflict. For an analysis of nonfiction, you might look at word choice and meaning.

Use a graphic organizer like the one below to collect information and organize your literary response essay.

Literary Response Essay

Text Title: "Gettysburg Address"

Author: Abraham Lincoln

Date Written: November, 1863

Publishing Information:
first published in newspapers

My Overall Impression of the Text:
powerful speech!

Main Idea 1 about Text:
nation founded on equality
Supporting Detail:
"soldiers gave their lives" for this

Main Idea 2 about Text:
other founding principles
Supporting Detail:
"of the people, by the people, for the people"

My Responses to Main Idea 1:
Soldiers' sacrifices keep us free.

My Responses to Main Idea 2:
I, too, have responsibilities to my country.

The text a writer responds to is called *a source text*. Read the source text below. Then note how the reader responded to it.

The Gettysburg Address
By Abraham Lincoln

Four score and seven years ago our fathers brought forth on this continent a new nation, conceived in liberty, and dedicated to the proposition that all men are created equal.

Now we are engaged in a great civil war, testing whether that nation, or any nation so conceived and so dedicated, can long endure. We are met on a great battle-field of that war. We have come to dedicate a portion of that field as a final resting place for those who here gave their lives that this nation might live. It is altogether fitting and proper that we should do this.

But, in a larger sense, we can not dedicate—we can not consecrate—we can not hallow—this ground. The brave men, living and dead, who struggled here, have consecrated it, far above our poor power to add or detract. . . . It is rather for us to be here dedicated to the great task remaining before us—that from these honored dead we take increased devotion to that cause for which they gave the last full measure of devotion— that we here highly resolve that these dead shall not have died in vain—that this nation, under God, shall have a new birth of freedom—and that government of the people, by the people, for the people, shall not perish from the earth.

The Message of Gettysburg

In 1863, President Abraham Lincoln traveled to Pennsylvania. The occasion was the dedication of a cemetery for the soldiers who had died at the Battle of Gettysburg. Lincoln's brief comments are today known as "The Gettysburg Address," and they present a new vision of the founding principles of the United States.

Lincoln begins his speech by noting that our nation was founded on the idea of equality just eighty-seven years prior to his speech. He then notes that the men buried at Gettysburg "gave their lives that this nation might live." This point makes me think of all the wars since then and the ways that soldiers' sacrifices allow me to enjoy the benefits of a democratic society.

Most powerfully, Lincoln ends his speech by restating the founding principles of the Declaration of Independence and the U.S. Constitution. Ours is a government "of the people, by the people, for the people." It was the brave sacrifice of those people and the ones who died at Gettysburg that Lincoln so beautifully honors in his speech. It reminds me that I have responsibilities to be a part of the government that so many have fought to keep alive.

In the introductory paragraph, identify the author and date.

State controlling idea of the text.

Include quotations from the text.

Describe reaction to a main idea.

Describe reaction to a main idea.

Narratives

Narratives can be either fiction or nonfiction. Fiction narratives tell stories featuring characters, settings, and plots. The forms of nonfiction narrative include:

- autobiographical essays/personal essays
- biographical essays
- diary or journal entries

Personal Essay or Autobiographical Narrative

In a personal essay, a writer describes events that he or she actually experienced. The purpose is often to entertain readers or to teach them.

Personal/Autobiographical Narrative Overview

> **Beginning**
> Introduce the people, setting, and situation. State why the event or experience was important.

> **Middle**
> Give details about what happened in the order that it happened. Share your thoughts and feelings. Use lively details and dialogue.

> **End**
> Explain how the action came to an end or the problem was solved. Summarize why the event or experience was important.

Personal Narrative Model

> ### A Hard Lesson Learned
>
> When Marie invited me to her birthday party, I was thrilled. She was the most popular girl in school. My best friend said, "Why do you want to go? Marie is not nice. She doesn't know how to be a friend." I wish I had listened, because my friend was right. The best I can say about my time with Marie is that it taught me a hard but valuable lesson about friendship.

Journal or Diary Entry

Journal entries are the least formal kind of nonfiction narrative. They are often used to record events from a person's life, but they can also be used as learning tools, such as when a person documents a research process or traces thoughts about something over time.

Journal Entry Model

> January 4, 2007
> I went to the library today to research my paper about hip-hop music. I was worried that I wouldn't find anything, but then I remembered a tip my teacher gave me: ask a librarian! So I did, and he was very helpful. We found three books, six magazine articles, and even a documentary film. I'm glad I thought to ask. It definitely made doing the assignment easier for me.

Short Story or Novel

Short stories and **novels** are common forms of narrative fiction. Novels are typically longer than short stories, with more developed characters and plots. Both of these forms usually include descriptive elements, such as figurative language and vivid word choice.

Plot Diagram for Fiction

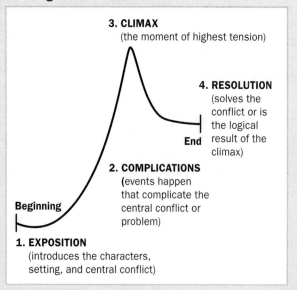

3. CLIMAX (the moment of highest tension)

4. RESOLUTION (solves the conflict or is the logical result of the climax)

End

2. COMPLICATIONS (events happen that complicate the central conflict or problem)

Beginning

1. EXPOSITION (introduces the characters, setting, and central conflict)

Using Persuasive Strategies

Good persuasive essays demonstrate effective use of persuasive strategies. Use persuasive strategies, such as appeals, to support your opinions. Note in the following examples how the writer's opinion statement changes depending on the appeal chosen.

Persuasive Essay

In a **persuasive essay**, you try to convince readers to agree with you or take a particular action. TV commercials, magazine ads, newspaper editorials, and campaign speeches are all kinds of persuasive media that begin as persuasive writing.

Persuasive Essay Planner

OPINION STATEMENT	I BELIEVE THAT WE SHOULD … KEEP OUR CATS INDOORS
Reason 1:	It's safe for the cat.
Evidence:	Many cats catch diseases outdoors.
Reason 2:	It's safer for wildlife.
Evidence:	Many animals are killed by outdoor cats each year.
Reason 3:	Cats lead happy lives indoors.
Evidence:	Experts say house cats are content.
Counter-argument	Cats like to be outside. However, they don't need to be.

Start a persuasive essay by stating an issue in a way that will make the audience care about it. Then state your opinion about the issue.

Keep Cats Indoors!

According to the American Bird Conservancy, pet cats kill thousands of birds each year. Now, I love cats. In fact, I own one. But I never let him go outdoors unless he is in his cat carrier. If you are a true animal lover, you will keep your cat indoors, too.

Support your opinion with reasons, evidence, and other appeals.

- An ethical appeal is directed at the reader's sense of right and wrong.

It's just plain wrong to let your cat hunt and hurt other animals. Birds, rabbits, and other wildlife animals have the right to live just as your cat does.

- A logical appeal is directed at the reader's common sense.

The fact is that it is dangerous for your cat to be outdoors. Your pet may be hit by a car. It may catch a serious disease from an infected animal. It may be chased by a dog or other larger animal.

- An emotional appeal is directed at the reader's feelings.

Do you really want your cat to be lost? Picture how cold, lonely, scared, and hungry your pet might become while it is looking for your home.

Now picture what it is like for a bird or a rabbit to be chased by a cat. Can you feel the terror of these little animals?

Additional things to remember:

- A personal anecdote, case study, or analogy validates your opinion.
- Think of questions or concerns your reader might have and address them.

Position Paper

In a **position paper**, you state your opinion, or position, on an issue that has at least two sides to it. You also give reasons and evidence to support your position. The purpose of position papers is to persuade, or convince, your readers to agree with you.

Unlike a persuasive essay, a position paper does not necessarily include a call to action. A position paper also does not necessarily contain counter-arguments. The main purpose of a position paper is to state and support an opinion.

Position Paper Overview

Beginning
Introduce the issue. Show readers why they should care about it; then state your position, the controlling idea of the paper.

Middle
Support your position with reasons that will convince your audience. Organize the reasons strategically. Use transitions to help readers move smoothly from one reason to another.

End
Restate your position in a memorable way.

Check your position paper for the following elements:

- an attention-grabbing introduction with a clear statement of opinion
- supporting reasons with evidence for each reason
- clear organization and transition words, such as *first*, *next*, and *most important*

Play Your Way to Good Health

Recently, I joined the swim team. I had never been particularly interested in sports before. However, I have always been interested in having good health and making new friends. I received these benefits and many more from being on the swim team. Therefore, I think that all students should become involved in sports.

The first big benefit of becoming involved in a sport is that it will improve your health.

Persuasive Speech

A **persuasive speech** tries to convince the audience to take an action or believe something.

Persuasive Speech Overview

Beginning
Introduce the topic. Get listeners' attention. You might tell a story from your own experience or describe a case study of someone else's experience. Give necessary background information. End by stating your opinion. It is your controlling idea.

Middle
Support your position. Give reasons readers or listeners should agree with you. Also use ethical or emotional appeals when appropriate. Then state at least one possible objection, or counterargument, to your opinion and respond to it respectfully.

End
Sum up your reasons and give a call to action. Tell readers what action you want them to take or what belief you want them to have.

Check your persuasive speech for the following elements:

- An attention-grabbing introduction with a clear statement of opinion.
- Paragraphs organized by reason.
- Strong appeals appropriate to the topic and audience.
- A counterargument with reasons and evidence against that argument.
- A summary of your opinion and a call to action.
- Respectful tone throughout.

Problem-Solution Essay

A **problem-solution essay** informs readers about a problem and suggests one or more ways to solve it. A problem-solution essay has five main parts:

Problem-Solution Essay Planner

1. PROBLEM	Clearly state the problem. Where does it take place? When does it happen? Why does it matter?
2. CAUSES	Why does the problem happen? Who or what is to blame?
3. EFFECTS	Who is affected? How?
4. SOLUTIONS	Think about possible solutions. What has already been done? Has it helped? Think of new solutions. What are the benefits and risks of each idea?
5. CONCLUSION	Which solution is best? What makes it best? How could it be carried out? What do you want your reader or listener to understand? What do you want your reader or listener to do?

Watch Educational Television

Can watching TV actually be good for you? Surprisingly, a recent university study suggests that it can. However, there's a catch. You have to watch educational TV, like nature shows and history programs. According to the study, watching shows like these can help improve your scores on standardized tests. Based on this study, I urge you to examine your TV habits and, if necessary, form a new habit: watching educational TV.

Though you may not at first believe it, watching educational TV shows can be fun. They can make a dry subject come alive for you. And when that happens, you learn and remember more. Let me give you an example. I had a hard time remembering anything I read about World War II. For me, the war happened so long ago that it did not seem real or interesting. When I watched a Public Broadcasting System series about the war, however, I began to feel differently. The subject became interesting to me when I watched and listened to interviews with people who lived through World War II. After watching the series, I reread my history book, and it made a lot more sense to me.

Reduce, Reuse, and Recycle

The United States is running out of land—land for landfills, that is. Landfills are where trash is taken and buried after workers collect it from homes or businesses and haul it away. Our landfill system is a good one. Or it would be, if we did not generate so much trash. Unfortunately, the average American throws away more than four pounds of paper, packaging, meal scraps, and other kinds of garbage each day. Multiply four pounds by the number of Americans, and you can see why we have a problem. Fortunately, there are simple solutions that anyone can put into effect. They are the "Three *Rs*": Reduce, Reuse, and Recycle.

Summary or Abstract

A **summary** is a brief restatement of the main points of a text or visual medium, such as plays or books. An **abstract** is a summary of a research report that appears before the report. It tells the reader what your report is about. Begin a summary by giving information about the original work. Then present the main ideas and the most important supporting details. Use quotations and proper citation when necessary. (For sample citations, see the model research report on pp. 727–728.)

Summary Model

> William Shakespeare wrote the tragic play *Hamlet* in about 1600. Since then, it has become one of the most famous plays in the English language.
>
> As the play opens, Hamlet, the Prince of Denmark, is visited by the ghost of his father, the king. The king's ghost tells Hamlet that the king was murdered, and Hamlet decides to find out by whom. He suspects that his uncle Claudius, who has married his mother and taken over the role of king, is the murderer.
>
> Hamlet's behavior grows stranger over the course of the play, as he is tormented by the idea of his father's murder and his mother's betrayal. He decides to create a play that he believes will show that Claudius is guilty. When Claudius does indeed show himself to be guilty, Hamlet's words and actions grow increasingly violent.
>
> In the end, Hamlet, his mother, and Claudius are all killed during a duel. An invading army stumbles upon the bloody scene, and Hamlet is carried away to be buried.

Research Reports

A **research report** is a presentation of information about a topic. In a research report, you combine and organize facts from different sources of information. You put the information in your own words and let your readers know where you found the information you cite, or use, in your report.

Research reports are typically researched, written, and cited using either the Modern Language Association (MLA) style or the American Psychological Association (APA) style. The style is often determined by the subject matter.

To learn more about research, see the **Language and Learning Handbook**, pp. 639–644.

Analysis of an Issue

To write an **analysis of an issue**, research a controversial situation—one that has at least two sides to it. Then use the information to write a report that answers the question *How?* or *Why?* In an analysis, the writer's personal opinion does not need to be included. The purpose of the analysis is to inform and explain, not to persuade.

Use the following graphic organizer to organize your report.

Issue Analysis Overview

Beginning
Start with an interesting fact or idea about the issue. Make readers care about it. Give background if necessary. Then state your controlling idea.

Middle
Analyze the issue. Take it apart, and examine each part. Answer the question *How?* or *Why?*

End
Sum up the results of your analysis. You might state the importance, or significance, of what you discovered. Or you might restate your controlling idea in an interesting way.

Works Cited
List the sources of information you used.

The following pages show a Research Report with citations done in MLA style.

J. Smith
Mrs. Walker
English 100
January 10, 2013

This section gives the name of the writer, the name of the writer's teacher, the name of the class, and the date.

An Analysis of the Global Warming Debate

The issue of global warming has divided the scientific community. Some scientists believe that carbon dioxide and other greenhouse gases are warming Earth, causing dangerous changes in the climate. Other scientists disagree. They believe that there is no proof of global warming or its effects on the climate. Is global warming real? And if it is, should we be worried about it?

The introductory paragraph is clear and effective and states the controlling idea.

The analysis focuses on these controlling ideas.

The theory of global warming is not new. It was first proposed in 1896 by Svante Arrhenius, a Swedish scientist. He said that people were unknowingly causing Earth's temperature to rise. The rise, he believed, was caused by people releasing carbon dioxide into the atmosphere when they burned coal and other carbon-based fuels. The carbon dioxide, he believed, raised Earth's temperature (Maslin 24).

Parenthetical citations like this one tell readers where the student found information.

Over the years, other scientists further developed Arrhenius's theory, which has evolved into a scientific model called the "greenhouse effect." According to the effect, Earth's atmosphere is like the glass in a greenhouse. Glass lets sunlight in and re-reflects it, bouncing heat from sunrays back into the house and trapping it there. Similarly, carbon dioxide and other greenhouse gases re-reflect rays from the sun, trapping heat in the atmosphere around Earth.

Background helps readers understand the issue.

The greenhouse effect is a natural process that protects us and our planet. Without the greenhouse effect, it would not be warm enough on Earth for plants and animals to live (Fridell 25). However, many scientists believe that problems occur when the level of greenhouse gases rises, causing the amount of heat energy trapped around Earth also to rise. This process, it is believed, may cause Earth to become warmer than it has ever been.

The student uses a variety of sentence structures.

Most scientists believe that this temperature change has already happened. For example, scientists at the U.S. Environmental Protection Agency (EPA) say that over the past century Earth's surface temperature has increased about 1.4 degrees F ("Basic Information"). The EPA believes that the rise has been caused by carbon dioxide produced by the burning of gasoline, oil, and coal.

Does such a small rise in temperature really matter? Many scientists believe it does. They think that the higher surface temperature of Earth is causing dangerous changes to our planet. Temperature changes will result in changes in rainfall patterns like drought and flooding. As ice in the north and south poles melts, global sea levels will rise. People living near

The student develops the analysis by explaining a main viewpoint on global warming.

Smith 2

the ocean may lose land or experience more severe storms. People and animals will be impacted. ("Global Warming"). These changes will impact citizens across the globe, including people in the United States (Karl, J.M. et al).

Kerry Emanuel, a scientist at the Massachusetts Institute of Technology (MIT) is a strong believer in global warming. He thinks that global warming has caused hurricanes to be more powerful and destructive. After studying about 5,000 hurricanes, he found that storms increased in intensity during the same period that Earth's temperature began to rise. The number of big storms has increased since 1923 (Tollefson 2012). Emanuel believes that warmer ocean temperatures are to blame for the increase in storms' destructive power (Kluger 92).

Not all scientists agree that global warming is causing climate changes. Physicist S. Fred Singer is representative of this group. In an interview for the Public Broadcasting System (PBS), Singer said that "whether or not human beings can produce a global climate change is an important question [that] is not at all settled. It can only be settled by actual measurements, data. And the data are ambiguous.... Since 1979, our best measurements show that the climate has been cooling just slightly. Certainly, it has not been warming" ("What's up?"). Singer bases his conclusion on measurements from weather satellites, which he believes to be more accurate than measurements from ground-based thermometers.

Dr. Richard Lindzen, a scientist at MIT, shares Singer's doubts about global warming and climate change. According to Dr. Lindzen, rises in Earth's temperature and carbon dioxide levels "neither constitute support for alarm nor establish man's responsibility for the small amount of global warming that has occurred" (Lindzen). He believes that the computer models on which global warming forecasts have been made are flawed and incorrect.

> The student develops the analysis by explaining a different main viewpoint on global warming.

Why, then, do so many scientists believe in global warming? Lindzen believes the answer has more to do with money than with science. He believes that government money is more often given to scientists whose work appears to predict and prevent disasters than to scientists whose work does not predict gloom and doom. Lindzen feels that because these kinds of projects tend to attract funding, some scientists have exaggerated the effects of global warming to get government grants (Lindzen).

> The student answers the question *Why?*

And so the debate continues. Perhaps this is for the best. As James Hansen of the National Aeronautics and Space Administration (NASA) put it, "Science thrives on repeated challenges . . . and there is even special pleasure in trying to find something wrong with well-accepted theory. Such challenges eventually strengthen our understanding of the subject" (Hansen).

> In the conclusion, the student effectively sums up the report.

Works Cited

"Basic Information." *Climate Change*. 14 Dec. 2006. U.S. Environmental

Protection Agency. 5 Jan. 2007

<http://www.epa.gov/climatechange/basicinfo.html>.

Fridell, Ron. *Global Warming*. New York: Franklin Watts, 2002.

"Global Warming: A Way Forwrad: Facing Climate Change." National

Geographic. Video and Audio. 30 Nov. 2012.

<http://video.nationalgeographic.com/video/environment/

global-warming-environment/way-forward-climate/>.

Hansen, James. "The Global Warming Debate." Education. Jan. 1999. NASA

Goddard Institute for Space Studies. 7 Jan. 2007

<http://www.giss.nasa.gov/edu/gwdebate>.

Karl, T.R, Melillo, J.M, and Peterson T.C. *U.S. Global Change Research Program.*

2009. Global climate change impacts in the United States. Cambridge:

Cambridge University Press, 2009.

Kluger, Jeffrey. "The Man Who Saw Katrina Coming." *Time* 8 May 2006: 92.

Lindzen, Richard. "Climate of Fear." Opinion Journal from the Wall Street

Journal Editorial Page. 12 April 2006. WSJ.com. 2 Jan. 2007

<http://www.opinionjournal.com/extra/?id=110008220&mod=RSS_O>.

Maslin, Mark. *Global Warming: A Very Short Introduction*. Oxford: Oxford

University Press, 2004.

Tollefson, J. "Hurricane Sandy Spins Up Climate Change Discussion."

Nature. October 2012.

<http://www.nature.com/news/hurricane-sandy-spins-up-climate-

discussion-1.11706>. Accessed November 23, 2012.

"What's up with the Weather?" NOVA Frontline. 2000. WGBH/NOVA/

FRONTLINE. 4 Jan. 2007

<http://www.pbs.org/wgbh/warming>.

The student lists all the sources of information cited in the research report.

Career and Workplace Communication

In the world of work, there are expectations about the form and style of written communications. The following writing forms will help you at your workplace.

Business Letter

Business letters serve many purposes. You might write a business letter to make a request or to register a complaint with a business or other organization. The example below is a cover letter, a type of business letter in which the sender introduces himself or herself to an employer and states his or her qualifications for a job. Business letters should be typed on a computer or other word processor and should sound and look professional. Follow the business letter format below, and always check your letters carefully for grammatical or spelling errors.

Adam Russell
1297 Newport Ave.
Chicago, IL 79910
(555) 212-9402
May 18, 2013

Ms. Carlita Ortiz
Ortiz Corner Grocery
2480 North Lincoln Ave.
Chicago, IL 79919

Dear Ms. Ortiz:

I recently read in the *Chicago Tribune* that you are taking applications for the position of full-time checkout clerk. I am very interested in interviewing for this position.

I worked for supermarkets for the previous two summers in similar positions, first at Green Grocers and then at The Grainery Foods. My managers always gave me good performance reviews, and I truly enjoy the work.

I currently attend Julius Jones High School, but I am available for work in the evenings and will be available in the summer after June 10, 2013. I can be reached after 4 p.m. on weekdays. I look forward to hearing from you about this opportunity and thank you for your consideration.

Sincerely,

Adam Russell

Adam Russell

Insert contact information for yourself followed by the person you are writing to.

Insert a space between the date and the contact information.

Use a formal greeting, addressing a specific person. Use formal titles and last names to show respect in business letters.

Do not indent paragraphs.

Use single-spaced paragraphs. Separate paragraphs with an extra space.

Always thank recipients for their attention.

Include a traditional closing with a handwritten and typed signature.

Résumé

A résumé is a document that describes your qualifications for a job. A well-written résumé includes the kind of information a potential employer would like to know about you. Examples include previous work experience, skills, and achievements. It is very important that résumés be free of errors, so that the employer can see that you would take a job seriously and pay attention to detail. Use the format below to set apart your résumé from all the résumés of other applicants.

Adam Russell

1297 Newport Ave.

Chicago, IL 79910

(555) 212-9402

Objective

To obtain full-time, seasonal work in the food service industry.

Work History

2012, Grainery Foods

Full-time checkout and stock clerk at a busy supermarket

- Used a standard register and invoice-tracking equipment

- Trained new employees

- Met and exceeded cash handling accuracy reviews

2011, Green Grocers

Full-time retail assistant at a local outdoor market

- Set up and closed market stalls

- Supervised volunteer staff

- Assisted customers with pricing and selection

Education

Currently enrolled at Julius Jones High School.

Awards

Student of the Month, April 2013.

References

Available upon request.

Include your contact information clearly at the top of the page.

Use boldface type, italics, or underlining to make important information or headings stand out.

List your experience, starting with your most recent job.

Use bullet points to draw attention to specific skills or responsibilities.

Include information about your education and any information that would show what you have done well in the past.

Keep a list of 3 to 5 references available. Check with your references before you give their names out.

Job Application

Many jobs require you to fill out an **application**. Follow the instructions closely and write as neatly as possible or type the information. You will often need to provide reference information for your work ability or character. It is important to have personal identification with you when completing job applications. Ask a manager if you have any questions.

Please type or print neatly.

Today's Date: 5 / 1 / 13

First Name: Adam   Last Name: Russell

Address: 1297 Newport Ave.

City: Chicago   State: IL   Zip: 79910

Phone: (555) 212-9402   Birth date: 7 / 20 / 99

Sex: M ☑ F ☐

Follow instructions.

Education

High School Name: Currently attending Julius Jones High School.

Employment History (List each job, starting with most recent.)

1. Employer: The Grainery Foods   Phone: (555) 436-0090

   Dates: 5/2013 – 9/2013   Position: Full-time checkout and stock clerk

   Duties: Check out orders and stock inventory.

Provide complete and accurate information.

References

1. Name: Consuela Ybarra   Relationship: supervisor

   Company: The Grainery Foods

   Address: 123 Main Street, Chicago   Phone: (555) 436-0092

2. Name: Roman Hrbanski   Relationship: teacher/coach

   Company: Julius Jones High School

   Address: 321 N. Elm Street, Chicago   Phone: (555) 233-0765

Provide contact information for people who can tell the employer that you are a good and dependable worker.

Business Memo

A memo, or memorandum, provides employees with information concerning the business or organization.

Date: June 28, 2013
From: Carlita Ortiz, General Manager
To: All Full-Time and Part-Time Staff
Re: Independence Day Sale Hours

Please remember that all employees scheduled to work the morning of Sunday, July 1, should report at 7:00 A.M., one hour earlier than usual, as we will need special help setting up the Independence Day Sale.

Thank you for your attention.

Give information regarding date, sender, recipients, and the topic.

State the purpose of the memo and any supporting information.

Be short and specific.

Creative Writing

Your imagination is the most important tool in building the forms of creative writing. Some of these forms, such as plays and some kinds of poetry, have set structures. Others, such as parody, are defined by their purpose rather than their structure. Creative writing allows you to describe people, things, and events in new and interesting ways.

To learn more about these forms, see the **Literary Terms**.

Poetry

Poetry is a literary form in which special emphasis is given to ideas through the use of style and rhythm. In poetry, lines of text are called verses, and groups of verses are called stanzas. Rhyme and other sound effects within and among lines and words are popular elements of poetic style.

Some poems are written in conventional poetic forms. The number of lines, rhythm, and rhyme patterns are defined by the form. Other poems have a style all their own. These are called free verse:

Friendship

To never judge
To accept your true self
Through all your faults
Still loyal and caring.
That is the making,
An act of giving and taking,
of what we call a true friend.

Song Lyrics

A **song lyric** is text set to music and meant to be sung. Like lyric poetry, song lyrics often express personal feelings using rhythm and sound effects. These effects provide musical qualities similar to those often found in lyric poetry. In fact, the word *lyric* comes from the ancient Greek word for *lyre*, a musical instrument with strings.

Parody

A **parody** makes fun of, imitates, or exaggerates another creation or work. The parody can be sarcastic, and it is often used to make a point in a funny way. A parody can be in any form, from plays to essays to poems.

Twinkle, Twinkle?

Twinkle, twinkle unseen star,
Covered in our smog you are.
Up above our town once bright,
Now we cannot see your light.

Play/Skit

A **play** is a narrative that is meant to be performed before an audience. The text of a play consists of dialogue spoken by the characters and brief descriptions of sets, lighting, stage movements, and vocal tone. A **skit** is a very short play:

James. You mean I won? [*grabbing Paula's hands*]

Paula. Yes, you did. You won the Battle of the Singers competition!

James. [*shocked, then jumps, screaming and hooting*] I can't believe it!

Poster

A **poster** is used to get people's attention and give information in a visually appealing way. Posters should have the following:

- a purpose: What do you want people to know or think?
- attention-grabbing colors or pictures
- a large heading that tells people what the poster is about
- large print so people can read the poster from a distance
- just enough details to convey your message

Electronic Communication

More and more, people are writing to each other using electronic forms of communication. Computers and portable devices, such as cell phones, offer a number of ways to research school assignments, conduct business, and keep in contact with friends and family. You need to protect your identity and stay safe online. Check your school's Acceptable Use Policy for guidance on how to protect your hardware and, more importantly, yourself.

E-mail

Electronic mail, or **e-mail**, allows users to exchange written messages and digital files over the Internet. Like traditional mail, e-mail requires an address to enable users to send and receive messages. This address is attached to an account that a user accesses through the Internet or through an e-mail software program. Keep the following rules in mind when writing e-mail:

- Carefully check the address of your recipient.
- Include the subject of the e-mail.
- Include a greeting.
- Be sure to supply enough background information to help the reader understand the topic and purpose of your e-mail.
- Unless you are writing to a peer, such as a friend or classmate, use a formal tone, proper punctuation, and grammar.
- Include a closing, and give your name.

> **From**: student@studentweb.edu
> **To**: n.patterson@njc.library.org
> **Subject**: Library Books
>
> Dear Ms. Patterson:
>
> I have returned the books that you asked me about. I put the books in the return box. Please let me know if you don't receive them.
>
> Thank you,
> Jamie

Instant Messaging and Text Messaging

Instant messaging, or **IM**, allows two users to exchange messages instantly over the Internet. **Text messages** are sent over cell phone lines. Like e-mail, these messages require each user to have an account. Messaging is used most frequently by peers, so the writing style may be very casual. Abbreviations are often used to shorten the amount of time and space needed for the message.

Blogs

Web logs, or **blogs**, are Internet newsletters. Many individuals and organizations use blogs to communicate their ideas to a wide audience. Some blogs offer articles on a particular topic, much like a newspaper or magazine. Others are more like journals, with individuals documenting their interests or events from their lives. Most blogs are updated regularly.

Listserves

A **listserve** is an electronic forum in which users discuss and share information about a particular topic. Users sign up for the listserve, then post and respond to questions using their e-mail account. Many experts use listserves to exchange information with others in their field.

Message Boards

A **message board**, or **forum**, allows users to post thoughts and questions about a topic to a Web site and then see what others have to say about it. The site is usually organized by individual topics, called threads.

Social Media

There are many different kinds of tools and web sites that connect individuals to friends or groups. Individuals choose whether to subscribe, follow, or "like" an individual or group. This gives you access to that group. After you have access to a group, messages can be created or shared. You can join study groups, or connect with other readers or authors.

Media and Feature Writing

Many forms of **media and feature writing** are used in newspapers, magazines, radio, and television programs. Some of these forms are like narration because they tell a story. Other forms are types of persuasive writing. The most common forms are described below.

Advertisement

Advertisements, or **ads**, are meant to persuade readers to buy a product or service. Ad text should make an immediate impact on the reader and be easily remembered. Usually, advertisements appeal to people's emotions rather than to logic. Advertising messages are usually presented in visually interesting ways. Ads on TV may use visual techniques and background music to increase their effectiveness.

News Article and Feature Article

The purpose of a **news article** is to provide information. It should provide well-researched facts about a current event. It answers the questions: *Who? What? Where? When? Why?* and *How?* The first paragraph of a news article introduces the main facts, and the following paragraphs provide supporting details.

The purpose of a **feature article** is to provide information and points of view about something fun, entertaining, or important in people's daily lives. Feature articles are lively, fact-based discussions. Magazines contain many examples of feature writing, such as "Great Prom Ideas" or "The Year's Best Music." One characteristic of feature articles is a strong lead, or first paragraph, that draws readers into the piece.

Because they are based in fact, both news articles and feature articles can be considered narrative nonfiction.

Editorial/Letter to the Editor

Editorials are common features of most newspapers. These articles give newspaper staff writers the chance to voice their opinions on important issues. Many periodicals also publish letters to the editor, in which the public can voice opinions on a periodical's content or other topics of interest to its readers. When writing a letter to the editor, be sure to support your opinion with facts and evidence. Editorials and letters to the editor are usually persuasive in tone.

Critique or Review

A **critique**, or **review**, presents the author's opinion of a book, movie, or other work. The review usually includes a brief plot summary or description of the work of art. A critique does more than just summarize the main ideas of a work, however. Details about performances or the author's opinion of the quality of the work supports the author's opinion. In an effective review, the author's opinions about the work are always supported by specific details. The purpose of critiques and reviews is to help readers decide whether to experience the work for themselves.

Worth Seeing?

The Fellowship of the Ring is a movie version of the epic J. R. R. Tolkien novel about a mythical world threatened by the power of an evil ring. Director Peter Jackson uses beautiful computer graphics to show the struggle of a small group of adventurers who set out to destroy the ring. The rich characters, exciting action scenes, and incredible music make *The Fellowship of the Ring* a must-see for all fans of fantasy and adventure films.

Speech

A **speech** is a type of spoken message, often planned in advance and later delivered to a group of people. A speech can have many purposes:

- **to inform or explain,** as when a community leader speaks to a group of news reporters about a new neighborhood program

- **to argue,** as when a political candidate makes a speech on TV to convince people to vote for him or her

- **to tell a story** and build relationships, as when a business leader makes a humorous after-dinner speech at a business convention, or tells their life story to inspire others to reach success.

Before planning a speech, identify the occasion for speaking, the audience, and your purpose. These three elements will help you select an appropriate tone, words, and details. For example, if you are planning a speech about computers for the members of a computer club, you will not need to define computer terms for your audience. If you were to give the same speech to a general audience, however, you might need to define the terms because some members of the audience may not know what the words mean.

> ### Computer Speech for Computer Club
>
> I am here to give you tips on creating Web pages. I will speak to you about the asynchronous qualities of Ajax and the advantages and disadvantages of pulling content with it.

> ### Computer Speech for General Audience
>
> I am here to give you tips on creating Web pages. I will speak to you about Ajax, which stands for "Asynchronous JavaScript and XML." Simply put, Ajax is a way to put content on a Web page by using codes that pull information from a server for you.

Script or Transcript

A **nonfiction script** is the prewritten text for a presentation or broadcast program. Like a news story, a nonfiction script contains the five Ws, but no unnecessary details. A **transcript** is a written record of a live discussion or broadcast.

Scripts and transcripts usually follow the written conventions of plays. The names of the speakers are followed by their dialogue and brief descriptions of movement, visual material, and other information necessary to describe how the presentation should look when it happens or how it looked when it happened.

> ### Transcript of WXQV TV Interview
>
> **MARCY RAY, INTERVIEWER:** Coach, you must be very excited about the big win today. Can you describe your feelings for me and our viewers?
>
> **COACH:** It's hard to put my feelings into words right now, Marcy. I guess what I'm feeling most is pride. The team worked so hard this year. Every one of those kids earned this win, and I'm very, very proud of the entire team.
>
> [*Background cheers from team members*]
>
> **RAY:** How will you and the team celebrate, Coach?
>
> **COACH:** We won't be celebrating alone. This win belongs to the whole school. So there will be a celebration and ceremony in the school gym Monday morning at 9 a.m. Students, parents, faculty, staff— everyone in the school community— are invited.

Social Communication

The forms of **social communication** help people establish and maintain relationships with friends and family. When you communicate socially, always think about the occasion for writing and how well you know the recipients. For example, if the occasion is informal and you know the recipients well, your tone and word choice can be informal. However, if the occasion is formal and you are not well acquainted with the recipients, a formal tone and formal language are more appropriate.

Friendly Letter

Before the development of electronic forms of communication, **friendly letters** were the most common way of exchanging ideas with friends and family. Today, the conventions of friendly letters are still used to write e-mail messages. The extra time and effort it takes to write and mail a letter show the recipient how much you care. Use the following rules to develop your friendly letters.

- Friendly letters can be handwritten or typed.
- Include the date.
- Include a salutation, or greeting, such as "Dear Joe."
- Indent the paragraphs.
- End the letter with a complimentary closing like "Sincerely," and your signature.
- Be sure to include the proper address and postage on the envelope.

November 3, 2007
Dear Grandfather,

    I want you to know how much we are all looking forward to your visit. It's been so long since we've seen you! Dad has already planned some special events for us, but I hope that we can go fishing.

Yours truly,
Carlos

Thank-You Letter

A **thank-you letter** is a brief, friendly letter in which the sender expresses appreciation for a gift or an act of kindness.

September 4, 2007
Dear Janita,

    Thank you so much for your help on the school newsletter. Your attention to detail and hard work were a big part of our success.

Thanks again,
Mr. Hahn

Invitation

An **invitation** gives the date, time, place, and purpose of a social event. An invitation often includes an RSVP. This is an abbreviation of *répondez, s'il vous plaît,* a French phrase for "please respond." Including an RSVP can help you plan for the number of people attending your event.

Come One, Come All!

Come celebrate Crystal's sixteenth birthday!

Where: Elm Park
1900 Elm Street

When: Friday, May 25
6:00–8:30 p.m.

RSVP: Please let Crystal know by Wednesday, May 23, whether you can attend.

Grammar, Usage, Mechanics, and Spelling

Parts of Speech Overview

All the words in the English language can be put into one of eight groups. These groups are the eight **parts of speech**. You can tell a word's part of speech by looking at how it functions, or the way it is used, in a sentence. Knowing about the functions of words can help you become a better writer.

The Eight Parts of Speech	Examples
A **noun** names a person, place, thing, or idea.	**Erik Weihenmayer** climbed the highest **mountain** in the **world**. The **journey** up **Mount Everest** took **courage**.
A **pronoun** takes the place of a noun.	**He** made the journey even though **it** was dangerous.
An **adjective** describes a noun or a pronoun.	Erik is a **confident** climber. He is **strong**, too.
A **verb** can tell what the subject of a sentence does or has. A **verb** can also link a noun or an adjective in the predicate to the subject.	Erik also **skis** and **rides** a bike. He **has** many hobbies. Erik **is** an athlete. He **is** also blind.
An **adverb** describes a verb, an adjective, or another adverb.	Illness **slowly** took his eyesight, but it **never** affected his spirit. His accomplishments have made him **very** famous. He has been interviewed **so** often.
A **preposition** shows how two things or ideas are related. It introduces a prepositional phrase.	Erik speaks **to** people **around** the world. **In** his speeches, he talks **about** his life.
A **conjunction** connects words or groups of words.	Courage **and** skill have carried him far. He has one disability, **but** he has many abilities.
An **interjection** expresses strong feeling.	**Wow**! What an amazing person he is. **Hurray**! He reached the mountain top.

Grammar and Usage

Grammar and **usage** rules tell us how to correctly identify and use the parts of speech and types of sentences.

Nouns

A **noun** names a person, place, thing, or idea. There are different kinds of nouns.

Common and Proper Nouns	Examples
A **common noun** names a general person, place, thing, or idea.	A **teenager** sat by the **ocean** and read a **magazine**.
Capitalize a common noun only when it begins a sentence.	**Magazines** are the perfect thing to read at the beach.
A **proper noun** names a specific person, place, thing, or idea. Always capitalize a proper noun.	**Jessica** sat by the **Pacific Ocean** and read *Teen Talk Magazine*.

Count and Noncount Nouns	Examples
Count nouns name things that you can count. The singular form of a count noun names one thing. The plural form names more than one thing.	<table><tr><td>**Singular**</td><td>**Plural**</td></tr><tr><td>one desk</td><td>two desks</td></tr><tr><td>one book</td><td>many books</td></tr><tr><td>one teacher</td><td>several teachers</td></tr></table>
You can count some food items by using a measurement word like **cup**, **slice**, or **glass** followed by the word **of**. To show the plural form, make the measurement word plural.	Jessica drank **a glass of water** after school. Jessica drank **two glasses of water** while she was reading her book.
Noncount nouns name things that you cannot count. They can be divided into different categories.	

Activities and Sports:	baseball, camping, dancing, golf, singing, soccer
Category Nouns:	clothing, equipment, furniture, machinery, mail
Food:	bread, cereal, cheese, lettuce, meat, milk, soup, tea
Ideas and Feelings:	democracy, enthusiasm, freedom, honesty, health
Materials:	air, fuel, gasoline, metal, paper, water, dust, soil
Weather:	fog, hail, heat, rain, smog, snow, humidity, sunshine

Some nouns can be either count or noncount nouns. It depends on how the nouns are used.	Jessica has read the book two **times**. She is fascinated by the idea of traveling through **time**.

Plural Nouns	Examples
Plural nouns name more than one person, place, thing, or idea. Add **-s** to most count nouns to make them plural. Other count nouns follow simple rules to form the plural.	My favorite **guitar** was made in Spain, but I also like my two American **guitars**.

Forming Noun Plurals

When a Noun Ends in:	Form the Plural by:	Examples
ch, **sh**, **s**, **x**, or **z**	adding **-es**	box—box**es** brush—brush**es**
a consonant + **y**	changing the **y** to **i** and adding **-es**	story—stor**ies**
a vowel + **y**	just adding **-s**	boy—boy**s**
f or **fe**	changing the **f** to **v** and adding **-es**, in most cases for some nouns that end in **f** or **fe**, just add **-s**	leaf—leav**es** knife—kni**ves** cliff—cliff**s** safe—safe**s**
a vowel + **o**	adding **-s**	radio—radio**s** kangaroo—kangaroo**s**
a consonant + **o**	adding **-s**, in most cases; other times adding **-es** some nouns take either **-s** or **-es**	photo—photo**s** potato—potato**es** zero—zero**s**/zero**es**

A few count nouns are **irregular**. These nouns do not follow the rules to form the plural.

Forming Plurals of Irregular Count Nouns

For some irregular count nouns, change the spelling to form the plural.	one child many **children** one foot many **feet**	one man several **men** one ox ten **oxen**	one person a few **people** one woman most **women**
For other irregular count nouns, keep the same form for the singular and the plural.	one deer two **deer**	one fish many **fish**	one sheep twelve **sheep**

Possessive Nouns	Examples
Possessive nouns show ownership or relationship of persons, places, or things.	**Ted's** daughter made the guitar. The **guitar's** tone is beautiful.
Follow these rules to make a noun possessive: • Add **'s** to a singular noun or a plural noun that does not end in **s**.	When she plays the piano, it attracts **people's** attention.
• If the owner's name ends in **s**, form the possessive by adding **'s** or just an apostrophe. Either is correct.	**Louis's** music is playful and funny. **Louis'** music is playful and funny.
• Add an apostrophe after the final **s** in a plural noun that ends in **s**.	Three **musicians'** instruments were left on the bus.

Noun Phrases and Clauses	Examples
A **noun phrase** is made up of a noun and its modifiers. Modifiers are words that describe, such as adjectives.	**The flying frog** does not actually fly. It glides on **special skin flaps**. Thailand is **a frog-friendly habitat**.
A **noun clause** is a group of words that functions as a noun and has a subject and a verb. It may begin with *that*, *how*, or a *wh-* word such as *why*, *what*, or *when*.	**How any animal flies** is hard to understand. He explained **that it is called a flying frog**. Its name makes sense to **whoever sees it**.

Articles

An **article** is a word that helps identify a noun.

Articles	Examples
A, **an**, and **the** are **articles**. An article often comes before a count noun. Do not use the articles **a** or **an** before a noncount noun.	It is **an** amazing event when **a** flying frog glides in **the** forest.
A and **an** are **indefinite articles**. Use **a** or **an** before a noun that names a nonspecific thing.	**A flying frog** stretched its webbed feet. **An owl** watched from a nearby tree.
• Use **a** before a word that starts with a consonant sound.	a **f**oot a **r**ainforest a **p**ool a **u**nion (*u* is pronounced like *y*, a **n**est a consonant)
• Use **an** before a word that starts with a vowel sound.	an **e**gg an **a**nimal an **a**dult an **a**mount an **o**cean an **h**our (The *h* is silent.)
The is a **definite article**. Use **the** before a noun that names a specific thing.	Leiopelmids are **the** oldest kind of frog in **the** world. They are survivors of **the** Jurassic period.

Pronouns

A **pronoun** is a word that takes the place of a noun. **Case** refers to the form that a pronoun takes to show how it is used in a sentence.

Subjective Case Pronouns	Examples
Use a **subject pronoun** as the subject of a sentence.	**Antonio** is looking forward to the homecoming dance. **He** is trying to decide what to wear.

Subject Pronouns

Singular	Plural
I	we
you	you
he, she, it	they

The pronoun **it** can be used as a **subject** to refer to a noun.	The **dance** starts at 7:00. **It** ends at 10:00.
But: The pronoun **it** can be the subject without referring to a specific noun.	**It** is important to arrive on time. **It** is fun to see your friends in formal clothes.

Objective Case Pronouns	Examples
Use an **object pronoun** after an **action verb**.	Tickets are on sale, so buy **them** now.

Object Pronouns

Singular	Plural
me	us
you	you
him, her, it	them

Use an **object pronoun** after a **preposition**.	Antonio invited Caryn. He ordered flowers for **her**.
Use **reciprocal pronouns** to show a two-way action between two or more people.	Mary and Juan tossed the ball to **each other**. Mary, Juan, and Lorenzo tested **one another** on the new math skills.

Possessive Words	Examples
A **possessive pronoun** tells who or what owns something.	**His** photograph of a tree won an award.
Possessive pronouns take the place of a **possessive noun and the person**, **place**, **or thing it owns**. Possessive pronouns always stand alone.	Which camera is Aleina's? The expensive camera is **hers**. **Mine** is a single-use, disposable camera.

Possessive Pronouns	
Singular	**Plural**
mine	ours
yours	yours
his, hers	theirs

Some possessive words act as **adjectives**, so they are called **possessive adjectives**. Possessive adjectives always come before a noun.	Aleina's photographs are beautiful because of **her** eye for detail.

Possessive Adjectives	
Singular	**Plural**
my	our
your	your
his, her, its	their

Demonstrative Words	Examples
A **demonstrative pronoun** points out a specific person, place, or thing. It can point to something near or far away.	**That** is a good photo of my grandparents. **These** are good photos, too.

Demonstrative Words		
	Singular	**Plural**
Near	this	these
Far	that	those

A demonstrative word can **act as an adjective**, answering the question *Which one?* or *Which ones?*	**This** photo album has pictures of my family. **These** photographs are of my grandparents.

Indefinite Pronouns	Examples
Use an **indefinite pronoun** when you are not talking about a specific person, place, or thing.	**Someone** has to lose the game. **Nobody** knows who the winner will be.

Some Indefinite Pronouns

These **indefinite pronouns** are always singular and need a **singular verb**.

another	either	nobody	someone
anybody	everybody	no one	something
anyone	everyone	nothing	
anything	everything	one	
each	neither	somebody	

Something is happening on the playing field.

We hope that **everything goes** well for our team.

These **indefinite pronouns** are always plural and need a **plural verb**.

both	few	many	several

Many of us **are** hopeful.

These **indefinite pronouns** can be either singular or plural.

all	any	most	none	some

Look at the phrase that follows the indefinite pronoun. If the noun or pronoun in the phrase is plural, use a **plural verb**. If the noun or pronoun is singular, use a **singular verb**.

Most of the players **are** tired.

Most of the game **is** over.

Relative Pronouns	Examples
A **relative pronoun** introduces **a relative clause**. It connects, or relates, the clause to a word in the sentence. Relative pronouns are used in restrictive and nonrestrictive clauses.	

Relative Pronouns

who	whoever	whosoever
whom	whomever	whomsoever
whose	which	whichever
what	whatever	whatsoever

> **Grammar Tip**
>
> In informal speech, it is acceptable to say "**Who** did you ask?" In formal writing, use the correct form, "**Whom** did you ask?"

Use **who**, **whom**, or **whose** for people. The pronouns **whoever**, **whomever**, **whosoever**, and **whomsoever** also refer to people.	The student **who** was injured is Joe. We play **whomever** we are scheduled to play.
Use **which**, **whichever**, **what**, **whatever**, and **whatsoever** for things.	Joe's wrist, **which** is sprained, will heal.
Use **that** for people or things.	The trainer **that** examined Joe's wrist is sure. The injury **that** Joe received is minor.

Reflexive and Intensive Pronouns	Examples
Reflexive and **intensive pronouns** refer to nouns or other pronouns in a sentence. These pronouns end with -**self** or -**selves**.	I will go to the store by **myself**.
Use a **reflexive pronoun** when the object **refers back to the subject**.	To surprise her technology teacher, **Kim** taught **herself** how to create a Web site on the computer.

Reflexive and Intensive Pronouns

Singular	Plural
myself	ourselves
yourself	yourselves
himself, herself, itself	themselves

Use an **intensive pronoun** when you want **to emphasize a noun or a pronoun** in a sentence.	The technology **teacher himself** learned some interesting techniques from Kim.

Agreement and Reference	Examples
When nouns and pronouns **agree**, they both refer to the same person, place, or thing. The **noun** is the **antecedent**, and the **pronoun** refers to it.	**Rafael and Felicia** visited a local college. **They** toured the campus. *antecedent pronoun*
A pronoun must agree (match) in **number** with the noun it refers to. • **Singular pronouns** refer to one person. • **Plural pronouns** refer to more than one person.	**Rafael** plays violin. **He** enjoyed the music school. **The teenagers** were impressed. **They** liked this college.
Pronouns and adjectives must agree in **gender** with the nouns they refer to. Use **she**, **her**, and **hers** to refer to females. Use **he**, **him**, and **his** to refer to males.	Felicia told **her** uncle about the college visit. **Her** uncle told **her** that **he** received **his** graduate degree from that school.

Editing Tip

Find each pronoun in your paper. Find the noun it is replacing. Do they match?

Adjectives

An **adjective** describes, or modifies, a noun or a pronoun. It can tell what kind, which one, how many, or how much.

Adjectives	Examples
Adjectives provide more detailed information about a noun. Usually, an adjective comes before the noun it describes.	Deserts have a **dry** climate.
But an adjective can also come after the noun.	The climate is also **hot**.

Adjectives That Compare	Examples
Comparative adjectives help show the similarities or differences between two nouns.	Deserts are **more fun** to study than forests are.
To form the comparative of one-syllable adjectives and two-syllable adjectives that end in a consonant + **y**, add -**er**, and use **than**. Use **more … than** if the adjective has three or more syllables.	The Sechura Desert in South America is small**er than** the Kalahari Desert in Africa. Is that desert **more interesting than** this one?
Superlative adjectives help show how three or more nouns are alike or different.	Of the Sechura, Kalahari, and Sahara, which is the **largest**?
To form the superlative of one-syllable adjectives and two-syllable adjectives that end in a consonant + **y**, add -**est**. Use **most** if the adjective has three or more syllables.	Which of the three deserts is the **smallest**? I think the Sahara is the **most beautiful**.
Irregular adjectives form the comparative and superlative differently. good better best some more most bad worse worst little less least	I had the **best** time ever visiting the desert. But the desert heat is **worse** than city heat.
Some two-syllable adjectives form the comparative with either -**er** or **more** and superlative with either -**est** or **most**. **Do not form a double comparison by using both.**	Most desert animals are **more lively** at night than during the day. Most desert animals are **livelier** at night than during the day.

Adjective Phrases and Clauses	Examples
An **adjective phrase** is a group of words that work together to modify a noun or a pronoun. A phrase has no verb.	Plants **in the desert** have developed adaptations.
An **adjective clause** is also a group of words that work together to modify a noun or a pronoun. Unlike a phrase, however, a clause has both a subject and a verb.	Desert plants **that have long roots** tap into water deep in the earth.

Verbs

Every sentence has two parts: a subject and a predicate. The subject tells who or what the sentence is about. The predicate tells something about the subject. For example:
The dancers / **performed** on stage.

The **verb** is the key word in the predicate because it tells what the subject does or has. Verbs can also link words.

Action Verbs	Examples
An **action verb** tells what the subject of a sentence does. Most verbs are action verbs.	Dancers **practice** for many hours. They **stretch** their muscles and **lift** weights.
Some **action verbs** tell about an action that you cannot see.	The dancers **recognize** the rewards that come from their hard work.

Linking Verbs	Examples
A **linking verb** connects, or links, the subject of a sentence to a word in the predicate.	**Linking Verbs** **Forms of the Verb *Be*** am is are / was were **Other Linking Verbs** appear feel look / seem smell / become taste
The word in the predicate can describe the subject.	Their feet **are** calloused.
Or the word in the predicate can rename the subject.	These dancers **are** athletes.

Conditional Verbs	Examples
Conditional verbs show, in the present, how one event depends on another event in the future.	Dancers **should** stretch to prevent injuries. An injury **might** prevent a dancer from performing.
Some Conditional Verbs can could might must shall should will would	
Sentences with conditional verbs often use **if** and **then** to show how two events are connected. Conditional verbs are sometimes called **modal verbs**.	**If** a principal dancer is unable to perform, **then** the understudy will perform the role.

Helping Verbs	Examples
Verb phrases have more than one verb: helping verbs and a main verb.	Ballet **is considered** a dramatic art form. *helping verb* *main verb*
The action word is called the **main verb**. It shows what the subject does, has, or is.	This dance form **has been evolving** over the years. *helping verbs* *main verb*
Any verbs that come before the main verb are the **helping verbs**.	Ballet **must have been** very different in the 1500s. *helping verbs* *main verb*
Helping verbs agree with the subject.	Baryshnikov **has performed** around the world. Many people **have praised** this famous dancer.
Adverbs can be in several places in a sentence. The adverb **not** always comes between the **helping verb** and the **main verb**.	If you **have** not **heard** of him, you can watch the film *Dancers* to see him perform. He sometimes **has danced** in films. Usually, he dances on stage.
In questions, the subject comes between the **helping verb** and the **main verb**.	**Have** you **heard** of Mikhail Baryshnikov?

Helping Verbs

Forms of the Verb *Be*		Forms of the Verb *Do*		Forms of the Verb *Have*	
am	was	do	did	have	had
is	were	does		has	
are					

Other Helping Verbs

To express ability: 　**can**, **could**	I **can** dance.
To express possibility: 　**may**, **might**, **could**	I **might** dance tonight.
To express necessity or desire: 　**must**, **would like**	I **must** dance more often. I **would like** to dance more often.
To express certainty: 　**will**, **shall**	I **will** dance more often.
To express obligation: 　**should**, **ought to**	I **should** practice more often. I **ought to** practice more often.

Verb Tense

The **tense** of a verb shows when an action happens.

Present Tense Verbs	Examples
The **present tense** of a verb tells about an action that happens now.	Greg **checks** his watch to see if it is time to leave. He **starts** work at 5:00 today.

Habitual Present Tense Verbs	Examples
The **habitual present tense** of a verb tells about an action that happens regularly or all the time.	Greg **works** at a pizza shop on Saturdays and Sundays. He **makes** pizzas and **washes** dishes.

Past Tense Verbs (Regular and Irregular)	Examples
The **past tense** of a verb tells about an action that happened earlier, or in the past. • The past tense form of **regular verbs** ends with -**ed**. • **Irregular verbs** have **special forms** to show the past tense. For more irregular verbs, see the **Troubleshooting Guide**, page 773.	Yesterday, Greg **worked** until the shop closed. He **made** 50 pizzas. He **learned** how to make a stuffed-crust pizza. Then Greg **chopped** onions and peppers. Greg **cut** the pizza. It **was** delicious. We **ate** all of it!

Some Irregular Verbs

Present Tense	Past Tense
cut	cut
is	was
eat	ate

Future Tense Verbs	Examples
The **future tense** of a verb tells about an action that will happen later, or in the future. To talk about the future, use: • the helping verb **will** plus a main verb. • the phrase **am going to**, **is going to**, or **are going to** plus a **main verb**.	Greg **will ride** the bus home after work tonight. Greg's mother **will drive** him to work tomorrow. On Friday, he **will get** his first paycheck. He **is going to take** a pizza home to his family. They **are going to eat** the pizza for dinner.

Perfect Tense Verbs

All verbs in the **perfect tenses**—**present**, **past**, and **future**—have a helping verb and a form of the main verb that is called the **past participle**.

Present Perfect Tense Verbs	Examples
For **regular verbs**, the past tense and the past participle end in -**ed**. To form the present perfect, use **has** or **have** with the past participle.	
Present Tense like	I **like** the Internet.
Past Tense liked	I **liked** the Internet.
Present Perfect has/have liked	I **have** always **liked** the Internet.
Irregular verbs have **special forms** for the past tense and past participle. Always use **has** or **have** with the past participle. See page 773.	
Present Tense know	I **know** a lot about the Internet.
Past Tense knew	I **knew** very little about the Internet last year.
Present Perfect has/have known	I **have known** about the Internet for a long time.
The **present perfect tense** of a verb can tell about an action that began in the past and is still going on.	The public **has used** the Internet since the 1980s. **Have** you **done** research on the Internet?

Past Perfect Tense Verbs	Examples
The **past perfect tense** of a verb tells about an action that was completed before some other action in the past. It uses the helping verb **had** and the past participle of the main verb.	Before the Internet became popular, people **had done** their research in the library.

Future Perfect Tense Verbs	Examples
The **future perfect tense** of a verb tells about an action that will be completed at a specific time in the future. It uses the helping verbs **will have** and the past participle of the main verb.	By the end of next year, 100,000 people **will have visited** our Web site.

Contractions

A **contraction** is a shortened form of a verb or verb and pronoun combination.

Contractions	Examples	
Use an **apostrophe** to show which letters have been left out of the contraction.	I would = I'd they are = they're	is not = isn't can not = can't
In contractions made up of a verb and the word **not**, the word **not** is usually shortened to **n't**.	I **can't** stop eating these cookies!	

Verb Forms

The **form** a verb takes changes depending on how it is used in a sentence, phrase, or clause.

Progressive Verbs	Examples
The **progressive verb** form tells about an action that occurs over a period of time.	
The **present progressive tense** of a verb tells about an action as it is happening.	They **are expecting** a big crowd for the fireworks show this evening.
• It uses the helping verb **am**, **is**, or **are**. The main verb ends in -**ing**.	**Are** you **expecting** the rain to end before the show starts?
The **past progressive tense** of a verb tells about an action that was happening over a period of time in the past.	They **were thinking** of canceling the fireworks.
• It uses the helping verb **was** or **were** and a main verb. The main verb ends in -**ing**.	A tornado **was heading** in this direction.
The **future progressive tense** of a verb tells about an action that will be happening over a period of time in the future.	The weather forecasters **will be watching** for the path of the tornado.
• It uses the helping verbs **will be** plus a main verb. The main verb ends in -**ing**.	I hope that they **will** not **be canceling** the show.

Transitive and Intransitive Verbs	Examples
Action verbs can be transitive or intransitive. A **transitive verb** needs an **object** to complete its meaning and to receive the action of the verb.	**Not complete:** **Complete:** Many cities **use** Many cities **use** fireworks.
The object can be a **direct object**. A direct object answers the question *Whom?* or *What?*	**Whom**: The noise **surprises** the audience. **What**: The people in the audience **cover** their ears.
An **intransitive verb** does not need an object to complete its meaning.	**Complete:** The people in our neighborhood **clap**. They **shout**. They **laugh**.
An **intransitive verb** may end the sentence, or it may be followed by other words that tell how, where, or when. These words are not objects since they do not receive the action of the verb.	The fireworks **glow** brightly. Then, slowly, they **disappear** in the sky. The show **ends** by midnight.

Active and Passive Voice	Examples
A verb is in **active voice** if the **subject** is doing the action.	Many cities **hold** fireworks displays for the Fourth of July.
A verb is in **passive voice** if the **subject** is not doing the action. A verb in passive voice always includes a form of the verb **be**, plus the past participle of the main verb. Use active voice to emphasize the subject. Use passive voice to put less emphasis on the subject, such as when:	Fireworks displays **are held** by many cities for the Fourth of July.
• the object, or receiver of the action, is more important than the doer	Our celebration **was held** after the winds died down.
• you don't know who the doer is	The fireworks **were made** in the U.S.
• you don't want to name the doer or place blame	The start time **is listed** incorrectly in the newspaper.

Two-Word Verbs

A **two-word verb** is a verb followed by a preposition. The meaning of the two-word verb is different from the meaning of the verb by itself.

Some Two-Word Verbs

Verb	Meaning	Example
break	to split into pieces	I didn't **break** the window with the ball.
break down	to stop working	Did the car **break down** again?
break up	to end	The party will **break up** before midnight.
	to come apart	The ice on the lake will **break up** in the spring.
bring	to carry something with you	**Bring** your book to class.
bring up	to suggest	She **brings up** good ideas at every meeting.
	to raise children	**Bring up** your children to be good citizens.
check	to make sure you are right	We can **check** our answers at the back of the book.
check in	to stay in touch with someone	I **check in** with my mom at work.
check up	to see if everything is okay	The nurse **checks up** on the patient every hour.
check off	to mark off a list	Look at your list and **check off** the girls' names.
check out	to look at something carefully	Hey, Marisa, **check out** my new bike!

Verb	Meaning	Example
fill	to place as much as can be held	**Fill** the pail with water.
fill in	to color or shade in a space	Please **fill in** the circle.
fill out	to complete	Marcos **fills out** a form to order a book.
get	to go after something	I'll **get** some milk at the store.
	to receive	I often **get** letters from my pen pal.
get ahead	to go beyond what is expected	She worked hard to **get ahead** in math class.
get along	to be on good terms with	Do you **get along** with your sister?
get out	to leave	Let's **get out** of the kitchen.
get over	to feel better	I hope you'll **get over** the flu soon.
get through	to finish	I can **get through** this book tonight.
give	to hand something to someone	We **give** presents to the children.
give out	to stop working	If she runs ten miles, her energy will **give out**.
give up	to quit	I'm going to **give up** eating candy.
go	to move from place to place	Did you **go** to the mall on Saturday?
go on	to continue	Why do the boys **go on** playing after the bell rings?
go out	to go someplace special	Let's **go out** to lunch on Saturday.
look	to see or watch	Don't **look** directly at the sun.
look over	to review	She **looks over** her test before finishing.
look up	to hunt for and find	We **look up** information on the Internet.
pick	to choose	I'd **pick** Lin for class president.
pick on	to bother or tease	My older brothers always **pick on** me.
pick up	to go faster	Business **picks up** in the summer.
	to gather or collect	**Pick up** your clothes!
run	to move quickly	Juan will **run** in a marathon.
run into	to see someone unexpectedly	Did you **run into** Chris at the store?
run out	to suddenly have nothing left	The cafeteria always **runs out** of nachos.
stand	to be on one's feet	I have to **stand** in line to buy tickets.
stand for	to represent	A heart **stands for** love.
stand out	to be easier to see	You'll **stand out** with that orange cap.
turn	to change direction	We **turn** right at the next corner.
turn up	to raise the volume	Please **turn up** the radio.
turn in	to give back	You didn't **turn in** the homework yesterday.
turn off	to make something stop	Please **turn off** the radio.

Forms of Irregular Verbs

Irregular verbs form the past tense and the past participle in a different way than regular verbs. These verb forms have to be memorized.

Some Irregular Verbs

Irregular Verb	Past Tense	Past Participle	Irregular Verb	Past Tense	Past Participle
be: am, is be: are	was were	been been	eat	ate	eaten
beat	beat	beaten	fall (*intr.*)	fell	fallen
become	became	become	feed	fed	fed
begin	began	begun	feel	felt	felt
bend	bent	bent	fight	fought	fought
bind	bound	bound	find	found	found
bite	bit	bitten	fly	flew	flown
blow	blew	blown	forget	forgot	forgotten
break	broke	broken	forgive	forgave	forgiven
bring	brought	brought	freeze	froze	frozen
build	built	built	get	got	got, gotten
burst	burst	burst	give	gave	given
buy	bought	bought	go	went	gone
catch	caught	caught	grow	grew	grown
choose	chose	chosen	have	had	had
come	came	come	hear	heard	heard
cost	cost	cost	hide	hid	hidden
creep	crept	crept	hit	hit	hit
cut	cut	cut	hold	held	held
dig	dug	dug	hurt	hurt	hurt
do	did	done	keep	kept	kept
draw	drew	drawn	know	knew	known
dream	dreamed, dreamt	dreamed, dreamt	lay (*tr.*)	laid	laid
drink	drank	drunk	lead	led	led
drive	drove	driven	leave	left	left

Irregular Verb	Past Tense	Past Participle	Irregular Verb	Past Tense	Past Participle
lend	lent	lent	sing	sang	sung
lie (*intr.*)	lay	lain	sink	sank	sunk
let	let	let	sit	sat	sat
light	lit	lit	sleep (*intr.*)	slept	slept
lose	lost	lost	slide	slid	slid
make	made	made	speak	spoke	spoken
mean	meant	meant	spend	spent	spent
meet	met	met	stand	stood	stood
pay	paid	paid	steal	stole	stolen
prove	proved	proved, proven	stick	stuck	stuck
put	put	put	sting	stung	stung
quit	quit	quit	strike	struck	struck
read	read	read	swear	swore	sworn
ride	rode	ridden	swim	swam	swum
ring	rang	rung	swing	swung	swung
rise (*intr.*)	rose	risen	take	took	taken
run	ran	run	teach	taught	taught
say	said	said	tear	tore	torn
see	saw	seen	tell	told	told
seek	sought	sought	think	thought	thought
sell	sold	sold	throw	threw	thrown
send	sent	sent	understand	understood	understood
set	set	set	wake	woke, waked	woken, waked
shake	shook	shaken	wear	wore	worn
show	showed	shown	weep	wept	wept
shrink	shrank	shrunk	win	won	won
shut	shut	shut	write	wrote	written

Verbals

A **verbal** is a word made from a verb but used as another part of speech.

Gerunds	Examples
A **gerund** is a verb form that ends in -**ing** and that is used as a noun. Like all nouns, a gerund can be the subject of a sentence or an object.	<u>**Cooking**</u> is Mr. Jimenez's favorite hobby. *subject* Mr. Jimenez truly enjoys **cooking**. *direct object* Mr. Jimenez is very talented at **cooking**. *object of preposition*

Infinitives	Examples
An **infinitive** is a verb form that begins with **to**. It can be used as a noun, an adjective, or an adverb.	Mr. Jimenez likes **to cook**. *noun* Mr. Jimenez's beef tamales are a sight **to see**. *adjective* Mr. Jimenez cooks **to relax**. *adverb*

Participial Phrases	Examples
A **participle** is a verb form that is used as an adjective. For regular verbs, it ends in -**ing** or -**ed**. Irregular verbs take the past participle form.	His **sizzling** fajitas taste delicious. Mr. Jimenez also makes tasty **frozen** desserts.
A **participial phrase** begins with a participle. Place the phrase next to the noun it describes.	**Standing by the grill**, he cooked meat. **Not**: He cooked meat, standing by the grill.

Absolutes

An **absolute** is a sentence-like phrase. It is usually formed with a subject and a participle.

Absolutes	Examples
An **absolute** modifies all the remaining parts of the sentence.	**More guests having arrived,** Mr. Jimenez added burgers to the grill.
Use a comma to set off the **absolute** from the rest of the sentence.	Mr. Jimenez, **his plans for a good party accomplished**, smiled broadly.

A phrase that utilizes a gerund, an infinitive, a participle, or an absolute is known as a **verbal phrase**.

Adverbs

An **adverb** describes a verb, an adjective, or another adverb.

Adverbs	Examples
Adverbs answer one of the following questions: • How? • Where? • When? • How often?	**Carefully** aim the ball. Kick the ball **here**. Try again **later** to make a goal. Cathy **usually** scores.
Adverbs that tell how often usually come before the main verb or after a form of **be**. Other adverbs often come after the verb.	Our team **always wins**. The whole team **plays well**.
An adverb can strengthen the meaning of an **adjective** or another **adverb**.	Gina is **really good** at soccer. She plays **very well**.

> **Grammar Tip**
>
> Use an adjective, rather than an adverb, after a linking verb.
>
> *My teacher **is** fair~~ly~~.*

Adverbs That Compare	Examples
Some **adverbs** compare actions. Add -**er** to compare the actions of two people. Add -**est** to compare the actions of three or more people.	Gina runs **fast**. Gina runs **faster** than Maria. Gina runs **the fastest** of all the players.
If the adverb ends in -**ly**, use **more** or **less** to compare two actions.	Gina aims **more carefully** than Jen. Jen aims **less carefully** than Gina.
Use **the most** or **the least** to compare three or more actions.	Gina aims **the most carefully** of all the players. Jen aims **the least carefully** of all the players.

Adverbial Phrases and Clauses	Examples
An **adverb phrase** is a prepositional phrase that modifies a verb, an adjective, or another adverb.	When Gina kicked the ball, it **went into the net**. The coach was **happy about the score**. Gina plays **best under pressure**.
An **adverb clause** has a subject and a verb. It modifies an independent main clause and cannot stand alone. Adverb clauses can tell when, why, or where.	**After the team won**, the coach praised the players. Everyone was muddy **because it had rained**. Soccer is popular **wherever there are fields available**.

Prepositions

A **preposition** comes at the beginning of a prepositional phrase. **Prepositional phrases** add details to sentences.

Uses of Prepositions	Examples
Some prepositions show **location**.	The Chávez Community Center is **by my house**. The pool is **behind the building**.
Some prepositions show **time**.	The Teen Club's party will start **after lunch**.
Some prepositions show **direction**.	Go **through the building** and **around the fountain** to get **to the pool**. The snack bar is **down the hall**.
Some prepositions have **multiple uses**.	We might see Joshua **at the party**. Meet me **at my house**. Come **at noon**.

Prepositional Phrases	Examples
A **prepositional phrase** starts with a preposition and ends with a noun or a pronoun. It includes all the words in between. The noun or pronoun is the **object of the preposition**.	I live **near the Chávez Community Center**. *object of preposition* Tom wants to walk there **with you and me**. *objects of preposition*
Prepositional phrases are often consecutive.	The Community Center is **up the street** and **on the right**.

Some Prepositions

Location		Time	Direction	Other Prepositions	
above	near	after	across	about	for
behind	next to	before	around	against	from
below	off	during	down	along	of
beside	on	till	into	among	to
between	out	until	out of	as	with
by	outside		through	at	without
in	over		toward	except	
inside	under		up		

Conjunctions and Interjections

A **conjunction** connects words or groups of words. An **interjection** expresses strong feeling or emotion.

Conjunctions	Examples
A **coordinating conjunction** connects words, phrases, or clauses.	
To show similarity: **and**	Irena **and** Irving are twins.
To show difference: **but**, **yet**	I know Irena, **but** I do not know Irving.
To show choice: **or**	They will celebrate their birthday Friday **or** Saturday night.
To show cause/effect: **so**, **for**	I have a cold, **so** I cannot go to the party.
To put negative ideas together: **nor**	My mother will not let me go, **nor** will my father.
Correlative conjunctions are used in pairs. The pair connects phrases or words.	**Some Correlative Conjunctions** both … and not only … but also either … or whether … or neither … nor
A **subordinating conjunction** introduces a **dependent clause** in a complex sentence. It connects the **dependent clause** to the main clause.	**Some Subordinating Conjunctions** after before till although if until as in order that when as if since where as long as so that while because though
A **conjunctive adverb** joins two independent clauses. Use a semicolon before the conjunction and a comma after it.	**Some Conjunctive Adverbs** besides meanwhile then consequently moreover therefore however nevertheless thus

Grammar Tip

When you use paired words, make sure you use both words in the sentence. Don't leave one out!

Interjections	Examples
An **interjection** shows emotion. If an interjection stands alone, follow it with an exclamation point.	**Help!** **Oops!** **Oh boy!**
An interjection used in a sentence can be followed by a comma or an exclamation mark. Use a comma after a weak interjection. Use an exclamation mark after a strong interjection.	**Oh**, it's a baby panda! **Hooray!** The baby panda has survived!

Sentences

A **sentence** is a group of words that expresses a complete thought. Every sentence has a subject (a main idea) and a predicate that describes what the main idea is, has, or does. Sentences can be classified according to their function and structure.

Sentence Types	Examples
A **declarative sentence** makes a statement. It ends with a period.	The football game was on Friday. The coach made an important announcement.
An **interrogative sentence** asks a question. It ends with a question mark.	Who heard the announcement? What did the coach say?
An **exclamatory sentence** shows surprise or strong emotion. It ends with an exclamation point.	That's fantastic news! I can't believe it!
An **imperative sentence** gives a command.	Give the team my congratulations.
• An imperative sentence usually begins with a verb and ends with a period.	**Be** on time.
• If an imperative sentence shows strong emotion, it ends with an exclamation point.	Beat the opponent!

Grammar Tip

Use **please** to make a command more polite:

Please call me if you have any questions.

Negative Sentences	Examples
A **negative sentence** uses a **negative word** to say "no."	The game in Hawaii was **not** boring! **Nobody** in our town missed it on TV. Our team **never** played better.

Negative Words			
no	none	no one	not
nowhere	never	nobody	nothing

Use only one negative word in a sentence. Using two negatives in one sentence is called a **double negative**. Two negatives cancel each other out. **I did not see no one**, means **I saw someone.**	anything The other team could not do ~~nothing~~ right. any Their team never scored ~~no~~ points.

Conditional Sentences	Examples
Conditional sentences tell how one action depends on another. These sentences often use conditional or modal verbs, such as **can**, **will**, **could**, **would**, or **might**.	**If** our team returns today, **then** we **will** have a party. **Unless** it rains, we **can** have the party outside.
Sometimes a conditional sentence tells about an imaginary condition and its imaginary result.	If my dog **could talk**, he **would tell** me his thoughts.

Sentence Structure

Phrases	Examples
A **phrase** is a group of related words that does not have both a subject and a verb. English can have noun phrases, verb phrases, adjective phrases, adverb phrases, prepositional phrases, and more.	The football team has won many games in overtime. *noun phrase* *verb phrase* *noun phrase* *prepositional phrase*

Clauses	Examples
A **clause** is a group of words that has both a **subject** and a **predicate**. A clause can be a complete sentence.	California's population / grew during the 1840s. *subject* *predicate*
An **independent clause** can stand alone as a complete sentence.	California's population / increased. *subject* *predicate*
A **dependent clause** cannot stand alone as a complete sentence.	**because** gold / was found there during that time
An **adjective clause** gives more details about the noun or pronoun that it describes.	The news **that gold had been found** spread fast.
An **adverb clause** can tell when, where, or why.	**When someone found gold**, people celebrated.
A **noun clause** can function as a subject, a direct object, or an object of a preposition.	The reporter knew **why the miners were celebrating.**
A **nonrestrictive clause** is a clause that adds non-essential detail to your sentence. Set it off with commas.	The miners, **who were happy to hear the news,** leaped for joy.

Simple Sentences	Examples
A **simple sentence** is one independent clause with a subject and a predicate. It has no dependent clauses.	Supplies / were scarce. The miners / needed goods and services.

Compound Sentences	Examples
When you join two independent clauses, you make a **compound sentence**.	
Use a comma and a **coordinating conjunction** or a **semicolon** to join independent clauses.	People opened stores, **but** supplies were scarce.
Or use a **conjunctive adverb** with a semicolon before it and a comma after it.	People opened stores; supplies slowly arrived. Miners made money; **however**, merchants made more money.

Complex Sentences	Examples
To make a **complex sentence**, join an independent clause with one or more dependent clauses.	Many writers visited camps **where miners worked**. *independent* *dependent*
If the dependent clause comes first, put a **comma** after it.	**While the writers were there**, they wrote stories about the miners.
Use a comma or commas to separate the nonrestrictive clause from the rest of the sentence.	The writers, **who were from California,** lived in the same tents as the miners.

Compound-Complex Sentences	Examples
You can make a **compound-complex sentence** by joining two or more independent clauses and one or more dependent clauses.	Many miners never found gold, **but** they stayed in California **because they found other jobs there**. *dependent*

Properly Placed Modifiers and Clauses	Examples
Place **modifiers** as closely as possible to the word or words that they describe. The meaning of a clause may be unclear if a modifier is not placed properly.	Unclear: Some miners **only** found fool's gold. (Does *only* describe *found* or *fool's gold*?) Clear: Some miners found **only** fool's gold.
A **misplaced clause** may make a sentence unclear and accidentally funny.	Unclear: I read that miners traveled by mule **when I studied American history**. (Did the miners travel while you studied?)
When the clause is placed properly, it makes the meaning of the sentence clear.	Clear: **When I studied American history**, I read that miners traveled by mule.
A **misplaced modifier** is a phrase placed too far away from the word or words it describes.	Unclear: The stream rushed past the miners, **splashing wildly**. (Did the miners or the stream splash wildly?)
Correct a misplaced modifier by placing it closer to the word or words it describes.	Clear: **Splashing wildly**, the stream rushed past the miners.
A **dangling modifier** occurs when you accidentally forget to include the word being described.	**Standing in rushing streams**, the search for gold was dangerous. (Who stood in the streams?)
Correct a dangling modifier by adding the missing word being described, adding words to the modifier, or rewording the sentence.	The search for gold was dangerous for **miners** standing in rushing streams.

Parenthetical Phrases and Appositives

Parenthetical Phrases and Appositives	Examples
A **parenthetical phrase** adds nonessential information to a sentence. You can leave out a nonessential phrase without changing the meaning of the sentence. Use commas to set off a nonessential phrase.	Most miners did not, **in fact**, find gold. Gold, **every miner's dream**, lay deeply buried.
An **appositive phrase** renames the noun next to it. An appositive phrase usually comes after the noun or pronoun it refers to. Use commas to set off an appositive.	James Marshall, **a mill worker**, started the Gold Rush when he found gold nuggets in 1848.

Clauses with Missing Words	Examples
In an **elliptical clause**, a word or words are left out to shorten a sentence and avoid repetition. You can tell what word is missing by reading the rest of the sentence.	Henry found six nuggets; **James**, **eight**. (You can tell that the missing word is "found.")
You may also combine two or more sentences that are similar and include related information. Some words, usually any pronouns that refer back to the subject, can be left out of the combined sentence. This is called **structural omission**.	James counted his gold nuggets. He put them away. He counted them again later.
In this example, the three sentences are combined, using commas and the conjunction **and**. The pronoun *he* is omitted from the final two sentences.	James counted his gold nuggets, put them away, **and** counted them again later.

Restrictive Relative Clauses	Examples
A **restrictive relative clause** is a clause that begins with a relative pronoun, such as **who**, **whom**, **which**, or **that**. You cannot remove the clause without changing its meaning. Do not use commas.	Only people **who have a ticket** can come in. The man **who found the dog** received a reward.

Coordination and Subordination	Examples
Use **coordination** to join clauses of equal weight, or importance.	Gold was often found next to streams, **and** it was also found deep beneath the earth.
Use **subordination** to join clauses of unequal weight, or importance.	The miners were called '49ers. *main idea*
	Many miners arrived in 1849. *less important detail*
Put the main idea in the main clause and the less important detail in the dependent clause.	The miners were called '49ers because many miners arrived in 1849.

Subjects and Predicates

A **subject** tells who or what the sentence is about. A **predicate** tells something about the subject.

Complete and Simple Subjects	Examples
The **complete subject** includes all the words in the subject.	**Many people** visit our national parks. **My favorite parks** are in the West.
The **simple subject** is the most important word in the complete subject.	Many <u>people</u> visit our national parks. My favorite <u>parks</u> are in the West.

Understood Subject	Examples
When you give a command, you do not state the subject. The subject **you** is understood in an imperative sentence.	Watch the geysers erupt. Soak in the hot springs. See a petrified tree.

It as the Subject	Examples
As the subject of a sentence, the pronoun *it* may refer to a specific noun. Or *it* can be the subject without referring to a specific noun.	See that **stone structure**? **It** is a natural bridge. **It** is amazing to see the natural wonders in these parks.

Complete and Simple Predicate	Examples
The predicate of a sentence tells what the subject is, has, or does. The **complete predicate** includes all the words in the predicate.	People **explore caves in Yellowstone Park**. Many flowers **grow wild throughout the park**. Some people **climb the unusual rock formations**.
The **simple predicate** is the **verb**. It is the most important word in the predicate.	People <u>explore</u> caves in Yellowstone Park. Many flowers <u>grow</u> wild throughout the park. Some people <u>climb</u> the unusual rock formations.

Compound Subject	Examples
A **compound subject** is two or more simple subjects joined by **and** or **or**.	<u>Yosemite</u> and <u>Yellowstone</u> are both in the West. Either <u>spring</u> or <u>fall</u> is a good time to visit.

Compound Predicate	Examples
A **compound predicate** has two or more verbs joined by **and** or **or**.	At Yosemite, some people **fish and swim**. My family **hikes** to the river **or stays** in the cabin. I **have seen** the falls **and have ridden** the trails.

Complete Sentences and Fragments

A **complete sentence** has both a **subject** and a **predicate** and expresses a complete thought. A **fragment** is written like a sentence but is not a complete thought.

Sentences and Fragments	Examples
Begin a complete sentence with a capital letter, and end it with a period or other end mark.	These parks / have many tourist attractions. subject predicate
A **fragment** is a sentence part that is incorrectly used as a complete sentence. For example, the fragment may be missing a subject. Add a subject to correct the problem.	**Incorrect:** Fun to visit because they have many attractions. **Correct:** Parks are fun to visit because they have many attractions.
Writers sometimes use fragments on purpose to emphasize an idea or for another effect.	I did not camp in bear country. **No way. Too dangerous**.

Subject-Verb Agreement

The number of a subject and the number of a verb must agree.

Subject-Verb Agreement	Examples
Use a **singular subject** with a **singular verb**.	Another popular **park is** the Grand Canyon.
Use a **plural subject** with a **plural verb**.	We **were amazed** by the colors of its cliffs.
If the simple subjects in a **compound subject** are connected by **and**, use a plural verb. If the compound subject is connected by **or**, look at the last simple subject. If it is singular, use a **singular verb**. If it is plural, use a **plural verb**.	A **mule** and a **guide are** available for a trip down the canyon. These **rafts** or this **boat is** the best way to go. This **boat** or these **rafts are** the best way to go.
The **subject** and **verb** must agree, even when other words come between them.	The **bikers** in the park **are looking** for animals.
The **subject** and **verb** must agree even if the subject comes after the verb.	There **are** other amazing **parks** in Arizona. Here **is** a **list** of them.

> **Editing Tip**
>
> Read your writing aloud to find mistakes in subject-verb agreement.

> **Grammar Tip**
>
> Subjects and verbs are not in prepositional phrases. Drop these phrases to find the subject and verb more easily.

Parallel Structure

A sentence is **parallel** when all of its parts have the same form.

Parallel Structure	Examples
The parts of a sentence must be **parallel**. Words, phrases, or clauses in a sentence that do the same job should have the same form.	They went hik**ing**, raft**ing**, and horseback rid**ing**. I know **that we must be** in shape to hike the Canyon, **that we have to carry** plenty of water, and **that we need to take and eat** salty snacks.

Mechanics

Proper use of capital letters and correct punctuation is important to effective writing.

Capitalization

Knowing when to use capital letters is an important part of clear writing.

First Word in a Sentence	Examples
Capitalize the first word in a sentence.	**W**e are studying the Lewis and Clark Expedition.

In Direct Quotations	Examples
Capitalize the first word in a **direct quotation**.	Clark said, "**There is great joy in camp**." "**We are in view of the ocean**," he said. "**It's the Pacific Ocean**," he added.

In Letters	Examples
Capitalize the first word used in the **greeting** or in the **closing** of a letter.	**D**ear Kim, **Y**our friend,

In Titles of Works	Examples
All important words in a **title** begin with a capital letter. Articles (**a, an, the**), short conjunctions (**and, but, or, so**), and short prepositions (**at, for, from, in, of, with**, etc.) are not capitalized unless they are the first or last word in the title.	**book:** *The Longest Journey* **poem:** "Leaves of Grass" **magazine:** *Flora and Fauna of Arizona* **newspaper:** *The Denver Post* **song:** "Star-Spangled Banner" **game:** Exploration! **TV series:** "The Gilmore Girls" **movie:** *The Lion King*

Pronoun *I*	Examples
Capitalize the pronoun *I* no matter where it is located in a sentence.	**I** was amazed when **I** learned that Lewis and Clark's expedition was over 8,000 miles.

Proper Nouns and Adjectives	Examples
Common nouns name a general person, place, thing, or idea. Proper nouns name a particular person, place, thing, or idea. All the important words in a **proper noun** start with a capital letter.	**Common Noun:** **t**eam **Proper Noun:** **C**orps of **D**estiny

Proper Nouns and Adjectives, continued	Examples
Proper nouns include the following: • names of people and their titles	**S**tephanie **E**ddins **C**aptain **M**eriwether **L**ewis
Do not capitalize a title if it is used without a name.	The **captain's** co-leader on the expedition was William Clark.
• family titles like **Mom** and **Dad** when they are used as names.	"William Clark is one of our ancestors," **Mom** said. I asked my **mom** whose side of the family he was on, hers or my **dad's**.
• names of organizations	United Nations History Club Wildlife Society
• names of languages and religions	Spanish Christianity
• months, days, special days, and holidays	April Sunday Thanksgiving
Names of geographic places are proper nouns. Capitalize street, city, and state names in mailing addresses.	**Cities and States**: Dallas, Texas **Streets and Roads**: Main Avenue **Bodies of Water**: Pacific Ocean **Countries**: Ecuador **Landforms**: Sahara Desert **Continents**: North America **Public Spaces**: Muir Camp **Buildings, Ships, and Monuments**: *Titanic* **Planets and Heavenly Bodies**: Neptune
A **proper adjective** is formed from a **proper noun**. Capitalize proper adjectives.	Napoleon Bonaparte was from **Europe**. He was a **European** leader in the 1800s.

Grammar Tip

If the family title is preceded by a possessive pronoun, always use lower case.

Abbreviations of Proper Nouns

Abbreviations of geographic places are also capitalized.

Geographic Abbreviations

Words Used in Addresses				Some State Names Used in Mailing Addresses			
Avenue	Ave.	Highway	Hwy.	California	CA	Michigan	MI
Boulevard	Blvd.	Lane	Ln.	Florida	FL	Ohio	OH
Court	Ct.	Place	Pl.	Georgia	GA	Texas	TX
Drive	Dr.	Street	St.	Illinois	IL	Virginia	VA

Abbreviations of Personal Titles

Capitalize abbreviations for a personal title. Follow the same rules for capitalizing a personal title.

Mr. . . . . Mister		**Mrs.** . . . . . . Mistress		**Dr.** . . . . Doctor	
Jr. . . . . Junior		**Capt.** . . . . . Captain		**Sen.** . . . . . . Senator	

Punctuation

Punctuation marks are used to emphasize or clarify meanings.

Apostrophe	Examples
Use an **apostrophe** to punctuate a **possessive noun**. If there is one owner, add **'s** to the owner's name. If the owner's name ends in s, it is correct to add **'s** *or* just the apostrophe. If there is more than one owner, add **'** if the plural noun ends in **s**. Add **'s** if it does not end in **s**.	Mrs. Ramos**'s** sons live in New Mexico. Mrs. Ramos**'** sons live in New Mexico. Her sons**'** birthdays are both in January. She sends cards for her children**'s** birthdays.
Use an **apostrophe** to replace the letters left out of a contraction.	could n~~o~~t = couldn**'t** he w~~oul~~d = he**'d**

> **Grammar Tip**
>
> Never use an apostrophe to form a plural—only to show possession or contraction.

End Marks	Examples
Use a **period** at the end of a statement or a polite command. Use a period after an indirect question. An indirect question tells about a question you asked.	Georgia read the paper to her mom**.** Tell me if there are any interesting articles**.** She asked if there were any articles about the new restaurant on Stone Street near their house**.**
Use a **question mark** at the end of a question. Use a question mark after a tag question that comes at the end of a statement.	What kind of food do they serve**?** The food is good, isn't it**?**
Use an **exclamation point** after an interjection. Use an exclamation point at the end of a sentence to show you feel strongly about something.	Wow**!** The chicken parmesan is delicious**!**

Comma	Examples
Use a comma:	
• before the **coordinating conjunction** in a compound sentence	Soccer is a relatively new sport in the United States, **but** it has been popular in England for a long time.
• to set off words that interrupt a sentence, such as an **appositive phrase** or a **nonrestrictive clause** that is not needed to identify the word it describes	Mr. Okada, **the soccer coach,** had the team practice skills like passing, **for example,** for the first hour. Passing, **which is my favorite skill,** was fun.
• to separate three or more items in a **series**	Shooting, passing, and dribbling are important skills.
• between two or more adjectives that tell equally about the same noun	The midfielder's quick, unpredictable passes made him the team's star player.
• after an **introductory phrase or clause**	**In the last game,** he made several goals.
• to separate a **nonrestrictive phrase** or **clause,** or a **nonrestrictive relative clause.**	The cook, **who used to be a teacher,** made enough soup to feed all of us.
• before someone's exact words and after them if the sentence continues	Mr. Okada said, "Meet the ball after it bounces," as we practiced our half-volleys.
• before and after a **nonrestrictive clause**	At the end of practice, **before anyone left,** Mr. Okada handed out revised game schedules.
• to set off a short phrase at the beginning of a sentence	**At last,** we could go home.
• to separate contrasting phrases	I like to watch movies, **not plays.**
Use a comma in these places in a letter:	
• between the city and the state	Milpas, AK
• between the date and the year	July 3, 2008
• after the greeting of a personal letter	Dear Mr. Okada,
• after the closing of a letter	Sincerely,

Dash	Examples
Use a **dash** to show a break in an idea or the tone in a sentence.	Water—a valuable resource—is often taken for granted.
Or use a dash to emphasize a word, a series of words, a phrase, or a clause.	It is easy to conserve water—wash full loads of laundry, use water-saving devices, fix leaky faucets.

Ellipsis	Examples
Use an **ellipsis** to show that you have left out words.	A recent survey documented ... water usage.
Or use an ellipsis to show an idea that trails off.	The survey reported the amount of water wasted ...

Hyphen	Examples
Use a **hyphen** to:	
• connect words in a number and in a fraction	**One-third** of the people wasted water every day.
• join some words to make a compound word	A **15-year-old boy** and his **great-grandmother** have started an awareness campaign.
• connect a letter to a word	They designed a **T-shirt** for their campaign.
• divide words at the end of a line. Always divide the word between two syllables.	Please join us in our awareness cam-paign.

Italics and Underlining	Examples
When you are using a computer, use **italics** for the names of:	
• magazines and newspapers	I like to read *Time Magazine* and the *Daily News*.
• books	They help me understand our history book, *The U.S. Story*.
• plays	Did you see the play *Abraham Lincoln in Illinois*?
• movies	It was made into the movie *Young Abe*.
• musicals	The musical *Oklahoma!* is about Southwest pioneers.
• music albums	*Greatest Hits from Musicals* is my favorite album.
• TV series	Do you like the singers on the TV show *American Idol*?
If you are using handwriting, underline.	

Parentheses	Examples
Use **parentheses** around extra information in a sentence.	The new story (in the evening paper) is very interesting.

Quotation Marks	Examples
Use **quotation marks** to show:	
• a speaker's exact words	"Listen to this!" Jim said.
• the exact words quoted from a book or other printed material	The announcement in the paper was: "The writer Josie Ramón will be at Milpas Library on Friday."
• the title of a song, poem, short story, magazine article, or newspaper article	Her famous poem "Speaking" appeared in the magazine article "How to Talk to Your Teen."
• the title of a chapter from a book	She'll be reading "Getting Along," a chapter from her new book.
• words used in a special way	We will be "all ears" at the reading.

Grammar Tip

Always put **periods** and **commas** inside quotation marks.

Semicolon	Examples
Use a **semicolon**:	
• to separate two simple sentences used together without a conjunction	A group of Jim's classmates plan to attend the reading; he hopes to join them.
• before a **conjunctive adverb** that joins two simple sentences. Use a comma after the adverb.	Jim wanted to finish reading Josie Ramón's book this evening; **however,** he forgot it at school.
• to separate a group of words in a series if the words in the series already have commas	After school, Jim has to study French, health, and math; walk, feed, and brush the dog; and eat dinner.

Colon	Examples
Use a **colon**:	
• after the greeting in a business letter	Dear Sir or Madam:
• to separate hours and minutes	The restaurant is open until 11:30 p.m.
• to start a list	If you decide to hold your banquet here, we can: 1. Provide a private room 2. Offer a special menu 3. Supply free coffee and lemonade.
• to set off a quotation	According to the review in *The Gazette:* El Gato Azul is *the* best place for tapas.
• to set off a list in running text	Among their best tapas are: fried goat cheese, caprece, and crab quesadilla.
• after a signal word like "the following" or "these"	Be sure to try these: black bean cakes, wontons con queso, and calamari frita.

Spelling

Correct spelling is important for clarity.

How to Be a Better Speller
To learn a new word: • Study the word and look up its meaning.   • Say the word aloud. Listen as you repeat it.   • Picture how the word looks.   • Spell the word aloud several times.   • Write the word several times for practice.   • Use the word often in writing until you are sure of its spelling.   • Keep a notebook of words that are hard for you to spell.   • Use a dictionary to check your spelling.   Knowing spelling rules can help you when you get confused. Use the rules shown in the boxes to help improve your spelling.

Memorize Reliable Generalizations	Examples
Always put a **u** after a **q**.	The **qu**ick but **qu**iet **qu**arterback asked **qu**antities of **qu**estions. *Exceptions:* Iraq Iraqi
Use **i** before **e** except after **c**.	The f**ie**rce rec**ei**ver was ready to catch the ball. *Exceptions:* • **ei**ther, h**ei**ght, th**ei**r, w**ei**rd, s**ei**ze • w**ei**gh, n**ei**ghbor (and other words where **ei** has the long **a** sound)

Spell Correctly	Examples
If a word ends in a consonant plus **y**, change the **y** to **i** before you add -**es**, -**ed**, -**er**, or -**est**.	The coach was the happ**iest** when his players tried their best.
For words that end in a vowel plus **y**, just add -**s** or -**ed**.	For five days before the game, the team sta**yed** at practice an extra 30 minutes.
If you add -**ing** to a verb that ends in -**y**, do not change the **y** to **i**.	The players learned a lot from stud**ying** the videos of their games.

Troubleshooting Guide

In this section you will find helpful solutions to common problems with grammer, usage, and sentences. There is also an alphabetical list of words that are often misused in English. Use these to help improve your writing skills.

Grammar and Usage: Problems and Solutions

Use these solutions to fix grammar and usage problems.

Problems with Nouns

Problem: The sentence has the wrong plural form of an irregular noun.	**Incorrect:** Many deers live there.
Solution: Rewrite the sentence using the correct plural form. (Check a dictionary.)	**Correct:** Many deer live there.
Problem: The noun should be possessive, but it is not.	**Incorrect:** The beginning should capture the readers interest.
Solution: Add an apostrophe to make the noun possessive.	**Correct:** The beginning should capture the readers' interest.

Problems with Pronouns

Problem: The pronoun does not agree in number or gender with the noun it refers to.	**Incorrect:** Mary called Robert, but they did not answer him.
Solution: Match a pronoun's number and gender to the number and gender of the noun it is replacing.	**Correct:** Mary called Robert, but he did not answer her.
Problem: A pronoun does not agree in number with the indefinite pronoun it refers to.	**Incorrect:** Everyone brought their book to class.
Solution: Make the pronoun and the word it refers to agree in number, so that both are singular or plural.	**Correct:** Everyone brought his or her book to class. All the students brought their books to class.
Problem: A reciprocal pronoun does not agree with the number of nouns it refers to.	**Incorrect:** The three boys gave presents to each other.
Solution: Use *each other* when referring to two people, and use *one another* when referring to more than two people.	**Correct:** The three boys gave presents to one another.

Troubleshooting Guide

Grammar and Usage: Problems and Solutions, continued

Problems with Pronouns, continued

Problem: It is hard to tell which noun in a compound subject is referred to or replaced. **Solution:** Replace the unclear pronoun with the noun it refers to.	**Incorrect:** Ana and Dawn own a car, but only she drives it. **Correct:** Ana and Dawn own a car, but only Dawn drives it.
Problem: It is unclear which antecedent a pronoun refers to. **Solution:** Rewrite the sentence to make it clearer.	**Incorrect:** The kitten's mother scratched its ear. **Correct:** The mother cat scratched her kitten's ear.
Problem: The object pronoun *them* is used as a demonstrative adjective. **Solution:** Replace *them* with the correct demonstrative adjectives.	**Incorrect:** Were any of them packages delivered? **Correct:** Were any of those packages delivered?
Problem: An object pronoun is used in a compound subject. *Remember that subjects do actions and objects receive actions.* **Solution:** Replace the object pronoun with a subject pronoun.	**Incorrect:** My brother and me rebuild car engines. **Correct:** My brother and I rebuild car engines.
Problem: A subject pronoun is used in a compound object. **Solution:** Replace the subject pronoun with an object pronoun.	**Incorrect:** Leticia asked my brother and I to fix her car. **Correct:** Leticia asked my brother and me to fix her car.
Problem: A subject pronoun is used as the object of a preposition. **Solution:** Replace the subject pronoun with an object pronoun.	**Incorrect:** Give your timesheet to Colin or I. **Correct:** Give your timesheet to Colin or me.
Problem: The subject pronoun *who* is used as an object. **Solution:** Replace *who* with the object pronoun *whom*.	**Incorrect:** Who am I speaking to? **Correct:** Whom am I speaking to?
Problem: The object pronoun *whom* is used as a subject. **Solution:** Replace *whom* with the subject pronoun *who*.	**Incorrect:** Whom shall I say is calling? **Correct:** Who shall I say is calling?

Problems with Verbs

Problem:	Incorrect:
In a sentence with two verbs, the tense of the second verb doesn't match the first.	Yesterday, Alberto called me and says he has tickets for the game.
Solution:	**Correct:**
Keep the verb tense the same unless there is a change in time, such as from past to present.	Yesterday, Alberto called me and said he had tickets for the game.
Problem:	**Incorrect:**
The -*ed* ending is missing from a regular past-tense verb.	This morning, I ask my brother to go with us.
Solution:	**Correct:**
Add the -*ed* ending.	This morning, I asked my brother to go with us.
Problem:	**Incorrect:**
The wrong form of an irregular verb is used.	We brang our portable TV to the game.
Solution:	**Correct:**
Replace the wrong form with the correct one. (Check a dictionary.)	We brought our portable TV to the game.
Problem:	**Incorrect:**
The participle form is used when the past-tense form is required.	After the game, we run over to Marcia's house.
Solution:	**Correct:**
Replace the wrong form with the correct one. (Check a dictionary.)	After the game, we ran over to Marcia's house.
Problem:	**Poor:**
The passive voice is overused.	A new activity schedule will be created by the camp counselors. Several fun activities are being considered by the counselors.
Solution:	**Better:**
Put the sentence in the active voice so that the subject does the action instead of receiving it.	The camp counselors are creating a new activity schedule. The counselors are considering several fun activities.
Problem:	**Poor:**
The sentence has a split infinitive.	The boy wanted to slowly walk to school.
Solution:	**Better:**
Rewrite the sentence to keep the infinitive as a single unit.	The boy wanted to walk to school slowly.

Problems with Adjectives

Problem: The sentence contains a double comparison, using both an *-er* ending and the word *more*, for example.	**Incorrect:** Joseph is more older than he looks.
Solution: Delete the incorrect comparative form.	**Correct:** Joseph is older than he looks.
Problem: The wrong form of an irregular adjective appears in a sentence that makes a comparison.	**Incorrect:** Cal feels worser since he ran out of medicine.
Solution: Replace the wrong form with the correct one. (Check a dictionary.)	**Correct:** Cal feels worse since he ran out of medicine.
Problem: The wrong demonstrative adjective is used.	**Incorrect:** That car here is really fast. This car there is not as fast.
Solution: Use *this* or the plural *these* for things that are near or "here." Use *that* or the plural *those* for things that are farther away or "there."	**Correct:** This car here is really fast. That car there is not as fast.
Problem: The adjective *good* is used to modify a verb.	**Incorrect:** Julia did good on her test.
Solution: Rewrite the sentence using the adverb *well*, or add a noun for the adjective to describe.	**Correct:** Julia did well on her test. Julia did a good job on her test.

Problems with Adverbs

Problem: An adverb is used to modify a noun or pronoun after the linking verb *feel*.	**Incorrect:** I feel badly about the mistake.
Solution: Rewrite the sentence using an adjective.	**Correct:** I feel bad about the mistake.
Problem: An adverb is used but does not modify anything in the sentence.	**Incorrect:** Hopefully, I didn't make too many mistakes on the test.
Solution: Rewrite the sentence changing the adverb to a verb.	**Correct:** I hope I didn't make too many mistakes on the test.
Problem: Two negative words are used to express one idea.	**Incorrect:** We don't have no aspirin.
Solution: Change one negative word to a positive word.	**Correct:** We don't have any aspirin.

Sentences: Problems and Solutions

Some problems with sentences in English are the result of missing parts of speech or incorrect punctuation. Two common problems are sentence fragments and run on sentences.

Problems with Sentence Fragments

Problem: An infinitive phrase is punctuated as a complete sentence. **Solution:** Add a complete sentence to the phrase.	**Incorrect:** To show students alternative ways to learn. **Correct:** To show students alternative ways to learn, Mr. Harris organized the trip.
Problem: A clause starting with a relative pronoun is punctuated as a complete sentence. **Solution:** Add a subject and predicate to the sentence.	**Incorrect:** Who might be interested in going on the trip. **Correct:** Anyone who might be interested in going on the trip should see Mr. Harris.
Problem: A participial phrase is punctuated as a complete sentence. **Solution:** Add a sentence to the participial phrase.	**Incorrect:** When traveling overseas. **Correct:** When traveling overseas, always try to speak to people in their native language.

Problems with Run On Sentences

Problem: Two main clauses are separated by a comma. This is known as a comma splice. **Solution:** Add a semicolon between the clauses.	**Incorrect:** Many music students fail to practice regularly, this is frustrating for teachers. **Correct:** Many music students fail to practice regularly; this is frustrating for teachers.
Problem: Two or more main clauses are run together with no punctuation. This is known as a fused sentence. **Solution:** Change one of the clauses into a subordinate clause. Rewrite the sentence as two sentences.	**Incorrect:** I started playing guitar when I was twelve I thought I was great I knew very little. **Correct:** I thought I was great when I started playing guitar at age twelve. I knew very little!
Problem: Two or more main clauses are joined with a conjunction, but without a comma. **Solution:** Use a comma after the first main clause and before the conjunction.	**Incorrect:** I continued to take lessons and I realized that I had much to learn to become a good guitarist. **Correct:** I continued to take lessons, and I realized that I had much to learn to become a good guitarist.

Words Often Confused

This section will help you to choose between words that are often confused.

a lot, allot

A lot means "many" and is always written as two words, never as one word. *Allot* means "to assign."

> I have **a lot** of friends who like to run.

> We are **allotted** 30 minutes for lunch.

a while, awhile

The two-word form *a while* is a noun phrase and is often preceded by the prepositions *after*, *for*, or *in*. The one-word form *awhile* is an adverb and cannot be used with a preposition.

> Let's stop here for **a while**.

> Let's stop here **awhile**.

accept, except

Accept is a verb that means "to receive." *Except* can be a verb meaning "to leave out" or a preposition meaning "excluding."

> I **accept** everything you say, **except** your point about music.

advice, advise

Advice is a noun that means "ideas about how to solve a problem." *Advise* is a verb and means "to give advice."

> I will give you **advice** about your problem today, but do not ask me to **advise** you again tomorrow.

affect, effect

Affect is a verb. It means "to cause a change in" or "to influence." *Effect* as a verb means "to bring about." As a noun, *effect* means "a result."

> The sunshine will **affect** my plants.

> The governor is working to **effect** change.

> The rain had no **effect** on our spirits.

aren't

Ain't is not used in formal English. Use the correct form of the verb *be* with the word *not*: *is not, isn't; are not,* or *aren't.*

> We **are not going to sing** in front of you.

> I **am not going to practice** today.

all ready, already

Use the two-word form, *all ready*, to mean "completely finished." Use the one-word form, *already*, to mean "before."

> We waited an hour for dinner to be **all ready**.

> It is a good thing I have **already** eaten today.

all right

The expression *all right* means "OK" and should be written as two words. The one-word form, *alright*, is not used in formal writing.

> I hope it is **all right** that I am early.

all together, altogether

The two-word form, *all together*, means "in a group." The one-word form, *altogether*, means "completely."

> It is **altogether** wrong that we will not be **all together** this holiday.

among, between

Use *among* when comparing more than two people or things. Use *between* when comparing a person or thing with one other person, thing, or group.

> You are **among** friends.

> We will split the money **between** Sal and Jess.

amount of, number of

Amount of is used with nouns that cannot be counted. *Number of* is used with nouns that can be counted.

> The **amount of** pollution in the air is increasing.

> A record **number of** people attended the game.

assure, ensure, insure

Assure means "to make feel better." *Ensure* means "to guarantee." *Insure* means "to cover financially."

> I **assure** you that he is OK.

> I will personally **ensure** his safety.

> If the car is **insured,** the insurance company will pay to fix the damage.

being as, being that

Neither of these is used in formal English. Use *because* or *since* instead.

> I went home early **because** I was sick.

beside, besides

Beside means "next to." *Besides* means "plus" or "in addition to."

> Located **beside** the cafeteria is a vending machine.

> **Besides** being the fastest runner, she is also the nicest team member.

bring, take

Bring means "to carry closer." *Take* means "to grasp." *Take* is often used with the preposition *away* to mean "carry away from."

> Please **bring** the dictionary to me and **take** the thesaurus from my desk.

bust, busted

Neither of these is used in formal English. Use *broke* or *broken* instead.

> I **broke** the vase by accident.

> The **broken** vase cannot be fixed.

can't; hardly; scarcely

Do not use *can't* with *hardly* or *scarcely*. That would be a double negative. Use only *can't*, or use *can* plus a negative word.

> I **can't** get my work done in time.

> I **can scarcely** get my work done in time.

capital, capitol

A *capital* is a place where a government is located. A *capitol* is an actual government building.

> The **capital** of the U.S. is Washington, D.C.

> The senate met at the **capitol** to vote.

cite, site, sight

To *cite* means "to quote a source." A *site* is "a place." *Sight* can mean "the ability to see" or it can mean "something that can be seen."

> Be sure to **cite** all your sources.

> My brother works on a construction **site**.

> Dan went to the eye doctor to have his **sight** checked.

> The sunset last night was a beautiful **sight**.

complement, compliment

Complement means "something that completes" or "to complete." *Compliment* means "something nice someone says about another person" or "to praise."

> The colors you picked really **complement** each other.

> I would like to **compliment** you on your new shoes.

could have, should have, would have, might have

Be sure to use "have," not "of," with words like *could*, *should*, *would*, and *might*.

> I **would have** gone, but I didn't feel well.

council, counsel

A *council* is a group that gives advice. To *counsel* is to give advice to someone.

> The city **council** met to discuss traffic issues.

> Mom, please **counsel** me on how to handle this situation.

coup d'état, coup de grâce

A *coup d'état* ("stroke of state") usually refers to the overthrow of a government. A coup de *grâce* ("stroke, or blow, or mercy") refers to a final action that brings victory.

different from, different than

Different from is preferred in formal English and is used when the comparison is between two persons or things. *Different than*, when used, is used with full clauses.

> My interest in music is **different from** my friend's.

> Movies today are **different than** they used to be in the 1950s.

each other, one another

Each other refers to two people. *One another* refers to more than two people.

> Mika and I gave **each other** presents for Christmas.

The five of us looked out for **one another** on the field trip.

farther, further

Farther refers to a physical distance. *Further* refers to time or amount.

If you go down the road a little **farther**, you will see the sign.

We will discuss this **further** at lunch.

fewer, less

Fewer refers to things that can be counted individually. *Less* refers to things that cannot be counted individually.

The farm had **fewer** animals than the zoo, so it was **less** fun to visit.

good, well

The adjective *good* means "kind." The adjective *well* means "healthy." The adverb *well* means "ably."

She is a **good** person.

I am glad to see that you are **well** again after that illness.

You have performed **well**.

immigrate to, emigrate from

Immigrate to means "to move to a country." *Emigrate from* means "to leave a country."

I **immigrated to** America in 2001 from Panama.

I **emigrated from** El Salvador because of the war.

it's, its

It's is a contraction of *it is*. *Its* is a possessive word meaning "belonging to it."

It's going to be a hot day.

The dog drank all of **its** water already.

kind of, sort of

These words mean "a type of." In formal English, do not use them to mean "partly." Use *somewhat* or *rather* instead.

The peanut is actually a **kind of** bean.

I feel **rather** silly in this outfit.

lay, lie

Lay means "to put in a place." It is used to describe what people do with objects. *Lie* means "to recline." People can *lie* down, but they *lay* down objects. Do not confuse this use of *lie* with the noun that means "an untruth."

I will **lay** the book on this desk for you.

She **lay** the baby in his crib.

I'm tired and am going to **lie** on the couch.

If you **lie** in court, you will be punished.

learn, teach

To *learn* is "to receive information." To *teach* is "to give information."

If we want to **learn**, we have to listen.

She will **teach** us how to drive.

leave (alone), let

Leave alone means "not to disturb someone." *Let* means "to allow or permit."

Leave her **alone**, and she will be fine.

Let them go.

like, as

Like can be used either as a preposition or as a verb meaning "to care about something." *As* is a conjunction and should be used to introduce a subordinate clause.

She sometimes acts **like** a princess. But I still **like** her.

She acts **as** if she owns the school.

loose, lose

Loose can be used as an adverb or adjective meaning "free" or "not securely attached." The verb *lose* means "to misplace" or "not to win."

I let the dog **loose** and he is missing.

Did you **lose** your homework?

Did they **lose** the game by many points?

passed, past

Passed is a verb that means "moved ahead of" or "succeeded." *Past* is a noun that means "the time before the present."

The car **passed** us quickly.

I **passed** my English test.

Poor grades are in the **past** now.

precede, proceed

Precede means "to come before." *Proceed* means "to go forward."

> Prewriting **precedes** drafting in the writing process.

> Turn left; then **proceed** down the next street.

principal, principle

A *principal* is "a person of authority." Principal can also mean "main." A *principle* is "a general truth or belief."

> The **principal** of our school makes an announcement every morning.

> The **principal** ingredient in baking is flour.

> The essay was based on the **principles** of effective persuasion.

raise, rise

The verb *raise* takes an object and means "to lift" or "to be brought up." The verb *rise* means "to lift oneself up." People can *rise*, but objects are *raised*.

> **Raise** the curtain for the play.

> She **raises** baby rabbits on her farm.

> I **rise** from bed every morning at six.

real, really

Real means "actual." It is an adjective used to describe nouns. *Really* means "actually" or "truly." It is an adverb used to describe verbs, adjectives, or other adverbs.

> The diamond was **real**.

> The diamond was **really** beautiful.

set, sit

The verb *set* usually means "to put something down." The verb *sit* means "to go into a seated position."

> I **set** the box on the ground.

> Please **sit** while we talk.

than, then

Than is used to compare things. *Then* means "next" and is used to tell when something took place.

> She likes fiction more **than** nonfiction.

> First, we will go to town; **then** we will go home.

they're, their, there

They're is the contraction of *they are*. *Their* is the possessive form of the pronoun *they*. *There* is used to indicate location.

> **They're** all on vacation this week.

> I want to use **their** office.

> The library is right over **there**.

> **There** are several books I want to read.

this, these, that, those

This indicates something specific that is near someone. *These* is the plural form. *That* indicates something specific that is farther from someone. *Those* is the plural form of *that*.

> **This** book in my hand belongs to me. **These** pens are also mine.

> **That** book is his. **Those** notes are his, too.

where

Do not use *at* or *to* after *where*. Simply use *where*.

> The restaurant is **where** I am right now.

> **Where** is Ernesto?

who, whom

Who is a subject. *Whom* is an object.

> **Who** is going to finish first?

> My grandmother is a woman to **whom** I owe many thanks.

who's, whose

Who's is a contraction of *who is*. *Whose* is the possessive form of *who*.

> **Who's** coming to our dinner party?

> **Whose** car is parked in the garage?

you're, your

You're is a contraction of *you are*. *Your* is a possessive adjective meaning "belonging to you."

> **You're** going to be late if you don't hurry.

> Is that **your** backpack under the couch?

Grammar Tip

If you can replace *who* or *whom* with *he*, *she*, or *they*, use *who*. If you can replace the word with *him*, *her*, or *them*, use *whom*.

Literary Terms

A

Alliteration The repetition of the same sounds (usually consonants) at the beginning of words that are close together. *Example:* Molly makes magnificent mousse, though Pablo prefers pecan pie.

See *also* **Assonance; Consonance; Repetition**

Allusion A key form of literary language, in which one text makes the reader think about another text that was written before it. Allusion can also mean a reference to a person, place, thing, or event that is not specifically named. *Example:* When Hannah wrote in her short story that vanity was the talented main character's "Achilles heel," her teacher understood that Hannah was referring to a character in a Greek myth. So, she suspected that the vanity of the main character in Hannah's short story would prove to be the character's greatest weakness.

See *also* **Connotation; Literature; Poetry**

Analogy A way of illustrating a thing or an idea by comparing it with a more familiar thing or idea. *Example: Blogs* are to the *Internet* as *journals* are to *paper.*

See *also* **Illustration; Metaphor; Rhetorical device; Simile**

Antagonist A major character who opposes the main character, or protagonist, in a fictional narrative or a play. *Example:* In many fairy tales, a wolf is the antagonist.

See *also* **Protagonist**

Argument A type of writing or speaking that supports a position or attempts to convince the reader or listener. Arguments include a claim that is supported by reasons and evidence.

See *also* **Claim; Reason; Evidence**

Article A short piece of nonfiction writing on a specific topic. Articles usually appear in newspapers and magazines.

See *also* **Nonfiction; Topic**

Assonance The repetition of the same or similar vowel sounds between consonants in words that are close together. *Example:* The expression, "mad as a hatter."

See *also* **Alliteration; Consonance; Repetition**

Autobiography The story of a person's life, written by that person. *Example:* Mahatma Gandhi wrote an autobiography titled *Gandhi: An Autobiography: The Story of My Experiments With Truth.*

See *also* **Biography; Diary; Journal; Memoir; Narration; Personal narrative**

B

Biography The story of a person's life, written by another person.

See *also* **Autobiography; Narration**

Blank verse A form of unrhymed verse in which each line normally has 10 syllables divided into five pairs of one unstressed and one stressed syllable. Of all verse forms, blank verse comes closest to the natural rhythms of English speech. Consequently, it has been used more often, in more ways than any other verse form in English. *Example:* Today she darts from the room with delight./Bizarre she does seem, like a haughty queen./I long to make her hot cinnamon tea/ One day, she will love me as I do her./

See *also* **Meter; Rhyme; Stress; Verse**

C

Character A person, an animal, or an imaginary creature in a work of fiction.

See *also* **Characterization; Character traits; Fiction**

Characterization The way a writer creates and develops a character. Writers use a variety of ways to bring a character to life: through descriptions of the character's appearance, thoughts, feelings, and actions; through the character's words; and through the words or thoughts of other characters.

See *also* **Character; Character traits; Dynamic character; Motive; Point of view; Short story; Static character**

Character traits The special qualities of personality that writers give their characters.

    See also **Character; Characterization**

Claim A statement that clearly identifies an author's ideas or opinion.

    See also **Argument, Reason, Evidence**

Climax The turning point or most important event in a plot.

    See also **Falling action; Plot; Rising action**

Comedy A play or a fictional story written mainly to amuse an audience. Most comedies end happily for the leading characters.

    See also **Drama; Narration; Play**

Complication *See* **Rising action**

Conflict The main problem faced by the protagonist in a story or play. The protagonist may be involved in a struggle against nature, another character (usually the *antagonist*), or society. The struggle may also be between two elements in the protagonist's mind.

    See also **Plot**

Connotation The feelings suggested by a word or phrase, apart from its dictionary meaning. *Example:* The terms "used car" and "previously owned vehicle" have different connotations. To most people, the phrase "previously owned vehicle" sounds better than "used car."

    See also **Denotation; Poetry**

Consonance The repetition of the same or similar consonant sounds that come after different vowel sounds in words that are close together. *Example:* Sid did bid on a squid, he did.

    See also **Alliteration; Assonance; Repetition**

D

Denotation The dictionary meaning of a word or phrase. Denotation is especially important in functional texts and other types of nonfiction used to communicate information precisely.

    See also **Connotation; Functional text; Nonfiction**

Description Writing that creates a "picture" of a person, place, or thing—often using language that appeals to the five senses: sight, hearing, touch, smell, and taste. *Example:* The bright, hot sun beat down on Earth's surface. Where once a vibrant lake cooled the skin of hippos and zebras, only thin, dry cracks remained, reaching across the land like an old man's fingers, as far as the eye could see. The smell of herds was gone, and only silence filled the space.

    See also **Imagery**

Dialect A form of a language commonly spoken in a certain place or by a certain group of people—especially a form that differs from the one most widely accepted. Dialect includes special words or phrases as well as particular pronunciations and grammar. Writers use dialect to help make their characters and settings lively and realistic. *Example:* While someone from the southern United States might say "ya'll" when referring to several friends, someone from the Northeast or Midwest might say "you guys."

    See also **Diction; Jargon**

Dialogue What characters say to each other. Writers use dialogue to develop characters, move the plot forward, and add interest. In most writing, dialogue is set off by quotation marks; in play scripts, however, dialogue appears without quotation marks.

Diary A book written by a person about his or her own life as it is happening. Unlike an autobiography, a diary is not usually meant to be published. It is made up of entries that are written shortly after events occur. The person writing a diary often expresses feelings and opinions about what has happened.

    See also **Autobiography; Journal**

Drama A kind of writing, in verse or prose, in which a plot unfolds in the words and actions of characters performed by actors. Two major genres of drama are comedy and tragedy.

    See also **Comedy; Genre; Play; Plot; Tragedy**

Dramatic conventions The usual ways of making drama seem real. Dramatic conventions include imagining that actors really are the characters they pretend to be and that a stage really is the place it represents.

Dynamic character A character who changes because of actions and experiences.

> *See also* **Character; Static character**

E

Editorial An article in a newspaper or magazine that gives the opinions of the editors or publishers. *Example:* Rather than just reporting the facts, a newspaper editorial might argue that the city government should not clear preserved woodlands in order to build a shopping mall.

Electronic text Writing that a computer can store or display on a computer screen. Forms of electronic text include *Web sites* (groupings of World Wide Web pages that usually contain hyperlinks), *blogs* (Web logs—sites maintained by an individual or organization that contain various kinds of informal writing, such as diaries, opinion pieces, and stories), and *e-mail*.

Epic A long, fictional, narrative poem, written in a lofty style, that celebrates the great deeds of one or more heroes or heroines. *Example:* Homer's *The Odyssey* is a famous epic poem of over 12,000 lines. The hero, Odysseus, spends ten years overcoming various obstacles in order to return home to his wife and son after the end of the Trojan War.

> *See also* **Fiction; Hero** or **Heroine; Poetry**

Essay A short piece of nonfiction, normally in prose, that discusses a single topic without claiming to do so thoroughly. Its purpose may be to inform, entertain, or persuade.

> *See also* **Exposition; Nonfiction; Persuasion; Photo-essay; Review; Topic**

Evidence Information provided to support a claim. Facts, statistics, and quotes from experts are commonly used as evidence.

> *See also* **Argument; Claim; Reasons**

Exposition The rising action of a story in which characters and the problems they face are introduced.

> *See also* **Description; Functional text; Narration; Persuasion; Rising action**

F

Fable A brief fictional narrative that teaches a lesson about life. Many fables have animals instead of humans as characters. Fables often end with a short, witty statement of their lesson. *Example:* "The Tortoise and the Hare" is a famous fable in which a boastful, quick-moving hare challenges a slow-moving tortoise to a race. Because the overconfident hare takes a nap during the race, the tortoise wins. The moral of the fable is that slow and steady wins the race.

> *See also* **Fiction; Folk tale; Narration**

Falling action The actions and events in a plot that happen after the climax. Usually, the major problem is solved in some way, so the remaining events serve to bring the story to an end.

> *See also* **Climax; Conflict; Plot, Rising action**

Fantasy Fiction in which imaginary worlds differ from the "real" world outside the text. Fairy tales, science fiction, and fables are examples of fantasy.

> *See also* **Fable; Fiction; Science fiction**

Fiction Narrative writing about imaginary people, places, things, or events.

> *See also* **Fable; Fantasy; Folk tale; Historical fiction; Myth; Narration; Nonfiction; Novel; Realistic fiction; Science fiction; Short story; Tall tale**

Figurative language The use of a word or phrase to say one thing and mean another. Figurative language is especially important in literature and poetry because it gives writers a more effective way of expressing what they mean than using direct, literal language. *Example:* Upon receiving her monthly bills, Victoria complained that she was "drowning in debt."

> *See also* **Hyperbole; Idiom; Imagery; Irony; Literature; Metaphor; Personification; Poetry; Simile; Symbol**

Flashback An interruption in the action of a narrative to tell about something that happened earlier. It is often used to give the reader background information about a character or situation.

> *See also* **Character; Narration**

Folk literature The collection of a people's literary works shared mainly orally rather than in writing. Such works include spells, songs, ballads (songs that tell a story), jokes, riddles, proverbs, nursery rhymes, and folk tales.

> *See also* **Folk tale; Folklore; Literature; Song lyrics**

Folk tale A short, fictional narrative shared orally rather than in writing, and thus partly changed through its retellings before being written down. Folk tales include myths, legends, fables, tall tales, ghost stories, and fairy tales.

> *See also* **Fable; Folk literature; Myth; Tall tale**

Folklore The collection of a people's beliefs, customs, rituals, spells, songs, sayings, and stories as shared mainly orally rather than in writing.

> *See also* **Folk literature; Folk tale**

Foreshadowing A hint that a writer gives about an event that will happen later in a story. *Example:* In a story about a teenage girl who starts getting into trouble, an early scene may show her friend stealing earrings from a jewelry store. Later the girl herself begins stealing. Based on the earlier scene, the reader might guess this is what the girl would do.

Free verse Writing that is free of meter, and thus not really verse at all. It is closer to rhythmic prose or speech. But like verse, and unlike prose or speech, it is arranged in lines, which divide the text into units of rhythm. Free verse may be rhymed or unrhymed.

> *See also* **Meter; Prose; Rhyme; Rhythm; Verse**

Functional text Writing in which the main purpose is to communicate the information people need to accomplish tasks in everyday life. *Examples:* résumés, business letters, instruction manuals, and the help systems of word-processing programs.

G

Genre A type or class of literary works grouped according to form, style, and/or topic. Major genres include fictional narrative prose (such as short stories and most novels), nonfiction narrative prose (such as autobiographies, historical accounts, and memoirs), drama (such as comedies and tragedies), verse (such as lyrics and epics), and the essay.

> *See also* **Essay; Fiction; Literature; Narration; Nonfiction; Prose; Style; Topic; Verse**

H

Haiku A form of short, unrhymed poetry that expresses a moment of sudden, intensely felt awareness. The words in haiku focus on what can be seen, smelled, tasted, touched, or heard. The haiku was invented in Japan, and it traditionally consists of 17 syllables in three lines of 5, 7, and 5 syllables. *Example:*

Gold, red leaves rustle
A baby cries somewhere near
Blue sky fades to gray.

> *See also* **Imagery; Lyric; Poetry**

Hero or **Heroine** In myths and legends, a man or woman of great courage and strength who is celebrated for his or her daring feats; also, any protagonist, or main character.

> *See also* **Myth; Protagonist**

Historical account A piece of nonfiction writing about something that happened in the past.

> *See also* **Memoir; Nonfiction**

Historical fiction Fiction based on events that actually happened or on people who actually lived. It may be written from the point of view of a "real" or an imaginary character, and it usually includes invented dialogue.

> *See also* **Fiction**

Humor A type of writing meant to be funny in a good-natured way. It often makes what characters look like, say, or do seem serious to them but ridiculous to the reader.

> *See also* **Parody**

Hyperbole Figurative language that exaggerates, often to the point of being funny, to emphasize something. *Example:* When his mother asked how long he had waited for the school bus that morning, Jeremy grinned and said, "Oh, not long. Only about a million years."

See also **Figurative language; Tall tale**

I

Idiom A phrase or expression that means something different from the word or words' dictionary meanings. Idioms cannot be translated word for word into another language because an idiom's meaning is not the same as that of the individual words that make it up. *Example:* "Mind your p's and q's" in English means to be careful, thoughtful, and behave properly.

Illustration Writing that uses examples to support a main idea. Illustration is often used to help the reader understand general, abstract, or complex ideas.

Imagery Figurative language that communicates sensory experience. Imagery can help the reader imagine how people, places, and things look, sound, taste, smell, and feel. It can also make the reader think about emotions and ideas that commonly go with certain sensations. Because imagery appeals to the senses, it is sometimes called *sensory language*.

See also **Description; Figurative language; Symbol**

Interview A discussion between two or more people in which questions are asked and answered so that the interviewer can get information. The record of such a discussion is also called an interview.

Irony A type of figurative language that takes three forms: (1) *verbal irony* means the opposite of what is said, or it means both what is said and the opposite of what is said, at once; (2) *dramatic irony* (a) contrasts what a speaker or character says with what the writer means or thinks, or (b) in a story, presents a speech or an action that means more to the audience than to the character who speaks or performs it, because the audience knows something the character does not; (3)

situational irony (a) contrasts an actual situation with what would seem appropriate, or (b) contrasts what one expects with what actually happens. *Examples:* 1. Verbal Irony: After having her car towed, getting drenched in a thunderstorm, and losing her wallet, Kate told her friend, "Let me tell you, today has been a real picnic."
2. Dramatic Irony: In the final scene of William Shakespeare's play *Romeo and Juliet*, Romeo finds Juliet drugged. While the audience knows that she is still alive, Romeo presumes that she is dead and decides to kill himself. Juliet shortly thereafter awakes and, upon finding Romeo dead, kills herself.
3. Situational Irony: In O. Henry's short story "The Gift of the Magi," a husband and wife each want to buy a Christmas present for the other. The wife buys her husband a chain for his watch; the husband buys the wife combs for her hair. To get enough money to buy these gifts, the wife cuts and sells her hair, and the husband sells his watch.

See also **Figurative language**

J

Jargon Specialized language used by people to describe things that are specific to their group or subject. *Example: Mouse* in a computer class means "part of a computer system," not "a rodent."

See also **Dialect; Diction**

Journal A personal record, similar to a diary. It may include accounts of actual events, stories, poems, sketches, thoughts, essays, a collection of interesting information, or just about anything the writer wishes to include.

See also **Diary**

L

Literature A body of written works in prose or verse.

See also **Functional text; Poetry; Prose; Verse**

Literary criticism The careful study and discussion of works of literature, mainly to understand them and judge their effectiveness.

See also **Literature**

Lyric One of the main types of poetry. Lyrics tend to be short and songlike, and express the state of mind—or the process of observing, thinking, and feeling—of a single "speaker."

See also **Haiku; Poetry; Song lyrics; Sonnet**

M

Memoir A written account of people the author has known and events he or she has witnessed. *Example:* Elie Wiesel's novel *Night* is a memoir. It documents his personal experiences in a concentration camp during World War II.

See also **Autobiography; Historical account**

Metaphor A type of figurative language that compares two unlike things by saying that one thing is the other thing. *Example:* Dhara says her grandfather can be a real mule when he doesn't get enough sleep.

See also **Figurative language; Simile; Symbol**

Meter The patterning of language into regularly repeating units of rhythm. Language patterned in this way is called *verse*. Most verse in English has been written in one of two main types of meter: (1) *accentual*, which depends on the number of stressed syllables in a line; (2) *accentual-syllabic*, which depends on the number of stressed and unstressed syllables in a line. By varying the rhythm within a meter, the writer can heighten the reader's attention to what is going on in the verse and reinforce meaning.

See also **Poetry; Rhythm; Stress; Verse**

Mood The overall feeling or atmosphere a writer creates in a piece of writing.

See also **Tone**

Motive The reason a character has for his or her thoughts, feelings, actions, or words. *Example:* Maria's motive for bringing cookies to her new neighbors was to learn what they were like.

See also **Characterization**

Myth A fictional narrative, often a folk tale, that tells of supernatural events as a way of explaining natural events and their relation to human life. Myths commonly involve gods, goddesses, monsters, and superhuman heroes or heroines.

See also **Folk tale; Hero** or **Heroine**

N

Narration The telling of events (a story), mostly through explanation and description, rather than through dialogue.

See also **Narrator; Point of view; Story**

Narrative Writing that gives an account of a set of real or imaginary events (the story), which the writer selects and arranges in a particular order (the plot). Narrative writing includes nonfiction works such as news articles, autobiographies, and historical accounts, as well as fictional works such as short stories, novels, and epics.

See also **Autobiography; Fiction; Historical account; Narrator; Nonfiction; Plot; Story**

Narrator Someone who gives an account of events. In fiction, the narrator is the teller of a story (as opposed to the real author, who invented the narrator as well as the story). Narrators differ in how much they participate in a story's events. In a first-person narrative, the narrator is the "I" telling the story. In a third-person narrative, the narrator is not directly involved in the events and refers to characters by name or as *he, she, it,* or *they.* Narrators also differ in how much they know and how much they can be trusted by the reader.

See also **Character; Narration; Point of view; Voice**

Nonfiction Written works about events or things that are not imaginary; writing other than fiction.

See also **Autobiography; Biography; Diary; Encyclopedia; Essay; Fiction; Historical account; Journal; Memoir; Personal narrative; Photo-essay; Report; Textbook**

Novel A long, fictional narrative, usually in prose. Its length enables it to have more characters, a more complicated plot, and a more fully developed setting than shorter works of fiction.

See also **Character; Fiction; Narration; Plot; Prose; Setting; Short story**

O

Onomatopoeia The use of words that imitate the sounds they refer to. *Examples: buzz, slam, hiss*

P

Paradox A statement or an expression that seems to contradict itself but may, when thought about further, begin to make sense and seem true. Paradox can shock the reader into attention, thus underscoring the truth of what is being said. *Example:* The Time Paradox: A man travels back in time and kills his grandfather. The paradox is that if he killed his grandfather, the man himself never would have been born.

Parody A piece of writing meant to amuse by imitating the style or features of another (usually serious) piece. It makes fun of the original by taking the elements it imitates to extreme or ridiculous lengths or by applying them to a lowly or comically inappropriate subject. *Example:* In 1729, Jonathan Swift wrote a pamphlet titled "A Modest Proposal." In it, he outrageously recommends that the poor sell their children as food to the wealthy in order to make money. "A Modest Proposal" is a parody of similar pamphlets distributed by the wealthy business class, whose practices, Swift believed, neglected human costs and made it difficult for the poor to overcome poverty.

> *See also* **Genre; Humor; Style**

Personal narrative An account of a certain event or set of events in a person's life, written by that person.

> *See also* **Autobiography; Narration**

Personification Figurative language that describes animals, things, or ideas as having human traits. *Examples:* in the movie *Babe* and in the book *Charlotte's Web*, the animals are all personified

> *See also* **Figurative language**

Persuasion Writing that attempts to get someone to do or agree to something by appealing to logic or emotion. Persuasive writing is used in advertisements, editorials, sermons, and political speeches.

> *See also* **Description; Editorial; Exposition; Narration; Rhetorical device**

Photo-essay A short nonfiction piece made up of photographs and captions. The photographs are as important as the words in giving information to the reader.

> *See also* **Essay; Nonfiction**

Play A work of drama, especially one written to be performed on a stage. *Example:* Lorraine Hansberry's *A Raisin in the Sun*

> *See also* **Drama**

Plot The pattern of events and situations in a story or play. Plot is usually divided into four main parts: *conflict* (or *problem*), *rising action* (or *exposition* or *complication*), *climax*, and *falling action* (or *resolution*).

> *See also* **Climax; Conflict; Drama; Falling action; Fiction; Narration; Rising action; Story**

Poetry A form of literary expression that uses line breaks for emphasis. Poems often use connotation, imagery, metaphor, symbol, paradox, irony, allusion, repetition, and rhythm. Word patterns in poetry include rhythm or meter, and often rhyme and alliteration. The three main types of poetry are narrative, dramatic, and lyric.

> *See also* **Alliteration; Connotation; Figurative language; Literature; Lyric; Meter; Narration; Repetition; Rhyme; Rhythm; Verse**

Point of view The position from which the events of a story seem to be observed and told. A first-person point of view tells the story through what the narrator knows, experiences, concludes, or can find out by talking to other characters. A third-person point of view may be *omniscient*, giving the narrator unlimited knowledge of things, events, and characters, including characters' hidden thoughts and feelings. Or it may be *limited* to what one or a few characters know and experience. *Example* of First-Person Point of View: I'm really hungry right now, and I can't wait to eat my lunch. *Example* of Third-Person Limited Point of View: Olivia is really hungry right now and she wants to eat her lunch. *Example* of Third-Person Omniscient Point of View: Olivia is really hungry right now and she wants to eat her lunch. The other students are thinking about their weekend plans. The teacher is wondering how she will finish the lesson before the bell rings.

> *See also* **Character; Fiction; Narration; Narrator; Voice**

Prose A form of writing in which the rhythm is less regular than that of verse and more like that of ordinary speech.

> *See also* **Rhythm; Verse**

Protagonist The main character in a fictional narrative or a play. He or she may be competing with an antagonist; sometimes called the hero or heroine. *Example:* Although the Tin Man, the Cowardly Lion, and the Scarecrow are important characters in *The Wizard of Oz*, Dorothy is the protagonist.

> *See also* **Antagonist; Hero** or **Heroine**

Pun An expression, used for emphasis or humor, in which two distinct meanings are suggested by one word or by two similar-sounding words. *Example:* The following joke uses a pun on the way that the word "lettuce" sounds similar to "let us":

Q: Knock, knock.　　**A**: Who's there?
Q: Lettuce.　　**A**: Lettuce who?
Q: Lettuce in, it's cold out here!

> *See also* **Humor**

R

Realistic fiction Fiction in which detailed handling of imaginary settings, characters, and events produces a lifelike illusion of a "real" world. *Example:* Although Upton Sinclair's *The Jungle* is a work of fiction, the author's graphic, detailed descriptions of the slaughterhouse workers' daily lives led to real changes in the meat packing industry.

> *See also* **Fiction**

Reason A logical explanation that connects a piece of evidence to a writer or speaker's claim.

> *See also* **Argument; Claim; Evidence**

Refrain A line, group of lines, or part of a line repeated (sometimes with slight changes) at various points in poetry or song.

> *See also* **Poetry; Repetition; Song lyrics**

Repetition The repeating of individual vowels and consonants, syllables, words, phrases, lines, or groups of lines. Repetition can be used because it sounds pleasant, to emphasize the words in which it occurs, or to help tie the parts of a text into one structure. It is especially important in creating the musical quality of poetry, where it can take such forms as alliteration, assonance, consonance, rhyme, and refrain.

> *See also* **Alliteration; Assonance; Consonance; Poetry; Refrain; Rhyme**

Report A usually short piece of nonfiction writing on a particular topic. It differs from an essay in that it normally states only facts and does not directly express the writer's opinions.

> *See also* **Essay; Nonfiction; Topic**

Resolution *See* **Falling action**

Review An essay describing a work or performance and judging its effectiveness.

> *See also* **Description; Essay**

Rhetorical device A use of language that differs from ordinary use in order to emphasize a point. It achieves its effects mainly by arranging words in a special way rather than by changing the meaning of the words themselves. Rhetorical devices include *analogy*, *antithesis* (placing words in contrast with one another), *anaphora* (repeating the same word or phrase in a series of lines, clauses, or sentences), the *rhetorical question* (asking a question not to request information, but to make a point more forcefully than simply stating it would do), and *apostrophe* (directly addressing an absent person, nonhuman, or an idea).

> *See also* **Analogy; Figurative language**

Rhyme The repetition of ending sounds in different words. Rhymes usually come at the end of lines of verse, but they may also occur within a line. If rhymed sounds are exactly the same, they make a *perfect rhyme*. If the endings of rhyming words are spelled the same but sound different, they make an *eye rhyme*. And if the last stressed vowels of rhyming words are only similar but the rhyming consonants are the same (or nearly so), the words make a *partial rhyme* (also called *slant rhyme*, *near rhyme*, or *imperfect rhyme*). *Examples:* The words "look" and "brook" and "shook" are perfect rhymes. The words "slaughter" and "laughter" are an eye rhyme. The words "ought" and "fault" form a partial rhyme.

> *See also* **Poetry; Repetition; Rhyme scheme; Stress; Verse**

Rhyme scheme The pattern of rhymed line endings in a work of verse or a stanza. It can be represented by giving a certain letter of the alphabet to each line ending on the same rhyme. *Example:* Because the end word of every other line rhymes in the following poem, the rhyme scheme is *abab*:

Winter night falls quick (a)
The pink sky gone, blackness overhead (b)
Looks like the snow will stick (a)
Down the street and up the hill I tread (b)

See also **Rhyme; Stanza; Verse**

Rhythm The natural rise and fall, or "beat," of language. In English it involves a back-and-forth movement between stressed and unstressed syllables. Rhythm is present in all language, including ordinary speech and prose, but it is most obvious in verse.

See also **Meter; Prose; Stress; Verse**

Rising action The part of a plot that presents actions or events that lead to the climax.

See also **Climax; Conflict; Exposition; Falling action; Plot**

S

Science fiction A genre of fantasy writing based on real or imaginary scientific discoveries. It often takes place in the future.

See also **Fantasy; Fiction**

Script The text of a play, radio or television broadcast, or movie.

Setting The time and place in which the events of a story occur.

See also **Drama; Narration**

Short story A brief, fictional narrative in prose. Like the novel, it organizes the action, thought, and dialogue of its characters into a plot. But it tends to focus on fewer characters and to center on a single event, which reveals as much as possible about the protagonist's life and the traits that set him or her apart.

See also **Character; Fiction; Narration; Novel; Plot; Prose; Protagonist; Story**

Simile A type of figurative language that compares two unlike things by using a word or phrase such as *like, as, than, similar to, resembles,* or *seems. Examples:* The tall, slim man had arms as willowy as a tree's branches. The woman's temper is like an unpredictable volcano.

See also **Figurative language; Metaphor**

Song lyrics Words meant to be sung. Lyrics have been created for many types of songs, including love songs, religious songs, work songs, sea chanties, and children's game songs. Lyrics for many songs were shared orally for generations before being written down. Not all song lyrics are lyrical like poems; some are the words to songs that tell a story. Not all poems called songs were written to be sung.

See also **Folk literature; Lyric; Narration; Poetry; Refrain**

Sonnet A major form of poetry made up of 14 rhyming lines of equal length. Most sonnets in English take one of two basic patterns: (1) The Italian, or Petrarchan, sonnet consists of two parts: a group of eight lines rhyming *abbaabba*, followed by a group of six lines usually rhyming *cdecde*; (2) The English, or Shakespearean, sonnet is divided into three groups of four lines rhyming *abab cdcd efef* and a pair rhyming *gg*.

See also **Lyric; Meter; Rhyme; Rhyme scheme; Verse**

Speech A message on a specific topic, spoken before an audience; also, spoken (not written) language.

Stanza A group of lines that forms a section of a poem and has the same pattern (including line lengths, meter, and usually rhyme scheme) as other sections of the same poem. In printed poems, stanzas are separated from each other by a space.

See also **Meter; Rhyme scheme; Verse**

Static character A character who changes little, if at all. Things happen *to*, rather than *within*, him or her. *Example:* In Charles Dickens's novel *Great Expectations*, Joe Gargery is a static character. He is a poor, uneducated blacksmith who endures the cruelty of his wife and Pip, the main character. Throughout the novel, Joe remains humble, loyal, and supportive of those he loves.

See also **Character; Characterization; Dynamic character**

Story A series of events (actual or imaginary) that can be selected and arranged in a certain order to form a narrative or dramatic plot. It is the raw material from which the finished plot is built. Although there are technical differences, the word *story* is sometimes used in place of *narrative*.

See also **Drama; Narration; Plot**

Stress The force with which a syllable is spoken compared with neighboring syllables in a line of verse. A stressed syllable is spoken more forcefully than an unstressed one.

See also **Meter; Rhythm; Verse**

Style The way a writer uses language to express the feelings or thoughts he or she wants to convey. Just as no two people are alike, no two styles are exactly alike. A writer's style results from his or her choices of vocabulary, sentence structure and variety, imagery, figurative language, rhythm, repetition, and other resources.

See also **Diction; Figurative language; Genre; Imagery; Parody; Repetition; Rhythm; Voice**

Suspense A feeling of curiosity, tension, or excitement a narrative creates in the reader about what will happen next. Mystery novels, like horror movies, are often full of suspense.

See also **Narration**

Symbol A word or phrase that serves as an image of some person, place, thing, or action but that also calls to mind some other, usually broader, idea or range of ideas. *Example:* An author might describe doves flying high in the sky to symbolize a peaceful setting.

See also **Figurative language; Imagery**

T

Tall tale A kind of folk tale that wildly exaggerates a character's strength and ability, usually for comic effect. *Example:* Stories about Paul Bunyan, the enormous lumberjack whose footprints created Minnesota's 10,000 lakes, are considered tall tales.

See also **Hyperbole**

Textbook A book prepared for use in schools for the study of a subject.

Theme The underlying message or main idea of a piece of writing. It expresses a broader meaning than the topic of the piece.

See also **Topic**

Tone A writer's or speaker's attitude toward his or her topic or audience or toward him- or herself. A writer's tone may be positive, negative, or neutral. The words the writer chooses, the sentence structure, and the overall pattern of words convey the intended tone.

See also **Connotation; Figurative language; Literature; Mood; Rhythm; Topic**

Topic What or who is being discussed in a piece of writing; the subject of the piece.

See also **Theme**

Tragedy A play or a fictional narrative about the disastrous downfall of the protagonist, usually because of a flaw in his or her moral character. Though brought to ruin, the protagonist comes to understand the meaning of his or her actions and to accept the consequences. *Example:* William Shakespeare's play *Hamlet* is about the downfall and eventual death of the protagonist, Hamlet, so it is considered a tragedy.

See also **Drama; Narration; Protagonist**

V

Verse Language that differs from prose and ordinary speech by being arranged in regular units of rhythm called *meter*. The meter, in turn, occurs within a larger unit of rhythm and meaning: the *line*. In written verse, unlike written prose, the writer rather than the printer decides where one line ends and the next begins. Not all poetry is written in verse (poetry can even be written in prose), and not all verse is poetry (even skillfully written verse can be ineffective in communicating experience).

See also **Blank verse; Free verse; Meter; Poetry; Prose; Rhythm; Sonnet**

Voice The specific group of traits conveyed by the narrator or "speaker" in a literary work.

See also **Narrator**

Vocabulary Glossary

The definitions in this glossary are for words as they are used in the selections in this book. Use the Pronunciation Key below to help you use each word's pronunciation. Then read about the parts of an entry.

Pronunciation Key

Symbols for Consonant Sounds				Symbols for Short Vowel Sounds		Symbols for R-controlled Sounds		Symbols for Variant Vowel Sounds	
b	box	**p**	pan	**a**	hat	**ar**	barn	**ah**	father
ch	chick	**r**	ring	**e**	bell	**air**	chair	**aw**	ball
d	dog	**s**	bus	**i**	chick	**ear**	ear	**oi**	boy
f	fish	**sh**	fish	**o**	box	**īr**	fire	**ow**	mouse
g	girl	**t**	hat	**u**	bus	**or**	corn	**oo**	book
h	hat	**th**	earth			**ur**	girl	**ü**	fruit
j	jar	**th**	father	Symbols for Long Vowel Sounds					
k	cake	**v**	vase	**ā**	cake			Miscellaneous Symbols	
ks	box	**w**	window	**ē**	key			**shun**	fraction
kw	queen	**wh**	whale	**ī**	bike			**chun**	question
l	bell	**y**	yarn	**ō**	goat			**zhun**	division
m	mouse	**z**	zipper	**yū**	mule				
n	pan	**zh**	treasure						
ng	ring								

Academic Vocabulary

Certain words in this glossary have a red dot indicating that they are academic vocabulary words. These are the words that are necessary for you to learn in order to understand the concepts being taught in school.

Parts of an Entry

The **entry** shows how the word is spelled and how it is broken into syllables.

The **pronunciation** shows you how to say the word.

part of speech
n. for noun
v. for verb
adj. for adjective
adv. for adverb.

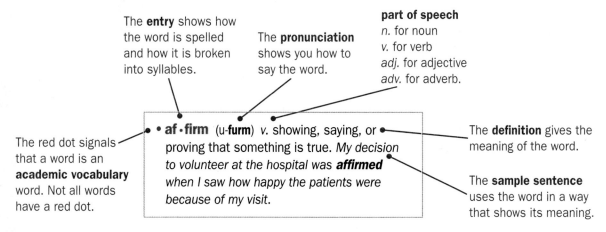

The red dot signals that a word is an **academic vocabulary** word. Not all words have a red dot.

• **af·firm** (u-**furm**) *v.* showing, saying, or proving that something is true. *My decision to volunteer at the hospital was **affirmed** when I saw how happy the patients were because of my visit.*

The **definition** gives the meaning of the word.

The **sample sentence** uses the word in a way that shows its meaning.

A

- **achieve** (u-**chēv**) *v.* to succeed or do well. *If you work hard, you can **achieve** your goals.*

  advertising (**ad**-vur-tīz-ing) *n.* media that encourages people to buy, do, or use things. *The company uses **advertising** like TV commercials and Internet ads to sell its new product.*

- **affect** (u-**fekt**) *v.* to change something in some way. *You can **affect** the environment by using more or less water.*

  affirm (u-**furm**) *v.* showing, saying, or proving that something is true. *My decision to volunteer at the hospital was **affirmed** when I saw how happy the patients were because of my visit.*

  aggressive (u-**gre**-siv) *adj.* forceful, bold, and willing to take strong action. *She is an **aggressive** soccer player who scores lots of goals.*

  alien (**ā**-lē-un) *adj.* a person who comes from another country. *When she moved to the U.S., she was an **alien** in a strange, new culture.*

- **alternative** (awl-**tur**-nu-tiv) *adj.* offering a choice that is different from what is usual or expected. *The **alternative** movie was created and filmed in a unique way.*

  ambitious (am-**bi**-shus) *adj.* having big goals that you want to achieve. *The **ambitious** student studied day and night to win the science prize.*

  anxiety (ang-**zī**-ut-ē) *n.* worry, concern. *I felt great **anxiety** before I started my new job.*

  appeal (u-**pēl**) *v.* to ask for a good reaction. *That commercial **appeals** to my love of cars.*

  arrogant (**ar**-u-gunt) *adj.* overly proud; thinking you are very smart or talented. *The **arrogant** girl acts like she is better than everyone else.*

  ashamed (u-**shāmd**) *adj.* guilty or embarassed. *I felt **ashamed** about the way I had treated my friend when I was angry.*

- **assemble** (u-**sem**-bul) *v.* to put something together. ***Assemble** the model car out of the pieces in the box.*

- **assume** (u-**sūm**) *v.* to think that something is true even if you do not know that it is. *He **assumes** that I am poor because my clothes are old.*

- **authority** (u-**thor**-u-tē) *n.* power over others. *Government leaders have the **authority** to make laws.*

B

- **bias** (**bī**-us) *n.* opinions that affect the way you see or present things. *He couldn't be partial because he is too **biased**.*

- **bond** (**bond**) *n.* a kind of connection between people or things. *My sister and I are held together by the strong **bonds** of family and love.*

  boundary (**bown**-du-rē) *n.* a line that separates two places. *This fence marks the **boundary** between our yard and yours.*

  boycott (**boi**-kot) *n.* a way to punish an organization by refusing to use its product or service. *We will hold a **boycott** of the company's products because we don't like the way it treats its workers.*

  burden (**bur**-din) *n.* a heavy thing that you must carry or something difficult you have to do or know about. *Keeping my brother's secret was a great **burden** to me.*

C

- **capable** (**kā**-pu-bul) *adj.* able to do something. *We are all **capable** of doing good and bad things with our lives.*

  career (ku-**rear**) *n.* the kind of work a person does. *The artist began her **career** by drawing comics in high school.*

  cause (**kawz**) *n.* an idea you believe in and are willing to fight for. *I volunteer my time and money to the **cause** of helping the homeless.*

- **cease** (**cēs**) *v.* to stop. *The voices **ceased** when he entered the room, and it got completely quiet.*

  circumstances (**sur**-kum-stans-uz) *n.* the situation a person is in. *There are many **circumstances** that cause people to make bad choices.*

collaborate (ku-**lab**-u-rāt) *v.* to work together with one or more people on a specific task or project. *My friends and I* ***collaborate*** *on group projects for class.*

• **collapse** (ku-**laps**) *v.* to fall down suddenly. *The man* ***collapsed*** *to the floor when he heard the bad news about his son's accident.*

• **commit** (ku-**mit**) *v.* to perform, do, or carry out something, often a crime. *She* ***committed*** *the crime of robbery.*

• **commitment** (ku-**mit**-mint) *n.* something that you continue to work on even when it's difficult. *He shows his* ***commitment*** *to work by coming early every day.*

compassion (kum-**pash**-un) *n.* deep concern about other's suffering and troubles. *I felt* ***compassion*** *for the sad, lonely girl.*

compose (kum-**pōz**) *v.* to create something by writing it. *If you compose a poem, I'll* ***compose*** *music to go with it.*

confession (kun-**fe**-shun) *n.* something private or secret that you tell. *The boy made a* ***confession*** *to his mother, because he felt badly about what he had done.*

• **conflict** (**kahn**-flikt) *n.* disagreement, problem, or argument. *A story's* ***conflict*** *is the main problem.*

• **conquer** (**kon**-kur) *v.* to beat, to defeat. *The army* ***conquered*** *its enemy after a long battle.*

• **conscientiously** (kon-shē-en-shus-lē) *adv.* carefully and thoroughly. *Maribel* ***conscientiously*** *researched all the facts before writing her history essay.*

• **consequence** (**kon**-su-kwens) *n.* something that happens as the result of another action. *If you lie to a friend, you may have to face a* ***consequence***, *like losing your friendship.*

• **constant** (**kon**-stunt) *adj.* stays the same; without any change. *No matter what changes, my love for my family will always stay* ***constant***.

• **consumer** (kun-**sū**-mur) *n.* someone who buys or uses something. *Stores want* ***consumers*** *to buy their products.*

• **contact** (**kon**-takt) *n.* connection. *I am still in* ***contact*** *with my friends from first grade.*

• **contribute** (kun-**tri**-byūt) *v.* to give. *Students* ***contribute*** *ideas to a group discussion.*

• **convince** (kun-**vins**) *v.* to make someone believe something. *My friend tried to* ***convince*** *me to buy the expensive magazine.*

D

desperately (**des**-pur-it-lē) *adv.* a feeling of great need. *The doctors worked* ***desperately*** *to save the child's life.*

• **detect** (di-**tekt**) *v.* to discover or notice something that was not clear. *I* ***detected*** *uneasiness in her voice.*

• **device** (di-**vīs**) *n.* machine or tool that is used to do a particular job. *A cell phone is a* ***device*** *that makes it easy to communicate.*

devotion (di-**vō**-shun) *n.* love and dedication you feel toward someone or something. *Her poetry tells about the great* ***devotion*** *she feels for her family and friends.*

discourage (dis-**kur**-ej) *v.* to make someone not want to do something. *His laughter* ***discouraged*** *me from painting any more pictures.*

• **discrimination** (dis-kri-mu-**nā**-shun) *n.* unfair treatment to people in a particular group. *Racism is a form of* ***discrimination*** *that focuses on a person's ethnicity.*

disgusted (di-**skus**-tid) *adj.* to feel turned off or very upset. *I felt* ***disgusted*** *when I saw the rude way he treated others.*

disrespect (dis-ri-**spekt**) *n.* rudeness, lack of respect. *When children yell at their parents, they show* ***disrespect***.

distracted (di-**strakt**-id) *adj.* unable to pay attention. *If you are* ***distracted*** *by too many activities after school, you may not have time for homework.*

- **diversity** (di-**vur**-si-tē) *n.* a variety of different people or things. *Having students from different countries creates **diversity** at our school.*

  dread (**dred**) *n.* great fear. *The thought of death fills me with **dread**.*

E

efficient (i-**fi**-shunt) *adj.* working well without wasting energy. *My **efficient** car gets 35 miles per gallon of gas.*

empathy (**em**-pu-thē) *n.* understanding someone else's feelings or behavior. *I felt **empathy** for the lonely boy and could feel his sadness.*

endure (in-**dyūr**) *v.* to continue to exist for a long time. *Some old stories **endure** for centuries because people love to read and hear them.*

entreat (in-**trēt**) *v.* to ask, beg. *I **entreated** her to let me retake the test.*

- **environment** (in-**vī**-ru-munt) *n.* all of the things that surround you. *The race car driver's work **environment** is noisy and stressful.*

euphoria (ū-**for**-ē-u) *n.* great joy and happiness. *Our team was filled with **euphoria** after we won the art contest.*

- **evaluate** (i-**val**-ū-āt) *v.* to decide how good or valuable something is. *The teacher will **evaluate** your presentation and then give you a final grade.*

- **evidence** (**e**-vu-duns) *n.* information that helps prove something. *The detective looks for **evidence** that supports her ideas.*

- **expand** (ik-**spand**) *v.* to increase or grow larger. *Our group will **expand** if more members join.*

expectation (ek-spek-**tā**-shun) *n.* belief about how things will turn out. *If you have high **expectations**, you expect something to turn out well.*

- **expression** (eks-**pre**-shun) *n.* the ability to communicate in a creative way. *Poetry is one form of creative **expression**.*

F

fate (**fāt**) *n.* the future that is expected to happen. *Many people believe that you cannot change your **fate**, while others think that you can change it with hard work.*

- **feature** (**fē**-cher) *n.* the parts of your face. *His big, brown eyes are his best **feature**.*

feud (**fyūd**) *n.* an argument between two people, groups, families, or tribes. *The **feud** between our families lasted for years.*

G

- **generation** (je-nu-**rā**-shun) *n.* people who are about the same age. *We can learn a lot from our parents' **generation**.*

genuine (**jen**-yū-win) *adj.* real and not fake. *He thought that the statue was **genuine** gold, but it was really made of brass.*

- **grant** (**grant**) *v.* to give or allow. *My teacher **granted** us extra time to complete the project.*

grief (**grēf**) *n.* deep sadness or sorrow. *He felt great **grief** when his good friend died.*

- **guarantee** (gar-un-**tē**) *n.* a promise. *I'll make you a **guarantee** that you'll enjoy the movie.*

H

heritage (**her**-u-tij) *n.* background, race, or ethnic group you belong to. *Your **heritage** includes the traditions and beliefs given to you by your family, culture, and society.*

historian (hi-**stor**-ē-un) *n.* person who studies the events of the past and interprets them. *The **historian** wrote an article about World War II.*

humiliating (hyū-**mi**-lē-ā-ting) *adj.* very embarrassing. *A **humiliating** experience hurts your pride.*

I

identification (ī-den-tu-fu-**kā**-shun) *n.* a feeling that you understand a person or group of people. *I felt an **identification**, with the characters in the movie.*

imitation (im-u-**tā**-shun) *n.* something that looks or acts like something else. *I thought the painting was real, but it was just an **imitation**.*

- **impact** (**im**-pakt) *n.* to have an influence or effect. *Do movies and celebrities **impact** the things you choose to buy?*

- **impose** (im-**pōz**) *v.* to intrude. *After a few days with them, they felt he was beginning to **impose**.*

improvisation (im-prah-vi-**zā**-shun) *n.* something done without pre-planning. *When I forgot to prepare a speech for class, **improvisation** was my only option.*

influence (**in**-flū-uns) *v.* to affect a person in some way. *Some people believe that violence on TV can **influence** teens in harmful ways.*

- **inherent** (in-**hir**-unt) *adj.* something that you are born with. *She has always had an **inherent** sense of courage.*

- **inhibit** (in-**hib**-it) *v.* to stop or hold you back from doing something. *I want to swim, but my fear of water **inhibits** me.*

- **insight** (**in**-sīt) *n.* a new or special understanding about something. *The instruction sheet gave me **insight** into how to use the machine.*

- **inspire** (in-**spīr**) *v.* to encourage someone to take action. *A movie about an Olympic athlete **inspired** me to start exercising.*

- **integrity** (in-**te**-gru-tē) *n.* honest and trustworthy. *I trust her because she shows **integrity** in everything she says and does.*

- **interpret** (in-**ter**-prut) *v.* to translate something from one language to another. *I often **interpret** letters and notices for my parents, who don't read English.*

- **invest** (in-**vest**) *v.* to provide time, money, or attention to help something grow. *I **invest** money in this business because I know it will earn more money later.*

- **investigation** (in-ves-ti-**gā**-shun) *n.* careful search or study that looks for facts. *We only found out the truth about the event after we conducted our own **investigation**.*

issue (**i**-shoo) *n.* an important topic or idea that people are concerned about. *How to stop school violence is an important **issue** that affects many teens.*

J

just (**just**) *adj.* guided by truth and fairness. *I admire leaders who make decisions that are reasonable, fair, and **just**.*

juvenile (**joo**-vu-nīl) *adj.* young. *The **juvenile** court is for people younger than eighteen.*

L

literacy (**li**-tu-ru-sē) *n.* ability to read and write. *Without **literacy**, it is difficult to complete a job application, use the Internet, or read a map.*

loyalty (**loi**-ul-tē) *n.* being faithful to someone or something. *The friends showed **loyalty** to each other by staying together no matter what happened.*

luxury (**luk**-shu-rē) *n.* expensive things that you do not really need. *Is it a **luxury** to have two pairs of dress shoes?*

M

- **major** (**mā**-jur) *adj.* great in size or importance. *We have a **major** problem that is too big for us to solve without help.*

majority (mu-**jar**-u-tē) *n.* a greater number of the whole. *Based on the results of the elections, you can tell the **majority** has spoken.*

- **manipulate** (mu-**ni**-pyu-lāt) *v.* to influence or control someone or something in a negative way. *That toy commercial uses popular cartoon characters to **manipulate** kids into wanting new toys.*

maturity (mu-**choor**-u-tē) *n.* the time when a person has all the abilities of an adult. *The girl's serious and responsible actions showed **maturity**.*

- **media** (**mē**-dē-u) *n.* different ways people use to communicate, inform, and entertain. *Newspapers, radio, and TV are **media** that provide news and entertainment to many people.*

melodious (me-**lō**-dē-us) *adj.* pleasant to hear, like music. *Whenever she sings, everyone enjoys her **melodious** songs.*

- **minor** (**mī**-nur) *adj.* small or unimportant. *My twin and I differ in **minor** ways, but we think alike and are interested in the same things.*

minority (mu-**nor**-u-tē) *n.; adj.* a group that has fewer members than most of the people. [*noun*] *Many **minority** groups feel they are treated unfairly by groups with more people.*

- **motivation** (mō-tu-**vā**-shun) *n.* reason for doing something or thinking a certain way. *My **motivation** for volunteering is to help my neighbors.*

N

neglect (ni-**glekt**) *n., v.* to ignore or disregard. *I saved the kittens from the **neglect** they suffered from the people who did not take care of them.*

O

- **objectivity** (ub-jek-**tiv**-u-tē) *n.* view or judgment that is not influenced by personal opinions. *We could trust his ideas because of his **objectivity**.*

obstacle (**ahb**-sti-kul) *n.* something that gets in the way or causes trouble. *The fallen tree was an **obstacle** on a road.*

- **obvious** (**ob**-vē-us) *adj.* easy to see or understand. *The answer to the riddle is **obvious** because everyone knows it.*

ominous (**ah**-mu-nus) *adj.* threatening. *The dark, cloudy sky looked **ominous**.*

- **option** (**op**-shun) *n.* a choice. *He had several **options** for lunch.*

P

- **perceive** (per-**sēv**) *v.* to see something in a certain way. *People with different points of view **perceive** things differently.*

- **persistent** (pur-**sis**-tunt) *adj.* continuing, unchanging. *The **persistent** woman kept asking for help even though everyone ignored her.*

persuasive (pur-**swā**-siv) *adj.* believable enough to make you do or believe something. *The **persuasive** man always gets people to help him.*

- **phenomenon** (fi-**nahm**-i-nahn) *n.* something different that people get really excited about. *The new music video is a real **phenomenon**; people everywhere are watching it.*

ponder (**pon**-dur) *v.* to think carefully about. *I **pondered** the meaning of the poem for hours.*

portrayal (por-**trā**-ul) *n.* a representation or picture. *The movie was a realistic **portrayal** of his life.*

poverty (**pov**-er-tē) *n.* the situation of being very poor. *People without enough money for food, shelter, or clothing live in **poverty**.*

- **precision** (pri-**si**-zhun) *n.* exactness and correctness. *A stopwatch keeps track of time with great **precision**.*

prejudiced (**prej**-u-dist) *adj.* to form negative opinions about others without thinking about the facts. *I try not to be **prejudiced** about people who are different than me.*

pretense (**prē**-tens) *n.* the act of pretending to do or be something. *Some people try to act tough, but my brother never shows any **pretense**.*

privilege (**pri**-vu-lij) *n.* something special that someone is allowed to have, be, or do. *The football team gets the **privilege** of leaving school early on game days.*

prodigy (**prah**-du-jē) *n.* young person who has unusual skills for his or her age. *They called the girl a **prodigy** because she could play the violin when she was four years old.*

- **profession** (pru-**fe**-shun) *n.* type of job that you need special training to do. *Because he chose the medical **profession**, he spent years studying to be a doctor.*

profit (**prah**-fut) *n.* the money you make when you sell something, after expenses are subtracted. *The bookstore increased its **profits** by selling more books and magazines this year.*

prophet (**pro**-fut) *n.* someone who can predict what will happen in the future. *The **prophet** warned us about the coming disaster.*

protest (**prō**-test) *v.* to say or show you are against something. *We **protest** the unfair way the students are being treated.*

provider (pru-**vī**-dur) *n.* someone who gives necessary things to someone else. *My mother is an excellent **provider**, because she gives us food, shelter, and love.*

provoke (pru-**vōk**) *v.* to force a person or thing to act. *We hope our protests against the unfair law will **provoke** the government to make a change.*

R

racism (**rā**-si-zum) *n.* belief that some races, or ethnic groups, are better than others. *The man shows **racism** when he judges others because of their ethnicity.*

recall (**rē**-kawl) *v.* to remember something from the past. *I **recall** many happy memories from my childhood.*

recitation (re-si-**tā**-shun) *n.* speaking a poem or other text aloud in front of other people. *For my class project, I will give a poetry **recitation**.*

reconciliation (re-kun-si-lē-**ā**-shun) *n.* agreement to make up after an arguement. *The men reached a **reconciliation** by talking about their problem.*

refuge (**re**-fyūj) *n.* a place of safety. *My bedroom is my **refuge** when I want to be alone.*

• **release** (rē-**lēs**) *v.* to let something go or set free. *Our teacher said he would **release** us from class as soon as the work was finished.*

• **relevance** (**re**-lu-vents) *n.* an idea that is important and connects to another thing. *The news story has **relevance** to my own life.*

• **rely** (ri-**lī**) *v.* to depend on. *Do you **rely** on your alarm clock to wake you up in the morning?*

reputation (re-pyu-**tā**-shun) *n.* the way people think about you. *He had a **reputation** as a shy person because he was always so quiet in class.*

resist (ri-**zist**) *v.* fight against. *I **resisted** the urge to scream during the scary movie.*

responsible (ri-**spon**-su-bul) *adj.* able to take care of. *If you borrow a pen, you are **responsible** for returning it when you are done.*

restore (ri-**stor**) *v.* to return something to the way it was before. *After we talked about our problems, our friendship was **restored** to the way it used to be.*

• **reveal** (ri-**vēl**) *v.* to show or display. *He would never **reveal** the secret of the magic trick.*

• **revolution** (re-vu-**lū**-shun) *n.* major or total change. *The American **Revolution** changed the government of our country.*

ritual (**ri**-chu-wul) *n.* set plan for or formal way of doing something. *Many cultures have **rituals** to protect children from danger.*

S

salvage (**sal**-vuj) *v.* to save or rescue. *I **salvaged** my friendship by telling my friend I was sorry.*

segregation (se-gri-**gā**-shun) *n.* separation of some people from others because of race. *In the past, **segregation** didn't allow black and white children to go to the same schools.*

self-esteem (**self** es-**tēm**) *n.* feeling that you are valuable; confidence in yourself. *The confident girl has high **self-esteem**.*

shame (**shām**) *n.* a painful feeling that is caused by embarrassment or guilt. *He felt **shame** about a mistake that he had made.*

• **significant** (sig-**ni**-fi-kint) *adj.* of great value or importance. *My friends and family are a **significant** part of my life.*

skeptic (**skep**-tik) *n.* someone who doubts beliefs that are generally accepted by others. *My friends believe in the legend, but I'm a **skeptic** who needs more proof.*

solution (su-**lū**-shun) *n.* the answer that solves or fixes a problem. *My team found a **solution** to our problem with the project.*

standard (**stan**-durd) *adj.* way people judge or measure things. *According to the teacher's high **standards**, Mary was a great student.*

stereotype (**ster**-ē-u-tīp) *n.* an idea people have about an entire group of people. *People say that all teens are lazy and rude, but that **stereotype** doesn't fit me.*

• **structure** (**struk**-chur) *n.* way something is set up or organized. *My poem has a **structure** that includes lots of rhyme.*

subside (sub-**sīd**) *v.* to become less strong. *When a storm **subsides** the wind and rain slow down.*

successful (suk-**ses**-ful) *adj.* having done well. *The parents at the graduation were proud of their **successful** children.*

- **survivor** (sur-**vī**-vur) *n.* a person who overcomes some hardship or manages to live through a disaster. *The police rescued the **survivors** of the car accident.*

suspect (su-**spekt**) *v.* to believe that something may be different from what it seems. *I **suspect** that she is lying.*

- **symbol** (**sim**-bul) *n.* something that represents or stands for something else. *An eagle is a **symbol** of the United States. A dove is a **symbol** of peace.*

T

talent (**tal**-unt) *n.* special ability or skill. *She has a wonderful **talent** in music.*

technology (tek-**nah**-lu-jē) *n.* scientific knowledge as it is used in the world. *The car doesn't run on gas; it uses a battery-powered **technology**.*

territory (**ter**-u-tor-ē) *n.* a specific area of land that belongs to you. *A long fence marks the edges of our farm's **territory**.*

terror (**ter**-rur) *n.* feeling of great fear. *The actress in the horror movie had a look of **terror** on her face.*

token (**tō**-kun) *adj.* one person or thing that is included to supposedly represent a larger group. *A **token** female on the all-male team was supposed to show that the group included both sexes.*

- **trace** (**trās**) *n.* small sign that shows that someone or something has been in a place. *The police searched for fingerprints or any other **trace** of the man at the crime scene.*

tragedy (**tra**-ju-dē) *n.* a terrible event or disaster. *The earthquake **tragedy** left people homeless, and many children became orphans.*

transcend (tran-**send**) *v.* to rise above or go beyond. *Art is something that **transcends** the limits of language.*

- **transform** (trans-**form**) *v.* to change something in an important way. *I **transformed** my sketch into a painting.*

U

unite (yū-**nīt**) *v.* to bring together. *When neighbors **unite**, they can change their community.*

V

value (**val**-yū) *v.* to think something is important or useful. *I **value** friends more than money.*

variety (vu-**rī**-u-tē) *n.* representation of many different things. *The people in the group represent a **variety** of backgrounds from all over the world.*

vulnerable (**vul**-nu-ru-bul) *adj.* weak and easily hurt; helpless. *The small child was lost and **vulnerable** without his mother.*

Beginning-Middle-End

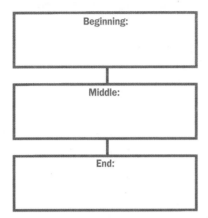

Character-Setting-Plot

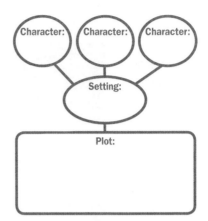

Character Description

Character	What the Character Does	What This Shows About the Character

Goal-and-Outcome

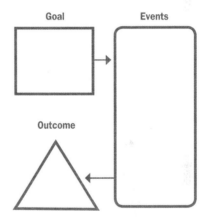

Problem-and-Solution

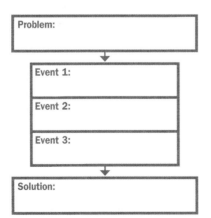

Cause-and-Effect Chart

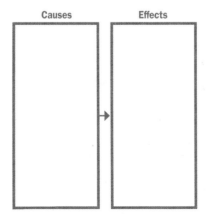

Cycle Diagram

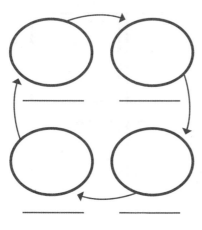

Sequence Chain

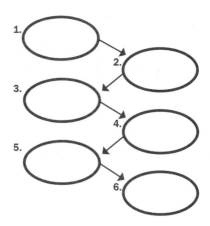

Time Line

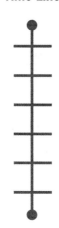

Main-Idea Diagram

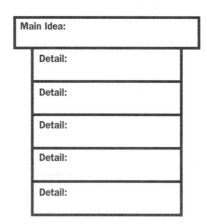

Idea Web

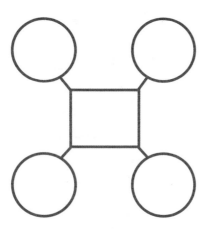

Topic Triangle

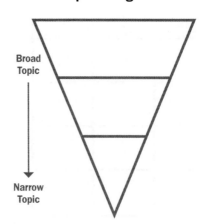

Venn Diagram

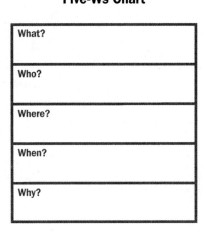

Classification Chart

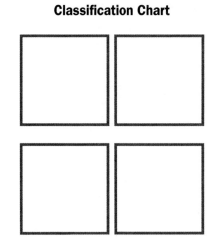

Five-Ws Chart

What?	
Who?	
Where?	
When?	
Why?	

KWL Chart

K What Do I Know?	W What Do I Want to Learn?	L What Did I Learn?

Table

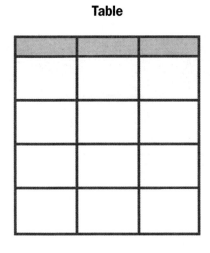

Outline

I. _____

    A. _____

    B. _____

II. _____

    A. _____

    B. _____

III. _____

    A. _____

    B. _____

Graph

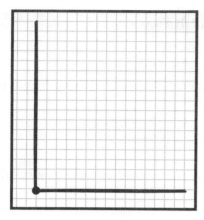

T Chart

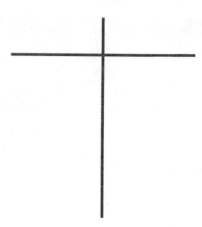

Word Map

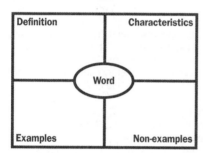

Common Core State Standards

UNIT 1: Choices

SE Pages	Lesson	Code	Standards Text
0–1	Discuss the Essential Question	SL.9-10.1.b	Work with peers to set rules for collegial discussions and decision-making, clear goals and deadlines, and individual roles as needed.
		SL.9-10.3	Evaluate a speaker's point of view, reasoning, and use of evidence and rhetoric, identifying any fallacious reasoning or exaggerated or distorted evidence.
2	Analyze and Debate	SL.9-10.4	Present information, findings, and supporting evidence clearly, concisely, and logically such that listeners can follow the line of reasoning and the organization, development, substance, and style are appropriate to purpose, audience, and task.
3	Plan a Project	SL.9-10.1.b	Work with peers to set rules for collegial discussions and decision-making, clear goals and deadlines, and individual roles as needed.
3	Choose More to Read	RL.9-10.10	By the end of grade 10, read and comprehend literature, including stories, dramas, and poems, at the high end of the grades 9–10 text complexity band independently and proficiently.
		RI.9-10.10	By the end of grade 10, read and comprehend literary nonfiction at the high end of the grades 9–10 text complexity band independently and proficiently.
4-5	How to Read Using Reading Strategies	RI.9-10.10	By the end of grade 10, read and comprehend literary nonfiction at the high end of the grades 9–10 text complexity band independently and proficiently.
		L.9-10.6	Acquire and use accurately general academic and domain-specific words and phrases, sufficient for reading, writing, speaking, and listening at the college and career readiness level; demonstrate independence in gathering vocabulary knowledge when considering a word or phrase important to comprehension or expression.
6-9	How to Read Short Stories	RL.9-10.3	Analyze how complex characters develop over the course of a text, interact with other characters, and advance the plot or develop the theme.
		RL.9-10.10	By the end of grade 10, read and comprehend literature, including stories, dramas, and poems, at the high end of the grades 9–10 text complexity band independently and proficiently.
		L.9-10.6	Acquire and use accurately general academic and domain-specific words and phrases, sufficient for reading, writing, speaking, and listening at the college and career readiness level; demonstrate independence in gathering vocabulary knowledge when considering a word or phrase important to comprehension or expression.

Cluster 1

SE Pages	Lesson	Code	Standards Text
10	Prepare to Read	RI.9-10.4	Determine the meaning of words and phrases as they are used in a text, including figurative, connotative, and technical meanings; analyze the cumulative impact of specific word choices on meaning and tone.
		SL.9-10.1	Initiate and participate effectively in a range of collaborative discussions (one-on-one, in groups, and teacher-led) with diverse partners on grades 9–10 topics, texts, and issues, building on others' ideas and expressing their own clearly and persuasively.
		L.9-10.6	Acquire and use accurately general academic and domain-specific words and phrases, sufficient for reading, writing, speaking, and listening at the college and career readiness level; demonstrate independence in gathering vocabulary knowledge when considering a word or phrase important to comprehension or expression.

SE Pages	Lesson	Code	Standards Text
11	**Before Reading: The Good Samaritan**	RL.9-10.5	Analyze how an author's choices concerning how to structure a text, order events within it, and manipulate time create such effects as mystery, tension, or surprise.
		RL.9-10.10	By the end of grade 10, read and comprehend literature, including stories, dramas, and poems, at the high end of the grades 9–10 text complexity band independently and proficiently.
12–25	**Read The Good Samaritan**	RL.9-10.1	Cite strong and thorough textual evidence to support analysis of what the text says explicitly as well as inferences drawn from the text.
		RL.9-10.2	Determine a theme or central idea of a text and analyze in detail its development over the course of the text, including how it emerges and is shaped and refined by specific details; provide an objective summary of the text.
		RL.9-10.3	Analyze how complex characters develop over the course of a text, interact with other characters, and advance the plot or develop the theme.
		RL.9-10.4	Determine the meaning of words and phrases as they are used in a text, including figurative, connotative, and technical meanings; analyze the cumulative impact of specific word choices on meaning and tone.
		RL.9-10.5	Analyze how an author's choices concerning how to structure a text, order events within it, and manipulate time create such effects as mystery, tension, or surprise.
		RL.9-10.10	By the end of grade 10, read and comprehend literature, including stories, dramas, and poems, at the high end of the grades 9–10 text complexity band independently and proficiently.
		W.9-10.9.a	Apply grades 9–10 Reading standards to literature.
		W.9-10.10	Write routinely over extended time frames (time for research, reflection, and revision) and shorter time frames (a single sitting or a day or two) for a range of tasks, purposes, and audiences.
		L.9-10.1.b	Use various types of phrases (noun, verb, adjectival, adverbial, participial, prepositional, absolute) and clauses (independent, dependent; noun, relative, adverbial) to convey specific meanings and add variety and interest to writing or presentations.
		L.9-10.2	Demonstrate command of the conventions of standard English capitalization, punctuation, and spelling when writing.
		L.9-10.3	Apply knowledge of language to understand how language functions in different contexts, to make effective choices for meaning or style, and to comprehend more fully when reading or listening.
		L.9-10.6	Acquire and use accurately general academic and domain-specific words and phrases, sufficient for reading, writing, speaking, and listening at the college and career readiness level; demonstrate independence in gathering vocabulary knowledge when considering a word or phrase important to comprehension or expression.
26–27	**Postscript: Don't Go Gentle Into That Good Expressway**	RL.9-10.2	Determine a theme or central idea of a text and analyze in detail its development over the course of the text, including how it emerges and is shaped and refined by specific details; provide an objective summary of the text.

Common Core State Standards, continued

Cluster 1, continued

SE Pages	Lesson	Code	Standards Text
26–27	Postscript: Don't Go Gentle Into That Good Expressway continued	SL.9-10.1	Initiate and participate effectively in a range of collaborative discussions (one-on-one, in groups, and teacher-led) with diverse partners on grades 9–10 topics, texts, and issues, building on others' ideas and expressing their own clearly and persuasively.
		L.9-10.4	Determine or clarify the meaning of unknown and multiple-meaning words and phrases based on grades 9–10 reading and content, choosing flexibly from a range of strategies.
		L.9-10.5	Demonstrate understanding of figurative language, word relationships, and nuances in word meanings.
28	Before Reading: The World Is in Their Hands	RI.9-10.2	Determine a central idea of a text and analyze its development over the course of the text, including how it emerges and is shaped and refined by specific details; provide an objective summary of the text.
		RI.9-10.7	Analyze various accounts of a subject told in different mediums, determining which details are emphasized in each account.
		RI.9-10.10	By the end of grade 10, read and comprehend literary nonfiction at the high end of the grades 9–10 text complexity band independently and proficiently.
29–33	Read The World Is in Their Hands	RI.9-10.1	Cite strong and thorough textual evidence to support analysis of what the text says explicitly as well as inferences drawn from the text.
		RI.9-10.2	Determine a central idea of a text and analyze its development over the course of the text, including how it emerges and is shaped and refined by specific details; provide an objective summary of the text.
		RI.9-10.5	Analyze in detail how an author's ideas or claims are developed and refined by particular sentences, paragraphs, or larger portions of a text.
		RI.9-10.7	Analyze various accounts of a subject told in different mediums, determining which details are emphasized in each account.
		RI.9-10.10	By the end of grade 10, read and comprehend literary nonfiction at the high end of the grades 9–10 text complexity band independently and proficiently.
		W.9-10.9.b	Apply grades 9–10 Reading standards to literary nonfiction.
		L.9-10.1.b	Use various types of phrases (noun, verb, adjectival, adverbial, participial, prepositional, absolute) and clauses (independent, dependent; noun, relative, adverbial) to convey specific meanings and add variety and interest to writing or presentations.
		L.9-10.6	Acquire and use accurately general academic and domain-specific words and phrases, sufficient for reading, writing, speaking, and listening at the college and career readiness level; demonstrate independence in gathering vocabulary knowledge when considering a word or phrase important to comprehension or expression.
34	Postscript: Making a Difference	RI.9-10.2	Determine a central idea of a text and analyze its development over the course of the text, including how it emerges and is shaped and refined by specific details; provide an objective summary of the text.
		RI.9-10.7	Analyze various accounts of a subject told in different mediums, determining which details are emphasized in each account.

SE Pages	Lesson	Code	Standards Text
34	**Postscript: Making a Difference** continued	RI.9-10.10	By the end of grade 10, read and comprehend literary nonfiction at the high end of the grades 9–10 text complexity band independently and proficiently.
35	**Reflect and Assess Critical Thinking**	RL.9-10.1	Cite strong and thorough textual evidence to support analysis of what the text says explicitly as well as inferences drawn from the text.
		RL.9-10.3	Analyze how complex characters develop over the course of a text, interact with other characters, and advance the plot or develop the theme.
	Write About Literature	W.9-10.1	Write arguments to support claims in an analysis of substantive topics or texts, using valid reasoning and relevant and sufficient evidence.
	Key Vocabulary Review	L.9-10.6	Acquire and use accurately general academic and domain-specific words and phrases, sufficient for reading, writing, speaking, and listening at the college and career readiness level; demonstrate independence in gathering vocabulary knowledge when considering a word or phrase important to comprehension or expression.
	Read with Ease: Expression	RL.9-10.10	By the end of grade 10, read and comprehend literature, including stories, dramas, and poems, at the high end of the grades 9–10 text complexity band independently and proficiently.
36	**Grammar: Write Complete Sentences**	L.9-10.1.b	Use various types of phrases (noun, verb, adjectival, adverbial, participial, prepositional, absolute) and clauses (independent, dependent; noun, relative, adverbial) to convey specific meanings and add variety and interest to writing or presentations.
36	**Language Development: Ask and Answer Questions**	SL.9-10.1.b	Work with peers to set rules for collegial discussions and decision-making, clear goals and deadlines, and individual roles as needed.
36	**Literary Analysis: Analyze Theme**	RL.9-10.2	Determine a theme or central idea of a text and analyze in detail its development over the course of the text, including how it emerges and is shaped and refined by specific details; provide an objective summary of the text.
36	**Language Development: Give and Follow Instructions**	SL.9-10.1.b	Work with peers to set rules for collegial discussions and decisions-making, clear goals and deadlines, and individual roles as needed.
37	**Vocabulary Study: Prefixes**	L.9-10.4.c	Consult general and specialized reference materials, both print and digital, to find the pronunciation of a word or determine or clarify its precise meaning, its part of speech, or its etymology.
37	**Writing: Write a Definition Paragraph**	W.9-10.2	Write informative/explanatory texts to examine and convey complex ideas, concepts, and information clearly and accurately through the effective selection, organization, and analysis of content.
37	**Research/Speaking: Oral Report**	W.9-10.7	Conduct short as well as more sustained research projects to answer a question (including a self-generated question) or solve a problem; narrow or broaden the inquiry when appropriate; synthesize multiple sources on the subject, demonstrating understanding of the subject under investigation.
		SL.9-10.4	Present information, findings, and supporting evidence clearly, concisely, and logically such that listeners can follow the line of reasoning and the organization, development, substance, and style are appropriate to purpose, audience, and task.

Common Core State Standards, continued

Cluster 1, continued

SE Pages	Lesson	Code	Standards Text
38	Workplace Workshop: Inside a Law Office	W.9-10.7	Conduct short as well as more sustained research projects to answer a question (including a self-generated question) or solve a problem; narrow or broaden the inquiry when appropriate; synthesize multiple sources on the subject, demonstrating understanding of the subject under investigation.
		SL.9-10.1	Initiate and participate effectively in a range of collaborative discussions (one-on-one, in groups, and teacher-led) with diverse partners on grades 9–10 topics, texts, and issues, building on others' ideas and expressing their own clearly and persuasively.
		L.9-10.6	Acquire and use accurately general academic and domain-specific words and phrases, sufficient for reading, writing, speaking, and listening at the college and career readiness level; demonstrate independence in gathering vocabulary knowledge when considering a word or phrase important to comprehension or expression.
39	Vocabulary Workshop: Use Word Parts	L.9-10.4.b	Identify and correctly use patterns of word changes that indicate different meanings or parts of speech.
		L.9-10.4.c	Consult general and specialized reference materials, both print and digital, to find the pronunciation of a word or determine or clarify its precise meaning, its part of speech, or its etymology.
		L.9-10.4.d	Verify the preliminary determination of the meaning of a word or phrase.

Cluster 2

SE Pages	Lesson	Code	Standards Text
40	Prepare to Read	RI.9-10.4	Determine the meaning of words and phrases as they are used in a text, including figurative, connotative, and technical meanings; analyze the cumulative impact of specific word choices on meaning and tone.
		SL.9-10.1	Initiate and participate effectively in a range of collaborative discussions (one-on-one, in groups, and teacher-led) with diverse partners on grades 9–10 topics, texts, and issues, building on others' ideas and expressing their own clearly and persuasively.
		L.9-10.6	Acquire and use accurately general academic and domain-specific words and phrases, sufficient for reading, writing, speaking, and listening at the college and career readiness level; demonstrate independence in gathering vocabulary knowledge when considering a word or phrase important to comprehension or expression.
41	Before Reading: Thank You, Ma'am	RL.9-10.2	Determine a theme or central idea of a text and analyze in detail its development over the course of the text, including how it emerges and is shaped and refined by specific details; provide an objective summary of the text.
		RL.9-10.3	Analyze how complex characters develop over the course of a text, interact with other characters, and advance the plot or develop the theme.
42–51	Read Thank You, Ma'am	RL.9-10.1	Cite strong and thorough textual evidence to support analysis of what the text says explicitly as well as inferences drawn from the text.
		RL.9-10.2	Determine a theme or central idea of a text and analyze in detail its development over the course of the text, including how it emerges and is shaped and refined by specific details; provide an objective summary of the text.
		RL.9-10.3	Analyze how complex characters develop over the course of a text, interact with other characters, and advance the plot or develop the theme.

SE Pages	Lesson	Code	Standards Text
42–51 **Read Thank You, Ma'am** continued		RL.9-10.4	Determine the meaning of words and phrases as they are used in a text, including figurative, connotative, and technical meanings; analyze the cumulative impact of specific word choices on meaning and tone.
		RL.9-10.7	Analyze the representation of a subject or a key scene in two different artistic mediums, including what is emphasized or absent in each treatment.
		RL.9-10.10	By the end of grade 10, read and comprehend literature, including stories, dramas, and poems, at the high end of the grades 9–10 text complexity band independently and proficiently.
		W.9-10.9	Draw evidence from literary or informational texts to support analysis, reflection, and research.
		L.9-10.1	Demonstrate command of the conventions of standard English grammar and usage when writing or speaking.
		L.9-10.2.c	Spell correctly.
		L.9-10.6	Acquire and use accurately general academic and domain-specific words and phrases, sufficient for reading, writing, speaking, and listening at the college and career readiness level; demonstrate independence in gathering vocabulary knowledge when considering a word or phrase important to comprehension or expression.
52	**Before Reading: Juvenile Justice**	RI.9-10.2	Determine a central idea of a text and analyze its development over the course of the text, including how it emerges and is shaped and refined by specific details; provide an objective summary of the text.
		RI.9-10.3	Analyze how the author unfolds an analysis or series of ideas or events, including the order in which the points are made, how they are introduced and developed, and the connections that are drawn between them.
53–58	**Read Juvenile Justice**	RI.9-10.1	Cite strong and thorough textual evidence to support analysis of what the text says explicitly as well as inferences drawn from the text.
		RI.9-10.2	Determine a central idea of a text and analyze its development over the course of the text, including how it emerges and is shaped and refined by specific details; provide an objective summary of the text.
		RI.9-10.3	Analyze how the author unfolds an analysis or series of ideas or events, including the order in which the points are made, how they are introduced and developed, and the connections that are drawn between them.
		RI.9-10.4	Determine the meaning of words and phrases as they are used in a text, including figurative, connotative, and technical meanings; analyze the cumulative impact of specific word choices on meaning and tone.
		RI.9-10.8	Delineate and evaluate the argument and specific claims in a text, assessing whether the reasoning is valid and the evidence is relevant and sufficient; identify false statements and fallacious reasoning.
		RI.9-10.10	By the end of grade 10, read and comprehend literary nonfiction at the high end of the grades 9–10 text complexity band independently and proficiently.

Common Core State Standards, continued

Cluster 2, continued

SE Pages	Lesson	Code	Standards Text
53–58	**Read Juvenile Justice** continued	W.9-10.9	Draw evidence from literary or informational texts to support analysis, reflection, and research.
		L.9-10.1	Demonstrate command of the conventions of standard English grammar and usage when writing or speaking.
		L.9-10.6	Acquire and use accurately general academic and domain-specific words and phrases, sufficient for reading, writing, speaking, and listening at the college and career readiness level; demonstrate independence in gathering vocabulary knowledge when considering a word or phrase important to comprehension or expression.
59	**Reflect and Assess Critical Thinking**	RL.9-10.1	Cite strong and thorough textual evidence to support analysis of what the text says explicitly as well as inferences drawn from the text.
		RI.9-10.1	Cite strong and thorough textual evidence to support analysis of what the text says explicitly as well as inferences drawn from the text.
	Write About Literature	RI.9-10.1	Cite strong and thorough textual evidence to support analysis of what the text says explicitly as well as inferences drawn from the text.
	Key Vocabulary Review	W.9-10.1	Write arguments to support claims in an analysis of substantive topics or texts, using valid reasoning and relevant and sufficient evidence.
		L.9-10.6	Acquire and use accurately general academic and domain-specific words and phrases, sufficient for reading, writing, speaking, and listening at the college and career readiness level; demonstrate independence in gathering vocabulary knowledge when considering a word or phrase important to comprehension or expression.
	Read with Ease: Phrasing	RI.9-10.10	By the end of grade 10, read and comprehend literary nonfiction at the high end of the grades 9–10 text complexity band independently and proficiently.
60	**Grammar: Make Subjects and Verbs Agree**	RL.9-10.1	Cite strong and thorough textual evidence to support analysis of what the text says explicitly as well as inferences drawn from the text.
60	**Language Development: Express Ideas and Opinions**	SL.9-10.1.a	Come to discussions prepared, having read and researched material under study; explicitly draw on that preparation by referring to evidence from texts and other research on the topic or issue to stimulate a thoughtful, well-reasoned exchange of ideas.
60	**Literary Analysis: Analyze Dialogue**	L.9-10.3.a	Write and edit work so that it conforms to the guidelines in a style manual appropriate for the discipline and writing type.
61	**Vocabulary Study: Word Roots**	L.9-10.4.c	Consult general and specialized reference materials, both print and digital, to find the pronunciation of a word or determine or clarify its precise meaning, its part of speech, or its etymology.
61	**Writing on Demand: Write a Short Comparison Essay**	W.9-10.2	Write informative/explanatory texts to examine and convey complex ideas, concepts, and information clearly and accurately through the effective selection, organization, and analysis of content.
		W.9-10.9.a	Apply grades 9–10 Reading standards to literature.
61	**Listening/Speaking: Interview**	SL.9-10.4	Present information, findings, and supporting evidence clearly, concisely, and logically such that listeners can follow the line of reasoning and the organization, development, substance, and style are appropriate to purpose, audience, and task.

Cluster 2, continued

SE Pages	Lesson	Code	Standards Text
62–63	Listening and Speaking Workshop: Oral Response to Literature	SL.9-10.1.a	Come to discussions prepared, having read and researched material under study; explicitly draw on that preparation by referring to evidence from texts and other research on the topic or issue to stimulate a thoughtful, well-reasoned exchange of ideas.
		SL.9-10.3	Evaluate a speaker's point of view, reasoning, and use of evidence and rhetoric, identifying any fallacious reasoning or exaggerated or distorted evidence.
		SL.9-10.4	Present information, findings, and supporting evidence clearly, concisely, and logically such that listeners can follow the line of reasoning and the organization, development, substance, and style are appropriate to purpose, audience, and task.
		L.9-10.3	Apply knowledge of language to understand how language functions in different contexts, to make effective choices for meaning or style, and to comprehend more fully when reading or listening.

Cluster 3

SE Pages	Lesson	Code	Standards Text
64	Prepare to Read	RI.9-10.4	Determine the meaning of words and phrases as they are used in a text, including figurative, connotative, and technical meanings; analyze the cumulative impact of specific word choices on meaning and tone.
		SL.9-10.1	Initiate and participate effectively in a range of collaborative discussions (one-on-one, in groups, and teacher-led) with diverse partners on grades 9–10 topics, texts, and issues, building on others' ideas and expressing their own clearly and persuasively.
		L.9-10.6	Acquire and use accurately general academic and domain-specific words and phrases, sufficient for reading, writing, speaking, and listening at the college and career readiness level; demonstrate independence in gathering vocabulary knowledge when considering a word or phrase important to comprehension or expression.
65	Before Reading: The Necklace	RL.9-10.3	Analyze how complex characters develop over the course of a text, interact with other characters, and advance the plot or develop the theme.
		RL.9-10.4	Determine the meaning of words and phrases as they are used in a text, including figurative, connotative, and technical meanings; analyze the cumulative impact of specific word choices on meaning and tone.
		L.9-10.4.a	Use context as a clue to the meaning of a word or phrase.
66–79	Read The Necklace	RL.9-10.1	Cite strong and thorough textual evidence to support analysis of what the text says explicitly as well as inferences drawn from the text.
		RL.9-10.2	Determine a theme or central idea of a text and analyze in detail its development over the course of the text, including how it emerges and is shaped and refined by specific details; provide an objective summary of the text.
		RL.9-10.3	Analyze how complex characters develop over the course of a text, interact with other characters, and advance the plot or develop the theme.
		RL.9-10.4	Determine the meaning of words and phrases as they are used in a text, including figurative, connotative, and technical meanings; analyze the cumulative impact of specific word choices on meaning and tone.
		RL.9-10.5	Analyze how an author's choices concerning how to structure a text, order events within it, and manipulate time create such effects as mystery, tension, or surprise.

Common Core State Standards, continued

Cluster 3, continued

SE Pages	Lesson	Code	Standards Text
66–79	**Read The Necklace** continued	RL.9-10.6	Analyze a particular point of view or cultural experience reflected in a work of literature from outside the United States, drawing on a wide reading of world literature.
		RL.9-10.7	Analyze the representation of a subject or a key scene in two different artistic mediums, including what is emphasized or absent in each treatment.
		RL.9-10.10	By the end of grade 10, read and comprehend literature, including stories, dramas, and poems, at the high end of the grades 9–10 text complexity band independently and proficiently.
		W.9-10.9	Draw evidence from literary or informational texts to support analysis, reflection, and research.
		W.9-10.10	Write routinely over extended time frames (time for research, reflection, and revision) and shorter time frames (a single sitting or a day or two) for a range of tasks, purposes, and audiences.
		L.9-10.1	Demonstrate command of the conventions of standard English grammar and usage when writing or speaking.
		L.9-10.4.a	Use context as a clue to the meaning of a word or phrase.
		L.9-10.5.a	Interpret figures of speech in context and analyze their role in the text.
		L.9-10.5.b	Analyze nuances in the meaning of words with similar denotations.
		L.9-10.6	Acquire and use accurately general academic and domain-specific words and phrases, sufficient for reading, writing, speaking, and listening at the college and career readiness level; demonstrate independence in gathering vocabulary knowledge when considering a word or phrase important to comprehension or expression.
80	**Before Reading: The Fashion Show**	RI.9-10.4	Determine the meaning of words and phrases as they are used in a text, including figurative, connotative, and technical meanings; analyze the cumulative impact of specific word choices on meaning and tone.
		RI.9-10.6	Determine an author's point of view or purpose in a text and analyze how an author uses rhetoric to advance that point of view or purpose.
		L.9-10.4.a	Use context as a clue to the meaning of a word or phrase.
81–86	**Read The Fashion Show**	RI.9-10.1	Cite strong and thorough textual evidence to support analysis of what the text says explicitly as well as inferences drawn from the text.
		RI.9-10.2	Determine a central idea of a text and analyze its development over the course of the text, including how it emerges and is shaped and refined by specific details; provide an objective summary of the text.
		RI.9-10.4	Determine the meaning of words and phrases as they are used in a text, including figurative, connotative, and technical meanings; analyze the cumulative impact of specific word choices on meaning and tone.
		RI.9-10.6	Determine an author's point of view or purpose in a text and analyze how an author uses rhetoric to advance that point of view or purpose.

SE Pages	Lesson	Code	Standards Text
81–86	**Read The Fashion Show** continued	RI.9-10.7	Analyze various accounts of a subject told in different mediums, determining which details are emphasized in each account.
		RI.9-10.10	By the end of grade 10, read and comprehend literary nonfiction at the high end of the grades 9–10 text complexity band independently and proficiently.
		W.9-10.10	Write routinely over extended time frames (time for research, reflection, and revision) and shorter time frames (a single sitting or a day or two) for a range of tasks, purposes, and audiences.
		L.9-10.1	Demonstrate command of the conventions of standard English grammar and usage when writing or speaking.
		L.9-10.4.a	Use context as a clue to the meaning of a word or phrase.
		L.9-10.6	Acquire and use accurately general academic and domain-specific words and phrases, sufficient for reading, writing, speaking, and listening at the college and career readiness level; demonstrate independence in gathering vocabulary knowledge when considering a word or phrase important to comprehension or expression.
87	**Reflect and Assess Critical Thinking**	RL.9-10.1	Cite strong and thorough textual evidence to support analysis of what the text says explicitly as well as inferences drawn from the text.
		RI.9-10.1	Cite strong and thorough textual evidence to support analysis of what the text says explicitly as well as inferences drawn from the text.
		RL.9-10.2	Determine a theme or central idea of a text and analyze in detail its development over the course of the text, including how it emerges and is shaped and refined by specific details; provide an objective summary of the text.
		RI.9-10.2	Determine a central idea of a text and analyze its development over the course of the text, including how it emerges and is shaped and refined by specific details; provide an objective summary of the text.
		RL.9-10.3	Analyze how complex characters develop over the course of a text, interact with other characters, and advance the plot or develop the theme.
		RL.9-10.6	Analyze a particular point of view or cultural experience reflected in a work of literature from outside the United States, drawing on a wide reading of world literature.
	Write About Literature	W.9-10.3	Write narratives to develop real or imagined experiences or events using effective technique, well-chosen details, and well-structured event sequences.
	Key Vocabulary Review	L.9-10.6	Acquire and use accurately general academic and domain-specific words and phrases, sufficient for reading, writing, speaking, and listening at the college and career readiness level; demonstrate independence in gathering vocabulary knowledge when considering a word or phrase important to comprehension or expression.
	Read with Ease: Intonation	RI.9-10.10	By the end of grade 10, read and comprehend literary nonfiction at the high end of the grades 9–10 text complexity band independently and proficiently.

Common Core State Standards, continued

Cluster 3, continued

SE Pages	Lesson	Code	Standards Text
88	**Grammar: Fix Sentence Fragments**	L.9-10.1	Demonstrate command of the conventions of standard English grammar and usage when writing or speaking.
88	**Language Development: Express Feelings and Intentions**	SL.9-10.4	Present information, findings, and supporting evidence clearly, concisely, and logically such that listeners can follow the line of reasoning and the organization, development, substance, and style are appropriate to purpose, audience, and task.
88	**Literary Analysis: Analyze Setting and Theme**	RL.9-10.2	Determine a theme or central idea of a text and analyze in detail its development over the course of the text, including how it emerges and is shaped and refined by specific details; provide an objective summary of the text.
		RL.9-10.6	Analyze a particular point of view or cultural experience reflected in a work of literature from outside the United States, drawing on a wide reading of world literature.
89	**Vocabulary Study: Suffixes**	L.9-10.4.b	Identify and correctly use patterns of word changes that indicate different meanings or parts of speech.
89	**Writing Trait: Focus and Unity: Thesis or Central Idea**	W.9-10.5	Develop and strengthen writing as needed by planning, revising, editing, rewriting, or trying a new approach, focusing on addressing what is most significant for a specific purpose and audience.
89	**Research/Writing: Research Report**	W.9-10.2	Write informative/explanatory texts to examine and convey complex ideas, concepts, and information clearly and accurately through the effective selection, organization, and analysis of content.
		W.9-10.7	Conduct short as well as more sustained research projects to answer a question (including a self-generated question) or solve a problem; narrow or broaden the inquiry when appropriate; synthesize multiple sources on the subject, demonstrating understanding of the subject under investigation.
		W.9-10.8	Gather relevant information from multiple authoritative print and digital sources, using advanced searches effectively; assess the usefulness of each source in answering the research question; integrate information into the text selectively to maintain the flow of ideas, avoiding plagiarism and following a standard format for citation.

Close Reading

SE Pages	Lesson	Code	Standards Text
90–93	**Read The Grapes of Wrath**	RL.9-10.10	By the end of grade 10, read and comprehend literature, including stories, dramas, and poems, at the high end of the grades 9–10 text complexity band independently and proficiently.

Unit Wrap-Up

SE Pages	Lesson	Code	Standards Text
94	**Present Your Project**	SL.9-10.1.c	Propel conversations by posing and responding to questions that relate the current discussion to broader themes or larger ideas; actively incorporate others into the discussion; and clarify, verify, or challenge ideas and conclusions.
		SL.9-10.6	Adapt speech to a variety of contexts and tasks, demonstrating command of formal English when indicated or appropriate.
	Reflect on Your Reading	SL.9-10.1.a	Come to discussions prepared, having read and researched material under study; explicitly draw on that preparation by referring to evidence from texts and other research on the topic or issue to stimulate a thoughtful, well-reasoned exchange of ideas.

Unit Wrap-Up, continued

SE Pages	Lesson	Code	Standards Text
94	**Present Your Project** continued **Respond to the Essential Question**	SL.9-10.1.a	Come to discussions prepared, having read and researched material under study; explicitly draw on that preparation by referring to evidence from texts and other research on the topic or issue to stimulate a thoughtful, well-reasoned exchange of ideas.

Writing Project: Autobiographical Narratives

SE Pages	Lesson	Code	Standards Text
95–99	**Study Autobiographical Narratives and Prewrite**	W.9-10.3.c	Use a variety of techniques to sequence events so that they build on one another to create a coherent whole.
		W.9-10.5	Develop and strengthen writing as needed by planning, revising, editing, rewriting, or trying a new approach, focusing on addressing what is most significant for a specific purpose and audience.
100–101	**Autobiographical Narrative: Draft**	W.9-10.3	Write narratives to develop real or imagined experiences or events using effective technique, well-chosen details, and well-structured event sequences.
		W.9-10.3.d	Use precise words and phrases, telling details, and sensory language to convey a vivid picture of the experiences, events, setting, and/or characters.
		W.9-10.4	Produce clear and coherent writing in which the development, organization, and style are appropriate to task, purpose, and audience.
		W.9-10.6	Use technology, including the Internet, to produce, publish, and update individual or shared writing products, taking advantage of technology's capacity to link to other information and to display information flexibly and dynamically.
102–105	**Autobiographical Narrative: Revise Trait: Focus and Unity**	W.9-10.3.a	Engage and orient the reader by setting out a problem, situation, or observation, establishing one or multiple point(s) of view, and introducing a narrator and/or characters; create a smooth progression of experiences or events.
		W.9-10.3.b	Use narrative techniques, such as dialogue, pacing, description, reflection, and multiple plot lines, to develop experiences, events, and/or characters.
		W.9-10.3.c	Use a variety of techniques to sequence events so that they build on one another to create a coherent whole.
		W.9-10.3.e	Provide a conclusion that follows from and reflects on what is experienced, observed, or resolved over the course of the narrative.
		W.9-10.5	Develop and strengthen writing as needed by planning, revising, editing, rewriting, or trying a new approach, focusing on addressing what is most significant for a specific purpose and audience.
		SL.9-10.1	Initiate and participate effectively in a range of collaborative discussions (one-on-one, in groups, and teacher-led) with diverse partners on grades 9–10 topics, texts, and issues, building on others' ideas and expressing their own clearly and persuasively.
		SL.9-10.1.d	Respond thoughtfully to diverse perspectives, summarize points of agreement and disagreement, and, when warranted, qualify or justify their own views and understanding and make new connections in light of the evidence and reasoning presented.

Common Core State Standards, continued

Student Handbooks, continued

Writing Project: Autobiographical Narratives, continued

SE Pages	Lesson	Code	Standards Text
106–108	Autobiographical Narrative: Edit and Proofread Capitalization: Proper Nouns and Adjectives Punctuation: Quotations Spelling Complete Sentences	W.9-10.6	Use technology, including the Internet, to produce, publish, and update individual or shared writing products, taking advantage of technology's capacity to link to other information and to display information flexibly and dynamically.
		L.9-10.1	Demonstrate command of the conventions of standard English grammar and usage when writing or speaking.
		L.9-10.2	Demonstrate command of the conventions of standard English capitalization, punctuation, and spelling when writing.
		L.9-10.2.c	Spell correctly.
		L.9-10.3.a	Write and edit work so that it conforms to the guidelines in a style manual appropriate for the discipline and writing type.
109	Autobiographical Narrative: Publish and Present	W.9-10.6	Use technology, including the Internet, to produce, publish, and update individual or shared writing products, taking advantage of technology's capacity to link to other information and to display information flexibly and dynamically.
		SL.9-10.1	Initiate and participate effectively in a range of collaborative discussions (one-on-one, in groups, and teacher-led) with diverse partners on grades 9–10 topics, texts, and issues, building on others' ideas and expressing their own clearly and persuasively.
		SL.9-10.6	Adapt speech to a variety of contexts and tasks, demonstrating command of formal English when indicated or appropriate.
UNIT 2: The Art of Expression			
110–111	Discuss the Essential Question	SL.9-10.1.b	Work with peers to set rules for collegial discussions and decision-making (e.g., informal consensus, taking votes on key issues, presentation of alternate views), clear goals and deadlines, and individual roles as needed.
		SL.9-10.3	Evaluate a speaker's point of view, reasoning, and use of evidence and rhetoric, identifying any fallacious reasoning or exaggerated or distorted evidence.
112	Analyze and Debate	SL.9-10.4	Present information, findings, and supporting evidence clearly, concisely, and logically such that listeners can follow the line of reasoning and the organization, development, substance, and style are appropriate to purpose, audience, and task.
113	Plan a Project	SL.9-10.1.b	Work with peers to set rules for collegial discussions and decision-making (e.g., informal consensus, taking votes on key issues, presentation of alternate views), clear goals and deadlines, and individual roles as needed.
113	Choose More to Read	RL.9-10.10	By the end of grade 10, read and comprehend literature, including stories, dramas, and poems, at the high end of the grades 9–10 text complexity band independently and proficiently.
		RI.9-10.10	By the end of grade 10, read and comprehend literary nonfiction at the high end of the grades 9–10 text complexity band independently and proficiently.
114–117	How to Read Nonfiction	RI.9-10.2	Determine a central idea of a text and analyze its development over the course of the text, including how it emerges and is shaped and refined by specific details; provide an objective summary of the text.

UNIT 2: The Art of Expression, continued

SE Pages	Lesson	Code	Standards Text
114–117	**How to Read Nonfiction** continued	RI.9-10.6	Determine an author's point of view or purpose in a text and analyze how an author uses rhetoric to advance that point of view or purpose.
		RI.9-10.10	By the end of grade 10, read and comprehend literary nonfiction at the high end of the grades 9–10 text complexity band independently and proficiently.
		L.9-10.6	Acquire and use accurately general academic and domain-specific words and phrases, sufficient for reading, writing, speaking, and listening at the college and career readiness level; demonstrate independence in gathering vocabulary knowledge when considering a word or phrase important to comprehension or expression.
Cluster 1			
118	**Prepare to Read**	RI.9-10.4	Determine the meaning of words and phrases as they are used in a text, including figurative, connotative, and technical meanings; analyze the cumulative impact of specific word choices on meaning and tone.
		SL.9-10.1	Initiate and participate effectively in a range of collaborative discussions (one-on-one, in groups, and teacher-led) with diverse partners on grades 9–10 topics, texts, and issues, building on others' ideas and expressing their own clearly and persuasively.
		L.9-10.4	Determine or clarify the meaning of unknown and multiple-meaning words and phrases based on grades 9–10 reading and content, choosing flexibly from a range of strategies.
		L.9-10.4.c	Consult general and specialized reference materials, both print and digital, to find the pronunciation of a word or determine or clarify its precise meaning, its part of speech, or its etymology.
		L.9-10.6	Acquire and use accurately general academic and domain-specific words and phrases, sufficient for reading, writing, speaking, and listening at the college and career readiness level; demonstrate independence in gathering vocabulary knowledge when considering a word or phrase important to comprehension or expression.
119	**Before Reading: Creativity at Work**	RI.9-10.2	Determine a central idea of a text and analyze its development over the course of the text, including how it emerges and is shaped and refined by specific details; provide an objective summary of the text.
		RI.9-10.6	Determine an author's point of view or purpose in a text and analyze how an author uses rhetoric to advance that point of view or purpose.
120–127	**Read Creativity at Work**	RI.9-10.1	Cite strong and thorough textual evidence to support analysis of what the text says explicitly as well as inferences drawn from the text.
		RI.9-10.2	Determine a central idea of a text and analyze its development over the course of the text, including how it emerges and is shaped and refined by specific details; provide an objective summary of the text.
		RI.9-10.6	Determine an author's point of view or purpose in a text and analyze how an author uses rhetoric to advance that point of view or purpose.
		RI.9-10.10	By the end of grade 10, read and comprehend literary nonfiction at the high end of the grades 9–10 text complexity band independently and proficiently.

Common Core State Standards, continued

SE Pages	Lesson	Code	Standards Text
120–127	Read Creativity at Work continued	W.9-10.2.b	Develop the topic with well-chosen, relevant, and sufficient facts, extended definitions, concrete details, quotations, or other information and examples appropriate to the audience's knowledge of the topic.
		W.9-10.10	Write routinely over extended time frames (time for research, reflection, and revision) and shorter time frames (a single sitting or a day or two) for a range of tasks, purposes, and audiences.
		L.9-10.1	Demonstrate command of the conventions of standard English grammar and usage when writing or speaking.
		L.9-10.6	Acquire and use accurately general academic and domain-specific words and phrases, sufficient for reading, writing, speaking, and listening at the college and career readiness level; demonstrate independence in gathering vocabulary knowledge when considering a word or phrase important to comprehension or expression
128	Before Reading: Hidden Secrets of the Creative Mind	RI.9-10.2	Determine a central idea of a text and analyze its development over the course of the text, including how it emerges and is shaped and refined by specific details; provide an objective summary of the text.
		RI.9-10.3	Analyze how the author unfolds an analysis or series of ideas or events, including the order in which the points are made, how they are introduced and developed, and the connections that are drawn between them.
		L.9-10.1.b	Use various types of phrases (noun, verb, adjectival, adverbial, participial, prepositional, absolute) and clauses (independent, dependent; noun, relative, adverbial) to convey specific meanings and add variety and interest to writing or presentations.
129–132	Read Hidden Secrets of the Creative Mind	RI.9-10.2	Determine a central idea of a text and analyze its development over the course of the text, including how it emerges and is shaped and refined by specific details; provide an objective summary of the text.
		RI.9-10.3	Analyze how the author unfolds an analysis or series of ideas or events, including the order in which the points are made, how they are introduced and developed, and the connections that are drawn between them.
		RI.9-10.10	By the end of grade 10, read and comprehend literary nonfiction at the high end of the grades 9–10 text complexity band independently and proficiently.
		W.9-10.9	Draw evidence from literary or informational texts to support analysis, reflection, and research.
		W.9-10.10	Write routinely over extended time frames (time for research, reflection, and revision) and shorter time frames (a single sitting or a day or two) for a range of tasks, purposes, and audiences.
		L.9-10.1	Demonstrate command of the conventions of standard English grammar and usage when writing or speaking.
		L.9-10.4.a	Use context as a clue to the meaning of a word or phrase.

SE Pages	Lesson	Code	Standards Text
129–132	**Read Hidden Secrets of the Creative Mind** continued	L.9-10.6	Acquire and use accurately general academic and domain-specific words and phrases, sufficient for reading, writing, speaking, and listening at the college and career readiness level; demonstrate independence in gathering vocabulary knowledge when considering a word or phrase important to comprehension or expression.
133	**Reflect and Assess** **Critical Thinking**	RI.9-10.1	Cite strong and thorough textual evidence to support analysis of what the text says explicitly as well as inferences drawn from the text.
		RI.9-10.10	By the end of grade 10, read and comprehend literary nonfiction at the high end of the grades 9–10 text complexity band independently and proficiently.
		SL.9-10.1	Initiate and participate effectively in a range of collaborative discussions (one-on-one, in groups, and teacher-led) with diverse partners on grades 9–10 topics, texts, and issues, building on others' ideas and expressing their own clearly and persuasively.
	Write About Literature	W.9-10.1	Write arguments to support claims in an analysis of substantive topics or texts, using valid reasoning and relevant and sufficient evidence.
	Key Vocabulary Review	L.9-10.6	Acquire and use accurately general academic and domain-specific words and phrases, sufficient for reading, writing, speaking, and listening at the college and career readiness level; demonstrate independence in gathering vocabulary knowledge when considering a word or phrase important to comprehension or expression.
	Read with Ease: Phrasing	RI.9-10.10	By the end of grade 9, read and comprehend literary nonfiction in the grades 9–10 text complexity band proficiently, with scaffolding as needed at the high end of the range. By the end of grade 10, read and comprehend literary nonfiction at the high end of the grades 9–10 text complexity band independently and proficiently.
134	**Grammar: Use Subject Pronouns**	L.9-10.1	Demonstrate command of the conventions of standard English grammar and usage when writing or speaking.
134	**Language Development: Describe People, Places, and Things**	SL.9-10.4	Present information, findings, and supporting evidence clearly, concisely, and logically such that listeners can follow the line of reasoning and the organization, development, substance, and style are appropriate to purpose, audience, and task.
134	**Literary Analysis: Analyze Description**	RI.9-10.4	Determine the meaning of words and phrases as they are used in a text, including figurative, connotative, and technical meanings; analyze the cumulative impact of specific word choices on meaning and tone.
134	**Listening/ Speaking: Interview**	SL.9-10.4	Present information, findings, and supporting evidence clearly, concisely, and logically such that listeners can follow the line of reasoning and the organization, development, substance, and style are appropriate to purpose, audience, and task.
135	**Vocabulary Study: Context Clues**	L.9-10.4.a	Use context as a clue to the meaning of a word or phrase.
135	**Writing on Demand: Writing a Test Essay**	W.9-10.1	Write arguments to support claims in an analysis of substantive topics or texts, using valid reasoning and relevant and sufficient evidence.

Common Core State Standards, continued

Cluster 1, continued

SE Pages	Lesson	Code	Standards Text
135	**Research/Speaking: Oral Presentation**	W.9-10.6	Use technology, including the Internet, to produce, publish, and update individual or shared writing products, taking advantage of technology's capacity to link to other information and to display information flexibly and dynamically.
		W.9-10.7	Conduct short as well as more sustained research projects to answer a question (including a self-generated question) or solve a problem; narrow or broaden the inquiry when appropriate; synthesize multiple sources on the subject, demonstrating understanding of the subject under investigation.
		SL.9-10.5	Make strategic use of digital media in presentations to enhance understanding of findings, reasoning, and evidence and to add interest.
136	**Workplace Workshop: Inside an Art Museum**	W.9-10.7	Conduct short as well as more sustained research projects to answer a question (including a self-generated question) or solve a problem; narrow or broaden the inquiry when appropriate; synthesize multiple sources on the subject, demonstrating understanding of the subject under investigation.
		W.9-10.10	Write routinely over extended time frames (time for research, reflection, and revision) and shorter time frames (a single sitting or a day or two) for a range of tasks, purposes, and audiences.
		SL.9-10.1	Initiate and participate effectively in a range of collaborative discussions (one-on-one, in groups, and teacher-led) with diverse partners on grades 9–10 topics, texts, and issues, building on others' ideas and expressing their own clearly and persuasively.
		L.9-10.6	Acquire and use accurately general academic and domain-specific words and phrases, sufficient for reading, writing, speaking, and listening at the college and career readiness level; demonstrate independence in gathering vocabulary knowledge when considering a word or phrase important to comprehension or expression.
137	**Vocabulary Workshop: Use Context Clues**	L.9-10.4.a	Use context as a clue to the meaning of a word or phrase.
		L.9-10.4.c	Consult general and specialized reference materials, both print and digital, to find the pronunciation of a word or determine or clarify its precise meaning, its part of speech, or its etymology.
		L.9-10.4.d	Verify the preliminary determination of the meaning of a word or phrase.

Cluster 2

SE Pages	Lesson	Code	Standards Text
138	**Prepare to Read**	RI.9-10.4	Determine the meaning of words and phrases as they are used in a text, including figurative, connotative, and technical meanings; analyze the cumulative impact of specific word choices on meaning and tone.
		SL.9-10.1	Initiate and participate effectively in a range of collaborative discussions (one-on-one, in groups, and teacher-led) with diverse partners on grades 9–10 topics, texts, and issues, building on others' ideas and expressing their own clearly and persuasively.
		L.9-10.6	Acquire and use accurately general academic and domain-specific words and phrases, sufficient for reading, writing, speaking, and listening at the college and career readiness level; demonstrate independence in gathering vocabulary knowledge when considering a word or phrase important to comprehension or expression.

SE Pages	Lesson	Code	Standards Text
139	**Before Reading: Hip-Hop as Culture**	RI.9-10.2	Determine a central idea of a text and analyze its development over the course of the text, including how it emerges and is shaped and refined by specific details; provide an objective summary of the text.
		RI.9-10.6	Determine an author's point of view or purpose in a text and analyze how an author uses rhetoric to advance that point of view or purpose.
140–149	**Read Hip-Hop as Culture**	RI.9-10.1	Cite strong and thorough textual evidence to support analysis of what the text says explicitly as well as inferences drawn from the text.
		RI.9-10.2	Determine a central idea of a text and analyze its development over the course of the text, including how it emerges and is shaped and refined by specific details; provide an objective summary of the text.
		RI.9-10.4	Determine the meaning of words and phrases as they are used in a text, including figurative, connotative, and technical meanings; analyze the cumulative impact of specific word choices on meaning and tone.
		RI.9-10.6	Determine an author's point of view or purpose in a text and analyze how an author uses rhetoric to advance that point of view or purpose.
		RI.9-10.10	By the end of grade 10, read and comprehend literary nonfiction at the high end of the grades 9–10 text complexity band independently and proficiently.
		W.9-10.9.b	Apply grades 9–10 Reading standards to literary nonfiction.
		W.9-10.10	Write routinely over extended time frames (time for research, reflection, and revision) and shorter time frames (a single sitting or a day or two) for a range of tasks, purposes, and audiences.
		L.9-10.1	Demonstrate command of the conventions of standard English grammar and usage when writing or speaking.
		L.9-10.2	Demonstrate command of the conventions of standard English capitalization, punctuation, and spelling when writing.
		L.9-10.2.c	Spell correctly.
		L.9-10.4.a	Use context as a clue to the meaning of a word or phrase.
		L.9-10.6	Acquire and use accurately general academic and domain-specific words and phrases, sufficient for reading, writing, speaking, and listening at the college and career readiness level; demonstrate independence in gathering vocabulary knowledge when considering a word or phrase important to comprehension or expression.
150	**Before Reading: I Am Somebody**	RL.9-10.2	Determine a theme or central idea of a text and analyze in detail its development over the course of the text, including how it emerges and is shaped and refined by specific details; provide an objective summary of the text.
		RL.9-10.5	Analyze how an author's choices concerning how to structure a text, order events within it, and manipulate time create such effects as mystery, tension, or surprise.

Common Core State Standards, continued

SE Pages	Lesson	Code	Standards Text
151–154	**Read I Am Somebody**	RL.9-10.1	Cite strong and thorough textual evidence to support analysis of what the text says explicitly as well as inferences drawn from the text.
		RL.9-10.2	Determine a theme or central idea of a text and analyze in detail its development over the course of the text, including how it emerges and is shaped and refined by specific details; provide an objective summary of the text.
		RL.9-10.4	Determine the meaning of words and phrases as they are used in the text, including figurative and connotative meanings; analyze the cumulative impact of specific word choices on meaning and tone.
		RL.9-10.5	Analyze how an author's choices concerning how to structure a text, order events within it, and manipulate time create such effects as mystery, tension, or surprise.
		RL.9-10.10	By the end of grade 10, read and comprehend literature, including stories, dramas, and poems, at the high end of the grades 9–10 text complexity band independently and proficiently.
		RI.9-10.2	Determine a central idea of a text and analyze its development over the course of the text, including how it emerges and is shaped and refined by specific details; provide an objective summary of the text.
		W.9-10.9.a	Apply grades 9–10 Reading standards to literature.
		W.9-10.10	Write routinely over extended time frames (time for research, reflection, and revision) and shorter time frames (a single sitting or a day or two) for a range of tasks, purposes, and audiences.
		L.9-10.1.b	Use various types of phrases (noun, verb, adjectival, adverbial, participial, prepositional, absolute) and clauses (independent, dependent; noun, relative, adverbial) to convey specific meanings and add variety and interest to writing or presentations.
		L.9-10.6	Acquire and use accurately general academic and domain-specific words and phrases, sufficient for reading, writing, speaking, and listening at the college and career readiness level; demonstrate independence in gathering vocabulary knowledge when considering a word or phrase important to comprehension or expression.
155	**Reflect and Assess Critical Thinking**	RL.9-10.1	Cite strong and thorough textual evidence to support analysis of what the text says explicitly as well as inferences drawn from the text.
		RI.9-10.1	Cite strong and thorough textual evidence to support analysis of what the text says explicitly as well as inferences drawn from the text.
		SL.9-10.1	Initiate and participate effectively in a range of collaborative discussions (one-on-one, in groups, and teacher-led) with diverse partners on grades 9–10 topics, texts, and issues, building on others' ideas and expressing their own clearly and persuasively.
	Write About Literature	RL.9-10.2	Determine a theme or central idea of a text and analyze in detail its development over the course of the text, including how it emerges and is shaped and refined by specific details; provide an objective summary of the text.
		RI.9-10.2	Determine a central idea of a text and analyze its development over the course of the text, including how it emerges and is shaped and refined by specific details; provide an objective summary of the text.

SE Pages	Lesson	Code	Standards Text
155	**Reflect and Assess** continued	W.9-10.10	Write routinely over extended time frames (time for research, reflection, and revision) and shorter time frames (a single sitting or a day or two) for a range of tasks, purposes, and audiences.
	Key Vocabulary Review	L.9-10.6	Acquire and use accurately general academic and domain-specific words and phrases, sufficient for reading, writing, speaking, and listening at the college and career readiness level; demonstrate independence in gathering vocabulary knowledge when considering a word or phrase important to comprehension or expression.
	Read with Ease: Intonation	RI.9-10.10	By the end of grade 10, read and comprehend literary nonfiction at the high end of the grades 9–10 text complexity band independently and proficiently.
156	**Grammar: Use Action Verbs in the Present**	L.9-10.1.b	Use various types of phrases (noun, verb, adjectival, adverbial, participial, prepositional, absolute) and clauses (independent, dependent; noun, relative, adverbial) to convey specific meanings and add variety and interest to writing or presentations.
156	**Language Development: Describe Experiences**	SL.9-10.1	Initiate and participate effectively in a range of collaborative discussions (one-on-one, in groups, and teacher-led) with diverse partners on grades 9–10 topics, texts, and issues, building on others' ideas and expressing their own clearly and persuasively.
156	**Literary Analysis: Analyze Style and Word Choice**	RL.9-10.4	Determine the meaning of words and phrases as they are used in the text, including figurative and connotative meanings; analyze the cumulative impact of specific word choices on meaning and tone.
		RI.9-10.4	Determine the meaning of words and phrases as they are used in a text, including figurative, connotative, and technical meanings; analyze the cumulative impact of specific word choices on meaning and tone.
156	**Research/Speaking: Oral Presentation**	W.9-10.7	Conduct short as well as more sustained research projects to answer a question (including a self-generated question) or solve a problem; narrow or broaden the inquiry when appropriate; synthesize multiple sources on the subject, demonstrating understanding of the subject under investigation.
		SL.9-10.4	Present information, findings, and supporting evidence clearly, concisely, and logically such that listeners can follow the line of reasoning and the organization, development, substance, and style are appropriate to purpose, audience, and task.
157	**Vocabulary Study: Context Clues for Idioms**	L.9-10.4.a	Use context as a clue to the meaning of a word or phrase.
		L.9-10.5.a	Interpret figures of speech in context and analyze their role in the text.
157	**Writing Trait: Focus and Unity**	W.9-10.5	Develop and strengthen writing as needed by planning, revising, editing, rewriting, or trying a new approach, focusing on addressing what is most significant for a specific purpose and audience.
158–159	**Listening and Speaking Workshop: Descriptive Presentation**	SL.9-10.3	Evaluate a speaker's point of view, reasoning, and use of evidence and rhetoric, identifying any fallacious reasoning or exaggerated or distorted evidence.
		SL.9-10.4	Present information, findings, and supporting evidence clearly, concisely, and logically such that listeners can follow the line of reasoning and the organization, development, substance, and style are appropriate to purpose, audience, and task.
		L.9-10.3	Apply knowledge of language to understand how language functions in different contexts, to make effective choices for meaning or style, and to comprehend more fully when reading or listening.

Common Core State Standards, continued

Cluster 3

SE Pages	Lesson	Code	Standards Text
160	**Prepare to Read**	RI.9-10.4	Determine the meaning of words and phrases as they are used in a text, including figurative, connotative, and technical meanings; analyze the cumulative impact of specific word choices on meaning and tone.
		SL.9-10.1	Initiate and participate effectively in a range of collaborative discussions (one-on-one, in groups, and teacher-led) with diverse partners on grades 9–10 topics, texts, and issues, building on others' ideas and expressing their own clearly and persuasively.
		L.9-10.5.b	Analyze nuances in the meaning of words with similar denotations.
		L.9-10.6	Acquire and use accurately general academic and domain-specific words and phrases, sufficient for reading, writing, speaking, and listening at the college and career readiness level; demonstrate independence in gathering vocabulary knowledge when considering a word or phrase important to comprehension or expression.
161	**Before Reading: Slam: Performance Poetry Lives On**	RI.9-10.2	Determine a central idea of a text and analyze its development over the course of the text, including how it emerges and is shaped and refined by specific details; provide an objective summary of the text.
		RI.9-10.6	Determine an author's point of view or purpose in a text and analyze how an author uses rhetoric to advance that point of view or purpose.
162–173	**Read Slam: Performance Poetry Lives On**	RI.9-10.1	Cite strong and thorough textual evidence to support analysis of what the text says explicitly as well as inferences drawn from the text.
		RI.9-10.2	Determine a central idea of a text and analyze its development over the course of the text, including how it emerges and is shaped and refined by specific details; provide an objective summary of the text.
		RI.9-10.4	Determine the meaning of words and phrases as they are used in a text, including figurative, connotative, and technical meanings; analyze the cumulative impact of specific word choices on meaning and tone.
		RI.9-10.6	Determine an author's point of view or purpose in a text and analyze how an author uses rhetoric to advance that point of view or purpose.
		RI.9-10.10	By the end of grade 10, read and comprehend literary nonfiction at the high end of the grades 9–10 text complexity band independently and proficiently.
		W.9-10.9.b	Apply grades 9–10 Reading standards to literary nonfiction.
		W.9-10.10	Write routinely over extended time frames (time for research, reflection, and revision) and shorter time frames (a single sitting or a day or two) for a range of tasks, purposes, and audiences.
		L.9-10.1.b	Use various types of phrases (noun, verb, adjectival, adverbial, participial, prepositional, absolute) and clauses (independent, dependent; noun, relative, adverbial) to convey specific meanings and add variety and interest to writing or presentations.
		L.9-10.4.c	Consult general and specialized reference materials, both print and digital, to find the pronunciation of a word or determine or clarify its precise meaning, its part of speech, or its etymology.
		L.9-10.5.b	Analyze nuances in the meaning of words with similar denotations.

SE Pages	Lesson	Code	Standards Text
162–173	**Read Slam: Performance Poetry Lives On** continued	L.9-10.6	Acquire and use accurately general academic and domain-specific words and phrases, sufficient for reading, writing, speaking, and listening at the college and career readiness level; demonstrate independence in gathering vocabulary knowledge when considering a word or phrase important to comprehension or expression.
174	**Before Reading: Euphoria**	RL.9-10.2	Determine a theme or central idea of a text and analyze in detail its development over the course of the text, including how it emerges and is shaped and refined by specific details; provide an objective summary of the text.
		RL.9-10.5	Analyze how an author's choices concerning how to structure a text, order events within it, and manipulate time create such effects as mystery, tension, or surprise.
175–176	**Read Euphoria**	RL.9-10.2	Determine a theme or central idea of a text and analyze in detail its development over the course of the text, including how it emerges and is shaped and refined by specific details; provide an objective summary of the text.
		RL.9-10.4	Determine the meaning of words and phrases as they are used in the text, including figurative and connotative meanings; analyze the cumulative impact of specific word choices on meaning and tone.
		RL.9-10.5	Analyze how an author's choices concerning how to structure a text, order events within it, and manipulate time create such effects as mystery, tension, or surprise.
		RL.9-10.10	By the end of grade 10, read and comprehend literature, including stories, dramas, and poems, at the high end of the grades 9–10 text complexity band independently and proficiently.
		W.9-10.9.a	Apply grades 9–10 Reading standards to literature.
		L.9-10.6	Acquire and use accurately general academic and domain-specific words and phrases, sufficient for reading, writing, speaking, and listening at the college and career readiness level; demonstrate independence in gathering vocabulary knowledge when considering a word or phrase important to comprehension or expression.
177	**Reflect and Assess Critical Thinking**	RL.9-10.2	Determine a theme or central idea of a text and analyze in detail its development over the course of the text, including how it emerges and is shaped and refined by specific details; provide an objective summary of the text.
		RI.9-10.2	Determine a central idea of a text and analyze its development over the course of the text, including how it emerges and is shaped and refined by specific details; provide an objective summary of the text.
		RI.9-10.10	By the end of grade 10, read and comprehend literary nonfiction at the high end of the grades 9–10 text complexity band independently and proficiently.
		SL.9-10.1	Initiate and participate effectively in a range of collaborative discussions (one-on-one, in groups, and teacher-led) with diverse partners on grades 9–10 topics, texts, and issues, building on others' ideas and expressing their own clearly and persuasively.
	Write About Literature	RL.9-10.5	Analyze how an author's choices concerning how to structure a text, order events within it, and manipulate time create such effects as mystery, tension, or surprise.

Common Core State Standards, continued

Cluster 3, continued

SE Pages	Lesson	Code	Standards Text
177	**Reflect and Assess** continued	W.9-10.10	Write routinely over extended time frames (time for research, reflection, and revision) and shorter time frames (a single sitting or a day or two) for a range of tasks, purposes, and audiences.
	Key Vocabulary Review	L.9-10.6	Acquire and use accurately general academic and domain-specific words and phrases, sufficient for reading, writing, speaking, and listening at the college and career readiness level; demonstrate independence in gathering vocabulary knowledge when considering a word or phrase important to comprehension or expression.
	Read with Ease: Expression	RI.9-10.10	By the end of grade 10, read and comprehend literary nonfiction at the high end of the grades 9–10 text complexity band independently and proficiently.
178	**Grammar: Use Verbs to Talk About the Present**	L.9-10.1.b	Use various types of phrases (noun, verb, adjectival, adverbial, participial, prepositional, absolute) and clauses (independent, dependent; noun, relative, adverbial) to convey specific meanings and add variety and interest to writing or presentations.
178	**Language Development: Give and Follow Commands**	SL.9-10.6	Adapt speech to a variety of contexts and tasks, demonstrating command of formal English when indicated or appropriate.
178	**Literary Analysis: Literary Movements**	RI.9-10.1	Cite strong and thorough textual evidence to support analysis of what the text says explicitly as well as inferences drawn from the text.
178	**Media Study: Judging Panel**	SL.9-10.1.d	Respond thoughtfully to diverse perspectives, summarize points of agreement and disagreement, and, when warranted, qualify or justify their own views and understanding and make new connections in light of the evidence and reasoning presented.
179	**Vocabulary Study: Context Clues for Idioms**	L.9-10.4.a	Use context as a clue to the meaning of a word or phrase.
		L.9-10.5.a	Interpret figures of speech in context and analyze their role in the text.
179	**Writing: Write a How-To Paragraph**	W.9-10.2	Write informative/explanatory texts to examine and convey complex ideas, concepts, and information clearly and accurately through the effective selection, organization, and analysis of content.

Close Reading

180–183	**Read The Creativity Crisis**	RI.9-10.10	By the end of grade 10, read and comprehend literary nonfiction at the high end of the grades 9–10 text complexity band independently and proficiently.

Unit Wrap-Up

184	**Unit Wrap-Up Present Your Project**	SL.9-10.4	Present information, findings, and supporting evidence clearly, concisely, and logically such that listeners can follow the line of reasoning and the organization, development, substance, and style are appropriate to purpose, audience, and task.
	Reflect on Your Reading	SL.9-10.1.a	Come to discussions prepared, having read and researched material under study; explicitly draw on that preparation by referring to evidence from texts and other research on the topic or issue to stimulate a thoughtful, well-reasoned exchange of ideas.
	Respond to the Essential Question	SL.9-10.1.a	Come to discussions prepared, having read and researched material under study; explicitly draw on that preparation by referring to evidence from texts and other research on the topic or issue to stimulate a thoughtful, well-reasoned exchange of ideas.

Writing Project: Position Paper

SE Pages	Lesson	Code	Standards Text
185–189	**Study Position Papers and Prewrite**	W.9-10.1.a	Introduce precise claim(s), distinguish the claim(s) from alternate or opposing claims, and create an organization that establishes clear relationships among claim(s), counterclaims, reasons, and evidence.
		W.9-10.1.b	Develop claim(s) and counterclaims fairly, supplying evidence for each while pointing out the strengths and limitations of both in a manner that anticipates the audience's knowledge level and concerns.
190–191	**Position Paper: Draft**	W.9-10.1.a	Introduce precise claim(s), distinguish the claim(s) from alternate or opposing claims, and create an organization that establishes clear relationships among claim(s), counterclaims, reasons, and evidence.
		W.9-10.1.b	Develop claim(s) and counterclaims fairly, supplying evidence for each while pointing out the strengths and limitations of both in a manner that anticipates the audience's knowledge level and concerns.
		W.9-10.1.d	Establish and maintain a formal style and objective tone while attending to the norms and conventions of the discipline in which they are writing.
		W.9-10.4	Produce clear and coherent writing in which the development, organization, and style are appropriate to task, purpose, and audience.
192–195	**Position Paper: Revise** **Trait: Focus and Unity**	W.9-10.1	Write arguments to support claims in an analysis of substantive topics or texts, using valid reasoning and relevant and sufficient evidence.
		W.9-10.1.a	Introduce precise claim(s), distinguish the claim(s) from alternate or opposing claims, and create an organization that establishes clear relationships among claim(s), counterclaims, reasons, and evidence.
		W.9-10.1.b	Develop claim(s) and counterclaims fairly, supplying evidence for each while pointing out the strengths and limitations of both in a manner that anticipates the audience's knowledge level and concerns.
		W.9-10.1.c	Use words, phrases, and clauses to link the major sections of the text, create cohesion, and clarify the relationships between claim(s) and reasons, between reasons and evidence, and between claim(s) and counterclaims.
		W.9-10.1.d	Establish and maintain a formal style and objective tone while attending to the norms and conventions of the discipline in which they are writing.
		W.9-10.5	Develop and strengthen writing as needed by planning, revising, editing, rewriting, or trying a new approach, focusing on addressing what is most significant for a specific purpose and audience.
		SL.9-10.1	Initiate and participate effectively in a range of collaborative discussions (one-on-one, in groups, and teacher-led) with diverse partners on grades 9-10 topics, texts, and issues, building on others' ideas and expressing their own clearly and persuasively.
		SL.9-10.1.d	Respond thoughtfully to diverse perspectives, summarize points of agreement and disagreement, and, when warranted, qualify or justify their own views and understanding and make new connections in light of the evidence and reasoning presented.

Common Core State Standards, continued

Writing Project: Position Paper, continued

SE Pages	Lesson	Code	Standards Text
196–198	Position Paper: Edit and Proofread	L.9-10.1	Demonstrate command of the conventions of standard English grammar and usage when writing or speaking.
	Capitalization: Names of Groups Colons Spelling Present Tense Verbs	L.9-10.2	Demonstrate command of the conventions of standard English capitalization, punctuation, and spelling when writing.
		L.9-10.2.b	Use a colon to introduce a list or quotation.
		L.9-10.2.c	Spell correctly.
		L.9-10.3.a	Write and edit work so that it conforms to the guidelines in a style manual appropriate for the discipline and writing type.
199	Position Paper: Publish and Present	W.9-10.6	Use technology, including the Internet, to produce, publish, and update individual or shared writing products, taking advantage of technology's capacity to link to other information and to display information flexibly and dynamically.
		SL.9-10.3	Evaluate a speaker's point of view, reasoning, and use of evidence and rhetoric, identifying any fallacious reasoning or exaggerated or distorted evidence.
		SL.9-10.4	Present information, findings, and supporting evidence clearly, concisely, and logically such that listeners can follow the line of reasoning and the organization, development, substance, and style are appropriate to purpose, audience, and task.
		SL.9-10.6	Adapt speech to a variety of contexts and tasks, demonstrating command of formal English when indicated or appropriate.
UNIT 3: The Hero Within			
200–201	Discuss the Essential Question	SL.9-10.1.b	Work with peers to set rules for collegial discussions and decision-making (e.g., informal consensus, taking votes on key issues, presentation of alternate views), clear goals and deadlines, and individual roles as needed.
		SL.9-10.3	Evaluate a speaker's point of view, reasoning, and use of evidence and rhetoric, identifying any fallacious reasoning or exaggerated or distorted evidence.
202	Debate and Vote	SL.9-10.4	Present information, findings, and supporting evidence clearly, concisely, and logically such that listeners can follow the line of reasoning and the organization, development, substance, and style are appropriate to purpose, audience, and task.
203	Plan a Project	SL.9-10.1.b	Work with peers to set rules for collegial discussions and decision-making (e.g., informal consensus, taking votes on key issues, presentation of alternate views), clear goals and deadlines, and individual roles as needed.
203	Choose More to Read	RL.9-10.10	By the end of grade 10, read and comprehend literature, including stories, dramas, and poems, at the high end of the grades 9–10 text complexity band independently and proficiently.
		RI.9-10.10	By the end of grade 10, read and comprehend literary nonfiction at the high end of the grades 9–10 text complexity band independently and proficiently.
204–207	How to Read Short Stories	RL.9-10.1	Cite strong and thorough textual evidence to support analysis of what the text says explicitly as well as inferences drawn from the text.
		RL.9-10.6	Analyze a particular point of view or cultural experience reflected in a work of literature from outside the United States, drawing on a wide reading of world literature.

UNIT 3: The Hero Within, continued

SE Pages	Lesson	Code	Standards Text
204–207	**How to Read Short Stories** continued	RL.9-10.10	By the end of grade 10, read and comprehend literature, including stories, dramas, and poems, at the high end of the grades 9–10 text complexity band independently and proficiently.
		SL.9-10.1	Initiate and participate effectively in a range of collaborative discussions (one-on-one, in groups, and teacher-led) with diverse partners on grades 9-10 topics, texts, and issues, building on others' ideas and expressing their own clearly and persuasively.
		L.9-10.6	Acquire and use accurately general academic and domain-specific words and phrases, sufficient for reading, writing, speaking, and listening at the college and career readiness level; demonstrate independence in gathering vocabulary knowledge when considering a word or phrase important to comprehension or expression.

Cluster 1

SE Pages	Lesson	Code	Standards Text
208	**Prepare to Read**	RL.9-10.4	Determine the meaning of words and phrases as they are used in the text, including figurative and connotative meanings; analyze the cumulative impact of specific word choices on meaning and tone.
		SL.9-10.1	Initiate and participate effectively in a range of collaborative discussions (one-on-one, in groups, and teacher-led) with diverse partners on grades 9-10 topics, texts, and issues, building on others' ideas and expressing their own clearly and persuasively.
		L.9-10.4.c	Consult general and specialized reference materials, both print and digital, to find the pronunciation of a word or determine or clarify its precise meaning, its part of speech, or its etymology.
		L.9-10.6	Acquire and use accurately general academic and domain-specific words and phrases, sufficient for reading, writing, speaking, and listening at the college and career readiness level; demonstrate independence in gathering vocabulary knowledge when considering a word or phrase important to comprehension or expression.
209	**Before Reading: The Sword in the Stone**	RL.9-10.1	Cite strong and thorough textual evidence to support analysis of what the text says explicitly as well as inferences drawn from the text.
		RL.9-10.6	Analyze a particular point of view or cultural experience reflected in a work of literature from outside the United States, drawing on a wide reading of world literature.
210–221	**Read The Sword in the Stone**	RL.9-10.1	Cite strong and thorough textual evidence to support analysis of what the text says explicitly as well as inferences drawn from the text.
		RL.9-10.3	Analyze how complex characters (e.g., those with multiple or conflicting motivations) develop over the course of a text, interact with other characters, and advance the plot or develop the theme.
		RL.9-10.4	Determine the meaning of words and phrases as they are used in the text, including figurative and connotative meanings; analyze the cumulative impact of specific word choices on meaning and tone.
		RL.9-10.6	Analyze a particular point of view or cultural experience reflected in a work of literature from outside the United States, drawing on a wide reading of world literature.
		RL.9-10.10	By the end of grade 10, read and comprehend literature, including stories, dramas, and poems, at the high end of the grades 9–10 text complexity band independently and proficiently.
		W.9-10.9.a	Apply grades 9–10 Reading standards to literature.

Common Core State Standards, continued

Cluster 1, continued

SE Pages	Lesson	Code	Standards Text
210–221	**Read The Sword in the Stone** continued	W.9-10.10	Write routinely over extended time frames (time for research, reflection, and revision) and shorter time frames (a single sitting or a day or two) for a range of tasks, purposes, and audiences.
		L.9-10.1.a	Use parallel structure.
		L.9-10.2.c	Spell correctly.
		L.9-10.4.a	Use context as a clue to the meaning of a word or phrase.
		L.9-10.4.b	Identify and correctly use patterns of word changes that indicate different meanings or parts of speech.
		L.9-10.4.c	Consult general and specialized reference materials, both print and digital, to find the pronunciation of a word or determine or clarify its precise meaning, its part of speech, or its etymology.
		L.9-10.6	Acquire and use accurately general academic and domain-specific words and phrases, sufficient for reading, writing, speaking, and listening at the college and career readiness level; demonstrate independence in gathering vocabulary knowledge when considering a word or phrase important to comprehension or expression.
222	**Before Reading: Was There a Real King Arthur?**	RI.9-10.1	Cite strong and thorough textual evidence to support analysis of what the text says explicitly as well as inferences drawn from the text.
		RI.9-10.5	Analyze in detail how an author's ideas or claims are developed and refined by particular sentences, paragraphs, or larger portions of a text.
223–230	**Read Was There a Real King Arthur?**	RI.9-10.1	Cite strong and thorough textual evidence to support analysis of what the text says explicitly as well as inferences drawn from the text.
		RI.9-10.2	Determine a central idea of a text and analyze its development over the course of the text, including how it emerges and is shaped and refined by specific details; provide an objective summary of the text.
		RI.9-10.5	Analyze in detail how an author's ideas or claims are developed and refined by particular sentences, paragraphs, or larger portions of a text.
		RI.9-10.10	By the end of grade 10, read and comprehend literary nonfiction at the high end of the grades 9–10 text complexity band independently and proficiently.
		W.9-10.9.b	Apply grades 9–10 Reading standards to literary nonfiction.
		W.9-10.10	Write routinely over extended time frames (time for research, reflection, and revision) and shorter time frames (a single sitting or a day or two) for a range of tasks, purposes, and audiences.
		L.9-10.1	Demonstrate command of the conventions of standard English grammar and usage when writing or speaking.
		L.9-10.6	Acquire and use accurately general academic and domain-specific words and phrases, sufficient for reading, writing, speaking, and listening at the college and career readiness level; demonstrate independence in gathering vocabulary knowledge when considering a word or phrase important to comprehension or expression.

SE Pages	Lesson	Code	Standards Text
231	**Reflect and Assess Critical Thinking**	RL.9-10.1	Cite strong and thorough textual evidence to support analysis of what the text says explicitly as well as inferences drawn from the text.
		RI.9-10.1	Cite strong and thorough textual evidence to support analysis of what the text says explicitly as well as inferences drawn from the text.
		SL.9-10.1	Initiate and participate effectively in a range of collaborative discussions (one-on-one, in groups, and teacher-led) with diverse partners on grades 9–10 topics, texts, and issues, building on others' ideas and expressing their own clearly and persuasively.
	Write About Literature	W.9-10.1	Write arguments to support claims in an analysis of substantive topics or texts, using valid reasoning and relevant and sufficient evidence.
	Key Vocabulary Review	L.9-10.6	Acquire and use accurately general academic and domain-specific words and phrases, sufficient for reading, writing, speaking, and listening at the college and career readiness level; demonstrate independence in gathering vocabulary knowledge when considering a word or phrase important to comprehension or expression.
	Read with Ease: Phrasing	RL.9-10.10	By the end of grade 10, read and comprehend literature, including stories, dramas, and poems, at the high end of the grades 9–10 text complexity band independently and proficiently.
232	**Grammar: Use Verb Tenses**	L.9-10.1.a	Use parallel structure.
232	**Language Development: Ask for and Give Information**	SL.9-10.1.a	Come to discussions prepared, having read and researched material under study; explicitly draw on that preparation by referring to evidence from texts and other research on the topic or issue to stimulate a thoughtful, well-reasoned exchange of ideas.
232	**Literary Analysis: Compare Character's Motives and Traits**	RL.9-10.3	Analyze how complex characters develop over the course of a text, interact with other characters, and advance the plot or develop the theme.
233	**Vocabulary Study: Word Families**	L.9-10.4.b	Identify and correctly use patterns of word changes that indicate different meanings or parts of speech.
		L.9-10.4.d	Verify the preliminary determination of the meaning of a word or phrase.
233	**Writing on Demand: Write a Test Essay**	W.9-10.1	Write arguments to support claims in an analysis of substantive topics or texts, using valid reasoning and relevant and sufficient evidence.
233	**Media Study: Compare Visuals**	W.9-10.7	Conduct short as well as more sustained research projects to answer a question (including a self-generated question) or solve a problem; narrow or broaden the inquiry when appropriate; synthesize multiple sources on the subject, demonstrating understanding of the subject under investigation.
234	**Workplace Workshop: Inside an Airport**	W.9-10.7	Conduct short as well as more sustained research projects to answer a question (including a self-generated question) or solve a problem; narrow or broaden the inquiry when appropriate; synthesize multiple sources on the subject, demonstrating understanding of the subject under investigation.
		L.9-10.6	Acquire and use accurately general academic and domain-specific words and phrases, sufficient for reading, writing, speaking, and listening at the college and career readiness level; demonstrate independence in gathering vocabulary knowledge when considering a word or phrase important to comprehension or expression.

Common Core State Standards, continued

Cluster 1, continued

SE Pages	Lesson	Code	Standards Text
235	**Vocabulary Workshop: Find Familiar Words**	L.9-10.4.b	Identify and correctly use patterns of word changes that indicate different meanings or parts of speech.
		L.9-10.4.c	Consult general and specialized reference materials, both print and digital, to find the pronunciation of a word or determine or clarify its precise meaning, its part of speech, or its etymology.
		L.9-10.4.d	Verify the preliminary determination of the meaning of a word or phrase.

Cluster 2

SE Pages	Lesson	Code	Standards Text
236	**Prepare to Read**	RL.9-10.4	Determine the meaning of words and phrases as they are used in the text, including figurative and connotative meanings; analyze the cumulative impact of specific word choices on meaning and tone.
		SL.9-10.1	Initiate and participate effectively in a range of collaborative discussions (one-on-one, in groups, and teacher-led) with diverse partners on grades 9–10 topics, texts, and issues, building on others' ideas and expressing their own clearly and persuasively.
		L.9-10.6	Acquire and use accurately general academic and domain-specific words and phrases, sufficient for reading, writing, speaking, and listening at the college and career readiness level; demonstrate independence in gathering vocabulary knowledge when considering a word or phrase important to comprehension or expression.
237	**Before Reading: A Job for Valentin**	RL.9-10.1	Cite strong and thorough textual evidence to support analysis of what the text says explicitly as well as inferences drawn from the text.
		RL.9-10.6	Analyze a particular point of view or cultural experience reflected in a work of literature from outside the United States, drawing on a wide reading of world literature.
238–250	**Read A Job or Valentin**	RL.9-10.1	Cite strong and thorough textual evidence to support analysis of what the text says explicitly as well as inferences drawn from the text.
		RL.9-10.2	Determine a theme or central idea of a text and analyze in detail its development over the course of the text, including how it emerges and is shaped and refined by specific details; provide an objective summary of the text.
		RL.9-10.3	Analyze how complex characters develop over the course of a text, interact with other characters, and advance the plot or develop the theme.
		RL.9-10.4	Determine the meaning of words and phrases as they are used in the text, including figurative and connotative meanings; analyze the cumulative impact of specific word choices on meaning and tone.
		RL.9-10.6	Analyze a particular point of view or cultural experience reflected in a work of literature from outside the United States, drawing on a wide reading of world literature.
		RL.9-10.7	Analyze the representation of a subject or a key scene in two different artistic mediums, including what is emphasized or absent in each treatment.
		RL.9-10.10	By the end of grade 10, read and comprehend literature, including stories, dramas, and poems, at the high end of the grades 9–10 text complexity band independently and proficiently.
		W.9-10.9.a	Apply grades 9–10 Reading standards to literature.

SE Pages	Lesson	Code	Standards Text
238–250	**Read A Job or Valentin** continued	W.9-10.10	Write routinely over extended time frames (time for research, reflection, and revision) and shorter time frames (a single sitting or a day or two) for a range of tasks, purposes, and audiences.
		L.9-10.1.b	Use various types of phrases (noun, verb, adjectival, adverbial, participial, prepositional, absolute) and clauses (independent, dependent; noun, relative, adverbial) to convey specific meanings and add variety and interest to writing or presentations.
		L.9-10.2.c	Spell correctly.
		L.9-10.5.a	Interpret figures of speech in context and analyze their role in the text.
		L.9-10.6	Acquire and use accurately general academic and domain-specific words and phrases, sufficient for reading, writing, speaking, and listening at the college and career readiness level; demonstrate independence in gathering vocabulary knowledge when considering a word or phrase important to comprehension or expression.
251	**Postscript: Hero**	RL.9-10.2	Determine a theme or central idea of a text and analyze in detail its development over the course of the text, including how it emerges and is shaped and refined by specific details; provide an objective summary of the text.
		SL.9-10.1	Initiate and participate effectively in a range of collaborative discussions (one-on-one, in groups, and teacher-led) with diverse partners on grades 9–10 topics, texts, and issues, building on others' ideas and expressing their own clearly and persuasively.
252	**Before Reading: In the Heart of a Hero**	RI.9-10.1	Cite strong and thorough textual evidence to support analysis of what the text says explicitly as well as inferences drawn from the text.
		RI.9-10.5	Analyze in detail how an author's ideas or claims are developed and refined by particular sentences, paragraphs, or larger portions of a text.
253–256	**Read In the Heart of a Hero**	RI.9-10.1	Cite strong and thorough textual evidence to support analysis of what the text says explicitly as well as inferences drawn from the text.
		RI.9-10.5	Analyze in detail how an author's ideas or claims are developed and refined by particular sentences, paragraphs, or larger portions of a text.
		RI.9-10.7	Analyze various accounts of a subject told in different mediums, determining which details are emphasized in each account.
		RI.9-10.10	By the end of grade 10, read and comprehend literary nonfiction at the high end of the grades 9–10 text complexity band independently and proficiently.
		W.9-10.1.b	Develop claim(s) and counterclaims fairly, supplying evidence for each while pointing out the strengths and limitations of both in a manner that anticipates the audience's knowledge level and concerns.
		W.9-10.10	Write routinely over extended time frames (time for research, reflection, and revision) and shorter time frames (a single sitting or a day or two) for a range of tasks, purposes, and audiences.
		L.9-10.1.a	Use parallel structure.
		L.9-10.1.b	Use various types of phrases (noun, verb, adjectival, adverbial, participial, prepositional, absolute) and clauses (independent, dependent; noun, relative, adverbial) to convey specific meanings and add variety and interest to writing or presentations.

Common Core State Standards, continued

Cluster 2, continued

SE Pages	Lesson	Code	Standards Text
253–256	**Read In the Heart of a Hero** continued	L.9-10.4.a	Use context (e.g., the overall meaning of a sentence, paragraph, or text; a word's position or function in a sentence) as a clue to the meaning of a word or phrase.
		L.9-10.4.b	Identify and correctly use patterns of word changes that indicate different meanings or parts of speech.
		L.9-10.6	Acquire and use accurately general academic and domain-specific words and phrases, sufficient for reading, writing, speaking, and listening at the college and career readiness level; demonstrate independence in gathering vocabulary knowledge when considering a word or phrase important to comprehension or expression.
257	**Reflect and Assess Critical Thinking**	RL.9-10.1	Cite strong and thorough textual evidence to support analysis of what the text says explicitly as well as inferences drawn from the text.
		RI.9-10.1	Cite strong and thorough textual evidence to support analysis of what the text says explicitly as well as inferences drawn from the text.
		SL.9-10.1.a	Come to discussions prepared, having read and researched material under study; explicitly draw on that preparation by referring to evidence from texts and other research on the topic or issue to stimulate a thoughtful, well-reasoned exchange of ideas.
		SL.9-10.6	Adapt speech to a variety of contexts and tasks, demonstrating command of formal English when indicated or appropriate.
	Write About Literature	W.9-10.9.a	Apply grades 9–10 Reading standards to literature.
	Key Vocabulary Review	L.9-10.6	Acquire and use accurately general academic and domain-specific words and phrases, sufficient for reading, writing, speaking, and listening at the college and career readiness level; demonstrate independence in gathering vocabulary knowledge when considering a word or phrase important to comprehension or expression.
	Read with Ease: Expression	RL.9-10.10	By the end of grade 10, read and comprehend literature, including stories, dramas, and poems, at the high end of the grades 9–10 text complexity band independently and proficiently.
258	**Grammar: Use Verb Tenses**	L.9-10.1.a	Use parallel structure.
		L.9-10.1.b	Use various types of phrases (noun, verb, adjectival, adverbial, participial, prepositional, absolute) and clauses (independent, dependent; noun, relative, adverbial) to convey specific meanings and add variety and interest to writing or presentations.
258	**Language Development: Engage in Discussion**	SL.9-10.1.b	Work with peers to set rules for collegial discussions and decision-making (e.g., informal consensus, taking votes on key issues, presentation of alternate views), clear goals and deadlines, and individual roles as needed
258	**Literary Analysis: Multiple Themes in Text**	RL.9-10.2	Determine a theme or central idea of a text and analyze in detail its development over the course of the text, including how it emerges and is shaped and refined by specific details; provide an objective summary of the text.
259	**Vocabulary Study: Borrowed Words**	L.9-10.4.c	Consult general and specialized reference materials (e.g., dictionaries, glossaries, thesauruses), both print and digital, to find the pronunciation of a word or determine or clarify its precise meaning, its part of speech, or its etymology.

Cluster 2, continued

SE Pages	Lesson	Code	Standards Text
259	Research/Writing: Profile	W.9-10.2.b	Develop the topic with well-chosen, relevant, and sufficient facts, extended definitions, concrete details, quotations, or other information and examples appropriate to the audience's knowledge of the topic.
		W.9-10.7	Conduct short as well as more sustained research projects to answer a question (including a self-generated question) or solve a problem; narrow or broaden the inquiry when appropriate; synthesize multiple sources on the subject, demonstrating understanding of the subject under investigation.
259	Writing Trait: Voice and Style	W.9-10.5	Develop and strengthen writing as needed by planning, revising, editing, rewriting, or trying a new approach, focusing on addressing what is most significant for a specific purpose and audience.
260–261	Listening and Speaking Workshop: Panel Discussion	SL.9-10.1.b	Work with peers to set rules for collegial discussions and decision-making (e.g., informal consensus, taking votes on key issues, presentation of alternate views), clear goals and deadlines, and individual roles as needed.
		SL.9-10.1.c	Propel conversations by posing and responding to questions that relate the current discussion to broader themes or larger ideas; actively incorporate others into the discussion; and clarify, verify, or challenge ideas and conclusions.
		SL.9-10.1.d	Respond thoughtfully to diverse perspectives, summarize points of agreement and disagreement, and, when warranted, qualify or justify their own views and understanding and make new connections in light of the evidence and reasoning presented.
		SL.9-10.3	Evaluate a speaker's point of view, reasoning, and use of evidence and rhetoric, identifying any fallacious reasoning or exaggerated or distorted evidence.
		L.9-10.3	Apply knowledge of language to understand how language functions in different contexts, to make effective choices for meaning or style, and to comprehend more fully when reading or listening.

Cluster 3

SE Pages	Lesson	Code	Standards Text
262	Prepare to Read	RI.9-10.4	Determine the meaning of words and phrases as they are used in a text, including figurative, connotative, and technical meanings; analyze the cumulative impact of specific word choices on meaning and tone.
		SL.9-10.1	Initiate and participate effectively in a range of collaborative discussions (one-on-one, in groups, and teacher-led) with diverse partners on grades 9–10 topics, texts, and issues, building on others' ideas and expressing their own clearly and persuasively.
		L.9-10.4.b	Identify and correctly use patterns of word changes that indicate different meanings or parts of speech.
		L.9-10.6	Acquire and use accurately general academic and domain-specific words and phrases, sufficient for reading, writing, speaking, and listening at the college and career readiness level; demonstrate independence in gathering vocabulary knowledge when considering a word or phrase important to comprehension or expression.
263	Before Reading: The Woman in the Snow	RL.9-10.1	Cite strong and thorough textual evidence to support analysis of what the text says explicitly as well as inferences drawn from the text.
		RL.9-10.6	Analyze a particular point of view or cultural experience reflected in a work of literature from outside the United States, drawing on a wide reading of world literature.

Common Core State Standards, continued

Cluster 3, continued

SE Pages	Lesson	Code	Standards Text
264–277	**Read The Woman in the Snow**	RL.9-10.1	Cite strong and thorough textual evidence to support analysis of what the text says explicitly as well as inferences drawn from the text.
		RL.9-10.4	Determine the meaning of words and phrases as they are used in the text, including figurative and connotative meanings; analyze the cumulative impact of specific word choices on meaning and tone.
		RL.9-10.6	Analyze a particular point of view or cultural experience reflected in a work of literature from outside the United States, drawing on a wide reading of world literature.
		RL.9-10.7	Analyze the representation of a subject or a key scene in two different artistic mediums, including what is emphasized or absent in each treatment.
		RL.9-10.10	By the end of grade 10, read and comprehend literature, including stories, dramas, and poems, at the high end of the grades 9–10 text complexity band independently and proficiently.
		W.9-10.9.a	Apply grades 9–10 Reading standards to literature.
		W.9-10.10	Write routinely over extended time frames (time for research, reflection, and revision) and shorter time frames (a single sitting or a day or two) for a range of tasks, purposes, and audiences.
		L.9-10.1	Demonstrate command of the conventions of standard English grammar and usage when writing or speaking.
		L.9-10.6	Acquire and use accurately general academic and domain-specific words and phrases, sufficient for reading, writing, speaking, and listening at the college and career readiness level; demonstrate independence in gathering vocabulary knowledge when considering a word or phrase important to comprehension or expression.
278	**Before Reading: Rosa Parks**	RI.9-10.1	Cite strong and thorough textual evidence to support analysis of what the text says explicitly as well as inferences drawn from the text.
		RI.9-10.3	Analyze how the author unfolds an analysis or series of ideas or events, including the order in which the points are made, how they are introduced and developed, and the connections that are drawn between them.
279–284	**Read Rosa Parks**	RI.9-10.1	Cite strong and thorough textual evidence to support analysis of what the text says explicitly as well as inferences drawn from the text.
		RI.9-10.2	Determine a central idea of a text and analyze its development over the course of the text, including how it emerges and is shaped and refined by specific details; provide an objective summary of the text.
		RI.9-10.3	Analyze how the author unfolds an analysis or series of ideas or events, including the order in which the points are made, how they are introduced and developed, and the connections that are drawn between them.
		RI.9-10.10	By the end of grade 10, read and comprehend literary nonfiction at the high end of the grades 9–10 text complexity band independently and proficiently.
		W.9-10.10	Write routinely over extended time frames (time for research, reflection, and revision) and shorter time frames (a single sitting or a day or two) for a range of tasks, purposes, and audiences.
		L.9-10.1	Demonstrate command of the conventions of standard English grammar and usage when writing or speaking.

SE Pages	Lesson	Code	Standards Text
279–284	**Read Rosa Parks** continued	L.9-10.6	Acquire and use accurately general academic and domain-specific words and phrases, sufficient for reading, writing, speaking, and listening at the college and career readiness level; demonstrate independence in gathering vocabulary knowledge when considering a word or phrase important to comprehension or expression.
285	**Reflect and Assess Critical Thinking**	RL.9-10.1	Cite strong and thorough textual evidence to support analysis of what the text says explicitly as well as inferences drawn from the text.
		RL.9-10.2	Determine a theme or central idea of a text and analyze in detail its development over the course of the text, including how it emerges and is shaped and refined by specific details; provide an objective summary of the text.
		RL.9-10.6	Analyze a particular point of view or cultural experience reflected in a work of literature from outside the United States, drawing on a wide reading of world literature.
		RL.9-10.10	By the end of grade 10, read and comprehend literature, including stories, dramas, and poems, at the high end of the grades 9–10 text complexity band independently and proficiently.
		RI.9-10.1	Cite strong and thorough textual evidence to support analysis of what the text says explicitly as well as inferences drawn from the text.
		RI.9-10.2	Determine a central idea of a text and analyze its development over the course of the text, including how it emerges and is shaped and refined by specific details; provide an objective summary of the text.
		SL.9-10.1	Initiate and participate effectively in a range of collaborative discussions (one-on-one, in groups, and teacher-led) with diverse partners on grades 9–10 topics, texts, and issues, building on others' ideas and expressing their own clearly and persuasively.
	Write About Literature	W.9-10.2	Write informative/explanatory texts to examine and convey complex ideas, concepts, and information clearly and accurately through the effective selection, organization, and analysis of content.
	Key Vocabulary Review	L.9-10.6	Acquire and use accurately general academic and domain-specific words and phrases, sufficient for reading, writing, speaking, and listening at the college and career readiness level; demonstrate independence in gathering vocabulary knowledge when considering a word or phrase important to comprehension or expression.
	Read with Ease: Intonation	RL.9-10.10	By the end of grade 10, read and comprehend literature, including stories, dramas, and poems, at the high end of the grades 9–10 text complexity band independently and proficiently.
286	**Grammar: Use Subject and Object Pronouns**	L.9-10.1	Demonstrate command of the conventions of standard English grammar and usage when writing or speaking.
286	**Language Development: Elaborate During a Discussion**	SL.9-10.1.a	Come to discussions prepared, having read and researched material under study; explicitly draw on that preparation by referring to evidence from texts and other research on the topic or issue to stimulate a thoughtful, well-reasoned exchange of ideas.
286	**Literary Analysis: Compare Themes**	RL.9-10.2	Determine a theme or central idea of a text and analyze in detail its development over the course of the text, including how it emerges and is shaped and refined by specific details; provide an objective summary of the text.
287	**Vocabulary Study: Word Families**	L.9-10.4.b	Identify and correctly use patterns of word changes that indicate different meanings or parts of speech.
		L.9-10.4.d	Verify the preliminary determination of the meaning of a word or phrase.

Common Core State Standards, continued

Cluster 3, continued

SE Pages	Lesson	Code	Standards Text
287	Writing: Write an Opinion Paragraph	W.9-10.1	Write arguments to support claims in an analysis of substantive topics or texts, using valid reasoning and relevant and sufficient evidence.
		W.9-10.5	Develop and strengthen writing as needed by planning, revising, editing, rewriting, or trying a new approach, focusing on addressing what is most significant for a specific purpose and audience.
287	Listening/Speaking: Oral Interpretation	SL.9-10.6	Adapt speech to a variety of contexts and tasks, demonstrating command of formal English when indicated or appropriate.

Close Reading

288–289	Read The American Promise	RI.9-10.10	By the end of grade 10, read and comprehend literary nonfiction at the high end of the grades 9–10 text complexity band independently and proficiently.

Unit Wrap-Up

290	Unit Wrap-Up Present Your Project	SL.9-10.5	Make strategic use of digital media in presentations to enhance understanding of findings, reasoning, and evidence and to add interest.
	Reflect on Your Reading	SL.9-10.1.a	Come to discussions prepared, having read and researched material under study; explicitly draw on that preparation by referring to evidence from texts and other research on the topic or issue to stimulate a thoughtful, well-reasoned exchange of ideas.
	Respond to the Essential Question	SL.9-10.1.a	Come to discussions prepared, having read and researched material under study; explicitly draw on that preparation by referring to evidence from texts and other research on the topic or issue to stimulate a thoughtful, well-reasoned exchange of ideas.

Writing Project: Response to Literature

291–295	Study a Response to Literature and Prewrite	W.9-10.2.a	Introduce a topic; organize complex ideas, concepts, and information to make important connections and distinctions; include formatting, graphics, and multimedia when useful to aiding comprehension.
		W.9-10.2.b	Develop the topic with well-chosen, relevant, and sufficient facts, extended definitions, concrete details, quotations, or other information and examples appropriate to the audience's knowledge of the topic.
		W.9-10.5	Develop and strengthen writing as needed by planning, revising, editing, rewriting, or trying a new approach, focusing on addressing what is most significant for a specific purpose and audience.
		W.9-10.6	Use technology, including the Internet, to produce, publish, and update individual or shared writing products, taking advantage of technology's capacity to link to other information and to display information flexibly and dynamically.
296–297	Response to Literature: Draft	W.9-10.2	Write informative/explanatory texts to examine and convey complex ideas, concepts, and information clearly and accurately through the effective selection, organization, and analysis of content.
		W.9-10.2.a	Introduce a topic; organize complex ideas, concepts, and information to make important connections and distinctions; include formatting, graphics, and multimedia when useful to aiding comprehension.
		W.9-10.4	Produce clear and coherent writing in which the development, organization, and style are appropriate to task, purpose, and audience.

Writing Project: Response to Literature, continued

SE Pages	Lesson	Code	Standards Text
296–297	**Response to Literature: Draft** continued	W.9-10.6	Use technology, including the Internet, to produce, publish, and update individual or shared writing products, taking advantage of technology's capacity to link to other information and to display information flexibly and dynamically.
		W.9-10.9	Draw evidence from literary or informational texts to support analysis, reflection, and research.
298–301	**Response to Literature: Revise Trait: Voice and Style**	W.9-10.2.a	Introduce a topic; organize complex ideas, concepts, and information to make important co nnections and distinctions; include formatting, graphics, and multimedia when useful to aiding comprehension.
		W.9-10.2.b	Develop the topic with well-chosen, relevant, and sufficient facts, extended definitions, concrete details, quotations, or other information and examples appropriate to the audience's knowledge of the topic.
		W.9-10.2.d	Use precise language and domain-specific vocabulary to manage the complexity of the topic.
		W.9-10.2.f	Provide a concluding statement or section that follows from and supports the information or explanation presented.
		W.9-10.4	Produce clear and coherent writing in which the development, organization, and style are appropriate to task, purpose, and audience.
		W.9-10.5	Develop and strengthen writing as needed by planning, revising, editing, rewriting, or trying a new approach, focusing on addressing what is most significant for a specific purpose and audience.
		SL.9-10.1	Initiate and participate effectively in a range of collaborative discussions (one-on-one, in groups, and teacher-led) with diverse partners on grades 9–10 topics, texts, and issues, building on others' ideas and expressing their own clearly and persuasively.
		SL.9-10.1.d	Respond thoughtfully to diverse perspectives, summarize points of agreement and disagreement, and, when warranted, qualify or justify their own views and understanding and make new connections in light of the evidence and reasoning presented.
		L.9-10.1.b	Use various types of phrases (noun, verb, adjectival, adverbial, participial, prepositional, absolute) and clauses (independent, dependent; noun, relative, adverbial) to convey specific meanings and add variety and interest to writing or presentations.
302–304	**Response to Literature: Edit and Proofread Capitalization: Days of the Week and Months Punctuation: Appositives and Nouns of Direct Address Active Voice Verb Tense Consistency**	L.9-10.1	Demonstrate command of the conventions of standard English grammar and usage when writing or speaking.
		L.9-10.2	Demonstrate command of the conventions of standard English capitalization, punctuation, and spelling when writing.
		L.9-10.3.a	Write and edit work so that it conforms to the guidelines in a style manual appropriate for the discipline and writing type.

Common Core State Standards, continued

Writing Project: Response to Literature, continued

SE Pages	Lesson	Code	Standards Text
305	**Response to Literature: Publish and Present**	W.9-10.2.a	Introduce a topic; organize complex ideas, concepts, and information to make important connections and distinctions; include formatting, graphics, and multimedia when useful to aiding comprehension.
		W.9-10.6	Use technology, including the Internet, to produce, publish, and update individual or shared writing products, taking advantage of technology's capacity to link to other information and to display information flexibly and dynamically.
		SL.9-10.1	Initiate and participate effectively in a range of collaborative discussions (one-on-one, in groups, and teacher-led) with diverse partners on grades 9–10 topics, texts, and issues, building on others' ideas and expressing their own clearly and persuasively.

UNIT 4: Opening Doors

SE Pages	Lesson	Code	Standards Text
306–307	**Discuss the Essential Question**	SL.9-10.1.b	Work with peers to set rules for collegial discussions and decision-making (e.g., informal consensus, taking votes on key issues, presentation of alternate views), clear goals and deadlines, and individual roles as needed.
		SL.9-10.3	Evaluate a speaker's point of view, reasoning, and use of evidence and rhetoric, identifying any fallacious reasoning or exaggerated or distorted evidence.
308	**Analyze and Debate**	SL.9-10.4	Present information, findings, and supporting evidence clearly, concisely, and logically such that listeners can follow the line of reasoning and the organization, development, substance, and style are appropriate to purpose, audience, and task.
309	**Plan a Project**	SL.9-10.1.b	Work with peers to set rules for collegial discussions and decision-making (e.g., informal consensus, taking votes on key issues, presentation of alternate views), clear goals and deadlines, and individual roles as needed.
309	**Choose More to Read**	RL.9-10.10	By the end of grade 10, read and comprehend literature, including stories, dramas, and poems, at the high end of the grades 9–10 text complexity band independently and proficiently.
		RI.9-10.10	By the end of grade 10, read and comprehend literary nonfiction at the high end of the grades 9–10 text complexity band independently and proficiently.
310–313	**How to Read Nonfiction**	RI.9-10.1	Cite strong and thorough textual evidence to support analysis of what the text says explicitly as well as inferences drawn from the text.
		RI.9-10.5	Analyze in detail how an author's ideas or claims are developed and refined by particular sentences, paragraphs, or larger portions of a text.
		RI.9-10.10	By the end of grade 10, read and comprehend literary nonfiction at the high end of the grades 9–10 text complexity band independently and proficiently.
		SL.9-10.1	Initiate and participate effectively in a range of collaborative discussions (one-on-one, in groups, and teacher-led) with diverse partners on grades 9–10 topics, texts, and issues, building on others' ideas and expressing their own clearly and persuasively.
		L.9-10.6	Acquire and use accurately general academic and domain-specific words and phrases, sufficient for reading, writing, speaking, and listening at the college and career readiness level; demonstrate independence in gathering vocabulary knowledge when considering a word or phrase important to comprehension or expression.

Cluster 1

SE Pages	Lesson	Code	Standards Text
314	**Prepare to Read**	RI.9-10.4	Determine the meaning of words and phrases as they are used in a text, including figurative, connotative, and technical meanings; analyze the cumulative impact of specific word choices on meaning and tone.
		SL.9-10.1	Initiate and participate effectively in a range of collaborative discussions (one-on-one, in groups, and teacher-led) with diverse partners on grades 9–10 topics, texts, and issues, building on others' ideas and expressing their own clearly and persuasively.
		L.9-10.6	Acquire and use accurately general academic and domain-specific words and phrases, sufficient for reading, writing, speaking, and listening at the college and career readiness level; demonstrate independence in gathering vocabulary knowledge when considering a word or phrase important to comprehension or expression.
315	**Before Reading: Curtis Aikens and the American Dream**	RI.9-10.1	Cite strong and thorough textual evidence to support analysis of what the text says explicitly as well as inferences drawn from the text.
		RI.9-10.5	Analyze in detail how an author's ideas or claims are developed and refined by particular sentences, paragraphs, or larger portions of a text.
316–328	**Read Curtis Aikens and the American Dream**	RI.9-10.1	Cite strong and thorough textual evidence to support analysis of what the text says explicitly as well as inferences drawn from the text.
		RI.9-10.5	Analyze in detail how an author's ideas or claims are developed and refined by particular sentences, paragraphs, or larger portions of a text.
		RI.9-10.10	By the end of grade 10, read and comprehend literary nonfiction at the high end of the grades 9–10 text complexity band independently and proficiently.
		W.9-10.9.b	Apply grades 9–10 Reading standards to literary nonfiction.
		W.9-10.10	Write routinely over extended time frames (time for research, reflection, and revision) and shorter time frames (a single sitting or a day or two) for a range of tasks, purposes, and audiences.
		L.9-10.1.b	Use various types of phrases (noun, verb, adjectival, adverbial, participial, prepositional, absolute) and clauses (independent, dependent; noun, relative, adverbial) to convey specific meanings and add variety and interest to writing or presentations.
		L.9-10.2.c	Spell correctly.
		L.9-10.4	Determine or clarify the meaning of unknown and multiple-meaning words and phrases based on grades 9–10 reading and content, choosing flexibly from a range of strategies.
		L.9-10.6	Acquire and use accurately general academic and domain-specific words and phrases, sufficient for reading, writing, speaking, and listening at the college and career readiness level; demonstrate independence in gathering vocabulary knowledge when considering a word or phrase important to comprehension or expression.
329	**Postscript: Think You Don't Need an Education?**	RI.9-10.1	Cite strong and thorough textual evidence to support analysis of what the text says explicitly as well as inferences drawn from the text.
		RI.9-10.3	Analyze how the author unfolds an analysis or series of ideas or events, including the order in which the points are made, how they are introduced and developed, and the connections that are drawn between them.

Common Core State Standards, continued

Cluster 1, continued

SE Pages	Lesson	Code	Standards Text
330	**Before Reading: Go For It!**	RI.9-10.1	Cite strong and thorough textual evidence to support analysis of what the text says explicitly as well as inferences drawn from the text.
		RI.9-10.7	Analyze various accounts of a subject told in different mediums, determining which details are emphasized in each account.
331–334	**Read Go For It!**	RI.9-10.1	Cite strong and thorough textual evidence to support analysis of what the text says explicitly as well as inferences drawn from the text.
		RI.9-10.4	Determine the meaning of words and phrases as they are used in a text, including figurative, connotative, and technical meanings; analyze the cumulative impact of specific word choices on meaning and tone.
		RI.9-10.7	Analyze various accounts of a subject told in different mediums, determining which details are emphasized in each account.
		RI.9-10.10	By the end of grade 10, read and comprehend literary nonfiction at the high end of the grades 9–10 text complexity band independently and proficiently.
		W.9-10.9.b	Apply grades 9–10 Reading standards to literary nonfiction.
		W.9-10.10	Write routinely over extended time frames (time for research, reflection, and revision) and shorter time frames (a single sitting or a day or two) for a range of tasks, purposes, and audiences.
		L.9-10.1	Demonstrate command of the conventions of standard English grammar and usage when writing or speaking.
		L.9-10.6	Acquire and use accurately general academic and domain-specific words and phrases, sufficient for reading, writing, speaking, and listening at the college and career readiness level; demonstrate independence in gathering vocabulary knowledge when considering a word or phrase important to comprehension or expression.
335	**Reflect and Assess** **Critical Thinking**	RI.9-10.1	Cite strong and thorough textual evidence to support analysis of what the text says explicitly as well as inferences drawn from the text.
		RI.9-10.2	Determine a central idea of a text and analyze its development over the course of the text, including how it emerges and is shaped and refined by specific details; provide an objective summary of the text.
		RI.9-10.8	Delineate and evaluate the argument and specific claims in a text, assessing whether the reasoning is valid and the evidence is relevant and sufficient; identify false statements and fallacious reasoning.
		RI.9-10.10	By the end of grade 10, read and comprehend literary nonfiction at the high end of the grades 9–10 text complexity band independently and proficiently.
	Write About Literature	W.9-10.10	Write routinely over extended time frames (time for research, reflection, and revision) and shorter time frames (a single sitting or a day or two) for a range of tasks, purposes, and audiences.
	Key Vocabulary Review	L.9-10.6	Acquire and use accurately general academic and domain-specific words and phrases, sufficient for reading, writing, speaking, and listening at the college and career readiness level; demonstrate independence in gathering vocabulary knowledge when considering a word or phrase important to comprehension or expression.
	Read with Ease: Phrasing	RI.9-10.10	By the end of grade 10, read and comprehend literary nonfiction at the high end of the grades 9–10 text complexity band independently and proficiently.

Cluster 1, continued

SE Pages	Lesson	Code	Standards Text
336	Grammar: Show Possession	L.9-10.1.b	Use various types of phrases (noun, verb, adjectival, adverbial, participial, prepositional, absolute) and clauses (independent, dependent; noun, relative, adverbial) to convey specific meanings and add variety and interest to writing or presentations.
336	Language Development: Define and Explain	SL.9-10.1.a	Come to discussions prepared, having read and researched material under study; explicitly draw on that preparation by referring to evidence from texts and other research on the topic or issue to stimulate a thoughtful, well-reasoned exchange of ideas.
336	Research/ Writing: Visual Presentation	W.9-10.7	Conduct short as well as more sustained research projects to answer a question (including a self-generated question) or solve a problem; narrow or broaden the inquiry when appropriate; synthesize multiple sources on the subject, demonstrating understanding of the subject under investigation.
336	Media Study: Evaluate Public Service Announcements	W.9-10.7	Conduct short as well as more sustained research projects to answer a question (including a self-generated question) or solve a problem; narrow or broaden the inquiry when appropriate; synthesize multiple sources on the subject, demonstrating understanding of the subject under investigation.
		SL.9-10.3	Evaluate a speaker's point of view, reasoning, and use of evidence and rhetoric, identifying any fallacious reasoning or exaggerated or distorted evidence.
337	Vocabulary Study: Dictionary and Jargon	L.9-10.4.c	Consult general and specialized reference materials, both print and digital, to find the pronunciation of a word or determine or clarify its precise meaning, its part of speech, or its etymology.
337	Writing Trait: Development of Ideas	W.9-10.2	Write informative/explanatory texts to examine and convey complex ideas, concepts, and information clearly and accurately through the effective selection, organization, and analysis of content.
		W.9-10.5	Develop and strengthen writing as needed by planning, revising, editing, rewriting, or trying a new approach, focusing on addressing what is most significant for a specific purpose and audience.
338	Workplace Workshop: Inside a Restaurant	W.9-10.2	Write informative/explanatory texts to examine and convey complex ideas, concepts, and information clearly and accurately through the effective selection, organization, and analysis of content.
		W.9-10.4	Produce clear and coherent writing in which the development, organization, and style are appropriate to task, purpose, and audience.
		W.9-10.10	Write routinely over extended time frames (time for research, reflection, and revision) and shorter time frames (a single sitting or a day or two) for a range of tasks, purposes, and audiences.
339	Vocabulary Workshop: Access Words During Reading	L.9-10.4.d	Verify the preliminary determination of the meaning of a word or phrase.

Cluster 2

SE Pages	Lesson	Code	Standards Text
340	Prepare to Read	RI.9-10.4	Determine the meaning of words and phrases as they are used in a text, including figurative, connotative, and technical meanings; analyze the cumulative impact of specific word choices on meaning and tone.
		SL.9-10.1	Initiate and participate effectively in a range of collaborative discussions (one-on-one, in groups, and teacher-led) with diverse partners on grades 9-10 topics, texts, and issues, building on others' ideas and expressing their own clearly and persuasively.

Common Core State Standards, continued

SE Pages	Lesson	Code	Standards Text
340	**Prepare to Read** continued	L.9-10.4.c	Consult general and specialized reference materials, both print and digital, to find the pronunciation of a word or determine or clarify its precise meaning, its part of speech, or its etymology.
		L.9-10.6	Acquire and use accurately general academic and domain-specific words and phrases, sufficient for reading, writing, speaking, and listening at the college and career readiness level; demonstrate independence in gathering vocabulary knowledge when considering a word or phrase important to comprehension or expression.
341	**Before Reading: Superman and Me**	RI.9-10.1	Cite strong and thorough textual evidence to support analysis of what the text says explicitly as well as inferences drawn from the text.
		RI.9-10.5	Analyze in detail how an author's ideas or claims are developed and refined by particular sentences, paragraphs, or larger portions of a text.
342–349	**Read Superman and Me**	RI.9-10.1	Cite strong and thorough textual evidence to support analysis of what the text says explicitly as well as inferences drawn from the text.
		RI.9-10.4	Determine the meaning of words and phrases as they are used in a text, including figurative, connotative, and technical meanings; analyze the cumulative impact of specific word choices on meaning and tone.
		RI.9-10.5	Analyze in detail how an author's ideas or claims are developed and refined by particular sentences, paragraphs, or larger portions of a text.
		RI.9-10.10	By the end of grade 10, read and comprehend literary nonfiction at the high end of the grades 9–10 text complexity band independently and proficiently.
		W.9-10.1	Write arguments to support claims in an analysis of substantive topics or texts, using valid reasoning and relevant and sufficient evidence.
		W.9-10.9.b	Apply grades 9–10 Reading standards to literary nonfiction.
		W.9-10.10	Write routinely over extended time frames (time for research, reflection, and revision) and shorter time frames (a single sitting or a day or two) for a range of tasks, purposes, and audiences.
		L.9-10.1.b	Use various types of phrases (noun, verb, adjectival, adverbial, participial, prepositional, absolute) and clauses (independent, dependent; noun, relative, adverbial) to convey specific meanings and add variety and interest to writing or presentations.
		L.9-10.6	Acquire and use accurately general academic and domain-specific words and phrases, sufficient for reading, writing, speaking, and listening at the college and career readiness level; demonstrate independence in gathering vocabulary knowledge when considering a word or phrase important to comprehension or expression.
350	**Before Reading: A Smart Cookie/It's Our Story, Too**	RI.9-10.1	Cite strong and thorough textual evidence to support analysis of what the text says explicitly as well as inferences drawn from the text.
		RI.9-10.5	Analyze in detail how an author's ideas or claims are developed and refined by particular sentences, paragraphs, or larger portions of a text.
351–356	**Read A Smart Cookie/It's Our Story, Too**	RL.9-10.1	Cite strong and thorough textual evidence to support analysis of what the text says explicitly as well as inferences drawn from the text.
		RL.9-10.5	Analyze how an author's choices concerning how to structure a text, order events within it, and manipulate time create such effects as mystery, tension, or surprise.

SE Pages	Lesson	Code	Standards Text
351–356	Read A Smart Cookie/It's Our Story, Too continued	RI.9-10.1	Cite strong and thorough textual evidence to support analysis of what the text says explicitly as well as inferences drawn from the text.
		RI.9-10.5	Analyze in detail how an author's ideas or claims are developed and refined by particular sentences, paragraphs, or larger portions of a text.
		RI.9-10.6	Determine an author's point of view or purpose in a text and analyze how an author uses rhetoric to advance that point of view or purpose.
		RI.9-10.10	By the end of grade 10, read and comprehend literary nonfiction at the high end of the grades 9–10 text complexity band independently and proficiently.
		W.9-10.9.a	Apply grades 9–10 Reading standards to literature.
		W.9-10.10	Write routinely over extended time frames (time for research, reflection, and revision) and shorter time frames (a single sitting or a day or two) for a range of tasks, purposes, and audiences.
		L.9-10.1.b	Use various types of phrases (noun, verb, adjectival, adverbial, participial, prepositional, absolute) and clauses (independent, dependent; noun, relative, adverbial) to convey specific meanings and add variety and interest to writing or presentations.
		L.9-10.6	Acquire and use accurately general academic and domain-specific words and phrases, sufficient for reading, writing, speaking, and listening at the college and career readiness level; demonstrate independence in gathering vocabulary knowledge when considering a word or phrase important to comprehension or expression.
357	Reflect and Assess Critical Thinking	RI.9-10.1	Cite strong and thorough textual evidence to support analysis of what the text says explicitly as well as inferences drawn from the text.
		RI.9-10.10	By the end of grade 10, read and comprehend literary nonfiction at the high end of the grades 9–10 text complexity band independently and proficiently.
	Write About Literature	W.9-10.9.a	Apply grades 9–10 Reading standards to literature.
	Key Vocabulary Review	W.9-10.9.b	Apply grades 9–10 Reading standards to literary nonfiction.
		L.9-10.6	Acquire and use accurately general academic and domain-specific words and phrases, sufficient for reading, writing, speaking, and listening at the college and career readiness level; demonstrate independence in gathering vocabulary knowledge when considering a word or phrase important to comprehension or expression.
	Read with Ease: Intonation	RI.9-10.10	By the end of grade 10, read and comprehend literary nonfiction at the high end of the grades 9–10 text complexity band independently and proficiently.
358	Grammar: Use Pronouns in Prepositional Phrases	L.9-10.1.b	Use various types of phrases (noun, verb, adjectival, adverbial, participial, prepositional, absolute) and clauses (independent, dependent; noun, relative, adverbial) to convey specific meanings and add variety and interest to writing or presentations.
358	Language Development: Clarify	SL.9-10.1.c	Propel conversations by posing and responding to questions that relate the current discussion to broader themes or larger ideas; actively incorporate others into the discussion; and clarify, verify, or challenge ideas and conclusions.

Common Core State Standards, continued

Cluster 2, continued

SE Pages	Lesson	Code	Standards Text
358	Literary Analysis: Analyze Imagery	RL.9-10.4	Determine the meaning of words and phrases as they are used in the text, including figurative and connotative meanings; analyze the cumulative impact of specific word choices on meaning and tone.
		RI.9-10.4	Determine the meaning of words and phrases as they are used in a text, including figurative, connotative, and technical meanings; analyze the cumulative impact of specific word choices on meaning and tone.
359	Vocabulary Study: Multiple-Meaning Words	L.9-10.4.c	Consult general and specialized reference materials, both print and digital, to find the pronunciation of a word or determine or clarify its precise meaning, its part of speech, or its etymology.
359	Writing: Social Science: Write a Case Study	W.9-10.2	Write informative/explanatory texts to examine and convey complex ideas, concepts, and information clearly and accurately through the effective selection, organization, and analysis of content.
		W.9-10.5	Develop and strengthen writing as needed by planning, revising, editing, rewriting, or trying a new approach, focusing on addressing what is most significant for a specific purpose and audience.
359	Listening/Speaking: Oral Presentation	SL.9-10.1.a	Come to discussions prepared, having read and researched material under study; explicitly draw on that preparation by referring to evidence from texts and other research on the topic or issue to stimulate a thoughtful, well-reasoned exchange of ideas.
		SL.9-10.4	Present information, findings, and supporting evidence clearly, concisely, and logically such that listeners can follow the line of reasoning and the organization, development, substance, and style are appropriate to purpose, audience, and task.
360–361	Listening and Speaking Workshop: Oral Report	W.9-10.7	Conduct short as well as more sustained research projects to answer a question (including a self-generated question) or solve a problem; narrow or broaden the inquiry when appropriate; synthesize multiple sources on the subject, demonstrating understanding of the subject under investigation.
		SL.9-10.2	Integrate multiple sources of information presented in diverse media or formats evaluating the credibility and accuracy of each source.
		SL.9-10.3	Evaluate a speaker's point of view, reasoning, and use of evidence and rhetoric, identifying any fallacious reasoning or exaggerated or distorted evidence.
		SL.9-10.4	Present information, findings, and supporting evidence clearly, concisely, and logically such that listeners can follow the line of reasoning and the organization, development, substance, and style are appropriate to purpose, audience, and task.
		L.9-10.3	Apply knowledge of language to understand how language functions in different contexts, to make effective choices for meaning or style, and to comprehend more fully when reading or listening.

Cluster 3

SE Pages	Lesson	Code	Standards Text
362	Prepare to Read	RI.9-10.4	Determine the meaning of words and phrases as they are used in a text, including figurative, connotative, and technical meanings; analyze the cumulative impact of specific word choices on meaning and tone.
		SL.9-10.1	Initiate and participate effectively in a range of collaborative discussions (one-on-one, in groups, and teacher-led) with diverse partners on grades 9–10 topics, texts, and issues, building on others' ideas and expressing their own clearly and persuasively.

SE Pages	Lesson	Code	Standards Text
	Prepare to Read continued	L.9-10.6	Acquire and use accurately general academic and domain-specific words and phrases, sufficient for reading, writing, speaking, and listening at the college and career readiness level; demonstrate independence in gathering vocabulary knowledge when considering a word or phrase important to comprehension or expression.
363	**Before Reading: The Fast and the Fuel-Efficient**	RI.9-10.1	Cite strong and thorough textual evidence to support analysis of what the text says explicitly as well as inferences drawn from the text.
		RI.9-10.5	Analyze in detail how an author's ideas or claims are developed and refined by particular sentences, paragraphs, or larger portions of a text.
364–374	**Read The Fast and the Fuel-Efficient**	RI.9-10.1	Cite strong and thorough textual evidence to support analysis of what the text says explicitly as well as inferences drawn from the text.
		RI.9-10.2	Determine a central idea of a text and analyze its development over the course of the text, including how it emerges and is shaped and refined by specific details; provide an objective summary of the text.
		RI.9-10.5	Analyze in detail how an author's ideas or claims are developed and refined by particular sentences, paragraphs, or larger portions of a text.
		RI.9-10.10	By the end of grade 10, read and comprehend literary nonfiction at the high end of the grades 9–10 text complexity band independently and proficiently.
		W.9-10.9.b	Apply grades 9–10 Reading standards to literary nonfiction.
		W.9-10.10	Write routinely over extended time frames (time for research, reflection, and revision) and shorter time frames (a single sitting or a day or two) for a range of tasks, purposes, and audiences.
		L.9-10.1.b	Use various types of phrases (noun, verb, adjectival, adverbial, participial, prepositional, absolute) and clauses (independent, dependent; noun, relative, adverbial) to convey specific meanings and add variety and interest to writing or presentations.
		L.9-10.4.a	Use context as a clue to the meaning of a word or phrase.
		L.9-10.4.b	Identify and correctly use patterns of word changes that indicate different meanings or parts of speech.
		L.9-10.6	Acquire and use accurately general academic and domain-specific words and phrases, sufficient for reading, writing, speaking, and listening at the college and career readiness level; demonstrate independence in gathering vocabulary knowledge when considering a word or phrase important to comprehension or expression.
375	**Postscript: Cartoon**	RL.9-10.10	By the end of grade 10, read and comprehend literature, including stories, dramas, and poems, at the high end of the grades 9–10 text complexity band independently and proficiently.
376	**Before Reading: Teens Open Doors**	RI.9-10.1	Cite strong and thorough textual evidence to support analysis of what the text says explicitly as well as inferences drawn from the text.
		RI.9-10.3	Analyze how the author unfolds an analysis or series of ideas or events, including the order in which the points are made, how they are introduced and developed, and the connections that are drawn between them.

Common Core State Standards, continued

SE Pages	Lesson	Code	Standards Text
377–380	**Read Teens Open Doors**	RI.9-10.1	Cite strong and thorough textual evidence to support analysis of what the text says explicitly as well as inferences drawn from the text.
		RI.9-10.3	Analyze how the author unfolds an analysis or series of ideas or events, including the order in which the points are made, how they are introduced and developed, and the connections that are drawn between them.
		RI.9-10.10	By the end of grade 10, read and comprehend literary nonfiction at the high end of the grades 9–10 text complexity band independently and proficiently.
		W.9-10.4	Produce clear and coherent writing in which the development, organization, and style are appropriate to task, purpose, and audience.
		W.9-10.10	Write routinely over extended time frames (time for research, reflection, and revision) and shorter time frames (a single sitting or a day or two) for a range of tasks, purposes, and audiences.
		L.9-10.1	Demonstrate command of the conventions of standard English grammar and usage when writing or speaking.
		L.9-10.6	Acquire and use accurately general academic and domain-specific words and phrases, sufficient for reading, writing, speaking, and listening at the college and career readiness level; demonstrate independence in gathering vocabulary knowledge when considering a word or phrase important to comprehension or expression.
381	**Reflect and Assess** **Critical Thinking**	RI.9-10.1	Cite strong and thorough textual evidence to support analysis of what the text says explicitly as well as inferences drawn from the text.
		RI.9-10.2	Determine a central idea of a text and analyze its development over the course of the text, including how it emerges and is shaped and refined by specific details; provide an objective summary of the text.
		RI.9-10.10	By the end of grade 10, read and comprehend literary nonfiction at the high end of the grades 9–10 text complexity band independently and proficiently.
	Write About Literature	W.9-10.1	Write arguments to support claims in an analysis of substantive topics or texts, using valid reasoning and relevant and sufficient evidence.
		W.9-10.9.b	Apply grades 9–10 Reading standards to literary nonfiction.
	Key Vocabulary Review	L.9-10.6	Acquire and use accurately general academic and domain-specific words and phrases, sufficient for reading, writing, speaking, and listening at the college and career readiness level; demonstrate independence in gathering vocabulary knowledge when considering a word or phrase important to comprehension or expression.
	Read with Ease: Expression	RI.9-10.10	By the end of grade 10, read and comprehend literary nonfiction at the high end of the grades 9–10 text complexity band independently and proficiently.
382	**Grammar: Use the Correct Pronoun**	L.9-10.1	Demonstrate command of the conventions of standard English grammar and usage when writing or speaking.
382	**Language Development: Verify or Confirm Information**	SL.9-10.1.a	Come to discussions prepared, having read and researched material under study; explicitly draw on that preparation by referring to evidence from texts and other research on the topic or issue to stimulate a thoughtful, well-reasoned exchange of ideas.

Cluster 3, continued

SE Pages	Lesson	Code	Standards Text
382	Research/Writing: Descriptive Diagram	W.9-10.2	Write informative/explanatory texts to examine and convey complex ideas, concepts, and information clearly and accurately through the effective selection, organization, and analysis of content.
		W.9-10.7	Conduct short as well as more sustained research projects to answer a question (including a self-generated question) or solve a problem; narrow or broaden the inquiry when appropriate; synthesize multiple sources on the subject, demonstrating understanding of the subject under investigation.
382	Listening/Speaking: Speech	SL.9-10.4	Present information, findings, and supporting evidence clearly, concisely, and logically such that listeners can follow the line of reasoning and the organization, development, substance, and style are appropriate to purpose, audience, and task.
		SL.9-10.6	Adapt speech to a variety of contexts and tasks, demonstrating command of formal English when indicated or appropriate.
383	Vocabulary Study: Multiple-Meaning Words	L.9-10.4.c	Consult general and specialized reference materials, both print and digital, to find the pronunciation of a word or determine or clarify its precise meaning, its part of speech, or its etymology.
383	Writing on Demand: Write a Problem-Solution Essay	W.9-10.1	Write arguments to support claims in an analysis of substantive topics or texts, using valid reasoning and relevant and sufficient evidence.
		W.9-10.4	Produce clear and coherent writing in which the development, organization, and style are appropriate to task, purpose, and audience.

Close Reading

384–387	Read The Sky Is Not the Limit	RI.9-10.10	By the end of grade 10, read and comprehend literary nonfiction at the high end of the grades 9–10 text complexity band independently and proficiently.

Unit Wrap-Up

388	Unit Wrap-Up Present Your Project	W.9-10.2	Write informative/explanatory texts to examine and convey complex ideas, concepts, and information clearly and accurately through the effective selection, organization, and analysis of content.
		W.9-10.4	Produce clear and coherent writing in which the development, organization, and style are appropriate to task, purpose, and audience.
		W.9-10.6	Use technology, including the Internet, to produce, publish, and update individual or shared writing products, taking advantage of technology's capacity to link to other information and to display information flexibly and dynamically.
	Reflect on Your Reading	SL.9-10.1.a	Come to discussions prepared, having read and researched material under study; explicitly draw on that preparation by referring to evidence from texts and other research on the topic or issue to stimulate a thoughtful, well-reasoned exchange of ideas.
	Respond to the Essential Question	SL.9-10.1.a	Come to discussions prepared, having read and researched material under study; explicitly draw on that preparation by referring to evidence from texts and other research on the topic or issue to stimulate a thoughtful, well-reasoned exchange of ideas.

Common Core State Standards, continued

Writing Project: Research Report

SE Pages	Lesson	Code	Standards Text
389–393	Study Research Reports and Prewrite	W.9-10.2.a	Introduce a topic; organize complex ideas, concepts, and information to make important connections and distinctions; include formatting, graphics, and multimedia when useful to aiding comprehension.
		W.9-10.5	Develop and strengthen writing as needed by planning, revising, editing, rewriting, or trying a new approach, focusing on addressing what is most significant for a specific purpose and audience.
		W.9-10.7	Conduct short as well as more sustained research projects to answer a question (including a self-generated question) or solve a problem; narrow or broaden the inquiry when appropriate; synthesize multiple sources on the subject, demonstrating understanding of the subject under investigation.
		W.9-10.8	Gather relevant information from multiple authoritative print and digital sources, using advanced searches effectively; assess the usefulness of each source in answering the research question; integrate information into the text selectively to maintain the flow of ideas, avoiding plagiarism and following a standard format for citation.
394–395	Research Report: Draft	W.9-10.2.a	Introduce a topic; organize complex ideas, concepts, and information to make important connections and distinctions; include formatting, graphics, and multimedia when useful to aiding comprehension.
		W.9-10.4	Produce clear and coherent writing in which the development, organization, and style are appropriate to task, purpose, and audience.
		W.9-10.8	Gather relevant information from multiple authoritative print and digital sources, using advanced searches effectively; assess the usefulness of each source in answering the research question; integrate information into the text selectively to maintain the flow of ideas, avoiding plagiarism and following a standard format for citation.
		L.9-10.3.a	Write and edit work so that it conforms to the guidelines in a style manual appropriate for the discipline and writing type.
396–399	Research Report: Revise Trait: Development of Ideas	W.9-10.2.a	Introduce a topic; organize complex ideas, concepts, and information to make important connections and distinctions; include formatting, graphics, and multimedia when useful to aiding comprehension.
		W.9-10.2.b	Develop the topic with well-chosen, relevant, and sufficient facts, extended definitions, concrete details, quotations, or other information and examples appropriate to the audience's knowledge of the topic.
		W.9-10.2.c	Use appropriate and varied transitions to link the major sections of the text, create cohesion, and clarify the relationships among complex ideas and concepts.
		W.9-10.2.d	Use precise language and domain-specific vocabulary to manage the complexity of the topic.
		W.9-10.2.e	Establish and maintain a formal style and objective tone while attending to the norms and conventions of the discipline in which they are writing.
		W.9-10.5	Develop and strengthen writing as needed by planning, revising, editing, rewriting, or trying a new approach, focusing on addressing what is most significant for a specific purpose and audience.
		W.9-10.7	Conduct short as well as more sustained research projects to answer a question (including a self-generated question) or solve a problem; narrow or broaden the inquiry when appropriate; synthesize multiple sources on the subject, demonstrating understanding of the subject under investigation.

Writing Project: Research Report, continued

SE Pages	Lesson	Code	Standards Text
396–399 **Research Report: Revise** **Trait: Development of Ideas** continued		SL.9-10.1	Initiate and participate effectively in a range of collaborative discussions (one-on-one, in groups, and teacher-led) with diverse partners on grades 9–10 topics, texts, and issues, building on others' ideas and expressing their own clearly and persuasively.
		L.9-10.3.a	Write and edit work so that it conforms to the guidelines in a style manual appropriate for the discipline and writing type.
		L.9-10.2	Demonstrate command of the conventions of standard English capitalization, punctuation, and spelling when writing.
		L.9-10.3.a	Write and edit work so that it conforms to the guidelines in a style manual appropriate for the discipline and writing type.
400–402 **Research Report: Edit and Proofread Capitalization: Titles of Publications Parentheses Verb Tense Consistency Pronoun-Antecedent Agreement**		L.9-10.1	Demonstrate command of the conventions of standard English grammar and usage when writing or speaking.
		L.9-10.2	Demonstrate command of the conventions of standard English capitalization, punctuation, and spelling when writing.
		L.9-10.3.a	Write and edit work so that it conforms to the guidelines in a style manual appropriate for the discipline and writing type.
403 **Research Report: Publish and Present**		W.9-10.2.a	Introduce a topic; organize complex ideas, concepts, and information to make important connections and distinctions; include formatting, graphics, and multimedia when useful to aiding comprehension.
		W.9-10.6	Use technology, including the Internet, to produce, publish, and update individual or shared writing products, taking advantage of technology's capacity to link to other information and to display information flexibly and dynamically.
		SL.9-10.1	Initiate and participate effectively in a range of collaborative discussions (one-on-one, in groups, and teacher-led) with diverse partners on grades 9–10 topics, texts, and issues, building on others' ideas and expressing their own clearly and persuasively.
		SL.9-10.4	Present information, findings, and supporting evidence clearly, concisely, and logically such that listeners can follow the line of reasoning and the organization, development, substance, and style are appropriate to purpose, audience, and task.

UNIT 5: Fear This!

SE Pages	Lesson	Code	Standards Text
404–405	**Discuss the Essential Question**	SL.9-10.1.b	Work with peers to set rules for collegial discussions and decision-making (e.g., informal consensus, taking votes on key issues, presentation of alternate views), clear goals and deadlines, and individual roles as needed.
		SL.9-10.3	Evaluate a speaker's point of view, reasoning, and use of evidence and rhetoric, identifying any fallacious reasoning or exaggerated or distorted evidence.
406	**Analyze and Vote**	SL.9-10.4	Present information, findings, and supporting evidence clearly, concisely, and logically such that listeners can follow the line of reasoning and the organization, development, substance, and style are appropriate to purpose, audience, and task.
407	**Plan a Project**	SL.9-10.1.b	Work with peers to set rules for collegial discussions and decision-making (e.g., informal consensus, taking votes on key issues, presentation of alternate views), clear goals and deadlines, and individual roles as needed.

Common Core State Standards, continued

UNIT 5: Fear This!, continued

SE Pages	Lesson	Code	Standards Text
407	**Choose More to Read**	RL.9-10.10	By the end of grade 10, read and comprehend literature, including stories, dramas, and poems, at the high end of the grades 9–10 text complexity band independently and proficiently.
		RI.9-10.10	By the end of grade 10, read and comprehend literary nonfiction at the high end of the grades 9–10 text complexity band independently and proficiently.
408–411	**How to Read Short Stories**	RL.9-10.10	By the end of grade 10, read and comprehend literature, including stories, dramas, and poems, at the high end of the grades 9–10 text complexity band independently and proficiently.
		SL.9-10.1.a	Come to discussions prepared, having read and researched material under study; explicitly draw on that preparation by referring to evidence from texts and other research on the topic or issue to stimulate a thoughtful, well-reasoned exchange of ideas.
		L.9-10.6	Acquire and use accurately general academic and domain-specific words and phrases, sufficient for reading, writing, speaking, and listening at the college and career readiness level; demonstrate independence in gathering vocabulary knowledge when considering a word or phrase important to comprehension or expression.
Cluster 1			
412	**Prepare to Read**	RI.9-10.4	Determine the meaning of words and phrases as they are used in a text, including figurative, connotative, and technical meanings; analyze the cumulative impact of specific word choices on meaning and tone.
		SL.9-10.1	Initiate and participate effectively in a range of collaborative discussions (one-on-one, in groups, and teacher-led) with diverse partners on grades 9–10 topics, texts, and issues, building on others' ideas and expressing their own clearly and persuasively.
		L.9-10.6	Acquire and use accurately general academic and domain-specific words and phrases, sufficient for reading, writing, speaking, and listening at the college and career readiness level; demonstrate independence in gathering vocabulary knowledge when considering a word or phrase important to comprehension or expression.
413	**Before Reading: The Interlopers**	RL.9-10.5	Analyze how an author's choices concerning how to structure a text, order events within it, and manipulate time create such effects as mystery, tension, or surprise.
		RL.9-10.10	By the end of grade 10, read and comprehend literature, including stories, dramas, and poems, at the high end of the grades 9–10 text complexity band independently and proficiently.
414–423	**Read The Interlopers**	RL.9-10.1	Cite strong and thorough textual evidence to support analysis of what the text says explicitly as well as inferences drawn from the text.
		RL.9-10.5	Analyze how an author's choices concerning how to structure a text, order events within it, and manipulate time create such effects as mystery, tension, or surprise.
		RL.9-10.10	By the end of grade 10, read and comprehend literature, including stories, dramas, and poems, at the high end of the grades 9–10 text complexity band independently and proficiently.
		W.9-10.9.a	Apply grades 9–10 Reading standards to literature.
		W.9-10.10	Write routinely over extended time frames (time for research, reflection, and revision) and shorter time frames (a single sitting or a day or two) for a range of tasks, purposes, and audiences.

SE Pages	Lesson	Code	Standards Text
414–423	**Read The Interlopers** continued	L.9-10.1.b	Use various types of phrases (noun, verb, adjectival, adverbial, participial, prepositional, absolute) and clauses (independent, dependent; noun, relative, adverbial) to convey specific meanings and add variety and interest to writing or presentations.
		L.9-10.4.b	Identify and correctly use patterns of word changes that indicate different meanings or parts of speech.
		L.9-10.4.c	Consult general and specialized reference materials, both print and digital, to find the pronunciation of a word or determine or clarify its precise meaning, its part of speech, or its etymology.
		L.9-10.6	Acquire and use accurately general academic and domain-specific words and phrases, sufficient for reading, writing, speaking, and listening at the college and career readiness level; demonstrate independence in gathering vocabulary knowledge when considering a word or phrase important to comprehension or expression.
424	**Before Reading: An Interview with the King of Terror**	RI.9-10.4	Determine the meaning of words and phrases as they are used in a text, including figurative, connotative, and technical meanings; analyze the cumulative impact of specific word choices on meaning and tone.
		RI.9-10.10	By the end of grade 10, read and comprehend literary nonfiction at the high end of the grades 9–10 text complexity band independently and proficiently.
425–430	**Read An Interview with the King of Terror**	RI.9-10.1	Cite strong and thorough textual evidence to support analysis of what the text says explicitly as well as inferences drawn from the text.
		RI.9-10.2	Determine a central idea of a text and analyze its development over the course of the text, including how it emerges and is shaped and refined by specific details; provide an objective summary of the text.
		RI.9-10.3	Analyze how the author unfolds an analysis or series of ideas or events, including the order in which the points are made, how they are introduced and developed, and the connections that are drawn between them.
		RI.9-10.4	Determine the meaning of words and phrases as they are used in a text, including figurative, connotative, and technical meanings; analyze the cumulative impact of specific word choices on meaning and tone.
		RI.9-10.10	By the end of grade 10, read and comprehend literary nonfiction at the high end of the grades 9–10 text complexity band independently and proficiently.
		W.9-10.9.b	Apply grades 9–10 Reading standards to literary nonfiction.
		W.9-10.10	Write routinely over extended time frames (time for research, reflection, and revision) and shorter time frames (a single sitting or a day or two) for a range of tasks, purposes, and audiences.
		L.9-10.1.b	Use various types of phrases (noun, verb, adjectival, adverbial, participial, prepositional, absolute) and clauses (independent, dependent; noun, relative, adverbial) to convey specific meanings and add variety and interest to writing or presentations.
		L.9-10.4.a	Use context as a clue to the meaning of a word or phrase.
		L.9-10.6	Acquire and use accurately general academic and domain-specific words and phrases, sufficient for reading, writing, speaking, and listening at the college and career readiness level; demonstrate independence in gathering vocabulary knowledge when considering a word or phrase important to comprehension or expression.

Common Core State Standards

SE Pages	Lesson	Code	Standards Text
431	**Reflect and Assess Critical Thinking**	RL.9-10.1	Cite strong and thorough textual evidence to support analysis of what the text says explicitly as well as inferences drawn from the text.
		RL.9-10.2	Determine a theme or central idea of a text and analyze in detail its development over the course of the text, including how it emerges and is shaped and refined by specific details; provide an objective summary of the text.
		RL.9-10.5	Analyze how an author's choices concerning how to structure a text, order events within it, and manipulate time create such effects as mystery, tension, or surprise.
		RL.9-10.10	By the end of grade 10, read and comprehend literature, including stories, dramas, and poems, at the high end of the grades 9–10 text complexity band independently and proficiently.
		RI.9-10.2	Determine a central idea of a text and analyze its development over the course of the text, including how it emerges and is shaped and refined by specific details; provide an objective summary of the text.
		L.9-10.6	Acquire and use accurately general academic and domain-specific words and phrases, sufficient for reading, writing, speaking, and listening at the college and career readiness level; demonstrate independence in gathering vocabulary knowledge when considering a word or phrase important to comprehension or expression.
	Write About Literature	W.9-10.3	Write narratives to develop real or imagined experiences or events using effective technique, well-chosen details, and well-structured event sequences.
	Key Vocabulary Review	L.9-10.6	Acquire and use accurately general academic and domain-specific words and phrases, sufficient for reading, writing, speaking, and listening at the college and career readiness level; demonstrate independence in gathering vocabulary knowledge when considering a word or phrase important to comprehension or expression.
	Read with Ease: Phrasing	RL.9-10.10	By the end of grade 10, read and comprehend literature, including stories, dramas, and poems, at the high end of the grades 9–10 text complexity band independently and proficiently.
432	**Grammar: Use Adjectives to Elaborate**	L.9-10.1.b	Use various types of phrases (noun, verb, adjectival, adverbial, participial, prepositional, absolute) and clauses (independent, dependent; noun, relative, adverbial) to convey specific meanings and add variety and interest to writing or presentations.
432	**Language Development: Tell a Story**	SL.9-10.6	Adapt speech to a variety of contexts and tasks, demonstrating command of formal English when indicated or appropriate.
432	**Literary Analysis: Analyze Irony**	RL.9-10.5	Analyze how an author's choices concerning how to structure a text, order events within it, and manipulate time create such effects as mystery, tension, or surprise.
433	**Vocabulary Study: Synonyms**	L.9-10.5.b	Analyze nuances in the meaning of words with similar denotations.
433	**Writing: Write a Character Sketch**	W.9-10.3	Write narratives to develop real or imagined experiences or events using effective technique, well-chosen details, and well-structured event sequences.
		W.9-10.5	Develop and strengthen writing as needed by planning, revising, editing, rewriting, or trying a new approach, focusing on addressing what is most significant for a specific purpose and audience.

Cluster 1, continued

SE Pages	Lesson	Code	Standards Text
433	Listening/ Speaking: Dramatization	RL.9-10.7	Analyze the representation of a subject or a key scene in two different artistic mediums, including what is emphasized or absent in each treatment.
		SL.9-10.6	Adapt speech to a variety of contexts and tasks, demonstrating command of formal English when indicated or appropriate.
434	Workplace Workshop: Inside a Newspaper Office	W.9-10.2	Write informative/explanatory texts to examine and convey complex ideas, concepts, and information clearly and accurately through the effective selection, organization, and analysis of content.
		W.9-10.7	Conduct short as well as more sustained research projects to answer a question (including a self-generated question) or solve a problem; narrow or broaden the inquiry when appropriate; synthesize multiple sources on the subject, demonstrating understanding of the subject under investigation.
		W.9-10.10	Write routinely over extended time frames (time for research, reflection, and revision) and shorter time frames (a single sitting or a day or two) for a range of tasks, purposes, and audiences.
435	Vocabulary Workshop: Make Word Connections	L.9-10.4.c	Consult general and specialized reference materials, both print and digital, to find the pronunciation of a word or determine or clarify its precise meaning, its part of speech, or its etymology.
		L.9-10.4.d	Verify the preliminary determination of the meaning of a word or phrase.
		L.9-10.5	Demonstrate understanding of figurative language, word relationships, and nuances in word meanings.

Cluster 2

SE Pages	Lesson	Code	Standards Text
436	Prepare to Read	RI.9-10.4	Determine the meaning of words and phrases as they are used in a text, including figurative, connotative, and technical meanings; analyze the cumulative impact of specific word choices on meaning and tone.
		SL.9-10.1	Initiate and participate effectively in a range of collaborative discussions (one-on-one, in groups, and teacher-led) with diverse partners on grades 9–10 topics, texts, and issues, building on others' ideas and expressing their own clearly and persuasively.
		L.9-10.6	Acquire and use accurately general academic and domain-specific words and phrases, sufficient for reading, writing, speaking, and listening at the college and career readiness level; demonstrate independence in gathering vocabulary knowledge when considering a word or phrase important to comprehension or expression.
437	Before Reading: The Baby-Sitter	RL.9-10.4	Determine the meaning of words and phrases as they are used in the text, including figurative and connotative meanings; analyze the cumulative impact of specific word choices on meaning and tone.
		RL.9-10.5	Analyze how an author's choices concerning how to structure a text, order events within it, and manipulate time create such effects as mystery, tension, or surprise.
		RL.9-10.10	By the end of grade 10, read and comprehend literature, including stories, dramas, and poems, at the high end of the grades 9–10 text complexity band independently and proficiently.

Common Core State Standards, continued

SE Pages	Lesson	Code	Standards Text
438–450	**Read The Baby-Sitter**	RL.9-10.1	Cite strong and thorough textual evidence to support analysis of what the text says explicitly as well as inferences drawn from the text.
		RL.9-10.3	Analyze how complex characters develop over the course of a text, interact with other characters, and advance the plot or develop the theme.
		RL.9-10.4	Determine the meaning of words and phrases as they are used in the text, including figurative and connotative meanings; analyze the cumulative impact of specific word choices on meaning and tone.
		RL.9-10.5	Analyze how an author's choices concerning how to structure a text, order events within it, and manipulate time create such effects as mystery, tension, or surprise.
		RL.9-10.7	Analyze the representation of a subject or a key scene in two different artistic mediums, including what is emphasized or absent in each treatment.
		RL.9-10.10	By the end of grade 10, read and comprehend literature, including stories, dramas, and poems, at the high end of the grades 9–10 text complexity band independently and proficiently.
		W.9-10.9.a	Apply grades 9–10 Reading standards to literature.
		W.9-10.10	Write routinely over extended time frames (time for research, reflection, and revision) and shorter time frames (a single sitting or a day or two) for a range of tasks, purposes, and audiences.
		L.9-10.1.b	Use various types of phrases (noun, verb, adjectival, adverbial, participial, prepositional, absolute) and clauses (independent, dependent; noun, relative, adverbial) to convey specific meanings and add variety and interest to writing or presentations.
		L.9-10.2.c	Spell correctly.
		L.9-10.4.a	Use context (e.g., the overall meaning of a sentence, paragraph, or text; a word's position or function in a sentence) as a clue to the meaning of a word or phrase.
		L.9-10.4.c	Consult general and specialized reference materials, both print and digital, to find the pronunciation of a word or determine or clarify its precise meaning, its part of speech, or its etymology.
		L.9-10.6	Acquire and use accurately general academic and domain-specific words and phrases, sufficient for reading, writing, speaking, and listening at the college and career readiness level; demonstrate independence in gathering vocabulary knowledge when considering a word or phrase important to comprehension or expression.
451	**Postscript: Cartoon**	RL.9-10.4	Determine the meaning of words and phrases as they are used in the text, including figurative and connotative meanings; analyze the cumulative impact of specific word choices on meaning and tone.
		RL.9-10.7	Analyze the representation of a subject or a key scene in two different artistic mediums, including what is emphasized or absent in each treatment.
452	**Before Reading: Beware: Do Not Read This Poem**	RL.9-10.4	Determine the meaning of words and phrases as they are used in the text, including figurative and connotative meanings; analyze the cumulative impact of specific word choices on meaning and tone.
		RL.9-10.10	By the end of grade 10, read and comprehend literature, including stories, dramas, and poems, at the high end of the grades 9–10 text complexity band independently and proficiently.

SE Pages	Lesson	Code	Standards Text
453–456	**Read Beware: Do Not Read This Poem**	RL.9-10.1	Cite strong and thorough textual evidence to support analysis of what the text says explicitly as well as inferences drawn from the text.
		RL.9-10.4	Determine the meaning of words and phrases as they are used in the text, including figurative and connotative meanings; analyze the cumulative impact of specific word choices on meaning and tone.
		RL.9-10.10	By the end of grade 10, read and comprehend literature, including stories, dramas, and poems, at the high end of the grades 9–10 text complexity band independently and proficiently.
		W.9-10.9.a	Apply grades 9–10 Reading standards to literature.
		W.9-10.10	Write routinely over extended time frames (time for research, reflection, and revision) and shorter time frames (a single sitting or a day or two) for a range of tasks, purposes, and audiences.
		L.9-10.1.b	Use various types of phrases (noun, verb, adjectival, adverbial, participial, prepositional, absolute) and clauses (independent, dependent; noun, relative, adverbial) to convey specific meanings and add variety and interest to writing or presentations.
		L.9-10.6	Acquire and use accurately general academic and domain-specific words and phrases, sufficient for reading, writing, speaking, and listening at the college and career readiness level; demonstrate independence in gathering vocabulary knowledge when considering a word or phrase important to comprehension or expression.
457	**Reflect and Assess Critical Thinking**	RL.9-10.2	Determine a theme or central idea of a text and analyze in detail its development over the course of the text, including how it emerges and is shaped and refined by specific details; provide an objective summary of the text.
		RL.9-10.3	Analyze how complex characters develop over the course of a text, interact with other characters, and advance the plot or develop the theme.
		RL.9-10.4	Determine the meaning of words and phrases as they are used in the text, including figurative and connotative meanings; analyze the cumulative impact of specific word choices on meaning and tone.
		RL.9-10.10	By the end of grade 10, read and comprehend literature, including stories, dramas, and poems, at the high end of the grades 9–10 text complexity band independently and proficiently.
	Write About Literature	W.9-10.1	Write arguments to support claims in an analysis of substantive topics or texts, using valid reasoning and relevant and sufficient evidence.
		W.9-10.9	Draw evidence from literary or informational texts to support analysis, reflection, and research.
	Key Vocabulary Review	L.9-10.6	Acquire and use accurately general academic and domain-specific words and phrases, sufficient for reading, writing, speaking, and listening at the college and career readiness level; demonstrate independence in gathering vocabulary knowledge when considering a word or phrase important to comprehension or expression.
	Read with Ease: Expression	RL.9-10.10	By the end of grade 10, read and comprehend literature, including stories, dramas, and poems, at the high end of the grades 9–10 text complexity band independently and proficiently.

Common Core State Standards, continued

Cluster 2, continued

SE Pages	Lesson	Code	Standards Text
458	Grammar: Compare Adjectives	L.9-10.1.b	Use various types of phrases (noun, verb, adjectival, adverbial, participial, prepositional, absolute) and clauses (independent, dependent; noun, relative, adverbial) to convey specific meanings and add variety and interest to writing or presentations.
458	Language Development: Make Comparisons	SL.9-10.1	Initiate and participate effectively in a range of collaborative discussions (one-on-one, in groups, and teacher-led) with diverse partners on grades 9–10 topics, texts, and issues, building on others' ideas and expressing their own clearly and persuasively.
458	Literary Analysis: Analyze Foreshadowing	RL.9-10.5	Analyze how an author's choices concerning how to structure a text, order events within it, and manipulate time create such effects as mystery, tension, or surprise.
459	Vocabulary Study: Thesaurus	L.9-10.4.c	Consult general and specialized reference materials (e.g., dictionaries, glossaries, thesauruses), both print and digital, to find the pronunciation of a word or determine or clarify its precise meaning, its part of speech, or its etymology.
459	Writing on Demand: Write a Literary Analysis	W.9-10.1	Write arguments to support claims in an analysis of substantive topics or texts, using valid reasoning and relevant and sufficient evidence.
459	Listening/Speaking: Storytelling	Sl.9-10.3	Evaluate a speaker's point of view, reasoning, and use of evidence and rhetoric, identifying any fallacious reasoning or exaggerated or distorted evidence.
460–461	Listening and Speaking Workshop: Dramatic Reading	SL.9-10.6	Adapt speech to a variety of contexts and tasks, demonstrating command of formal English when indicated or appropriate.

Cluster 3

SE Pages	Lesson	Code	Standards Text
462	Prepare to Read	RL.9-10.4	Determine the meaning of words and phrases as they are used in the text, including figurative and connotative meanings; analyze the cumulative impact of specific word choices on meaning and tone.
		SL.9-10.1	Initiate and participate effectively in a range of collaborative discussions (one-on-one, in groups, and teacher-led) with diverse partners on grades 9–10 topics, texts, and issues, building on others' ideas and expressing their own clearly and persuasively.
		L.9-10.4.c	Consult general and specialized reference materials, both print and digital, to find the pronunciation of a word or determine or clarify its precise meaning, its part of speech, or its etymology.
		L.9-10.6	Acquire and use accurately general academic and domain-specific words and phrases, sufficient for reading, writing, speaking, and listening at the college and career readiness level; demonstrate independence in gathering vocabulary knowledge when considering a word or phrase important to comprehension or expression.
463	Before Reading: The Tell-Tale Heart	RL.9-10.5	Analyze how an author's choices concerning how to structure a text, order events within it, and manipulate time (e.g., pacing, flashbacks) create such effects as mystery, tension, or surprise.
		RL.9-10.10	By the end of grade 10, read and comprehend literature, including stories, dramas, and poems, at the high end of the grades 9–10 text complexity band independently and proficiently.
464–473	Read The Tell-Tale Heart	RL.9-10.1	Cite strong and thorough textual evidence to support analysis of what the text says explicitly as well as inferences drawn from the text.
		RL.9-10.3	Analyze how complex characters develop over the course of a text, interact with other characters, and advance the plot or develop the theme.

SE Pages	Lesson	Code	Standards Text
464–473	**Read The Tell-Tale Heart** continued	RL.9-10.5	Analyze how an author's choices concerning how to structure a text, order events within it, and manipulate time create such effects as mystery, tension, or surprise.
		RL.9-10.7	Analyze the representation of a subject or a key scene in two different artistic mediums, including what is emphasized or absent in each treatment.
		RL.9-10.10	By the end of grade 10, read and comprehend literature, including stories, dramas, and poems, at the high end of the grades 9–10 text complexity band independently and proficiently.
		W.9-10.3	Write narratives to develop real or imagined experiences or events using effective technique, well-chosen details, and well-structured event sequences.
		W.9-10.10	Write routinely over extended time frames (time for research, reflection, and revision) and shorter time frames (a single sitting or a day or two) for a range of tasks, purposes, and audiences.
		L.9-10.1.b	Use various types of phrases (noun, verb, adjectival, adverbial, participial, prepositional, absolute) and clauses (independent, dependent; noun, relative, adverbial) to convey specific meanings and add variety and interest to writing or presentations.
		L.9-10.2.c	Spell correctly.
		L.9-10.6	Acquire and use accurately general academic and domain-specific words and phrases, sufficient for reading, writing, speaking, and listening at the college and career readiness level; demonstrate independence in gathering vocabulary knowledge when considering a word or phrase important to comprehension or expression.
474	**Before Reading: The Raven**	RL.9-10.4	Determine the meaning of words and phrases as they are used in the text, including figurative and connotative meanings; analyze the cumulative impact of specific word choices on meaning and tone.
		RL.9-10.10	By the end of grade 10, read and comprehend literature, including stories, dramas, and poems, at the high end of the grades 9–10 text complexity band independently and proficiently.
475–481	**Read The Raven**	RL.9-10.1	Cite strong and thorough textual evidence to support analysis of what the text says explicitly as well as inferences drawn from the text.
		RL.9-10.4	Determine the meaning of words and phrases as they are used in the text, including figurative and connotative meanings; analyze the cumulative impact of specific word choices on meaning and tone.
		RL.9-10.10	By the end of grade 10, read and comprehend literature, including stories, dramas, and poems, at the high end of the grades 9–10 text complexity band independently and proficiently.
		W.9-10.9.a	Apply grades 9–10 Reading standards to literature.
		W.9-10.10	Write routinely over extended time frames (time for research, reflection, and revision) and shorter time frames (a single sitting or a day or two) for a range of tasks, purposes, and audiences.
		L.9-10.1.b	Use various types of phrases (noun, verb, adjectival, adverbial, participial, prepositional, absolute) and clauses (independent, dependent; noun, relative, adverbial) to convey specific meanings and add variety and interest to writing or presentations.

Common Core State Standards, continued

SE Pages	Lesson	Code	Standards Text
475–481	**Read The Raven** continued	L.9-10.5	Demonstrate understanding of figurative language, word relationships, and nuances in word meanings.
		L.9-10.6	Acquire and use accurately general academic and domain-specific words and phrases, sufficient for reading, writing, speaking, and listening at the college and career readiness level; demonstrate independence in gathering vocabulary knowledge when considering a word or phrase important to comprehension or expression.
482	**Postscript: The Mysterious Edgar Allan Poe**	RI.9-10.2	Determine a central idea of a text and analyze its development over the course of the text, including how it emerges and is shaped and refined by specific details; provide an objective summary of the text.
		RI.9-10.6	Determine an author's point of view or purpose in a text and analyze how an author uses rhetoric to advance that point of view or purpose.
483	**Reflect and Assess Critical Thinking**	RL.9-10.1	Cite strong and thorough textual evidence to support analysis of what the text says explicitly as well as inferences drawn from the text.
		RL.9-10.4	Determine the meaning of words and phrases as they are used in the text, including figurative and connotative meanings; analyze the cumulative impact of specific word choices on meaning and tone.
		RL.9-10.5	Analyze how an author's choices concerning how to structure a text, order events within it, and manipulate time create such effects as mystery, tension, or surprise.
		RL.9-10.10	By the end of grade 10, read and comprehend literature, including stories, dramas, and poems, at the high end of the grades 9–10 text complexity band independently and proficiently.
	Write About Literature	W.9-10.9.a	Apply grades 9–10 Reading standards to literature.
	Key Vocabulary Review	L.9-10.6	Acquire and use accurately general academic and domain-specific words and phrases, sufficient for reading, writing, speaking, and listening at the college and career readiness level; demonstrate independence in gathering vocabulary knowledge when considering a word or phrase important to comprehension or expression.
	Read with Ease: Intonation	RL.9-10.10	By the end of grade 10, read and comprehend literature, including stories, dramas, and poems, at the high end of the grades 9–10 text complexity band independently and proficiently.
484	**Grammar: Use Adverbs Correctly**	L.9-10.1.b	Use various types of phrases (noun, verb, adjectival, adverbial, participial, prepositional, absolute) and clauses (independent, dependent; noun, relative, adverbial) to convey specific meanings and add variety and interest to writing or presentations.
484	**Language Development: Compare and Contrast**	W.9-10.9.a	Apply grades 9–10 Reading standards to literature.
		SL.9-10.1.a	Come to discussions prepared, having read and researched material under study; explicitly draw on that preparation by referring to evidence from texts and other research on the topic or issue to stimulate a thoughtful, well-reasoned exchange of ideas.
484	**Literary Analysis: Analyze Mood and Tone**	RL.9-10.4	Determine the meaning of words and phrases as they are used in the text, including figurative and connotative meanings; analyze the cumulative impact of specific word choices on meaning and tone.
484	**Literary Analysis: Analyze Symbolism**	RL.9-10.4	Determine the meaning of words and phrases as they are used in the text, including figurative and connotative meanings; analyze the cumulative impact of specific word choices on meaning and tone.

Cluster 3, continued

SE Pages	Lesson	Code	Standards Text
485	Vocabulary Study: Analogies	L.9-10.5	Demonstrate understanding of figurative language, word relationships, and nuances in word meanings.
485	Writing Trait: Organization	W.9-10.4	Produce clear and coherent writing in which the development, organization, and style are appropriate to task, purpose, and audience.
485	Listening/Speaking: Dramatization	SL.9-10.6	Adapt speech to a variety of contexts and tasks, demonstrating command of formal English when indicated or appropriate.

Close Reading

SE Pages	Lesson	Code	Standards Text
486–489	Read Puddle	RL.9-10.10	By the end of grade 10, read and comprehend literature, including stories, dramas, and poems, at the high end of the grades 9–10 text complexity band independently and proficiently.

Unit Wrap-Up

SE Pages	Lesson	Code	Standards Text
490	Unit Wrap-Up Present Your Project	SL.9-10.2	Integrate multiple sources of information presented in diverse media or formats evaluating the credibility and accuracy of each source.
		SL.9-10.4	Present information, findings, and supporting evidence clearly, concisely, and logically such that listeners can follow the line of reasoning and the organization, development, substance, and style are appropriate to purpose, audience, and task.
		SL.9-10.5	Make strategic use of digital media in presentations to enhance understanding of findings, reasoning, and evidence and to add interest.
		SL.9-10.6	Adapt speech to a variety of contexts and tasks, demonstrating command of formal English when indicated or appropriate.
	Reflect on Your Reading	SL.9-10.1.a	Come to discussions prepared, having read and researched material under study; explicitly draw on that preparation by referring to evidence from texts and other research on the topic or issue to stimulate a thoughtful, well-reasoned exchange of ideas.
	Respond to the Essential Question	SL.9-10.1.a	Come to discussions prepared, having read and researched material under study; explicitly draw on that preparation by referring to evidence from texts and other research on the topic or issue to stimulate a thoughtful, well-reasoned exchange of ideas.

Unit 5 Writing Project: Short Story

SE Pages	Lesson	Code	Standards Text
491–495	Study Short Stories and Prewrite	W.9-10.3.c	Use a variety of techniques to sequence events so that they build on one another to create a coherent whole.
		W.9-10.5	Develop and strengthen writing as needed by planning, revising, editing, rewriting, or trying a new approach, focusing on addressing what is most significant for a specific purpose and audience.
496–497	Short Story: Draft	W.9-10.3.d	Use precise words and phrases, telling details, and sensory language to convey a vivid picture of the experiences, events, setting, and/or characters.
		W.9-10.4	Produce clear and coherent writing in which the development, organization, and style are appropriate to task, purpose, and audience.

Common Core State Standards, continued

Unit 5 Writing Project: Short Story, continued

SE Pages	Lesson	Code	Standards Text
498–501	Short Story: Revise Trait: Organization	W.9-10.3.a	Engage and orient the reader by setting out a problem, situation, or observation, establishing one or multiple point(s) of view, and introducing a narrator and/or characters; create a smooth progression of experiences or events.
		W.9-10.3.b	Use narrative techniques, such as dialogue, pacing, description, reflection, and multiple plot lines, to develop experiences, events, and/or characters.
		W.9-10.3.c	Use a variety of techniques to sequence events so that they build on one another to create a coherent whole.
		W.9-10.3.d	Use precise words and phrases, telling details, and sensory language to convey a vivid picture of the experiences, events, setting, and/or characters.
		W.9-10.3.e	Provide a conclusion that follows from and reflects on what is experienced, observed, or resolved over the course of the narrative.
		W.9-10.5	Develop and strengthen writing as needed by planning, revising, editing, rewriting, or trying a new approach, focusing on addressing what is most significant for a specific purpose and audience.
		SL.9-10.1.d	Respond thoughtfully to diverse perspectives, summarize points of agreement and disagreement, and, when warranted, qualify or justify their own views and understanding and make new connections in light of the evidence and reasoning presented.
502-504	Short Story: Edit and Proofread Capitalization: Quotations Punctuation Paragraph Structure Adjectives and Adverbs	L.9-10.1	Demonstrate command of the conventions of standard English grammar and usage when writing or speaking.
		L.9-10.1.b	Use various types of phrases and clauses to convey specific meanings and add variety and interest to writing or presentations.
		L.9-10.2	Demonstrate command of the conventions of standard English capitalization, punctuation, and spelling when writing.
		L.9-10.3.a	Write and edit work so that it conforms to the guidelines in a style manual appropriate for the discipline and writing type.
505	Short Story: Publish and Present	W.9-10.6	Use technology, including the Internet, to produce, publish, and update individual or shared writing products, taking advantage of technology's capacity to link to other information and to display information flexibly and dynamically.
		SL.9-10.5	Make strategic use of digital media in presentations to enhance understanding of findings, reasoning, and evidence and to add interest.
		SL.9-10.6	Adapt speech to a variety of contexts and tasks, demonstrating command of formal English when indicated or appropriate.

UNIT 6: Are You Buying It?

SE Pages	Lesson	Code	Standards Text
506–507	Discuss the Essential Question	SL.9-10.1.b	Work with peers to set rules for collegial discussions and decision-making, clear goals and deadlines, and individual roles as needed.
		SL.9-10.3	Evaluate a speaker's point of view, reasoning, and use of evidence and rhetoric, identifying any fallacious reasoning or exaggerated or distorted evidence.
508	Analyze and Debate	SL.9-10.4	Present information, findings, and supporting evidence clearly, concisely, and logically such that listeners can follow the line of reasoning and the organization, development, substance, and style are appropriate to purpose, audience, and task.

UNIT 6: Are You Buying It?, continued

SE Pages	Lesson	Code	Standards Text
509	Plan a Project	SL.9-10.1.b	Work with peers to set rules for collegial discussions and decision-making (e.g., informal consensus, taking votes on key issues, presentation of alternate views), clear goals and deadlines, and individual roles as needed.
509	Choose More to Read	RL.9-10.10	By the end of grade 10, read and comprehend literature, including stories, dramas, and poems, at the high end of the grades 9–10 text complexity band independently and proficiently.
		RI.9-10.10	By the end of grade 10, read and comprehend literary nonfiction at the high end of the grades 9–10 text complexity band independently and proficiently.
510–513	How to Read Nonfiction	RI.9-10.8	Delineate and evaluate the argument and specific claims in a text, assessing whether the reasoning is valid and the evidence is relevant and sufficient; identify false statements and fallacious reasoning.
		L.9-10.6	Acquire and use accurately general academic and domain-specific words and phrases, sufficient for reading, writing, speaking, and listening at the college and career readiness level; demonstrate independence in gathering vocabulary knowledge when considering a word or phrase important to comprehension or expression.

Cluster 1

SE Pages	Lesson	Code	Standards Text
514	Prepare to Read	RI.9-10.4	Determine the meaning of words and phrases as they are used in a text, including figurative, connotative, and technical meanings; analyze the cumulative impact of specific word choices on meaning and tone.
		SL.9-10.1	Initiate and participate effectively in a range of collaborative discussions (one-on-one, in groups, and teacher-led) with diverse partners on grades 9–10 topics, texts, and issues, building on others' ideas and expressing their own clearly and persuasively.
		L.9-10.6	Acquire and use accurately general academic and domain-specific words and phrases, sufficient for reading, writing, speaking, and listening at the college and career readiness level; demonstrate independence in gathering vocabulary knowledge when considering a word or phrase important to comprehension or expression.
515	Before Reading: Ad Power	RI.9-10.8	Delineate and evaluate the argument and specific claims in a text, assessing whether the reasoning is valid and the evidence is relevant and sufficient; identify false statements and fallacious reasoning.
		RI.9-10.10	By the end of grade 10, read and comprehend literary nonfiction at the high end of the grades 9–10 text complexity band independently and proficiently.
516–526	Read Ad Power	RI.9-10.1	Cite strong and thorough textual evidence to support analysis of what the text says explicitly as well as inferences drawn from the text.
		RI.9-10.2	Determine a central idea of a text and analyze its development over the course of the text, including how it emerges and is shaped and refined by specific details; provide an objective summary of the text.
		RI.9-10.8	Delineate and evaluate the argument and specific claims in a text, assessing whether the reasoning is valid and the evidence is relevant and sufficient; identify false statements and fallacious reasoning.
		RI.9-10.10	By the end of grade 10, read and comprehend literary nonfiction at the high end of the grades 9–10 text complexity band independently and proficiently.
		W.9-10.1	Write arguments to support claims in an analysis of substantive topics or texts, using valid reasoning and relevant and sufficient evidence.

Common Core State Standards, continued

Cluster 1, continued

SE Pages	Lesson	Code	Standards Text
516–526	**Read Ad Power** continued	W.9-10.9.b	Apply grades 9–10 Reading standards to literary nonfiction.
		W.9-10.10	Write routinely over extended time frames (time for research, reflection, and revision) and shorter time frames (a single sitting or a day or two) for a range of tasks, purposes, and audiences.
		L.9-10.1.b	Use various types of phrases (noun, verb, adjectival, adverbial, participial, prepositional, absolute) and clauses (independent, dependent; noun, relative, adverbial) to convey specific meanings and add variety and interest to writing or presentations.
		L.9-10.4.a	Use context as a clue to the meaning of a word or phrase.
		L.9-10.6	Acquire and use accurately general academic and domain-specific words and phrases, sufficient for reading, writing, speaking, and listening at the college and career readiness level; demonstrate independence in gathering vocabulary knowledge when considering a word or phrase important to comprehension or expression.
527–529	**Postscript: Without Commercials**	RL.9-10.2	Determine a theme or central idea of a text and analyze in detail its development over the course of the text, including how it emerges and is shaped and refined by specific details; provide an objective summary of the text.
		RL.9-10.4	Determine the meaning of words and phrases as they are used in the text, including figurative and connotative meanings; analyze the cumulative impact of specific word choices on meaning and tone.
		RL.9-10.10	By the end of grade 10, read and comprehend literature, including stories, dramas, and poems, at the high end of the grades 9–10 text complexity band independently and proficiently.
530	**Before Reading: What's Wrong with Advertising?**	RI.9-10.4	Determine the meaning of words and phrases as they are used in a text, including figurative, connotative, and technical meanings; analyze the cumulative impact of specific word choices on meaning and tone.
		RI.9-10.6	Determine an author's point of view or purpose in a text and analyze how an author uses rhetoric to advance that point of view or purpose.
		RI.9-10.10	By the end of grade 10, read and comprehend literary nonfiction at the high end of the grades 9–10 text complexity band independently and proficiently.
531–536	**Read What's Wrong with Advertising?**	RI.9-10.1	Cite strong and thorough textual evidence to support analysis of what the text says explicitly as well as inferences drawn from the text.
		RI.9-10.2	Determine a central idea of a text and analyze its development over the course of the text, including how it emerges and is shaped and refined by specific details; provide an objective summary of the text.
		RI.9-10.4	Determine the meaning of words and phrases as they are used in a text, including figurative, connotative, and technical meanings; analyze the cumulative impact of specific word choices on meaning and tone.
		RI.9-10.6	Determine an author's point of view or purpose in a text and analyze how an author uses rhetoric to advance that point of view or purpose.
		RI.9-10.10	By the end of grade 10, read and comprehend literary nonfiction at the high end of the grades 9–10 text complexity band independently and proficiently.
		W.9-10.9.b	Apply grades 9–10 Reading standards to literary nonfiction.

SE Pages	Lesson	Code	Standards Text
531–536	**Read What's Wrong with Advertising?** continued	W.9-10.10	Write routinely over extended time frames (time for research, reflection, and revision) and shorter time frames (a single sitting or a day or two) for a range of tasks, purposes, and audiences.
		L.9-10.1.b	Use various types of phrases (noun, verb, adjectival, adverbial, participial, prepositional, absolute) and clauses (independent, dependent; noun, relative, adverbial) to convey specific meanings and add variety and interest to writing or presentations.
		L.9-10.4.a	Use context as a clue to the meaning of a word or phrase.
		L.9-10.6	Acquire and use accurately general academic and domain-specific words and phrases, sufficient for reading, writing, speaking, and listening at the college and career readiness level; demonstrate independence in gathering vocabulary knowledge when considering a word or phrase important to comprehension or expression.
537	**Reflect and Assess Critical Thinking**	RI.9-10.1	Cite strong and thorough textual evidence to support analysis of what the text says explicitly as well as inferences drawn from the text.
		RI.9-10.6	Determine an author's point of view or purpose in a text and analyze how an author uses rhetoric to advance that point of view or purpose.
		RI.9-10.10	By the end of grade 10, read and comprehend literary nonfiction at the high end of the grades 9–10 text complexity band independently and proficiently.
	Write About Literature	W.9-10.2	Write informative/explanatory texts to examine and convey complex ideas, concepts, and information clearly and accurately through the effective selection, organization, and analysis of content.
	Key Vocabulary Review	L.9-10.6	Acquire and use accurately general academic and domain-specific words and phrases, sufficient for reading, writing, speaking, and listening at the college and career readiness level; demonstrate independence in gathering vocabulary knowledge when considering a word or phrase important to comprehension or expression.
	Read with Ease: Expression	RI.9-10.10	By the end of grade 10, read and comprehend literary nonfiction at the high end of the grades 9–10 text complexity band independently and proficiently.
538	**Grammar: Vary Your Sentences**	L.9-10.1.b	Use various types of phrases (noun, verb, adjectival, adverbial, participial, prepositional, absolute) and clauses (independent, dependent; noun, relative, adverbial) to convey specific meanings and add variety and interest to writing or presentations.
538	**Language Development: Persuade**	SL.9-10.4	Present information, findings, and supporting evidence clearly, concisely, and logically such that listeners can follow the line of reasoning and the organization, development, substance, and style are appropriate to purpose, audience, and task.
538	**Literary Analysis: Compare Authors' Purposes and Viewpoints**	RI.9-10.6	Determine an author's point of view or purpose in a text and analyze how an author uses rhetoric to advance that point of view or purpose.
539	**Vocabulary Study: Latin and Greek Roots**	L.9-10.4.d	Verify the preliminary determination of the meaning of a word or phrase (e.g., by checking the inferred meaning in context or in a dictionary).

Common Core State Standards, continued

Cluster 1, continued

SE Pages	Lesson	Code	Standards Text
539	**Writing: Write a Letter to the Editor**	W.9-10.1	Write arguments to support claims in an analysis of substantive topics or texts, using valid reasoning and relevant and sufficient evidence.
		W.9-10.5	Develop and strengthen writing as needed by planning, revising, editing, rewriting, or trying a new approach, focusing on addressing what is most significant for a specific purpose and audience.
540	**Workplace Workshop: Inside a Department Store**	W.9-10.4	Produce clear and coherent writing in which the development, organization, and style are appropriate to task, purpose, and audience.
		W.9-10.7	Conduct short as well as more sustained research projects to answer a question (including a self-generated question) or solve a problem; narrow or broaden the inquiry when appropriate; synthesize multiple sources on the subject, demonstrating understanding of the subject under investigation.
		W.9-10.10	Write routinely over extended time frames (time for research, reflection, and revision) and shorter time frames (a single sitting or a day or two) for a range of tasks, purposes, and audiences.
541	**Vocabulary Workshop: Build Word Knowledge**	L.9-10.4	Determine or clarify the meaning of unknown and multiple-meaning words and phrases based on grades 9–10 reading and content, choosing flexibly from a range of strategies.

Cluster 2

SE Pages	Lesson	Code	Standards Text
542	**Prepare to Read**	RI.9-10.4	Determine the meaning of words and phrases as they are used in a text, including figurative, connotative, and technical meanings; analyze the cumulative impact of specific word choices on meaning and tone.
		SL.9-10.1	Initiate and participate effectively in a range of collaborative discussions (one-on-one, in groups, and teacher-led) with diverse partners on grades 9–10 topics, texts, and issues, building on others' ideas and expressing their own clearly and persuasively.
		L.9-10.6	Acquire and use accurately general academic and domain-specific words and phrases, sufficient for reading, writing, speaking, and listening at the college and career readiness level; demonstrate independence in gathering vocabulary knowledge when considering a word or phrase important to comprehension or expression.
543	**Before Reading: A Long Way to Go: Minorities and the Media**	RI.9-10.8	Delineate and evaluate the argument and specific claims in a text, assessing whether the reasoning is valid and the evidence is relevant and sufficient; identify false statements and fallacious reasoning.
		RI.9-10.10	By the end of grade 10, read and comprehend literary nonfiction at the high end of the grades 9–10 text complexity band independently and proficiently.
544–551	**Read A Long Way to Go: Minorities and the Media**	RI.9-10.1	Cite strong and thorough textual evidence to support analysis of what the text says explicitly as well as inferences drawn from the text.
		RI.9-10.2	Determine a central idea of a text and analyze its development over the course of the text, including how it emerges and is shaped and refined by specific details; provide an objective summary of the text.
		RI.9-10.4	Determine the meaning of words and phrases as they are used in a text, including figurative, connotative, and technical meanings; analyze the cumulative impact of specific word choices on meaning and tone.
		RI.9-10.8	Delineate and evaluate the argument and specific claims in a text, assessing whether the reasoning is valid and the evidence is relevant and sufficient; identify false statements and fallacious reasoning.

Cluster 2, continued

SE Pages	Lesson	Code	Standards Text
544–551	**Read A Long Way to Go: Minorities and the Media** continued	RI.9-10.10	By the end of grade 10, read and comprehend literary nonfiction at the high end of the grades 9–10 text complexity band independently and proficiently.
		W.9-10.1.b	Develop claim(s) and counterclaims fairly, supplying evidence for each while pointing out the strengths and limitations of both in a manner that anticipates the audience's knowledge level and concerns.
		W.9-10.10	Write routinely over extended time frames (time for research, reflection, and revision) and shorter time frames (a single sitting or a day or two) for a range of tasks, purposes, and audiences.
		L.9-10.1.b	Use various types of phrases (noun, verb, adjectival, adverbial, participial, prepositional, absolute) and clauses (independent, dependent; noun, relative, adverbial) to convey specific meanings and add variety and interest to writing or presentations.
		L.9-10.4	Determine or clarify the meaning of unknown and multiple-meaning words and phrases based on grades 9–10 reading and content, choosing flexibly from a range of strategies.
		L.9-10.6	Acquire and use accurately general academic and domain-specific words and phrases, sufficient for reading, writing, speaking, and listening at the college and career readiness level; demonstrate independence in gathering vocabulary knowledge when considering a word or phrase important to comprehension or expression.
552	**Before Reading: Reza: Warrior of Peace**	RI.9-10.8	Delineate and evaluate the argument and specific claims in a text, assessing whether the reasoning is valid and the evidence is relevant and sufficient; identify false statements and fallacious reasoning.
		RI.9-10.10	By the end of grade 10, read and comprehend literary nonfiction at the high end of the grades 9–10 text complexity band independently and proficiently.
553–556	**Read Reza: Warrior of Peace**	RI.9-10.8	Delineate and evaluate the argument and specific claims in a text, assessing whether the reasoning is valid and the evidence is relevant and sufficient; identify false statements and fallacious reasoning.
		RI.9-10.10	By the end of grade 10, read and comprehend literary nonfiction at the high end of the grades 9–10 text complexity band independently and proficiently.
		W.9-10.1.b	Develop claim(s) and counterclaims fairly, supplying evidence for each while pointing out the strengths and limitations of both in a manner that anticipates the audience's knowledge level and concerns.
		W.9-10.10	Write routinely over extended time frames (time for research, reflection, and revision) and shorter time frames (a single sitting or a day or two) for a range of tasks, purposes, and audiences.
		L.9-10.1.b	Use various types of phrases (noun, verb, adjectival, adverbial, participial, prepositional, absolute) and clauses (independent, dependent; noun, relative, adverbial) to convey specific meanings and add variety and interest to writing or presentations.
		L.9-10.6	Acquire and use accurately general academic and domain-specific words and phrases, sufficient for reading, writing, speaking, and listening at the college and career readiness level; demonstrate independence in gathering vocabulary knowledge when considering a word or phrase important to comprehension or expression.

Common Core State Standards, continued

Cluster 2, continued

SE Pages	Lesson	Code	Standards Text
557	**Reflect and Assess Critical Thinking**	RI.9-10.1	Cite strong and thorough textual evidence to support analysis of what the text says explicitly as well as inferences drawn from the text.
		RI.9-10.2	Determine a central idea of a text and analyze its development over the course of the text, including how it emerges and is shaped and refined by specific details; provide an objective summary of the text.
		RI.9-10.8	Delineate and evaluate the argument and specific claims in a text, assessing whether the reasoning is valid and the evidence is relevant and sufficient; identify false statements and fallacious reasoning.
		RI.9-10.10	By the end of grade 10, read and comprehend literary nonfiction at the high end of the grades 9–10 text complexity band independently and proficiently.
	Write About Literature	W.9-10.1	Write arguments to support claims in an analysis of substantive topics or texts, using valid reasoning and relevant and sufficient evidence.
		L.9-10.6	Acquire and use accurately general academic and domain-specific words and phrases, sufficient for reading, writing, speaking, and listening at the college and career readiness level; demonstrate independence in gathering vocabulary knowledge when considering a word or phrase important to comprehension or expression.
	Read with Ease: Intonation	RI.9-10.10	By the end of grade 10, read and comprehend literary nonfiction at the high end of the grades 9–10 text complexity band independently and proficiently.
558	**Grammar: Use Compound Sentences**	L.9-10.1.b	Use various types of phrases (noun, verb, adjectival, adverbial, participial, prepositional, absolute) and clauses (independent, dependent; noun, relative, adverbial) to convey specific meanings and add variety and interest to writing or presentations.
558	**Language Development: Evaluate**	SL.9-10.1.a	Come to discussions prepared, having read and researched material under study; explicitly draw on that preparation by referring to evidence from texts and other research on the topic or issue to stimulate a thoughtful, well-reasoned exchange of ideas.
558	**Literary Analysis: Persuasive Text Structures**	RI.9-10.5	Analyze in detail how an author's ideas or claims are developed and refined by particular sentences, paragraphs, or larger portions of a text.
558	**Media Study: Report on Minorities and the Media**	SL.9-10.1	Initiate and participate effectively in a range of collaborative discussions (one-on-one, in groups, and teacher-led) with diverse partners on grades 9–10 topics, texts, and issues, building on others' ideas and expressing their own clearly and persuasively.
		SL.9-10.3	Evaluate a speaker's point of view, reasoning, and use of evidence and rhetoric, identifying any fallacious reasoning or exaggerated or distorted evidence.
559	**Vocabulary Study: Latin and Greek Roots**	L.9-10.4	Determine or clarify the meaning of unknown and multiple-meaning words and phrases based on grades 9–10 reading and content, choosing flexibly from a range of strategies.
559	**Writing Trait: Organization**	W.9-10.5	Develop and strengthen writing as needed by planning, revising, editing, rewriting, or trying a new approach, focusing on addressing what is most significant for a specific purpose and audience.
560–561	**Listening and Speaking Workshop: Debate**	SL.9-10.1.a	Come to discussions prepared, having read and researched material under study; explicitly draw on that preparation by referring to evidence from texts and other research on the topic or issue to stimulate a thoughtful, well-reasoned exchange of ideas.

Cluster 2, continued

SE Pages	Lesson	Code	Standards Text
560–561	**Listening and Speaking Workshop: Debate** continued	SL.9-10.1.b	Work with peers to set rules for collegial discussions and decision-making (e.g., informal consensus, taking votes on key issues, presentation of alternate views), clear goals and deadlines, and individual roles as needed.
		SL.9-10.1.c	Propel conversations by posing and responding to questions that relate the current discussion to broader themes or larger ideas; actively incorporate others into the discussion; and clarify, verify, or challenge ideas and conclusions.
		SL.9-10.1.d	Respond thoughtfully to diverse perspectives, summarize points of agreement and disagreement, and, when warranted, qualify or justify their own views and understanding and make new connections in light of the evidence and reasoning presented.
		SL.9-10.3	Evaluate a speaker's point of view, reasoning, and use of evidence and rhetoric, identifying any fallacious reasoning or exaggerated or distorted evidence.
		SL.9-10.4	Present information, findings, and supporting evidence clearly, concisely, and logically such that listeners can follow the line of reasoning and the organization, development, substance, and style are appropriate to purpose, audience, and task.
		L.9-10.3	Apply knowledge of language to understand how language functions in different contexts, to make effective choices for meaning or style, and to comprehend more fully when reading or listening.

Cluster 3

SE Pages	Lesson	Code	Standards Text
562	**Prepare to Read**	RI.9-10.4	Determine the meaning of words and phrases as they are used in a text, including figurative, connotative, and technical meanings; analyze the cumulative impact of specific word choices on meaning and tone.
		SL.9-10.1	Initiate and participate effectively in a range of collaborative discussions (one-on-one, in groups, and teacher-led) with diverse partners on grades 9–10 topics, texts, and issues, building on others' ideas and expressing their own clearly and persuasively.
		L.9-10.4.c	Consult general and specialized reference materials, both print and digital, to find the pronunciation of a word or determine or clarify its precise meaning, its part of speech, or its etymology.
		L.9-10.6	Acquire and use accurately general academic and domain-specific words and phrases, sufficient for reading, writing, speaking, and listening at the college and career readiness level; demonstrate independence in gathering vocabulary knowledge when considering a word or phrase important to comprehension or expression.
563	**Before Reading: What Is News?**	RI.9-10.4	Determine the meaning of words and phrases as they are used in a text, including figurative, connotative, and technical meanings; analyze the cumulative impact of specific word choices on meaning and tone.
		RI.9-10.6	Determine an author's point of view or purpose in a text and analyze how an author uses rhetoric to advance that point of view or purpose.
564–573	**Read What Is News?**	RI.9-10.1	Cite strong and thorough textual evidence to support analysis of what the text says explicitly as well as inferences drawn from the text.
		RI.9-10.2	Determine a central idea of a text and analyze its development over the course of the text, including how it emerges and is shaped and refined by specific details; provide an objective summary of the text.

Common Core State Standards, continued

Cluster 3, continued

SE Pages	Lesson	Code	Standards Text
564–573	**Read What Is News?** continued	RI.9-10.3	Analyze how the author unfolds an analysis or series of ideas or events, including the order in which the points are made, how they are introduced and developed, and the connections that are drawn between them.
		RI.9-10.4	Determine the meaning of words and phrases as they are used in a text, including figurative, connotative, and technical meanings; analyze the cumulative impact of specific word choices on meaning and tone.
		RI.9-10.6	Determine an author's point of view or purpose in a text and analyze how an author uses rhetoric to advance that point of view or purpose.
		RI.9-10.7	Analyze various accounts of a subject told in different mediums, determining which details are emphasized in each account.
		RI.9-10.8	Delineate and evaluate the argument and specific claims in a text, assessing whether the reasoning is valid and the evidence is relevant and sufficient; identify false statements and fallacious reasoning.
		RI.9-10.10	By the end of grade 10, read and comprehend literary nonfiction at the high end of the grades 9–10 text complexity band independently and proficiently.
		W.9-10.1	Write arguments to support claims in an analysis of substantive topics or texts, using valid reasoning and relevant and sufficient evidence.
		W.9-10.9.b	Apply grades 9–10 Reading standards to literary nonfiction.
		W.9-10.10	Write routinely over extended time frames (time for research, reflection, and revision) and shorter time frames (a single sitting or a day or two) for a range of tasks, purposes, and audiences.
		L.9-10.1.b	Use various types of phrases (noun, verb, adjectival, adverbial, participial, prepositional, absolute) and clauses (independent, dependent; noun, relative, adverbial) to convey specific meanings and add variety and interest to writing or presentations.
		L.9-10.6	Acquire and use accurately general academic and domain-specific words and phrases, sufficient for reading, writing, speaking, and listening at the college and career readiness level; demonstrate independence in gathering vocabulary knowledge when considering a word or phrase important to comprehension or expression.
574	**Before Reading: How to Detect Bias in the News**	RI.9-10.5	Analyze in detail how an author's ideas or claims are developed and refined by particular sentences, paragraphs, or larger portions of a text.
		RI.9-10.10	By the end of grade 10, read and comprehend literary nonfiction at the high end of the grades 9–10 text complexity band independently and proficiently.
575–578	**Read How to Detect Bias in the News**	RI.9-10.1	Cite strong and thorough textual evidence to support analysis of what the text says explicitly as well as inferences drawn from the text.
		RI.9-10.2	Determine a central idea of a text and analyze its development over the course of the text, including how it emerges and is shaped and refined by specific details; provide an objective summary of the text.
		RI.9-10.5	Analyze in detail how an author's ideas or claims are developed and refined by particular sentences, paragraphs, or larger portions of a text.
		RI.9-10.10	By the end of grade 10, read and comprehend literary nonfiction at the high end of the grades 9–10 text complexity band independently and proficiently.

SE Pages	Lesson	Code	Standards Text
575–578	**Read How to Detect Bias in the News** continued	W.9-10.1	Write arguments to support claims in an analysis of substantive topics or texts, using valid reasoning and relevant and sufficient evidence.
		W.9-10.10	Write routinely over extended time frames (time for research, reflection, and revision) and shorter time frames (a single sitting or a day or two) for a range of tasks, purposes, and audiences.
		L.9-10.1.a	Use parallel structure.
		L.9-10.1.b	Use various types of phrases (noun, verb, adjectival, adverbial, participial, prepositional, absolute) and clauses (independent, dependent; noun, relative, adverbial) to convey specific meanings and add variety and interest to writing or presentations.
		L.9-10.6	Acquire and use accurately general academic and domain-specific words and phrases, sufficient for reading, writing, speaking, and listening at the college and career readiness level; demonstrate independence in gathering vocabulary knowledge when considering a word or phrase important to comprehension or expression.
579	**Reflect and Assess Critical Thinking**	RI.9-10.1	Cite strong and thorough textual evidence to support analysis of what the text says explicitly as well as inferences drawn from the text.
		RI.9-10.8	Delineate and evaluate the argument and specific claims in a text, assessing whether the reasoning is valid and the evidence is relevant and sufficient; identify false statements and fallacious reasoning.
		RI.9-10.10	By the end of grade 10, read and comprehend literary nonfiction at the high end of the grades 9–10 text complexity band independently and proficiently.
	Write About Literature	RI.9-10.1	Cite strong and thorough textual evidence to support analysis of what the text says explicitly as well as inferences drawn from the text.
		W.9-10.1	Write arguments to support claims in an analysis of substantive topics or texts, using valid reasoning and relevant and sufficient evidence.
	Key Vocabulary Review	L.9-10.6	Acquire and use accurately general academic and domain-specific words and phrases, sufficient for reading, writing, speaking, and listening at the college and career readiness level; demonstrate independence in gathering vocabulary knowledge when considering a word or phrase important to comprehension or expression.
	Read with Ease: Phrasing	RI.9-10.10	By the end of grade 10, read and comprehend literary nonfiction at the high end of the grades 9–10 text complexity band independently and proficiently.
580	**Grammar: Use Complex Sentences**	L.9-10.1.b	Use various types of phrases (noun, verb, adjectival, adverbial, participial, prepositional, absolute) and clauses (independent, dependent; noun, relative, adverbial) to convey specific meanings and add variety and interest to writing or presentations.
580	**Language Development: Justify**	RI.9-10.8	Delineate and evaluate the argument and specific claims in a text, assessing whether the reasoning is valid and the evidence is relevant and sufficient; identify false statements and fallacious reasoning.
		SL.9-10.4	Present information, findings, and supporting evidence clearly, concisely, and logically such that listeners can follow the line of reasoning and the organization, development, substance, and style are appropriate to purpose, audience, and task.

Common Core State Standards, continued

Cluster 3, continued

SE Pages	Lesson	Code	Standards Text
580	**Media Study: Evaluate Bias in the Media**	RI.9-10.7	Analyze various accounts of a subject told in different mediums (e.g., a person's life story in both print and multimedia), determining which details are emphasized in each account.
		SL.9-10.2	Integrate multiple sources of information presented in diverse media or formats (e.g., visually, quantitatively, orally) evaluating the credibility and accuracy of each source.
581	**Vocabulary Study: Denotations and Connotations**	L.9-10.5.b	Analyze nuances in the meaning of words with similar denotations.
581	**Writing on Demand: Write a Response**	W.9-10.1	Write arguments to support claims in an analysis of substantive topics or texts, using valid reasoning and relevant and sufficient evidence.
581	**Listening/ Speaking: Oral Report**	SL.9-10.4	Present information, findings, and supporting evidence clearly, concisely, and logically such that listeners can follow the line of reasoning and the organization, development, substance, and style are appropriate to purpose, audience, and task.
		SL.9-10.5	Make strategic use of digital media in presentations to enhance understanding of findings, reasoning, and evidence and to add interest.

Close Reading

SE Pages	Lesson	Code	Standards Text
582–585	**Read Is Google Making Us Stupid?**	RI.9-10.10	By the end of grade 10, read and comprehend literary nonfiction at the high end of the grades 9–10 text complexity band independently and proficiently.

Unit Wrap-Up

SE Pages	Lesson	Code	Standards Text
586	**Unit Wrap-Up Present Your Project**	SL.9-10.3	Evaluate a speaker's point of view, reasoning, and use of evidence and rhetoric, identifying any fallacious reasoning or exaggerated or distorted evidence.
		SL.9-10.4	Present information, findings, and supporting evidence clearly, concisely, and logically such that listeners can follow the line of reasoning and the organization, development, substance, and style are appropriate to purpose, audience, and task.
		SL.9-10.5	Make strategic use of digital media (e.g., textual, graphical, audio, visual, and interactive elements) in presentations to enhance understanding of findings, reasoning, and evidence and to add interest.
	Reflect on Your Reading	SL.9-10.1.a	Come to discussions prepared, having read and researched material under study; explicitly draw on that preparation by referring to evidence from texts and other research on the topic or issue to stimulate a thoughtful, well-reasoned exchange of ideas.
	Respond to the Essential Question	SL.9-10.1.a	Come to discussions prepared, having read and researched material under study; explicitly draw on that preparation by referring to evidence from texts and other research on the topic or issue to stimulate a thoughtful, well-reasoned exchange of ideas.

Unit 6 Writing Project: Persuasive Essay

SE Pages	Lesson	Code	Standards Text
587–591	**Study Persuasive Essays and Prewrite**	W.9-10.1.a	Introduce precise claim(s), distinguish the claim(s) from alternate or opposing claims, and create an organization that establishes clear relationships among claim(s), counterclaims, reasons, and evidence.
		W.9-10.1.b	Develop claim(s) and counterclaims fairly, supplying evidence for each while pointing out the strengths and limitations of both in a manner that anticipates the audience's knowledge level and concerns.
		W.9-10.5	Develop and strengthen writing as needed by planning, revising, editing, rewriting, or trying a new approach, focusing on addressing what is most significant for a specific purpose and audience.

Unit 6 Writing Project: Persuasive Essay, continued

SE Pages	Lesson	Code	Standards Text
587–591	**Study Persuasive Essays and Prewrite** continued	W.9-10.7	Conduct short as well as more sustained research projects to answer a question (including a self-generated question) or solve a problem; narrow or broaden the inquiry when appropriate; synthesize multiple sources on the subject, demonstrating understanding of the subject under investigation.
		W.9-10.8	Gather relevant information from multiple authoritative print and digital sources, using advanced searches effectively; assess the usefulness of each source in answering the research question; integrate information into the text selectively to maintain the flow of ideas, avoiding plagiarism and following a standard format for citation.
592–593	**Persuasive Essay: Draft**	W.9-10.1	Write arguments to support claims in an analysis of substantive topics or texts, using valid reasoning and relevant and sufficient evidence.
		W.9-10.4	Produce clear and coherent writing in which the development, organization, and style are appropriate to task, purpose, and audience.
		W.9-10.6	Use technology, including the Internet, to produce, publish, and update individual or shared writing products, taking advantage of technology's capacity to link to other information and to display information flexibly and dynamically.
594–597	**Persuasive Essay: Revise Trait: Voice and Style**	W.9-10.1.a	Introduce precise claim(s), distinguish the claim(s) from alternate or opposing claims, and create an organization that establishes clear relationships among claim(s), counterclaims, reasons, and evidence.
		W.9-10.1.b	Develop claim(s) and counterclaims fairly, supplying evidence for each while pointing out the strengths and limitations of both in a manner that anticipates the audience's knowledge level and concerns.
		W.9-10.1.d	Establish and maintain a formal style and objective tone while attending to the norms and conventions of the discipline in which they are writing.
		W.9-10.3.e	Provide a conclusion that follows from and reflects on what is experienced, observed, or resolved over the course of the narrative.
		W.9-10.5	Develop and strengthen writing as needed by planning, revising, editing, rewriting, or trying a new approach, focusing on addressing what is most significant for a specific purpose and audience.
		SL.9-10.1	Initiate and participate effectively in a range of collaborative discussions (one-on-one, in groups, and teacher-led) with diverse partners on grades 9–10 topics, texts, and issues, building on others' ideas and expressing their own clearly and persuasively.
		SL.9-10.1.d	Respond thoughtfully to diverse perspectives, summarize points of agreement and disagreement, and, when warranted, qualify or justify their own views and understanding and make new connections in light of the evidence and reasoning presented.

Common Core State Standards, continued

Unit 6 Writing Project: Persuasive Essay

SE Pages	Lesson	Code	Standards Text
598–600	**Persuasive Essay:**	L.9-10.1.a	Use parallel structure.
	Edit and Proofread	L.9-10.1.b	Use various types of phrases (noun, verb, adjectival, adverbial, participial, prepositional, absolute) and clauses (independent, dependent; noun, relative, adverbial) to convey specific meanings and add variety and interest to writing or presentations.
	Capitalization: Specific School Courses		
	Semicolons and Commas	L.9-10.2	Demonstrate command of the conventions of standard English capitalization, punctuation, and spelling when writing.
	Precise Language		
	Effective Sentences	L.9-10.3.a	Write and edit work so that it conforms to the guidelines in a style manual appropriate for the discipline and writing type.
		L.9-10.6	Acquire and use accurately general academic and domain-specific words and phrases, sufficient for reading, writing, speaking, and listening at the college and career readiness level; demonstrate independence in gathering vocabulary knowledge when considering a word or phrase important to comprehension or expression.
601	**Persuasive Essay: Publish and Present**	W.9-10.6	Use technology, including the Internet, to produce, publish, and update individual or shared writing products, taking advantage of technology's capacity to link to other information and to display information flexibly and dynamically.
		SL.9-10.1.a	Come to discussions prepared, having read and researched material under study; explicitly draw on that preparation by referring to evidence from texts and other research on the topic or issue to stimulate a thoughtful, well-reasoned exchange of ideas.
		SL.9-10.3	Evaluate a speaker's point of view, reasoning, and use of evidence and rhetoric, identifying any fallacious reasoning or exaggerated or distorted evidence.
		SL.9-10.4	Present information, findings, and supporting evidence clearly, concisely, and logically such that listeners can follow the line of reasoning and the organization, development, substance, and style are appropriate to purpose, audience, and task.
UNIT 7: Where We Belong			
602–603	**Discuss the Essential Question**	SL.9-10.1.b	Work with peers to set rules for collegial discussions and decision-making (e.g., informal consensus, taking votes on key issues, presentation of alternate views), clear goals and deadlines, and individual roles as needed.
		SL.9-10.3	Evaluate a speaker's point of view, reasoning, and use of evidence and rhetoric, identifying any fallacious reasoning or exaggerated or distorted evidence.
604	**Compare and Discuss**	SL.9-10.4	Present information, findings, and supporting evidence clearly, concisely, and logically such that listeners can follow the line of reasoning and the organization, development, substance, and style are appropriate to purpose, audience, and task.
605	**Plan a Project**	SL.9-10.1.b	Work with peers to set rules for collegial discussions and decision-making (e.g., informal consensus, taking votes on key issues, presentation of alternate views), clear goals and deadlines, and individual roles as needed.
605	**Choose More to Read**	RL.9-10.10	By the end of grade 10, read and comprehend literature, including stories, dramas, and poems, at the high end of the grades 9–10 text complexity band independently and proficiently.
		RI.9-10.10	By the end of grade 10, read and comprehend literary nonfiction at the high end of the grades 9–10 text complexity band independently and proficiently.

UNIT 7: Where We Belong, continued

SE Pages	Lesson	Code	Standards Text
606–609	**How to Read Drama**	RL.9-10.4	Determine the meaning of words and phrases as they are used in the text, including figurative and connotative meanings; analyze the cumulative impact of specific word choices on meaning and tone (e.g., how the language evokes a sense of time and place; how it sets a formal or informal tone).
		RL.9-10.10	By the end of grade 10, read and comprehend literature, including stories, dramas, and poems, at the high end of the grades 9–10 text complexity band independently and proficiently.
610–611	**How to Read Poetry**	RL.9-10.7	Analyze the representation of a subject or a key scene in two different artistic mediums, including what is emphasized or absent in each treatment.
		L.9-10.6	Acquire and use accurately general academic and domain-specific words and phrases, sufficient for reading, writing, speaking, and listening at the college and career readiness level; demonstrate independence in gathering vocabulary knowledge when considering a word or phrase important to comprehension or expression.
Cluster 1			
612	**Prepare to Read**	RL.9-10.4	Determine the meaning of words and phrases as they are used in the text, including figurative and connotative meanings; analyze the cumulative impact of specific word choices on meaning and tone.
		SL.9-10.1	Initiate and participate effectively in a range of collaborative discussions (one-on-one, in groups, and teacher-led) with diverse partners on grades 9–10 topics, texts, and issues, building on others' ideas and expressing their own clearly and persuasively.
		L.9-10.6	Acquire and use accurately general academic and domain-specific words and phrases, sufficient for reading, writing, speaking, and listening at the college and career readiness level; demonstrate independence in gathering vocabulary knowledge when considering a word or phrase important to comprehension or expression.
613	**Before Reading: A Raisin in the Sun**	RL.9-10.4	Determine the meaning of words and phrases as they are used in the text, including figurative and connotative meanings; analyze the cumulative impact of specific word choices on meaning and tone.
		RL.9-10.7	Analyze the representation of a subject or a key scene in two different artistic mediums, including what is emphasized or absent in each treatment.
614–633	**Read A Raisin in the Sun**	RL.9-10.1	Cite strong and thorough textual evidence to support analysis of what the text says explicitly as well as inferences drawn from the text.
		RL.9-10.2	Determine a theme or central idea of a text and analyze in detail its development over the course of the text, including how it emerges and is shaped and refined by specific details; provide an objective summary of the text.
		RL.9-10.3	Analyze how complex characters develop over the course of a text, interact with other characters, and advance the plot or develop the theme.
		RL.9-10.4	Determine the meaning of words and phrases as they are used in the text, including figurative and connotative meanings; analyze the cumulative impact of specific word choices on meaning and tone.
		RL.9-10.7	Analyze the representation of a subject or a key scene in two different artistic mediums, including what is emphasized or absent in each treatment.

Common Core State Standards

Cluster 1, continued

SE Pages	Lesson	Code	Standards Text
614–633	**Read A Raisin in the Sun** continued	RL.9-10.10	By the end of grade 10, read and comprehend literature, including stories, dramas, and poems, at the high end of the grades 9–10 text complexity band independently and proficiently.
		W.9-10.9.a	Apply grades 9–10 Reading standards to literature.
		W.9-10.10	Write routinely over extended time frames (time for research, reflection, and revision) and shorter time frames (a single sitting or a day or two) for a range of tasks, purposes, and audiences.
		L.9-10.1.b	Use various types of phrases (noun, verb, adjectival, adverbial, participial, prepositional, absolute) and clauses (independent, dependent; noun, relative, adverbial) to convey specific meanings and add variety and interest to writing or presentations.
		L.9-10.5.a	Interpret figures of speech in context and analyze their role in the text.
		L.9-10.6	Acquire and use accurately general academic and domain-specific words and phrases, sufficient for reading, writing, speaking, and listening at the college and career readiness level; demonstrate independence in gathering vocabulary knowledge when considering a word or phrase important to comprehension or expression.
634	**Before Reading: Family Bonds**	RL.9-10.4	Determine the meaning of words and phrases as they are used in the text, including figurative and connotative meanings; analyze the cumulative impact of specific word choices on meaning and tone.
635–640	**Read Family Bonds**	RL.9-10.1	Cite strong and thorough textual evidence to support analysis of what the text says explicitly as well as inferences drawn from the text.
		RL.9-10.2	Determine a theme or central idea of a text and analyze in detail its development over the course of the text, including how it emerges and is shaped and refined by specific details; provide an objective summary of the text.
		RL.9-10.4	Determine the meaning of words and phrases as they are used in the text, including figurative and connotative meanings; analyze the cumulative impact of specific word choices on meaning and tone.
		RL.9-10.10	By the end of grade 10, read and comprehend literature, including stories, dramas, and poems, at the high end of the grades 9–10 text complexity band independently and proficiently.
		W.9-10.9.a	Apply grades 9–10 Reading standards to literature.
		W.9-10.10	Write routinely over extended time frames (time for research, reflection, and revision) and shorter time frames (a single sitting or a day or two) for a range of tasks, purposes, and audiences.
		SL.9-10.1.a	Come to discussions prepared, having read and researched material under study; explicitly draw on that preparation by referring to evidence from texts and other research on the topic or issue to stimulate a thoughtful, well-reasoned exchange of ideas.
		L.9-10.1.b	Use various types of phrases (noun, verb, adjectival, adverbial, participial, prepositional, absolute) and clauses (independent, dependent; noun, relative, adverbial) to convey specific meanings and add variety and interest to writing or presentations.
		L.9-10.2.c	Spell correctly.

SE Pages	Lesson	Code	Standards Text
635–640	**Read Family Bonds** continued	L.9-10.6	Acquire and use accurately general academic and domain-specific words and phrases, sufficient for reading, writing, speaking, and listening at the college and career readiness level; demonstrate independence in gathering vocabulary knowledge when considering a word or phrase important to comprehension or expression.
641	**Reflect and Assess Critical Thinking**	RL.9-10.1	Cite strong and thorough textual evidence to support analysis of what the text says explicitly as well as inferences drawn from the text.
		RL.9-10.2	Determine a theme or central idea of a text and analyze in detail its development over the course of the text, including how it emerges and is shaped and refined by specific details; provide an objective summary of the text.
		RL.9-10.3	Analyze how complex characters develop over the course of a text, interact with other characters, and advance the plot or develop the theme.
		RL.9-10.10	By the end of grade 10, read and comprehend literature, including stories, dramas, and poems, at the high end of the grades 9–10 text complexity band independently and proficiently.
	Write About Literature	W.9-10.9.a	Apply grades 9–10 Reading standards to literature.
	Key Vocabulary Review	L.9-10.6	Acquire and use accurately general academic and domain-specific words and phrases, sufficient for reading, writing, speaking, and listening at the college and career readiness level; demonstrate independence in gathering vocabulary knowledge when considering a word or phrase important to comprehension or expression.
	Read with Ease: Phrasing	RL.9-10.10	By the end of grade 10, read and comprehend literature, including stories, dramas, and poems, at the high end of the grades 9–10 text complexity band independently and proficiently.
642	**Grammar: Write in the Present Perfect Tense**	L.9-10.1.b	Use various types of phrases (noun, verb, adjectival, adverbial, participial, prepositional, absolute) and clauses (independent, dependent; noun, relative, adverbial) to convey specific meanings and add variety and interest to writing or presentations.
		L.9-10.2.c	Spell correctly.
642	**Language Development: Negotiate**	SL.9-10.1.d	Respond thoughtfully to diverse perspectives, summarize points of agreement and disagreement, and, when warranted, qualify or justify their own views and understanding and make new connections in light of the evidence and reasoning presented.
642	**Literary Analysis: Analyze and Compare Poetry**	RL.9-10.10	By the end of grade 10, read and comprehend literature, including stories, dramas, and poems, at the high end of the grades 9–10 text complexity band independently and proficiently.
643	**Vocabulary Study: Interpret Figurative Language**	L.9-10.4.a	Use context as a clue to the meaning of a word or phrase.
		L.9-10.5.a	Interpret figures of speech in context and analyze their role in the text.
643	**Writing on Demand: Write About Theme**	W.9-10.4	Produce clear and coherent writing in which the development, organization, and style are appropriate to task, purpose, and audience.
		W.9-10.9.a	Apply grades 9–10 Reading standards to literature.

Common Core State Standards, continued

Cluster 1, continued

SE Pages	Lesson	Code	Standards Text
643	Listening/ Speaking: Dramatization	RL.9-10.7	Analyze the representation of a subject or a key scene in two different artistic mediums, including what is emphasized or absent in each treatment.
		SL.9-10.6	Adapt speech to a variety of contexts and tasks, demonstrating command of formal English when indicated or appropriate.
644	Workplace Workshop: Inside a Real Estate Agency	W.9-10.1	Write arguments to support claims in an analysis of substantive topics or texts, using valid reasoning and relevant and sufficient evidence.
		W.9-10.10	Write routinely over extended time frames (time for research, reflection, and revision) and shorter time frames (a single sitting or a day or two) for a range of tasks, purposes, and audiences.
645	Vocabulary Workshop: Interpret Figurative Language	RL.9-10.4	Determine the meaning of words and phrases as they are used in the text, including figurative and connotative meanings; analyze the cumulative impact of specific word choices on meaning and tone.
		L.9-10.5.a	Interpret figures of speech in context and analyze their role in the text.

Cluster 2

SE Pages	Lesson	Code	Standards Text
646	Prepare to Read	RI.9-10.4	Determine the meaning of words and phrases as they are used in a text, including figurative, connotative, and technical meanings; analyze the cumulative impact of specific word choices on meaning and tone.
		SL.9-10.1	Initiate and participate effectively in a range of collaborative discussions (one-on-one, in groups, and teacher-led) with diverse partners on grades 9–10 topics, texts, and issues, building on others' ideas and expressing their own clearly and persuasively.
		L.9-10.6	Acquire and use accurately general academic and domain-specific words and phrases, sufficient for reading, writing, speaking, and listening at the college and career readiness level; demonstrate independence in gathering vocabulary knowledge when considering a word or phrase important to comprehension or expression.
647	Before Reading: Pass It On	RL.9-10.3	Analyze how complex characters develop over the course of a text, interact with other characters, and advance the plot or develop the theme.
		RL.9-10.4	Determine the meaning of words and phrases as they are used in the text, including figurative and connotative meanings; analyze the cumulative impact of specific word choices on meaning and tone.
648–665	Read Pass It On	RL.9-10.1	Cite strong and thorough textual evidence to support analysis of what the text says explicitly as well as inferences drawn from the text.
		RL.9-10.3	Analyze how complex characters develop over the course of a text, interact with other characters, and advance the plot or develop the theme.
		RL.9-10.4	Determine the meaning of words and phrases as they are used in the text, including figurative and connotative meanings; analyze the cumulative impact of specific word choices on meaning and tone.
		RL.9-10.10	By the end of grade 10, read and comprehend literature, including stories, dramas, and poems, at the high end of the grades 9–10 text complexity band independently and proficiently.
		RI.9-10.4	Determine the meaning of words and phrases as they are used in a text, including figurative, connotative, and technical meanings; analyze the cumulative impact of specific word choices on meaning and tone.

SE Pages	Lesson	Code	Standards Text
648–665	**Read Pass It On** continued	RI.9-10.6	Determine an author's point of view or purpose in a text and analyze how an author uses rhetoric to advance that point of view or purpose.
		W.9-10.9.a	Apply grades 9–10 Reading standards to literature.
		W.9-10.10	Write routinely over extended time frames (time for research, reflection, and revision) and shorter time frames (a single sitting or a day or two) for a range of tasks, purposes, and audiences.
		L.9-10.1.b	Use various types of phrases (noun, verb, adjectival, adverbial, participial, prepositional, absolute) and clauses (independent, dependent; noun, relative, adverbial) to convey specific meanings and add variety and interest to writing or presentations.
		L.9-10.5	Demonstrate understanding of figurative language, word relationships, and nuances in word meanings.
		L.9-10.6	Acquire and use accurately general academic and domain-specific words and phrases, sufficient for reading, writing, speaking, and listening at the college and career readiness level; demonstrate independence in gathering vocabulary knowledge when considering a word or phrase important to comprehension or expression.
666	**Before Reading: Standing Together**	RL.9-10.4	Determine the meaning of words and phrases as they are used in the text, including figurative and connotative meanings; analyze the cumulative impact of specific word choices on meaning and tone.
		RL.9-10.5	Analyze how an author's choices concerning how to structure a text, order events within it, and manipulate time create such effects as mystery, tension, or surprise.
667–672	**Read Standing Together**	RL.9-10.2	Determine a theme or central idea of a text and analyze in detail its development over the course of the text, including how it emerges and is shaped and refined by specific details; provide an objective summary of the text.
		RL.9-10.4	Determine the meaning of words and phrases as they are used in the text, including figurative and connotative meanings; analyze the cumulative impact of specific word choices on meaning and tone.
		RL.9-10.5	Analyze how an author's choices concerning how to structure a text, order events within it, and manipulate time create such effects as mystery, tension, or surprise.
		RL.9-10.10	By the end of grade 10, read and comprehend literature, including stories, dramas, and poems, at the high end of the grades 9–10 text complexity band independently and proficiently.
		W.9-10.9.a	Apply grades 9–10 Reading standards to literature.
		W.9-10.10	Write routinely over extended time frames (time for research, reflection, and revision) and shorter time frames (a single sitting or a day or two) for a range of tasks, purposes, and audiences.
		L.9-10.1.b	Use various types of phrases (noun, verb, adjectival, adverbial, participial, prepositional, absolute) and clauses (independent, dependent; noun, relative, adverbial) to convey specific meanings and add variety and interest to writing or presentations.
		L.9-10.4.b	Identify and correctly use patterns of word changes that indicate different meanings or parts of speech.

Common Core State Standards, continued

SE Pages	Lesson	Code	Standards Text
667–672	**Read Standing Together** continued	L.9-10.6	Acquire and use accurately general academic and domain-specific words and phrases, sufficient for reading, writing, speaking, and listening at the college and career readiness level; demonstrate independence in gathering vocabulary knowledge when considering a word or phrase important to comprehension or expression.
673	**Reflect and Assess Critical Thinking**	RL.9-10.1	Cite strong and thorough textual evidence to support analysis of what the text says explicitly as well as inferences drawn from the text.
		RL.9-10.2	Determine a theme or central idea of a text and analyze in detail its development over the course of the text, including how it emerges and is shaped and refined by specific details; provide an objective summary of the text.
		RL.9-10.10	By the end of grade 10, read and comprehend literature, including stories, dramas, and poems, at the high end of the grades 9–10 text complexity band independently and proficiently.
	Write About Literature	W.9-10.9.a	Apply grades 9–10 Reading standards to literature.
	Key Vocabulary Review	L.9-10.6	Acquire and use accurately general academic and domain-specific words and phrases, sufficient for reading, writing, speaking, and listening at the college and career readiness level; demonstrate independence in gathering vocabulary knowledge when considering a word or phrase important to comprehension or expression.
	Read with Ease: Expression	RL.9-10.10	By the end of grade 10, read and comprehend literature, including stories, dramas, and poems, at the high end of the grades 9–10 text complexity band independently and proficiently.
674	**Grammar: Write with the Perfect Tenses**	L.9-10.1.b	Use various types of phrases (noun, verb, adjectival, adverbial, participial, prepositional, absolute) and clauses (independent, dependent; noun, relative, adverbial) to convey specific meanings and add variety and interest to writing or presentations.
674	**Language Development: Use Appropriate Language**	SL.9-10.6	Adapt speech to a variety of contexts and tasks, demonstrating command of formal English when indicated or appropriate.
674	**Literary Analysis/ Research: Literary Criticism**	RL.9-10.10	By the end of grade 10, read and comprehend literature, including stories, dramas, and poems, at the high end of the grades 9–10 text complexity band independently and proficiently.
675	**Vocabulary Study: Denotation and Connotation**	L.9-10.5.b	Analyze nuances in the meaning of words with similar denotations.
675	**Writing: Write a Literary Critique**	W.9-10.1	Write arguments to support claims in an analysis of substantive topics or texts, using valid reasoning and relevant and sufficient evidence.
		W.9-10.5	Develop and strengthen writing as needed by planning, revising, editing, rewriting, or trying a new approach, focusing on addressing what is most significant for a specific purpose and audience.
675	**Listening/Speaking: Compare Media**	RL.9-10.7	Analyze the representation of a subject or a key scene in two different artistic mediums, including what is emphasized or absent in each treatment.
676-677	**Listening and Speaking Workshop: Narrative Presentation**	SL.9-10.3	Evaluate a speaker's point of view, reasoning, and use of evidence and rhetoric, identifying any fallacious reasoning or exaggerated or distorted evidence.
		SL.9-10.4	Present information, findings, and supporting evidence clearly, concisely, and logically such that listeners can follow the line of reasoning and the organization, development, substance, and style are appropriate to purpose, audience, and task.

Cluster 2, continued

SE Pages	Lesson	Code	Standards Text
676-677	**Listening and Speaking Workshop: Narrative Presentation** continued	SL.9-10.6	Adapt speech to a variety of contexts and tasks, demonstrating command of formal English when indicated or appropriate.
		L.9-10.3	Apply knowledge of language to understand how language functions in different contexts, to make effective choices for meaning or style, and to comprehend more fully when reading or listening.

Cluster 3

SE Pages	Lesson	Code	Standards Text
678	**Prepare to Read**	RI.9-10.4	Determine the meaning of words and phrases as they are used in a text, including figurative, connotative, and technical meanings; analyze the cumulative impact of specific word choices on meaning and tone.
		SL.9-10.1	Initiate and participate effectively in a range of collaborative discussions (one-on-one, in groups, and teacher-led) with diverse partners on grades 9-10 topics, texts, and issues, building on others' ideas and expressing their own clearly and persuasively.
		L.9-10.6	Acquire and use accurately general academic and domain-specific words and phrases, sufficient for reading, writing, speaking, and listening at the college and career readiness level; demonstrate independence in gathering vocabulary knowledge when considering a word or phrase important to comprehension or expression.
679	**Before Reading: Voices of America**	RL.9-10.4	Determine the meaning of words and phrases as they are used in the text, including figurative and connotative meanings; analyze the cumulative impact of specific word choices on meaning and tone.
680–689	**Read Voices of America**	RL.9-10.1	Cite strong and thorough textual evidence to support analysis of what the text says explicitly as well as inferences drawn from the text.
		RL.9-10.2	Determine a theme or central idea of a text and analyze in detail its development over the course of the text, including how it emerges and is shaped and refined by specific details; provide an objective summary of the text.
		RL.9-10.4	Determine the meaning of words and phrases as they are used in the text, including figurative and connotative meanings; analyze the cumulative impact of specific word choices on meaning and tone.
		RL.9-10.10	By the end of grade 10, read and comprehend literature, including stories, dramas, and poems, at the high end of the grades 9–10 text complexity band independently and proficiently.
		W.9-10.9.a	Apply grades 9–10 Reading standards to literature.
		W.9-10.10	Write routinely over extended time frames (time for research, reflection, and revision) and shorter time frames (a single sitting or a day or two) for a range of tasks, purposes, and audiences.
		SL.9-10.1	Initiate and participate effectively in a range of collaborative discussions (one-on-one, in groups, and teacher-led) with diverse partners on grades 9-10 topics, texts, and issues, building on others' ideas and expressing their own clearly and persuasively.
		L.9-10.1.b	Use various types of phrases (noun, verb, adjectival, adverbial, participial, prepositional, absolute) and clauses (independent, dependent; noun, relative, adverbial) to convey specific meanings and add variety and interest to writing or presentations.

Common Core State Standards, continued

SE Pages	Lesson	Code	Standards Text
680–689	**Read Voices of America** continued	L.9-10.6	Acquire and use accurately general academic and domain-specific words and phrases, sufficient for reading, writing, speaking, and listening at the college and career readiness level; demonstrate independence in gathering vocabulary knowledge when considering a word or phrase important to comprehension or expression.
690	**Before Reading: Human Family**	RL.9-10.4	Determine the meaning of words and phrases as they are used in the text, including figurative and connotative meanings; analyze the cumulative impact of specific word choices on meaning and tone.
		RL.9-10.5	Analyze how an author's choices concerning how to structure a text, order events within it, and manipulate time create such effects as mystery, tension, or surprise.
691–694	**Read Human Family**	RL.9-10.1	Cite strong and thorough textual evidence to support analysis of what the text says explicitly as well as inferences drawn from the text.
		RL.9-10.2	Determine a theme or central idea of a text and analyze in detail its development over the course of the text, including how it emerges and is shaped and refined by specific details; provide an objective summary of the text.
		RL.9-10.4	Determine the meaning of words and phrases as they are used in the text, including figurative and connotative meanings; analyze the cumulative impact of specific word choices on meaning and tone.
		RL.9-10.5	Analyze how an author's choices concerning how to structure a text, order events within it, and manipulate time create such effects as mystery, tension, or surprise.
		RL.9-10.10	By the end of grade 10, read and comprehend literature, including stories, dramas, and poems, at the high end of the grades 9–10 text complexity band independently and proficiently.
		W.9-10.9.a	Apply grades 9–10 Reading standards to literature.
		W.9-10.10	Write routinely over extended time frames (time for research, reflection, and revision) and shorter time frames (a single sitting or a day or two) for a range of tasks, purposes, and audiences.
		L.9-10.1.b	Use various types of phrases (noun, verb, adjectival, adverbial, participial, prepositional, absolute) and clauses (independent, dependent; noun, relative, adverbial) to convey specific meanings and add variety and interest to writing or presentations.
		L.9-10.6	Acquire and use accurately general academic and domain-specific words and phrases, sufficient for reading, writing, speaking, and listening at the college and career readiness level; demonstrate independence in gathering vocabulary knowledge when considering a word or phrase important to comprehension or expression.
695	**Reflect and Assess Critical Thinking**	RL.9-10.1	Cite strong and thorough textual evidence to support analysis of what the text says explicitly as well as inferences drawn from the text.
		RL.9-10.2	Determine a theme or central idea of a text and analyze in detail its development over the course of the text, including how it emerges and is shaped and refined by specific details; provide an objective summary of the text.
		RL.9-10.6	Analyze a particular point of view or cultural experience reflected in a work of literature from outside the United States, drawing on a wide reading of world literature.
		RL.9-10.10	By the end of grade 10, read and comprehend literature, including stories, dramas, and poems, at the high end of the grades 9–10 text complexity band independently and proficiently.

Cluster 3, continued

SE Pages	Lesson	Code	Standards Text
	Reflect and Assess continued **Write About Literature**	W.9-10.9.a	Apply grades 9–10 Reading standards to literature.
	Key Vocabulary Review	L.9-10.6	Acquire and use accurately general academic and domain-specific words and phrases, sufficient for reading, writing, speaking, and listening at the college and career readiness level; demonstrate independence in gathering vocabulary knowledge when considering a word or phrase important to comprehension or expression.
	Read with Ease: Intonation	RL.9-10.10	By the end of grade 10, read and comprehend literature, including stories, dramas, and poems, at the high end of the grades 9–10 text complexity band independently and proficiently.
696	**Grammar: Enrich Your Sentences**	L.9-10.1.b	Use various types of phrases (noun, verb, adjectival, adverbial, participial, prepositional, absolute) and clauses (independent, dependent; noun, relative, adverbial) to convey specific meanings and add variety and interest to writing or presentations.
696	**Literary Analysis: Allusions**	RL.9-10.9	Analyze how an author draws on and transforms source material in a specific work.
696	**Language Development: Use Appropriate Language**	SL.9-10.6	Adapt speech to a variety of contexts and tasks, demonstrating command of formal English when indicated or appropriate.
697	**Vocabulary Study: Figurative Language**	L.9-10.5	Demonstrate understanding of figurative language, word relationships, and nuances in word meanings.
697	**Writing Trait: Voice and Style**	W.9-10.5	Develop and strengthen writing as needed by planning, revising, editing, rewriting, or trying a new approach, focusing on addressing what is most significant for a specific purpose and audience.
697	**Research/Writing: Historical Figure Biography**	W.9-10.2	Write informative/explanatory texts to examine and convey complex ideas, concepts, and information clearly and accurately through the effective selection, organization, and analysis of content.
		W.9-10.7	Conduct short as well as more sustained research projects to answer a question (including a self-generated question) or solve a problem; narrow or broaden the inquiry when appropriate; synthesize multiple sources on the subject, demonstrating understanding of the subject under investigation.
		W.9-10.8	Gather relevant information from multiple authoritative print and digital sources, using advanced searches effectively; assess the usefulness of each source in answering the research question; integrate information into the text selectively to maintain the flow of ideas, avoiding plagiarism and following a standard format for citation.

Close Reading

698–699	**Read Mending Wall**	RL.9-10.10	By the end of grade 10, read and comprehend literature, including stories, dramas, and poems, at the high end of the grades 9–10 text complexity band independently and proficiently.

Unit Wrap-Up

700	**Unit Wrap-Up Present Your Project**	W.9-10.8	Gather relevant information from multiple authoritative print and digital sources, using advanced searches effectively; assess the usefulness of each source in answering the research question; integrate information into the text selectively to maintain the flow of ideas, avoiding plagiarism and following a standard format for citation.

Common Core State Standards, continued

Unit Wrap-Up, continued

SE Pages	Lesson	Code	Standards Text
700	**Unit Wrap-Up** continued **Reflect on Your Reading**	SL.9-10.1.a	Come to discussions prepared, having read and researched material under study; explicitly draw on that preparation by referring to evidence from texts and other research on the topic or issue to stimulate a thoughtful, well-reasoned exchange of ideas.
	Respond to the Essential Question	SL.9-10.1.a	Come to discussions prepared, having read and researched material under study; explicitly draw on that preparation by referring to evidence from texts and other research on the topic or issue to stimulate a thoughtful, well-reasoned exchange of ideas.

Language and Learning Handbook

SE Pages	Lesson	Code	Standards Text
703–712	**Strategies for Learning and Developing Language**	SL.9-10.1.c	Propel conversations by posing and responding to questions that relate the current discussion to broader themes or larger ideas; actively incorporate others into the discussion; and clarify, verify, or challenge ideas and conclusions.
		SL.9-10.3	Evaluate a speaker's point of view, reasoning, and use of evidence and rhetoric, identifying any fallacious reasoning or exaggerated or distorted evidence.
		SL.9-10.4	Present information, findings, and supporting evidence clearly, concisely, and logically such that listeners can follow the line of reasoning and the organization, development, substance, and style are appropriate to purpose, audience, and task.
		SL.9-10.6	Adapt speech to a variety of contexts and tasks, demonstrating command of formal English when indicated or appropriate.
		L.9-10.1	Demonstrate command of the conventions of standard English grammar and usage when writing or speaking.
		L.9-10.4	Determine or clarify the meaning of unknown and multiple-meaning words and phrases based on grades 9–10 reading and content, choosing flexibly from a range of strategies.
		L.9-10.4.c	Consult general and specialized reference materials, both print and digital, to find the pronunciation of a word or determine or clarify its precise meaning, its part of speech, or its etymology.
		L.9-10.5.a	Interpret figures of speech in context and analyze their role in the text.
		L.9-10.6	Acquire and use accurately general academic and domain-specific words and phrases, sufficient for reading, writing, speaking, and listening at the college and career readiness level; demonstrate independence in gathering vocabulary knowledge when considering a word or phrase important to comprehension or expression.
713–716	**Listening and Speaking**	SL.9-10.1	Initiate and participate effectively in a range of collaborative discussions (one-on-one, in groups, and teacher-led) with diverse partners on grades 9–10 topics, texts, and issues, building on others' ideas and expressing their own clearly and persuasively.
		SL.9-10.1.c	Propel conversations by posing and responding to questions that relate the current discussion to broader themes or larger ideas; actively incorporate others into the discussion; and clarify, verify, or challenge ideas and conclusions.
		SL.9-10.1.d	Respond thoughtfully to diverse perspectives, summarize points of agreement and disagreement, and, when warranted, qualify or justify their own views and understanding and make new connections in light of the evidence and reasoning presented.
		L.9-10.1.a	Use parallel structure.

Language and Learning Handbook, continued

SE Pages	Lesson	Code	Standards Text
713–716	**Listening and Speaking** continued	L.9-10.5	Demonstrate understanding of figurative language, word relationships, and nuances in word meanings.
717–720	**Viewing and Representing**	RI.9-10.7	Analyze various accounts of a subject told in different mediums (e.g., a person's life story in both print and multimedia), determining which details are emphasized in each account.
		W.9-10.8	Gather relevant information from multiple authoritative print and digital sources, using advanced searches effectively; assess the usefulness of each source in answering the research question; integrate information into the text selectively to maintain the flow of ideas, avoiding plagiarism and following a standard format for citation.
		SL.9-10.2	Integrate multiple sources of information presented in diverse media or formats (e.g., visually, quantitatively, orally) evaluating the credibility and accuracy of each source.
		SL.9-10.5	Make strategic use of digital media in presentations to enhance understanding of findings, reasoning, and evidence and to add interest.
721–724	**Technology and Media**	W.9-10.6	Use technology, including the Internet, to produce, publish, and update individual or shared writing products, taking advantage of technology's capacity to link to other information and to display information flexibly and dynamically.
		SL.9-10.5	Make strategic use of digital media in presentations to enhance understanding of findings, reasoning, and evidence and to add interest.
725–730	**Research**	W.9-10.7	Conduct short as well as more sustained research projects to answer a question (including a self-generated question) or solve a problem; narrow or broaden the inquiry when appropriate; synthesize multiple sources on the subject, demonstrating understanding of the subject under investigation.
		W.9-10.8	Gather relevant information from multiple authoritative print and digital sources, using advanced searches effectively; assess the usefulness of each source in answering the research question; integrate information into the text selectively to maintain the flow of ideas, avoiding plagiarism and following a standard format for citation.
		L.9-10.3.a	Write and edit work so that it conforms to the guidelines in a style manual appropriate for the discipline and writing type.

Reading Handbook

SE Pages	Lesson	Code	Standards Text
734–746	**Reading Strategies**	RL.9-10.1	Cite strong and thorough textual evidence to support analysis of what the text says explicitly as well as inferences drawn from the text.
		RI.9-10.1	Cite strong and thorough textual evidence to support analysis of what the text says explicitly as well as inferences drawn from the text.
747–771	**Reading Fluency**	RL.9-10.10	By the end of grade 10, read and comprehend literature, including stories, dramas, and poems, at the high end of the grades 9–10 text complexity band independently and proficiently.
		RI.9-10.10	By the end of grade 10, read and comprehend literary nonfiction at the high end of the grades 9–10 text complexity band independently and proficiently.

Common Core State Standards, continued

Reading Handbook, continue

SE Pages	Lesson	Code	Standards Text
772–775	**Study Skills and Strategies**	SL.9-10.1.a	Come to discussions prepared, having read and researched material under study; explicitly draw on that preparation by referring to evidence from texts and other research on the topic or issue to stimulate a thoughtful, well-reasoned exchange of ideas.
		SL.9-10.2	Integrate multiple sources of information presented in diverse media or formats evaluating the credibility and accuracy of each source.
776–783	**Vocabulary**	L.9-10.4	Determine or clarify the meaning of unknown and multiple-meaning words and phrases based on grades 9–10 reading and content, choosing flexibly from a range of strategies.
		L.9-10.4.a	Use context as a clue to the meaning of a word or phrase.
		L.9-10.4.b	Identify and correctly use patterns of word changes that indicate different meanings or parts of speech.
		L.9-10.4.c	Consult general and specialized reference materials, both print and digital, to find the pronunciation of a word or determine or clarify its precise meaning, its part of speech, or its etymology.
		L.9-10.4.d	Verify the preliminary determination of the meaning of a word or phrase.
		L.9-10.5	Demonstrate understanding of figurative language, word relationships, and nuances in word meanings.
		L.9-10.6	Acquire and use accurately general academic and domain-specific words and phrases, sufficient for reading, writing, speaking, and listening at the college and career readiness level; demonstrate independence in gathering vocabulary knowledge when considering a word or phrase important to comprehension or expression.

Writing Handbook

SE Pages	Lesson	Code	Standards Text
785–791	**The Writing Process**	W.9-10.4	Produce clear and coherent writing in which the development, organization, and style are appropriate to task, purpose, and audience.
		W.9-10.6	Use technology, including the Internet, to produce, publish, and update individual or shared writing products, taking advantage of technology's capacity to link to other information and to display information flexibly and dynamically.
792–801	**Writing Traits**	RI.9-10.10	By the end of grade 10, read and comprehend literary nonfiction at the high end of the grades 9–10 text complexity band independently and proficiently.
		W.9-10.1.c	Use words, phrases, and clauses to link the major sections of the text, create cohesion, and clarify the relationships between claim(s) and reasons, between reasons and evidence, and between claim(s) and counterclaims.
		W.9-10.2.c	Use appropriate and varied transitions to link the major sections of the text, create cohesion, and clarify the relationships among complex ideas and concepts.
		W.9-10.2.e	Establish and maintain a formal style and objective tone while attending to the norms and conventions of the discipline in which they are writing.
		W.9-10.2.f	Provide a concluding statement or section that follows from and supports the information or explanation presented.
		W.9-10.3.d	Use precise words and phrases, telling details, and sensory language to convey a vivid picture of the experiences, events, setting, and/or characters.

SE Pages	Lesson	Code	Standards Text
792–801	**Writing Traits** continued	W.9-10.4	Produce clear and coherent writing in which the development, organization, and style are appropriate to task, purpose, and audience.
		L.9-10.1	Demonstrate command of the conventions of standard English grammar and usage when writing or speaking.
802–823	**Writing Purposes, Modes, and Forms**	W.9-10.1	Write arguments to support claims in an analysis of substantive topics or texts, using valid reasoning and relevant and sufficient evidence.
		W.9-10.4	Produce clear and coherent writing in which the development, organization, and style are appropriate to task, purpose, and audience.
		W.9-10.5	Develop and strengthen writing as needed by planning, revising, editing, rewriting, or trying a new approach, focusing on addressing what is most significant for a specific purpose and audience.
		W.9-10.6	Use technology, including the Internet, to produce, publish, and update individual or shared writing products, taking advantage of technology's capacity to link to other information and to display information flexibly and dynamically.
		SL.9-10.2	Integrate multiple sources of information presented in diverse media or formats evaluating the credibility and accuracy of each source.
		L.9-10.3.a	Write and edit work so that it conforms to the guidelines in a style manual appropriate for the discipline and writing type.
824–858	**Grammar, Usage, Mechanics, and Spelling**	L.9-10.1	Demonstrate command of the conventions of standard English grammar and usage when writing or speaking.
		L.9-10.1.a	Use parallel structure.
		L.9-10.1.b	Use various types of phrases (noun, verb, adjectival, adverbial, participial, prepositional, absolute) and clauses (independent, dependent; noun, relative, adverbial) to convey specific meanings and add variety and interest to writing or presentations.
		L.9-10.2	Demonstrate command of the conventions of standard English capitalization, punctuation, and spelling when writing.
		L.9-10.2.a	Use a semicolon (and perhaps a conjunctive adverb) to link two or more closely related independent clauses.
		L.9-10.2.b	Use a colon to introduce a list or quotation.
		L.9-10.2.c	Spell correctly.
		L.9-10.3	Apply knowledge of language to understand how language functions in different contexts, to make effective choices for meaning or style, and to comprehend more fully when reading or listening.
859–867	**Troubleshooting Guide**	L.9-10.1	Demonstrate command of the conventions of standard English grammar and usage when writing or speaking.
		L.9-10.3	Apply knowledge of language to understand how language functions in different contexts, to make effective choices for meaning or style, and to comprehend more fully when reading or listening.

INDEX OF SKILLS

in poetry 642

question mark 748, 846, 854

quotation mark 60, 106, 108, 376, 502, 504, 857

semicolon 598, 600, 749, 845, 847, 857

underlining 394, 856

Purpose for writing 98, 188, 294, 392, 590, 786

see also Author's purpose

Q

Question 786

Question mark 748, 846, 854

Quickwrite 64, 160, 208, 462

Quotation marks 60, 106, 108, 376, 502, 504, 852, 857

Quotations 106, 108, 252, 254, 304, 376, 400, 502, 504, 515, 716, 729, 786, 852, 857

punctuation and capitalization of 106, 108, 502, 504, 852

R

Reading fluency 751–771

accuracy and rate 13, 35, 43, 59, 67, 121, 133, 141, 155, 163, 211, 231, 238, 257, 265, 285, 317, 335, 357, 365, 381, 415, 431, 439, 457, 465, 483, 517, 537, 545, 557, 565, 579, 615, 641, 673, 681, 695, 736, 747

expression 35, 177, 257, 381, 457, 537, 673, 750–751, 756, 759, 761, 765, 767, 769

intonation 87, 155, 285, 357, 483, 557, 695, 748, 753, 755, 757, 762, 764, 766, 770

phrasing 59, 133, 231, 335, 431, 579, 641, 749, 752, 754, 758, 760, 763, 768, 771

Reading handbook 764–783

Reading journal 174

Reading selections *see Index of Authors and Titles*

Reading strategies

use 4–5, 94, 734

use graphic organizers 737

see also Ask questions; Connections, make (reading strategy); Determine importance; Draw conclusions; Emotional responses, identify; Generalizations, form; Inferences, make; Monitor reading; Plan and monitor; Predictions; Preview; Sensory images, identify; Set a purpose; Summarize; Synthesize; Visualize

Reasons 590, 591

support of position/argument 186, 187, 512, 552, 558, 567, 588, 809, 875

Rebuttal 588

Reference tools 259, 705, 781, 789

see also Dictionary; Style guide (manual); Thesaurus

Reflective essay 803–804

Relate words 776

Report 875

oral report 37, 156, 360–361, 581

research 89, 390–403, 558, 728–730, 812

Representations 719

script compared to performance 613, 617, 618, 623, 626, 628, 632, 633, 675

Research 786

assistive technology 382

Good Samaritan laws 37

historical figure biography 697

historical hero 259

jobs/careers 136, 234

literacy in the United States 336

literary criticism 674

part of the brain 135

peers under pressure 89

process 391–403, 725–730

questions 725, 730

research report 391–403

sources 786

teens and trends 156

using media 722

Research report 89, 180–183, 728–730, 812

Research tip 391

Resolution 11, 384–385, 410, 492, 496, 875

see also Plot diagram

Resources 726, 786

evaluation of 391

for help with studying 775

primary/secondary 391

Résumé 817

Reviewing strategies 774

Revise *see Writing process*

Revising tip 298, 594

Revision checklist 104, 194, 300, 398, 500, 596

Rhetorical devices 296, 875

alliteration 716, 868

analogy 190, 424, 425, 429, 430, 485, 716, 809, 868

irony 106, 432, 502, 716, 872

mood 716

parallelism 599, 716, 851

pun 716, 875

quotations 252, 254, 304, 376, 716, 729, 786, 857

repetition 716

tone 716

see also Mood; Repetition; Tone

Rhetorical fallacy 55, 57, 530

Rhyme 150, 174, 610, 642, 666, 690, 692, 694, 875, 876

Rhymed couplet 666

Rhythm 174, 611, 642, 690, 692, 694, 876

Rising action 410, 492, 496, 869, 876

see also Plot diagram

Root words 61, 235

Anglo-Saxon 541

Greek, Latin 539, 541, 559, 779

S

Sarcasm 106

Science fiction 876

Script 822, 876

see also Drama

Secondary sources 391, 727

Semicolon 598, 600, 749, 845, 847, 857

Sensory images, identify 634, 679, 682, 686, 689, 690, 692, 693, 694, 746

Sensory words 15, 27

Sentences

active and passive voice 303, 304

capitalization of first word 852

combining 598, 599, 600

complete 36, 107, 800, 851

complex 580, 599, 845, 848

compound 558, 598, 847, 848

conditional 846

fragments 88, 107, 108, 851, 863

negative 71, 846

parallel structure 599, 716, 851

participles in 696

punctuation 857

run-on 863

simple 847

structure of 847–848

subject-verb agreement 851

types of 846

use a variety 538

Sequence 312, 313, 315, 328, 574, 737

Series 855, 857

Set a purpose 14, 28, 33, 44, 68, 212, 239, 267, 416, 440, 447, 466, 616, 629, 650, 661, 734, 736

Setting 8, 43, 65, 68, 69, 70, 72, 76, 77, 79, 88, 93, 413, 608

Short fiction 350, 356

Short story *see Genre*

see also Characters/characterization; Setting; Writing forms

Sight words 574

Signal words 857

INDEX OF AUTHORS AND TITLES

INDEX OF ART AND ARTISTS

Acknowledgments, continued from page ii

TEXT

Teresa Palomo Acosta: "My Mother Pieced Quilts" by Teresa Palomo Acosta from *Festival de Flor y Canto*. Copyright © by Teresa Paloma Acosta. Used by permission of the author.

Alfred Publishing Co., Inc.: " I Am Somebody" words and music by Joseph Saddler, Nathaniel Glover, and Larry Dukes. Copyright © 1987 by WB Music Corp., E/A Music, Inc. and Grandmaster Flash Publishing, Inc. All rights administered by WB Music Corp. All rights reserved. Used by permission of Alfred Publishing Co., Inc.

Annick Press: "Ad Power" from *Made You Look* by Shari Graydon. Copyright © 2003 by Shari Graydon. Published by Annick Press. Reprinted with permission.

Arte Publico Press: "Legal Alien" from *Chants* by Pat Mora. Copyright © 1985 by Pat Mora. Recorded with permission from Arte Publico Press-University of Houston.

Susan Bergholz Literary Services: "A Smart Cookie" from *The House on Mango Street* by Sandra Cisneros. Copyright © 1984 by Sandra Cisneros. Published by Vintage Books, a division of Random House, Inc., New York, and in hardcover by Alfred A. Knopf in 1994. Reprinted by permission of Susan Bergholz Literary Services, New York. All rights reserved.

"My Father Is a Simple Man" by Luis Omar Salinas from *The Sadness of Days*. Copyright © 1987. Reprinted by permission of Susan Bergholz Literary Services, New York. All rights reserved.

Cartoonbank: "Guilt-Powered Car" by Mick Stevens. Copyright © 2001 Mick Stevens; "Shouldn't Willis be…" by Gahan Wilson. Copyright © 1999 Gahan Wilson. All cartoons copyright *The New Yorker* Collection from cartoonbank.com. All rights reserved. Reprinted with permission.

Center for Media Literacy: "A Long Way to Go: Minorities and the Media" by Carlos Cortes, from *Media 7 Values*, Issue 38, Winter, 1987. Copyright © 1987 by the Center for Media Literacy, www.media-lit.org. Used by permission.

Curtis Brown: "The Baby-Sitter" by Jane Yolen from *Things That Go Bump in the Night*. Copyright © 1989 by Jane Yolen, published by HarperCollins. Reprinted by permission of Curtis Brown, Ltd.

Excerpt from *The Creativity Crisis* by Po Bronson and Ashley Merryman. Copyright © 2010 by Po Bronson and Ashley Merryman. Used by permission of Curtis Brown, Ltd.

Enslow Publishers: Adapted from *Advertising Information of Manipulation?* by Nancy Day. Copyright © 1999 by Nancy Day. Published by Enslow Publishers, Inc., Berkeley Heights, NJ. All rights reserved. Reprinted with permission.

Eric Feil: "The World Is in Their Hands" by Eric Feil from *Inspire Your World*. Used by permission of the author.

Farrar, Straus and Giroux: "Thank You, M'am" by Langston Hughes from *Short Stories*. Copyright © 1996 by Ramona Bass and Arnold Rampersad. Reprinted by permission of Hill and Wang, a division of Farrar, Starus and Giroux, Inc.

HarperCollins: "Curtis G. Aikens Sr." by Dan Rather from *The American Dream*. Copyright © 2001 by Dan Rather. Reprinted by permission of HarperCollins Publishers.

Joel Hoffmam: "Puddle" by Arthur Porges from *Alfred Hitchcock's Mystery Magazine*. Copyright © 1972 by Arthur Porges. Reprinted by permission of Joel Hoffman.

Henry Holt: "Nothing Gold Can Stay" by Robert Frost from the *Poetry of Robert Frost*, edited by Edward Connery Lathem. Copyright © 1987 by Henry Holt and Company By permission.

Houghton Mifflin Harcourt: "Without Commercials" by Alice Walker from *Horses Make a Landscape Look More Beautiful: Poems by Alice Walker*. Copyright © 1984 by Alice Walker, reprinted by permission of Houghton Mifflin Harcourt Publishing Corporation. All rights reserved.

Learning Seed: "How to Detect Bias in the News" by Jeffrey Schank/Learning Seed. Reprinted by permission of Learning Seed LLC.

Hal Leonard: "If There Be Pain" by Tupac Shakur. Copyright © 2000 Microhits Music Corp. Reprinted by permission of Hal Leonard.

"Hero," words and music by Walter Afanasieff and Mariah Carey. Copyright © 1993 WB Music Corp., Wallyworld Music, Songs of Universal, Inc., and Rye Songs. All rights on behalf of itself and Wallyworld Music administered by WB Music Corp. All rights for Rye Songs administered by Songs of Universal, Inc. All rights reserved. Used by permission.

Life: "In the Heart of a Hero" by Johnny Dwyer from *Life*, November 2005. Copyright © 2005 Life Inc. Reprinted with permission. All rights reserved.

Lowe Worldwide: "Got Milk?" by permission of the National Fluid Milk Processor Promotion Board and Lowe Worldwide, Inc.

Lowenstein-Yost Associates: "Beware: Do Not Read This Poem" from *Ishmael Reed: New and Collected Poems,1964–2006*. Copyright © 1988 by Ishmael Reed. Permission granted by Lowenstein-Yost Associates, Inc.

Katy Murphy: "Never a Dull Friday Night" by Katy Murphy from the *Oakland Tribune*, March 27, 2006. Reprinted by permission.

McClatchy-Tribune Information Services: "Miami Pilot Dubbed 'Emerging Explorer' by National Geographic" from the *Miami Herald*, June 5, 2012, Copyright © 2012 the McClatchy Company. Used by permission of The McClatchy Company.

"Author Brings Back Memories of Not So Long Ago" by Yvette Cabrera from the *Orange County Register*, April 15, 2002. Copyright © 2002 by the McClatchy-Tribune Information Services. All rights reserved. Reprinted with permission.

National Geographic Society: "Was There a Real King Arthur?" by Robert Steward from *Mysteries of History*. Copyright © 2003 by the National Geographic Society. Reprinted with permission of the National Geographic Society.

Pearson Education, Inc.: "The Tell-Tale Heart" from *Great American Short Stories* retold by Emily Hutchinson. Copyright © 1994 by Pearson Education, Inc., publishing as AGS Globe. Used by permission.

Penguin Group (USA) Inc.: "Euphoria" by Lauren Brown. Copyright © 2000 by 17th Street Productions. by permission of Viking Penguin, A Division of Penguin Young Readers Group, A Member of Penguin Group (USA) Inc., 345 Hudson Street, New York, NY 10014. All rights reserved.

What Is Slam Poetry?" by Cecily Von Ziegesar, copyright © 2000, from *Slam*, edited by Cecily Von Ziegesar. Used by permission of Viking Penguin, a division of Penguin Group (USA) Inc.

Excerpt from *The Grapes of Wrath* by John Steinbeck. Copyright © 1939, renewed 1967 by John Steinbeck. Used by permission of Viking Penguin, a division of Penguin Group (USA) Inc.

"The Sword in the Stone," from *King Arthur and the Legends of Camelot* by Molly Perham. Copyright © 1993 by Molly Perham. Used by permission of Viking Penguin, A Division of Penguin Young Readers Group, A Member of Penguin Group (USA) Inc., 345 Hudson Street, New York, NY 10014. All rights reserved.

Philadelphia Inquirer: "The Fast and the Fuel Efficient" by Akweli Parker from the Philadelphia Inquirer, April 16, 2006. Copyright © 2006 by the *Philadelphia Inquirer*. Reprinted with permission of the Philadelphia Inquirer, all rights reserved.

Public Broadcasting Service: "What Is News?" from Greater Washington Educational Telecommunications Association, source: pbs.org.

Random House: "Human Family" from *I Shall Not Be Moved* by Maya Angelou Copyright © 1990 by Maya Angelou. Used by permission of Random House, Inc.

"The Good Samaritan" from *Finding Our Way* by René Saldaña, Jr. Copyright © 2003 by René Saldaña Jr. Used by permission of Random House Children's Books, a division of Random House, Inc.

"I, Too" by Langston Hughes from *The Collected Poems of Langston Hughes*. Copyright © 1994 by the Estate of Langston Hughes. Used by permission of Random House, Inc.

"A Message for Black Teenagers" from *Magic Johnson: My Life* by Earvin "Magic" Johnson. Copyright © 1992 by June Bug Enterprises. Used by permission of Random House, Inc.

Excerpt from *A Raisin in the Sun* by Lorraine Hansberry. Copyright © 1958 by Robert Nemiroff, as an unpublished work. Copyright © 1959, 1966, 1984 by Robert Nemiroff. Copyright renewed 1986, 1987 by Robert Nemiroff. Caution: Professionals and amateurs are hereby warned that A Raisin in the Sun, being fully protected under the Copyright Laws of the United States of America, the British Empire, including the Dominion of Canada, and all other countries of the Universal Copyright and Berne Conventions, is subject to royalty. All rights, including professional, amateur, motion picture, recitation, lecturing, public reading, radio and television broadcasting, and the rights of translation into foreign languages, are strictly reserved. Particular emphasis is laid on the question of readings, permission for which must be secured in writing. All inquiries should be addressed to the William Morris Agency, 1350 Avenue of the Americas, New York, NY 10019, authorized agents for the Estate of Lorraine Hansberry and for Robert Nemiroff, Executor. Used by permission of Random House, Inc.

"What's Wrong with Advertising" from *Ogilvy on Advertising* by David Ogilvy. Copyright © 1985 by David Ogilvy. Reprinted by permission of Carlton Publishing Group. Used by permission of Random House, Inc.

"The Woman in the Snow" from *The Dark Thirty* by Patricia C. McKissack. Copyright © 1992 by Patricia C. McKissack. Used by permission of Alfred A. Knopf, an imprint of Random House Children's Books, a division of Random House, Inc. Used by permission of Random House, Inc.

Scholastic: "A Job for Valentín" from *An Island Like You* by Judith Ortiz Cofer. Copyright © 1995 by Judith Ortiz Cofer. Reprinted by permission of Scholastic Inc.

"A Raisin in the Sun" by Lorraine Hansberry, adapted by Rachel Waugh, *Scholastic Scope*, September 20, 2004. Reprinted by permission of Scholastic Inc.

Interview excerpted from "Interview with Stephen King" by Byron Cahill, from *Writing*. Copyright © 2005 by Weekly Reader. Used by permission of Scholastic Inc.

"Slam: Performance Poetry Lives On" from *Writing*, April/May 2005. Copyright © 2005 by Weekly Reader. Special permission granted by Scholastic Inc. All rights reserved.

Simon & Schuster: "The Fashion Show" adapted from *The Other Side of the Sky* by Farah Ahmedi with Tamim Ansary. Text © 2005 Nestegg Productions LLC. Used with the permission of Simon Spotlight Entertainment, an imprint of Simon & Schuster Children's Publishing Division.

Efrem Smith: "Hip-Hop as Culture" by Reverend Efrem Smith. Reprinted by permission of the author.

Nancy Stauffer Associates: "Superman and Me" by Sherman Alexie from *The Most Wonderful Books: Writers on Discovering the Pleasures of Reading*, edited by Michael Dorris and Emilie Buchwald. Copyright © 1997 by Sherman Alexie. All rights reserved. Reprinted by permission.

Richard Thompson: "Teens Open Doors" by Richard Thompson from the *Boston Globe*, June 29, 2006. Copyright © 2006 by Richard Thompson. Reprinted by permission of the author.

Time: "The Hidden Secrets of the Creative Mind" by Francine Russo from *Time*, January 16, 2006. Copyright © 2006 by Time Inc. Reprinted by permission.

"Rosa Parks" by Rita Dove from "Time's 100 Most Important People of the Century" from *Time*, June 14, 1999. Copyright © 1999 Time Inc. Reprinted by permission.

Tribune Media Services: "Is Google Making Us Stupid?" by Nicholas Carr from *The Atlantic*, July 1, 2008. Copyright © 2008 by the Atlantic Media Co. Used by permission of Tribune Media Services. Reprinted by permission.

WGBH/Boston: "Juvenile Justice" from Frontline/WGBH Educational Foundation. Copyright © 2005 WGBH/Boston. Used by permission.

What Kids Can Do: "Creativity at Work" by Abe Louise Young, from the website "What Kids Can Do." Reprinted by permission of What Kids Can Do, Inc.

Nellie Wong: "Where Is My Country?" by Nellie Wong from *Chinese American Poetry: An Anthology*, edited by L. Ling-Chi Wang and Henry Yiheng Zhao. Copyright © 1987 by Nellie Wong. Reprinted by permission of the author.

Youth Philanthropy Worldwide: "Schools for Indigenous Children" from *Youth Philanthropy Worldwide*, April 2006. Reprinted by permission of Youth Philanthropy Worldwide.

PHOTO CREDITS

iv Rene Saldana. **vii** Magical Assortment, 2005 Peter Anton. Mixed media sculpture, private collection. **ix** Ethan Miller/Getty Images. **xi** The Life Line, 1864, Winslow Homer. Oil on canvas, Philadelphia Museum of Art/Superstock. **xiii** Trigal, 2004, Homero Aguilar. Oil on linen, private collection. **xv** George Tooker (1920-2011) Voice II, 1972 Tempera on panel National Academy Museum, New York, USA/The Bridgeman Art Library Courtesy of The Estate of George Tooker and DC Moore Gallery, New York. **xvii** John Eder/Getty Images. **xix** Dale Kennington/SuperStock. **xxiii** Lester Lefkowitz/CORBIS. **1** Magical Assortment, 2005 Peter Anton. Mixed media sculpture, private collection. **0-1** Amy Helene Johansson. **3** Sandpiper; Graphic Universe; Speak. **6** g215/Shutterstock. **7** Best View Stock/Shutterstock; David Katzenstein/CORBIS. **9** djem/Shutterstock. **10** Tetra Images/CORBIS; Ariel Skelley/CORBIS. **11** George Doyle/Getty Images. **12** Rene Saldana. **13** George Doyle/Getty Images. **14-15** Donald Gruener/Getty Images. **16** 2013/Polka Dot Images/Jupiterimages Corporation. **19** Emil Jacobsen/iStockphoto. **20** Stockbyte/Getty Images. **23** 2013 Fuse/CORBIS/Jupiterimages Corporation. **24** Donald Gruener/Getty Images. **26** William Whitehurst/CORBIS. **27** Damian Dovarganes/AP Images. **29** Tony Freeman/PhotoEdit, Inc. **31** Youth Service America 2007. **32** Michelle D. Bridwell/PhotoEdit, Inc. **34** XNR Productions; Shawn Henry; Youth Philanthropy Worldwide. **38** Jose Luis Pelaez, Inc./CORBIS; Bryan F. Peterson/CORBIS; RF/CORBIS. **40** Flying Colours Ltd; Rob Lewine/Getty Images. **41** 2013 The Jacob and Gwendolyn Lawrence Foundation, Seattle/Artists Rights Society (ARS), New York/Art Resource. **42** CORBIS. **43** 2013 The Jacob and Gwendolyn Lawrence Foundation, Seattle/Artists Rights Society (ARS), New York/Art Resource. **45** The City from Greenwich Village -John Sloan,1922 oil on canvas, National Gallery of Art, Washington D.C. **47** The Window, 1970, Bernard Safran. Oil on masonite, private collection; The Window, 1970, Bernard Safran. Oil on masonite, private collection. **49** Smithsonian American Art Museum, Washington, DC/Art Resource, NY; Liz Garza Williams. **52** From FRONTLINE Juvenile Justice website (http://www.pbs.org/wgbh/pages/frontline/shows/juvenile/bench/adulttime.html) 1995–2011 WGBH Educational Foundation; Ken Hurst/Shutterstock.com. **53** 2013 Comstock/JupiterImages Corporation. **54** Courtesy of FRONTLINE/WGBH Educational Foundation. Copyright 2005. WGBH/Boston/WGBH Media Library. **55** Courtesy of FRONTLINE/WGBH Educational Foundation. Copyright 2005. WGBH/Boston/WGBH Media Library. **56** Courtesy of FRONTLINE/WGBH Educational Foundation. Copyright 2005. WGBH/Boston/WGBH Media Library. **57** Courtesy of FRONTLINE/WGBH Educational Foundation. Copyright 2005. WGBH/Boston/WGBH Media Library. **58** From FRONTLINE Juvenile Justice website (http://www.pbs.org/wgbh/pages/frontline/shows/juvenile/bench/adulttime.html) 1995–2011 WGBH Educational Foundation. **60** Charles Barsotti/Cartoonbank. **63** Cleve Bryant/PhotoEdit, Inc. **64** Roger Tidman/CORBIS. **65** Karen Struthers/Shutterstock; Margherita Goldsmid, later Mrs Raphael (oil on canvas), Sargent, John Singer (1856-1925)/Private Collection/The Bridgeman Art Library. **66** Henry Guttmann/Getty Images. **67** Karen Struthers/Shutterstock.com; Margherita Goldsmid, later Mrs Raphael (oil on canvas), Sargent, John Singer (1856-1925)/Private Collection/The Bridgeman Art Library. **69** The Salon of Princess Mathilde (1820-1904) 1883 (oil on canvas), Nittis, Giuseppe or Joseph de (1846–84)/Pinacoteca Giuseppe de Nittis, Barletta, Italy/Alinari/The Bridgeman Art Library. **70** Alexander Mak/Shutterstock; Elio Ciol/CORBIS. **71** Elio Ciol/CORBIS; Elio Ciol/CORBIS. **73** Comstock/JupiterImages Corporation. **75** Scala/Art Resource, NY. **76** A Woman Ironing, 1873, Edgar Degas. Oil on canvas, The Metropolitan Museum of Art/Alamy. **77** Art Resource, NY. **81** Alyce Lytz. **82** Alyce Lytz. **84** Krisanne Johnson/White House via Getty Images. **86** Alyce Lytz. **90** John Vachon/Farm Security Administration/Office of War Information Photograph Collection/Library of Congress. **91, 92** Ralph Foster Archive, College of the Ozarks/VAGA. **93** Dorothea Lange/Farm Security Administration/Office of War Information Photograph Collection/Library of Congress. **94** Sandpiper; Graphic Universe; Speak. **95** Jeremy Walker/Getty Images; Christian Wheatley/iStockphoto; VisionsofAmerica/Joe Sohm/Getty Images. **101** Christian Wheatley/iStockphoto. **102-103** VisionsofAmerica/Joe Sohm/Getty Images. **110-111** REUTERS/Julie Adnam. **111** Ethan Miller/Getty Images. **112** Judie Long/Alamy. **113** Farrar, Straus and Giroux; Scholastic Paperbacks. **114** Digital Image The Museum of Modern Art/Licensed by SCALA/Art Resource, NY. **118** Maria Dryhout/Shutterstock. **119** Abe Louise Young/WKCD. **120** Ralph Freso/East Valley Tribune. **121** Abe Louise Young/WKCD. **122** Abe Louise Young/WKCD. **123** Abe Louise Young/WKCD; Abe Louise Young/WKCD. **124** Abe Louise Young/WKCD. **125** Abe Louise Young/WKCD; 2004 MJ Maloney. **126** Abe Louise Young/WKCD; Abe Louise Young/WKCD. **129** Ocean/CORBIS. **130** Matthias Kulka/zefa/CORBIS; Mark Harmel/Getty Images. **136** AP Photo/Plain Dealer, Lynn Ischay; Kelly-Mooney Photography/CORBIS; Alain Nogues/CORBIS. **138** Ocean/CORBIS; Ocean/CORBIS. **139** 2013 Thinkstock/JupiterImages Corporation. **140** 2013 Thinkstock/JupiterImages Corporation. **142** James Leynse/CORBIS; 2013 JupiterImages Corporation. **143** Wendell Metzen/Getty Images; 2013 Thinkstock/JupiterImages Corporation; GEMS/Redferns/MUSICPICTURES.COM; Reuters/CORBIS. **144** Ingram Publishing; Nicky J. Sims/Redferns/Getty Images; Wendell Metzen/Getty Images; Ebet Roberts. **145** Ebet Roberts; AP Photo/Lennox McLendon. **146** Robert Knight; Scott Gries/Getty Images. **147** Wendell Metzen/Getty Images; Tim Mosenfelder/Getty Images; AP Photo/Reed Saxon. **148** Wendell Metzen/Getty Images; David Bergman/CORBIS. **149** Carlo Allegri/Getty Images. **151** Frank Micelotta/I/Getty ImagesageDirect. **154** Alexis Maryon/Retna UK. **158** Hill Street Studios/Getty Images. **160** Lito C. Uyan/CORBIS. **161** 3RI. **163** 3RI. **164** Courtesy of Kai Zhang. **165** 3RI; 3RI; 3RI; 3RI. **167** Joe McCary/Shakespeare Theatre Company. **168** Allen Ginsberg/CORBIS. **169** Guido Schiefer/Alamy. **170** James Lance/CORBIS. **171** Neville Elder/CORBIS. **172** Lawrence Lucier/Stringer/Getty Images. **173** Robyn Twomey. **174** 3RI. **175** Image Source/CORBIS. **176** Image Source/CORBIS. **180** John Hersey/theispot.com; Farrar, Straus and Giroux; Scholastic Paperbacks. **182** Iker Ayestaran/theispot.com. **183** Doggygraph/Shutterstock. **184** Penguin Group. **185** John Harper/CORBIS. **186** Jeff Greenberg/PhotoEdit, Inc. **191**

Acknowledgments, continued

Andy Sacks/Getty Images. **192** Andy Sacks/Getty Images. **200** The Life Line, 1864, Winslow Homer. Oil on canvas, Philadelphia Museum of Art/Superstock. **200-201** Ashley Cooper/CORBIS. **203** Graphic Universe; Candlewick; Harper Perennial. **204** Joe Cornish/Getty Images. **209** Pete Turner/Getty Images; Richard T. Nowitz/CORBIS. **211** Pete Turner/Getty Images; Richard T. Nowitz/CORBIS. **212** Pete Turner/Getty Images. **213** Mountain Dragon, 1992, Bob Eggleton. Acrylic on illustration board, private collection of Pat Wilshire, Pennsylvania. **217** Merlin and Arthur (bronze), John, Sir William Goscombe (1860-1952)/National Museum Wales/The Bridgeman Art Library ; Pete Turner/Getty Images. **219** The British Museum/Topham/The Image Works. **220** King Arthur, 1903 (oil on canvas), Butler, Charles Ernest (1864-c.1918)/Private Collection/Christopher Wood Gallery, London, UK/The Bridgeman Art Library. **221** Pete Turner/Getty Images. **223** CORBIS; Scala/Art Resource, NY. **224** The Trustees of The British Museum; Roger Bamber/Alamy; Werner Forman/Art Resource, NY; Tokyo National Museum. **225** heraldryclipart.com; Ric Ergenbright/CORBIS; Alfred the Great (849-99), after a painting in the Bodleian Gallery (colour litho), English School, (19th century)/Private Collection/The Stapleton Collection/The Bridgeman Art Library ; Scala/Art Resource, NY. **228** Michael Jenner/Alamy. **229** Skyscan Photolibrary/Alamy; Roy Rainford/Getty Images. **234** Simon Marcus/CORBIS; Park Street/PhotoEdit, Inc. Inc.; AGStockUSA/Alamy. **236** Zave Smith/CORBIS. **237** Girl in Miami, 1999 (oil on panel) (see also 118567), Ferguson, Max/Private Collection/The Bridgeman Art Library. **238** Girl in Miami, 1999 (oil on panel) (see also 118567), Ferguson, Max/Private Collection/The Bridgeman Art Library ; University of Georgia, Peter Frey. **238-239** Verba/Shutterstock. **240** Verba/Shutterstock. **242** Verba/Shutterstock. **244** Verba/Shutterstock. **243** Trembling Hands, 2007, Andres Medrano Thompson, Ink on Paper, collection of the artist. **245** Elephant, 2006, Elephant rubber bands. Rubber bands and mixed media. **247** Verba/Shutterstock. **248** Reaching hands, 2007, Jerry Lindemann. Digital Illustration. **250** Verba/Shutterstock. **251** PhotoDisc/Getty Images. **253** AP Photo/Albany Times Union, Skip Dickstein, File; Colin Archer/Getty Images. **254** AP Photo/Mary Altaffer; AP Photo/The Post Star,T.J. Hooker. **258** Alan Schein/CORBIS. **260** Steve Skjold/Alamy. **263** Lonny Kalfus/Getty Images. **262** Benn Mitchell/Getty Images; Comstock/Thinkstock/JupiterImages. **264** JFK Presidential Library and Museum, Education Department. **265** Lonny Kalfus/Getty Images ; David Finn; Lonny Kalfus/Getty Images. **266** Pools of Defiance, 2001 (oil on canvas), Bootman, Colin (Contemporary Artist)/Private Collection/The Bridgeman Art Library. **267** John Ferrell, Farm Security Administration collection, Prints & Photographs Division, Library of Congress,LC-USF34-011465-D. **268** The Country Girl (oil on canvas), Ambrose, Lester J. (1879-1949)/Private Collection/Lawrence Steigrad Fine Arts, New York/The Bridgeman Art Library. **271** John Ferrell, Farm Security Administration collection, Prints & Photographs Division, Library of Congress,LC-USF34-011465-D; The Metropolitan Museum of Art. Image source: Art Resource, NY. **273** John Ferrell, Farm Security Administration collection, Prints & Photographs Division, Library of Congress,LC-USF34-011465-D. **279** AP Photo/Montgomery

County Sheriff's office. **280** AP Photo/Horace Cort. **281** AP Photo/Gene Herrick. **283** Don Cravens//Time Life Pictures/Getty Images. **284** Fred Viebahn. **286** Bettmann/CORBIS. **288** Bruce Davidson/Magnum Photos. **289** Lori Ferber/Lori Ferber Collectibles. **290** Graphic Universe; Candlewick; Harper Perennial. **291** Jack Hollingsworth/PhotoDisc/Getty Images. **297** Rudi von Briel/PhotoEdit, Inc.; Frank Siteman/Getty Images. **306-307** Tino Soriano/National Geographic/Getty Images. **309** Yuri Arcurs/Shutterstock; Dover Publications; Rayo; Speak. **310** Photographer's Choice/Punchstock. **311** Bud Endress; Felix Mizioznikov/iStockphoto. **314** Punchstock. **315** Josh Westrich/CORBIS. **316** Josh Westrich/CORBIS. **319** Matthias Kulka/CORBIS. **322** Matthias Kulka/CORBIS. **321** dibrova/Shutterstock. **323** GeoffBlack/iStockphoto. **324** Lannis Waters/CORBIS. **326** Matthias Kulka/CORBIS. **327** William Morrow & Company. **330** The Enterprise Center. **331** Gregg Newton/CORBIS. **333** The Enterprise Center. **338** Michael Newman/PhotoEdit, Inc. **339** Digital Vision/Superstock. **340** The Andy Warhol Foundation for the Visual Arts/CORBIS; Courtesy Ronald Feldman Fine Arts, New York. **342** Ulf Andersen/Getty Images. **343** The Andy Warhol Foundation for the Visual Arts/CORBIS; Courtesy Ronald Feldman Fine Arts, New York. **351** Alicia Wagner Calzada/ZUMA. **352** The Dreamer, 2002, Patssi Valdez, Acrylic on canvas. Courtesy of Patricia Correia Gallery, Santa Monica, California. **353** Ray Laskowitz/Lonely Planet Images. **354** East on the 10, 2001. Frank Romero. Oil on wood, private collection.; Random House. **356** Ulf Andersen/Getty Images. **358** Ray Laskowitz/Lonely Planet Images. **360-361** Jonathon Nourok/PhotoEdit, Inc. **362** Roy McMahon/Stock Image/Getty Images; Louis DeLuca/Dallas Morning News/CORBIS. **363** Jose Luis Pelaez; Inc./CORBIS; Michael Perez/The Philadelphia Inquirer. **365** Michael Perez/The Philadelphia Inquirer. **366** Michael Perez/The Philadelphia Inquirer. **367** The Philadelphia Inquirer Graphics and Animation: Alan Baseden/Inquirer Staff Artist. **368** Gerald S. Williams/The Philadelphia Inquirer. **369** Michael Perez/The Philadelphia Inquirer. **371** Michael Perez/The Philadelphia Inquirer. **373** Michael Perez/The Philadelphia Inquirer. **375** Mick Stevens/The New Yorker Collection/www.cartoonbank.com. **376** 2013 Comstock Images/Jupiterimages Corporation; GINA GAYLE/INDEPENDENCE TECHNOLOGY/PRN/Newscom. **378** Feature Photo Service/Newscom. **379** Mark Wilson/The Boston Globe/Getty Images. **384-387** iStockphoto. **385** Jon Ross Photography. **386** Jon Ross Photography. **388** Dover Publications; Rayo; Speak. **389** Blend Images/Ariel Skelley/Getty Images. **396** Hemera Technologies/Getty Images. **404-405** Brian J. Skerry/National Geographic Stock. **406** Album/Art Resource, NY. **407** Dutton Juvenile; Harper; Graphia. **408** Judith Wagner/CORBIS. **413** Michael A. Keller/zefa/CORBIS. **413** Sherrie Nickol/CORBIS; Christoph Burki/Getty Images. **414** Time Life Pictures/Mansell/Time Life Pictures/Getty Images. **414-415** Christoph Burki/Getty Images. **416** Christie's Images/SuperStock. **420** Untitled, 1910, Emily Carr. Watercolor, graphite on paper, Collection of the Vancouver Art Gallery, Emily Carr Trust, VAG 42.3.87, Photo: Trevor Mills, Vancouver Art Gallery. **425** Amy Guip/CORBIS Outline. **426** Cat's Collection/CORBIS. **429** Simon & Schuster; Simon & Schuster; Arthur Tilley/Getty Images. **434** Elaine Thompson/ASSOCIATED PRESS;

Ocean/CORBIS; Spencer Grant/PhotoEdit, Inc. **436** Adrianna Williams/CORBIS; Randy Faris/CORBIS; Jason Stemple Photographer. **437** Patricia McDonough/Getty Images; Digital Vision/Getty Images; W. EUGENE SMITH/Getty Images. **438** Patricia McDonough/Getty Images; Digital Vision/Getty Images. **439** W. EUGENE SMITH/Getty Images. **440** Bertrand Demée/Getty Images. **441** Amelie Sourget/Beateworks/CORBIS; John Slater/Getty Images; Per Gustafon/Getty Images. **442** Ryan McVay/Getty Images; Lena Sergeeva/Getty Images; Image Source/Thinkstock; Tim O'Leary/zefa/CORBIS; 2013 Image Source/Jupiterimages Corporation. **444** Bertrand Demée/Getty Images. **445** xyno/iStockphoto. **446** InnervisionArt/Shutterstock. **447** Bertrand Demée/Getty Images. **448** xyno/iStockphoto. **449** Donata Pizzi/Getty Images; Susanne Borges/A.B./CORBIS; Digital Vision/Getty Images. **451** Gahan Wilson/The New Yorker Collection/www.cartoonbank.com. **453** Julian Andrew Holtom/Getty Images; Peter Beavis/Getty Images; Vincent Besnault/Getty Images; Thomas Barwick/Getty Images; Digital Vision/Getty Images; Gandee Vasan/Getty Images; Gus Wedge/Getty Images; Olaf Tiedje/Getty Images; Christoph Wilhelm/Getty Images; Per Gustafon/Getty Images. **454** Nathan Griffith/CORBIS. **456** Christopher Felver/CORBIS. **458** Mick Stevens/The New Yorker Collection/www.cartoonbank.com. **460** Cleve Bryant/PhotoEdit, Inc. **462** Louis Moses/CORBIS; Owen Franken/CORBIS. **463** Mark Summers. **464** Time & Life Pictures/Getty Images ; Mark Summers. **466** Theodore Gericault (1791-1824) Dying, 1824 (oil on canvas), Correard, Alexandre (1788-1857)/Musee des Beaux-Arts, Rouen, France/Giraudon/The Bridgeman Art Library. **469** 2013 The Estate of Francis Bacon. All rights reserved./ARS, New York/DACS, London/Bridgeman Art Library. **471** George Marks/Retrofile/Getty Images. **472** Images.com/CORBIS. **475** Collier Campbell Lifeworks/CORBIS. **476** Collier Campbell Lifeworks/CORBIS. **478** Collier Campbell Lifeworks/CORBIS; Australian Raven, 2005, Kate Breakley. Handcolored silver gelatin photograph, Courtesy of Stephen Clark Gallery. **480** Collier Campbell Lifeworks/CORBIS. **482** Bettmann/CORBIS; Charles O'Rear/CORBIS. **486** Vetta/Getty Images. **486, 488, 489** Vittorio Bruno/Shutterstock. **489** Chase Jarvis. **490** Graphia; Judith Wagner/CORBIS. **491** Paul Mason/Getty Images. **492** Ryan McVay/Getty Images. **496-497** Todd Keith/Getty Images. **498** Vintage Image/Alamy. **497** James Strachan/Getty Images. **506-507** Stu Smucker/Lonely Planet Images/Getty Images. **507** John Eder/Getty Images. **509** Simon Pulse; University of Washington Press; Candlewick. **510** Hans Neleman/Getty Images. **511** PhotoDisc/Getty Images; PhotoDisc/Getty Images. **514** lightpoet/Shutterstock; CORBIS. **515** Alan Schein Photography/CORBIS. **516-517** Alan Schein Photography/CORBIS. **519** Harrison Eastwood/Getty Images; Harrison Eastwood/Getty Images; Harrison Eastwood/Getty Images; Karen Moskowitz/Getty Images. **520** CORBIS. **521** Liz Garza Williams; MacArt by Ray G; MacArt by 3RI; National Geographic. **522** The name and character of Smokey Bear are the property of the United States, as provided by 16 U.S.C. 580P-1 and 18 U.S.C 711, and are used with the permission of the Forest Service, U.S. Department of Agriculture. OR "16 U.S.A. 580P-1 and 18 U.S.C 711.". **523** AP Photo/Diane Bondareff. **525** Got Milk Ad. **529** Frank Capri/Hulton Archive/Getty Images. **531** 2013 John Lund/